THE EXPOSITOR'S BIBLE COMMENTARY

General Editor:

FRANK E. GAEBELEIN
Headmaster Emeritus, Stony Brook School;
Former Coeditor, *Christianity Today*

Associate Editor:

RICHARD P. POLCYN
Zondervan Publishing House

Consulting Editors, Old Testament:

WALTER C. KAISER, JR.
Professor of Semitic Languages
and Old Testament,
Trinity Evangelical Divinity School

BRUCE K. WALTKE
(Consulting Editor, 1972–1984)
Professor of Old Testament,
Regent College

RALPH H. ALEXANDER
(Consulting Editor, 1984—)
Professor of Hebrew Scripture
Western Seminary, Portland, Oregon

Consulting Editors, New Testament:

JAMES MONTGOMERY BOICE
Pastor, Tenth Presbyterian Church,
Philadelphia, Pennsylvania

MERRILL C. TENNEY
Professor of Bible and Theology, Emeritus,
Wheaton College

THE EXPOSITOR'S BIBLE COMMENTARY

with

The New International Version
of
The Holy Bible

IN TWELVE VOLUMES

VOLUME 2

(GENESIS–NUMBERS)

Regency
Reference Library
Zondervan Publishing House
Grand Rapids, Michigan

THE EXPOSITOR'S BIBLE COMMENTARY, VOLUME 2

REGENCY REFERENCE LIBRARY is an imprint of
Zondervan Publishing House,
1415 Lake Drive, S.E., Grand Rapids, Michigan 49506.

Library of Congress Cataloging in Publication Data
(Revised for Volume 2)

The Expositor's Bible commentary.
Includes bibliographies.
Contents: v. 1. Introductory articles.—v.2.
Genesis-Numbers— —v. 7. Daniel-Minor
Prophets.—(etc.)—v. 12. Hebrews-Revelation.
1. Bible–Commentaries. I. Gaebelein, Frank Ely, 1899-
. II. Douglas, J. D. (James Dixon) III. Bible. English.
New International 1976.
BS491.2.E96 220.7'7 76-41334
ISBN 0-310-36440-X (v.2)

Printed in the United States of America

90 91 92 93 94 95 / DH / 10 9 8 7 6 5 4 3 2 1

CONTENTS

Contributors to Volume 2 vi
Preface vii
Abbreviations ix
Transliterations xv
Genesis 1
Exodus 285
Leviticus 499
Numbers 655

CONTRIBUTORS TO VOLUME 2

GENESIS: John H. Sailhamer

B.A., California State University (Long Beach); Th.M., Dallas Theological Seminary; M.A., Ph.D., University of California (Los Angeles)

Associate Professor of Old Testament and Semitic Languages, Trinity Evangelical Divinity School

EXODUS: Walter C. Kaiser, Jr.

A.B., Wheaton College; B.D., Wheaton Graduate School of Theology; M.A., Ph.D., Brandeis University

Academic Dean and Senior Vice President of Education, Trinity Evangelical Divinity School

LEVITICUS: R. Laird Harris

B.S., University of Delaware; Th.B.,Th.M., Westminster Theological Seminary; M.A., University of Pennsylvania; Ph.D., Dropsie College

Professor Emeritus of Old Testament, Covenant Theological Seminary

NUMBERS: Ronald B. Allen

B.A., California State University (Los Angeles); Th.M., Th.D., Dallas Theological Seminary

Professor of Hebrew Scripture, Western Baptist Seminary

PREFACE

The title of this work defines its purpose. Written primarily by expositors for expositors, it aims to provide preachers, teachers, and students of the Bible with a new and comprehensive commentary on the books of the Old and New Testaments. Its stance is that of a scholarly evangelicalism committed to the divine inspiration, complete trustworthiness, and full authority of the Bible. Its seventy-eight contributors come from the United States, Canada, England, Scotland, Australia, New Zealand, and Switzerland, and from various religious groups, including Anglican, Baptist, Brethren, Free, Independent, Methodist, Nazarene, Presbyterian, and Reformed churches. Most of them teach at colleges, universities, or theological seminaries.

No book has been more closely studied over a longer period of time than the Bible. From the Midrashic commentaries going back to the period of Ezra, through parts of the Dead Sea Scrolls and the Patristic literature, and on to the present, the Scriptures have been expounded. Indeed, there have been times when, as in the Reformation and on occasions since then, exposition has been at the cutting edge of Christian advance. Luther was a powerful exegete, and Calvin is still called "the prince of expositors."

Their successors have been many. And now, when the outburst of new translations and their unparalleled circulation have expanded the readership of the Bible, the need for exposition takes on fresh urgency.

Not that God's Word can ever become captive to its expositors. Among all other books, it stands first in its combination of perspicuity and profundity. Though a child can be made "wise for salvation" by believing its witness to Christ, the greatest mind cannot plumb the depths of its truth (2 Tim. 3:15; Rom. 11:33). As Gregory the Great said, "Holy Scripture is a stream of running water, where alike the elephant may swim, and the lamb walk." So, because of the inexhaustible nature of Scripture, the task of opening up its meaning is still a perennial obligation of biblical scholarship.

How that task is done inevitably reflects the outlook of those engaged in it. Every Bible scholar has presuppositions. To this neither the editors of these volumes nor the contributors to them are exceptions. They share a common commitment to the supernatural Christianity set forth in the inspired Word. Their purpose is not to supplant the many valuable commentaries that have preceded this work and from which both the editors and contributors have learned. It is rather to draw on the resources of contemporary evangelical scholarship in producing a new reference work for understanding the Scriptures.

A commentary that will continue to be useful through the years should handle contemporary trends in biblical studies in such a way as to avoid becoming outdated when critical fashions change. Biblical criticism is not in itself inadmissable, as some have mistakenly thought. When scholars investigate the authorship, date, literary characteristics, and purpose of a biblical document, they are practicing biblical criticism. So also when, in order to ascertain as nearly as possible the original form of the text, they deal with variant readings, scribal errors, emendations, and other phenomena in the manuscripts. To do these things is essential to responsible exegesis and exposition. And always there is the need to distinguish hypothesis from fact, conjecture from truth.

The chief principle of interpretation followed in this commentary is the grammatico-historical one—namely, that the primary aim of the exegete is to make clear the meaning of the text at the time and in the circumstances of its writing. This endeavor to understand what in the first instance the inspired writers actually said must not be confused with an inflexible literalism. Scripture makes lavish use of symbols and figures of speech; great portions of it are poetical. Yet when it speaks in this way, it speaks no less truly than it does in its historical and doctrinal portions. To understand its message requires attention to matters of grammar and syntax, word meanings, idioms, and literary forms—all in relation to the historical and cultural setting of the text.

The contributors to this work necessarily reflect varying convictions. In certain controversial matters the policy is that of clear statement of the contributors' own views followed by fair presentation of other ones. The treatment of eschatology, though it reflects differences of interpretation, is consistent with a general premillennial position. (Not all contributors, however, are premillennial.) But prophecy is more than prediction, and so this commentary gives due recognition to the major lode of godly social concern in the prophetic writings.

THE EXPOSITOR'S BIBLE COMMENTARY is presented as a scholarly work, though not primarily one of technical criticism. In its main portion, the Exposition, and in Volume 1 (General and Special Articles), all Semitic and Greek words are transliterated and the English equivalents given. As for the Notes, here Semitic and Greek characters are used but always with transliterations and English meanings, so that this portion of the commentary will be as accessible as possible to readers unacquainted with the original languages.

It is the conviction of the general editor, shared by his colleagues in the Zondervan editorial department, that in writing about the Bible, lucidity is not incompatible with scholarship. They are therefore endeavoring to make this a clear and understandable work.

The translation used in it is the New International Version (North American Edition). To the International Bible Society thanks are due for permission to use this most recent of the major Bible translations. It was chosen because of the clarity and beauty of its style and its faithfulness to the original texts.

To the associate editor, Richard P. Polcyn, and to the contributing editors—Dr. Walter C. Kaiser, Jr., Dr. Bruce K. Waltke, and Dr. Ralph H. Alexander for the Old Testament, and Dr. James Montgomery Boice and Dr. Merrill C. Tenney for the New Testament—the general editor expresses his gratitude for their unfailing cooperation and their generosity in advising him out of their expert scholarship. And to the many other contributors he is indebted for their invaluable part in this work. Finally, he owes a special debt of gratitude to Dr. Robert K. DeVries, publisher, The Zondervan Corporation, and Miss Elizabeth Brown, secretary, for their assistance and encouragement.

Whatever else it is—the greatest and most beautiful of books, the primary source of law and morality, the fountain of wisdom, and the infallible guide to life—the Bible is above all the inspired witness to Jesus Christ. May this work fulfill its function of expounding the Scriptures with grace and clarity, so that its users may find that both Old and New Testaments do indeed lead to our Lord Jesus Christ, who alone could say, "I have come that they may have life, and have it to the full" (John 10:10).

FRANK E. GAEBELEIN

ABBREVIATIONS

A. General Abbreviations

A	Codex Alexandrinus
Akkad.	Akkadian
א	Codex Sinaiticus
Ap. Lit.	Apocalyptic Literature
Apoc.	Apocrypha
Aq.	Aquila's Greek Translation of the Old Testament
Arab.	Arabic
Aram.	Aramaic
b	Babylonian Gemara
B	Codex Vaticanus
C	Codex Ephraemi Syri
c.	*circa*, about
cf.	*confer*, compare
ch., chs.	chapter, chapters
cod., codd.	codex, codices
D	Codex Bezae
DSS	Dead Sea Scrolls (see E.)
ed., edd.	edited, edition, editor; editions
e.g.	*exempli gratia*, for example
Egyp.	Egyptian
et al.	*et alii*, and others
EV	English Versions of the Bible
fem.	feminine
ff.	following (verses, pages, etc.)
fl.	flourished
ft.	foot, feet
gen.	genitive
Gr.	Greek
Heb.	Hebrew
Hitt.	Hittite
ibid.	*ibidem*, in the same place
id.	*idem*, the same
i.e.	*id est*, that is
impf.	imperfect
infra.	below
in loc.	*in loco*, in the place cited
j	Jerusalem or Palestinian Gemara
Lat.	Latin
LL.	Late Latin
LXX	Septuagint
M	Mishnah
masc.	masculine
mg.	margin
Mid	Midrash
MS(S)	manuscript(s)
MT	Masoretic text
n.	note
n.d.	no date
Nestle	Nestle (ed.) *Novum Testamentum Graece*
no.	number
NT	New Testament
obs.	obsolete
OL	Old Latin
OS	Old Syriac
OT	Old Testament
p., pp.	page, pages
par.	paragraph
Pers.	Persian
Pesh.	Peshitta
Phoen.	Phoenician
pl.	plural
Pseudep.	Pseudepigrapha
Q	Quelle ("Sayings" source in the Gospels)
qt.	quoted by
q.v.	*quod vide*, which see
R	Rabbah
rev.	revised, reviser, revision
Rom.	Roman
RVm	Revised Version margin
Samar.	Samaritan recension
SCM	Student Christian Movement Press
Sem.	Semitic
sing.	singular
SPCK	Society for the Promotion of Christian Knowledge
Sumer.	Sumerian
s.v.	*sub verbo*, under the word
Syr.	Syriac
Symm.	Symmachus
T	Talmud
Targ.	Targum
Theod.	Theodotion
TR	Textus Receptus
tr.	translation, translator, translated
UBS	Tha United Bible Societies' Greek Text
Ugar.	Ugaritic
u.s.	*ut supra*, as above
v., vv.	verse, verses
viz.	*videlicet*, namely
vol.	volume
vs.	versus
Vul.	Vulgate
WH	Westcott and Hort, *The New Testament in Greek*

B. Abbreviations for Modern Translations and Paraphrases

AmT	Smith and Goodspeed, *The Complete Bible, An American Translation*
ASV	American Standard Version, American Revised Version (1901)
Beck	Beck, *The New Testament in the Language of Today*
BV	Berkeley Version (The Modern Language Bible)
JB	The Jerusalem Bible
JPS	*Jewish Publication Society Version of the Old Testament*
KJV	King James Version
Knox	R.G. Knox, *The Holy Bible: A Translation from the Latin Vulgate in the Light of the Hebrew and Greek Original*
LB	The Living Bible
Mof	J. Moffatt, *A New Translation of the Bible*
NAB	The New American Bible
NASB	New American Standard Bible
NEB	The New English Bible
NIV	The New International Version
Ph	J. B. Phillips *The New Testament in Modern English*
RSV	Revised Standard Version
RV	Revised Version — 1881–1885
TCNT	Twentieth Century New Testament
TEV	Today's English Version
Wey	*Weymouth's New Testament in Modern Speech*
Wms	C. B. Williams, *The New Testament: A Translation in the Language of the People*

C. Abbreviations for Periodicals and Reference Works

AASOR	*Annual of the American Schools of Oriental Research*
AB	*Anchor Bible*
AIs	de Vaux: *Ancient Israel*
AJA	*American Journal of Archaeology*
AJSL	*American Journal of Semitic Languages and Literatures*
AJT	*American Journal of Theology*
Alf	Alford: *Greek Testament Commentary*
ANEA	*Ancient Near Eastern Archaeology*
ANEP	Pritchard: *Ancient Near Eastern Pictures*
ANET	Pritchard· *Ancient Near Eastern Texts*
ANF	Roberts and Donaldson: *The Ante-Nicene Fathers*
A-S	Abbot-Smith: *Manual Greek Lexicon of the New Testament*
AThR	*Anglican Theological Review*
BA	*Biblical Archaeologist*
BAG	Bauer, Arndt, and Gingrich: *Greek-English Lexicon of the New Testament*
BAGD	Bauer, Arndt, Gingrich, and Danker: *Greek-English Lexicon of the New Testament* 2nd edition
BASOR	*Bulletin of the American Schools of Oriental Research*
BC	Foakes-Jackson and Lake: *The Beginnings of Christianity*
BDB	Brown, Driver, and Briggs: *Hebrew-English Lexicon of the Old Testament*
BDF	Blass, Debrunner, and Funk: *A Greek Grammar of the New Testament and Other Early Christian Literature*
BDT	Harrison: *Baker's Dictionary of Theology*
Beng.	Bengel's *Gnomon*
BETS	*Bulletin of the Evangelical Theological Society*
BH	*Biblia Hebraica*
BHS	*Biblia Hebraica Stuttgartensia*
BJRL	*Bulletin of the John Rylands Library*
BS	*Bibliotheca Sacra*
BT	*Babylonian Talmud*
BTh	*Biblical Theology*
BW	*Biblical World*
CAH	*Cambridge Ancient History*
CanJTh	*Canadian Journal of Theology*
CBQ	*Catholic Biblical Quarterly*
CBSC	*Cambridge Bible for Schools and Colleges*
CE	*Catholic Encyclopedia*
CGT	*Cambridge Greek Testament*

CHS	Lange: *Commentary on the Holy Scriptures*
ChT	*Christianity Today*
DDB	*Davis' Dictionary of the Bible*
Deiss BS	Deissmann: *Bible Studies*
Deiss LAE	Deissmann: *Light From the Ancient East*
DNTT	*Dictionary of New Testament Theology*
EBC	*The Expositor's Bible Commentary*
EBi	*Encyclopaedia Biblica*
EBr	*Encyclopaedia Britannica*
EDB	*Encyclopedic Dictionary of the Bible*
EGT	Nicoll: *Expositor's Greek Testament*
EQ	*Evangelical Quarterly*
ET	*Evangelische Theologie*
ExB	*The Expositor's Bible*
Exp	*The Expositor*
ExpT	*The Expository Times*
FLAP	Finegan: *Light From the Ancient Past*
GKC	Gesenius, Kautzsch, Cowley, *Hebrew Grammar*, 2nd Eng. ed.
GR	*Gordon Review*
HBD	*Harper's Bible Dictionary*
HDAC	Hastings: *Dictionary of the Apostolic Church*
HDB	Hastings: *Dictionary of the Bible*
HDBrev.	Hastings: *Dictionary of the Bible*, one-vol. rev. by Grant and Rowley
HDCG	Hastings: *Dictionary of Christ and the Gospels*
HERE	Hastings: *Encyclopedia of Religion and Ethics*
HGEOTP	Heidel: *The Gilgamesh Epic and Old Testament Parallels*
HJP	Schurer: *A History of the Jewish People in the Time of Christ*
HR	Hatch and Redpath: *Concordance to the Septuagint*
HTR	*Harvard Theological Review*
HUCA	*Hebrew Union College Annual*
IB	*The Interpreter's Bible*
ICC	*International Critical Commentary*
IDB	*The Interpreter's Dictionary of the Bible*
IEJ	*Israel Exploration Journal*
Int	*Interpretation*
INT	E. Harrison: *Introduction to the New Testament*
IOT	R. K. Harrison: *Introduction to the Old Testament*
ISBE	*The International Standard Bible Encyclopedia*
ITQ	*Irish Theological Quarterly*
JAAR	*Journal of American Academy of Religion*
JAOS	*Journal of American Oriental Society*
JBL	*Journal of Biblical Literature*
JE	*Jewish Encyclopedia*
JETS	*Journal of Evangelical Theological Society*
JFB	Jamieson, Fausset, and Brown: *Commentary on the Old and New Testament*
JNES	*Journal of Near Eastern Studies*
Jos. Antiq.	Josephus: *The Antiquities of the Jews*
Jos. War	Josephus: *The Jewish War*
JQR	*Jewish Quarterly Review*
JR	*Journal of Religion*
JSJ	*Journal for the Study of Judaism in the Persian, Hellenistic and Roman Periods*
JSOR	*Journal of the Society of Oriental Research*
JSS	*Journal of Semitic Studies*
JT	*Jerusalem Talmud*
JTS	*Journal of Theological Studies*
KAHL	Kenyon: *Archaeology in the Holy Land*
KB	Koehler-Baumgartner: *Lexicon in Veteris Testament Libros*
KD	Keil and Delitzsch: *Commentary on the Old Testament*
LSJ	Liddell, Scott, Jones: *Greek-English Lexicon*
LTJM	Edersheim: *The Life and Times of Jesus the Messiah*
MM	Moulton and Milligan: *The Vocabulary of the Greek Testament*
MNT	Moffatt: *New Testament Commentary*

MST	McClintock and Strong: *Cyclopedia of Biblical, Theological, and Ecclesiastical Literature*
NBC	Davidson, Kevan, and Stibbs: *The New Bible Commentary*, 1st ed.
NBCrev.	Guthrie and Motyer: *The New Bible Commentary*, rev. ed.
NBD	J. D. Douglas: *The New Bible Dictionary*
NCB	*New Century Bible*
NCE	*New Catholic Encyclopedia*
NIC	*New International Commentary*
NIDCC	Douglas: *The New International Dictionary of the Christian Church*
NovTest	*Novum Testamentum*
NSI	Cooke: *Handbook of North Semitic Inscriptions*
NTS	*New Testament Studies*
ODCC	*The Oxford Dictionary of the Christian Church*, rev. ed.
Peake	Black and Rowley: *Peake's Commentary on the Bible*
PEQ	*Palestine Exploration Quarterly*
PNFl	P. Schaff: *The Nicene and Post-Nicene Fathers* (1st series)
PNF2	P. Schaff and H. Wace: *The Nicene and Post-Nicene Fathers* (2nd series)
PTR	*Princeton Theological Review*
RB	*Revue Biblique*
RHG	Robertson's *Grammar of the Greek New Testament in the Light of Historical Research*
RTWB	Richardson: *A Theological Wordbook of the Bible*
SBK	Strack and Billerbeck: *Kommentar zum Neuen Testament aus Talmud und Midrash*
SHERK	*The New Schaff-Herzog Encyclopedia of Religious Knowledge*
SJT	*Scottish Journal of Theology*
SOT	Girdlestone: *Synonyms of Old Testament*
SOTI	Archer: *A Survey of Old Testament Introduction*
ST	*Studia Theologica*
TCERK	Loetscher: *The Twentieth Century Encyclopedia of Religious Knowledge*
TDNT	Kittel: *Theological Dictionary of the New Testament*
TDOT	*Theological Dictionary of the Old Testament*
THAT	*Theologisches Handbuch zum Alten Testament*
ThT	*Theology Today*
TNTC	*Tyndale New Testament Commentaries*
Trench	Trench: *Synonyms of the New Testament*
TWOT	*Theological Wordbook of the Old Testament*
UBD	*Unger's Bible Dictionary*
UT	Gordon: *Ugaritic Textbook*
VB	Allmen: *Vocabulary of the Bible*
VetTest	*Vetus Testamentum*
Vincent	Vincent: *Word-Pictures in the New Testament*
WBC	*Wycliffe Bible Commentary*
WBE	*Wycliffe Bible Encyclopedia*
WC	*Westminster Commentaries*
WesBC	*Wesleyan Bible Commentaries*
WTJ	*Westminster Theological Journal*
ZAW	*Zeitschrift für die alttestamentliche Wissenschaft*
ZNW	*Zeitschrift für die neutestamentliche Wissenschaft*
ZPBD	*The Zondervan Pictorial Bible Dictionary*
ZPEB	*The Zondervan Pictorial Encyclopedia of the Bible*
ZWT	*Zeitschrift für wissenschaftliche Theologie*

D. Abbreviations for Books of the Bible, the Apocrypha, and the Pseudepigrapha

OLD TESTAMENT

Gen	2 Chron	Dan
Exod	Ezra	Hos
Lev	Neh	Joel
Num	Esth	Amos
Deut	Job	Obad
Josh	Ps(Pss)	Jonah
Judg	Prov	Mic
Ruth	Eccl	Nah
1 Sam	S of Songs	Hab
2 Sam	Isa	Zeph
1 Kings	Jer	Hag
2 Kings	Lam	Zech
1 Chron	Ezek	Mal

NEW TESTAMENT

Matt	1 Tim
Mark	2 Tim
Luke	Titus
John	Philem
Acts	Heb
Rom	James
1 Cor	1 Peter
2 Cor	2 Peter
Gal	1 John
Eph	2 John
Phil	3 John
Col	Jude
1 Thess	Rev
2 Thess	

APOCRYPHA

1 Esd	1 Esdras
2 Esd	2 Esdras
Tobit	Tobit
Jud	Judith
Add Esth	Additions to Esther
Wisd Sol	Wisdom of Solomon
Ecclus	Ecclesiasticus (Wisdom of Jesus the Son of Sirach)
Baruch	Baruch
Ep Jer	Epistle of Jeremy
S Th Ch	Song of the Three Child. (or Young Men)
Sus	Susanna
Bel	Bel and the Dragon
Pr Man	Prayer of Manasseh
1 Macc	1 Maccabees
2 Macc	2 Maccabees

PSEUDEPIGRAPHA

As Moses	Assumption of Moses
2 Baruch	Syriac Apocalypse of Baruch
3 Baruch	Greek Apocalypse of Baruch
1 Enoch	Ethiopic Book of Enoch
2 Enoch	Slavonic Book of Enoch
3 Enoch	Hebrew Book of Enoch
4 Ezra	4 Ezra
JA	Joseph and Asenath
Jub	Book of Jubilees
L Aristeas	Letter of Aristeas
Life AE	Life of Adam and Eve
Liv Proph	Lives of the Prophets
MA Isa	Martyrdom and Ascension of Isaiah
3 Macc	3 Maccabees
4 Macc	4 Maccabees
Odes Sol	Odes of Solomon
P Jer	Paralipomena of Jeremiah
Pirke Aboth	Pirke Aboth
Ps 151	Psalm 151
Pss Sol	Psalms of Solomon
Sib Oracles	Sibylline Oracles
Story Ah	Story of Ahikar
T Abram	Testament of Abraham
T Adam	Testament of Adam
T Benjamin	Testament of Benjamin
T Dan	Testament of Dan
T Gad	Testament of Gad
T Job	Testament of Job
T Jos	Testament of Joseph
T Levi	Testament of Levi
T Naph	Testament of Naphtali
T 12 Pat	Testaments of the Twe Patriarchs
Zad Frag	Zadokite Fragments

E. Abbreviations of Names of Dead Sea Scrolls and Related Texts

CD	Cairo (Genizah text of the) Damascus (Document)
DSS	Dead Sea Scrolls
Hev	Nahal Hever texts
Mas	Masada Texts
Mird	Khirbet mird texts
Mur	Wadi Murabba'at texts
P	Pesher (commentary)
Q	Qumran
1Q, 2Q, etc.	Numbered caves of Qumran, yielding written material; followed by abbreviation of biblical or apocryphal book.
QL	Qumran Literature
1QapGen	Genesis Apocryphon of Qumran Cave 1
1QH	*Hodayot* (Thanksgiving Hymns) from Qumran Cave 1
1QIsa a,b	First or second copy of Isaiah from Qumran Cave 1
1QpHab	Pesher on Habakkuk from Qumran Cave 1
1QM	*Milhamah* (War Scroll)
1QpMic	Pesher on portions of Micah from Qumran Cave 1
1QS	*Serek Hayyahad* (Rule of the Community, Manual of Discipline)
1QSa	Appendix A (Rule of the Congregation) to 1Qs
1QSb	Appendix B (Blessings) to 1QS
3Q15	Copper Scroll from Qumran Cave 3
4QExod a	Exodus Scroll, exemplar "a" from Qumran Cave 4
4QFlor	Florilegium (or Eschatological Midrashim) from Qumran Cave 4
4Qmess ar	Aramaic "Messianic" text from Qumran Cave 4
4QpNah	Pesher on portions of Nahum from Qumran Cave 4
4QPrNab	Prayer of Nabonidus from Qumran Cave 4
4QpPs37	Pesher on portions of Psalm 37 from Qumran Cave 4
4QTest	Testimonia text from Qumran Cave 4
4QTLevi	Testament of Levi from Qumran Cave 4
4QPhyl	Phylacteries from Qumran Cave 4
11QMelch	Melchizedek text from Qumran Cave 11
11QtgJob	Targum of Job from Qumran Cave 11

TRANSLITERATIONS

Hebrew

א = ʾ	ד = ḏ	י = y	ס = s	ר = r
בּ = b	ה = h	כּ = k	ע = ʿ	שׂ = ś
ב = ḇ	ו = w	ך כ = ḵ	פּ = p	שׁ = š
גּ = g	ז = z	ל = l	ף פ = p̄	תּ = t
ג = ḡ	ח = ḥ	ם מ = m	ץ צ = ṣ	ת = ṯ
דּ = d	ט = ṭ	ן נ = n	ק = q	

(ה)ָ = â (h)	ָ = ā	ַ = a	ֲ = ^{a}
ֵי = ê	ֵ = ē	ֶ = e	ֱ = ^{e}
ִי = î	ֹ = ō	ִ = i	ְ = ^{e} (*if vocal*)
וֹ = ô		ָ = o	ֳ = ^{o}
וּ = û		ֻ = u	

Aramaic

ʾ b g d h w z ḥ ṭ y k l m n s ʿ p ṣ q r ś š t

Arabic

ʾ b t ṯ ǧ ḥ ḫ d ḏ r z s š ṣ ḍ ṭ ẓ ʿ ġ f q k l m n h w y

Ugaritic

ʾ b g d ḏ h w z ḥ ḫ ṭ ẓ y k l m n s ś ʿ ǵ ṗ ṣ q r š t ṯ

Greek

α	*a*	π	*p*	αι	*ai*
β	*b*	ρ	*r*	αὐ	*au*
γ	*g*	σ,ς	*s*	ει	*ei*
δ	*d*	τ	*t*	εὐ	*eu*
ε	*e*	υ	*y*	ηὐ	*ēu*
ζ	*z*	φ	*ph*	οι	*oi*
η	*ē*	χ	*ch*	οὐ	*ou*
θ	*th*	ψ	*ps*	υι	*hui*
ι	*i*	ω	*ō*		
κ	*k*			ῥ	*rh*
λ	*l*	γγ	*ng*	῾	*h*
μ	*m*	γκ	*nk*		
ν	*n*	γξ	*nx*	ᾳ	*ā*
ξ	*x*	γχ	*nch*	ῃ	*ē*
ο	*o*			ῳ	*ō*

GENESIS

John H. Sailhamer

GENESIS

Introduction

1. Background
2. Unity
3. Authorship, Date, and Place of Origin
4. Purpose
    a. Compositional analysis of the Pentateuch
    b. Narrative/poetic seams in the Pentateuch
    c. A narrative typology
    d. Summary
5. Literary Form
    a. Assessing the structure
    b. The principle of selectivity
6. Bibliography
7. Outline

1. Background

Little is known today about the origin and authorship of the Book of Genesis. The book is a part of the Pentateuch, which Jewish tradition and the NT have ascribed to Moses (cf. John 1:17; 5:46; 7:19, 23). Though many modern biblical scholars doubt the Mosaic authorship of most of the book, there is little evidence within the book itself to warrant such skepticism. Generally, the question of the authorship of Genesis is taken up within the context of theories regarding the literary history of the narratives found within the Pentateuch as a whole. Similarly, questions of the authorship of Genesis have been bound up with doubts regarding the historicity of many of the narratives as well as varying assessments of the nature and purpose of the narratives themselves. Fortunately, an understanding and an appreciation of the book are not dependent on a final answer to these and other introductory questions. In the final analysis, an understanding of the book and its message comes from reading the book itself. No amount of historical and literary scholarship can replace the simple reading of the text as the primary means for determining the book's nature and purpose.

We must distinguish at least two forms of background material in the study of Genesis: (1) the historical background or context within which the book was written and (2) the historical background or context of the events recorded in the book. In the first we have in mind a specific time and place in which the book was composed. We look for the occasion of the writing of the book, who wrote it, and for whom it was written. In the second we must look over a wide-ranging array of settings for the events of the book itself, taking us from the Garden of Eden to the Flood, to the building of the city of Babylon, to the land of the patriarchs, and, finally, to the land of Egypt. In the present section we will discuss the background of Genesis in the second sense of the term—the background of the events of the book. Below, under the Authorship of Genesis, we will discuss the background and context within which the book was written.

For purposes of historical background, the events of Genesis can be divided into two types. On the one hand are the events that happened on a global or even cosmic scale: e.g., the Creation (chs. 1–2) and the Flood (chs. 6–8). On the other hand are the events that happened only in a very isolated, localized way: e.g., Noah's drunkenness (ch. 9) and Abraham's vision (ch. 15). By far the great majority of events in Genesis happened within a limited sphere of time and location and can best be described simply as "family matters." The narratives of the book turn from major catastrophies, such as the Flood or the destruction of Sodom and Gomorrah, to seemingly incidental encounters between private individuals. Significantly, both the major and the individual types of events are the most difficult historical events to reconstruct by modern historical methods. On the whole, events such as the Creation and the Flood do not belong to the field of historical research at all. They rather fall in the domain of the natural sciences: astronomy, geology, and biology. A study of the Flood, which evidentially appears to have been global in scope, would be the task of the science of geology, not history. On the other hand, isolated events in the lives of a few individuals like Abraham and his family can be studied only in the general terms of historical and cultural anthropology.

2. Unity

The Book of Genesis is characterized by both an easily discernible unity and a noticeable lack of uniformity. The history of the study of the book is marked by the tendency to stress one of these characteristics over against the other. Critical scholarship tends to see the lack of uniformity of style and vocabulary as a sign of the lack of unity in the structure and message of the book. Conservatives, on the other hand, often ignore the rough edges in the narratives, thinking that in so doing they are safeguarding the unity of the book. What appears to be necessary to sustain a realistic understanding of the unity of the book is an appreciation of the nature of its composition and an understanding of its structure.

Much like the writers of the NT Gospels and the later historical books of the OT (e.g., Kings and Chronicles), the writer of the Book of Genesis appears to have composed his work from "archival" records of God's great deeds in the past. We know from references within the early historical books that such records were maintained at an early stage in Israel's history (Exod 17:14; Num 21:14; Josh 10:13); so it is not unlikely that similar records were kept at far earlier stages within the individual households of the patriarchs and their tribal ancestors. In any event, the narratives within the Book of Genesis appear to be largely made up of small, self-contained stories worked together into larger units by means of various geographical and genealogical tables. If such is, in fact, the case, one should not expect to find absolute uniformity of style, etc., among all the individual narratives any more than an absolute uniformity can be expected in the later historical books (e.g., Kings, Chronicles, or the Gospels). Indeed, we would more likely expect the writer, working under the direction of God, to have preserved his records just as he had received them, sacrificing uniformity for the sake of historical faithfulness.

The unity of the Book of Genesis, therefore, should be seen in its compositional strategy as a whole rather than in an absolutely smooth and uniform narrative. For example, the short narrative about building the city of Babylon (11:1–9) is almost entirely self-contained and shows little external relationship with other narratives within its immediate context. Yet the narrative plays a strategic role in the development of one of the major themes in the book: the restoration of the primeval blessing through the call of Abraham. How does the author bring about this theme using the Babylon narrative? By placing the narrative between two genealogies of "Shem," the author establishes a relationship between the central point of the narrative—"Let us make a name ['Shem'] for ourselves" (11:4)—and the central point of the patriarchal narratives—"and God said, 'I will make your name ["Shem"] great' " (12:2a). Thus the genealogies of "Shem" provide a narrative link between the story of the city of Babylon and the account of the call of Abraham. The picture of the narratives of Genesis that emerges from such observations is that of a carefully wrought account of Israel's early history fashioned from the narratives and genealogical tables of Israel's own ancestral archives.

3. Authorship, Date, and Place of Origin

The question naturally arises as to who wrote or composed the final account of the Book of Genesis. Who was responsible for putting all the narratives together into the larger picture? As part of the Pentateuch, the composer of Genesis likely would be the same as that of the Pentateuch as a whole. Like most biblical books, however, the name of the author of the entire Pentateuch is not stated, leaving us little to go on for the Book of Genesis. Nowhere in the work does the author refer to himself or identify himself.

Early and reliable tradition has ascribed the authorship of the Pentateuch to Moses; and it is a fact that throughout the pentateuchal narratives it is Moses who is most closely associated with the writing of the material that is contained in the Pentateuch. For example, Moses recorded the details of the battle with the Amalekites (Exod 17:14). Also, most—if not all—of the laws recorded in the Pentateuch were written down by Moses as they were dictated to him by the Lord (e.g., Exod 20:1). Later biblical texts such as Joshua 8:31–32 likewise speak of the literary contribution of Moses in the laws contained in the Pentateuch. It appears relatively certain that Jesus and the writers of the NT believed that Moses was the author of the Pentateuch (e.g., John 5:46). While we may concur with these later biblical authors, we should not lose sight of the fact that the Pentateuch itself comes to us as an anonymous work and was apparently intended to be read as such.

4. Purpose[1]

Since the purpose of the Book of Genesis is intricately bound up with the purpose of the Pentateuch, we shall address briefly the question of the overall purpose of the Pentateuch.

a. *Compositional analysis of the Pentateuch*

Whatever one's view of the origin and diversity of the individual parts of the Pentateuch, it is widely held today that the canonical Pentateuch exhibits a unified structure with a common purpose. The task of discovering the purpose of a work as large and diverse as the Pentateuch is best achieved by means of compositional analysis, which basically describes the method and techniques used by an author. What large units of text did he use to build the final text? What functions do the individual units play in light of the completed whole? What final touches did the author give to the text that determine how it is to be read and received? What is the religious and theological viewpoint of the final text? These are just some of the probing questions that are used to determine the structure of a text.

It has been long recognized that the final shaping of the canonical Pentateuch involved the sorting and placement of material consisting of at least four distinct literary types: narrative, poetry, law, and genealogy. The genealogical texts play an important role in the early sections of the Pentateuch, especially in the Book of Genesis, but do not lead to fruitful conclusions about the shape or structure of the Pentateuch as a whole. A similar verdict can be drawn from a consideration of the large legal collections within the Pentateuch. The importance of such collections is beyond dispute, but they do not appear to be the means by which the whole of the Pentateuch has been shaped.

A close study of the author's use of narrative and poetic texts, however, sheds considerable light on the final shape of the work. The technique of using a poetic speech and a short epilogue to conclude a narrative is well known in biblical literature and occurs frequently within recognizable segments of the Pentateuch itself.[2] The Creation account in Genesis 1 and 2 concludes with the short poetic

---

[1] The material presented in this section can be found in an expanded form in the author's article "The Canonical Approach to the OT: Its Effect on Understanding Prophecy," JETS 30 (September 1987): 307ff.

[2] The stylistic features of the narrative in chs. 1–4 are as follows: The beginning of a new narrative section is marked by a waw + subject + perfect (QATAL) (cf. 3:1; 4:1; see Walter Gross, *Syntaktische Erscheinungen am Anfang Althebräischer Erzählungen: Hintergrund und Vordergrund*, Supplements to Vetus Testamentum [Leiden: E.J. Brill, 1981], pp. 131–45). The sequence within a narrative unit is maintained with WAYYIQTOL verbs. The conclusion of a unit is marked by the waw + subject + perfect that begins the next unit as well as the presence of poetic texts followed by a short epilogue (2:23–24; 3:14–24; 4:23–26). This stylistic feature also marks the conclusion of the Book of Genesis as a whole (chs. 49–50) and the conclusion of the Pentateuch (Deut 32–34). On the basis of such boundary markers, chapters 1 and 2 are part of a single unit, leaving only 1:1 outside this unit. The relationship of 1:1 to the rest of the narrative has become a vexing question (see Notes on 1:1).

The grammatical and syntactical analysis throughout this commentary will proceed on the grounds that the Hebrew clause is the most basic unit of the text. The system for describing the verbal clause consists of marking the presence or absence of the conjunction "waw," the type of verbal predicate (QATAL, YIQTOL, etc.), and the position of the verb. In the last case the position of the verb is marked only for whether or not it falls at the beginning of the clause. Thus the clause *berē'šîṯ bārā' 'elōhîm* can be described as 0 + X + QATAL, which means the clause does not have the conjunction "waw," the verbal predicate is QATAL (a perfect), and the verb does not fall at the beginning of the clause. This last feature is marked with the "X". It simply signals that a clause constituent other than a verb occupies the first position in the clause.

discourse of Adam (2:23) followed by an epilogue (v.24). The account of the Fall in chapter 3 concludes with a poetic discourse (vv.14–19) and an epilogue (vv.20–24). The account of Cain in chapter 4 concludes with a poetic discourse (vv.23–24) and an epilogue (vv.25–26). The fact that this same pattern can be found throughout Genesis (see Notes on 1:1) suggests that it was an important part of the compositional technique of the author of the book. Most notably is the occurrence of this pattern in the Joseph story (chs. 37–48), which concludes with the poetic discourse of Jacob's blessing of Ephraim and Manasseh (48:15–16, 20).

More importantly, however, the poetic speech–short epilogue pattern recurs at a much higher level within the entire Pentateuch, suggesting that the technique was extended as part of the structure embracing the whole of the book. First, the pattern is found in the inclusion of the large poetic text (49:1–27) at the close of the patriarchal narratives, along with the epilogue of chapter 50. Second, the two major narrative units that follow that of Genesis—the Exodus narratives and the wilderness narratives—are both concluded by a similar poetic section, Exodus 15 and Numbers 23–24. Finally, the pattern can be seen to embrace the whole of the Pentateuch in that the whole of the narrative of the Pentateuch, which stretches from Genesis 1 through Deuteronomy, is concluded by the poetic "Song of Moses" (Deut 32–33) and the epilogue of chapter 34.

If such a compositional scheme lies behind the final shaping of the Pentateuch, as it appears, it would be wise to begin here with the question of the compositional purpose of the book. Are there any clues lying along the seams of these large units that point to the author's ultimate purpose? If so, we should be guided by them in any further probings into the author's purpose at a lower level in the text. We will begin our investigation of the compositional purpose of the Pentateuch with a closer look along the seams of these large units of narrative and poetry. Here we will attempt to uncover the basic hermeneutic of the author of the Pentateuch and from there demonstrate the use of that hermeneutic at lower levels in the text.

b. *Narrative/poetic seams in the Pentateuch*

At three macro-structural junctures in the Pentateuch, the author has spliced a major poetic discourse onto the end of a large unit of narrative (Gen 49; Num 24; Deut 31). A close look at the material lying between and connecting the narrative and poetic sections reveals the presence of a homogeneous compositional stratum. It is most noticeably marked by the recurrence of the same terminology and narrative motifs. In each of the three segments, the central narrative figure (Jacob, Balaam, Moses) calls an audience together (imperative: "Gather around" [*hē'āsᵉp̱û*], Gen 49:1; "Come" [*lᵉḵāh*], Num 24:14; "Assemble" [*haqhîlû*], Deut 31:28) and proclaims (cohortative: "so I can tell you" [*wᵉ'aggîḏāh*], Gen 49:1; "let me warn you" [*'î'āṣᵉḵā*], Num 24:14; "so that I can speak" [*wa'ᵃḏabbᵉrāh*], Deut 31:28) what will happen (*yiqrā'*, Gen 49:1; "will do" [*ya'ᵃśeh*], Num 24:14; "will fall" [*wᵉqārā'ṯ*], Deut 31:29) in "days to come" (*bᵉ'aḥᵃrîṯ hayyāmîm*, Gen 49:1; Num 24:14; Deut 31:29).

The brief narrative prologue to the poetic text in Genesis 49 tells us that the central figure, Jacob, had called together (*hē'āsᵉp̱û*, "gather") his sons to announce to them "what will happen to you in days to come" (*'ēṯ 'ᵃšer-yiqrā' 'eṯḵem bᵉ'aḥᵃrîṯ hayyāmîm*, 49:1). Thus, however we may want to translate the terminology he used in this seam introducing the poetic discourse of Jacob, the author has provided the reader with an indispensable clue to its meaning. Jacob's poetic discourse was about "what will happen" (*yiqrā'*) "in days to come" (*b*[e]*'aḥ*[a]*rîṯ hayyāmîm*).

In an identical macro-structural position within the seam connecting the poetic text of Deuteronomy 32 with the whole preceding narrative of the Pentateuch, we find another narrative prologue with the same terminology and motif. The central figure, Moses, had called together (*haqhîlû*, Deut 31:28 [NIV, "Assemble"]) the elders of the tribes to announce to them the "disaster" (v.29) that "will fall upon you in the end of days" (*w*[e]*qārā'ṯ '*[e]*ṯkem b*[e]*'aḥ*[a]*rîṯ hayyāmîm*, Deut 31:29, lit. tr.). Again the reader is afforded an all-important clue to the meaning of the poetic text. It was about "what will happen" (*w*[e]*qārā'ṯ;* NIV, "will fall") in the "days to come" (*b*[e]*'aḥ*[a]*rîṯ hayyāmîm*). In the seams connecting both poetic texts, Genesis 49 and Deuteronomy 32, to the preceding narrative segments, and using the same terminology (*qārā' b*[e]*'aḥ*[a]*rîṯ hayyāmîm*), the author has inserted an identical message to the reader as a clue that the poetic discourses are to be read "eschatologically."

At one other crucial juncture connecting the large units of poetic and narrative texts in the Pentateuch (Num 24:14), the same terminology (*b*[e]*'aḥ*[a]*rîṯ hayyāmîm*, "in days to come") occurs. Here, in the narrative prologue to the last words of Balaam, the author again provides the reader with the necessary hermeneutical clue to the meaning of the poetic texts. Again it has to do with the "days to come" (*b*[e]*'aḥ*[a]*rîṯ hayyāmîm*). As in the other two passages, the events that lie ahead in the future days are revealed in the last words of the central narrative figure, Balaam.

Such convergence of macro-structure, narrative motifs, and terminology among these three strategically important parts of the Pentateuch can hardly be accidental. The fact that *b*[e]*'aḥ*[a]*rîṯ hayyāmîm* occurs only one other time in the Pentateuch, and that also within a macro-structural seam (Deut 4), argues strongly for our taking these connecting segments to be part of the final work that went into giving the Pentateuch its present shape. To state it clearly, these connecting segments reveal the work of the final composer or author of the Pentateuch. As such they are also a clear indication of the hermeneutic of this author. Not only does he show throughout his work an intense interest in events of the past. The further fact that he repeatedly and strategically returns to the notion of the *b*[e]*'aḥ*[a]*rîṯ hayyāmîm* in giving his work its final shape reveals that his interest lies in the future as well as in the past.

To summarize what appears to be the overall strategy of the author in these three segments, we might say that one of the central concerns lying behind the final shape of the Pentateuch is an attempt to uncover an inherent relationship between the past and the future. That which happened to God's people in the past portends of events that still lie in the future (*b*[e]*'aḥ*[a]*rîṯ hayyāmîm*, "in days to come"). Or to say it another way, the past is seen as a lesson of the future. For our purposes these observations lead to the following conclusion. A consideration of the macro-structural strategy lying behind the final shape of the Pentateuch suggests the author worked within a clearly defined hermeneutic. Because of the terminology he uses (viz., *b*[e]*'aḥ*[a]*rîṯ hayyāmîm*), we could call it an eschatological reading of his historical narratives. The narrative texts of past events are presented as pointers to events that are yet future. Past events foreshadow the future. Thus we can see that such a hermeneutic leads to a form of "narrative typology." We should, then, look for signs of such a typology in the composition of the smaller units of narrative in the Pentateuch and the Book of Genesis.

c. *A narrative typology*

A small narrative segment that has attracted an extraordinary amount of attention over the years is the account of Abraham's visit to Egypt in Genesis 12:10–20. The similarities between this narrative and that of Genesis 20 and 26 are well known. Such similarities are most often taken to be a sign of historical or literary dependency. Another way to view the similarities, however, is to see them as part of a larger typological scheme intending to show that future events are often foreshadowed in events of the past (see quote by Cassuto in commentary on 12:1–10). In fact, many of the similarities in the patriarchal narratives may have originated out of such a scheme of narrative typology. Further evidence suggesting that this may be the case comes from a comparison between Genesis 12:10–20 and the large narrative unit that deals with the Israelites' sojourn in Egypt (Gen 41–Exod 12). The chart there suggests that the composition of Genesis 12:10–20 has been intentionally structured to prefigure or foreshadow the events of Israel's sojourn in Egypt.

If the similarities between these two narratives are not merely accidental, then it is clear that some sort of "narrative typology" lies behind their composition. The author wants to show that the events of the past are pointers to those of the future. One interesting confirmation that this particular text was in fact intended to be read in such a way is the role played by Lot within the narrative. It can hardly be accidental that Genesis 12:10–20, which forms the frontispiece to the Lot narratives, is virtually duplicated, as a kind of *inclusio*, in Genesis 20, which comes after the last of the narratives dealing with Lot. This is especially noticeable in light of the fact that chapter 20 is both chronologically and geographically out of place in its narrative context. The positioning of the Lot narratives between these two remarkably similar narratives about Abraham is apparently a reflection of the narrative strategy.

Of special interest is the fact that in Genesis 12:10–13:4, Lot occupies the same position as that of the "mixed multitude" (*ʿēreḇ*, Exod 12:38; NIV, "other people") in the narrative of Genesis 41–Exodus 12. In other words, the author appears to want to draw the reader's attention to the identification of Lot with the *ʿēreḇ*. It is as if Lot is seen as a prefiguration of the *ʿēreḇ* that comes out of Egypt with the Israelites. Along this same line it is significant that the last narrative dealing with Lot shows us that he is the father of the Moabites and the Ammonites (Gen 19:36–38), the very group that is prohibited from taking part in the congregational worship (Deut 23:3–4). Thus, as Lot is finally excluded from the assembly of Abraham, the reader is reminded that there is to be no *ʿēreḇ* in the Israelite assembly.

The question that naturally arises is whether such a typological reading of these narratives was ever appreciated by the original or early readers of the book. Fortunately, in this case we have a clear witness to the fact that it was. In Nehemiah 13:1–3, the problem of marriage to foreign wives was handled by an appeal to Deuteronomy 23:3–4, where the Ammonites and Moabites were restricted from the worship assembly. The author of the Book of Nehemiah then remarks that when they heard this, they separated out from them "all who were of foreign descent" (*ʿēreḇ*, Neh 13:3). Since this is the only other occurrence of the term *ʿēreḇ* in the Hebrew Bible, and since the use of *ʿēreḇ* in Exodus 12:38 has no association with the Moabites and Ammonites, the association between the *ʿēreḇ* and the Moabites and Ammonites could only have come from an association of the term with Lot and his two daughters. In other words, Nehemiah appears to have read the Genesis narratives "typologically," identifying Lot, the father of the Moabites and the Ammonites, with the *ʿēreḇ*.

Such evidence offers a very early assessment of how the original readers of the Pentateuch understood and read the Pentateuchal narratives.

d. *Summary*

The final shape of the Pentateuch reflects an interest in reading the historical narratives both typologically and eschatologically. The events of the past are read as pointers to the future. The future is portrayed as "like" the past. Second, the internal composition of smaller narrative units also reflects this same interest in typology. For example, Abraham was presented as a picture or type of the future Israel, and Lot was presented as a type of the future "mixed multitude."

5. Literary Form[3]

Except for the scattered poetic sections in the Book of Genesis, the overall literary form of the book is historical narrative, which is the re-presentation of past events for the purpose of instruction. Two dimensions are always at work in shaping such narratives: (1) the course of the historical event itself and (2) the viewpoint of the author who recounts the events. This dual aspect of historical narrative means that one must not only look at the course of the event in its historical setting, but one must also look for the purpose and intention of the author in recounting the event. In what follows we will outline briefly some general principles on how we will go about the task of finding the author's intent and purpose in recounting the events of the Book of Genesis in historical narrative.

a. *Assessing the structure*

The most influential yet subtle feature of an author's work in relating historical events is the overall framework within which he arranges his account. Some would call this the literary context. Perhaps a more usable term would be to talk about the "structure" of the passage. What this means is that there is always an internal relationship of each segment of a narrative to the other segments of the narrative and to the narrative viewed as a whole. When we speak of structure, then, we are speaking of "the total set of relationships within a given narrative unit."

General structural elements to look for in every historical narrative are simple but nonetheless important. They include an introduction, a conclusion, sequence, disjuncture, repetition, deletion, description, and dialogue. These elements combine to form the building blocks of the larger narrative units. For example, Genesis 1:1–2:4a is clearly recognizable as a unit of historical narrative. It has an introduction (1:1), a body (1:2–2:3), and a conclusion (2:4a). These three segments form a unit. Within this unit several structural elements combine to tie this passage (Gen 1:1–2:4a) together and give it a specific meaning. One of the more obvious elements is the repetition of the phrase "evening and morning," which divides the passage into a seven-day scheme. Creation forms a period of one work week concluding with a rest day. Already in this simple structural framework is the tilting of the account that

[3] The material presented in this section can be found in an expanded form in the author's article "Exegetical Notes: Genesis 1:1–2:2a," *Trinity Journal* 5, New Series 1 (Spring 1984): 73–82.

betrays the interests of the author—Creation is viewed in terms of man's own work week.

Another, more subtle, structural element tying the passage together is the tight sentence pattern (or sequence) within which the events of Creation are recorded. This is apparent in the almost monotonous string of "ands" in the EVs of chapter 1. In contrast to this smooth sequence, however, is an abrupt disjuncture at 1:2, in effect shoving this verse outside the regular sequence of the chapter. A study of the author's style in Genesis shows that when he wants to begin a specific topic much narrower than the preceding subject matter, he uses such a technique of disjuncture.[4]

Here, then, at the beginning of the account, the structure reveals the aim of the author: to narrow the scope of his narrative from the universe (1:1) to the land (1:2–31).[5] This is quite a remarkable turning point in the account of Creation and should not be overlooked by anyone attempting to follow the author's intent in this chapter. Structure, then, implies purpose, and that in turn suggests a central concern or integration point that gives a passage its meaning and direction.

In the two examples just cited, it is suggested that the central concern of Genesis 1 focuses on man and the land. Certainly we need more than these two examples to be convinced that this is the central concern; but the cumulative effect of further observations confirms that this is the direction or purpose behind the framework of the account. When we have observed the internal structure of a passage, as we briefly have done with Genesis 1:1–2:4a, we have not completed the task of assessing the total structural relationship of the passage to the broader context within which it is found. There may indeed be a whole series of further structural ties between the passage and its literary environment.

Here we are faced with the problem of where to fix the outside limits to a passage within a historical narrative. It is very often the case in the OT narratives that the division of the narrative into "books" cuts across very tightly constructed segments (e.g., Gen 1–Exod 1:7 is a structurally complete unit not recognized by those who divided the Pentateuch into five parts). Beyond these literary units there lie, as well, the larger borders of the OT canon and the subsequent canon of the Old and New Testaments.

In working with Genesis 1:1–2:4a, we can safely set out perimeters around the Pentateuch (Genesis–Deuteronomy) as the largest meaningful unit (literarily). Since it comes first, it also seems safe to say that Genesis 1:1–2:4a is to be considered an introduction to the Pentateuch. Once the largest unit of historical narrative has been drawn, a twofold task remains: (1) to determine the central concern of this unit and (2) to develop the contribution of the smaller unit (Gen 1:2–4a) to the concern of the whole. The central concern of the large narrative unit is not always immediately apparent but usually becomes clearer with a trial-and-error effort to relate the parts to the whole. This amounts, in practice, to reading through the entire unit and formulating a general statement of the overall theme. This theme is then checked against further readings of the text. Each reading should produce a clearer idea of the whole, which in turn should cast more light on the parts or segments.

---

[4]See Gen 3:1. See also Gross, *Syntaktische*, pp. 131–45.

[5]For this commentary the English word "earth" will be retained in its use in the collocation "the heavens and the earth," but otherwise it will be rendered "land," the English word more consonant with the Hebrew *'ereṣ*. In this way the full range of meaning of *'ereṣ* is left intact, and the text remains open to important interpretive options (see Notes on 1:2).

Since we have drawn the Pentateuch as the largest unit with a meaningful structural relationship to Genesis 1:1–2:4a, the question we should now ask is whether there is a center to the Pentateuch. We suggest that the central concern of the Pentateuch should be described in the following way.

First, it should be pointed out that the most prominent event and the most far-reaching theme in the Pentateuch, viewed entirely on its own, is the covenant between God and Israel established at Mount Sinai. The meaning of this event as it is described in the Pentateuch can be summarized in the following cluster of themes: (1) God comes to dwell with Israel, (2) Israel is a chosen people, (3) God gives Israel the land, (4) Israel must obey God's will, and (5) salvation or judgment is contingent on Israel's obedience.

If we leave these ideas in their original dress, we find that they are clothed in the metaphor of the ancient Near Eastern monarch: God, the Great King, grants to his obedient vassal-prince the right to dwell in his land and promises protection from his enemies. Somewhat more generally, this cluster of ideas may go by the name "theocracy," or the kingdom of God. However we may state it, this rule of God among his people Israel is the central concern of the Pentateuch.

There is, however, more that can be said about the intention of the author of the Pentateuch. We can say, namely, something about what he is telling his readers about the covenant at Sinai. This can be summarized in the following three points:

1. The author of the Pentateuch wants to draw a connecting link between God's original plan of blessing for mankind and his establishment of the covenant with Israel at Sinai (this will be developed in the commentary). Put simply, the author sees the covenant at Sinai as God's plan to restore his blessing to mankind through the descendants of Abraham (Gen 12:1–3; Exod 2:24).

2. The author of the Pentateuch wants to show that the covenant at Sinai failed to restore God's blessing to mankind because Israel failed to trust God and obey his will.

3. The author of the Pentateuch wants to show that God's promise to restore the blessing would ultimately succeed because God himself would one day give to Israel a heart to trust and obey him (Deut 30:1–10).

The outlook of the Pentateuch, then, might be described as "eschatological," for it looks to the future as the time when God's faithful promise (blessing) would be fulfilled. The past, Mount Sinai, had ended in failure from the author's perspective. The message of the Pentateuch, however, is hope: God's people should trust and obey him and, like Abraham, have faith in his promises. Thus the primary subject matter of the Pentateuch is the Sinai covenant. The author saw God's election of Israel and the establishment of the covenant at Sinai as the central religious and theological concern. The Pentateuch was his answer to the concern raised by the covenant in the same way that Galatians was the apostle Paul's answer to the same concern. The Pentateuch, therefore, was both the author's explanation of the place Sinai occupied in God's plan and his explication of the lessons to be drawn from the experience.

It is important to see that while the Pentateuch is about the Sinai covenant, it is not the document of that covenant. The Pentateuch does contain documents that were a part of the Sinai covenant, e.g., the Ten Commandments (Exod 20), the covenant code (Exod 21–23), tabernacle instruction (Exod 25–31), and the law of sacrifice (Lev 1–7); but the Pentateuch, as a literary document, is fundamentally different from a document of the Sinai covenant. What this means is that the Pentateuch is a document that looks at the Sinai covenant as an object under consideration. It was attempting to evaluate the Sinai covenant from a perspective that was not the same as that of the covenant itself. Like the other historical books of the OT, the Prophets, and the NT, the Pentateuch represents a look back at the failure of Sinai and a look forward to a time of fulfillment (e.g., Deut 30).

This brings us to the question of the contribution of the smaller narrative unit (Gen 1:1–2:4a) to the central concern of the whole (the Pentateuch). In other words, if we are right in saying that Genesis 1 is an introduction to the Pentateuch, then we should ask what it introduces about the Pentateuch's central concern, that is, what it introduces about the covenant at Sinai. The following principles are intended to show how a segment of historical narrative can contribute to the central concern of the larger narrative of which it is a part.

b. *The principle of selectivity*

No historical narrative is a complete account of all that occurred in a given event or series of events. The author must select those events that most effectively relate not only what happened but also the meaning and significance of what happened. We can formulate a working description of this principle of selection in this way: The author selects and arranges those features of a historical event that most characteristically portray the meaning of the event as conceived by him.

A close study of Genesis 1:1–2:4a shows that a careful and purposeful selection has been made in the composition of the Creation account and that the features selected do, in fact, provide an introduction to the Sinai covenant—that is, the Creation account tells the reader information that makes the author's view of the Sinai covenant understandable.

One way to ferret out this selection is to ask, What general features of Creation (the subject matter) would I expect to find in Genesis 1:1–2:4a that are not found in the narrative? Where, for example, is the account of the creation of the angels? Where, for that matter, is the account of the creation of the stars and the galaxies? Certainly the creation of these bodies is stated as a brute fact in v.1 and is editorially alluded to in v.16; but relative to the detail of the rest of the account in chapter 1, we could almost say that the author has passed them by. He has chosen rather to concentrate on the creation and preparation of the land. If we judge from the topics selected in Genesis 1:1–2:4a, we can say that the author has only three specific subjects in his account of Creation: God, man, and the land. Having said that there is little mention of the creation of the rest of the universe, we should notice that the creation of the sun and moon is given considerable attention. But we should be quick to note, as well, that neither of these celestial bodies is mentioned in its own right. Rather their creation is recounted in terms of the role they play in the affairs of men on the land: "to separate the day from the night, and let them serve as signs to mark seasons and days and years" (1:14–15).

At this point we need to show how the two principles of structure and selectivity work together to give a narrative passage its meaning. First, we have already noted that an internal structural element has defined the scope of the Genesis 1:1–2:4a Creation account. That is, the disjuncture at 1:2 is used by the author to focus his Creation account on the land. This is consistent with what our analysis of the selection showed: one of the author's three specific topics is the land.

Now we can turn to the external structural relationship of Genesis 1:1–2:4a to the Pentateuch and ask, What does the land as a subject have to do with the Sinai covenant? Or, more precisely stated, How does what Genesis 1:1–2:4a records about the land serve as an introduction to the author's view of the covenant at Sinai? When Genesis 1:1–2:4a speaks of God's creation and preparation of the land, we are, in fact, introduced to one of the central elements of the Sinai covenant, namely the promise of God to give the land to Israel: "If you obey me fully and keep my covenant, then out of all nations you will be my treasured possession among all the nations because all the land is mine" (Exod 19:5, pers. tr.; cf. Jer 27:5). What, then, does Genesis 1:1–2:4a tell us about the land? It tells us that God is its owner. He created and prepared the land, and he can give it to whomever he chooses (Jer 27:5). In the ancient world—as in our own—the right to own land and grant it to others formed the basis of an ordered society. The author of the Pentateuch, then, is quick to point out that the promise of the land to Israel, made effective in the Sinai covenant, was in every way a right justly belonging to God.

Another example of the interrelationship between structure and selection can be seen in the view of God in Genesis 1:1–2:4a. When viewed as an introduction (structural relationship) to the covenant at Sinai, we can see that Genesis 1 presents a very important view of the covenant God: he is the Creator of the universe (Gen 1:1). Because Israel had come to know God through the covenant in a close and personal way, a certain theological pressure existed that, if left unchecked, could—and at times did—erode a proper view of God. This pressure was the tendency to localize and nationalize God as the God of Israel alone (Mic 3:11)—a God who exists solely for Israel and for their blessing.

Over against this lesser view of God stands the message of Genesis 1 with its clear introduction to the God who created the universe and who has blessed all humanity. From the point of view of the author of the Pentateuch, the God of the covenant is the Creator of the universe; and he has a plan of blessing for all people. This is the theological foundation of all subsequent missionary statements in the Bible.

We can conclude this section with a summary of Genesis 1:1–2:4a. The author of the Pentateuch intends his Creation account to relate to his readers that God, the Creator of the universe, has prepared the land as a home for his special creature, man, and that he has a plan of blessing for all of his creatures.[6]

[6] Brevard S. Childs ("The Exegetical Significance of Canon for the Study of the Old Testament," *Supplements to Vetus Testamentum* [Leiden: E.J. Brill, 1978], pp. 66–80) has pointed to the fact that the literary-canonical function of the "*toledoth*" (NIV, "account of") heading in 2:4a is to join the Creation account of chapter 1 with that of chapter 2. The formula functions throughout Genesis to bind the deeds of the father to those of the son(s)—5:1; 6:9; 10:1; 11:10. Just as there is continuity between the deeds of the father and those of the sons, so also in Creation God's works follow in orderly succession (Gunkel). The use of the "*toledoths*" in Genesis is part of an overall plan of the writer to stress the "likeness" between events and persons (cf. 5:1–3). Here in 2:4a the events of chapter 1 are drawn into a relationship of "likeness" with those of chapter 2 as a way of explicating the central theme of 1:2–2:3 ("man in God's image") by the narrative of 2:4b–25. The writer's point in drawing a connection between the two accounts is to show that the purpose of man's creation, as it is portrayed in chapter 2, is to reflect God's "likeness." In thus drawing the analogy between God and man, the writer has prepared the way for the development of a central theme in the Pentateuch and in Genesis 2, the relationship of work and worship (see comments on 2:2–3 and 2:15).

6. Bibliography

Commentaries

Aalders, G. Charles. *Genesis.* Bible Student's Commentary. Grand Rapids: Zondervan, 1981.
Calvin, John. *Commentaries on the First Book of Moses Called Genesis.* Grand Rapids: Baker Book House, 1979.
Cassuto, U. *A Commentary on the Book of Genesis.* Jerusalem: Magnes, 1961.
Delitzsch, Franz. *A New Commentary on Genesis.* Translated by Sophia Taylor. Edinburgh: T. & T. Clark, 1888.
Dillmann, A. *Genesis Critically and Exegetically Expounded.* Translated by Wm. B. Stevenson. Edinburgh: T. & T. Clark, 1897.
Gunkel, Hermann. *Genesis Übersetzt und Erklärt.* 9th edition. Göttingen: Vandenhoeck & Ruprecht, 1977.
Heinisch, Paul. *Das Buch Genesis Übersetzt und Erklärt.* Verlag von Peter Hanstein, 1930.
Hoberg, Gottfried. *Die Genesis nach dem Literalsinn Erklärt.* Herdersche Verlagshandlung, 1908.
Holzinger, H. *Genesis.* Kurzer Handkommentar zum Alten Testament. Freiburg, 1898.
Jacob, Benno. *Das erste Buch der Tora Genesis: Übersetzt und Erklärt.* Berlin: Schocken Verlag, 1934.
Keil, Carl Friedrich. *Genesis und Exodus.* 3d edition. Brunnen Verlag, 1878.
———. *Biblical Commentary on the Old Testament.* KD. Reprint edition. Grand Rapids: Eerdmans, 1971.
Kidner, Derek. *Genesis: An Introduction and Commentary.* London: Tyndale, 1967.
König, Eduard. *Die Genesis: Eingeleitet, Übersetzt und Erklärt.* Gütersloh: Bertelsmann, 1919.
Lamy, Thomas J. *Commentarium in Librum Geneseos.* Mecheln: Dessain, 1883.
Leupold, H.C. *Exposition of Genesis.* 2 vols. Grand Rapids: Baker, 1942.
Procksch, D. Otto. *Die Genesis Übersetzt und Erklärt.* Kommentar zum Alten Testament. Deichertsche Verlagsbuchhandlung, 1913.
Rad, Gerhard von. *Genesis: A Commentary.* Philadelphia: Westminster, 1961.
Skinner, John. *A Critical and Exegetical Commentary on Genesis.* Edinburgh: T. & T. Clark, 1910.
Speiser, E.A. *Genesis: Introduction, Translation, and Notes.* Garden City, N.Y.: Doubleday, 1964.
Thomas, W.H. Griffith. *Genesis: A Devotional Commentary.* Grand Rapids: Eerdmans, 1946.
Wenham, Gordon J. *Genesis 1–15.* Word Biblical Commentary. Waco: Word, 1987.
Westermann, Claus. *Genesis.* 2 vols. Neukirchener Vluyn: Neukirchener, 1981–83.

Special Studies

Alter, Robert. *The Art of Biblical Narrative.* New York: Basic Books, 1981.
Blum, Erhard. *Die Komposition der Vätergeschichte.* Neukirchener Vluyn: Neukirchener Verlag, 1984.
König, Eduard. *Historisch-Comparative Syntax der Hebräischen Sprache.* Leipzig: J.C. Hinrichs, 1897.

7. Outline

I. Introduction to the Patriarchs and the Sinai Covenant (1:1–11:26)
  A. The Land and the Blessing (1:1–2:25)
    1. The God of creation (1:1)
    2. Preparation of the land (1:2–2:3)
      a. First day (1:2–5)
      b. Second day (1:6–8)
      c. Third day (1:9–13)
      d. Fourth day (1:14–19)
      e. Fifth day (1:20–23)
      f. Sixth day (1:24–31)
      g. Seventh day (2:1–3)
    3. The gift of the land (2:4–24)
      a. Creation of man (2:4–7)
      b. Preparation of the garden (2:8–14)
      c. Man's place in the garden (2:15–24)
  B. The Land and the Exile (2:25–4:26)
    1. Disobedience (2:25–3:7)
      a. The transition (2:25)
      b. The tempter (3:1)
      c. The temptation (3:2–7)
    2. Judgment (3:8–20)
      a. The scene (3:8)
      b. The trial (3:9–13)
      c. The verdict (3:14–20)
    3. Protection (3:21)
    4. Exile (3:22–24)
  C. Life in Exile (4:1–26)
    1. Worship (4:1–8)
    2. Repentance (4:9–15a)
    3. Protection (4:15b–24)
    4. Blessing (4:25–26)
  D. The Story of Noah (5:1–10:32)
    1. Prologue (5:1–3)
    2. The sons of Adam (5:4–32)
    3. Epilogue (6:1–4)
    4. The Flood (6:5–9:17)
      a. The decree (6:5–12)
      b. The command to build the ark (6:13–22)
      c. The command to enter the ark (7:1–5)
      d. The floods (7:6–24)
      e. The floods abate (8:1–14)
      f. The command to exit the ark (8:15–19)
      g. The altar and the covenant (8:20–9:17)
    5. Noah's drunkenness (9:18–29)
    6. The line of Noah (10:1–32)
      a. The sons of Noah (10:1)
      b. The sons of Japheth (10:2–5)
      c. The sons of Ham (10:6–20)

d. The sons of Shem (10:21–31)
e. Epilogue (10:32)
E. The City of Babylon (11:1–9)
F. The Line of Shem (11:10–26)

II. Abraham (11:27–25:10 [11])
A. The Line of Abraham (11:27–32)
B. The Call of Abraham (12:1–9)
C. Abraham in Egypt (12:10–13:4)
D. The Lot Narratives (13:5–19:38)
1. Abraham and Lot (13:5–18)
2. Abraham and the nations (14:1–24)
3. Abraham and the covenant (15:1–21)
4. Hagar (16:1–16)
5. Abraham, Sarah, and Ishmael (17:1–27)
6. Three visitors (18:1–33)
a. Abraham's hospitality (18:1–8)
b. The promise of a son (18:9–15)
c. Sodom in the balance (18:16–22)
d. Abraham's intercession (18:23–33)
7. Lot and Sodom (19:1–38)
a. Two angels at Sodom (19:1–14)
b. Lot's deliverance (19:15–28)
c. Lot's incest (19:29–38)
E. Abraham and Abimelech (20:1–18)
F. Abraham and Isaac (21:1–25:11)
1. The birth of Isaac (21:1–7)
2. Hagar and Ishmael (21:8–21)
3. Abraham and Abimelech (21:22–34)
4. The binding of Isaac (22:1–14)
5. The angel of the Lord (22:15–19)
6. The relatives of Abraham (22:20–24)
7. Machpelah and Sarah's death (23:1–20)
8. A bride for Isaac (24:1–67)
9. Abraham's death (25:1–10 [11])

III. The Account of Ishmael (25:12–18)

IV. The Account of Isaac (25:19–35:29)
A. The Birth of Jacob and Esau (25:19–28)
B. Selling the Birthright (25:29–34)
C. Isaac and Abimelech (26:1–35)
D. The Stolen Blessing (27:1–40)
E. Jacob's Flight From Beersheba (27:41–28:5)
F. Esau's Bitterness (28:6–9)
G. Jacob at Bethel (28:10–22)
H. Jacob and Rachel (29:1–14a)
I. Jacob's Marriages (29:14b–30)
J. The Birth of Jacob's Sons (29:31–30:24)
K. Jacob and Laban's Sheep (30:25–43)
L. Jacob's Flight From Laban (31:1–21)

M. Jacob Overtaken by Laban (31:22–55)
N. Jacob's Meeting With Angels (32:1–2)
O. Messengers Sent to Esau (32:3–22)
P. Jacob's Wrestling Match (32:23–32)
Q. Jacob's Meeting With Esau (33:1–17)
R. Jacob at Shechem (33:18–34:31)
S. Jacob's Return to Bethel (35:1–15)
T. Benjamin's Birth and Rachel's Death (35:16–20)
U. The Sons of Jacob (35:21–26)
V. The Death of Isaac (35:27–29)

V. The Account of Esau (36:1–43)
A. Esau's Journey to Seir (36:1–8)
B. Esau in Seir (36:9–43)
1. The sons of Esau (36:9–19)
2. The sons of Seir the Horite (36:20–30)
3. Rulers in Edom (36:31–43)

VI. The Account of Jacob (37:1–49:33)
A. Jacob in the Land (37:1)
B. Joseph's Dreams (37:2–11)
C. Joseph's Journey to Egypt (37:12–36)
D. Judah and Tamar (38:1–30)
E. Joseph in the House of Potiphar (39:1–23)
F. Joseph in Jail (40:1–23)
G. Joseph's Interpretation of Pharaoh's Dreams (41:1–36)
H. Joseph's Exaltation Over Egypt (41:37–57)
I. Joseph's Brothers in Egypt (42:1–28)
J. Joseph's Brothers Return for Benjamin (42:29–38)
K. Joseph's Identity (43:1–45:28)
1. The second trip to Egypt (43:1–34)
2. The silver cup (44:1–34)
3. Joseph's revelation (45:1–28)
L. Jacob's Journey to Egypt (46:1–7)
M. Jacob's Sons in Egypt (46:8–27)
N. Settling in Goshen (46:28–47:12)
O. Joseph's Rule in Egypt (47:13–27)
P. Jacob's Deathbed (47:28–49:33)
1. Jacob's burial instructions (47:28–31)
2. Ephraim and Manasseh blessed (48:1–22)
3. Jacob's sons blessed (49:1–28)
4. Jacob's burial instructions repeated (49:29–33)
Q. Jacob's Death and Burial (50:1–14)

VII. The Final Joseph Narrative (50:15–26)
A. Joseph's Forgiveness (50:15–21)
B. Summary of Joseph's Life and Death (50:22–26)

Text and Exposition

I. Introduction to the Patriarchs and the Sinai Covenant (1:1–11:26)

Chapters 1–11 form an introduction to both the Book of Genesis and the Pentateuch as a whole. These chapters should be read with this dual purpose in mind. They set the stage for the narratives of the patriarchs (Gen 12–50) as well as provide the appropriate background for understanding the central topic of the Pentateuch: the Sinai covenant (Exodus–Deuteronomy).

The author of the Pentateuch has carefully selected and arranged Genesis 1–11 to serve its function as an introduction. Behind the present shape of the narrative lies a clear theological program. In nearly every section of the work, the author's theological interest can be seen. His theological perspective can be summarized in two points. First, the author intends to draw a line connecting the God of the Fathers and the God of the Sinai covenant with the God who created the world. Second, the author intends to show that the call of the patriarchs and the Sinai covenant have as their ultimate goal the reestablishment of God's original purpose in Creation. In a word, the biblical covenants are marked off as the way to a new Creation.

A. *The Land and the Blessing (1:1–2:25)*

A close look at the narrative style of the opening chapters of Genesis suggests that the first two chapters form a single unit. This unit has three primary sections. The first section is 1:1, which stands apart from the rest of chapter 1. The remaining two sections are 1:2–2:3 and 2:4b–25. The heading entitled *tôl^{e}d̲ôt̲* ("generations"; NIV, "the account of") in 2:4a serves to connect these last two sections. Two primary themes dominate the Creation account: the land and the blessing. In recounting the events of Creation, the author has selected and arranged his narrative so that these themes are allowed full development. The preparation of the "land" and the divine "blessing" are important to the author of Genesis (and the Pentateuch) because these two themes form the basis of his treatment of the patriarchal narratives and the Sinai covenant. In translating the Hebrew word *'ereṣ* "earth" in 1:1 and 1:2, the EVs have blurred the connection of these early verses of Genesis to the central theme of the "land" (*'ereṣ*) in the Pentateuch. Although *'ereṣ* can be translated by either "earth" or "land," the general term "land" in English more closely approximates the use of *'ereṣ* in chapter 1. Thus from the start the author betrays his interest in the covenant by concentrating on the *'ereṣ* in the account of Creation (see fn. 5, p. 11). "Nothing is here by chance; everything must be considered carefully, deliberately, and precisely" (von Rad, in loc.).

1. *The God of creation*

1:1

[1]In the beginning God created the heavens and the earth.

1 The account opens with a clear, concise statement about the Creator and the Creation. Its simplicity belies the depth of its content. These seven words are the foundation of all that is to follow in the Bible. The purpose of the statement is threefold: to identify the Creator, to explain the origin of the world, and to tie the work of God in the past to the work of God in the future. The Creator is identified in 1:1 as "God," that is, "Elohim" (*'ᵉlōhîm*). Although God is not further identified in v.1 (e.g., 15:7; Exod 20:2), the author appears confident that there will be no mistaking this God with any other than the God of the Fathers and the God of the covenant at Sinai. The proper context for understanding 1:1, in other words, is the whole of the Book of Genesis and the Pentateuch. Already in Genesis 2:4b, God (Elohim) is identified with the Lord (Yahweh), the God who called Abraham (Gen 12:1) and delivered Israel from Egypt (Exod 3:15).

The God of 1:1, then, is far from a faceless deity. From the perspective of the Pentateuch as a whole, he is the God who has called the Fathers into his good "land" (*'ereṣ*), redeemed them from Egypt, and led them again to the borders of the *'ereṣ*, a "land" he provided and now calls on them to enter and possess. He is the "Redeemer-Shepherd" of Jacob's blessing in 48:15. The purpose of 1:1 is not to identify this God as such but to identify him as the Creator of the universe.

It is not difficult to detect a polemic against idolatry behind the words of 1:1. By identifying God as the Creator, a crucial distinction is introduced between the God of the Fathers and the gods of the nations, gods that to the biblical authors were mere idols. God alone created the heavens and the earth. The sense of 1:1 is similar to the message in the Book of Jeremiah that Israel was to carry to all the nations: "Tell them this," Jeremiah said. " 'These gods, who did not make the heavens and the earth, will perish from the earth and from under the heavens' " (Jer 10:11). Psalm 96:5 shows that the full impact of Genesis 1:1 was appreciated by later biblical writers as well: "For all the gods of the nations are idols, but the LORD [Yahweh] made the heavens."

The statement in 1:1 not only identifies the Creator, it also explains the origin of the world. According to the sense of 1:1 (see Notes), the narrative states that God created all that exists in the universe. As it stands, the statement is an affirmation that God alone is eternal and that all else owes its origin and existence to him. The influence of this verse is reflected throughout the work of later biblical writers (e.g., Ps 33:6; John 1:3; Heb 11:3).

Equally important in 1:1 is the meaning of the phrase "In the beginning" (*bᵉrē'šîṯ*) within the framework of the Creation account and the Book of Genesis. The term "beginning" (*rē'šîṯ*) in biblical Hebrew marks a starting point of a specific duration as in "the beginning of the year" (*rē'šîṯ haššānāh*; Deut 11:12). The end of a specific period is marked by its antonym, "its end" (*'aḥᵃrîṯ*), as in Deuteronomy 11:12: "the end of the year" (lit. tr. of *'aḥᵃrîṯ šānāh*) (H.-P. Müller, THAT, p. 709).

In opening the account of Creation with the phrase "in the beginning" (*bᵉrē'šîṯ*), the author has marked Creation as the starting point of a period of time. "Hence will here be the beginning of the history which follows. . . . The history to be related from this point onwards has heaven and earth for its object, its scenes, its factors. At the head of this history stands the creation of the world as its commencement, or at all events its foundation" (Delitzsch, p. 76). By commencing this history with a "beginning" (*rē'šîṯ*), a word often paired with its antonym "end" (*'aḥᵃ rîṯ*), the author has not only commenced a history of God and his people, he has also prepared the way for the consummation of that history at "the end of time" (*'aḥᵃrîṯ*) ("Already in Gn 1:1 the concept of 'the last days' fills the mind of the reader," Procksch, p. 425).

The growing focus within the biblical canon on the "times of the end" (*'aḥᵃrîṯ hayyāmîm*) was an appropriate extension to the "end" (*'aḥᵃrîṯ*) already anticipated in the "beginning" (*rē'šîṯ*) of Genesis 1:1. The fundamental principle reflected in Genesis 1:1 and the prophetic vision of the times of the end in the rest of Scripture is that the "last things will be like the first things" (Ernst Böklen, *Die Verwandtschaft der jüdisch-christlichen mit der Parsischen Eschatologie* [Göttingen: Vandenhoeck & Ruprecht, 1902], p. 136): "Behold, I will create new heavens and a new earth" (Isa 65:17); "Then I saw a new heaven and a new earth" (Rev 21:1). The allusions to Genesis 1 and 2 in Revelation 22 illustrate the role these early chapters of Genesis played in shaping the form and content of the scriptural vision of the future (*'aḥᵃrîṯ hayyāmîm*).

Notes

1 The interpretation given to v.1 rests on the traditional reading of בְּרֵאשִׁית (*bᵉrē'šîṯ*) in the absolute state: "In the beginning." A strong case, however, can be made for reading the phrase as a construct and subordinating v.1 to vv.2–3: "When God set about to create the heavens and the earth—the world being then a formless waste . . . —God said, 'Let there be light' " (Speiser, p. 3). The implication of reading the phrase as a construct is that v.1 would then be a circumstantial clause and would no longer carry the traditional sense of "creation from nothing" (*creatio ex nihilo*). According to such a reading, the world, as unformed material, would have been present when the first act of Creation was performed, that being God's command in v.3: "Let there be light." The first act of Creation would have been the creation of light from darkness, and vv.1–3 would say nothing of an original Creation. The principle argument for this view is the lack of an article with רֵאשִׁית (*rē'šîṯ*, "beginning") in v.1. Without the article, it is maintained, *bᵉrē'šîṯ* cannot be read as an absolute ("in the beginning"); it must be read as a construct ("in beginning") (Speiser, p. 3).

In defense of the traditional view (that *bᵉrē'šîṯ* is in the absolute state), it can be said that *rē'šîṯ*, along with several other adverbials, does occur in the absolute state *without an article* (e.g., Isa 46:10; cf. König, *Syntax*, par. 294g). Thus the argument that the article *must* be with *bᵉrē'šîṯ* for it to be absolute does not hold in every case. There are other arguments that *bᵉrē'šîṯ* should not be read as an absolute (see Westermann, pp. 94ff.), but none of them is sufficient to stand against the traditional view without the central grammatical argument of the absence of the article in *bᵉrē'šîṯ* just referred to. An example such as Isa 46:10, then, is crucial in that it shows that the article is *not* necessary for the absolute state.

The examples of König (*Syntax*, par. 294g) have been contested on the grounds that they are all from poetic texts, where the use of the article varies from that of prose texts such as Gen 1 (Gross, *Syntaktische*, p. 144). But, although König has cited examples from prose texts (e.g., 3:22; 6:4), Gross's insistence that examples be cited from prose texts alone, though methodologically sound, is too demanding in light of the frequent occurrence of the article in biblical poetry. The traditional reading has in its favor both the simplicity of its style, which is consistent with the remainder of the chapter, and the finite form of the verb בָּרָא (*bārā'*, "to create"). Some have proposed that *bārā'* be vocalized as *bᵉrō'*; but 5:1, which does in fact have *bᵉrō'* following a construct, shows both that lengthy circumstantial clauses are not a feature of the style of the writer of Gen 1, and that the infinitive (*bᵉrō'*), not the perfect (*bārā'*), is the expected form for such subordinate clauses (contrasted with that of the style of Hos 1:2, where the construct is used with the perfect). Genesis 2:4b cannot be used to show that lengthy circumstantial clauses are a feature of the style of the writer because of the marked contrast between the style of 1:1–2:4a and 2:4bff.

It has long been recognized that the stylistic features of the "framework" of the Pentateuch vary markedly from that of the narrative within it. Such variations should be considered in any comparisons of style with the Pentateuch. The interpretations of the medieval Jewish scholars Rashi (השלם רשי תורה חומשי חמשה [Jerusalem: Ariel, 1986], p. 2) and Ibn Ezra (מקראות גדולות [New York: Abraham Isaac Fieldman, n.d.], p. 2) are often appealed to against the traditional view. Both scholars read *bᵉrē'šîṯ* as a construct phrase. It should be noted, however, that grammatical considerations did not motivate Rashi and Ibn Ezra in their choice. It was their own understanding about the order of Creation that led them to reject the traditional reading. Rashi, who was, as far as is known, the first to suggest the construct reading, recognized in the מֵרֵאשִׁית (*mērē'šîṯ*) of Isa 46:10 an exception to his rule that *rē'šîṯ* always occurred in the construct state. He explained this as an exception by assuming (in the guise of an interlocutor) the *rē'šîṯ* in Isa 46:10 was in fact in the construct state and was an elliptical expression for בְּרֵאשִׁית דָּבָר (*bᵉrē'šîṯ dāḇār*, lit., "in the beginning of the thing, of history, of the matter," etc.). Thus Rashi could say that the *rē'šîṯ* in the *mērē'šîṯ* of Isa 46:10 was in fact a construct phrase.

Rashi, however, would not allow for a similar reading in Gen 1:1—"In the very beginning," viz., the traditional reading—because he believed the מַיִם (*mayim*, "waters") of v.2 had already been created before the creation of the heavens and the earth in v.1. Thus v.1 could not be the "very beginning of all things" (traditional view), and consequently reading *bᵉrē'šîṯ* as an absolute was impossible.

Though the argument is subtle, it is clear that Rashi himself did not oppose the traditional reading *on grammatical grounds* but rather on the basis of the subject matter. He did not understand "the heavens and the earth" (v.1) as an expression of "totality." Rather he held the two words to refer specifically and solely to the "heavens" and "the earth" as two limited and distinct entities. He also believed that the "heavens" (שָׁמַיִם [*šāmayim*]) were created from "fire" (אֵשׁ ['*ēš*]) and "water" (מַיִם [*mayim*]). Rashi reasoned quite simply that if the "heavens" were created from fire and water in v.1, the *water* must have already been in existence prior to v.1. If such were the case, v.1 could not refer to an absolute beginning (traditional view) and so had to be read as a construct (circumstantial clause).

Ibn Ezra, who also was an early advocate of the view that *bᵉrē'šîṯ* is a construct phrase, like Rashi, held to the construct view because of the mention of water in v.2. He assumed that the water must have been created before 1:1 since "heavens" meant only "expanse" (v.8) and "earth" meant "dry land" (v.9), and since the water, which was neither a part of the "expanse" or the "dry land," was already present in v.2. Neither Rashi nor Ibn Ezra appears to have rejected the traditional view on grammatical grounds, thinking the construct reading was the better reading. Rather they believed it was the only reading that would solve the apparent difficulty of the "water" in v.2 not being accounted for in v.1. In fact, Ibn Ezra warned his readers not to be "astonished" at the suggestion of a construct before a verb, which suggests that he himself felt some difficulty in reading *bᵉrē'šîṯ* before a finite verb as a construct and that he anticipated the same reaction in his readers.

Both Rashi and Ibn Ezra produced examples to show that a finite verb after a construct noun was permissible. But both the fact and the nature of their defense of their reading in 1:1 betrays their own uneasiness with such a reading. The use of the accent *tifcha* in *bᵉrē'šîṯ* is sometimes used as an argument for the traditional view, suggesting that a construct noun could not or would not have a disjunctive accent. However, not only do construct forms commonly take a disjunctive accent (e.g., זֲהַב [*zᵃhaḇ*, "the gold of"], 2:12; עֵץ ['*ēṣ*, "the tree of"], 2:17), but also since אֱלֹהִים (*'ᵉlōhîm*, "God") has been given the *athnach*, a dichotomy must divide its line either where it does in *bᵉrē'šîṯ* or in *bārā'*, thus breaking the connection of subject and verb. The position of the dichotomy in either case is permissible and does not affect the grammatical relationship between the members of such a small line.

Notice the contrast between v.1a and the accentuation of the short *athnach* lines in nominal clauses (2:11a, 13a) where the *tifcha* divides the subject and predicate and the subject is conjoined with its adjuncts. The accentuation of 2:6a is also consistent with this distinction since the clause is a nominal clause (see R. Meyer, *Hebräische Grammatik*, vol. 3 [Berlin: Satzlehre, 1972], par. 92, 4b). In the verbal clauses in 3:2a, 4a, however, the subject and predicate are kept together in the short *athnach* lines and the adverbial adjunct is separated. Genesis 3:12 shows that in verbal clauses subject and verb can be separated in very short *athnach* lines.

The above examples are *not* given as "rules" of the accentuation system but only to show that various combinations of accents (conjunctive and disjunctive) are possible within *athnach* lines of three words or less and that the combinations do not carry grammatical importance. In light of these examples, it is not possible to argue that the accent in *b^e^rē'šîṯ* implies the Masoretes read it as an absolute.

Indications within Genesis itself suggest that the author intentionally chose רֵאשִׁית (*rē'šîṯ*) in v.1 because of its close association with אַחֲרִית (*'aḥ^a^rîṯ*) and thus had the "end" in view when he wrote of the "beginning." For example, *rē'šîṯ* as an adverbial of time meaning "beginning" or "first" occurs only in v.1 in the Pentateuch (Gen 10:10—substantival, not temporal). Elsewhere in the Pentateuch the author uses בַּתְּחִלָּה (*batt^e^ḥillāh,* lit., "at the first"; four times, all in Genesis: 13:3; 41:21; 43:18, 20) and בָּרִאשֹׁנָה (*bāri'šōnāh,* lit., "at the first"; ten times, three in Genesis: 13:4; 28:19; 38:28). Both *t^e^ḥillāh* and *ri'šōnāh* differ from *rē'šîṯ* in that they mark a "beginning" of a series in opposition to the "second" or "next" member of the series (see 13:3–4). *Rē'šîṯ,* on the other hand, marks the "beginning" in opposition to the "end" (*'aḥ^a^rîṯ;* cf. Job 8:7; 42:12; Eccl 7:8; Isa 46:10).

As Rashi argued, if the author had wanted only to say that the heavens and the earth were created first in a series, he would have used *bāri'šōnāh.* The use of *rē'šîṯ* in 1:1 strongly suggests that the author's choice of this word was motivated by its association with *'aḥ^a^rîṯ.* If that is so, it suggests that an intentional anticipation of the "end" (*'aḥ^a^rîṯ*) lies behind the author's choice of the word "beginning." In other words, the author's depiction of Creation appears to be controlled by an eschatological anticipation of the "end times" (*'aḥ^a^rîṯ*).

Another indication that *rē'šîṯ* was used for its association with *'aḥ^a^rîṯ* comes from a consideration of the structure of Genesis and the Pentateuch. It has been noted that, in the narrative style of much of the Pentateuch, the conclusions of minor and major units are marked by poetic texts followed by a brief epilogue (see Introduction: Compositional analysis of the Pentateuch). On these stylistic grounds, the conclusion of the Book of Genesis is chapters 49–50 and the conclusion of the Pentateuch is Deuteronomy 32–34. Both narratives consist of poetic texts with an epilogue. In both of these "conclusions," the poetic texts are framed by a short prologue (Gen 49:1; Deut 31:28–30) in which the "patriarch" (Jacob and Moses) called together the "elders" (Gen 49:1; Deut 31:28) and spoke his final words to them (cf. O. Eissfeldt, "Die Umrahmung des Mose-Liedes Dtn 32, 1–43 und des Mose-Gesetzes Dtn 1–30 in Dtn 31, 9–32, 47," *Kleine Schriften* [Tübingen: J.C.B. Mohr, n.d.], 3:322ff.).

The function of both prologues is to situate the poetic texts within the framework of the "end times" (*b^e^'aḥ^a^rîṯ hayyāmîm,* Gen 49:1c; Deut 31:29; NIV, "in days to come"). It is not important at this moment whether the *'aḥ^a^rîṯ* is intended to be read as eschatological (Hugo Gressmann, *Der Messias* [Göttingen: Vandenhoeck & Ruprecht, 1929], p. 223) or only historically future (Joseph Klausner, *The Messianic Idea in Israel* [London: Allen and Unwin, 1956], p. 30). The important point here is that the author of Genesis turns directly to the theme and terminology of "the end times" (*'aḥ^a^rîṯ*) when he draws his narrative to a close in Genesis and in the Pentateuch as a whole. If the use of *'aḥ^a^rîṯ* is intentional at the conclusion of the narrative, which it surely must be, then it is likely that the use of its semantic antipode, *rē'šîṯ,* is also intentional at the beginning of the narrative. Thus, again, it seems apparent that the choice of *rē'šîṯ* in 1:1 is intended to introduce an anticipation of the "end" into the "beginning." In thus consciously grounding the future in the past, the author of Genesis follows a "fundamental principle" in biblical eschatology: the last things are like the first things (Böklen, *Die Verwandtschaft,* p. 136).

The phrase הַשָּׁמַיִם וְאֵת הָאָרֶץ (*haššāmayim w^e^'ēṯ hā'āreṣ,* "the heavens and the earth") is a figure of speech (merism) for the expression of "totality." Its use in the Bible appears to be restricted to the totality of the present world order and is equivalent to the "all things" in Isa 44:24 (cf. Ps 103:19; Jer 10:16). Particularly important to notice is that its use elsewhere in Scripture suggests that the phrase includes the sun and the moon as well as the stars (e.g., Joel 3:15–16).

2. *Preparation of the land (1:2–2:3)*

As a praise of God's grace, the theme of the remainder of the Creation account (1:2–2:25) is God's gift of the land. First, God prepared the land for men and women by dividing the waters and furnishing its resources (1:2–27). Then he gave the land and its resources as a blessing to be safeguarded by obedience (2:16–17). Since a similar pattern is reflected in the Psalm of Moses (Exod 15:1–18), where God leads his people to the Promised Land through the divided waters of the Red Sea, the Creation account appears to be the narrative equivalent to such a hymn. The purpose is the same in both texts: "He is my God, and I will praise him,/ my father's God, and I will exalt him" (Exod 15:2b). In the poem in Deuteronomy 32, the author draws a similar connection between God's gracious work of Creation and his gracious covenant with Israel. There, in terminology clearly reminiscent of Genesis 1, Moses portrayed God's loving care for Israel over against Israel's chronic disobedience. In that poem the loss of the land, which was to come in the future exile, was portrayed as the height of folly over against God's gracious and loving provision for his people. We will see throughout these early chapters that the viewpoint reflected in Moses' final song plays a major role in the theological shaping of these narratives.

a. *First day*

1:2–5

2Now the earth was formless and empty, darkness was over the surface of the deep, and the Spirit of God was hovering over the waters.

3And God said, "Let there be light," and there was light. 4God saw that the light was good, and he separated the light from the darkness. 5God called the light "day," and the darkness he called "night." And there was evening, and there was morning—the first day.

2a Verse 2 describes the condition of the land just before God prepared it for man. The sense of the phrase "formless and empty" (*tōhû wāḇōhû*) must be gained from the context alone. The immediate context (vv.2a, 9) suggests that the land was described as "formless and empty" because there was "darkness" over the land and because the land was covered with water. The general context of chapter 1 suggests that the author meant the terms "formless and empty" to describe the condition of the land *before* God made it "good." Before God began his work, the land was "formless" (*tōhû*), and God then made it "good" (*ṭôḇ*). Thus the expression "formless and empty" ultimately refers to the condition of the land in its "not-yet" state—the state it was in before God made it "good." In this sense the description of the land in 1:2 is similar to that in 2:5–6. Both describe the land as "not-yet" what it shall be.

In light of the fact that the remainder of the chapter pictures God preparing the land as a place for man to dwell, we should understand v.2 to focus our attention on the land as a place not yet inhabitable for man (Ibn Ezra). Having described the land as uninhabitable, the remainder of the account is a portrayal of God's preparing the land for man. The meaning of the word *tōhû* is identical to that of Isaiah 45:18: "[God] did not create it [the land] to be empty [*tōhû*], but formed it to be inhabited." The term "empty" in the Isaiah passage stands in opposition to the phrase "to be inhabited." This is the same meaning of the word *tōhû* in Deuteronomy 32:10. There "formless" (*tōhû*) is parallel to "desert" (*miḏbār*), an uninhabitable wasteland.

The description of the land as "formless and empty" in v.2a, then, plays a central role in the Creation account because it shows the condition of the land before God's gracious work has prepared it for man's well being (*ṭôḇ*). Deuteronomy 32 draws on the same imagery (v.10) in depicting Israel's time of waiting in the wilderness before their entry into the good land. The prophets also have drawn from the same source to depict God's judgment of exile. When Israel disobeyed God, the land (*hā'āreṣ*) became again "uninhabitable" (*tōhû*), and the people were sent into exile: "I looked at the earth, and it was formless and empty [*tōhû wāḇōhû*] and at the heavens and their light was gone. . . . the fruitful land was a desert" (Jer 4:23–26). The *land* after the Exile was depicted in its state before God's gracious preparation of the land in Creation. The description of the land in Genesis 1:2, then, fits well into the prophet's vision of the future. The land lies empty, dark, and barren, awaiting God's call to light and life. Just as the light of the sun broke in upon the primeval darkness heralding the dawn of God's blessing (1:3), so also the prophets and the apostles mark the beginning of the new age of salvation with the light that shatters the darkness (Isa 8:22–9:2; Matt 4:13–17; John 1:5, 8–9).

Similar ideas are already at work in the composition of the first chapter of Genesis. Just as the future messianic salvation would be marked by a flowering of the desert (Isa 35:1–2), so also God's final acts of salvation are foreshadowed in Creation. The wilderness waits for its restoration. Henceforth the call to prepare for the coming day of salvation while yet waiting in the wilderness would become the hallmark of the prophets' vision of the future (Isa 40:3; Mark 1:4–5; Rev 12:6, 14–15).

2b The second part of v.2 has received remarkably diverse interpretations. The central question is whether the last clause in v.2 ("The Spirit of God was hovering over the waters") belongs with the first two clauses, and hence further describes the state of the uninhabitable land, or whether it belongs to the following verse (3) and describes the work of God, or the Spirit of God, in the initial stages of Creation. In the first instance it would be translated "a mighty wind," while in the second instance it would be translated "the Spirit of God," as in most EVs.

Although many modern interpreters have read the clause as "a mighty wind," the traditional reading "Spirit of God" seems the only reading compatible with the verb "hovering" (*mᵉraḥep̱eṯ*), a verb not suited to describing the blowing of a wind. Moreover, the image of the Spirit of God hovering over the waters is similar to the depiction of God in Deuteronomy 32:11 as an eagle "hovering" (*yᵉraḥēp̱*) over the nest of its young, protecting and preparing their nest. The use of the similar image of God both at the beginning of the Pentateuch and at the end suggests that it is the picture of the Spirit of God that is intended here.

Another observation in support of the meaning "Spirit of God" in v.2 comes from the parallels between the Creation account (Gen 1) and the account of the construction of the tabernacle in Exodus. Although many lines of comparison can be drawn between the two accounts, showing that the writer had intended a thematic identity between the two narratives, it will suffice here to note that in both accounts the work of God (*mᵉlā'ḵāh*, Gen 2:2; Exod 31:5) is to be accomplished by the "Spirit of God" (*rûᵃḥ 'ᵉlōhîm*). As God did his "work" (*mᵉlā'ḵāh*) of creation by means of the "Spirit of God" (*rûᵃḥ 'ᵉlōhîm*), so Israel was to do their "work" (*mᵉlā'ḵāh*) by means of the "Spirit of God."

3–5 Verse 3 has often been taken to mean that God created light before he had created the sun, since here he said, "Let there be light," but not until v.16 does the narrative speak of God making the sun. It should be noted, however, that the sun, moon, and stars are all to be included in the usual meaning of the phrase "heavens and the earth" (*haššāmayim wᵉhā'āreṣ*), and thus according to the present account these celestial bodies were all created in v.1. Verse 3 then does not describe the creation of the sun but the appearance of the sun through the darkness, much the way the sunrise is described in 44:3; Exodus 10:23; and Nehemiah 8:3, where the Hebrew word *'ôr* refers to the light of the sun. The narrative does not explain the cause of the darkness in v.2, just as it does not explain the cause of the similar darkness in the land of Egypt in Exodus 10:22. The absence of an explanation in either case is, however, insufficient grounds for assuming that the sun had not yet been created. The expression "heavens and the earth" does not easily permit that assumption (see further on 1:14–18).

The division between "the day" and "the night" in v.4 also leaves little room for an interpretation of the "light" in v.3 as other than that of the light from the sun. In consideration of the frequent repetitions of the phrase "And God saw that it was good" (vv.4, 10, 12, 18, 21, 25, 31), we may assume that this is an element that the narrative intends to emphasize. In view of such an emphasis at the beginning of the book, it is hardly accidental that throughout the Book of Genesis and the Pentateuch the activity of "seeing" is continually put at the center of the author's conception of God. The first name given to God within the book is that of Hagar's: "El Roi" (*'ēl rᵒ'î*), the "God who sees" (16:13). Also, in 22:1–19, a central chapter dealing with the nature of God in Genesis, the narrative concludes on the theme that God is the one who "sees." Thus the place where the Lord appeared to Abraham is called "The LORD will see" (22:14). (Though the EVs often translate the verb "to see" in this passage as "to provide," as it should be, the Hebrew word *rā'āh* ["to see"] only comes to mean "to provide" secondarily [cf. TWOT, p. 823].)

The close connection between the notion of "seeing" and "providing," which is brought out so clearly in chapter 22, likely plays an important role in the sense of the verb "to see" in chapter 1. In a tragic reversal of his portrayal of God's "seeing" the "good" in Creation, the author subsequently returns to the notion of God's "seeing" at the opening of the account of the Flood. Here too the biblical God is the God who "sees"; but at that point in the narrative, after the Fall, God no longer "saw" the "good" (*ṭôḇ*), but he "saw how great man's wickedness [*rā'āh*] on the earth had become" (6:5). The verbal parallels suggest that the two narratives are to be read as a contrast of the state of man before and after the Fall (O. Eissfeldt, "Die kleinste literarische Einheit in den Erzählungsbüchern des Alten Testaments," *Kleine Schriften*, vol. 1 [Tübingen: J.C.B. Mohr, 1962], p. 144).

The "good" that the author had in view has a very specific range of meaning in chapter 1—the "good" is that which is *beneficial* for man. Notice, for example, how in the description of the work of the second day (vv.6–8), the narrative does not say that "God saw that it was good." The reason is that on that day there was nothing created or made that was, in fact, "good" or beneficial for man. The heavens were made and the waters divided, but the land, where man was to dwell, still remained hidden under the "deep." The land was still *tōhû;* it was not yet a place where man could dwell. It was only when, on the third day, the sea was parted and the dry land appeared that the text could say, "God saw that it was good" (v.10). When and only when the land was ready for man could God call it good.

Throughout this opening chapter God is depicted as the one who both knows what is "good" for man and is intent on providing the good for him. In this way the author has prepared the reader for the tragedy that awaits in chapter 3. It is in light of an understanding of God as the one who knows "good" (*ṭô<u>b</u>*) from "evil" (*ra'*), and who is intent on providing man with the good, that man's rebellious attempt to gain the knowledge of "good and evil" for himself can be seen clearly for the folly that it was. The author seems bent on portraying the "fall of man," not merely as a sin, but also as the work of fools. When we read the portrayal of God in chapter 1 as the Provider of all that is good and beneficial (*wayyar' 'ᵉlōhîm kî-ṭô<u>b</u>*, "And God saw that it was good"), we cannot help but see in this an anticipation of the author's depiction of the hollowness of that first rebellious thought: "The woman saw that the fruit of the tree was good [*ṭô<u>b</u>*] . . . and desirable for gaining wisdom" (3:6). Here again the verbal parallels between God's "seeing the good" in chapter 1 and the woman's "seeing the good" in chapter 3 cannot be without purpose in the text. In drawing a parallel between the woman's "seeing" and God's "seeing," the author has given a graphic picture of the limits of human wisdom and has highlighted the tragic irony of the Fall.

Notes

---

2 The English translation of תֹהוּ וָבֹהוּ (*tōhû wā<u>b</u>ōhû*) as "formless and empty" (NIV), or "without form and void" (RSV), often leads to an understanding of the description of the earth as a chaotic, amorphous mass, rather than calling to mind an uninhabitable stretch of wasteland, a wilderness not yet inhabitable for man, as is suggested in the first chapter. The translation often stirs up images of the earth and the universe in a primeval stage of existence, much like the view of the origin of the universe in the physical sciences, a mass of cooling gases, not yet in its present spherical shape, whirling aimlessly through space (e.g., "an original formless matter in the first stage of the creation of the universe," The New Scofield Bible, p. 1). Though such a picture could find support in the English expession "without form and void," it is not an image likely to arise out of the Hebrew *tōhû wā<u>b</u>ōhû*.

The origin of the English translation is apparently the Greek version (LXX) that translates *tōhû* with ἀόρατος (*aoratos*, "unseen") and *<u>b</u>ōhû* with ἀκατασκεύαστος (*akataskeuastos*, "unformed"). Since both terms play an important role in the Hellenistic cosmologies at the time of the LXX translation, it is likely that the choice of these terms, and others within the LXX of Genesis, was motivated by an attempt to harmonize the biblical account with accepted views in the translators' own day rather than a strict adherence to the sense of the Hebrew text (Armin Schmitt, "Interpretation der Genesis aus hellenistischem Geist," ZAW 86 [1974]: 150–51). It is of special interest then that the later Greek versions—e.g., Aquila ("empty and nothing"), Symmachus ("fallow and indistinct")—decidedly move away from the early Greek version (LXX). It is also important to notice that the early Semitic versions have no trace of the concepts found in the LXX: e.g., Neophyti I appropriately paraphrases *tōhû wā<u>b</u>ōhû* with "desolate without human beings or beast and void of all cultivation of plants and of trees." The Vulgate ("*inanis et vacua*") also shows little relationship to the LXX.

Within the EVs the influence of the LXX is at least as old as the Geneva Bible ("without forme and void," 1599), reflecting Calvin's own translation: "*informis et inanis*" (p. 67). However, his understanding of *informis et inanis* is quite different from the image suggested to the modern reader in the English equivalent "formless and void," as his commentary on these words shows: "Were we now to take away, I say, from the earth all that God added after the time here alluded to, then we should have this rude and unpolished, or rather shapeless chaos" (p. 73). In the days of the early EVs, the terms "formless" and "void" would not have suggested the same cosmological images as those same terms do in a scientific age such as our own.

5 יוֹם אֶחָד (*yôm 'eḥā<u>d</u>*, lit., "one day") should not be read as if it were "first day" (Exod 12:15–16; Lev 23 *passim*), as the uses of *yôm 'eḥā<u>d</u>* elsewhere in Genesis demonstrate (27:45; 33:13; cf. 1 Sam 27:1; Isa 9:13; Jonah 3:4). Cassuto's (with Nachmanides) explanation is forced—"There was only *one day*, for the second had not yet been created" (p. 30)—since he has to make an exception to his rule immediately for שֵׁם הָאֶחָד (*šēm hā'eḥā<u>d</u>*, "name of the first") in 2:11. Why would the writer have avoided the use of *yôm 'eḥā<u>d</u>* in this chapter? There are two possible solutions.

First, the grammatical construction of Gen 1 allows potentially for two "first days" at the beginning of the chapter. The day that begins in v.3—וַיְהִי־אוֹר (*way^ehî-'ôr*, "and there was light")—and the day that begins in v.1—בְּרֵאשִׁית (*b^erē'šî<u>t</u>*). In his conception of the narrative of chapter 1, the author may not have wanted to convey the idea that the day that begins in v.3 was actually יוֹם רִאשׁוֹן (*yôm ri'šôn*, "the first day"). He may have wanted to reserve the notion of "the first day" for the day that began with *b^erē'šî<u>t</u>* in v.1. Thus *yôm 'eḥā<u>d</u>* could have been used to avoid the misconception. In the same way the author does not say "the first river" (הַנָּהָר הָרִאשׁוֹן [*hannāhār hāri'šôn*]) in 2:11 (the NIV doesn't bring out this distinction) but rather "one (river)" (הָאֶחָד [*hā'eḥā<u>d</u>*]), because the river (*nāhār*, 2:10) that divides into four heads has already been mentioned.

A second possible motive for avoiding the mention of a "first day" is that throughout the Torah יוֹם רִאשׁוֹן (*yôm ri'šôn*) is used to denote the "first day" of a special feast, a day in which there is to be no מְלָאכָה (*m^elā'<u>k</u>āh*, "work"; cf. Exod 12:16; Lev 23:7, 35, 39; Num 28:18). The use of *yôm 'eḥā<u>d</u>* may have been intended to avoid a possible objection to the work (*m^elā'<u>k</u>āh*) of God on one such *yôm ri'šôn* in chapter 1. The well-known textual problem in 2:2 (q.v.) is centered on a similar objection.

---

b. *Second day*

1:6–8

6 And God said, "Let there be an expanse between the waters to separate water from water." 7 So God made the expanse and separated the water under the expanse from the water above it. And it was so. 8 God called the expanse "sky." And there was evening, and there was morning—the second day.

6–8 The sense of the account of the second day of Creation is largely determined by one's understanding of the author's perspective. The central question is how the author understood and used the term "expanse" (*rāqî^a'*). Was the term used from a cosmological perspective, that is, was it intended to describe a major component of the structured universe (e.g., Delitzsch: "the higher ethereal region, the so-called atmosphere, the sky, is here meant; it is represented as the semi-spherical vault of heaven stretched over the earth and its water" [p. 86])? Or did the term describe something immediate in the everyday experience of the author, e.g., the "clouds" that hold the rain?

We must be careful neither to let our own view of the structure of the universe nor what we might think to have been the view of ancient men (Gunkel, p. 107) control our understanding of the biblical author's description of the "expanse" (*rāqî^a'*). We must seek what clues there are from the biblical text itself. One such clue is the purpose that the author assigns to the "expanse" in v.6: it is "to separate water from water." The "expanse" holds water above the land; that much is certain. A second clue is the name given to the *rāqîaʿ*. In v.8 it is called the "sky" (*šāmāyim*). Finally, we should look at the uses of "expanse" within chapter 1. Here the the term refers not only to the place where God put the sun, moon, and stars (v.14) but also to that place where the birds fly (v.20: "across the expanse of the sky").

Is there a single word or idea that would accommodate such uses of the term "expanse"? Cosmological terms such as "ceiling," "vault," or "global ocean," which are often used for "expanse" in chapter 1, do not suit the use of the term in v.20. Such explanations, though drawn from analogies of ancient Near Eastern cosmologies, appear too specific for the present context. Thus it would be unlikely that the narrative would have in view here a "solid partition or vault that separates the earth from the waters above" (Westermann, p. 116). It appears more likely that the narrative has in view something within the everyday experience of the natural world, in a general way, that place where the birds fly and where God placed the lights of heaven (cf. v.14). In English the word "sky" appears to cover this sense well.

The "waters above" the sky is likely a reference to the clouds. That is at least the view that appears to come from the reflections on this passage in later biblical texts. For example, in the author's account of the Flood in chapter 7, reference is made to the "floodgates of the heavens [*haššāmayim*]," which, when opened, pour forth rain (vv.11–12; cf. 2 Kings 7:2; Pss 104:3; 147:8; 148:4). The writer of Proverbs 8:28 has read the term "expanse" in Genesis 1 as a reference to the "clouds" (*šeḥāqîm*).

In recent years it has become customary to point to a subtle but significant tension between the accounts of v.6 and v.7. Whereas v.6 recounts the creation of the "expanse" by God's "word" alone ("And God said"), it is maintained that v.7 presents an alternative recounting of the creation of the "expanse" by God's "act" ("So God made," Westermann). It is apparent that throughout chapter 1 there is a consistent alternation between accounts of God's speaking and acting, often giving the impression of duplication (cf. v.11 with v.12; v.14 with v.16; v.24 with v.25). This impression is heightened by the presence of the recurring expression "and it was so" (*wayehî-ḵēn*), which suggests that what God had commanded had been accomplished.

A close reading of chapter 1 could make it appear that the author at first recounted God's creative work as the result of his speaking ("And God said . . . and it was so") and then recounted God's work as an act or deed that he carried out to completion ("And God made . . ."). If such observations are correct, we are left with the impression that the Creation account of chapter 1 has very little internal consistency and coherence. Though such an outcome cannot be ruled out, it is worth asking whether there is another explanation for the apparent duplicity that runs throughout the whole of the chapter.

A possible explanation lies in a consideration of the nature of narrative texts such as the present account of Creation. A twofold task lies before the authors of narrative texts such as this. It is not only their responsibility to recount and report events of the past, that is, to maintain a consistent and continuous flow of narrated events within the world of the narrative text. Often it is necessary for them to supply the reader with more than the bare facts about those events; it is necessary to supply the reader with a measure of commentary on the events recorded, that is, to "monitor" the reader's understanding and then to "manage" his appreciation of those events. Such is the case for the author of Genesis, for example, in 2:24. There he momentarily set aside the flow of narrative to address the reader directly with a word of advice and application: "For this reason a man will leave his father and mother and be united to his wife, and they will become one flesh." At that point in the narrative, the author is directly managing the reader's response to the events of the narrative. Although in the past little attention was paid to such features of narrative texts, it has become increasingly apparent that narratives have such features to one degree or another (see Robert de Beaugrade and Wolfgang Dressler, *Introduction to Text Linguistics* [London: Longman, 1981], pp. 163ff.).

It may be possible to explain difficulties and irregularities in Genesis by looking for such "reader conscious" techniques in the narrative. For example, in 1:24 the author recounted the fact that God spoke and the animals came into being: "And God said, . . . And it was so [*way^{e}hî-ḵēn*]." But then he followed that description of God's work by a "reader-oriented" comment: God made the animals according to their own kind, and he saw that it was good (v.25). (Presumably the purpose of such a comment was to assure the reader that it was, in fact, God who made the animals and not *anyone* else and, as well, to underscore the fact that God made the animals "according to their kinds," a key theme in this chapter that has its ultimate focal point in the one major exception, the creation of man "in the image of God" (v.27).

In other words, behind the Creation account of Genesis 1, there appears to lie the same concern as that found in Psalm 104, especially vv.27–30:

> These all look to you
> . . . .
> when you take away their breath,
> they die and return to the dust.
> When you send your Spirit,
> they are created,
> and you renew the face of the earth.

God is the Creator of all life, both animal and human. Such a reading of chapter 1 not only accounts for the duplications within the whole of the chapter, but more importantly it allows for a more explicit reckoning of the overall intention of the author. The author, by monitoring his own text, reveals his chief interest in the events he is recounting and can be seen at each point along the way preparing the reader for a proper understanding of the narrative.

Notes

---

7 The MT reads וַיְהִי־כֵן (*way^{e}hî-ḵēn*, "and it was so") at the end of v.7, but in the LXX its equivalent, *καὶ ἐγένετο οὕτως* (*kai egeneto houtōs*), occurs at the end of v.6. Throughout the rest of the chapter, *way^{e}hî-ḵēn* occurs between God's spoken word—וַיֹּאמֶר אֱלֹהִים (*wayyō'mer '^{e}lōhîm*, "and God said")—and the narration of God's action—וַיַּעַשׂ אֱלֹהִים (*wayya'aś '^{e}lōhîm*, "and God made"; cf. vv.9b, 11b, 15b, 24b, 30b). In the two places where the MT does not follow that scheme, vv.6 and 20, the LXX reads *καὶ ἐγένετο οὕτως* (*kai egeneto outōs*, "and it was so"), suggesting that the LXX readings are an attempt to correct the imbalance of the MT. In keeping with that tendency, the LXX also reads *καὶ εἶδεν ὁ θεὸς ὅτι καλόν* (*kai eiden ho theos hoti kalon*) in v.8, filling in the lack of the expression "and God saw that it was good" for the second day. The overall impression given by the LXX in these instances is of a secondary attempt to provide a balanced, consistent text. Thus the MT is to be taken as the more original.

c. *Third day*

1:9–13

[9]And God said, "Let the water under the sky be gathered to one place,
and let dry ground appear." And it was so. [10]God called the dry
ground "land," and the gathered waters he called "seas." And
God saw that it was good.
[11]Then God said, "Let the land produce vegetation: seed-
bearing plants and trees on the land that bear fruit with seed in it,
according to their various kinds." And it was so. [12]The land
produced vegetation: plants bearing seed according to their kinds
and trees bearing fruit with seed in it according to their kinds. And
God saw that it was good. [13]And there was evening, and there was
morning—the third day.

9–13 There are two distinct acts of God on the third day: (1) the preparation of the dry land and the seas and (2) the furnishing of the dry land with bushes and fruit trees. Unlike the work of the second day, both acts are called "good" (*ṭôḇ*). They are "good" because they are created for man's benefit. Both acts relate to the preparation of the land, a central concern of the author of Genesis (cf. 12:7; 13:15; 15:18; 26:4). The separation of the waters and the preparation of the dry land is to be read in light of the subsequent accounts of the Flood (chs. 6–9) and the parting of the "Red Sea" (Exod 14–15). In all three accounts the waters are an obstacle standing in the way of man's inhabiting the dry land. The water must be removed for man to enjoy God's gift of the land. But as we learn in the accounts of the Flood and the Red Sea, the waters are also God's instrument of judgment on those who do not follow his way.

The author of chapter 1 was not merely recounting past events, he was building a case for the importance of obedience to the will of God. In the Creation account of chapter 1, the author began with the simple picture of God's awesome power at work harnessing the great sea (*t^{e}hôm,* v.2; NIV, "the deep"). It is a picture of God's work on behalf of man's "good." But in the Flood account, when the narrative returns to the picture of God's power over the waters of the great sea (*t^{e}hôm,* 7:11; NIV, "deep"), it is a bitter reminder of the other side of God's power. The sea (*t^{e}hôm*) has become an instrument of God's judgment.

In his second act on the third day, God furnished the land (*hā'āreṣ*) with bushes and fruit trees. In the present shape of the narrative, it is likely that the author intended a connection to be drawn between God's furnishing the land with fruit trees in chapter 1 and his furnishing the "garden" with trees "good for food" in chapter 2. Whatever our opinion may be about whether the two accounts of Creation in chapters 1 and 2 originally belonged together, there is little doubt that as they are put together in the narrative before us, they are meant to be read as one account.

The implications of reading the two chapters together are greater than has been acknowledged. For one, if the two accounts are, in fact, about the same act of Creation, then the narrative has identified the "land" (*hā'āreṣ*) of chapter 1 with the "garden" of chapter 2. The focus of the Creation account in chapter 1, then, is on the part of God's creation that ultimately becomes the location of the Garden of Eden. We will have more to say about the location of Eden in chapter 2, but for now it is enough to point to the connection between "the land" and its "fruit trees" in chapter 1 and the trees of the garden in chapter 2. The selectivity of the Creation account can be seen in the fact that it focuses only on the "seed-bearing plants" and "fruit trees." Those are the plants that are for man's food. No other forms of vegetation are mentioned (see Notes).

Notes

9 The LXX reading *συναγωγὴν* (*synagōgēn*, "be gathered") has suggested to many exegetes a Hebrew text that read מִקְוֵה (*miqweh*, "gathering") rather than the MT's מָקוֹם (*māqôm*, "place"). Westermann (p. 79), following Cassuto (p. 35), has favored the MT over the LXX on the grounds that אֶחָד (*'eḥāḏ*, "one") would not likely be used with *miqweh*: "The number *one* can readily be understood in connection with *place* . . . but it is not appropriate to *pool*, for there were no other pools in existence" (Cassuto, in loc.). Such an argument is inappropriate in a textual decision. What has to be explained is which reading appears more original, not whether one reading can more readily be understood than the other. The LXX version was more likely guided in its rendering by a desire to assimilate the far object (*συναγωγὴν*) to the verb (*συναχθήτω*, *synachthētō*). The last half of v.9 in the LXX—"and the water that was under the heaven gathered together into their pools and the dry land appeared"—does not commend itself as more original than the shorter MT by virtue of the tendency already observed in the LXX (or its *Vorlage*) to fill out and balance the marred symmetry of the MT.

11 The MT accentuation makes it clear that the Masoretes read דֶּשֶׁא (*deše'*, "vegetation") as the main idea that is explicated by the two kinds of plants, עֵשֶׂב (*'ēśeḇ*, "plants") and עֵץ (*'ēṣ*, "trees"). Westermann (p. 79) correctly says that if such is the sense of the verse, the lack of a waw between *'ēśeḇ* and *'ēṣ* is difficult. But to suggest on those grounds that the waw form (*we'ēṣ*) of the versions is the better text overlooks the fact that in most cases the difficult reading is to be taken as the more original. Certainly the *we'ēṣ* of v.12 shows that the narrative envisions two kinds of plants, *'ēśeḇ* and *'eṣ*. But the *we'ēṣ* of v.12 can also explain why the versions would have added the *we'ēṣ* in v.11. It is best to leave the MT intact and read v.11 as a single sentence. The first clause—תַּדְשֵׁא הָאָרֶץ דֶּשֶׁא (*taḏeše' hā'āreṣ deše'*, "Let the land produce vegetation")—is in apposition (F.I. Andersen, *The Sentence in Biblical Hebrew* [Hawthrone, N.J.: Mouton, 1974], p. 46) to the sentence that follows—עֵשֶׂב מַזְרִיעַ זֶרַע עֵץ פְּרִי (*'ēśeḇ mazrîa' zera' 'ēṣ perî*, "seed-bearing plants and fruit trees"), which consists of two clauses in "asyndetic coordination" (ibid., p. 57). The *we'ēṣ* in v.12, then, can be viewed as a repetition and explication of God's words in v.11. The waw in *we'ēṣ* makes explicit the "asyndetic coordination" of the *'ēṣ* in v.11.

Another way to read the *'ēṣ* of the MT in v.11 is as an apposition sentence, the second clause of the sentence *'ēṣ perî* explaining the first clause *'ēśeḇ mazrîa' zera'* (Andersen, *Sentence in Biblical Hebrew*, p. 46). Thus there is only one kind of vegetation (*deše'*) in v.11, the "seed-bearing plants, namely (apposition) the fruit trees." Such a reading would explain why לְמִינוֹ (*lemînô*, "according to their various kinds") occurs only once in v.11. It would also illustrate the close relationship between chapters 1 and 2 of Genesis. Already the notion of "fruit trees," so prominent in chapter 2, is made the central focus in chapter 1. The major obstacle to the appositional sentence reading is the *we'ēṣ* in v.12 and v.29—וְאֵת־כָּל־הָעֵץ (*we'et-kol-hā'ēṣ*, "and every tree")—which seems to see, not one kind of vegetation in v.11, but two. Jacob (p. 45) states that עֵץ פְּרִי (*'ēṣ perî*) in v.11 does not refer to "fruit trees," specifically, but to trees generally. Westermann (p. 125) concurs. According to Jacob "fruit trees" are called עֵץ מַאֲכָל (*'ēṣ ma'ᵃḵāl*; cf. Lev 19:23, Deut 20:20; Neh 9:25; Ezek 47:12).

While it is true that the term *'ēṣ perî* is rare (Gen 1:11; Ps 148:9; Eccl 2:5), it is explicitly explained and qualified in v.12 ("trees bearing fruit"). In Ps 148:9 *'ēṣ perî* occurs with *kol-'ᵃrāzîm* in a series of contrasts—"mountains and all hills, fruit trees [*'ēṣ perî*] and all cedars [*'ᵃrāzîm*], wild animals and all cattle, small creatures and flying birds"—suggesting that the expression does not refer to trees in general but to a specific type of tree. At the end of chapter 1 (v.29), the narrative looks back to the two kinds of plants brought forth on the third day—*'ēśeḇ* ("plant") and *hā'ēṣ 'ᵃšer-bô p̱erî-'ēṣ* ("every tree that has fruit in it")—stating that they are the food for man. The animals, on the other hand, are given a different diet in v.30: יֶרֶק עֵשֶׂב (*yereq ʿēśeb*, "every green plant"). This suggests that the description of the land sprouting plants on the third day had only man's nourishment in view.

---

d. *Fourth day*

1:14–19

[14]And God said, "Let there be lights in the expanse of the sky to separate the day from the night, and let them serve as signs to mark seasons and days and years, [15]and let them be lights in the expanse of the sky to give light on the earth." And it was so. [16]God made two great lights—the greater light to govern the day and the lesser light to govern the night. He also made the stars. [17]God set them in the expanse of the sky to give light on the earth, [18]to govern the day and the night, and to separate light from darkness. And God saw that it was good. [19]And there was evening, and there was morning—the fourth day.

14 The narration of events on the fourth day raises several questions. Does the text state that the sun, moon, and stars were created on the fourth day? If so, how could "the heavens and the earth," which would have included the sun, moon, and stars, have been created "in the beginning" (v.1)? Could there have been a "day and night" during the first three days of Creation if the sun had not yet been created? Were there plants and vegetation on the land (created on the third day) before the creation of the sun? Keil represents a common evangelical viewpoint when he suggests that though "the heavens and the earth" were created "in the beginning" (v.1), it was not until the fourth day that they were "completed" (p. 59). Keil's explanation can be seen already in Calvin, who states that "the world was not perfected at its very commencement, in the manner in which it is now seen, but that it was created an empty chaos of heaven and earth." According to Calvin, this "empty chaos" was then filled on the fourth day with the sun, moon, and stars. Calvin's view is similar to that of Rashi: "[The sun, moon, and stars] were created on the first day, but on the fourth day [God] commanded that they be placed in the sky."

Another common line of interpretation (the "Restitution Theory" or "Gap Theory") is reflected in the Scofield Bible, though it can be found much earlier in the history of interpretation (cf. O. Zöckler, "Schöpfung," *Real-Encyklopädie für protestantische Theologie und Kirche,* 20 [Gotha: Verlag von Rudolf Besser, 1866], pp. 735–36): "The sun and moon were created 'in the beginning.' The 'light' of course came from the sun, but the vapour diffused the light. Later the sun appeared in an unclouded sky." According to this view the sun, moon, and stars were all created in 1:1, but they could not be seen from the earth until the fourth day. Both of the above approaches to the questions raised by this passage seek to avoid what appears to be the obvious sense of the text, that is, that the sun, moon, and stars were created on the fourth day. Both views modify the sense of the verb "created" so that it harmonizes with the statement of the first verse: God created the world in the beginning.

There is, however, another way to look at this text that provides a coherent reading of 1:1 and 1:14–18. First, we must decide on the meaning of the phrase "the heavens and the earth" in v.1 (see Notes). If the phrase means "universe" or "cosmos," as is most probable (H.H. Schmid, THAT, 1:229), then it must be taken with the same sense it has throughout its uses in the Bible (e.g., Joel 3:15–16); thus it would include the sun, moon, and stars. So the starting point of an understanding of vv.14–18 is the view that the whole of the universe, including the sun, moon, and stars, was created "in the beginning" (v.1) and thus not on the fourth day.

The second step is a consideration of the syntax of v.14 (see Notes). When the syntax of v.14 is compared to that of the creation of the expanse in v.6, the two verses have a quite different sense. The syntax of v.6 suggests that when God said, "Let there be an expanse," he was, in fact, creating an expanse where there was none previously ("creation out of nothing"). So clearly the author intended to say that God created the expanse on the first day. In v.14, however, the syntax is different, though the translations are often similar in English. In v.14 God does not say, "Let there be lights . . . to separate," as if there were no lights before this command and afterward the lights were created. Rather the Hebrew text reads, "And God said, 'Let the lights in the expanse of the sky separate.'" In other words, unlike the syntax of v.6, in v.14 God's command assumes that the lights were already in the expanse and that in response to his command they were given a purpose, "to separate the day from the night" and "to mark seasons and days and years." If the difference between the syntax of v.6 (the use of *hāyāh* alone) and v.14 (*hāyāh* + *l* infinitive; cf. GKC, 114h) is significant, then it suggests that the author did not understand his account of the fourth day as an account of the creation of the lights; but, on the contrary, the narrative assumes that the heavenly lights have been created already "in the beginning."

15–19 A third observation comes from the structure of vv.15–16. At the end of v.15, the author recounts, "and it was so" (*way^{e}hî-ḵēn*). This expression marks the end of the author's "report" and the beginning of his "comment" in v.16 (see comment on vv.6–7). Thus v.16 is not an account of the creation of the sun, moon, and stars on the fourth day. Rather it is a remark directed to the reader drawing out the significance of that which has previously been recounted: "So God [and not anyone else] made the lights and put them into the sky" (pers. tr.). Behind this narrative, in other words, is a concern on the part of the author to emphasize that God alone created the lights of the heavens, and thus no one else is to be given the glory and honor due only to him. The passage also states that God created the light in the heavens for a purpose, namely, to divide day and night, and to mark the "seasons and days and years" (vv.17–18). Both of these concerns form the heart of the whole of chapter 1, namely, the lesson that God alone is the Creator of all things and worthy of the worship of his people.

Notes

14 יְהִי רָקִיעַ בְּתוֹךְ הַמָּיִם (*y^{e}hî rāqî^{a}ʿ b^{e}ṯôḵ hammāyim,* "Let there be an expanse between the waters") in v.6 is to be distinguished from the similar clause in v.14—יְהִי מְאֹרֹת בִּרְקִיעַ הַשָּׁמַיִם לְהַבְדִּיל (*y^{e}hî m^{e}ʾōrōṯ birqî^{a}ʿ haššāmayim l^{e}haḇdîl,* "Let the lights in the expanse of the sky separate"). The verb הָיָה (*hāyāh*) in v.6 is a simple predicate: "Let there be," whereas in v.14, *hāyāh* has a complementary infinitive, *l^{e}haḇdîl,* which expresses a purpose: "Let the lights be for separating." GKC (par. 114h) remarks: "Just as clearly the idea of aiming at a definite purpose or turning towards an object may be seen in the combination of the verb הָיָה [*hāyāh*] *to be,* with ל [*l*] and an infinitive."

e. *Fifth day*

1:20–23

[20]And God said, "Let the water teem with living creatures, and let birds fly above the earth across the expanse of the sky." [21]So God created the great creatures of the sea and every living and moving thing with which the water teems, according to their kinds, and every winged bird according to its kind. And God saw that it was good. [22]God blessed them and said, "Be fruitful and increase in number and fill the water in the seas, and let the birds increase on the earth." [23]And there was evening, and there was morning—the fifth day.

20–23 The creation of living creatures is divided into two days. On the fifth day, as the account reads, God created the creatures of the sea and the sky. On the sixth day (vv.24–28), God created the land creatures—which included man. In v.20 God spoke ("And God said," *wayyō'mer*), and then in v.21 God acted ("So God created," *wayyiḇrā'*). The word for "created" (*bārā'*) is used six times in the Creation account (1:1, 21, 27; 2:3). Elsewhere the word "to make" (*'āśāh*) is used to describe God's actions.

Why is *bārā'* used with reference to the "great creatures of the sea" (v.21)? Are these "great creatures" singled out by the use of a special term? One suggestion is that the use of the word *bārā'* just at this point in the narrative is intended to mark the beginning of a new stage in the Creation, namely, the creation of the "living beings," a group distinct from the vegetation and physical world of the previous days (von Rad, Westermann). Each new step in the account is marked by the use of *bārā'*: the universe (v.1), the living creatures (v.2), and man (v.26). The orderliness of the account is evident, as is its lack of specificity. The primary interest of the author is to show the creation of all living creatures in three distinct groups: on the fifth day, sea creatures and sky creatures, and on the sixth day, land creatures.

For the first time in the Creation account, the notion of "blessing" appears (v.22). The blessing of the creatures of the sea and sky is identical with the blessing of man, with the exception of the notion of "dominion," which is given only to man. As soon as "living beings" are created, the notion of "blessing" is appropriate because the blessing relates to the giving of life.

Notes

21 The choice of the verb בָּרָא (*bārā'*, "to create") here is also related to the development of the theme of the "blessing" since there is an alliteration between "to create" (*bārā'*) and "to bless" (*bāraḵ*) throughout the account:

וַיְבָרֶךְ	. . .	וַיִּבְרָא	1:21–22[1]
וַיְבָרֶךְ	. . .	וַיִּבְרָא	1:27–28[2]
בָּרָא	. . .	וַיְבָרֶךְ	2:3a, b[3]
בְּרָאָם	. . .	וַיְבָרֶךְ	5:2b, a[4]

In the same way the choice of *bārā'* at the beginning of the chapter (1:1) appears to be related to an alliteration with *berē'šîṯ*.

[1] *wayyibrā'. . . way^ebārek.*
[2] *wayyibrā'. . . way^ebārek.*
[3] *way^ebārek. . . bārā'.*
[4] *way^ebārek. . . b^erā'ām.*

---

f. *Sixth day*

1:24–31

24 And God said, "Let the land produce living creatures according to
their kinds: livestock, creatures that move along the ground, and
wild animals, each according to its kind." And it was so. 25 God
made the wild animals according to their kinds, the livestock
according to their kinds, and all the creatures that move along the
ground according to their kinds. And God saw that it was good.
26 Then God said, "Let us make man in our image, in our
likeness, and let them rule over the fish of the sea and the birds of
the air, over the livestock, over all the earth, and over all the
creatures that move along the ground."

27 So God created man in his own image,
in the image of God he created him;
male and female he created them.

28 God blessed them and said to them, "Be fruitful and increase
in number; fill the earth and subdue it. Rule over the fish of the
sea and the birds of the air and over every living creature that
moves on the ground."
29 Then God said, "I give you every seed-bearing plant on the
face of the whole earth and every tree that has fruit with seed in it.
They will be yours for food. 30 And to all the beasts of the earth and
all the birds of the air and all the creatures that move on the
ground—everything that has the breath of life in it—I give every
green plant for food." And it was so.
31 God saw all that he had made, and it was very good. And there
was evening, and there was morning—the sixth day.

24–25 The account of the creation of the land creatures on the sixth day distinguishes two types: the "living creatures" that dwell on the land and mankind. In turn the "living creatures" of the land are divided into three groups: "livestock," "creatures that move along the ground," and "wild animals" (v.24). Mankind is distinguished as "male" and "female" (v.27).

Once again the author begins with the divine command—"And God said" (*wayyō'mer 'elōhîm*)—in v.24 and then follows with the comment to the reader in v.25: "God made" (*wayya'aś 'elōhîm*). At first reading the comment in v.25 does not appear to add significantly to what was reported of the command of v.24. However, a comparison of these verses with similar verses (vv.11–12) shows that v.25 does add an important clarification to the report of v.24. In v.11 God said, "Let the land produce vegetation" (*tad^ešē' hā'āreṣ deše'*); and, in the comment that follows, the author added (v.12), "The land produced vegetation" (*tôṣē' hā'āreṣ deše'*).

The point of the comment was apparently that the land, not God, produced the vegetation. In vv.24–25, however, there is a shift in emphasis. Verse 24 reports a command similar to v.11: "Let the land produce living creatures" (*tôṣē' hā'āreṣ nepeš ḥayyāh*); but the comment that follows in v.25 stresses that it was God who made the living creatures: "God made the wild animals" (*wayya'aś 'elōhîm 'et-ḥayyat hā'āreṣ*).

Apparently the author wanted to show that though the command was the same for the creation of both the vegetation and the living creatures on land, there was a distinction between the origin of the two forms of life. Vegetation was produced from the land, but the living creatures were made by God himself. Life stems from God and is to be distinguished from the rest of the physical world (cf. the creation of man and the animals in ch. 2).

26–27 The creation of man is set apart from the previous acts of creation by a series of subtle contrasts with the earlier accounts of God's acts. For example, in v.26 the beginning of the creation of man is marked by the usual "And God said." However, God's command that follows is not an impersonal (third person) "Let there be . . . " but rather the more personal (first person) "Let us make." Second, whereas throughout the previous account the making of each creature is described as "according to its kind" (*lᵉmînēhû*), in the account of the creation of man it is specified that the man and the woman were made "in our [God's] image" (*bᵉṣalmēnû*), not merely "according to his own kind." Man's image is not simply of himself; he also shares a likeness to his Creator. Third, the creation of man is specifically noted as a creation of man as "male and female" (v.27). The author has not considered gender to be an important feature to stress in his account of the creation of the other forms of life, but for humanity it is of some importance. Thus the narrative puts stress on the fact that God created man as "male and female." Fourth, only man has been given dominion in God's creation. This dominion is expressly stated to be over all other living creatures: sky, sea, and land creatures.

If we ask why the author has singled out the creation of man in this way, one obvious answer is that he intended to portray him as a special creature, marked off from the rest of God's works. But the author's purpose seems not merely to mark man as different from the rest of the creatures; the narrative seems just as intent on showing that man is like God as well. It is important not to lose sight of the fact that behind the portrayal of the creation of man in this narrative lies the purpose of the author of Genesis and the Pentateuch. The reader is given certain facts that are to serve as the starting point for the larger purposes of the author within the Pentateuch. Man is a creature. But man is a special creature. He is made in the image and likeness of God.

There have been many attempts to explain the plural forms: "Let *us* make [*na'ᵃśeh*] man in *our* image [*bᵉṣalmēnû*], in *our* likeness [*kiḏmûṯēnû*]" (see Westermann, 1:144–45; König, *Genesis,* p. 153). Westermann (pp. 144–45) summarizes the explanations given to the plurals under four headings: (1) the plural is a reference to the Trinity; (2) the plural is a reference to God and his heavenly court of angels; (3) the plural is an attempt to avoid the idea of an immediate resemblance of humans to God; (4) the plural is an expression of deliberation on God's part as he sets out to create man. The singulars in v.27 (*bᵉṣalmô* ["in his own image"] and *bᵉṣelem 'ᵉlōhîm* ["in the image of God"]; cf. 5:1) rule out explanation 2 above, that the plural refers to a heavenly court of angels, since in the immediate context man's creation is said to be "in *his* image" with no mention of man in the image of the angels.

Explanations 3 and 4 above are both possible within the context, but neither explanation is specifically supported by the context. It is not convincing to point to Genesis 11:7 in support of the notion of deliberation since the use of the plural in that passage is motivated by the chiastic wordplay between *nāḇᵉlāh* ("let us confuse," 11:7) and *nilbᵉnāh* ("let us make," 11:3) (see J.P. Fokklemann, *Narrative Art in*

Genesis [Assen: Van Gorcum, 1975]). Where we do find unequivocal deliberation (as in 18:17), it is not the plural that is used but rather the singular: "Shall I hide from Abraham what I am about to do?" As Westermann has stated, explanation 1 is "a dogmatic judgment," though we could add that it is not a judgment that runs counter to the passage itself. However, if we seek an answer from the immediate context, we should turn to the next verse for our clues.

In v.27 it is stated twice that man was created (*bārā'*) in God's image and a third time that man was created (*bārā'*) "male and female." The same pattern is found in Genesis 5:1–2a: "When God created [*bārā'*] man, . . . he created [*bārā'*] them male and female." The singular man (*'āḏām*) is created as a plurality, "male and female" (*zāḵār ûnᵉqēḇāh*). In a similar way the one God (*wayyō'mer 'ᵉlōhîm*, "And God said") created man through an expression of his plurality (*na'ᵃśeh 'āḏām bᵉṣalmēnû*, "Let us make man in our image"). Following this clue the divine plurality expressed in v.26 is seen as an anticipation of the human plurality of the man and woman, thus casting the human relationship between man and woman in the role of reflecting God's own personal relationship with himself. "Could anything be more obvious than to conclude from this clear indication that the image and likeness of the being created by God signifies existence in confrontation, i.e., in this confrontation, in the juxtaposition and conjunction of man and man which is that of male and female, and then to go on to ask against this background in what the original and prototype of the divine existence of the Creator consists?" (K. Barth, *Church Dogmatics* [New York: Scribner, 1956], 3/1, p. 195).

28 The importance of the blessing in v.28 cannot be overlooked. Throughout the remainder of the Book of Genesis and the Pentateuch, the "blessing" remains a central theme. The living creatures have already been blessed on the fifth day (v.22); thus the author's view of the blessing extends beyond man to that of the whole of God's living creatures. In v.28 man is also included in God's blessing. The blessing itself in these verses is primarily "posterity": "Be fruitful and increase in number; fill the earth." Thus already the fulfillment of the blessing is tied to man's "seed" and the notion of "life"—two themes that will later dominate the narratives of the Book of Genesis. The imperatives "Be fruitful," "increase," and "fill" are not to be understood as commands in this verse since the introductory statement identifies them as a "blessing" (*wayᵉḇāreḵ*). The imperative, along with the jussive, is the common mood of the blessing (cf. Gen 27:19).

g. *Seventh day*

2:1–3

1 Thus the heavens and the earth were completed in all their vast array.
2 By the seventh day God had finished the work he had been doing; so
on the seventh day he rested from all his work. 3 And God blessed
the seventh day and made it holy, because on it he rested from all
the work of creating that he had done.

2:1–3 The author has set the seventh day apart from the first six, not only by stating specifically that God "sanctified" it, but also by changing the style of the account markedly. On this day God does not "speak" (*wayyō'mer*), nor does he "work" (*wayya'aś*) as he had on the previous days. On this day he "blessed" (*wayᵉḇāreḵ*, v.3) and "sanctified" (*wayᵉqaddēš*; NIV, "made it holy"), but he did not "work." The reader is left with a somber and repetitive reminder of only one fact: God did not work on the seventh day. While little else is recounted, it is repeated three times that God did not work. The author surely intended by this to put the emphasis on God's "rest" (vv.2–3).

It is likely, as well, that the author intended the reader to understand the account of the seventh day in light of the "Image of God" theme of the sixth day. If the purpose of pointing to the "likeness" between man and his Creator was to call on the reader to be more like God (e.g., Lev 11:45), then it is significant that the account of the seventh day stresses the very thing that the writer elsewhere so ardently calls on the reader to do: "rest" on the seventh day (cf. Exod 20:8–11). If, as we have earlier suggested, the author's intention was to point to the past as a picture of the future, then the emphasis on God's "rest" forms an important part of the author's understanding of what lies in the future. At important points along the way, the author will return to the theme of God's "rest" as a reminder of what yet lies ahead (2:15; 5:29; 8:4; Exod 20:11; Deut 5:14; 12:10; 25:19). Later biblical writers continued to see a parallel between God's "rest" in Creation and the future "rest" that awaits the faithful (Ps 95:11; Heb 3:11).

Notes

1 The threefold expression הַשָּׁמַיִם וְהָאָרֶץ וְכָל־צְבָאָם (*haššāmayim wᵉhā'āreṣ wᵉkol-ṣᵉḇā'ām*, "the heavens and the earth . . . in all their vast array") refers to the "sky" (*haššāmayim*) of 1:8 and the "land" (*hā'āreṣ*) of 1:10, which were made and then filled with "their array" (*ṣᵉḇā'ām*, lit., "their hosts") in the remainder of the chapter (as in Deut 4:19, where the *ṣᵉḇā' haššāmayim* refers to the "the sun, the moon and the stars"), rather than to the hendiadys of 1:1—אֵת הַשָּׁמַיִם וְאֵת הָאָרֶץ (*'eṯ haššāmayim wᵉ'eṯ hā'āreṣ*)—which refers to the whole of the "universe." The NIV, however, overlooks this distinction and takes the verse as a reference back to 1:1. In so doing it must resort to an unlikely paraphrase of *wᵉkol-ṣᵉḇā'ām* as "in all their vast array."

2 The NIV translation of וַיְכַל אֱלֹהִים בַּיּוֹם הַשְּׁבִיעִי מְלַאכְתּוֹ (*wayᵉḵal 'ᵉlōhîm bayyôm haššᵉḇî'î mᵉla'ḵtô*, "By the seventh day God had finished the work") superficially glosses over a serious question. As is evident in the versions (Samar., LXX, Syr.), the thought of God "finishing his work" on the Sabbath, or seventh day, gave rise to a secondary reading of הַשִּׁשִּׁי (*haššiššî*, "the sixth"): viz., "God finished his work on the sixth day." However, as the parallel in Exod 40:33b shows, *wayᵉḵal mᵉla'ḵtô* simply states that God's work was finished on the seventh day. The second half of the verse states it in the positive: "So on the seventh day he rested from all his work."

3 Unlike the other days of Creation, the seventh day does not conclude with "and there was evening, and there was morning—the seventh day." In this respect the seventh day stands apart from the other six days in not having an account of its conclusion. It is this feature of the narrative that has suggested a picture of an eternal, divine "Sabbath." The addition of the infinitive לַעֲשׂוֹת (*la'ᵃśôṯ*, "had done") is important in that it identifies and equates the two verbs used to describe the work of God in chapter 1: בָּרָא (*bārā'*) and עָשָׂה (*'āśāh*). Consequently, immediately after the narrative of the Fall (3:21), where it occurs with God as the subject, the verb *'āśāh* points to an interruption of God's "Sabbath": "The LORD God made [*wayya'aś*] garments of skin for Adam and his wife and clothed them."

3. *The gift of the land (2:4–24)*

It is important to read chapter 2 as an integral part of the first chapter. (The chapter divisions are, of course, not original and sometimes very arbitrary. They are referred to here only for the sake of convenience.) It seems apparent that the author intended the second chapter to be read closely with the first and that the events in each chapter be identified as part of the same event. Thus the author explicitly returned to the place and time of chapter 1 at the beginning of chapter 2: "When the LORD God made the earth and the heavens" (v.4). It is likely that the author's central theological interests in chapter 1 would be continued in chapter 2 as well: the theme of man's creation in the "image of God." Thus we may expect to find in chapter 2 a continuation of the theme of the "likeness" between man and the Creator.

a. *Creation of man*

2:4–7

4 This is the account of the heavens and the earth when they were created.
When the LORD God made the earth and the heavens—5 and no shrub of the field had yet appeared on the earth and no plant of the field had yet sprung up, for the LORD God had not sent rain on the earth and there was no man to work the ground, 6 but streams came up from the earth and watered the whole surface of the ground—7 the LORD God formed the man from the dust of the ground and breathed into his nostrils the breath of life, and the man became a living being.

4–6 Chapter 2 begins with a description of the condition of the land (*hāʾāreṣ*) before the creation of man. In this respect it resembles the description of the land in 1:2. The focus of the description is on those parts of the land that were to be directly affected by the Fall (3:8–24). The narrative points to the fact that before man was created (in v.7), the effects of man's rebellion and the Fall had "not yet" been felt on the land. In the subsequent narratives, each of the parts of the description of the land in vv.4–6 is specifically identified as a result of the fall of man. The "shrub of the field" (*śî^{a}ḥ haśśāḏeh*) and "plant of the field" (*ʿēśeḇ haśśāḏeh*) are not a reference to the "vegetation" of chapter 1 but rather anticipate the "thorns and thistles" (*qôṣ w^{e}ḏardar*) and "plants of the field" (*ʿēśeḇ haśśāḏeh*) that were to come (in 3:18) as a result of the curse (Cassuto). Similarly, when the narrative states that the Lord God had not yet "sent rain on the earth" (*himṭîr . . . ʿal-hāʾāreṣ*, v.5), we can sense the allusion to the Flood narratives, at which time the Lord explicitly stated, "I will send rain on the earth [*mamṭîr ʿal-hāʾāreṣ*]" (7:4).

The reference to "no man to work the ground [*laʿ^{a}ḇōḏ ʾeṯ-hāʾ^{a}ḏāmāh*]" (v.5) points to the time when the man and the woman were to be cast from the garden "to work the ground [*laʿ^{a}ḇōḏ ʾeṯ-hāʾ^{a}ḏāmāh*]" (3:23). Thus as an introduction to the account of man's creation, we are told that a land had been prepared for him: "streams came up from the earth and watered the whole surface of the ground" (v.6). In the description of that land, however, we can already see the coming of the time when man would become an alien and a stranger in a foreign land.

7 At first glance the description of the creation of man here is quite different from that of chapter 1. Man was made "from the dust of the ground" rather than "in the image of God" as in chapter 1. No two descriptions could be more distinct. However, we should not overlook the fact that the topic of the "creation of man" in chapter 2 is not limited merely to v.7. In fact, the topic of the creation of the man and the woman is the focus of the whole of chapter 2. What the author had stated as a simple fact in chapter 1 (man, male and female, was created in God's likeness) is explained and developed throughout the narrative of chapter 2. We cannot contrast the depiction of the creation of man in chapter 1 with only one verse in chapter 2; we must compare it to the whole of the chapter.

The first point the author is intent on making is that man, though a special creature made in God's image, was nevertheless a creature like the other creatures that God had made. Man did not begin as a "heavenly creature"; he was made of the "dust [*'āp̱ār*] of the ground." In light of the special treatment given to man's creation in chapter 1, the emphasis in chapter 2 on man's "creatureliness" is not without its importance. The notion that man's origin might somehow be connected with that of the divine is deliberately excluded by this narrative. Man's origin was the dust of the ground. One can also see in this picture of man's origin an anticipation of his destiny in the Fall, when he would again return to the "dust" (*'āp̱ār*, 3:19). In Creation man arose out of the dust, but in the Fall he returned to the dust. Thus the author graphically pictures the contrast between the work of God and the work of man.

Chapter 2 makes still another contribution to the picture of man's creation in God's image. It can be seen in the author's depiction of the land that was prepared for man's dwelling. The description of the Garden of Eden appears to be deliberately cast to foreshadow the description of the tabernacle found later in the Pentateuch. The garden, like the tabernacle, was the place where man could enjoy the fellowship and presence of God.

b. *Preparation of the garden*

2:8–14

> 8 Now the LORD God had planted a garden in the east, in Eden; and there he put the man he had formed. 9 And the LORD God made all kinds of trees grow out of the ground—trees that were pleasing to the eye and good for food. In the middle of the garden were the tree of life and the tree of the knowledge of good and evil.
>
> 10 A river watering the garden flowed from Eden; from there it was separated into four headwaters. 11 The name of the first is the Pishon; it winds through the entire land of Havilah, where there is gold. 12 (The gold of that land is good; aromatic resin and onyx are also there.) 13 The name of the second river is the Gihon; it winds through the entire land of Cush. 14 The name of the third river is the Tigris; it runs along the east side of Asshur. And the fourth river is the Euphrates.

8 An inordinate amount of attention has been given in chapter 2 to the description of the "garden." We must pay attention to these details. First, we are told that the Lord God planted the garden and "put" (*wayyāśem*) man there. Later in the same narrative this is repeated, though, as we shall see, with significant differences. We should also notice that the garden was planted "in the east [*miqqeḏem*], in Eden." The word "Eden" (*'ēḏen*) appears to be a specific place; and since, in the Hebrew Bible, the word means "delight," we may assume that the name was intended to evoke a picture of idyllic delight and rest.

The fact that the garden was "in the east" in Eden is somewhat striking. Elsewhere in the Book of Genesis, the notion of "eastward" (e.g., *miqqeḏem*) is associated with judgment and separation from God (e.g., 3:24; 11:2; 13:11). Also, when the man and woman were expelled from the garden, the cherubim were placed "on the east side" (*miqqeḏem,* 3:24) of the Garden of Eden, giving the impression that the garden itself was not in the east. Such an apparent difficulty in the coherence of the passage may account for the fact that in v.8 the garden is not actually called the "garden *of* Eden," as it is elsewhere, but rather the "garden *in* Eden" (*gan-beʿēḏen*), a designation found only in this verse. Thus, according to v.8, the garden was planted in Eden, which was apparently to be taken as a location larger than the garden itself; and, if "in the east" is taken with reference to Eden itself, the garden was on its eastern side.

It is still unclear how the reference to "east" (*miqqeḏem*) in v.8, which seems positive, is to be associated with the other references to "east" in the subsequent narratives, which are all to be taken negatively. One solution may be that of the early versions. The Targum of Onkelos translates *miqqeḏem* as *milqaḏmîn* ("long ago") rather than as "eastward" (cf. the Vulgate's *a principio*). Both meanings are possible for *miqqeḏem*. In any event, if a geographical direction is meant here, the author is apparently establishing an important distinction between "east" and "west" that will be of great thematic importance throughout the remainder of the book (see below). For now we are given only a hint that the location of the garden may be important.

9–10 In the garden were beautiful, lush trees, including the elusive "tree of life" and "tree of the knowledge of good and evil" (v.9), as well as a river that divided into four "headwaters" (v.10). Special care is given to locate the rivers and to describe the character of the lands through which they flowed. The lands were rich in gold and precious jewels (v.12), and their location was closely aligned with the land later promised to Abraham and his descendants (see Ibn Ezra, Rashi)—another example of the author's continual interest in drawing comparisons between the early events in primeval history and specific events and places in the life of Israel.

Later biblical prophets also made an association between the Garden of Eden and the land promised to the fathers (cf. Ezek 36:35: "This land that was laid waste has become like the garden of Eden"; Joel 2:3: "Before them the land is like the garden of Eden, behind them, a desert waste"; Isa 51:3: "The LORD will surely comfort Zion and will look with compassion on all her ruins; he will make her deserts like Eden, her wastelands like the garden of the LORD"; Zech 14:8: "On that day living water will flow out from Jerusalem"; Rev 22:1–2: "Then the angel showed me the river of the water of life, as clear as crystal, flowing from the throne of God and of the Lamb down the middle of the great street of the city. On each side of the river stood the tree of life, bearing twelve crops of fruit, yielding its fruit every month").

11–14 The location of the Garden of/in Eden has long been a topic of debate. Two of the rivers mentioned in association with the garden can be identified with certainty, the Euphrates (*perāṯ*) and the Tigris (*ḥiddeqel*) (v.14). It is difficult to identify the other two, the "Pishon" (*pîšôn*) and the "Gihon" (*gîḥôn*) (vv.11, 13). Since the "land of Cush" (*ʾereṣ kûš*) is identified in the Bible as Ethiopia, the "Gihon" is most likely to be taken as the river that passes through the land of Ethiopia. This suggests that the river the author had in mind was the "river of Egypt." The land of "Havilah," however, cannot be identified. It should be noted that the amount of description given to each of the four rivers is in inverse proportion to the certainty of the identification of each of the rivers.

Most of the attention in the narrative is given to the river "Pishon" (v.11), but there is least certainty regarding that river's identification and location. On the other hand, the narrative merely states that the River Euphrates is the fourth river (v.14). The author's attention to detail with the two lesser-known rivers (e.g., the gold and jewels) can be tied to the parallels between the role of the garden and that of the tabernacle later in the Pentateuch. The mention of the Euphrates and Tigris rivers, on the other hand, can be linked to the identification of the Garden of Eden and the Promised Land. It can hardly be a coincidence that these rivers, along with the "River of Egypt," again play a role in marking boundaries of the land promised to Abraham (15:18).

Another important detail in the description of the Garden of Eden in chapter 2 is the close similarity between the appearance and role of the garden and that of the tabernacle in Exodus 25–27. We have already called attention to the similarities between the account of Creation in chapter 1 (see comments there) and the account of the building of the tabernacle in Exodus 25–27. Thus it is no surprise to find that the description of the "garden" erected by God in chapter 2 should also suggest similarities to the tabernacle. In describing the garden the author's primary interest lay in stressing the beauty of the gold and precious stones throughout the lands encompassed by the garden. If the purpose of such descriptions in the later literature is taken as a guide, the point of the description of the garden is to show the glory of God's presence through the beauty of the physical surroundings.

The prophet Haggai later proclaimed the glory of God's presence in the new temple with a description of the gold and precious metals of that temple (Hag 2:7–8): " 'I will fill this house with glory,' says the LORD Almighty. 'The silver is mine and the gold is mine,' declares the LORD Almighty." So also John's description of the New Jerusalem stressed the gold and precious stones that pictured the glorious presence of God among his people (Rev 21:18): "The wall [of New Jerusalem] was made of jasper, and the city of pure gold, as pure as glass. The foundations of the city walls were decorated with every kind of precious stone." If there was, in fact, an attempt to depict the garden as a foreshadowing of the tabernacle of God, then it is of further interest to find that the description of God's placing man in the garden also bears strong resemblance to the later establishment of the priesthood for the tabernacle and the temple.

Notes

---

8 The pluperfect translation of וַיִּטַּע (*wayyiṭṭa'*)—"Now the LORD God had planted a garden"—is not warranted by the immediate context or Hebrew syntax (see Paul Joüon, *Grammaire de L'Hébreu Biblique* [Rome: Pontifical Bible Institute, 1923], par. 118d; König, *Syntax*, par. 142; S.R. Driver, *A Treatise On the Use of the Tenses in Hebrew* [Oxford: Oxford University Press, 1892], pp. 84ff.). The difficulty lies in the apparent conflict between this account and that in chapter 1, where the plants are first created and then man. The English translators have attempted to solve the problem by means of a past-perfect translation for *wayyiṭṭa'*. Even if the past perfect were possible for the waw-consecutive form, which the grammarians deny, the waw consecutive וַיָּשֶׂם (*wayyāśem*, "and he put") that follows it, on any reckoning, is to be read as continuing the action of *wayyiṭṭa'*; and that clause contains the reference to the creation of the man. Rather than attempting to sort out the relative chronologies of the two accounts, it is better to recognize that 2:4b–14 is a

summary of the events of chapter 1 and thus is not to be read in chronological harmony with it. The verses say, simply, before there were any wild plants, before there was any rain, before man had to work the ground, God made man from the ground, planted a garden for him, and put him in the garden. After an extensive description of the garden, the narrative gets under way in v.15 by returning to the act of God's placing man in the garden.

9 The expression כָּל־עֵץ נֶחְמָד לְמַרְאֶה וְטוֹב לְמַאֲכָל (*kol-ʿēṣ neḥmāḏ lemar'eh weṭôḇ lema'aḵāl*) should be understood as "every tree that is beautiful and edible"; thus the garden is depicted as an orchard of fruit trees, not merely a garden of every kind of tree. The translation "all kinds of trees" (NIV) gives the erroneous impression that every type of tree was to be found in the garden. The syntax of v.9b suggests that there were two special trees to be found there, the "tree of life" and the "tree of the knowledge of good and evil." In this verse the "tree of life" is said to be בְּתוֹךְ הַגָּן (*beṯôḵ haggān*, "in the middle of the garden"). In 3:3, however, it is the "tree of the knowledge of good and evil" that is in the "middle of the garden" (*beṯôḵ-haggān*). The natural inference from the larger context is that both trees were in the "middle of the garden."

---

c. *Man's place in the garden*

2:15–24

[15] The LORD God took the man and put him in the Garden of Eden to work it and take care of it. [16] And the LORD God commanded the man, "You are free to eat from any tree in the garden; [17] but you must not eat from the tree of the knowledge of good and evil, for when you eat of it you will surely die."

[18] The LORD God said, "It is not good for the man to be alone. I will make a helper suitable for him."

[19] Now the LORD God had formed out of the ground all the beasts of the field and all the birds of the air. He brought them to the man to see what he would name them; and whatever the man called each living creature, that was its name. [20] So the man gave names to all the livestock, the birds of the air and all the beasts of the field.

But for Adam no suitable helper was found. [21] So the LORD God caused the man to fall into a deep sleep; and while he was sleeping, he took one of the man's ribs and closed up the place with flesh. [22] Then the LORD God made a woman from the rib he had taken out of the man, and he brought her to the man.

[23] The man said,

"This is now bone of my bones
  and flesh of my flesh;
she shall be called 'woman,'
  for she was taken out of man."

[24] For this reason a man will leave his father and mother and be united to his wife, and they will become one flesh.

15–24 The author had already noted that God "put" (*wayyāśem*) man into the garden (v.8b). In v.15 he returned to this point and recounted the purpose for God's putting man there. Two important points from v.15 are in danger of being obscured by the English translations. The first is the change from v.8 in the Hebrew word for "put." Unlike v.8, where a common term for "put" is used, in v.15 the author uses a term (*wayyanniḥēhû*) that he elsewhere has reserved for two special uses: God's "rest" or "safety," which he gives to man in the land (e.g., Gen 19:16; Deut 3:20; 12:10; 25:19), and the "dedication" of something in the presence of the Lord (Exod 16:33–34; Lev

16:23; Num 17:4; Deut 26:4, 10). Both senses of the term appear to lie behind the author's use of the word in v.15. Man was "put" into the garden where he could "rest" and be "safe," and man was "put" into the garden "in God's presence" where he could have fellowship with God (3:8).

A second point from v.15 that has often been overlooked in the EVs is the specific purpose for God's putting man in the garden. In most EVs man is "put" in the garden "to work it and take care of it" (*leʿobdāh ûlešomrāh*). Although that translation was as early as the LXX (2d cent. B.C.), there are serious objections to it. For one, the suffixed pronoun in the Hebrew text rendered "it" in English is feminine, whereas the noun "garden," which the pronoun refers to in English, is a masculine noun in Hebrew. Only by changing the pronoun to a masculine singular, as the LXX has done, can it have the sense of the EVs, namely "to work" and "to keep." Moreover, later in this same narrative (3:23) "to work the ground" (*laʿabōḏ*) is said to be a result of the Fall, and the narrative suggests that the author had intended such a punishment to be seen as an ironic reversal of man's original purpose (see comments on 3:22–24). If such was the case, then "working" and "keeping" the garden would not provide a contrast to "working the ground."

In light of these objections, which cannot easily be overlooked, a more suitable translation of the Hebrew *leʿobdāh ûlešomrāh* would be "to worship and to obey" (Cassuto). Man is put in the garden to worship God and to obey him. Man's life in the garden was to be characterized by worship and obedience; he was a priest, not merely a worker and keeper of the garden. Such a reading not only answers the objections raised against the traditional English translation, it also suits the larger ideas of the narrative. Throughout chapter 2 the author has consistently and consciously developed the idea of man's "likeness" to God along the same lines as the major themes of the Pentateuch as a whole, namely, the theme of worship and Sabbath rest.

A further confirmation of our reading *leʿobdāh ûlešomrāh* as "to worship and to obey" is the fact that in v.16 we read for the first time that "God commanded" (*wayeṣaw*) the man whom he had created. Just as in the remainder of the Torah, enjoyment of God's good land is made contingent on "keeping" (*lišmōr*) God's commandments (*miṣwōṯ*) (cf. Deut 30:16). The similarity between this condition for enjoyment of God's blessing and that laid down for Israel at Sinai and in Deuteronomy is clear. Indeed, one can hardly fail to hear in these words of God to the first man the words of Moses to Israel: "See, I set before you today life and blessing [lit., 'the good' (*haṭṭôḇ*; NIV, 'prosperity')], death and calamity [lit., 'the evil' (*hārāʿ*; NIV, 'destruction')]. For I command you today to love the LORD your God, to walk in his ways, and to keep [*lišmōr*] his commands [*miṣwōṯāyw*], decrees and laws; then you will live [*ḥāyāh*] and increase [*rāḇāh*], and the LORD your God will bless you in the land you are entering to possess. But if your heart turns away and you are not obedient, . . . You will not live long in the land you are crossing the Jordan to enter and possess" (Deut 30:15–18).

The inference of God's commands in vv.16–17 is that God alone knows what is good (*ṭôḇ*) for man and that God alone knows what is not good (*raʿ*) for him. To enjoy the "good" man must trust God and obey him. If man disobeys, he will have to decide for himself what is good (*ṭôḇ*) and what is not good (*raʿ*). While to modern man such a prospect may seem desirable, to the author of Genesis it is the worst fate that could have befallen him. Only God knows what is good (*ṭôḇ*) for man. Only God can know what is good.

Having put this in general terms in vv.16–17, the author turns in the remainder of the chapter to set forth a specific example of God's knowledge of the "good": the creation of the woman. Not only has the first chapter stressed that God knows the good (e.g., "and God saw that it was good [*ṭôḇ*]"), but now in the present narrative the creation of the woman has become an archetypal example of God's knowledge of the good. When He sees man alone, God says, "It is not good [*ṭôḇ*] for the man to be alone" (v.18). At the close of chapter 2, the author put the final touches on his account of what it means for man to be "in God's image and likeness." In the first chapter the author had intimated that man's creation in the "image of God" somehow entailed his creation as male and female: "In the image of God he created him;/ male and female he created them" (1:27). In the narrative of the creation of the woman in chapter 2, the author has returned to develop this theme by showing that man's creation "in God's image" also entails a "partnership" (*ʿēzer kᵉnegdô*; NIV, "a suitable helper") with his wife. The "likeness" that the man and the woman share with God in chapter 1 finds an analogy in the "likeness" between the man and his wife in chapter 2. Here also, as in the first chapter, man's likeness to God is shown against the background of his distinction from the other creatures.

For the first time since the account of the creation of the man and the woman in chapter 1, there is divine deliberation (Wenham, p. 68). The plural "Let us make" (*naʿᵃśeh,* 1:26) is replaced by the singular "I will make" (*ʾeʿᵉśeh,* 2:18) perhaps because only the woman is being created. In chapter 1 the divine plurality found its analogy in the creation of "male and female," just as here the divine singular appears to be a curious reflection of man's being alone (*lᵉḇaddô,* 2:18). The divine intention for the woman is that she be a "partner," an *ʿēzer kᵉnegḏô* (2:18, 20). The term *ʿēzer kᵉnegḏô* occurs only two times in the Bible, once at the beginning and once at the conclusion of the account of God's making the animals. The preposition *negeḏ* means "in front of" and with the further preposition *k* means "corresponding to" (BDB, p. 617) or "exact correspondence" (Jacob, p. 94). The point of the narrative is that there was no helper who corresponded to man among the animals. A special act of creation of the woman was necessary.

In what sense was the woman created to be a "helper"? Augustine suggested that she was to help in the task of bringing forth children (Delitzsch, p. 140). According to Delitzsch, she was to help "till and keep" the garden (ibid.). Westermann seeks a more comprehensive interpretation: the woman is to provide "support in a wide sense" (p. 309). Although each of these approaches to the question has validity, in light of the importance of the blessing ("Be fruitful and increase") in the creation of the man and the woman in 1:28, it appears most likely that the "help" envisioned is tied to the bearing of children. Further support for such an interpretation comes from the narrative of the next chapter. Not only does the woman's judgment relate specifically to her role in bearing children (3:16), but also in the promise of the "offspring" (*zeraʿ*, lit., "seed," 3:15) there is an apparent wordplay on the woman's role as a "helper" (*ʿēzer kᵉnegḏô*).

Just as at other crucial points in the narrative, when a new relationship is initiated (e.g., the covenant with Abraham, 15:12; the covenant with Jacob, 28:11), the recipient of God's provision sleeps while God acts. Within these narratives the purpose of the sleep is not merely anesthetic, though in the present narrative that surely plays a part. As in the other narratives listed above, the man's sleep in the face of the divine activity appears to be intended to portray a sense of passivity and acceptance of the divine provision (cf. Ps 127:2).

Much discussion has centered on the mention of the "rib" from which the woman was created. At first glance nothing in the narrative seems to take up and develop this detail. It is difficult to say why the mention of the rib was included in the story. A homiletic midrash often quoted by commentators says that "just as the rib is found at the side of the man and is attached to him, even so the good wife, the rib of her husband, stands at his side to be his helper-counterpart, and her soul is bound up with his" (Cassuto, p. 134). The same ambiguity lies in the last remark in 2:21: "And [he] closed up the place with flesh," which is often taken as an attempt to preserve the beauty of the scene by summarily removing any images of bodily mutilation (cf. Cassuto, p. 134).

Finally, the man's jubilant response—"bone of my bones and flesh of my flesh"—appears to go beyond the narrative account in vv.21–22, where there is only mention of the "rib." This last detail has prompted Cassuto to suggest that "He did not take the bone alone, as the exegetes usually understand the verse . . . the Creator took together with the bone also the flesh attached to it, and from the flesh He formed the woman's flesh, and from the bone her bones" (p. 134). Cassuto's comment serves more to point out the nature of the problem than to solve it, though it points the way to a solution.

In the mention of "one of the ribs" (*'aḥaṯ miṣṣal'ōṯāyw*), the narrative anticipates the words of the man—"bone of my bones [*mē'ᵃṣāmay*]"—by the wordplay between "ribs" and "bones" (*mṣl'* reverses *'ṣm*). Such a wordplay explains why the rib is first called "one of the ribs" (*'aḥaṯ miṣṣal'ōṯāyw*) and not simply "the rib" as in the next verse.

Moreover, in the mention of the closing of the "flesh" (*bāśār*) over the rib, the narrative further anticipates the response of the man in 3:23: "flesh [*bāśār*] of my flesh." It appears, then, that in the mention of the rib from which the woman was created, no particular meaning is to be attached to the rib as such but rather to "the rib and the flesh" as showing the woman to be in substance the same as the man. Westermann's statement regarding this narrative aptly describes its purpose: "Gen 2 is unique among the creation myths of the whole of the Ancient Near East in its appreciation of the meaning of woman, i.e., that human existence is a partnership of man and woman" (p. 232).

There can be no doubt that the author intended the account of the naming of the animals to be read as a part of the story of the creation of the woman. This is made certain in v.20, where at the conclusion of the man's naming the animals the author remarks, "But for Adam, no suitable helper was found." The clear implication is that the author saw in man's naming the animals also his search for a suitable partner. In recounting that no suitable partner had been found, the author has assured the reader that man was *not like* the other creatures. In contrast to this, the author recorded in graphic detail the words of the man when he discovered the woman who was one like himself: "This is now bone of my bone and flesh of my flesh" (v.23). The man recognized his own likeness in the woman.

Notes

---

15 As Cassuto has pointed out (p. 122), infinitives with a final he and without the *mappiq*—e.g., לְעָבְדָהּ וּלְשָׁמְרָה (*lᵉ'oḇdāh ûlᵉšomrāh*, "to serve him and to obey him" [see comments]; NIV, "to work it and take care of it")—are common in biblical Hebrew (GKC, par. 45d;

Joüon, *Grammaire*, par. 49d). The importance of these two infinitives can be seen in the fact that the narrative returns to precisely them in its summary conclusion of the state of mankind after the Fall. The man and the woman were created "for worship" (*l^e'obdāh*, 2:15), but after the Fall they were thrown out of the garden "to work the ground" (*la'^abōḏ 'eṯ-hā'^aḏāmāh*, 3:23). In the same way they were created "for obedience" (*l^ešomrāh*, 2:15), but after the Fall they were "kept" (*lišmōr*, 3:24; NIV, "guard") from the tree of life.

17 In the remainder of the Pentateuch, the expression מוֹת תָּמוּת (*môṯ tāmûṯ*, "you will surely die") means that one has come under the verdict of the death penalty (cf. 20:7; Exod 31:14; Lev 24:16). It is a pronouncement of a judge on one who has been condemned to die. In the Leviticus passage the sentence is to be carried out by stoning the guilty party. In the present narrative the verdict is carried out by expulsion from the garden and the "tree of life" (3:22–24). The narrative thus suggests that the picture of man's "immortality" before the Fall is not that of an inherent human quality but rather a gift from God in the access to the tree of life given to him (cf. 1 Tim 6:16).

18 The expression עֵזֶר כְּנֶגְדּוֹ (*'ēzer k^enegdô*) has the general sense of "a suitable helper." The specific sense of these terms should be drawn from the immediate context. That the woman (wife) is a "helper" (*'ēzer*) is to be understood from the "commission" given to man in both 1:28 ("Be fruitful and increase in number") and 2:15 ("for worship and obedience"; see comments in loc.). The implication of the narrative is that in both of these areas of life, the family and worship, man stands in need of the woman's help. It is not good that he should be alone.

19–20 A straightforward reading of וַיִּצֶר יהוה אֱלֹהִים (*wayyiṣer yhwh 'elōhîm*, "And the LORD God formed") suggests that in chapter 2 the creation of the animals follows that of the creation of man. In chapter 1, however, the animals are created first and then man (vv.24–26). This has long been pointed to as evidence of an internal contradiction within the Genesis account of Creation. The NIV has offered an untenable solution in its rendering the waw consecutive in *wayyiṣer* by a pluperfect: "Now the LORD God *had* formed." Not only is such a translation for the waw consecutive hardly possible (see the Hebrew grammars, Joüon, *Grammaire*, par. 118d; König, *Syntax*, par. 142; Driver, *Tenses in Hebrew*, pp. 84ff.), but it misses the very point of the narrative, namely, that the animals were created in response to God's declaration that it was not good that man should be alone (2:18).

Cassuto has shown (p. 129), however, that the difficulty posed by the lack of coherence between the two accounts of the creation of man has a simple solution: only two kinds of animals are said to be created in 2:19, "the beasts of the field" (חַיַּת הַשָּׂדֶה, *ḥayyaṯ haśśāḏeh*) and "all the birds of the air" (כָּל־עוֹף הַשָּׁמַיִם, *kol-'ôp̱ haššāmayim*); yet in 2:20 Adam names three kinds of animals: "the livestock [הַבְּהֵמָה, *habb^ehēmāh*], the birds of the air and all the beasts of the field." Elsewhere in the Torah (Lev 17:13), the "beasts of the field and the birds of the air" are distinguished from "the livestock" by the fact that they can be caught only by hunting them. Thus "of all the species of beasts and flying creatures that had already been created and had spread over the face of the earth and the firmament of the heavens, the Lord God now formed particular specimens for the purpose of presenting them all before man in the midst of the Garden" (Cassuto, p. 129). Such a reading of the text not only resolves the apparent difficulty between the two accounts of man's creation, but it also points out how carefully the Genesis narratives have been worked into the narratives of the Pentateuch as a whole. Both the LXX (ἔτι [*eti*] = *'ôḏ*, "yet," "still") and the Samaritan Pentateuch (*'ôḏ*) show that Cassuto's explanation was sensed very early in the history of interpretation.

B. *The Land and the Exile (2:25–4:26)*

If chapter 2 had in fact portrayed man's earliest state as a "prototype" of God's gift of the good land to Israel, then it should come as no surprise that the account of the

Fall should also be recounted in terms that bring to mind Israel's future exile from the land.

1. *Disobedience (2:25–3:7)*

A more-studied attempt to treat the problem of evil and temptation to sin cannot be found in all the Scriptures. With few exceptions the author has left the reader completely alone with the events of the story. He does not reflect on the events that transpire. There are no comments. We, the readers, are left to ourselves and our sense of the story for an answer to the questions it raises. We must seek our clues to the story's meaning from the few signs of the author's own shaping of the story.

a. *The transition*

2:25

25 The man and his wife were both naked, and they felt no shame.

25 Verse 25 is clearly intended to link the account of the land and the blessing (1:1–2:24) with that of the Fall (2:25–3:24). The reference to the "two of them" (NIV, "both") looks back to the previous narrative, while their description as "naked, . . . and no shame" anticipates the central problem of the narrative that follows. It is important to notice that two different but related words are used to describe the "nakedness" of the man and his wife in this narrative. Apart from the obvious meaning of *ʿārôm* (i.e., "naked"), the nuanced sense can be gained from the immediate context: "they were not ashamed."

The choice of *ʿārôm* ("naked") at the beginning of the narrative is likely motivated by two considerations. First, there is an alliteration between *ʿārôm* and *ʿārûm* ("crafty," 3:1). There is an obvious play on the two words. The effect of such a pun is both to draw the reader into the story by providing an immediate connecting link with the previous narrative and to provide a presage to the events and outcome of the subsequent story. The link provides an immediate clue to the potential relationship between the serpent's "cunning" and the innocence implied in the "nakedness" of the couple. The story unfolds the nature of that relationship.

Second, there is a difference in meaning between *ʿārôm* ("naked") in 2:25 and *ʿêrōm* ("naked") in 3:7. Whereas both terms are infrequently used in the Pentateuch, *ʿêrōm* is distinguished by its use in Deuteronomy 28:48, where it depicts the state of Israel's exiles who have been punished for their failure to trust and obey God's word: "Because you did not serve the LORD your God joyfully and gladly in the time of prosperity, therefore in hunger and thirst, in nakedness [*ûḇeʿêrōm*] and dire poverty, you will serve the enemies the LORD sends against you." In distinguishing the first state of man's nakedness (*ʿārûm*) from the second (*ʿêrōm*), the author has introduced a subtle yet perceptible clue to the story's meaning. The effect of the Fall was not simply that the man and the woman come to know they were "naked" (*ʿārûm*). The effect is rather that they come to know that they were "naked" (*ʿêrōm*) in the sense of being "under God's judgment," as in Deuteronomy 28:48 (cf. Ezek 16:39; 23:29).

b. *The tempter*

3:1

[1]Now the serpent was more crafty than any of the wild animals the LORD God had made. He said to the woman, "Did God really say, 'You must not eat from any tree in the garden'?"

1 The author has chosen to disclose a small but important clue to the story by revealing a detail about the snake: he was more "crafty" (*'ārûm*) than any of the creatures. The word *'ārûm* is not primarily a negative term in the Bible but suggests wisdom and adroitness (besides its use here, it occurs eight times in Proverbs and twice in Job). The description of the serpent as "crafty" is in keeping with the fact that there are several features of this story that suggest the author wanted to draw a relationship between the Fall and man's quest for wisdom. Man's disobedience is not so much depicted as an act of great wickedness or a great transgression as much as it is an act of great folly. He had all the "good" (*ṭôḇ*) he would have needed, but he wanted more—he wanted to be like God.

The forbidden tree is the tree of the knowledge of "good and evil" (*ṭôḇ wārā'*, 2:9). When the woman and the man took of the tree and ate, it was because she "saw that the tree was desirable for gaining wisdom [*lᵉhaśkîl*]" (v.6). Thus even the serpent is represented as a paragon of wisdom, an archetypical wiseman (*'ārûm*). However, the serpent and his wisdom (*'ārûm*) lead ultimately to the curse (*'ārûr*, v.14).

It should not be overlooked that the serpent is said to be one of the "wild animals" (*ḥayyaṯ haśśāḏeh*) that the Lord God had made (cf. 1:25; 2:19). The purpose of this statement is to exclude the notion that the serpent was a supernatural being (Procksch, p. 32). "The serpent is none other than a serpent" (Jacob, p. 102).

Notes

1 The clause structure W + X + QATAL—וְהַנָּחָשׁ הָיָה (*wᵉhannāḥāš hāyāh*, "Now the serpent was") indicates that a new section of narrative has begun. Verse 1 gives the background information for the narrative that follows.

The מִן (*min*) preposition can have the sense of either the partitive ("subtil as none other of the beasts," GKC, par. 119w) or the comparative ("subtil above all beasts of the field," BDB, p. 582), as the NIV's "more crafty than." In favor of the partitive sense is the use of *min* in v.14: "Cursed are you from all the cattle and from all the beasts of the field" (pers. tr.). In v.14 it is the serpent who is cursed and not the other animals; so the comparative use of *min* is not suitable. The added phrase in v.14—"from all the livestock" (*mikkol-habbᵉhēmāh*)—shows that the sense of the *min* is partitive in that verse ("cursed are you as none of the livestock and as none of the wild animals") in that, according to v.1, the serpent was not included in both groups of animals but only among the "wild animals." The close ties between v.14 and v.1 suggest that the partitive sense of the *min* should be read there also.

The net effect of reading the *min* as a partitive is to suggest that the serpent was not in every respect an ordinary animal. He was not "craftier than" the other beasts of the field. Rather, he was crafty "and the wild animals were not." Thus Westermann's statement (p. 239) that "the serpent is not outside the circle of those already mentioned in the narrative" needs to be expanded to include the idea that the serpent was not totally within the circle of those already mentioned in the narrative. There is certainly no mention yet of the identification of the serpent with Satan, but the narrative has not closed the door on that interpretation as some commentators have supposed.

---

c. *The temptation*

3:2–7

> [2]The woman said to the serpent, "We may eat fruit from the trees in the garden, [3]but God did say, 'You must not eat fruit from the tree that is in the middle of the garden, and you must not touch it, or you will die.' "
> [4]"You will not surely die," the serpent said to the woman. [5]"For God knows that when you eat of it your eyes will be opened, and you will be like God, knowing good and evil."
> [6]When the woman saw that the fruit of the tree was good for food and pleasing to the eye, and also desirable for gaining wisdom, she took some and ate it. She also gave some to her husband, who was with her, and he ate it. [7]Then the eyes of both of them were opened, and they realized they were naked; so they sewed fig leaves together and made coverings for themselves.

2–7 The story of the temptation is told with subtle simplicity. The snake speaks only twice, but that is enough to offset the balance of trust and obedience between the man and the woman and their Creator. The centerpiece of the story is the question of the knowledge of the "good and evil" (*ṭôḇ wārā'*). The snake implied by his questions that God was keeping this knowledge *from* the man and the woman (v.5), while the sense of the narratives in the first two chapters has been that God was keeping this knowledge *for* the man and the woman (e.g., 1:4, 10, 12, 18, 21, 25, 31; 2:18). In other words, the snake's statements are a direct challenge to the central theme of the narrative of chapters 1 and 2: God will provide the "good" (*ṭôḇ*) for man if he will only trust him and obey him.

However, a narrative clue already points to the woman's assuming God's role of "knowing the good" even before she ate of the fruit—that is, the description of the woman's thoughts in the last moments before the Fall. The narrative (v.6) states that "the woman saw that the . . . tree was good" (*wattēre' hā'iššāh kî ṭôḇhā'ēṣ*). Up until now in the narrative, the expression "and he saw that it was good" (*wayyar' kî ṭôḇ*) has only been used of God. Now, instead of God, it is the woman who "saw that it was good." Precisely at this point the author raises the issue of becoming "wise" (*l^ehaśkîl*): "When the woman saw that the fruit of the tree was . . . also desirable for gaining wisdom." Thus the temptation is not presented as a general rebellion from God's authority. It is rather portrayed as a quest for wisdom and "the good" apart from God's provision.

Having thus shown the temptation to be a quest for "wisdom" apart from God, the story comes to an abrupt conclusion in the act of the transgression: "she took some and ate it. She also gave some to her husband, who was with her, and he ate it" (v.6b). How quickly the transgression comes once the decision has been made! The thrust of the story, with all its simplicity, lies in its tragic and ironic depiction of the search for wisdom. Ironically, that which the snake promised did, in fact, come about: the man and the woman became "like God" as soon as they ate of the fruit. The irony, however, lies in the fact that they were already "like God" because they had been created in his image (1:26).

In the temptation the serpent promised that the man and the woman would know "good and evil" (v.5), just as God knew "good and evil." It goes without question in the story that the man and the woman had believed that when they obtained the knowledge of "good and evil," they would, on their own, enjoy the "good." The possibility that they would know only the "evil" and not the "good" is not raised in the narrative prior to their eating the fruit. Yet when they ate of the fruit and their eyes were opened, it was not the "good" that they saw and enjoyed. Their new knowledge was that of their own nakedness (*wayyēḏeʿû kî ʿêrummim,* "and they realized they were naked," v.7). Their knowledge of "good and evil" that was to make them "like God" resulted in the knowledge that they were no longer even like each other: they were ashamed of their nakedness, and they sewed leaves together to hide their differences from each other. Like the Preacher of Ecclesiastes, they sought wisdom but found only vanity and toil. As the next segment of the narrative shows, not only did the man and his wife attempt to cover their shame from each other in their making clothing from the trees of the garden, they also tried to hide themselves from God at the first sound of his coming.

2. *Judgment (3:8–20)*

a. *The scene*

3:8

> 8 Then the man and his wife heard the sound of the LORD God as he was walking in the garden in the cool of the day, and they hid from the LORD God among the trees of the garden.

8 The judgment scene opens with the "sound" (*qôl*) of the Lord's coming. Again there is irony in the author's depiction of the scene. The expression "the sound of the LORD God" (*qôl yhwh ʾelōhîm*) is common in the Pentateuch, especially Deuteronomy (5:25; 8:20; 13:18; 15:5; 18:16; 26:14; 27:10; 28:1, 2, 15, 45, 62; 30:8, 10) where—along with the verb "to hear/obey" and the preposition *b* (*šāmaʿ beqôl yhwh ʾelōhîm*)—it is the common form of expression for the Lord's call to obedience. It can hardly be without purpose that the author opens the scene of the curse with a subtle but painful reminder of the single requirement for obtaining God's blessing: "to hear/obey the voice of the LORD God" (*lišmōʿ ʾeṯ-qôl yhwh ʾelōhênû*; cf. v.8).

Also, the coming of the Lord at the mountain of Sinai is foreshadowed in this scene of the Lord God's coming to the first disobedient couple. In Deuteronomy 5:25 and 18:16 (cf. Exod 20:18–21), when the Lord came to Sinai, the people "heard the sound of the LORD our God" (*lišmōʿ ʾeṯ-qôl yhwh ʾelōhênû*). The response of Adam in the garden was much the same as that of Israel at the foot of Sinai. When the people heard the sound of the Lord at Sinai, they were afraid "and stayed at a distance and said . . . , 'Do not have God speak to us or we will die' " (Exod 20:18–19). So also Adam and his wife fled at the first sound of the Lord in the garden.

The time of the Lord's visit is often translated as "the cool of the day" or "the time of the evening," but the text reads "the wind of the day." There is nothing in the context to suggest that it refers to a time of day (Jacob). In light of the general context of the picture of God's coming in judgment and power, the "wind" (*rûaḥ*) that the author envisioned resembles that "great and powerful wind" (*rûaḥ geḏôlāh weḥāzāq*) that blew on the "mountain . . . of the LORD" in 1 Kings 19:11. Thus the viewpoint of the narrative would be much the same as that in Job 38:1, where the Lord answered Job "out of the storm."

It is not without significance that the author calls our attention to the hiding place. They fled to the trees. Throughout this chapter and the previous one, the trees play a central role in depicting man's changing relationship with God. First, in chapters 1 and 2 the fruit trees are the sign of God's bountiful provision. Then, at the beginning of the third chapter, the trees become the ground for inciting the man and the woman to rebellion and the place where the rebellious man and woman seek to hide from God. Finally, when the man and the woman are cast out of the garden, their way is barred from "the way to the tree of life" (v.24). The full sense of this focus on the trees should perhaps be understood in light of the role of the tree as the place of the punishment of death (Deut 21:22–23) and also in light of the later role of the tree as the place of the gift of life (Gal 3:13).

Notes

8 The expression קוֹל יהוה אֱלֹהִים מִתְהַלֵּךְ בַּגָּן (*qôl yhwh 'elōhîm mithallēk baggān*) can be read in two ways. It may refer to the "sound" made by the LORD's walking through the garden (e.g., "the sound of the LORD God as he was walking in the garden," NIV), or it may refer to the "voice" of the Lord that echoed (*mithallēk;* cf. Jer 46:22) throughout the garden. In the latter view the "sound" (*qôl*) can refer to the actual "voice" of God or, as in Deut 5:25, it can refer to the "noise" of a theophany, e.g., thunder (cf. Exod 20:18). The statement of the man in v.10—"I heard you [*qōlekā,* lit., 'your voice'] in the garden"—suggests that the "sound" they heard was not the sound of the Lord's footsteps; also, the fact that it is only in v.9 that the narrative says, "But the LORD God called" suggests that the "sound" in v.8 is not yet the sound of his voice (Cassuto, p. 151). The close association between this passage and other theophanies in Scripture supports the interpretation that sees the "sound of the LORD God" as part of a theophany.

b. *The trial*

3:9–13

9But the LORD God called to the man, "Where are you?"
10He answered, "I heard you in the garden, and I was afraid because I was naked; so I hid."
11And he said, "Who told you that you were naked? Have you eaten from the tree that I commanded you not to eat from?"
12The man said, "The woman you put here with me—she gave me some fruit from the tree, and I ate it."
13Then the LORD God said to the woman, "What is this you have done?"
The woman said, "The serpent deceived me, and I ate."

9–13 Before meting out the judgment, God's only words to the rebellious man and woman come in the form of questions: "Where are you?" (v.9); "Who told you that you were naked? Have you eaten from the tree?" (v.11); "What is this you have done?" (v.13). The picture of God's questioning before his act of judgment recalls the proceedings of a court session much like that of 4:9–10: "Where is your brother Abel? . . . What have you done? Listen! Your brother's blood cries out [*ṣō'aqîm*] to me from the ground"; and 18:21: "I will go down and see if what they have done is as bad as the outcry [*hakkeṣaʿăqāṯāh*] that has reached me." Skillfully, by the repetition of the word "naked" (vv.7, 10, 11), the author allows the man to be convicted with his own words: "I was afraid because I was naked" (*ʿêrōm*, v.10). Then, as though to show that alienation between the man and the woman went far beyond the shame that each now felt in the presence of the other, the author recounts the petty attempt on the man's part to cast blame on the woman ("she gave me," v.12) and, obliquely, on God ("the woman you put here with me"). In the man's words there is an ironic reminder of God's original intention: "It is not good for the man to be alone. I will make a helper suitable for him" (2:18). As an index of the extent of man's fall, the author shows that the man saw God's good gift as the source of his trouble.

c. *The verdict*

3:14–20

[14]So the LORD God said to the serpent, "Because you have done this,

"Cursed are you above all the livestock
  and all the wild animals!
You will crawl on your belly
  and you will eat dust
  all the days of your life.
[15]And I will put enmity
  between you and the woman,
  and between your offspring and hers;
he will crush your head,
  and you will strike his heel."

[16]To the woman he said,

"I will greatly increase your pains in childbearing;
  with pain you will give birth to children.
Your desire will be for your husband,
  and he will rule over you."

[17]To Adam he said, "Because you listened to your wife and ate from the tree about which I commanded you, 'You must not eat of it,'

"Cursed is the ground because of you;
  through painful toil you will eat of it
  all the days of your life.
[18]It will produce thorns and thistles for you,
  and you will eat the plants of the field.
[19]By the sweat of your brow
  you will eat your food
until you return to the ground,
  since from it you were taken;
for dust you are
  and to dust you will return."

[20]Adam named his wife Eve, because she would become the mother of all the living.

Although much can be said about the curse of the snake, the woman, and the man, it is important to notice that very little is actually written. This passage shows most clearly the artful composition that produced the Book of Genesis. There are no long discourses on the appearance of the snake before and after the curse. Did he have feet? Did he have wings? The thoughts of the snake, if there were such, or the thoughts of the man and woman are left completely out of the picture. The narrative gives nothing to help understand their plight as individuals. The snake, the woman, and the man are not depicted as individuals involved in a personal crisis; rather they are representatives. We are left with the impression that this is not their story so much as it is our story, the story of mankind. With great skill the author presents these three participants as the "heads" of their race. The snake, on the one hand, and the man and the woman, on the other, are as two great nations embarking on a great struggle, a struggle that will find its conclusion only by an act of some distant "seed" or "offspring."

14–15 Whereas once the snake was "crafty" (*'ārûm*, v.1), now he was "cursed" (*'ārûr*, v.14). His "curse" distinguished him "above all the livestock and all the wild animals," that is, he must "crawl on [his] belly and . . . eat dust all the days of [his] life" (v.14). This curse does not necessarily suggest that the snake had previously walked with feet and legs as the other land animals. The point is rather that for the rest of his life, as a result of the curse, when the snake crawls on his belly, as snakes do, he will "eat dust." The emphasis lies in the snake's "eating dust," an expression that elsewhere carries the meaning of "total defeat" (cf. Isa 65:25; Mic 7:17).

The curse of the snake, then, as a result of his part in the Fall, is to be the perennial reminder of the ultimate defeat of the rebellious "seed." So strongly was this imagery of the snake's defeat felt by later biblical writers that in their description of the ultimate victory and reign of the righteous "seed," when peace and harmony are restored to creation, the serpent remains under the curse: "dust will [still] be the serpent's food" (Isa 65:25).

As representatives the snake and the woman embody the fate of their seed, and that fate is their fate as well. The author has brought about this "headship" of the snake and the woman by means of a careful but consistent identification of the snake and his "seed." At first in v.15 the "enmity" is said to have been put between the snake and the woman and between the "seed" of the snake and the "seed" of the woman. The second half of v.15, however, says that the "seed" of the woman ("he") will crush the head of the snake ("your head"). The woman's "seed" is certainly intended to be understood as a group (or individual) that lies the same temporal distance from the woman as the "seed" of the snake does from the snake itself. Yet in this verse it is the "seed" of the woman who crushes the head of the snake. Though the "enmity" may lie between the two "seeds," the goal of the final crushing blow is not the "seed" of the snake but rather the snake itself; *his* head will be crushed. In other words, it appears that the author seems intent on treating the snake and his "seed" together, as one.

What happens to the snake's "seed" in the distant future can be said to happen to the snake as well. This suggests that the author views the snake in terms that extend beyond this particular snake of the garden. The snake, for the author, is representative of someone or something else. The snake is represented by his "seed." When that "seed" is crushed, the head of the snake is crushed. Consequently more is at stake in this brief passage than the reader is at first aware of. A program is set forth. A plot is established that will take the author far beyond this or that snake and his "seed." It is what the snake and his "seed" represent that lies at the center of the author's focus. With that "one" lies the "enmity" that must be crushed.

No attempt is made to answer the ancillary question of the snake's role in the temptation over against the role of a higher being, e.g., Satan. This was, however, the drama that later biblical writers saw behind the deed of the snake (cf. Rom 16:20; Rev 12:9: "That ancient serpent called the devil or Satan, who leads the whole world astray"). From what has been said, such a reading of this passage does not lie outside the narrative implications of the verse. In the last analysis the reader is left with only the words of the Lord to the snake. It is, however, unlikely that at such a pivotal point in the narrative the author would intend no more than a mere reference to snakes and their offspring and the fear of them among humanity.

Looking at the passage within the larger scope of the purpose of the book and the pains taken by the author to construct a whole narrative out of just these small segments of discourse, much more seems to lie in these words (the Lord's first spoken words after the Fall). In light of the fact that such programmatic discourses are strategically important throughout the remainder of the book, it seems likely that the author intended these words to be read as programmatic and foundational for the establishment of the plot and characterization of the remainder of the book. In the narrative to follow, there is to be war ("enmity"). The two sides are represented by two seeds, the "seed" of the snake and the "seed" of the woman. In the ensuing battle the "seed" of the woman will crush the head of the snake. Though wounded in the struggle, the woman's "seed" will be victorious.

Verse 15 still contains a puzzling yet important ambiguity: Who is the "seed" of the woman? It seems obvious that the purpose of his verse has not been to answer that question but rather to raise it. The remainder of the book is the author's answer.

16 The judgment against the woman relates first to her sons and then to her husband. She would now bear sons (children) in increased pain or toil (*'iṣṣᵉḇônēḵ*). Her "desire" (*tᵉšûqāṯēḵ*) will be for her husband, and he will "rule over" her. The sense of this judgment within the larger context of the book lies in the role of the woman that is portrayed in chapters 1 and 2. The woman and her husband were to have enjoyed the blessing of children (1:28) and the harmonious partnership of marriage (2:18, 21–25). The judgment relates precisely to these two points. What the woman once was to do as a blessing—be a marriage partner and have children—had become tainted by the curse. In those moments of life's greatest blessing—marriage and children—the woman would sense most clearly the painful consequences of her rebellion from God.

We should not overlook the relationship between the promise of v.15 and the words to the woman in v.16. In that promise the final victory was to be through the "seed" of the woman. In the beginning, when the man and the woman were created, childbirth was at the center of the blessing that their Creator had bestowed on them ("Be fruitful and increase in number; fill the earth," 1:28). Now, after the Fall, childbirth is again to be the means through which the snake would be defeated and the blessing restored. In the pain of the birth of every child, there was to be a reminder of the hope that lay in God's promise. Birthpangs are not merely a reminder of the futility of the Fall; they are as well a sign of an impending joy: "We know that the whole creation has been groaning as in the pains of childbirth right up to the present time. Not only so, but we ourselves, who have the firstfruits of the Spirit, groan inwardly as we wait eagerly for our adoption as sons, the redemption of our bodies. For in this hope we were saved" (Rom 8:22–24; cf. Matt 24:8).

17–20 As man's judgment the "good land" provided by the Creator (chs. 1–2) was cursed. Man could no longer "freely eat" of the produce of the land. Throughout chapters 2 and 3, the author has carefully monitored the man's ongoing relationship with his Creator by means of the theme of "eating" (*'āḵal*). At first God's blessing and provision for man are noted in the words "you are free to eat [*'āḵōl tō'ḵēl*, 2:16] from any tree in the garden," recalling the good gifts in chapter 1 and the pronouncement that all was then "very good" (1:31). Then, in chapter 3, it was precisely over the issue of "eating" (*'āḵal*) that the tempter raised doubts about God's ultimate goodness and care for the man and his wife (3:1–3). Finally, the man and the woman's act of disobedience in chapter 3 is simply though thoughtfully described as "she ate it [*wattō'ḵal*]. . . . and he ate it [*wayyō'ḵal*]" (v.6).

It is not surprising, then, to find that the author calls our attention to precisely the aspect of "eating" in his description of the judgment on the man: "Cursed is the ground because of you; through painful toil you will eat of it [*tō'ḵᵃlennāh*] all the days of your life" (v.17). Such a focus on "eating," which seems to dominate the author's depiction of the Fall, is connected with the author's interest elsewhere on the importance of "eating" and its association with man's relationship to God, that is, in the Torah's teaching regarding the clean and the unclean food (Lev 11; Deut 14) and the regulations for annual "feasts" to celebrate God's gift of the "good land" in the covenant (Lev 23). To this could also be added the larger context of the role of "feasts" and "eating" in the biblical eschaton: Revelation 19:9 (cf. SBK, 4:2, p. 1154o).

The description of the "land" in v.18 ("you will eat the plants of the field," *'ēśeḇ haśśāḏeh*) is a reversal of the state of the land as it was described in chapter 2. There it is stated, "No shrub of the field had yet appeared on the earth and no plant of the field [*'ēśeḇ haśśāḏeh*] had yet sprung up" (2:5). In drawing a contrast between the condition of the "land" (*hā'āreṣ*) before and after the Fall, the author shows that the present condition of the land is not the way it was intended to be. Rather the state of the land is the result of man's rebellion. Thus the author has paved the way for a central motif in the structure of biblical eschatology, the hope of "a new heaven and a new earth" (Rev 21:1; cf. Isa 65:17; Rom 8:22–24).

Just as v.18 was intended to show the reversal of the state of the "land" before and after the Fall, so v.19 intends to show the same for the condition of man himself. Before the Fall man was taken from the ground and given the "breath of life" (2:7). As a result of the Fall, however, man must return to the ground and the dust from which he was taken (3:19). The author's point in showing such a reversal was to stress that the verdict of death, warned of before the Fall (2:17), had come about.

As a constant reminder of the effect of the Fall, the author draws a connection between the man's name, "Adam" (*'āḏām*, v.20), and the "ground" (*'ᵃḏāmāh*) from which he was taken. Adam, curiously enough, named his wife Eve "because she would become the mother of all the living." This was the second time Adam named his wife (cf. 2:23). Her first name pointed to her origin ("out of man"), whereas her second name pointed to her destiny ("the mother of all the living").

Notes

14–19 The divine words to the three guilty individuals are carefully presented as a single syntactical unit. It begins with the waw consecutive—וַיֹּאמֶר (*wayyō'mer*, "and [the LORD God] said")—and follows with an 0 + X + QATAL—אֶל־הָאִשָּׁה אָמַר (*'el-hā'iššāh 'āmar*, "To the woman he said")—and then a W + X + QATAL—וּלְאָדָם אָמַר (*ûlᵉ'āḏām 'āmar*, "To Adam he said").

16 The expression עִצְּבוֹנֵךְ וְהֵרֹנֵךְ (*'iṣṣᵉḇônēḵ wᵉhērōnēḵ*, "your pains in childbearing") is a hendiadys: "your pain and your conception." Both *hērôn* and *'iṣṣᵉḇôn* are *qiṭṭālôn* nouns

(H. Bauer and P. Leander, *Historische Grammatik der Hebräischen Sprache des Alten Testaments* [Heldesheim: George Olms Verlagsbuchhandlung, 1962], pp. 498–99). *Hērôn* may be a mixed form (ibid., p. 499i) or a contraction of הֵרָיוֹן (*hērāyôn*, BDB, p. 248). The LXX reading *τὸν στεναγμόν* (*ton stenagmon*, "groaning") perhaps reflects an underlying Hebrew variant וְהֶגְיֹנֵךְ (*wᵉhegyōnēḵ*) for וְהֵרֹנֵךְ (*wᵉhērōnēḵ*) (BHS), but there is little or no evidence to support this. Elsewhere in the Pentateuch and the rest of the LXX *stenagmos* is not used for rendering any form of הָגָה (*hāg̱āh*, "to murmur, groan").

The word תְּשׁוּקָה (*tᵉšûqāh*, "longing"; NIV, "desire") is "unusual and striking" (BDB, p. 1003). Apart from 3:16, it occurs only in Gen 4:7 and S of Songs 7:10. Its use in S of Songs shows that the "longing" can refer to physical attraction, but in Gen 4:7 the "longing" carries the sense of a desire to overcome or defeat another. It is unwise to read too much into the word itself. The way that the whole of this section of the curse—וְאֶל־אִישֵׁךְ תְּשׁוּקָתֵךְ וְהוּא יִמְשָׁל־בָּךְ (*wᵉ'el-'îšēḵ tᵉšûqāṯēḵ wᵉhû' yimšol-bāḵ*, "Your desire will be for your husband, and he will rule over you")—foreshadows the Lord's words to Cain in 4:7—וְאֵלֶיךָ תְּשׁוּקָתוֹ וְאַתָּה תִּמְשָׁל־בּוֹ (*wᵉ'ēleykā tᵉšûqāṯô wᵉ'attāh timšol-bô*, "it desires to have you but you must master it")—suggests that the author intended the two passages to be read together. If so, the sense of "desiring" in 3:16 should be understood as the wife's desire to overcome or gain the upper hand over her husband. In the same way, the sense of *yimšol-bāḵ* is as in the NIV: "he will rule over you." Within the context of the Creation account in chapters 2 and 3, this last statement stands in sharp contrast to the picture of the man and the woman as "one flesh" (*lᵉḇāśār 'eḥāḏ*, 2:24) and the picture of the woman as a "helper suitable for him" (*'ēzer kᵉnegkô*, 2:18). The Fall has had its effect on the relationship of the husband and wife.

20 The name "Eve" (חַוָּה, *ḥawwāh*) is a wordplay on the Hebrew word for "life" (חַי, *ḥay*). Ironically, in this same section of text the man and his wife are forbidden access to the "tree of life [*haḥayyîm*]" lest they "live [*ḥay*] forever" (v.22).

---

3. *Protection*

3:21

> [21]The Lord God made garments of skin for Adam and his wife and clothed them.

21 In striking contrast to God's rest from work in chapter 2, immediately after the statement of God's judgment, the author returns to the description of God's work: "The Lord God made [*wayya'aś*] garments of skin for Adam and his wife and clothed them." After—and because of—the Fall, there was more work to be done. The mention of the type of clothing that God made—"garments of skin [*'ôr*]," i.e., tunics—is perhaps intended to recall the state of the man and the woman before the Fall: they "were both naked [*'ᵃrûmmîm*], and they felt no shame" (2:25). The author may also be anticipating the notion of sacrifice in the slaying of the animals for the making of the skin garments, though he has given no clues of this meaning in the narrative itself.

Later in the Pentateuch the Lord instructed the people to make tunics for the priests who were to enter into the presence of God at the tabernacle. The purpose of the tunics was to cover the priests' nakedness (*'erwāh*) lest they incur guilt and die (Exod 28:42). The author may be anticipating this "lasting ordinance" (Exod 28:43) in drawing our attention to God's covering the nakedness of the man and the woman. In this way the role of the priests, developed later in the Pentateuch, is foreshadowed by God's work in ages past—his work of restoring to man the blessing of his presence and fellowship.

4. *Exile*

3:22–24

> 22 And the LORD God said, "The man has now become like one of us, knowing good and evil. He must not be allowed to reach out his hand and take also from the tree of life and eat, and live forever." 23 So the LORD God banished him from the Garden of Eden to work the ground from which he had been taken. 24 After he drove the man out, he placed on the east side of the Garden of Eden cherubim and a flaming sword flashing back and forth to guard the way to the tree of life.

22–23 The verdict of death now brought against the man and the woman consisted of their being cast out of the garden and barred from access to the tree of life. The penalty is identical to that established by the Mosaic law: to "be put to death" (*môṯ yûmāṯ*, lit., "he shall surely die") is to be "cut off from his people" (Exod 31:14). In this sense the transgression of Adam and Eve means they must be cast off from the protective presence of the community in the garden (cf. Gen 4:14).

The author uses irony to show the folly of man's fall. He shows that even though man's quest to "be like God" (vv.5–7) was obtained, the goal itself proved to be undesirable. Man, who had been created "like God" in the beginning (1:26), found himself after the Fall curiously "like God"—but no longer "with God" in the garden (v.22). In this subtle verbal interchange, the author has shown that man's happiness (*ṭôḇ*, "good") does not consist of his being "like God" so much as it does his being "with God," enjoying the blessings of his presence (Ps 16:11).

To underscore the reversals that man suffered in his rebellion, the author uses a wordplay on two key terms from his earlier depiction of man's blessing in the garden. In 2:15 man was put into the garden for "worship" (*leʿoḇdāh*) and "obedience" (*lešomrāh*); but here in v.23, after the Fall, man was cast out of the garden "to work [*laʿaḇōḏ*] the ground," and he is "kept" (*lišmōr*, NIV, "to guard") from "the way to the tree of life" (v.24).

24 In his depiction of the garden and the tree of life after the Fall, the author has again anticipated God's plan to restore man's blessing and life in the covenant at Sinai and the Torah. The tree of life stands guarded by the "cherubim" just as in the Sinai covenant the Torah lies in the ark of the covenant guarded by the "cherubim" (Exod 25:10–22; cf. Deut 31:24–26). Only through the covenant can man's fellowship with God be restored: "There, above the cover between the two cherubim that are over the ark of the Testimony, I will meet with you and give you all my commands for the Israelites" (Exod 25:22). In the covenant man was returned to the state he enjoyed in Genesis 2:15—one who serves God, obeys his will, and enjoys his blessing.

The author's mention of the direction "east" is not a mere geographical detail. Throughout the Book of Genesis, the author carefully apprises the reader of the direction of man's movement. In doing so he drops a narrative clue to the meaning of the events he is recounting. At this point in the narrative, "east" has only the significance of "outside the garden." Later in the book the author will carry this significance further by showing "east" to be the direction of the "city of Babylon" (11:2) and the "cities of Sodom and Gomorrah" (13:11). At the same time he will show that to return from the east is to return to the Promised Land and to return to the city of "Salem" (14:17–20).

C. *Life in Exile (4:1–26)*

In chapter 4 the author gives a brief glimpse of life outside the Garden of Eden. The woman bore sons (cf. 3:16), and the sons became both workers of the ground (cf. 3:23) and tenders of sheep. Thus the narrative assumes the effects of the Fall recorded in chapter 3 ("by the sweat of your brow you will eat your food"). The chapter is framed by the accounts of the births of Adam's sons at the beginning (vv.1–2), in the center (vv.17–22), and at the conclusion (vv.25–26). Many diverse events are included within the small space of the chapter, giving it an appearance of being a transition and staging narrative connecting the preceding events to those that are to follow. On the basis of Jude 11 ("Woe to them! They have taken the way of Cain") and Hebrews 11:4 ("By faith Abel offered God a better sacrifice than Cain did"), Cain has often been taken as a "type" of a godless humanity and Abel as a "type" of the spiritual man (cf. The Scofield Bible: "Cain . . . is a type of the mere man of the earth. . . . Abel . . . is a type of the spiritual man" [p. 8, nn. 3–4]; and Augustine: "Cain then was the first-born . . . who belonged to the city of men; Abel . . . belonged to the city of God"). Though there is no doubt truth in seeing both Cain and Abel as narrative examples of godlessness and godliness, there are hints in the text that the author also sees in Cain an example of repentance and forgiveness. The central question in the narrative is the meaning of Cain's words in 4:13 (see discussion in loc.). If his words are to be understood as an expression of remorse and repentance, then Cain's city (v.17) and the line of Cain's descendants (vv.17–24) are cast in a new light.

1. *Worship*

4:1–8

1 Adam lay with his wife Eve, and she became pregnant and gave birth
to Cain. She said, "With the help of the LORD I have brought forth a
man." 2 Later she gave birth to his brother Abel.
Now Abel kept flocks, and Cain worked the soil. 3 In the course of time
Cain brought some of the fruits of the soil as an offering to the LORD.
4 But Abel brought fat portions from some of the firstborn of his flock.
The LORD looked with favor on Abel and his offering, 5 but on Cain and
his offering he did not look with favor. So Cain was very angry, and his
face was downcast.
6 Then the LORD said to Cain, "Why are you angry? Why is your face
downcast? 7 If you do what is right, will you not be accepted? But if you
do not do what is right, sin is crouching at your door; it desires to have
you, but you must master it."
8 Now Cain said to his brother Abel, "Let's go out to the field." And
while they were in the field, Cain attacked his brother Abel and killed
him.

1–2 Eve's first words after the Fall raise many questions. The translation that reads "With the help of the LORD I have brought forth [or 'acquired'] a man" (v.1) leaves the impression that her words are positive. Her acknowledging God's help makes it look as though she were hopeful that the promise of a "seed" to crush the head of the serpent (3:15) might find its fulfillment in this son. Her words, however, can also be read in a less positive light: e.g., "I have created a man equally with the Lord" (Cassuto, p. 196). In this sense Eve's words are taken as a boast that just as the Lord had created a man, so now she had created a man. Within the immediate context it would be difficult to decide between two such diverse readings of the passage. Two considerations, however, suggest that the latter interpretation of Eve's words is more likely.

First, throughout the narratives that make up the Book of Genesis, a recurring theme is that of the attempt and failure of human effort in obtaining a blessing that only God can give. God continuously promised man a blessing, and man pushed it aside in favor of his own attempts at the blessing. The story of the building of the city of Babylon (ch. 11) is the most familiar of such narratives. In particular, Eve's situation brings to mind that of Sarah's attempt to achieve the blessing through her handmaiden Hagar. Just as Sarah had tried to bring about the fulfillment of God's promised "seed" (16:1–4) on her own, so also Eve's words give expression to her confidence in her own ability to fulfill the promise of 3:15.

The second consideration is Eve's later words about the birth of Seth ("God has granted me another child [*zera'*, lit., 'seed'] in place of Abel," v.25), which shed a great deal of light on her words in v.1. The contrast between her words at the beginning of the narrative and at the close is striking and revealing. At the beginning Eve said, "I have brought forth a man [*'îš*]," whereas at the close of the narrative she acknowledged, "God has granted me another seed [*zera'*]." Moreover Eve did not say that Seth was given to replace Cain, but he was to replace Abel. This suggests that within the story Eve had not placed her hope in Cain but in Abel. True to the plot of the remaining narratives in Genesis, Cain, the older son, did not stand to inherit the blessing, but rather the younger son was to inherit the blessing. Also true to the plot of the remaining narratives, it was God himself who provided the other "seed" (*zera'*) through yet another younger son.

3–4 In light of the parallels between the previous scene (3:21–24) and the worship of God in the Sinai covenant (see above), it is appropriate that the author has turned immediately to the question of God's acceptance of the "offering" (*minḥāh*) and worship of Cain and his brother. The author's purpose seems to be to use the narrative of Cain and Abel to teach a lesson on the kind of worship that is pleasing to God. Worship that pleases God springs from a pure heart. How does the narrative teach a lesson about a pure heart? It does so by allowing the reader to see, behind the scenes, the response of Cain to God's rejection. In his response we see the heart that lay behind the unaccepted offering. Cain's worship was not acceptable, whereas Abel's worship was. The difference between the two offerings is not explicitly drawn out by the author. Contrary to the popular opinion that Cain's offering was not accepted because it was not a blood sacrifice, it seems clear from the narrative that both offerings, in themselves, were acceptable—they are both described as "offerings" (*minḥāh*) and not "sacrifices" (*zeḇaḥ*). The narrative suggests, as well, that they were both "firstfruits" offerings (*mibbᵉḵōrôṯ*, v.4); thus as a farmer Cain's offering of "fruits of the soil" (v.3) was as appropriate for his occupation as Abel's "firstborn of his flock" (v.4) was for his occupation as a shepherd.

5–7 Rather than attempting to discover what was wrong with Cain's offering, we would be better advised simply to take notice that the author has omitted any explanation. He was apparently less concerned about Cain's offering than he was Cain's response to the Lord's rejection of his offering. Whatever the cause of God's rejection of Cain's offering, the narrative itself focuses our attention to Cain's response. It is there that the narrative seeks to make its point. Cain's response was twofold: (1) anger against God (v.4b) and (2) anger against his brother (v.8). By stating the problem in this way, the author surrounds his lesson on "pleasing offerings" with a subtle narrative warning: "by their fruit you will recognize them" (Matt 7:20). In his understanding of the importance of a pure heart in worship, the author is very close in his ideas to those expressed by Jeremiah against the false and hypocritical worshipers in his day. Just as Jeremiah pleaded with his people "to do well [*'im-hêṭêḇ têṭîḇû*, NIV, 'if you really change'] . . . and do not shed innocent blood," lest they be exiled from their land (Jer 7:5–7), so God pleaded with Cain to "do what is right" (*'im-têṭîḇ*) or face the consequences of shedding innocent blood and exile from the land (v.7; cf. v.12).

8 It is possible that the author intended the present narrative to be read in light of the Deuteronomic legislation of the "cities of refuge." There is a similarity between the terse description of Cain's offense against Abel and the description of an intentional homicide in Deuteronomy 19:11. The similarity appears to play into the purpose of the author. The purpose of the cities of refuge was to insure that "innocent blood will not be shed in your land" (Deut 19:10). That, of course, is the central point of the Cain and Abel narrative: "Your brother's blood cries out to me from the ground" (v.10).

In setting out the types of offenses for which the "cities of refuge" are to be used, Deuteronomy 19:11 specifies that a guilty murderer is one who lies in wait for his neighbor, "rises up" (*weqām;* NIV, "assaults") against him, and slays him. In the narrative of Genesis 4, it states that "while they were in the field, Cain attacked [*wayyāqom*, lit., 'rose up (against)'] Abel and killed him" (v.8). According to the law in Deuteronomy, Cain's offense was punishable by death, though, of course, he would still have had recourse to the cities of refuge. In any event, the fact that God showed mercy on Cain and the fact that later in the story God's mercy was connected with Cain's building a city suggest that a more than coincidental relationship exists between the story of Cain and the later Deuteronomic legislation dealing with the cities of refuge. The narrative may be suggesting not only that Cain's offense was punishable by death but also that the city Cain built (v.17) was an early "prototype" of the cities of refuge.

Notes

1–2 The syntax of וְהָאָדָם יָדַע (*wehā'āḏām yāḏa'*, lit., "And Adam knew") (W + X + QATAL) suggests that a new section has begun and that vv.1–2 give the background for the events of the following narrative. The fact that Cain is described as one who "works the ground" (עֹבֵד אֲדָמָה, *'ōḇēḏ 'aḏāmāh;* NIV, "worked the soil") suggests that the time period intended is subsequent to the expulsion of the man and woman at the close of chapter 3. Thus when the narrative states that Cain "went out from the LORD's presence" (v.16) and "lived in the land of Nod, east of Eden," it should not be assumed that up to that time he had been in the Garden of Eden.

The woman's use of קָנִיתִי (*qānîṯî*) for "I have brought forth" is motivated by the wordplay on the name of the first son, "Cain" (קַיִן [*qayin*]). But why does she say, "I have brought forth a man [אִישׁ, *'îš*]," and why does she add, "with . . . the LORD" (אֶת־יהוה [*'eṯ-yhwh*])? If, as is suggested in the commentary to this verse, Eve's words mean that she sees this birth as an attempt to rival God's intended blessing, the choice of the word *'îš* can be explained with reference to the creation of the woman in chapter 2. The use of *'îš* reverses the wordplay of *'îš* and *'iššāh* (אִשָּׁה ["woman"]) in 2:23. A wordplay between *'îš* and *'enôš* (אֱנוֹשׁ ["Enosh"], 4:26) may also be behind the choice of words here. Thus a literary connection is established between the first son born (*'îš*) in the chapter and the last son (*'enôš*).

Grammatically, on the analogy of Gen 26:34 (אִשָּׁה אֶת־יְהוּדִית [*'iššāh 'eṯ-yehûḏîṯ*, lit., "a woman, Judith"), the אִישׁ אֶת־יהוה (*'îš 'eṯ-yhwh*, lit., "a man, the LORD") could be read as an accusative object: "I have brought forth a man, the LORD" (cf. Luther's "*Ich habe den mann, den Herrn*"). The evidence from the versions (LXX, *dia tou theou*; Vul., *per deum*) suggests that the accusative sense of "I have brought forth a man, the LORD," was not acceptable to the early translators, and they avoided that sense by means of a free translation. The modern translation "with the help of the LORD" (NIV)—which would seem to require עִם־יהוה (*'im-yhwh*, "with the LORD") rather than אֶת־יהוה (*'eṯ-yhwh*, lit., "the LORD")—makes good sense; but, according to Westermann (p. 291), such a meaning is not attested elsewhere in Scripture. If וְאֵת שַׁדַּי (*we'ēṯ šadday*, "the Almighty") is correct in Gen 49:25, however, there may be some evidence there for the sense of "with the help of" for the preposition *'eṯ*.

3 The Scofield Bible represents the popular view that Cain's offering was faulted because it was not a blood sacrifice: "Cain's unbloody offering was a refusal of the divine way," or "His [Abel's] sacrifice, in which atoning blood was shed (Heb. 9:22), was therefore at once his confession of sin and the expression of his faith in the interposition of a substitute (Heb. 11:4)" (pp. 10–11). However, the word מִנְחָה (*minḥāh*, "offering") refers to any type of offering, whether grain or animal (KB, s.v.). By itself *minḥāh* would not imply that the offering should be a slaughtered animal, as would זֶבַח (*zeḇah*). KB (p. 251) describes the latter term as "an offering of sheep, goat, cattle, the aim of which is communion between the giver of the offering and the deity to whom the offering is given." Since Cain was a farmer, his *minḥāh* was appropriately from the "fruits of the soil"; and since Abel was a shepherd, his *minḥāh* was appropriately from "the firstborn of his flock." The fact that the writer of Hebrews (11:4) refers to Cain's and Abel's offerings each as a θυσία (*thysia*) does not imply that he saw them as essentially to be blood sacrifices since the LXX renders *minḥāh* in Gen 4:3–4 with θυσία. The LXX distinguishes between the *minḥāh* (= *thysia*) of Cain and the *minḥāh* (= δῶρον [*dōron*, "gift"]) of Abel, but *thysia* does not represent a "blood sacrifice."

8 The standard Hebrew texts have simply, "And Cain spoke [וַיֹּאמֶר, *wayyō'mer*] to Abel his brother; and when they were in the field, Cain rose up against Abel his brother and killed him." Many Hebrew texts and editions leave a space in the middle of the verse, and most of the ancient versions (Samar. , LXX, Targum [Neophyti 1], Syr., Vul.) have "And Cain said to Abel his brother, 'Let's go out to the field' [נֵלְכָה הַשָּׂדֶה, *nēlekāh haśśāḏeh*]." There is little doubt that these versions do not represent the original text (Gunkel) but rather are later attempts to fill in a laconic text. The question is whether the text as it stands is original (Jacob, p. 140) or textually corrupt (Skinner, p. 107). Jacob points to a similar construction (*'āmar* without an object) in Exod 19:25; but, in fact, the object of that clause is supplied by the following clause in 20:1: וַיְדַבֵּר אֱלֹהִים אֵת כָּל־הַדְּבָרִים הָאֵלֶּה (*wayeḏabbēr 'elōhîm 'ēṯ kol-haddeḇārîm hā'ēlleh*, "And God spoke all these words"). Second Chron 32:24b has *'āmar* without an object but is itself textually suspect. The use of *wayyō'mer* (without an object) in Gen 22:7 does not support the present reading in Gen 4:8 because, like Exod 19:25 and 2 Chron 2:10, the object of *wayyō'mer* is contained in the following clause (e.g., וַיֹּאמֶר אָבִי [*wayyō'mer 'āḇî*, lit., "he said, 'My father' "]); Hos 13:2 and Ps 71:10 are poetic texts and thus do not provide an appropriate analogy. In Esth 1:18 וְהַיּוֹם הַזֶּה (*wehayyôm hazzeh*, "this day") is the object of תֹּאמַרְנָה (*tō'marnāh*, "[they] will respond"; cf. KJV).

Cassuto (p. 215) retains the form of the Hebrew text (*wayyō'mer*) but suggests that the root is not "to speak" but "to fix a place for meeting," the meaning of *'amarun* in Arabic. That such a sense could have been completely lost by the time of the earliest versions (e.g., Samar., LXX) is not likely. It is more likely that a textual problem lies behind the passage. The reading suggested by the versions (e.g., "Let's go out into the field") does not commend itself as original since it merely fills in the missing object clause without making any contribution to the sense of the narrative. Gunkel (p. 44) proposes the reading וַיֵּמֶר

(*wayyemer*) from מָרָה (*mārāh*, "to begin a struggle") or וַיֵּמַר (*wayyēmar*) from מָרַר (*mārar*, "to be bitter"). Others have suggested וַיִּשְׁמֹר (*wayyišmōr*, "and he watched"), which would then be a wordplay on הֲשֹׁמֵר אָחִי (*hašōmēr 'āḥî*, "my brother's keeper") in v.9. There is, however, no explanation for such textual corruption. The matter may best be left unresolved, or with Delitzsch to conclude that "the narrator, hastening past what Cain said, forthwith informs us of its being carried into execution" (p. 183).

The relationship of this passage to the rest of the Pentateuch, however, may point the way toward yet another textual solution. As the commentary to v.8 (above) has suggested, there are striking similarities between Cain's murder of Abel in 4:8 and the description of intentional homicide in Deut 19:11. There are also similarities between the role of the city as a refuge for Cain in chapter 4 and the description of the cities of refuge in Deut 19. If such intertextuality exists between these two passages, a close comparison of Gen 4:8—וַיֹּאמֶר . . . וַיָּקָם . . . וַיַּהַרְגֵהוּ (*wayyō'mer . . . wayyāqom . . . wayyahargēhû*, lit., "and he said, . . . and he rose up, . . . and he killed him")—and Deut 19:11—וְאָרַב . . . וְקָם . . . וְהִכָּהוּ (*we'ārab . . . weqām . . . wehikkāhû*, lit., "he lies in wait, . . . he rises up, . . . and he strikes") gives a possible explanation for the origin of the reading *wayyō'mer*. Owing to the frequent interchange of *wayyō'mer* within the narrative (each change of action is marked by *wayyō'mer*: 4:6, 7, 9a, 9b, 10, 13), *'ārab* could have been read as *'āmar*. Both the interchange of the letters beth and mem and the frequent transposition of letters are common scribal errors. Judges 9:43—וַיֶּאֱרֹב . . . בַּשָּׂדֶה . . . וַיָּקָם . . . וַיַּכֵּם (*wayye'erōb . . . baśśādeh . . . wayyāqom . . . wayyakkēm*, lit., "and he set ambush . . . in the field, . . . and he rose up, . . . and he attacked them")—shows that the Deuteronomic legislation did have its influence on the description of similar events within the biblical narratives. Thus the original text of Gen 4:8 may have been even more similar to the Deuteronomic passage dealing with the cities of refuge.

---

2. *Repentance*

4:9–15a

9 Then the LORD said to Cain, "Where is your brother Abel?"

"I don't know," he replied. "Am I my brother's keeper?"

10 The LORD said, "What have you done? Listen! Your brother's blood cries out to me from the ground. 11 Now you are under a curse and driven from the ground, which opened its mouth to receive your brother's blood from your hand. 12 When you work the ground, it will no longer yield its crops for you. You will be a restless wanderer on the earth."

13 Cain said to the LORD, "My punishment is more than I can bear. 14 Today you are driving me from the land, and I will be hidden from your presence; I will be a restless wanderer on the earth, and whoever finds me will kill me."

15 But the LORD said to him, "Not so; if anyone kills Cain, he will suffer vengeance seven times over."

9–12 Again, as in chapter 3, when he came in judgment, the Lord first asked questions—"Where is Abel your brother?" (v.9)—then meted out the punishment: "You are under a curse ['*ārûr*] and driven from the ground. . . . When you work the ground, it will no longer yield its crops to you. You will be a restless wanderer on the earth" (vv.11–12). The picture of Cain's judgment is remarkably similar to the exile Israel was warned of in Deuteronomy: "You will be cursed ['*ārûr*] in the city and cursed in the country [*baśśādeh*, lit., 'in the field']. Your basket and your kneading trough will be cursed. The fruit of your womb will be cursed, and the crops of your land, and the calves of your herds and the lambs of your flocks" (28:16–18).

The imagery of God's judgment against Cain appears to have become a metaphor to the prophets (Isa 26:21) in picturing the judgment of God against Israel in the Exile: "See, the LORD is coming out of his dwelling to punish the people of the earth for their sins. The earth will disclose the blood shed upon her [*wᵉgillᵉṯāh hā'āreṣ 'eṯ-dāmeyhā*]; she will conceal her slain no longer." (Isaiah 27 continues with images drawn from the early chapters of Genesis, of God's final victory over the "serpent" [*nāḥāš*] and God's watchful care over his "fruitful vineyard" where no "briers and thorns" are allowed to grow.)

13–14 The meaning of this passage turns on how we understand Cain's reply in v.13. Did Cain complain that his "punishment" was too great to bear? Or should we understand his reply to be that his "iniquity" was too great to forgive? Although most EVs read "punishment" for *'ᵃwōnî*, both the sense of *'ᵃwōnî* with *nᵉśō'* ("bear") and the Lord's response to Cain's words in v.15 suggest that Cain's words are not to be understood as a complaint about his punishment but rather as an expression of remorse over the extent of his "iniquity" (*'ᵃwōnî*, see Cassuto). In v.14 Cain acknowledged that God's punishment (v.12) would result in his own death since he would not have the protection of an established community. Like his parents, Adam and Eve, who were driven out (*wayᵉḡāreš*, 3:24) of their home, the penalty of death was to be carried out against Cain by banishment from a protective community: "Today you are driving [*gēraštā*] me from the land, and I will be hidden from your presence; I will be a restless wanderer on the earth, and whoever [or 'whatever'] finds me will kill me."

15a The fact that the Lord's response was one of mercy and protection suggests that the author understood Cain's words as those of a repentant sinner. By themselves Cain's words do not necessarily suggest repentance, but the Lord's response ("Very well; if anyone kills Cain, he will suffer vengeance seven times over," NIV mg.) implies that Cain's words in v.13 are words of repentance.

Notes

13 The word עֲוֹנִי (*'ᵃwōnî*) usually means "iniquity" or "guilt" but can occasionally mean "punishment." The early versions understood the word in the former sense (LXX, ἡ αἰτία [*hē aitia*]; notice also the variant ἡ ἁμαρτία [*hē hamartia*]; Targum Onkelos, חוֹבִי [*ḥôḇî*]; Vul., *iniquitas mea*) and most modern versions in the latter sense (cf. NIV). The reason for the modern translation is Cain's words in v.14. There he complains of his punishment, not of his guilt (Skinner, p. 109). There are, however, compelling reasons for retaining the sense of "iniquity," "guilt" found in the older versions. First, the sense of נָשָׂא עָוֹן (*nāśā' 'ᵃwōn*) as "to bear one's punishment" is, at best, rare (cf. BDB, pp. 730–31, who lists many examples that could be read as either "guilt" or "punishment"; F. Buhl, however, in his 17th edition of William Gesenius's *Hebräisches und aramäisches Handwörterbuch* [Berlin: Springer Verlag, 1962, p. 572], gives only two examples for *'ᵃwōn* as "punishment" apart from Gen 4:13, namely, Isa 5:18; Ps 40:13; but neither passage has *nāśā' 'ᵃwōn;* rather they have only *'ᵃwōn*. William Gesenius's *Thesaurus Philologicus Criticus Linguae Hebraeae et Chaldaeae*

Veteris Testamenti [Lipsiae: F.C.G. Vogelii, 1835, p. 1000] lists only Isa 5:18 as "punishment [*poena peccati*]." In KB [p. 689] only two of the six examples listed apart from Gen 4:13 have *nāśā' 'ᵃwōn*, Ezek 44:10, 12). Second, v.14 can also be read as simply a request for mitigation of punishment in addition to the confession of guilt in v.13. There is no reason why v.14 must be read as an explanation of v.13. Third, if *'ᵃwōn* is to refer unequivocally to Cain's "punishment," which *he* must bear, we would expect that to be marked grammatically, e.g., מִנְּשֹׂאִי (*minnoś'î;* Jacob, p. 143).

---

3. *Protection*

4:15b–24

Then the LORD put a mark on Cain so that no one who found him would kill him. 16 So Cain went out from the LORD's presence and lived in the land of Nod, east of Eden.

17 Cain lay with his wife, and she became pregnant and gave birth to Enoch. Cain was then building a city, and he named it after his son Enoch. 18 To Enoch was born Irad, and Irad was the father of Mehujael, and Mehujael was the father of Methushael, and Methushael was the father of Lamech.

19 Lamech married two women, one named Adah and the other Zillah. 20 Adah gave birth to Jabal; he was the father of those who live in tents and raise livestock. 21 His brother's name was Jubal; he was the father of all who play the harp and flute. 22 Zillah also had a son, Tubal-Cain, who forged all kinds of tools out of bronze and iron. Tubal-Cain's sister was Naamah.

23 Lamech said to his wives,

"Adah and Zillah, listen to me;
  wives of Lamech, hear my words.
I have killed a man for wounding me,
  a young man for injuring me.
24 If Cain is avenged seven times,
  then Lamech seventy-seven times."

15b–18 The major issues at stake in this narrative seem identical to those that lie behind the narrative of the "cities of refuge" (Num 35:9–34). In both narratives God provides protection against the "avenger of blood." The question is not first whether one was actually guilty of the crime of murder—that could be settled by due process (Num 35:12). The more basic question lying behind Cain's statement and the provision of the cities of refuge (in Num 35) was the protection of the accused against the threat of a blood avenger. In both narratives God's provision was intended to put an end to the further bloodshed that even an unintentional killing engenders: "Bloodshed pollutes the land" (Num 35:33).

The background of the cities of refuge may provide a clue to the sense of the "sign" or "mark" (v.15b) given to Cain in this passage. It is clear that the purpose of the mark was to provide Cain with protection from vengeance. It is often said that the "mark" was put "on" Cain (cf. EVs), though the passage states that the sign was given "to" or "for" Cain (*wayyāśem leqayin 'ôt*, lit., "and he appointed to Cain a sign"; cf. 21:13, 18; 27:37; 45:7, 9; 46:3 with 21:14; 44:21).

What was the "mark" given to Cain for his protection? Though the narrative does not explicitly identify the sign (many attempts have been made to identify it, e.g., a dog, a bright-colored coat, a horn on his forehead [L. Diestel, *Geschichte des Alten Testaments in der christliche Kirche* (Jena: Mauke's Verlage [Hermann Dufft], 1869),

p. 497]), we should note that after the mention of the sign, the narrative continues with an account of Cain's departure to the land of Nod, "east of Eden," where he built a city. In light of the parallels with those texts relating to the cities of refuge, it may be significant that in this text the "sign narrative" is followed by the "city narrative." In the present shape of the text, Cain's city may have been intended as the "sign" that gave divine protection to Cain.

One element of the narrative that seems to be in favor of such a reading is the fact that, within the narrative itself, the purpose of the "sign" was to provide protection for Cain from anyone who might attempt to avenge Abel's death. Such was the express goal of the "cities of refuge": "They will be places of refuge from the avenger [*lᵉmiqlāṭ miggō'ēl*], so that a person accused of murder may not die before he stands trial before the assembly" (Num 35:12). The subsequent narrative testifies to the association of Cain's sign and the cities of refuge in that even in Lamech's day Cain's city was a place of refuge for the "manslayer" (see comments below). Thus within the narrative as a whole, Cain's city may be viewed as a "city of refuge" given to him by God to protect him and his descendants from blood revenge (see Deut 19:11–13). The importance the author attaches to the "city" that Cain built can be seen in the fact that the remainder of the chapter is devoted to the "culture" that developed in the context of that city.

19–24 In vv.20–24 the author names the originators of the primary components of city life: animal husbandry (Jabal, v.20), arts (Jubal, v.21), craftsmanship (Tubal-Cain, v.22), and, it appears, law (Lamech, vv.23–24). Lamech's words to his two wives have been interpreted many ways; they are frequently read as an example of a boasting arrogance and rebellion. When read in the context of the Mosaic law and in the context of the teaching regarding the cities of refuge, however, Lamech's words appear to be an appeal to a system of legal justice (see form critical remarks in Notes). The Mosaic law provided for the safe refuge of any "manslayer" until a just trial could be held (Num 35:12). Lamech, by referring to the "avenging of Cain" (cf. v.24), made it known that in his city he, too, had been "avenged."

To show that he had not shed innocent blood, Lamech appealed to the fact that he killed a man "for wounding" (*lᵉp̱iṣ'î*) and "for injuring" (*lᵉḥabburāṯî*) him (v.23). He did not "hate his neighbor, lie in wait for him, rise up against him, and kill him" (cf. Deut 19:11) as Cain had done, but rather he based his appeal on a plea of self-defense. Lamech's appeal to the law of lex talionis bears striking resemblances to the Mosaic law that provided for a just penalty with the principle of lex talionis (Exod 21:25). On the basis of this principle, one could appeal to an "eye for an eye and a tooth for a tooth."

The classic statement of the principle of lex talionis is given in Exodus 21:24–25, where it concludes with the same words used by Lamech: "a wound [*peṣa'*] for a wound [*pāṣa'*] and a bruise [*ḥabbûrāh*] for a bruise [*ḥabbûrāh*]." The purpose of the principle was not to allow for revenge but rather to prevent it. The force of the principle was to insure that a given crime was punished only by a just penalty. It prohibited a penalty that went in excess of the severity of the offense. Like the laws establishing the cities of refuge, the principle of lex talionis was to prevent the escalation of an offense in blood revenge. Thus Lamech killed a man for wounding him, not because he "hated him" (Deut 19:4–6). If Cain, who killed his brother with malice, could be avenged, then Lamech would surely be avenged for a killing in self-defense, that is, for "wounding" him.

The point of the narrative is not so much to show that Lamech's sense of justice was correct or even exemplary. Rather, it is to show that Cain's city and descendants had a system of law and justice representative of an ordered society. Not only did Cain's city have agriculture, music, and craftsmen, it also had an ordered base from which man could run his affairs by law. The picture of Lamech is reminiscent of that of many ancient monarchs whose contribution to the peace and order of their realms was epitomized in their legal decisions (e.g., Hammurabi's "Laws").

Notes

17 Unlike the clause structure of v.1 (W + X + QATAL), the WAYYIQTOL clause here—וַיֵּדַע קַיִן (*wayyēḏa' qayin,* lit., "And Cain knew") indicates that the narrative continues on through this portion of the story. The building of the city is to be understood as part of the same story and thus in close proximity to God's words to Cain in v.15.

23–24 Lamech's words not only show lexical similarities with the Mosaic law, they also show close form-critical similarities. The presence of the two כִּי (*kî*) clauses in Lamech's song has long been a source of difficulty (e.g., "It is rather clumsy to begin the third line too with כִּי," Westermann, p. 335). Form critically, the *kî* clause is the expected introduction to the main clause of the casuistic law (Gerhard Liedke, *Gestalt und Bezeichnung alttestamentlicher Rechtssätze* [Neukirchen: Neukirchener Verlag, 1971], pp. 29–35). The *kî* clause in v.24 also follows the pattern of casuistic law in its verb form: (1) the initial *kî* (2) followed by the verb (3) in the third person (4) imperfect (ibid., pp. 34–35). Westermann has pointed out that v.24 stands off from the song of Lamech and serves to link his words to the preceding narrative, suggesting that "it could well be that this verse is a later addition which links the old song with the Cain and Abel narrative" (p. 335). If v.24 were not the words of Lamech but rather those of the author of the Pentateuch (as an inserted comment along the lines of 2:24), then the form-critical considerations of v.24 reveal an intentional link, not only with its immediate context, but also with the whole of the rest of the Torah. The *kî* clause in v.25b shows just how easily and imperceptively the author moves from discourse (someone speaking in the narrative) to narrative itself (the recounting of events within the text). The only clue that the words "God has granted me another child" are the words of the woman and not those of the author is the first person pronoun לִי (*lî*, "to me"). Thus the change in person between Lamech's first person discourse in v.23 ("I have killed a man") and the reference to Lamech in the third person in v.24 ("Lamech seventy-seven times") may be a similar clue to the switch from discourse to narrative in vv.23–24.

4. *Blessing*

4:25–26

25 Adam lay with his wife again, and she gave birth to a son and named him Seth, saying, "God has granted me another child in place of Abel, since Cain killed him." 26 Seth also had a son, and he named him Enosh. At that time men began to call on the name of the LORD.

25–26 The scene at the conclusion of the chapter returns to that of the beginning. A new son is born (v.25). Though Cain's sons have prospered and have become the founders of the new world after the Fall, the focus of the narrative turns from the line of Cain to that of the new son born "in place of Abel." The woman called him "Seth" (*šēṯ*) because, she said, "God has granted [*šāṯ*] me another child."

In such narratives as these, the author clearly betrays his interest in the "seed" (*zera'*, 3:15) of the woman. Chapter 5 shows just how seriously the author takes the promise in 3:15. The focus is on the "seed" and the one who will crush the head of the snake. A pattern is established in chapter 4 that will remain the thematic center of the book. The one through whom the promised seed will come is not the heir apparent, that is, the eldest son, but the one whom God chooses. Abel, the younger of the two sons, received God's favor (4:4); Seth, still the younger son, replaced Abel. Cain takes his place in the narrative as one who was not to become a part of the line of the "seed." With him throughout the remainder of the Book of Genesis are Japheth (10:2–5), Ham (10:6–20), Nahor (11:29; 22:20–24), Ishmael (17:20), Lot (19:19–38), and Esau (ch. 36).

To underscore the importance of the line of Seth, the author notes that in his days people already practiced true worship of the God of the covenant: "At that time men began to call on the name of the LORD" (v.26). Such a note signifies that for the author of the Book of Genesis the worship of the Lord established at the time of Moses was not something new but rather a return to the worship of the only and true God. In light of such statements in the Pentateuch as Deuteronomy 31:27–29, where the focus is on the failure of the people to properly worship the God of the covenant, it is remarkable that the author does not take a similar view of the patriarchs before the Flood. At least as far as the line of Seth was concerned, these men, like Abraham after them, are described as true worshipers of the covenant God.

D. *The Story of Noah (5:1–10:32)*

At the beginning of chapter 5, a major break in the narrative is signaled by the new heading: "This is the written account of Adam's line." This section of narrative, which concludes in 9:29, is built around a list of the descendants of Adam. The list focuses on ten men. The first is Adam, the last Noah. The list continues until the death of Noah is recorded (9:29), at which time a new list of the sons of Noah begins (10:1–11:26). The second list ends with the birth of Abraham (11:26). Several narrative passages, varying greatly in size, are interspersed within these lists of names. The largest is the account of the Flood in the days of Noah (6:5–9:19), but there are other important narratives as well: Enoch's translation (5:24); Lamech's naming of Noah (5:29); the sons of God (6:1–4); Noah's drunkenness (9:20–27); Nimrod the mighty hunter (10:8–10); the Philistines (10:14); the division of the land (10:25); and the city of Babylon (11:1–9). The interweaving of bits of narrative and genealogical lists is one of the most characteristic features of the narrative technique of the author of Genesis. Often the genealogical lists are taken to be mere interludes in the course of events being described in the narratives. A close reading of the text, however, suggests that the author has something more specific in mind in including these lists of names and that they play an important role in shaping the context within which the narratives of the book are to be read.

1. *Prologue*

5:1–3

1 This is the written account of Adam's line.

When God created man, he made him in the likeness of God. [2]He created them male and female and blessed them. And when they were created, he called them "man."

[3]When Adam had lived 130 years, he had a son in his own likeness, in his own image; and he named him Seth.

The first question that must be asked is the relationship of chapter 5 to the first four verses of chapter 6. As our outline shows, we have taken 6:1–4 to be the "epilogue" to the list of names in chapter 5. When read with chapter 5 rather than the remainder of chapter 6, these four verses (6:1–4) take on a specific meaning within the narrative. They form a conclusion to the author's list of the sons of Adam, summarizing the main points of the passage before moving on to the story of the Flood (see discussion on these verses below).

1–3 The effect of this prologue on the genealogical list that follows in chapter 5 is striking. The prologue first redirects the reader's attention back to the course of events in the first chapter: the creation of the man and the woman (v.1). In so doing the prologue reiterates the central point of that earlier account: the creation of the man and the woman in the "image and likeness" of God. Second, the prologue ties chapter 5 together with the preceding verses in chapter 4 (vv.25–26) by continuing the pattern of "birth" and "naming." Just as the first parents named their sons (4:25–26), so also in the prologue to chapter 5 God named Adam (v.2); and he, in turn, named his son (Seth, v.3).

There is a similarity between the picture of the first parents and their sons and that of God and Adam. This is most readily seen in the fact that God's naming Adam appears here for the first time in Genesis. It was not a feature of the earlier account of man's creation in chapters 1 and 2. It appears that the author brings it in here specifically to heighten the comparison between 4:25–26 and the role of God in the prologue. In other words, the effect of the prologue is to cast God in the role of a father who has named Adam as his son.

Third, the role of God as a father is heightened even further by the parallels between his creating Adam "in the image of God" and Adam's giving birth to a son "in his own likeness, in his own image" (v.3). The author has gone to great lengths to depict God's creation of man in terms of a patriarch's establishment and overseeing of his family. The motive behind drawing such a parallel lies in the purpose of the list of patriarchs in chapter 5. Not only is Adam the father of Seth and Seth the father of Enosh, etc., but God is the Father of them all. If we follow the lines of these genealogical lists throughout the subsequent chapters of Genesis, two important points emerge: (1) God is shown to be the Father of all humanity (ch. 10), and (2) God is specifically shown to be the Father of Abraham and his seed.

The point of the prologue in vv.1–3 is much the same as that of the Song of Moses in Deuteronomy 32:6b. In that song Moses addresses a disobedient people with the rebuke, "Is he not your Father, your Creator"? Given such a purpose behind the prologue to chapter 5, it is not surprising that the author should return to the theme of the "sons of God" at the conclusion of this section in 6:1–2 (cf. Luke 3:38, where Adam is called the "son of God").

The author's return to the theme of God's "blessing" man (cf. v.2) is also a part of his overall scheme to cast God's purposes for man in terms that will recall a father's care for his children. Throughout the remainder of the Book of Genesis, a recurring theme is that of the father's blessing his children (9:26–27; 27:27; 48:15; 49:1–28). In keeping with such a theme, the author shows at each crucial turning point in the narrative that God himself renewed his blessing to the next generation of sons (1:28; 5:2; 9:1; 12:3; 24:11). Seen as a whole, the picture that emerges is that of a loving father insuring the future well-being of his children through the provision of an inherited blessing. In this way the author has laid a theological foundation for the rest of Scripture. God's original plan of blessing for all humanity, though thwarted by human folly, will nevertheless be restored through the seed of the woman (3:15), the seed of Abraham (12:3), and the "Lion of the tribe of Judah" (49:8–12; cf. Rev 5:5–13). It is on this same foundation that the apostle Paul built his view of Jesus as the one through whom God has "blessed us" (Eph 1:3) and "adopted us as his sons" (v.5) so that "we have obtained an inheritance" (v.11, KJV) from the one we may call "*Abba,* Father" (Rom 8:15).

Notes

3–32 The five formal elements listed below represent the structure of the list of names in chapter 5:

a: Name (X) lived (וַיְחִי, *way*^{e}*ḥî*) ‹nn› years/begat (וַיּוֹלֶד, *wayyôleḏ*) Name (Y)

b: Name (X) lived (וַיְחִי, *way*^{e}*ḥî*) ‹nn› years/after he begat (אַחֲרֵי הוֹלִידוֹ, *'aḥ*^{a}*rê hôlîḏô*) Name (Y)

c: begat sons and daughters (וַיּוֹלֶד בָּנִים וּבָנוֹת, *wayyôleḏ bānîm ûḇānôṯ*)

d: all the days of (וַיִּהְיוּ כָּל־יְמֵי, *wayyihyû kol-y*^{e}*mê*) Name (X) are ‹nn› years

e: and he (Name [X]) died (וַיָּמֹת, *wayyāmoṯ*).

The occurrence of each of the above elements for each of the ten names is charted below:

	a	b	c	d	e
1. Adam	x(+)	x	x	x	x
2. Seth	x	x	x	x	x
3. Enosh	x	x	x	x	x
4. Kenan	x	x	x	x	x
5. Mahalalel	x	x	x	x	x
6. Jared	x	x	x	x	x
7. Enoch	x	+	x	x	–
8. Methuselah	x	x	x	x	x
9. Lamech	x(+)	x	x	x	x
10. Noah	(x)	–	6:1	–	–
11. Noah (9:28)		x	–	x	x

The strict uniformity of the list suggests that the following deviations from the pattern deserve special attention.

1. At the beginning of the list (5:3b), there is an addition that mentions the naming of the next son: וַיִּקְרָא אֶת־שְׁמוֹ שֵׁת (*wayyiqrā' 'eṯ-š*^{e}*mô šēṯ,* "and he named him Seth"). Symmetrically, at the close of the list (5:29), there is an identical addition mentioning the naming of the next son: וַיִּקְרָא אֶת־שְׁמוֹ נֹחַ (*wayyiqrā' 'eṯ-š*^{e}*mô nō*^{a}*ḥ,* "and he named him Noah").

2. There is no mention of the deaths of Enoch and Noah in the list of chapter 5. It is important that for each of these two men the narrative specifically notes that "he walked with God" (הִתְהַלֵּךְ אֶת־הָאֱלֹהִים [*hiṯhallēḵ 'eṯ-hā'*^{e}*lōhîm*]). Traces of a similar formal pattern can be detected: compare 5:22—"and Enoch walked with God [וַיִּתְהַלֵּךְ חֲנוֹךְ אֶת־הָאֱלֹהִים (*wayyiṯhallēḵ ḥ*^{a}*nôḵ 'eṯ-hā'*^{e}*lōhîm*)] . . . and he begat sons [וַיּוֹלֶד בָּנִים (*wayyôleḏ bānîm;* NIV, 'and had other sons')]"—with 6:9–10—"and Noah walked with God [נֹחַ אֶת־הָאֱלֹהִים הִתְהַלֶּךְ־

(*'eṯ-hā'ᵉlōhîm hiṯhallek-nōᵃḥ*)] . . . and Noah begat three sons [וַיּוֹלֶד נֹחַ שְׁלֹשָׁה בָנִים (*wayyôleḏ nōᵃḥ šᵉlōšāh bānîm*)]."

3. Elements b through e are missing for Noah in chapter 5. Three of the elements are found at the close of the Noah narratives (b, d, e) and are in the same form as the rest of the names in chapter 5 (see 9:28–29). The only missing element in Noah's case is the mention that he "begat sons and daughters" (c). As the table above has indicated, it is just that element that is taken up in the first verse of chapter 6.

The relative chronologies and ages of the ten men. By adding the age of each patriarch at the time of the birth of the son who continues the line, a complete chronology from Adam to Noah can be established in which (according to the MT) "the Flood began in the year 1656 after the creation and ended in 1657" (Cassuto, p. 252). If taken as such it would seem that the time periods during which each of the patriarchs lived overlapped to a large extent. Adam, for example, would have lived until after the birth of Lamech, the ninth patriarch, and Methuselah, the eighth patriarch (the oldest and last to die), would have lived until the year of the Flood. Though many diverse attempts have been made to explain the relative chronologies and long ages of the ten men in this list, there are essentially only three approaches to the problem.

1. One may read the ages and relative chronologies recorded throughout this chapter as an idealization of a "long lost" age when life was not as it is today. Just as Isaiah envisioned the future rule of the Messiah as a time when "he who dies at a hundred will be thought a mere youth" (Isa 65:20), so the writer of Genesis may also be idealizing the past with a symbolic exaggeration of the number of years of their lives. Though such an approach provides insight into the narrative purpose behind the listing of the long lives, it falls short of a complete explanation in that there is little or no indication in the text that the numbers are to be taken any way other than realistically.

2. Another approach is to insist on a straightforward reading of the list as an actual chronology of the pre-Flood era. Though such long ages are considered improbable in today's world, it may be argued that before the Flood conditions were such that unusually long lives were not impossible. The strength of such an approach is that it appears to take seriously the actual statements of the text. On the face of it, the chapter suggests that there were 1656 years from Adam to the Flood and that these ten men did, in fact, live lives that spanned much of that time period. The problem with reading the text this way is that it leaves us with an extremely short time span in which to place not only all the events and civilizations recorded in the early chapters of Genesis but also all those events known to us from the study of history and archaeology. If from Adam to the Flood is only 1656 years and from the Flood to Abraham 365 years (cf. Gen 11), then all of the known history of human civilization and all of the prehistory of man must be put within a time period of only two thousand years. In the earlier commentaries, e.g., Calvin, such a chronology was taken at face value without difficulty; but most today would allow for some "gaps" in the chronology, thus not insisting on a time period of only 1656 years from Adam to the Flood (cf. Henry Morris and John Whitcomb, *The Genesis Flood* [Grand Rapids: Baker, 1961]).

3. A further approach is to see the ten individuals listed as representative of whole family units. The individuals themselves did not live to such old ages but rather the families and tribes that they represent extended throughout those years. One could point to the account of "Judah" and "Simeon" in Judges 1 as a similar example. Though the text speaks as if Judah and Simeon are individuals (lit., "And Judah said to Simeon his brother," Judg 1:3), they clearly represent the activities of whole tribal units.

---

2. *The sons of Adam*

5:4–32

4 After Seth was born, Adam lived 800 years and had other sons and daughters. 5 Altogether, Adam lived 930 years, and then he died.

6 When Seth had lived 105 years, he became the father of Enosh. 7 And
after he became the father of Enosh, Seth lived 807 years and had other
sons and daughters. 8 Altogether, Seth lived 912 years, and then he died.
9 When Enosh had lived 90 years, he became the father of Kenan.
10 And after he became the father of Kenan, Enosh lived 815 years and
had other sons and daughters. 11 Altogether, Enosh lived 905 years, and
then he died.
12 When Kenan had lived 70 years, he became the father of Mahalalel.
13 And after he became the father of Mahalalel, Kenan lived 840 years
and had other sons and daughters. 14 Altogether, Kenan lived 910 years,
and then he died.
15 When Mahalalel had lived 65 years, he became the father of Jared.
16 And after he became the father of Jared, Mahalalel lived 830 years and
had other sons and daughters. 17 Altogether, Mahalalel lived 895 years,
and then he died.
18 When Jared had lived 162 years, he became the father of Enoch.
19 And after he became the father of Enoch, Jared lived 800 years and
had other sons and daughters. 20 Altogether, Jared lived 962 years, and
then he died.
21 When Enoch had lived 65 years, he became the father of Methuselah. 22 And after he became the father of Methuselah, Enoch walked with
God 300 years and had other sons and daughters. 23 Altogether, Enoch
lived 365 years. 24 Enoch walked with God; then he was no more,
because God took him away.
25 When Methuselah had lived 187 years, he became the father of
Lamech. 26 And after he became the father of Lamech, Methuselah lived
782 years and had other sons and daughters. 27 Altogether, Methuselah
lived 969 years, and then he died.
28 When Lamech had lived 182 years, he had a son. 29 He named him
Noah and said, "He will comfort us in the labor and painful toil of our
hands caused by the ground the LORD has cursed." 30 After Noah was
born, Lamech lived 595 years and had other sons and daughters.
31 Altogether, Lamech lived 777 years, and then he died.
32 After Noah was 500 years old, he became the father of Shem, Ham
and Japheth.

4–32 The genealogical list in chapter 5 is nearly identical in form to that of 11:10–26, the genealogy (*tôlᵉḏōṯ, Toledoth*; NIV, "the account of") of Shem. A comparison of the formal elements of the two genealogies shows that the only difference between them is the inclusion of the clause "and then he died" (*wayyāmōṯ*) at the end of each of the names in chapter 5. Why would the author have felt it important to remind the reader specifically of the death of each of these patriarchs, whereas in the other genealogical lists he allows the matter of the death of the individual to remain implicit in the statement of the total number of the years of his life? The answer is not hard to find in chapter 5, because in this chapter alone one of the patriarchs, Enoch, *did not die*. The total number of the years of his life is given, as with the other genealogies, but only here is there an exception. Enoch "was no more, because God took him away" (v.24). In other words, the author purposefully underscores the death of each patriarch in chapter 5 to highlight and focus the reader's attention to the exceptional case of Enoch.

Why does the author want to point to Enoch so specifically as an exception? It is not merely because he did not die. That in itself is reason enough to merit special attention, but it does not sufficiently explain the purpose of the author in this case. The author's purpose can better be seen in the way he has emphasized, through repetition, that Enoch "walked with God" (vv.22, 24). The phrase "walked with God" (*wayyiṯhallēḵ 'eṯ-hā'ᵉlōhîm*) clearly means something to the author, for he uses the same expression to describe Noah as "a righteous man, blameless among the people of his time" (6:9), and Abraham and Isaac as faithful servants of God (17:1; 24:40; 48:15). Its use here shows that the author views it as the reason why Enoch did not die. Enoch is pictured as one who did not suffer the fate of Adam ("you will die") because, unlike the others, he "walked with God."

The sense of the author is clear. Enoch is an example of one who found *life* amid the curse of death. In Enoch the author is able to show that the pronouncement of death is not the last word that need be said about a man's life. One can find life if one "walks with God." For the author, then, a door is left open for a return to the tree of life in the garden. Enoch found that door in his "walking with God" and in so doing has become a paradigm for all who seek to find life. It is significant that the author returns to this theme at the opening of chapter 17, where God establishes his covenant promise with Abraham. Here the meaning is clear: "Walk before me and be blameless. I will confirm my covenant between me and you" (17:1–2). To "walk with God" is to fulfill one's covenant obligations.

For the author of Genesis, "walking with God" is the way to life. As Moses says to the people in the wilderness, "See, I set before you today life and prosperity, death and destruction. For I command you today to love the LORD your God, to walk in his ways, and to keep his commands . . . and the LORD your God will bless you in the land you are entering to possess" (Deut 30:15–16). It is important to see that for the author of the Pentateuch, "walking with God" could not have meant a mere "keeping" of a set of laws. Rather, it is just with those men who could not have had a set of "laws" that the author associates the theme of "walking with God." By choosing such men to exemplify "walking with God," the author shows his desire to teach a better way to live than merely a legalistic adherence to the law. We must not lose sight of the fact that from the author's perspective the way of the law at Sinai had not proved successful (e.g., Deut 31:27). A better way lay still in the future (Deut 30:5–6). For him the way to life was exemplified best in men like Enoch ("Enoch walked with God," 5:22), Noah ("he walked with God," 6:9), and Abraham ("Abram believed the LORD, and he credited it to him as righteousness," 15:6). It is to these patriarchs who lived long before the giving of the law at Sinai that the author of Genesis turns for a model of faith and trust in God.

The second of the ten patriarchs to be singled out for special attention by the author is Noah. The genealogical list in chapter 5 has been purposefully restructured at its conclusion to accommodate the Flood narrative (see Notes). The Flood narrative has been inserted into the genealogy between the notation of Noah's age at the time he begat his three sons (*wayᵉhî-nōᵃḥ*, 5:32; lit., "And Noah was") and the notation of the total length of his life (*wayᵉḥî-nōᵃḥ*, 9:28) and his death (*wayyāmōṯ*, 9:29; "and he died"). As a result the material relating to Noah varies greatly from that of the rest of these early patriarchs.

Two points in particular call for attention. First, in a section that breaks into the formal pattern of the list of names and shows clear lines of affinity with the structure and content of the prologue (5:1–3), we are told that Noah will bring comfort from the labor and painful toil of the curse (*wayyiqrā' 'eṯ-šᵉmô nōᵃḥ . . . zeh yᵉnaḥᵃmēnû*, "He named him Noah. . . . He will comfort us," v.29). In light of Genesis 8:21, it is likely that the comfort that Noah brought was the salvation of mankind in the ark as well as the reinstitution of the sacrifice after the Flood. In so doing Noah averted any future destruction of mankind (cf. 8:21).

Second, it is then significant that the narrative of the Flood, in which Noah and his family were the sole survivors, is inserted into the genealogical list just before the final word about his death. Thus the final word about Noah's death (*wayyāmōṯ*) does not appear until 9:28–29, where it, in effect, has become a part of the following table of nations (ch. 10). The reason for this adjustment of the genealogy of Noah and the insertion of the account of the Flood is clear from the way in which the author has reintroduced part of the genealogy of Noah into the Flood account (6:9–10). The same explanation for Enoch's rescue from death ("he walked with God") is made the basis for Noah's rescue from death in the Flood: "he walked with God" (6:9). Thus in the story of Noah and the Flood, the author was able to repeat the lesson of Enoch: *Life* comes through "walking with God."

At the close of the Flood account, by means of a brief genealogical note, the author appends the story of Noah's drunkenness (9:18–27). It is a strikingly different picture of Noah than that of the account of the Flood. However, it is a picture of Noah that well serves the author's purpose, because it provides a basis for the final word he has to give concerning Noah: viz., "and he died" (*wayyāmōṯ*, v.29). In other words, while Noah, along with Enoch, provided a lesson in the way of life that pleases God ("he walked with God"), Noah also provided the opposite lesson. Whatever the actual nature of his conduct might have been (see comments on 9:18–27), the author presents Noah's deed as one of disgrace and shame ("nakedness," as in ch. 3); and he seems intent on depicting the scene in such a way as to establish parallels between Noah's disgrace (he took of the fruit of his orchard and became naked) and that of Adam and Eve (who took of the fruit of the garden and saw that they were naked). Having thus depicted Noah, the narrative concludes with the remaining sections of Noah's genealogy and the account of his death (vv.28–29).

3. *Epilogue*

6:1–4

1 When men began to increase in number on the earth and daughters
were born to them, 2 the sons of God saw that the daughters of men
were beautiful, and they married any of them they chose. 3 Then the LORD
said, "My Spirit will not contend with man forever, for he is mortal; his
days will be a hundred and twenty years."

4 The Nephilim were on the earth in those days—and also afterward—
when the sons of God went to the daughters of men and had children by
them. They were the heroes of old, men of renown.

1–2 At the conclusion of the list of patriarchs and before the account of the Flood, the author gives a summary of the state of affairs of Adam's descendants. (For similar summaries at the close of a genealogical list, see 10:31–32; 11:27–32; Exod 1:7.) This small passage has had many diverse interpretations. In most cases the interpretations have arisen out of the viewpoint that these verses introduce the story of the Flood. If the events of these verses are an introduction to the Flood account, then they must be about the wickedness of mankind and the horrendous deeds that caused the Flood (e.g., Calvin: "For, in order to make a transition to the history of the deluge, he prefaces it by declaring the whole world to have been so corrupt, that scarcely anything was left to God, out of the widely spread defection"). Such a starting point for reading these verses, then, has led to a number of interpretations of the supposed wickedness depicted in them.

Historically there have been three primary interpretations of vv.1–4. The "sons of God" are (1) angels (the oldest view, e.g., codex Alexandrinus: *angeloi* ["angels"]); (2) royalty (also very old, e.g., Targum Onkelos: *b^enê rab̲r^eb̲ayā'* ["sons of lords"], though Jacob Levy [*Chaldäisches Wörterbuch über die Targumim* (Leipzig: Baumgaertner's Buchhandlung, 1881), 2:403] suggests that these may be "angels" in Onkelos; see also codex Neophyti I: "sons of judges," though a marginal reading has "kings," or possibly "angels" [see Alejandro Diez-Macho, *Neophyti I,* Targum Palestinense MS de la Biblioteca Vaticana (Madrid: Consejo Superior de Investigaciones Cientificas, 1968), 1:33]); and (3) pious men from the "line of Seth" (see Diestel, *Geschichte,* p. 499).

The first view has not been widely held since it appears to contradict the statement in Matthew 22:30: "At the resurrection people will neither marry nor be given in marriage; they will be like the angels in heaven" (cf. Diestel, *Geschichte,* p. 499). The commonly accepted view is that the "sons of God" refer to the godly, pious line of Seth (Calvin: "It was, therefore, base ingratitude in the posterity of Seth, to mingle themselves with the children of Cain"; The Scofield Bible: "verse 2 marks the breaking down of the separation between the godly line of Seth and the godless line of Cain"). All such interpretations, however, originate from the assumption that vv.1–4 are an introduction to the account of the Flood and are therefore to be understood as the cause of the Flood. If, on the other hand, we read vv.1–4 as a summary of chapter 5, there is little to arouse our suspicion that the events recounted are anything out of the ordinary. As a summary of the preceding chapter, this little narrative is a reminder that the sons and daughters of Adam had greatly increased in number, had married, and had continued to have children. The impression it gives is that of an interlude, a calm before the storm. For a brief moment we see a picture of man in the midst of his everyday affairs: "marrying and giving in marriage, up to the day Noah entered the ark; and they knew nothing about what would happen until the flood came and took them all away" (Matt 24:38–39).

Just as in 2:24, where the author turned briefly to the theme of marriage before moving on to the account of the Fall, so also in 6:1–4, on the eve of the Flood, the narrative turns briefly again to the theme of marriage. It is interesting to notice that the description of the marriages hinges on several key terms already well-developed by the author of the book. For example, in the statement that "men began to increase [*lārōb̲*] on the face of the earth" (v.1), the author recalls the blessing of God in 1:28: "Be fruitful and increase in number" (*ûr^eb̲û*; cf. Exod 1:7).

3 What is the meaning of the Lord's statement "My Spirit will not remain [*yād̲ôn;* NIV, 'contend'] with man forever, for he is mortal; his days will be a hundred and twenty years"? Though the statement is terse and open to several interpretations, its sense is clear if read within the context of what precedes and follows. It is interesting to notice that this is the first time the Lord has spoken since 5:2, where, after creating man male and female, he "called them man [Adam]." In that context the term "man" (Adam) clearly had a wider scope ("mankind") than the personal individual ("Adam") of chapter 4. In the remainder of chapter 5, the focus of the author was on the lives of individual men again, and thus in 5:3 he turned immediately to the genealogy of Adam, the individual. So it is only in v.3, as God speaks a second time, that the focus of the term "man" (Adam) is again on "mankind" as a whole. The point is that between these two statements of God about mankind, the author has put the list of ten

great individual men, men whose length of life stands in stark contrast to the "one hundred and twenty years" of the life of "mankind."

The inference of such an arrangement of the narrative is that it was God's Spirit dwelling (*yāḏôn*) with these men that gave them their long lives and not their own "flesh." The sad reality of the narrative, however, is that such long lives do not belong to mankind as a whole but belonged to another age. The long lives of the ten great men in chapter 5 are thus shown to be exceptions rather than the rule. Henceforth man's life would be "a hundred and twenty years" only. Such a short life, in comparison with the long lives of the previous chapter, marks man's fall and separation from his Creator.

In keeping with this point, the author continues to show the ages of the men of the book and notes that generally their ages grow increasingly shorter (cf. 11:10–26). It is only at the close of the Pentateuch that we finally reach an individual who is specifically mentioned as dying at the age of 120 years, Moses, who was in the wilderness and who died as a result of unbelief and divine punishment (Num 20)—he died though he was still in good strength (Deut 34:7).

The 120 years was taken by Luther (also Calvin and The Scofield Bible) to refer to a time of reprieve granted by God to mankind before sending the Flood ("I want to give to them yet a reprieve of 120 years," Luther Bible). Such an interpretation is apparently an attempt to resolve the discrepancy between the limit put on man's life of 120 years and the record of the length of the human lives in 11:10–26 that exceeded 120 years (cf. Augustine: "They cannot be taken as foretelling that thereafter men would not live beyond a hundred and twenty years, since we find that after the Flood, as before, men lived even beyond five hundred years," *City of God*, 15.24), a discrepancy that does not exist in the above interpretation.

The reprieve interpretation may also reflect the influence of 1 Peter 3:20—"when God waited patiently in the days of Noah while the ark was being built"—which has been taken by many (see Gustav Wohlenberg, *Der erste und zweite Petrusbrief und der Judasbrief* [Leipzig: A. Deichert'sche Verlagsbuchhandlung Werner Scholl, 1915], p. 114) to refer to the period of 120 years in Genesis 6:3. Such an understanding of the 120 years can already be found in the Onkelos Targum ("A reprieve ['*arḵā*'] will be given to them") and Targum Neophyti I ("Behold I have given you the space ['*arḵā*'] of a hundred and twenty years [hoping that] perhaps they might do repentance and they did not do [it]"), but it is not in the LXX or the Vulgate.

4 The author uses the term "Nephilim" (*hannᵉp̱ilîm*) elsewhere in the Pentateuch to refer to the great men ('*anšê-middôṯ*; NIV, "people . . . of great size") who were in the land of Canaan at the time of the Exodus (Num 13:32–33). Here in v.4 the term "Nephilim" also appears to refer to the great men ('*anšê haššēm*, lit., "men of name") of antiquity. In light of the fact that the author has just completed a list of the names of ten great men from antiquity (ch. 5), it is possible that he has these ten men in mind in referring to the "men of renown." The mention of the "Nephilim" in Numbers 13:33, however, indicates that there were still survivors of the "Nephilim" in the days of the Exodus, which would appear to be in conflict with our taking them as the ten great men of chapter 5 (see, however, the Notes).

Notes

1–4 There are several formal indications in the narrative that vv.1–4 belong to the preceding account and thus are not to be read as a prologue to the account of the Flood. The opening clause—וַיְהִי (*wayᵉhî*, "and it was"; NIV, "When")—follows the string of similar clauses at the end of chapter 5 (5:31–32). In 5:32 the *wayᵉhî* clause is continued by *wayyôleḏ* (וַיּוֹלֶד ["and he became the father of"], 5:32b), just as *wayᵉhî* in 6:1a is continued by *yullᵉḏû* (יֻלְּדוּ ["and they were born"], 6:1b). The line of WAYYIQTOL clauses continues from chapter 5 to 6:3, whereas in 6:4a the narrative line is interrupted by an asyndetic, inverted verbal clause with the perfect: הַנְּפִלִים הָיוּ בָאָרֶץ (*hannᵉp̄ilîm hāyû ḇā'āreṣ*, "The Nephilim were on the earth"). Such clauses have marked the conclusion of the Genesis narratives since the first chapter.

2 The identity of בְּנֵי־הָאֱלֹהִים (*bᵉnê-hā'ᵉlōhîm*, "the sons of God") and בְּנוֹת הָאָדָם (*bᵉnôṯ hā'āḏām*, "the daughters of men [lit., 'man']") is the subject of a longstanding debate among biblical scholars. Three views are prominent: the sons of God are (1) angels, (2) the godly seed of Seth, (3) the royal line of kings. All three views share the supposition that 6:1–4 is a prologue to the account of the Flood and hence primarily negative in its outlook. However, if these verses are read as a summary conclusion to chapter 5, the description of the sons of God choosing wives from the daughters of men in that context does not point to a particularly horrendous act. The only negative connotation that may be suggested comes from the contrast between God's exercise of "the knowledge of good and evil" in choosing a wife for Adam—וַיֹּאמֶר יהוה אֱלֹהִים לֹא־טוֹב הֱיוֹת הָאָדָם לְבַדּוֹ (*wayyō'mer yhwh 'ᵉlōhîm lō'-ṭôḇ hᵉyôṯ hā'āḏām lᵉḇaddô*, "The LORD God said, 'It is not good for the man to be alone,'" 2:18)—and the sons of God now taking on themselves the same exercise of that knowledge: וַיִּרְאוּ בְנֵי־הָאֱלֹהִים . . . כִּי טֹבֹת (*wayyir'û ḇᵉnê-hā'ᵉlōhîm . . . kî ṭōḇōṯ*, lit., "and the sons of God saw that they were good").

Why then are the men specifically called the "sons of God" and the women the "daughters of men"? Such a designation of the men and the women in this summary is in keeping with the earlier description of the origin of the man and the woman. Though the description of the creation of the man and the woman in chapter 1 is clear that both have been created in God's image, chapters 2 and 3 specify that the man was created by the breath of God (נִשְׁמַת חַיִּים, *nišmaṯ ḥayyîm*, 2:7) and that the woman was created (וַיִּבֶן, *wayyiḇen*) from the "side" (הַצֵּלָע, *haṣṣēlā'*) of the man. Thus men are called the "sons" (*bᵉnê*) of God—denoting their origin from God—and women are called the "daughters" (*bᵉnôṯ*) of man—denoting their origin from man. In the case of the "daughters" (*bᵉnôṯ*), at least, there is a direct wordplay on the woman's origin in 2:22: "Then the LORD God made [וַיִּבֶן, *wayyiḇen*]," that is, the relation between *bᵉnôṯ* and *bānāh*.

3 The translation "My Spirit will not contend with man forever" rests on reading יָדוֹן (*yāḏôn*, "to prevail") as a form of דִּין (*dîn*, "to rule"), which is unlikely (see BDB, p. 192) since it would then have been *yāḏîn* rather than *yāḏôn*, or taking *yāḏôn* as a form of the otherwise unknown root דּוֹן (*dôn*) (Bauer and Leander, *Historische Grammatik*, p. 398; cf. KB, p. 208). It is generally agreed that the LXX's *καταμείνῃ* (*katameinēi*, "stay," "abide") is an attempt to gain a sense from the context alone and thus does not reflect an early understanding of the word itself. However, in light of the complete lack of a consensus on the philological meaning of the term, it is best to follow the lead of the LXX and seek a sense for the word from within the immediate context. The LXX's "shall not abide with" (*οὐ μὴ καταμείνῃ, ou mē katameinēi*) adequately reflects the sense of contrast with the second part of the verse: "his days will be a hundred and twenty years."

4 The author has assumed his readers would not understand the term הַנְּפִלִים (*hannᵉp̄ilîm*, "the Nephilim") since he identified them within the narrative itself as the הַגִּבֹּרִים (*haggibbōrîm*, "the heroes"), namely, the אַנְשֵׁי הַשֵּׁם (*'anšê haššēm*, "men of renown"). The antecedent of הֵמָּה (*hēmmāh*, "they") is *hannᵉp̄ilîm* (Skinner, p. 147). The *hannᵉp̄ilîm* were in the land "in those days" and "also afterward [וְגַם אַחֲרֵי־כֵן אֲשֶׁר, *wᵉg̱am 'aḥᵃrê-ḵēn 'ᵃšer*]—when the sons of God went to the daughters of men and had children by them." The sense of the phrase *wᵉg̱am 'aḥᵃrê-ḵēn 'ᵃšer* is that the *hannᵉp̱ilîm* were not the offspring of the union of the sons of God with the daughters of man. Thus the *hannᵉp̱ilîm* were in the land "while" (בַּיָּמִים הָהֵם [*bayyāmîm hāhēm*, lit., "in those days"]) and "also after" (*wᵉg̱am 'aḥᵃrê-ḵēn*) the time of the union of the sons of God and the daughters of men. The remark in Num 13:33, which identifies the *hannᵉp̱ilîm* that the spies saw in the land with the "sons of Anak" and the *hannᵉp̱ilîm* in Gen 6:3, is not in the LXX and thus may not have been in the original text. On the face of it, the remark presents a problem to the view that only Noah and his sons survived the Flood, since it suggests that the "sons of Anak" were descendants of the "Nephilim" (*min hannᵉp̱ilîm*, lit., "from the Nephilim") who lived before the Flood. In Num 13:22, 28, the "Anakim" are called יְלִדֵי הָעֲנָק (*yᵉliḏê hā'ᵃnāq*, "descendants of Anak") rather than בְּנֵי עֲנָק (*bᵉnê 'ᵃnāq*, "sons of Anak") as here in Num 13:33 (NIV has "descendants") (cf. G.B. Gray, *A Critical and Exegetical Commentary on Numbers* [Edinburgh: T. & T. Clark, 1903], p. 151). However, in Deut 9:2 they are called the *bᵉnê 'ᵃnāq* (NIV, "Anakites") (cf. Gray). If the remark in Num 13:33 is secondary, it may have been motivated by the sense of "and also afterward" (*wᵉg̱am 'aḥᵃrê-ḵēn*) here in Gen 6:4.

---

4. *The Flood (6:5–9:17)*

The account of the Flood gives every indication of being a carefully wrought and intricately complex narrative. There are seven principle stages in the narrative: (1) the decision to send the Flood and rescue Noah (6:5–12), (2) the command to build the ark (6:13–22), (3) the command to enter the ark (7:1–5), (4) the floods come (7:6–24), (5) the floods abate (8:1–14), (6) the command to exit the ark (8:15–19), and (7) the building of the altar and the covenant (8:20–9:17). Within each stage the author has arranged a whirling array of activities in which the reader himself is caught up in the fury of the Flood and the sense of the impending wrath of God.

It is significant to notice how the author guides the readers' participation in the narrative by keeping a tight control on the point of view from which the story is told. At the beginning of the story, the reader follows the course of events from a divine perspective. We, the readers, are allowed to look down from heaven over all the earth and see what the Lord himself sees; we are allowed to listen in on his conversations and follow his judgments (6:5–7:5). With the onset of the Flood, however, we lose our privileged position. We no longer see what God sees. We see only what the characters of the story themselves see as the heavens pour forth rain and the fountains of the deep break apart. Our perspective as readers is "horizontal." The floods rise up around us; we cannot stand alongside God and look down on those in the narrative who are experiencing God's judgment.

As the Flood progresses God becomes strangely absent. Only the waters and those fleeing the waters are kept in narrative view. The author refuses to allow the reader to stand in a neutral corner and watch while God judges the world. We are forced to take sides like those in the narrative itself. Like Lot's wife (19:26), we cannot look on while others experience God's judgment. We are left either to enter the ark with Noah or to remain outside in the Flood. The only glimpse of God we are allowed as the waters of the Flood close in around "all flesh" is his closing of the door behind those who have entered the ark (7:16). After 150 days of flood waters (8:1–4), the reader catches a brief glimpse of God's actions (God remembered Noah and sent a wind to dry up the waters); but, here again, we are not allowed to continue to view the rest of the story from such a lofty perspective. Immediately the narrative returns us to the ark where, with Noah, we must wait for the waters to recede and rely only on the return of the raven and the dove sent out through the little window of the ark (8:5–14). Once the dry land has appeared (8:14), the reader's perspective returns to that of the Lord in heaven, and we hear and see his point of view again as at the beginning of the story.

a. *The decree*

6:5–12

5The LORD saw how great man's wickedness on the earth had become, and that every inclination of the thoughts of his heart was only evil all the time. 6The LORD was grieved that he had made man on the earth, and his heart was filled with pain. 7So the LORD said, "I will wipe mankind, whom I have created, from the face of the earth—men and animals, and creatures that move along the ground, and birds of the air—for I am grieved that I have made them." 8But Noah found favor in the eyes of the LORD.

9This is the account of Noah.

Noah was a righteous man, blameless among the people of his time, and he walked with God. 10Noah had three sons: Shem, Ham and Japheth.

11Now the earth was corrupt in God's sight and was full of violence. 12God saw how corrupt the earth had become, for all the people on earth had corrupted their ways.

5–7 These verses form the introduction proper to the Flood story. As such they tie the story together with previous narratives and provide the central themes of the narrative to follow. Here and throughout the Flood story, there are numerous ties established with the Creation account in chapter 1. The effect is to show that the Flood was a reversal of God's good work of Creation. In chapter 1 God is shown as the one who prepared the *good land* for man and his family. In the account of the Flood, on the other hand, God is shown as the one who takes this good land from man when he acts corruptly and does not walk in God's way. The central themes introduced in these opening verses are God's judgment of man's wickedness and his gracious salvation of the righteous (von Rad).

The cause for the Flood is tied directly to the earlier account of the fall of man in chapter 3. As a result of the Fall, man had obtained the "knowledge of good and evil" (*ṭôḇ wārāʿ*, 3:22). It is clear from the previous narratives that the author does not consider man's having obtained a knowledge of "good and evil" to be beneficial for man. From the author's perspective, man was far better off when he had to trust God for "the good" (*ṭôḇ*). One of the ways the author is able to teach this lesson in chapter 1 is through the recurring expression "and God saw [*wayyarʾ*] that it was good" (*ṭôḇ*). The central theme of "God's good provisions for man" is embodied in the recurring picture of God's "seeing" what is good (*ṭôḇ*). After the Fall, when man had to find the "good" on his own, what God "saw" (*wayyarʾ*, v.5) was not that his Creation was *good* (*ṭôḇ*); but, rather, "the LORD saw [*wayyarʾ*] how great man's wickedness [*rāʿaṯ*] on the earth had become, and that every inclination of the thoughts of his heart was only evil [*raʿ*]."

In v.6—"the LORD was grieved [*wayyinnāḥem*] that he had made man on the earth, and his heart was filled with pain [*wayyitʿassēḇ*]"—the author describes the Lord's response to man's wickedness by making a curious wordplay on Lamech's naming

Noah: "He will comfort us [*yᵉnaḥᵃmēnû*] in . . . the painful toil of our hands" (*ûmē'iṣṣᵉḇôn*, 5:29). Thus in both passages Noah is introduced with wordplays associating his name, "Noah" (*nōᵃḥ*), with the "comfort" (*niḥam*) from the grief and pain (*'āṣaḇ*) caused by man's rebellion (cf. Cassuto). By making God the subject of the verbs in v.6, the author has shown that the grief and pain of man's sin was not something that only man felt. God himself was grieved over man's sin (v.7). In returning in this way to the role of "comforter" invested in the significance of Noah's name, the author suggests that not only did Noah bring comfort to mankind in his grief, but also he brought comfort to God.

8 Noah alone among all the others "found favor [*ḥēn*, i.e., 'grace'] in the eyes of the LORD." Here again the narrative makes a play on Noah's name in that the word *ḥēn* is a reversal of the consonants of the name "Noah" (*nōᵃḥ*) (Cassuto). The purpose of v.8 is to say no more than that Noah found favor with God. In the following section (vv.9–12) the author explains why God found Noah to be an exception. In that explanation lies the central purpose of the Flood account in the Book of Genesis.

9–12 The Flood account begins in v.9 with the description of Noah's righteousness. It seems clear from the way the author begins the account that the main purpose of the story of the Flood is not to show why God sent a flood but rather to show why God saved Noah. In this opening section Noah's "righteousness" is contrasted with the "violence" of "all flesh." The message of the narrative is quite straightforward. The reason God saved Noah was that he "walked with God" and did not "corrupt" God's way (v.12). In describing Noah in this way, the author intentionally draws a parallel between the deliverance of Noah from the Flood and Enoch's deliverance from death (5:22–24). The point is clear enough: God delivers those who "walk with" him and who do not "corrupt his way."

In the account of Enoch's deliverance, as here in vv.9–10, the author is not specific about the nature of Enoch's "righteousness" or what it means to "walk with God." In the following section, however, the author allows the reader to peer much closer into the nature of Noah's righteousness. We are allowed to see him at work. The picture of Noah (*nōᵃḥ*) that emerges from the Flood story thus becomes a model of the kind of life that finds grace (*ḥēn*) in the sight of God. It is a picture of simple obedience to God's commands and trust in his provision. In light of the predominance of the concept of "faith" elsewhere in the Pentateuch (cf. Hans-Christoph Schmidt, "Redaktion des Pentateuch im Geiste der Prophetie, Beobachtungen zur Bedeutung der 'Glaubens'—Thematik innerhalb der Theologie des Pentateuch," VetTest 32, 2 [1983]: 170–89), it is appropriate to say that the author has in mind a picture of Noah very much like that of the writer of Hebrews, one who "by his faith . . . condemned the world and became heir of the righteousness that comes by faith" (Heb 11:7).

Notes

---

5 The expression וַיַּרְא יהוה כִּי רַבָּה רָעַת הָאָדָם (*wayyar' yhwh kî rabbāh rā'aṯ hā'āḏām*, "The LORD saw how great man's wickedness on the earth had become") is an allusion back to the Creation account in chapter 1: וַיַּרְא אֱלֹהִים אֶת־הָאוֹר כִּי־טוֹב (*wayyar' 'ᵉlōhîm 'eṯ-hā'ôr kî-ṭôḇ*,

"And God saw that the light was good," v.4), just as 6:12—וַיַּרְא אֱלֹהִים אֶת־הָאָרֶץ וְהִנֵּה נִשְׁחָתָה (*wayyar' 'elōhîm 'eṯ-hā'āreṣ wehinnēh nišḥāṯāh,* "God saw how corrupt the earth had become")—appears to allude to 1:32 [31 MT]—וַיַּרְא אֱלֹהִים אֶת־כָּל־אֲשֶׁר עָשָׂה וְהִנֵּה טוֹב מְאֹד (*wayyar' 'elōhîm 'eṯ-kol-'ašer 'āśāh wehinnēh ṭôḇ me'ōḏ,* "And God saw all that he had made, and it was very good"). Such allusions show that the whole of the narrative has been carefully shaped according to a master plan (see O. Eissfeldt, "Die kleinste literarische Einheit in den Erzählungsbüchern des Alten Testaments," *Kleine Schriften,* vol. 1 [Tübingen: J.C.B. Mohr, 1962], p. 144).

---

b. *The command to build the ark*

6:13–22

13 So God said to Noah, "I am going to put an end to all people, for the earth is filled with violence because of them. I am surely going to destroy both them and the earth. 14 So make yourself an ark of cypress wood; make rooms in it and coat it with pitch inside and out. 15 This is how you are to build it: The ark is to be 450 feet long, 75 feet wide and 45 feet high. 16 Make a roof for it and finish the ark to within 18 inches of the top. Put a door in the side of the ark and make lower, middle and upper decks. 17 I am going to bring floodwaters on the earth to destroy all life under the heavens, every creature that has the breath of life in it. Everything on earth will perish. 18 But I will establish my covenant with you, and you will enter the ark—you and your sons and your wife and your sons' wives with you. 19 You are to bring into the ark two of all living creatures, male and female, to keep them alive with you. 20 Two of every kind of bird, of every kind of animal and of every kind of creature that moves along the ground will come to you to be kept alive. 21 You are to take every kind of food that is to be eaten and store it away as food for you and for them."

22 Noah did everything just as God commanded him.

13 There are important similarities between the account of the building of the ark and two other narratives in the Pentateuch, viz., the account of Creation in Genesis 1 and the building of the "tabernacle" in Exodus 25ff. Each account has a discernible pattern: God speaks (*wayyō'mer/wayeḏabbēr*), an action is commanded (imperative/jussive), and the command is carried out (*wayya'aś*) according to God's will (*wayehî kēn/ka'ašer ṣiwwāh 'elōhîm*). The key to these similarities lies in the observation that each narrative concludes with a divine blessing (*wayeḇāreḵ,* Gen 1:28; 9:1; Exod 39:43) and, in the case of the tabernacle and Noah's ark, a divinely ordained *covenant* (Gen 6:8; Exod 34:27; in this regard it is of some importance that later biblical tradition also associated the events of Gen 1–3 with the making of a divine covenant; cf. Hos 6:7). Noah, like Moses, followed closely the commands of God and in so doing found salvation and blessing in his *covenant.*

It is not hard to see in these examples the lesson intended by the author of the Pentateuch. It is stated directly to the readers in Deuteronomy 30:2–3: "When you and your children return to the LORD your God and obey him with all your heart and with all your soul according to everything I command you today [*keḵōl 'ašer-'ānōḵî meṣawweḵā*], then the LORD your God will restore your fortunes and have compassion on you and gather you again from all the nations where he scattered you." The author's purpose in drawing out the list of specifications for the ark in chapter 6, as with the details of the building of the tabernacle, is not so much that the reader might be able to see what the ark or the tabernacle looked like, but rather that we might appreciate the meticulous care with which these godly and exemplary men went about their tasks of obedience to God's will. They obeyed God with "all their hearts."

14 The size and shape of the ark are described only in the most general terms. The word "ark" (*tēḇāh*), an Egyptian loan word, means "palace" (not "chest" or "coffin" as in BDB [see KB, p. 1017], thus a different word than "ark" in Exod 2:3, 5, though the uses seem very similar, and no doubt a link is intended between the two passages). Thus the sense of the term focuses on the structure as an abode rather than its shape or size. It was not unusual in ancient literature for a large ship to be called a palace (see J.B. Pritchard, ANET, p. 94; Riekele Borger, *Babylonisch-Assyrische Lesestuecke*, No. 2 [Rome: Pontifical Bible Institute, 1963], p. 97). Perhaps a parallel to this is the use of the English nautical term "castle" (cf. *Oxford English Dictionary*, II [Oxford: Oxford University Press, 1971], p. 162). The English translation "ark" is taken directly from the Latin Vulgate (*arca*, meaning "box") and hence derived ultimately from the LXX (*kibōtos*, "chest"; cf. Matt 24:38; Luke 17:27; Heb 11:7).

The exact nature of the material from which the structure was made is unknown (see KB, p. 193). The NIV's "cypress wood" rests on the doubtful association of the consonants of the Latin word *cupressus* and those of the Hebrew *gpr* as well as on the fact that such wood was commonly used for shipbuilding in the ancient world. It may be that the term "gopher" describes the shape of the wood (the LXX read it as *tetragōnos* ["square"]) rather than the kind. In any event, the term is used without further comment; and like so many of the terms in this section, its meaning remains a mystery. This wood was then sealed with "pitch" (*kōp̱er*), another rare word found only here in v.14.

The art of shipbuilding was a skill known and practiced already in the earliest civilizations in the Near East. The city of Byblos, located along the Syrian coastline and one of the oldest continuously occupied cities in the Near East, was well-known throughout the region for its maritime trade. The forests that grew nearby the city were a continuous source of supply, not only for ships, but for construction projects of all kinds. According to the Palermo Stone (a copy of the annals of predynastic Egyptian kings, see James H. Breasted, *A History of Egypt* [London: Hodder and Stoughton, 1945], p. 47), the Egyptian king Sneferu brought forty shiploads of lumber from Byblos and built forty-four boats ranging up to 170 feet (100 cubits) in length (ANET, p. 227). The Egyptians called the inhabitants of Byblos "the woodcutters," and their name for large ocean-going ships was "Byblos-boats" (J. Bottero, "Syria Before 2200 B.C.," CAH, 1.2:347–48). Drower says of the shipyards of Byblos during the mid-second millennium B.C.: "This was an age of heavy freighters capable of transporting bulky cargoes. They carried timber, livestock and agricultural produce, salt, wine and oil in large jars. Ugarit had grain-ships capable of carrying a hundred and fifty tons of grain" (M.S. Drower, "Syria c. 1550–1400 B.C.," CAH, 2.1:508).

15 For a wooden vessel, the size of the ark was enormous by ancient as well as modern standards. It would have been about two and a half times the size of the large "Byblos-boats" used by the Egyptians during the Early Dynastic Period and would even have been larger than the largest wooden ships in the modern period of sailing. The Cutty Sark, a three-masted clipper ship launched in 1869, was just over 212 feet (New EBr, 3:814). Oceanliners of the twentieth century, however, being constructed of steel, are much larger. The Queen Elizabeth, the largest passenger liner ever built, measured over 1000 feet in length (New EBr, 9:850). By modern standards Noah's ocean vessel is comparable to a small cargo ship, thus still of considerable size.

16 As far as the layout of the ark is concerned, we learn from the narrative that it was constructed with three stories, or decks, of "rooms" (v.14) or separate compartments (*qinnîm,* lit., "nests"); it had an opening for light (*ṣōhar;* NIV, "roof") and a door in its side. We cannot assume that the structure consisted only of those features enumerated in this brief description. Only the faintest outline is given here.

We should not conclude from the brevity of the narrative that Noah and his sons built such a vessel on their own any more than we would assume that only Bezalel and Oholiab built the tabernacle by themselves (Exod 31:2–6). As Exodus 36:6 shows, there were other men who worked with them, even though elsewhere only Bezalel is mentioned (Exod 37:1; 38:22). What is important to notice, however, is that there is ample evidence from the earliest stages of civilization in the Near East of the requisite skills in architectual design and woodworking for making such a structure. What we know as the earliest examples of architecture on a grand scale, e.g., the funerary monuments of archaic Egypt, are in fact later replicas of prototype wooden structures. Though nothing of these earlier structures have survived, we can learn a great deal about their design and craftsmanship from the later stone and brick copies (Walter B. Emery, *Archaic Egypt* [Middlesex: Penguin, 1972], pp. 176ff.).

Notes

13–22 The formal similarities between the three passages are shown below:

	Gen 1	Gen 6	Exod 25ff.
וַיֹּאמֶר[1]	1:3, 6, 9, 11, 20, 24, 26	6:13; 7:1	
וַיְדַבֵּר[2]			25:1
Imperative/ Jussive	1:3, 6, 9, 11, 14, 20, 24	6:14ff.; 7:1	25:2ff.
וַיַּעַשׂ[3]	1:7, 16, 25	6:22; 7:5	36:8ff.
כֵּן[4]	1:7, 9, 11, 15, 24		
כַּאֲשֶׁר[5]		6:22; 7:5, 9, 16	38:22; 39:1, 5, 7, 21, 26, 29, 31, 32, 42, 43

[1] (*wayyō'mer,* "and he said").
[2] (*way^e^dabbēr,* "and he said").
[3] (*wayya'aś,* "and he made").
[4] (*kēn,* "so").
[5] (*ka'^a^šer,* "just as").

c. *The command to enter the ark*

7:1–5

[1]The LORD then said to Noah, "Go into the ark, you and your whole family, because I have found you righteous in this generation. [2]Take with you seven of every kind of clean animal, a male and its mate, and two of every kind of unclean animal, a male and its mate, [3]and also seven of every kind of bird, male and female, to keep their various kinds alive throughout the earth. [4]Seven days from now I will send rain on the earth for forty days and forty nights, and I will wipe from the face of the earth every living creature I have made."

[5]And Noah did all that the LORD commanded him.

1–5 The command to make the ark had been given and followed to its completion (6:22). The next scene opens with the command to enter the ark before the coming rains (v.1). The emphasis of the section lies in its mention of the special provisions for the "clean animals" to be taken into the ark (v.2). The section follows the same pattern as the previous one in which we saw important parallels with the provisions for the building of the tabernacle. It is noteworthy that there are parallels between this narrative of Noah's entering the ark and the narrative of the provisions for making ready the tabernacle in the wilderness. Both narratives, for example, emphasize that entry into the ark/tabernacle is to be accompanied by an animal offering. At the close of the description of the building of the tabernacle (Exod 35–39), when the completion of the tabernacle has been recorded (Exod 39:43), the command is given for it to be set up and readied for use (Exod 40:1–33). When it is readied and the glory of the Lord has filled the tabernacle (Exod 40:34–38), provisions are made for "drawing near" to the tabernacle (Lev). One may "draw near" only by bringing an animal offering that is "unblemished" (*tāmîm,* Lev 1:3; NIV, "without defect"). Thus just as the completed tabernacle can be entered only with the "unblemished animals" as an offering, so Noah's entry into the ark is tied to his taking with him "seven pairs" of every clean animal.

The specific mention of the "clean animals" (*habbᵉhēmāh haṭṭᵉhôrāh,* v.2) that Noah took with him into the ark is perhaps intended to suggest that while in the ark he ate only "clean meat," as is the requirement in the tabernacle (Lev 7:19–21). Such parallels suggest that the author has intentionally drawn a comparison between the salvation that lies in the ark of Noah during the impending "forty days and forty nights" of rain (v.4) and the salvation in the presence of the tabernacle during the impending "forty years" in the wilderness. Again it is the centrality of the idea of a covenant relationship that lies behind the author's work.

In light of such parallels it is significant that the author makes direct reference to the sacrificial importance of these "clean animals" taken into the ark when at the close of the Flood account he shows that these animals were in fact to be used for an offering to the Lord (8:20–21). In describing the Lord's acceptance of these offerings (*wayyāraḥ yhwh 'eṯ-rêᵃḥ hannîḥōᵃḥ,* "the pleasing aroma," 8:21), the author uses the specific terminology used in Leviticus 1:17 (*rêᵃḥ nîḥōᵃḥ layhwh,* "an aroma pleasing to the LORD"), and again it is tied to the notion of a covenant (9:8, 11). Such "typological" shaping of the Flood narrative by the author of the Pentateuch is remarkably similar to the later reading of this passage in 1 Peter 3:21. In that passage the ark is seen to prefigure the saving work of Christ as it is pictured in NT baptism.

Notes

Gunkel lists several repetitions throughout the Flood account that in his judgment point to multiple sources lying behind the present account of the Flood:

1. God saw man's wickedness:	(6:5)	[1]וַיַּרְא יהוה
	(6:12)	[2]וַיַּרְא אֱלֹהִים
2. God announced the Flood:	(6:17)	[3]וַאֲנִי הִנְנִי מֵבִיא אֶת־הַמַּבּוּל
	(7:4)	[4]אָנֹכִי מַמְטִיר עַל־הָאָרֶץ
3. Command to enter the ark:	(6:18)	[5]וּבָאתָ אֶל־הַתֵּבָה
	(7:1)	[6]בֹּא־אַתָּה וְכָל־בֵּיתְךָ אֶל־הַתֵּבָה
4. Number of animals:	(6:19)	[7]וּמִכָּל־הָחַי מִכָּל־בָּשָׂר שְׁנַיִם מִכֹּל
	(7:2)	[8]מִכֹּל הַבְּהֵמָה הַטְּהוֹרָה תִּקַּח־לְךָ שִׁבְעָה שִׁבְעָה
5. Entrance into the ark:	(7:7)	[9]וַיָּבֹא נֹחַ וּבָנָיו וְאִשְׁתּוֹ וּנְשֵׁי־בָנָיו אִתּוֹ אֶל־הַתֵּבָה
	(7:13)	[10]בָּא נֹחַ . . . אֶל־הַתֵּבָה
6. Onset of the Flood:	(7:10)	[11]וַיְהִי לְשִׁבְעַת הַיָּמִים וּמֵי הַמַּבּוּל הָיוּ
	(7:11)	[12]בִּשְׁנַת שֵׁשׁ־מֵאוֹת . . . נִבְקְעוּ כָּל־מַעְיְנֹת תְּהוֹם
7. Flood waters prevailed:	(7:17)	[13]וַיְהִי הַמַּבּוּל אַרְבָּעִים יוֹם . . . וַיִּשְׂאוּ אֶת־הַתֵּבָה
	(7:18)	[14]וַיִּגְבְּרוּ הַמַּיִם . . . וַתֵּלֶךְ הַתֵּבָה
8. All life died:	(7:21)	[15]וַיִּגְוַע כָּל־בָּשָׂר
	(7:22)	[16]כֹּל אֲשֶׁר נִשְׁמַת־רוּחַ חַיִּים בְּאַפָּיו . . . מֵתוּ
9. Flood waters ceased:	(8:2a)	[17]וַיִּסָּכְרוּ מַעְיְנֹת תְּהוֹם
	(8:2b)	[18]וַיִּכָּלֵא הַגֶּשֶׁם מִן־הַשָּׁמָיִם
10. Noah's knowledge that the Flood had ceased:	(8:11)	[19]וַיֵּדַע נֹחַ כִּי־קַלּוּ הַמַּיִם
	(8:15–16)	[20]וַיְדַבֵּר אֱלֹהִים אֶל־נֹחַ . . . צֵא מִן־הַתֵּבָה
11. God's promise not to destroy man again:	(8:21)	[21]לֹא־אֹסִף עוֹד לְהַכּוֹת אֶת־כָּל־חַי
	(9:11)	[22]וְלֹא־יִהְיֶה עוֹד מַבּוּל לְשַׁחֵת הָאָרֶץ

When examined along with the variations in the use of *yhwh* and *'ᵉlōhîm* and other points of style, Gunkel (p. 137) and others distinguished two primary sources behind the account: a "P" account of the Flood (6:9–22; 7:6, 11, 13–16a, 17a, 18–21, 24; 8:1, 2a, 3b, 4, 5, 13a, 14–19; 9:1–17, 28, 29) and a "J" account (6:5–8; 7:1, 2, 3b, 4, 5, 7, 10, 12, 16b, 17b, 22, 23a, 23b; 8:2b, 3a, 6a, 6b, 7–12, 13b, 20–22). This discovery he called the "masterpiece" ("*Meisterstück*," p. 137) of modern biblical criticism. According to Skinner (p. 147) the critical unraveling of the Flood account "is justly reckoned amongst the most brilliant achievements of purely literary criticism, and affords a particularly instructive lesson in the art of documentary analysis." Westermann and other modern critical scholars continue to accept the analysis of the Flood account represented in the work of Gunkel and Skinner ("We can accept therefore the present results of source criticism," Westermann, p. 396). More recently, however, there has been a tendency to see in these repetitions a mark of the style and technique of the biblical writers. Rather than being a clue to the existence of a variant source, repetition can be viewed as an essential element in the structure of biblical narrative. R.N. Whybray ("The Making of the Pentateuch," JSOT, Supplement Series 53 [1987]: 83), for example, has shown that not only is virtually every element in the Flood account repeated, as the documentary analysis has shown, but also in most cases the repetition is not simply twice but three and four times:

> God's intention to destroy the inhabitants of the earth is stated four times (Gen. 6.5–7, 11–13, 17; 7.4). Four times it is recorded that Noah and his companions entered the Ark (7.7–9, 13–14, 15, 16). Three times the coming of the rain is recorded (7.6, 10, 11–12). The prevailing or increasing of the waters of the Flood is mentioned five times (7.17, 18, 19, 20, 24), and their abatement similarly five times (8.1, 2, 3, 4, 5). It is

illogical on the basis of these repetitions to analyze the story into *two* documents (J and P). On the other hand the dramatic effect of this portentous constant repetition in the text as it stands cannot be denied.

See also Meir Sternberg, *The Poetics of Biblical Narrative* (Bloomington, Ind.: Indiana University Press, 1985), pp. 365–440; Wolfgang Richter, *Exegese als Literaturwissenschaft* (Göttingen: Vandenhoeck & Ruprecht, 1971), pp. 51–55; G.J. Wenham, "The Coherence of the Flood Narrative," VetTest 28 (1978): 336–48.

Andersen has shown that much of the repetition in the Flood account stems from the writer's use of a type of sentence he has called "epic repetition" and "chiastic coordination." Thus, far from being a haphazard mixture of two divergent accounts of the Flood, the end result of the narrative composition "looks as if it has been made out of whole cloth" (*Sentence in Biblical Hebrew*, p. 40).

[1](*wayyar' yhwh,* "and the LORD saw").
[2](*wayyar' 'elōhîm,* "and God saw").
[3](*wa'anî hinnî mēḇî' 'eṯ-hammabbûl,* "I am going to bring flood[waters]").
[4]('*ānōḵî mamṭîr 'al-hā'āreṣ,* "I will send rain on the earth").
[5](*ûḇā'ṯā 'el-hattēḇāh,* "and you will enter the ark").
[6](*bō'-'attāh wekol-bêṯekā 'el-hattēḇāh,* "Go into the ark, you and your whole family").
[7](*ûmikkol-hāḥay mikkol-bāśār šenayim mikkōl,* "of all living creatures").
[8](*mikkōl habbehēmāh haṭṭehôrāh tiqqaḥ-lekā šiḇ'āh šiḇ'āh,* "Take with you seven of every kind of clean animal").
[9](*wayyāḇō' nōaḥ ûḇānāyw we'ištô ûnešê-ḇānāyw 'ittô 'el-hattēḇāh,* "And Noah and his sons and his wife and his sons' wives entered the ark").
[10](*bā' nōaḥ . . . 'el-hattēḇāh,* "Noah . . . entered the ark").
[11](*wayehî lešiḇ'aṯ hayyāmîm ûmê hammabbûl hāyû,* "And after the seven days, the floodwaters came").
[12](*bišnaṯ šēš-mē'ôṯ . . . niḇqe'û kol-ma'yenōṯ tehôm,* "In the six hundredth year, . . . all the springs of the great deep burst forth").
[13](*wayehî hammabbûl 'arbā'îm yôm . . . wayyiś'û 'eṯ-hattēḇāh,* "For forty days the flood kept coming . . . they lifted the ark").
[14](*wayyigberû hammayim . . . wattēlek hattēḇāh,* "The waters rose . . . and the ark floated").
[15](*wayyigwa' kol-bāśār,* "every living thing . . . perished").
[16](*kōl 'ašer nišmaṯ-ruaḥ ḥayyîm be'appāyw . . . mēṯû,* "Everything . . . that had the breath of life in its nostrils died").
[17](*wayyissākerû ma'yenōṯ tehôm,* "Now the springs of the deep . . . had been closed").
[18](*wayyikkālē' haggešem min-haššāmāyim,* "and the rain had stopped falling from the sky").
[19](*wayyēḏā' nōaḥ kî-qāllû hammayim,* "Then Noah knew that the water had receded").
[20](*wayeḏabbēr 'elōhîm 'el-nōaḥ . . . ṣē' min-hattēḇāh,* "Then God said to Noah, 'Come out of the ark' ").
[21](*lō'-'ōsip̱ 'ōḏ lehakkôṯ 'eṯ-kol-ḥay,* "never again will I destroy all living creatures").
[22](*welō'-yihyeh 'ôḏ mabbûl lešaḥēṯ hā'āreṣ,* "never again will there be a flood to destroy the earth").

---

d. *The floods*

7:6–24

[6]Noah was six hundred years old when the floodwaters came on the
earth. [7]And Noah and his sons and his wife and his sons' wives entered
the ark to escape the waters of the flood. [8]Pairs of clean and unclean
animals, of birds and of all creatures that move along the ground, [9]male
and female, came to Noah and entered the ark, as God had commanded
Noah. [10]And after the seven days the floodwaters came on the earth.
[11]In the six hundredth year of Noah's life, on the seventeenth day of
the second month—on that day all the springs of the great deep burst
forth, and the floodgates of the heavens were opened. [12]And rain fell on
the earth forty days and forty nights.
[13]On that very day Noah and his sons, Shem, Ham and Japheth,
together with his wife and the wives of his three sons, entered the ark.

14 They had with them every wild animal according to its kind, all
livestock according to their kinds, every creature that moves along the
ground according to its kind and every bird according to its kind,
everything with wings. 15 Pairs of all creatures that have the breath of life
in them came to Noah and entered the ark. 16 The animals going in were
male and female of every living thing, as God had commanded Noah.
Then the LORD shut him in.

17 For forty days the flood kept coming on the earth, and as the waters
increased they lifted the ark high above the earth. 18 The waters rose and
increased greatly on the earth, and the ark floated on the surface of the
water. 19 They rose greatly on the earth, and all the high mountains
under the entire heavens were covered. 20 The waters rose and covered
the mountains to a depth of more than twenty feet. 21 Every living thing
that moved on the earth perished—birds, livestock, wild animals, all the
creatures that swarm over the earth, and all mankind. 22 Everything on
dry land that had the breath of life in its nostrils died. 23 Every living
thing on the face of the earth was wiped out; men and animals and the
creatures that move along the ground and the birds of the air were
wiped from the earth. Only Noah was left, and those with him in the ark.

24 The waters flooded the earth for a hundred and fifty days.

6–24 What is most apparent in the description of the onset of the Flood is the focus of the author on the occupants of the ark. With great detail the procession of those entering the ark passes by the impatient eyes of the modern reader. Noah's age, the month and the day of the beginning of the rain, the source of the waters, the kinds of animals and their number—no bit of information is too insignificant if it can contribute to the author's purpose of holding this picture before the reader as long as literarily possible. It is first and foremost this picture of Noah's salvation that the author wants his readers to take a long look at. It is only at the conclusion of chapter 7, when the ark is resting safely over the highest mountains in the surging flood, that the author cast his glance in the direction of those who did not seek refuge in the ark (vv.21–23). But even then the author's attention on those who did not survive the Flood is motivated less by an interest in what happened to them specifically ("[they] died," v.22) than the reason why they perished: "Only Noah was left [*wayiššā'er*], and those with him in the ark" (v.23).

It is in the repetitions that the author's message comes through most clearly. Thus when it is repeated four times that those who survived the Flood were those who had done "as God had commanded" (*ka'ašer ṣiwwāh 'elōhîm,* 7:9, 16: cf. v.5; 6:22), the author's point is clear. Obedience to the Lord is the way to salvation. In the same way as Noah is here an example of obedience and salvation, later narrative figures, such as Abraham (*ka'ašer ṣiwwāh . . . 'elōhîm,* "as God commanded," 21:4) and the sons of Israel (*ka'ašer ṣiwwāh yhwh,* "just what the LORD commanded," Exod 12:28), are called on to exhibit the same lesson.

e. *The floods abate*

8:1–14

1 But God remembered Noah and all the wild animals and the livestock
that were with him in the ark, and he sent a wind over the earth, and the
waters receded. 2 Now the springs of the deep and the floodgates of the
heavens had been closed, and the rain had stopped falling from the sky.
3 The water receded steadily from the earth. At the end of the hundred
and fifty days the water had gone down, 4 and on the seventeenth day of

the seventh month the ark came to rest on the mountains of Ararat. 5 The
waters continued to recede until the tenth month, and on the first day of
the tenth month the tops of the mountains became visible.
6 After forty days Noah opened the window he had made in the ark
7 and sent out a raven, and it kept flying back and forth until the water
had dried up from the earth. 8 Then he sent out a dove to see if the water
had receded from the surface of the ground. 9 But the dove could find no
place to set its feet because there was water over all the surface of the
earth; so it returned to Noah in the ark. He reached out his hand and
took the dove and brought it back to himself in the ark. 10 He waited
seven more days and again sent out the dove from the ark. 11 When the
dove returned to him in the evening, there in its beak was a freshly
plucked olive leaf! Then Noah knew that the water had receded from the
earth. 12 He waited seven more days and sent the dove out again, but this
time it did not return to him.
13 By the first day of the first month of Noah's six hundred and first
year, the water had dried up from the earth. Noah then removed the
covering from the ark and saw that the surface of the ground was dry.
14 By the twenty-seventh day of the second month the earth was
completely dry.

1 While those in the ark may have been safe, they had not yet been saved. The author does not finish his story until Noah and his family are back on dry ground (v.14). But those in the ark had to wait ("a hundred and fifty days," 7:24) before God sent his deliverance. Just as the author later passes over the four hundred years that Israel waited in Egypt (Exod 1:7) and then the forty years of waiting in the wilderness (Num 14:33–34) in order to focus on God's deliverance, so now the story passes over the time of waiting in the ark and proceeds immediately to the decisive moment when "God remembered [*wayyizkōr 'elōhîm*] Noah and all . . . that were with him in the ark."

The description of God's rescue of Noah foreshadows God's deliverance of Israel in the Exodus. Just as later "God remembered [*wayyizkōr 'elōhîm*] his covenant" (Exod 2:24) and sent "a strong east wind" (*berûaḥ qāḏîm 'azzāh*) to dry up the waters before his people (Exod 14:21) so that they "went through . . . on dry ground [*bayyabbāšāh*, v.22]," so also in the story of the Flood we read that "God remembered" (*wayyizkōr 'elōhîm*) those in the ark and sent a "wind" (*rûaḥ 'al-hā'āreṣ*) over the waters so that his people might come out on "dry ground" (*yāḇešāh hā'āreṣ*, vv.13–14).

It hardly seems likely that so many verbal and thematic parallels within the Pentateuch could be a mere coincidence. The author of Genesis, who frequently seizes on wordplays (e.g., 11:9) and recounts wordplays within narratives (e.g., 21:6), would not have been unaware of the parallels suggested by his narratives. We must reckon with the fact that the author is deliberately recounting these various events in such a way to highlight their similarity. God's dealings in the past prefigure his work in the present and the future.

2–14 Again it is noticeable how the author has prolonged the picture of God's deliverance. God is depicted at work stopping the flow of the waters and removing the sources of the floods (v.2). But it still takes time before Noah can be back on dry land (v.3). He still has to wait. With this picture of God at work as background, the author turns his attention to Noah inside the ark. The narrative now focuses on the patience of Noah as he waited on God's deliverance. At the end of forty days, Noah began to look for signs of his impending deliverance. He sent out a raven (v.7) and a dove (vv.8–12), but no signs of dry land appeared. Noah continued to wait (vv.10, 12). When the sign of the return of the dry lands finally appeared and the dove did not return (v.12), the author reminds us that Noah had waited exactly one year (cf. 7:6, 11 and 8:13–14). But even then Noah could only open the window to look out of the ark. He still had to wait for God's command to go out before leaving the ark (vv.15–17).

The image that emerges from this portrait of Noah in the narrative is that of a righteous and faithful *remnant* (*wayiššā'er 'ak-nōaḥ*, 7:23; "Only Noah was left") patiently waiting for God's deliverance. It is a common image in later biblical literature (e.g., Isa 8:17–18; 40:31; James 5:7–11), and its development here in the Flood narrative has contributed greatly to its later use. Henceforth, within the biblical text, "the Flood" is synonymous with eschatological judgment (e.g., Isa 8:7–8), and Noah's deliverance is an image of the salvation of the faithful (e.g., Matt 24:37–39).

Notes

---

1 Most recently J.W. Wenham (*Genesis 1–15*, Word Biblical Commentary [Waco: Word, 1987]) has shown how the structure of the Flood story centers the reader's attention on the וַיִּזְכֹּר אֱלֹהִים אֶת־נֹחַ (*wayyizkōr 'elōhîm 'et-nōaḥ*, "But God remembered Noah") of 8:1. Particularly important is the way that the structural patterns noted by Wenham help explain the author's careful attention to the time periods of each event. Wenham points to the following pattern of "mirror-image" repetition in the use of numbers:

7 days of waiting for flood (7:4)
  7 days of waiting for flood (7:10)
    40 days of flood (7:17a)
      150 days of water triumphing (7:24)
      150 days of water waning (8:3)
    40 days of waiting (8:6)
  7 days of waiting (8:10)
7 days of waiting (8:12)

One can clearly see the importance of the "7 days" in this pattern. It is the same 7-day pattern that plays a central role in the Creation account of chapter 1. The period of "40 days" is also significant later in the Torah as the time of waiting and watching in the "40 days" of spying out the land and the corresponding "40 years" of waiting in the wilderness (Num 14:33–35). In the Numbers passage the "40 years" are specifically said to correspond to the "40 days."

---

f. *The command to exit the ark*

8:15–19

15Then God said to Noah, 16"Come out of the ark, you and your wife and your sons and their wives. 17Bring out every kind of living creature that is with you—the birds, the animals, and all the creatures that move along the ground—so they can multiply on the earth and be fruitful and increase in number upon it."

18So Noah came out, together with his sons and his wife and his sons' wives. 19All the animals and all the creatures that move along the ground and all the birds—everything that moves on the earth—came out of the ark, one kind after another.

15–19 In the same epic style of the description of the entry of the ark (cf. the sentence structure of 7:7–9 with 8:18–19; both are examples of "epic repetition" [Andersen, *Sentence in Biblical Hebrew*, p. 39]), the author depicts the exit. He is careful to show that even here Noah left the ark only at God's command (vv.15–16). The description, though condensed, closely follows the Creation pattern in Genesis 1 (e.g., "let them swarm upon the earth, and let them be fruitful and multiply upon the earth," v.17, pers. tr.). The picture given is that of a return to the work of Creation "in the beginning." It is significant that right at this point in the narrative the author takes up a lengthy account of the *covenant* (8:20–9:17). The restoration of God's Creation was founded on the establishment of a covenant.

There is a striking thematic parallel between the picture of God's calling Noah out of the ark (8:15–20) and the call of Abraham (12:1–7).

Genesis 8:15–20	Genesis 12:1–7
a. Then God said to Noah (8:15)	a. The Lord had said to Abram (12:1)
b. Come out from the ark (8:16)	b. Leave your country (12:1)
c. So Noah came out (8:18)	c. So Abram left (12:4)
d. Then Noah built an altar to the LORD (8:20)	d. So [Abram] built an altar there to the LORD (12:7)
e. Then God blessed Noah (9:1)	e. "And I [God] will bless you" (12:2)
f. "Be fruitful and increase" (9:1)	f. "I will make you into a great nation" (12:2)
g. "I now establish my covenant with you and with your descendants" (9:9)	g. "To your offspring, I will give this land" (12:7)

Both Noah and Abraham represent new beginnings in the course of events recorded in Genesis. Both are marked by God's promise of blessing and his gift of the covenant.

Notes

16–19 The sentence structure follows that described by Andersen as "epic repetition" (*Sentence in Biblical Hebrew*, pp. 39ff.).

In Discourse:

8:16 [1]צֵא מִן־הַתֵּבָה אַתָּה וְאִשְׁתְּךָ וּבָנֶיךָ וּנְשֵׁי־בָנֶיךָ אִתָּךְ

8:17 [2]כָּל־הַחַיָּה אֲשֶׁר־אִתְּךָ מִכָּל־בָּשָׂר . . . הַוְצֵא אִתָּךְ

In Narrative:

8:18 [3]וַיֵּצֵא־נֹחַ וּבָנָיו וְאִשְׁתּוֹ וּנְשֵׁי־בָנָיו אִתּוֹ

8:19 [4]כָּל־הַחַיָּה כָּל־הָרֶמֶשׂ וְכָל־הָעוֹף כֹּל . . . יָצְאוּ מִן־הַתֵּבָה

Andersen says of this type of sentence, "The rhetorical effect of this kind of epic repetition is to slow down the pace of the narrative. It holds the picture a little longer and enforces it on the mind" (*Sentence in Biblical Hebrew*, p. 40).

17 Compare Gen 8:17 and Gen 1:21.

8:17 [5]כָּל־הַחַיָּה אֲשֶׁר־אִתְּךָ מִכָּל־בָּשָׂר בָּעוֹף וּבַבְּהֵמָה וּבְכָל־הָרֶמֶשׂ הָרֹמֵשׂ

1:21 [6]כָּל־נֶפֶשׁ הַחַיָּה הָרֹמֶשֶׂת אֲשֶׁר שָׁרְצוּ הַמַּיִם לְמִינֵהֶם וְאֵת כָּל־עוֹף כָּנָף לְמִינֵהוּ

Compare Gen 8:17b and Gen 1:20a.

8:17b [7]וְשָׁרְצוּ בָאָרֶץ

1:20a	[8]יִשְׁרְצוּ הַמַּיִם שֶׁרֶץ נֶפֶשׁ
Compare Gen 8:17b and Gen 1:22	
8:17b	[9]וּפָרוּ וְרָבוּ עַל־הָאָרֶץ
1:22	[10]פְּרוּ וּרְבוּ וּמִלְאוּ אֶת־הַמַּיִם

[1](*ṣēʾ min-hattēḇāh ʾattāh weʾišteḵā ûḇāneyḵā ûnešê-ḇāneyḵā ʾittāḵ,* "Come out of the ark, you and your wife and your sons and their wives").
[2](*kol-haḥayyāh ʾašer-ʾitteḵā mikkol-bāśār . . . hawṣēʾ ʾittāḵ,* "Bring out every kind of living creature that is with you").
[3](*wayyēṣēʾ-nōaḥ ûḇānāyw weʾištô ûnešê-ḇānāyw ʾittô,* "So Noah came out, together with his sons and his wife and his sons' wives").
[4](*kol-haḥayyāh kol-hāremeś weḵol-hāʿôp̄ kōl . . . yāṣeʾû min-hattēḇāh,* "All the animals and all the creatures that move along the ground and all the birds . . . came out of the ark").
[5](*kol-haḥayyāh ʾašer-ʾitteḵā mikkol-bāśār bāʿôp̄ ûḇabbehēmāh ûḇeḵol-hāremeś hārōmēś,* "every kind of living creature that is with you—the birds, the animals, and all the creatures that move along the ground").
[6](*kol-nep̄eš haḥayyāh hārōmeśeṯ ʾašer šāreṣû hammayim leminēhem weʾeṯ kol-ʿôp̄ kānāp̄ leminēhû,* "every living and moving thing with which the water teems, according to their kinds, and every winged bird according to its kind").
[7](*wešāreṣû ḇāʾāreṣ,* "so they can multiply on the earth").
[8](*yišreṣû hammayim šereṣ nep̄eš,* "Let the water teem with living creatures").
[9](*ûp̄ārû werāḇû ʿal-hāʾāreṣ,* "be fruitful and increase in number upon [the earth]").
[10](*perû ûreḇû ûmilʾû ʾeṯ-hammayim,* "Be fruitful and increase in number and fill the water").

---

g. *The altar and the covenant*

8:20–9:17

20 Then Noah built an altar to the LORD and, taking some of all the clean animals and clean birds, he sacrificed burnt offerings on it. 21 The LORD smelled the pleasing aroma and said in his heart: "Never again will I curse the ground because of man, even though every inclination of his heart is evil from childhood. And never again will I destroy all living creatures, as I have done.

22 "As long as the earth endures,
seedtime and harvest,
cold and heat,
summer and winter,
day and night
will never cease."

9:1 Then God blessed Noah and his sons, saying to them, "Be fruitful and increase in number and fill the earth. 2 The fear and dread of you will fall upon all the beasts of the earth and all the birds of the air, upon every creature that moves along the ground, and upon all the fish of the sea; they are given into your hands. 3 Everything that lives and moves will be food for you. Just as I gave you the green plants, I now give you everything.

4 "But you must not eat meat that has its lifeblood still in it. 5 And for your lifeblood I will surely demand an accounting. I will demand an accounting from every animal. And from each man, too, I will demand an accounting for the life of his fellow man.

6 "Whoever sheds the blood of man,
by man shall his blood be shed;
for in the image of God
has God made man.

7 As for you, be fruitful and increase in number; multiply on the earth and increase upon it."

8 Then God said to Noah and to his sons with him: 9 "I now establish
my covenant with you and with your descendants after you 10 and with
every living creature that was with you—the birds, the livestock and all
the wild animals, all those that came out of the ark with you—every
living creature on earth. 11 I establish my covenant with you: Never again
will all life be cut off by the waters of a flood; never again will there be a
flood to destroy the earth."
12 And God said, "This is the sign of the covenant I am making
between me and you and every living creature with you, a covenant for
all generations to come: 13 I have set my rainbow in the clouds, and it
will be the sign of the covenant between me and the earth. 14 Whenever I
bring clouds over the earth and the rainbow appears in the clouds, 15 I
will remember my covenant between me and you and all living creatures
of every kind. Never again will the waters become a flood to destroy all
life. 16 Whenever the rainbow appears in the clouds, I will see it and
remember the everlasting covenant between God and all living creatures of every kind on the earth."
17 So God said to Noah, "This is the sign of the covenant I have
established between me and all life on the earth."

8:20–9:17 In the account of Noah's altar and the covenant, the author continues his close associations with Genesis 1. As a result of Noah's altar and offering, the whole of the state of mankind before the Flood is reestablished. Man is still fallen (9:21); but through an offering on the altar, he may yet find God's blessing (8:21–9:3). It is significant that just as in Genesis 1, the focus of the author's interest in man after the Flood is his creation in God's image (9:6).

Just as significant as the associations of this passage with the Creation account, however, are the several close associations between Noah's altar and Moses' altar at Mount Sinai following the Exodus (Exod 24:4–18). A brief list of some key parallels gives a sense of the verbal and thematic similarities: (1) The building of the altar in both accounts follows a major act of God's salvation—God's rescue of Noah from the Flood and God's deliverance of the Israelites from bondage in Egypt; (2) the altar and the offering in both accounts mark the establishment of a "covenant" (*berîṯ*) with God (Gen 9:9; Exod 24:7); (3) the outcome of both covenants is God's "blessing" (*wayebāreḵ*, Gen 9:1; *ûḇēraḵ*, Exod 23:25); (4) the central provision in both covenants is protection from "beasts of the field" or "wild animals" (*ḥayyaṯ hā'āreṣ*, Gen 9:2; *ḥayyaṯ haśśāḏeh*, Exod 23:29) and human enemies (Gen 9:5–6; Exod 23:22); (5) specific mention is made that the "earth" will be preserved from destruction (Gen 9:11; Exod 23:29); (6) in Genesis the visible "sign" of the establishment of the covenant is the rainbow in the "clouds" (*be'ānān*, 9:13–17), and in Exodus the conclusion of the covenant making is marked by the appearance of the glory of God in the "cloud" (*he'ānān*, 24:15) that covered the mountain; (7) in both covenants stipulations are given to which the people must be obedient (Gen 9:4; Exod 24:3).

What these observations suggest is that the author is intentionally drawing out the similarities between God's covenant with Noah and the covenant at Sinai. Why? The answer that best fits with the author's purposes is that he wants to show that God's covenant at Sinai is not a new act of God. The covenant is rather a return to God's original promises. Once again at Sinai, as he had done in the past, God is at work restoring his fellowship with man and bringing man back to himself. The covenant with Noah plays an important role in the author's development of God's restoration of blessing. It lies midway between God's original blessing of all mankind (1:28) and God's promise to bless "all peoples on the earth" through Abraham (12:1–3).

Notes

8:20–9:17 It has already been noted that the Creation account of Gen 1 has been composed to foreshadow the giving of the covenant at Mount Sinai. One of the clearest indications of this is the pattern of the "ten words." Just as the whole of the covenant could be stated in "ten words" (עֲשֶׂרֶת הַדְּבָרִים [*ʿaśereṯ haddeḇārîm*, NIV, "the Ten Commandments"], Exod 34:28), so the whole of the universe could be created in "ten words" (וַיֹּאמֶר אֱלֹהִים [*wayyōʾmer ʾelōhîm*, "And God said"] occurs ten times in ch. 1—vv.3, 6, 9, 11, 14, 20, 24, 26, 28, 29). The same pattern lies behind the account of the Flood. Throughout the whole of the account, there is the same tenfold repetition of "and God/the LORD said."

6:7a	וַיֹּאמֶר יהוה[1]
6:13a	וַיֹּאמֶר אֱלֹהִים[2]
7:1a	וַיֹּאמֶר יהוה[1]
8:15	וַיְדַבֵּר אֱלֹהִים[3]
8:15	לֵאמֹר[4]
8:21a	וַיֹּאמֶר יהוה[1]
9:1a	וַיֹּאמֶר[5]
9:8a	וַיֹּאמֶר אֱלֹהִים[2]
9:12a	וַיֹּאמֶר אֱלֹהִים[2]
9:17	וַיֹּאמֶר אֱלֹהִים[2]

Such patterns are a part of the whole of the compositional scheme of the book. Within the structure of Genesis, the number 10 is unusually dominant, e.g., ten individuals in the lists of names in chapter 5 and chapter 11, and the tenfold reiteration of the promised blessing throughout the book.

9:1 The similarities between 9:1 and 1:28 are transparent:

9:1	וַיְבָרֶךְ אֱלֹהִים אֶת־נֹחַ וְאֶת־בָּנָיו וַיֹּאמֶר לָהֶם פְּרוּ וּרְבוּ וּמִלְאוּ אֶת־הָאָרֶץ[6]
1:28	וַיְבָרֶךְ אֹתָם אֱלֹהִים וַיֹּמֶר לָהֶם אֱלֹהִים פְּרוּ וּרְבוּ וּמִלְאוּ אֶת־הָאָרֶץ[7]

6 The use of the third person reference to God—בְּצֶלֶם אֱלֹהִים (*beṣelem ʾelōhîm*, "in the image of God")—suggests that v.6b is to be understood as a comment of the narrator and not the words of God speaking to Noah. Thus at this point in the narrative the author has inserted an important explanation (כִּי [*kî*, "for"]) for the prohibition of manslaughter—namely, a reference back to the creation of man in God's image (M. Fishbane, ***Biblical Interpretation in Ancient Israel*** [Oxford: Clarendon, 1985], p. 320). Already the narrative has become the basis for the development of the law.

7 The blessing of v.1—פְּרוּ וּרְבוּ וּמִלְאוּ אֶת־הָאָרֶץ (*perû ûreḇû ûmilʾû ʾeṯ-hāʾāreṣ*, "Be fruitful and increase in number and fill the earth")—is reiterated, though with a significant modification, in v.7—פְּרוּ וּרְבוּ שִׁרְצוּ בָאָרֶץ וּרְבוּ־בָהּ (*perû ûreḇû širṣû ḇāʾāreṣ ûreḇû-ḇāh*, "be fruitful and increase in number; multiply on the earth and increase upon it"): v.7 has *širṣû bāʾāreṣ* in place of v.1's *milʾû ʾeṯ-hāʾāreṣ*. Thus the text of v.1, which follows 1:28 (*milʾû ʾeṯ-hāʾāreṣ*), is made to conform to its future reference in Exod 1:7—פָּרוּ וַיִּשְׁרְצוּ וַיִּרְבּוּ (*pārû wayyišreṣû wayyirbû*, "[they] were fruitful and multiplied greatly") (which is summarized in the second half of the verse by וַתִּמָּלֵא הָאָרֶץ אֹתָם [*wattimmālēʾ hāʾāreṣ ʾōṯām*, "so that the land was filled with them").

[1](*wayyōʾmer yhwh*, "And the LORD said").

[2](*wayyōʾmer ʾelōhîm*, "And God said").

[3](*wayedabbēr ʾelōhîm*, "And God said").

[4](*lēʾmōr*, "saying"; untr. in NIV).

[5](*wayyōʾmer*, "and he said").

[6](*wayeḇāreḵ ʾelōhîm ʾeṯ-nōaḥ weʾeṯ-bānāyw wayyōʾmer lāhem perû ûreḇû ûmilʾû ʾeṯ-hāʾāreṣ*, "Then God blessed Noah and his sons, saying to them, 'Be fruitful and increase in number and fill the earth' ").

[7](*wayeḇāreḵ ʾōṯām ʾelōhîm wayyōʾmer lāhem ʾelōhîm perû ûreḇû ûmilʾû ʾeṯ-hāʾāreṣ*, "God blessed them and said to them, 'Be fruitful and increase in number; fill the earth' ").

5. *Noah's drunkenness*

9:18–29

18The sons of Noah who came out of the ark were Shem, Ham and
Japheth. (Ham was the father of Canaan.) 19These were the three sons
of Noah, and from them came the people who were scattered over the
earth.

20Noah, a man of the soil, proceeded to plant a vineyard. 21When he
drank some of its wine, he became drunk and lay uncovered inside his
tent. 22Ham, the father of Canaan, saw his father's nakedness and told
his two brothers outside. 23But Shem and Japheth took a garment and
laid it across their shoulders; then they walked in backward and covered
their father's nakedness. Their faces were turned the other way so that
they would not see their father's nakedness.

24When Noah awoke from his wine and found out what his youngest
son had done to him, 25he said,

"Cursed be Canaan!
The lowest of slaves
will he be to his brothers."

26He also said,

"Blessed be the LORD, the God of Shem!
May Canaan be the slave of Shem.
27May God extend the territory of Japheth;
may Japheth live in the tents of Shem,
and may Canaan be his slave."

28After the flood Noah lived 350 years. 29Altogether, Noah lived 950
years, and then he died.

18–19 These verses conclude the Flood story but at the same time introduce the short episode of Noah's drunkenness. They aptly demonstrate the author's style of composition throughout the Book of Genesis. By means of these short transitional units, the author ties together individual, self-contained narratives into a larger line of stories. The clue that should not be overlooked in this particular transitional unit is the identification of Canaan as one of the sons of Ham (v.18). That bit of information is crucial to the meaning of the narrative to follow (cf. vv.22, 25).

20–21 In placing the story of Noah's drunkenness at this point in the story line, the author continues to follow the plan of casting the Flood narrative as a recursion of the Creation account. Just as in the account of Creation, in the early chapters of Genesis, God planted (*wayyiṭṭaʿ*, 2:8) a garden for man to enjoy, so now as the narrative has returned the reader's attention back to the point of God's "blessing" (9:1) and covenant relationship (v.17), the story of Noah picks up with the planting (*wayyiṭṭaʿ*, v.20) of an orchard. The outcome is remarkably similar to the outcome of the story of the Garden of Eden. Noah ate of the fruit of his orchard and became naked (v.21). The author, in pointing out the similarities of Noah and Adam, wants to show even here, too, after the salvation from the Flood, that man's enjoyment of God's good gifts could not be sustained. Noah, like Adam, sinned, and the effects of that sin were to be felt in the generations of sons and daughters to follow. As in chapter 3, the effect of Noah's sin is seen in his "nakedness" (v.22; cf. 2:25; 3:7). When read in the context of the events of the Garden of Eden (ch. 3), the allusive details of Noah's drunkenness become quite transparent. In a subtle parody of man's original state ("[They] were both naked, and they felt no shame," 2:25), Noah in his drunkenness "uncovered himself in his tent" (lit. tr.).

22–26 Ham looked on his father's nakedness (v.22), but Shem and Japheth did not. They instead covered their father's nakedness without looking on him (v.23). The actions of the three sons as they are described in this narrative have been regarded by many as the mere outline of a much more sinister deed. Whatever the details of the actual act might have been, taken at face value the sons' actions suit the author's purpose quite well. What he apparently wants to show is simply the contrast between the deeds of Ham and those of Shem and Japheth. That contrast becomes the basis for the curse and the blessing that follow (vv.25–26).

The significance of the contrast between the actions of the sons is seen from the author's account of the Fall in chapter 3. In covering their father's nakedness, Shem and Japheth (cf. *šᵉnêhem*, v.23, lit., "the two of them"; NIV, "their"; cf. 2:25; 3:7) were like Adam and Eve (3:7) and God (3:21) who did not look on man's nakedness but covered it with coats of skin (cf. 2:25). Ham, on the other hand, did not follow that lead. His actions were more like those of whom God warned later in the Torah who "expose their own nakedness" before God and man (cf. Exod 20:26). Since some scholars have interpreted Exodus 20:24–26 as a prohibition of Canaanite forms of worship (see Brevard S. Childs, *The Book of Exodus* [Philadelphia: Westminster, 1974], p. 466), there may be an intended link between Ham and the Canaanites in the notion of "nakedness." So important was this matter to the author of the Torah that he included among the rules for the priest that they should wear "linen undergarments" as a covering for their "naked flesh" when they go near the presence of God at the altar (Exod 28:42–43). The sons of Noah are here shown to belong to two groups of mankind, those who like Adam and Eve hide the shame of their nakedness, and those who like Ham, or rather the Canaanites, have no sense of their shame before God. To the one group, the line of Shem, there will be blessing (v.26); but to the other, the Canaanites (not the Hamites), there can only be curse (v.25).

It is important to see how the author uses these narratives to teach a larger lesson, that of the importance of acknowledging the guilt of one's sin. His point is not simply that all Canaanites are cursed. That would certainly not fit what he later writes about Abraham as the one through whom "all peoples on earth [including the Canaanites] will be blessed" (12:3). Rather his point is simply that these three sons, as later the "seed of Abraham" and the "nations," represent two responses to human guilt and disobedience. Ultimately the author will show that it is not simply because one is born into a certain family line that he is blessed or cursed. In the figure of Abraham, the author will set forth his final case for the way of blessing: "Abraham believed the LORD, and he credited it to him as righteousness" (15:6).

Notes

25 Why was Canaan cursed rather than Ham? It is common in the narratives of Genesis to anticipate the deeds of later generations in the acts of their fathers. For example, the narratives of Jacob and Esau foreshadow the affairs of Israel and Edom; the Lot narratives foreshadow Israel's relationship to the Ammonites and Moabites; the narratives of Joseph and Judah anticipate the relationships between the later kingdoms of Israel and Judah. Thus it is not unusual that this narrative should anticipate and foreshadow the wickedness of the Canaanites (e.g., 19:5–9) in the sin of Ham as well as their subsequent service to the Israelites from the time of Joshua (Josh 16:10: וַיְהִי לְמַס־עֹבֵד [*wayehî lemas-'ōḇēḏ*, "but are required to do forced labor"]) to the kings (1 Kings 9:21: *lemas-'ōḇēḏ*, "for his labor force").

It should be noted that the form of the verb יִהְיֶה (*yihyeh*) is imperfect and not jussive (as וִיהִי [*wîhî*] in vv.26–27); so the sense is more likely that of a prediction ("he will be") rather than a malediction ("May he be"). Thus Noah's words anticipate a central theme of the following narratives—separation of the chosen seed from the seed of the Canaanites (cf. 24:3; 27:46).

26 Several questions arise in this verse. We should first note that it begins with a new introduction—וַיֹּאמֶר (*wayyō'mer*, "He also said")—thus marking it off from v.25. This suggests that some significance may lie behind the change from the imperfect יִהְיֶה (*yihyeh*, "he will be") in v.25 to the jussive וִיהִי (*wîhî*, "May he be") in vv.26–27. In opposition to the jussive, the imperfect signals an indicative statement regarding the future of Canaan, whereas the jussive signals a wish. But what is wished for in 26b and 27b? If read along with v.25, as most commentators do, the wish appears to be that of a curse—"May Canaan be a slave to them [his brothers]/to him [Shem]." Consequently the suggestion of Ibn Ezra and others that the plural suffix לָמוֹ (*lāmô*) refers to God as well as Shem has been discounted since "service to the true God cannot be thought of as a curse" (Jacob, p. 266). However, if a curse of Canaan is not intended in vv.26–27, as the change in verbal forms and the additional *wayyō'mer* in v.26 may suggest, then Ibn Ezra's reading is acceptable. But to whom does the suffix *lāmô* refer? By form *lāmô* is a contraction of לָהֻמוֹ (*lāhumô*), which yields לָהֶם (*lāhem*), thus third masculine plural "to them" (Bauer and Leander, *Historische Grammatik*, p. 215). Joüon (*Grammaire*, 103f.), GKC (103g), and König (*Genesis*, p. 388) suggest that here *lāmô* may be a rare pausal form of לוֹ (*lô*; cf. LXX *αὐτοῦ* [*autou*]), as in Isa 44:15. In any event, if *lāmô* is read as a plural, its antecedent may be "his brothers" (לְאֶחָיו, *le'eḥāyw*) in the preceding verse (cf. Targums Onkelos and Neophyti I), though this is unlikely in that each line seems to present a sense complete in itself (König, *Genesis*, p. 388); or the antecedent may be "Shem," read as a collective referring to the descendants of Shem (Rashi, Keil), an explanation that does not commend itself.

It is possible that the plural *lāmô* has its antecedent in the plural אֱלֹהֵי (*'elôhê*, "God of") of v.26a, since the plural *'elōhîm* has on other occasions been treated as a plural though the sense is clearly singular (cf. Eccl 12:1; König, *Syntax*, par. 263c). If that is the case, and if vv.26–27 are not a curse (see above), then the sense of this verse would be "May Canaan serve him (the God of Shem)," a sense very much in line with the scope of the blessing in the narratives that follow—"all peoples on earth will be blessed through you" (Gen 12:3). Thus both the wickedness of the Canaanites and God's intended blessing for them are anticipated in Noah's words.

27 Who will dwell in the tents of Shem? Grammatically there are two equally acceptable answers. Either God (אֱלֹהִים, *'elōhîm*) or Japheth may be the subject of וְיִשְׁכֹּן (*weyiškōn*, "may live"). It is not unusual for the object of a clause to become the subject of the following clause (cf. 4:17; 16:6b; 40:4). The fact that יהוה (*yhwh*, "the LORD") is always the subject of שָׁכַן (*šāḵan*, "to rest"), and never *'elōhîm*, however, is a strong argument for reading Japheth as the subject: "May [Japheth] live in the tents of Shem"—meaning, May Japheth enjoy the blessing along with Shem. Thus the hope of future blessing for the family of Noah is depicted in the same imagery found in the later narratives—the future ideal of brothers living together in harmony (cf. Gen 13:8; 33:4; 36:6–8; Ps 133:1), an ideal not yet realized in the Genesis narratives.

---

6. *The line of Noah (10:1–32)*

The author's purpose in giving a list of names at this point in the narrative can be seen in the statement at the end of chapter 10: "From these the nations [*haggôyim*] spread out over the earth after the flood" (v.32). In these names the reader is given a panoramic view of the nations as a backdrop for the remainder of the events of the Book of Genesis and the Torah. The list is complex and shows many signs of selection and shaping to fit a pattern. The pattern that emerges is determined by the number "seventy." There are exactly seventy nations (*gôyim*) represented in the list. Thus, like other biblical "genealogies" (e.g., Matthew 1; see D.A. Carson, EBC, 8:68–69), the present list of names owes its shape to a kind of "numerical symbolism" in which the concept of a totality of nations (*gôyim*) is expressed in the number "seventy." In other words, "all nations" (*gôyim*) find their ultimate origins in the three sons of Noah. Humanity in its totality is closely circumscribed. There is a unity among men that the author does not want the reader to lose sight of. It is out of this one humanity that Abraham will be called.

Though he is on the verge of narrowing his focus to the "seed of Abraham" and the "sons of Israel," the author first lays a solid foundation for his ultimate purpose in God's choice of Abraham: through his "seed" God's blessing will be restored to "all people on earth" (12:3). It is not without purpose that the author reminds his readers that the total number of Abraham's "seed" at the close of the Book of Genesis is also "seventy" (46:27; cf. Exod 1:5). Before Abraham, the nations (*gôyim*) numbered "seventy." After Abraham, at the close of the book, the seed of Abraham numbered "seventy," the same as that of the nations. He who was taken from the nations has reached the number of the nations. Such careful attention to detail suggests that the author of the book has in mind a specific understanding of the role of the "seed" of Abraham. By correlating the number of nations with the number of the seed of Abraham, he holds Abraham's "seed" before the reader as a "new humanity" and Abraham himself as a kind of "second Adam," the "father of many nations [*gôyim*]" (17:5). In this chosen "seed" God's original blessing will be restored.

There is, then, much theological reflection behind the shaping of these earlier sections of Genesis. In Deuteronomy 32:8, Moses alluded to this chapter by saying, "When the Most High gave the nations their inheritance, when he divided all mankind, he set up boundaries for the peoples according to the number of the sons of Israel" (cf. Paul's view of Abraham in Rom 4:16: "He is the father of us all").

Chapter 10 is not simply a list of seventy names. Throughout the list the author has inserted several historical notes (vv.8–12, 14, 19, 25) as well. Each of these notes is of special relevance to a particular event yet to be recorded in the Book of Genesis. The note about Nimrod and his kingdom in Babylon, for example, provides a wider context for the narrative of the "tower of Babel" in chapter 11. By and large the notes focus on those nations that are the subject of God's judgment in the remainder of the book (e.g., Babylon, vv.8–12; the Philistines, v.14; the Canaanites, including Sodom and Gomorrah, v.19).

a. *The sons of Noah*

10:1

1This is the account of Shem, Ham and Japheth, Noah's sons, who themselves had sons after the flood.

1 Chapter 10 is bracketed at either end (vv.1, 32) with an identification of the list of names as "Noah's sons" and the temporal marker "after the flood." It is clear that the author was concerned that the list in chapter 10 not be read outside its context within the line of narrative coming out of the Flood. Such conspicuous attention to context is another indication that the author has a plan to unfold in this narrative and that he did not want the reader to lose sight of it.

Notes

1–32 Cassuto notes that if Nimrod is counted along with the others, there are seventy-one names and not an even seventy. Thus he excludes Nimrod from the list. While it is true that his name occurs as part of a narrative insertion (vv.8–12) and the introduction to the Nimrod narrative—וְכוּשׁ יָלַד (*w^e^k̲ûš yālad̲,* "Cush was the father of," v.8)—is really a duplication of the list of the sons of Cush in v.7—וּבְנֵי כוּשׁ (*ûb̲^e^nê k̲ûš,* "The sons of Cush")—the construction *w^e^k̲ûš yālad̲* is continued by וּמִצְרַיִם יָלַד (*ûmiṣrayim yālad̲,* "Mizraim was the father of," v.13) and וּכְנַעַן יָלַד (*ûk̲^e^na'an yālad̲,* "Canaan was the father of," v.15) and thus appears to be an integral part of the narrative. It is more likely, however, that it is the Philistines (v.14) who are not to be counted since they are not genealogically connected to any of the sons of Noah in this chapter. The reference to the Philistines in v.14 is not understood as part of the reckoning of the sons of Noah but a historical and geographical footnote. We should also notice that the cities of Nimrod's kingdom (vv.10–12) and the cities that mark the borders of Canaan (v.19) are not reckoned as part of the seventy nations, and Assyria (v.11) is only to be counted once, that is, in v.22.

The key words that provide the framework for the arrangement of this list of names are מִשְׁפְּחֹת (*mišp^e^ḥōt̲,* "clans"), אַרְצֹת (*'arṣōt̲,* "territory"), and לְשֹׁנֹת (*l^e^šōnōt̲,* language") (vv.5, 20, 31–32). These words link chapter 10 with chapters 11 and 12. Chapter 11 picks up the theme of the *l^e^šōnōt̲* but uses the term שָׂפָה (*śāp̄āh,* "language"). Chapter 12 picks up the theme of both the *'arṣōt̲* (12:1: לֶךְ־לְךָ מֵאַרְצְךָ [*lek̲-l^e^k̲ā mē'arṣ^e^k̲ā,* "Leave your country"]) and the *mišp^e^ḥōt̲* (12:3: כֹּל מִשְׁפְּחֹת הָאֲדָמָה [*kōl mišp^e^ḥōt̲ hā'^a^d̲āmāh,* "all peoples on earth"]).

---

b. *The sons of Japheth*

10:2–5

2 The sons of Japheth:
Gomer, Magog, Madai, Javan, Tubal, Meshech and Tiras.
3 The sons of Gomer:
Ashkenaz, Riphath and Togarmah.
4 The sons of Javan:
Elishah, Tarshish, the Kittim and the Rodanim. 5 (From these
the maritime peoples spread out into their territories by their
clans within their nations, each with its own language.)

2–5 The list begins with those nations that are considered the "Islands of the Nations" (cf. v.5). They are the nations that make up the geographical horizon of the author, the outer fringe of the known world, a kind of "third world" over against the nations of Ham (Canaan) and Shem. In later biblical literature, when the focus is on the establishment of God's universal kingdom, these nations again come into view to show that God's plan includes all mankind: "He will rule from sea to sea. . . . The kings of Tarshish and of distant shores will bring tribute to him" (Ps 72:8, 10).

A pattern in the author's selection is clearly discernible in the list of the sons of Japheth. Fourteen names are listed in all: seven sons of Japheth (v.2), then seven grandsons (vv.3–4). The author has omitted the sons of five of the seven sons of Japheth (Magog, Madai, Tubal, Meshech, and Tiras). He lists only the sons of Gomer and Javan (vv.3–4). Thus his intention is not to give an exhaustive list but rather a "complete" list, one that for him is obtained in the number "seven."

c. *The sons of Ham*

10:6–20

6The sons of Ham:
Cush, Mizraim, Put and Canaan.
7The sons of Cush:
Seba, Havilah, Sabtah, Raamah and Sabteca.
The sons of Raamah:
Sheba and Dedan.
8Cush was the father of Nimrod, who grew to be a mighty warrior on
the earth. 9He was a mighty hunter before the LORD; that is why it is said,
"Like Nimrod, a mighty hunter before the LORD." 10The first centers of
his kingdom were Babylon, Erech, Akkad and Calneh, in Shinar. 11From
that land he went to Assyria, where he built Nineveh, Rehoboth Ir,
Calah12and Resen, which is between Nineveh and Calah; that is the
great city.

13Mizraim was the father of
the Ludites, Anamites, Lehabites, Naphtuhites, 14Pathrusites,
Casluhites (from whom the Philistines came) and Caphtorites.
15Canaan was the father of
Sidon his firstborn, and of the Hittites, 16Jebusites, Amorites,
Girgashites, 17Hivites, Arkites, Sinites, 18Arvadites, Zemarites
and Hamathites.
Later the Canaanite clans scattered 19and the borders of Canaan
reached from Sidon toward Gerar as far as Gaza, and then toward
Sodom, Gomorrah, Admah and Zeboiim, as far as Lasha.
20These are the sons of Ham by their clans and languages, in their
territories and nations.

6–12 The author has given the list of the sons of Ham a thorough working over. It begins in the same way as the list of the sons of Japheth, with the simple naming of Ham's four sons: Cush, Mizraim, Put, and Canaan (v.6). Then, as also in the Japheth list, the grandsons of the first listed (Cush) are given (v.7a). But before going on to the next son (Mizraim, v.13), he lists the great grandsons (sons of Raamah, v.7a). The end result is a list of names that again numbers "seven sons"—thus a complete list. Immediately following these seven names, a narrative on the exploits of Nimrod and his cities is inserted (vv.8–12), which breaks into the pattern of "sevens" that has characterized the lists thus far. The importance of this small narrative lies in its introduction of the city of Babylon (v.10), which is the subject of the following chapter (11:1–9).

The deliberate association of Assyria with Babylon (vv.10–12) is also significant; otherwise in the lists of names that follow, Assyria is associated with the sons of Shem. By means of this narrative insertion, then, the author has not only introduced a key city, Babylon, but has taken Assyria out of its natural associations with Shem and given it a new identification with the city of Babylon. Thus the author has opened the way for an association and identification of any city with the city of Babylon. These appear to be the initial stirrings of a "larger than life" symbolic value for the city of Babylon, one known in the Book of Isaiah (chs. 13–14, where Assyria is identified with Babylon) and fully developed in the image of "MYSTERY BABYLON THE GREAT" in Revelation 17:5. The prophet Micah can already speak of Assyria as the "land of Nimrod" (Mic 5:6).

13–20 The author returns to the genealogy of the sons of Ham with a list of the sons of Mizraim, once again containing seven names (vv.13–14). This is the last list to be shaped by the numerical pattern "seven." The remainder of the lists of names appear to be influenced by no particular numerical pattern except that of the total number of "seventy nations" that dominates the list of names as a whole. Since it is clear that the author of the "list of the sons of Noah" has intentionally worked out a final pattern of seventy names, it is likely that, where it is found, the pattern of the smaller lists of seven names is also intentional. As with the number "seventy," the idea of "completeness" likely lies behind the number "seven." Thus for those lists that contain seven names, we may conclude that the author intends to give a "complete" accounting of the sons of that group, without actually listing all the sons. He is, as it were, passing them by without further comment.

With the lists that now occupy the attention of the author (those that do not number in the "sevens," vv.15–29), however, the focus is more comprehensive because these sons, the Canaanites and the sons of Shem, play more prominently in the narratives of the Book of Genesis and the Pentateuch. The author was especially interested in the exact boundaries of the area of Canaan (v.19) since that area of land lay at the heart of his purpose in writing the book. This was the land promised to Abraham, though "at that time the Canaanites were in the land" (12:6).

d. *The sons of Shem*

10:21–31

21 Sons were also born to Shem, whose older brother was Japheth; Shem was the ancestor of all the sons of Eber.

22 The sons of Shem:
Elam, Asshur, Arphaxad, Lud and Aram.
23 The sons of Aram:
Uz, Hul, Gether and Meshech.
24 Arphaxad was the father of Shelah,
and Shelah the father of Eber.
25 Two sons were born to Eber:
One was named Peleg, because in his time the earth was divided; his brother was named Joktan.
26 Joktan was the father of
Almodad, Sheleph, Hazarmaveth, Jerah, 27 Hadoram, Uzal,
Diklah, 28 Obal, Abimael, Sheba, 29 Ophir, Havilah and Jobab.
All these were sons of Joktan.

30 The region where they lived stretched from Mesha toward Sephar, in the eastern hill country.

31 These are the sons of Shem by their clans and languages, in their territories and nations.

21–31 The author begins the list of the sons of Shem with a prosaic introduction (v.21). The purpose of the introduction is to draw out the major lines of continuity running through chapter 10. The author calls attention to the relationship of Shem and Japheth: "Shem, the older brother of Japheth" (NIV mg.) and the relationship of Shem to the following generations: "Shem was the ancestor of all the sons of Eber." The reference to Shem and Japheth together without Ham may be significant, possibly intended to recall Noah's blessing of Shem and Japheth in 9:26–27, where there also Canaan is excluded. If so, it is another reminder of the ways in which the author uses allusions to past narratives to retain the reader's focus on the major points of the narrative—in this case the line of the blessing. The mention of the "sons of Eber" anticipates the genealogy that yet lies ahead, that one that results in the birth of Abraham (11:10–26). So, before moving on to complete the list of the sons of Noah, the author inserts this short summary to tie the list to the preceding and following narrative contexts.

The list of descendants of Shem is also highly selective, though it does not follow any particular numerical scheme as the earlier lists. Rather, the line of Shem is traced up to the two sons of Eber and from there continues to follow the line of the second son, Joktan (vv.26–29). It is significant that another genealogy of Shem is repeated after the account of the building of Babylon (11:1–9), and there the line is continued to Abraham through the first son of Eber, Peleg (11:10–26). In arranging the genealogy of Shem in such a way, the author draws a dividing line through the descendants of Shem on either side of the city of Babylon. The dividing line falls between the two sons of Eber, that is, Peleg and Joktan. One line leads to the building of Babylon and the other to the family of Abraham. The author supplies a hint to this division of the line of Shem with the comment that in Peleg's day "the earth was divided" (v.25). As throughout the biblical text, the "earth" is a reference to the "inhabitants of the land." Thus not only is the land divided in the confusion of languages (11:1), but, more fundamentally, two great lines of humanity diverge from the midst of the sons of Shem: those who seek to make a name (Shem) for themselves in the building of the city of Babylon (11:4) and those for whom God will make a name in the call of Abraham (Shem, 12:2).

Notes

25 The notice "in his [פֶּלֶג (*peleg̱*, 'Peleg's')] time the earth [הָאָרֶץ (*hā'āreṣ*)] was divided [נִפְלְגָה (*nip̱lᵉgāh*)]" provides the narrative clue to the structure of the genealogies of chapters 10 and 11. The genealogy of Shem in 10:21–31 is traced from Shem to the sons of Joktan, the brother of Peleg. After the account of the building of the city of Babylon, the genealogy of Shem is taken up again and traced through Peleg to Abraham (11:10–26). Thus the one line of Shem ends in Babylon and the other in the land with Abraham.

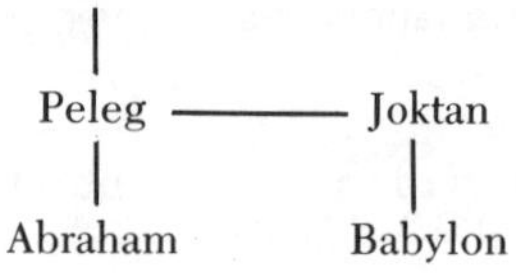

30 What is the function of this obscure note regarding the homeland of those from the line of Joktan? Obstensively it is to give the location of the settlement of the line, but narratively it serves to connect the line of Joktan with the account of the building of Babylon that follows. The link is made by means of the key term הַר הַקֶּדֶם (*har haqqeḏem,* lit., "mountain of the east"; NIV, "eastern hill country"). The narrative is less interested in the exact location than it is in the association with the מִקֶּדֶם (*miqqeḏem,* "eastward") of 11:2, the location of the "plain of Shinar" where the city of Babylon was built.

---

e. *Epilogue*

10:32

[32]These are the clans of Noah's sons, according to their lines of descent, within their nations. From these the nations spread out over the earth after the flood.

32 In the subscription to chapter 10, the author again takes up the theme of the division of the nations: "From these the nations spread out over the earth." His purpose is to provide a context for the narrative of the city of Babylon that follows. What he has described "geographically and linguistically" in chapter 10, he will describe "theologically" in chapter 11, namely, God's judgment of Babylon and dispersion of the nations.

E. *The City of Babylon*

11:1–9

[1]Now the whole world had one language and a common speech. [2]As men moved eastward, they found a plain in Shinar and settled there.

[3]They said to each other, "Come, let's make bricks and bake them thoroughly." They used brick instead of stone, and tar for mortar. [4]Then they said, "Come, let us build ourselves a city, with a tower that reaches to the heavens, so that we may make a name for ourselves and not be scattered over the face of the whole earth."

[5]But the LORD came down to see the city and the tower that the men were building. [6]The LORD said, "If as one people speaking the same language they have begun to do this, then nothing they plan to do will be impossible for them. [7]Come, let us go down and confuse their language so they will not understand each other."

[8]So the LORD scattered them from there over all the earth, and they stopped building the city. [9]That is why it was called Babel—because there the LORD confused the language of the whole world. From there the LORD scattered them over the face of the whole earth.

1–9 As was stated in the above comments, it is important to notice the position of the account of the building of Babylon within the lists of names that form the subject matter of chapters 10 and 11. It is located between the two lines that are traced from Shem: first, the line that extends from Shem (10:22) through Eber (v.24) through Joktan (vv.26–29), and, second, the line extending from Shem (11:10) through Eber (v.14), through Peleg (v.17). As it is presently situated in the text, the account of the founding of the city of Babylon falls at the end of the list of fourteen names from the line of Joktan (10:26–29). At the end of the list of the ten names of the line of Peleg, however, is the account of the call of Abraham (11:27–12:10). So there are two great lines of the descendants of Shem that divide in the two sons of Eber (10:25). One ends in Babylon, the other in the Promised Land. It is hard not to see this positioning of the account of Babylon as deliberate on the part of the author of Genesis, especially in light of the continuous interplay between the name Shem (*šēm*) and the quest for making "a name" (*šēm*) both in the account of the building of Babylon (11:4) and in the account of God's election of Abraham (12:2).

The first scene of the story of the building of Babylon opens outside the "plain in Shinar" (v.2). The narrative specifically notes that the builders "moved eastward" (*miqqeḏem*) to the plain where they founded the city. It seems important that we picture the starting point of the events of the story as a "land" (see Notes) west of Babylon. The builders started out in the land and moved eastward to build Babylon. It can hardly be without importance that the author has provided the story with such a geographical orientation. As early as Genesis 3, the author has shown his interest in marking the directions of travel taken in man's search for a home. When the man and his wife were driven from the garden because they had chosen the knowledge of good and evil for themselves, they were made to settle in a land "eastward" (*miqqeḏem*) from the garden (3:24). When Cain was cast out from the presence of God because he refused God's instruction, he went to dwell in a land "east of Eden" (*qiḏmaṯ*, 4:16). When Lot divided from Abraham and sought for himself a land "like the garden of the LORD," he moved "toward the east" (*miqqeḏem*) while Abraham remained in the land (13:10–12).

In light of such intentional uses of the notion of "eastward" within the Genesis narratives, we can see that here too the author intentionally draws the story of the founding of Babylon into the larger scheme at work throughout the book. It is a scheme that contrasts God's way of blessing (e.g., Eden and the Promised Land) with man's own attempt to find the "good." In the Genesis narratives, when man goes "east," he leaves the land of blessing (Eden and the Promised Land) and goes to a land where the greatest of his hopes will turn to ruin (Babylon and Sodom).

The central question surrounding this story is why God judged the builders of the city. Though the story is quite brief, the author has left the reader with definite, though subtle, indications of the story's meaning. The clues lie in the repetition of key words within the story, key words that also tie the story to the larger narrative context. We have already made note of the importance of the word "name" (*šēm*) within the larger context of chapters 10 through 12. Within the story itself, the word *šēm* also plays a central role. First, according to the builders of the city, the reason for building a city was "to make a name [*šēm*]" for themselves (v.4). Second, the conclusion of the story returns to the "name" (*šēm*) of the city, ironically associating it (Babylon/Babel) with the confusion (*bālal*) of their language (v.9). Thus the builders' attempt to make a name for themselves is a central feature of the story both in terms of the internal structure of the story and its linking with the surrounding narratives.

The term "scattered" (*pûṣ*, v.4) is another key word that ties the story together internally and externally with the surrounding narratives. The purpose of the city was so that its inhabitants would not "be scattered [*pûṣ*] over the face of the whole earth" (v.4). Ironically, at the conclusion of the story it is the Lord who "scattered" (*pûṣ*) the builders from the city "over the face of the whole earth" (v.8), a fact repeated twice at the conclusion (vv.8–9).

The expression "the whole land" (*kol-hā'āreṣ*) is a third key term in the story. The people had left "the whole land [NIV, 'world']" (v.1) to build a city in the east. The purpose of the city was to keep them from being scattered throughout "the whole land" (*kol hā'āreṣ,* v.4). But in response the Lord reversed their plan and scattered them over "all the land" (*kol-hā'āreṣ,* vv.8–9).

The story of the founding of the city of Babylon has been carefully constructed around key terms and ideas. The people of the land are at first united as one people sharing one language and living in the "land" (v.1). They moved "eastward" (v.2) and built a city to make a name for themselves so as not to be scattered over the land. When God saw their plan, he initiated a counterplan, one that resulted in the very thing the city builders were attempting to prevent: "the LORD scattered them over the face of the whole land" (v.8).

Although by itself the story of the building of Babylon makes good enough sense as the story of man's plans thwarted in God's judgment, its real significance lies in its ties to the themes developed in the surrounding narratives. The focus of the author since the beginning chapters of the Book of Genesis has been both on God's plan to bless mankind by providing him with that which is "good" and on man's failure to trust God and enjoy the "good" God had provided. The characteristic mark of man's failure up to this point in the book has been his attempt to grasp the "good" on his own rather than trust God to provide it for him. The author has centered his description of God's blessing on the gift of the land: "Be fruitful and increase in number; fill the earth" (1:28). The good land is the place of blessing. To leave this land and to seek another is to forfeit the blessing of God's good provisions. It is to live "east of Eden."

Within this context the events of the story of the building of the city of Babylon take on a greater range of significance. As Cain left the land and went eastward (*qiḏmaṯ-'ēḏen,* 4:16) and there built a city (4:17), the people, who were once united in the land (the last-mentioned location of the sons of Noah was the garden planted by Noah, 9:20), left the land, moved "eastward," and founded their own (*lānû,* v.4; NIV, "ourselves") city, there to make a name *for themselves* (*lānû*). God, who saw that their plans would succeed, moved to rescue them from those very plans and return them to the land and the blessing that awaited there.

The story of the building of Babylon ends with only a hint of a return to the land of blessing; but in the continuation of the Genesis narratives (chs. 12ff.), the next series of events brings God's plans into sharp focus: "The LORD had said to Abram, 'Leave your country, your people and your father's household and go to the land I will show you. . . . I will make your name great and you will be a blessing' " (12:1–2).

Notes

---

1 The meaning of כָּל־הָאָרֶץ (*kol-hā'āreṣ,* "the whole land [NIV, 'world']") is limited here to a particular geographical location since in the following verse it says that the "men moved eastward" and found the valley where they built the city of Babylon. Thus the narrative pictures the founding of the city of Babylon at the end of a migration of people from the west.

The sense of שָׂפָה אֶחָת (*śāp̄āh 'eḥāṯ,* "one language") appears to parallel דְּבָרִים אֲחָדִים (*d*[e]*ḇārîm '*[a]*ḥāḏîm*), namely, that these people all spoke the same language (NIV, "a common speech"). That, of course, is the premise of the narrative that follows. The expression *d*[e]*ḇārîm '*[a]*ḥāḏîm* could also mean "few words"; but since the narrative does not develop any further in that direction, it is better to take it in the sense of "one language," a theme that is further developed (e.g., עַם אֶחָד [*'am 'eḥāḏ,* "one people"], v.6). This also appears to be the sense of later interbiblical allusions to this narrative, e.g., שְׂפַת כְּנַעַן (*śᵉpaṯ kᵉnaʿan*, "the language of Canaan," Isa 19:18).

1–9 There are many wordplays and alliterations in this small narrative.

1. Same consonants

    v.2b: [1]שִׁנְעָר וַיֵּשְׁבוּ שָׁם
    v.3a: [2]נִלְבְּנָה לְבֵנִים
    v.3a: [3]נִשְׂרְפָה לִשְׂרֵפָה
    v.3b: [4]הַלְּבֵנָה לְאָבֶן
    v.3b: [5]הַחֵמָר . . . לַחֹמֶר
    v.4a: [6]נִבְנֶה־לָּנוּ
    v.4a: [7]בַשָּׁמַיִם . . . שֵׁם
    v.5a: [8]וַיֵּרֶד יהוה לִרְאֹת אֶת־הָעִיר
    v.5b: [9]בָּנוּ בְּנֵי
    v.7b: [10]שָׁם שְׂפָתָם אֲשֶׁר לֹא יִשְׁמְעוּ אִישׁ שְׂפַת
    v.9a: [11]בָּבֶל . . . בָּלַל

2. Similar consonants

    v.3b: [12]הַחֵמָר הָיָה לָהֶם לַחֹמֶר
    v.4a: [13]רֹאשׁוֹ בַשָּׁמַיִם וְנַעֲשֶׂה־לָּנוּ שֵׁם
    v.7a: [14]שָׁם שְׂפָתָם
    v.8a: [15]אֹתָם מִשָּׁם
    v.9b: [16]מִשָּׁם הֱפִיצָם

3. Reversed same consonants

    v.4: [17]פֶּן־נָפוּץ
    v.3a, v.7: [19]נָבְלָה, [18]נִלְבְּנָה

4. Reversed similar consonants

    v.2b: [20]וַיִּמְצְאוּ . . . בְאֶרֶץ
    v.7b, v.8a: [22]וַיָּפֶץ, [21]שְׂפַת

Cassuto (pp. 232ff.) has noted other plays on words as well as the fact that throughout the narrative the central theme of Babylon (בָּבֶל [*bāḇel*]) is echoed in the recurrence of the consonants ב (*ḇ*) and ל (*l*). This is similar to the recurrence of the name "Isaac" (יִצְחָק [*yiṣḥāq*]) throughout the patriarchal narratives (see comments on ch. 17).

[1](*šinʿār wayyēšᵉḇû šām*, "Shinar and settled there").
[2](*nilbᵉnāh lᵉḇēnîm*, "let's make bricks").
[3](*niśrᵉpāh liśrēpāh*, "[let's] bake them thoroughly [lit., 'with fire']").
[4](*hallᵉḇēnāh lᵉʾāḇen*, "brick instead of stone").
[5](*haḥēmār . . . laḥōmer*, "tar instead of mortar").
[6](*niḇneh-lānû*, "let us build ourselves").
[7](*ḇaššāmayim . . . šēm*, "to the heavens . . . a name").
[8](*wayyēreḏ yhwh lirʾōṯ ʾeṯ-hāʿîr*, "But the LORD came down to see the city").
[9](*bānû bᵉnê*, "the men were building" [lit., "they built, the men"]).
[10](*šām śᵉpāṯām ʾᵃšer lōʾ yišmᵉʿû ʾîš śᵉpaṯ*, "confuse their language so they will not understand each other").
[11](*bāḇel . . . bālal*, "Babel . . . [he] confused").
[12](*haḥēmār hāyāh lāhem laḥōmer*, "tar instead of mortar").
[13](*rōʾšô ḇaššāmayim wᵉnaʿᵃśeh-lānû šēm*, "reaches to the heavens, so that we may make a name for ourselves").
[14](*šām śᵉpāṯām*, "[there] confuse their language").
[15](*ʾōṯām miššām*, "them from there").
[16](*miššām hᵉpîṣām*, "from there [he] scattered them").
[17](*pen-nāpûṣ*, "not [lit., 'lest'] be scattered").
[18](*nilbᵉnāh*, "let's make").
[19](*nāḇᵉlāh*, "[let's] confuse").
[20](*wayyimṣᵉʾû . . . bᵉʾereṣ*, lit., "and they found . . . in the land of [untr. NIV]").
[21](*śᵉpaṯ*, "language").
[22](*wayyāpeṣ*, "so [he] scattered").

F. *The Line of Shem*

11:10–26

[10]This is the account of Shem.
Two years after the flood, when Shem was 100 years old, he became the father of Arphaxad. [11]And after he became the father of Arphaxad, Shem lived 500 years and had other sons and daughters.
[12]When Arphaxad had lived 35 years, he became the father of Shelah.
[13]And after he became the father of Shelah, Arphaxad lived 403 years and had other sons and daughters.
[14]When Shelah had lived 30 years, he became the father of Eber.
[15]And after he became the father of Eber, Shelah lived 403 years and had other sons and daughters.
[16]When Eber had lived 34 years, he became the father of Peleg. [17]And after he became the father of Peleg, Eber lived 430 years and had other sons and daughters.
[18]When Peleg had lived 30 years, he became the father of Reu. [19]And after he became the father of Reu, Peleg lived 209 years and had other sons and daughters.
[20]When Reu had lived 32 years, he became the father of Serug. [21]And after he became the father of Serug, Reu lived 207 years and had other sons and daughters.
[22]When Serug had lived 30 years, he became the father of Nahor.
[23]And after he became the father of Nahor, Serug lived 200 years and had other sons and daughters.
[24]When Nahor had lived 29 years, he became the father of Terah.
[25]And after he became the father of Terah, Nahor lived 119 years and had other sons and daughters.
[26]After Terah had lived 70 years, he became the father of Abram, Nahor and Haran.

10–26 This list of ten descendants of Shem performs a function similar to that of the list of ten descendants of Adam in chapter 5. It draws the line of the "faithful" from Noah to Abraham and bypasses the line of the "unfaithful" (10:26–30). The list of the ten descendants of Shem (11:10–26) closely resembles the list of the ten descendants of Adam (5:1–32). A comparison of the use of the two lists within the larger narrative complex suggests that they both are a result of the careful attention given by the author to the final shape of the text. In chapter 5, the list of ten patriarchs from Adam to Noah provided the necessary linkage between the "offspring" promised to the woman (3:15) and the offspring of Noah, the survivor of the Flood (7:23). Not only does the list mark the "line of the promise," it also is the means for bypassing the other line that occupies the attention of the author of Genesis, the line of Cain (4:17–22), which also consists of a list of ten names. Cain's line represents the builders of the city (4:17) and the civilization (vv.20–24) that was destroyed in the Flood.

The list in chapter 5, then, reveals a highly developed theological reflection on the promise that had been made concerning the seed of the woman in 3:15. It shows the author was conscious of the impending failure of the line of Cain and the city they had built. The judgment and destruction that awaited that city, however, would not mean the end of God's promise. Noah would survive and his offspring would carry the hope of the promise. Such theological reflection achieves full expression in the words of the woman at the birth of Seth: "God has granted me another child [*zera' 'aḥēr*, lit., 'another seed'] in place of Abel, since Cain killed him" (4:25). There are two seeds, that of Cain and that of the woman. The line of Cain may rise up against the seed of the woman, but God had provided another seed in place of the one who was slain. The line of Cain may lead to judgment and destruction, but God would preserve the line of Seth through whom the promise would be fulfilled.

The same theological reflection on God's promise lies behind the list of ten names in vv.10–26. Here the author's aim is to show that God's promise concerning the seed of the woman cannot be thwarted by the confusion and scattering of the nations at Babylon. Though the seed of Noah were scattered at Babylon, God has preserved a line of ten great men from Noah to the chosen seed of Abraham. Out of the ruins of two great cities, the city of Cain and the city of Babylon, God has preserved his promised seed. By beginning the list of names over again with Shem, the author shows his intention to bypass the other line that had been traced to Shem in the previous chapter (10:26–30).

Notes

---

26 Numbering from Shem to Terah, the list has only nine names. The LXX has a tenth name in the list (*Καιναν*, *Kainan*), the father of שֶׁלַח (*šelaḥ*, "Shelah," v.12). This appears to be a secondary attempt to adapt the list to the scheme of ten names. Jacob (p. 304) suggests that the number ten was intended by reading Noah with both the list in chapter 5 and (from 9:28) the list in chapter 11. The number ten is also obtainable by reading Abraham as the last name (11:26b). That, of course, appears to arbitrarily exclude Nahor and Haran, who are listed after Abram at the close of the list.

As is often the case with the numerical symmetry of the Genesis lists, the numbers are close, but some adding and subtracting is often necessary in the end. One might be tempted to draw the conclusion that if the numbers are not always perfect, it means that the apparent symmetry was not intentional. However, the fact that some adding and subtracting is necessary even when the narrative itself does the final counting (e.g., 46:27) shows that a purpose lies behind such numerical symmetry, even though that symmetry is not always perfect.

II. Abraham (11:27–25:10[11])

A. *The Line of Abraham*

11:27–32

27 This is the account of Terah.
Terah became the father of Abram, Nahor and Haran. And Haran
became the father of Lot. 28 While his father Terah was still alive, Haran
died in Ur of the Chaldeans, in the land of his birth. 29 Abram and Nahor
both married. The name of Abram's wife was Sarai, and the name of
Nahor's wife was Milcah; she was the daughter of Haran, the father of
both Milcah and Iscah. 30 Now Sarai was barren; she had no children.
31 Terah took his son Abram, his grandson Lot son of Haran, and his
daughter-in-law Sarai, the wife of his son Abram, and together they set
out from Ur of the Chaldeans to go to Canaan. But when they came to
Haran, they settled there.
32 Terah lived 205 years, and he died in Haran.

27–32 Another genealogy precedes the narrative of Abraham. The function of this genealogy is not so much to connect Abraham with the preceding events, as the previous genealogies have done, but to provide the reader with the necessary background for understanding the events in the life of Abraham. The list includes eight names. All the individuals named are relevant for understanding the events of the following narrative except "Iscah" (v.29). The inclusion of this otherwise insignificant name in the list suggests that the author is seeking to achieve a specific number of names. Thus far in the Book of Genesis, the author has followed a pattern of listing ten names between important individuals in the narrative. In this short list only eight names are given, hence if we are expecting ten names, the number of individuals in this list appears to be short by two names. By listing only eight names, the author leaves the reader uncertain who the ninth and, more importantly, the tenth name will be. It is only as the narrative unfolds that the ninth and tenth names are shown to be the two sons of Abraham, "Ishmael" (16:15) and "Isaac" (21:3).

In his genealogical introduction, then, the author anticipates the central event in the forthcoming narrative: the birth of Isaac, who will mark the tenth name. This is one of many ways the author carefully guides the reader toward the focus of his narrative—yet also holds the reader back in anticipation. The same concern can be seen in the initial reminder that "Sarai was barren; she had no child" (*wālāḏ*, v.30) and in the prominence given in the following narrative to the wordplay on Isaac's name ("he laughs," 17:17; 18:12–13, 15; 19:14; 21:3, 6). The unusual spelling of the word "child" (*wālāḏ*) in v.30 may be due to an attempt to call attention to this important element of the introduction. Later in the narrative in Abraham's response to the announcement of the birth of this child (*wālāḏ*), there appears to be a deliberate allusion to this unusual spelling, as well as to the name ("Isaac") of the child: "Abraham fell facedown; he laughed [*wayyiṣḥāq* = *yiṣḥāq* = 'Isaac'] and said to himself, 'Will a son be born [*yiwwālēḏ*; cf. *wālāḏ*] to a man a hundred years old?' " (17:17).

Interspersed in the list of names is the brief notice that Terah and his family, including Abraham and Lot, had left Ur of the Chaldeans and traveled as far as Haran, enroute to the land of Canaan (v.32). There is no mention of the call of God until 12:1, and that appears to be after the death of Terah (v.32b). The initial impression is that while in Haran Abraham was called to leave his homeland—after the death of his father, Terah, and not while in Ur of the Chaldeans. That impression is further sustained by the narrative in 12:4–5, which recounts Abraham's obedient response to the call of God and explicitly states that he "set out from Haran," not mentioning Ur of the Chaldeans. A second look, however, suggests that the author intended us to understand the narrative differently.

In vv.27–32 we are explicitly shown that Ur of the Chaldeans, not Haran, was the place of Abraham's birth (vv.28, 31). Thus when the command is given Abraham to leave the place of his birth (12:1; NIV, "your country"), only Ur of the Chaldeans can be understood, despite the fact that the narrative of chapter 12 makes no mention of it. The role of 11:27–32 in providing the "geographical context" of chapter 12, then, should not be overlooked, especially in light of the author's close attention to "geography" in working out his key themes, e.g., his emphasis on traveling "eastward" (see comment on 11:2). Even though the narrative of chapter 12 would suggest otherwise, the author seems clearly intent on having the reader understand Abraham's call as a call to leave "Ur of the Chaldeans." That this is the view of the author is confirmed by the later reference to Abraham's call in 15:7. There the author looks back to the call of Abraham and sees it as a call from "Ur of the Chaldeans" rather than from Haran. This is also the view of the author of the Book of Nehemiah (9:7) and the author of Acts (7:2–3) in the NT.

The importance of this detail goes far beyond the question of harmonizing the biblical accounts. By putting the call of Abraham within the setting of Ur of the Chaldeans, the author aligns his narrative with themes that will prove central in the later prophetic literature. For Isaiah the "glory of the Chaldeans" (Isa 13:19, NIV mg.) is the city of Babylon that God will overturn "like Sodom and Gomorrah" (cf. 48:14b). In Jeremiah (cf. NIV mg. of 24:5; 25:12; 50:1, 8, 35, 45; 51:24, 54) and Ezekiel (1:3; 12:13; 23:15, 23), the Chaldeans are those who live in the city of Babylon and who have taken God's people into captivity. So it is in harmony with these prophets that the author of Genesis puts Abraham's call in the context of "Ur of the Chaldeans," drawing a line connecting the call of Abraham (12:1–3) with the dispersion of the city of Babylon (11:1–9) and thus making Abraham prefigure all those future exiles who, in faith, wait for the return to the Promised Land. In much the same way the prophet Micah pictured the remnant who awaited the return from exile as descendants of Abraham faithfully trusting in God's promise (Mic 7:18–20).

Marked similarities are evident between this introduction to the narrative of Abraham and the introduction to the narrative of Isaac (25:19–26), indicating that the author sees the two narratives as related. Abraham's brother, Haran, died "before" his father (*'al-pᵉnê teraḥ,* lit., "in the face of Terah"; v.28a) just as Isaac's brother Ishmael died "before his brothers" (*'al-pᵉnê kol-'eḥāyw,* lit., "in the faces of all his brothers"; 25:18b). At the beginning of the Abraham narrative, there is a brief introduction of Nahor (v.29), who is to become a key character in the subsequent narratives concerning the quest for a bride for Abraham's son (24:24). So also at the beginning of the Isaac narrative, Laban (25:20), the father of the bride of Isaac's son Jacob, is given a brief introduction (28:2). In both the Abraham and the Isaac narratives, the introductions turn quickly to the key characters: Abraham and Lot in the Abraham narratives and Isaac-Jacob and Esau in the Isaac narratives.

As an introduction to the Abrahamic narrative, it is recounted that Abraham took a wife, Sarai, and that she was barren (*'ᵃqārāh,* vv.29–30). So also in the Isaac narrative, we read that Isaac took a wife, Rebekah, and that she was barren (*'ᵃqārāh,* 25:20–21). Unlike the Abraham narratives, where the motive of barrenness occupies center stage throughout, the barrenness of Isaac's wife is treated in a single verse (25:21); and the narrative moves on to the theme of the struggle between the brothers, Jacob and Esau. Both narratives, however, contain an element of struggle between brothers; and the introductions to both narratives are centrally concerned with setting forth the necessary background of that struggle. Abraham was accompanied by Lot from birth (v.27), and Jacob was accompanied by Esau from birth (25:22–24). In the struggles that ensued from Abraham's companionship with Lot (13:7) and Jacob's companionship with Esau (chs. 25–28), Abraham must be "separated" from Lot (13:9, 11, 14) and Jacob must be "separated" from Esau (25:23).

There are striking verbal parallels between the accounts of the struggle that arose between Abraham and Lot and the struggle between Jacob and Esau. In 13:6 the narrative reads, "the land could not support them while they stayed together" (*wᵉlō'-nāśā' 'ōṯām hā'āreṣ lāšeḇeṯ yaḥdāw*), "for their possessions were so great" (*kî-hāyāh rᵉḵûšām rāḇ*) "that they were not able to stay together" (*wᵉlō' yāḵᵉlû lāšeḇeṯ yaḥdāw*). In the same manner, in 36:7 the narrative reads, "Their possessions were too great" (*kî-hāyāh reḵûšām rāḇ miššeḇeṯ yaḥdāw*); "the land where they were staying could not support them both because of their livestock" (*wᵉlō' yāḵᵉlāh 'ereṣ mᵉḡûrêhem lāśē'ṯ 'ōṯām*). Such parallels have the effect of drawing the themes of the two narratives together so that they reinforce a central theme. The theme in this case is that of the fulfillment of the blessing: "Be fruitful and increase in number; fill the earth" (1:28).

Along with the theme of "blessing," the theme of "separation" (*pāraḏ*), so prominent in chapter 10 (vv.5, 32), continues to play a central role in the author's purpose. The ideas that lie behind such a theme can be seen clearly in the final words of the Pentateuch: "When the Most High gave the nations their inheritance, when he divided [*pāraḏ*] all mankind, he set up boundaries for the peoples. . . . For the LORD's portion is his people, Jacob his allotted inheritance" (Deut 32:8–9).

B. *The Call of Abraham*

12:1–9

1 The LORD had said to Abram, "Leave your country, your people and your father's household and go to the land I will show you.

> 2 "I will make you into a great nation
> and I will bless you;
> I will make your name great,
> and you will be a blessing.
> 3 I will bless those who bless you,
> and whoever curses you I will curse;
> and all peoples on earth
> will be blessed through you."

4 So Abram left, as the LORD had told him; and Lot went with him. Abram was seventy-five years old when he set out from Haran. 5 He took his wife Sarai, his nephew Lot, all the possessions they had accumulated and the people they had acquired in Haran, and they set out for the land of Canaan, and they arrived there.

6 Abram traveled through the land as far as the site of the great tree of Moreh at Shechem. At that time the Canaanites were in the land. 7 The LORD appeared to Abram and said, "To your offspring I will give this land." So he built an altar there to the LORD, who had appeared to him.

8 From there he went on toward the hills east of Bethel and pitched his tent, with Bethel on the west and Ai on the east. There he built an altar to the LORD and called on the name of the LORD. 9 Then Abram set out and continued toward the Negev.

1–5 We have already suggested that by placing the call of Abraham after the dispersion of the nations at Babylon (11:1–9), the author intended to picture Abraham's call as God's gift of salvation in the midst of judgment. As a way of sustaining this theme even further, the author has patterned the account of Abraham's call and blessing after an earlier account of a similar gift of salvation in the midst of judgment, the conclusion of the Flood narrative (see comments on 8:15–19). The similarities between the two narratives are striking, showing that Abraham, like Noah, marks a new beginning as well as a return to God's original plan of blessing "all mankind" (cf. 1:28).

The theme of Abraham and his descendants marking a new beginning in God's plan of blessing is developed in a number of other ways as well in Genesis. Most notable is the frequent reiteration of God's "blessing" in 1:28 (and 9:1) throughout the narratives of Abraham and his descendants (e.g., 12:1–3; 13:15–16; 15:5, 18; 17:6–8; 22:17–18;

25:11; 26:2–4; 27:27–29; 49:28). The "Promise to the Fathers" is none other than a reiteration of God's original blessing of mankind (1:28). To make this clear the author has given a representative list of "all mankind" in chapter 10 according to their "families" (v.32; NIV, "clans") and has shown how their dispersion was the result of the rebellion of the city of Babylon (11:1–9). These same "families of the earth" (NIV, "peoples on earth") are to be blessed in Abraham and his seed (12:3). Abraham is here represented as a "new Adam," the "seed of Abraham" as a "second Adam," a new humanity. Those who "bless" him, God will bless; those who "curse" him, God will curse. The way of *life and blessing,* which was once marked by the "tree of the knowledge of good and evil" (2:17) and then by the ark (7:23b), is now marked by identification with Abraham and his seed.

The identity of the "seed" of Abraham is one of the chief themes of the following narratives. At the close of the book (49:8–12), a curtain on the future is drawn back and a glimpse of the future seed of Abraham is briefly allowed. This one "seed" who is to come, to whom the right of kingship belongs, will be the "lion of the tribe of Judah" (cf. 49:9); and "the obedience of the nations is his" (49:10). The importance the author attaches to the connection of the fulfillment of the "blessing" and coming of this one from the tribe of Judah can be seen in the narrative framework given to the prophetic poem of Jacob in chapter 49. At the conclusion of Jacob's words, the author has repeated three times that his words are to be understood as a renewal of the theme of the blessing: "and he blessed [*way*^{e}*ḇāreḵ*] them each according to his blessing [*k*^{e}*ḇirḵāṯô*] he blessed [*bēraḵ*] them" (49:28, pers. tr.).

6–9 The account of Abraham's entry into the land of Canaan is selective. Only three sites in the land are mentioned: Shechem (v.6), between Bethel and Ai (v.8), and the Negev (v.9). As Cassuto has pointed out, it can hardly be accidental that these are the same three locations visited by Jacob when he returned to Canaan from Haran (chs. 34–35) as well as the same sites occupied in the account of the conquest of the land under Joshua:

> The Torah does not recount its narrative simply to instruct about ancient history. Rather, its aim is that of teaching religion and heritage and it uses ancient tradition for this purpose. By carefully choosing its words, the Torah signals to the reader key relationships within the ancient tradition that show its meaning. Already in the first section of chapter 12 of Genesis it is possible to recognize this method. Abram comes up out of the north and passes through all the land of Canaan in three journeys. In the first journey he goes to the place of Shechem and there he builds an altar to the Lord, marking the "ideal conquest" of the land and its sanctification to the Lord (12:6–7). In the second journey he arrives on the east of Bethel, with Bethel on the west and Ai on the east. Again he builds an altar at this place and calls on the name of the Lord (12:8). In the third journey he travels to the Negev (12:9) and there, in Hebron, he purchased later the field of Machpelah (Gen 23). Jacob's return from the east and his journeys in the land are like those of Abraham. First, he goes to Shechem and purchases a section of a field where he puts his tent and erects an altar to the God of Israel (33:18–20). Before he leaves this site, he commands his household to put away the foreign gods which are in their midst (35:2) and hides all of the idols he has received from Shechem beneath the oak tree which is there (35:4). Then he journeys to Bethel and sets up there a pillar to the glory of his God (35:14–15). Finally, he travels on to the south, which is the Negev, and comes to Hebron (35:27). The key points in the journeys of Abraham, then, parallel those of Jacob and both of these, in turn, parallel the key points in the conquest of the land

as it is recounted in the Book of Joshua. There it is noted that the first city which they themselves conquered was Ai, and it uses the same expression as Genesis 12:8—east of Bethel, between Bethel and Ai, west of Ai (Joshua 7:2, 8:9, cf. also verse 12). Immediately after this the Book of Joshua recounts that Joshua built an altar at Mount Ebal, that is, next to Shechem (Joshua 8:30). From there, the Israelites spread out into two further regions: south of Bethel and Ai (Joshua 10) and north of Shechem (Joshua 11). This is precisely the same three regions which we see with Abraham and Jacob. In Shechem Joshua commanded the Israelites to put away the foreign gods which were in their midst (Joshua 24:23) using almost the same words as those of Jacob in his day. There Joshua erected a large stone under the oak which was in the sanctuary of the Lord (Joshua 24:26)—under the oak as in Genesis 35:4. These parallels show clearly the method of demonstrating that the deeds of the fathers in former times prefigure those of their descendants in the present. Its intention is to show that what happened to Abraham also happened to Jacob and then also to their descendants. This is to show that the conquest of the land had already been accomplished in a symbolic way in the times of the fathers, demonstrated by means of their building their altars and purchasing property. Thus it shows that in the deeds of the fathers there is a source of trust that the Lord has cared for them from the very start and that he will still remain trustworthy in the days of the descendants of the fathers later on. (EBi, 1:65–66)

Notes

---

1 It is only from the larger context, i.e., 11:27–32, that we can identify מוֹלַדְתְּךָ (*môladtekā*, "your people") with אוּר כַּשְׂדִּים (*'ûr kaśdîm*, "Ur of the Chaldeans")—viz., in 11:28 בְּאֶרֶץ מוֹלַדְתּוֹ (*be'ereṣ môladtô*, "in the land of his birth") is identified as בְּאוּר כַּשְׂדִּים (*be'ûr kaśdîm*, "in Ur of the Chaldeans"). It is apparent, then, that the author of the wider context intended the *môladtekā* of 12:1 to be understood as *'ûr kaśdîm*. Thus the reading of Gen 12:1 in Acts 7:2, in which God called Abraham "before he lived in Haran," follows the logic of the larger context. In Gen 24:7–10, however, אֶרֶץ מוֹלַדְתִּי (*'ereṣ môladtî*, "native land") is identified as אֲרַם נַהֲרַיִם (*'aram naharayim*, "Aram Naharaim," i.e., "Northwestern Mesopotamia" [NIV mg.]).

2 The imperative with waw—וֶהְיֵה בְּרָכָה (*wehyēh berākāh*, "will be blessed") following a cohortative—וַאֲגַדְּלָה (*wa'agaddelāh*, "and I will make great") is to be read as a "consequence which is intended, or in fact an intention" (GKC, par. 110i). Thus the purpose of God's call is not only that Abraham might become a great nation, but also that he might be a blessing (*berākāh*).

3 The singular מְקַלֶּלְךָ (*meqallelkā*, "whoever curses you") may be motivated by the intended association of this divine word with specific individuals in later narrative events (see comments on ch. 16).

Much discussion (see Walter C. Kaiser, Jr., *Toward An Old Testament Theology* [Grand Rapids: Zondervan, 1978], p. 13; and Westermann, *Genesis*, 2:175) has centered on the meaning of the Niphal (וְנִבְרְכוּ [*wenibrekû*, "(they) will be blessed"]) here in v.3 (and 18:18; 28:14), particularly in opposition to the Hithpael (וְהִתְבָּרֲכוּ [*wehitbārakû*, "they will be blessed"]) found elsewhere (22:18; 26:4). There is general agreement that both should have the same meaning, but is the Niphal to be understood in light of the Hithpael or the Hithpael in light of the Niphal? The usual meaning of the Niphal is passive (cf. Oskar Grether, *Hebraeische Grammatik fuer den akademischen Unterricht* [Muenchen: Claudius Verlag, 1967], p. 67) and the Hithpael is reflexive. If taken as passive, the sense of this clause is "through you will all the families of the earth be blessed." If reflexive, the sense is that the nations henceforth will bless themselves by evoking the name of Abraham. As Rashi (p. 123) explained it, "A man will say to his son, 'May you be like Abraham.'" Thus if *nib̲rek̲û* is passive, there is a broader, more theological sense to the passage. God has a plan of blessing for all nations that was to be effected through the seed of Abraham. If reflexive, Abraham appears to be little more than a reminder of God's blessing.

More recently Westermann, who takes *nib̲rek̲û* as reflexive, has suggested that in the final analysis there is little difference between the passive and reflexive sense: "When the 'families of the earth' bless themselves 'in Abraham,' that is, wish themselves well by naming Abraham's name (as in Psalm 72:17 and still more clearly in Genesis 48:20), it is thus naturally presupposed that they then will also receive a blessing" (*Genesis,* 2:176).

Most explanations of *wenib̲rek̲û* share the view that the Niphal is used interchangeably with the Hithpael in the Genesis passages. Thus the forms collectively are read as either passive or reflexive. There is reason to doubt, however, that the two forms are used in Genesis with identical meaning. The Niphal *wenib̲rek̲û* occurs three times (12:3; 18:18; 28:14), which are its only occurrences in the Hebrew Bible. The Hithpael *hit̲bārak̲û* occurs twice (22:18; 26:4). There is an important difference in the clauses where these two verbal stems occur. Although each takes an adverbial modifier with the ב (*b*) preposition, the Niphal forms occur with the pronominal object (e.g., בְּךָ [*bek̲ā,* "through you"]):

12:3: [1]וְנִבְרְכוּ בְךָ
18:18: [2]וְנִבְרְכוּ בוֹ
28:14: [3]וְנִבְרֲכוּ בְךָ

(The antecedent of the pronominal object of the preposition is the individual patriarch who, at that point, is the one addressed. Note that in 28:14, the only occurrence of this promise given to Jacob, the adverbial phrase וּבְזַרְעֶךָ [*ûb̲ezar'ek̲ā,* "and your offspring"] is added to the end of the clause.)

The Hithpael forms occur with the nominal object, viz., זַרְעֲךָ (*zar'ak̲ā,* "offspring"):

22:18: [4]וְהִתְבָּרֲכוּ בְזַרְעֲךָ
26:4: [4]וְהִתְבָּרֲכוּ בְזַרְעֲךָ

Such variation should lead us to suspect that the alternation of Niphal and Hithpael is purposeful. Is there a feature of either the Niphal or the Hithpael that could explain this alternation? There are examples of what may be an "iterative" sense to the Hithpael (R.H. Williams, *Hebrew Syntax: An Outline* [Toronto: University of Toronto Press, 1967], pp. 28–31) that would explain the Hithpael *hit̲bārak̲û* in 22:18 and 26:4 as extending the promised blessing into the future as an on-going blessing. In Gen 5:22, for example, the Hithpael וַיִּתְהַלֵּךְ (*wayyit̲hallēk̲,* "[he] walked"; cf. 6:9: הִתְהַלֶּךְ [*hit̲hallek,* "he walked"], Perf.; 17:1: הִתְהַלֵּךְ (*hit̲hallēk̲,* "walk"], Impv.; 3:8: מִתְהַלֵּךְ [*mit̲hallēk̲,* "walking"], Part.) expresses an on-going walk with God (iterative). Also, if the Hithpael in Gen 3:24—הַמִּתְהַפֶּכֶת (*hammit̲happek̲et̲,* "flashing back and forth")—expresses a "turning to and fro," that would imply an iterative sense for the stem. In Gen 37:34b the Hithpael has a clear iterative sense: וַיִּתְאַבֵּל עַל־בְּנוֹ יָמִים רַבִּים (*wayyit̲'abbēl 'al-benô yāmîm rabbîm,* "and he lamented over his son many days"). The use of the Hithpael, then, in the expression of the blessing of Abraham may not be a duplication of the Niphal, nor the Niphal a duplication of the Hithpael. Each may have its own contribution to make to an understanding of the promise. The Niphal can be read as passive, which it most likely is in its own right, and the Hithpael as iterative when the promise is envisioned with respect to the future "seed"—the blessing will continue (iterative) to be offered to the nations through the seed of Abraham.

5 The verbal parallels between Abraham's leaving Ur in chapter 11 and his response to God's call in chapter 12 are striking:

1. 11:31: [5]וַיִּקַּח תֶּרַח אֶת־אַבְרָם
   12:5: [6]וַיִּקַּח אַבְרָם אֶת־שָׂרַי
2. 11:31b: [7]וַיֵּצְאוּ אִתָּם מֵאוּר כַּשְׂדִּים לָלֶכֶת אַרְצָה כְּנַעַן
   12:5b: [8]וַיֵּצְאוּ לָלֶכֶת אַרְצָה כְּנַעַן

3. 11:31b: [9]וַיָּבֹאוּ עַד־חָרָן
12:5b: [10]וַיָּבֹאוּ אַרְצָה כְּנָעַן

The similarities are perhaps designed to play down the distinction between the two events, merging them into one continuous journey.

6 The clause structure of וְהַכְּנַעֲנִי אָז בָּאָרֶץ (*w^{e}hakk^{e}na'^{a}nî 'āz bā'āreṣ,* "The Canaanites were then in the land") suggests that it is to be understood as background to what follows, namely the promise of the land. As the promise of the land is first given, we are reminded that the Canaanites were at that time dwelling there.

[1](*w^{e}niḇr^{e}ḵû ḇ^{e}ḵā,* "[they] will be blessed through you").
[2](*w^{e}niḇr^{e}ḵû ḇô,* "will be blessed through him").
[3](*w^{e}niḇr^{a}ḵû ḇ^{e}kā,* "will be blessed through you").
[4](*w^{e}hiṯbār^{a}ḵû ḇ^{e}zar'^{a}ḵā,* "and through your offspring [they] will be blessed").
[5](*wayyiqqaḥ teraḥ 'eṯ-'aḇrām,* "Terah took . . . Abram").
[6](*wayyiqqaḥ 'aḇrām 'eṯ-śāray,* lit., "Abram took Sarai").
[7](*wayyēṣ^{e}'û 'ittām mē'ûr kaśdîm lāleḵeṯ 'arṣāh k^{e}na'an,* "together they set out from Ur of the Chaldeans to go to Canaan").
[8](*wayyēṣ^{e}'û lāleḵeṯ 'arṣāh k^{e}na'an,* "and they set out for the land of Canaan").
[9](*wayyāḇō'û 'aḏ-ḥārān,* "they came to Haran").
[10](*wayyāḇō'û 'arṣāh k^{e}nā'an,* lit., "and they arrived in the land of Canaan").

C. *Abraham in Egypt*

12:10–13:4

[10]Now there was a famine in the land, and Abram went down to Egypt
to live there for a while because the famine was severe. [11]As he was
about to enter Egypt, he said to his wife Sarai, "I know what a beautiful
woman you are. [12]When the Egyptians see you, they will say, 'This is his
wife.' Then they will kill me but will let you live. [13]Say you are my sister,
so that I will be treated well for your sake and my life will be spared
because of you."

[14]When Abram came to Egypt, the Egyptians saw that she was a very
beautiful woman. [15]And when Pharaoh's officials saw her, they praised
her to Pharaoh, and she was taken into his palace. [16]He treated Abram
well for her sake, and Abram acquired sheep and cattle, male and
female donkeys, menservants and maidservants, and camels.

[17]But the LORD inflicted serious diseases on Pharaoh and his
household because of Abram's wife Sarai. [18]So Pharaoh summoned
Abram. "What have you done to me?" he said. "Why didn't you tell me
she was your wife? [19]Why did you say, 'She is my sister,' so that I took
her to be my wife? Now then, here is your wife. Take her and go!"
[20]Then Pharaoh gave orders about Abram to his men, and they sent him
on his way, with his wife and everything he had.

[13:1]So Abram went up from Egypt to the Negev, with his wife and
everything he had, and Lot went with him. [2]Abram had become very
wealthy in livestock and in silver and gold.

[3]From the Negev he went from place to place until he came to Bethel,
to the place between Bethel and Ai where his tent had been earlier [4]and
where he had first built an altar. There Abram called on the name of the
LORD.

12:10–13:4 Verse 10 opens a new episode with a notice that a famine forced Abraham to seek refuge in Egypt. Almost as if to justify Abraham's somewhat incongruous journey to Egypt, it is emphasized at the end of the verse that the "famine was severe." The narrative continues to 13:4 where we are returned to our point of departure, with Abraham worshiping God at the altar that he had built between Bethel and Ai.

A recurring theme can be traced throughout the subsequent narratives in Genesis, one that is first noted in the present story. That theme is the threat to God's promise in 12:1–3 (Westermann). In nearly every episode that follows, the promise of a "numerous seed," "blessing to all peoples on earth," or the "gift of the land" is placed in jeopardy by the actions of the characters of the narrative. The promise looks as if it will fail. In the face of such a threat, however, the narratives show that God always remains faithful to his word and that he himself enters the arena and safeguards the promise. The purpose of such a recurring narrative theme is to show that only God can bring about his promise. Man's failure cannot stand in the way of God's promise.

The account of Abraham's "sojourn" in Egypt bears the stamp of having been intentionally shaped to parallel the later account of God's deliverance of Israel from Egypt (Gen 41–Exod 12). Both passages have a similar message as well. Thus here, at the beginning of the narratives dealing with Abraham and his seed, we find an anticipation of the events that will occur at the end. As with other sections of the book, the parallels are striking:

	Abraham		*Joseph*
12:10	- There was a famine in the land	41:54b	- There was a famine in all the lands
12:11	- When he drew near to go into Egypt . . .	46:28	- When they came toward the land of Goshen . . .
12:11	- He said to Sarai his wife	46:31	- Joseph said to his brothers . . .
12:11	- I know that . . .	46:31	- I will go up and say to Pharaoh . . .
12:12	- And it shall come to pass when the Egyptians see you, they will say . . .	46:33	- And it shall come to pass when Pharaoh calls you, he will say . . .
12:13	- Say . . .	46:34a	- Say . . .
12:13	- That it might be well with me on account of you	46:34b	- That you might dwell in the land of Goshen
12:13	- And the officers of Pharaoh saw her and declared it to Pharaoh	47:1	- And Joseph came and declared to Pharaoh . . .
12:15	- And the wife was taken into the house of Pharaoh	47:5	- And Pharaoh said . . . "settle your father and brothers in the best part of the land."
12:15	- And Abraham acquired sheep and cattle . . .	47:6	- Put them in charge of my livestock.
		47:27	- They acquired property and were fruitful and increased greatly
12:17	- And the Lord struck Pharaoh with great plagues	Exod 11:1	- One more plague I will bring against Pharaoh

12:18	- And Pharaoh called to Abram and said	12:31	- And Pharaoh called to Moses and Aaron and said
12:19	- Take and go	12:32	- Take and go
12:20	- and sent them away	12:33	- to send them away
13:1	- And Abram went up from Egypt toward the Negev	12:37	- And the sons of Israel traveled from Rameses toward Succoth.
13:1	- And Lot went with him	12:38	- And also a great mixed multitude went with him
13:2	- And Abram was very rich with livestock, silver, and gold	12:38	- And they had very much livestock,
		12:35	- silver, and gold
13:4	- Returned to altar and worshiped God	12:4	- Passover

By shaping the account of Abraham's sojourn in Egypt to parallel the events of the Exodus, the author permits the reader to see the implications of God's past deeds with his chosen people. The past is not allowed to remain in the past. Its lessons are drawn for the future. Behind the pattern stands a faithful, loving God. What he has done with Abraham, he will do for his people today and tomorrow.

The whole of God's plan, from beginning to end, is thus contained within the scope of this simple story. It is in light of such parallels as these that we should also understand the close similarity between the account of Abraham's sojourn in Egypt in chapter 12, the account of his sojourn in Gerar in chapter 20, and the account of Isaac's sojourn in Gerar in chapter 26. The similarities between these texts have long been recognized, though not always appreciated. We must avoid two extremes. We cannot be content to reduce the importance of the similarities to evidence of a "common tradition." Nor is it enough to attribute the similarities to mere coincidence. It is more likely that the similarities are intentional and part of the larger scheme of "parallels" found throughout the Pentateuch.

For example, within the Joseph narratives there are "sets" of parallel dreams recounted with marked similarities. Though different in their details, each "set" of dreams is about the same thing (37:5–7, 9; 40:5–19; 41:17–21, 22–24). In his interpretation of the Pharaoh's dreams, Joseph voiced the meaning not only lying behind the repetition of the dreams but, apparently, also to all the repetitions and parallels within the Pentateuch as well: "The reason the dream was given to Pharaoh in two forms is that the matter has been firmly decided by God, and God will do it soon" (41:32). The reason there are repetitions and recursions of similar narratives throughout the Pentateuch is to show that the matter has been firmly decided by God and that God will act quickly to bring about his promise.

Notes

1 The position of וְלוֹט עִמּוֹ (*welôṭ ʿimmô*, "and Lot went with him"), which is a nominal clause, between the preceding clause and the adverbial הַנֶּגְבָּה (*hannegḇāh*, "to the Negev") is unusual and shows that the narrative is explicitly setting Lot apart from the family and

household of Abraham. The preceding narrative of Abraham's sojourn in Egypt was silent regarding Lot; so it was necessary here to reinstate him into the narrative. The Samaritan Pentateuch and the LXX have *w^elôṭ ʿimmô* already in 12:20, which appears to be an assimilation to 13:1. The expression in v.14—אַחֲרֵי הִפָּרֶד־לוֹט מֵעִמּוֹ (*'aḥ^arê hippāreḏ-lôṭ mēʿimmô*, "after Lot had parted from him")—presupposes the presence of *w^elôṭ ʿimmô* in v.1.

D. *The Lot Narratives (13:5–19:38)*

1. *Abraham and Lot*

13:5–18

5 Now Lot, who was moving about with Abram, also had flocks and herds and tents. 6 But the land could not support them while they stayed together, for their possessions were so great that they were not able to stay together. 7 And quarreling arose between Abram's herdsmen and the herdsmen of Lot. The Canaanites and Perizzites were also living in the land at that time.

8 So Abram said to Lot, "Let's not have any quarreling between you and me, or between your herdsmen and mine, for we are brothers. 9 Is not the whole land before you? Let's part company. If you go to the left, I'll go to the right; if you go to the right, I'll go to the left."

10 Lot looked up and saw that the whole plain of the Jordan was well watered, like the garden of the LORD, like the land of Egypt, toward Zoar. (This was before the LORD destroyed Sodom and Gomorrah.) 11 So Lot chose for himself the whole plain of the Jordan and set out toward the east. The two men parted company: 12 Abram lived in the land of Canaan, while Lot lived among the cities of the plain and pitched his tents near Sodom. 13 Now the men of Sodom were wicked and were sinning greatly against the LORD.

14 The LORD said to Abram after Lot had parted from him, "Lift up your eyes from where you are and look north and south, east and west. 15 All the land that you see I will give to you and your offspring forever. 16 I will make your offspring like the dust of the earth, so that if anyone could count the dust, then your offspring could be counted. 17 Go, walk through the length and breadth of the land, for I am giving it to you."

18 So Abram moved his tents and went to live near the great trees of Mamre at Hebron, where he built an altar to the LORD.

5–18 A new section begins at 13:5, though its connections with the preceding section are clear. The narrative is governed by the theme of "struggle" and shaped around the "separation" (*pāraḏ*, vv.9, 11, 14) that results from the struggle. At its conclusion stands the second statement of the "promise" (vv.14–17). Just as the first statement of the "promise" was preceded by Abraham's separation from among the nations (*pāraḏ*, 10:32) and his father's house (12:1), so the second statement of the "promise" is put in the context of Abraham's separation (*pāraḏ*) from his closest kin, Lot (13:14). It is not without purpose that the final statement of the "promise" to Abraham comes immediately after he has demonstrated his willingness to be separated from his only son and heir, Isaac (22:15–18).

Abraham's separation from Lot also carries on the theme of the "promise in jeopardy." As the story reads, Abraham is on the verge of giving the Promised Land to Lot ("If you go to the left, I'll go to the right; if you go to the right, I'll go to the left," v.9). What is particularly striking about Abraham's offer is that in the subsequent narrative (19:37–38) Lot is shown to be the father of the Ammonites and the Moabites. Abraham is about to hand the Promised Land over to the same people who, in the author's own day (e.g., Num 22–25) and throughout Israel's subsequent history (Deut 23:3–6; Ezra 9:1), were the primary obstacle to the fulfillment of the promise. Thanks to Abraham the promise seems to teeter on the whim of the father of the Moabites. But, as the narrative shows, Lot "chose" (*wayyibḥar*) to go "east" (*miqqeḏem*, v.11); so Abraham remained in the land (v.12). Thus God's promise was secure, in spite of Abraham's passivity.

Even the plans of the nations are shown to fit into the will of God for his people. Nothing can stand in the way of God's promise to Abraham. The same viewpoint that is reflected in this narrative is found in the later prophetic literature. In Isaiah 45 the prophet describes the rise of the Persian king Cyrus as the work of God's own hand. All of Cyrus's plans and military campaigns had only one purpose, according to Isaiah. That purpose was that God's people Israel might return and dwell safely in the Promised Land: "He will rebuild my city and set my exiles free" (Isa 45:13).

The author provides the reader with a subtle foreshadowing of the fatal results of Lot's choice. The land he chose was "like the garden of the LORD" and "like the land of Egypt" (v.10), a positive description within the context of Genesis. But the author then adds that the land chosen by Lot is found in the area "toward Zoar." As the subsequent narrative will show, Zoar was the city where Lot had to flee for safety from the destruction of Sodom and Gomorrah (19:22). Already in Lot's choice of a land "to the east" that was "like the garden of the LORD," we can see anticipated in the reference to "Zoar" the final outcome of that choice.

Definite ties can be seen within this narrative connecting Lot's "separation" (*pāraḏ*) to the "separation" (*pāraḏ*, 10:32) of the nations at Babylon (11:1–9) and the judgment of the nations at Sodom (19:1–29). The ties between chapter 13 and the destruction of Sodom (ch. 19) can be seen in v.10b—"before the LORD destroyed Sodom and Gomorrah"—and vv.12b–13: "And Lot lived among the cities of the plain and pitched his tents near Sodom. Now the men of Sodom were wicked and were sinning greatly against the LORD." This is the same information restated at the beginning of chapter 19. The ties between chapter 13 and the account of the destruction of Babylon stem from the fact that Lot's separation from Abraham and journey eastward appears to have been consciously shaped by the account of the Fall of Babylon.

In 10:32 the author closes the account of the dispersion of the nations with the following statement: "From these the nations spread out [*pāraḏ*; i.e., 'separated'] over the earth after the flood." Then the narrative of the dispersion of Babylon opens with the account of the people of the land "traveling eastward" (*nāsaʿ miqqeḏem*) into "the plain [*biqʿāh*] in Shinar" where they set out to build the city of Babylon (11:1–2). In the same way Lot is said to have "traveled eastward" (*nāsaʿ miqqeḏem*, 13:11) from the land into "the cities of the plain" (*kikkar*) of the Jordan when he "parted" (*pāraḏ*) from Abraham.

Following the "separation" of the nations at Babylon, the narrative resumes with Abraham traveling throughout the land of Canaan, receiving it as a promise, and then building an altar in response to God's promise (12:1–9). So also, after Lot "separated" to Sodom, Abraham traveled throughout the land of Canaan, received it a second time as a promise, and built an altar in response (vv.14–18).

Lot, then, is the link connecting the author's treatment of the two cities, Babylon and Sodom. The close parallels between the two that are created in the narrative of chapter 13 suggest that the author intended both cities to tell the same story. As in the case of parallels and repetitions throughout the book, the double account of God's destruction of the "city in the east" is intended to drive home the point that God's judgment of the wicked is certain and imminent (cf. 41:32).

2. *Abraham and the nations*

14:1–24

1At this time Amraphel king of Shinar, Arioch king of Ellasar,
Kedorlaomer king of Elam and Tidal king of Goiim 2went to war against
Bera king of Sodom, Birsha king of Gomorrah, Shinab king of Admah,
Shemeber king of Zeboiim, and the king of Bela (that is, Zoar). 3All these
latter kings joined forces in the Valley of Siddim (the Salt Sea). 4For
twelve years they had been subject to Kedorlaomer, but in the thirteenth
year they rebelled.
5In the fourteenth year, Kedorlaomer and the kings allied with him
went out and defeated the Rephaites in Ashteroth Karnaim, the Zuzites
in Ham, the Emites in Shaveh Kiriathaim 6and the Horites in the hill
country of Seir, as far as El Paran near the desert. 7Then they turned
back and went to En Mishpat (that is, Kadesh), and they conquered the
whole territory of the Amalekites, as well as the Amorites who were
living in Hazazon Tamar.
8Then the king of Sodom, the king of Gomorrah, the king of Admah,
the king of Zeboiim and the king of Bela (that is, Zoar) marched out and
drew up their battle lines in the Valley of Siddim 9against Kedorlaomer
king of Elam, Tidal king of Goiim, Amraphel king of Shinar and Arioch
king of Ellasar—four kings against five. 10Now the Valley of Siddim was
full of tar pits, and when the kings of Sodom and Gomorrah fled, some
of the men fell into them and the rest fled to the hills. 11The four kings
seized all the goods of Sodom and Gomorrah and all their food; then
they went away. 12They also carried off Abram's nephew Lot and his
possessions, since he was living in Sodom.
13One who had escaped came and reported this to Abram the Hebrew.
Now Abram was living near the great trees of Mamre the Amorite, a
brother of Eshcol and Aner, all of whom were allied with Abram. 14When
Abram heard that his relative had been taken captive, he called out the
318 trained men born in his household and went in pursuit as far as Dan.
15During the night Abram divided his men to attack them and he routed
them, pursuing them as far as Hobah, north of Damascus. 16He
recovered all the goods and brought back his relative Lot and his
possessions, together with the women and the other people.
17After Abram returned from defeating Kedorlaomer and the kings
allied with him, the king of Sodom came out to meet him in the Valley of
Shaveh (that is, the King's Valley).
18Then Melchizedek king of Salem brought out bread and wine. He
was priest of God Most High, 19and he blessed Abram, saying,

"Blessed be Abram by God Most High,
  Creator of heaven and earth.
20And blessed be God Most High,
  who delivered your enemies into your hand."

Then Abram gave him a tenth of everything.
21The king of Sodom said to Abram, "Give me the people and keep
the goods for yourself."
22But Abram said to the king of Sodom, "I have raised my hand to the
LORD, God Most High, Creator of heaven and earth, and have taken an
oath 23that I will accept nothing belonging to you, not even a thread or

the thong of a sandal, so that you will never be able to say, 'I made Abram rich.' [24] I will accept nothing but what my men have eaten and the share that belongs to the men who went with me—to Aner, Eshcol and Mamre. Let them have their share."

1–11 At first glance the ties between chapters 13 and 14 seem meager. With respect to both the time and the place, the two narratives seem only distantly related. Somewhat abruptly the narrative begins in the time frame marked as "In the days of Amraphel" (v.1; NIV, "At this time Amraphel"), with no point of reference to the time of the preceding chapter. Just as abruptly the location of the narrative moves from Abraham's tent in Hebron (13:18) to that of an event of international importance, the wars of the four kings (14:1–11). There are several indications within the narrative, however, that suggest the author intended chapter 14 to be read closely with what has preceded. In 14:12 the focus of the account of the war between nations is quickly reduced to the scope of chapter 13 by recounting that Lot had been captured along with the sack of Sodom. Immediately following the report of Lot's capture, the narrative returns to the scene of 13:18, with Abraham dwelling at the "great trees of Mamre" in Hebron (14:13b). At that point Abraham is brought into the center of the account of the battle with the four kings and, somewhat surprisingly, is capable of marshalling his forces to defeat the kings (vv.14–17). With the mention of "Mamre" at the end of the account (v.24), the reader is returned to the scene at the close of chapter 13.

In putting these two narratives together in this way, the author has allowed an event of international importance to sweep past Abraham's tent in Hebron and thus to involve Abraham in an event that will show on an enormous scale the implications of Abraham's faith—yet without losing its simple and "everyday" character. "Yahweh" (i.e., the LORD), the God Abraham worshiped at his altar in Hebron (13:18), is the "Creator of heaven and earth" (14:22) who delivers the four kings of the east into Abraham's hands. Abraham, who asks nothing and wants nothing from the kings of this world (vv.22–23), is the only one who proves able to dwell peacefully in the land. As 12:3 has forecast, those who join with Abraham (v.13b) will enjoy his blessing (v.24b); but those who separate from him, as Lot had done (13:12), will suffer the same fate as Sodom and Gomorrah (14:11–12).

Another feature of the composition of chapter 14 shows clearly the author's intent to link this chapter with the themes of the preceding narratives. At the outset of the account of the war of the four kings, the reader is reminded that the events of chapter 14 "happened in the days of Amraphel, king of Shinar" (lit. tr.). Shinar has already been clearly and consciously identified by the author as Babylon (10:10; 11:2, 9). The author appears to have deliberately arranged the opening of this narrative so that the king of Shinar's name would come first, thus aligning the narrative with the theme of "Babylon" introduced in chapters 10 (v.10) and 11 (v.2). The intention of the author can be seen in the fact that he has deliberately put the king of Shinar's name first in the narrative. This can be seen from the fact that the list of kings in v.1 is different than the lists of the names of these four kings throughout the remainder of the chapter. Whereas in v.1 Amraphel, king of Shinar, comes first in the list, throughout the chapter Kedorlaomer, king of Elam, is first among the four kings (vv.4, 5, 9, 17). In v.9 where the list of the kings is given, Kedorlaomer begins the list and Amraphel is third, but in v.1 Amraphel is first and Kedorlaomer is third. When the sequence of the names in both lists is compared, it can be seen that Kedorlaomer is followed by Tidal in the lists, and Amraphel is followed by Arioch; thus the break in the sequence of the names comes only at Amraphel's name.

14:9 Kedorlaomer, Tidal,	Amraphel, Arioch
14:1 Amraphel, Arioch,	Kedorlaomer, Tidal

If the sequence in v.9 is the original one, as is suggested by the fact that elsewhere in the lists Kedorlaomer is always first (as simply "Kedorlaomer, " v.4, or "Kedorlaomer and the kings allied with him," vv.5, 17), then at the beginning of the narrative the author has apparently broken the list into two sections, putting the section beginning with Amraphel first and the other section second.

What immediately strikes the reader in this account of the conquest of Canaan by the four kings is that very little information is given about the actual battles while the account is overladen with geographical and political details. The author is apparently more interested in the geographical extent of the warfare than in the actual course of the battles. What emerges as certain from this feature of the narrative is that the events recounted were global in scope and ended in the disgraceful defeat of the kings of Sodom and Gomorrah. The kings were completely routed (vv.10–11).

12 At this point in the account, the perspective of the narrative changes markedly. The reader's field of vision is directed from the global scope of the war with the four eastern kings to the sudden change in the fate of Lot. Lot, who departed from Abraham to pitch his tent in Sodom, was taken captive along with the possessions of Sodom and Gomorrah. In the midst of the harried description of the deteriorating course of events, the reader is reminded of the ultimate cause of Lot's unfortunate fate: "he was living in Sodom." Thus again the narrative is brought into the larger context of the blessing in the land (12:1–3; 13:14–17) and the fate of all those who separate themselves from Abraham.

Lot's fate is a lesson, or, rather, the first stage in a lesson, that will bring him still further in need of the intercession of Abraham (18:23–32). Twice, by means of Abraham, Lot's welfare is restored: first here in the war with Babylon and then later (chs. 18–19) in the destruction of Sodom. Here Abraham and his band of 318 men rescued Lot. Later it was Abraham's intercession (18:23–32; 19:29) that effected Lot's rescue. The picture of Abraham that emerges from these narratives is the same as that given voice in 20:7: "he is a prophet, and he will pray for you and you will live."

13–16 The focus of the narrative returns to the scene at the close of chapter 13. Abraham was dwelling with his three friends at Hebron, strangely unaffected by the events recorded in the previous narrative. In this brief scene, strikingly similar to Job 1:17, Abraham was able to muster a select army, defeat the four kings, and return Lot with the rest of the captives.

17–20 After his return from battle, Abraham was met by two kings in the "Valley of Shaveh" (lit., "the King"). It has been suggested that the present shape of this narrative is disheveled and in disarray owing to the insertion of the section on Melchizedek (vv.18–20). It appears to have been inserted into the section dealing with the king of Sodom. It is true that Melchizedek appears in the narrative as if out of nowhere and just as quickly is gone, not to be encountered again nor subsequently explained. But the structure of the narrative is not unusual. (The Hebrew construction is a chiastic coordination with the WAYYIQTOL [*wayyēṣē'*] of *yāṣā'* [v.17] followed by the QATAL [*hôṣî'*] of *yāṣā'* [v.18] and the word order of predicate-subject [v.17] followed by subject-predicate [v.18]; cf. Andersen, *Sentence in Biblical Hebrew*, pp. 123ff.) The insertion of the encounter with Melchizedek (vv.18–20) into the section dealing with the king of Sodom is done in such a way as to suggest that it is to be read as the background to the encounter with the king of Sodom (the pattern W + X + QATAL, when it precedes the main clause, e.g., WAYYIQTOL, depicts background; cf. Gross, *Syntaktische*, pp. 131–45). Thus a contrast is established between Abraham's response to the king of Salem and his response to the king of Sodom. The response to the one is positive, but to the other it is negative.

Lying behind Abraham's response to both kings is the contrast between the offer of the king of Salem and that of the king of Sodom. The king of Salem brings "bread and wine" as a priestly act (v.18) and acknowledges that it was the "God Most High, Creator of heaven and earth," who delivered the adversaries into Abraham's hand (v.19). In other words, the perspective of the king of Salem is precisely that of the author of the Pentateuch himself who has also acknowledged at the start of his work that the God who delivered Israel from the hand of the Egyptians (Exod 20:2) is the Creator of heaven and earth (Gen 1:1). Abraham's response to the king of Salem, then, is an appropriate recognition of the validity of Melchizedek's offer as well as his priesthood: Abraham paid a tithe (v.20; see Num 18:21).

21–24 The offer of the king of Sodom, on the other hand, was quite different. He offered to give Abraham all the "goods" (*hārekuš*) recovered in the battle (v.21). Abraham's response shows how the author viewed this gesture. Abraham would have nothing to do with an offer of reward from the king of Sodom. As his solemn speech at the close of the narrative shows, Abraham's reward would not come from the kings of this world but from Yahweh, "the LORD, the Creator of heaven and earth" (v.22). Any "goods" or "possessions" he was to have would come from the LORD, as the following chapter sets out to show (e.g., 15:1, 14b).

In a number of points, the events of chapter 14 reflect the same concerns of Deuteronomy 20:1–15, the instructions concerning carrying out wars with foreign nations. Abraham's actions are described in ways reminiscent of the conduct of warfare against "cities that are at a distance from you and do not belong to the nations nearby" (Deut 20:15). Abraham did not hesitate to go into battle with an army greater than his (cf. Deut 20:1). Thus the author informs us that Abraham took with him only 318 men, a number that brings to mind Gideon's 300 men in Judges 7:6. Abraham went into battle specifically with only the "trained men born in his household" (v.14). The Hebrew expression used here for "trained" (*hanîkāyw*) is not found elsewhere in the Bible; nor is its meaning clear within the context of ancient history and customs. The use of the word here, however, provides another link with Deuteronomy 20:5 where it is said that one who goes into battle should be only one who has already "dedicated" (*ḥānak*) his house. Since within the Pentateuch the verb *ḥānak* occurs only in this passage of Deuteronomy, a link between the two texts seems likely.

Though he rejected the offer of a reward from the king of Sodom, Abraham laid claim to rightfully own that which his young men had eaten (*'ākelû*, v.24). In Deuteronomy 20:14b it is explicitly said that those who go into war with nations afar off may "eat" (*we'ākaltā;* NIV, "use"; viz., to "devour," i.e., "to confiscate [for themselves]") of the spoils taken in battle. Abraham also recognized that his three friends had their own rightful share in the spoil (v.24), which corresponds to the provisions of Deuteronomy 20:14. On the other hand, the offer to take from the possessions of the king of Sodom was flatly rejected by Abraham (v.23), as was prescribed in Deuteronomy 20:17 for the spoils of those nations who live within the boundaries of the land of inheritance.

Along these same lines it is to be noted that in Deuteronomy 20:2 the "priest" (*hakkōhēn*) was assigned the role of reminding the people that "the LORD your God is the one who goes with you to fight for you against your enemies to give you victory" (Deut 20:4; cf. v.13: "When the LORD your God delivers it into you hand" [*b*^{e}*yāḏeḵā*]). In much the same way, Abraham was met by Melchizedek, a "priest" (*kōhēn*, v.18) of the Most High God, who proclaimed to him that it was the "God Most High, who delivered your enemies into your hand" (*b*^{e}*yāḏeḵā*, v.20).

In light of such similarities it appears that the author had intended to show that Abraham lived a life in harmony with God's will even though he lived long before the revelation at Sinai. Abraham was one who pictured God's Law written on his heart. He obeyed the Law, though the law had not yet been given. Such an understanding of the life of Abraham is not foreign to the author of Genesis. Indeed, one of the last statements made about Abraham in the Book of Genesis is that he kept God's "commands [*miṣwōṯay*], . . . decrees [*ḥuqqôṯay*] and . . . laws [*tôrōṯāy*]" (26:5). These terms are well-known from the pages of Deuteronomy (e.g., 11:1; 26:17), where they are the stock vocabulary for describing the keeping of the Torah revealed at Sinai. The author's point appears to have been to show that Abraham, as a man of faith, "kept the law." He did not have the law written out before him; nevertheless he kept it. In this respect the picture of Abraham that emerges from chapters 14 and 26 is much like that of the "new covenant" promise in Jeremiah 31:33, in which God has promised to write the Torah on the heart of his covenant people so that they will obey it from the heart. It is the picture of Abraham that later emerges as the central figure in the NT writers' portrayal of life under the new covenant (e.g., Rom 4; Gal 3).

Notes

1 The syntax of v.1 is difficult. As it stands אַמְרָפֶל מֶלֶךְ־שִׁנְעָר (*'amrāp̱el meleḵ-šin'ār*, "Amraphel king of Shinar") is the genitive of בִּימֵי (*bîmê*, "At this time") following וַיְהִי (*wayhî*, lit., "and he was"; NIV, untr.), a clause type not uncommon in Genesis: "And it came about in the days of Amraphel" (cf. 8:13a1; 12:11a1; 15:17a1; 24:15a1, 22a1, 52a1, 26:8a1; 27:1a1, 30a1 [bis], 30a3; 29:10a1; 30:25a1; 37:23a1; 39:5a1; 43:2a1). The problem, however, is what to do with the remainder of the verse—the names of the other three kings. It would appear that they simply follow *'amrāp̱el*: "And it came about in the days of Amraphel king of Shinar, Arioch. . . ." If that is the case, however, then we are left without a subject for the following clause—עָשׂוּ מִלְחָמָה (*'āśû milḥāmāh*, "went to war")—in v.2 (cf. RSV, "These kings made war"). Examples of such clause types (0 + QATAL + X) are rare in the narrative of Genesis (18:11b1; 21:14a4; 48:14b1). The early versions (e.g., LXX: "And it came about during the Amraphite reign of the king of Shinar, Arioch, the king of Ellasar and Kedorlaomer, the king of Elam . . . made war with"; the Vul.: "*factum est autem in illo tempore, ut Amrafel . . . inirent bellum*") show that the difficulty has long been felt.

Syntactically, the LXX offers the best reading of the Hebrew text as it stands, in that it separates Amraphel from the names of the other kings. In the present shape of the narrative, it was evidently important that the events of this chapter be read in the context of the rule of the "king of Shinar." The Genesis Apocryphon from Qumran has כְּדָרְלָעֹמֶר מֶלֶךְ עֵילָם

(*keḏorlā'ōmer meleḵ 'êlām*, "Kedorlaomer king of Elam") first and then *'amrāp̱el*, and in this follows the Book of Jubilees. It appears to be merely an adjustment of the opening list to conform to the remaining lists where Kedorlaomer is first (J.A. Fitzmyer, *The Genesis Apocryphon of Qumran Cave 1, A Commentary* [Rome: Biblical Institute, 1971], p. 159). In the Palestinian targums, *šin'ār* is identified as Babylon in accordance with Gen 10:10 and 11:1–9, and *'amrāp̱el* is Nimrod.

2–11 The numerous explanations throughout this short narrative—הִיא־צֹעַר (*hî'-ṣō'ar*, "that is, Zoar," v.2), הוּא יָם הַמֶּלַח (*hû' yām hammelaḥ*, "the Salt Sea," v.3), אֲשֶׁר עַל־הַמִּדְבָּר (*'ašer 'al-hammiḏbār*, "near the desert," v.6), הִוא קָדֵשׁ (*hiw' qāḏēš*, "that is, Kadesh," v.7), הַיֹּשֵׁב בְּחַצְצֹן תָּמָר (*hayyōšēḇ beḥaṣeṣōn tāmār*, "who were living in Hazezon Tamar," v.7b)—suggest that at the time of the composition of Genesis, this account already contained many obscure—or at least not readily identifiable—elements. However, the fact that בֶּלַע (*bela'*, "Bela") is twice identified as *ṣō'ar* (vv.2, 8), whereas עֵמֶק הַשִּׂדִּים (*'ēmeq haśśiddîm*, "the Valley of Siddim") is identified only once (v.3), though it is mentioned three times (vv.3, 8, 10), also suggests that the added information was not always merely to fill a lack of knowledge but also sought to draw a clear connection between the events of this chapter and those of later narratives. In chapter 19 *ṣō'ar* is again important (19:22), whereas *'ēmeq haśśiddîm* plays no further role outside of chapter 14.

10 Notice the chiastic coordination: וַיָּנֻסוּ . . . נָסוּ (*wayyānusû . . . nāsû*, "when [they] fled . . . [they] fled") (see Andersen, *Sentence in Biblical Hebrew*, p. 123). Chiastic coordination, like its appositional counterpart epic repetition, slows a narrative at its close.

11–12 The similarities between v.11 and v.12 suggest the presence of the technique of "*Wiederaufnahme*" ("resumption") (Fishbane, *Biblical Interpretation*, p. 85):

11: וַיִּקְחוּ[1] אֶת־כָּל־רְכֻשׁ . . . וַיֵּלֵכוּ

12: וַיִּקְחוּ[2] אֶת־לוֹט וְאֶת־רְכֻשׁוֹ . . . וַיֵּלֵכוּ

Its use here is to link the two narratives together into a whole story.

The fact that the identification of Lot as בֶּן־אֲחִי אַבְרָם (*ben-'aḥî 'aḇrām*, lit., "the son of the brother of Abram"; NIV, "Abram's nephew Lot") is placed after רְכֻשׁוֹ (*reḵušô*, "possessions") rather than after לוֹט (*lôṭ*, "Lot"), where we might have expected it, appears to be an attempt to ensure that the third person pronoun with *reḵušô* was not understood as referring to Abram. The narrative wishes to give no grounds for the proposal of the king of Sodom later in the narrative: "keep the goods [*hāreḵuš*] for yourself" (v.21). The *reḵušô* belonged to Lot, not Abraham.

13–24 There are numerous verbal links between chapters 14 and 15:

14:13: הָאֱמֹרִי[3]	15:16, 21: הָאֱמֹרִי[3]
14:13b: בְּרִית[4]	15:18a: בְּרִית[4]
14:14b: 318 men	15:2b: אֱלִיעֶזֶר[5] = 318
14:14c: דָּן[6]	15:14a: דָּן[6]
14:15: דַּמָּשֶׂק[7]	15:2b: דַּמֶּשֶׂק[8]
14:16a: הָרְכֻשׁ[9]	15:14b: בִּרְכֻשׁ[10]
14:18a: צֶדֶק[11]	15:6b: צְדָקָה[12]
14:18a: שָׁלֵם[13]	15:15a: בְּשָׁלוֹם,[14] 16b: שָׁלֵם[15]
14:19b, 22b: שָׁמַיִם[16]	15:5a: הַשָּׁמַיְמָה[17]
14:20a: מִגֵּן[18]	15:1b: מָגֵן[19]
14:21: הָרְכֻשׁ[9]	15:1b: שְׂכָרְךָ[20] (רכשׁ reverses שׂכר)

[1](*wayyiqḥû 'eṯ-kol-reḵuš . . . wayyēlēḵû*, "seized all the goods . . . then they went away").

[2](*wayyiqḥû 'eṯ-lôṭ we'eṯ-reḵušô . . . wayyēlēḵû*, "They also carried off Lot . . . and his possessions . . . and they left [untr. NIV]").

[3](*hā'emōrî*, "the Amorite").

[4](*berîṯ*, "were allied/[made] a covenant").

[5](*'elî'ezer*, "Eliezer") (= 318: ר [*r*] = 200, ז [*z*] = 7, ע ['] = 70, י [*y*] = 10, ל [*l*] = 30, א [']= 1).

[6](*dān*, "Dan/will punish").

[7](*dammāśeq*, "Damascus").

[8](*dammeśeq*, “Damascus”).
[9](*hār^{e}ḵuš*, “the goods”).
[10](*birḵuš*, “with . . . possessions”).
[11](*ṣeḏeq*, “[Melchi]zedek”).
[12](*ṣ^{e}ḏāqāh*, “righteousness”).
[13](*šālēm*, “Salem”).
[14](*b^{e}šālôm*, “in peace”).
[15](*šālēm*, “full”).
[16](*šāmayim*, “heaven”).
[17](*haššāmay^{e}māh*, “at the heavens”).
[18](*miggēn*, “delivered”).
[19](*māg̱ēn*, “shield”).
[20](*ś^{e}ḵā̄r^{e}ḵā*, “your . . . reward”).

---

3. *Abraham and the covenant*

15:1–21

1 After this, the word of the LORD came to Abram in a vision:

“Do not be afraid, Abram.
I am your shield,
your very great reward.”

2 But Abram said, “O Sovereign LORD, what can you give me since I
remain childless and the one who will inherit my estate is Eliezer of
Damascus?” 3 And Abram said, “You have given me no children; so a
servant in my household will be my heir.”
4 Then the word of the LORD came to him: “This man will not be your
heir, but a son coming from your own body will be your heir.” 5 He took
him outside and said, “Look up at the heavens and count the stars—if
indeed you can count them.” Then he said to him, “So shall your
offspring be.”
6 Abram believed the LORD, and he credited it to him as righteousness.
7 He also said to him, “I am the LORD, who brought you out of Ur of the
Chaldeans to give you this land to take possession of it.”
8 But Abram said, “O Sovereign LORD, how can I know that I will gain
possession of it?”
9 So the LORD said to him, “Bring me a heifer, a goat and a ram, each
three years old, along with a dove and a young pigeon.”
10 Abram brought all these to him, cut them in two and arranged the
halves opposite each other; the birds, however, he did not cut in half.
11 Then birds of prey came down on the carcasses, but Abram drove
them away.
12 As the sun was setting, Abram fell into a deep sleep, and a thick and
dreadful darkness came over him. 13 Then the LORD said to him, “Know
for certain that your descendants will be strangers in a country not their
own, and they will be enslaved and mistreated four hundred years. 14 But
I will punish the nation they serve as slaves, and afterward they will
come out with great possessions. 15 You, however, will go to your
fathers in peace and be buried at a good old age. 16 In the fourth
generation your descendants will come back here, for the sin of the
Amorites has not yet reached its full measure.”
17 When the sun had set and darkness had fallen, a smoking firepot
with a blazing torch appeared and passed between the pieces. 18 On that
day the LORD made a covenant with Abram and said, “To your
descendants I give this land, from the river of Egypt to the great river,
the Euphrates— 19 the land of the Kenites, Kenizzites, Kadmonites,

[20]Hittites, Perizzites, Rephaites, [21]Amorites, Canaanites, Girgashites and Jebusites."

1–4 Later on Abraham is explicitly called a "prophet" (*nāḇî'*, 20:7). In chapter 15 the author goes to great lengths to cast him in that role. The central subject of the chapter deals with the announcement of events that lie far in the future (vv.13–16), and thus it is of utmost importance to the author that Abraham's credentials as a prophet be clearly set forth and defended. As is characteristic of the later prophetic literature, God's address to Abraham is introduced in an elevated style typical of the later prophetic literature: "the word of the LORD came to Abram" (vv.1, 4; cf. Jer 34:12). To this is added the fact that, like the seer Balaam (Num 24:4, 16), Abraham saw the word of the Lord "in a vision" (*bammaḥᵃzeh*). The word *maḥᵃzeh* occurs only here and in Numbers 24 (the prophecies of Balaam) in the Pentateuch.

Such an introduction to the events of this chapter is intended to show that the events recorded in chapter 15 are, in fact, those that Abraham saw in the vision (Jacob, in loc.). Thus like prophetic visions elsewhere in Scripture, there may be more than a little symbolic value to the events. This is especially likely to be true of the visual display that Abraham saw in v.17.

It may also be of significance to notice that here, *for the first time*, it is recorded that Abraham spoke to God. Up to this point in the narrative of Genesis, when God spoke to him, Abraham obeyed but did not speak to God in return. Abraham, in fact, spoke to God only on rare occasions (vv.2–3, 8; 17:18; 18:23–33; 22:11). In the vision of chapter 15, however, Abraham not only replied to God's promise but raised a question of how the promise would be fulfilled. In fact, Abraham raised so many questions in this chapter that the author seems compelled to remind the reader of his unwavering faith (v.6).

Abraham's questions, however, provide the necessary backdrop for the central issue of the chapter: God's apparent delay in fulfilling his promises. The issue at stake in this chapter is the same as that faced by the prophet Jeremiah in his own day. God's people, who should have been enjoying the promised blessing, instead find themselves about to enter captivity in Babylon. The promise appears to have come to naught: "This whole country will become a desolate wasteland, and these nations will serve [*'āḇᵉḏû*] the king of Babylon seventy years" (Jer 25:11). But in Jeremiah's warning of impending judgment, there is, as well, the promise of ultimate blessing. The time of exile in a foreign land has a limit: "When the seventy years are fulfilled," the Lord told Jeremiah, "I will punish the king of Babylon and his nation, the land of the Babylonians [NIV mg., 'Chaldeans'], for their guilt" (Jer 25:12). Thus the faithful in exile can, like Daniel (9:2), wait in hope that in spite of the present affliction in Babylon, God would remain faithful to his promise: "I, Daniel, understood from the Scriptures, according to the word of the LORD given to Jeremiah [*hāyāh ḏᵉḇar-yhwh 'el-yirmiyāh*] the prophet, that the desolation of Jerusalem would last seventy years. So I turned to the Lord God and pleaded with him in prayer and petition, in fasting, and in sackcloth and ashes" (Dan 9:2–3).

The limit to God's judgment is set at seventy years. In much the same way, the present chapter of Genesis addresses an audience awaiting the fulfillment of the promises to the fathers but who can see no present evidence of the fulfillment. They are like those whom Isaiah calls on to "hope in the LORD" (Isa 40:31) and who Habakkuk says will ultimately "live" (*yiḥyeh*) through the present affliction only because they have been made "righteous by their faith" (cf. Hab 2:4).

As the author of Genesis 15 has shown, Abraham's predicament is not too far from that of later generations of God's people. Abraham too must wait in faith for the fulfillment of the promise, being counted righteous in his faith (v.6), but realizing that the promise was afar off to another generation (vv.15–16). "All these people were still living by faith when they died. They did not receive the things promised; they only saw them and welcomed them from a distance" (Heb 11:13). So the message to the reader is to stand fast. When people ask, "Where is this 'coming' he promised?" remember, "the Lord is not slow in keeping his promise, as some understand slowness. He is patient with you, not wanting any to perish, but everyone to come to repentance" (2 Peter 3:4, 9).

The statement "Do not be afraid. . . . I am your shield, your very great reward" (v.1b) raises a number of questions. What was Abraham afraid of? What "reward" (*śᵉḵārᵉḵā*) did God have in mind? Were the military events in chapter 14 still posing a threat to Abraham? Since chapter 15 opens by making a major break with the preceding chapter ("after this"; cf. 22:1; 39:7; 40:1), God's first words to Abraham are probably not to be understood within the immediate context of chapter 14. We are left, then, with the subject matter of chapter 15 itself to determine the sense of these first words to Abraham. From that perspective it becomes apparent that Abraham had begun to fear for the final outcome of God's promise to make his "offspring like the dust of the earth" in number (13:16).

The questions Abraham raised betray the fact that such a fear lay behind God's first words of comfort. Abraham asked, "What can you give me since I remain childless?" (v.2). Then he accused, "You have given me no children" (v.3). Finally, as he was again reminded that his "offspring" (v.5) would be greater than one could number and would inherit the Land of Promise, he asked, "How can I know that I will gain possession of it?" (v.8). Not only do his questions betray the fear that lay within him, but also the Lord's continued assurances point in the same direction: "A son coming from your own body will be your heir" (v.4). In the present shape of the narrative, then, Abraham is portrayed as one who has reason to fear that God's promises will not be fulfilled. From all appearances around about him, Abraham has little to give him hope that God will remain faithful to his word. Abraham was still childless, and all his possessions one day would be again in the hands of one from "Damascus" (v.2).

The mention of "Damascus" (v.2) apparently was intended to draw a connection to Abraham's victory near "Damascus" in chapter 14, tying the themes behind the events of chapter 15 to those of chapter 14. In this chapter it is shown that the fulfillment of God's promises lay not in the strength of "Damascus," where Abraham defeated the four kings, but in the "faith" (*he'ᵉmin,* v.6; NIV, "[Abram] believed") of his chosen "offspring." In much the same way, the prophet Isaiah warned the weakhearted of his day, "Don't be afraid ['*al-tîrā*']. . . . 'It will not take place, it will not happen, for the head of Aram is Damascus, and the head of Damascus is only Rezin. . . . If you do not stand firm in your faith [*ṯa'ᵃmînû*], you will not stand [*ṯē'āmēnû*] at all' " (Isa 7:4–9).

At the close of the narrative, Abraham was given a vision of the distant future. It was to be a source of comfort in the face of the apparent unfulfilled promises of God. The events in the vision fit precisely those that actually occurred to Abraham's seed—events that are recorded in Exodus 1–12. The importance of the vision lies not so much in the assurances it may have given Abraham in his own day but rather in the assurances it was to give the reader. The reader knows, from reading the rest of the Pentateuch, that the vision was to be fulfilled in the days of Moses. Thus, within the narrative of the Book of Genesis and the Pentateuch, the vision and its fulfillment confirm the prophetic words of Abraham. He was given a true vision. What he saw in the vision, did, in fact, come to pass and has been recorded within the Pentateuch itself. Thus for the readers who know that the vision is true, Abraham is shown to be a true prophet according to the test in Deuteronomy 18:22: "If what a prophet proclaims in the name of the LORD does not take place or come true, that is a message that the LORD has not spoken." Abraham, like Jeremiah after him (Jer 27–29), was a true prophet even though he spoke of exile and not blessing. But also like Jeremiah (chs. 30–31), Abraham's vision looked beyond the coming exile to the time when God would restore his people and "punish" (*dān*) their oppressors: "But I will punish the nation they serve as slaves, and afterward they will come out with great possessions" (15:14).

It is in light of this vision, then, that God's first words to Abraham in chapter 15 are to be understood. With these same words Jeremiah comforted those awaiting exile in his day: "Do not fear ['*al-tîrā*'], O Jacob my servant; do not be dismayed, O Israel. . . . I will surely save you out of a distant place, your descendants from the land of their exile" (Jer 30:10). It is significant that the next words Abraham spoke to the Lord are those in 17:18: "If only Ishmael might live under your blessing," spoken after he had said to himself in laughter, "Will a son be born to a man a hundred years old?" Throughout the Genesis narratives, when Abraham speaks he gives expression to questions that appear to reveal doubt. On the other hand, when, in the narratives, he is silent, his actions always exhibit faith.

5 The appeal to the number of the stars of "the heavens" harkens back to Abraham's own words in 14:22, where his hope for reward was based solely on the "Creator of heaven and earth." If Yahweh was the Creator of the great multitude of the stars in heaven, it follows that he was able to give Abraham an equal number of descendants ("offspring"). Thus God's faithfulness in the past was made the basis for Abraham's trust in the future.

The comparison of the number of Abraham's descendants to that of the stars of the heavens occurs several times in the Pentateuch: twice as the promise was reiterated to Isaac (22:17; 26:4), and then again by Moses at a crucial moment when God was on the verge of destroying the whole nation (Exod 32:13). In Deuteronomy 1:10 there is an allusion to this promise in reference to the great multitude that came out of Egypt; but as Deuteronomy 28:62 makes clear, the promise remained to be fulfilled in yet a future generation. It is possible that the image of the "star" that was to arise out of the house of Jacob in Numbers 24:17 owes its inspiration to this particular feature of the promise to the fathers.

6 The syntax of v.6 suggests that it is to be read as "background" information for the scene that unfolds in v.7. God was about to enter a "covenant" with Abraham that would lie at the base of all God's future dealings with him and his seed (vv.7–21). Verse 6 opens the scene by setting the record straight: Abraham had believed in Yahweh and had been accounted righteous. The "covenant" did not make him "righteous"; rather it was through his "faith" that he was reckoned righteous. Only after he had been counted righteous through his faith could Abraham enter into God's covenant. The precise location and use of the concept of "faith" here in chapter 15 is no more accidental than its use throughout the remainder of the Pentateuch. At key moments along the course of the book, the author returns to the notion of "faith" and points to it as the decisive factor in God's dealings with Abraham's descendants (e.g., Exod 4:5, 31; 14:31; 19:9; cf. H.-C. Schmitt, "Redaktion des Pentateuch im Geiste der Prophetie," VetTest 2 [1982]: 170ff.).

7–16 These verses, as v.18 shows, recount the establishment of a covenant (*b^e^rîṯ*) between the Lord and Abram. Thus it is fitting that in many respects the account should foreshadow the making of the covenant at Sinai. The opening statement "I am the LORD, who brought you out of Ur of the Chaldeans" (v.7) is virtually identical to the opening statement of the Sinai covenant (Exod 20:2): "I am the LORD your God, who brought you out of Egypt." The expression "Ur of the Chaldeans" is a reference back to 11:28 and 31, grounding the present covenant in a past act of divine salvation from "Babylon," just as Exodus 20:2 grounds the Sinai covenant in an act of divine salvation from Egypt. The coming of God's presence in the awesome fire and darkness of Mount Sinai (Exod 19:18; 20:18; Deut 4:11) appears to be intentionally foreshadowed in Abram's pyrotechnic vision (vv.12, 17). In the Lord's words to Abram (vv.13–16), the connection between Abram's covenant and the Sinai covenant is explicitly made by means of the reference to the four hundred years of bondage of Abram's descendants and their subsequent "exodus" ("and afterward they will come out [*yēṣ^e^'û*]," v.14).

17 The act of dividing the animals and walking through the parts was apparently an ancient form of contractual agreement. Very little is actually known of this custom from records of the ancient world, though commentators have frequently pointed to some possible parallels. Two notable such are Jeremiah 34:18—"The men who have violated my covenant and have not fulfilled the terms of the covenant they made before me, I will treat like the calf they cut in two and then walked between its pieces"—and a treaty between Ashurnirari V of Assyria and Mati'ilu of Arpad—"If Mati'ilu sins against (this) treaty made under oath by the gods, then, just as this spring lamb, brought from its fold, will not return to its fold, . . . alas, Mati'ilu . . . will not return to his country" (ANET, p. 532). In neither of these examples, however, is there an extended parallel, though the Jeremiah passage shows close similarity in terminology.

While the meaning of the details may remain a mystery to us, fortunately the writer of Genesis has explained the custom: "On that day the LORD made a covenant with Abram." The narrative is perhaps intentionally ambivalent about the meaning of the details since it is only the formal nature of the contract that it wishes to stress, and also because it may wish to avoid any notion of a self-imprecation on God's part. Wenham notes that the animals mentioned fall into the category of animals acceptable for sacrifice and thus interprets the events within the context of the OT rituals in Leviticus and later events in the Torah. The animals represent Israel or its priestly leaders. The birds of prey represent the nations that Abraham symbolically defends Israel against—perhaps Egypt and God's deliverance of Israel. God's walking through the parts represents his presence with his people (p. 332).

In support of such an interpretation of these events is the fact that they are explicitly reported as a "vision" at the beginning of the chapter, leading the reader to expect the possibility of symbolism. However, such a one-to-one correlation of the details of the narrative and specific future events does not find immediate support from within the narrative. What the narrative offers is merely a general adumbration of the events that lie yet in the future of the offspring of Abraham—an adumbration that is prefaced by a foreboding sense of darkness: "a thick and dreadful darkness came over him" (v.12).

The sudden and solitary image of the birds of prey that Abram must drive away (v.11) give a fleeting glimpse of the impending doom that awaits Abraham's seed, but in the same moment it points to the protective care of God's promises—"Then birds of prey came down upon the carcasses, and Abram drove them away." The imagery is remarkably similar to the words of Christ in Matthew 24:28: "Wherever there is a carcass, there the vultures will gather." In both contexts the imagery of the birds of prey surrounding the carcass is followed by a reference to the darkening of the sun (Gen 15:12; Matt 24:29) and the promise of future redemption (Gen 15:14; Matt 24:30). Perhaps the imagery of this passage provided the code for Matthew's portrayal of the "last days" (cf. Luke 17:37).

18–21 The author again draws the promise of the land back into the narrative by concluding with a description of the geographical boundaries of the covenant land. It has been pointed out that the borders of the Promised Land appear to coincide with those of the Garden of Eden (cf. 2:10–14).

The preceding considerations lead to the conclusion that the author has intentionally sought to draw the reader's attention to the events at Sinai in his depiction of the covenant with Abraham. If we ask why the author has sought to do this, the answer lies in the larger purpose of the book. It is part of the overall strategy of Genesis to show that what God did at Sinai was part of a larger plan that had already been put into action with the patriarchs. Thus the Exodus and the Sinai covenant serve as reminders, not only of God's power and grace, but also of God's faithfulness. What he sets out to accomplish with his people, he will carry through to the end.

Notes

There are several features of the picture of Abraham in this chapter that distinguish it from the picture of him found thus far in the patriarchal narratives:

1. For the first time Abraham answers (speaks to) the Lord when the Lord speaks to him (vv.2, 8).
2. The introductory phrase "the word of the LORD came to Abram/him" (vv.1, 4) is unique.
3. The Lord appears to Abraham in a vision (v.1).
4. Abraham "believed" (v.6).
5. When he spoke to Abraham, God identified himself (v.7).
6. Explicit future events are revealed to Abraham (vv.13–16).

1 אַחַר הַדְּבָרִים הָאֵלֶּה הָיָה דְבַר־יהוה (*'aḥar haddeḇārîm hā'ēlleh hāyāh deḇar-yhwh,* "After this the word of the LORD came") marks a major break in the narrative in that it signals a change in subject, time, and place. At the same time, however, the pronoun *hā'ēlleh* (lit., "these") links these events with what preceded.

2 The meaning of מֶשֶׁק (*mešeq;* NIV, "inherit") is unknown (see KB, s.v.). The fact that the LXX has merely transliterated it (Μασεκ, "Masek") suggests that already at an early date the meaning of the term was unknown. The phrase הוּא דַּמֶּשֶׂק (*hû' dammeśeq;* NIV, "of Damascus") appears to be an explanation of the obscure phrase בֶּן־מֶשֶׁק בֵּיתִי (*ben-mešeq bêṯî,* lit., "son of my estate"). The motive of the explanation is to link Abraham's words to the events of the preceding chapter by means of the wordplay of *mešeq* with *dammeśeq* in 14:15. דַּמֶּשֶׂק אֱלִיעֶזֶר (*dammeśeq 'elî'ezer,* "Eliezer of Damascus") may be a clue to the significance of the number 318 in 14:14 since Eliezer's name adds up to 318 (see Notes on ch. 14). This could hardly be a coincidence (see further in next note).

3 נָתַתָּה זָרַע (*nāṯattāh zāra'*, lit., "you gave no child") appears to explain the obscure מַה־תִּתֶּן־לִי . . . עֲרִירִי (*mah-titten-lî . . . '^{a}rîrî*, "what can you give to me . . . childless") in the preceding verse. This can be seen from the repetition of key elements of v.2 in v.3:

15:2: [1]וַיֹּאמֶר אַבְרָם . . . מַה־תִּתֶּן־לִי . . . עֲרִירִי

15:3: [2]וַיֹּאמֶר אַבְרָם הֵן לִי לֹא נָתַתָּה זָרַע

The key term *zera'* (vv.3, 5, 13) explains the rare *'^{a}rîrî* by reversing the two consonants ער and רע (see הפך, W. Bacher, *Die Exegetische Terminologie der Jüdischen Traditionslitera-tur*, 2 [Hildessheim: Georg Olms Verlagsbuchhandlung, 1905], p. 56). Notice that in Jer 22:30 *'^{a}rîrî* is again explained by *zera'*. In Lev 20:20–21, the only other occurrence of the term, *'^{a}rîrî* is explained by עֶרְוָה (*'erwāh*, lit., "nakedness"; NIV, "dishonored"), that is, by a word link: ער = ער.

זֶרַע (*zera'*, lit., "seed") may also be linked to the name אֱלִיעֶזֶר (*'^{e}lî'ezer*, "Eliezer"): זרע reverses עזר. The בֶן־בֵּיתִי (*ben-bêṯî*, "a servant in my household") is surely an explanation of בֶן־מֶשֶׁק בֵּיתִי (*ben-mešeq bêṯî*, "the one who will inherit my estate") and may also be a further link to the previous chapter by linking *ben-bêṯî* with יְלִידֵי בֵיתוֹ (*y^{e}lîḏê bêṯô*, "born in his household," 14:14b). There are thus close narrative ties between the explanations of obscure words and phrases in both chapters 14 and 15.

6 The syntax of וְהֶאֱמִן בַּיהוה (*w^{e}he'^{e}min bayhwh*, "[Abram] believed the LORD") (W + QATAL + X; cf. 2:6b, 10b, 24 [bis]; 15:6a; 21:25a; 29:3 [quat]; 30:41a [bis], 42b; 34:5b; 37:3b; 38:5b, 9b; 47:22b) suggests that this is a comment within the narrative and is not to be understood as an event within the framework of the other events of the narrative. The narrator "updates" the reader's understanding of the events by informing him of Abraham's faith.

18 The mention of נְהַר מִצְרַיִם (*n^{e}har miṣrayim*, "the river of Egypt") in the boundaries of the promise of the land provides a link with the narrative that follows: Hagar is called a שִׁפְחָה מִצְרִית (*šipḥāh miṣrîṯ*, "an Egyptian maidservant," 16:1).

19 Three names are included in this list that do not occur elsewhere in similar lists: הַקֵּינִי (*haqqênî*, "the Kenites"), הַקְּנִזִּי (*haqq^{e}nizzî*, "the Kenizzites"), הַקַּדְמֹנִי (*haqqaḏmōnî*, "the Kadmonites"). It may be coincidental that the names are quite similar and that each begins with the letter *q*. However, since the addition of these three names makes a total of ten names, it is more likely that the list is intended to fit within the previous pattern of lists with ten names (chs. 5, 11).

[1](*wayyō'mer 'aḇrām . . . mah-titten-lî . . . '^{a}rîrî*, "But Abram said, 'What can you give me . . . ?' ").
[2](*wayyō'mer 'aḇrām hēn lî lō' nāṯattāh zāra'*, "And Abram said, 'You have given me no seed [NIV, "children"]' ").

---

4. *Hagar*

16:1–16

1 Now Sarai, Abram's wife, had borne him no children. But she had an Egyptian maidservant named Hagar; 2 so she said to Abram, "The LORD has kept me from having children. Go, sleep with my maidservant; perhaps I can build a family through her."

Abram agreed to what Sarai said. 3 So after Abram had been living in Canaan ten years, Sarai his wife took her Egyptian maidservant Hagar and gave her to her husband to be his wife. 4 He slept with Hagar, and she conceived.

When she knew she was pregnant, she began to despise her mistress. 5 Then Sarai said to Abram, "You are responsible for the wrong I am suffering. I put my servant in your arms, and now that she knows she is pregnant, she despises me. May the LORD judge between you and me."

6"Your servant is in your hands," Abram said. "Do with her whatever
you think best." Then Sarai mistreated Hagar; so she fled from her.
7The angel of the LORD found Hagar near a spring in the desert; it was
the spring that is beside the road to Shur. 8And he said, "Hagar, servant
of Sarai, where have you come from, and where are you going?"
"I'm running away from my mistress Sarai," she answered.
9Then the angel of the LORD told her, "Go back to your mistress and
submit to her." 10The angel added, "I will so increase your descendants
that they will be too numerous to count."
11The angel of the LORD also said to her:

"You are now with child
and you will have a son.
You shall name him Ishmael,
for the LORD has heard of your misery.
12He will be a wild donkey of a man;
his hand will be against everyone
and everyone's hand against him,
and he will live in hostility
toward all his brothers."

13She gave this name to the LORD who spoke to her: "You are the God
who sees me," for she said, "I have now seen the One who sees me."
14That is why the well was called Beer Lahai Roi; it is still there, between
Kadesh and Bered.
15So Hagar bore Abram a son, and Abram gave the name Ishmael to
the son she had borne. 16Abram was eighty-six years old when Hagar
bore him Ishmael.

1–6 Chapter 16 appears to contain allusions to three other important passages in the Pentateuch: Genesis 3:6; 12:3; and Deuteronomy 7:1–6. By bringing the events of Hagar and Abram into the larger context of these other passages, the author enlarges the reference of the story beyond Abram and Hagar as individuals and ties their actions to the themes of the book as a whole. The first sign of an intentional interdependence of the Hagar story on surrounding texts is the notice at the beginning of the narrative that Hagar was an "Egyptian" (*miṣrîṯ*) maidservant of Sarai (vv.1, 3). Only at the beginning of the story is Hagar identified as an "Egyptian maidservant," however. Throughout the remainder of the story she is known only by name or as the "servant" (*šip̱ḥāh*).

The second reference to Hagar as "the Egyptian" (*miṣrîṯ*, v.3) is strikingly different from the first (v.1). The adjective *miṣrîṯ* does not modify "the maidservant" (*šip̱ḥāh*) as in v.1 ("Egyptian maidservant") but stands alone as a substantive along with "maidservant" in apposition to the personal name, Hagar ("Hagar, the Egyptian, her maidservant"). In v.3, then, "the Egyptian" serves as a conspicuous reminder of Hagar's identity in v.1, "an Egyptian maidservant."

The mention of Hagar's geographical origin (*miṣrîṯ*, "Egyptian") appears to function as a connecting link with the geographical list immediately preceding the story (15:18b–21), since in that list the first geographical name is "Egypt" (*miṣrayim*, 15:18). If such a connection is intentional, then it appears the author is attempting to position the account of Hagar (ch. 16) so that her story is representative of those nations in the preceding list. A way is thus opened for the events in the life of Hagar and Abram to be interpreted within the larger theological context of Genesis and the Pentateuch where these lists of names occur. Particularly important in this regard are the similarities between Genesis 16 and Deuteronomy 7:1–6, the prohibition of taking foreign wives, a text that had enormous importance to later generations of Israelites (cf. Ezra 9; cf. Fishbane, *Biblical Interpretation,* pp. 114ff.).

The account of Sarai's plan to have a son has not only been connected with the list of nations in chapter 15; it also appears to have been intentionally shaped with reference to the account of the Fall in Genesis 3. Each of the main verbs (WAYYIQTOL forms) and key expressions in 16:2–3 finds a parallel in Genesis 3:

16:2a: *wattō'mer śāray 'el* ("so she said [Sarai] to")	3:2: *wattō'mer hā'iššāh 'el* ("The woman said to")
16:2b: *wayyišma' 'aḇrām l^{e}qôl śārāy* ("Abram agreed to what Sarai said")	3:17: *šāma'tā l^{e}qôl 'išteḵā* ("you listened to your wife")
16:3a: *wattiqqaḥ śāray* ("Sarai . . . took")	3:6a: *wattiqqaḥ mippiryô* ("she took some")
16:3b: *wattittēn 'ōṯāh l^e'aḇrām 'îšāh* ("and [she] gave her to her husband [Abram]")	3:6b: *wattittēn gam-l^e'îšāh* ("she also gave some to her husband")

At the same time that these parallels have established an association between the Hagar narrative and the Fall (Gen 3), the repeated use of the verb "to curse" (*qālal*) in 16:4–5 appears also to mark an intentional association of the passage with the patriarchal blessing in 12:3 since *qālal* occurs with a similar meaning only in these two passages in Genesis. It is mentioned twice within 16:4–5 that Hagar, *the Egyptian,* "despised" (*qālal*) Sarai, the very thing that 12:3 warned would end in God's curse: "Whoever curses [*m^{e}qallel^{e}ḵā*] you I will curse [*'ā'ōr*]." (It is noteworthy that one of the few other occurrences of the verb is Deut 23:5, a passage with long-standing association with Deut 7:1–6 and the theme of "foreign wives" within the OT canon.)

As a consequence of her despising Sarai, Hagar was forced into the "desert" (*bammiḏbār*, v.7) where she was to stay until she submitted herself again to Sarai. It is only in association with her return to Sarai and her submission to her that the Lord offered Hagar a blessing: "I will so increase [*'arbeh*] your descendants that they will be too numerous to count" (v.10). This was the same "blessing" that Abram himself was to receive (17:2: "I will increase" [*'arbeh*]) and which Ishmael was to receive in 17:20: "I will make him fruitful and will greatly increase his numbers." The association of this blessing with the primeval blessing in 1:26 is unmistakable. In other words, just as the author has positioned the Hagar narrative as representative of the list of nations in 15:18b–21, so also within the narrative Hagar's actions have become exemplary of the nations who will find either blessing or curse in their relationship with the family of Abram.

The first section (vv.1–6) of the Hagar narrative is concerned with Sarai's well-known plan to deal with her barrenness. Sarai's plan of offering her maid to Abram to bear him a child was apparently acceptable within the social custom of the day. There is reason to doubt, however, whether the biblical author looks approvingly at the scheme. From his vantage point Sarai's plan was one more example of the futility of human efforts to achieve God's blessing—not to mention the difficulties his approval of Sarai's plan would pose in light of the fact that he had already extolled the virtues of monogamy in previous sections of his narrative (Gen 2:24). His overall disapproval is suggested by the observation made above that the author has recounted the story in a way that associates Sarai's action with that of Eve in Genesis 3, showing her plan, like Eve's scheme to be like God, to be an attempt to circumvent God's plan of blessing in favor of gaining a blessing on her own. Another indication that the author does not approve of the plan is the fact that in the subsequent narrative (Gen 17), Sarai's plan does not meet with God's approval (17:15–19).

Finally, there is the matter of the position of this narrative immediately following the establishment of a covenant to affirm the promise of a child (15:4). By placing the Hagar story here, the author suggests that Sarai's scheme was intended to head off that divine promise by supplying it with a human solution. Thus the story falls in line with the theme of the stories that preceded it in demonstrating the unacceptability of human effort in fulfilling the divine promise. Sarai's plan, though successful, does not meet with divine approval (17:15–19), just as the unsuccessful plans and schemes of those in the previous narratives (11:1–9; 12:10–20; 13:1–12; 14:21–24).

7–12 The location of the narrative shifts in vv.7–12 from the household of Abram to the wilderness. The author's identification of the spring as the "spring that is beside the road to Shur" (*beḏereḵ šûr,* v.7) assures the reader of what might otherwise only be suspected: Hagar was returning to Egypt (see 25:18).

The associations between chapter 16 and chapter 3 continue in this section of the narrative as well. Just as the Lord sought Adam and Eve after the Fall (3:9: "Where are you?" [*'ayyekkāh*]), so the angel of the Lord found Hagar in the wilderness and greeted her with the similar question (16:8): "Where [*'ê-mizzeh*] have you come from, and where are you going?"

Finally, as in 3:15, where a renewed hope of blessing was sounded amid the chords of despair, so also in 16:10–12, the angel of the Lord offers a blessing to a distraught Hagar found wandering through the wilderness. The child to be born will be named "Ishmael" (*yišmā'ē'l*), because "the LORD has heard" (*kî-šāma' yhwh*) her "misery" (*'onyēḵ*). The key term throughout the chapter is "misery" (*'onî*), which occurs as a noun in v.11b and as a verb in v.6 (*watteʿannehā,* "mistreated") and v.9 (*wehiṯ'annî,* "submit"). Hagar was afflicted by Sarai (v.6); she was told to put herself back under that affliction (v.9); and the Lord heard her affliction (v.11).

The second half of Hagar's "blessing" did not portend well for her son. The text says that he would be a "wild donkey of a man" (v.12). There is a wordplay between "donkey" (*pere'*) and "Paran" (*pā'rān;* cf. 21:21), the location of the tribes of Ishmael in later history, that is, "his hand will be against everyone and everyone's hand against him" (v.12). The sense of the last statement in the blessing is uncertain, but its meaning can perhaps be gained from the final statement of the author regarding Ishmael in 21:21, where it is said that he "was living in the Desert." That would suggest that the literal Hebrew sense of "he shall dwell upon the face of all his brothers" would be "he shall dwell over against all his kinsmen" (RSV; cf. NIV mg.). He was to dwell on the outskirts of civilization, that is, in the wilderness.

13–16 The final section of the narrative consists of Hagar's naming of God and the birth of Ishmael. The two events go together in that the birth of the child was the confirmation of the name given to God in this section: "the God of seeing" (see note on v.13).

Notes

12 וְהוּא יִהְיֶה פֶּרֶא אָדָם יָדוֹ בַכֹּל וְיַד כֹּל בּוֹ (*wᵉhû' yihyeh pere' 'āḏām yāḏô ḇakkōl wᵉyaḏ kōl bô,* "He will be a wild donkey of a man;/ his hand will be against everyone") is an appositional sentence (see Andersen, *Sentence in Biblical Hebrew*, pp. 36ff.), which suggests that the second clause (*yāḏô ḇakkōl wᵉyaḏ kōl bô*) is an explanation of the first (*wᵉhû' yihyeh pere' 'āḏām*).

13 אֵל רֳאִי (*'ēl rᵒ'î*) is not "the God who sees me," as the LXX and the NIV, which would be אֵל רֹאִי (*'ēl rō'î*). Keil suggests that the participle would be רֹאָנִי (*rō'ānî*) (as in Isa 47:10) rather than *rō'î*. However, *rᵒ'î* is a QUTL noun from רָאָה (*rā'āh*, "to see"; cf. Bauer and Leander, *Historische Grammatik*, p. 577). The explanation given the name *'ēl rᵒ'î* in the second half of the verse calls on the similar sounding perfect רָאִיתִי (*rā'îṯî*, "I saw") and participle *rō'î*. The participle is also the basis of the name given the well in v.14: לַחַי רֹאִי (*laḥay rō'î*, "Lahai Roi").

The words רָאִיתִי אַחֲרֵי (*rā'îṯî 'aḥᵃrê*, "I have seen the back of" [NIV mg.]) in Hagar's explanation of רֹאִי (*rō'î*, "the One who sees me") appear to be related to רָאִיתָ אֶת־אֲחֹרָי (*rā'îṯā 'eṯ-'ᵃḥōrāy*, "you will see my back") in Exod 33:23.

---

5. *Abraham, Sarah, and Ishmael*

17:1–27

1 When Abram was ninety-nine years old, the Lord appeared to him
and said, "I am God Almighty; walk before me and be blameless. 2 I will
confirm my covenant between me and you and will greatly increase your
numbers."

3 Abram fell facedown, and God said to him, 4 "As for me, this is my
covenant with you: You will be the father of many nations. 5 No longer
will you be called Abram; your name will be Abraham, for I have made
you a father of many nations. 6 I will make you very fruitful; I will make
nations of you, and kings will come from you. 7 I will establish my
covenant as an everlasting covenant between me and you and your
descendants after you for the generations to come, to be your God and
the God of your descendants after you. 8 The whole land of Canaan,
where you are now an alien, I will give as an everlasting possession to
you and your descendants after you; and I will be their God."

9 Then God said to Abraham, "As for you, you must keep my covenant,
you and your descendants after you for the generations to come. 10 This
is my covenant with you and your descendants after you, the covenant
you are to keep: Every male among you shall be circumcised. 11 You are
to undergo circumcision, and it will be the sign of the covenant between
me and you. 12 For the generations to come every male among you who
is eight days old must be circumcised, including those born in your
household or bought with money from a foreigner—those who are not
your offspring. 13 Whether born in your household or bought with your
money, they must be circumcised. My covenant in your flesh is to be an
everlasting covenant. 14 Any uncircumcised male, who has not been
circumcised in the flesh, will be cut off from his people; he has broken
my covenant."

15 God also said to Abraham, "As for Sarai your wife, you are no longer
to call her Sarai; her name will be Sarah. 16 I will bless her and will surely
give you a son by her. I will bless her so that she will be the mother of
nations; kings of peoples will come from her."

17 Abraham fell facedown; he laughed and said to himself, "Will a son
be born to a man a hundred years old? Will Sarah bear a child at the age

of ninety?" [18]And Abraham said to God, "If only Ishmael might live under your blessing!"

[19]Then God said, "Yes, but your wife Sarah will bear you a son, and you will call him Isaac. I will establish my covenant with him as an everlasting covenant for his descendants after him. [20]And as for Ishmael, I have heard you: I will surely bless him; I will make him fruitful and will greatly increase his numbers. He will be the father of twelve rulers, and I will make him into a great nation. [21]But my covenant I will establish with Isaac, whom Sarah will bear to you by this time next year." [22]When he had finished speaking with Abraham, God went up from him.

[23]On that very day Abraham took his son Ishmael and all those born in his household or bought with his money, every male in his household, and circumcised them, as God told him. [24]Abraham was ninety-nine years old when he was circumcised, [25]and his son Ishmael was thirteen; [26]Abraham and his son Ishmael were both circumcised on that same day. [27]And every male in Abraham's household, including those born in his household or bought from a foreigner, was circumcised with him.

1a The report of Abram's age serves as a connecting link to the preceding narrative of Ishmael's birth. At the close of chapter 16, Abram was eighty-six years old when Ishmael was born. At the beginning of chapter 17, Abram's age is put at ninety-nine years. The close attention to Abram's age comes up again at the conclusion of the chapter where the reader is reminded that Abram was ninety-nine years old when he was circumcised and Ishmael was thirteen (vv.24–27). Thus the age of Abram functions as a framework for the events of the chapter as well as a link to the preceding context. The next note concerning the age of Abram after chapter 17 comes with the account of the birth of Isaac (21:5). There it is reported that Abraham was one hundred years old. Between these two points the text contains a diverse collection of narratives with little close attention to their chronological coherence. The notices regarding the age of Abram/Abraham, however, provide the outside chronological boundaries for the events of the narratives, showing that they all are to be understood as taking place within the year before the birth of Isaac.

1b–2 Chapter 17 is one of a small group of narratives in which the author explicitly states that the "LORD appeared" (*wayyērā'*) to someone (12:7; 18:1; 26:2, 24; 35:9). Unlike the similar statement in chapter 18 (*wayyērā'*, v.1), where the author devotes special attention to the actual nature of the Lord's appearance, here the interest of the author seems solely in what the Lord said, not in the nature of the appearance itself. The Lord's first speech to Abram is brief and serves mainly as a summary introduction to the second speech, which by comparison is long. As a summary, however, the first speech establishes the interpretive boundaries for the rest of the chapter. Most importantly, it establishes the fact that the events of the chapter represent the making of a covenant between the Lord and Abram. The substance of the covenant is the promise of abundant descendants.

The author has immediately identified God as the LORD (*yhwh*, v.1b), the God of the covenant at Sinai (Exod 3:15). Within the narrative, however, God identified himself to Abram as "God Almighty" (*'ēl šadday*). In so doing, the author has removed all doubt regarding the faith of Abram at this stage in the narrative. Abram worshiped the covenant God, Yahweh (*yhwh*), but he knew him as "God Almighty." (See Exod 6:3: "I appeared [*wā'ērā'*] to Abraham, to Isaac and to Jacob as God Almighty [*'ēl šadday*], but by my name the LORD [*yhwh*, 'Yahweh'] I did not make myself known to them.")

After identifying himself, the Lord gives a brief synopsis of the covenant, stressing Abram's obligation: "Walk before me and you will be blameless" (lit. tr.)—the imperative (*wehyēh*), since it is dependent on a preceding imperative (*hiṯhallēḵ*, "walk"), should not be read as an English imperative (as NIV: "be") but as a "consequence" that follows from an initial condition (GKC, p. 325)—and the divine promise: "[I] will greatly increase your numbers" (v.2). The choice of words in v.2—"I will make [*weʾettenāh*] my covenant" (RSV)—poses a question of the coherence of chapter 17 with the preceding narrative. Had not God already "made" (*kāraṯ*) a covenant with Abraham in 15:18? Why did he establish a covenant with Abram a second time? Several solutions to this problem have been proposed. The simplest answer lies in seeing the two covenants as, in fact, two distinct aspects of God's covenant with Abraham—the one stressing the promise of the land (15:18–21) and the other stressing the promise of a great abundance of descendants (17:2).

3a The report of Abram's response to the Lord's words is also brief. The author simply recounts that Abram "fell facedown" (*wayyippōl ʿal-pānāyw*), a sign of deep respect. The significance of this brief description of Abram's response can be seen in the similarities between it and the account of Abram's response to the Lord's second speech. At that point (v.17) he not only "fell facedown" (*wayyippōl ʿal-pānāyw*) but also "laughed" (*wayyiṣḥāq*). In other words, when Abram heard that God would greatly increase his descendants, he responded with respect and submission. But when he heard *how* God would carry out his plan, his respect contained a tinge of laughter. The notion of "laughter" (*yiṣḥāq*) and the announcement of the birth of "Isaac" (*yiṣḥāq*, 21:4), an obvious wordplay, plays an important role in the composition of the next several chapters (see commentary below).

3b–16 The second divine speech is divided into three sections (3b–8, 9–14, 15–16), each marked by the reintroduction of the clause "and God said" (*wayedabbēr ʾittô ʾelōhîm*, v.3b; *wayyōʾmer ʾelōhîm*, vv.9, 15). Each section deals respectively with one of the parties of the covenant (the Lord, Abram, and Sarai), each of whom is specifically named or identified at the beginning of each section: the Lord ("As for me [*ʾanî*]," v.4a), Abram ("As for you [*weʾattāh*]," v.9a), and Sarai ("As for Sarai your wife [*śāray ʾišteḵā*]," v.15a). The substance of each section of the covenant is memorialized by a specific sign within that section: the change of Abram's name in the first section (v.5), the circumcision of all males of the family in the second section (vv.10–14), and the change of Sarai's name in the third section (v.15).

God's part of the covenant (vv.3b–8) consists of two promises: abundant descendants (vv.4–6) and eternal faithfulness (vv.7–8). As the narratives have already stressed, the descendants of Abraham who belong to this covenant will owe their existence to God alone: "You will be a father of many nations." They will be "children born not of natural descent, nor of human decision or a husband's will, but born of God" (John 1:13). The promise of abundant descendants is memorialized in the change of Abram's name to "Abraham" (*ʾaḇrāhām*, v.5), which is interpreted to mean "father of many nations" (*ʾaḇ-hamôn gôyim*, v.4b).

The choice of the word "be fruitful" (*prh*) in v.6 (*hip̄rēṯî ʾōṯeḵā*, "I will make you fruitful") and "multiply" (*rḇh*) in v.2 (*weʾarbeh ʾôṯeḵā*, "increase your numbers") seems intended to recall the blessing of all mankind in 1:28: "Be fruitful [*perû*] and increase in number [*ûreḇû*]; fill the earth" and its reiteration in 9:1: "Be fruitful [*perû*] and increase in number [*ûreḇû*] and fill the earth," showing the covenant with

Abraham to be the means through which God's original blessing would again be channeled to all mankind.

A new element is added in v.6b: "kings will come forth from you." This seems to anticipate not only the subsequent history of Abraham's descendants as it is recorded in the later historical books (e.g., Samuel and Kings); but, more importantly, it provides a link between the general promise of blessing through the seed of Abraham and the author's subsequent focus of that blessing in the royal house of Judah (Gen 49:8–12; Num 24:7–9). The notion that the blessing would come from a king is not new to the author's argument (cf. 14:18–19). What is here being developed for the first time, however, is the idea that this king would come from the seed of Abraham. At work here is the same theological planning as that lying behind the structure of the genealogy of Matthew 1: "A record of the genealogy of Jesus Christ the son of David, the son of Abraham." Keeping in mind the close association of the term "messiah" (*christos*) with the kingship elsewhere in biblical literature (e.g., 1 Sam 24:6, 10), it is not too far from the truth to speak of a "christology" of Genesis in such passages.

The focus of vv.7–8 lies in the repetition of the term "everlasting" (*'ôlām*). The covenant promised is an "everlasting covenant" (*b^erî<u>t</u> 'ôlām*, v.7) and the possession of the land an "everlasting possession" (*'^ahuzza<u>t</u> 'ôlām*, v.8). The promises contained in these verses are not given here for the first time (cf. 13:14–15; 15:18–21); rather it is the everlasting (*'ôlām*) nature of the covenant—that which is to assure the fulfillment of the promises—that is in view. The eternality of the land-covenant was certainly implied in the "forever" (*'a<u>d</u>-'ôlām*) of the promise (13:15); but when the covenant was granted in chapter 15, there was not yet a mention of its being "eternal." Thus as God reiterated his role in the covenant, the focus was centered on his everlasting faithfulness: "I will establish my covenant as an everlasting covenant. . . . The whole land of Canaan, . . . I will give as an everlasting possession" (vv.7–8).

Abram's part in the covenant consisted of his obedience to the covenant: "You must keep my covenant" (*'e<u>t</u>-b^erî<u>t</u>î tišmōr*, v.9). What this meant was immediately explained: "This is my covenant [*b^erî<u>t</u>î*] . . . you are to keep [*tišm^erû*]. . . . Every male among you shall be circumcised" (v.10). To keep (*šāmar*) the covenant was to faithfully practice circumcision; to "break" (*hē<u>p</u>ar*, cf. v.14b) the covenant was to be "uncircumcised" (*'ārēl zā<u>k</u>ār*, v. 14a). Lest the reader conclude that the whole of the covenant was simply the rite of circumcision, the author has included the words "and it will be the sign of the covenant" (*w^ehāyāh l^e'ô<u>t</u> b^erî<u>t</u>*, v.11b).

Sarai's part in the covenant was to be the one through whom the offspring of Abraham was born. She was to be the mother of nations, and "kings of peoples will come from her" (v.16b). She, in her old age, was to be the one through whom it would be demonstrated that God alone could fulfill his covenanted promise. As with Abraham, Sarai's new name was to be a sign of her part in the covenant. She would no longer be called "Sarai" (*śārāy*) but would be called "Sarah" (*śārāh*) (v.15). The author does not explain the meaning of Sarah's new name as he had with the renaming of Abraham (v.5b). He apparently takes it for granted that the reader will understand v.16 as an explanation of her name. Since in Hebrew "Sarah" self-evidently means "princess," the reader could easily recognize that she was to be called "princess" because "kings of peoples will come from her" (v.16b).

17–18 Abraham's response to God's promise is not what the reader would expect: "Abraham fell facedown" and "laughed" (*wayyiṣḥāq*, v.17a). In light of the author's portrayal of Abraham thus far in Genesis (e.g., 15:6), it does not seem likely that his laughter is intended to point to a lack of faith—although one must admit that the text itself leaves that impression. However, without commenting directly on Abraham's surprising reaction to God's promise, the author allows Abraham's own words in v.17b to uncover the motivation behind his laughter—"Will a son be born to a man a hundred years old? Will Sarah bear a child at the age of ninety?"—leaving a final verdict on the nature of his laughter somewhat in the lurch.

In 18:12, when Sarah also responded to God's promise with laughter, the author shows that her laughter was met with divine disapproval: "Then the LORD said, 'Why did Sarah laugh?' " The absence of such a rebuke of Abraham's laughter here in chapter 17 suggests that his laughter does not so much reflect a total lack of faith as it does a limitation of his faith in what God must do to fulfill his promise. Abraham is not depicted here as one whose faith in God has reached full maturity; rather he is one whose faith must still be pushed beyond its present limits. His faith must grow if he is to continue to put his trust in God's promise. In any event, one clear purpose of the author in including the note about Abraham's laughter can be seen in the fact that the Hebrew expression "he laughed" (*wayyiṣḥāq*, v.17) foreshadows the name "Isaac" (*yiṣḥāq*).

The irony of Abraham's response is evident. Even in his surprising response of laughter in the face of God's promise, Abraham's laughter became a verbal sign marking the ultimate fulfillment of the promise in Isaac. Throughout the remainder of the narratives surrounding the birth of Isaac (*yiṣḥāq*), a key word within each major section is "laughter" (*ṣāḥaq*). Sarah "laughed" (*wattiṣḥaq*, 18:12); Lot's sons-in-law laughed (*ḵimṣaḥēq*, 19:14; NIV, "[thought he was] joking"); all who heard of Sarah's birth to Isaac would "laugh" (*yiṣḥāq*, 21:6); the son of Hagar laughed (*meṣaḥēq*, 21:9b; NIV, "was mocking") at Isaac. Finally, Isaac's own failure to trust in God (26:7) was uncovered when the Philistine king saw him "laughing" (*meṣaḥēq*, 26:8b; NIV, "caressing") with Rebekah. Thus, for the author of the book, both the power of God and the limitations of human faith are embodied in that most ambiguous of human acts, laughter.

For the first time the name "Abraham," rather than "Abram," is used as the subject of a verb: "Abraham fell facedown; he laughed" (v.17; cf. v.3). The author's irony can be seen in the fact that Abraham was laughing at the very thing that his new name was intended to mark: "You will be the father of many nations" (v.4b).

19–22 The content of the third divine speech extends the covenant to include Isaac, who is to be born of Sarah, and consequently excludes Ishmael, the son of Hagar. Thus Isaac was not to be one of the anonymous "offspring" who was to receive the benefits of the covenant. He is here brought to the level of a participant in the original covenant: "I will establish my covenant with him as an everlasting covenant for his descendants after him" (v.19b). Thus the identification of the covenant "offspring" of Abraham is made more specific. The descendants of Abraham who are heirs of the covenant are those through Sarah, that is, the "offspring" of Isaac. In this respect God's words to Abraham concerning Isaac in chapter 17 ("I will establish my covenant with him," v.19b) already anticipated the reiteration of these words in the covenant with Isaac in 26:3b: "[I] will confirm the oath I swore to your father Abraham."

The descendants of Hagar, on the other hand, are consequently excluded from the covenant. However, in this final speech the author is careful to show that although Ishmael has been excluded from the covenant with Abraham, Ishmael and his descendants are still to live under the blessing of God (v.20). In fact, in his blessing of Ishmael, God reiterated both his original blessing of all mankind in 1:28 ("I will surely bless him; I will make him fruitful and will greatly increase his numbers," v.20a) and his blessing of Abraham in 12:2 ("I will make him into a great nation," v.20b). Just as the "offspring" of Isaac would form a great nation of twelve tribes (49:1–27), so the "offspring" of Ishmael, under God's blessing, would form a great nation of twelve rulers (v.20b). The list of these twelve rulers is given in 25:13–15.

23 Abraham's final response shows that he obeyed the covenant as was commanded in v.9; that is, he circumcised all male members of his household "as God told him." This final remark about Abraham's obedience carries the reader back to the beginning of the narrative where the injunction was given: "Walk before me and be blameless" (v.1). This portrait of an obedient Abraham is reminiscent of the picture of Noah who also "walked with God" and was "blameless" (6:9). In light of the sparsity of these terms in Genesis, it seems likely that the author expected an association to be made between these two great men based on the close recurrence of both terms. "Blameless" (*tāmîm*) occurs in Genesis only in these two texts; "walk before God" (*hiṯhallēḵ*) occurs more frequently but in carefully planned contexts (Enoch, 5:22, 24; Noah, 6:9; Abram, 17:1; 24:40; and 48:15 [with Isaac]). Thus Abraham and Noah are presented as examples of those who have lived in obedience to the covenant and were therefore "blameless" before God because both obeyed God (v.23b; cf. 6:22; 7:5, 9, 16).

24–27 The ages of Abraham and Ishmael mark an *inclusio* to the narrative, which opened with the age of Abraham and, by implication, the age of Ishmael. The final word at the close restates Abraham's obedient response to the covenant. The chiastic structure of vv.26–27 adds a certain formality to the conclusion as well as stresses the major topic of the chapter: Abraham obeyed God's will in carrying out his covenant obligations.

Notes

5 The wordplay between אַבְרָהָם (*'aḇrāhām*, "Abraham") and אַב־הֲמוֹן גּוֹיִם (*'aḇ-hamôn gôyim*, "a father of many nations") illustrates the nature of the paronomasia found throughout these narratives. It is not intended to be a strict etymological derivation but a simple play on the similar sounds of the two words.

15 Notice the chiastic alliteration in שְׁמָהּ שָׂרָי כִּי שָׂרָה שְׁמָהּ (*šemāh śāray kî śārāh šemāh*, "[her name] Sarai; her name will be Sarah"). The two names *śāray* and *śārāh* appear to be two forms of the same name. The change to *śārāh*, however, makes clearer the link between this name and the word meaning "princess" (*śārāh*).

6. *Three visitors (18:1–33)*

a. *Abraham's hospitality*

18:1–8

1 The LORD appeared to Abraham near the great trees of Mamre while
he was sitting at the entrance to his tent in the heat of the day.

[2]Abraham looked up and saw three men standing nearby. When he saw them, he hurried from the entrance of his tent to meet them and bowed low to the ground.

[3]He said, "If I have found favor in your eyes, my lord, do not pass your servant by. [4]Let a little water be brought, and then you may all wash your feet and rest under this tree. [5]Let me get you something to eat, so you can be refreshed and then go on your way—now that you have come to your servant."

"Very well," they answered, "do as you say."

[6]So Abraham hurried into the tent to Sarah. "Quick," he said, "get three seahs of fine flour and knead it and bake some bread."

[7]Then he ran to the herd and selected a choice, tender calf and gave it to a servant, who hurried to prepare it. [8]He then brought some curds and milk and the calf that had been prepared, and set these before them. While they ate, he stood near them under a tree.

1a Chapter 18 is an extensively developed narrative showing clear signs of theological reflection at several key points. What appear to be the central issues of the chapter (the announcement of the birth of Isaac and the question of the fate of the righteous amid divine judgment) are not only dealt with in this chapter but are also treated in chapters 17 (announcement of Isaac's birth) and 19 (fate of the righteous amid divine judgment). The author's treatment of these two themes in chapter 18, however, shows his concern to push beyond a mere reporting of the events to develop them into a lesson in theology. The narrative begins, in the same way as chapter 17, with the author's report that "the LORD [*yhwh*] appeared [*wayyērā'*] to Abraham." The importance of this comment at the beginning of the narrative should not be overlooked. Its effect is to help clarify one of the most puzzling features of the narrative, namely, who were the three men who visited Abraham and what was their mission?

In opening the narrative with the statement that the Lord "appeared" to Abraham, the author leaves no doubt that in some (albeit unexplained) way the three men represented the Lord's appearance to Abraham. Not all questions are answered by beginning the narrative in this way, however. In fact, such an opening gives rise to several new questions. But opening the narrative with a reference to the Lord's "appearing" to Abraham provides an important context to guide the reading of the remainder of the chapter. However the details of the story are sorted out, the fact remains that, in sum, the events of the chapter constitute an account of the Lord's *appearance* to Abraham.

The mention of the "great trees of Mamre" reestablishes the location of Abraham during these events. When last noted he had moved his tents near the "trees of Mamre" (13:18). It appears that the author wants us to see that Abraham has not moved since he settled near the "Mamre at Hebron"; thus, at the beginning of chapter 18, he updates the reader on Abraham's whereabouts. Perhaps the purpose is to reestablish the scene at the close of chapter 13, where Abraham was dwelling in the land God had promised to him, and Lot had turned away and "pitched his tents near Sodom" (13:12). At that time the reader had already been apprised of the condition of the people of Sodom: "Now the men of Sodom were wicked and were sinning greatly against the LORD" (13:13).

The Hebrew text does not have "to Abraham" in v.1 as the NIV but rather "to him" (*'ēlāyw*). The antecedent of "him" is "Abraham" in 17:26. The identification of Abraham within chapter 18 does not occur until v.6. Thus the opening section of chapter 18 is closely bound with the end of chapter 17 and the account of the circumcision of Abraham and his household.

The final verse (33)—which recounts that after the Lord had finished speaking, "he left" (*wayyēlek̲*)—shows that the whole chapter is to be understood within the context of the Lord's appearance to Abraham. Elsewhere the conclusion of the expression "the LORD/God appeared" is marked by a brief notice of the Lord's departure (cf. 17:1 and 22; 35:9 and 13). Consequently, we are to understand the whole of chapter 18 to fit within the account of the Lord's appearance to Abraham.

1b–8 The narrative of the arrival of three men at Abraham's tent is complicated by several uncertainties within the text. First, the relationship between the three men and the appearance of the Lord (18:1a) is not explicit; second, there appears to be a conscious shift in the verbal forms between v.3 and vv.4–9. In v.3 the verbs and pronouns are all singular masculine, whereas in vv.4–9 the forms are plural masculine. Also, there is uncertainty about the ultimate value of the vowel points in the MT, which in v.3 have rendered Abraham's greeting (*'ᵃd̲ōnāy*, "my l/Lord"; cf. NIV mg.) as an address to God: "O Lord" (by lengthening the final vowel to a qamaṣ—*'ᵃd̲ōnāy*—rather than a pathaḥ—*'ᵃd̲ōnay*, as in 19:2a).

Finally, there is the question of the nature of the relationship between the uncertainties just raised in chapter 18 and their apparent counterparts in chapter 19 where, for example, the relationship between the "two angels" (or "messengers," *hammal'āk̲îm*, 19:1a) and the Lord (*yhwh*) remains unexplained (e.g., the two "men" [19:12] tell Lot they will destroy Sodom [19:13], but the text states that "the LORD rained down burning sulfur on Sodom and Gomorrah" [19:24]). The verbs and pronouns in Lot's greeting are all plural masculine (19:2) and continue to be so until the end of the story, where the same sort of unevenness found in chapter 18 reappears (e.g., 19:17: "as soon as they [plural masculine] had brought them out, one of them said [singular masculine]"; or 19:18: "Lot said to them [plural masculine], . . . Your servant ['your' is singular masculine]"). Also, unlike 18:3b, the Masoretes' vocalization of "my lords" (NIV) in 19:2 reflects an address to persons other than God (*'ᵃd̲ōnay* rather than *'ᵃd̲ōnāy*), whereas when the same persons are addressed in 19:18, the Masoretic form of "my lords" (NIV) is again the form used only to address God (*'ᵃd̲ōnāy*).

Such features as those mentioned above have left the impression that the text of these chapters has come down to us in a highly irregular and uneven form, leading many to suppose that more than one version of the story lies behind the present narrative. Gunkel, for example, concluded that the "interchange of the singular and plural forms does not follow a recognizable principle but is rather completely unmotivated" (Hermann Gunkel, *Genesis übersetzt und erklärt* [Göttingen: Vandenhoeck and Ruprecht, 1977], p. 194). Over against such an evaluation, however, it can confidently be said that the text as it presently stands does evoke a singular and coherent interpretation if it is read with an eye for the importance of every detail and apparent irregularity. As the following comments will attempt to demonstrate, throughout the narrative the apparent irregularities in the text can be seen, not as the end result of a haphazard weaving together of divergent stories, but as the result of the author's careful balancing of two central theological positions with respect to the divine presence and power. Such irregularities as exist in the narrative are best understood as the result of a conscious attempt to stress at one and the same time the theological relevance of the promise of God's *presence* along with his transcendent, sovereign *power*. Thus the final unevenness of the narrative should not be traced to its diverse origin (however much that may have played a part in its present shape), or to a careless disregard for cohesion, but to the struggle of the author to remain faithful to the central theological constraints of his task, namely, the need to reconcile two equally important views of God.

The close similarities between the account of Abraham's visit by "three men" (18:1–3) and that of Lot's visit by the "two angels/men" (19:1–2) suggest that the narratives should be explored further for clues regarding their interrelationship. The scene in chapter 18 opens with Abraham sitting "at the entrance to his tent" (*yōšē<u>b</u> pe<u>t</u>aḥ-hā'ōhel,* v.1), just as in the opening of chapter 19 Lot is found "sitting in the gateway of [Sodom]" (*yōšē<u>b</u> beša'ar-se<u>d</u>ōm,* v.1). Second, just as when Abraham "saw" (*wayyar'*) the men, he ran "to meet them" (*liqrā'<u>t</u>ām*) and "bowed low to the ground" (*wayyištaḥû 'ārṣāh*) and said, "O Lord, if now" (*'a<u>d</u>ōnāy 'im-nā'*; NIV, "If . . . my lord"), so also in the account of Lot in chapter 19, when he "saw" (*wayyar'*) the angels/men, he got up "to meet them" (*liqrā'<u>t</u>ām*) and "bowed down with his face to the ground" (*wayyištaḥû 'appayim 'āreṣāh*) and said, "Behold now, O lords" (*hinneh nā'-'a<u>d</u>ōnay;* NIV, "My lords"). The effect of these unmistakable similarities between the two accounts is to highlight the one primary difference between them, namely, the way the visitors are greeted. Abraham addressed them as "Lord" (*'a<u>d</u>ōnāy*) and appropriately used the singular to address all three men in v.3 (see above). Lot, however, addressed the visitors as "lords" (*'a<u>d</u>ōnay*) and thus used the plural to address the two angels/men. What is the reader to make of this contrast? The most apparent explanation is that the author wanted us to see that Abraham, who had just entered the covenant (ch. 17), recognized the Lord when he appeared to him, whereas Lot, who then lived in Sodom, did not recognize the Lord. The lives of the two men continue to offer a contrast. Abraham knew God, but Lot did not.

We should notice that in light of the statement in 18:1 that "the LORD appeared to Abraham," it can be seen that the reader has been prepared for Abraham's greeting the three men as "the Lord." In the case of Lot's greeting the three men as simply "my lords," the reader is also in a position to judge Lot's response. In 18:21 the reader had been informed that the Lord was on his way to Sodom; thus when the two angels/men arrived, the most likely inference is that they represented the Lord's visit. That such is the case is later confirmed within the narrative. As the narrative progresses, Lot comes to the point of recognizing his visitors as emissaries of the Lord. This can be seen in the fact that the last time he addressed these same two angels/men (19:18), he called "them" (notice the plural *'alēhem*) "Lord" (*'a<u>d</u>ōnāy;* NIV, "my lords" but cf. mg.); and, appropriately, like Abraham, he addressed them both with the singular. In keeping with Lot's recognition of the identity of the two angels/men, in 19:19 Lot stated his requests to them in the same words as Abraham (in 18:3b) had addressed his three visitors: compare Lot's words in 19:19—"[If] your servant has found favor in your eyes" (*hinnēh-nā' māṣā' 'a<u>b</u>de<u>k</u>ā ḥēn be'êney<u>k</u>ā*)—with those of Abraham in 18:3b—"If I have found favor in your eyes" (*'im-nā' māṣā'<u>t</u>î ḥēn be'êney<u>k</u>ā*).

The interchange between the singular and plural verbs and pronouns in v.3 (where the singular is used) and vv.4ff. (where the plural is used) appears to be one of the ways that the author attempted to clarify a crucial point in the narrative, namely, the nature of the divine-human relationship. The biblical God is one who makes himself known intimately and concretely to his covenant people. He can make himself known through "speaking" (*wayyō'mer,* 1:3 et al.), "in a vision" (*bammaḥazeh,* 15:1), or through his "angel" (*mal'āḵ*, 16:7) who speaks for him. He even can "appear" (*wayyērā'*) to individuals, as in 12:7; 17:1; and 18:1. Those narratives that speak of God's making himself known through words, visions, and angels would not be expected to pose a difficulty to the reader of the Pentateuch who was familiar with the strict prohibition against the presentation of God in any physical form in passages such as Deuteronomy 4:15 ("You saw no form of any kind the day the LORD spoke to you at Horeb"). But passages where it is expressly stated that God "appeared" (*wayyērā'*) to someone (12:7; 17:1; 18:1) would naturally raise difficult questions. How is it that God can "appear" and yet his form not be seen (Deut 4:15)? How can God "appear" and yet say "my face must not be seen" (Exod 33:23)? Such questions appear to lie behind the apparent unevenness of the narrative in chapter 18.

By carefully identifying and distinguishing the characters in the narrative by means of the singular and plural verbal forms, the author is able to show that the Lord's appearing to Abraham and the visit of the three men are one and the same event. God appeared to Abraham, but not "face to face" in his own physical form. Rather the author has so arranged the singular and plural forms that the three men always represent God's presence and can be identified with his presence but yet at the same time remain clearly distinct from him.

A reading of the narrative with an eye for the alternations between singular and plural reveals the remarkable skill and timing of the author and makes clear his theological program. First, we should not overlook the fact that the author has identified the scene as a visit from the Lord ("And the Lord appeared to him," 18:1). Second, Abraham saw the three men, greeted them, and then addressed them as the Lord (*'ᵃḏōnāy*), using the singular throughout v.3. Once established as a visit from the Lord, the three men are addressed by Abraham in the plural; and the author follows his lead by using the plural in the description of the three men in vv.4–9 ("and they answered" [*wayyō'mᵉrû*], vv.5b, 9a).

At v.10, without reidentifying the speaker, the author picks up the narrative again with the singular "and he said" (the NIV has correctly added "the LORD" in its translation, but it should be kept in mind that the Hebrew text does not have this "reidentification" of the subject). By not identifying the speaker in v.10 ("and he said"), the author has minimized the break that naturally would arise from the alternation between the plural "and they said" (*wayyō'mᵉrû*, vv.5, 9) and the singular "and he said" (*wayyō'mer*, v.10), but the break remains intact. First the men spoke (*wayyō'mᵉrû*), then an unidentified "he" spoke (*wayyō'mer*, later identified as the Lord), leaving the impression within the narrative as a whole that this "he" has spoken in behalf of the men and, consequently, the men spoke for "him." The reader is left the task of "filling the gaps" with the most contextually appropriate explanation.

The explanation seems to be that the three men, as such, are to be understood as the physical "appearance" of the Lord to Abraham. In other words, though God himself did not appear to Abraham in physical form, the three men are to be seen as representative of his presence. In much the same way the Burning Bush of Exodus 3:2–3 was a physical representation of God's presence but yet was not actually the physical presence of God. In such a way the actual presence of God among his covenant people was assured but without leaving the impression that God may have a physical form.

The identity of the "he" (*wayyō'mer*) is explicitly recovered in vv.13–14, where the author supplies "the LORD" as the speaking subject (*wayyō'mer yhwh*), and his words are the same as those of v.10: "I will return to you at the appointed time next year and

Sarah will have a son" (v.14b). Thus the "he" of v.10 can be none other than the Lord; yet he was not at that point in the narrative identified as such in order to maintain the close connection between his words and those of the three men. This same interweaving of the three men and the Lord continues throughout the narrative. In v.16 the men made their way toward Sodom, and Abraham accompanied them; but in v.17 it is the Lord who spoke (first to himself, vv.17–19, and then to Abraham, vv.20–21). But as the Lord finished speaking, the men (*hā'ᵃnāšîm*) departed from Abraham to go toward Sodom (v.22); and the Lord remained with Abraham (*wayhwh 'ôḏennû 'ōmēḏ lip̱nê 'aḇrāhām,* as in the *tiqqune sopherim;* cf. NIV mg.), departing finally in v.33 (*wayyēleḵ yhwh*). Thus the narrative teaches that the Lord can speak with Abraham with or without the men, but he had appeared (*wayyērā',* v.1) to Abraham in the form of the three men (*šᵉlōšāh 'ᵃnāšîm,* v.2).

In a similar way the "two angels" (*šᵉnê hammal'āḵîm*) of 19:1 (later called simply "the men," e.g., *hā'ᵃnāšîm,* v.10) are addressed with the plural at the beginning of the narrative because Lot did not recognize their true identity—emissaries of the Lord. But after he learned who they were and who had sent them, he addressed "them," in the plural (*'ᵃlēhem,* v.18a), as "the Lord" (*'ᵃḏōnāy,* v.18b; cf. NIV mg.), using the singular (e.g., "your servant" [*'aḇdᵉḵā,* v.19a]), and was followed also in this by the author in the narrative: "He said" (*wayyō'mer,* v.21). (The MT already has the singular [*wayyō'mer*] in v.17a.)

The plural pronoun in v.18 along with the plural verbal forms in v.16 make the singular form of the MT very difficult and thus to be preferred. The plural of the LXX, Peshitta, and Vulgate are likely the translators' attempts to smooth out the difficulty of the singular in light of the plurals in v.16 and the "to them" (*'ᵃlēhem*) in v.18a, though it is not impossible that they represent an early Hebrew text with the same intention. In v.21 also the identity of the "he" (*wayyō'mer,* "he said") is concealed by the author to smooth over (but not eliminate) the break caused by the change from plural to singular. As in 18:13, the "he" in 19:21 is finally identified as "the LORD" in 19:24, some distance from the switch to the singular, so as not to disturb further the already difficult break caused by the shift to the singular. The reader, however, has already been given advance notice that the "two angels/men" in chapter 19 are the Lord in that in 18:21 the Lord had said (*wayyō'mer,* v.20a), "I will go down [*'ērᵃḏāh-nā'*] and see [*wᵉ'er'eh*] . . . the outcry that has reached me." After such a statement the reader is led to draw the obvious conclusion at the beginning of chapter 19 that the "two angels/men" are the Lord's visit to the city spoken of in 18:21—a conclusion Lot himself failed to draw. When Lot failed to see this, the reader is given an advance insight into Lot's own state of awareness of the Lord's presence.

Notes

3 אֲדֹנָי (*'ᵃḏōnāy,* "Lord") with the lengthened final dipthong is used by the MT only to refer to God. The Masoretes marked *'ᵃḏōnāy* in this verse as "holy" (קֹדֶשׁ [*qōḏeš*]; see S. Baer, *Liber Genesis* [Lipsiae: Bernahardi Tauchnitz, 1869], p. 20). Several Masoretic MSS read *yhwh* in place of *'ᵃḏōnāy* in this verse (J.C. Doederlein and J.H. Meisner, *Biblica Hebraica* [Halle: Libraria Orphanotrophei, 1818], p. 21), so also Targum Onkelos and the LXX.

The plurals in the Samaritan Pentateuch—בְּעֵינֵיכֶם . . . תַּעַבֹרוּ . . . עַבְדֵּיךָ (*bᵉ'êneyḵem . . . ta'ᵃḇōrû . . . 'aḇdeyḵā,* "in your eyes . . . pass by . . . your servant") appear secondary.

b. *The promise of a son*

18:9–15

9 "Where is your wife Sarah?" they asked him.
"There, in the tent," he said.
10 Then the LORD said, "I will surely return to you about this time next year, and Sarah your wife will have a son."
Now Sarah was listening at the entrance to the tent, which was behind him. 11 Abraham and Sarah were already old and well advanced in years, and Sarah was past the age of childbearing. 12 So Sarah laughed to herself as she thought, "After I am worn out and my master is old, will I now have this pleasure?"
13 Then the LORD said to Abraham, "Why did Sarah laugh and say, 'Will I really have a child, now that I am old?' 14 Is anything too hard for the LORD? I will return to you at the appointed time next year and Sarah will have a son."
15 Sarah was afraid, so she lied and said, "I did not laugh."
But he said, "Yes, you did laugh."

Although the announcement of the birth of a son is made to Abraham, the focus of the narrative is clearly on Sarah's response. In her laughter ("she laughed" [*wattiṣḥaq*], v.12), the name of the son ("Isaac" [*yiṣḥāq*]) is foreshadowed. But the significance of Sarah's laughter goes beyond that. Her laughter becomes the occasion to draw an important theological point from the narrative, namely, that what the Lord was about to do to fulfill his promise to Abraham was a matter "too wonderful" (*h^ayippālē'*, v.14; NIV, "too hard") even for his own people to imagine.

9–11 Verses 9–10 set the stage for the brief but intricate narrative that follows. The three men inquired about Sarah, but they spoke only to Abraham. Sarah remained "off camera" through most of the narrative, though the reader is kept abreast of her thoughts and motives as she listened in on the conversation. Only in v.15b is she finally addressed directly, but she was given no opportunity to respond.

As background to Sarah's response, the author inserts an explanation in v.11. Abraham and Sarah were too old to have children. Sarah, as all women her age, no longer was physically capable of even conceiving a child. The structure of the Hebrew sentence suggests that the last statement ("Sarah was past the age of childbearing") is a restatement of the sense of the first (see Anderson, *Sentence in Biblical Hebrew*, pp. 46ff.). In such a statement one may detect an attempt to ensure a harmony between this passage and that of 25:1–4. There it is stated that Abraham took another wife, apparently after the death of Sarah, and that she bore him sons. Thus, although Abraham's age was a factor to be reckoned with, the primary obstacle to the fulfillment of the promise was Sarah's old age. The primary importance of Sarah's age can also be seen in her own restatement of the obstacle in v.12, where she put her old age first and then that of Abraham's: "After I am worn out and my master is old, will I now have this pleasure?" Finally there is the restatement of Sarah's thoughts in v.13, where the Lord rephrases them as "Will I really have a child, now that I am old?" with no mention of Abraham's old age.

The point of the above verses is that they bring the promise to the brink of failure, pushing the obstacle to its fulfillment far beyond the previous levels. It was not only that Sarah was barren (11:30; 16:1) or that Abraham was old (since he later had children without any apparent divine intervention, 25:1–4). These obstacles in themselves are great enough to demonstrate that the promise, when fulfilled, came from God alone. But the author takes the reader one step further. Sarah was even past the physical age of bearing children. For her to have a child was not simply unlikely; it was impossible (*hᵃyippālē'*, v.14; NIV, "too hard")!

12–15 The key to the sense of this short passage lies in the Lord's question to Abraham about Sarah's laughter. The subtle changes in the wording of Sarah's thoughts reveal that the Lord was not simply restating her thoughts but was interpreting them as well. First, the Lord restated Sarah's somewhat ambiguous statement—"After I am worn out, . . . will I now have this pleasure?" (v.12)—as simply "Will I really have a child?" (*ha'ap̱ 'umnām 'ēlēḏ*, v.13). Then he took Sarah's statement about her husband—"my master is old" (*wa'ḏōnî zāqēn*, v.12)—and reshaped it into a statement about herself: "now that I am old" (*wa'ᵃnî zāqantî*, v.13). Finally, he went beyond her actual words to their intent: "Is anything too hard for the LORD?" (*hᵃyippālē'*, v.14a). The underlying issue at stake in the narrative then is brought to the surface in these questions to Abraham. That is, they demonstrate the physical impossibility of the fulfillment of the promise through Sarah.

Once the obstacle of the physical impossibility of Sarah's giving birth to a son was firmly established, the Lord repeated his promise to Abraham, "I will return to you at the appointed time next year and Sarah will have a son" (v.14b). At this point Sarah, who had only been "listening at the entrance to the tent" (v.10), entered the conversation with a terse reply: "I did not laugh" (v.15a). The author then quickly puts her response aside as a lie and goes on to explain that she lied because "she was afraid" (v.15). This brief narrative then concludes with the Lord's reiteration of what the reader by now certainly knows to be the truth, namely, that Sarah did, in fact, laugh.

In the course of this brief but important narrative, the reader has come to a new level of understanding regarding the promise of a son and its potential fulfillment. The promise was beyond all physical possibility. No one could know this more than Sarah herself, and through the course of the narrative the author has artfully and delicately revealed her most intimate knowledge to the reader. Having made that point, the author immediately brings the narrative to a close and moves on to a new section of the story.

Notes

11 The syntax (W + nominal clause) suggests that the information is to be understood as background for what follows, namely, Sarah's laughter.

c. *Sodom in the balance*

18:16–22

16 When the men got up to leave, they looked down toward Sodom,
and Abraham walked along with them to see them on their way. 17 Then
the LORD said, "Shall I hide from Abraham what I am about to do?
18 Abraham will surely become a great and powerful nation, and all
nations on earth will be blessed through him. 19 For I have chosen him,

so that he will direct his children and his household after him to keep the way of the LORD by doing what is right and just, so that the LORD will bring about for Abraham what he has promised him."
20 Then the LORD said, "The outcry against Sodom and Gomorrah is so great and their sin so grievous 21 that I will go down and see if what they have done is as bad as the outcry that has reached me. If not, I will know."
22 The men turned away and went toward Sodom, but Abraham remained standing before the LORD.

16 As the three men arose and looked out toward Sodom, Abraham accompanied them to send them off. The men have been strangely out of the picture for most of the immediately preceding narrative, but the author brings them back into view just before the Lord speaks in v.17. In so doing the author once again establishes an association between the Lord's presence and the appearance of the three men. In the middle of v.16 the author skillfully begins to turn the narrative in the direction of chapter 19. The reader's attention is directed to a seemingly insignificant gesture on the part of the three men as they rise to leave: "They looked down [*wayyašqipû*, v.16] toward Sodom." As the men's heads turned to look down over the doomed city, so also the reader's attention is directed toward that city in anticipation of the events of the next chapter. The intense preoccupation with the events surrounding the announcement of the birth of Isaac, which has played such a dominant role in the narrative thus far, suddenly vanishes and is not again seen until the time of its fulfillment two chapters later (21:1).

17–19 The syntax of v.17 suggests that the Lord's words are intended to be read as the background to what follows. Without these verses the narrative would read smoothly from v.6 to v.20. The intervening verses, however, provide an important context for the discourse between the Lord and Abraham because, like the direct discourse throughout the Book of Genesis, the words of the Lord here reveal the inner motivation for his actions ("what I am about to do," v.17). The Lord's words are concise but have far-reaching consequences. Verse 18 looks back to the original promise that Abraham would become a "great . . . nation" (cf. 12:2a) and that "all the nations on earth will be blessed through him" (cf. 12:3b).

Verse 19 seems to be an expansion on the ideas of 17:1 ("walk before me and be blameless"). Nowhere else in the book, however, do we have such a reflective perspective on the events of the whole of the Abrahamic narratives. First, the Lord puts into words that which has been a central part of the narrative but has not yet been expressly verbalized, namely, Abraham's election: "I have chosen him" (*yᵉḏaʿtîw*). Second, the Lord went on to express his purpose (*lᵉmaʿan*) in choosing Abraham; and, as it turns out, this purpose goes beyond that revealed in the preceding narratives. Here the attention is directed internally ("to keep the way of the LORD") with the end in view that Abraham and his descendants do "what is right and just." Only then (*lᵉmaʿan*) will the Lord fulfill what he had promised to Abraham ("so that [*lᵉmaʿan*] the LORD will bring about for Abraham what he has promised"). The notion of an internalized obedience found in this verse is remarkably close to the terms of the "new covenant" found in the prophetic literature ("I will put my law in their minds and write it in their hearts," Jer 31:33) and is deeply rooted in the theology of Deuteronomy ("The LORD your God will circumcise your hearts and the hearts of your descendants, so that you may love him with all your heart and all your soul, and [*l^e ma'an*] live," 30:6).

20–21 Although v.20 is a continuation of the Lord's speaking, the syntax of the verse suggests that his words are to be set in a different setting than those preceding. In vv.17–19 it appears that the Lord was speaking to himself or that the author was simply recalling what the Lord had said on another occasion, not within the immediate sequence of events. In any case, Abraham was not the one addressed in those verses. In vv.20–21, however, Abraham was most certainly the one addressed. The Lord's words to Abraham were the answer to the question posed by the Lord in v.17 ("Shall I hide from Abraham what I am about to do?"). Thus in vv.20–21, the Lord revealed to Abraham what he was about to do: he would go down to investigate the wickedness of the cities of Sodom and Gomorrah.

22 It should be noted that the narrative first states that the Lord (*yhwh*) said, "I will go down and see" (v.21); then the narrative continues by stating that "the men [*hā'anāšîm*] turned away and went toward Sodom." Thus once again the Lord and the men are brought into close association so that the actions of the one are identified with the actions of the other. It is important to notice the inherent logic of the narrative at this point since this same logic follows the reader into the next chapter. If "the men" (*hā'anāšîm*) are the emissaries of the Lord and represent his presence amid everyday affairs, then when they journey to Sodom and Gomorrah, as here, it can rightly be said that the Lord himself was visiting these cities, as in v.21 ("I will go down and see").

As has been the case throughout this narrative, "the men" (*hā'anāšîm*) represent the Lord's appearance but are not actually identified as the Lord. Thus the fact that the Lord remained behind after two of "the men" had left is no more a surprise than the fact that the Lord was again present with Lot in Sodom along with two of "the men" (19:12, 16) (see discussion above). So when the Lord said, "I will go down and see," the reader is led to conclude that, as in chapter 18, "the men" in chapter 19 represented the Lord's presence with Lot.

One question remains, however. If the three men left Abraham, why did only "two messengers" (*š^e nê hammal'āk̲îm*, 19:1) arrive in Sodom? It seems reasonably clear that the two messengers who visited Lot are two of the "three men" who visited Abraham, especially in light of the fact that in chapter 19 the "messengers" are subsequently referred to simply as "the men" (*hā'anāšîm*). But what happened to the other "man"? This question has given rise to several speculations about the identity of the one man who does not visit Sodom. The most common explanation is that the "man" is a "christophany," that is, an appearance of the Second Person of the Trinity in human form, before the Incarnation. Thus when the text says that "the men [*hā'anāšîm*] turned away and went toward Sodom" and that the Lord remained with Abraham, and then further that only "two messengers" (19:1) came to Sodom, it seems to follow that one of the men must have stayed behind with Abraham. Since we know that the Lord stayed behind, that man must have been the Lord. Abraham was then visited by the preincarnate Christ who was accompanied by two "angels" (19:1).

Although this interpretation has many features of the narrative in its favor, the primary difficulty with such an explanation is that it overlooks the fairly certain fact that although Lot failed to appreciate it, the author of the narrative sees the "two messengers" as representative of the presence of the Lord (e.g., "And Lot said to them, 'No, Lord,' " 19:18 [NIV mg.]), just as the three men in chapter 18. Thus the fact that the men in chapter 18 are referred to as "the Lord" does not mean that one of them is actually the Lord; rather it means that all three represent the Lord's presence. If the two men in chapter 19 can be addressed as "the Lord" even though they merely represent the Lord, so also can the three men in chapter 18 (e.g., v.3). Hence, after calling attention to the fact that Lot is visited by only two messengers, the author subsequently refers to them simply as "the men" (*hā'ᵃnāšîm*) as in chapter 18.

The question still remains, however, that if all three men left Abraham and traveled toward Sodom, why then is Lot visited by only two men rather than the three men of chapter 18? Where did the third man go, if not to Sodom? The answer to that question is readily at hand in chapter 18. It seems quite clear that the two men in Sodom represent the carrying out of the Lord's intention to "go down and see if what they have done is as bad as the outcry." But how did the Lord investigate the "outcry of Gomorrah"? Did he not also say he was going down to Gomorrah to see their deeds as well? Since the narrative records only the events of the men's visit to Sodom, because that is where Lot dwelt (13:12), and since at the conclusion of chapter 19 the mention is made not only of the Lord's destruction of Sodom but also of Gomorrah (v.24a), the question is left open whether the Lord also investigated the "outcry of Gomorrah" as he said he would. Thus within the inner logic—the "outcry" that had reached the Lord was the "outcry against Sodom and Gomorrah" (*za'ᵃqaṯ sᵉḏōm wa'ᵃmōrāh*, 18:20), and the Lord destroyed both Sodom and Gomorrah (19:24)—of the narrative of chapters 18 and 19, it seems apparent that the author would have us conclude that the third man went to Gomorrah and carried out a similar task in that city.

In other words, by specifying the number of men who visited Lot, the author leaves the narrative of chapter 19 open to a reading that harmonizes at all points. By specifying the number of men who visited Sodom, the author has left the reader with an answer to the question of the Lord's righteous and just treatment of Gomorrah. Although unstated, the solution is ready at hand: the third man visited Gomorrah and thus "the Judge of all the earth" (v.25) has "dealt justly" (cf. 19:15b). It is precisely that theme that is dealt with in the intervening narrative.

Notes

19 It is not unusual to render יְדַעְתִּיו (*yāḏa'tîw*) as "I have chosen" in light of the common meaning of יָדַע (*yāḏa'*, "to take notice of, regard"; cf. 39:6; Deut 33:9). This is the same use as Hos 13:5 and Amos 3:2. The reading for *yāḏa'tîw* reflected in the LXX—יָדַעְתִּי כִּי (*yāḏa'tî kî*, "I know that")—is likely the translator's own solution to the use of *yāḏa'* in this context since he resorts to a similar solution for *yāḏa'* in Gen 39:6.

22 The הָאֲנָשִׁים (*hā'ᵃnāšîm*, "the men") referred to here are the שְׁלֹשָׁה אֲנָשִׁים (*šᵉlōšāh 'ᵃnāšîm*, "three men") of v.2, just as in v.16. It is the customary style in narrative to give the number of entities first and then to refer to them without the number. For example, once it is stated that "Noah had three sons"—וַיּוֹלֶד נֹחַ שְׁלֹשָׁה בָנִים (*wayyôleḏ nōᵃḥ šᵉlōšāh ḇānîm*, 6:10)—they are subsequently referred to simply as "your/his sons" (בָּנֶיךָ [*ḇāneykā*], 6:18; 8:16; בָּנָיו [*ḇānāyw*], 7:7; 8:18; בְּנֵי־נֹחַ [*ḇᵉnê-nōᵃḥ*], 9:18). Notice how in 7:13 the wives of Noah's three sons, who have not yet been numbered, are numbered—שְׁלֹשֶׁת נְשֵׁי־בָנָיו (*šᵉlōšeṯ nᵉšê-ḇānāyw*, "the wives of his three sons").

d. *Abraham's intercession*

18:23–33

[23]Then Abraham approached him and said: "Will you sweep away the righteous with the wicked? [24]What if there are fifty righteous people in the city? Will you really sweep it away and not spare the place for the sake of the fifty righteous people in it? [25]Far be it from you to do such a thing—to kill the righteous with the wicked, treating the righteous and the wicked alike. Far be it from you! Will not the Judge of all the earth do right?"

[26]The LORD said, "If I find fifty righteous people in the city of Sodom, I will spare the whole place for their sake."

[27]Then Abraham spoke up again: "Now that I have been so bold as to speak to the Lord, though I am nothing but dust and ashes, [28]what if the number of the righteous is five less than fifty? Will you destroy the whole city because of five people?"

"If I find forty-five there," he said, "I will not destroy it."

[29]Once again he spoke to him, "What if only forty are found there?"

He said, "For the sake of forty, I will not do it."

[30]Then he said, "May the Lord not be angry, but let me speak. What if only thirty can be found there?"

He answered, "I will not do it if I find thirty there."

[31]Abraham said, "Now that I have been so bold as to speak to the Lord, what if only twenty can be found there?"

He said, "For the sake of twenty, I will not destroy it."

[32]Then he said, "May the Lord not be angry, but let me speak just once more. What if only ten can be found there?"

He answered, "For the sake of ten, I will not destroy it."

[33]When the LORD had finished speaking with Abraham, he left, and Abraham returned home.

23–33 The central issue of the discourse between Abraham and the Lord is expressed in Abraham's question, "Will not the Judge of all the earth do right?" (v.25). The Lord's answer, which is echoed throughout the narrative, is a resounding yes. Abraham persisted with the question until it was conclusively dealt with. The sequence Abraham followed has been variously interpreted. He started with a question about fifty righteous men in a city and concluded with the question of ten righteous men. Why did he stop at ten men? Why not ask if there were nine men, eight men, and so on? Did he not care about Lot and his family who only numbered four? The narrative of 19:29 shows that the author considers Lot to have been the central "righteous" one under discussion (cf. 2 Peter 2:7). Why then did Abraham not continue his line of questions down to four righteous ones in the city? One possible solution is that the sequence fifty down to ten, in units of ten, would naturally end with ten—the next question would have been, "Were there no righteous left in the city?" The answer to that question is not the concern of Abraham since he was interested only in the salvation of the righteous amid the unrighteous, not the destruction of the wicked. Thus Abraham had his answer in general terms and did not need to pursue the question to the exact number. So the author of the narrative cuts off the questioning at this point to allow the issue to remain at a more general level.

In Abraham's concern for Lot, the narrative addresses the larger issue of God's treatment of any righteous one (not merely Lot) in his judgment of the wicked. It is also important to notice that in the narrative that follows (ch. 19), the city of Sodom was not spared on Lot's behalf. The city was destroyed, and Lot was taken out of the city—a scenario not anticipated in Abraham's line of questions. It may then be that within the narrative at the close of chapter 18, Abraham's abrupt conclusion to his questions is intended to suit the events of the narrative in chapter 19. By ending the questions at ten righteous in the city, the narrative leaves open the question of what God would do if less than ten righteous were found in there. Thus Abraham's questions and God's reply are shown to harmonize with the actual course of events in chapter 19 where the city was not spared on Lot's behalf. It should be pointed out, however, that as the narrative continues in chapter 19, though Sodom was not spared for Lot's sake, the little city of Zoar was spared on Lot's behalf (see comments on 19:17–22).

7. *Lot and Sodom (19:1–38)*

a. *Two angels at Sodom*

19:1–14

1 The two angels arrived at Sodom in the evening, and Lot was sitting in the gateway of the city. When he saw them, he got up to meet them and bowed down with his face to the ground. 2 "My lords," he said, "please turn aside to your servant's house. You can wash your feet and spend the night and then go on your way early in the morning."

"No," they answered, "we will spend the night in the square."

3 But he insisted so strongly that they did go with him and entered his house. He prepared a meal for them, baking bread without yeast, and they ate. 4 Before they had gone to bed, all the men from every part of the city of Sodom—both young and old—surrounded the house. 5 They called to Lot, "Where are the men who came to you tonight? Bring them out to us so that we can have sex with them."

6 Lot went outside to meet them and shut the door behind him 7 and said, "No, my friends. Don't do this wicked thing. 8 Look, I have two daughters who have never slept with a man. Let me bring them out to you, and you can do what you like with them. But don't do anything to these men, for they have come under the protection of my roof."

9 "Get out of our way," they replied. And they said, "This fellow came here as an alien, and now he wants to play the judge! We'll treat you worse than them." They kept bringing pressure on Lot and moved forward to break down the door.

10 But the men inside reached out and pulled Lot back into the house and shut the door. 11 Then they struck the men who were at the door of the house, young and old, with blindness so that they could not find the door.

12 The two men said to Lot, "Do you have anyone else here—sons-in-law, sons or daughters, or anyone else in the city who belongs to you? Get them out of here, 13 because we are going to destroy this place. The outcry to the LORD against its people is so great that he has sent us to destroy it."

14 So Lot went out and spoke to his sons-in-law, who were pledged to marry his daughters. He said, "Hurry and get out of this place, because the LORD is about to destroy the city!" But his sons-in-law thought he was joking.

1a According to vv.10, 12, 16, the two "angels" of v.1 were "men" (*hā'ᵃnāšîm*). The definite article on the word "angels" (*hammal'āḵîm* or "messengers") suggests that the two men have already been identified and thus must have been the men (*hā'ᵃnāšîm*) who visited Abraham in the previous chapter (18:3). The mention of the fact that only two of the three men (18:2) were sent to investigate the "outcry" of Sodom (18:20) suggests that the third man was sent to investigate the "outcry" of the city of Gomorrah (18:20; see previous discussion on ch. 18). We hear nothing more about the third man. After v.1 the "angels" are referred to both as "the men" (*hā'ªnāšîm*, vv.10, 12, 16) and as "the angels" (*hammal'āḵîm*, v.15). What is of more importance is the fact that toward the end of the narrative, the men, as in chapter 18, are represented as a visitation of the Lord (v.18: "But Lot said to *them*, 'No, Lord ['ª*ḏōnāy*]' "; cf. NIV mg.) (see previous discussion on ch. 18). The men came to carry out the Lord's retribution against the wickedness of the city (v.13b); but in response to Abraham's prayer for the righteous (18:23–32), they also had come to rescue Lot (19:29).

1b–11 The depiction of the events at Lot's house on the eve of the destruction of Sodom and Gomorrah is intended to give justification for the divine judgment on the two cities. Even Lot, the righteous one who was ultimately rescued, is shown to have been tainted by his association with Sodom. Unlike Abraham, who immediately recognized God's presence in the visit of the men (18:2), Lot appears quite insensitive to God's presence with the messengers, addressing them only as "sirs" ('ª*ḏōnay*, v.2; NIV, "lords"). Though Lot was just as hospitable as Abraham and can certainly not be put in the same class as the men of Sodom, Lot's suggestion that the men of the city take his own daughters and do with them what they please can hardly be taken within the narrative as a sign of his good character (v.8). In fact, at the close of the narrative, in an ironic turn of events, Lot himself inadvertently carried out his own horrible proposal by lying with his own daughters (vv.30–38).

The contrasting picture of Abraham and Lot, then, appears to show the consequences of Lot's earlier decision to "pitch his tents near Sodom" (13:12). At the close of the narrative, Lot is pictured as the father of the Moabites and Ammonites. Thus the fate of Lot was the fate of Moab (v.37) and the sons of Ammon (v.38). Though they lived on the border of the Promised Land, they would not enjoy its blessings (Num 24:17).

12–14 The messengers clearly stated their twofold purpose. They had been sent to destroy the city and to rescue Lot and his family (vv.12–13). The response of the two "sons-in-law" (v.14) shows that they are at one with the rest of the men of the city. This provides a further vindication of the divine punishment that was to follow. There is a curious wordplay in the response of the two sons-in-law that provides a connecting link with the previous chapter. When they heard of the impending divine judgment on their city, the sons saw Lot's words as an occasion for "laughter" (*wayᵉhî ḵimṣaḥēq*, v.14; NIV, "thought they were joking"). The wordplay between their "laughter" (*mᵉṣaḥēq*), the "laughter" of Sarah (*wattiṣḥaq*, 18:12; *ṣāḥªqāh*, 18:13; *ṣāḥaqtî*, 18:15a; *ṣāḥāqtᵉ*, 18:15b), and the "laughter" of Abraham (*wayyiṣḥāq*, 17:17) is obvious and provides a bridge across these narratives to the ultimate fulfillment of God's promise in the birth of Isaac, whose name means "laughter" (*yiṣḥāq*).

Notes

2 This is the only occurrence of אֲדֹנַי ('ª*ḏōnay*, "my lords"), with short final dipthong, in the MT. Its use here shows clearly that אֲדֹנָי ('ª*ḏōnāy*) in 18:3 is intentional. The Masoretes have

marked it as חול (*ḥwl*), meaning it should not be taken as a reference to God (Baer, *Liber Genesis*, p. 22). It is consistent then that the plural verbs (e.g., סורו נָא [*sûrû nā'*, "please turn"]) and pronouns (e.g., עַבְדְּכֶם [*'aḇdᵉḵem*, "your servant's"]) are used with it. This suggests that the distinction between *'ᵃḏōnāy* in 18:3, which has singular verbs, and *'ᵃḏōnay* here is not merely a Masoretic tradition but rather preserves an important element in the narrative itself.

6 The singular סָגַר (*sāḡar*, "[he] shut"; cf. *sgrw* of the Samar.) shows the same interchange between singular and plural as chapter 18 (see Notes in loc.). As the identity of the two messengers becomes clearer within the narrative, the interchange between their being referred to as singular and as plural increases (see וַיֹּאמֶר [*wayyō'mer*, "one . . . said"] in v.17). Notice that in vv.18–19, once Lot knew that the men were from God, he spoke "to them" (אֲלֵהֶם [*'ᵃlēhem*]) with singular verbs (e.g., עָשִׂיתָ [*'āśîṯā*, "you have shown") and pronouns (e.g., עַבְדְּךָ [*'aḇdᵉḵā*, "your servant"]).

12 The הַמַּלְאָכִים (*hammal'āḵîm*, "the angels") of the Samaritan Pentateuch is an adjustment to v.1 and v.15. Notice that the הָאֲנָשִׁים (*hā'ᵃnāšîm*, "the men") in v.5 is written as הָאַנָשִׁים (*hā'anāšîm*)—aleph with pathaḥ rather than composite shewa—in the Leningrad text (B19). This may also be an adjustment to v.1 in that these are the vowels of *mal'āḵîm*.

13–14 The כִּי־מַשְׁחִתִים אֲנַחְנוּ אֶת־הַמָּקוֹם הַזֶּה (*kî-mašḥiṯîm 'ᵃnaḥnû 'eṯ-hammāqôm hazzeh*, "because we are going to destroy this place") of v.13 is repeated by Lot as כִּי־מַשְׁחִית יהוה אֶת־הָעִיר (*kî-mašḥîṯ yhwh 'eṯ-hā'îr*, "because the LORD is about to destroy the city") in v.14, showing the close association between the men and the Lord.

14 כִּמְצַחֵק (*ḵimṣaḥēq*, "joking") is a wordplay on "Isaac" (יִצְחָק [*yiṣḥāq*]).

---

b. *Lot's deliverance*

19:15–28

15 With the coming of dawn, the angels urged Lot, saying, "Hurry! Take your wife and your two daughters who are here, or you will be swept away when the city is punished."

16 When he hesitated, the men grasped his hand and the hands of his wife and of his two daughters and led them safely out of the city, for the
LORD was merciful to them. 17 As soon as they had brought them out, one
of them said, "Flee for your lives! Don't look back, and don't stop anywhere in the plain! Flee to the mountains or you will be swept away!"

18 But Lot said to them, "No, my lords, please! 19 Your servant has
found favor in your eyes, and you have shown great kindness to me in sparing my life. But I can't flee to the mountains; this disaster will
overtake me, and I'll die. 20 Look, here is a town near enough to run to,
and it is small. Let me flee to it—it is very small, isn't it? Then my life will be spared."

21 He said to him, "Very well, I will grant this request too; I will not
overthrow the town you speak of. 22 But flee there quickly, because I
cannot do anything until you reach it." (That is why the town was called Zoar.)

23 By the time Lot reached Zoar, the sun had risen over the land.
24 Then the LORD rained down burning sulfur on Sodom and Gomorrah—
from the LORD out of the heavens. 25 Thus he overthrew those cities and
the entire plain, including all those living in the cities—and also the
vegetation in the land. 26 But Lot's wife looked back, and she became a
pillar of salt.

27 Early the next morning Abraham got up and returned to the place
where he had stood before the LORD. 28 He looked down toward Sodom
and Gomorrah, toward all the land of the plain, and he saw dense smoke rising from the land, like smoke from a furnace.

15–16 In contrast to the account of the wickedness of the city of Sodom, which was placed in the darkness of night (vv.2, 4–5), the setting of the rescue of Lot occurs at the break of day (v.15). In turning the reader's attention to such details, the writer draws on a common biblical image that pictures salvation as a sunrise dispelling the evil darkness (see comment on 1:2) and consequently provides a larger context for viewing the events of this chapter. In contrast to the men of Sodom who blindly groped for the door of Lot's house, Lot and his family were taken by the hand and led out of the city to safety (v.16). To show that the rescue of Lot was in response to the prayer of Abraham, the angels' words explicitly recall Abraham's prayer in behalf of the righteous in the previous chapter. Abraham had prayed, "Will you sweep away the righteous with the wicked?" (*ha'ap̱ tispeh ṣaddîq 'im-rāšā'*, 18:23); and similarly the messengers warned Lot and his family to leave the city, "or you will be swept away when the city is punished" (*pen-tissāp̱eh ba'ᵃwōn hā'îr*, 19:15), and again in v.17: "or you will be swept away" (*pen-tissāp̱eh*). In fact, we are explicitly reminded by the narrator that Lot's rescue was an answer to Abraham's prayer in the previous chapter: "[God] remembered Abraham, and he brought Lot out of the catastrophe that overthrew the cities where Lot had lived" (v.29).

The picture of Lot then is that of a righteous man living amid the unrighteous—a righteous man who has been rescued from the fate of the wicked through the intercession of God's chosen one. One further important detail is added to the picture of Lot's rescue. Surprisingly the basis of God's saving Lot was not Lot's righteousness but the Lord's compassion. When the men took hold of Lot and lead him and his family out of the doomed city, the writer is careful to note that this was because "the LORD was merciful to them" (v.16). Lot's righteousness is not apparent from the narrative of chapter 19. It comes only from the connection established by the writer between Abraham's prayer "for the righteous" in chapter 18 and the events of Lot's rescue in chapter 19. When it is said in v.29 that God remembered Abraham and rescued Lot from the destruction of the cities, the natural inference is that Lot was the "righteous one" Abraham had in mind in his prayer in chapter 18. In the account of the rescue itself, however, the emphasis is on God's compassion. Lot's words to the messengers (v.19) reinforce the role of God's grace in the rescue of Lot. Lot acknowledged that he had found "favor" (*ḥēn*) and "kindness" (*ḥasdᵉḵā*) before God.

17–22 A brief episode is recounted at the conclusion of Lot's rescue that prolongs further the reader's attention to it. Lot requested shelter in the nearby city of Zoar (v.20); and granting the request the Lord saved the city of Zoar from destruction (v.21). The effect of this short episode is to further strengthen the author's point that Lot's rescue is a result of prayer, both Abraham's and his own (*hinnēh-nā'*, v.19, lit., "behold now"; untr. in NIV). A reminder of the importance of Abraham's prayer in chapter 18 can be seen in the fact that with Lot's request the actual circumstances envisioned in Abraham's prayer are realized when God saved the city on account of the righteous ones in it. God had promised not to destroy the city "on behalf of" the righteous in it (18:26, 28, 29, 30, 31, 32). So now, though Sodom was destroyed, Zoar was saved from the destruction on account of Lot (v.21). Thus by including this episode the writer has headed off an interpretive problem between chapters 18 and 19: namely, if Lot was the "righteous one" whom Abraham had in mind in his prayer in chapter 18, why did the Lord not save the city of Sodom on his behalf? Whatever the specific answer given to that question (see discussion on ch. 18), the point of vv.17–22 is that Abraham's prayer was specifically answered, and God did save the city of Zoar on account of the righteous one living in it.

23–28 The perspective of the narrative widens in scope as it recounts the destruction of the cities. The scope is that of 18:20–21, where both Sodom and Gomorrah and the surrounding cities are in view. We are reminded of two things before the onset of the description of God's judgment. First, "the sun had arisen over the land" (v.23b), and second, "Lot reached Zoar [safely]" (19:23a). The mention of the sun ties this section together with Lot's early morning rescue (v.15) as well as with the larger biblical picture of the "sunrise" as an image of divine salvation for the righteous and divine judgment on the wicked (Isa 9:2; Mal 4:1–2). With that as an introduction, the author depicts the scene that will become the classic image of the fate of every wicked one: "The LORD rained down burning sulfur on Sodom and Gomorrah" (vv.24–25).

As in the story of the Flood (chs. 6–8), the narrative does not dwell on the destruction of the cities. Rather our attention is centered on the response of two individuals, Lot's wife and Abraham, both of whom "looked" at the destruction of the cities, but with very differing consequences. Few details are given about either. Lot's wife became a "pillar of salt" (*neṣîḇ melaḥ*) because she "looked back" (*wattabbēṭ mē'aḥarāyw*, v.26). Apparently she suffered the same fate as the wicked on whom it rained burning sulfur because she disobeyed the words of the men ("Don't look back" [*'al-tabbîṭ 'aḥareyḵā*]; "don't stop anywhere in the plain! Flee to the mountains," v.17).

The double warning—i.e., "don't look; don't tarry"—that the men gave to Lot and his family may provide a narrative clue to the exact nature of the misdeed of Lot's wife. In light of the warning, we are perhaps to infer that she did not simply look behind her but rather "tarried to look in the valley" and hence was swept away with the wicked. Abraham, on the other hand, looked from a vantage point consistent with the men's words in v.17. They said, "Don't stop anywhere in the plain" (*we'al-ta'amōḏ beḵol-hakkikkār*), and so the writer reminds us that Abraham "was returned to the place where he had stood [*'āmaḏ*] before the LORD" (v.27) and "looked down toward Sodom and Gomorrah, toward all the land of the plain" (v.28). In any event, Abraham, though obviously unaware of the words of the men to Lot and his family, still obeyed the words and escaped the destruction.

This picture of Abraham is consistent with the overall picture of him as one who obeys and pleases God, though with little external instruction. Lot's wife, on the other hand, knew what to do but failed to do it. It is important to note that the narrative allows us to view the smoldering ruins from Abraham's perspective rather than Lot's. Clearly the central figure in the narrative is Abraham. It was his intercession that resulted in Lot's rescue; so we return to the perspective of Abraham to the place where he was at the time of the intercession to see a final glimpse of the effect of that prayer.

The reader is not told what Abraham might have been thinking as he watched the smoke billow up from the ruined cities. Abraham was silent. His thoughts were his own. But in view of the fact that the writer has deliberately turned our attention back to the scene of Abraham's prayer in chapter 18, it is hard not to see in this final scene a reminder of the central question of that prayer: "Will not the Judge of all the earth do right?" (v.25). At this point in the narrative, the answer to Abraham's question is made graphically clear. Sodom, in its wickedness, has been shown to be truly deserving of divine wrath. Lot has been rescued and Abraham himself spared from the destruction.

Only the disobedient among them, Lot's sons-in-law and wife, have perished along with the wicked. The whole of the narrative seems carefully planned to focus the reader's attention just on these points.

Notes

---

17 The plural for וַיֹּאמֶר (*wayyō'mer*, "one . . . said") in the old versions (LXX, Syr., Vul.) is a secondary adjustment to הָאֲנָשִׁים (*hā'ᵃnāšîm*, "the men") in v.16. In light of the אֲדֹנָי (*'ᵃḏōnāy*, "Lord") in v.18, the singulars in v.19, and the *wayyō'mer* in v.21, *wayyō'mer* here does not appear without purpose.

18 There are no textual grounds for changing אֲלֵהֶם (*'ᵃlēhem*, "to them") to אֵלָיו (*'ēlāyw*, "to him") as Eissfeldt suggests in BHS.

אֲדֹנָי (*'ᵃḏōnāy*, "Lord") is marked as "holy" (קֹדֶשׁ [*qōḏeš*]) by the Masoretes (Baer, *Liber Genesis*, p. 23), thus the long dipthong is not merely the result of its pausal position. There are no textual grounds for changing it to אֲדֹנִי (*'ᵃḏōnî*, "my lord").

22 עַל־כֵּן קָרָא שֵׁם־הָעִיר צוֹעַר (*ʿal-kēn qārā' šēm-hā'îr ṣôʿar*, "That is why the town was called Zoar") is a reference back to 14:2 (see Notes in loc.).

24 The syntax W + X + QATAL suggests that this verse is background to the main clause of v.25. Notice that the reference to both סְדֹם (*sᵉḏōm*, "Sodom") and עֲמֹרָה (*ʿᵃmōrāh*, "Gomorrah") aligns the narrative with 18:20, as does the הֶעָרִים הָאֵל (*heʿārîm hā'ēl*, "those cities") in v.25.

24–28 There is a curious similarity in clause structure, verbal forms, and reversal of themes between these verses and 1:2–5.

---

c. *Lot's incest*

19:29–38

29 So when God destroyed the cities of the plain, he remembered
Abraham, and he brought Lot out of the catastrophe that overthrew the
cities where Lot had lived.

30 Lot and his two daughters left Zoar and settled in the mountains, for
he was afraid to stay in Zoar. He and his two daughters lived in a cave.
31 One day the older daughter said to the younger, "Our father is old,
and there is no man around here to lie with us, as is the custom all over
the earth. 32 Let's get our father to drink wine and then lie with him and
preserve our family line through our father."

33 That night they got their father to drink wine, and the older daughter
went in and lay with him. He was not aware of it when she lay down or
when she got up.

34 The next day the older daughter said to the younger, "Last night I
lay with my father. Let's get him to drink wine again tonight, and you go
in and lie with him so we can preserve our family line through our
father." 35 So they got their father to drink wine that night also, and the
younger daughter went and lay with him. Again he was not aware of it
when she lay down or when she got up.

36 So both of Lot's daughters became pregnant by their father. 37 The
older daughter had a son, and she named him Moab; he is the father of
the Moabites of today. 38 The younger daughter also had a son, and she
named him Ben-Ammi; he is the father of the Ammonites of today.

29–38 The writer returns to Lot in the concluding narrative of chapter 19. Verse 29 is a clear reminder of Abraham's role in Lot's rescue: "[God] remembered Abraham, and he brought Lot out of the catastrophe." It is obvious that any merit on Lot's part that may have resulted in his rescue has been subordinated to the central importance of Abraham's intercession on his behalf. As such the writer is carrying through with the theme of God's promise—in Abraham and his offspring, "all people on earth will be blessed" (12:3). With that reminder the writer is free to recount the events of the final days of Lot, events that cast Lot in a very different light.

Ironically, in his own drunkenness Lot carried out the shameful act that he himself had suggested to the men of Sodom (19:8): he lay with his own daughters (vv.32–36). The account is remarkably similar to the story of the last days of Noah after his rescue from the Flood (9:20–27). There, as here, the father becomes drunk with wine and uncovers himself in the presence of his children with negative consequences. Thus at the close of the two great narratives of divine judgment, the Flood and the destruction of Sodom, those who were saved from God's wrath subsequently fell into a form of sin reminiscent of those who died in the judgment. Such is a common theme in the prophetic literature (e.g., Isa 56–66; Mal 1).

The introduction and body of this last Lot story is characterized by numerous wordplays and repetitions (see Notes on vv.29–30). Its purpose has been taken to be both positive (Westermann, p. 384) and negative (Delitzsch, p. 62). The positive characteristics of the story rest primarily on its relationship to other narratives in Genesis where the focus rests on preservation of the "seed" at all costs (e.g., Tamar in ch. 38). The negative aspects of the story stem from the drunkenness and incest that plays a central role in the plan of the daughters: "If it was not lust, therefore, which impelled them to this shameful deed, their conduct was worthy of Sodom, and shows quite as much as their previous betrothal to men of Sodom, that they were deeply imbued with the sinful character of that city" (Keil, p. 237). In light of such narratives as Genesis 38, where the equally shameful deed of Tamar is marked as "righteous" (v.26) in light of its purpose, we should probably look beyond the moral aspects of this narrative for our final assessment. Through the clever plan of the daughters, the line of Lot is preserved. Deuteronomy 2:9 and 19, which speak of the "sons of Lot" (NIV, "descendants") in warm and accepting terms, show that this narrative is not likely a mere polemic against the Moabites and Ammonites. However, the same ambiguity in this narrative regarding the actions of Lot's daughters can also be found in the Torah's view of the Moabites and the Ammonites. Though they are considered Israel's relatives, they are excluded from Israel's worship (Deut 23:3–4). Keil is correct in pointing out that the Moabites and the Ammonites' exclusion from the Holy Place in Deuteronomy 23 was based on their mistreatment of Israel during the time of the Conquest. They did not meet them with bread and water as brothers, and they hired Balaam to curse the Israelites (Num 22:4–20; Deut 23:4).

Lot is mentioned as the father of the Moabites and the Ammonites in Deuteronomy 2:9, 19, the passage that stresses their relationship to Israel, and not in Deuteronomy 23, where they are excluded from the congregation. Thus the present narrative is probably not to be taken as the basis of Israel's conflict with her neighbors. It rather pictures them as the survivors of God's judgment and the benefactors of his mercy. Both the Moabites and the Ammonites continued to play an important role in later biblical history. Located southeast of the Israelite territory, in Transjordan area, these two kingdoms frequently came into conflict with the Israelites (see Judg 3:12–30; 11:4–33; 1 Sam 11:1–11; 2 Sam 8:2; 10:1–19; 2 Kings 3). In the Book of Ruth, Ruth the Moabitess personifies the question of the inclusion of Gentiles in the covenant promises to Abraham. During the Babylonian exile, the Moabites and Ammonites provided a safe refuge for the Jews who had fled Judah (Jer 40:11; cf. J.R. Bartlett, "The Moabites and Edomites," *Peoples of Old Testament Times,* ed. by D.J. Wiseman [Oxford: Oxford University Press, 1973], pp. 229–58; Martin Noth, "Die Nachbarn der israelitischen Staemme im Ostjordanland," *Aufsaetze zur biblischen Landes- und Altertumskunde,* ed. Hans Walter Wolff [Neukirchen-Vluyn: Neukirchen Verlag, 1971], pp. 63–75).

Notes

29–30 Notice the wordplays in these two verses:

וַיְהִי בְּשַׁחֵת¹ (v.29a)   with וַיְשַׁלַּח² (v.29b)
הַכִּכָּר³ (v.29a)   with וַיִּזְכֹּר⁴ (v.29a)
הַהֲפֵכָה⁵ (v.29b)   with בַּהֲפֹךְ⁶ (v.29b)
מִצּוֹעַר ... בְּצוֹעַר⁷ (vv.30a,b)   with בַּמְּעָרָה⁸ (v.30c)

And the repetitions:

אֱלֹהִים⁹ (v.29a)   אֱלֹהִים⁹ (v.29a)
עָרֵי¹⁰ (v.29a)   הֶעָרִים¹¹ (v.29b)
לוֹט¹² (v.29b)   לוֹט¹² (v.30a)
וַיֵּשֶׁב¹³ (v.30a)   לָשֶׁבֶת ... וַיֵּשֶׁב¹⁴ (v.30b,c)
וּשְׁתֵּי בְנֹתָיו¹⁵ (v.30a)   וּשְׁתֵּי בְנֹתָיו¹⁵ (v.30c)

34–37 There may be a wordplay intended between מֵאָבִינוּ (*mēʾābînû,* "our father," v.34b), מֵאֲבִיהֶן (*mēʾăbîhen,* "their father," v.36b), מוֹאָב (*môʾāḇ,* "Moab," v.37a), and אֲבִי־מוֹאָב (*ʾăbî-môʾāḇ,* "father of the Moabites," v.37b).

37–38 Notice the chiastic coordination in הוּא יָלְדָה בֵן ... וַתֵּלֶד הַבְּכִירָה בֵן (*wattēleḏ habbᵉḵîrāh bēn ... hiwʾ yālᵉḏāh bēn,* "The older daughter had a son ... [she] had a son"; see Andersen, *Sentence in Biblical Hebrew,* p. 122).

¹ *wayᵉhî bᵉšaḥēṯ* ("So when").
² *wayᵉšallaḥ* ("he brought").
³ *hakkikkār* ("the plain").
⁴ *wayyizkōr* ("he remembered").
⁵ *hahᵃpēḵāh* ("the catastrophe").
⁶ *bahᵃpōḵ* ("that overthrew").
⁷ *miṣṣôʿar ... bᵉṣôʿar* (lit., "from Zoar ... in Zoar").
⁸ *bammᵉʿārāh* ("in a cave").
⁹ *ʾelōhîm* ("God").
¹⁰ *ʿārê* ("cities of").
¹¹ *heʿārîm* ("the cities").
¹² *lôṭ* ("Lot").
¹³ *wayyēšeḇ* ("and [he] settled").
¹⁴ *lāšeḇeṯ ... wayyēšeḇ* ("to stay ... lived").
¹⁵ *ûštê bᵉnōṯāyw* ("and his two daughters").

E. Abraham and Abimelech
20:1–18

¹ Now Abraham moved on from there into the region of the Negev and lived between Kadesh and Shur. For a while he stayed in Gerar, ² and

there Abraham said of his wife Sarah, "She is my sister." Then
Abimelech king of Gerar sent for Sarah and took her.
3 But God came to Abimelech in a dream one night and said to him,
"You are as good as dead because of the woman you have taken; she is
a married woman."
4 Now Abimelech had not gone near her, so he said, "Lord, will you
destroy an innocent nation? 5 Did he not say to me, 'She is my sister,'
and didn't she also say, 'He is my brother'? I have done this with a clear
conscience and clean hands."
6 Then God said to him in the dream, "Yes, I know you did this with a
clear conscience, and so I have kept you from sinning against me. That
is why I did not let you touch her. 7 Now return the man's wife, for he is a
prophet, and he will pray for you and you will live. But if you do not
return her, you may be sure that you and all yours will die."
8 Early the next morning Abimelech summoned all his officials, and
when he told them all that had happened, they were very much afraid.
9 Then Abimelech called Abraham in and said, "What have you done to
us? How have I wronged you that you have brought such great guilt
upon me and my kingdom? You have done things to me that should not
be done." 10 And Abimelech asked Abraham, "What was your reason for
doing this?"
11 Abraham replied, "I said to myself, 'There is surely no fear of God in
this place, and they will kill me because of my wife.' 12 Besides, she
really is my sister, the daughter of my father though not of my mother;
and she became my wife. 13 And when God had me wander from my
father's household, I said to her, 'This is how you can show your love to
me: Everywhere we go, say of me, "He is my brother." ' "
14 Then Abimelech brought sheep and cattle and male and female
slaves and gave them to Abraham, and he returned Sarah his wife to
him. 15 And Abimelech said, "My land is before you; live wherever you
like."
16 To Sarah he said, "I am giving your brother a thousand shekels of
silver. This is to cover the offense against you before all who are with
you; you are completely vindicated."
17 Then Abraham prayed to God, and God healed Abimelech, his wife
and his slave girls so they could have children again, 18 for the LORD had
closed up every womb in Abimelech's household because of Abraham's
wife Sarah.

The focus of the narrative of chapters 20 and 21 is on the relationship between Abraham and the nations. Abraham's role is that of a prophetic intercessor, as in the promise "all peoples on earth will be blessed through you" (12:3). He prayed for the Philistines (20:7), and God healed them (v.17). In the narrative Abimelech plays the role of a "righteous Gentile" with whom Abraham could live in peace and blessing. There is, then, an implied contrast in the narratives between chapters 19 (Lot, the one who pictures the mixed multitude) and 20 (Abimelech, the righteous sojourner).

1 Abraham left the "great trees of Mamre" (18:1, 33) and traveled into "the Negev" (*hannegeḇ*, i.e., "southward") to sojourn in Gerar. The fact that the author has reminded us in chapter 21 (vv.23b, 34a) that Abraham was still sojourning in Gerar suggests that the events of these two chapters are intended to be understood as having taken place in the "land of the Philistines" (v.34; see Notes).

2 Sarah was taken into Abimelech's house. Notice how truncated this part of the narrative is compared to the story of a similar event in chapter 12. What was there developed into a full story is here condensed into a single verse. Clearly the interest of the author is not so much the fate of Sarah as it is that of the Philistines. Many of the details of the event recorded here (e.g., Abraham's motive and intention in the deception, as well as a partial rationalization of the deception itself) are withheld until Abraham is given an opportunity to speak on his own behalf (vv.11–13). At that point his actions cast more light on the Philistines' inner motives than on his own. Abraham's words serve to show that he had mistakenly judged the Philistines to be a wicked people, something that the actions of the Philistines proved false.

3–16 The narrative goes to great lengths to demonstrate the innocence of the Philistine Abimelech. Before Abimelech pled his own innocence (v.4b), the author makes certain that we get the facts straight by informing us that "Abimelech had not gone near her" (v.4a). Thus when Abimelech claimed to be "innocent" (*ṣaddîq*, lit., "righteous") and appealed to his innocence in the face of Abraham's deception, the reader can do no other than side with him. All the information in the narrative itself points in his favor. Indeed, the matter is finally settled when God himself concurred with Abimelech's plea of innocence, saying, "I know you did this with a clear conscience" (v.6).

Having shown Abimelech to be innocent, the narrative then points to a feature of Abimelech's relationship with Abraham that threatens disaster. Abimelech was in immediate need of a warning lest he lose his innocence by his mistreatment of Abraham's household. Abraham's wife was to be returned, and Abraham the prophet must pray in behalf of the life of Abimelech (v.7). The surprising outcome of God's visit of Abimelech is that he responded immediately by rising early in the morning (v.8) and declaring his dream to his servants and then to Abraham. The last statement in v.8 shows the mood of the Philistines: "the men were very much afraid." Like the sailors and the king of Nineveh in the Book of Jonah (1:16; 3:6–9), the Philistines responded quickly and decisively to God's warning. Like Jonah, however, Abraham in this narrative was a reluctant prophet.

Abraham's reply (vv.11–13) seems intended not only to justify his action with Sarah in the present narrative but also to provide a larger picture for understanding his similar actions while in Egypt in chapter 12. At the same time, by tracing the plan back to the very beginnings of his sojourning from his father's house, he showed that the plan in this instance was not based on an actual assessment of the Philistines' religious life; rather it was simply a part of a larger scheme. Thus an explanation is given as to why Abraham misjudged the Philistines. The reader is somewhat at a loss to evaluate Abraham's explanation. Though we have followed the life of Abraham closely since he left his father's house in chapter 11, this is the first we have heard of such an overarching strategy on Abraham's part or of this aspect of his relationship with Sarah. In the last analysis we are left only with the opinion of Abimelech himself, who undoubtedly accepted Abraham's explanation and faulted only himself in this unfortunate situation. Just how sincerely Abimelech accepted Abraham's story can be seen in the fact that in speaking to Sarah he called Abraham "your brother" (v.16), showing that he accepted the explanation and in turn was attempting to restore the broken relationship with expensive gifts.

17–18 Abraham, on his part, accepted the gifts from the Philistines and offered a prayer on their behalf in return (v.17). Only at this point do we discover the nature of God's words to Abimelech in v.7 ("You may be sure that you and all yours will die"). The Lord had "closed up every womb in Abimelech's household" (v.18).

Notes

1 There appears to be a conscious attempt to draw out the similarities between the event recounted in 12:9–20 and the one here in chapter 20. Notice, for example, the way both narratives are introduced:

12:9: וַיִּסַּע אַבְרָם הָלוֹךְ וְנָסוֹעַ הַנֶּגְבָּה[1]
20:1: וַיִּסַּע מִשָּׁם אַבְרָהָם אַרְצָה הַנֶּגֶב[2]

The two similar narratives have been placed on either side of the Lot narratives. The motivation behind such an arrangement of the narratives may have been to reinitiate the theme of "the promise in jeopardy" that had been interrupted by the judgment theme in the Lot narratives.

There are also parallels and similarities between this chapter and the narrative in chapter 38, Judah and Tamar. Both narratives concentrate on the "righteousness" of those not yet a part of the line of promise.

Just at this point in the book, there is a cluster of narratives that focus the reader's attention on the Gentile nations:

1. 19:29–38: Moabites, Ammonites
2. 20:1–18: Philistines
3. 21:1–8: Isaac
4. 21:9–21: Ishmaelites
5. 21:22–34: Philistines

1–2 וַיָּגָר בִּגְרָר (*wayyāg̲or big̲rār*, "he stayed in Gerar") locates the events of this chapter (and the next) in Gerar, where אֲבִימֶלֶךְ (*'ᵃb̲îmelek̲*, "Abimelech") the "king of Gerar" lived. It is assumed, but not explicitly stated, that at the end of chapter 21 Abraham was still in Gerar—וַיָּגָר אַבְרָהָם בְּאֶרֶץ פְּלִשְׁתִּים (*wayyāg̲or 'ab̲rāhām bᵉ'ereṣ pᵉlištîm*, "And Abraham stayed in the land of the Philistines," 21:34). There is, however, some ambiguity regarding Abraham's settlement throughout the narratives. In 21:22 Abraham is in Beersheba sojourning with *'ᵃb̲îmelek̲* (21:31–32), but in 21:32 *'ᵃb̲îmelek̲* leaves to return to the "land of the Philistines." Keil (pp. 247f.) is no doubt correct in assuming that the discrepancy is only apparent due to the lack of absolute boundaries marking the Philistine territory at this time. The remark in 21:34, however, plays an important role as an introduction to the events of chapter 22. The net effect of 21:34 is to prepare the way for chapter 22 in which there is an analogy with Abraham leaving "Ur of the Chaldeans" to go "to the land which God would show him" (cf. 12:1).

15–16 Notice the chiastic coordination in וַיֹּאמֶר אֲבִימֶלֶךְ . . . וּלְשָׂרָה אָמַר (*wayyō'mer 'ᵃb̲îmelek̲ . . . ûlᵉśārāh 'āmar*, "And Abimelech said. . . . To Sarah he said"; cf. Andersen, *Sentence in Biblical Hebrew*, p. 122).

17–18 Since וַיֵּלֵדוּ (*wayyēlēd̲û*, "so they could have children again") means "to bear" or "to beget" (BDB, s.v.), it would at first appear that the Philistines began to bear children after God had healed them. That implies that their illness had resulted in their not being able to bear children. It is often assumed that the detection and effects of such an illness would necessitate a time period longer than the period of time that could be placed between the announcement of Isaac's birth in chapter 18 and the birth itself in chapter 21. But, as Jacob has suggested (p. 474), *wayyēlēd̲û* does not mean that they all, at that point in time, begat children in answer to Abraham's prayer. Rather it means that as a result of their being well, they went on to have children again. Thus v.18 explains *wayyēlēd̲û* as infertility—עָצֹר עָצַר יהוה בְּעַד כָּל־רֶחֶם (*'āṣōr 'āṣar yhwh bᵉ'ad̲ kol-reḥem*, "The Lord had closed up every womb"; cf. עֲצָרַנִי יהוה מִלֶּדֶת [*'ᵃṣāranî yhwh milled̲et̲*, "the Lord has kept me from having children," 16:2]).

[1](*wayyissa' 'ab̲rām hālôk̲ wᵉnāsôᵃ' hanneg̲bāh*, "Then Abram set out and continued toward the Negev").
[2](*wayyissa' miššām 'ab̲rāhām 'arṣāh hannег̲eb̲*, "Now Abraham moved on from there into the region of the Negev").

F. *Abraham and Isaac (21:1–25:11)*

1. *The birth of Isaac*

21:1–7

> [1] Now the LORD was gracious to Sarah as he had said, and the LORD did for Sarah what he had promised. [2] Sarah became pregnant and bore a son to Abraham in his old age, at the very time God had promised him. [3] Abraham gave the name Isaac to the son Sarah bore him. [4] When his son Isaac was eight days old, Abraham circumcised him, as God commanded him. [5] Abraham was a hundred years old when his son Isaac was born to him.
>
> [6] Sarah said, "God has brought me laughter, and everyone who hears about this will laugh with me." [7] And she added, "Who would have said to Abraham that Sarah would nurse children? Yet I have borne him a son in his old age."

1–7 Verse 1 picks up a central line of narrative from 18:10: "I will surely return to you about this time next year, and Sarah your wife will have a son." The stories of Lot and Abraham's sojourn with the Philistines have occupied most of the narrator's attention for the last three chapters, and only now does he return to the promise of a son. One can hardly fail to ask why the news of the birth of Isaac has been delayed and treated so anticlimactically by the writer. Certainly more attention was paid to the *announcement* of the birth of the son in chapter 18 than here in the report of the *accomplished fact.*

If we look for an answer to this question in the clues that come out of the text, we may find it in the emphasis given in the narrative to the Lord's faithfulness to his word. The birth of Isaac came about "as [the LORD] had said," a fact stressed three times within the first two verses. The plan not only came about, but, more importantly, it happened as it was announced. Thus the narrative calls attention to God's faithfulness to his word and to his careful attention to the details of his plan.

The importance of the announcement of Isaac's birth can be seen in the choice of the verb *pāqaḏ* ("visited"; NIV, "was gracious") in v.1. Often this verb is used in contexts where the focus is on God's attentive care and concern (W. Schottroff, THAT, 2:470ff.). In Exodus 3:16 the same word is translated "I have watched." Frequently the word finds its parallel in the verb "to remember" (e.g., Isa 23:16–17) and may be meant here as a complement to passages such as Genesis 8:1 ("But God remembered Noah") and Exodus 2:24 ("God . . . remembered his covenant with Abraham, with Isaac and with Jacob"). Also important is the reminder that Isaac was the "son . . . in [Abraham's] old age" (v.2) and that he was born "at the very time [*lammô'ēḏ*] God had promised him." Thus the key themes of the earlier promise narratives (e.g., 18:10–14) are reiterated with the announcement of the fulfillment. While stressing the divine side of the fulfillment, the narrative also emphasizes Abraham's obedience: "When his son Isaac was eight days old, Abraham circumcised him, as God commanded him" (v.4; cf. 17:12).

Abraham was a hundred years old at the time Isaac was born (cf. 17:1, 24). Sarah's words—"Who would have said to Abraham that Sarah would nurse children? Yet I have borne him a son in his old age" (v.7)—serve to emphasize his age.

Notes

---

1 The syntax W + X + QATAL suggests that וַיהוה פָּקַד (*wayhwh pāqad*, "Now the LORD was gracious") begins a new section and provides background for the events that follow.

4 כַּאֲשֶׁר צִוָּה אֹתוֹ אֱלֹהִים (*ka'ᵃšer ṣiwwāh 'ōṯô 'ᵉlōhîm,* "as God commanded him") refers back to the making of the covenant in 17:12.

5 The chronological notice that "Abraham was a hundred years old" refers to 17:24—"Abraham was ninety-nine years old"—and shows that the events of the intervening chapters (18–20) happened within a period of one year. It also reveals the age of Ishmael at this point. He was thirteen years old in 17:25; so at this point he was fourteen.

---

2. *Hagar and Ishmael*

21:8–21

8 The child grew and was weaned, and on the day Isaac was weaned
Abraham held a great feast. 9 But Sarah saw that the son whom Hagar
the Egyptian had borne to Abraham was mocking, 10 and she said to
Abraham, "Get rid of that slave woman and her son, for that slave woman's son will never share in the inheritance with my son Isaac."

11 The matter distressed Abraham greatly because it concerned his
son. 12 But God said to him, "Do not be so distressed about the boy and your maidservant. Listen to whatever Sarah tells you, because it is
through Isaac that your offspring will be reckoned. 13 I will make the son
of the maidservant into a nation also, because he is your offspring."

14 Early the next morning Abraham took some food and a skin of water and gave them to Hagar. He set them on her shoulders and then sent her off with the boy. She went on her way and wandered in the desert of Beersheba.

15 When the water in the skin was gone, she put the boy under one of
the bushes. 16 Then she went off and sat down nearby, about a bowshot away, for she thought, "I cannot watch the boy die." And as she sat there nearby, she began to sob.

17 God heard the boy crying, and the angel of God called to Hagar from heaven and said to her, "What is the matter, Hagar? Do not be
afraid; God has heard the boy crying as he lies there. 18 Lift the boy up
and take him by the hand, for I will make him into a great nation."

19 Then God opened her eyes and she saw a well of water. So she went and filled the skin with water and gave the boy a drink.

20 God was with the boy as he grew up. He lived in the desert and
became an archer. 21 While he was living in the Desert of Paran, his
mother got a wife for him from Egypt.

8–21 The celebration of Isaac's coming of age was the occasion for the account of the expulsion of Ishmael. The similarities between this chapter and the events in chapter 16 can hardly escape the attention of even the casual reader. The writer's close attention to the similarities in the details of the two chapters is perhaps best explained by his frequent use of "foreshadowing" to draw connections between important narratives. In this case the Lord's promise to Hagar (16:11–12) was recounted in a strikingly similar fashion to that of the fulfillment of the promise (vv.18–21). The promise foreshadows the fulfillment.

Notes

9 מְצַחֵק (*meṣaḥāq*, “mocking”) is a wordplay on יִצְחָק (*yiṣḥāq*, “Isaac”).

17 Although Ishmael’s name is not mentioned in this chapter—he is בֶּן־הָגָר (*ben-hāg̱ār*, “the son of Hagar,” v.9a), בְּנָהּ (*bᵉnāh*, “her son,” v.10a), בֶּן־הָאָמָה (*ben-hā’āmāh*, “the slavewoman’s son,” vv.10b, 13a), הַנַּעַר (*hanna‘ar*, “the boy,” vv.12a, 17a, 17b, 18a, 19b, 20a), הַיֶּלֶד (*hayyeleḏ*, “the boy,” vv.14a, 15b, 16a)—there is a clear wordplay on his name (יִשְׁמָעֵאל [*yišmā‘ē’l*, “Ishmael”]) in וַיִּשְׁמַע אֱלֹהִים (*wayyišma‘ ’ᵉlōhîm*, “God heard,” v.17) and כִּי־שָׁמַע אֱלֹהִים (*kî-šāma‘ ’ᵉlōhîm*, “God has heard”) in this verse.

3. *Abraham and Abimelech*

21:22–34

22 At that time Abimelech and Phicol the commander of his forces said to Abraham, “God is with you in everything you do. 23 Now swear to me here before God that you will not deal falsely with me or my children or my descendants. Show to me and the country where you are living as an alien the same kindness I have shown to you.”

24 Abraham said, “I swear it.”

25 Then Abraham complained to Abimelech about a well of water that Abimelech’s servants had seized. 26 But Abimelech said, “I don’t know who has done this. You did not tell me, and I heard about it only today.”

27 So Abraham brought sheep and cattle and gave them to Abimelech, and the two men made a treaty. 28 Abraham set apart seven ewe lambs from the flock, 29 and Abimelech asked Abraham, “What is the meaning of these seven ewe lambs you have set apart by themselves?”

30 He replied, “Accept these seven lambs from my hand as a witness that I dug this well.”

31 So that place was called Beersheba, because the two men swore an oath there.

32 After the treaty had been made at Beersheba, Abimelech and Phicol the commander of his forces returned to the land of the Philistines. 33 Abraham planted a tamarisk tree in Beersheba, and there he called upon the name of the LORD, the Eternal God. 34 And Abraham stayed in the land of the Philistines for a long time.

22–34 The reoccurrence of Abimelech in v.22, though something of a surprise in the narrative, shows that the setting of these narratives had not changed and that Abraham was still living with the Philistines. This judgment is confirmed at the conclusion of the narrative where it explicitly says that Abraham continued to sojourn with the Philistines “for a long time” (v.34). The reader is forced to ask why his attention is constantly being drawn to the fact that Abraham was dwelling with the Philistines during this time. Perhaps it was to present a picture of Abraham as someone who had yet to experience the fulfillment of God’s promises. Without the continuing accounts of Abraham’s dealings with Abimelech, the other events in these narratives might easily have been read within the context of the Promised Land. Thus what we are forced to see is a picture of Abraham who did not live out all his days in the Land of Promise but spent many of his days in exile. Even Isaac, the son of the promise, was not born in the Land of Promise. He was, rather, born in exile and had to sojourn there with his father who “wandered from nation to nation, from one kingdom to another” (Ps 105:13). The intention of the narrative seems very close to that which the writer of the Book of Hebrews saw in these narratives. In Hebrews 11:8–13, where it is recalled that though Abraham had left his father's land and had come to the Land of Promise, he lived there "like a stranger in a foreign country. . . . they were aliens and strangers on earth."

The picture of Abraham in exile is exemplary of God's caring for the righteous who must suffer while waiting to enter the land. The servants of Abimelech had stolen Abraham's wells. But because God was with Abraham in all that he did (v.22), he made a covenant with their king (v.27); and all was restored to him (v.32).

4. *The binding of Isaac*

22:1–14

1Some time later God tested Abraham. He said to him, "Abraham!"
"Here I am," he replied.
2Then God said, "Take your son, your only son, Isaac, whom you love,
and go to the region of Moriah. Sacrifice him there as a burnt offering
on one of the mountains I will tell you about."
3Early the next morning Abraham got up and saddled his donkey. He
took with him two of his servants and his son Isaac. When he had cut
enough wood for the burnt offering, he set out for the place God had
told him about. 4On the third day Abraham looked up and saw the place
in the distance. 5He said to his servants, "Stay here with the donkey
while I and the boy go over there. We will worship and then we will come
back to you."
6Abraham took the wood for the burnt offering and placed it on his
son Isaac, and he himself carried the fire and the knife. As the two of
them went on together, 7Isaac spoke up and said to his father Abraham,
"Father?"
"Yes, my son?" Abraham replied.
"The fire and wood are here," Isaac said, "but where is the lamb for
the burnt offering?"
8Abraham answered, "God himself will provide the lamb for the burnt
offering, my son." And the two of them went on together.
9When they reached the place God had told him about, Abraham built
an altar there and arranged the wood on it. He bound his son Isaac and
laid him on the altar, on top of the wood. 10Then he reached out his
hand and took the knife to slay his son. 11But the angel of the LORD
called out to him from heaven, "Abraham! Abraham!"
"Here I am," he replied.
12"Do not lay a hand on the boy," he said. "Do not do anything to him.
Now I know that you fear God, because you have not withheld from me
your son, your only son."
13Abraham looked up and there in a thicket he saw a ram caught by its
horns. He went over and took the ram and sacrificed it as a burnt
offering instead of his son. 14So Abraham called that place The LORD
Will Provide. And to this day it is said, "On the mountain of the LORD it
will be provided."

1–14 The first verse of this narrative provides a necessary preliminary understanding of the events of the chapter. Without it God's request that Abraham offer up Isaac as a "burnt offering" would be inexplicable. By stating clearly at the start that "God tested Abraham" (v.1), the writer quickly allays any doubt about God's real purpose. There is, then, no thought of an actual sacrifice of Isaac in the narrative, though in the mind of Abraham within the narrative that, of course, was the only thought that was entertained. The whole structure of the narrative focuses so strongly on the Lord's request that the writer apparently sensed the need to dispel any suspense or suspicion about the Lord's real intention.

Several features of the narrative serve to keep the reader's attention focused directly on the inward struggle of Abraham as he carried out the Lord's request—all, we might add, without any mention of the actual thoughts of Abraham's mind. First, there is the abruptness of the Lord's request within the narrative. Apart from the remark in v.1 that the narrative represented a test of Abraham, the reader is given no advanced warning of the nature of the request nor of its severity. Nothing in the preceding narratives would have hinted at this sort of request. The reader, in other words, is as surprised and shocked by the Lord's request as Abraham himself would have been. Second, the reader is given no further explanation of the request. The whole of the request is made up of three simple imperatives (v.2): "Take" (*qaḥ-nā'*), "go" (*wᵉlek*), and "sacrifice him" (*wᵉha'ᵃlēhû*). Furthermore, the reader is given no reason to believe that Abraham himself had any further explanation.

Like many biblical narratives, the reader often knows information that the characters in the narrative do not. In this case the reader knows that this was a test. But apart from this, we know no more about God's plans and ways than the characters within the narrative itself. We are as much in the dark about the intention of God's ways as Abraham. Thus we, the readers, are forced to rely on the assessment of Abraham himself, within the narrative, and to view the events of the narrative through his eyes and by means of his response. At the same time, in the absence of any explanation from the narrator, we are forced to read our own thoughts and feelings into those of Abraham. In the case of this narrative, the reader is given ample opportunity to do that as the ensuing events are narrated. What is particularly noticeable is how the writer of this story prolongs the narrative with excessive and deliberate details of Abraham's preparation for the journey and the journey itself. By allowing or, indeed, forcing the reader to follow one incidental and perfunctory act after the other (e.g., "[he] saddled his donkey" [v.3a], "he took with him two of his servants" [v.3b], "he had cut enough wood" [v.3c]—none of these acts prove relevant to the narrative in the end), the writer forces the reader to look beyond these narratively meaningless external events to ponder the thoughts of Abraham himself as he so matter-of-factly carried them out.

The writer gives no hints as to the nature of Abraham's inner thoughts, but this is certainly only because no hints were necessary. Who cannot imagine what Abraham felt? When, at last, someone in the narrative speaks, it is Isaac, not God, who breaks the silence; and the question he raises—"Where is the lamb for the burnt offering?"—served only to heighten the anguish that the Lord's request brought to Abraham and by now the reader. When Abraham finally ends his narrative silence and speaks in his reply to Isaac, for the first time, a hint at an answer is given: he said, "God himself will provide [*'ᵉlōhîm yir'eh-llô*] the lamb for the burnt offering, my son" (v.8). Such a reply is not anticipated within the narrative thus far, but the reply itself anticipates precisely the final outcome of the story: "The LORD will provide" (*yhwh yir'eh*, v.14). Thus midway through the narrative, the writer allows the final words of the story to appear and foreshadow the end. The reader is assured thereby both of the outcome of the narrative and of the quality of Abraham's faith.

Abraham's words cast a new light on his silence. Amid the anguish that the reader has read into Abraham's silence, there is now also a silent confidence in the Lord who will provide. Abraham's words should not be understood as merely an attempt to calm the curious Isaac; but in light of the fact that they anticipate the actual outcome of the narrative, they are to be read as a confident expression of his trust in God. Few narratives in Genesis can equal this story in dramatic tension. The writer seems deliberately to prolong the tension of both Abraham and the reader in his depiction of the last moments before God interrupted the action and called the test to a halt. Abraham's every action is described in exaggerated detail. At the last dramatic moment—"[Abraham] reached out his hand and took the knife to slay his son" (v.10)—the Lord intervened and, as Abraham had already anticipated, provided a fit substitute for the burnt offering. Abraham therefore named the altar he had built "The LORD will provide" (*yhwh yir'eh*, v.14); and the writer adds, "And to this day it is said, 'On the mountain of the LORD it will be provided'" (*yhwh yērā'eh*).

Notes

---

1 The two uses of וַיְהִי אַחַר הַדְּבָרִים הָאֵלֶּה (*wayᵉhî 'aḥar haddᵉḇārîm hā'ēlleh*, lit., "and after these things"; NIV, "Some time later") in vv.1, 20 show the author's conscious attempt to link the events into a definite chronological scheme (cf. 15:1).

The syntax of וְהָאֱלֹהִים נִסָּה אֶת־אַבְרָהָם (*wᵉhā'ᵉlōhîm nissāh 'eṯ-'aḇrāhām*, "God tested Abraham") (W + X + QATAL) suggests that the clause contains background information for the following story.

2 לֶךְ־לְךָ (*leḵ-lᵉḵā*, "go") and אֶל־אֶרֶץ הַמֹּרִיָּה (*'el-'ereṣ hammōrîyāh*, "to the region of Moriah") appear to be allusions back to 12:1: לֶךְ־לְךָ (*leḵ-lᵉḵā*, "leave") and אֶל־הָאָרֶץ אֲשֶׁר אַרְאֶךָּ (*'el-hā'āreṣ 'ᵃšer 'ar'eḵā*, "to the land I will show you"). This suggests a wordplay between *hammōrîyāh* and *rā'āh* (רָאָה, "to see"). The word *hammōrîyāh* is a place name for a site later identified with the location where the temple was built (cf. 2 Chron 3:1). The Samaritan Pentateuch (המוראה [*hmwr'h*]) and some early versions (e.g., Samar. Targ., Symm.) associate *hammōrîyāh* with *rā'āh*. In light of the central role played in this chapter by the verb *rā'āh* (see אֱלֹהִים יִרְאֶה [*'ᵉlōhîm yir'eh*, "God . . . will provide"], v.8a; יהוה יִרְאֶה [*yhwh yir'eh*, "the LORD will provide"], v.14a; יהוה יֵרָאֶה [*yhwh yērā'eh*], v.14b), the association of *hammōrîyāh* and *rā'āh* may have been intentional. In 2 Chron 3:1, the only other occurrence of הַמּוֹרִיָּה (*hammôrîyāh*) in the Bible, there is also a wordplay between *hammôrîyāh* and *rā'āh* in אֲשֶׁר נִרְאָה לְדָוִיד אָבִיהוּ (*'ᵃšer nir'āh lᵉḏāwîḏ 'āḇîhû*, "where [the LORD] had appeared to David his father"). The Syriac (= הָאֱמֹרִי [*hā'ᵉmōrî*, "the Amorites"]) reflects a different attempt to explain *hammōrîyāh* by means of a wordplay (מרא [*mr'*] reverses אמר [*'mr*]), but also suggests a reading with א (', aleph) like that of the Samaritan Pentateuch. The parallel of *'el-'ereṣ hammōrîyāh* in 2b, namely, אֲשֶׁר אֹמַר אֵלֶיךָ (*'ᵃšer 'ōmar 'ēleyḵā*, "I will tell you about") suggests a similar wordplay of *mr'* and *'mr*. None of these wordplays on *hammōrîyāh* should lead us to change the present MT. They may simply represent the narrative's own efforts to provide a wider context for these events by means of an interbiblical link.

14 יִרְאֶה (*yir'eh*, "will provide") is Qal imperfect whereas יֵרָאֶה (*yērā'eh*, "it will be provided") is Niphal imperfect. The Niphal in v.14b is an explanation of Abraham's statement in v.14a (אֲשֶׁר ['ᵃ*šer*] functions as כִּי [*kî*]; cf. 30:18; 31:49; BDB, p. 83) and links the statement to the appearance of the Lord in worship (cf. Lev 9:4: הַיּוֹם יהוה נִרְאָה אֲלֵיכֶם [*hayyôm yhwh nir'āh 'ᵃlêḵem*, "For today the LORD will appear to you"]).

---

5. *The angel of the Lord*

22:15–19

15 The angel of the LORD called to Abraham from heaven a second time
16 and said, "I swear by myself, declares the LORD, that because you have

done this and have not withheld your son, your only son, 17 I will surely
bless you and make your descendants as numerous as the stars in the
sky and as the sand on the seashore. Your descendants will take
possession of the cities of their enemies, 18 and through your offspring
all nations on earth will be blessed, because you have obeyed me."
19 Then Abraham returned to his servants, and they set off together for
Beersheba. And Abraham stayed in Beersheba.

15–19 Attached to the end of the narrative is an account of a "second" (*šēnîṯ*, v.15) encounter between Abraham and the angel of the Lord. Since in v.19 Abraham returned to the two young men who had accompanied him, it appears that this "second" encounter with the angel is to be understood as having occurred on the same occasion as the first. Why then does the writer call attention to it as a "second" meeting? Perhaps the purpose is to draw attention to the fact that this second discourse came at a separate time and thus after Abraham had finished the burnt offering. By drawing attention to this fact, the writer has subtly but intentionally separated the account of the renewed promise (vv.16–18) from the narrative of Abraham's test (vv.1–15). Perhaps this feature of the narrative is intended to show that the renewal of God's original promises to Abraham was not based on Abraham's specific actions in carrying out the test but rather was based on the faith and obedience of Abraham that showed through this test. This interpretation would account for the general expression "this thing" (*haddāḇār hazzeh;* NIV, "this") in v.16. However, as Jacob (in loc.) has suggested, the general statement "because you have done this" is explained by the more specific reference to the deed of Abraham in fulfilling the test: "and have not withheld your son." Against Jacob it could be pointed out that the second of the two clauses—"and have not withheld your son"—is connected with a waw and thus is more likely a further reason for the promise (cf. Andersen, *Sentence in Biblical Hebrew,* pp. 99–101), rather than a more specific explanation of "this thing."

The promise reiterated here is similar to that of chapters 12, 13, 15, 17, and 18. The promise of "blessing" (v.17) is similar to 12:2. The increase of Abraham's "descendants" is similar to 13:16; 15:5; and 17:2. The view of the "nations'" enjoyment of and participation in Abraham's blessing (v.18) is similar to 12:3 and 18:18. The reference to Abraham's act of obedience as the basis of the promise is similar to 18:19. Perhaps, also, the reference to Abraham's descendants possessing the "cities of their enemies" (v.17) is to be taken as a reference to the gift of the "land" that is found throughout the earlier narratives (e.g., 12:7; 13:15; 15:18; 17:8).

Notes

17 וְיִרַשׁ זַרְעֲךָ אֵת שַׁעַר אֹיְבָיו (*w^{e}yiraš zar'^{a}ḵā 'ēṯ ša'ar 'ōy^{e}ḇāyw,* "Your descendants will take possession of the cities of their enemies") anticipates וְיִירַשׁ זַרְעֵךְ אֵת שַׁעַר שֹׂנְאָיו (*w^{e}yîraš zar'ēḵ 'ēṯ ša'ar śōn^e'āyw,* "May your offspring possess the gates of their enemies," 24:60).

19 Abraham returned to בְּאֵר שָׁבַע (*b^e'ēr šāḇa',* "Beersheba") as in 21:33.

6. *The relatives of Abraham*

22:20–24

[20]Some time later Abraham was told, "Milcah is also a mother; she has borne sons to your brother Nahor: [21]Uz the firstborn, Buz his brother, Kemuel (the father of Aram), [22]Kesed, Hazo, Pildash, Jidlaph and Bethuel." [23]Bethuel became the father of Rebekah. Milcah bore these eight sons to Abraham's brother Nahor. [24]His concubine, whose name was Reumah, also had sons: Tebah, Gaham, Tahash and Maacah.

20–24 Immediately after the reiteration of the promise of a great multitude of descendants, the writer attaches a notice regarding the increase of the family that Abraham and Sarah had left behind in their homeland. The fact that the number of names in the list is twelve suggests that the writer intended to draw a comparison with the twelve sons of Jacob or the twelve sons of Ishmael in 25:12–15. In any event, the central purpose of listing the names is to introduce into the flow of the narrative the source of the future bride of Isaac, Rebekah (v.23), and to show that she was of the lineage of Milcah and not of her concubine (v.24).

Notes

---

23 The syntax W + X + QATAL with inverted word order and the fact that רִבְקָה (*ri<u>b</u>qāh*, "Rebekah") is not counted in the total (שְׁמֹנָה אֵלֶּה [*šᵉmōnāh 'ēlleh*, "these eight"]) shows that this is an explanation inserted within the list anticipating the narrative of chapter 24 (cf. vv.15, 24). There is no reason to suppose it is a later gloss.

---

7. *Machpelah and Sarah's death*

23:1–20

[1]Sarah lived to be a hundred and twenty-seven years old. [2]She died at Kiriath Arba (that is, Hebron) in the land of Canaan, and Abraham went to mourn for Sarah and to weep over her.

[3]Then Abraham rose from beside his dead wife and spoke to the Hittites. He said, [4]"I am an alien and a stranger among you. Sell me some property for a burial site here so I can bury my dead."

[5]The Hittites replied to Abraham, [6]"Sir, listen to us. You are a mighty prince among us. Bury your dead in the choicest of our tombs. None of us will refuse you his tomb for burying your dead."

[7]Then Abraham rose and bowed down before the people of the land, the Hittites. [8]He said to them, "If you are willing to let me bury my dead, then listen to me and intercede with Ephron son of Zohar on my behalf [9]so he will sell me the cave of Machpelah, which belongs to him and is at the end of his field. Ask him to sell it to me for the full price as a burial site among you."

[10]Ephron the Hittite was sitting among his people and he replied to Abraham in the hearing of all the Hittites who had come to the gate of his city. [11]"No, my lord," he said. "Listen to me; I give you the field, and I give you the cave that is in it. I give it to you in the presence of my people. Bury your dead."

[12]Again Abraham bowed down before the people of the land [13]and he
said to Ephron in their hearing, "Listen to me, if you will. I will pay the
price of the field. Accept it from me so I can bury my dead there."
[14]Ephron answered Abraham, [15]"Listen to me, my lord; the land is
worth four hundred shekels of silver, but what is that between me and
you? Bury your dead."
[16]Abraham agreed to Ephron's terms and weighed out for him the
price he had named in the hearing of the Hittites: four hundred shekels
of silver, according to the weight current among the merchants.
[17]So Ephron's field in Machpelah near Mamre—both the field and the
cave in it, and all the trees within the borders of the field—was deeded
[18]to Abraham as his property in the presence of all the Hittites who had
come to the gate of the city. [19]Afterward Abraham buried his wife Sarah
in the cave in the field of Machpelah near Mamre (which is at Hebron) in
the land of Canaan. [20]So the field and the cave in it were deeded to
Abraham by the Hittites as a burial site.

1–20 Sarah died in Hebron, and Abraham came there to mourn her death (v.2). Although the text is not clear, it appears that he came from Beersheba where he had been dwelling at the close of chapter 22 (v.19). The point of the narrative of chapter 23 is to show how Abraham first came into legal possession of a parcel of land in Canaan. Through what appears to be a hard bargain, Abraham bought not only a cave in which to bury his wife but also a large field with many trees. The chapter shows that Abraham came by this property fair and square. The field and particularly the cave in it became an important burial site for the patriarchs and their wives. According to 49:30–32, this is not only where Sarah and Abraham were buried but also Isaac, Rebekah, Leah, and Jacob (50:13).

The sense of chapter 23 within the larger context of the Book of Genesis can be seen in the similarity between Abraham's response to the offers of the sons of Heth and to those of the king of Sodom in chapter 14. In both cases the writer wants to show that Abraham would not accept a gift from the Canaanites. When the king of Sodom offered to reward Abraham, he replied that it should never be said that the king of Sodom made Abraham wealthy (14:23). In the same way Abraham adamantly refused to accept the parcel of land as a gift. Apparently against the wishes of the Hethites, he paid the full price for the land.

If viewed from the perspective of God's covenant promises to Abraham, both these narratives fit well within the overall themes of the book. God, not man, was the source of Abraham's hope of blessing. He would not seek to become wealthy or to own land apart from the promises of God. The same purpose also lies behind the note in 33:19, that when Jacob returned to the land, after his sojourn in the East, he purchased a portion of a field to pitch his tent. Wherever possible the writer seizes the opportunity to show that the patriarchs came by their possession of the land fairly and that it was a gift from God and not from those who were dwelling in the land at the time.

Still another idea that lies in this narrative can be seen in the Book of Jeremiah. In Jeremiah 32:6–15, on the eve of the Babylonian captivity, Jeremiah's trust in God's promise of the land was expressed in his purchase of a parcel of land. Though the people would soon be removed from the land in captivity, Jeremiah purchased a plot of ground because he was confident that they would one day return and enjoy the good land God had given them. The writer of Genesis appears to have a similar idea in mind in the picture of Abraham in chapter 23. He purchased only a portion of the land that would some day belong to his seed. In this small purchase was embodied the hope in God's promise that one day in the future it would all belong to him and his descendants. In the same way Joseph's last request was that his bones be returned to the land promised to Abraham, Isaac, and Jacob (50:24). His request was carried out when the Israelites buried his bones in the parcel of land purchased by Jacob from the sons of Hamor (Josh 24:32).

Notes

1 שְׁנֵי חַיֵּי שָׂרָה (šᵉnê ḥayyê śārāh, lit., "years of years the lives of Sarah") is omitted in the LXX and Vulgate. It is likely a later textual gloss to וַיִּהְיוּ חַיֵּי שָׂרָה (wayyihyû ḥayyê śārāh, "Sarah lived"). That is not sufficient reason, however, to insert šᵉnê after wayyihyû as in BHS.

2 Both the ancient name for the city of Sarah's death—קִרְיַת אַרְבַּע (Qiryat 'arba', "Kiriath Arba")—and its more recent name—חֶבְרוֹן (Ḥebrôn, "Hebron")—are given, as in Gen 35:27 (cf. Josh 14:15; 15:13, 54; Judg 1:10). Elsewhere the narrative gives only the more recent name, Hebron (cf. 13:18b). Later in the narrative the place where Abraham buried Sarah—מְעָרַת שְׂדֵה הַמַּכְפֵּלָה עַל־פְּנֵי מַמְרֵא (mᵉ'āraṯ śᵉḏēh hammakpēlāh 'al-pᵉnê mamrē', "the cave in the field of Machpelah near Mamre")—is also identified as Hebron (v.19). The narrative is clearly concerned to maintain a uniform location for the events. Hebron plays an important role in the later narratives of David. It is at Hebron that David is first anointed king over Judah (2 Sam 5:3).

17 The subject of וַיָּקָם (wayyāqom, "was deeded") is שְׂדֵה עֶפְרוֹן (śᵉḏēh 'eprôn, "Ephron's field," as in v.20 and Lev 25:30) with the ל (l) marking the possessor—לְאַבְרָהָם (lᵉ'aḇrāhām, "to Abraham," v.18a). The expression means that Abraham was given possession of the land with all its responsibilities (cf. Lev 25:30).

20 The waw consecutive—וַיָּקָם (wayyāqom, "So was deeded")—summarizes the events of the preceding narrative; cf. וַיִּבֶז עֵשָׂו אֶת־הַבְּכֹרָה (wayyiḇez 'ēśāw 'eṯ-habbᵉḵōrāh, "So Esau despised his birthright," 25:34).

8. A bride for Isaac

24:1-67

¹Abraham was now old and well advanced in years, and the LORD had blessed him in every way. ²He said to the chief servant in his household, the one in charge of all that he had, "Put your hand under my thigh. ³I want you to swear by the LORD, the God of heaven and the God of earth, that you will not get a wife for my son from the daughters of the Canaanites, among whom I am living, ⁴but will go to my country and my own relatives and get a wife for my son Isaac."

⁵The servant asked him, "What if the woman is unwilling to come back with me to this land? Shall I then take your son back to the country you came from?"

⁶"Make sure that you do not take my son back there," Abraham said. ⁷"The LORD, the God of heaven, who brought me out of my father's household and my native land and who spoke to me and promised me on oath, saying, 'To your offspring I will give this land'—he will send his angel before you so that you can get a wife for my son from there. ⁸If the woman is unwilling to come back with you, then you will be released from this oath of mine. Only do not take my son back there." ⁹So the servant put his hand under the thigh of his master Abraham and swore an oath to him concerning this matter.

10 Then the servant took ten of his master's camels and left, taking
with him all kinds of good things from his master. He set out for Aram
Naharaim and made his way to the town of Nahor. 11 He had the camels
kneel down near the well outside the town; it was toward evening, the
time the women go out to draw water.
12 Then he prayed, "O LORD, God of my master Abraham, give me
success today, and show kindness to my master Abraham. 13 See, I am
standing beside this spring, and the daughters of the townspeople are
coming out to draw water. 14 May it be that when I say to a girl, 'Please
let down your jar that I may have a drink,' and she says, 'Drink, and I'll
water your camels too'—let her be the one you have chosen for your
servant Isaac. By this I will know that you have shown kindness to my
master."
15 Before he had finished praying, Rebekah came out with her jar on
her shoulder. She was the daughter of Bethuel son of Milcah, who was
the wife of Abraham's brother Nahor. 16 The girl was very beautiful, a
virgin; no man had ever lain with her. She went down to the spring, filled
her jar and came up again.
17 The servant hurried to meet her and said, "Please give me a little
water from your jar."
18 "Drink, my lord," she said, and quickly lowered the jar to her hands
and gave him a drink.
19 After she had given him a drink, she said, "I'll draw water for your
camels too, until they have finished drinking." 20 So she quickly emptied
her jar into the trough, ran back to the well to draw more water, and
drew enough for all his camels. 21 Without saying a word, the man
watched her closely to learn whether or not the LORD had made his
journey successful.
22 When the camels had finished drinking, the man took out a gold
nose ring weighing a beka and two gold bracelets weighing ten shekels.
23 Then he asked, "Whose daughter are you? Please tell me, is there
room in your father's house for us to spend the night?"
24 She answered him, "I am the daughter of Bethuel, the son that
Milcah bore to Nahor." 25 And she added, "We have plenty of straw and
fodder, as well as room for you to spend the night."
26 Then the man bowed down and worshiped the LORD, 27 saying,
"Praise be to the LORD, the God of my master Abraham, who has not
abandoned his kindness and faithfulness to my master. As for me, the
LORD has led me on the journey to the house of my master's relatives."
28 The girl ran and told her mother's household about these things.
29 Now Rebekah had a brother named Laban, and he hurried out to the
man at the spring. 30 As soon as he had seen the nose ring, and the
bracelets on his sister's arms, and had heard Rebekah tell what the man
said to her, he went out to the man and found him standing by the
camels near the spring. 31 "Come, you who are blessed by the LORD," he
said. "Why are you standing out here? I have prepared the house and a
place for the camels."
32 So the man went to the house, and the camels were unloaded.
Straw and fodder were brought for the camels, and water for him and
his men to wash their feet. 33 Then food was set before him, but he said,
"I will not eat until I have told you what I have to say."
"Then tell us," Laban said.
34 So he said, "I am Abraham's servant. 35 The LORD has blessed my
master abundantly, and he has become wealthy. He has given him
sheep and cattle, silver and gold, menservants and maidservants, and
camels and donkeys. 36 My master's wife Sarah has borne him a son in
her old age, and he has given him everything he owns. 37 And my master
made me swear an oath, and said, 'You must not get a wife for my son

from the daughters of the Canaanites, in whose land I live, 38 but go to
my father's family and to my own clan, and get a wife for my son.'
39 "Then I asked my master, 'What if the woman will not come back
with me?'
40 "He replied, 'The Lord, before whom I have walked, will send his
angel with you and make your journey a success, so that you can get a
wife for my son from my own clan and from my father's family. 41 Then,
when you go to my clan, you will be released from my oath even if they
refuse to give her to you—you will be released from my oath.'
42 "When I came to the spring today, I said, 'O Lord, God of my master
Abraham, if you will, please grant success to the journey on which I have
come. 43 See, I am standing beside this spring; if a maiden comes out to
draw water and I say to her, "Please let me drink a little water from your
jar," 44 and if she says to me, "Drink, and I'll draw water for your camels
too," let her be the one the Lord has chosen for my master's son.'
45 "Before I finished praying in my heart, Rebekah came out, with her
jar on her shoulder. She went down to the spring and drew water, and I
said to her, 'Please give me a drink.'
46 "She quickly lowered her jar from her shoulder and said, 'Drink, and
I'll water your camels too.' So I drank, and she watered the camels also.
47 "I asked her, 'Whose daughter are you?'
"She said, 'The daughter of Bethuel son of Nahor, whom Milcah bore
to him.'
"Then I put the ring in her nose and the bracelets on her arms, 48 and I
bowed down and worshiped the Lord. I praised the Lord, the God of my
master Abraham, who had led me on the right road to get the
granddaughter of my master's brother for his son. 49 Now if you will
show kindness and faithfulness to my master, tell me; and if not, tell me,
so I may know which way to turn."
50 Laban and Bethuel answered, "This is from the Lord; we can say
nothing to you one way or the other. 51 Here is Rebekah; take her and
go, and let her become the wife of your master's son, as the Lord has
directed."
52 When Abraham's servant heard what they said, he bowed down to
the ground before the Lord. 53 Then the servant brought out gold and
silver jewelry and articles of clothing and gave them to Rebekah; he also
gave costly gifts to her brother and to her mother. 54 Then he and the
men who were with him ate and drank and spent the night there.
When they got up the next morning, he said, "Send me on my way to
my master."
55 But her brother and her mother replied, "Let the girl remain with us
ten days or so; then you may go."
56 But he said to them, "Do not detain me, now that the Lord has
granted success to my journey. Send me on my way so I may go to my
master."
57 Then they said, "Let's call the girl and ask her about it." 58 So they
called Rebekah and asked her, "Will you go with this man?"
"I will go," she said.
59 So they sent their sister Rebekah on her way, along with her nurse
and Abraham's servant and his men. 60 And they blessed Rebekah and
said to her,

"Our sister, may you increase
  to thousands upon thousands;
may your offspring possess
  the gates of their enemies."

61 Then Rebekah and her maids got ready and mounted their camels
and went back with the man. So the servant took Rebekah and left.

62Now Isaac had come from Beer Lahai Roi, for he was living in the
Negev. 63He went out to the field one evening to meditate, and as he
looked up, he saw camels approaching. 64Rebekah also looked up and
saw Isaac. She got down from her camel 65and asked the servant, "Who
is that man in the field coming to meet us?"
"He is my master," the servant answered. So she took her veil and
covered herself.
66Then the servant told Isaac all he had done. 67Isaac brought her into
the tent of his mother Sarah, and he married Rebekah. So she became
his wife, and he loved her; and Isaac was comforted after his mother's
death.

1–9 The story begins with an account of the oath made between Abraham and his servant. The point of the section is to show Abraham's concern for God's promise that was to come to the descendants of Isaac. In this sense the story picks up from 21:1 the theme of Isaac the promised offspring. Though Isaac is a central figure in chapter 22, he is not portrayed there as the promised offspring but rather as the beloved son of Abraham. Abraham's faith was tested, and Isaac's role within that narrative was directed toward that end. The focus on Isaac as the chosen descendant, which is at the center of chapter 24, however, takes the reader back to the account of his birth in chapter 21 and to the announcement of his birth in chapter 18. At the end of the Abrahamic narratives, then, the writer returns to the themes that loomed large at the beginning—the promised descendants and the blessing.

Two important points are made regarding the future of Abraham's descendants in this opening section. First, they were not to be mixed with the inhabitants of Canaan (v.3). Though no explanation is given, Abraham's desire that Isaac not take a wife from the Canaanites appears to be a further expression of the notion of the two lines of blessing and curse seen in Genesis 9:25–27: "Cursed be Canaan!" but "Blessed be the LORD, the God of Shem." As has been the case throughout the narratives thus far, the inhabitants of Canaan are considered to be under a divine curse for their iniquity (e.g., 15:16). The seed of Abraham is to be kept separate from the seed of Canaan. Second, the point is made in this section that Abraham's descendants are not to return to the land of their fathers. The Promised Land is their home, and Abraham is careful to ensure that Isaac not be taken back to the place of his father.

Finally, this section allows the writer once more to portray the faith of Abraham. The questions raised by the servant provide the occasion. What if the young woman does not want to return (v.5)? What then? As so many times before, Abraham's reply proves to be both prophetic—it anticipates the final outcome of the story—and thematic—it provides the central motive of the narrative—"The LORD, the God of heaven, . . . will send his angel before you so that you can get a wife for my son from there" (v.7). Consequently the key word in the narrative is *haqrēh* ("give [me] success," v.12), and the key idea is that of God's going before the servant to prepare his way. The primary means of getting this message across in the narrative is the words of the loquacious servant.

10–27 The servant spelled out very specifically the nature of the sign he sought from the Lord (vv.12–14). To add force to the picture of God's preparing the way, the writer informs us that even before the servant had finished speaking, the young girl in question arrived on the scene (v.15a). The reader is given all the details of the background of the young girl as soon as she enters the picture (vv.15b–16). While the servant himself must wait to find out the actual identity of the girl, the reader already knows that this is Rebekah, the daughter of Bethuel, the son of Milcah. The point is to show from the start that the Lord has answered the servant's prayer. Thus the writer has sacrificed a certain amount of narrative suspense for the sake of his main idea. Indeed, judging from the type of information given about the girl in v.16 (e.g., she was beautiful, she was a virgin, no man had known her), the writer leaves us in no doubt that this was the girl the servant had asked for and that God had indeed sent his messenger out ahead of him to prepare the way. The rest of the story only confirms what the writer has given away here at the beginning. This is the girl. Thus when the writer continues to recount all the details that show this was in fact the girl, it only serves to underscore the extent to which the Lord had prepared this wife for Isaac.

What is unusual about this particular narrative, and also what makes it unusually long, is the fact that even though we, the readers, already know who the young girl was and what family she was from, we still must wait for the servant to inquire of the girl and find out for himself. Rather than finding out such information at the same time as the character in the narrative, the reader's part in the story is to look on as the servant himself discovers who the girl is and how the Lord had prepared his way. The point of the narrative is not so much the reader's discovery of what God has done but rather the servant's response to it. The purpose of this, apparently, is to give due attention to the Lord's role in the events. The writer is not content with leaving the reader alone with such an amazing picture of God's work. Rather, in the character of the servant and in his response, the reader is shown the proper response to such events. Such divine preparation for the descendants of Abraham and the line of the blessing must be accompanied by the kind of appreciation seen in the servant: "Then the man bowed down and worshiped the LORD, saying, 'Praise be to the LORD, the God of my master Abraham, who has not abandoned his kindness and faithfulness to my master' " (vv.26–27).

28–48 Another striking feature of this story is that after introducing the new characters of Laban and his household, the writer allows the servant again to retell the narrative (vv.34–49). But as with most repetitions in biblical narrative, the retelling is not a mere repeating. It is rather a reassertion of the central points of the first narrative. The point of the retelling can be seen in the fact that the servant adds to what was originally reported by Abraham (v.7). Originally we heard Abraham say, only generally, that God would send a messenger and that the servant would find a wife for Isaac (v.7). When he retold the story to Laban, however, the servant included the idea that God would send the angel and also added that the angel would make his journey a success by gaining a wife for Isaac from his own family (v.40). As we overhear the servant recount more details, we see that the miracle of God's provision was even more grand than that suggested in the narrative itself.

50–61 Again, at the conclusion of the servant's account of the events, Laban and Bethuel express their view of the events. They too acknowledge that it was the Lord who prepared the way for the servant to meet Rebekah. Thus the reader has been given three witnesses that these events have been the work of God: the narrator (vv.15–16), the servant (vv.26–27), and Laban (v.50). The final witness is Rebekah herself, who, against the wishes of her brother and her mother, returned with the servant to Isaac. The simplicity of her response ("I will go," v.58) reveals the nature of her trust in the God of Abraham. The fact that Rebekah's response (*'ēlēḵ*, "I will go," v.58) is identical to Ruth's (*'ēlēḵ*, "I will go," Ruth 1:16) suggests that there may be more than a mere coincidental relationship between the narratives of the two women.

62–67 The importance of the blessing of Rebekah by her family lies in the similarity of this blessing to that given to Abraham by the Lord in 22:17: "Your descendants will take possession of the cities of their enemies." The purpose is once again to show just what careful attention to detail the Lord has shown in choosing this wife for Isaac. In God's plan the same blessing has been given to both Isaac and his bride.

Isaac, for the first time in the story, enters the narrative just as the servant was bringing the young woman to him. They both lift up their eyes and see the other in the distance (vv.63–64). The narrator, along with the readers, knows who it is that Isaac and Rebekah see, but they themselves do not. Notice how the narrator writes "she saw Isaac"; yet it is not until the next verse that Rebekah herself learns that it was Isaac. Here is another example of the curious perspective of the reader throughout the narrative. The readers learn nothing new as the narrative progresses. It is only the characters that continue to discover the providential ordering of the events; we, the readers, merely watch as the characters discover the greatness of God's leading.

Verse 66 shows that the writer knows just how long to tell the story and stops short of going beyond that point. He says merely that the servant "told Isaac all he had done." A lesser writer might have allowed the servant to retell the story one more time, but by this time the events of the story are so clear that even the casual reader could have supplied Isaac with most of the details. The final remarks (v.67) again show that God's guidance in the mundane areas of life is good for those who put their trust in him. When Isaac took Rebekah as his wife, he loved her and was comforted with her after the death of his mother. In other words, Rebekah had taken the place of Sarah in the line of the descendants of Abraham.

Notes

---

1 The syntax W + X + QATAL suggests this verse is to be read as background to the narrative that follows (cf. 1:2–3).

12 הִקְרֵה (*haqrēh*, "give . . . success," Hiphil of קָרָה [*qārāh*, "to meet, happen"]) is a word found in some texts stressing the salvation-historical aspect of divine guidance and help (e.g., Num 11:23; Ruth 2:3; Jer 32:23; cf. E. Jenni, THAT, 2:684). In some contexts the word appears to mean little more than "to chance upon" (see BDB). However, such contexts may even more subtly stress divine guidance. Regarding Ruth 2:3, Hals says, "The labeling of Ruth's meeting with Boaz as 'chance' is nothing more than the author's way of saying that no human intent was involved. For Ruth and Boaz it was an accident, but not for God. . . . It is a kind of underplaying for effect. By calling this meeting an accident, the writer enables himself subtly to point out that even the 'accidental' is directed by God" (quoted in Jack M. Sasson, *Ruth* [Baltimore: The Johns Hopkins University Press, 1979], p. 44). In the present passage יהוה (*yhwh*, "the LORD") is expressly the subject of *haqrēh;* so "chance" is hardly adequate as a translation.

27 אָנֹכִי (*'ānōḵî*, "I") is the subject of a compound nominal clause (R. Meyer, *Hebräische Grammatik* [Berlin: Walter de Gruyter, n.d.], 3:13). There is no need to emend it to כִּי (*kî*, "for") as in the BHS apparatus.

67 הָאֹהֱלָה שָׂרָה אִמּוֹ (hāʾōhᵉlāh śārāh ʾimmô, "into the tent of Sarah his mother") is difficult in that it is unusual for nouns in construct to have an article as hāʾōhᵉlāh. There are, however, several examples of such constructions: e.g., Num 21:14: הַנְּחָלִים אַרְנוֹן (hannᵉḥālîm ʾarnôn, "the ravines of Arnon"); 2 Kings 23:17: הַמִּזְבַּח בֵּית־אֵל (hammizbaḥ bêṯ-ʾēl, "the altar of Bethel"); Isa 36:16: הַמֶּלֶךְ אַשּׁוּר (hammeleḵ ʾaššûr, "the king of Assyria") (König, Syntax, par. 303a). GKC explains the anomaly by suggesting śārāh ʾimmô is a later insertion (par. 127f). The examples cited by König show such a solution to be unnecessary.

---

9. Abraham's death

25:1–10[11]

¹Abraham took another wife, whose name was Keturah. ²She bore him Zimran, Jokshan, Medan, Midian, Ishbak and Shuah. ³Jokshan was the father of Sheba and Dedan; the descendants of Dedan were the Asshurites, the Letushites and the Leummites. ⁴The sons of Midian were Ephah, Epher, Hanoch, Abida and Eldaah. All these were descendants of Keturah.
⁵Abraham left everything he owned to Isaac. ⁶But while he was still living, he gave gifts to the sons of his concubines and sent them away from his son Isaac to the land of the east.
⁷Altogether, Abraham lived a hundred and seventy-five years. ⁸Then Abraham breathed his last and died at a good old age, an old man and full of years; and he was gathered to his people. ⁹His sons Isaac and Ishmael buried him in the cave of Machpelah near Mamre, in the field of Ephron son of Zohar the Hittite, ¹⁰the field Abraham had bought from the Hittites. There Abraham was buried with his wife Sarah. ¹¹After Abraham's death, God blessed his son Isaac, who then lived near Beer Lahai Roi.

Chapter 25 is a transition chapter. Abraham dies, and the blessing is renewed with Isaac. Ishmael passes from the scene, and the new generation—Jacob and Esau—is born.

1–6 The narrative reads as though after the death of Sarah, Abraham took another wife (wayyōsep̄ ʾaḇrāhām wayyiqqaḥ ʾiššāh) by the name Keturah (v.1). There is little basis in the Hebrew text for the translation "Abraham had taken a wife" (NIV mg.), as though Keturah had been a wife or "concubine" of Abraham in his younger days at the same time he was married to Sarah. Some have suggested that Keturah was one of the "concubines" mentioned in v.6 and hence these sons were born to Abraham and Keturah while Sarah was alive. Support for that interpretation appears to come from the fact that the Chronicler called Keturah a "concubine" (1 Chron 1:32). Though Keturah is called a "concubine" in Chronicles, she is called a "wife" here in v.1, which would seem to preclude her from being a mere concubine during the time Sarah was alive.

The picture that emerges of Abraham's life after the death of Sarah is that of a complete rejuvenation of the old man of the previous narratives. He continued to be rewarded with the blessing of many offspring. The writer, however, is careful to point out that none of these sons, except Isaac, had any share in the promised blessing: Abraham gave gifts to the other sons and sent them away, but he "left everything he owned to Isaac" (v.5). The focus on Isaac is reasserted clearly in v.11 where the writer shows that God himself blessed Isaac after the death of Abraham.

7–10 Surprisingly little attention is given to the details of the death of Abraham. The length of his life is given (v.7), which serves to connect him to the patriarchs listed at length in the previous chapters (cf. 11:32). The narrative adds the epitaph that Abraham died "at a good old age" (*beśēḇāh ṭôḇāh,* v.8), which recalls the word of the Lord to Abraham in 15:15: "You, however, will go to your fathers in peace and be buried at a good old age [*beśêḇāh ṭôḇāh*]." The mention of Abraham's "good [*ṭôḇāh*] old age" also serves as a contrast to Jacob's years that are characterized in 47:9 as "few and difficult" (*rāʿîm,* lit., "evil"). Thus, within the context of the Book of Genesis, Abraham and Jacob provide a narrative example of the contrast of "good" (*ṭôḇ*) and "evil" (*raʿ*), a theme begun in the first chapters of the book and carried through to the end (cf. 50:20). The emphasis of the narrative in this section lies in the fact that Abraham was buried in the field that he purchased from Ephron the Hittite (vv.9–10). The final resting place of Abraham was in a portion of the Promised Land that he rightfully owned.

11 Verse 11 opens the portion of Genesis that deals specifically with Isaac, and it gives this important but simple introduction: "After Abraham's death, God blessed his son Isaac." There are relatively few narratives devoted to the theme of "blessing" in the life of Isaac. Most of them are woven into the busy tapestry of chapter 26. All the more important then is this brief statement that God blessed Isaac. Such a reminder shows again the overarching purpose of the writer to draw out the line through which the divine blessing would come and to show it as a part of God's plan announced long before (cf. 17:21).

Notes

---

1 The verb וַיֹּסֶף (*wayyōsep̱*) means "again" and should be translated "took another wife" (so NIV). The past perfect ("had taken") is not appropriate for the WAYYIQTOL form that expresses the idea of succession (Joüon, *Grammaire*, par. 118; cf. Gen 38:5; 1 Sam 19:21; cf. BDB, p. 415). Keil (p. 261) says there is "no firm ground" for supposing that Abraham took Keturah as a wife after the death of Sarah. However, the presence of *wayyōsep̱* is certainly grounds enough.

2 The descendants of מִדְיָן (*miḏyān,* "Midian") and מְדָן (*meḏān,* "Medan") play a further role in the Genesis narratives in that they take part in the rescue of Joseph from his brothers (cf. 37:28: מִדְיָנִים [*miḏyānîm,* "Midianites"] and 37:36: הַמְּדָנִים [*hammeḏānîm,* "Medanities"; NIV, "Midianites"]).

5–10 The end of the Abrahamic narrative is marked by chiastic coordination (vv.5–6: וַיִּתֵּן אַבְרָהָם . . . וְלִבְנֵי . . . נָתַן אַבְרָהָם [*wayyittēn 'aḇrāhām . . . welibnê . . . nāṯan 'aḇrāhām,* "Abraham left . . . to his sons . . . Abraham gave"]) and epic repetition (vv.9–10: וַיִּקְבְּרוּ אֹתוֹ . . . שָׁמָּה קֻבַּר אַבְרָהָם [*wayyiqberû 'ōṯô . . . šāmmāh qubbar 'aḇrāhām,* "(they) buried him. . . . There Abraham was buried"]) (cf. Andersen, *Sentence in Biblical Hebrew*, pp. 39ff.; 122ff.).

11 וַיְהִי אַחֲרֵי מוֹת אַבְרָהָם (*wayehî 'aharê môṯ 'aḇrāhām,* "After Abraham's death") is a common syntactical form at the beginning of a large narrative segment (cf. Josh 1:1; Judg 1:1).

III. The Account of Ishmael

25:12–18

[12]This is the account of Abraham's son Ishmael, whom Sarah's maidservant, Hagar the Egyptian, bore to Abraham.

13 These are the names of the sons of Ishmael, listed in the order of
their birth: Nebaioth the firstborn of Ishmael, Kedar, Adbeel, Mibsam,
14 Mishma, Dumah, Massa, 15 Hadad, Tema, Jetur, Naphish and Kede-
mah. 16 These were the sons of Ishmael, and these are the names of the
twelve tribal rulers according to their settlements and camps. 17 Altogether, Ishmael lived a hundred and thirty-seven years. He breathed his
last and died, and he was gathered to his people. 18 His descendants
settled in the area from Havilah to Shur, near the border of Egypt, as you
go toward Asshur. And they lived in hostility toward all their brothers.

12–18 At the opening of the Isaac stories, there is a final statement regarding the line of Ishmael (v.12). It consists of a genealogy of the twelve leaders of Ishmael's clan, a report of the length of Ishmael's life, and, finally, a report of his death. As with other lists of names throughout the book, the number twelve appears to be a deliberate attempt to set these individuals off as founders of a new and separate people (cf. comment on 22:20). The mention of "twelve tribal rulers" (*šenêm-ʿāśār neśîʾim*) recalls the word of the Lord regarding the future of the line of Ishmael from 17:20, where it was promised that he too would be blessed and that "twelve rulers" (*šenêm-ʿāśār neśîʾim*) would be born to him and become a great nation. It is apparently enough for the writer to recall only Ishmael's blessing by way of this allusion to the earlier promise. Perhaps a mention of a blessing promised to Ishmael at this point in the narrative would have been too easily confused with the larger theme of the blessings of the Abrahamic covenant. In any case, no further mention is made of the blessing of Ishmael that was recounted in 17:20, and henceforth we hear nothing more about him in Genesis. The writer's interest turns quickly to Isaac.

Notes

12–18 The descendants of Ishmael continue to play a part in the Genesis narratives (28:9; 36:3; 37:27–28; 39:1).

18 The verb נָפַל (*nāpal*, "they lived in hostility," NIV), which takes the place of יִשְׁכֹּן (*yiškōn*, "he will live [in hostility]," NIV) in the similar expression in 16:12b, is best explained from נֹפְלִים (*nōpelîm*, "had settled") in Judg 7:12. The *yiškōn* has apparently been represented in the וַיִּשְׁכְּנוּ (*wayyiškenû*, "[they] settled") of the first part of the verse (Jacob, p. 539). The NIV's translation of עַל־פְּנֵי כָל־אֶחָיו נָפָל (*ʿal-penê kol-ʾeḥāyw nāpal* ("lived in hostility toward all their brothers") is apparently influenced by יָדוֹ בַכֹּל וְיַד כֹּל בּוֹ (*yādô bakkōl weyad kōl bô*, "and everyone's hand against him") in 16:12. The more neutral "he settled over against all his people" (RSV) is preferable.

IV. The Account of Isaac (25:19–35:29)

A. *The Birth of Jacob and Esau*

25:19–28

19 This is the account of Abraham's son Isaac.
Abraham became the father of Isaac, 20 and Isaac was forty years old
when he married Rebekah daughter of Bethuel the Aramean from
Paddan Aram and sister of Laban the Aramean.

21Isaac prayed to the LORD on behalf of his wife, because she was
barren. The LORD answered his prayer, and his wife Rebekah became
pregnant. 22The babies jostled each other within her, and she said,
"Why is this happening to me?" So she went to inquire of the LORD.
23The LORD said to her,

"Two nations are in your womb,
and two peoples from within you will be separated;
one people will be stronger than the other,
and the older will serve the younger."

24When the time came for her to give birth, there were twin boys in her
womb. 25The first to come out was red, and his whole body was like a
hairy garment; so they named him Esau. 26After this, his brother came
out, with his hand grasping Esau's heel; so he was named Jacob. Isaac
was sixty years old when Rebekah gave birth to them.
27The boys grew up, and Esau became a skillful hunter, a man of the
open country, while Jacob was a quiet man, staying among the tents.
28Isaac, who had a taste for wild game, loved Esau, but Rebekah loved
Jacob.

19 The narratives that have the life of Isaac for their backdrop are introduced as "the account of Abraham's son Isaac." Almost immediately, however, the narratives themselves turn out to be about the sons of Isaac rather than Isaac himself. Isaac is an important link in the line of Abraham; but as an individual character within the narratives, he is given little attention. Only in chapter 26 does the narrative turn specifically to him. In most other narratives he plays a secondary role.

20–28 There are several similarities between the Isaac narratives and other patriarchal narratives. Isaac, like Esau (26:34), was forty years old when he took Rebekah (v.20). Like Sarah (11:30), Rebekah was barren. Like Abraham (20:17), Isaac prayed for his wife; and the Lord answered, and she bore two sons. The concentration on the barrenness of both Sarah and Rebekah, as well as Rachel (29:31) and Leah (29:35), enables the writer to reiterate the point that the promised blessing through the chosen seed of Abraham is not to be accomplished merely by human effort. The fulfillment of the promise is only possible at each crucial juncture because of a specific act of God. The struggle that ensues between Jacob and Esau was already anticipated in the womb of their mother (25:22).

A central theme of the remainder of the book—the struggle between brothers—is introduced in the brief account of the wrestling of the twins in the womb. The conflict between brothers is not a new motif in Genesis. Already in chapter 4 the struggle between Cain and Abel has foreshadowed a whole series of such conflicts within the book: the sons of Noah (9:20–27), Abraham and Lot (13:7–12), Isaac and Ishmael (21:9), Jacob and Laban (29–31), and Joseph and his brothers (37–50). Such an emphasis on "enmity" and struggle appears to stem from the first words of judgment in the book, namely God's statement: "I will put enmity between . . . your offspring and hers" (3:15). The writer of the book patiently waits until the end to thematically express the lesson behind these struggles, using the words of Joseph to his brothers: "You intended it to harm me, but God intended it for good" (50:20). Out of each of the struggles, God's will was accomplished. The point is not so much that the struggles were necessary for the accomplishment of the will of God, but rather that God's will was accomplished in spite of the conflict.

Another important motif is present in this account: "the older will serve the younger" (v.23). As far back as chapter 4, the narrative has portrayed God choosing and approving the younger and the weaker through whom he would accomplish his purpose and bring about his blessing. The offering of Cain, the older brother, was rejected, whereas the offering of the younger brother, Abel, was accepted. The line of Seth, the still younger brother, was the chosen line (4:26–5:8); Isaac was chosen over his older brother Ishmael (17:18–19); Rachel was chosen over her older sister Leah (29:18); Joseph, the younger brother, was chosen over all the rest (37:3); and Judah was chosen over his older brothers (49:8). The intention behind each of these "reversals" was the recurring theme of God's sovereign plan of grace. The blessing was not a natural right, as a right of the firstborn son would be. Rather, God's blessing is extended to those who have no other claim to it. They all received what they did not deserve (cf. Mal 1:1–5; Rom 9:10–13).

Notes

25–26 Notice the chiastic coordination: וַיֵּצֵא הָרִאשׁוֹן. . . . וְאַחֲרֵי־כֵן יָצָא אָחִיו (*wayyēṣē' hāri'šôn . . . w^{e}'aḥ^{a}rê-k̲ēn yāṣā' 'āḥîw*, "The first to come out. . . . After this, his brother came out"; cf. Andersen, *Sentence in Biblical Hebrew*, p. 122).

There is a wordplay in both of the sons' names. "Esau" (עֵשָׂו [*'ēśāw*]) was "red" (אַדְמוֹנִי [*'^{a}d̲mônî*], which is a play on אֱדוֹם [*'^{e}d̲ôm*, "Edom"; cf. v.30; 36:1]), and his body was "hairy" (שֵׂעָר [*śē'ār*]), a play on his name *'ēśāw*. "Jacob" (יַעֲקֹב [*ya'^{a}qōb̲*]) grasped the "heel" (עָקֵב [*'^{a}qēb̲*]) of Esau.

B. *Selling the Birthright*

25:29–34

29 Once when Jacob was cooking some stew, Esau came in from the open country, famished. 30 He said to Jacob, "Quick, let me have some of that red stew! I'm famished!" (That is why he was also called Edom.)

31 Jacob replied, "First sell me your birthright."

32 "Look, I am about to die," Esau said. "What good is the birthright to me?"

33 But Jacob said, "Swear to me first." So he swore an oath to him, selling his birthright to Jacob.

34 Then Jacob gave Esau some bread and some lentil stew. He ate and drank, and then got up and left.

So Esau despised his birthright.

29–34 The story of Esau's rejection of his birthright is purposefully attached to the end of the narrative that introduces the motif of the older serving the younger. It is a narrative example that God's choice of Jacob over Esau did not run contrary to the wishes of either of the two brothers. It is clear from the narrative that Esau was one who "despised" his birthright, while Jacob is portrayed as one who would go to great lengths to gain it. The importance of the contrast between the two brothers can best be seen in the fact that the writer himself explicitly states the point of the narrative in the conclusion of the story: "So Esau despised his birthright" (v.34). In few cases in Genesis do we find such a clear and forthright statement of the writer's own understanding of the sense of the individual stories. We are left with no doubt that the writer saw in this story of Jacob's trickery a larger lesson, that Esau, though he had the right of the firstborn, did not value it over a small bowl of soup. Thus, when in God's plan Esau lost his birthright and consequently his blessing, there was no injustice dealt him. The narrative has shown that he did not want the birthright. He despised it.

Notes

---

30 There is a wordplay between "red stew" (אָדֹם [*'āḏōm*]) and the name "Edom" (אֱדוֹם [*'ᵉḏôm*]).

31–34 The term בְּכֹרָה (*bᵉḵōrāh,* "birthright") occurs four times in these verses and few times elsewhere. In 27:36 Esau alludes to *bᵉḵōrāh* in these verses and makes a wordplay on the idea of God's "blessing" (בְּרָכָה [*bᵉrāḵāh*]) as well as Jacob's name: וַיַּעְקְבֵנִי זֶה פַעֲמַיִם אֶת־בְּכֹרָתִי לָקָח וְהִנֵּה עַתָּה לָקַח בִּרְכָתִי (*wayya'qᵉḇēnî zeh p̱a'ᵃmayim 'eṯ-bᵉḵōrāṯî lāqāḥ wᵉhinnēh 'attāh lāqaḥ birḵāṯî,* "He has deceived me these two times, and now he has taken my blessing").

34 A link between the narratives of chapters 25 and 26 can be seen in 25:34 (וַיֵּלַךְ [*wayyēlaḵ,* "(he) left"]) and 26:1 (וַיֵּלֶךְ [*wayyēleḵ,* "(he) went"]).

C. *Isaac and Abimelech*

26:1–35

1 Now there was a famine in the land—besides the earlier famine of
Abraham's time—and Isaac went to Abimelech king of the Philistines in
Gerar.
2 The LORD appeared to Isaac and said, "Do not go down to Egypt;
live in the land where I tell you to live.
3 Stay in this land for a while, and I
will be with you and will bless you. For to you and your descendants I
will give all these lands and will confirm the oath I swore to your father
Abraham.
4 I will make your descendants as numerous as the stars in the
sky and will give them all these lands, and through your offspring all
nations on earth will be blessed,
5 because Abraham obeyed me and
kept my requirements, my commands, my decrees and my laws."
6 So
Isaac stayed in Gerar.

7 When the men of that place asked him about his wife, he said, "She
is my sister," because he was afraid to say, "She is my wife." He
thought, "The men of this place might kill me on account of Rebekah,
because she is beautiful."

8 When Isaac had been there a long time, Abimelech king of the
Philistines looked down from a window and saw Isaac caressing his wife
Rebekah.
9 So Abimelech summoned Isaac and said, "She is really your
wife! Why did you say, 'She is my sister'?"

Isaac answered him, "Because I thought I might lose my life on
account of her."

10 Then Abimelech said, "What is this you have done to us? One of the
men might well have slept with your wife, and you would have brought
guilt upon us."

11 So Abimelech gave orders to all the people: "Anyone who molests
this man or his wife shall surely be put to death."

12 Isaac planted crops in that land and the same year reaped a
hundredfold, because the LORD blessed him.
13 The man became rich,
and his wealth continued to grow until he became very wealthy.
14 He
had so many flocks and herds and servants that the Philistines envied

him. 15 So all the wells that his father's servants had dug in the time of his father Abraham, the Philistines stopped up, filling them with earth.

16 Then Abimelech said to Isaac, "Move away from us; you have become too powerful for us."

17 So Isaac moved away from there and encamped in the Valley of Gerar and settled there. 18 Isaac reopened the wells that had been dug in the time of his father Abraham, which the Philistines had stopped up after Abraham died, and he gave them the same names his father had given them.

19 Isaac's servants dug in the valley and discovered a well of fresh water there. 20 But the herdsmen of Gerar quarreled with Isaac's herdsmen and said, "The water is ours!" So he named the well Esek, because they disputed with him. 21 Then they dug another well, but they quarreled over that one also; so he named it Sitnah. 22 He moved on from there and dug another well, and no one quarreled over it. He named it Rehoboth, saying, "Now the LORD has given us room and we will flourish in the land."

23 From there he went up to Beersheba. 24 That night the LORD appeared to him and said, "I am the God of your father Abraham. Do not be afraid, for I am with you; I will bless you and will increase the number of your descendants for the sake of my servant Abraham."

25 Isaac built an altar there and called on the name of the LORD. There he pitched his tent, and there his servants dug a well.

26 Meanwhile, Abimelech had come to him from Gerar, with Ahuzzath his personal adviser and Phicol the commander of his forces. 27 Isaac asked them, "Why have you come to me, since you were hostile to me and sent me away?"

28 They answered, "We saw clearly that the LORD was with you; so we said, 'There ought to be a sworn agreement between us'—between us and you. Let us make a treaty with you 29 that you will do us no harm, just as we did not molest you but always treated you well and sent you away in peace. And now you are blessed by the LORD."

30 Isaac then made a feast for them, and they ate and drank. 31 Early the next morning the men swore an oath to each other. Then Isaac sent them on their way, and they left him in peace.

32 That day Isaac's servants came and told him about the well they had dug. They said, "We've found water!" 33 He called it Shibah, and to this day the name of the town has been Beersheba.

34 When Esau was forty years old, he married Judith daughter of Beeri the Hittite, and also Basemath daughter of Elon the Hittite. 35 They were a source of grief to Isaac and Rebekah.

There are several similarities between the events of this chapter and those in the life of Abraham (12:10–20; 20:1–18). The writer is not only fully conscious of the similarities, but he also appears to be using them to advance the theme of God's faithfulness to his promises. While the stories and narratives of this chapter appear at first glance to be only loosely related, without a clear guiding theme, when seen from the perspective of the life of Abraham, the chapter shows a remarkable unity of structure and purpose. Each of the brief narratives that make up chapter 26 portrays Isaac in a situation or circumstance that has a parallel in the life of Abraham. In the short span of one chapter, the writer shows how the whole of the life of Isaac was a rehearsal of that which happened to Abraham. Thus the lesson that is conveyed is that God's faithfulness in the past can be counted on in the present and the future. What he has done for the fathers, he will also do for the sons.

1 The account opens with a reminder that the present famine was a new one, not the same famine that forced Abraham to go to Egypt (12:10). By including this reminder, the writer calls attention to the connection between the two passages. God's dealings with Abraham had foreshadowed his dealings with Isaac just as his dealings with the patriarchs in general had foreshadowed his ongoing ways with Israel. At first we are told only that Isaac went down to Gerar to Abimelech; but in the warning Isaac received in the vision of v.2, the reader is informed that he was on his way to Egypt. No explanation is given why he should not go to Egypt, except that he is to "live in the land" (v.2). We are apparently to read this in light of the promise that "the land" is to be given to the descendants of Abraham. Thus immediately following this word from the Lord, there is the first major reiteration of the Abrahamic covenant and of the promise that "the land" is to be given to Isaac and his descendants (v.3).

It is at first surprising that Isaac remained with Abimelech (v.6). Was this not also outside of "the land" promised to Abraham? Apparently in anticipation of this problem, the writer notes that the gift of the land included also the land of the Philistines. He does this by showing that the Lord's promise was to give "all these lands" (*kol-hā'ᵃrāṣōṯ hā'ēl*, v.4) to Abraham's descendants, not just "in the land" (*hā'āreṣ*) where there was famine. The use of the plural expands the notion of the land to include all those places where the patriarchs sojourned. The picture of the Promised Land in this narrative is consistent with that of 15:18–19, where the border of "the land" is the "river of Egypt" and the Euphrates.

2–5 The Lord's warning to Isaac that he should remain in the land became the occasion for a formal restatement of the blessing (v.2). In the face of the impending famine, the Lord promised to be with Isaac, to bless him, and to bring about all that had been promised to his father, Abraham. Essentially the same promise given to Abraham was given to Isaac. His seed would be great in number (cf. 12:2), the land would be his (12:7), and all the nations of the land would be blessed in him (12:3).

The Lord then added a remarkable note: Abraham "kept my requirements [*mišmartî*], my commands [*miṣwōṯay*], my decrees [*ḥuqqôṯay*] and my laws [*wᵉṯôrōṯāy*]" (v.5). It is remarkable that this is precisely the way in which obedience to the Sinai covenant is expressed in Deuteronomy 11:1: "Love the LORD your God and keep his requirements [*mišmartô*], his decrees [*ḥuqqōṯāyw*], his laws [*mišpāṭāyw*] and his commands [*miṣwōṯāyw*]."

Did Abraham know the law? If so how? If not, what was the meaning of the Lord's words? There is no indication in these narratives that Abraham had an actual copy of the laws of the Pentateuch or of any oral tradition. Thus it would seem unlikely that the writer would expect the reader to understand the Lord's words in such a way. The solution, rather, lies in the writer's portrayal of Abraham throughout the book. We have already seen that at several points in the narrative, Abraham acted in accordance with the law, particularly Deuteronomy; yet there has never been the assumption that he actually had a knowledge of the law itself. In chapter 14, when Abraham fought with the kings who were from a far country, his actions followed quite closely the stipulations of Deuteronomy 20. The same can be said in that same chapter regarding his treatment of the nations who were nearby (e.g., the king of Sodom). In his dealings with them he also followed the stipulation of Deuteronomy 20. He obeyed the law from the heart, much as the ideal picture given in Deuteronomy 30:6 would have it. Thus Abraham is an example of one who shows the law written on his heart (Jer 31:33). He is the writer's ultimate example of true obedience to the law, the one about whom the Lord could say, "Abraham obeyed me" (v.5). Thus, by showing Abraham to be an example of "keeping the law," the writer has shown the nature of the relationship between the law and faith. Abraham, a man who lived in faith, could be described as one who kept the law.

The view of faith and the law reflected in this narrative is the same as that in Deuteronomy 30:11–14, where Moses said, "What I am commanding you [*hammiṣwāh hazzō'ṯ,* lit., 'this command'] is not too difficult for you or beyond your reach. . . . it is in your mouth and in your heart so you may obey it [*ûḇilḇāḇeḵā la'ᵃśōṯô*]." It is also in keeping with the apostle Paul's understanding of Deuteronomy 30 in Romans 10, where he writes that the "word" that Moses says is "in your heart" is "the word of faith we are proclaiming" (Rom 10:8).

6–11 There are several similarities between Isaac and Abraham in this section. Just as Abraham "stayed in Gerar" (20:1), so also did Isaac (26:6). Just as Abraham once devised a scheme with his wife Sarah, calling her his sister (20:2), so also did Isaac with Rebekah (26:7). Just as Abraham was rebuked by the Philistine king, Abimelech, for the great shame he might have brought on his people (20:9), so also was Isaac (26:10). Such similarities can hardly be coincidental. The writer wants to portray to the reader that the lives of the two patriarchs did in fact run a similar course. Unlike the same incident in the life of Abraham, however, it was not God who warned Abimelech not to touch (*lingōᵃ'*) Abraham's wife (20:6), but rather Abimelech himself forbade anyone to touch (*hannōḡēᵃ'*, 26:11; NIV, "molest") the wife; it was not God who protected the wife with the threat of capital punishment (*môṯ tāmûṯ,* lit., "will surely die"; 20:7), but Abimelech said that anyone who molested Isaac or his wife "shall surely be put to death" (*môṯ yûmāṯ,* 26:11).

In light of the similarities between the two narratives, we would do well to ask why there is a change in perspective on the two similar events. The intention of the writer is perhaps best uncovered by the effect these differences have on the reader's understanding of the characters themselves. Though Abimelech is said to have been "pure of heart" (*tām-leḇāḇeḵā,* 20:6; NIV, "clear conscience"), in chapter 26 his actions alone show that his heart was right. Abimelech did not need to be warned in the dream. All that was necessary was to discover that Rebekah was not Isaac's sister (v.8). That was enough for him to fear that a great shame (*'āšām,* v.10; NIV, "guilt") may come upon his people. Clearly the picture of the Philistine king that emerges at this point in chapter 26 is that of a righteous, even pious, Gentile, one who did what was right and, by contrast, showed Isaac to be less righteous than he. Such a view of the nations around about the patriarchs is a far cry from the picture given of Sodom and Gomorrah and of Lot and his daughters. Apparently at this point in the book the writer wanted to portray a wider picture of the nations as both wicked and deserving judgment and as righteous and capable of entering into covenant with the chosen offspring (21:27, 32; 26:28). This, however, is not the full picture of the Philistines to be gained from chapter 26. They also caused great hardship for Isaac in the controversies over the wells (vv.14–22).

12–13 Just as Abraham prospered while sojourning among the Gentiles (12:16; 20:14), so now Isaac prospered while sojourning with Abimelech. Lest we fail to see the significance of Isaac's prosperity, by way of explanation the writer adds: "the LORD blessed him" (*wayeḇārᵃḵēhû yhwh*). This is the second time the writer has spoken of Isaac's blessing. Its repetition is apparently to underscore the connection between

Isaac's prosperity and God's promise to Abraham in chapter 12: "I will make you into a great nation and I will bless you [*wa'ᵃbārekᵉkā*]" (v.2). What God had promised to Abraham was fulfilled with Isaac.

14–22 Just as Abraham's prosperity became the occasion for the conflict between his shepherds and those of Lot (13:5–7), so also Isaac's wealth angered the Philistines; and they became jealous and contention arose. Again the writer seems intent on drawing a line of comparison between Abraham and Lot (ch. 13), on the one hand, and Isaac and Abimelech, on the other. Thus this section relates that "the herdsmen [*rō'ê*] of Gerar quarreled [*wayyārîbû*] with Isaac's herdsmen [*rō'ê*]" (v.20) in virtually the identical terms used in the narrative of contention (*wayᵉhî-rîb;* NIV, "And quarreling arose," 13:7) that broke out between the herdsmen (*rō'ê*) of Abram and the herdsmen (*rō'ê*) of Lot. As the name given to the well—"Rehoboth"—shows, there was a progressive resolution of the conflict as Isaac continued to move away from the Philistines and dug new wells. After finding no conflict at Rehoboth, they said, "We will flourish in the land" (*ûpārînû bā'āreṣ,* v.22), which recalls in identical terms the original blessing of chapter 1:28: "Be fruitful [*pᵉrû*] . . . and fill the earth [*hā'āreṣ*]."

The whole depiction of Isaac in this narrative, then, shows that he, like Abraham, enjoyed the firstfruits of God's blessing—even though it resulted in and took place amid bitter contention with those among whom they lived. Clearly the narrative intends to point to the patriarchs as those whose lives most clearly pictured the kind of blessing God intended his people to enjoy. At the same time, these narratives point to the stark reality that even the fathers did not enjoy the full blessing. They too had to face adversity; but they trusted God, and he blessed them amid the conflict.

23–25 Just as the Lord had spoken to Abraham after he had separated from Lot (13:14–17) and renewed his promise of land and great prosperity, so now with Isaac, after he had returned to Beersheba, the Lord appeared and renewed the promise (vv.23–24). For a third time it is said that the Lord would bless Isaac (*ûbēraktîkā,* vv.2, 12). Like his father, Abraham (12:7; 13:3–4), Isaac responded by building an altar and worshiping God (v.25).

26–31 Just as Abimelech and his people came to Abraham and acknowledged to him, "God is with you" (21:22), seeking to enter into a covenant with him, so now Abimelech has come to Isaac, acknowledging that "the LORD [is] with you," and seeking to enter a covenant (26:28). Isaac, like Abraham before him, was the source of blessing to those nations who sought him out. Isaac, like Abraham, trusted God and lived "in peace" (*bᵉšālôm*) with his neighbors (v.31).

32–33 As a final picture of Isaac in this brief collage of images, the writer concludes with the account of the news of the discovery of a new well. The point of the brief notice can be seen in the fact that the writer emphasizes that the announcement was made "on the same day" (*bayyôm hahû',* v.32; NIV, "that day") that Isaac had made peace with his neighbors. Consequently the writer associated the name of the city, "Beersheba" (*bᵉ'ēr šeba',* lit. "well of the seven/oath"; cf. 21:31), with the "oath" (*wayyiššābᵉ'û,* v.31; NIV, "[they] swore an oath").

34–35 At first glance it may appear that the short notice of Esau's marriage to two Hittite women does not play a significant role within the larger narrative context.

However, when read as an introduction to chapter 27, it casts quite a different light on the events of that chapter. Just before the account of the mischievous blessing of Jacob, we are told that Esau, from whom the blessing was stolen, had married Hittite women and that they were a source of grief to both Isaac and Rebekah. These verses, then, take their place along with vv.29–34 as background to the central event of chapter 27, the blessing of Jacob. These preliminary notices put into perspective the cunning deed of Jacob and Rebekah. They demonstrate that Esau was not fit to inherit the blessing.

Notes

---

1 The phrase מִלְּבַד הָרָעָב . . . אֲשֶׁר הָיָה בִּימֵי אַבְרָהָם (*millᵉḇaḏ hārā'āḇ . . . 'ᵃšer hāyāh bîmê 'aḇrāhām,* "besides the . . . famine of Abraham's time") is a remarkable reference back to 12:10 and clearly shows that the author is interested in the larger flow of the narratives and their interconnectedness.

The dagesh in אֲבִימֶּלֶךְ (*'ᵃḇîmmeleḵ,* "Abimelech"; found only in some MSS and B19) may be an attempt to distinguish this king from the אֲבִימֶלֶךְ (*'ᵃḇîmeleḵ,* "Abimelech") in chapter 20. The name is *'ᵃḇîmeleḵ* (without dagesh) throughout the remainder of the chapter.

5 עֵקֶב אֲשֶׁר־שָׁמַע אַבְרָהָם בְּקֹלִי (*'ēqeḇ 'ᵃšer-šāma' 'aḇrāhām bᵉqōlî,* "Because Abraham obeyed me") is the same as עֵקֶב אֲשֶׁר שָׁמַעְתָּ בְּקֹלִי (*'ēqeḇ 'ᵃšer šāma'tā bᵉqōlî,* "because you have obeyed me") in 22:18.

The terms מִשְׁמַרְתִּי מִצְוֹתַי חֻקּוֹתַי וְתוֹרֹתָי (*mišmartî miṣwōṯay ḥuqqôṯay wᵉṯôrōṯāy,* "my requirements, my commandments, my decrees and my laws") are common technical terms in Deuteronomy. They are a summary description of the content of the whole of the law (cf. Deut 11:1: וְחֻקֹּתָיו וּמִשְׁפָּטָיו וּמִצְוֹתָיו [*wᵉḥuqqōṯāyw ûmišpāṭāyw ûmiṣwōṯāyw,* "his decrees, his laws and his commands"] and also וְשָׁמַרְתָּ מִשְׁמַרְתּוֹ [*wᵉšāmartā mišmartô,* "and keep his requirements"]; cf. Deut 4:40; 8:11, 20; 9:23; 26:17; 1 Kings 2:3; 6:12; 8:58; 9:4–6; Dan 9:10).

8 There is a wordplay between the name "Isaac" (יִצְחָק [*yiṣḥāq*]) and "caressing" (מְצַחֵק [*mᵉṣaḥēq*]).

13 Notice the epic repetition in וַיִּגְדַּל הָאִישׁ . . . עַד כִּי־גָדַל מְאֹד (*wayyigdal hā'îš . . . 'aḏ kî-gāḏal mᵉ'ōḏ,* "The man became rich . . . until he became very wealthy"; cf. Andersen, *Sentence in Biblical Hebrew,* p. 39).

15 The mention of wells dug by Abraham appears to be a reference to 21:25–30, where Abraham had made a contract with אֲבִימֶלֶךְ (*'ᵃḇîmeleḵ,* "Abimelech") regarding a well he had dug (כִּי חָפַרְתִּי אֶת־הַבְּאֵר הַזֹּאת [*kî ḥāp̱artî 'eṯ-habbᵉ'ēr hazzō'ṯ,* "that I dug this well"]). On that occasion the name of the place (בְּאֵר שָׁבַע [*bᵉ'ēr šāḇa',* "Beersheba"]) is derived from the "seven" (שֶׁבַע [*šeḇa'*]) lambs that Abraham gave to *'ᵃḇîmeleḵ* as a witness to the contract. In the present context the name *bᵉ'ēr šāḇa'* (v.23) is derived from the name of the last well (שִׁבְעָה [*šiḇ'āh,* "Shibah"], v.33), which is itself derived from the fact that the two men took an oath (וַיִּשָּׁבְעוּ [*wayyiššāḇᵉ'û,* "(they) swore an oath"], v.31) and/or that this is the seventh (שִׁבְעָה [*šib'āh*]) well dug in this chapter (vv.15, 18, 19, 20, 21, 22, 25, 33). Such multiple derivations of names is not uncommon in these narratives (e.g., 30:23–24).

D. *The Stolen Blessing*

27:1–40

1 When Isaac was old and his eyes were so weak that he could no longer see, he called for Esau his older son and said to him, "My son."

"Here I am," he answered.
2 Isaac said, "I am now an old man and don't know the day of my
death. 3 Now then, get your weapons—your quiver and bow—and go
out to the open country to hunt some wild game for me. 4 Prepare me the
kind of tasty food I like and bring it to me to eat, so that I may give you
my blessing before I die."
5 Now Rebekah was listening as Isaac spoke to his son Esau. When
Esau left for the open country to hunt game and bring it back, 6 Rebekah
said to her son Jacob, "Look, I overheard your father say to your brother
Esau, 7 'Bring me some game and prepare me some tasty food to eat, so
that I may give you my blessing in the presence of the LORD before I die.'
8 Now, my son, listen carefully and do what I tell you: 9 Go out to the flock
and bring me two choice young goats, so I can prepare some tasty food
for your father, just the way he likes it. 10 Then take it to your father to
eat, so that he may give you his blessing before he dies."
11 Jacob said to Rebekah his mother, "But my brother Esau is a hairy
man, and I'm a man with smooth skin. 12 What if my father touches me?
I would appear to be tricking him and would bring down a curse on
myself rather than a blessing."
13 His mother said to him, "My son, let the curse fall on me. Just do
what I say; go and get them for me."
14 So he went and got them and brought them to his mother, and she
prepared some tasty food, just the way his father liked it. 15 Then
Rebekah took the best clothes of Esau her older son, which she had in
the house, and put them on her younger son Jacob. 16 She also covered
his hands and the smooth part of his neck with the goatskins. 17 Then
she handed to her son Jacob the tasty food and the bread she had
made.
18 He went to his father and said, "My father."
"Yes, my son," he answered. "Who is it?"
19 Jacob said to his father, "I am Esau your firstborn. I have done as
you told me. Please sit up and eat some of my game so that you may
give me your blessing."
20 Isaac asked his son, "How did you find it so quickly, my son?"
"The LORD your God gave me success," he replied.
21 Then Isaac said to Jacob, "Come near so I can touch you, my son, to
know whether you really are my son Esau or not."
22 Jacob went close to his father Isaac, who touched him and said,
"The voice is the voice of Jacob, but the hands are the hands of Esau."
23 He did not recognize him, for his hands were hairy like those of his
brother Esau; so he blessed him. 24 "Are you really my son Esau?" he
asked.
"I am," he replied.
25 Then he said, "My son, bring me some of your game to eat, so that I
may give you my blessing."
Jacob brought it to him and he ate; and he brought some wine and he
drank. 26 Then his father Isaac said to him, "Come here, my son, and kiss
me."
27 So he went to him and kissed him. When Isaac caught the smell of
his clothes, he blessed him and said,

"Ah, the smell of my son
is like the smell of a field
that the LORD has blessed.
28 May God give you of heaven's dew
and of earth's richness—
an abundance of grain and new wine.
29 May nations serve you
and peoples bow down to you.

Be lord over your brothers,
and may the sons of your mother bow down to you.
May those who curse you be cursed
and those who bless you be blessed."

30 After Isaac finished blessing him and Jacob had scarcely left his
father's presence, his brother Esau came in from hunting. 31 He too
prepared some tasty food and brought it to his father. Then he said to
him, "My father, sit up and eat some of my game, so that you may give
me your blessing."
32 His father Isaac asked him, "Who are you?"
"I am your son," he answered, "your firstborn, Esau."
33 Isaac trembled violently and said, "Who was it, then, that hunted
game and brought it to me? I ate it just before you came and I blessed
him—and indeed he will be blessed!"
34 When Esau heard his father's words, he burst out with a loud and
bitter cry and said to his father, "Bless me—me too, my father!"
35 But he said, "Your brother came deceitfully and took your blessing."
36 Esau said, "Isn't he rightly named Jacob? He has deceived me these
two times: He took my birthright, and now he's taken my blessing!"
Then he asked, "Haven't you reserved any blessing for me?"
37 Isaac answered Esau, "I have made him lord over you and have
made all his relatives his servants, and I have sustained him with grain
and new wine. So what can I possibly do for you, my son?"
38 Esau said to his father, "Do you have only one blessing, my father?
Bless me too, my father!" Then Esau wept aloud.
39 His father Isaac answered him,

"Your dwelling will be
away from the earth's richness,
away from the dew of heaven above.
40 You will live by the sword
and you will serve your brother.
But when you grow restless,
you will throw his yoke
from off your neck."

We can hardly overlook the fact that in this narrative the writer not only wants to convey an important lesson, but he also wants to tell an interesting and suspenseful story. One can see that he has gone to great lengths to make the story what it is. What is particularly noticeable is the way in which the characters of the story are developed. As we shall see, at several points along the way helpful characterizations of those in the narrative are provided to enable the reader to see behind the mere events of the narrative to the underlying story that develops. In telling a good story, however, the writer has not lost sight of his primary purpose, which is to maintain and further develop the themes of the book. At the climactic end of the central portion of the story, as the disheartened father, Isaac, and the rejected son, Esau, reflect upon Jacob's successful plan to steal the blessing, the writer allows their words of dismay and anger to express the central theme of the story: Isaac: "I blessed him—and indeed he will be blessed" (v.33); Esau: "He has deceived me these two times: He took my birthright, and now he's taken my blessing" (v.36). Jacob had obtained that which belonged to Esau; and Isaac, his father, had given him the blessing. In the course of it all, the will of God, expressed before the two sons were born, was brought to full realization: "The older will serve the younger" (25:23).

1–26 In recounting the story the writer pays close attention to all those elements that heighten the suspense and highlight the deception of Jacob. In this regard the writer demonstrates that Jacob's name, which means "the deceiver" (cf. v.36: *wayya'qᵉḇēnî*, "he has deceived me"), has been appropriately chosen. It is only one of several stories that bring out this aspect of Jacob's character. Isaac is depicted as one too old and too blind to distinguish between his two sons. In some respects the writer's drawing out these details may be an attempt to ameliorate Isaac's culpability in the story. However, Isaac's insistence on a "good meal" before the blessing recalls all too clearly Esau's own trading of the birthright for a pot of stew and thus casts Isaac in a similar role to that of Esau. The purpose of telling the reader about Isaac's blindness was perhaps to make the story more believable and, consequently, more suspenseful. If Isaac were old and blind, the events of the story make sense and the suspense in the story itself is real. The point of telling the reader such information at the beginning of the story is to ensure that the question of the success of the plan is not settled beforehand. The writer's interest in a truly suspenseful story is carried right to the end, where Jacob is shown leaving "at the same moment as" (cf. v.30) his brother Esau returned from the hunt. The plan is in danger of not succeeding right up to the end.

27–29 As the story has stressed throughout, the goal of Jacob's strategy had been to wrestle the blessing from Isaac. Although Isaac did not appear completely convinced, in the end he blessed Jacob (*wayᵉḇārᵃḵēhû*, lit., "he blessed him"; v.27). The theme of "blessing" within this story points out the relationship of this narrative both to the preceding narratives and to the narratives that follow. The promise to Abraham (12:2–3) is alluded to in the final words of the blessing: "May those who curse you be cursed and those who bless you be blessed" (v.29; cf. 12:3). In a similar fashion Isaac's blessing foreshadows Jacob's later prophecy concerning the kingship of the house of Judah: "Be lord over your brothers, and may the sons of your mother bow down to you" (cf. 49:8). Thus the words of Isaac are a crucial link in the development of the theme of the blessing of the seed of Abraham. In what may appear only as a selfish attempt to rob his brother's blessing, Jacob's daring scheme turns out to be a link in the chain connecting the blessing of the offspring of Abraham with the rise of the kingship in the house of Judah.

30–40 The reverse side of the blessing of Jacob is the disappointment and anger of Esau. There is no attempt in this narrative to revel in Esau's misfortune. He is presented merely as a tragic figure, a victim of his brother who was more resourceful and daring than he. Upon hearing of his misfortune, "he burst out with a loud and bitter cry" (v.34); and immediately his words turn the reader's attention back to the events of 25:21–34 and his loss of the birthright: "He has deceived me these two times: He took [*lāqāḥ*] my birthright [*bᵉḵōrāṯî*], and now he's taken [*lāqaḥ*] my blessing [*birḵāṯî*]!" (v.36). The chiastic structure of this last remark (X + *lāqāḥ*//*lāqaḥ* + X) as well as the wordplay (*bᵉḵōrāṯî*//*birḵāṯî*) suggests that the writer intended Esau's remarks as a concise summary of the sense of the narrative thus far. Esau had lost everything, and Jacob had gained it all. Within the narrative, Isaac recounted the main points of the blessing a second time: "I have made him lord over you and have made all his relatives his servants, and I have sustained him with grain and new wine" (v.37). This underscores the fact that Isaac had blessed Jacob rather than Esau.

Finally, weepingly, Isaac answered Esau's pleas for a blessing with a third reiteration of the central point of Jacob's blessing: "You will serve your brother" (v.40).

The point of these reiterations of the effect of the blessing is primarily to underscore the irretrievability of the lost blessing and hence the certainty of the fulfillment of the blessing itself. By showing that the blessing was irrevocable, even by the father who gave the blessing, the writer underscores an important feature of the blessing. It is out of man's hands. It cannot even be revoked. It will come to pass, just as it was given.

Notes

1 The mention of יִצְחָק (*yiṣḥāq*, "Isaac") in 26:35 is a link to *yiṣḥāq* in 27:1.

2ff. The central word of this story is בֵּרֵךְ (*bērēḵ*, "to bless"), just as in 25:27–34 the central word was בְּכֹרָה (*b^{e}ḵōrāh*, "birthright"). The theme of the two stories is the same; and the two stories are linked by the words of Esau, which make a clear association between *b^{e}ḵōrāh* and *b^{e}rāḵāh* (v.36).

20 Jacob's use of הִקְרָה (*hiqrāh*, "gave success," as in 24:12) appears intended to reveal, albeit ironically, the ultimate purpose behind these events. As in the case of Esau at the close of the story (see note on v.36), Jacob's words express an underlying theme that links this story with the themes in the book as a whole.

29 The content of the blessing not only alludes to the central themes of the earlier narratives but also anticipates those that will follow.

Compare

27:29: אֹרְרֶיךָ אָרוּר וּמְבָרְכֶיךָ בָּרוּךְ[1]

12:3: וַאֲבָרְכָה מְבָרְכֶיךָ וּמְקַלֶּלְךָ אָאֹר[2]

Compare

27:29: וְיִשְׁתַּחֲווּ לְךָ בְּנֵי אִמֶּךָ[3]

49:8: יִשְׁתַּחֲווּ לְךָ בְּנֵי אָבִיךָ[4]

36 The statement of Esau that Jacob had deceived him "these two times" (פַּעֲמַיִם [*pa'^{a}mayim*]) is part of a larger theme in the Genesis narratives that is stated expressly by Joseph in 41:32: "The reason the dream was given to Pharaoh twice [פַּעֲמָיִם (*pa'^{a}māyim*); NIV, "in two forms"] is that the matter has been firmly decided by God, and God will do it soon." Thus Esau's words play an important role in linking this story to the major themes of the book.

[1](*'ōr^{e}reyḵā 'ārûr ûm^{e}ḇār^{a}ḵeyḵā bārûḵ*, "May those who curse you be cursed and those who bless you be blessed").

[2](*wa'^{a}ḇār^{a}ḵāh m^{e}ḇār^{e}ḵeyḵā ûm^{e}qallelḵā 'ā'ōr*, "I will bless those who bless you, and whoever curses you I will curse").

[3](*w^{e}yištaḥ^{a}wwû l^{e}ḵā b^{e}nê 'immeḵā*, "may the sons of your mother bow down to you").

[4](*yištaḥ^{a}wwû l^{e}ḵā b^{e}nê 'āḇîḵā*, "your father's sons will bow down to you").

E. *Jacob's Flight From Beersheba*

27:41–28:5

41 Esau held a grudge against Jacob because of the blessing his father had given him. He said to himself, "The days of mourning for my father are near; then I will kill my brother Jacob."

42 When Rebekah was told what her older son Esau had said, she sent for her younger son Jacob and said to him, "Your brother Esau is consoling himself with the thought of killing you. 43 Now then, my son, do what I say: Flee at once to my brother Laban in Haran. 44 Stay with

him for a while until your brother's fury subsides. 45 When your brother
is no longer angry with you and forgets what you did to him, I'll send
word for you to come back from there. Why should I lose both of you in
one day?"
46 Then Rebekah said to Isaac, "I'm disgusted with living because of
these Hittite women. If Jacob takes a wife from among the women of this
land, from Hittite women like these, my life will not be worth living."
28:1 So Isaac called for Jacob and blessed him and commanded him:
"Do not marry a Canaanite woman. 2 Go at once to Paddan Aram, to the
house of your mother's father Bethuel. Take a wife for yourself there,
from among the daughters of Laban, your mother's brother. 3 May God
Almighty bless you and make you fruitful and increase your numbers
until you become a community of peoples. 4 May he give you and your
descendants the blessing given to Abraham, so that you may take
possession of the land where you now live as an alien, the land God
gave to Abraham." 5 Then Isaac sent Jacob on his way, and he went to
Paddan Aram, to Laban son of Bethuel the Aramean, the brother of
Rebekah, who was the mother of Jacob and Esau.

27:41–28:5 Jacob's scheme not only resulted in his obtaining the blessing that Isaac had intended for Esau, it also became the occasion for Jacob's journey to the house of Laban in search of a wife. The picture of Esau at the conclusion of this story is that of a bitter, spiteful brother and son. He made plans to slay Jacob and regain by force his birthright and blessing (v.41). Again it was Rebekah who thwarted the plans by having Isaac send Jacob back to her own homeland to find a wife (vv.42–45). As has been the case in many of the narratives of Genesis, Isaac's words of blessing to the departing Jacob precisely anticipated the eventual outcome of the ensuing story: Jacob would visit Laban "for a while," Esau's anger would subside, and Jacob would find a wife and return as a great assembly of people (28:1–3). Within Isaac's farewell blessing is a final reiteration of the central theme of the preceding narrative: The blessing of Abraham was to rest on the family of Jacob. The promises of Abraham and the promises of Isaac were now the promises of Jacob.

Notes

---

44 Notice how Rebekah's words foreshadow and anticipate the events of the following narrative. Compare יָשַׁבְתָּ עִמּוֹ יָמִים אֲחָדִים (*yāšab̲tā ʿimmô yāmîm ʾaḥād̲îm,* "Stay with him for awhile," v.44) with 29:14: וַיֵּשֶׁב עִמּוֹ חֹדֶשׁ יָמִים (*wayyēšeb̲ ʿimmô ḥōd̲eš yāmîm,* "[and he] stayed with him for a whole month") and 29:20: כְּיָמִים אֲחָדִים (*keyāmîm ʾaḥād̲îm,* "only a few days").

28:1 There is not a major break in the narrative at this point. The narrative continues until v.9, at which time a new segment begins.

F. *Esau's Bitterness*

28:6–9

6 Now Esau learned that Isaac had blessed Jacob and had sent him to
Paddan Aram to take a wife from there, and that when he blessed him he
commanded him, "Do not marry a Canaanite woman," 7 and that Jacob
had obeyed his father and mother and had gone to Paddan Aram. 8 Esau

then realized how displeasing the Canaanite women were to his father Isaac; [9]so he went to Ishmael and married Mahalath, the sister of Nebaioth and daughter of Ishmael son of Abraham, in addition to the wives he already had.

6–9 The final picture of Esau in this narrative is that of a bitter son seeking to spite his parents through deliberate disobedience. The writer's purpose, however, is not merely to dwell on Esau's bitterness but to prepare the reader for the events that lay ahead in the narrative and to tie the present narrative to that which has preceded. Esau was a bitter man when Jacob left; but, just as Rebekah had said (27:45), when Jacob returned, Esau had changed. The point of the narrative is to highlight the changing relationship between the two brothers. Though at first Esau was angry, in the end, when Jacob returned, Esau "ran to meet Jacob and embraced him; he threw his arms around his neck and kissed him. And they wept" (33:4). The brothers are reconciled, and Esau partook of the blessing (*birkāṯî;* NIV, "the present") that Jacob had received (33:11). Such a view of the reconciliation between Jacob and Esau, Israel and Edom, is an important element in the future hope of the later prophetic books (cf. Amos 9:12/Acts 15:17). It is a picture of the ultimate fulfillment of God's promise to Abraham: "all peoples on earth will be blessed through you" (12:3). Such a view seems firmly rooted in the theological structure of the present narrative.

In the marriage of Esau to the daughter of Ishmael, there is a reminder that the promised offspring of Abraham was determined, not by the will of man, but ultimately by the will of God. The families of the two "older" sons (Ishmael and Esau) were united in the marriage, but by now neither had received the blessing promised to Abraham. The families of the "younger" sons (Isaac and Jacob), however, had and continued to receive the promise of the blessing.

Notes

9 The names of the wives of Esau vary considerably in the three references to them (26:34; 28:9; 36:2–3). For example, מָחֲלַת בַּת־יִשְׁמָעֵאל (*māḥ^alaṯ baṯ-yišmā'ē'l,* "Mahalath . . . daughter of Ishmael") is called בָּשְׂמַת בַּת־יִשְׁמָעֵאל (*bāś^emaṯ baṯ-yišmā'ē'l,* "Basemath daughter of Ishmael") in 36:3. Moreover, in 26:34 another of Esau's wives is named בָּשְׂמַת בַּת־אֵילֹן (*bāś^emaṯ baṯ-'êlōn,* "Basemath daughter of Elon"). The Samaritan Pentateuch has *māḥ^alaṯ* for *bāś^emaṯ* in 36:3, which is not likely the original reading. Keil suggests that the "difference arose from the fact that Moses availed himself of genealogical documents for Esau's family and tribe, and inserted them without alteration" (p. 321). Following a common interpretation (known already from Rashi), he says the variations in name come from an ancient custom in the East of giving surnames founded upon some important event in one's life. Though there is nothing improbable in Keil's explanation, it must remain merely an explanation of the difficulty and not the final answer. Keil does appear to be correct, however, in supposing that the difference ultimately stems from the records used by the writer and not from a later hand.

G. *Jacob at Bethel*

28:10–22

[10]Jacob left Beersheba and set out for Haran. [11]When he reached a certain place, he stopped for the night because the sun had set. Taking

one of the stones there, he put it under his head and lay down to sleep.
[12]He had a dream in which he saw a stairway resting on the earth, with
its top reaching to heaven, and the angels of God were ascending and
descending on it. [13]There above it stood the LORD, and he said: "I am the
LORD, the God of your father Abraham and the God of Isaac. I will give
you and your descendants the land on which you are lying. [14]Your
descendants will be like the dust of the earth, and you will spread out to
the west and to the east, to the north and to the south. All peoples on
earth will be blessed through you and your offspring. [15]I am with you
and will watch over you wherever you go, and I will bring you back to
this land. I will not leave you until I have done what I have promised
you."

[16]When Jacob awoke from his sleep, he thought, "Surely the LORD is
in this place, and I was not aware of it." [17]He was afraid and said, "How
awesome is this place! This is none other than the house of God; this is
the gate of heaven."

[18]Early the next morning Jacob took the stone he had placed under
his head and set it up as a pillar and poured oil on top of it. [19]He called
that place Bethel, though the city used to be called Luz.

[20]Then Jacob made a vow, saying, "If God will be with me and will
watch over me on this journey I am taking and will give me food to eat
and clothes to wear [21]so that I return safely to my father's house, then
the LORD will be my God and [22]this stone that I have set up as a pillar will
be God's house, and of all that you give me I will give you a tenth."

10–22 Jacob, like Abraham in chapter 15, received a confirmation of the promised blessing while asleep in the night (*bā' haššemeš;* NIV, "because the sun had set"; cf. 15:12; 28:11). Abraham received God's word "in a vision" (*bammaḥ*^{a}*zeh,* 15:1), and Jacob saw the Lord in a dream (*wayyaḥ*^{a}*lōm,* v.12; NIV, "he had a dream"). In both narratives, however, a divine confirmation was given regarding the establishment of the same covenant of promise: (1) the gift of the land, (2) the promise of great posterity, and (3) blessing to all the nations. In a remarkably similar fashion, the viewpoint of both chapters turns to the future "exile" of Abraham's descendants and the promise of a "return." Abraham's vision looked forward to the sojourn of God's people in Egypt and also to the Lord's deliverance in the Exodus. Jacob's dream looked forward to his own sojourn to Haran and to the Lord's eventual return of Jacob to the land promised to Abraham. In both cases the promise was that God would not forsake them and would return them to their land. Just as Abraham's vision anticipated narratives from the latter part of the Pentateuch, so Jacob's vision anticipated the events that were to come in the next several chapters. The purpose, then, of the account of Jacob's dream in this chapter is to show that in all the events of the narratives that follow we are to see a fulfillment of the promise made here to Jacob.

The Lord said, "I am with you and will watch over you wherever you go, and I will bring you back to this land" (v.15). Within this carefully constructed narrative, those words become the guiding motif and principle that governs the course of the narrated events. So when Jacob returned from Laban's house after many years, he returned to the same place, Bethel, where God again blessed him and promised to give him the land he had already promised to Abraham (35:12); and God reaffirmed his promise to make his descendants into a great nation (35:11). Just as Jacob erected a "pillar" (*maṣṣēḇāh*) at the outset of his journey and then named the place "Bethel" (28:18–19), so also when he returned, he erected another "pillar" (*maṣṣēḇāh*) and named the place "Bethel" (35:14–15). At either end of the Jacob narratives, then, the writer has placed the reminder that God was with Jacob in all that he did and that God was faithful to his promises.

Notes

---

12 The story is linked together with the key word מֻצָּב (*muṣṣāḇ*, "resting"); cf. נִצָּב (*niṣṣāḇ*, "stood," v.13) and מַצֵּבָה (*maṣṣēḇāh*, "pillar," v.22).

H. *Jacob and Rachel*

29:1–14a

[1]Then Jacob continued on his journey and came to the land of the eastern peoples. [2]There he saw a well in the field, with three flocks of sheep lying near it because the flocks were watered from that well. The stone over the mouth of the well was large. [3]When all the flocks were gathered there, the shepherds would roll the stone away from the well's mouth and water the sheep. Then they would return the stone to its place over the mouth of the well.

[4]Jacob asked the shepherds, "My brothers, where are you from?"

"We're from Haran," they replied.

[5]He said to them, "Do you know Laban, Nahor's grandson?"

"Yes, we know him," they answered.

[6]Then Jacob asked them, "Is he well?"

"Yes, he is," they said, "and here comes his daughter Rachel with the sheep."

[7]"Look," he said, "the sun is still high; it is not time for the flocks to be gathered. Water the sheep and take them back to pasture."

[8]"We can't," they replied, "until all the flocks are gathered and the stone has been rolled away from the mouth of the well. Then we will water the sheep."

[9]While he was still talking with them, Rachel came with her father's sheep, for she was a shepherdess. [10]When Jacob saw Rachel daughter of Laban, his mother's brother, and Laban's sheep, he went over and rolled the stone away from the mouth of the well and watered his uncle's sheep. [11]Then Jacob kissed Rachel and began to weep aloud. [12]He had told Rachel that he was a relative of her father and a son of Rebekah. So she ran and told her father.

[13]As soon as Laban heard the news about Jacob, his sister's son, he hurried to meet him. He embraced him and kissed him and brought him to his home, and there Jacob told him all these things. [14]Then Laban said to him, "You are my own flesh and blood."

1–14a In keeping with the picture of Jacob's sojourn as an exile from the Promised Land, the writer opens the account with the words "Jacob continued on his journey and came to the land of the eastern peoples" (v.1). Jacob's journey to find a wife was similar to that of Abraham's servant who sought a wife for Isaac. In chapter 24 the writer uses the words of the servant to guide the narrative and to show that it was God alone who directed the servant to the right young woman for Isaac. In this chapter Jacob is relatively silent. He does not reflect on God's guidance nor on the Lord's promise to be with him wherever he goes (28:15). It was Jacob's actions, not his words, that tell the story of God's help and guidance. First, as with the servant in chapter 24, God directed Jacob to the well where Rachel watered her flocks.

One gets the impression early in the story that Jacob was going to do a mighty deed because of the special care with which the writer describes the size of the rock covering the well and the number of shepherds already on hand. Only when all the shepherds are present are the men able to lift the rock from the well and water the flocks (vv.3, 8), because the rock was big (v.2). When Jacob saw Rachel, however, and the shepherds identified her as the daughter of Laban, he single-handedly removed the rock and watered her sheep (v.10). Then in a great show of emotion, Jacob kissed Rachel and cried with a loud voice (v.11). Clearly the writer wants us to see in this emotional response that, though he did not say it specifically as Abraham's servant had done (24:27), Jacob saw in these circumstances the guiding hand of God. We are apparently also expected to see Jacob's physical strength as further evidence that God was with Jacob and that he had not forsaken his promises (28:15; cf. 24:27).

Throughout the Jacob narratives, God's guidance is shown in the superhuman strength and cunning of the patriarch. No attempt is made to glory in that strength as such but rather to use it as a sign of God's protective presence. It was the fulfillment of God's promise to be with Jacob in all that he did (28:15). The account is very similar to that of Exodus 2:17, where Moses meets his wife by fighting off the shepherds who have driven away the seven daughters of the priest of Midian and then waters their sheep.

I. *Jacob's Marriages*

29:14b–30

After Jacob had stayed with him for a whole month, 15 Laban said to him, "Just because you are a relative of mine, should you work for me for nothing? Tell me what your wages should be."

16 Now Laban had two daughters; the name of the older was Leah, and the name of the younger was Rachel. 17 Leah had weak eyes, but Rachel was lovely in form, and beautiful. 18 Jacob was in love with Rachel and said, "I'll work for you seven years in return for your younger daughter Rachel."

19 Laban said, "It's better that I give her to you than to some other man. Stay here with me." 20 So Jacob served seven years to get Rachel, but they seemed like only a few days to him because of his love for her.

21 Then Jacob said to Laban, "Give me my wife. My time is completed, and I want to lie with her."

22 So Laban brought together all the people of the place and gave a feast. 23 But when evening came, he took his daughter Leah and gave her to Jacob, and Jacob lay with her. 24 And Laban gave his servant girl Zilpah to his daughter as her maidservant.

25 When morning came, there was Leah! So Jacob said to Laban, "What is this you have done to me? I served you for Rachel, didn't I? Why have you deceived me?"

26 Laban replied, "It is not our custom here to give the younger daughter in marriage before the older one. 27 Finish this daughter's bridal week; then we will give you the younger one also, in return for another seven years of work."

28 And Jacob did so. He finished the week with Leah, and then Laban gave him his daughter Rachel to be his wife. 29 Laban gave his servant girl Bilhah to his daughter Rachel as her maidservant. 30 Jacob lay with Rachel also, and he loved Rachel more than Leah. And he worked for Laban another seven years.

14b–30 For the first time in the narratives, Jacob was the object of deception. Laban had turned the tables on him. The similarity between what Laban did to Jacob and what Jacob had done to Isaac (ch. 27) is patent. Jacob was able to exchange the younger for the older, whereas Laban reversed the trick and exchanged the older for the younger. Jacob was getting what he deserved. In this light the seven extra years that Jacob had to serve Laban appear as a repayment for his treatment of Esau. By calling such situations to the attention of the reader, the writer begins to draw an important lesson from these narratives. Jacob's deceptive schemes for obtaining the blessing did not meet with divine approval. Through Jacob's plans God's will had been accomplished; but the writer is intent on pointing out, as well, that the schemes and tricks were not of God's design.

Jacob was indignant: "Why have you deceived me?" (v.25). But he was left speechless by Laban's reply: "It is not our custom here to give the younger daughter in marriage before the older one." After that the narrative says only that Jacob conceded: "and Jacob did so" (v.28). Unbeknown to him, Laban's words had deftly expressed the very circumstances that had led Jacob on his present journey.

The irony of such a circumstance speaks for itself. Certainly the biblical reader was expected to interpret such irony as the work of a divine plan. Jacob's past had caught up with him, and he could do no more than accept the results and serve Laban seven more years. At first it had looked as if Jacob's journey was in fact following the course that Rebekah had anticipated, saying, "Stay with him [Laban] for a while [*yāmîm ʾᵃḥāḏîm*, lit., 'a few days']" (27:44). Thus we are not surprised to read that Jacob's first seven years of working for Laban seemed as if they were "only a few days" (*kᵉyāmîm ʾᵃḥāḏîm*, v.20). But with the discovery of Laban's trick, seven more years are added to Rebekah's "few days"; and Jacob's—and Rebekah's—plans begin to unravel.

J. *The Birth of Jacob's Sons*

29:31–30:24

[31]When the LORD saw that Leah was not loved, he opened her womb,
but Rachel was barren. [32]Leah became pregnant and gave birth to a
son. She named him Reuben, for she said, "It is because the LORD has
seen my misery. Surely my husband will love me now."
[33]She conceived again, and when she gave birth to a son she said,
"Because the LORD heard that I am not loved, he gave me this one too."
So she named him Simeon.
[34]Again she conceived, and when she gave birth to a son she said,
"Now at last my husband will become attached to me, because I have
borne him three sons." So he was named Levi.
[35]She conceived again, and when she gave birth to a son she said,
"This time I will praise the LORD." So she named him Judah. Then she
stopped having children.
[30:1]When Rachel saw that she was not bearing Jacob any children, she
became jealous of her sister. So she said to Jacob, "Give me children, or
I'll die!"
[2]Jacob became angry with her and said, "Am I in the place of God,
who has kept you from having children?"
[3]Then she said, "Here is Bilhah, my maidservant. Sleep with her so
that she can bear children for me and that through her I too can build a
family."
[4]So she gave him her servant Bilhah as a wife. Jacob slept with her,
[5]and she became pregnant and bore him a son. [6]Then Rachel said,

"God has vindicated me; he has listened to my plea and given me a
son." Because of this she named him Dan.
7Rachel's servant Bilhah conceived again and bore Jacob a second
son. 8Then Rachel said, "I have had a great struggle with my sister, and I
have won." So she named him Naphtali.
9When Leah saw that she had stopped having children, she took her
maidservant Zilpah and gave her to Jacob as a wife. 10Leah's servant
Zilpah bore Jacob a son. 11Then Leah said, "What good fortune!" So
she named him Gad.
12Leah's servant Zilpah bore Jacob a second son. 13Then Leah said,
"How happy I am! The women will call me happy." So she named him
Asher.
14During wheat harvest, Reuben went out into the fields and found
some mandrake plants, which he brought to his mother Leah. Rachel
said to Leah, "Please give me some of your son's mandrakes."
15But she said to her, "Wasn't it enough that you took away my
husband? Will you take my son's mandrakes too?"
"Very well," Rachel said, "he can sleep with you tonight in return for
your son's mandrakes."
16So when Jacob came in from the fields that evening, Leah went out
to meet him. "You must sleep with me," she said. "I have hired you with
my son's mandrakes." So he slept with her that night.
17God listened to Leah, and she became pregnant and bore Jacob a
fifth son. 18Then Leah said, "God has rewarded me for giving my
maidservant to my husband." So she named him Issachar.
19Leah conceived again and bore Jacob a sixth son. 20Then Leah
said, "God has presented me with a precious gift. This time my husband
will treat me with honor, because I have borne him six sons." So she
named him Zebulun.
21Some time later she gave birth to a daughter and named her Dinah.
22Then God remembered Rachel; he listened to her and opened her
womb. 23She became pregnant and gave birth to a son and said, "God
has taken away my disgrace." 24She named him Joseph, and said, "May
the LORD add to me another son."

29:31–30:24 In a way that calls to mind the beginning of the Abrahamic narratives (11:30), the writer introduces the central problem of the narrative: the Lord opened Leah's womb, "but Rachel was barren" (29:31). It is at first surprising to read that it was the Lord who was behind Rachel's barrenness. In the preceding chapter (28:14) God had promised that Jacob's descendants would be more numerous than the "dust of the earth." Now Rachel, Jacob's intended wife (29:30), was barren; and it appeared to be the Lord's doing (v.31). By means of such a twist in the narrative, the writer shows again that Jacob's plans have come to naught. Jacob had planned to take Rachel as his wife, but God intended him to have Leah. Thus in two major reversals in Jacob's life, we can begin to see the writer's theme taking shape. Jacob sought to marry Rachel, but Laban tricked him. Then Jacob sought to build a family through Rachel, but she was barren; and God opened Leah's womb.

Jacob's schemes, which had brought him fortune thus far, were beginning to crumble. Such schemes will not be sufficient to carry out the further plans of God. Jacob, too, will have to depend on God to bring about the divine blessing. Though Jacob had chosen Rachel, God had chosen Leah. In the conflict that ensued between Jacob and his two wives over the birth of their sons, the pattern is set for the remainder of the narratives in Genesis. One of Leah's sons was Judah (v.35), while Rachel was the mother of Joseph (30:24).

Though all twelve sons are important, Joseph and Judah stand out markedly in the narratives that follow. Both are used by God in important ways, but each has a different role to play in the accomplishment of God's blessing. Here, at the beginning, it appeared that ultimately Judah, the son of Leah, was given the place of preeminence. Counter to Jacob's plans, God had opened the womb of Leah and not Rachel. In the end the Lord harkened to Rachel, and her son Joseph was born (30:22). But as Jacob's words to Rachel underscore (30:2), God had withheld sons from Rachel so that the descendants of Abraham would be built from Leah. Even after Leah had ceased bearing children (29:35), she managed to have two more sons and a daughter by Jacob (30:14–21). Just as Jacob had purchased the birthright for a pot of stew (25:29–34), so also Leah purchased the right to more children by Jacob with the mandrakes of her son Reuben (30:14–16). All the conflict and tension that existed between Joseph and his brothers—and particularly Joseph and Judah—in the narratives that follow are anticipated and foreshadowed here at the beginning in this narrative of their births.

Notes

32 The name רְאוּבֵן (*re'ûḇēn*, "Reuben") is a wordplay on כִּי־רָאָה יהוה בְּעָנְיִי (*kî-rā'āh yhwh be'onyî*, "the LORD has seen my misery") and thus a combination of *rā'āh* and *bēn* (בֵּן ["son"]) from *be'onyî*. The nature of the wordplay is instructive for the appreciation of wordplays generally in the biblical narratives. They are not intended as etymological statements on the nature of the language; but rather, like all wordplays, they reflect a desire to see connections in the similarities reflected in language.

33 שִׁמְעוֹן (*šim'ôn*, "Simeon") is linked to שָׁמַע יהוה כִּי־שְׂנוּאָה אָנֹכִי (*šāma' yhwh kî-śenû'āh 'ānōḵî*, "the LORD heard that I am not loved"), thus שָׁמַע plus וֹן from נוּ in שְׂנוּאָה.

34 לֵוִי (*lēwî*, "Levi") is linked to יִלָּוֶה אִישִׁי (*yillāweh 'îšî*, "my husband will become attached"), thus לָוָה with the final "i" of אִישִׁי.

35 יְהוּדָה (*yehûḏāh*, "Judah") is linked to אוֹדֶה אֶת־יהוה (*'ôḏeh 'eṯ-yhwh*, "I will praise the LORD"), thus אוֹדֶה with יְהוּ for יהוה.

30:6 דָּן (*dān*, "Dan") is linked to דָּנַנִּי אֱלֹהִים (*dānanni 'elōhîm*, "God has vindicated me").

8 נַפְתָּלִי (*napṯālî*, "Naphtali") is linked to נַפְתּוּלֵי אֱלֹהִים נִפְתַּלְתִּי (*napṯûlê 'elōhîm nipṯaltî*, "I have wrestled mighty wrestlings [wrestlings of God]"; cf. BDB, p. 836; NIV, "I have had a great struggle").

11 גָּד (*gāḏ*, "Gad") is linked to בְּגָד (*begāḏ*, Kethiv; Qere is בָּא גָד [*bā' gāḏ*]). The Kethiv *begāḏ* is probably the ב (*b*) preposition with *gaḏ* ("good fortune"). The Qere *bā' gāḏ* means "good fortune has come."

13 אָשֵׁר (*'āšēr*, "Asher") is linked to both בְּאָשְׁרִי (*be'ošrî*, "How happy I am!") and אִשְּׁרוּנִי בָּנוֹת (*'iššerûnî bānôṯ*, "women will call me happy").

18 יִשָּׂשכָר (*yiśśāḵār*, "Issachar") is linked to לְאִישִׁי . . . שְׂכָרִי (*śeḵārî . . . le'îšî*, "rewarded me . . . to my husband").

20 זְבֻלוּן (*zeḇulûn*, "Zebulun") is linked to זְבָדַנִי אֱלֹהִים אֹתִי זֵבֶד טוֹב הַפַּעַם יִזְבְּלֵנִי אִישִׁי (*zeḇāḏanî 'elōhîm 'ōṯî zēḇeḏ ṭôḇ happa'am yizbelēnî 'îšî*, "God has presented me with a precious gift. This time my husband will honor me"), and thus זָבַד (*zāḇaḏ*, "to present with") and זָבַל (*zāḇal*, "to honor").

21 There is no link given for דִּינָה (*dînāh*, "Dinah").

23–24 יוֹסֵף (*yôsēp̱*, "Joseph") is linked to אָסַף (*'āsap̱*, "to take away")—viz., אָסַף אֱלֹהִים אֶת־חֶרְפָּתִי (*'āsap̱ 'elōhîm 'eṯ-ḥerpāṯî*, "God has taken away my disgrace")—and in the following verse to יֹסֵף (*yōsēp̱*, "add")—viz., יֹסֵף יהוה לִי בֵּן אַחֵר (*yōsēp̱ yhwh lî bēn 'aḥēr*, "may the LORD add to me another son").

K. *Jacob and Laban's Sheep*

30:25–43

[25]After Rachel gave birth to Joseph, Jacob said to Laban, "Send me
on my way so I can go back to my own homeland. [26]Give me my wives
and children, for whom I have served you, and I will be on my way. You
know how much work I've done for you."
[27]But Laban said to him, "If I have found favor in your eyes, please
stay. I have learned by divination that the LORD has blessed me because
of you." [28]He added, "Name your wages, and I will pay them."
[29]Jacob said to him, "You know how I have worked for you and how
your livestock has fared under my care. [30]The little you had before I
came has increased greatly, and the LORD has blessed you wherever I
have been. But now, when may I do something for my own household?"
[31]"What shall I give you?" he asked.
"Don't give me anything," Jacob replied. "But if you will do this one
thing for me, I will go on tending your flocks and watching over them:
[32]Let me go through all your flocks today and remove from them every
speckled or spotted sheep, every dark-colored lamb and every spotted
or speckled goat. They will be my wages. [33]And my honesty will testify
for me in the future, whenever you check on the wages you have paid
me. Any goat in my possession that is not speckled or spotted, or any
lamb that is not dark-colored, will be considered stolen."
[34]"Agreed," said Laban. "Let it be as you have said." [35]That same day
he removed all the male goats that were streaked or spotted, and all the
speckled or spotted female goats (all that had white on them) and all the
dark-colored lambs, and he placed them in the care of his sons. [36]Then
he put a three-day journey between himself and Jacob, while Jacob
continued to tend the rest of Laban's flocks.
[37]Jacob, however, took fresh-cut branches from poplar, almond and
plane trees and made white stripes on them by peeling the bark and
exposing the white inner wood of the branches. [38]Then he placed the
peeled branches in all the watering troughs, so that they would be
directly in front of the flocks when they came to drink. When the flocks
were in heat and came to drink, [39]they mated in front of the branches.
And they bore young that were streaked or speckled or spotted. [40]Jacob
set apart the young of the flock by themselves, but made the rest face
the streaked and dark-colored animals that belonged to Laban. Thus he
made separate flocks for himself and did not put them with Laban's
animals. [41]Whenever the stronger females were in heat, Jacob would
place the branches in the troughs in front of the animals so they would
mate near the branches, [42]but if the animals were weak, he would not
place them there. So the weak animals went to Laban and the strong
ones to Jacob. [43]In this way the man grew exceedingly prosperous and
came to own large flocks, and maidservants and menservants, and
camels and donkeys.

25–43 After the account of the birth of the sons, the writer turns immediately to the first mention of Jacob's departure from Haran (vv.25–26). Laban, seeking the Lord's blessing on behalf of Jacob (v.27), attempted to settle his account for the work Jacob had done for him over the years of his sojourn with him. So Laban asked Jacob to name his wages (v.28). Laban's offer apparently contained a request that he stay on with him and continue to watch over his herds. (Though the words "please stay" in the EVs are not in the MT, they represent an accurate picture of what Laban's words imply.) In any event, Jacob struck a bargain with Laban that resulted in great blessing and wealth for Jacob.

The point of the narrative is to show that such blessing did not come from Laban; rather it was a gift from God. As Abraham had rejected the offer of wealth from the king of Sodom (14:21), so now Jacob refused to take anything from Laban. What Jacob took instead was the right to stay on and shepherd Laban's flocks and to keep a part of the herd that he raised (v.31). After the deal was struck, Jacob was allowed to keep all the speckled or spotted goats and all the black sheep in Laban's herds. From this he would build his own herds.

Although the writer does not specifically state it within the narrative, the passage is surely to be read as an example of the Lord's promise in chapter 28 to be with Jacob during his sojourn in the East. Jacob's clever use of the peeled poplar branches was not so much intended to demonstrate his resourcefulness as it was to further the theme of God's continued faithfulness to his word. The clue to the meaning of the passage is the last verse of the chapter (v.43), where a summary of the whole narrative is given. The summary recalls quite clearly God's blessing of both Abraham (12:16) and Isaac (26:14) and thus puts the events of this chapter within the larger context of the themes developed throughout the book, namely, God's promise of blessing and his faithfulness to that promise. Jacob's wise dealings with Laban then are an example of the way God caused him to prosper during this sojourn. Further confirmation that such is the sense of the narrative comes from the words of Jacob himself in the next chapter. Looking back he told his wives that it was God who had taken Laban's herds and given them to him (31:9).

Notes

---

30 The words of Jacob—וַיִּפְרֹץ לָרֹב וַיְבָרֶךְ יהוה אֹתְךָ לְרַגְלִי (*wayyip̱rōṣ lārōḇ way^{e}ḇārēḵ yhwh 'ōṯ^{e}ḵā l^{e}raḡlî*, "[it] has increased greatly, and the LORD has blessed you wherever I have been")—provide the motivation of the story that follows, and they recur at the conclusion as a summary of the events: וַיִּפְרֹץ הָאִישׁ מְאֹד מְאֹד (*wayyip̱rōṣ hā'îš m^{e}'ōḏ m^{e}'ōḏ*, "the man grew exceedingly prosperous," v.43).

43 The final summary of the events of the chapter is reminiscent of the description of Abraham in 12:16.

Compare:

[1]וַיְהִי־לוֹ צֹאן רַבּוֹת וּשְׁפָחוֹת וַעֲבָדִים וּגְמַלִּים וַחֲמֹרִים

[2]וַיְהִי־לוֹ צֹאן־וּבָקָר וַחֲמֹרִים וַעֲבָדִים וּשְׁפָחֹת וַאֲתֹנֹת וּגְמַלִּים

[1](*way^{e}hî-lô ṣō'n rabbôṯ ûš^{e}p̱āḥôṯ wa'^{a}ḇāḏîm ûg^{e}mallîm waḥ^{a}mōrîm*, "and [he] came to own large flocks, and maidservants and menservants, and camels and donkeys," v.43).

[2](*way^{e}hî-lô ṣō'n-ûḇāqār waḥ^{a}mōrîm wa'^{a}ḇāḏîm ûš^{e}p̱āḥōṯ wa'^{a}ṯōnōṯ ûg^{e}mallîm*, "and [Abram] acquired sheep and cattle, male and female, donkeys, menservants and maidservants, and camels," 12:16).

L. *Jacob's Flight From Laban*

31:1–21

1 Jacob heard that Laban's sons were saying, "Jacob has taken
everything our father owned and has gained all this wealth from what

belonged to our father." 2And Jacob noticed that Laban's attitude
toward him was not what it had been.
3Then the LORD said to Jacob, "Go back to the land of your fathers and
to your relatives, and I will be with you."
4So Jacob sent word to Rachel and Leah to come out to the fields
where his flocks were. 5He said to them, "I see that your father's attitude
toward me is not what it was before, but the God of my father has been
with me. 6You know that I've worked for your father with all my strength,
7yet your father has cheated me by changing my wages ten times.
However, God has not allowed him to harm me. 8If he said, 'The
speckled ones will be your wages,' then all the flocks gave birth to
speckled young; and if he said, 'The streaked ones will be your wages,'
then all the flocks bore streaked young. 9So God has taken away your
father's livestock and has given them to me.
10"In breeding season I once had a dream in which I looked up and
saw that the male goats mating with the flock were streaked, speckled
or spotted. 11The angel of God said to me in the dream, 'Jacob.' I
answered, 'Here I am.' 12And he said, 'Look up and see that all the male
goats mating with the flock are streaked, speckled or spotted, for I have
seen all that Laban has been doing to you. 13I am the God of Bethel,
where you anointed a pillar and where you made a vow to me. Now leave
this land at once and go back to your native land.' "
14Then Rachel and Leah replied, "Do we still have any share in the
inheritance of our father's estate? 15Does he not regard us as foreigners? Not only has he sold us, but he has used up what was paid for
us. 16Surely all the wealth that God took away from our father belongs
to us and our children. So do whatever God has told you."
17Then Jacob put his children and his wives on camels, 18and he
drove all his livestock ahead of him, along with all the goods he had
accumulated in Paddan Aram, to go to his father Isaac in the land of
Canaan.
19When Laban had gone to shear his sheep, Rachel stole her father's
household gods. 20Moreover, Jacob deceived Laban the Aramean by
not telling him he was running away. 21So he fled with all he had, and
crossing the River, he headed for the hill country of Gilead.

1–3 Just as Isaac's wealth had made the Philistines jealous (26:14), so here Jacob learned that Laban was now angry and jealous of his wealth (vv.1–2). At this time the Lord also directed Jacob to return to the land of his fathers (v.3). We are again reminded of the Lord's promise to be "with" (*ʿimmāḵ,* 28:15) Jacob on his journey; and thus the direction of Jacob's life again points toward Bethel, the place of the original promise.

We seem to have reached the middle point, the turning point of the narrative and life of Jacob. He was on his way back to Bethel. It is interesting that later on (32:10), when Jacob looked back at this point in the narrative, he repeated the Lord's words of comfort and promise. However, instead of the promise "I will be with you" (*ʿimmāḵ,* 31:3), Jacob recalled God's words as "I will make you prosper" (*ʾêṭîḇāh,* 32:10). Thus Jacob's own words offer an expansion and commentary on the sense of God's promise to be "with" him. Such an understanding of the Divine Presence illustrates the writer's own expansion of the notion of God's promise of his presence to include the continual care and blessing of Abraham's seed.

4–13 Jacob's words of explanation to his wives repeat the primary events of the preceding chapter. It is as if the writer lets Jacob retell from his own perspective the confusing events of that chapter. Not only does this explanation help his wives understand the course of events that have transpired, but also his words are a helpful guide to the reader in understanding the narratives that precede and follow. Though the events of chapter 30 may look to the reader as though Jacob was getting the best of Laban, it appears that from another perspective Jacob's actions are to be understood as the Lord's enabling Jacob to be repaid for Laban's mistreatment of him. As Jacob explained the events of the preceding narratives to his wives, the reader himself begins to see the same events in a clearer light. The events were all a part of the outworking of God's plan, the plan that began with Jacob's vow at Bethel and the Lord's promise to be with him. Now even Laban's change of attitude toward Jacob and the jealousy of his sons are seen as part of the plan of God.

14–21 Like Rebekah (24:58) before them and Ruth (1:16) after them, Jacob's wives were willing to leave their own family and go back with him to the land of Canaan. More importantly, they were ready also to put their trust in God and seek his blessing (31:16). With such an apparent approval of the wives' response to Jacob, it is a curious fact then that the writer mentions Rachel's stealing of Laban's "household gods" (31:19). What point does this make within the narrative? Are we to view Rachel's actions favorably or do they reveal some weakness of character in the wife of Jacob? One element in the narrative that may point to a solution is the similarity and contrast between Rachel's stealing her father's "household gods" when fleeing home with her husband and Jacob's stealing his father's blessing when fleeing from home to find a wife (ch. 27). In both cases it was the younger who stole what rightfully belonged to the elder. Jacob's stealing the blessing appears to be consciously recast here in the form of Rachel's stealing her father's wealth. Yet in this case the writer is careful to absolve Jacob of any part in the deed. We are reminded that Jacob did not know that Rachel had taken the gods (31:32). It is through Rachel's resourcefulness alone that Laban's prized possessions were successfully taken.

Notes

3 God's words here—וְאֶהְיֶה עִמָּךְ (w^e'ehyeh 'immāk̲, "I will be with you")—and the way they are later interpreted by Jacob—יהוה הָאֹמֵר אֵלַי . . . וְאֵיטִיבָה עִמָּךְ (yhwh hā'ōmēr 'ēlay . . . w^e'êṭîb̲āh 'immāk̲, "O LORD, who said to me . . . I will make you prosper," 32:9 [10 MT])—is an example of the way the biblical narratives allow the characters of the narrative to offer their own interpretations of the meaning of the events. The most striking example of this in Genesis is the account of Abraham's servant seeking a bride for Isaac (Gen 24).

7–12 The theological interpretation given by Jacob to the preceding narrative can be seen in statements like וְלֹא־נְתָנוֹ אֱלֹהִים לְהָרַע (w^elō'-n^et̲ānô '^{e}lōhîm l^ehāra‛, "God has not allowed him to harm me," v.7), וַיַּצֵּל אֱלֹהִים אֶת־מִקְנֵה אֲבִיכֶם וַיִּתֶּן־לִי (wayyaṣṣēl '^{e}lōhîm 'et̲-miqnēh '^{a}b̲îk̲em wayyitten-lî, "So God has taken your father's livestock and has given them to me," v.9), and וַיֹּאמֶר אֵלַי מַלְאַךְ הָאֱלֹהִים בַּחֲלוֹם (wayyō'mer 'ēlay mal'ak̲ hā'^{e}lōhîm bah^{a}lôm, "The angel of God said to me in a dream," v.11).

13 אָנֹכִי הָאֵל בֵּית־אֵל ('ānōk̲î hā'ēl bêt̲-'ēl, "I am the God of Bethel") is difficult in that bêt̲-'ēl appears to be in apposition to hā'ēl, making it an appellation to hā'ēl. In 28:19, however, bêt̲-'ēl is a place name. The grammars explain such cases as ellipsis equivalent in this case to hā'ēl 'ēl bêt̲-'ēl ("the God, namely, the God of Bethel"; cf. GKC, par. 127f.; cf. also 2 Kings 23:17: הַמִּזְבֵּחַ בֵּית־אֵל [hammizbaḥ bêt̲-'ēl, lit., "the altar, namely, the altar of Bethel"]). It may also be that bêt̲-'ēl is a short form of b^eb̲êt̲-'ēl.

19 According to vv.30, 32, הַתְּרָפִים (*hatterāp̱îm,* "household gods") are אֱלֹהִים (*'elōhîm,* "gods"). Although a number of suggestions have been offered regarding the purpose of these "gods," v.37 indicates that the *hatterāp̱îm* may have represented Laban's wealth and possessions: מִכֹּל כְּלֵי־בֵיתֶךָ (*mikkōl kelê-ḇêṯeḵā,* lit., "from any of the goods of your household"). In any event, that is the sense given to them by the story.

M. *Jacob Overtaken by Laban*

31:22–55

22 On the third day Laban was told that Jacob had fled. 23 Taking his
relatives with him, he pursued Jacob for seven days and caught up with
him in the hill country of Gilead. 24 Then God came to Laban the
Aramean in a dream at night and said to him, "Be careful not to say
anything to Jacob, either good or bad."
25 Jacob had pitched his tent in the hill country of Gilead when Laban
overtook him, and Laban and his relatives camped there too. 26 Then
Laban said to Jacob, "What have you done? You've deceived me, and
you've carried off my daughters like captives in war. 27 Why did you run
off secretly and deceive me? Why didn't you tell me, so I could send you
away with joy and singing to the music of tambourines and harps?
28 You didn't even let me kiss my grandchildren and my daughters good-
by. You have done a foolish thing. 29 I have the power to harm you; but
last night the God of your father said to me, 'Be careful not to say
anything to Jacob, either good or bad.' 30 Now you have gone off
because you longed to return to your father's house. But why did you
steal my gods?"
31 Jacob answered Laban, "I was afraid, because I thought you would
take your daughters away from me by force. 32 But if you find anyone
who has your gods, he shall not live. In the presence of our relatives, see
for yourself whether there is anything of yours here with me; and if so,
take it." Now Jacob did not know that Rachel had stolen the gods.
33 So Laban went into Jacob's tent and into Leah's tent and into the
tent of the two maidservants, but he found nothing. After he came out of
Leah's tent, he entered Rachel's tent. 34 Now Rachel had taken the
household gods and put them inside her camel's saddle and was sitting
on them. Laban searched through everything in the tent but found
nothing.
35 Rachel said to her father, "Don't be angry, my lord, that I cannot
stand up in your presence; I'm having my period." So he searched but
could not find the household gods.
36 Jacob was angry and took Laban to task. "What is my crime?" he
asked Laban. "What sin have I committed that you hunt me down?
37 Now that you have searched through all my goods, what have you
found that belongs to your household? Put it here in front of your
relatives and mine, and let them judge between the two of us.
38 "I have been with you for twenty years now. Your sheep and goats
have not miscarried, nor have I eaten rams from your flocks. 39 I did not
bring you animals torn by wild beasts; I bore the loss myself. And you
demanded payment from me for whatever was stolen by day or night.
40 This was my situation: The heat consumed me in the daytime and the
cold at night, and sleep fled from my eyes. 41 It was like this for the
twenty years I was in your household. I worked for you fourteen years for
your two daughters and six years for your flocks, and you changed my
wages ten times. 42 If the God of my father, the God of Abraham and the
Fear of Isaac, had not been with me, you would surely have sent me

away empty-handed. But God has seen my hardship and the toil of my hands, and last night he rebuked you."

43 Laban answered Jacob, "The women are my daughters, the children are my children, and the flocks are my flocks. All you see is mine. Yet what can I do today about these daughters of mine, or about the children they have borne? 44 Come now, let's make a covenant, you and I, and let it serve as a witness between us."

45 So Jacob took a stone and set it up as a pillar. 46 He said to his relatives, "Gather some stones." So they took stones and piled them in a heap, and they ate there by the heap. 47 Laban called it Jegar Sahadutha, and Jacob called it Galeed.

48 Laban said, "This heap is a witness between you and me today." That is why it was called Galeed. 49 It was also called Mizpah, because he said, "May the LORD keep watch between you and me when we are away from each other. 50 If you mistreat my daughters or if you take any wives besides my daughters, even though no one is with us, remember that God is a witness between you and me."

51 Laban also said to Jacob, "Here is this heap, and here is this pillar I have set up between you and me. 52 This heap is a witness, and this pillar is a witness, that I will not go past this heap to your side to harm you and that you will not go past this heap and pillar to my side to harm me. 53 May the God of Abraham and the God of Nahor, the God of their father, judge between us."

So Jacob took an oath in the name of the Fear of his father Isaac. 54 He offered a sacrifice there in the hill country and invited his relatives to a meal. After they had eaten, they spent the night there.

55 Early the next morning Laban kissed his grandchildren and his daughters and blessed them. Then he left and returned home.

22–42 The dispute over the stolen household gods (v.30) gives an occasion for the writer to restate his central theme. The theme is expressed in Jacob's words to Laban: "If the God of my father, the God of Abraham and the Fear of Isaac, had not been with me, you would surely have sent me away empty-handed. But God has seen my hardship and the toil of my hands, and last night he rebuked you" (31:42). Jacob's wealth had not come through his association with Laban. On the contrary, it had come only through God's gracious care during his difficult sojourn.

43–55 The narrative concludes with an account of a covenant (*b^e^rîṯ*, v.44) between Jacob and Laban. Just as Isaac parted ways with Abimelech by entering into a covenant (26:28–31), so also Jacob and Laban parted ways with a covenant.

Notes

---

47 Notice the chiastic coordination in וַיִּקְרָא־לוֹ לָבָן . . . וְיַעֲקֹב קָרָא לוֹ (*wayyiqrā'-lô lāḇān . . . w^e^ya‘^a^qōḇ qārā' lô*, "Laban called it . . . Jacob called it" (Andersen, *Sentence in Biblical Hebrew*, p. 122).

Jacob's words are recorded in Aramaic: יְגַר שָׂהֲדוּתָא (*y^e^ḡar śāh^a^ḏûṯā'*, "Jegar Sahadutha," viz., "witness heap" [NIV mg.]).

48 The name "Galeed" (גַּלְעֵד [*gal‘ēḏ*]) is linked to "heap of witness" (*gal ‘ēḏ*).

49 A further link is made to the place of the contract by the wordplay between the name of the place "Mizpah" (הַמִּצְפָּה [*hammiṣpāh*, linked with יִצֶף יהוה (*yiṣep̱ yhwh*, "may the LORD keep watch")]) and the "pillar" (הַמַּצֵּבָה [*hamaṣṣēḇāh*]) that Jacob had set up in v.45 (cf. v.51).

N. *Jacob's Meeting With Angels*

32:1–2

1 Jacob also went on his way, and the angels of God met him. 2 When
Jacob saw them, he said, "This is the camp of God!" So he named that
place Mahanaim.

1–2 The events of this chapter are couched between two accounts of Jacob's encounter with angels (vv.1, 25). The effect of these two brief pictures of Jacob's meeting with angels on his return to the land is to align the present narrative with the similar picture of the Promised Land in the early chapters of Genesis. The land was guarded on its borders by angels. The same picture was suggested early in the Book of Genesis when Adam and Eve were cast out of the Garden of Eden and "cherubim" were positioned on the east of the garden to guard the way to the tree of life. It can hardly be accidental that as Jacob returned from the east, he was met by angels at the border of the Promised Land. This brief notice may also be intended to alert the reader to the meaning of Jacob's later wrestling with the "man" (*'îš*) at Peniel (vv.25–30). The fact that Jacob had met with angels here suggests that the man at the end of the chapter is also an angel.

Notes

1–2 The chiastic coordination—וַיֵּלֶךְ וַיָּשָׁב לָבָן לִמְקֹמוֹ וְיַעֲקֹב הָלַךְ לְדַרְכּוֹ (*wayyēlek̲ wayyāšob̲ lāb̲ān limqōmô wᵉyaʿᵃqōb̲ hālak̲ lᵉd̲arkô*, "Then [Laban] left and returned home. Jacob also went on his way") suggests that the Masorah is correct in reading 32:1–3 as the conclusion of the preceding narrative and not the opening of a new section, as in the English chapter divisions.

2 (3 MT) As throughout the preceding narrative, the place name מַחֲנָיִם (*maḥᵃnāyim*, "Mahanaim") is identified by means of a wordplay on "camp [מַחֲנֵה (*maḥᵃnēh*)] of God."

O. *Messengers Sent to Esau*

32:3–22

3 Jacob sent messengers ahead of him to his brother Esau in the land
of Seir, the country of Edom. 4 He instructed them: "This is what you are
to say to my master Esau: 'Your servant Jacob says, I have been staying
with Laban and have remained there till now. 5 I have cattle and donkeys,
sheep and goats, menservants and maidservants. Now I am sending this
message to my lord, that I may find favor in your eyes.' "
6 When the messengers returned to Jacob, they said, "We went to your
brother Esau, and now he is coming to meet you, and four hundred men
are with him."
7 In great fear and distress Jacob divided the people who were with
him into two groups, and the flocks and herds and camels as well. 8 He
thought, "If Esau comes and attacks one group, the group that is left
may escape."
9 Then Jacob prayed, "O God of my father Abraham, God of my father
Isaac, O LORD, who said to me, 'Go back to your country and your
relatives, and I will make you prosper,' 10 I am unworthy of all the

kindness and faithfulness you have shown your servant. I had only my staff when I crossed this Jordan, but now I have become two groups.
[11]Save me, I pray, from the hand of my brother Esau, for I am afraid he will come and attack me, and also the mothers with their children. [12]But you have said, 'I will surely make you prosper and will make your descendants like the sand of the sea, which cannot be counted.' "

[13]He spent the night there, and from what he had with him he selected a gift for his brother Esau: [14]two hundred female goats and twenty male goats, two hundred ewes and twenty rams, [15]thirty female camels with their young, forty cows and ten bulls, and twenty female donkeys and ten male donkeys. [16]He put them in the care of his servants, each herd by itself, and said to his servants, "Go ahead of me, and keep some space between the herds."

[17]He instructed the one in the lead: "When my brother Esau meets you and asks, 'To whom do you belong, and where are you going, and who owns all these animals in front of you?' [18]then you are to say, 'They belong to your servant Jacob. They are a gift sent to my lord Esau, and he is coming behind us.' "

[19]He also instructed the second, the third and all the others who followed the herds: "You are to say the same thing to Esau when you meet him. [20]And be sure to say, 'Your servant Jacob is coming behind us.' " For he thought, "I will pacify him with these gifts I am sending on ahead; later, when I see him, perhaps he will receive me." [21]So Jacob's gifts went on ahead of him, but he himself spent the night in the camp.

[22]That night Jacob got up and took his two wives, his two maidservants and his eleven sons and crossed the ford of the Jabbok.

3–12 The emphasis of this chapter is on the wealth of Jacob and the restoration of Jacob and Esau. Much suspense surrounds Jacob's reunion with his brother Esau. Like Jacob, we the readers are not sure of Esau's intentions in gathering four hundred (v.6) men to meet Jacob on his return. The last we have heard from Esau, his intention was to slay Jacob in revenge for the stolen blessing (27:41). Jacob's fear that Esau had now come to do just that seems to be well founded. In light of this, Jacob's prayer (vv.9–12) plays a crucial role in reversing the state of affairs. Jacob prayed, "Save me, I pray, from the hand of my brother" (v.11), and he then appealed to the promises God had made throughout the preceding chapters: "You have said, 'I will surely make you prosper and will make your descendants like the sand of the sea' " (v.12).

13–22 True to form, Jacob then made elaborate plans to save himself and his family in the face of Esau's potential threat. He provided his servants with abundant gifts for Esau and instructed them carefully on how to approach Esau when they met. In it all his thought was that he would "pacify" Esau and deliver his family from his hand. A very familiar picture of Jacob emerges in this narrative. It is Jacob the planner and the schemer. As he had taken Esau's birthright and blessing, as he had taken the best of Laban's herds, so now he had a plan to pacify Esau. As the narrative unfolds, however, it was not Jacob's plan that succeeded but his prayer. When he met with Esau, he found that Esau had had a change of heart. Running to meet Jacob, Esau embraced and kissed him and wept (33:4). All of Jacob's plans and schemes had come to naught. In spite of them all, God had prepared Jacob's way.

Notes

9 (10 MT) See Notes on 31:3.

P. *Jacob's Wrestling Match*

32:23–32

23 After he had sent them across the stream, he sent over all his
possessions. 24 So Jacob was left alone, and a man wrestled with him till
daybreak. 25 When the man saw that he could not overpower him, he
touched the socket of Jacob's hip so that his hip was wrenched as he
wrestled with the man. 26 Then the man said, "Let me go, for it is
daybreak."
But Jacob replied, "I will not let you go unless you bless me."
27 The man asked him, "What is your name?"
"Jacob," he answered.
28 Then the man said, "Your name will no longer be Jacob, but Israel,
because you have struggled with God and with men and have overcome."
29 Jacob said, "Please tell me your name."
But he replied, "Why do you ask my name?" Then he blessed him
there.
30 So Jacob called the place Peniel, saying, "It is because I saw God
face to face, and yet my life was spared."
31 The sun rose above him as he passed Peniel, and he was limping
because of his hip. 32 Therefore to this day the Israelites do not eat the
tendon attached to the socket of the hip, because the socket of Jacob's
hip was touched near the tendon.

23–32 There are many unanswered questions in this brief narrative of Jacob's wrestling with an angel. It is, however, clear that the picture of Jacob's struggle with God is meant to epitomize the whole of the Jacob narratives. Throughout the narratives Jacob's life has been characterized by struggle, particularly by a struggle to obtain a blessing from God—just as in this narrative. Jacob had struggled with his brother (chs. 25, 27), his father (ch. 27), his father-in-law (chs. 29–31), and God (ch. 32). Jacob's own words express the substance of these narratives about him: "I will not let you go unless you bless me" (v.26). Here we see a graphic picture of Jacob struggling for the blessing, struggling with God and with man (v.28).

Most significant is the fact that, according to this narrative, Jacob had emerged victorious in his struggle: "You have struggled with God and man and have overcome" (v.28). Jacob's victory, even in his struggle with God, came when, as the text says, the angel "blessed him" (v.29). The importance of Jacob's naming the site "Peniel" (v.30) is that it identified the one with whom Jacob was wrestling as God. Jacob said, "I saw God face to face" (v.30). Jacob's remark did not necessarily mean that the "man" (*'îš*) with whom he wrestled was in fact God. Rather, as with other similar statements (e.g., Judg 13:22), when one saw the "angel of the LORD," it was appropriate to say that he had seen the face of God (but cf. Hos 12:2–4).

Notes

28 (29 MT) The name יִשְׂרָאֵל (*yiśrā'ēl,* "Israel") is linked to שָׂרִיתָ עִם־אֱלֹהִים (*śārîṯā 'im-'ᵉlōhîm,* "you have struggled with God"), sounding a note that occurs in the later literature (e.g., Hos 12:2–6).

30 (31 MT) The place name פְּנִיאֵל (*p*^{e}*nî'ēl*, "Peniel"), or פְּנוּאֵל (*p*^{e}*nû'ēl*, "Penuel"), is linked to the phrase "face to face" (פָּנִים אֶל־פָּנִים [*pānîm 'el-pānîm*]). The difference between *p*^{e}*nî'ēl* and *p*^{e}*nû'ēl* is probably a survival of earlier case endings (Meyer, *Hebräische Grammatik*, 2:49).

Q. *Jacob's Meeting With Esau*

33:1–17

[1]Jacob looked up and there was Esau, coming with his four hundred
men; so he divided the children among Leah, Rachel and the two
maidservants. [2]He put the maidservants and their children in front, Leah
and her children next, and Rachel and Joseph in the rear. [3]He himself
went on ahead and bowed down to the ground seven times as he
approached his brother.
[4]But Esau ran to meet Jacob and embraced him; he threw his arms
around his neck and kissed him. And they wept. [5]Then Esau looked up
and saw the women and children. "Who are these with you?" he asked.
Jacob answered, "They are the children God has graciously given
your servant."
[6]Then the maidservants and their children approached and bowed
down. [7]Next, Leah and her children came and bowed down. Last of all
came Joseph and Rachel, and they too bowed down.
[8]Esau asked, "What do you mean by all these droves I met?"
"To find favor in your eyes, my lord," he said.
[9]But Esau said, "I already have plenty, my brother. Keep what you
have for yourself."
[10]"No, please!" said Jacob. "If I have found favor in your eyes, accept
this gift from me. For to see your face is like seeing the face of God, now
that you have received me favorably. [11]Please accept the present that
was brought to you, for God has been gracious to me and I have all I
need." And because Jacob insisted, Esau accepted it.
[12]Then Esau said, "Let us be on our way; I'll accompany you."
[13]But Jacob said to him, "My lord knows that the children are tender
and that I must care for the ewes and cows that are nursing their young.
If they are driven hard just one day, all the animals will die. [14]So let my
lord go on ahead of his servant, while I move along slowly at the pace of
the droves before me and that of the children, until I come to my lord in
Seir."
[15]Esau said, "Then let me leave some of my men with you."
"But why do that?" Jacob asked. "Just let me find favor in the eyes of
my lord."
[16]So that day Esau started on his way back to Seir. [17]Jacob, however,
went to Succoth, where he built a place for himself and made shelters
for his livestock. That is why the place is called Succoth.

1–17 When he saw Esau and the four hundred men approaching, Jacob divided his entourage again (cf. 32:7–8). Jacob showed his preference for Rachel and Joseph by putting them last after his wives' maidens and Leah and her sons. Neither Jacob nor the reader expected Esau's greeting. Right up to the present point in the narrative, Jacob had expected revenge from Esau, or, if not revenge, then heavy bargaining and appeasement. The reader has had no clue that Jacob's fears were not well founded. But, seemingly in response to Jacob's prayer (cf. 32:11), Esau had had a change of heart.

The change in Esau is depicted graphically in the contrast between Jacob's fearful approach ("[he] bowed down to the ground seven times as he approached his brother," v.3) and the eager excitement of Esau to see his brother ("But Esau ran to meet Jacob and embraced him; . . . and kissed him," v.4). All of Jacob's plans and preparations pale in the light of Esau's joy at his arrival. Ironically, the four hundred men accompanying Esau turned out, not to be for battle with Jacob's household and for taking his spoils, but rather for safeguarding the final stage of Jacob's journey (v.15). Once again Jacob is portrayed as one who has gone to great lengths to secure his own well being, but one whose efforts have proved pointless in light of the final outcome. Jacob continued to scheme and plan; yet God's own plans ultimately made Jacob's worthless.

The picture of Jacob and Esau in these narratives curiously foreshadows the relationship between the historical Israel of the Davidic monarchy and Esau's own descendants, Edom, as that relationship is depicted in the later prophetic books. Though often there was bitter resentment between the two nations, which God frequently used to chastise his disobedient people (e.g., 1 Kings 11:14; Obad 1–18), in the end God's kingdom was to be extended even to include the land of Edom (Obad 21).

Notes

1 The present chapter is linked to the last by means of the association of וַיִּשָּׂא (*wayyiśśā'*, "looked up") and הַנָּשֶׁה (*hannāšeh,* "the tendon").

4 The verb וַיִּשָּׁקֵהוּ (*wayyiššāqēhû,* "and he kissed him") is not in the LXX and is marked with "dots" in the MT. There is little understanding of the nature of these Masoretic dots, but in this case it may mean the word was not considered original (cf. Israel Yeivin, *Introduction to the Tiberian Masorah* [Missoula, Mont.: Scholars, n.d.], p. 45).

R. *Jacob at Shechem*

33:18–34:31

18 After Jacob came from Paddan Aram, he arrived safely at the city of
Shechem in Canaan and camped within sight of the city. 19 For a
hundred pieces of silver, he bought from the sons of Hamor, the father
of Shechem, the plot of ground where he pitched his tent. 20 There he
set up an altar and called it El Elohe Israel.

34:1 Now Dinah, the daughter Leah had borne to Jacob, went out to visit
the women of the land. 2 When Shechem son of Hamor the Hivite, the
ruler of that area, saw her, he took her and violated her. 3 His heart was
drawn to Dinah daughter of Jacob, and he loved the girl and spoke
tenderly to her. 4 And Shechem said to his father Hamor, "Get me this
girl as my wife."

5 When Jacob heard that his daughter Dinah had been defiled, his
sons were in the fields with his livestock; so he kept quiet about it until
they came home.

6 Then Shechem's father Hamor went out to talk with Jacob. 7 Now
Jacob's sons had come in from the fields as soon as they heard what
had happened. They were filled with grief and fury, because Shechem

had done a disgraceful thing in Israel by lying with Jacob's daughter—a thing that should not be done.

[8]But Hamor said to them, "My son Shechem has his heart set on your daughter. Please give her to him as his wife. [9]Intermarry with us; give us your daughters and take our daughters for yourselves. [10]You can settle among us; the land is open to you. Live in it, trade in it, and acquire property in it."

[11]Then Shechem said to Dinah's father and brothers, "Let me find favor in your eyes, and I will give you whatever you ask. [12]Make the price for the bride and the gift I am to bring as great as you like, and I'll pay whatever you ask me. Only give me the girl as my wife."

[13]Because their sister Dinah had been defiled, Jacob's sons replied deceitfully as they spoke to Shechem and his father Hamor. [14]They said to them, "We can't do such a thing; we can't give our sister to a man who is not circumcised. That would be a disgrace to us. [15]We will give our consent to you on one condition only: that you become like us by circumcising all your males. [16]Then we will give you our daughters and take your daughters for ourselves. We'll settle among you and become one people with you. [17]But if you will not agree to be circumcised, we'll take our sister and go."

[18]Their proposal seemed good to Hamor and his son Shechem. [19]The young man, who was the most honored of all his father's household, lost no time in doing what they said, because he was delighted with Jacob's daughter. [20]So Hamor and his son Shechem went to the gate of their city to speak to their fellow townsmen. [21]"These men are friendly toward us," they said. "Let them live in our land and trade in it; the land has plenty of room for them. We can marry their daughters and they can marry ours. [22]But the men will consent to live with us as one people only on the condition that our males be circumcised, as they themselves are. [23]Won't their livestock, their property and all their other animals become ours? So let us give our consent to them, and they will settle among us."

[24]All the men who went out of the city gate agreed with Hamor and his son Shechem, and every male in the city was circumcised.

[25]Three days later, while all of them were still in pain, two of Jacob's sons, Simeon and Levi, Dinah's brothers, took their swords and attacked the unsuspecting city, killing every male. [26]They put Hamor and his son Shechem to the sword and took Dinah from Shechem's house and left. [27]The sons of Jacob came upon the dead bodies and looted the city where their sister had been defiled. [28]They seized their flocks and herds and donkeys and everything else of theirs in the city and out in the fields. [29]They carried off all their wealth and all their women and children, taking as plunder everything in the houses.

[30]Then Jacob said to Simeon and Levi, "You have brought trouble on me by making me a stench to the Canaanites and Perizzites, the people living in this land. We are few in number, and if they join forces against me and attack me, I and my household will be destroyed."

[31]But they replied, "Should he have treated our sister like a prostitute?"

33:18–20 These last verses form a transition in the narrative between Jacob's sojourn in the east and events of the later years of his life in the land of Canaan. As he left Canaan in chapter 28, Jacob vowed that if God would be with him and watch over him so that he returned to the land "in peace" (*b^e šālôm;* NIV, "safely"), he would give to God a tenth of all he had (28:20–22). The narrative has been careful to follow the events in Jacob's life that have shown the Lord's faithfulness to this vow. Thus here we are told that Jacob returned "safely" (*šālēm,* v.18) to the land of Canaan. Though he was not yet back to Bethel, he was "in [the land of] Canaan"; thus God had been faithful.

Jacob returned to Bethel in chapter 35 and built an altar there (v.7). No mention is made in any of these texts of Jacob's giving a "tenth" of all he had to the Lord. Most assume that the erection of an altar here and in chapter 35 along with the offerings represented his "tenth" (Keil, p. 283). It may be also that the "hundred pieces of silver" (v.19) that he paid for the portion of land where an altar was built was intended to represent a part of that "tenth." The portion of land purchased by Jacob at Shechem plays an important role in the later biblical narratives. This was the portion of land where the Israelites buried the bones of Joseph (Josh 24:32) and thus represented their hope in God's ultimate fulfillment of his promise of the land.

34:1 The birth of Dinah was recorded without much comment in 30:21. But once Jacob and his descendants had departed from Paddan Aram and settled in the vicinity of Shechem (vv.18–20), Dinah became the center of the conflict between Jacob and the inhabitants of Canaan. The point of the narrative is to reiterate the portrait of Jacob that has been central throughout these stories. That portrait is of a man who planned and schemed for what appears to be his own ends, but who in the end actually accomplished God's purposes. In the present narrative God's purpose in setting apart the descendants of Abraham comes into jeopardy with the proposal of marriage between Dinah and Shechem.

Throughout the narrative we are reminded that the purpose of the marriage was that the family of Jacob should become "one people" (vv.16, 22) with the inhabitants of Canaan. The last time such a proposal was made was in the building of the city of Babylon (11:6). The wording of the proposal also runs counter to Abraham's admonition to the servant who sought a wife for his son Isaac: "Swear by the LORD, the God of heaven and the God of earth, that you will not get a wife for my son from the daughters of the Canaanites, among whom I am living" (24:3); or to Rebekah's fear in the case of Jacob: "If Jacob takes a wife from among the women of this land, from Hittite women like these, my life will not be worth living" (27:46); or finally to Isaac's command: "Do not marry a Canaanite woman" (28:1).

While the story in this chapter operates at a level of family honor and the brothers' concern for their ravaged sister, the story nevertheless also carries along the theme that runs so clearly through the Jacob narratives, namely, that God works through and often in spite of the limited self-serving plans of man. The writer's purpose was not to approve these human plans and schemes but rather to show how God, in his sovereign grace, could still achieve his purpose through them.

2–4 Though the narrative is clear that the Hivite son genuinely loved Dinah (v.3), the point of the story is that he had taken her and laid with her (v.2), apparently against her will, and had thus humiliated her. Simeon and Levi's final words about the incident express clearly how they viewed the situation: "Should he have treated our sister like a prostitute?" (v.31).

5–24 Jacob was curiously silent about the incident. When he heard of what had happened to Dinah, he waited for the return of his sons. The reason behind Jacob's silence is not clear at the beginning of the story. Could he have a plan and was he merely waiting for the right occasion? Or was he afraid to act in the absence of his sons? Was he afraid to act at all? Such questions remain unanswered in the narrative.

It is significant, however, that throughout the story it was the sons of Jacob, not Jacob himself, who carried out the deception; and at the end of the story Jacob admonished his sons for their actions. The plans and schemes no longer were Jacob's; they were the plans and schemes of his sons. The sons of Jacob have taken the place of their father in the thematic structure of the narratives. In his last words to the two sons Simeon and Levi, Jacob had very harsh words for them concerning the events of this chapter: "Let me not enter their council, let me not join their assembly, for they have killed men in their anger. . . . Cursed be their anger, so fierce, and their fury, so cruel!" (49:6–7). The present narrative does not linger to explain Jacob's passive role but goes on quickly to describe the cunning vengeance of Simeon and Levi who had taken up where their father had left off.

That Simeon and Levi had a plan of deception to repay the offense is already suggested in the report of their anger at hearing the news of Dinah (v.7). The reader knows from the bitterness of their anger that they would not let such an act go unpunished. The course of action they chose played remarkably well into the hands of the writer in the development of his themes. In chapter 17 it was the rite of circumcision that was to be a sign (*'ôṯ*, v.11) of the unity of the covenant people and their separation from the rest of the nations. Circumcision was not limited to Abraham's descendants but was rather given as a sign of one's joining in the hope of God's promises to Abraham. It was, in fact, a sign given of the covenant promise that Abraham would become the father of "many nations" (17:5). But in the way the sons of Jacob carried out the request that these Canaanites be circumcised, it offers a curious reversal of God's intention. They offered circumcision as a means for the two families to become "one people" (*'am 'ehāḏ*, v.16). The Canaanites were not joining the offspring of Abraham; rather, the descendants of Abraham were joining with the Canaanites. The importance of this point is stressed when Shechem repeats it to his countrymen: "Won't their livestock, their property and all their other animals become ours?" (v.23). A thematic interplay between chapters 17 and 34, then, lies behind the writer's reason for including this narrative in the book.

A further indication of this narrative interrelationship is the wordplay in the two chapters between the word "sign" (*'ôṯ*, 17:11) and the "consent" (*'ûṯ*; cf. vv.15, 22, 23) of the two families to live as "one people." What is the overall purpose of the association between the two chapters? What point is the writer making? Again the solution lies in the way the present narrative fits into the larger thematic development within the Jacob narratives. Jacob and his family have continuously been characterized as those who attempt to carry out God's intentions by means of their own plans and schemes. On the surface their plans work reasonably well, but they always involve cunning and deceit to be successful. The writer does not wish to suggest that in such plans God's own plans are represented. On the contrary, Jacob's plans and those of his family are always depicted as the plans of those who are far out ahead of God and his plans. But the ultimate purpose of these narratives is to show that in spite of the fact that such plans run counter to God's own, they cannot thwart the eventual outworking of his intentions.

25–31 When the sons of Jacob carried out their deception to the end, the writer is careful not to let their actions go unrebuked. Jacob's words apparently express the writer's own final judgment on the actions of the sons: "You have brought trouble on me by making me a stench to the Canaanites and Perizzites, the people living in this land" (v.30). The writer then lets the sons' reply stand as the last words of the narrative, apparently to show that their motive had not been mere plunder but the honor of their sister (v.31).

Notes

19 The "plot of ground" (חֶלְקַת הַשָּׂדֶה [*ḥelqaṯ haśśāḏeh*]) that Jacob purchased is later remembered as the place where Joseph's bones were buried (cf. 50:25; Josh 24:32).

34:1 With the introduction of Dinah, the narrative begins a new segment. The birth of Dinah was recorded in 30:21.

5 Though the syntax of וְהֶחֱרִשׁ יַעֲקֹב (*wᵉheḥᵉriš yaʿᵃqōḇ*, "so [Jacob] kept quiet") (W + QATAL + X) is unusual, it is not without example in the narrative portions of Genesis (cf. 2:6b, 10b, 24b[bis]; 15:6a; 21:25a; 26:13b; 29:3[quat]; 30:41[bis], 42b; 34:5b; 37:3b; 38:5b, 9b; 47:22b). The chiastic structure וְיַעֲקֹב שָׁמַע . . . וְהֶחֱרִשׁ יַעֲקֹב (*wᵉyaʿᵃqōḇ šāmaʿ . . . wᵉheḥᵉriš yaʿᵃqōḇ*, "When Jacob heard . . . so [Jacob] kept quiet") and the renominalization of *yaʿᵃqōḇ* suggests that *wᵉheḥᵉriš* is to be preferred to *wayyaḥᵃrēš* (or *wayyaḥᵃrêš*) (BHS mg.).

7 בְיִשְׂרָאֵל (*ḇᵉyiśrāʾēl*) can mean "in Israel" or "against Israel" (BDB, p. 89, II.4.a). In the first instance Israel would refer to a people, whereas in the second Israel would refer to the individual. Since the individual is called Jacob in this section, *ḇᵉyiśrāʾēl* likely refers to the people. From the perspective of the narrative, the sons of Jacob are already being thought of as a people.

25–27 Notice the accumulation of chiastic coordination and epic repetition at the close of the narrative:

(v.25b)[1] וַיָּבֹאוּ עַל־הָעִיר בֶּטַח . . . (v.27a)[2] בְּנֵי יַעֲקֹב בָּאוּ עַל־הַחֲלָלִים
(v.25c)[3] וַיַּהַרְגוּ כָּל־זָכָר . . . (v.26a)[4] הָרְגוּ לְפִי־חָרֶב
(v.26b)[5] וַיִּקְחוּ אֶת־דִּינָה . . . (v.28c)[6] וְאֶת־אֲשֶׁר בַּשָּׂדֶה לָקָחוּ

Perhaps also:

(v.27a)[7] וַיָּבֹזּוּ הָעִיר . . . (v.29)[8] וְאֶת־כָּל־חֵילָם וְאֶת־כָּל־טַפָּם וְאֶת־נְשֵׁיהֶם שָׁבוּ וַיָּבֹזּוּ

[1] (*wayyāḇōʾû ʿal-hāʿîr beṭaḥ*, lit., "they came into the city unexpected").
[2] (*bᵉnê yaʿᵃqōḇ bāʾû ʿal-hahᵃlālîm*, "The sons of Jacob came upon the dead bodies").
[3] (*wayyahargû kol-zāḵār*, "killing every male").
[4] (*hārᵉgû lᵉp̄î-ḥāreḇ*, lit., "they killed with the edge of the sword").
[5] (*wayyiqḥû ʾeṯ-dînāh*, "[they] took Dinah").
[6] (*wᵉʾeṯ-ʾᵃšer baśśāḏeh lāqāḥû*, lit., "and they seized whatever was in the field").
[7] (*wayyāḇōzzû hāʿîr*, "[they] looted the city").
[8] (*wᵉʾeṯ-kol-ḥêlām wᵉʾeṯ-kol-ṭappām wᵉʾeṯ-nᵉšêhem šāḇû wayyāḇōzzû*, "They carried off all their wealth and all their women and children, taking as plunder").

S. *Jacob's Return to Bethel*

35:1–15

[1]Then God said to Jacob, "Go up to Bethel and settle there, and build an altar there to God, who appeared to you when you were fleeing from your brother Esau."

[2]So Jacob said to his household and to all who were with him, "Get rid of the foreign gods you have with you, and purify yourselves and change your clothes. [3]Then come, let us go up to Bethel, where I will build an altar to God, who answered me in the day of my distress and who has been with me wherever I have gone." [4]So they gave Jacob all the foreign gods they had and the rings in their ears, and Jacob buried

them under the oak at Shechem. 5 Then they set out, and the terror of
God fell upon the towns all around them so that no one pursued them.
6 Jacob and all the people with him came to Luz (that is, Bethel) in the
land of Canaan. 7 There he built an altar, and he called the place El
Bethel, because it was there that God revealed himself to him when he
was fleeing from his brother.
8 Now Deborah, Rebekah's nurse, died and was buried under the oak
below Bethel. So it was named Allon Bacuth.
9 After Jacob returned from Paddan Aram, God appeared to him again
and blessed him. 10 God said to him, "Your name is Jacob, but you will
no longer be called Jacob; your name will be Israel." So he named him
Israel.
11 And God said to him, "I am God Almighty; be fruitful and increase in
number. A nation and a community of nations will come from you, and
kings will come from your body. 12 The land I gave to Abraham and Isaac
I also give to you, and I will give this land to your descendants after
you." 13 Then God went up from him at the place where he had talked
with him.
14 Jacob set up a stone pillar at the place where God had talked with
him, and he poured out a drink offering on it; he also poured oil on it.
15 Jacob called the place where God had talked with him Bethel.

1–5 The chapter opens with a reference back to 28:10–15, the appearance of the Lord to Jacob at Bethel. As Jacob had once fled to Bethel to escape the anger of his brother Esau, so now the Lord has told Jacob to return to Bethel and dwell there in the face of the trouble that his two sons, Simeon and Levi, had stirred up. When Jacob obeyed and went to Bethel, the Lord delivered him from the anger of the Canaanites who dwelt nearby (v.50). It is significant that Jacob called God the one "who answered me in the day of my distress and who has been with me wherever I have gone" (v.3). That epithet serves as a fitting summary of the picture of God that has emerged from the Jacob narratives. Jacob was in constant distress; yet in each instance God remained faithful to his promise and delivered him.

The only previous mention of the "gods" that Jacob's household might have had is to the "household gods" (*hatt^{e}rāp̱îm,* 31:19) that Rachel stole from her father. These may be included in the term "foreign gods" (*ʾ^{e}lōhê hannēḵār,* vv.2, 4); but in light of the fact that the writer mentions that they buried the "rings in their ears" (v.4) along with these "foreign gods," it is likely that Jacob's household had picked up other religious objects while they were living in Shechem. In any case, the point of the narrative is that Jacob and his family were leaving such things behind and purifying themselves in preparation for their journey to Bethel.

6–15 The arrival at Bethel marked the end of Jacob's journey and the final demonstration of the faithfulness of God. He had been with Jacob throughout his journey, and now Jacob had returned to Bethel in safety. As Abraham and Isaac had done on numerous occasions, Jacob built an altar and named it in commemoration of the Lord's appearing to him there when he left for Haran (v.7; cf. 28:10–22). In response the Lord appeared again to Jacob and "blessed him" (v.9). For a second time Jacob's name was changed to "Israel" (v.10; cf. 32:28). Why twice? It is significant that there is no explanation of the name "Israel" in this second naming. Thus it appears that the negative connotation of the name Israel ("struggled with God," 32:28) has been deliberately omitted. Perhaps the point of the second renaming was to erase the negative connotation of the name given in the first instance. At this point Jacob was not the same Jacob who "struggled with God and men."

The point of the second renaming, then, was to give the name "Israel" a more neutral or even positive connotation—that which it was to have for the remainder of the Torah. It does so by removing the notion of "struggle" associated with the wordplay in 32:28 and letting it stand in a positive light, contrasting it with the name "Jacob" (*ya'aqōḇ*), a name frequently associated throughout these narratives with Jacob's deceptions (cf. comment on 27:36). In Jacob's successive names, then, we can see the writer's assessment of Jacob's standing before God.

The importance of God's words to Jacob in vv.11–12 cannot be overemphasized. First, God's words "be fruitful and increase in number" recalled clearly the primeval blessing of Creation (1:28) and hence showed God to be still "at work" in bringing about the blessing to all mankind through Jacob. Second, for the first time since 17:16 ("kings of peoples will come from her"), the mention is made of royalty ("kings," v.11) in the promised line. Third, the promise of the land, first given to Abraham and then to Isaac, was renewed here with Jacob (v.12). Thus within these brief words several major themes of the book have come together. The primeval blessing of mankind was renewed through the promise of a royal offspring and the gift of the land.

In the course of the narrative, this section represents a major turning point and thematic focus. Two lines that have thus far run parallel are about to converge, and out of them both will emerge a single theme. Jacob has two wives, each representing a possible line through which the promise will be carried on: the line of Rachel, namely the house of Joseph, and the line of Leah, the house of Judah. Just as Abraham had two sons and only one was the son of promise, and just as Isaac had two sons and only one was the son of the blessing, so now Jacob, though he has twelve sons, has two wives (Leah and Rachel); and each has a son (Judah and Joseph) that can rightfully contend for the blessing. In the narratives that follow, the writer holds both sons, Joseph and Judah, before the readers as rightful heirs of the promise. As the Jacob narratives have already anticipated, in the end it was Judah, the son of Leah, not Joseph, the son of Rachel, that gained the blessing (49:8–12).

T. *Benjamin's Birth and Rachel's Death*

35:16–20

16 Then they moved on from Bethel. While they were still some distance from Ephrath, Rachel began to give birth and had great difficulty. 17 And as she was having great difficulty in childbirth, the midwife said to her, "Don't be afraid, for you have another son." 18 As she breathed her last—for she was dying—she named her son Ben-Oni. But his father named him Benjamin.

19 So Rachel died and was buried on the way to Ephrath (that is, Bethlehem). 20 Over her tomb Jacob set up a pillar, and to this day that pillar marks Rachel's tomb.

16–20 Rachel, Joseph's mother and Jacob's favorite wife, died giving birth to her second son, Benjamin. The account of the birth of the youngest son, Benjamin, is separated from the rest of the sons in 29:32–30:24, but it follows closely on that passage. The last son to have been born was Rachel's first son, Joseph. At the time of his birth, Rachel had said, "May the LORD add to me another son" (30:24). Apparently looking back to that request, Rachel's midwife said, "Don't be afraid, for you have another son" (35:17). Benjamin was the other son. As she was about to die, Rachel named the son "Ben-Oni," meaning "son of my trouble." Jacob, however, making a wordplay on "Oni," which can mean either "trouble" or "wealth" (cf. *'ônî* ["my strength"], 49:3), named him "Benjamin" (lit., "son of my right hand"), reinterpreting the name given by Rachel to mean "son of my wealth or good fortune" (Keil, p. 318; cf. Leupold, p. 924; Ramban, פירושי התורה לרבינו משה בן נחמן [*pyrwšy htwrh lrbynw mšh bn nḥmn*], edited by Ḥayyim Rab S'ww'l [Jerusalem: Mossad Harav Kook, 1984], p. 197).

It was important to the writer that the site of Rachel's burial, Ephrath, be clearly identified with the city of Bethlehem, an important place in later biblical history (cf. 1 Sam 17:12; Mic 5:2). This site is further identified by the pillar that Jacob set up to mark Rachel's grave (v.20). Some such identification of the burial place of Rachel was still known at the time of Samuel as can be seen from the fact that Samuel told Saul to look for two men "near Rachel's tomb" (1 Sam 10:2). Although only a brief allusion to this site is made in the further narratives of Genesis (48:7), this passage continued to play an important role in later biblical texts. The prophet Jeremiah alluded to this passage in his description of the destruction of Jerusalem: "Rachel weeping for her children and refusing to be comforted, because her children are no more" (Jer 31:15); and in Micah 5:2 (v.1 MT) the prophet perhaps alludes to this passage in his vision of the future Davidic King. It appears that Rachel's agony in the birth of Benjamin had later become a picture of the painful waiting of the sons of Israel for the promised Messiah (cf. Matt 2:18).

Notes

---

18 The name בִּנְיָמִין (*binyāmin*, "Benjamin") is linked to בֶּן־אוֹנִי (*ben-'ônî*, "Ben-Oni"). Notice also the chiastic coordination: וַתִּקְרָא שְׁמוֹ בֶּן־אוֹנִי וְאָבִיו קָרָא־לוֹ בִנְיָמִין (*wattiqrā' šemô ben-'ônî we'ābîw qārā'-lô binyāmîn*, "she named her son Ben-Oni. But his father named him Benjamin") (Andersen, *Sentence in Biblical Hebrew*, p. 122).

U. *The Sons of Jacob*

35:21–26

21 Israel moved on again and pitched his tent beyond Migdal Eder.
22 While Israel was living in that region, Reuben went in and slept with his father's concubine Bilhah, and Israel heard of it.

Jacob had twelve sons:
23 The sons of Leah:
Reuben the firstborn of Jacob,
Simeon, Levi, Judah, Issachar and Zebulun.
24 The sons of Rachel:
Joseph and Benjamin.
25 The sons of Rachel's maidservant Bilhah:
Dan and Naphtali.
26 The sons of Leah's maidservant Zilpah:
Gad and Asher.
These were the sons of Jacob, who were born to him in Paddan Aram.

21–26 The narrative is concerned to show that the oldest sons of Jacob fell from favor because of their horrendous conduct. The writer has already recounted the violence of Simeon and Levi (ch. 34), and now he briefly notes the misconduct of Reuben (v.22). As the list that follows shows (vv.23–26), the next brother in line was Judah, the son of Leah. With the older sons out of the way, the stage is then set for the development of the line of Judah and the line of Joseph. The narratives that follow are devoted primarily to Joseph, but that by no means is an indication of the final outcome. The last word regarding the future of these two lines of Abraham's descendants is not heard until chapters 48 and 49.

V. *The Death of Isaac*

35:27–29

27 Jacob came home to his father Isaac in Mamre, near Kiriath Arba (that is, Hebron), where Abraham and Isaac had stayed. 28 Isaac lived a hundred and eighty years. 29 Then he breathed his last and died and was gathered to his people, old and full of years. And his sons Esau and Jacob buried him.

27–29 The end of the Jacob narratives is marked by the death of his father, Isaac. The purpose of this notice is not simply to record Isaac's death but rather to show the complete fulfillment of God's promise to Jacob (28:21). According to Jacob's vow, he had asked that God watch over him during his sojourn and return him safely to the house of his father. Thus the conclusion of the narrative marks the final fulfillment of these words as Jacob returned to the house of his father, Isaac, before he died.

Notes

---

27 The back reference—אֲשֶׁר־גָּר־שָׁם אַבְרָהָם וְיִצְחָק (*'ašer-gār-šām 'aḇrāhām weyiṣḥāq*, "where Abraham and Isaac had stayed")—shows the author's concern for the whole text and the interconnectedness of the events.

29 The order of the two sons—עֵשָׂו וְיַעֲקֹב (*'ēśāw weya'aqōḇ*, "Esau and Jacob")—reflects the order of events in the following chapters. First the events relating to Esau are covered and then those relating to Jacob.

V. The Account of Esau (36:1–43)

A. *Esau's Journey to Seir*

36:1–8

1 This is the account of Esau (that is, Edom).

2 Esau took his wives from the women of Canaan: Adah daughter of Elon the Hittite, and Oholibamah daughter of Anah and granddaughter of Zibeon the Hivite— 3 also Basemath daughter of Ishmael and sister of Nebaioth.

4 Adah bore Eliphaz to Esau, Basemath bore Reuel, 5 and Oholibamah bore Jeush, Jalam and Korah. These were the sons of Esau, who were born to him in Canaan.

6 Esau took his wives and sons and daughters and all the
members of his household, as well as his livestock and all his other
animals and all the goods he had acquired in Canaan, and moved to
a land some distance from his brother Jacob. 7 Their possessions
were too great for them to remain together; the land where they
were staying could not support them both because of their
livestock. 8 So Esau (that is, Edom) settled in the hill country of Seir.

1–8 The separation of Jacob and Esau is cast in the same form as the separation of Abraham and Lot in chapter 13. The possessions of the two brothers were too great (v.7; cf. 13:6), and the land was not able to sustain both of them (v.7; cf. 13:6); so just as Lot parted from Abraham and went eastward, so Esau parted from Jacob and went to Seir. The heirs of the promise remained in the land, and the other sons moved eastward. The writer is careful to note that their parting of ways was beneficial to both Jacob and Esau. It was because of their great wealth that they had to part company.

In the remainder of this chapter, the writer goes to great lengths to show the progress and well being of the line of Esau. He is particularly careful to note that Esau is, in fact, "Edom." The name Esau is identified by "that is, Edom" (e.g., vv.1, 8), throughout the chapter. Why such a concern? The solution lies in the future importance of Edom during the later periods of Israel's history.

As in the Book of Obadiah, Edom became a small picture for Israel's relationship to the other nations at large. In the future reign of the messianic King, Edom would once again, as in the days of David, be a part of his kingdom: "Deliverers will go up on Mount Zion to govern the mountains of Esau. And the kingdom will be the LORD's" (Obad 21). So also within the Pentateuch, the possession of Edom is a mark of the strength and victorious reign of the "star" (*kôkāḇ*, Num 24:17) that is to arise or "come out of Jacob" (*miyyaʿaqōḇ*, Num 24:17). It is no wonder then that the NT writers can look to such passages and see in "Edom" (*ʾedôm*) a promise that relates to "all mankind" (*ʾāḏām*). Such a case is Acts 15:17, where James applies Amos 9:12's "the remnant of Edom" to "the remnant of men."

Notes

3 See the note on 28:9.

4 Notice the chiastic coordination: וַתֵּלֶד עָדָה לְעֵשָׂו . . . וּבָשְׂמַת יָלְדָה אֶת־רְעוּאֵל[1] (Andersen, *Sentence in Biblical Hebrew*, p. 122).

[1] (*wattēleḏ ʿāḏāh leʿēśāw . . . ûḇāśemaṯ yāleḏāh ʾeṯ-reʿûʾēl*, "Adah bore to Esau . . . and Basemath bare Reuel").

B. *Esau in Seir (36:9–43)*

1. *The sons of Esau*

36:9–19

9 This is the account of Esau the father of the Edomites in the hill
country of Seir.
10 These are the names of Esau's sons:

Eliphaz, the son of Esau's wife Adah, and Reuel, the son of Esau's wife Basemath.
11The sons of Eliphaz:
Teman, Omar, Zepho, Gatam and Kenaz.
12Esau's son Eliphaz also had a concubine named Timna, who bore him Amalek. These were grandsons of Esau's wife Adah.
13The sons of Reuel:
Nahath, Zerah, Shammah and Mizzah. These were grandsons of Esau's wife Basemath.
14The sons of Esau's wife Oholibamah daughter of Anah and granddaughter of Zibeon, whom she bore to Esau:
Jeush, Jalam and Korah.

15These were the chiefs among Esau's descendants:
The sons of Eliphaz the firstborn of Esau:
Chiefs Teman, Omar, Zepho, Kenaz,
16Korah, Gatam and Amalek. These were the chiefs descended from Eliphaz in Edom; they were grandsons of Adah.
17The sons of Esau's son Reuel:
Chiefs Nahath, Zerah, Shammah and Mizzah. These were the chiefs descended from Reuel in Edom; they were grandsons of Esau's wife Basemath.
18The sons of Esau's wife Oholibamah:
Chiefs Jeush, Jalam and Korah. These were the chiefs descended from Esau's wife Oholibamah daughter of Anah.
19These were the sons of Esau (that is, Edom), and these were their chiefs.

9–14 In the remainder of the chapter, the writer includes an unusually long list of the "genealogy" of Esau. The list is made up of several smaller lists. Together a meaningful structure is apparent, revealing a conscious effort on the part of the narrative to present the family of Esau as a coherent and distinct whole (Westermann, p. 686). There is first a list of the names of the sons of Esau (vv.9–14), largely dependent on the brief narratives regarding Esau's wives (26:34; 28:9; 36:3; see note on 28:9). Verse 10 divides the sons of Esau into two groups: the sons of Adah and the sons of Basemath. Adah's sons (and grandsons) are listed in vv.11–12, then Basemath's in v.13, and finally Oholibamah's in v.14. Oholibamah is not mentioned at the top of the list in v.10 but is named in v.5.

15–19 Verses 15–19 list the tribal "chiefs" of the sons of Esau, beginning with the eldest, Eliphaz, and again grouped according to their mothers: Adah (vv.15b–16), Basemath (v.17), and Oholibamah (v.18). The term "chief" (*'allûp̱*) is used in the Bible only for the tribal leaders of Edom, with the exception of Zechariah 12:5–6, where it is also used of the leaders of Judah. The word is found outside the Bible, however, where it refers to the leaders of foreign nations (U. Cassuto, *Encyclopaedia Biblica* [Jerusalem: Instituti Bialik, 1955], 1:332). The title "chief" then would have denoted primarily a political or military function (viz., "tribal chief," KB, p. 53; Westermann, p. 687). The names are virtually the same in both lists with the exception of Korah in v.16a, who is not in the first list (v.11), and the order of Kenaz and Gatam is reversed.

Notes

11–12 Again notice the chiastic coordination: וַיִּהְיוּ בְּנֵי אֱלִיפָז. . . . וְתִמְנַע הָיְתָה פִילֶגֶשׁ לֶאֱלִיפַז[1] (Andersen, *Sentence in Biblical Hebrew*, p.122).

[1] (*wayyihyû bᵉnê 'ᵉlîp̱āz. . . . wᵉṯimna' hāyᵉṯāh pîleg̱eš le'ᵉlîp̱az*, "The sons of Eliphaz. . . . Eliphaz also had a concubine named Timnah").

---

2. *The sons of Seir the Horite*

36:20–30

20 These were the sons of Seir the Horite, who were living in the region:
Lotan, Shobal, Zibeon, Anah, 21 Dishon, Ezer and Dishan. These sons of Seir in Edom were Horite chiefs.
22 The sons of Lotan:
Hori and Homam. Timna was Lotan's sister.
23 The sons of Shobal:
Alvan, Manahath, Ebal, Shepho and Onam.
24 The sons of Zibeon:
Aiah and Anah. This is the Anah who discovered the hot springs in the desert while he was grazing the donkeys of his father Zibeon.
25 The children of Anah:
Dishon and Oholibamah daughter of Anah.
26 The sons of Dishon:
Hemdan, Eshban, Ithran and Keran.
27 The sons of Ezer:
Bilhan, Zaavan and Akan.
28 The sons of Dishan:
Uz and Aran.
29 These were the Horite chiefs:
Lotan, Shobal, Zibeon, Anah, 30 Dishon, Ezer and Dishan. These were the Horite chiefs, according to their divisions, in the land of Seir.

20–30 To the two above lists is added a list of "the sons of Seir the Horite, who were living in the region" (vv.20–28), and then a list of their tribal "chiefs" (vv.29–30). Seir is ordinarily the name of the geographical territory occupied by the Edomites (BDB, p. 973), but here it refers to an individual. He and his descendants are listed here because they occupied the territory of Edom. In 2 Chronicles 25:11, 14, the "sons of Seir" are called "Edomites." The list identifies Seir as a "Horite," which earlier commentators interpreted as "cave dwellers"—deriving the sense from the similarity of the word "Horite" to the Hebrew word *ḥōr* ("Hor"), meaning "cave" (William Gesenius, *Thesaurus Philologicus Criticus Linguae Hebraeae et Chaldaeae Veteris Testamenti* [Lipsiae: F.C.G. Vogelii, 1835], p. 458). Though often rejected by modern lexicographers (KB, p. 339), there is a growing opinion among recent commentators that the older commentators may have been correct (Speiser, p. 283).

3. *Rulers in Edom*

36:31–43

31 These were the kings who reigned in Edom before any Israelite king reigned:

32 Bela son of Beor became king of Edom. His city was named Dinhabah.

33 When Bela died, Jobab son of Zerah from Bozrah succeeded him as king.

34 When Jobab died, Husham from the land of the Temanites succeeded him as king.

35 When Husham died, Hadad son of Bedad, who defeated Midian in the country of Moab, succeeded him as king. His city was named Avith.

36 When Hadad died, Samlah from Masrekah succeeded him as king.

37 When Samlah died, Shaul from Rehoboth on the river succeeded him as king.

38 When Shaul died, Baal-Hanan son of Acbor succeeded him as king.

39 When Baal-Hanan son of Acbor died, Hadad succeeded him as king. His city was named Pau, and his wife's name was Mehetabel daughter of Matred, the daughter of Me-Zahab.

40 These were the chiefs descended from Esau, by name, according to their clans and regions:

Timna, Alvah, Jetheth, 41 Oholibamah, Elah, Pinon, 42 Kenaz,
Teman, Mibzar, 43 Magdiel and Iram. These were the chiefs of
Edom, according to their settlements in the land they occupied.

This was Esau the father of the Edomites.

31–39 The list of Edomite kings in vv.31–39 is introduced by the heading "These were the kings who reigned in Edom before any Israelite king reigned" (see Notes).

40–43 The chapter closes with a final list of the tribal "chiefs" of Esau's clan. Several names in this list overlap with those in vv.10–14.

Notes

---

31 The expression לִפְנֵי מְלָךְ־מֶלֶךְ לִבְנֵי יִשְׂרָאֵל (*lip̠nê m^elok̠-melek̠ lib̠nê yiśrā'ēl*, "before any Israelite king reigned") presupposes a knowledge of the kingship in Israel, or at least an anticipation of the kingship. Thus it is a part of those texts (e.g., 17:6, 16; 35:11) that look forward to the promises of Gen 49:10; Num 24:7, 17–18; and Deut 17:14–20 (cf. 1 Sam 2:10). It should be noticed that there is no mention of the death (וַיָּמָת [*wayyāmot̠*]) of the last king in the list, הֲדַר (*h^ad̠ar*, "Hadar," v.39), or הֲדַד (*h^ad̠ad̠*, "Hadad"), as he is called in 1 Chron 1:50, whereas in the Chronicles passage וַיָּמָת הֲדָד (*wayyāmot̠ h^ad̠ād̠*, "Hadad also died") is added. This suggests that the Genesis list assumes that *h^ad̠ar* was still alive and that the Chronicles passage brings the list up to date.

VI. The Account of Jacob (37:1–49:33)

A. *Jacob in the Land*

37:1

1 Jacob lived in the land where his father had stayed, the land of Canaan.

1 Verse 1 belongs structurally to the preceding narrative as a conclusion to the Jacob story. It shows Jacob back in the Land of Promise but still dwelling there as a sojourner like his father before him. The writer's point is to show that the promises of God had not yet been completely fulfilled and that Jacob, as his fathers before him, was still awaiting the fulfillment. It is from a verse such as this that the NT writers read the lives of the patriarchs as "aliens and strangers on earth" (Heb 11:13). The verse also provides a fitting transition to the next section, the Joseph narratives, which trace the course of events by which the sons of Jacob left the Land of Promise and entered the land of Egypt. According to 25:11 Jacob's father, Isaac, dwelt in Beer Lahai Roi, which evidently is where Jacob lived at this time.

Notes

1–2 Notice the similarity in syntactical structure:

וַיֵּשֶׁב יַעֲקֹב בְּאֶרֶץ מְגוּרֵי אָבִיו בְּאֶרֶץ כְּנָעַן[1] (vv.1–2)
אֵלֶּה תֹּלְדוֹת

וַיֵּשֶׁב יִצְחָק עִם־בְּאֵר לַחַי רֹאִי[2] (25:11–12)
וְאֵלֶּה תֹּלְדֹת

Both clauses serve as transitions between two large narrative segments.

[1] (*wayyēšeb̲ ya'aqōb̲ be'ereṣ megûrê 'āb̲îw be'ereṣ kenā'an 'ēlleh tōled̲ôt̲*, "Jacob lived in the land where his father had stayed, the land of Canaan. This is the account").

[2] (*wayyēšeb̲ yiṣḥāq 'im-be'ēr laḥay rō'î we'ēlleh tōled̲ōt̲*, lit., "And Isaac lived near Beer Lahai Roi. And this is the account").

B. *Joseph's Dreams*

37:2–11

2 This is the account of Jacob.
Joseph, a young man of seventeen, was tending the flocks with his brothers, the sons of Bilhah and the sons of Zilpah, his father's wives, and he brought their father a bad report about them.
3 Now Israel loved Joseph more than any of his other sons, because he had been born to him in his old age; and he made a richly ornamented
robe for him. 4 When his brothers saw that their father loved him more
than any of them, they hated him and could not speak a kind word to him.
5 Joseph had a dream, and when he told it to his brothers, they hated
him all the more. 6 He said to them, "Listen to this dream I had: 7 We were
binding sheaves of grain out in the field when suddenly my sheaf rose and stood upright, while your sheaves gathered around mine and bowed down to it."
8 His brothers said to him, "Do you intend to reign over us? Will you actually rule us?" And they hated him all the more because of his dream and what he had said.
9 Then he had another dream, and he told it to his brothers. "Listen," he said, "I had another dream, and this time the sun and moon and eleven stars were bowing down to me."
10 When he told his father as well as his brothers, his father rebuked him and said, "What is this dream you had? Will your mother and I and

your brothers actually come and bow down to the ground before you?"
11 His brothers were jealous of him, but his father kept the matter in mind.

2–3a The formal title of the section is "This is the account of Jacob" (v.2a). As v.2b suggests, however, the remaining narrative is not about Jacob as such but about Joseph; and as we shall see, it is also about Judah. The writer immediately begins to tell the story of Joseph. Thus a number of pertinent details about him are given. He is seventeen years old. Along with his brothers, he is a shepherd of his father's sheep; and he is only a young lad (*na'ar*) compared with his other brothers. Most importantly, however, the writer introduces the fact that Joseph brought a "bad [*rā'āh*] report" about his brothers to his father and also that his father Jacob loved him more than the other brothers because he was the son born to him in his old age (v.3a).

In the context of the preceding narratives about Jacob and his wives, we can see that Jacob's special love for Rachel (*wayye'ehab gam-'et-rāḥēl millē'āh*, "And he loved Rachel more than Leah," 29:30) has carried over to that of her son, Joseph (*weyiśrā'ēl 'āhab 'et-yôsēp mikkol-bānāyw*, "Now Israel loved Joseph more than any of his other sons," v.3a). Since the story of Joseph is filled with wordplays and reversals, it seems likely that the reference to the "bad [*rā'āh*] report" in v.2 foreshadows the brothers' intended "evil" (*rā'āh;* NIV, "harm") spoken of in 50:20.

3b–11 The "richly ornamented robe" (v.3b) that Jacob made for Joseph visually illustrates the father's preferential love for Joseph. As such the writer continually returns to the coat throughout the remainder of the story as a way of reminding the reader of this central issue in the narrative (vv.23, 31, 32, 33). Jacob's preferential treatment of Joseph was the central problem that initiated the action of the story, for it angered Joseph's brothers and turned them against him (v.4). Eventually their anger resulted in a plan to do away with him altogether (v.18). But first, adding to their hatred, Joseph recounted to his brothers two dreams, both of which end with the image of his brothers "bowing down" (*wattištaḥaweynā*, v.7; *mištaḥawîm*, v.9; *lehištaḥawōt*, v.10) to him. The picture of the brothers bowing down to Joseph foreshadows the conclusion of the story where, because he is ruler of the land of Egypt, his brothers "bowed down" (*wayyištaḥawû*, 42:6) to him. Thus on that occasion the narrative reminds us that Joseph "remembered his dreams about them" (42:9).

Ironically, however, the manner in which the Book of Genesis was composed suggests that the picture of Joseph and his brothers foreshadows even further the relationship between Judah and his brothers as pictured in Jacob's words in 49:8: "Judah, . . . your father's sons will bow down to you" (*yištaḥawwû*). The picture of Joseph is transcended by that of Judah, just as the blessing that the sons of Joseph received in chapter 48 is transcended by that of Judah in chapter 49.

The fact that Joseph had two dreams that foreshadowed his future ascendancy over his brothers is to be understood in light of Joseph's own words in chapter 41. There he explained to the Pharaoh, "The reason the dream was given to Pharaoh in two forms [*pa'amāyim*, lit., 'twice'] is that the matter has been firmly decided by God, and God will do it soon" (41:32). So here the matter is already settled at the beginning of the story. God will surely bring to pass the fulfillment of Joseph's dream. The writer is careful to show throughout this narrative that Joseph's dreams do, in fact, come to pass.

The significance of the dreams is stated in the words of Joseph's brothers: "Will you actually rule us?" (*māšôl timšōl,* v.8). This reveals the sense of the "bowing down" (*l^{e}hištaḥ^{a}wōṯ,* v.10) to be an acknowledgement of royalty and kingship. The irony of the narrative composition is that in the end such royal honor does not reside in the house of Joseph but in the house of Judah ("The scepter will not depart from Judah," 49:10).

Notes

2–3 The syntax W + X + QATAL suggests that these clauses are describing the background of the events to follow. There is perhaps a wordplay between נַעַר (*na'ar,* "young man") and רָעָה (*rā'āh,* "bad") that serves to further link the clauses. The clause type—וְעָשָׂה לוֹ כְּתֹנֶת פַּסִּים (*w^{e}'āśāh lô k^{e}ṯōneṯ passîm,* "he made a richly ornamented robe for him") (W + QATAL + X)—is represented elsewhere in Genesis (2:6b, 10c, 24b[bis]; 15:6a; 21:25a; 26:13b; 29:3[quat]; 30:41a[bis], 42b; 34:5b; 37:3b; 38:5b, 9b; 47:22b) and thus need not be changed to follow the Samaritan Pentateuch (וַיַּעַשׂ [*wayya'aś,* "and he will make"]).

3 The meaning of כְּתֹנֶת פַּסִּים (*k^{e}ṯōneṯ passîm;* NIV, "richly ornamented robe") is "a coat of extended length," literally, a coat that extends to the hands and feet (*passîm*). The idea of a "coat of many colors" comes from the early versions: LXX (*χιτῶνα ποικίλον, chitōna poikilon*), Palestinian Targum (פַּרְגּוֹד מְצוּיָיר [*pargôḏ m^{e}ṣûyāyr,* "many colored coat" (J. Levy, *Chaldäisches Wörterbuch über die Targumim* [Leipzig: Baumgaertner's Buchhandlung, 1881], p. 286)]), Vulgate (*tunicam polymitam*). The only other occurrence of the term is 2 Sam 13:18–19, where it refers to the "kind of garment the virgin daughters of the king wore."

C. *Joseph's Journey to Egypt*

37:12–36

12 Now his brothers had gone to graze their father's flocks near
Shechem, 13 and Israel said to Joseph, "As you know, your brothers are
grazing the flocks near Shechem. Come, I am going to send you to
them."

"Very well," he replied.

14 So he said to him, "Go and see if all is well with your brothers and
with the flocks, and bring word back to me." Then he sent him off from
the Valley of Hebron.

When Joseph arrived at Shechem, 15 a man found him wandering
around in the fields and asked him, "What are you looking for?"

16 He replied, "I'm looking for my brothers. Can you tell me where they
are grazing their flocks?"

17 "They have moved on from here," the man answered. "I heard them
say, 'Let's go to Dothan.' "

So Joseph went after his brothers and found them near Dothan. 18 But
they saw him in the distance, and before he reached them, they plotted
to kill him.

19 "Here comes that dreamer!" they said to each other. 20 "Come now,
let's kill him and throw him into one of these cisterns and say that a
ferocious animal devoured him. Then we'll see what comes of his
dreams."

21 When Reuben heard this, he tried to rescue him from their hands.
"Let's not take his life," he said. 22 "Don't shed any blood. Throw him
into this cistern here in the desert, but don't lay a hand on him." Reuben
said this to rescue him from them and take him back to his father.
23 So when Joseph came to his brothers, they stripped him of his
robe—the richly ornamented robe he was wearing—24 and they took
him and threw him into the cistern. Now the cistern was empty; there
was no water in it.
25 As they sat down to eat their meal, they looked up and saw a
caravan of Ishmaelites coming from Gilead. Their camels were loaded
with spices, balm and myrrh, and they were on their way to take them
down to Egypt.
26 Judah said to his brothers, "What will we gain if we kill our brother
and cover up his blood? 27 Come, let's sell him to the Ishmaelites and
not lay our hands on him; after all, he is our brother, our own flesh and
blood." His brothers agreed.
28 So when the Midianite merchants came by, his brothers pulled
Joseph up out of the cistern and sold him for twenty shekels of silver to
the Ishmaelites, who took him to Egypt.
29 When Reuben returned to the cistern and saw that Joseph was not
there, he tore his clothes. 30 He went back to his brothers and said, "The
boy isn't there! Where can I turn now?"
31 Then they got Joseph's robe, slaughtered a goat and dipped the
robe in the blood. 32 They took the ornamented robe back to their father
and said, "We found this. Examine it to see whether it is your son's
robe."
33 He recognized it and said, "It is my son's robe! Some ferocious
animal has devoured him. Joseph has surely been torn to pieces."
34 Then Jacob tore his clothes, put on sackcloth and mourned for his
son many days. 35 All his sons and daughters came to comfort him, but
he refused to be comforted. "No," he said, "in mourning will I go down
to the grave to my son." So his father wept for him.
36 Meanwhile, the Midianites sold Joseph in Egypt to Potiphar, one of
Pharaoh's officials, the captain of the guard.

12–18 After a minor difficulty in which he temporarily lost his way and had to seek help from a stranger, Joseph found his brothers in Dothan. The purpose of this small account of Joseph's seeking his brothers can be seen by comparing it with the brief and similar prelude to the second part of the story where he met his brothers in Egypt (chs. 42–44). The symmetry of the two passages and the verbal and thematic parallels serve to reinforce the sense in the narrative that every event is providentially ordered. Here at the beginning of the Joseph story, when Joseph's brothers "saw him" (*wayyir'û 'ōṯô,* v.18) approaching, they "plotted" (*wayyiṯnakk^{e}lû*) "to kill him" (*lah^{a}mîṯô*). In the same way midway through the narrative, when Joseph first "saw his brothers" (*wayyar' 'eṯ-'eḥāyw,* 42:7) in Egypt, he eluded his brothers by "disguising himself" (*wayyiṯnakkēr,* 42:7; NIV, "pretended to be a stranger") so that they did not recognize him and then planned a scheme that, at least on the surface, looked as if he intended to kill them (*w^{e}lō' ṯāmûṯû,* 42:20; NIV, "that you may not die").

19–36 The details of the brother's plans are given as well as their motivation. Behind their plans lie Joseph's two dreams. Little did they suspect that the very plans that they were then scheming were to lead to the fulfillment of those dreams. In every detail of the narrative the writer's purpose shows through, that is, to demonstrate the truthfulness of Joseph's final words to his brothers: "You intended it to harm me, but

God intended it for good" (50:20). The first plan was simply "to kill him" (*wenahargēhû*, 37:20), throw his body in a pit, and then tell their father that an "evil" (*rā'āh;* NIV, "ferocious") animal had eaten him. Again, the brothers punctuated their plan with a reference to Joseph's dreams in an obviously ironic statement: "we'll see what comes of his dreams" (v.20; cf. 42:9). This initial plan, however, is interrupted by Reuben, who, the writer tells us, saved Joseph from their hands (vv.21–22).

The reference to Reuben is countered later in the narrative by a similar reference to Judah (v.26). The writer apparently wants to show that it was not merely Reuben who saved Joseph from the plan of his brothers but that Judah also played an important role. Again we can see the central importance of Jacob's last words regarding Judah in 49:8–12. In the end it is Judah who is placed at the center of the narrative's focus on the fulfillment of the divine blessing. It is the descendants of Judah who will ultimately figure in the coming of the Promised Seed. Reuben's plan is to persuade the brothers merely to throw Joseph into a pit and, apparently, leave him to die (vv.21–22a). We learn from the narrative, however, that his actual plan was to return later and rescue Joseph (v.22b). Reuben's plan was partly successful. The brothers threw Joseph into the pit alive and left him there. The reference to Joseph's coat, by turning our attention briefly back to the earlier events of the narrative, highlights the central point of the story, namely, that the present plan is all part of a larger divine plan foreshadowed in Joseph's dreams.

The story takes an important turn with the arrival of the "Ishmaelites" who were bearing spices down to Egypt (v.25). The "Ishmaelites" become the occasion for Judah to enter the story with the suggestion that, rather than letting Joseph die (*nahₐrōg*, v.26) in the pit, they could "sell him to the Ishmaelites" (v.27). Only a cursory account of Joseph's fate follows in the text. The Ishmaelites, who are also called "Midianites" in this narrative, arrive, and Joseph is sold to them for twenty shekels (v.28). They then take him to Egypt with them.

When the focus of the narrative returns to Reuben and to the outcome of his plan to deal with Joseph, ironically it serves only to underscore the role of Judah in the actual rescue of Joseph. Verse 29 suggests that Reuben had no part in the plan to sell Joseph to the Ishmaelites. He returned to the pit, expecting to find Joseph there and to rescue him, but Joseph was not there. Reuben's surprise is shown in his rage upon seeing that Joseph is gone. Thus in no uncertain terms we learn that it was Judah, not Reuben, who saved the life of Joseph. Ultimately the brothers must fall back on their original plan of telling their father that a "ferocious" (*rā'āh*, lit., "evil"; 37:33) animal had killed Joseph.

Once again the coat that Jacob had given to Joseph provides the narrative link in the story. The symbol of the brothers' original hatred for Joseph becomes the means of the father's recognition of his loss. In the end the blood-stained coat is all that remains of Joseph, and upon seeing it Jacob tore off his own coat and exchanged it for sackcloth (v.34). Thus Jacob's own fate and that of his sons is briefly sketched out in this opening narrative. What happens to Joseph foreshadows all that will happen to the sons of Jacob. They will be carried down into Egypt and will be put into slavery. In this sense, then, Jacob's final words set the focus of the narratives to follow: "in mourning will I go down ['*ērēd̲*] to the grave [Sheol] to my son" (v.35). Ironically, the Joseph narratives conclude with Jacob's going down (*mēred̲āh*, 46:3–4) to Egypt to see his son and then with his own death (50:24–26).

Notes

25–36 There are three groups of peoples mentioned in connection with Joseph's journey to Egypt: יִשְׁמְעֵאלִים (*yišmᵉʿēʾlîm*, "the Ishmaelites," vv.25, 27), מִדְיָנִים (*miḏyānîm*, "the Midianites," v.28), and הַמְּדָנִים (*hammᵉḏānîm*, "the Medanites," v.36 [NIV mg.]). The difference in spelling between *miḏyānîm* and *hammᵉḏānîm* is only slight; and following the LXX and other early versions, the *hammᵉḏānîm* is often read as *hammiḏyānîm* (e.g., NIV). According to 25:2, however, the *mᵉḏānîm* and the *miḏyānîm* are two distinct groups; and the early versions do not offer the better reading on textual critical grounds. To complicate the matter 39:1 credits the *hayyišmᵉʿēʾlîm* with bringing Joseph to Egypt rather than the *miḏyānîm* or the *mᵉḏānîm*. We should leave the text as it stands, with three groups, and see the variations in names in light of such texts as Judg 7:8–12, where the "camp of Midian" (מַחֲנֵה מִדְיָן [*mahᵃnēh miḏyān*]) is said to be made up of "The Midianites [*miḏyān*], the Amalekites and all the other eastern peoples [*wᵉḵol-bᵉnê-qeḏem*]," and Judg 8:24, where these same peoples are generically referred to as "Ishmaelites" (*yišmᵉʿēʾlîm*).

The term יִשְׁמְעֵאלִים (*yišmᵉʿēʾlîm*, "Ishmaelites") apparently was both a term to describe the descendants of Ishmael and a name for a broad category of tribal groups (cf. BDB, p. 1035). This last use appears to be the sense of the term in Genesis 37. The use of הַמְּדָנִים (*hammᵉḏānîm*, "the Medanites"), on the other hand, curiously lends support to the broader sense of the term "Ishmaelite." By showing the traders to have been both *miḏyānîm* and *mᵉḏānîm*, the narrative avoids the misunderstanding of reading the term "Ishmaelite" as merely the physical descendants of Abraham's son Ishmael. In the present state of the narrative, the term "Ishmaelites" more or less has to stand for a larger configuration of tribes consisting of both "Midianites" and "Medanites." See note on 45:4.

36 The mention of Potiphar, the captain of the guard, is intended as a link to chapter 39, where it is repeated again after the interruption of chapter 38. Verse 36, then, presupposes the existence of chapter 38 and prepares the reader for a smooth transition back into the story line of the Joseph narrative.

D. *Judah and Tamar*

38:1–30

1 At that time, Judah left his brothers and went down to stay with a
man of Adullam named Hirah. 2 There Judah met the daughter of a
Canaanite man named Shua. He married her and lay with her; 3 she
became pregnant and gave birth to a son, who was named Er.
4 She conceived again and gave birth to a son and named him Onan.
5 She gave birth to still another son and named him Shelah. It was at
Kezib that she gave birth to him.

6 Judah got a wife for Er, his firstborn, and her name was Tamar. 7 But
Er, Judah's firstborn, was wicked in the LORD's sight; so the LORD put him
to death.

8 Then Judah said to Onan, "Lie with your brother's wife and fulfill
your duty to her as a brother-in-law to produce offspring for your
brother." 9 But Onan knew that the offspring would not be his; so
whenever he lay with his brother's wife, he spilled his semen on the
ground to keep from producing offspring for his brother. 10 What he did
was wicked in the LORD's sight; so he put him to death also.

11 Judah then said to his daughter-in-law Tamar, "Live as a widow in
your father's house until my son Shelah grows up." For he thought, "He
may die too, just like his brothers." So Tamar went to live in her father's
house.

[12]After a long time Judah's wife, the daughter of Shua, died. When Judah had recovered from his grief, he went up to Timnah, to the men who were shearing his sheep, and his friend Hirah the Adullamite went with him.

[13]When Tamar was told, "Your father-in-law is on his way to Timnah to shear his sheep," [14]she took off her widow's clothes, covered herself with a veil to disguise herself, and then sat down at the entrance to Enaim, which is on the road to Timnah. For she saw that, though Shelah had now grown up, she had not been given to him as his wife.

[15]When Judah saw her, he thought she was a prostitute, for she had covered her face. [16]Not realizing that she was his daughter-in-law, he went over to her by the roadside and said, "Come now, let me sleep with you."

"And what will you give me to sleep with you?" she asked.

[17]"I'll send you a young goat from my flock," he said.

"Will you give me something as a pledge until you send it?" she asked.

[18]He said, "What pledge should I give you?"

"Your seal and its cord, and the staff in your hand," she answered. So he gave them to her and slept with her, and she became pregnant by him. [19]After she left, she took off her veil and put on her widow's clothes again.

[20]Meanwhile Judah sent the young goat by his friend the Adullamite in order to get his pledge back from the woman, but he did not find her. [21]He asked the men who lived there, "Where is the shrine prostitute who was beside the road at Enaim?"

"There hasn't been any shrine prostitute here," they said.

[22]So he went back to Judah and said, "I didn't find her. Besides, the men who lived there said, 'There hasn't been any shrine prostitute here.' "

[23]Then Judah said, "Let her keep what she has, or we will become a laughingstock. After all, I did send her this young goat, but you didn't find her."

[24]About three months later Judah was told, "Your daughter-in-law Tamar is guilty of prostitution, and as a result she is now pregnant."

Judah said, "Bring her out and have her burned to death!"

[25]As she was being brought out, she sent a message to her father-in-law. "I am pregnant by the man who owns these," she said. And she added, "See if you recognize whose seal and cord and staff these are."

[26]Judah recognized them and said, "She is more righteous than I, since I wouldn't give her to my son Shelah." And he did not sleep with her again.

[27]When the time came for her to give birth, there were twin boys in her womb. [28]As she was giving birth, one of them put out his hand; so the midwife took a scarlet thread and tied it on his wrist and said, "This one came out first." [29]But when he drew back his hand, his brother came out, and she said, "So this is how you have broken out!" And he was named Perez. [30]Then his brother, who had the scarlet thread on his wrist, came out and he was given the name Zerah.

1–11 The narrative of chapter 38 has only a loose connection with the Joseph story. The first verse notes only that these events occurred "at the same time" (*bā'ēṯ hahiw'*; NIV, "at that time"). Without this remark we would have little basis for relating these events to the story of Joseph. In the overall strategy of the book, however, this chapter plays a crucial role. The very fact that the narrative seems to lie outside the course of events of the Joseph story shows that the writer has put it here for a special purpose. It plays an important part in the development of the central themes of the book.

As before in the Book of Genesis, the narrative begins with the mention of three sons (cf. the three sons of Adam, Noah, and Terah). Two of the sons died because of the evil (*ra'*; NIV, "were wicked") they did; thus the offspring of Judah was put in jeopardy. Who would prolong the seed? The point of this introductory information is to show that the continuation of the house of Judah lay in Judah's hands.

The narrative that follows shows that Judah does nothing to further the offspring of his own household. It takes the "righteousness" (*ṣāḏ^eqāh*) of the woman Tamar (v.26) to preserve the seed of Judah. A nearly identical theme is found in the Book of Ruth (4:18), which itself alludes to this chapter of Genesis. The story of chapter 38, then, is much like the other "patriarchal" narratives outside the story of Joseph, which show the promised offspring in jeopardy and the patriarch showing little concern for its preservation. Just as in chapter 20 where the seed of Abraham was protected by the "righteous" (*ṣaddîq*, 20:4; NIV, "innocent") Abimelech (cf. also 26:9–11), it is the woman Tamar, not Judah the patriarch, who is ultimately responsible for the survival of the descendants of the house of Judah.

The text is not clear from whose house Jacob originally took Tamar for his son's wife (v.6). Since we are told that Judah's own wife was a Canaanite (v.2), had Tamar also been a Canaanite, it assumedly would have been mentioned in the narrative. If Tamar was not a Canaanite, as appears likely, then this introduction shows another point at which the promise to Abraham would have stood in jeopardy. By marrying the daughter of a Canaanite, Judah had realized the worst fears of Abraham (24:3) and Isaac (28:1); so, according to the logic of the narrative, the promise regarding the descendants of Abraham and Isaac was in danger of being unfulfillable. Through Tamar's clever plan, then, the seed of Abraham was preserved by not being allowed to continue through the sons of the Canaanite, the daughter of Shua. The line was continued through Judah and Tamar. The genealogy at the close of the narrative serves to underscore this point.

12–26 Tamar's plan resembles that of Jacob and Rebekah (ch. 27). Through a disguise she obtained a part in the blessing of the firstborn. In so doing, just as with Jacob and Rebekah, she obtained that which the patriarch should have rightfully given. Selah, the son of Judah, was of age (v.14), and Tamar should have been given to him for a wife (v.11). Thus, in the end, the continuation of the line of Judah was not due to the righteous actions of the patriarch Judah but rather lay in the hands of the "righteous" Tamar. Such has been a recurring theme throughout the patriarchal narratives.

27–30 The whole of the Jacob narratives reaches a fitting summary in this brief account of the birth of the two sons Perez and Zerah. As the Jacob narrative began with an account of the struggle of the twins Jacob and Esau (25:22), so now the conclusion of the Jacob narrative is marked by a similar struggle of twins. In both cases the struggle resulted in a reversal of the right of the firstborn and the right of the blessing. The result of both struggles was that the younger gained the upper hand over the elder. As Jacob struggled with Esau and overcame him, so Perez overcame Zerah, the elder, and gained the right of the firstborn (vv.28–29; cf. Num 26:20, where Perez is regarded as the firstborn). The brevity and austerity with which the narrative is recounted leaves the impression that the meaning of the passage is self-evident to the reader. Indeed, coming as it does on the heels of a long series of reversals in which the younger gains the upper hand on the elder, its sense is transparent.

Notes

---

1 The phrase בָּעֵת הַהִוא (*bā'ēṯ hahiw'*, "At that time") serves as a link to the surrounding narrative, though it does so only in a general way. The writer appears intent on not drawing the chronological context too closely around the story in chapter 38. The general sense of *bā'ēṯ hahiw'* can be seen in comparison with the more definite בְּעֶצֶם הַיּוֹם הַזֶּה (*beʿeṣem hayyôm hazzeh*, "on that same day") in 17:26 and אַחַר הַדְּבָרִים הָאֵלֶּה (*'aḥar haddeḇārîm hā'ēlleh*, "After this") in 15:1.

5 The location כְּזִיב (*keziḇ*, "Kezib"), mentioned only here in the Bible, may be associated with אַכְזָב (*'aḵzāḇ*, "Aczib"), as Keil and others have suggested, in which case it was located in the lowland of Judah (cf. Josh 15:44).

7 The only wordplay on any of the names in this narrative is that between עֵר (*ʿēr*, "Er") and רַע (*raʿ*, "evil").

15–18 The narrative at this point makes no effort to accuse or excuse the intention or action of Judah. The text says he considered Tamar to be a זוֹנָה (*zônāh*, "a prostitute"; cf. BDB, p. 275: "a harlot"); and she is later (vv.21–22) described as a קְדֵשָׁה (*qeḏēšāh*, "shrine prostitute," "harlot"). Both actions are clearly condemned in the Torah: *qeḏēšāh* (Deut 23:17–18: "temple prostitute") and *zônāh* (Deut 22:21: "by being promiscuous").

29–30 Notice the formal syntax of the conclusion of the story: וַיְהִי כְּמֵשִׁיב יָדוֹ וְהִנֵּה יָצָא אָחִיו. . . . וְאַחַר יָצָא אָחִיו (*wayehî kemēšîḇ yāḏô wehinnēh yāṣā' 'āḥîw. . . . we'aḥar yāṣā' 'āḥîw*, "But when he drew back his hand, his brother came out. . . . Then his brother . . . came out").

E. *Joseph in the House of Potiphar*

39:1–23

1 Now Joseph had been taken down to Egypt. Potiphar, an Egyptian who was one of Pharaoh's officials, the captain of the guard, bought him from the Ishmaelites who had taken him there.

2 The Lord was with Joseph and he prospered, and he lived in the house of his Egyptian master. 3 When his master saw that the Lord was with him and that the Lord gave him success in everything he did, 4 Joseph found favor in his eyes and became his attendant. Potiphar put him in charge of his household, and he entrusted to his care everything he owned. 5 From the time he put him in charge of his household and of all that he owned, the Lord blessed the household of the Egyptian because of Joseph. The blessing of the Lord was on everything Potiphar had, both in the house and in the field. 6 So he left in Joseph's care everything he had; with Joseph in charge, he did not concern himself with anything except the food he ate.

Now Joseph was well-built and handsome, 7 and after a while his master's wife took notice of Joseph and said, "Come to bed with me!"

8 But he refused. "With me in charge," he told her, "my master does not concern himself with anything in the house; everything he owns he has entrusted to my care. 9 No one is greater in this house than I am. My master has withheld nothing from me except you, because you are his wife. How then could I do such a wicked thing and sin against God?" 10 And though she spoke to Joseph day after day, he refused to go to bed with her or even be with her.

11 One day he went into the house to attend to his duties, and none of the household servants was inside. 12 She caught him by his cloak and said, "Come to bed with me!" But he left his cloak in her hand and ran out of the house.

13When she saw that he had left his cloak in her hand and had run out
of the house, 14she called her household servants. "Look," she said to
them, "this Hebrew has been brought to us to make sport of us! He
came in here to sleep with me, but I screamed. 15When he heard me
scream for help, he left his cloak beside me and ran out of the house."
16She kept his cloak beside her until his master came home. 17Then
she told him this story: "That Hebrew slave you brought us came to me
to make sport of me. 18But as soon as I screamed for help, he left his
cloak beside me and ran out of the house."
19When his master heard the story his wife told him, saying, "This is
how your slave treated me," he burned with anger. 20Joseph's master
took him and put him in prison, the place where the king's prisoners
were confined.
But while Joseph was there in the prison, 21the LORD was with him; he
showed him kindness and granted him favor in the eyes of the prison
warden. 22So the warden put Joseph in charge of all those held in the
prison, and he was made responsible for all that was done there. 23The
warden paid no attention to anything under Joseph's care, because the
LORD was with Joseph and gave him success in whatever he did.

1 Fully conscious of the intervening Judah narrative, the text resumes the account of Joseph, taking up where chapter 37 left off. As in 37:27, those who have brought Joseph into Egypt are called "Ishmaelites," while in 37:28, 36, they are known as "Midianites."

2–6 Verse 2 establishes the overall theme of the narrative: "The LORD was with Joseph and he prospered." Verses 3–6 relate the theme to the specific series of events to follow: Joseph's blessing from the Lord is recognized by his Egyptian master, and Joseph is put in charge of his household. Joseph's sojourn in Egypt, like that of his father, Jacob's (30:27), has resulted in an initial fulfillment of the Abrahamic promise that "all peoples on earth will be blessed through you" (12:3). Thus we are told that "the LORD blessed the house of the Egyptian because of Joseph" (v.5). Such a thematic introduction alerts the reader to the underlying lessons intended throughout the narrative. This is not a story of the success of Joseph; rather it is a story of God's faithfulness to his promises. The last note about Joseph in this introductory section ("Joseph was well-built and handsome," v.6) sets the stage for what follows.

7–20 This story about Joseph reverses a well-known plot in the patriarchal narratives. Whereas before it was the beautiful wife (*yᵉp̱aṯmar'eh,* 12:11; *ṭôḇaṯ-mar'eh,* 26:7) of the patriarch who was sought by the foreign ruler, now it was Joseph, the handsome patriarch (*yᵉp̱ēh-ṯō'ar wîp̱ēh mar'eh,* 39:6) himself who was sought by the wife of the foreign ruler. Whereas in the earlier narratives it was either the Lord (12:17; 20:3) or the moral purity of the foreign ruler (26:10) that rescued the wife rather than the patriarch, here it was Joseph's own moral courage that saved the day. Joseph's reply explicitly laid bare his motives: "How then could I do such a wicked thing [*rā'āh,* lit., 'evil'] and sin against God?" (v.9). The purpose of this reversal perhaps lies in a change of emphasis on the part of the writer in the Joseph narratives. Whereas in the preceding narratives, the focus of the writer had been on God's faithfulness in fulfilling his covenant promises, in the story of Joseph his attention is turned to the human response.

We have seen in the preceding narratives that Abraham, Isaac, and Jacob repeatedly fell short of God's expectations, though, of course, they continued to have faith in

God. In the Joseph narratives, however, we do not see him fall short. On the contrary, Joseph is a striking example of one who always responds in total trust and obedience to the will of God. Behind the Joseph narratives, then, lies an emphasis that has been little felt in the earlier stories where the stress has been on God's overriding commitment and faithfulness to his promises. The Joseph narratives, on the other hand, give expression to that part of the promise found in 18:19: "that they may do righteousness and justice [*ṣ*^{e}*ḏāqāh ûmišpāṭ*] so that the LORD may fulfill what he has promised to Abraham" (pers. tr.). There was a human part to be played in the fulfillment of God's plan. When God's people respond as Joseph responded, then their way and God's blessing will prosper.

The Joseph narratives are intended then to give balance to the narratives of Abraham, Isaac, and Jacob. Together the two sections show both God's faithfulness in spite of human failure as well as the necessity of an obedient and faithful response. The theological emphasis is remarkably similar to that of the "new covenant theology" of Jeremiah (Jer 31:31–34) and Ezekiel (Ezek 36:22–32) where the two themes of divine sovereignty and human responsibility are woven together by means of the concept of God's Spirit giving man a "new heart"—a heart given to man by God that responds with obedience and faith. It can hardly be accidental, then, that in all the Book of Genesis only Joseph is described as one who was filled with the Spirit of God (41:38). The same theological emphasis can be found in Deuteronomy 30:6–10, where Moses grounds his hope in the future of God's covenant promises in the divine work of giving man a new heart. Joseph was imprisoned through no fault of his own. In fact, the narrative is explicit in its emphasis on the total uprightness of Joseph throughout the attempted seduction by the Egyptian's wife. He was in jail because of false witness laid against him.

21–23 The epilogue to the story is clear in its emphasis. God has turned an intended evil against Joseph into a good. God was with Joseph (v.21) and prospered his way. Lying behind the course of events, then, is the lesson that the whole of the Joseph narratives teach: "You intended to harm me [*rā'āh*, lit., 'evil'], but God intended it for good [*ṭôḇ*]" (50:20). Like Daniel during the Exile, Joseph suffered for doing what was right, but God turned the evil done to him into a blessing.

Notes

1 On the relationship of the "Ishmaelites" and "Midianites," see Notes on 37:25–36. Verse 1 repeats much of 37:36 because of the intervening story of Judah and Tamar. The syntax of v.1 (W + X + QATAL) suggests that this is background information to the story that follows.

2 The וַיְהִי (*way*^{e}*hî*, "was") clauses in chapter 39 function essentially as W + X + QATAL clauses do in the rest of the biblical narratives, though with an additional sense of narrative summary. This stylistic feature is also known in other narratives, but it is particularly frequent in this narrative. See note on v.5 below.

5 Notice the chiastic coordination with וַיְהִי (*way*^{e}*hî*, lit., "and he was") in וַיְבָרֶךְ יהוה אֶת־בֵּית הַמִּצְרִי . . . וַיְהִי בִּרְכַּת יהוה בְּכָל־אֲשֶׁר יֶשׁ־לוֹ (*way*^{e}*ḇāreḵ yhwh 'eṯ-bêṯ hammiṣrî . . . way*^{e}*hî birkaṯ yhwh b*^{e}*ḵol-'*^{a}*šer yeš-lô*, "the LORD blessed the household of the Egyptian. . . . The blessing of the LORD was on everything [he] had").

14, 17 There may still be echoes of יִצְחָק (*yiṣḥāq*, "Isaac") in לְצַחֵק (*l^{e}ṣaḥeq*, "to make sport," vv.14, 17), though no obvious connection appears evident.

F. *Joseph in Jail*

40:1–23

[1]Some time later, the cupbearer and the baker of the king of Egypt offended their master, the king of Egypt. [2]Pharaoh was angry with his two officials, the chief cupbearer and the chief baker, [3]and put them in custody in the house of the captain of the guard, in the same prison where Joseph was confined. [4]The captain of the guard assigned them to Joseph, and he attended them.

After they had been in custody for some time, [5]each of the two men—the cupbearer and the baker of the king of Egypt, who were being held in prison—had a dream the same night, and each dream had a meaning of its own.

[6]When Joseph came to them the next morning, he saw that they were dejected. [7]So he asked Pharaoh's officials who were in custody with him in his master's house, "Why are your faces so sad today?"

[8]"We both had dreams," they answered, "but there is no one to interpret them."

Then Joseph said to them, "Do not interpretations belong to God? Tell me your dreams."

[9]So the chief cupbearer told Joseph his dream. He said to him, "In my dream I saw a vine in front of me, [10]and on the vine were three branches. As soon as it budded, it blossomed, and its clusters ripened into grapes. [11]Pharaoh's cup was in my hand, and I took the grapes, squeezed them into Pharaoh's cup and put the cup in his hand."

[12]"This is what it means," Joseph said to him. "The three branches are three days. [13]Within three days Pharaoh will lift up your head and restore you to your position, and you will put Pharaoh's cup in his hand, just as you used to do when you were his cupbearer. [14]But when all goes well with you, remember me and show me kindness; mention me to Pharaoh and get me out of this prison. [15]For I was forcibly carried off from the land of the Hebrews, and even here I have done nothing to deserve being put in a dungeon."

[16]When the chief baker saw that Joseph had given a favorable interpretation, he said to Joseph, "I too had a dream: On my head were three baskets of bread. [17]In the top basket were all kinds of baked goods for Pharaoh, but the birds were eating them out of the basket on my head."

[18]"This is what it means," Joseph said. "The three baskets are three days. [19]Within three days Pharaoh will lift off your head and hang you on a tree. And the birds will eat away your flesh."

[20]Now the third day was Pharaoh's birthday, and he gave a feast for all his officials. He lifted up the heads of the chief cupbearer and the chief baker in the presence of his officials: [21]He restored the chief cupbearer to his position, so that he once again put the cup into Pharaoh's hand, [22]but he hanged the chief baker, just as Joseph had said to them in his interpretation.

[23]The chief cupbearer, however, did not remember Joseph; he forgot him.

1–23 Chapter 40 represents an intermediary stage in the development of the plot of the Joseph story. Joseph has been cast into jail and has risen to a position of prominence there. We are apparently to assume that Joseph's position was responsible for his being assigned to wait on the two incarcerated royal officials (vv.1–4). They each had a dream, which Joseph then correctly interpreted, but ultimately to no avail, since the surviving official soon forgot the matter. What could have been the writer's purpose in including at such great length the events of this part of the narrative? It can first be said that later in the story, when the Pharaoh himself had a dream, the butler then remembered the events of this chapter and told the king about Joseph. From that perspective the events recorded here prove decisive. But is there more to it than that? Why so much detail regarding each dream? Why such an elevated style in the telling of the story? The writer clearly wants to impress on the reader the picture of Joseph that comes through these events. It is a Joseph who, like Daniel, is an interpreter of dreams and mysteries. He discerns the course of future events that to others lies in total darkness. Even when we, the readers, hear the dreams recounted, we are at a loss to find their meaning.

The sense of the cup-bearer's dream may seem self-evident, but as the sense of the baker's dream shows, such apparently self-evident meanings are by no means certain. Who could, on the face of it, discern between the meanings of the two dreams? One is favorable and the other not so. There is clearly more to the dreams than a plain reading of each would suggest. The picture of Joseph that emerges from this narrative is precisely that which the Pharaoh himself later expresses. Joseph is "one in whom is the spirit of God" (41:38). He knows the interpretations of dreams, which, in his own words, "belong to God" (40:8). The narrative serves then to set Joseph apart from all those who have preceded him in the book. He is "discerning and wise" (41:39), and "things turned out exactly as he interpreted them" (41:13). Whereas Abraham was a "prophet" (20:7), Joseph is a "wiseman" (cf. 41:39). Whereas Abraham sees the course of future events "in a vision" (15:1), Joseph discerns (41:39) the course of the future in the mysterious dreams of others.

What lies behind the writer's portrayal of Joseph in these terms? Why the contrast with Abraham? The answer may lie in the perspective of the Pentateuch in general. As the last chapters of Deuteronomy show, the Pentateuch addresses itself to an audience that has seen the passing of Moses, the great prophet (Deut 34:10), and yet has not seen the fulfillment of all his great prophecies. Much lay ahead yet to be fulfilled. It is to this audience that the leadership of Joshua is presented, not as a prophet, but as one "filled with the spirit of wisdom" (Deut 34:9), a "wiseman" like Joseph.

Joseph, then, represents the kind of leadership that the readers of the Pentateuch would be called on to follow. He is a leader like Daniel, who needed to "discern" (cf. Dan 9:2) the visions of the prophets to find the course of God's future dealings with his people, rather than to wait on new prophecies to come. Joseph, like Solomon, is a picture of a truly wise leader who understands and sees the will of God in the affairs of those around him. In this sense Joseph stands as a prototype of all the later wisemen of Israel. All future leaders must stand the test of measurement against him. It is hardly surprising then that one sees foreshadowed in the picture of Joseph elements that later resemble David, Solomon, and, ultimately, the Messiah himself.

Notes

---

1 וַיְהִי אַחַר הַדְּבָרִים הָאֵלֶּה (*wayᵉhî 'aḥar haddᵉḇārîm hā'ēlleh,* "Some time later") ties these events together in chronological succession to those of chapter 39. There are otherwise few internal links between the two chapters.

15 גֻּנַּבְתִּי מֵאֶרֶץ הָעִבְרִים (*gunnaḇtî me'ereṣ hā'iḇrîm,* "I was forcibly carried off from the land of the Hebrews") is a back-reference to the narrative of chapter 37 and shows the unity of the story. Such references are common in the story of Joseph.

G. *Joseph's Interpretation of Pharaoh's Dreams*

41:1–36

[1]When two full years had passed, Pharaoh had a dream: He was standing by the Nile, [2]when out of the river there came up seven cows, sleek and fat, and they grazed among the reeds. [3]After them, seven other cows, ugly and gaunt, came up out of the Nile and stood beside those on the riverbank. [4]And the cows that were ugly and gaunt ate up the seven sleek, fat cows. Then Pharaoh woke up.

[5]He fell asleep again and had a second dream: Seven heads of grain, healthy and good, were growing on a single stalk. [6]After them, seven other heads of grain sprouted—thin and scorched by the east wind. [7]The thin heads of grain swallowed up the seven healthy, full heads. Then Pharaoh woke up; it had been a dream.

[8]In the morning his mind was troubled, so he sent for all the magicians and wise men of Egypt. Pharaoh told them his dreams, but no one could interpret them for him.

[9]Then the chief cupbearer said to Pharaoh, "Today I am reminded of my shortcomings. [10]Pharaoh was once angry with his servants, and he imprisoned me and the chief baker in the house of the captain of the guard. [11]Each of us had a dream the same night, and each dream had a meaning of its own. [12]Now a young Hebrew was there with us, a servant of the captain of the guard. We told him our dreams, and he interpreted them for us, giving each man the interpretation of his dream. [13]And things turned out exactly as he interpreted them to us: I was restored to my position, and the other man was hanged."

[14]So Pharaoh sent for Joseph, and he was quickly brought from the dungeon. When he had shaved and changed his clothes, he came before Pharaoh.

[15]Pharaoh said to Joseph, "I had a dream, and no one can interpret it. But I have heard it said of you that when you hear a dream you can interpret it."

[16]"I cannot do it," Joseph replied to Pharaoh, "but God will give Pharaoh the answer he desires."

[17]Then Pharaoh said to Joseph, "In my dream I was standing on the bank of the Nile, [18]when out of the river there came up seven cows, fat and sleek, and they grazed among the reeds. [19]After them, seven other cows came up—scrawny and very ugly and lean. I had never seen such ugly cows in all the land of Egypt. [20]The lean, ugly cows ate up the seven fat cows that came up first. [21]But even after they ate them, no one could tell that they had done so; they looked just as ugly as before. Then I woke up.

[22]"In my dreams I also saw seven heads of grain, full and good, growing on a single stalk. [23]After them, seven other heads sprouted—withered and thin and scorched by the east wind. [24]The thin heads of grain swallowed up the seven good heads. I told this to the magicians, but none could explain it to me."

[25]Then Joseph said to Pharaoh, "The dreams of Pharaoh are one and the same. God has revealed to Pharaoh what he is about to do. [26]The seven good cows are seven years, and the seven good heads of grain are seven years; it is one and the same dream. [27]The seven lean, ugly cows that came up afterward are seven years, and so are the seven

worthless heads of grain scorched by the east wind: They are seven years of famine.

[28]"It is just as I said to Pharaoh: God has shown Pharaoh what he is about to do. [29]Seven years of great abundance are coming throughout the land of Egypt, [30]but seven years of famine will follow them. Then all the abundance in Egypt will be forgotten, and the famine will ravage the land. [31]The abundance in the land will not be remembered, because the famine that follows it will be so severe. [32]The reason the dream was given to Pharaoh in two forms is that the matter has been firmly decided by God, and God will do it soon.

[33]"And now let Pharaoh look for a discerning and wise man and put him in charge of the land of Egypt. [34]Let Pharaoh appoint commissioners over the land to take a fifth of the harvest of Egypt during the seven years of abundance. [35]They should collect all the food of these good years that are coming and store up the grain under the authority of Pharaoh, to be kept in the cities for food. [36]This food should be held in reserve for the country, to be used during the seven years of famine that will come upon Egypt, so that the country may not be ruined by the famine."

The central theme of chapter 41 is expressed clearly and forthrightly within the narrative itself by Joseph in v.32: "the matter has been firmly decided by God, and God will do it soon." As the narratives of this chapter show, the assurance that God will surely bring future events to pass comes from the fact that the dreams relating those events are repeated twice. "Two" dreams with the same meaning show that God will certainly bring about that which was foreseen in the dreams. Throughout the narrative this theme is kept alive by a continuous return to the pattern of "twos." In the previous chapter the "two" (*šᵉnê*, 40:2) officials of the king each had a dream. One dream was good, the other bad. The dreams and their interpretations are repeated twice, once by the writer in the narrative of chapter 40 and then again by the cupbearer before the Pharaoh in vv.9–13.

After "two years" (*šᵉnāṯayim*, v.1), the king himself had "two" (*šēnîṯ*, v.5) dreams, one part of each dream was good ("years of great abundance," v.29) and the other bad ("years of famine," vv.27, 30). Within the narrative, each of the two dreams is repeated twice, once by the writer (vv.1–7) and again by Pharaoh (vv.17–24). When the dream is "repeated" (*hiššānôṯ*, v.32), it is to show that the matter "has been firmly decided" and that "God will do it soon." The point of the narrative is that such symmetry in human events is evidence of a divine work. The writer, along with Joseph, is able to see the handiwork of God in the events that he recounts, and he passes them along to the readers in these subtle interplays within the text itself.

1–8 Pharaoh's two dreams are more transparent than those of the two officials. The sense of the two dreams can be seen in the elements of the dream. Seven good cows and seven good heads of grain are seven good years. Seven ugly cows and seven blighted heads of grain are seven bad years to follow. To show that the dreams' simplicity conceals rather than reveals their meaning, the writer tells us that all the king's magicians and wisemen were unable to give their meaning (v.8). The inability of the court officials to interpret the dreams prefigures the officials in the court of Nebuchadnezzar who also proved powerless in the face of the king's mysterious dreams (Dan 2:4–12). In their case, however, to insure against fraud, they had not only to interpret the dream but to recount it as well. Joseph's interpretation of Pharaoh's dreams differed from Daniel's in that not only did he have to forecast from the dreams what was to happen, but, more importantly, he advised Pharaoh how to prepare for what was to come. Thus Joseph's wisdom in dealing with the situation forecast in the dreams is portrayed as of equal importance to the interpretation of the dreams. His was a wisdom that consisted more in planning and administration than in a knowledge of secret mysteries.

9–13 In the words of the cup-bearer, the reader's attention is redirected to the first occasion of Joseph's interpretation of the dreams. Though he had forgotten, he now recalled that Joseph's interpretation had stood the test of time: "Things turned out exactly as he interpreted them to us" (v.13). As it turns out, even the cup-bearer's forgetfulness worked in Joseph's favor since, just at the opportune moment, he remembered Joseph and recounted his wisdom before the king. By drawing the reader's attention to the events of the previous passage, both the wisdom of Joseph and the sovereign workings of God are emphasized. Joseph's wisdom is highlighted by the fact that in contrast to the wisemen of Egypt, the interpretation of Joseph, "a young Hebrew" (v.12), proved true. God's sovereign power is highlighted in the fact that though he did forget Joseph at the time, the cup-bearer remembered just at the right moment and thus served as the means for Joseph's ultimate rise to power.

14–36 The Pharaoh repeated his two dreams to Joseph in virtually the same terms as the writer originally recounted them. Why then does the writer allow the dreams to be told twice? It is not unusual for him to include such repetitions, but in each case the reader should look for the reason behind it. As was suggested above, the writer has gone out of his way to present the whole of the narrative in a series of "pairs," all fitting within the notion of the emphasis given by means of the repetition: "the matter has been firmly decided by God, and God will do it soon" (v.32). The repetition of the dreams, then, fits this pattern. But there may be still more to it.

When the Pharaoh repeated the dreams, he added only two major parts, the comment in v.19b—"I had never seen such ugly [*lārō*ᵃ'] cows in all the land of Egypt"—and the whole of v.21, stating that these cows looked just as "ugly" (*ra'*) as before they ate the good cows. In both cases the repetition seems to stress the "evil" (*ra'*) of the appearance of the cows in contrast with the "good" (*haṭṭōḇōṯ*, v.26) cows of the first group.

The writer's emphasis on the "good" and "evil" represents Joseph's wisdom and discernment as an ability to distinguish between the "good" (*ṭôḇ*) and the "evil" (*ra'*). Such a picture suggests that in the story of Joseph the writer is returning to one of the central themes of the beginning of the book, the knowledge of "good" (*ṭôḇ*) and "evil" (*ra'*). While Joseph is able to discern between "good and evil," it is clear from this story that ultimately such knowledge comes only from God (v.39). Joseph is the embodiment of the ideal that true wisdom, the ability to discern between "good and evil," comes only from God. Thus the lesson of the early chapters of Genesis is artfully repeated in these last chapters. Consistent with such an intention is the fact that at the very end of the book (50:20) the writer returns to the picture of God so clearly portrayed at the beginning (1:1–31), namely, the covenant God who alone brings about all things for the "good" of his own. In light of such considerations, it can hardly be accidental that the following narrative picks up just on this point by recounting that Joseph's plan seemed "good" (*wayyîṭaḇ*, v.37) to the Pharaoh and all his servants.

Notes

1 The מִקֵּץ שְׁנָתַיִם יָמִים (*miqqēṣ šᵉnāṯayim yāmîm,* "When two full years had passed") shows that the narrated events are now being closely related to one another. See the note on 38:1.
The nominal clause וּפַרְעֹה חֹלֵם (*ûp̱ar'ōh ḥōlēm,* lit., "Pharaoh was dreaming"), which continues until וַיִּישָׁן וַיַּחֲלֹם שֵׁנִית (*wayyîšān wayyaḥᵃlōm šēnîṯ,* "He fell asleep again and had a second dream," v.5) and וַיִּיקַץ (*wayyîqaṣ,* "The [Pharaoh] woke up," v.7), is striking and suggests the whole of the first section (vv.1–7) is background for the narrative that follows.

8 וַתִּפָּעֶם (*wattippā'em,* "was troubled") anticipates and serves as a link to פַּעֲמָיִם (*pa'ᵃmāyim,* "two forms," v.32).

10 The cup-bearer begins his own narrative account with an 0 + X + QATAL clause—פַּרְעֹה קָצַף עַל־עֲבָדָיו (*par'ōh qāṣap̱ 'al-'ᵃḇāḏāyw,* "Pharaoh was once angry"). Verses 10–13 retell the events of chapter 40. Notice that the cup-bearer concludes his narrative with epic repetition—וַיְהִי כַּאֲשֶׁר פָּתַר־לָנוּ כֵּן הָיָה (*wayᵉhî ka'ᵃšer pāṯar-lānû kēn hāyāh,* "And things turned out exactly as he interpreted them to us," v.13)—and a contrastive coordinated sentence—אֹתִי הֵשִׁיב עַל־כַּנִּי וְאֹתוֹ תָלָה (*'ōṯî hēšîḇ 'al-kannî wᵉ'ōṯô ṯālāh,* "I was restored to my position, and the other man was hanged"; cf. Andersen, *Sentence in Biblical Hebrew,* p. 150).

32 See the note on 27:36. פַּעֲמָיִם (*pa'ᵃmāyim,* "two forms" or "two times") is repeated again in 43:10.

H. *Jacob's Exaltation Over Egypt*

41:37–57

37 The plan seemed good to Pharaoh and to all his officials. 38 So Pharaoh asked them, "Can we find anyone like this man, one in whom is the spirit of God?"

39 Then Pharaoh said to Joseph, "Since God has made all this known to you, there is no one so discerning and wise as you. 40 You shall be in charge of my palace, and all my people are to submit to your orders. Only with respect to the throne will I be greater than you."

41 So Pharaoh said to Joseph, "I hereby put you in charge of the whole land of Egypt." 42 Then Pharaoh took his signet ring from his finger and put it on Joseph's finger. He dressed him in robes of fine linen and put a gold chain around his neck. 43 He had him ride in a chariot as his second-in-command, and men shouted before him, "Make way!" Thus he put him in charge of the whole land of Egypt.

44 Then Pharaoh said to Joseph, "I am Pharaoh, but without your word no one will lift hand or foot in all Egypt." 45 Pharaoh gave Joseph the name Zaphenath-Paneah and gave him Asenath daughter of Potiphera, priest of On, to be his wife. And Joseph went throughout the land of Egypt.

46 Joseph was thirty years old when he entered the service of Pharaoh king of Egypt. And Joseph went out from Pharaoh's presence and traveled throughout Egypt. 47 During the seven years of abundance the land produced plentifully. 48 Joseph collected all the food produced in those seven years of abundance in Egypt and stored it in the cities. In each city he put the food grown in the fields surrounding it. 49 Joseph stored up huge quantities of grain, like the sand of the sea; it was so much that he stopped keeping records because it was beyond measure.

50 Before the years of famine came, two sons were born to Joseph by Asenath daughter of Potiphera, priest of On. 51 Joseph named his firstborn Manasseh and said, "It is because God has made me forget all

my trouble and all my father's household." 52 The second son he named
Ephraim and said, "It is because God has made me fruitful in the land of
my suffering."
53 The seven years of abundance in Egypt came to an end, 54 and the
seven years of famine began, just as Joseph had said. There was famine
in all the other lands, but in the whole land of Egypt there was food.
55 When all Egypt began to feel the famine, the people cried to Pharaoh
for food. Then Pharaoh told all the Egyptians, "Go to Joseph and do
what he tells you."
56 When the famine had spread over the whole country, Joseph
opened the storehouses and sold grain to the Egyptians, for the famine
was severe throughout Egypt. 57 And all the countries came to Egypt to
buy grain from Joseph, because the famine was severe in all the world.

37–57 The account of the king's appointment of Joseph over all his kingdom continues to present a picture of Joseph that recalls the portrait of Adam in Genesis 1. Just as Adam is seen in the Creation account as dependent on God for his knowledge of "good and evil," so Joseph also is portrayed here in the same terms (see above comments). Just as Adam is made God's "vicegerent" to rule over all the land, so similarly Joseph is portrayed here as the Pharaoh's "vicegerent" over all his land (vv.40–43). As Adam was made in God's image to rule over all the land, so the king here gave Joseph his "signet ring" and dressed him in royal garments (v.42). The picture of Joseph resembles the psalmist's understanding of Genesis 1 when, regarding that passage, he writes, "[You have] crowned him with glory and honor./ You made him ruler over the works of your hands;/ you put everything under his feet" (Ps 8:5–7). Just as God provided a wife for Adam in the garden and gave man all the land for his enjoyment, so the king gave a wife to Joseph and put him over all the land (v.45).

What is to be made of such correspondences between Adam and Joseph? Are they intentional or coincidental? While they may be merely accidental similarities, such patterns in the description of key characters are found often in biblical texts and would not be thematically out of place here. At many points in the story, Joseph appears to be represented as an "ideal" of what a truly wise and faithful man is like. He is a model of the ideal man or the ideal king. He accomplishes all that Adam failed to do. It seems likely then that a conscious purpose lies behind these similarities with Genesis 1 in the portrayal of Joseph. The story of Joseph is a reflection of what might have been had Adam remained obedient to God and trusted him for the "good." At the same time the picture of Joseph is an anticipation of what might yet still be, if only God's people would, like Joseph, live in complete obedience and trust in God.

The picture of Joseph, then, looks back to Adam; but more, it looks forward to one who was yet to come. It anticipates the coming of the one from the house of Judah to whom the kingdom belongs (cf. 49:10). Thus in the final shape of the narrative, the tension between the house of Joseph and the house of Judah, which lies within many of these texts, is resolved by making the life of Joseph into a picture of the one who is to reign from the house of Judah.

Notes

45 פּוֹטִי פֶרַע (*pôṭî p̱eraʿ*, "Potiphera"), the father-in-law of Joseph, should not be confused with פּוֹטִיפַר (*pôṭîp̱ar*, "Potiphar," 39:1), the Egyptian official who was Joseph's former master.

51 The name מְנַשֶּׁה (*mᵉnaššeh,* "Manasseh") is linked to נַשַּׁנִי אֱלֹהִים (*naššanî ʾᵉlōhim,* "God has made me forget").

51–54 There are again examples of epic repetition—וַיִּקְרָא יוֹסֵף אֶת־שֵׁם הַבְּכוֹר. . . . וְאֵת שֵׁם הַשֵּׁנִי קָרָא אֶפְרָיִם (*wayyiqrāʾ yôsēp̱ ʾeṯ-šēm habbᵉkôr. . . . wᵉʾēṯ šēm haššēnî qārāʾ ʾep̱rāyim,* "Joseph named his firstborn. . . . The second son he named Ephraim," vv.51–52)—and chiastic coordination—וַיְהִי רָעָב בְּכָל־הָאֲרָצוֹת וּבְכָל־אֶרֶץ מִצְרַיִם הָיָה לָחֶם (*wayᵉhî rāʿāḇ bᵉḵol-hāʾᵃrāṣôṯ ûḇᵉḵol-ʾereṣ miṣrayim hāyāh lāḥem,* "There was a famine in all the other lands, but in the whole land of Egypt there was food," v.54b)—at the conclusion of the narrative.

52 The name אֶפְרָיִם (*ʾep̱rayim,* "Ephraim") is linked to הִפְרַנִי אֱלֹהִים (*hip̱ranî ʾᵉlōhîm,* "God has made me fruitful").

54 The use of the plural הָאֲרָצוֹת (*hāʾᵃrāṣôṯ,* "the lands") explains the sense of the second line, וּבְכָל־אֶרֶץ מִצְרַיִם הָיָה לָחֶם (*ûḇᵉḵol-ʾereṣ miṣrayim hāyāh lāḥem,* "but in the whole land of Egypt there was food"). The plural "lands" refers to all the other lands (see NIV) except Egypt. The LXX has οὐκ ἦσαν (*ouk ēsan* = לֹא הָיָה [*lōʾ hāyāh*], "there was no"), but also λιμὸς ἐν πάσῃ τῇ γῇ (*limos en pasē tē gē* = הָאָרֶץ [*hāʾāreṣ*], "the land"), which on the face of it looks like an attempt to harmonize this verse with the following: וַתִּרְעַב כָּל־אֶרֶץ מִצְרַיִם (*wattirʿaḇ kol-ʾereṣ miṣrayim,* "When all Egypt began to feel the famine").

55 The verb וַתִּרְעַב (*wattirʿaḇ,* "feel the famine") was perhaps intended to be read, "And the famine came upon." It would not have been understood to contradict the preceding verse—וּבְכָל־אֶרֶץ מִצְרַיִם הָיָה לָחֶם (*ûḇᵉḵol-ʾereṣ miṣrayim hāyāh lāḥem,* "but in the whole land of Egypt there was food")—any more than it itself would be contradicted by v.56—וְהָרָעָב הָיָה עַל כָּל־פְּנֵי הָאָרֶץ (*wᵉhārāʿāḇ hāyāh ʿal kol-pᵉnê hāʾāreṣ,* "when the famine had spread over the whole country") and v.57—כִּי־חָזַק הָרָעָב בְּכָל־הָאָרֶץ (*kî-ḥāzaq hārāʿāḇ bᵉḵol-hāʾāreṣ,* "because the famine was severe in all the world"). In fact, *wattirʿaḇ* appears to have been deliberately inserted here in the narrative to alleviate the tension between v.54b and vv.56a–57.

56–57 The use of וַיִּשְׁבֹּר (*wayyišbōr,* "and [he] sold") and לִשְׁבֹּר (*lišbōr,* "to buy") anticipates the יֶשׁ־שֶׁבֶר (*yeš-šeḇer,* "there was grain") of 42:1, providing a link with that chapter.

I. *Joseph's Brothers in Egypt*

42:1–28

1 When Jacob learned that there was grain in Egypt, he said to his
sons, "Why do you just keep looking at each other?" 2 He continued, "I
have heard that there is grain in Egypt. Go down there and buy some for
us, so that we may live and not die."
3 Then ten of Joseph's brothers went down to buy grain from Egypt.
4 But Jacob did not send Benjamin, Joseph's brother, with the others,
because he was afraid that harm might come to him. 5 So Israel's sons
were among those who went to buy grain, for the famine was in the land
of Canaan also.
6 Now Joseph was the governor of the land, the one who sold grain to
all its people. So when Joseph's brothers arrived, they bowed down to
him with their faces to the ground. 7 As soon as Joseph saw his brothers,
he recognized them, but he pretended to be a stranger and spoke
harshly to them. "Where do you come from?" he asked.
"From the land of Canaan," they replied, "to buy food."
8 Although Joseph recognized his brothers, they did not recognize
him. 9 Then he remembered his dreams about them and said to them,
"You are spies! You have come to see where our land is unprotected."
10 "No, my lord," they answered. "Your servants have come to buy
food. 11 We are all the sons of one man. Your servants are honest men,
not spies."

12"No!" he said to them. "You have come to see where our land is
unprotected."
13But they replied, "Your servants were twelve brothers, the sons of
one man, who lives in the land of Canaan. The youngest is now with our
father, and one is no more."
14Joseph said to them, "It is just as I told you: You are spies! 15And
this is how you will be tested: As surely as Pharaoh lives, you will not
leave this place unless your youngest brother comes here. 16Send one
of your number to get your brother; the rest of you will be kept in prison,
so that your words may be tested to see if you are telling the truth. If you
are not, then as surely as Pharaoh lives, you are spies!" 17And he put
them all in custody for three days.
18On the third day, Joseph said to them, "Do this and you will live, for I
fear God: 19If you are honest men, let one of your brothers stay here in
prison, while the rest of you go and take grain back for your starving
households. 20But you must bring your youngest brother to me, so that
your words may be verified and that you may not die." This they
proceeded to do.
21They said to one another, "Surely we are being punished because of
our brother. We saw how distressed he was when he pleaded with us for
his life, but we would not listen; that's why this distress has come upon
us."
22Reuben replied, "Didn't I tell you not to sin against the boy? But you
wouldn't listen! Now we must give an accounting for his blood." 23They
did not realize that Joseph could understand them, since he was using
an interpreter.
24He turned away from them and began to weep, but then turned back
and spoke to them again. He had Simeon taken from them and bound
before their eyes.
25Joseph gave orders to fill their bags with grain, to put each man's
silver back in his sack, and to give them provisions for their journey.
After this was done for them, 26they loaded their grain on their donkeys
and left.
27At the place where they stopped for the night one of them opened
his sack to get feed for his donkey, and he saw his silver in the mouth of
his sack. 28"My silver has been returned," he said to his brothers. "Here
it is in my sack."
Their hearts sank and they turned to each other trembling and said,
"What is this that God has done to us?"

The preceding chapter has recorded Joseph's rise to power. The present chapter turns to the divine purpose behind his miraculous rise. At the conclusion of this long and complicated section, Joseph recounted to his brothers the ultimate purpose behind the narratives: "God sent me ahead of you to preserve for you a remnant on earth and to save your lives by a great deliverance" (45:7). Joseph is cast in the role of a savior of his people. Though that is the primary meaning of the narratives, there are still many subplots along the way. Indeed, this section of Genesis becomes extremely complex in both plot and motive; and, like chapter 24, it is complicated even further by numerous repetitions in the reporting of the events. Nearly every major event is told twice, once by means of the narration of the event itself and then by one of the chief characters in the narrative.

1–2 The narrative returns to Jacob, who has been out of the picture since 37:34. As is frequently the case in biblical narratives, the words spoken at the beginning of a story foreshadow the final outcome. Jacob, sending his sons to Egypt, said, "Go down there . . . so that we may live and not die [*w*^{e}*niḥyeh w*^{e}*lō' nāmûṯ*, v.2]" (cf. *l*^{e}*miḥyāh š*^{e}*lāḥani* *'elōhîm,* "it was to save lives that God sent me," 45:5). Jacob's words also serve to align the deeds of Joseph with the larger themes of the Torah, namely, the theme of "life" (*ḥayyîm*) and "death" (*māweṯ*) (2:7, 9; 3:22; Deut 30:15). In so doing the events that follow are cast as a narrative picture, showing the way to return to the gift of life that was lost in the garden.

3–13 The "twelve" (*šenêm 'āśār,* vv. 13, 32) sons of Jacob are divided into two groups throughout the narrative. There are the "ten [*'aśārāh*] of Joseph's brothers" (v.3) and then the "two" (*šenayim*) sons of Jacob by Rachel, Joseph and Benjamin. These two sons of Rachel are contrasted with the two sons of Leah, viz., Reuben and Judah. Both Reuben and Judah play an important and similar role in the narrative (cf. Reuben, vv.22, 37; Judah, 43:3, 8). They speak on behalf of the other brothers and are the catalysts in the resolution of the plots instigated by Joseph. It was Judah, however, who saved the day by offering himself as a pledge (*'e'erḇennû,* 43:9; NIV, "I . . . will guarantee") for the young lad Benjamin; and it was Judah who repeated Jacob's own thematic words "that we and you and our children may live and not die" (*wenihyeh welō' nāmûṯ,* 43:8; cf. 42:2). Finally, it was Judah who spoke before Joseph and offered himself as a substitute for Benjamin, lest he cause any evil (*ra'*) to come on his father, Jacob (44:33–34).

Throughout the narrative, then, the plot was woven around the interplay between Joseph and Judah, and in the end it was Judah who resolved the conflict. By the same token it was Joseph who created the conflict and tension throughout the narrative. When his brothers approached to buy grain, he "pretended to be a stranger" (v.7) and spoke harshly, accusing them of being spies. What motivated Joseph? Was it revenge? Was he trying to get even with his brothers for what they had done to him? The writer immediately pushes aside such a possibility with the comment that Joseph "remembered his dreams about them" (v.9). Thus the reader is advised that Joseph's schemes and plans against his brothers were motivated by the dreams of the earlier narratives and not by the events his brothers had done to him.

Little more is said specifically regarding the purpose that Joseph saw in his continuous schemes to perplex his brothers. But several subtle reminders throughout the narrative reveal further his intention. For example, in response to Joseph's accusation that the brothers were spies, the brothers defended their integrity by saying, "Your servants are twelve brothers" (*šenêm 'āśār 'aḇāḏeyḵā 'aḥîm,* 42:13; NIV, "Your servants were twelve brothers"); but lest their integrity be gainsaid, they were forced to add: "and one is no more" (*wehā'eḥāḏ 'ênennû*). Joseph's schemes have provoked the first hint that their evil deed, accomplished long past, may yet still rise up against them. As proof that this point was not lost on the brothers, the writer allows us to listen in on the brothers' own version of this event when they recount it to their father (v.32). On that occasion they reported their own words in a different order than that of the narrative in v.13. In the narrative account the brothers mentioned first the "one who is no more" (v.13); but when they tell their father about Joseph's accusations and their response, they mention last the "one [who] is no more" (v.32) and then tell of Benjamin who is home with their father. Though subtle, such a reversal appears to be a narrative hint that the memory of what they did to Joseph was beginning to rub on their conscience.

Another reminder in the narrative that serves to reveal Joseph's motives in perplexing his brothers is the conclusion the brothers draw from Joseph's trick of having their money returned to them in their grain sacks. When they saw their money returned, they asked, "What is this that God has done to us?" (v.28). However they might have meant it, in the logic of the narrative itself, their words have a ring of truth about them. Though we, the readers, know it was Joseph who had had the money put back into their sacks, their words point us to the work of God, serving to confirm the direction the narrative as a whole appears to be taking. God is at work in the schemes of Joseph, and we are allowed to see in this narrative a preliminary reminder of the ultimate theme: "God intended it for good" (50:20).

14–24 Joseph devised two plans to test his brothers. The first was that "one" (*'eḥāḏ*, v.16) of the brothers should return for the youngest and the rest remain in prison. After three days the second plan was announced, "one" (*'eḥāḏ*, v.19) of the brothers was to remain behind and the others were to return to get the youngest. The double plan fits into the overall narrative scheme of repetition in that for both plans it is the "one" (*'eḥāḏ*) brother who rescues the others that is central. Within the narrative this "one" (*'eḥāḏ*) brother appears to be an echo of the "one [who] is no more." It is no wonder then that the brothers' own conclusion from within the narrative is that their present distress had been caused by the distress that they had brought on Joseph (vv.21–22).

Joseph's explanation of the change in plans also ties the narrative to the larger themes of the book. He said about his plan, "Do this and you will live [*wiḥyû*, v.18]. . . . that you may not die" (*wᵉlō' ṯāmûṯû*, v.20), which aligns the narrative with the theme of "life" and "death" that runs throughout the Pentateuch (cf. 50:20: "the saving of lives" [*lᵉhaḥᵃyōṯ*, lit., "to keep alive"]; cf. Deut 30:15). Joseph also said, "For I fear God" (v.18), which again identifies Joseph's plans with the will of God (50:20: "God intended it for good").

When the brothers begin to talk among themselves about the distress they had brought on Joseph, the reader can again catch a glimpse of where Joseph's plans are leading. Reuben's words focus our attention on the central point of the narrative: "Now we must give an accounting for his blood" (v.22). At this point we can see that Joseph's plans were not in revenge for how his brothers once treated him; rather they were to show how, in God's world, the "guilt" (*'ᵃšēmîm;* NIV, "we are being punished," v.21) of the brothers came back on them and called for justice. The remarkable message of the narrative, however, is that Joseph had already forgiven his brothers of the evil they had done to him. As v.24 shows, Joseph had to turn away from them to hide his sorrow for the distress his plan now caused. What awaited the brothers was not the "evil" (*ra'*) they intended for Joseph but the "good" (*ṭôḇ*) God intended for them through Joseph (50:20).

25–28 Joseph's next plan was to fill the brothers' sacks with the money they had brought to buy grain. Though nothing was said about Joseph's intention, the words of the brothers as they discovered their money were all that the narrative required: "What is this that God has done to us?" (v.28). We, the readers, know that it was Joseph who put the money in their sacks, but the brothers give expression to the underlying point of the narrative. God was behind it all and through it all was working out his purposes (cf. 50:20).

Notes

---

1 תִּתְרָאוּ (*tiṯrā'û*) is not a common expression, as is witnessed by the diversity of translations among the versions. The versions appear to be attempts at rendering *tiṯrā'û* rather than

offering a different text. The Hithpael is usually explained as reciprocal, viz., "keep looking at each other" (NIV). Jacob (p. 761) points to the preceding וַיַּרְא (*wayyar'*, "When [he] learned") and sees a contrast between Jacob's seeing the solution to the famine in Egypt and the sons' seeing only one another. However, the Hithpael can also have an iterative sense (Williams, *Hebrew Syntax*, p. 29); thus the expression may mean simply, "Why do you go on merely looking? [Do something!]."

3 לִשְׁבֹּר (*lišbōr*, "to buy"; cf. vv.5, 6, 10) is a link to the preceding narrative (*lišbōr*, 41:57).

4 Essential background information for the narrative that follows is recounted in the W + X + QATAL clause—וְאֶת־בִּנְיָמִין אֲחִי יוֹסֵף לֹא־שָׁלַח יַעֲקֹב (*wᵉ'eṯ-binyāmîn 'aḥî yôsēp̱ lō'-šālaḥ ya'aqōḇ*, "But Jacob did not send Benjamin, Joseph's brother").

5 כִּי־הָיָה הָרָעָב בְּאֶרֶץ כְּנָעַן (*kî-hāyāh hārā'āḇ bᵉ'ereṣ kᵉnā'an*, "for the famine was in the land of Canaan also") is not redundant but identifies for the first time הָאָרֶץ (*hā'āreṣ*, "the land") as *'ereṣ kᵉnā'an* ("the land of Canaan"). The mention of *hārā'āḇ* ("the famine") carries the narrative along (cf. 43:1).

6 וְיוֹסֵף הוּא הַשַּׁלִּיט עַל־הָאָרֶץ (*wᵉyôsēp̱ hû' haššallîṭ 'al-hā'āreṣ*, "Now Joseph was the governor of the land") is a summary of the results of the preceding narratives; thus it takes the form W + nominal clause.

The clause וַיִּשְׁתַּחֲווּ־לוֹ אַפַּיִם אָרְצָה (*wayyištaḥᵃwû-lô 'appayim 'ārᵉṣāh*, "they bowed down to him with their faces to the ground") recalls Joseph's dreams—וַתִּשְׁתַּחֲוֶיןָ (*wattištaḥᵃweynā*, "and [they] bowed down," 37:7)—as well as anticipates further stages in the story: וַיִּשְׁתַּחֲווּ־לוֹ אָרְצָה (*wayyištaḥᵃwû-lô 'ārᵉṣāh*, "and they bowed down before him to the ground," 43:26).

7 At a crucial point in the narrative, the alliteration of the verbs focuses the reader's attention on the actions of Joseph: וַיַּרְא . . . וַיַּכִּרֵם וַיִּתְנַכֵּר (*wayyar' . . . wayyakkirēm wayyiṯnakkēr*, "As soon as [Joseph] saw [his brothers], he recognized them, but he pretended to be a stranger").

8 Notice the chiastic coordination in וַיַּכֵּר יוֹסֵף אֶת־אֶחָיו וְהֵם לֹא הִכִּרֻהוּ (*wayyakkēr yôsēp̱ 'eṯ-'eḥāyw wᵉhēm lō' hikkiruhû*, "Although Joseph recognized his brothers, they did not recognize him").

22 Reuben's words "Didn't I tell you" show how the perspective of the narrative includes the events recorded as far back as chapter 37.

23 וְהֵם לֹא יָדְעוּ (*wᵉhēm lō' yāḏᵉ'û*, "They did not realize") is a comment to the reader, hence W + X + QATAL.

J. *Joseph's Brothers Return for Benjamin*

42:29–38

29 When they came to their father Jacob in the land of Canaan, they told him all that had happened to them. They said, 30 "The man who is lord over the land spoke harshly to us and treated us as though we were spying on the land. 31 But we said to him, 'We are honest men; we are not spies. 32 We were twelve brothers, sons of one father. One is no more, and the youngest is now with our father in Canaan.'

33 "Then the man who is lord over the land said to us, 'This is how I will know whether you are honest men: Leave one of your brothers here with me, and take food for your starving households and go. 34 But bring your youngest brother to me so I will know that you are not spies but honest men. Then I will give your brother back to you, and you can trade in the land.' "

35 As they were emptying their sacks, there in each man's sack was his pouch of silver! When they and their father saw the money pouches, they were frightened. 36 Their father Jacob said to them, "You have deprived me of my children. Joseph is no more and Simeon is no more, and now you want to take Benjamin. Everything is against me!"

37 Then Reuben said to his father, "You may put both of my sons to death if I do not bring him back to you. Entrust him to my care, and I will bring him back."

38 But Jacob said, "My son will not go down there with you; his brother is dead and he is the only one left. If harm comes to him on the journey you are taking, you will bring my gray head down to the grave in sorrow."

29–38 The events of this chapter are now retold in the words of the brothers themselves but in an abbreviated form. Their focus was on the plan of Joseph for the return of the youngest son. We must again ask why the writer has allowed this portion of the narrative to be retold. It certainly is a part of his overall strategy in telling the story, but what specifically does he intend? The solution lies in Jacob's response: "You have deprived me of my children. Joseph is no more and Simeon is no more" (v.36). As if he knew all that had in fact happened between his sons and Joseph, Jacob's words ring truer than he would ever have suspected. To the sons, and to the reader, his words were curiously true. The brothers had deprived him of Joseph, and it was because of them that Simeon was not now with them and that Benjamin was to be taken away. Thus now, in the words of their father, there was a reminder of the guilt that lingered over their treatment of Joseph.

In the face of Jacob's words, Reuben's response was very unusual: "You may put both of my sons to death if I do not bring him back to you" (v.37). Reuben certainly meant his words to insure confidence in his own resolve to return Benjamin; but within the context of the narrative, it appears only to add insult to injury. Jacob's reply to Reuben not only summarily dismissed Reuben's pledge, but it raised one more time the matter of the loss of Joseph: "His brother [Joseph] is dead and he is the only one left" (v.38).

K. *Joseph's Identity (43:1–45:28)*

1. *The second trip to Egypt*

43:1–34

1 Now the famine was still severe in the land. 2 So when they had eaten
all the grain they had brought from Egypt, their father said to them, "Go
back and buy us a little more food."
3 But Judah said to him, "The man warned us solemnly, 'You will not
see my face again unless your brother is with you.' 4 If you will send our
brother along with us, we will go down and buy food for you. 5 But if you
will not send him, we will not go down, because the man said to us, 'You
will not see my face again unless your brother is with you.' "
6 Israel asked, "Why did you bring this trouble on me by telling the
man you had another brother?"
7 They replied, "The man questioned us closely about ourselves and
our family. 'Is your father still living?' he asked us. 'Do you have another
brother?' We simply answered his questions. How were we to know he
would say, 'Bring your brother down here'?"
8 Then Judah said to Israel his father, "Send the boy along with me
and we will go at once, so that we and you and our children may live and
not die. 9 I myself will guarantee his safety; you can hold me personally
responsible for him. If I do not bring him back to you and set him here
before you, I will bear the blame before you all my life. 10 As it is, if we
had not delayed, we could have gone and returned twice."

11 Then their father Israel said to them, "If it must be, then do this: Put
some of the best products of the land in your bags and take them down
to the man as a gift—a little balm and a little honey, some spices and
myrrh, some pistachio nuts and almonds. 12 Take double the amount of
silver with you, for you must return the silver that was put back into the
mouths of your sacks. Perhaps it was a mistake. 13 Take your brother
also and go back to the man at once. 14 And may God Almighty grant you
mercy before the man so that he will let your other brother and
Benjamin come back with you. As for me, if I am bereaved, I am
bereaved."

15 So the men took the gifts and double the amount of silver, and
Benjamin also. They hurried down to Egypt and presented themselves
to Joseph. 16 When Joseph saw Benjamin with them, he said to the
steward of his house, "Take these men to my house, slaughter an
animal and prepare dinner; they are to eat with me at noon."

17 The man did as Joseph told him and took the men to Joseph's
house. 18 Now the men were frightened when they were taken to his
house. They thought, "We were brought here because of the silver that
was put back into our sacks the first time. He wants to attack us and
overpower us and seize us as slaves and take our donkeys."

19 So they went up to Joseph's steward and spoke to him at the
entrance to the house. 20 "Please, sir," they said, "we came down here
the first time to buy food. 21 But at the place where we stopped for the
night we opened our sacks and each of us found his silver—the exact
weight—in the mouth of his sack. So we have brought it back with us.
22 We have also brought additional silver with us to buy food. We don't
know who put our silver in our sacks."

23 "It's all right," he said. "Don't be afraid. Your God, the God of your
father, has given you treasure in your sacks; I received your silver."
Then he brought Simeon out to them.

24 The steward took the men into Joseph's house, gave them water to
wash their feet and provided fodder for their donkeys. 25 They prepared
their gifts for Joseph's arrival at noon, because they had heard that they
were to eat there.

26 When Joseph came home, they presented to him the gifts they had
brought into the house, and they bowed down before him to the ground.
27 He asked them how they were, and then he said, "How is your aged
father you told me about? Is he still living?"

28 They replied, "Your servant our father is still alive and well." And
they bowed low to pay him honor.

29 As he looked about and saw his brother Benjamin, his own mother's
son, he asked, "Is this your youngest brother, the one you told me
about?" And he said, "God be gracious to you, my son." 30 Deeply
moved at the sight of his brother, Joseph hurried out and looked for a
place to weep. He went into his private room and wept there.

31 After he had washed his face, he came out and, controlling himself,
said, "Serve the food."

32 They served him by himself, the brothers by themselves, and the
Egyptians who ate with him by themselves, because Egyptians could not
eat with Hebrews, for that is detestable to Egyptians. 33 The men had
been seated before him in the order of their ages, from the firstborn to
the youngest; and they looked at each other in astonishment. 34 When
portions were served to them from Joseph's table, Benjamin's portion
was five times as much as anyone else's. So they feasted and drank
freely with him.

1–14 In keeping with the general motif of "pairs" of events throughout the Joseph narratives, the story now begins the "second" journey of the sons into Egypt. The famine was still in the land, and the grain purchased earlier was gone; so the father sent his sons back for more (vv.1–2). This time it was Judah who insisted on taking Benjamin back with them in accordance with Joseph's demands (vv.3–5). In the previous chapter it had been Reuben (42:37).

In persuading his father, Judah gave expression once more to the central themes of "life" and "death" that have been carefully interwoven throughout these narratives (v.8). In a way similar to Reuben (42:37), Judah offered to take full responsibility for Benjamin if he was allowed to accompany the brothers to Egypt: "I myself will guarantee [*'e'erḇenû*] his safety" (v.9). The fact that both Reuben and Judah had suggested ways in which Benjamin could be safely taken to Egypt provides another reminder that the events depicted here have already been foreshadowed in the events of chapter 37, the brothers' maltreatment of Joseph. In that narrative both Reuben and Judah attempted to save Joseph's life in the face of the brothers' evil plan (37:21, 26). Here both Reuben and Judah attempt to save Benjamin from the plan that Joseph had initiated against the brothers. Such reversals are commonplace by now throughout these narratives and serve to show that the whole series of events recorded here were part of a larger plan, a divine plan (cf. 50:20). As a further reminder to the reader of the "repetition" throughout the narrative, Judah is allowed to express his impatience with Jacob by making explicit reference to the fact that this was the "second" time a journey to Egypt had been made: "If we had not delayed, we could have gone and returned twice" (v.10; cf. 41:32).

Jacob, or Israel, as he is known throughout this chapter, gave in to Judah's plan. Just as it was Judah's plan in chapter 37 that ultimately saved the life of Joseph (37:26), so now it was Judah's plan that saved the life of Simeon. Jacob's farewell words provide the narrative key to what follows: "May God Almighty grant you mercy [*raḥ^a^mîm*] before the man" (v.14). As so often in the patriarchal narratives, the events that follow seem to be guided by just these words. At the conclusion of the narrative, when the sons reached Joseph and he saw Benjamin, we are told that "his mercy" (*raḥ^a^māyw*, v.30; untr. in NIV) was kindled toward his brother. It is important that in these words of Jacob the compassion (*raḥ^a^mîm*) that Joseph was to find toward his brothers was given by "God Almighty." Again in these subtle and indirect ways the writer informs the reader of the power of God in directing the lives of his people and in carrying his plans to completion.

15–25 Curiously, the whole problem of the brothers' being "spies" (42:9) is not raised again. The readers, of course, know the brothers were not spies; so the writer simply allows the whole issue to drop without further comment. We are left instead with the apprehensions of the brothers themselves as they were ushered into the royal house of Joseph. Their fears and misgivings reveal to the reader their conviction that nothing good was going to come of this. The reader, however, is told at the start that the brothers were being taken into the house for a great feast (v.16). We know that the brothers' fears in v.18 were misguided. They need not have feared becoming Joseph's slaves. But it is precisely that misguided fear that the writer wishes to draw our attention to.

To show the underlying cause of the brothers' misgivings and to show just how misguided they actually were, the writer allows them to repeat to the steward the account of their finding the money in their grain sacks (vv.19–21). The purpose of this is to get the steward's response. The picture that emerges is that of the brothers vainly trying to explain themselves to anyone who will listen and vainly trying to return the money they had found in their sacks. But no one seems to take their explanation seriously, nor will anyone take their money. Joseph's steward brushed off their explanation with the remark, "It's all right. . . . Your God, the God of your father, has given you treasure in your sacks; I received your silver" (v.23). The reader surely knows that the steward's words cannot be taken seriously. There has been no mention of money given to the steward. From the narrative itself we are apparently to understand that the steward has been in on Joseph's secret plan all along. But, as is often the case in these narratives, unwittingly the steward expresses one of the central themes of the book: "the God of your father has given you treasure" (v.23).

26–34 The writer goes to great lengths in depicting the scene of the banquet. Joseph was conspicuously careful to ask about the well being of the brothers' father and the lad, Benjamin, whom they had brought back with them (vv.26–29). The reader almost has to remind himself that the brothers still did not know it was Joseph who was entertaining them. It is only when we see Joseph hurry to another room to hide his tears (v.30) that we are sure his identity was still unknown. The question that naturally arises out of this passage is what the brothers themselves thought about Joseph's questions and their treatment in his house. They had come expecting to be made into servants, but it was they who were being served (vv.31–32). Did they not suspect something? Did they not have questions about Joseph's curiosity about their father and his special treatment of Benjamin? The writer answers all such questions by simply stating that the brothers were "dismayed" (*wayyiṯmehû*, v.33; NIV, "in astonishment"). They asked no questions and seemed to accept the words of Joseph's steward ("the God of your father has given you treasure," v.23) and Joseph's words to Benjamin ("God be gracious to you, my son," v.29) as the most plausible solution. For the writer, of course, Joseph's steward had unwittingly given the correct explanation, and Joseph's words have provided a cryptic confirmation.

Notes

1 וְהָרָעָב כָּבֵד בָּאָרֶץ (*wehārāʿāḇ kāḇēḏ bāʾāreṣ*, "Now the famine was still severe in the land") continues the background of famine from the earlier narratives (cf. 41:54–56; 42:5).

10 פַּעֲמָיִם (*paʿamāyim*, "twice") continues the theme of 41:32.

14 Jacob's final words to his sons—וְאֵל שַׁדַּי יִתֵּן לָכֶם רַחֲמִים (*weʾēl šadday yittēn lāḵem raḥamîm*, "And may God Almightly grant you mercy")—are literally fulfilled at the close of the narrative—נִכְמְרוּ רַחֲמָיו (*niḵmerû raḥamāyw*, "Deeply moved," v.30).

15 Chiastic coordination depicts the return journey to Egypt: וַיִּקְחוּ הָאֲנָשִׁים . . . וּמִשְׁנֶה־כֶּסֶף לָקְחוּ (*wayyiqḥû hāʾanāšîm . . . ûmišneh-kesep̱ lāqeḥû*, "So the men took . . . and double the amount of silver [they took]"; cf. Andersen, *Sentence in Biblical Hebrew*, p. 122).

26 Joseph's dream—לְהִשְׁתַּחֲוֹת לְךָ אָרְצָה (*lehištaḥawōṯ leḵā ʾāreṣāh*, "bow down to the ground before you," 37:10)—continues to motivate the course of events in the narrative: וַיִּשְׁתַּחֲווּ־לוֹ אָרְצָה (*wayyištaḥawû-lô ʾāreṣāh*, "and they bowed down before him to the ground"; cf. Notes on 42:6: וַיִּשְׁתַּחֲווּ־לוֹ אַפַּיִם אָרְצָה [*wayyištaḥawû-lô ʾappayim ʾāreṣāh*, "they bowed down to him with their faces to the ground"]). Notice the repetition again in v.28: וַיִּשְׁתַּחֲוּוּ (*wayyištaḥawwû*, "and they bowed low"; cf. 41:32).

2. *The silver cup*

44:1–34

[1]Now Joseph gave these instructions to the steward of his house: "Fill
the men's sacks with as much food as they can carry, and put each
man's silver in the mouth of his sack. [2]Then put my cup, the silver one,
in the mouth of the youngest one's sack, along with the silver for his
grain." And he did as Joseph said.
[3]As morning dawned, the men were sent on their way with their
donkeys. [4]They had not gone far from the city when Joseph said to his
steward, "Go after those men at once, and when you catch up with
them, say to them, 'Why have you repaid good with evil? [5]Isn't this the
cup my master drinks from and also uses for divination? This is a
wicked thing you have done.' "
[6]When he caught up with them, he repeated these words to them.
[7]But they said to him, "Why does my lord say such things? Far be it
from your servants to do anything like that! [8]We even brought back to
you from the land of Canaan the silver we found inside the mouths of
our sacks. So why would we steal silver or gold from your master's
house? [9]If any of your servants is found to have it, he will die; and the
rest of us will become my lord's slaves."
[10]"Very well, then," he said, "let it be as you say. Whoever is found to
have it will become my slave; the rest of you will be free from blame."
[11]Each of them quickly lowered his sack to the ground and opened it.
[12]Then the steward proceeded to search, beginning with the oldest and
ending with the youngest. And the cup was found in Benjamin's sack.
[13]At this, they tore their clothes. Then they all loaded their donkeys and
returned to the city.
[14]Joseph was still in the house when Judah and his brothers came in,
and they threw themselves to the ground before him. [15]Joseph said to
them, "What is this you have done? Don't you know that a man like me
can find things out by divination?"
[16]"What can we say to my lord?" Judah replied. "What can we say?
How can we prove our innocence? God has uncovered your servants'
guilt. We are now my lord's slaves—we ourselves and the one who was
found to have the cup."
[17]But Joseph said, "Far be it from me to do such a thing! Only the
man who was found to have the cup will become my slave. The rest of
you, go back to your father in peace."
[18]Then Judah went up to him and said: "Please, my lord, let your
servant speak a word to my lord. Do not be angry with your servant,
though you are equal to Pharaoh himself. [19]My lord asked his servants,
'Do you have a father or a brother?' [20]And we answered, 'We have an
aged father, and there is a young son born to him in his old age. His
brother is dead, and he is the only one of his mother's sons left, and his
father loves him.'
[21]"Then you said to your servants, 'Bring him down to me so I can see
him for myself.' [22]And we said to my lord, 'The boy cannot leave his
father; if he leaves him, his father will die.' [23]But you told your servants,
'Unless your youngest brother comes down with you, you will not see
my face again.' [24]When we went back to your servant my father, we told
him what my lord had said.
[25]"Then our father said, 'Go back and buy a little more food.' [26]But we
said, 'We cannot go down. Only if our youngest brother is with us will
we go. We cannot see the man's face unless our youngest brother is
with us.'
[27]"Your servant my father said to us, 'You know that my wife bore me
two sons. [28]One of them went away from me, and I said, "He has surely

been torn to pieces." And I have not seen him since. [29]If you take this one from me too and harm comes to him, you will bring my gray head down to the grave in misery.'

[30]"So now, if the boy is not with us when I go back to your servant my father and if my father, whose life is closely bound up with the boy's life,
[31]sees that the boy isn't there, he will die. Your servants will bring the gray head of our father down to the grave in sorrow. [32]Your servant guaranteed the boy's safety to my father. I said, 'If I do not bring him back to you, I will bear the blame before you, my father, all my life!'

[33]"Now then, please let your servant remain here as my lord's slave in place of the boy, and let the boy return with his brothers. [34]How can I go back to my father if the boy is not with me? No! Do not let me see the misery that would come upon my father."

1–13 Once more Joseph tricked his brothers by having his cup and Benjamin's money returned in Benjamin's sack of grain. The purpose of the act is clear from what Joseph instructed his men to say. When they overtook the brothers, they were to say, "Why have you repaid good [*ṭôḇāh*] with evil [*rā'āh*]?" (v.4), and "This is a wicked thing [*hᵃrē'ōṯem*] you have done" (v.5).

If we are to judge by the brothers' response when the servants reached them with Joseph's message, the word that the servants spoke was more detailed than what we are given in the narrative. The brothers immediately made reference to the silver and gold that was supposedly in their sacks (v.8). But why were Joseph's words reported only in such general terms? The solution lies in the fact that the words spoken by Joseph expressed the central question of the Joseph narratives: the contrast between the "evil" (*rā'āh*) done by the brothers and the "good" (*ṭôḇāh*) intended and accomplished by God (cf. 50:20).

When stated in such a general way, Joseph's question looks as if it included the question of the brothers' treatment of him in chapter 37. The question does, in fact, raise again within the narrative the matter of the brothers' guilt in their treatment of Joseph. Whether the brothers realized this or not, the function of Joseph's question within the narrative is to point out to the reader that a residue of guilt still hung over the brothers' heads. It seemed as if everywhere they turned, they heard an echo of their mistreatment of their brother Joseph. The effect of such narrative strategies is to present a picture of a world in which ultimately justice does prevail and where an "evil" once done will not go unnoticed or unattended.

Joseph's plan worked as if every detail had been carefully worked out ahead of time. Not knowing that the cup and money were in Benjamin's sack, the brothers made a rash vow, putting the life of Benjamin and their own freedom in jeopardy (v.9). When the cup was discovered, their response was one of complete hopelessness (v.13). "They tore their clothing in a rage" (lit. tr. of *wayyiqrᵉ'û śimlōṯām*) and returned to the city. There was nothing else to do. Curiously, their response was a mirror image of their father's response upon hearing their own report of the loss of Joseph (37:34: *wayyiqra' ya'ᵃqōḇ śimlōṯāyw*, "Then Jacob tore his clothes"). The grief they had caused their father had returned on their own heads. In a word, they were trapped.

14–17 As Joseph's plans turned out as if perfectly orchestrated, we begin to see what his purpose had been all along. While it had looked like he was working a slow revenge upon his brothers, we can now see that his purpose was not revenge but repentance. Through his schemes his brothers were coming to an awareness of their guilt and were now ready to acknowledge it. Their utter frustration was expressed in their repetition of the question, "What can we say?" (v.16). Finally comes their expression of guilt: "How can we prove our innocence?" The rhetorical answer to these questions is an implied negative: "We have nothing to say; we cannot show ourselves to be right." Thus the conclusion they drew was "God has uncovered your servants' guilt."

Though we can see clearly that the brothers have only the immediate issue of the lost "cup" in mind, within the compass of the whole of the Joseph narrative, their words take on the scope of a confession of their former guilt as well. We, the readers, know that the brothers have not taken the cup. Joseph had it put into Benjamin's sack. We also know that the brothers know they did not take the cup. So, when they speak of God "uncovering [their] guilt" (v.16), we are forced to generalize their sense of guilt within the context of the narrative as a whole. We, along with the author of the narrative, read their words with a broader significance than they might have intended on that occasion. We see the narrative interconnections that were, obviously, not a part of their own understanding within the situation itself. In his response Joseph steered the matter in a direction that even more closely resembles his brothers' treatment of him. The young lad was to be sold into slavery in Egypt, and the brothers were to return to their father.

18–34 In Judah's final speech, he retold the whole of the Joseph story. His own retelling of the story reveals the brothers' perception of the events, as well as the hopelessness of their situation. The overall sense of Judah's version of the story is that the brothers have been mistreated. The implication is that if anyone was to blame, it was Joseph. According to Judah's version, Joseph was the one who initiated the series of mishaps that had ended in the present predicament. All the brothers had done was follow his instructions and the instructions of their father. Judah's words, however, reveal something more to the reader than even he intended. His words show that the fault did not lie with Joseph but with the "evil" intention of the brothers toward Joseph. Once again his words raised the issue of the brothers' mistreatment of Joseph. Curiously, at this point Judah said of Joseph, "[he] is dead" (44:20), rather than what was said of Joseph on other occasions, namely, that "[he] is no more" (42:13). The meaning of the expression "he is no more" (*'ênennû*) within Genesis does not imply that one is dead (cf. 42:36: "Simeon is no more" [*'ênennû*]; Gen 5:24: "Enoch walked with God; then he was no more [*'ênennû*], because God took him away").

We can see, then, that in retelling the story Judah added a dimension to the brother's recounting of the events to Joseph that was not previously there. The net effect is that the story now resembles the original intention of the brothers, which was "to kill" (*lahᵃmîṯô,* 37:18) Joseph; and it corresponds to the story that the brothers gave to Jacob. What in real life would have perhaps been a "slip of the tongue" is now, within the narrative, a clue to the state of mind of the brothers as well as to their guilt. But Judah's account raises even further the issue of the brothers' guilt regarding Joseph when he recounted Jacob's response to the demand that Benjamin be taken to Egypt. On that occasion Jacob had said, "You know that my wife bore me two sons. One of them went away from me, and I said, 'He has surely been torn to pieces' " (vv.27–28).

How could Judah recount the story this way? He surely knew that Jacob's words were mistaken. It was not a wild animal that killed Joseph; it was the brothers themselves who had sold him into slavery. But could Judah have told the story any other way? Clearly he could not. To tell the story the way it actually happened would be to admit to a guilt even greater than that of which they were presently accused. Thus even when retelling the story to demonstrate his own innocence, Judah gave testimony, to the reader at least, of his own guilt and the guilt of his brothers. Though it is through Judah's speech that the reader is again reminded of the brothers' guilt, we should not lose sight of the fact that once again it was Judah who intervened on behalf of Benjamin and ultimately, within the narrative, his words that saved the day. After this speech Joseph could contain himself no longer. He felt compelled to unveil his identity to his brothers.

Notes

---

1 With וַיְצַו (*wayeṣaw*, "[Now Joseph] gave these instructions"; without a subject but supplied by NIV) the narrative flows without break into the next episode.

3 The real break in the narrative comes here with the 0 + nominal clause—הַבֹּקֶר אוֹר (*habbōqer 'ôr*, "As morning dawned")—and the inverted W + X + QATAL—וְהָאֲנָשִׁים שֻׁלְּחוּ (*wehā'anāšîm šulleḥû*, "the men were sent").

4 The clause structure is unusual for Genesis:
הֵם יָצְאוּ אֶת־הָעִיר (*hēm yāṣe'û 'et-hā'îr*, "They had . . . gone") (0 + X + QATAL)
לֹא הִרְחִיקוּ (*lō' hirḥîqû*, "not far") (0 + X + QATAL)
וְיוֹסֵף אָמַר לַאֲשֶׁר (*wayôsēp 'āmar la'ašer*, "when Joseph said to") (inverted W + X + QATAL).
Compare 27:30—וַיְהִי כַּאֲשֶׁר כִּלָּה יִצְחָק . . . וַיְהִי . . . יָצָא יַעֲקֹב . . . וְעֵשָׂו . . . בָּא (*wayehî ka'ašer killāh yiṣḥāq . . . wayehî . . . yāṣā' ya'aqōb . . . we'ēśāw . . . bā'*, "After Isaac finished . . . and Jacob had . . . left . . . Esau . . . came")—and 12:10—וַיְהִי כַּאֲשֶׁר הִקְרִיב לָבוֹא מִצְרָיְמָה (*wayehî ka'ašer hiqrîb lābô' miṣrāyemāh*, "As he was about to enter Egypt") for a more common syntax. For a syntax similar to that of the present verse, see Josh 11:18–20.
רָעָה (*rā'āh*, "evil," "misery") occurs at key moments throughout this narrative segment (vv.5 [הֲרֵעֹתֶם (*harē'ōtem*, lit., "you were wicked")], 29, 34).

14 Though the words are slightly different, וַיִּפְּלוּ לְפָנָיו אָרְצָה (*wayyippelû lepānāyw 'āreṣāh*, "they threw themselves to the ground before him") appears to continue the allusions to Joseph's dreams (37:10).

15 It is important to notice how the narrative protects Joseph from the charge of actually practicing divination. When he told his servants to say, וְהוּא נַחֵשׁ יְנַחֵשׁ בּוֹ (*wehû' naḥēš yenaḥēš bô*, "and [my master] also uses for divination," v.5), it was all part of a larger scheme to mislead his brothers and thus cannot be taken at face value; and when he said to his brothers, יְנַחֵשׁ אִישׁ אֲשֶׁר כָּמֹנִי (*yenaḥēš 'îš 'ašer kāmōnî*, "a man like me can find things out by divination"), he cautiously avoided saying that he in fact used the cup. All he said was "a man like me" used the cup for divination. This is not surprising in light of the fact that such a practice—מְנַחֵשׁ (*menaḥēš*, "interprets omens")—was strictly forbidden in Deut 18:10.

---

3. *Joseph's revelation*

45:1–28

1 Then Joseph could no longer control himself before all his attendants, and he cried out, "Have everyone leave my presence!" So there was no one with Joseph when he made himself known to his brothers.
2 And he wept so loudly that the Egyptians heard him, and Pharaoh's household heard about it.

[3]Joseph said to his brothers, "I am Joseph! Is my father still living?" But his brothers were not able to answer him, because they were terrified at his presence.

[4]Then Joseph said to his brothers, "Come close to me." When they had done so, he said, "I am your brother Joseph, the one you sold into Egypt! [5]And now, do not be distressed and do not be angry with yourselves for selling me here, because it was to save lives that God sent me ahead of you. [6]For two years now there has been famine in the land, and for the next five years there will not be plowing and reaping. [7]But God sent me ahead of you to preserve for you a remnant on earth and to save your lives by a great deliverance.

[8]"So then, it was not you who sent me here, but God. He made me father to Pharaoh, lord of his entire household and ruler of all Egypt. [9]Now hurry back to my father and say to him, 'This is what your son Joseph says: God has made me lord of all Egypt. Come down to me; don't delay. [10]You shall live in the region of Goshen and be near me—you, your children and grandchildren, your flocks and herds, and all you have. [11]I will provide for you there, because five years of famine are still to come. Otherwise you and your household and all who belong to you will become destitute.'

[12]"You can see for yourselves, and so can my brother Benjamin, that it is really I who am speaking to you. [13]Tell my father about all the honor accorded me in Egypt and about everything you have seen. And bring my father down here quickly."

[14]Then he threw his arms around his brother Benjamin and wept, and Benjamin embraced him, weeping. [15]And he kissed all his brothers and wept over them. Afterward his brothers talked with him.

[16]When the news reached Pharaoh's palace that Joseph's brothers had come, Pharaoh and all his officials were pleased. [17]Pharaoh said to Joseph, "Tell your brothers, 'Do this: Load your animals and return to the land of Canaan, [18]and bring your father and your families back to me. I will give you the best of the land of Egypt and you can enjoy the fat of the land.'

[19]"You are also directed to tell them, 'Do this: Take some carts from Egypt for your children and your wives, and get your father and come. [20]Never mind about your belongings, because the best of all Egypt will be yours.' "

[21]So the sons of Israel did this. Joseph gave them carts, as Pharaoh had commanded, and he also gave them provisions for their journey. [22]To each of them he gave new clothing, but to Benjamin he gave three hundred shekels of silver and five sets of clothes. [23]And this is what he sent to his father: ten donkeys loaded with the best things of Egypt, and ten female donkeys loaded with grain and bread and other provisions for his journey. [24]Then he sent his brothers away, and as they were leaving he said to them, "Don't quarrel on the way!"

[25]So they went up out of Egypt and came to their father Jacob in the land of Canaan. [26]They told him, "Joseph is still alive! In fact, he is ruler of all Egypt." Jacob was stunned; he did not believe them. [27]But when they told him everything Joseph had said to them, and when he saw the carts Joseph had sent to carry him back, the spirit of their father Jacob revived. [28]And Israel said, "I'm convinced! My son Joseph is still alive. I will go and see him before I die."

1–8 The narrative is clear that Joseph had taken no personal enjoyment in the deception of his brothers. When he could hold back no longer, he revealed his true identity (v.1). We are never told why he chose not to reveal his identity to his brothers immediately, but we can see from the narrative itself that the effect of his scheme has been to further the primary themes of the book. In his words of explanation and comfort to his brothers in this chapter, Joseph returned once again to the central theme of the narrative: though the brothers were responsible for Joseph's being sold into Egypt, and though they intended "harm," God was ultimately behind it all and had worked it out for the "good" (cf. 50:20). As he told his brothers, "It was to save lives [*l^e miḥ^e yāh*] that God sent me ahead of you" (v.5), and, "God sent me ahead of you to preserve for you a remnant on earth and to save [*ûl^e hah^a yôṯ*] your lives" (v.7). In the narrative thus far, this theme has been expressed by Jacob (42:2) and Judah (43:8) and has also been indirectly alluded to by Joseph himself (42:18). Here, however, and in 50:20, the theme is given its full expression in the words of Joseph.

Joseph's words pull back the narrative veil and allow the reader to see what has been going on behind the scenes. It was not the brothers who sent Joseph to Egypt; rather it was God. And God had a purpose for it all. We have seen numerous clues throughout the narrative that this has been the case; but now the central character, the one ultimately responsible for initiating the plots and subplots of the preceding narratives, reveals the divine plans and purpose behind it all. Joseph, who could discern the divine plan in the dreams of Pharaoh, also knew the divine plan in the affairs of his brothers. Through it all he saw God's plan to accomplish a "great deliverance" (v.7).

In describing God's care over him, Joseph made an allusion to the brothers' initial question regarding his dreams as a young lad. They had said, "Do you intend to reign over us?" (37:8). Now he reminded them that he had been made "ruler of all Egypt" (45:8).

9–20 In the second part of his speech to the brothers, Joseph made plans to bring his father to Egypt. He twice repeated that the brothers were to go to Jacob and with all haste bring him down to Egypt (vv.9, 13). He had set aside the "region of Goshen" (v.10) where they could continue to raise their families and livestock during the five remaining years of famine. In the midst of the famine, the sons of Israel were to be well-provided for in Goshen. It can hardly be without purpose that this picture of God's chosen people dwelling safely and prosperously in the land that Joseph provided for them comes at the close of the Book of Genesis and that it is a near replica of the way things were in the beginning. The writer appears intentionally to draw our attention to the connection between the end of the book and the beginning. Thus when the Pharaoh restated Joseph's offer and "twice" gave the brothers the "good" (*ṭûḇ*, vv.18, 20; NIV, "best") of the land of Egypt, it is hard not to see in the purpose of this narrative a conscious allusion to the "good" (*ṭôḇ*, 1:31) land given to Adam in the first chapter of the book. The picture of Joseph is a picture of restoration—not just the restoration of the good fortune of Jacob but, as a picture, the restoration of the blessing that was promised through the offspring of Jacob.

21–28 Jacob's response to the news of Joseph plays a key role in connecting these narratives to the message of the Pentateuch as a whole. Throughout the Pentateuch there is a focus on the response of God's people to the work of God. At important moments in the narrative, this response is interpreted as either one of "faith" (*he'^e mîn;* 15:6; Exod 4:31; 14:31; 19:9) or "no faith" (*lō'-he'^e mîn*, v.26; cf. Num 14:11; 20:12; cf. Hans-Christoph Schmitt, "Redaktion des Pentateuch im Geiste der Prophetie," VetTest 32, 2 [1982]: 170–89).

Jacob's response falls in with these other examples. Here, however, the writer gives a deeper insight into the nature of his faith. At first, when Jacob heard the news that

Joseph was alive, "his heart grew numb" (*wayyāp̱og libbô*, v.26; NIV, "Jacob was stunned") and "he did not believe" (*lō’-he’^{e}mîn*). But when he heard the words of Joseph and saw all that he had sent to take him back to Egypt, "the spirit . . . of Jacob revived" (v.27), and he set out to go to him (v.28).

The faith of Jacob bore the same marks as that of the other occurrences of faith throughout the Pentateuch, but in this text alone a different dimension is stressed. That new dimension in Jacob's faith is the contrast between his "numbed heart" and his "revived spirit." Jacob's lack of faith is identified with his "numbed heart." When his spirit was renewed, however, he believed. The viewpoint expressed here is very similar to that of the later prophetic literature where faith and the "new heart" are synonymous (cf. Jer 31:33–34; Ezek 36:26) and where lack of faith (*lō’ ṯa’^{a}mînû*, Hab 1:5; NIV, "not believe") is synonymous with "numbness" (*tāp̱ûg tôrāh*, Hab 1:4; NIV, "the law is paralyzed"). All these texts seem to be summed up in the words of David in Psalm 51: "Create in me a pure heart, O God,/ and renew a steadfast spirit within me" (v.10).

Notes

1 וְלֹא־יָכֹל יוֹסֵף לְהִתְאַפֵּק (*w^{e}lō’-yāḵōl yôsēp̱ l^{e}hiṯ’appēq*, "Then Joseph could no longer control himself") (W + X + QATAL) marks a transition to a new segment of narrative.

4–5 The מְכַרְתֶּם אֹתִי . . . הֵנָּה (*m^{e}ḵartem ’ōṯî . . . hēnnāh*, "the one you sold . . . here") gives a new perspective on the events of chapter 37. In Joseph's version of the events, it was neither the Ishmaelites nor the Midianites-Medanites who sold him into Egypt. It was his brothers. Joseph's words resolve an ambiguity in the text of 37:28. As it now stands the subject of the verbs וַיִּמְשְׁכוּ (*wayyimš^{e}ḵû*, "[they] pulled . . . up"), וַיַּעֲלוּ (*wayya‘^{a}lû*, lit., "and they lifted up" [untr. in NIV]), and וַיִּמְכְּרוּ (*wayyimk^{e}rû*, "and sold him") appears to be the אֲנָשִׁים מִדְיָנִים (*’^{a}nāšîm miḏyānîm*, lit., "men of Midian"), who are the subject of the immediately preceding verb וַיַּעַבְרוּ (*wayya‘aḇrû*, "[they] came by"). Thus 37:28 can be translated "The Midianite men passed by and drew Joseph up out of the pit and sold Joseph to the Ishmaelites" (lit. tr.). The way Joseph read it, however, the subject of these verbs is אֶחָיו (*’eḥāyw*, "his brothers"), who are the understood subject of the third masculine plural verbs throughout the narrative (cf. *’eḥāyw* in 37:23, 26, 27). Such a reading also suits Judah's statement to his brothers—לְכוּ וְנִמְכְּרֶנּוּ (*l^{e}ḵû w^{e}nimk^{e}rennû*, "Come, let's sell him")—in v.27.

14 The close of a segment is marked by chiastic coordination: וַיֵּבְךְּ וּבִנְיָמִן בָּכָה עַל־צַוָּארָיו (*wayyēḇk^{e} ûḇinyāmin bāḵāh ‘al-ṣawwā’rāyw*, "and wept, and Benjamin embraced him, weeping") (Andersen, *Sentence in Biblical Hebrew*, p. 122).

16–23 The theme of "the good" is marked throughout this segment by the repetition of forms of the root טוֹב (*ṭôḇ*; cf. וַיִּיטַב [*wayyîṭaḇ*, "pleased"], v.16; טוּב [*ṭûḇ*, "best"], vv.18, 20, 23).

L. *Jacob's Journey to Egypt*

46:1–7

1 So Israel set out with all that was his, and when he reached
Beersheba, he offered sacrifices to the God of his father Isaac.
2 And God spoke to Israel in a vision at night and said, "Jacob!
Jacob!"
"Here I am," he replied.

[3]"I am God, the God of your father," he said. "Do not be afraid to go
down to Egypt, for I will make you into a great nation there. [4]I will go
down to Egypt with you, and I will surely bring you back again. And
Joseph's own hand will close your eyes."
[5]Then Jacob left Beersheba, and Israel's sons took their father Jacob
and their children and their wives in the carts that Pharaoh had sent to
transport him. [6]They also took with them their livestock and the
possessions they had acquired in Canaan, and Jacob and all his
offspring went to Egypt. [7]He took with him to Egypt his sons and
grandsons and his daughters and granddaughters—all his offspring.

1–4 Before Jacob went to Egypt, he traveled to Beersheba and there built an altar and offered sacrifices to the God of his father, Isaac (v.1). The writer is careful to remind the reader in this way that the patriarchs all worshiped the same God. Jacob worshiped the God of his father, Isaac. In light of this fact, there appears to be a remarkable contrast between God's words to Jacob here in this chapter and his words to Isaac earlier in chapter 26. The Lord had said to Isaac, "Do not go down to Egypt" (26:2); but he now said to Jacob, "Do not be afraid to go down to Egypt" (v.3). Such a change in attitude toward the patriarchs' traveling to Egypt indicates that the Lord was following a specific plan with regard to his people. His instructions to Isaac in chapter 26 might have left the impression that he was opposed in principle to the seed of Abraham going into Egypt. That, in turn, might have left the impression that the whole of the Joseph story, which resulted in Jacob's going to Egypt, was running counter to God's purposes. When the Lord speaks to Jacob, however, it becomes clear that a sojourn in Egypt could play a part in God's plan. Such a perspective is consistent with the overall theme of the Joseph narrative, which is that God was working all things for the good of Jacob and his house (50:20).

God's words to Jacob in the night vision also reiterate the promise to Abraham that from his descendants would come a "great nation" (*l^{e}g̱ôy gāḏôl*, v.3; cf. 12:2), but they also add that God would do this in Egypt. Egypt was to be the place where the house of Jacob would become the nation of Israel. These words, then, anticipate all the great work of God that was yet to be recounted in the Torah. God would bring his people into Egypt and be with them there; and after they had become a great nation, he would bring them back to the Promised Land. This was the second "vision" in which God had revealed his future plans with the offspring of Abraham. In chapter 15, "in a vision" (v.1), God revealed to Abraham that his descendants would be taken into servitude for four hundred years (15:13) and after that would come out with "great wealth" (15:14; NIV, "possessions").

5–7 Special attention is given to the journey of Jacob and his household into Egypt. Just as Abraham had left Ur of the Chaldeans and journeyed to Canaan (12:4–5), so now Jacob left the land of Canaan and journeyed to Egypt (vv.5–6). Both men were leaving the land of their birth in obedience to the will of God, and the obedience of both men just at this point plays a pivotal role in God's election of the seed of Abraham. Thus vv.6–7 emphasize by repetition that "all his offspring" (*w^{e}ḵol-zarʿô*, vv.6–7; lit., "all his seed") went with Jacob into the land of Egypt. To graphically demonstrate the importance of this point, the writer now lists the names of "all his offspring" and numbers them at "seventy" (v.27).

Notes

---

3 לְגוֹי גָּדוֹל אֲשִׂימְךָ שָׁם (*l^{e}g̱ôy gāḏôl 'a^{a}śîm^{e}ḵā šām,* "I will make you into a great nation") is an allusion to וּקְהַל גּוֹיִם יִהְיֶה מִמֶּךָּ (*ûq^{e}hal g̱ôyim yihyeh mimmekkā,* "a community of nations will come from you") in 35:11.

4 אָנֹכִי אֵרֵד עִמְּךָ מִצְרַיְמָה וְאָנֹכִי אַעַלְךָ גַם־עָל91א+ה (*'ānōḵî 'ērēḏ 'imm^{e}ḵā miṣray^{e}māh w^e'ānōḵî 'a'alḵā g̱am-'ālōh,* "I will go down to Egypt with you, and I will surely bring you back again") anticipates the account of the exodus from Egypt in the Book of Exodus.

6–7 The narrative segment draws to a conclusion by means of epic repetition: וַיָּבֹאוּ מִצְרָיְמָה . . . הֵבִיא אִתּוֹ מִצְרָיְמָה (*wayyāḇō'û miṣrāy^{e}māh. . . . hēḇî' 'ittô miṣrāy^{e}māh,* "and [they] went to Egypt. He took with him to Egypt") (Andersen, *Sentence in Biblical Hebrew*, p. 39).

M. *Jacob's Sons in Egypt*

46:8–27

8 These are the names of the sons of Israel (Jacob and his descendants) who went to Egypt:

Reuben the firstborn of Jacob.

9 The sons of Reuben:
Hanoch, Pallu, Hezron and Carmi.

10 The sons of Simeon:
Jemuel, Jamin, Ohad, Jakin, Zohar and Shaul the son of a Canaanite woman.

11 The sons of Levi:
Gershon, Kohath and Merari.

12 The sons of Judah:
Er, Onan, Shelah, Perez and Zerah (but Er and Onan had died in the land of Canaan).
The sons of Perez:
Hezron and Hamul.

13 The sons of Issachar:
Tola, Puah, Jashub and Shimron.

14 The sons of Zebulun:
Sered, Elon and Jahleel.

15 These were the sons Leah bore to Jacob in Paddan Aram, besides his daughter Dinah. These sons and daughters of his were thirty-three in all.

16 The sons of Gad:
Zephon, Haggi, Shuni, Ezbon, Eri, Arodi and Areli.

17 The sons of Asher:
Imnah, Ishvah, Ishvi and Beriah.
Their sister was Serah.
The sons of Beriah:
Heber and Malkiel.

18 These were the children born to Jacob by Zilpah, whom Laban had given to his daughter Leah—sixteen in all.

19 The sons of Jacob's wife Rachel:
Joseph and Benjamin.
20 In Egypt, Manasseh and Ephraim were born to Joseph by Asenath daughter of Potiphera, priest of On.

21 The sons of Benjamin:
Bela, Beker, Ashbel, Gera, Naaman, Ehi, Rosh, Muppim, Huppim and Ard.

22These were the sons of Rachel who were born to Jacob—fourteen
in all.
23The son of Dan:
Hushim.
24The sons of Naphtali:
Jahziel, Guni, Jezer and Shillem.
25These were the sons born to Jacob by Bilhah, whom Laban had
given to his daughter Rachel—seven in all.
26All those who went to Egypt with Jacob—those who were his direct
descendants, not counting his sons' wives—numbered sixty-six persons. 27With the two sons who had been born to Joseph in Egypt, the
members of Jacob's family, which went to Egypt, were seventy in all.

8–27 The list of names in these verses appears to have been selected so that the total numbers "seventy" (*šiḇʿîm,* v.27). It can hardly be coincidental that the number of nations in Genesis 10 is also "seventy." Just as the "seventy nations" represent all the descendants of Adam, so now the "seventy sons" represent all the descendants of Abraham, Isaac, and Jacob, the sons of Israel. What we see here in narrative form is a demonstration of the theme in Deuteronomy 32:8, that God apportioned the boundaries of the nations (Gen 10) according to the number of the sons of Israel. Thus the writer has gone to great lengths to portray the new nation of Israel as a new humanity and Abraham as a second Adam. The blessing that is to come through Abraham and his offspring is a restoration of the original blessing of Adam, a blessing that was lost in the Fall.

The picture of God that emerges from these pages is not merely of a God who works with his own chosen people for their good alone but who works with the nations to bring about his plan of salvation and blessing. The picture is very similar to that of Isaiah 45, where the rise of the kingdom of Persia is portrayed as the handiwork of God, all for the sake of the universal salvation and blessing that God intended through his chosen seed.

In Deuteronomy 10:22 the number "seventy" is seen as a very small number in comparison to the fulfillment of God's promise of making the descendants of Abraham outnumber the stars of the heavens. Thus, in preparation for the idea of God's faithfulness to his promise to the patriarchs, we are reminded of the relatively few descendants of Israel who went into the land of Egypt. Exodus 1:5 returns to this same theme by reminding the reader of the "seventy" descendants of Jacob who went into Egypt and of their great increase during their sojourn there: "the Israelites were fruitful and multiplied greatly and became exceedingly numerous, so that the land was filled with them" (Exod 1:7)—a clear allusion to the promised blessing (cf. Gen 1:28).

Notes

8–27 The narrative is clear that the total number of the sons of Israel was "seventy" (שִׁבְעִים [*šiḇʿîm*], v.27). However, within the passage itself that number is arrived at in two different ways. First, there is a general list of the family of Jacob with subtotals: "thirty-three" (v.15), "sixteen" (v.18), "fourteen" (v.22), and "seven" (v.25), which totals seventy. This list includes Jacob himself (notice the addition of "Jacob and his descendants" to "These are the names of the Israelites," v.8) and includes Joseph (v.19) and his two sons born in Egypt (v.20) but not Er and Onan (v.12) who died in Canaan before the journey to Egypt. The subtotals in the list also include Dinah (v.15). The difficulty with this way of reading the list is the addition of "sons and daughters of his" (בָּנָיו וּבְנוֹתָיו [*bānāyw ûḇᵉnôṯāyw*]), which appears to exclude Jacob, but v.8 has dealt with that. Second, a further subtotal is given in vv.26–27: all those of the house of Jacob who came to Egypt equaled sixty-six (v.26). Since that number is said to include only "those who were [Jacob's] direct descendants" (v.26) and to exclude "[Jacob's] sons' wives" (נְשֵׁי בְנֵי־יַעֲקֹב [*nᵉšê ḇᵉnê-ya'ᵃqōḇ*]), Jacob, Dinah, and Serah are also not in the number. Jacob (pp. 832–33) has suggested that Shaul, the son of a Canaanite (v.10), is also to be excluded, which gives sixty-six. Keil (pp. 369–70) suggests that Joseph was not included in the sixty-six, but v.27 gives no grounds for this assumption. It appears certain that only Joseph's two sons were to be added to the subtotal of sixty-six. When Dinah and Serah and the two sons of Joseph, Ephraim and Manasseh, are added, the total is seventy. The final number of seventy is consistent with Exod 1:5 and Deut 10:22, both of which list seventy (*šiḇ'îm*) as the number of the sons of Israel who went down into Egypt.

The LXX lists five more names at the end of v.20. The names are derived from Num 26:29–36. Since the LXX also gives the number as seventy-five in Exod 1:5, the extra names appear to be intentional. Recently, Hebrew copies of Exod 1:5 have been found that also contain the number seventy-five (חמש ושבעים [*ḥmš wšḇ'ym*], 4QExoda). This was apparently the tradition followed by Stephen in Acts 7:14b. On textual grounds alone the LXX represents the better text in that the MT appears to be a harmonization to Deut 10:22. However, the compositional interest of the Pentateuch in the number seventy weighs in favor of the MT. It is not without importance that Hebrew texts from Qumran and the LXX vary considerably from the MT of Deut 32:8, where there is a thematic statement of the significance of the correspondence in number between the seventy nations in Gen 10 and the "members of Jacob's family." The Qumran texts and the LXX read "the number of the sons of God." On the other hand, in Gen 10 the tradition that lies behind the LXX may have included the four kingdoms of Nimrod (10:10) and the Philistines (14), thus making the total number of the table of nations equal seventy-five.

N. *Settling in Goshen*

46:28–47:12

28 Now Jacob sent Judah ahead of him to Joseph to get directions to Goshen. When they arrived in the region of Goshen, 29 Joseph had his chariot made ready and went to Goshen to meet his father Israel. As soon as Joseph appeared before him, he threw his arms around his father and wept for a long time.

30 Israel said to Joseph, "Now I am ready to die, since I have seen for myself that you are still alive."

31 Then Joseph said to his brothers and to his father's household, "I will go up and speak to Pharaoh and will say to him, 'My brothers and my father's household, who were living in the land of Canaan, have come to me. 32 The men are shepherds; they tend livestock, and they have brought along their flocks and herds and everything they own.' 33 When Pharaoh calls you in and asks, 'What is your occupation?' 34 you should answer, 'Your servants have tended livestock from our boyhood on, just as our fathers did.' Then you will be allowed to settle in the region of Goshen, for all shepherds are detestable to the Egyptians."

47:1 Joseph went and told Pharaoh, "My father and brothers, with their flocks and herds and everything they own, have come from the land of Canaan and are now in Goshen." 2 He chose five of his brothers and presented them before Pharaoh.

[3]Pharaoh asked the brothers, "What is your occupation?"
"Your servants are shepherds," they replied to Pharaoh, "just as our fathers were." [4]They also said to him, "We have come to live here awhile, because the famine is severe in Canaan and your servants' flocks have no pasture. So now, please let your servants settle in Goshen."
[5]Pharaoh said to Joseph, "Your father and your brothers have come to you, [6]and the land of Egypt is before you; settle your father and your brothers in the best part of the land. Let them live in Goshen. And if you know of any among them with special ability, put them in charge of my own livestock."
[7]Then Joseph brought his father Jacob in and presented him before Pharaoh. After Jacob blessed Pharaoh, [8]Pharaoh asked him, "How old are you?"
[9]And Jacob said to Pharaoh, "The years of my pilgrimage are a hundred and thirty. My years have been few and difficult, and they do not equal the years of the pilgrimage of my fathers." [10]Then Jacob blessed Pharaoh and went out from his presence.
[11]So Joseph settled his father and his brothers in Egypt and gave them property in the best part of the land, the district of Rameses, as Pharaoh directed. [12]Joseph also provided his father and his brothers and all his father's household with food, according to the number of their children.

28–34 Curiously, in the narrative itself it was Judah, not Joseph, who led the sons of Israel into the land of Goshen. Once again it appears as though the writer has singled out Judah for special attention over against Joseph. Although in the Joseph story as a whole it was Joseph who was responsible for the preservation of the sons in Egypt, here, within the detail of the passage, it was Judah who "pointed out the way" (*lehôrōṯ;* NIV, "to get directions," v.28) to the land of Goshen. Such a special focus on Judah is part of an overall strategy of the writer to highlight the crucial role of Judah in God's plan to bring about Israel's deliverance. The prominence of Judah is seen most clearly in Jacob's words of blessing to his twelve sons (49:8–12).

The chapter ends with Joseph's plan to secure the land of Goshen as a dwelling place for the sons of Israel (vv.31–34). The plan was simply to tell the Pharaoh that they were shepherds. As the writer informs us, the Egyptians hated shepherds and thus would allow the Israelites to dwell off by themselves in the land of Goshen. In the next chapter, Joseph's plan succeeded, and the people were given the land of Goshen. In these two brief narratives, Joseph and Judah are placed in marked contrast. Judah led the brothers to the land of Goshen, but it was Joseph's wise plan that resulted in their being able to live there.

47:1–12 Throughout the Joseph narratives the writer has been careful to allow the key events to be recounted twice. The events of chapters 46 and 47 are no exception. Joseph has recounted his plan to his brothers in chapter 46 and now, in chapter 47, the writer recounts the outcome of the events of the plan. The point is to show that Joseph's plan was successful and thereby reinforce a central theme of the narrative: "The LORD was with Joseph and he prospered" (39:2). Joseph's wisdom resulted in the sons of Israel dwelling safely in the land of Goshen while there was severe famine in the land of Canaan (vv.1–4). Pharaoh's response (vv.5–6) was even more generous than the previous narrative would have suggested. Not only did he grant their wish and allow Joseph's brothers to settle in Goshen, he also put the brothers in charge of his own livestock as well, a result curiously reminiscent of Joseph's own rise to power in the house of Pharaoh (cf. 41:41). Thus the narrative shows that Joseph's fortune was duplicated in the fortune of his brothers. The land of Goshen is called the "best part of the land" (*mêṭaḇ,* v.6), which perhaps is a wordplay on the "good" (*ṭôḇ*) that God intended in all of these recorded events (50:20).

Significantly, the central concern of the narrative is to show that Jacob "blessed Pharaoh" (*wayᵉḇāreḵ . . . 'eṯ-par'ōh,* vv.7, 10) when he was brought before him. Its importance can be seen from the fact that it was mentioned twice. Lying behind such an emphasis in the narrative is God's promise to Abraham that he would bless those who blessed the offspring of Abraham. The passage shows that in Joseph and Jacob, the promise to Abraham was being fulfilled with the nations round about them.

The words of Jacob to the Pharaoh in v.9—"My years have been few and difficult, and they do not equal the years of the pilgrimage of my fathers"—sound unusual in the way they contrast with the two accounts of his blessing of Pharaoh. What do Jacob's words mean? They appear to be a deliberate contrast to the later promise in Deuteronomy that one who honors his father and mother should "live long and that it may go well with you in the land" (Deut 5:16). Jacob, who deceived his father and thereby gained the blessing, must not only die outside the Promised Land, but also we learn here that his years were few and difficult. From his own words, then, we can see a final recompense for Jacob's actions earlier in the book. As Abraham obeyed God and lived long in the land (Gen 26:5), so Jacob's years were short and difficult. In spite of such a final verdict on the life of Jacob, the narrative goes on to show that he lived out his remaining years "in the good [*bᵉmêṭaḇ;* NIV, 'best part'] of the land" (v.11), though not the Promised Land; and Joseph, his son, provided for him and his household.

Notes

1 The narrative moves immediately into the next segment with only a change in time and place. The events follow closely what was spoken by Joseph at the conclusion of the preceding narrative. Again the words of the central character provide the outline of the events to follow.

6 A central theme—הָאָרֶץ הַטּוֹבָה (*hā'āreṣ haṭṭôḇāh,* "the good land")—is woven into the narrative by the repetition of בְּמֵיטַב הָאָרֶץ (*bᵉmêṭaḇ hā'āreṣ,* "the best part of the land," vv.6, 11).

7 וַיְבָרֶךְ יַעֲקֹב (*wayᵉḇāreḵ ya'ᵃqōḇ,* "Jacob blessed") takes up the theme of 12:3—"all peoples on earth will be blessed through you"—and is echoed later in Exod 12:32, where the Pharaoh asks, "And also bless me" (וּבֵרַכְתֶּם גַּם־אֹתִי [*ûḇēraḵtem gam-'ōṯî*]). The fact that it is repeated in v.10 (*wayᵉḇāreḵ ya'ᵃqōḇ*) shows that it plays an important role in the narrative.

O. *Joseph's Rule in Egypt*

47:13–27

13 There was no food, however, in the whole region because the famine was severe; both Egypt and Canaan wasted away because of the famine. 14 Joseph collected all the money that was to be found in Egypt and Canaan in payment for the grain they were buying, and he brought

it to Pharaoh's palace. [15]When the money of the people of Egypt and Canaan was gone, all Egypt came to Joseph and said, "Give us food. Why should we die before your eyes? Our money is used up."

[16]"Then bring your livestock," said Joseph. "I will sell you food in exchange for your livestock, since your money is gone." [17]So they brought their livestock to Joseph, and he gave them food in exchange for their horses, their sheep and goats, their cattle and donkeys. And he brought them through that year with food in exchange for all their livestock.

[18]When that year was over, they came to him the following year and said, "We cannot hide from our lord the fact that since our money is gone and our livestock belongs to you, there is nothing left for our lord except our bodies and our land. [19]Why should we perish before your eyes—we and our land as well? Buy us and our land in exchange for food, and we with our land will be in bondage to Pharaoh. Give us seed so that we may live and not die, and that the land may not become desolate."

[20]So Joseph bought all the land in Egypt for Pharaoh. The Egyptians, one and all, sold their fields, because the famine was too severe for them. The land became Pharaoh's, [21]and Joseph reduced the people to servitude, from one end of Egypt to the other. [22]However, he did not buy the land of the priests, because they received a regular allotment from Pharaoh and had food enough from the allotment Pharaoh gave them. That is why they did not sell their land.

[23]Joseph said to the people, "Now that I have bought you and your land today for Pharaoh, here is seed for you so you can plant the ground. [24]But when the crop comes in, give a fifth of it to Pharaoh. The other four-fifths you may keep as seed for the fields and as food for yourselves and your households and your children."

[25]"You have saved our lives," they said. "May we find favor in the eyes of our lord; we will be in bondage to Pharaoh."

[26]So Joseph established it as a law concerning land in Egypt—still in force today—that a fifth of the produce belongs to Pharaoh. It was only the land of the priests that did not become Pharaoh's.

[27]Now the Israelites settled in Egypt in the region of Goshen. They acquired property there and were fruitful and increased greatly in number.

13–27 The writer goes into great detail to show the final steps by which Joseph extended his authority and the authority of the Pharaoh over every region of Egypt. The narrative returns to the story line of 41:57 with an account of the affairs of Joseph in Egypt and his work on behalf of the Pharaoh. The brothers are no longer the center of attention. The writer, at least temporarily, leaves them behind to focus on Joseph and his sons. The narrative returns to the theme of the brothers in chapter 49, but there it is not Joseph and his brothers; rather it is Jacob and his sons—with Joseph simply being one of the brothers. It is only in the end, at 50:15, that we return to the theme of Joseph and his brothers.

We might ask what is the strategy of the writer in inserting the account of Joseph and his brothers (chs. 42–46) in the midst of the narratives dealing with Joseph's rise to power in Egypt (chs. 39–41, 47). The answer may lie in the way in which this final narrative resembles the story of Joseph and his brothers. Throughout those narratives the theme was repeatedly expressed that Joseph's wisdom and administrative skills saved the life of his brothers and father. Thus at the beginning of the story, Jacob had told his sons to go down to Egypt to buy grain "that we may live and not die" (*w^{e}niḥyeh w^{e}lō' nāmûṯ*, 42:2). Then Judah, "in the second year" (*š^{e}nāṯayim*, 45:6), told his father to let them return to Egypt "that we may live and not die" (*wᵉniḥyeh wᵉlō' nāmûṯ,* 43:8). Finally, when he revealed himself to them, Joseph told his brothers that God had sent him to Egypt "to save life" (*lᵉmiḥᵉyāh,* 45:5; NIV, "to save lives").

In keeping with that emphasis, the present narrative opens with the statement of the Egyptians to Joseph as they seek to buy grain from him: "Why should we die before your eyes?" (*wᵉlāmmāh nāmûṯ negdeḵā,* v.15). Then it continues with the account of their return to Joseph "the second year" (*baššānāh haššēnîṯ,* v.18; NIV, "the following year"), when they again said, "Why should we perish?" (*lāmmāh nāmûṯ,* v.19) and then again, "that we may live and not die" (*wᵉniḥyeh wᵉlō' nāmûṯ,* v.19). Such repetitions in the surface structure of the narrative suggest that a thematic strategy is at work. First with his brothers and then with the Egyptians, Joseph's wisdom is seen as the source of life for everyone in the land.

A further evidence of a distinct strategy behind the present narrative in chapter 47 can be seen in the ironic twist given the earlier narratives by the outcome of this chapter. The whole of the story of Joseph and his brothers began with Joseph being sold (*wayyimkᵉrû,* 37:28) into slavery (*'eḇeḏ,* 39:17) for twenty pieces of silver (*kāsep̱,* 37:28). Now, at the conclusion, Joseph is shown selling (*māḵᵉrû,* v.20) the whole of the land of Egypt into slavery (*'ᵃḇāḏîm,* vv.19, 25) and taking his family's "money" (*hākkesep̱,* lit., "silver," v.18). In the end, because of the wisdom of Joseph, the offspring of Abraham became "fruitful" (*wayyip̱rû,* v.27), "increased [*wayyirbû*] greatly in number," and were dwelling safely and prosperously in the "region" (*'ereṣ*) of Goshen. Such a picture appears to be an obvious replication of the intended blessing of the early chapters of Genesis: "Be fruitful [*pᵉrû*] and increase in number [*ûrᵉḇû*]; fill the earth [*hā'āreṣ*]" (1:28).

Notes

---

13 The syntax W + nominal clause suggests a new segment. Here the background is reestablished from 41:57.

P. *Jacob's Deathbed (47:28–49:33)*

1. *Jacob's burial instructions*

47:28–31

28 Jacob lived in Egypt seventeen years, and the years of his life were a hundred and forty-seven. 29 When the time drew near for Israel to die, he called for his son Joseph and said to him, "If I have found favor in your eyes, put your hand under my thigh and promise that you will show me kindness and faithfulness. Do not bury me in Egypt, 30 but when I rest with my fathers, carry me out of Egypt and bury me where they are buried."

"I will do as you say," he said.

31 "Swear to me," he said. Then Joseph swore to him, and Israel worshiped as he leaned on the top of his staff.

28 The thread of narrative continues from vv.8–12 where, at his last mention, Jacob's age had been given as 130 years. To return to the subject of Jacob, the writer bridges the narrative gap with a summation of all the years of his life, 17 years in Egypt and the 130 give a total of 147 years. The initial impression from this verse is that the Jacob narratives are coming to a close, but such is not the case. Two crucial chapters remain. The function of v.28 is twofold. It first provides continuity within the Jacob narrative that had been broken into by the account of Joseph's further rise to power (vv.13–27); and, second, it moves the narratives to a new time frame, 17 years later. Perhaps the underlying assumption intended is that by now the famine was over and Joseph's position in Egypt has been well established. With such matters behind, the writer moves to the last days of Jacob.

29–31 As he approached death, Jacob's only request was that he not be buried in the land of Egypt. The manner of the request suggests that it is intended as an allusion back to the sending of Abraham's servant for a bride for Isaac: "Put your hand under my thigh and promise" (v.29; cf. 24:2). The similarities between the two requests are transparent. As he approached death (24:1), Abraham did not want his son to take a wife from among the people in the land where he was then dwelling but rather to take a wife from among his own family (24:3–4). In the same way, as he approached death (v.29), Jacob did not want to be buried among the Egyptians but with his fathers (v.30) in his own land. The same theme is taken up in chapter 50 when Joseph makes his sons swear that they will carry his bones back to the Promised Land, a request carried out by the sons of Israel in Joshua 24:32.

What lies behind such requests? Do they give expression to any central themes in the book? The answer is yes. A central element of the promise to Abraham was the promise of the land. The request of the patriarchs to be buried in the land "with their fathers" brings to the fore their trust in the faithfulness of God to his word. Henceforth a key symbol of Israel's faith in the promises of God is the bones of the faithful offspring that lie buried in the Promised Land. One other chapter of the Bible pays specific attention to this symbol, Ezekiel 37, the prophecy of the "dry bones." There the hope embedded in the symbol is given full expression when the Lord says, "O my people, I am going to open your graves and bring you up from them; I will bring you into the land of Israel. . . . and you will live" (Ezek 37:12–14). It is no wonder then that in this same chapter Ezekiel returns directly to one of the central underlying issues of the Joseph narratives, namely, the rivalry between Joseph and Judah.

As early as the rivalry between Leah, Judah's mother, and Rachel, Joseph's mother (ch. 30), the question of the preeminence of one of the brothers over the other has occupied a central role in the narratives. In chapters 48 (the blessing of Joseph) and 49 (the blessing of Judah) the issue comes to a final resolution in the choice of one from the tribe of Judah who will reign over the rest of the brothers (Gen 49:8–10). So also in Ezekiel 37, the prophet returns to the theme of the Joseph narratives and the rivalry between the brothers. Here, as in Genesis, the brothers are reunited under the king from the tribe of Judah, David: "Son of man, take a stick of wood and write on it, 'Belonging to Judah'. . . . Then take another stick of wood and write on it, . . . 'Belonging to Joseph.'. . . Join them together into one stick so that they will become one in your hand. . . . There will be one king over all of them and they will never again be two nations or be divided into two kingdoms. . . . 'My servant David will be king over them, . . . They will live in the land I gave to my servant Jacob'" (Ezek 37:15–17, 22–24).

We can see then that the writer of Genesis has much the same concern underlying his narratives as the prophecies of Ezekiel. The concern is the fulfillment of God's promises to Jacob. Those whose faith is like that of Jacob's are those who look for the time when the "dry bones" will again be given life in the reign of the one from the tribe of Judah. Of further interest is the fact that Ezekiel's prophecy leads from this theme directly into his vision of the defeat of Gog and Magog (Ezek 38). In the same way the Book of Revelation weaves together the defeat of Gog and Magog (Ezek 38–39) with the victory of the "Lion of the tribe of Judah" (cf. Gen 49:8–12; cf. Num 24:7 [see Notes]; Rev 5:5; 19:11–16).

Notes

29–31 In the textual history of Num 24:7b, there is evidence of an eschatological interpretation of the Balaam oracles similar to that of Ezek 38 and 39. The MT reads מַלְכּוֹ (*malkô,* "his king") will be greater than אֲגַג (*'ᵃgag,* "Agag"), but the original reading surely was גּוֹג (*gôg,* "Gog"), a reading represented by most early witnesses apart from the MT.

31 The depiction of Jacob's death—וַיִּשְׁתַּחוּ יִשְׂרָאֵל (*wayyištaḥû yiśrā'ēl,* "and Israel worshiped")—may be an allusion to 37:10.

---

2. *Ephraim and Manasseh blessed*

48:1–22

1 Some time later Joseph was told, "Your father is ill." So he took his
two sons Manasseh and Ephraim along with him. 2 When Jacob was
told, "Your son Joseph has come to you," Israel rallied his strength and
sat up on the bed.
3 Jacob said to Joseph, "God Almighty appeared to me at Luz in the
land of Canaan, and there he blessed me 4 and said to me, 'I am going to
make you fruitful and will increase your numbers. I will make you a
community of peoples, and I will give this land as an everlasting
possession to your descendants after you.'
5 "Now then, your two sons born to you in Egypt before I came to you
here will be reckoned as mine; Ephraim and Manasseh will be mine, just
as Reuben and Simeon are mine. 6 Any children born to you after them
will be yours; in the territory they inherit they will be reckoned under the
names of their brothers. 7 As I was returning from Paddan, to my sorrow
Rachel died in the land of Canaan while we were still on the way, a little
distance from Ephrath. So I buried her there beside the road to
Ephrath" (that is, Bethlehem).
8 When Israel saw the sons of Joseph, he asked, "Who are these?"
9 "They are the sons God has given me here," Joseph said to his
father.
Then Israel said, "Bring them to me so I may bless them."
10 Now Israel's eyes were failing because of old age, and he could
hardly see. So Joseph brought his sons close to him, and his father
kissed them and embraced them.
11 Israel said to Joseph, "I never expected to see your face again, and
now God has allowed me to see your children too."
12 Then Joseph removed them from Israel's knees and bowed down
with his face to the ground. 13 And Joseph took both of them, Ephraim

on his right toward Israel's left hand and Manasseh on his left toward
Israel's right hand, and brought them close to him. 14 But Israel reached
out his right hand and put it on Ephraim's head, though he was the
younger, and crossing his arms, he put his left hand on Manasseh's
head, even though Manasseh was the firstborn.
15 Then he blessed Joseph and said,

"May the God before whom my fathers
  Abraham and Isaac walked,
the God who has been my shepherd
  all my life to this day,
16 the Angel who has delivered me from all harm
  —may he bless these boys.
May they be called by my name
  and the names of my fathers Abraham and Isaac,
and may they increase greatly
  upon the earth."

17 When Joseph saw his father placing his right hand on Ephraim's
head he was displeased; so he took hold of his father's hand to move it
from Ephraim's head to Manasseh's head. 18 Joseph said to him, "No,
my father, this one is the firstborn; put your right hand on his head."
19 But his father refused and said, "I know, my son, I know. He too will
become a people, and he too will become great. Nevertheless, his
younger brother will be greater than he, and his descendants will
become a group of nations." 20 He blessed them that day and said,

"In your name will Israel pronounce this blessing:
  'May God make you like Ephraim and Manasseh.' "

So he put Ephraim ahead of Manasseh.
21 Then Israel said to Joseph, "I am about to die, but God will be with
you and take you back to the land of your fathers. 22 And to you, as one
who is over your brothers, I give the ridge of land I took from the
Amorites with my sword and my bow."

The phrase "some time later" (v.1) suggests an important break in the narrative and separates this passage from the events that have preceded. Chapter 48 forms a fitting conclusion to the Joseph narratives. As in the earlier patriarchal narratives, the blessing of the father is passed along to the next generation. Two features of this passage stand out. First, as with the earlier instances of the patriarchal blessings, it was the younger son, Ephraim, who was blessed as the firstborn rather than the older, Manasseh (v.19). In this respect the passage continues the well-worn theme that the blessing did not follow the lines of natural descent or natural right. The blessing was a gift bestowed on those who could not claim it as a right. Second, the blessing recorded in this chapter is largely subordinated and superseded by the blessing of Jacob that follows in chapter 49.

It has been a curious feature of the whole of the Joseph narratives that Judah, rather than Joseph, ultimately prevailed in gaining the position of preeminence among his brothers. As important as Joseph is in the structure of the Genesis narratives, his role is subordinate to that of Judah. Consequently the blessings of the sons of Joseph recorded in this passage do not play an important role in the later biblical story. Rather, it is the blessing of Judah in chapter 49 that plays the dominant role in the continuing story of the promise and the blessing. From Judah comes the house of David, and from David comes the Messiah—that is the focus of the biblical story that follows. The two sons of Joseph, Ephraim and Manasseh, play an important role in the texts dealing with the divided northern kingdom; but the biblical writer's attention to that kingdom, which ultimately was exiled and lost in the Dispersion, pales quickly in the light of the rising star of David.

1–4 Once again we are reminded of the frailty of Jacob (v.1), and we can see that his life was drawing to a close. As soon as he saw Joseph and his two sons, however, Jacob was revived (v.2), and he prepared to bestow God's blessing on the house of Joseph. Jacob's recollection of God's promise to him at Bethel (35:9–13) is significant. He repeated the Lord's words almost verbatim; but in the minor alterations we can see not only Jacob's assessment of the promise but also the writer's perspective. As he had acknowledged in 35:9, so now Jacob recalled that God had "blessed him" (v.3). When he recounted what God had said, Jacob brought out a nuance to God's words that helps clarify the reader's understanding of the Lord's promised blessing.

In 35:11 the Lord had said, using the imperative mood, "Be fruitful [*p^{e}rēh*] and increase in number [*ûr^{e}ḇēh*]. A nation and a community of nations will come from your body." The use of the imperative in blessings is not unusual and should be understood, not as a command, but as a form of "well-wishing." The Lord was saying, "May you be fruitful and increase," just as in Genesis 1:28. But as Jacob retold the story to Joseph in this chapter, he did not use the imperative but rather changed the verbal forms to stress that God was the one who would bring about all that had been promised: "I am going to make you fruitful [*hinnî map̱r^{e}ḵā*] and will increase your numbers [*w^{e}hirbîṯiḵā*]. I will make you a community of peoples, and I will give this land as an everlasting possession to your descendants after you" (v.4).

As he reflected back on the blessing and recounted it to his sons, Jacob brought out just that aspect of the blessing that had been the theme of the Joseph narratives: God ultimately will bring about all that he has promised. All that had happened to the house of Jacob had been in God's plan and was intended by him "for good" (50:20).

A second nuance is noticeable in Jacob's recounting of the promise. When he recounted God's promise of the land, he again did so verbatim: "I will give this land . . . to your descendants after you" (cf. 35:11). But there is a significant addition to Jacob's retelling of the blessing. He has added "as an everlasting possession" (v.4), a statement that was not recorded in chapter 35. Only one other time is the promise of the land called an "everlasting possession" (cf. 13:15), in 17:8. There too when the promise was given to Abraham, the form of the blessing was not the imperative ("Be fruitful and increase") but the form of the verb denoting God as the subject of the action: The Lord says, "I . . . will greatly increase your numbers" (*w^{e}'arbeh 'ôṯ^{e}ḵā bim'ōḏ m^{e}'ōḏ*, 17:2) and "I will make you very fruitful" (*w^{e}hip̱rēṯî 'ōṯ^{e}ḵā bim'ōḏ m^{e}'ōḏ*, 17:6).

It may also be significant that Jacob omitted one of the key elements of the promise that the Lord had made to him in chapter 35. The Lord had said, "Kings will come from your body" (35:11; cf. 17:6, 16), but in the present chapter no mention of that part of the promise is made. Why is this part omitted in chapter 48? Likely the stress on the role of Judah with regard to the kingship in chapter 49 has precluded any mention of the promise of kings in reference to Joseph.

5–7 The two sons of Joseph, Ephraim and Manasseh, here were taken into the family of Jacob and were to be treated as his own (v.5). They, along with the other sons of Jacob, would inherit the promise of Abraham (v.6). Henceforth the families of Ephraim and Manasseh were counted among the sons of Jacob and later became two of the most important of the tribes of Israel. In later biblical texts these two names became synonymous with the northern kingdom of Israel, which stood in bitter opposition to the kingdom of Judah.

Verse 7 has long puzzled biblical interpreters. Why the mention of Rachel at this point in the narrative, and why the mention of her burial site? If we relate the verse to what precedes, then the mention of Rachel here could be prompted by the fact that just as she had borne Jacob "two sons" (44:27, Joseph and Benjamin) at a time when he was about to enter (48:7) the land, so also Joseph gave Jacob "two sons" (v.5) just at the time when he was about to enter Egypt. Such symmetry suggests that Ephraim and Manasseh are seen as replacements of Joseph and Benjamin, which serves to further the sense of divine providence behind the events of Jacob's life.

Furthermore, Jacob's recollection (v.7) is virtually verbatim to that of the account of Rachel's death in 35:16–19. In both passages the stress is laid on the site of "Ephrath," which the writer identifies in both passages as Bethlehem. As in the earlier cases of the concern for the burial of the patriarchs in the Promised Land, Jacob's mention of Rachel's burial is tied to the promise that the land would be an "eternal possession" of the seed of Abraham. Rachel's burial place, like that of Abraham and Sarah's and Jacob's own impending burial site (47:29–30), serves as a reminder of the faithfulness of God to his covenant promise.

8–14 The blessing of Ephraim and Manasseh is recounted in great detail. In the account of Jacob's blessing his sons (ch. 49), these two sons are not mentioned. The overall function of the present account then is to augment the blessings of chapter 49 with an account of the blessing of the two sons who have taken their place in the house of Jacob along with the other sons (vv.5–6). Great care is taken to emphasize that in the blessing of these two sons, Ephraim, the younger brother, was given the blessing of the firstborn over Manasseh (v.20b). As has been the case throughout the patriarchal narratives, it was the younger son who was chosen to carry the line of blessing.

The first blessing (vv.15–16) appears to be of Joseph rather than the two sons (*wayᵉḇārek̠ 'et̠-yôsēp̠,* "Then he blessed Joseph," v.15). In the blessing itself, however, reference is made to the "young sons" (v.16), and the blessing of Joseph ultimately focuses on them. Before Jacob went on to address the two sons specifically in the blessing, Joseph interrupted him, attempting to get his father to place his right hand on Manasseh rather than Ephraim (v.13), thus giving the right of the firstborn to Manasseh, the eldest son. After objecting to Joseph's attempt (v.19), Jacob went on to bless the two sons specifically (*wayᵉḇārᵃk̠ēm,* "He blessed them," v.20), thus giving Ephraim preeminence over Manasseh.

15–16 Jacob's blessing is a storehouse of key thematic terms that direct the reader's attention to several major themes at work in the book as a whole. God is identified as the "God before whom my fathers Abraham and Isaac walked [*hit̠hallᵉk̠û*]" (v.15). Not only does the mention of Abraham and Isaac connect Jacob's faith in God to his immediate forefathers, but it also helps tie together the faith of the earliest patriarchs in Genesis with that of Abraham, Isaac, and Jacob. At two earlier points in the book, the faith of the primeval patriarchs is described as those who "walked with God" (*hit̠hallek̠ 'et̠-hā'ᵉlōhîm,* 5:22, 24; 6:9). The faith of the early fathers was at one with that of the patriarchs—they walked with God.

At the same time this description of God also serves to link the faith of the fathers with that of the later generations of God's covenant people. As Moses said in

Deuteronomy 30:16, the essence of the covenant relationship was that God's people were to love God and "walk in his ways" (*lāleḵeṯ biḏrāḵāyw*); and as the prophets were later to say, "What does the LORD require of you? To act justly and to love mercy and to walk humbly with your God" (Mic 6:8).

Jacob's short catechism of faith, then, provides a theological link connecting and identifying the faith throughout all the ages. God is also described in Jacob's blessing as the "God who has been my shepherd all my life to this day" (v.15) and as the "Angel who has delivered me from all harm" (v.16). It is unusual that God himself should be described as "the Angel" (*hammal'āḵ*), since earlier in the book it is said that God sent "his angel" (*mal'āḵô*, 24:7) or simply that one of the patriarchs was visited by "the angel of the LORD" (*mal'aḵ yhwh*, 22:11).

The blessing of the two sons picks up the theme of the promise to Abraham. They are to be called by Jacob's "name" (*šᵉmî*, lit., "my name") and the "name" of Abraham and Isaac, just as God had promised Abraham: "I will make your name [*šᵉmeḵā*] great" (12:2). They were to "increase greatly" (v.16), just as God had promised Abraham, "I will make you into a great nation" (12:2).

17–20 The central concern of this section is to underscore the fact that Ephraim, the younger son, was given preeminence over Manasseh, the elder. There is an interesting reversal of the scene in which Jacob received the blessing from his father, Isaac, in chapter 27. Isaac, who was nearly blind, was deceived into blessing the younger son rather than the older. Though nearly blind himself (v.10), Jacob appeared to be making the same mistake. When Joseph attempted to correct him, however, he stated his intentions clearly: "His younger brother will be greater than he" (v.19). The writer reinforces his words by stating further that "he put Ephraim ahead of Manasseh" (v.20).

We may well ask why there is so much concern over whether Ephraim or Manasseh was put first, especially in light of the fact that in the next chapter it was Judah and neither Joseph nor his two sons who received the preeminent place. The answer is that the issue of preeminence in these texts is meant to address the larger question of who stands in a position to receive God's blessing. Over and over in these narratives, the answer to that question has been the same. Receiving the blessing that God offers does not rest with one's natural status in the world. On the contrary, the blessing of God is based solely on God's grace. The one to whom the blessing did not belong has become heir of the promise.

21–22 These last two verses are difficult to understand, not only in the immediate context, but also within the context of the entire picture of Jacob that emerges from the Genesis narratives. Throughout these narratives Jacob has been pictured, not as a man of "sword and ... bow" (v.22), but as "a quiet man, staying among the tents" (25:27). Elsewhere Jacob has said of the inhabitants of the land of Canaan, "If they join forces against me and attack me, I and my household will be destroyed" (34:30). Now, suddenly, on his deathbed, Jacob revealed another picture of himself as he bequeathed to Joseph the portion of land he had taken by force. Though he spoke to Joseph, his use of the plural pronouns ("with you," *'immāḵem*, v.21) shows that he was addressing a larger audience. In light of the fact that he spoke of a time when they would again return to the land of their fathers, that larger audience appears to be the house of Joseph that was to be represented in the tribes of Ephraim and Manasseh.

Notes

1 וַיְהִי אַחֲרֵי הַדְּבָרִים הָאֵלֶּה (*wayᵉhî 'aḥᵃrê haddᵉḇārîm hā'ēlleh,* "Some time later") marks the beginning of a major section. It is a transitional clause (cf. 22:1).

3 Jacob referred to the site of Bethel by the earlier name לוּז (*lûz,* "Luz"; cf. 28:19).

15 The LXX has αὐτοὺς (*autous,* "them") in place of אֶת־יוֹסֵף (*'eṯ-yôsēp̱,* "Joseph"). The MT is the more original in light of its difficulty, though the LXX is no doubt the proper sense of the passage. Though Joseph is the one blessed, it is the two sons—אֶת־הַנְּעָרִים (*'eṯ-hannᵉ'ārîm,* "these boys," v.16)—who are in fact the focus of the blessing.

3. *Jacob's sons blessed*

49:1–28

1 Then Jacob called for his sons and said: "Gather around so I can tell you what will happen to you in days to come.

2 "Assemble and listen, sons of Jacob;
listen to your father Israel.

3 "Reuben, you are my firstborn,
my might, the first sign of my strength,
excelling in honor, excelling in power.
4 Turbulent as the waters, you will no longer excel,
for you went up onto your father's bed,
onto my couch and defiled it.

5 "Simeon and Levi are brothers—
their swords are weapons of violence.
6 Let me not enter their council,
let me not join their assembly,
for they have killed men in their anger
and hamstrung oxen as they pleased.
7 Cursed be their anger, so fierce,
and their fury, so cruel!
I will scatter them in Jacob
and disperse them in Israel.

8 "Judah, your brothers will praise you;
your hand will be on the neck of your enemies;
your father's sons will bow down to you.
9 You are a lion's cub, O Judah;
you return from the prey, my son.
Like a lion he crouches and lies down,
like a lioness—who dares to rouse him?
10 The scepter will not depart from Judah,
nor the ruler's staff from between his feet,
until he comes to whom it belongs
and the obedience of the nations is his.
11 He will tether his donkey to a vine,
his colt to the choicest branch;
he will wash his garments in wine,
his robes in the blood of grapes.
12 His eyes will be darker than wine,
his teeth whiter than milk.

13 "Zebulun will live by the seashore
and become a haven for ships;
his border will extend toward Sidon.

14 "Issachar is a rawboned donkey
lying down between two saddlebags.
15 When he sees how good is his resting place
and how pleasant is his land,
he will bend his shoulder to the burden
and submit to forced labor.

16 "Dan will provide justice for his people
as one of the tribes of Israel.
17 Dan will be a serpent by the roadside,
a viper along the path,
that bites the horse's heels
so that its rider tumbles backward.

18 "I look for your deliverance, O LORD.

19 "Gad will be attacked by a band of raiders,
but he will attack them at their heels.

20 "Asher's food will be rich;
he will provide delicacies fit for a king.

21 "Naphtali is a doe set free
that bears beautiful fawns.

22 "Joseph is a fruitful vine,
a fruitful vine near a spring,
whose branches climb over a wall.
23 With bitterness archers attacked him;
they shot at him with hostility.
24 But his bow remained steady,
his strong arms stayed limber,
because of the hand of the Mighty One of Jacob,
because of the Shepherd, the Rock of Israel,
25 because of your father's God, who helps you,
because of the Almighty, who blesses you
with blessings of the heavens above,
blessings of the deep that lies below,
blessings of the breast and womb.

26 Your father's blessings are greater
than the blessings of the ancient mountains,
than the bounty of the age-old hills.
Let all these rest on the head of Joseph,
on the brow of the prince among his brothers.

27 "Benjamin is a ravenous wolf;
in the morning he devours the prey,
in the evening he divides the plunder."

28 All these are the twelve tribes of Israel, and this is what their father said to them when he blessed them, giving each the blessing appropriate to him.

1–2 The poetic discourse of chapter 49 plays a key role in the overall strategy of the patriarchal narratives as well as the strategy of the book as a whole (see Introduction, p. 7). Jacob's last words to his sons have become the occasion for a final statement of the book's major theme: God's plan to restore the lost blessing through the offspring of Abraham. The key to the writer's understanding of Jacob's last words lies in the narrative framework that surrounds them. In v.1 we are explicitly told that Jacob was speaking about those things that would happen "in the last days" (*b*ᵉ*'aḥ*ᵃ*rîṯ hayyāmîm;* NIV, "in days to come").

The same expression occurs in the Pentateuch as an introduction to two other poetic discourses, the oracles of Balaam (Num 24:14–24) and the last words of Moses (Deut 31:29). On all three occasions the subject matter introduced by the phrase "in days to come" is that of God's future deliverance of his chosen people. At the center of that deliverance stands a king (Gen 49:10; Num 24:7; Deut 33:5). In Genesis 49 that king is connected with the house of Judah.

At the close of Jacob's discourse (v.28), the writer goes to great lengths to draw a line connecting Jacob's words in this chapter to the theme of "the blessing" that has been a central concern of the book since 1:28. He does this by repeating the word "blessing" three times in the short span of v.28, which literally reads: "And he blessed [*way*ᵉ*ḇāreḵ*] them, each according to his blessing [*k*ᵉ*ḇirḵāṯô*] he blessed [*bēraḵ*] them." By framing Jacob's last words between v.1 and v.28, the writer shows where his interests lie. Jacob's words look to the future—"in days to come"—and draw on the past, viz., God's blessing of mankind. It is within that context we are to read and understand Jacob's words in this chapter. The order of the sons follows roughly the order of the record of their birth (chs. 29–30). The sons of Leah (Reuben, Simeon, Levi, Judah, Zebulun, Issachar) lead the list, followed by the sons of the handmaidens, Bilhah (Dan), Zilpah (Gad, Asher), and again Bilhah (Naphtali), and then the sons of Rachel (Joseph, Benjamin).

3–4 The key to the saying regarding Reuben is the statement "you will not excel" (*'al-tôṯar*, v.4; NIV, "no longer excel"). The word "excel" is a play on the two statements that have preceded it: "excelling in honor" (*yeṯer*) and "excelling in power" (*yeṯer*). Though Reuben has excelled, he will no longer excel. The reason given is brief but to the point: "for you went up onto . . . my couch and defiled it." This refers to an episode briefly noted in 35:22: "While Israel was living in that region, Reuben went in and slept with his father's concubine Bilhah, and Israel heard of it." As with the rest of these sayings, the message was terse and to the point. Reuben no longer had the right of the firstborn of the household of Jacob because he violated the honor of his father.

Ultimately, the purpose behind these initial sayings was the elimination of the otherwise rightful heirs to make room for Judah and Joseph at the top. Many years later the author of the Book of Chronicles offered the following explanation: "[Reuben] was the firstborn, but when he defiled his father's marriage bed, his rights as firstborn were given to the sons of Joseph son of Israel; so he could not be listed in the genealogical record in accordance with his birthright, and though Judah was the strongest of his brothers and a ruler came from him, the rights of the firstborn belonged to Joseph" (1 Chron 5:1–2). In his reference to the sons of Joseph taking the birthright, the Chronicler was no doubt thinking of Genesis 48:5, where Jacob said, "Ephraim and Manasseh [the two sons of Joseph] will be mine, just as Reuben and Simeon are mine."

5–7 Simeon and Levi are grouped together because they were the instigators of the bloodshed against the city of Shechem (34:25). At that time Jacob protested vehemently against the two sons and their attack on the defenseless city (34:30). Here Jacob gave his final verdict on their action: the two tribes of Levi and Simeon would not have their own portion in the inheritance of the land (cf. v.7). The fulfillment of Jacob's words can be found in the fact that the tribe of Simeon virtually disappears from the biblical narratives after the time of the Conquest and in the fact that the tribe of Levi was given the responsibility of the priesthood and hence was not given its own inheritance in the apportioning of the land.

8–12 Having eliminated the older brothers as rightful heirs of the blessing, Jacob foretold a future for the tribe of Judah that pictured him as the preeminent son. We have seen that the author of the Book of Chronicles did not read Jacob's words to mean that Judah was given the right of the firstborn, which, according to Genesis 48:5, belonged to Joseph (1 Chron 5:1–2). Though he did not have the right of the firstborn, Judah had been chosen over all the others as the royal tribe. According to the Book of Chronicles, Judah "prevailed" (1 Chron 5:2; NIV, "was the strongest") over his brothers and thus became heir to the throne. As the writer of Psalm 78 later put it, "[The LORD] rejected the tents of Joseph, he did not choose the tribe of Ephraim; but he chose the tribe of Judah, Mount Zion, which he loved" (vv.67–68). As is suggested in both of these later biblical texts, the words of Jacob regarding Judah in Genesis 49 anticipated in many details the future rise of David to Israel's throne.

Unlike the imagery used of the other sons, the words of Jacob regarding Judah are quite transparent, though they are, of course, made up of poetic images. Judah is described as a victorious warrior who returns home from battle and is greeted by the shouts of praise from his brothers. The parallelism of v.8 is extended by the statement "your father's sons will bow down [*yištaḥᵃwwû*] to you." It is difficult not to see in this an intentional allusion to the dream of Joseph (37:10) in which his father's sons would come to bow down before him. In other words, what was to happen to Joseph—and did, in fact, happen in the course of the narrative (e.g., 42:6)—has been picked up by way of this image and transferred to the future of the house of Judah. What had happened to Joseph is portrayed as a picture of what would happen to Judah "in days to come" (49:1; i.e., "in the last days").

The image of the victorious warrior is extended with the picture of Judah as a "young lion" (*gûr 'aryēh;* NIV, "lion's cub," v.9). The young lion is pictured as sleeping in its den after having just devoured its prey. The question at the end of v.9 speaks for itself: "Who dares to rouse him?" In v.10 the picture is filled out with a description of the young warrior as a king. He is the one who holds the "scepter" and the "ruler's staff." The point of Jacob's words is that Judah will hold such a status among the tribes of Israel until one comes "to whom it belongs." Those who reign from the house of Judah will do so in anticipation of the one to whom the kingship truly belongs. The word "Shiloh," found in some English versions, is simply an untranslated form of the Hebrew expression meaning "one to whom it belongs." It is not a name as such, nor is it to be associated with the site of the tabernacle in the days of Samuel (1 Sam 1:3).

The most startling aspect of the description of this one from the tribe of Judah comes next: "and the obedience of the nations is his" (v.10b). The use of the plural word "nations" (*'ammîm*) rather than the singular "nation" (*'am*) suggests that Jacob had in view a kingship that extended beyond the boundaries of the sons of Israel to include other nations as well. There may be an anticipation of this view in the promise of God to Jacob in 28:3 and 48:4: "I will make you a community of peoples" (*'ammîm*). In any case, later biblical writers were apparently guided by texts such as this in formulating their view of the universal reign of the future Davidic king, e.g., Psalm 2:8: "Ask of me, and I will make the nations [*gôyim*] your inheritance"; Daniel 7:13–14: "There before me was one like a son of man. . . . He was given authority, glory and sovereign power; all peoples, nations and men of every language worshiped him"; Revelation 5:5, 9: "See, the Lion of the tribe of Judah, the Root of David, has triumphed. . . . And they sang a new song: 'You are worthy . . . with your blood you purchased men for God from every tribe and language and people and nation.'"

Verses 11–12 draw an extended picture of the reign of this one from the tribe of Judah. In his day there will again be plenty for everyone. Poetically this idea of plentitude is expressed with the images of the donkey tethered to the choicest of vines and clothing washed in vintage wine (v.11). The sense of the imagery is that wine, the symbol of prosperity and blessing, will be so plentiful that even the choicest vines will be put to such everyday use as tethering the animals of burden and vintage wine will be as commonplace as wash water. Verse 12 returns to the picture of the king of Judah. His eyes are darker than wine and his teeth whiter than milk. He is a picture of strength and power.

Later biblical writers drew heavily from the imagery of this short text in their portrayal of the reign of the coming Messiah. Isaiah 63:1–6 envisions the coming of a conquering king whose clothes are like those of one who has tread the winepresses. His crimson clothing is then likened to the blood-stained garments of a victorious warrior. He is the one who has come to carry out the vengeance of God's wrath upon the ungodly nations (*'ammîm*, Isa 63:6). In the Book of Revelation, this same image is applied to the victorious return of Christ. He is the rider on "the white horse" who is "dressed in a robe dipped in blood" (Rev 19:11, 13). "Out of his mouth comes a sharp sword with which to strike down the nations. . . . He treads the winepress of the fury of the wrath of God Almighty" (Rev 19:15).

Jacob's words regarding the remaining sons, with the exception of Joseph, are noticeable, not only for their brevity, but also for their cryptic allusions to epic events that at the time lay yet in the future of the particular tribe. True to the poetic qualities of the text, the images of the destiny of the remaining sons are, in most cases, based on a wordplay of the son's name. The central theme uniting each image is that of prosperity. Just as in the image of the victorious king from the tribe of Judah who will reign over all nations in a time of rich blessing, so also each of the remaining brothers will experience the same sort of prosperity and blessing.

13 Zebulun, whose boundaries in Joshua 19:10–16 do not touch the sea, will extend its borders to the sea as far as Sidon. The Hebrew name Zebulun (*zᵉḇûlun*), which means "lofty abode," has become a cipher for the extension of the Promised Land into the "far recesses" (*yarḵāṯô;* NIV, "his border") of Sidon. There is apparently an intended wordplay between "abode" (*zᵉḇûlun*) and "abide" (*yiškōn;* NIV, "will live").

14–15 Issachar (*yiśśāḵār*), whose name is a play on the word "wages" (*śāḵār;* cf. 30:18), is pictured as a strong donkey who sees that his land of rest is good (*ṭôḇ*) and applies his back to the burden. The expression "he sees how good is his resting place" (*wayyar' mᵉnuḥāh kî ṭôḇ*) is perhaps an allusion to chapter 1 where the similar expression, "and God saw that it was good" (*wayyar' 'ᵉlōhîm kî-ṭôḇ*), is a constant reminder that God's purpose in Creation was to provide the "good" (*ṭôḇ*) for man. The use of the term "resting place" or "land of rest" (*mᵉnuḥāh*) aligns the words of Jacob with the theme of the future rest that God will give his people in the Promised Land (cf. Ps 95:11).

16–17 Dan (*dān*), whose name is a play on the expression "he will judge" (*yādîn*), is the one who will judge his people. He is likened to a snake along the path that attacks the heels of the horse and cunningly defeats the horseman. Though the sense of the image itself is unclear, Jacob's final words regarding Dan show that the image was meant in a positive way: "I look for your deliverance, O LORD" (v.18). Breaking in, as it does, on the increasingly terse poetic images, this expression of hope in the Lord's deliverance provides the much-needed clue to the meaning of Jacob's words. In the individual and future destiny of the sons is embodied the hope of all Israel. That hope is of a future prosperity for the nation and a future victory over their enemies. At the center of that hope is the king from the tribe of Judah.

19 The brief statement regarding Gad contains a wordplay on nearly every word: "Gad [*gād*] will be attacked [*yegûdennû*] by a band of raiders [*gedûd*], but he will attack [*yāgud*] them at their heels." Again, though it is very brief, the saying falls in line with the others following in the path of the prophecy regarding Judah in that it gives expression to the hope of the final defeat of the enemy.

20 The statement regarding Asher has no clear wordplays, and its meaning is self-evident. In the future Asher's sons will enjoy great abundance and rich delicacies.

21 The words regarding Naphtali are also brief. The picture they present, which is similar to the others, is of a time of great future prosperity and abundance.

22–26 As might be expected from the importance of Joseph in the earlier chapters, Jacob has much to say about the future of his tribe. In substance Jacob's statements regarding Joseph repeat much of what was said about the other brothers after Judah. The difference in the words to Joseph, however, is the repetition of the word "blessing" (*berākāh*). Whereas Jacob's words regarding the other brothers paint a picture of the future well being of the sons and thus figuratively speak of a future blessing, Jacob's words to Joseph explicitly refer to this future well being as a "blessing." As such the words to Joseph fall in line with all those earlier passages in the book that speak specifically of the promised "blessing" and prepare the way for the writer's final remarks about Jacob's words in v.28: "he blessed them, each according to his blessing, he blessed them" (lit. tr.). The reference to the "Shepherd" in v.24 appears to be an allusion to Jacob's earlier blessing of Ephraim and Manasseh (48:15).

27 The picture of Benjamin is similar to that of Judah. Both depict the patriarchs' future in terms expressing a victorious conquest over the enemy. In both the conqueror is a vicious predator, the lion and the wolf. The stark simplicity of these words to Benjamin, however, bring out the sense of sudden victory and conquest in much stronger terms than the imagery of Judah.

28 The writer sums up in uneqivocal terms the substance of Jacob's words to his sons. They are an expression of the theme of the blessing (*waybārek*, "when he blessed") that was to be passed along through the seed of Abraham, Isaac, and Jacob. Within Jacob's words to each of the sons (after Judah), the theme of blessing has been evident in two primary images. First, the reverse side of the blessing is stressed in the imagery of the victorious warrior. The defeat of the enemy is the prelude to the messianic peace. Second, the positive side of the blessing is stressed in the imagery of great prosperity and abundance. Behind such imagery of peace and prosperity lies the picture of the Garden of Eden—the Paradise lost. The focus of Jacob's words has been the promise that when the one comes to whom the kingship truly belongs, there will once again be the peace and prosperity that God intended all to have in the Garden of Eden.

Notes

---

1 See the discussion in the Introduction (pp. 7–8) on בְּאַחֲרִית הַיָּמִים (*beʾaḥarîṯ hayyāmîm*, "in days to come").

4 The פָּחַזְתָּ (*pāḥaztā*, "you are turbulent") of the Samaritan Pentateuch and apparently the versions is not to be preferred to פַּחַז (*paḥaz*, "[he is] turbulent") in the MT. Such elliptical clauses are not uncommon in poetic texts (König, *Genesis*, p. 725). The interchange of persons, as in חִלַּלְתָּ (*ḥillaltā*, "[you] defiled") and עָלָה (*ʿālāh*, "[he] went up"), is striking; but 24:27 shows it to be possible (ibid.).

5 The translation "their swords" for מְכֵרֹתֵיהֶם (*meḵērōṯêhem*) is derived from a midrash that connected it with the Greek μάχαιρα (*machaira*) because of the similarity of the consonants. More recently (KB) its meaning has been derived from the Ethiopic *mkr* meaning "to advise," thus "Weapons of violence are their counsels" (James Barr, *Comparative Philology and the Text of the Old Testament* [Oxford: Clarendon, 1968], p. 57).

8 There is a wordplay between the name יְהוּדָה (*yehûḏāh*, "Judah") and יוֹדוּךָ (*yôḏûḵā*, "will praise you"). The last clause—יִשְׁתַּחֲווּ לְךָ בְּנֵי אָבִיךָ (*yištaḥawwû leḵā benê ʾāḇîḵā*, "your father's sons will bow down to you")—breaks the pattern (3 x 3 bicola). It, however, plays an important role in linking the words about Judah to the dreams of Joseph in the preceding narratives (cf. 37:10; 42:6; 43:26, 28).

9 The words כָּרַע רָבַץ כְּאַרְיֵה וּכְלָבִיא מִי יְקִימֶנּוּ (*kāraʿ rāḇaṣ keʾaryēh ûḵelāḇîʾ mî yeqîmennû*, "Like a lion he crouches and lies down/ like a lioness, who dares rouse him?") are repeated in Balaam's oracle in Num 24:9 and applied to the future king from the house of Jacob (the plurals in the NIV of Num 24:9 are not in the Hebrew text). Thus within the Pentateuch Jacob's vision of the future is carried further along and developed. Balaam also links Gen 49:8–12 with the promise to Abraham in the statement, "May those who bless you be blessed and those who curse you be cursed!" which is an allusion to Gen 12:3.

10 Much discussion has centered on the meaning of the term "Shiloh." It is often taken as a proper name (cf. KJV), referring either to the place where the ark was kept during the days before the capture of Jerusalem (1 Sam 1–4) or to the future Messiah (cf. Scofield Reference Bible, p. 68: "Christ [first advent]"). The place of the ark in 1 Samuel and elsewhere, however, is written ה+א91שְׁל (*šilōh*) or שִׁלוֹ (*šilô*) or שִׁילוֹ (*šîlô*), not ה+א91שִׁיל (*šîlōh*), as in Genesis. The tradition was careful to distinguish the two forms, though it is not without exception—the Qere has *šîlô* for 49:10 (C.D. Ginsburg, *The Pentateuch* [London: British and Foreign Bible Society, 1926], p. 76), and some MSS have *šilōh* or *šîlô* in the text (see Doederlein and Meisner, *Biblica Hebraica*, p. 79). The tradition that *šîlōh* is the name of the Messiah is usually traced back to the Talmudic period (Jacob, p. 904), though it may already be reflected in Rev 19:11–13 where, amid numerous allusions to the imagery of Gen 49:8–12, the Messiah is described as one who "has a name written on him that no one knows but he himself." Others take *šîlōh* to be a noun (like נִיצוֹץ [*nîṣôṣ*, "spark"], König, *Genesis*, p. 730) from the root שָׁלָה (*šālāh*, "to be peaceful"). Thus *šîlōh* is the "man of peace" (e.g., שַׂר שָׁלוֹם [*śar šālôm*, Isa 9:6 (5 MT)]). If *šîlōh* is revocalized, it could be read as *šay lô* ("the one to whom tribute [*šay*] belongs") or *šellōh* ("the one [*šel*] to whom it belongs [*lōh*]"; cf. Jonah 1:12b: שֶׁלִּי [*šellî*, "fault"]). This last has the support of the Aramaic versions as well as some MSS of the LXX (cf. Ezek 21:27).

The term יִקְּהַת (*yiqq*ᵉ*hat̠*) is from יְקָהָה (*y*ᵉ*qāhāh*) or יִקְהָה (*yiqhāh*) and means "obedience" (KB, p. 411; cf. Prov 30:17).

11 The imagery of this verse appears to portray a time of great abundance. The donkey will be tied to the choicest vine, and vintage wine will be as plentiful as wash water. Later biblical interpretation, however, saw in the image of the "garments washed in the blood of grapes" (lit. tr.) the notion of the defeat of the enemies of God:

> Why are your garments red,
> like those of one treading the winepress?
> . . . .
> I trampled them in my anger
> and trod them down in my wrath;
> their blood spattered my garments,
> and I stained all my clothing.
>
> (Isa 63:2–3)

"He is dressed in a robe dipped in blood, and his name is the Word of God" (Rev 19:13).

12 The מִן (*min*) preposition is to be read in a comparative sense as in the NIV: "darker than [*min*] wine, . . . whiter than milk" (see BDB, p. 582).

28 Notice the epic repetition at the close of the segment: וַיְבָרֶךְ אוֹתָם אִישׁ אֲשֶׁר כְּבִרְכָתוֹ בֵּרַךְ אֹתָם (*way*ᵉ*b̲ārek̲ 'ôt̲ām 'îš 'ašer k*ᵉ*b̲irk̲āt̲ô bērak̲ 'ōt̲ām*) (Andersen, *Sentence in Biblical Hebrew*, pp. 39ff.).

---

4. *Jacob's burial instructions repeated*

49:29–33

29 Then he gave them these instructions: "I am about to be gathered to my people. Bury me with my fathers in the cave in the field of Ephron the Hittite, 30 the cave in the field of Machpelah, near Mamre in Canaan, which Abraham bought as a burial place from Ephron the Hittite, along with the field. 31 There Abraham and his wife Sarah were buried, there Isaac and his wife Rebekah were buried, and there I buried Leah. 32 The field and the cave in it were bought from the Hittites."

33 When Jacob had finished giving instructions to his sons, he drew his feet up into the bed, breathed his last and was gathered to his people.

29–33 As he lay dying, Jacob once more made a request that his sons bury him in the Land of Promise with his fathers (v.29). The specific place he had in mind was "Machpelah" (v.30), the burial place purchased by Abraham in chapter 23. Although Jacob had made a similar request in 47:29–30, this final one was far more specific. He wanted to be buried in the land with Abraham, Sarah, Isaac, Rebekah, and Leah (v.31), the central figures of the preceding narratives. The point of the request within the present narrative is the renewal of the reader's awareness of the promise of the land—the promise that Jacob's seed would live in peace in the land promised to Abraham and Isaac. It is to show that Jacob's faith in God's promises remained firm to the end. With such an expression of faith still on his lips, the narrative concludes with the fitting remark: "he . . . breathed his last and was gathered to his people" (v.33).

Q. *Jacob's Death and Burial*

50:1–14

1 Joseph threw himself upon his father and wept over him and kissed him. 2 Then Joseph directed the physicians in his service to embalm his father Israel. So the physicians embalmed him, 3 taking a full forty days, for that was the time required for embalming. And the Egyptians mourned for him seventy days.

4 When the days of mourning had passed, Joseph said to Pharaoh's court, "If I have found favor in your eyes, speak to Pharaoh for me. Tell him, 5 'My father made me swear an oath and said, "I am about to die; bury me in the tomb I dug for myself in the land of Canaan." Now let me go up and bury my father; then I will return.' "

6 Pharaoh said, "Go up and bury your father, as he made you swear to do."

7 So Joseph went up to bury his father. All Pharaoh's officials accompanied him—the dignitaries of his court and all the dignitaries of Egypt— 8 besides all the members of Joseph's household and his brothers and those belonging to his father's household. Only their children and their flocks and herds were left in Goshen. 9 Chariots and horsemen also went up with him. It was a very large company.

10 When they reached the threshing floor of Atad, near the Jordan, they lamented loudly and bitterly; and there Joseph observed a seven-day period of mourning for his father. 11 When the Canaanites who lived there saw the mourning at the threshing floor of Atad, they said, "The Egyptians are holding a solemn ceremony of mourning." That is why that place near the Jordan is called Abel Mizraim.

12 So Jacob's sons did as he had commanded them: 13 They carried him to the land of Canaan and buried him in the cave in the field of Machpelah, near Mamre, which Abraham had bought as a burial place from Ephron the Hittite, along with the field. 14 After burying his father, Joseph returned to Egypt, together with his brothers and all the others who had gone with him to bury his father.

1–14 Over half of the final chapter is occupied with a description of the mourning and burial of Jacob. Joseph himself mourned (v.1) and then the Egyptians (v.3). Great preparations were made both by Joseph and the Egyptians (v.2). A special request was granted by the Pharaoh to bury Jacob in his homeland (vv.4–5), and a large entourage (*hammaḥ*^{a}*neh kāḇēḏ m*^{e}*'ōḏ*, v.9; NIV, "a very large company") was provided by the Pharaoh as a burial processional to carry Jacob's body back to Canaan. "All [*kol*] Pharaoh's officials . . . and all [*kol*] the dignitaries of Egypt" (v.7) along with Pharaoh's chariots and horsemen accompanied Joseph on his journey back to Canaan. Even the Canaanites recognized this as "a very large [*kāḇēḏ*, lit., 'heavy'; NIV, 'solemn'] ceremony of mourning" (v.11). The writer himself seems to go out of his way to emphasize in detail the magnitude of the ceremony of mourning.

The question naturally arises why such detail over the burial of Jacob is given when in the death of the other patriarchs we are simply given the bare facts that they died and were buried. Even the account of the death of Joseph, which is also recorded in this chapter, consists only of the brief notice that he died and was embalmed and entombed in Egypt (v.26). Was his burial of any less magnitude than Jacob's? Surely it was not, but virtually no attention in the narrative is devoted to it. Why, then, the emphasis on Jacob's burial? Perhaps such a description is intended merely as a concluding flourish at the end of the book, or does it play a part in the ongoing strategy of the text? In light of the writer's careful attention to his larger themes throughout these narratives, it is appropriate to seek a motive for such an emphasis within the narrative. We can do that by asking what themes may be sustained or highlighted in such a full description of the burial party.

One theme that immediately comes to mind is that at a number of points throughout the narrative the writer's concern focuses on God's faithfulness to his promise of the land and the hope of God's people in the eventual return to the land. In the later prophetic literature, a recurring image of the fulfillment of the promise to return to the land pictures Israel returning to the land accompanied by many from among the nations. The prophets of Israel saw the return as a time when "all the nations [*kol-haggôyim*] will stream to" Jerusalem, and "many peoples [*'ammîm rabbîm*] will come and say, 'Come, let us go up to the mountain of the Lord, to the house of the God of Jacob' " (Isa 2:2–3); or, as Zechariah saw it, "In those days ten men from all languages and nations will take firm hold of one Jew by the hem of his robe and say, 'Let us go with you' " (Zech 8:23).

It is difficult not to see the same imagery at work in the present narrative. Jacob, in his final return to the Land of Promise, was accompanied by a great congregation of the officials and elders of the land of Egypt. With him was also the mighty army of the Egyptians. Thus the story of Jacob's burial in the land foreshadows the time when God "will bring Jacob back from captivity and will have compassion on all the people of Israel" (Ezek 39:25).

Notes

1 Chapter 50 follows closely on chapter 49. The two narrative segments are connected by a wordplay—וַיֶּאֱסֹף . . . וַיֵּאָסֶף (*wayye'esōp̱ . . . wayyē'āsep̱*, "he drew . . . and was gathered") with יוֹסֵף (*yôsēp̱*, "Joseph"; see Notes on 30:23).

VII. The Final Joseph Narrative (50:15–26)

A. *Joseph's Forgiveness*

50:15–21

15 When Joseph's brothers saw that their father was dead, they said,
"What if Joseph holds a grudge against us and pays us back for all the
wrongs we did to him?" 16 So they sent word to Joseph, saying, "Your
father left these instructions before he died: 17 'This is what you are to
say to Joseph: I ask you to forgive your brothers the sins and the wrongs
they committed in treating you so badly.' Now please forgive the sins of
the servants of the God of your father." When their message came to
him, Joseph wept.

18 His brothers then came and threw themselves down before him.
"We are your slaves," they said.

19 But Joseph said to them, "Don't be afraid. Am I in the place of God?
20 You intended to harm me, but God intended it for good to accomplish
what is now being done, the saving of many lives. 21 So then, don't be
afraid. I will provide for you and your children." And he reassured them
and spoke kindly to them.

15–21 The narrative turns once more to the scene of Joseph and his brothers and in so doing returns to the central theme of the Joseph narratives: "You intended to harm [*rāʿāh,* lit., 'evil'] me, but God intended it for good [*leṭōḇāh*] . . .[to] the saving of many lives [*lehahayōṯ ʿam-raḇ*]" (v.20). Behind all the events and human plans recounted in the story of Joseph lies the unchanging plan of God. It is the same plan introduced from the very beginning of the book where God looks out at what he has just created for man and sees that "it is good" (*ṭôḇ,* 1:4–31). Through his dealings with the patriarchs and Joseph, God had continued to bring about his good plan. He had remained faithful to his purposes, and it is the point of this narrative to show that his people can continue to trust him and to believe that "in all things God works for the good of those who love him, who have been called according to his purpose" (Rom 8:28).

The last description of Joseph's dealings with his brothers is the statement that "he comforted them [*wayenaḥēm ʾôṯām;* NIV, 'reassured'] and spoke kindly to them [*wayeḏabbēr ʿal-libbām*]" (v.21). It is again difficult not to see in this picture of Joseph and his brothers a foreshadowing of the future community of the sons of Israel in exile awaiting their return to the Promised Land. To that same community the call went out by the prophet Isaiah to "comfort [*naḥamû*], comfort [*naḥamû*] my people, says your God. Speak tenderly [*dabberû ʿal-lēḇ*] to Jerusalem, . . . she has received from the LORD's hand double for all her sins" (Isa 40:1–2).

B. *Summary of Joseph's Life and Death*

50:22–26

22 Joseph stayed in Egypt, along with all his father's family. He lived a hundred and ten years 23 and saw the third generation of Ephraim's children. Also the children of Makir son of Manasseh were placed at birth on Joseph's knees.

24 Then Joseph said to his brothers, "I am about to die. But God will surely come to your aid and take you up out of this land to the land he promised on oath to Abraham, Isaac and Jacob." 25 And Joseph made the sons of Israel swear an oath and said, "God will surely come to your aid, and then you must carry my bones up from this place."

26 So Joseph died at the age of a hundred and ten. And after they embalmed him, he was placed in a coffin in Egypt.

22–26 Though his words are few, the final statement of Joseph to his sons gives the clearest expression of the kind of hope taught in these narratives. Again, as had his father Jacob, Joseph wanted his bones returned to the Promised Land (v.25). Also like Jacob, he saw to it that his sons swore to return his bones when they returned to the land. Though he knew he would die and not see the time when his sons returned to the land, he nevertheless expressed clearly the hope and trust that he had in God's promise: "God will surely come to your aid [*pāqōḏ yip̄qōḏ*] and take you up out of this land to the land he promised on oath to Abraham, Isaac and Jacob" (v.24). As has been characteristic of the literary technique of the Joseph narratives, Joseph repeated a second time (cf. 41:32) his statement of trust in God's promise: "God will surely come to your aid [*pāqōḏ yip̄qōḏ*], and then you must carry my bones up from this place" (v.25).

Notes

25 The פָּקֹד יִפְקֹד אֱלֹהִים (*pāqōḏ yipqōḏ ʾᵉlōhîm*, "God will surely come to your aid") is perhaps an allusion to וַיהוה פָּקַד (*wayhwh pāqaḏ*, "Now the LORD was gracious") in 21:1.

26 The Book of Genesis ends with the Israelites "in Egypt" (בְּמִצְרָיִם [*bᵉmiṣrāyim*]). The narrative, however, does not end here. As in earlier segments of the book, the death of the patriarch is followed by a list of names that opens a new narrative of the events in the lives of the next generations (cf. Gen 50:26–Exod 1:5 with Gen 35:29–36:43).

EXODUS

Walter C. Kaiser, Jr.

EXODUS

Introduction

1. Title and Theme
2. Authorship and Unity
3. Date of Writing
4. Date of the Exodus
5. Route of the Exodus
6. Theology
7. Bibliography
8. Outline
9. Maps and Charts

1. Title and Theme

The name "Exodus," which is of Greek origin, comes from the LXX name for the second book of the Pentateuch. "Exodus" means "exit," "departure" (cf. its usage in Luke 9:31 [NIV, "departure"] and Heb 11:22). This name was retained also by the Vulgate, the Latin version; by the Jewish author Philo, who was a contemporary of Christ; and by the Syriac version.

The Hebrew name for the book derives from the first words of the text: "And these are the names of" (*wᵉʾēlleh šᵉmôṯ*), or simply *Shemoth.* This phrase occurs also in Genesis 46:8, where it likewise introduces a list of the names of those Israelites "who went to Egypt with Jacob" (1:1). This connecting phrase and the observation that the book begins with the conjunction "and" emphasize the fact that Exodus was never intended to exist separately but was thought of as a continuation of a narrative that began in Genesis and was completed in three more books, making up the first division of the Hebrew canon known as Torah (meaning "law," "instruction," "teaching"), or, since the second century A.D., "the Pentateuch" (i.e., "the five books").

In the Pentateuch as a whole, there are six major themes: (1) God's blessing on all nature and humanity; (2) God's promise to the patriarchs; (3) God's deliverance in the exodus from Egypt; (4) God's revelation of himself in covenant, law, and tabernacling presence at Sinai; (5) the wandering in the wilderness; and (6) preparation for entrance into Canaan. Three of these six major themes (3, 4, 5) are given extensive treatment in the second book of the Pentateuch, and thus Exodus forms the heart of the Torah.

2. Authorship and Unity

There are several internal claims in Exodus that directly ascribe authorship to Moses. He is told to record on a scroll the episode of Israel's victory over Amalek

(17:14). He is instructed to write down the Ten Commandments (34:4, 27–29). He "wrote down everything the LORD had said" (24:4), which included at least the Book of the Covenant (20:22–23:33).

These internal claims are supported by a strong association of Mosaic authorship with these same materials in other OT books such as Joshua 1:7; 8:31–32; 1 Kings 2:3; 2 Kings 14:6; Ezra 6:18; Nehemiah 13:1; Daniel 9:1–13; and Malachi 4:4.

The NT writers likewise support Mosaic authorship of the Book of Exodus. Mark 12:26 locates Exodus 3:6 in "the book of Moses," while Luke 2:22–23 assigns Exodus 13:2 to both "the Law of Moses" and "the Law of the Lord." Mark 7:10 attributes the fifth commandment (Exod 20:12) and one of the laws from the Book of the Covenant (Exod 21:17) to Moses. John (7:19) also joins in this chorus of witnesses who attribute the law to Moses. (For Mosaic authorship of other portions of the Pentateuch in the NT, see John 5:46–47; Acts 3:22; Rom 10:5.)

Traditionally many scholars assume the Book of Exodus derived from earlier editions of the story, which in turn used still earlier, mainly oral, material. Three major sources are hypothesized: J (Yahwistic, c. 950–850 B.C.), E (Elohistic, c. 750–850 B.C.), and P (Priestly, c. 500–540 B.C.).

In addition to these alleged three sources, the Ten Commandments and the Book of the Covenant are examples of material not found in any of these sources but which were known and therefore incorporated by the author(s) or editor(s).

Little or no agreement exists, however, on the precise boundaries of these subjectively devised sources; nor can the criteria for their detection be demonstrated to be functionally operative and legitimate for similar documents from epigraphic materials from periods of similar antiquity. Moreover, and most serious of all, these hypotheses directly oppose the clear internal claims of the Book of Exodus and the supporting external attributions of Mosaic authorship by other writers of Scripture. Even apart from the question of inspiration, it is best first to take a text (whether secular or sacred) on its own terms and claims. In other words, a text should be judged innocent until proven guilty rather than vice versa.

3. Date of Writing

Since Moses first became involved with leading the Israelites after his eightieth birthday (7:7), the date for the composition of the Book of Exodus must fall between his eightieth birthday and his one hundred and twentieth birthday, when he died, just as the wilderness wandering was drawing to a close (Deut 34:7). Thus the approximate date for the composition of this second book of the Pentateuch rests on the date set for the Exodus from Egypt.

4. Date of the Exodus

The Book of Exodus nowhere gives us specific enough data to definitely link biblical events with Egyptian chronology. We only know about "a new king, who did not know about Joseph" (1:8) or an anonymous "Pharaoh" (1:11, 19, 22; 2:15), or a "king of Egypt" (1:15; 2:23). It is noteworthy, however, that "Pharaoh," which means "great house" and designates the king's residence and household, became, for the first time in the Eighteenth Dynasty of Egypt, a title for the king himself. Thus even though Exodus 2:23 tells us that the king or "Pharaoh" of the Oppression died and therefore could not have been the Pharaoh of the Exodus (cf. 4:19), we have no internal evidence to specifically identify either of them.

The identity of these two Pharaohs has generally centered on two views: (1) placing the Exodus under Pharaohs of the Eighteenth Dynasty (c. 1580–1321 B.C.) and (2) placing it under Pharaohs of the Nineteenth Dynasty of the thirteenth century (c. 1321–1205 B.C.).

The two main pillars for the "late date" or thirteenth-century theory for the Exodus are (1) the two names for the store-cities built by the Israelites in Egypt—Pithom and Rameses (1:11)—and (2) the archaeological discoveries of many Palestinian sites that have been interpreted to favor an Israelite conquest toward the end of the thirteenth century.

The commonly held late-date view, that work on Pithom and Rameses must have been carried out in the Nineteenth Dynasty of Rameses II, and therefore must be dated in the thirteenth century, rests on two misconceptions: (1) the unnatural interpretation of Exodus 1:7–14, that the building of cities and the oppression commenced shortly before the Exodus rather than in the Middle Kingdom of Egypt, i.e., prior to the Eighteenth Dynasty, and (2) the name Rameses as one of the cities necessitates a late date.

Exodus 1:7–14, however, places the building of these cities as one of the first tasks these enslaved people accomplished. Since Israel's bondage spanned a number of centuries, not just decades, it is not difficult to assume that work on these cities was best remembered because it was among the first acts of their oppression.

Likewise, neither the name nor the location of these cities prevents an early date. Rameses is probably to be identified with Qantir (cf. map on p. 300; cf. also Hershel Shanks, "The Exodus and the Crossing of the Red Sea, According to Hans Goedicke," *Biblical Archaeologist Review* 7 [Sept.–Oct. 1981]: 44, for evidence of Syro-Palestinian remains from 1700–1500 B.C.), not Tanis. Pithom may be either Tell er-Retabeh (cf. map on p. 300), some nine miles west of the older suggested site of Tell el-Maskhuta, also in the Wadi Tumilat, or Heliopolis (see Uphill). Our MSS of Exodus 1:11 simply give the city's name in the later period—Rameses instead of Qantir, just as Genesis 47:11 knows the area where Jacob's family settled when they arrived in Egypt as "the district of Rameses" (another retrospective usage or modernization of an older term; cf. "Dan" in Gen 14:14 for the older name "Laish," which was not changed until the time of the judges [Judg 18:29]).

The second pillar for the late-date view is just as problematic. For example, Jericho continues to be an anomaly for this view; for in spite of all the redating of the previous excavation levels, there is absolutely no evidence for a thirteenth-century city. Likewise, the claim that certain burned levels at sites such as Lachish, Bethel, Debir, and Hazor were caused by an Israelite invasion mainly because they were followed by poor settlements alleged to be typical of earliest Israel, after its poverty ridden arrival from Egypt, is a very weak argument. Even the association of the innovative collared-rim ware type of pottery as an objective piece of evidence of a new Israelite presence is hazardous since no one similarly argues that the appearance of Palestinian imitations of Mycenaean ring ware from the earlier Grecian lands is objective evidence for a similar Mycenaean invasion.

Even more telling, Israel is recorded as deliberately burning very few sites—only Jericho, Ai, and Hazor. In fact, Joshua 11:13 specifically rules out Israel's burning any other sites than Hazor in her northern campaign. Thus the collapse of some of these sites with their burned levels may well indicate collapses attributable to Ammonite and Philistine encroachments (Judg 10:7) or forays from Egypt such as the one Pharaoh Merneptah boasted about on his stelae, not to mention the c. 1200 B.C. invasion of the Sea Peoples or the mutually destructive strife between tribes and cities as treated in Judges 19–20.

Likewise, the "early date" of the fifteenth century B.C. has two pillars: (1) the summarizing statement that there were 480 years (1 Kings 6:1) from the Exodus until the fourth year of Solomon (= 967 B.C. according to Thiele) and (2) the supporting data that three hundred years (Judg 11:26) had elapsed since Israel had entered Palestine until commencement of Judge Jephthah's rule. Both texts would set the Exodus at c. 1446 B.C., making Thutmose III the Pharaoh of the Oppression.[1]

The historicity of both of these biblical numbers, however, has frequently been rejected by noting that one MS tradition of the Greek translation (LXX^{BA}) has the figure 440 years instead of the 480 of the Hebrew text, or by explaining 480 as a round number involving twelve units or generations who are estimated to have used forty years for each generation. The first problem represents only a minor and therefore just a passing variant of textual tradition. Unfortunately for the twelve-generation theory, this too will be artificial on all counts: generations are more likely twenty than forty years, and there are actually eighteen generations, not just the stylized twelve generations, between the Exodus and the time of Solomon according to the priestly line in 1 Chronicles 6:33–37.

The three hundred years that Israel had occupied Canaan up to Jephthah's day mentioned in Judges 11:26 may be accounted for as follows:

Description	Judges	Years Duration
1. Oppression by Cushan-Rishathaim	3:8	8
Deliverance by Othniel and peace	3:11	40
2. Oppression by Moabites	3:14	18
Deliverance by Ehud and time of peace	3:30	80
3. Oppression by Canaanite King Jabin	4:3	20
Deliverance by Deborah/Barak and time of peace	5:31	40
4. Oppression by Midianites	6:1	7
Deliverance by Gideon and time of peace	8:28	40
Abimelech's reign	9:22	3
Tola's judgeship	10:2	23
Jair's judgeship	10:3	22
Years until Jephthah's time = 301		
(cf. Judg 11:26 = 300)		
5. Oppression by Ammonites	10:8	18
(on *east* side of the Jordan?)		
Deliverance by Jephthah	12:7	6
Ibzan's judgeship	12:9	7
Elon's judgeship	12:11	10
Abdon's judgeship	12:14	8

[1] Dated by W.F. Albright, G.E. Wright, and J. Pritchard as 1490–1436 B.C., but by the revised *Cambridge Ancient History* as 1504–1450 B.C.

Description	Judges	Years Duration
6. Oppression by Philistines (on *west* side of the Jordan?)	13:1	40
during which time Samson began to deliver Israel for 20 years	13:5; 15:20; 16:31	
(5 and 6 are parallel in time and contemporaneous)		

Judges 10:7–8 strongly suggests that the fifth and sixth oppressions occurred simultaneously; thus the 47 years of the Ammonite oppression and the subsequent judges do not continue the chronology since the story line continues into the Book of Samuel from the Philistine oppression.

Even when we allow some additional 15 to 20 years from Israel's entrance into the land and her division of the countryside among the tribes until the first oppression under Cushan-Rishathaim, the total for the first four oppressions, up to the time of Jephthah's judgeship, would be 301 years plus the estimated 15 to 20 years and 18 years of Ammonite oppression. Therefore 300 years as a round number is most acceptable. This fact warns us to take what would otherwise appear to be round numbers as fairly precise approximations of the actual time involved.

Our rough estimate of the total of 480 years from the Exodus until Solomon's fourth regal year could be outlined as follows:

Description	Years Expended
a. Entrance into and division of the land	15 (20)[?]
b. Oppressions 1–4 & deliverers (Cushan-Rishathaim to Judge Jair; Judg 11:26)	301
c. Philistine oppression	40
d. Samuel's judgeship	40
e. Saul's rule	40
f. David's rule	40
g. Solomon's fourth year	4
(1 Kings 6:1)	480 years total

Accordingly, the material from the Book of Judges is in keeping with the total years given in 1 Kings 6:1 and the general case made for the internal consistency of the biblical record for the early date of the Exodus as c. 1446 B.C.

5. Route of the Exodus

The wilderness itinerary actually begins in Exodus 12:37. Typically the itinerary formula consisted of two elements: (1) the departure place name with the verb "to journey" and the preposition "from" (e.g., 12:37; 13:20; 16:1; 17:1; 19:2) and (2) the arrival location with the preposition "at" or "to" (13:20; 15:22; 16:1; 17:1) and verbs such as "to camp" (13:20; 15:27) or "to come" (15:23, 27; 16:1).

The store-cities of Rameses (best identified with Qantir on the Bubastite-Pelusiac eastern arm of the Nile River delta; see map on p. 300) and Pithom (identified here as Tell-er Retabeh in the Wadi Tumilat)[2] were left behind. But there were three possible routes of escape: (1) a shorter northeast route going to Qantara through the land of the Philistines (a route Israel was warned against taking in 13:17); (2) a middle route heading across the Negeb to Beersheba (whose advocates incorrectly assume that Mount Sinai is Gebel Helal near Kadesh-Barnea); and (3) a southeastern route leading from the wilderness east of modern Ismailia to the southern extremities of the Sinai Peninsula. Israel took this southern route and headed for the "desert road toward the Red Sea" (13:18), presumably near the body of water by the same name that the Egyptians also called "The Sea of Reeds" (see comment on 13:18).

It is impossible to locate "Etham" exactly (13:20), but the region known as Atuma (a desert that begins at Lake Timsah and extends west and south of it, where the Egyptians knew that Asiatics grazed their flocks) is most likely (see Num 33:6–8). It would appear that Israel turned back to the west and then turned south to go around the bulging upper part of the large Bitter Lake only to go in a southeasterly direction between the mountain range of Jebel Jenefeh and the large and small Bitter Lakes.

The exact place Israel crossed the Red Sea is unknown, but it seems best to place this famous crossing somewhere between the southern end of the Bitter Lakes and the Gulf of Suez or even in the northern tip of the Gulf of Suez itself,[3] rather than across Lake Ballah (Kitchen, ZPEB, 2:430); the southern end of Lake Menzaleh (Hyatt, p. 159); or even the extreme suggestion of some that it was on the sandy strip of land that separates Lake Sirbonis (modern Lake Bardawil) from the Mediterranean Sea.

The wilderness itinerary begun in Exodus 12:37—and continued in 13:20; 14:2; and 15:22—resumes after the crossing on the shores of the Red Sea on the western side of the Sinai Peninsula (in 15:22–27; see comments and/or Notes on these passages). Thus we conclude that the southern route, not the northern or middle route, was chosen by Israel and ordered by God.

6. Theology

Exodus contains some of the richest, foundational theology of all the books in the OT. Preeminently, it lays the foundations for a theology of God's revelation of his person, his redemption, his law, and his worship. It also initiates the great institution of the priesthood and the role of the prophet and formalizes the covenant relationship between God and his people.

Detailed disclosures of the nature of God are found in Exodus 3, 6, 33, and 34. These texts focus on the fact and significance of his presence (as given by his name Yahweh and his glory). But his attributes of justice, truthfulness, mercy, faithfulness, and holiness are also highlighted. Thus to know God's "name" is to know him and his character (3:13–15; 6:3).

God is also the Lord of history, for there is no one like him, "majestic in holiness, awesome in glory, working wonders" (15:11). Thus neither the affliction of Israel nor the plagues in Egypt were outside his control. Pharaoh, the Egyptians, and all Israel would see the power of God.

---

[2] M. Havan, "The Exodus," IBD, sup. vol. (Nashville: Abingdon, 1976), p. 305, however, identifies Pithom with Tell el-Maskhuta and Rameses with the site nine miles west of that tell, viz., Tell er-Retabeh.

[3] Finegan, p. 85, or C. Bourdon, "La Route d l'Exode," *Revue Biblique* 41 (1932): 378–90.

Most reassuring of all is the fact that God remembers (2:24). What he had promised some four hundred to six hundred years earlier to Abraham, Isaac, and Jacob, he began to bring to fruition as Israel left Egypt for the Land of Promise. The covenant at Sinai was but another step in God's fulfillment of his promise to the patriarchs (3:15–17; 6:2–8; 19:3–6).

The theology of deliverance and salvation is likewise a strong emphasis of the book. The verb to "redeem" (*gā'al*, one who acts the part of a kinsman-redeemer) is used in 6:6 and 15:13. But the heart of redemption theology is best seen in the Passover narrative in chapter 12 along with the sealing of the covenant in chapter 24. The apostle Paul saw the death of the Passover lamb fulfilled in Christ (1 Cor 5:7). Indeed, John the Baptist called Jesus the "Lamb of God, who takes away the sin of the world" (John 1:29), just as the Last Supper was a celebration of the Passover meal. The Passover lamb, whose blood was applied to the doors of Israelite homes, (1) averted harm to that house, (2) provided a substitute that allowed the firstborn to live (12:13), and (3) propitiated the wrath of God so that the angel of death passed over the protected homes.

Exodus also tells us how we should live. The foundation of biblical ethics and morality is laid out for us first in the gracious character of God as revealed in the Exodus and then in the Ten Commandments and the ordinances of the Book of the Covenant. From the illustrations of the cases in chapters 21–23, we learn how to practically apply the principles of the ten words that in turn have their grounding in the permanency of the character of God.

The book concludes with an elaborate discussion on the theology of worship. The tabernacle was very costly in time, effort, and monetary value; yet in its significance and function it pointed to the chief end of man: to glorify God and to enjoy him forever. Above every other consideration was the fact that the omnipotent, unchanging, and transcendent God of all the universe had, by means of the tabernacle, graciously come to "dwell" or "tabernacle" with his people, thereby revealing his immanence as well. Therefore, not only was God mighty in their midst, but he was the God who had been, was, and would be present in their midst as well.

7. Bibliography

A. *Commentaries*

Bush, George. *Notes on Exodus.* 2 vols. Reprint. Minneapolis: James and Klock, 1976.

Cassuto, Umberto. *A Commentary on the Book of Exodus.* Translated by Israel Abrahams. Jerusalem: Magnes, 1967.

Childs, Brevard S. *The Book of Exodus: A Critical, Theological Commentary.* Philadelphia: Westminster, 1974.

Clements, Ronald E. *The Cambridge Bible Commentary: Exodus.* Cambridge: At the University Press, 1972.

Cole, R.A. *Exodus: An Introduction and Commentary.* Tyndale Old Testament Commentaries. Downers Grove, Ill.: Inter-Varsity, 1973.

Cook, F.C. *The Holy Bible: An Explanatory and Critical Commentary: Genesis-Exodus.* Vol. 1, Part 1. New York: Charles Scribner's Sons, 1899.

Davies, G. Henton. *Exodus.* Torch Bible Commentaries. London: SCM, 1967.

Driver, S.R. *The Book of Exodus.* Cambridge Bible for Schools and Colleges. Cambridge: University Press, 1911.

Durham, John I. *Exodus.* Word Biblical Commentary. Waco: Word, 1987.
Ellison, H.L. *Exodus.* The Daily Study Bible. Philadelphia: Westminster, 1982.
Gispen, W.H. *Exodus.* Bible Student's Commentary. Translated by E. van der Maas. Grand Rapids: Zondervan, 1982.
Greenberg, Moshe. *Understanding Exodus.* New York: Behrman House, 1969.
Hyatt, J. Philip. *Commentary on Exodus.* New Century Bible. Greenwood, S.C.: Attic, 1971.
Keil, C.F., and Delitzsch, Franz. *The Pentateuch.* KD. Translated by James Martin. Vols. 1 and 2. Reprint. Grand Rapids: Eerdmans, 1956.
Knight, George A.F. *Theology as Narration: A Commentary on the Book of Exodus.* Grand Rapids: Eerdmans, 1976.
Lange, John Peter. *Exodus.* Translated by Charles M. Mead. Reprint. Grand Rapids: Zondervan, 1960.
Lowenstamm, S.E. *The Tradition of Exodus in Its Development.* 2d edition. Jerusalem: Magnes, 1972.
McNeile, A.H. *The Book of Exodus.* Westminster Commentaries. 3d edition. London: Methuen and Co., 1931.
Meyer, Lester. *The Message of Exodus: A Theological Commentary.* Minneapolis: Augsburg, 1983.
Napier, B. Davie. *The Book of Exodus.* The Layman's Bible Commentary. Richmond: John Knox, 1963.
Noth, Martin. *Exodus: A Commentary.* Translated by J.S. Bowden. Philadelphia: Westminster, 1962.
Plastaras, J. *The God of Exodus.* Milwaukee: Bruce, 1966.
Ramm, B. *His Way Out: A Fresh Look at Exodus.* Glendale, Calif.: Regal, 1974.
Rawlinson, George. *Exodus.* The Pulpit Commentary. New York: Funk and Wagnalls, 1913.
Rylaarsdam, J. Coert. "Introduction and Exegesis to the Book of Exodus." *Interpreter's Bible.* Edited by G.A. Buttrick. Vol. 1. Nashville: Abingdon, 1952.
Youngblood, Ronald F. *Exodus.* Chicago: Moody, 1983.

B. Special Studies: Monographs

Beegle, Dewey. *Moses, the Servant of Yahweh.* Grand Rapids: Eerdmans, 1972.
Bimson, John J. *Redating the Exodus and Conquest.* Sheffield: University of Sheffield Press, 1978.
Boecker, Hans J. *Law and the Administration of Justice in the Old Testament and the Ancient Near East.* Minneapolis: Augsburg, 1980.
Buber, Martin. *Moses: The Revelation and the Covenant.* Reprint. New York: Harper and Row, 1958.
Coats, G.W. *Rebellion in the Wilderness: The Murmuring Motif in the Wilderness Traditions of the Old Testament.* Nashville: Abingdon, 1968.
Davidson, Joy. *Smoke on the Mountain: An Interpretation of the Ten Commandments in Terms of Today.* London: Hodder and Stoughton, 1966.
Davis, John J. *Moses and the Gods of Egypt: A Study in the Book of Exodus.* Grand Rapids: Baker, 1971.
Finegan, Jack. *Let My People Go: A Journey Through Exodus.* New York: Harper and Row, 1963.
Gilmer, Harry W. *The If-You Form of Israelite Law.* Missoula, Mont.: Scholars, 1975.
Hebert, Gabriel. *When Israel Came Out of Egypt.* Naperville, Ill.: SCM, 1961.
Jordan, James B. *The Law of the Covenant: An Exposition of Exodus 21–23.* Tyler, Tex.: Institute for Christian Economics, 1984.
Kevan, Ernest F. *Keep His Commandments: The Place of Law in the Christian Life.* London: Tyndale, 1964.
Kiene, Paul F. *The Tabernacle of God in the Wilderness of Sinai.* Translated by John S. Crandall. Grand Rapids: Zondervan, 1977.
McMillen, S.I. *None of These Diseases.* Old Tappan, N.J.: Revell, 1963.

Montet, Pierre. *Egypt and the Bible.* Translated by Leslie R. Keylock. Philadelphia: Fortress, 1968.
Morgan, G. Campbell. *The Ten Commandments.* Grand Rapids: Baker, 1974.
Motyer, J.A. *The Revelation of the Divine Name.* London: Tyndale, 1959.
Patrick, Dale. *Old Testament Law.* Atlanta: John Knox, 1985.
Paul, S.M. *Studies in the Book of the Covenant in the Light of Cuneiform and Biblical Law.* Leiden: Brill, 1970.
Pfeiffer, Charles F. *Egypt and the Exodus.* Grand Rapids: Baker, 1964.
Ridout, S. *Lectures on the Tabernacle.* New York: Loizeaux, 1952.
Robertson, C.C. *On the Track of the Exodus.* London: Gale and Polden, 1936.
Sanderson, Judith E. *An Exodus Scroll from Qumran: 4QpaleoExod^M and the Samaritan Tradition.* Decatur, Ga.: Scholars, 1986.
Segal, J.B. *The Hebrew Passover.* New York: Oxford University Press, 1963.
Slemming, C.W. *Made According to Pattern.* Fort Washington, Pa.: Christian Literature Crusade, 1971.
Soltau, Henry W. *The Tabernacle: The Priesthood and Offerings.* Grand Rapids: Kregel, n.d.
Sonsino, Rifat. *Motive Clauses in Hebrew Law.* Chico, Calif.: Scholars, 1980.
Stamm, Johann Jakob, and Andrew, Maurice Edward. *The Ten Commandments in Recent Research.* Naperville, Ill.: Allenson, 1967.

C. Special Studies: Articles

Alt, A. "The Origins of Israelite Law," in *Essays in Old Testament History and Religion.* Translated by R.A. Wilson. Oxford: Basil Blackwell, 1966, pp. 81–121.
Bimson, John J., and Livingston, David . "Redating the Exodus," *Biblical Archaeology Review* 13 (1987): 40–53.
Bodenheimer, L.S. "The Manna of Sinai," *Biblical Archaeologist* 10 (1947): 1–6.
Brekelmans, C. "Exodus XVIII and the Origins of Yahwism in Israel," *Old Testament Studies* 10 (1954): 215–54.
Craigie, Peter C. "Yahweh Is a Man of Wars," *Scottish Journal of Theology* 22 (1969): 183–88.
Cross, Frank M. "The Tabernacle," *Biblical Archaeologist* 10 (1947): 45–68.
———. "Yahweh and the God of the Fathers," *Harvard Theological Review* 55 (1962): 225–59.
Davies, G.I. "The Wilderness Itineraries: A Comparative Study," *Tyndale Bulletin* 25 (1974): 46–81.
Dyer, Charles H. "The Date of the Exodus Reexamined," *Bibliotheca Sacra* 140 (1983): 225–42.
Feinberg, Charles. "Tabernacle," in *The Zondervan Pictorial Encyclopedia of the Bible.* Edited by M.C. Tenney. 5 volumes. Grand Rapids: Zondervan, 1975, 5:572–83.
Ferris, Paul W. "Manna Narrative of Exodus 16:1–10," *Journal of Evangelical Theological Society* 18 (1975): 191–99.
Gardiner, A.H. "The Geography of the Exodus: An Answer," *Journal of Egyptian Archaeology* 10 (1924): 87–96.
———. "Tanis and Pi-Ramesse: A Retraction," *Journal of Egyptian Archaeology* 19 (1933): 122–28.
Gordon, Cyrus H. "He Is Who He Is," in *Joshua Finkel Festschrift.* New York: Yeshiva University, 1974, pp. 253–71.
Gronigen, G. Van. "That Final Question," in *The Law and the Prophets.* Edited by John H. Skilton. Nutley, N.J.: Presbyterian and Reformed, 1974, pp. 253–71.
Kitchen, K.A. "From the Brickfields of Egypt," *Tyndale Bulletin* (1976): 137–47.
Kline, M. "Lex Talionis and the Human Fetus," *Journal of Evangelical Theological Society* 20 (1977): 193–201.
Kuyper, L.J. "Hardness of Heart According to Biblical Perspective," *Scottish Journal of Theology* 27 (1974): 459–74.
Mendenhall, G. "Covenant Forms in Israelite Tradition," *Biblical Archaeologist* 17 (1954): 50–76.

Naville, E. "The Geography of the Exodus," *Journal of Egyptian Archaeology* 10 (1924): 18–39.
Oswalt, John. "The Golden Calves and the Egyptian Concept of Deity," *Evangelical Quarterly* 45 (1973): 13–20.
Perevolotsky, Aviram, and Finkelstein, Israel . "The Southern Sinai Exodus Route in Ecological Perspective," *Biblical Archaeology Review* 11 (1985): 27–41.
Ramm, B. "The Theology of the Book of Exodus: A Reflection on Exodus 12:12," Southwestern Journal of Theology 20 (1978): 59–68.
Uphill, E.P. "Pithom and Raamses: Their Location and Significance," *Journal of Near Eastern Studies* 27 (1968): 291–316.
———. "Pithom and Raamses: Their Location and Significance," *Journal of Near Eastern Studies* 28 (1969): 15–39.
Vriezen, T.C. "*'ehje 'ašer 'ehje," in The Festschrift for A. Bertholet.* Tübingen: J.C.B. Mohr, 1950, pp. 498–512.
———. "The Exegesis of Exodus XXIV, 9–11," *Old Testament Studies* 17 (1972): 100–133.
Wenham, Gordon J. "Legal Forms in the Book of the Covenant," *Tyndale Bulletin* 22 (1971): 95–102.
Woudstra, M.H. "The Tabernacle in Biblical-Theological Perspective," in *New Perspectives on the Old Testament.* Edited by J. Barton Payne. Waco: Word, 1970, pp. 83–103.
Zimmerli, W. "Ich bin Jahwe," *Geschichte und Altes Testament.* Tübingen: J.C.B. Mohr, 1953, pp. 179–209.

8. Outline

I. Divine Redemption (1:1–18:27)
  A. Fulfilled Multiplication and Forced Eradication (1:1–22)
    1. The promised increase (1:1–7)
    2. The first pogrom (1:8–14)
    3. The second pogrom (1:15–22)
  B. Preparations for Deliverance (2:1–4:26)
    1. Preparing a leader (2:1–10)
    2. Extending the time of preparation (2:11–22)
    3. Preparing a people for deliverance (2:23–25)
    4. Calling a deliverer (3:1–10)
    5. Answering inadequate objections (3:11–4:17)
      a. Who am I to go to Pharaoh? (3:11–12)
      b. What if they ask what your name is? (3:13–22)
      c. What if they will not believe me? (4:1–9)
      d. What about my slow tongue? (4:10–12)
      e. Why can you not find someone else? (4:13–17)
    6. Preparing a leader's family (4:18–26)
  C. First Steps in Leadership (4:27–7:5)
    1. Reinforced by a brother (4:27–31)
    2. Rebuffed by the enemy (5:1–14)
    3. Rebuffed by the enslaved (5:15–21)
    4. Revisited by old objections (5:22–23)
    5. Reinforced by the Name of God (6:1–8)
    6. Reminders of Moses' lowly origins (6:9–7:5)
  D. Judgment and Salvation Through the Plagues (7:6–11:10)
    1. Presenting the signs of divine authority (7:6–13)
    2. First plague: water turned to blood (7:14–24)
    3. Second plague: frogs (7:25–8:15)
    4. Third plague: gnats (8:16–19)
    5. Fourth plague: flies (8:20–32)
    6. Fifth plague: cattle murrain (9:1–7)
    7. Sixth plague: boils (9:8–12)
    8. Seventh plague: hail (9:13–35)
    9. Eighth plague: locusts (10:1–20)
    10. Ninth plague: darkness (10:21–29)
    11. Tenth plague: death of the firstborn (11:1–10)
  E. The Passover (12:1–28)
    1. Preparations for the Passover (12:1–13)
    2. Preparations for the Unleavened Bread (12:14–20)
    3. Celebration of the Passover (12:21–28)
  F. The Exodus From Egypt (12:29–51)
    1. Death at midnight (12:29–32)
    2. Preparations for the Exodus (12:33–36)
    3. The Exodus and the mixed multitude (12:37–51)
  G. The Consecration of the Firstborn (13:1–16)
  H. Journey to the Red Sea (13:17–15:21)
    1. Into the wilderness (13:17–22)
    2. At the Red Sea (14:1–14)

3. Across the Red Sea (14:15–31)
4. Song at the sea (15:1–21)

I. Journey to Sinai (15:22–18:27)
1. The waters of Marah (15:22–27)
2. The manna and the quail (16:1–36)
3. The waters of Meribah (17:1–7)
4. The war with Amalek (17:8–16)
5. The wisdom of Jethro (18:1–27)

II. Divine Morality (19:1–24:18)
A. The Eagles' Wings Speech (19:1–8)
B. The Advent of God on Sinai (19:9–25)
C. The Decalogue (20:1–17)
D. The Reaction of the People to the Theophany (20:18–21)
E. The Book of the Covenant (20:22–23:33)
1. The prologue (20:22–26)
2. Laws on slaves (21:1–11)
3. Laws on homicide (21:12–17)
4. Laws on bodily injuries (21:18–32)
5. Laws on property damages (21:33–22:15)
6. Laws on society (22:16–31)
7. Laws on justice and neighborliness (23:1–9)
8. Laws on sacred seasons (23:10–19)
9. Epilogue (23:20–33)
F. Ratification of the Covenant (24:1–18)

III. Divine Worship (25:1–40:38)
A. The Tabernacle (25:1–31:18)
1. Collection of materials (25:1–9)
2. Ark and mercy seat (25:10–22)
3. Table of the bread of the Presence (25:23–30)
4. Golden lampstand (25:31–40)
5. Curtains, framework, veil, and screen (26:1–37)
a. The tabernacle's curtains (26:1–14)
b. The tabernacle's framework (26:15–30)
c. The tabernacle's veil (26:31–35)
d. The tabernacle's screen (26:36–37)
6. Altar of burnt offering (27:1–8)
7. Court of the tabernacle (27:9–19)
8. Priesthood (27:20–28:5)
9. Garments of the priests (28:6–43)
10. Ordination of the priests (29:1–46)
11. Altar of incense (30:1–10)
a. Building instructions (30:1–6)
b. Operating instructions (30:7–10)
12. Census tax (30:11–16)
13. Bronze basin, anointing oil, and incense (30:17–38)
14. Appointment of craftsmen (31:1–11)
15. Sabbath rest (31:12–17)
16. Conclusion to the instructions (31:18)

B. False Worship of the Golden Calf (32:1–34:35)
   1. Golden calf (32:1–29)
   2. Mediation of Moses (32:30–35)
   3. Threatened separation and Moses' prayer (33:1–23)
   4. Renewal of the covenant (34:1–35)

C. Building the Tabernacle (35:1–40:38)
   1. Summons to build (35:1–19)
   2. Voluntary gifts (35:20–29)
   3. Bezalel and his artisans (35:30–36:7)
   4. Progress of the work and Moses' blessing (36:8–39:43)
   5. Erection of the tabernacle (40:1–33)
   6. Dedication of the tabernacle (40:34–38)

9. Maps and Charts

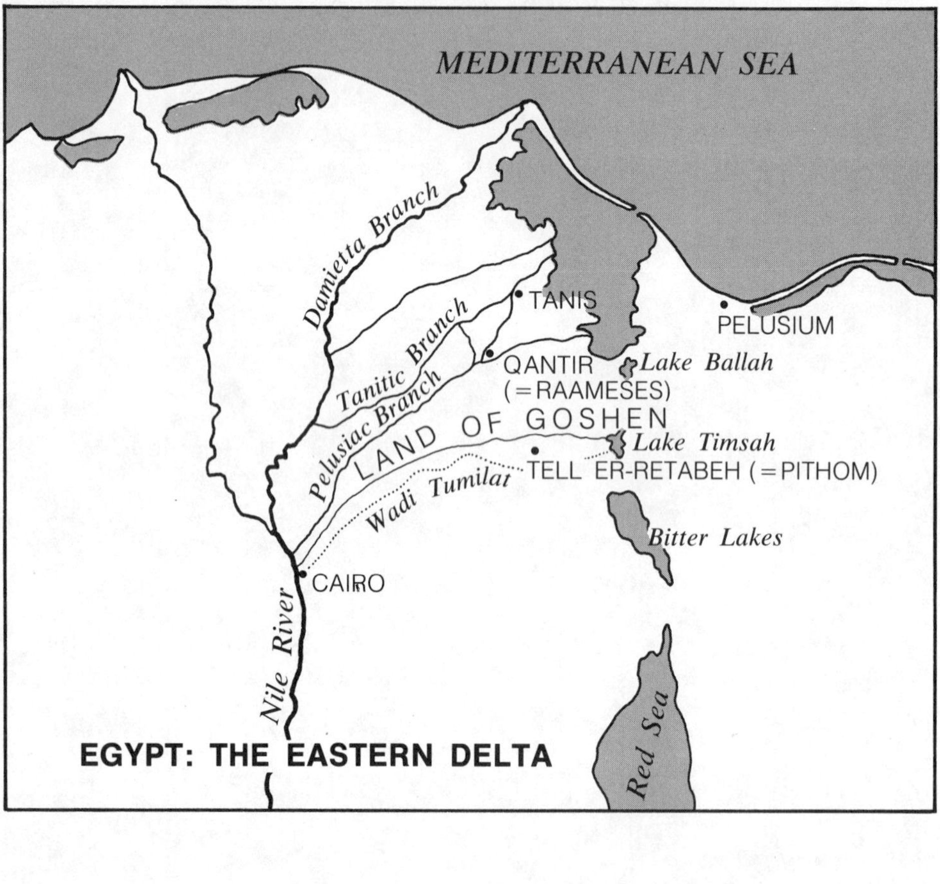

Synoptic Chart on the Tabernacle

Order: The Command to Build		*Order: The Execution of the Plans*
I. The Contribution to the Tabernacle	Exod 25:1–9	II. Exod 35:4–29
II. The Ark of the Covenant	Exod 25:10–22	VII. Exod 37:1–9
III. The Table of the Bread of Presence	Exod 25:23–30	VIII. Exod 37:10–16
IV. The Lampstand	Exod 25:31–40	IX. Exod 37:17–24
V. The Tabernacle and the Tent	Exod 26:1–14	IV. Exod 36:8–38
A. The Linen Curtains	Exod 26:1–6	A. Exod 36:8–13
B. The Goats' Hair Curtains	Exod 26:7–13	B. Exod 36:14–18
C. The Ram Skin Coverings	Exod 26:14	C. Exod 36:19
D. (The Silver Sockets)	(Exod 30:11–16)	D. (Exod 38:25–28)
VI. The Posts/Frames	Exod 26:15–30	V. Exod 36:20–34
VII. The [Inner] Curtain	Exod 26:31–37	VI. Exod 36:35–38
VIII. The Altar of Burnt Offering	Exod 27:1–8	XI. Exod 38:1–7
IX. The Courtyard of the Tabernacle	Exod 27:9–19	XIII. Exod 38:9–20
X. The Priesthood	Exod 27:20–28:5	
XI. The Priestly Garments	Exod 28:6–43	XVI. Exod 39:2–31
XII. The Consecration of the Priests	Exod 29:1–46	
XIII. The Altar of Incense	Exod 30:1–10, 34–38	X. Exod 37:25–29
XIV. The Atonement Money	Exod 30:11–16	XV. Exod 38:25–28
XV. The Bronze Basin (Laver)	Exod 30:17–21	XII. Exod 38:8
XVI. The Oil of Atonement	Exod 30:22–33	
XVII. The Incense of Spices	Exod 30:34–38	
XVIII. The Appointment of Workers	Exod 31:1–11	III. Exod 35:30–36:7
XIX. The Rest From Work on the Sabbath	Exod 31:12–17	I. Exod 35:1–3
XX. The Command to Erect the Tabernacle		XVII. Exod 40:1–16
XXI. The Erection of the Tabernacle		XVIII. Exod 40:17–33
XXII. Inventory of Materials Used		XIV. Exod 38:21–39:1

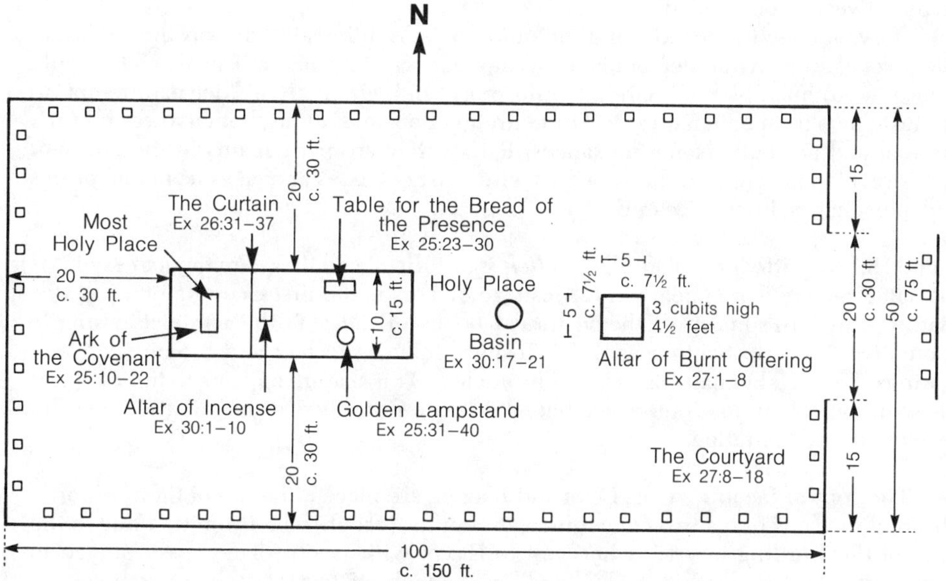

Text and Exposition

I. Divine Redemption (1:1–18:27)

A. *Fulfilled Multiplication and Forced Eradication (1:1–22)*

1. *The promised increase*

1:1–7

[1]These are the names of the sons of Israel who went to Egypt with Jacob, each with his family: [2]Reuben, Simeon, Levi and Judah; [3]Issachar, Zebulun and Benjamin; [4]Dan and Naphtali; Gad and Asher. [5]The descendants of Jacob numbered seventy in all; Joseph was already in Egypt.

[6]Now Joseph and all his brothers and all that generation died, [7]but the Israelites were fruitful and multiplied greatly and became exceedingly numerous, so that the land was filled with them.

The three prominent subjects of Exodus are (1) God's plan for deliverance, (2) God's guidance for morality, and (3) God's order for worship. As the writer begins his work, however, another prominent fact that governs the whole theology of Exodus is immediately set forth: vv.1–7 are a virtual commentary on the ancient promise made to Abraham, Isaac, and Jacob that their seed would be as numerous as the stars of heaven and the sands of the sea (e.g., Gen 15:5; 22:17). In fact, as if to underscore this connection with Genesis, vv.1–4 virtually repeat Genesis 35:22–26; v.5 is a reiteration of Genesis 46:27; v.6 of Genesis 50:26; and v.7 of Genesis 1:28. However, these repetitions were not without some new features. The reference to "families" or "households" in v.1 was new, as was the fact that Joseph was treated separately from his brothers in v.5; so also was the notice in v.6 that "all that generation" along with Jacob's twelve sons had died.

History, at once the scandal and the uniqueness of biblical faith, was the sphere of God's revelation. While heathenism and modern scientific naturalism affirm that only nature is ultimately real, Greek philosophy and Oriental mysticism attempt to extricate man from both nature and time. In this Book of Exodus, both nature and time are real and not bothersome nuisances. Rather they are participants in the fabric of God's revelation. Thus our book begins with a list of names and takes us to real places and personages in the Near East.

1 The Hebrew title for "Exodus" (*wᵉʾēlleh šᵉmôṯ*, lit., "And these are the names of") is the same phrase that appears in Genesis 46:8. This is the first example of a practice that appeared in almost all the historical books of the OT: the use of the simple copulative "and" to begin a book (cf. Joshua, Judges, Ruth, 1 and 2 Samuel, 1 and 2 Kings, Ezra, Nehemiah, Esther, 2 Chronicles). This feature appears to indicate that the writer was conscious of the fact that he was contributing to an ongoing sequence of revelation and narration.

2–4 The sons of Jacob's wives, Leah and Rachel, are placed in order of their seniority ahead of the sons of his two concubines, except for Joseph, who is omitted due to the form of the wording in v.1: "who went to Egypt with Jacob." They are arranged in three series that are marked off by "and" in the Hebrew text: (1) the first four sons of Leah (Gen 29:31–35) are linked together in v.2; (2) the last two sons of Leah (Gen

30:18–20), after she had temporarily ceased bearing children, along with Benjamin, the second son of Rachel (Gen 35:18), are separated by an "and" in v.3; and (3) the sons of the handmaid Bilhah and the sons of the handmaid Zilpah (Gen 30:6–13) are joined by "and" in v.4.

5 It is unnecessary to understand the number "seventy" as a symbol of perfection (so Cassuto, in loc.) or with the misunderstood phrase in Deuteronomy 32:8, that the total number of the nations should be "according to the number of the sons of Israel"; viz., the seventy in the table of nations of Genesis 10 (so Knight, in loc.). Instead the family list in Genesis 46 gives this tally: the six men of Leah had twenty-five sons and two grandsons totaling thirty-three; the two sons of Rachel had twelve sons totaling fourteen; Bilhah's two sons had five sons contributing seven to the sum, and Zilpah's two sons had eleven sons, one daughter (apparently counted here), and two grandsons, making sixteen; therefore, thirty-three plus fourteen plus seven plus sixteen equals seventy. Genesis 46:26–27 starts with the figure of sixty-six (apparently dropping out Er and Onan, since they died in Canaan, as well as deleting Joseph and his two sons, since they were already in Egypt, but adding Dinah, feeling she could not be deleted). To this total of sixty-six, it added Joseph, his two sons, and Jacob, himself for a total of seventy. The LXX, on the other hand, adds the names of Joseph's three grandsons and two great-grandsons in Genesis 46:20. Therefore, the total that version gives for Genesis 46:27 is seventy-five. Interestingly enough the LXX version for Exodus 1:5, Acts 7:14, and one Hebrew MS from Qumran (Frank M. Cross, Jr., *The Ancient Library of Qumran and Modern Biblical Studies* [Garden City, N.Y.: Doubleday, 1958; rev. ed., Anchor Books, 1961], p. 137) all have seventy-five as a total here as well. Regardless of which figure is used (seventy or seventy-five), the number is actual, not figurative. (See Notes on Gen 46:8–27, this vol.)

6–7 With the vocabulary of God's promised blessing of multiplication and increase as given to Adam (Gen 1:28), Noah (Gen 8:17; 9:1, 7), Abraham (Gen 17:2–6; 22:17), Isaac (Gen 26:4), and Jacob (Gen 28:3, 14; 35:11; 48:4), Moses recorded that God had been fulfilling his plan during the 430 years Israel was in Egypt.

Notes

---

1 See A. van Selms, "How Do Books of the Bible Commence?" *Biblical Essays: Proceedings of the Ninth Meetings Held in July 1966*, ed. by A.H. van Zyl (Stellenbosch: University of Stellenbosch, 1966), pp. 132–41.

5 כָּל־נֶפֶשׁ יֹצְאֵי יֶרֶךְ־יַעֲקֹב (*kol-nep̱eš yōṣeʾê yereḵ-yaʿaqōḇ*) is literally, "all the soul [collective singular] of the ones going out of the thigh of Jacob"—the usual expression for physical generation. The solidarity of the group is clear from the collective singular. The word "soul" here means "person."

7 וַיִּשְׁרְצוּ (*wayyišreṣû*, "multiplied," lit., "bred swiftly") is usually used only of the prolific marine life (Gen 1:20) and insects (Gen 7:21).

---

2. *The first pogrom*

1:8–14

[8]Then a new king, who did not know about Joseph, came to power in Egypt. [9]"Look," he said to his people, "the Israelites have become much too numerous for us. [10]Come, we must deal shrewdly with them or they will become even more numerous and, if war breaks out, will join our enemies, fight against us and leave the country."

[11]So they put slave masters over them to oppress them with forced labor, and they built Pithom and Rameses as store cities for Pharaoh. [12]But the more they were oppressed, the more they multiplied and spread; so the Egyptians came to dread the Israelites [13]and worked them ruthlessly. [14]They made their lives bitter with hard labor in brick and mortar and with all kinds of work in the fields; in all their hard labor the Egyptians used them ruthlessly.

8 The "new king" who was ignorant of Joseph's contribution to Egypt (rather than "had no personal acquaintance" with him) has been variously identified: the founder of the Hyksos dynasties (so Rea); the founder of the Eighteenth Dynasty who expelled the Hyksos, Amosis I (so Cook); the founder of the Nineteenth Dynasty, Rameses I, or even his son Seti I (so Rawlinson); or the first strong ruler of the Nineteenth Dynasty, Rameses II (so Rylaarsdam). The most logical choice favors the Hyksos king (see the Notes).

9–10 Israel was called "a people" (*'am*) for the first time in v.9. The situation called for an extremely delicate balance: Pharaoh needed to maintain the Israelite presence as an economic asset without thereby jeopardizing Egypt's national security.

11 The term "slave masters" is common to both Hebrew and Egyptian. The same official Egyptian name, *ser*, appears on the famous wall painting from the Thebean tomb of Rekhmire (see bibliography in Kitchen, "Brickfields of Egypt," p. 140, n. 17), the overseer of the brick-making slaves during the reign of Thutmose III. The painting shows such overseers armed with heavy whips. Their rank is denoted by the long staff held in their hands and by the Egyptian hieroglyphic determinative of the head and neck of a giraffe. This Egyptian title is found as early as the Sixth Dynasty under Pepi (Cook, p. 485). The two storehouse cities Israel built were for the storage of provisions and perhaps armaments (cf. 1 Kings 9:19; 2 Chron 8:4–5; 11:5, 11–12; 32:28). The location of one of those cities, Pithom (*Per-itm*, "House of [the god] Atum") in all probability may be equated with Tell er-Retabeh ("Broomhill"), which some equate with Heliopolis (cf. ZPEB, 4:803–4; the LXX of Exod 1:11 adds to the two storehouse cities, "and On, which is Heliopolis"), or less likely with another site eighty and one-half miles east, Tell el-Maskhuta ("Mound of Idols"), both in Wadi Tumilat (see the map on p. 300).

The other site, Rameses, has most recently been located at or near Qantir ("Bridge") instead of the more popular but remoter Tanis/Zoan site. (See the "Date of the Exodus" in the Introduction for further detail and Uphill, 27:291–316; 28:15–39; and Bimson, pp. 35–48.)

12–14 Cassuto notes how lopsided and foolish Pharaoh's challenge was: the king of Egypt said, "Or they will become even more numerous" (*pen-yirbeh*, lit., "or he will increase," v.10); but the God of the universe said, "The more they multiplied" (*kēn* *yirbeh,* lit., "more he multiplied," v.12). The result was that a frightful dread came over the Egyptians, just as it took hold of Moab in Numbers 22:3. Ironically, in both cases the God-intended instrument for the salvation of both nations (cf. Gen 12:3) became instead, through the hardness of men's hearts, the source of crippling fear. Thus the Egyptians "made [Israel's] lives bitter" (v.14)—a fact that would later be commemorated in the Passover meal, which was eaten "with bitter herbs" (12:8). The emphasis of vv.8–14 falls on the "ruthlessness" of the work and servitude imposed on Israel.

Notes

---

8 Since Gen 15:13 had predicted that Abraham's descendants would "be enslaved and mistreated four hundred years," and since the verb וַיָּקָם (*wayyāqom*) + עַל מִצְרָיִם (*'al miṣrāyim*) means "to rise up against (Egypt)" (e.g., Deut 19:11; 28:7; Judg 20:5; 2 Sam 18:31; 2 Kings 16:7), John Rea ("The Time of the Oppression and the Exodus," BETS 3 [1960]: 59–61) identifies the "new king" as the Hyksos ruler who arose in Egypt as king around 1730 B.C. The Hyksos were foreign invaders who drove the Egyptians south and did not use Egyptian hieroglyphic writing on their scarabs. They, too, were Semites. This also yields almost three hundred years of bondage (cf. again the four hundred years of Gen 15:13), instead of a brief time under one or more of the pharaohs who came after the Hyksos were expelled around 1575 B.C. The suggestion is good and is consistent with biblical data. Jacob's arrival in Egypt with his family is probably not to be equated with the arrival of the Hyksos around 1720 or 1730 B.C. (as many scholars argue) but is better placed a century and a half earlier, around 1880 B.C., if the dates of Exod 12:40 and 1 Kings 6:1 are to be judged as reliable indicators.

11 שָׂרֵי מִסִּים (*śārê missîm*) means "slave masters" or "taskmasters." The *mas* was the technical name for forced labor, corvée (cf. 1 Kings 5:13–18; 9:15–22; 12:4). Later (3:7; 5:6, 10, 13–14) Moses used נֹגְשִׂים (*nōg^e^śîm,* "slave drivers," from the root "to drive, press").

פַּרְעֹה (*par'ōh,* "Pharaoh") is not a personal name but comes from the Egyptian *pr-'o,* which literally means "great house." During the third millennium B.C. it meant the "royal palace," but it shifted in usage to an epithet for the king and became a royal title during the Eighteenth Dynasty. The use of "Pharaoh" indicates either that we are picking up on the story toward the end of the Oppression, which takes us into the Eighteenth Dynasty, or that it was a modernization of the ancient designation of "king" to help those understand who lived in the days of the Eighteenth Dynasty.

13–14 בְּפָרֶךְ (*b^e^pārek,* "ruthlessly") is a rare word that comes from a root meaning "to crush," "to break in pieces." The word may still contain a smack of the free use of the slave master's stick as Israel made bricks and worked in the fields tending royal flocks (Gen 47:6), worked on farms (Deut 11:10), and, perhaps, as Josephus suggested (Antiq. II, 203 [ix.1]), dug canals.

---

3. *The second pogrom*

1:15–22

15 The king of Egypt said to the Hebrew midwives, whose names were Shiphrah and Puah, 16 "When you help the Hebrew women in childbirth and observe them on the delivery stool, if it is a boy, kill him; but if it is a girl, let her live." 17 The midwives, however, feared God and did not do what the king of Egypt had told them to do; they let the boys live. 18 Then

the king of Egypt summoned the midwives and asked them, "Why have you done this? Why have you let the boys live?"
19The midwives answered Pharaoh, "Hebrew women are not like Egyptian women; they are vigorous and give birth before the midwives arrive."
20So God was kind to the midwives and the people increased and became even more numerous. 21And because the midwives feared God, he gave them families of their own.
22Then Pharaoh gave this order to all his people: "Every boy that is born you must throw into the Nile, but let every girl live."

15 The two midwives probably were representatives of or superintendents over the whole profession. Cook tries to argue that midwives seldom would be used by most women, especially those of the poorer classes, and therefore two midwives would be enough. But Rawlinson (p. 16) counters, "What impression could the monarch expect to make on a population of from one to two millions of souls by engaging the services of two persons only?"

16 The delivery stools were literally "two stones" (dual form), just as the potter's wheel in Jeremiah 18:3 had two stones. Older commentators (Lange, Bush) contended that the same word in Exodus 7:19 meant a stone watering trough, so that the midwives were advised to kill the male babies when they were laid on these stone troughs to be washed after birth. This suggestion may be safely rejected in light of consistent Egyptian evidence for the upright position for delivery on a type of birthing stool.

17–21 The midwives "feared God" (v.17) more than they feared the king of Egypt. If they were not Hebrews but Egyptians in nationality, their God-fearing ways reveal the presence of God's common grace and the residue of earlier divine revelation that their ancestors shared but had gradually left in whole or part (cf. "the fear of God" in Abraham with the Philistines, Gen 20:11; the Amalekites in their savage attack, Deut 25:18; and the wicked in general, Mal 3:5). The midwives were "religious" in that they had respect for life. But if the midwives were Hebrew women (see Notes), the "fear of God" was then a response of faith, just as Abraham's act of offering Isaac had been a response to the command of God in Genesis 22:8, 12. Even though these women lied to Pharaoh (which the Bible, as is often the case, does not stop to specifically condemn at this point), they are praised for their outright refusal to take infant lives. Their reverence for life reflected a reverence for God. Thus God gave them *bāttîm* ("houses" or "families," v.21; cf. Ruth 4:11; 2 Sam 7:11–12; 1 Kings 2:24 [NIV, "dynasty"], 33 for the same figurative expression). The midwives may also have attempted to avoid answering Pharaoh's question directly, and therefore they commented on what was true without giving all the details (vv.18–19).

22 A single concluding and transitional verse summarizes chapter 1. Pharaoh needed to openly command by decree what had proved abortive by mere speeches. "All his people" were made agents of this crime in order to nullify the divine work of increased Hebrew children. This clearly parallels Herod's action at the birth of Christ. Thus the third pogrom began.

Notes

15 Whether the midwives were Egyptians or Hebrews depends on the vocalization of לַמְיַלְּדֹת הָעִבְרִיֹּת (*lamᵉyallᵉdōt hāʿiḇrîyōt*, lit., "to the midwives, the Hebrews"). But the Greek translation of Josephus (Antiq. II, 206 [ix.2]), the reference to Exod 1:15, which separates the Egyptian midwives from the Hebrew women, and possibly Exod 1:22, which has Pharaoh's command going to *all* his people (as opposed to a few midwives), argue for the reading "to the midwives of the Hebrews" (*limᵉyallᵉdōt [ʾet] hāʿiḇriyyōt*). The only weight favoring the present vowel pointing of the MT is the Semitic names of the midwives, but it must be remembered that the Egyptian maid Hagar (Arabic *hajara*, "forsake") had a Semitic name as well.

Shiphrah and Puah appear to be Semitic and not Egyptian names. There is a *Sp-ra* ("fair one" or "beauty") in an eighteenth-century B.C. list of Egyptian slaves, and the Ugaritic word *pgt* ("girl") may be linked with Puah, meaning "splendid one" or "splendor." See W.F. Albright, "Northwest-Semitic Names in a List of Egyptian Slaves From the Eighteenth Century," *JAOS* 74 (1954): 222–33, esp. p. 229.

Whether "Hebrew" is connected (even if only partially) with the *Ḫabiru* of the third and second millennium B.C. is still vigorously debated without conclusive results. See Moshe Greenberg, *The Ḫab/piru* (New Haven: American Oriental Series, 1955).

16 הָאָבְנָיִם (*hāʾāḇᵉnāyim*, "delivery stools"; cf. Egypt. *db.ty*) are pictorially represented in A. Erman, *Die Religion der Ägypter* (Berlin: 1934), p. 55, and a discussion of the custom appears in W. Spiegelberg, *Ägypten Randglossen* (1904), pp. 19–25. In the Egyptian story of the Westcar Papyrus, the goddess Isis places herself in front of the seated woman Red-djedet, who proceeds to deliver triplets, while another goddess stands behind her. Notice also the Egyptian hieroglyphic determinative of the verb *mss* ("to give birth") with a woman delivering in a sitting position.

17 On the "fear of God" in Gen 20:11; 22:8, 12; Exod 1:17, 21; 18:21, see Hans Walter Wolff's discussion in *Vitality of Old Testament Traditions*, edd. Walter Brueggemann and Hans W. Wolff (Atlanta: John Knox, 1976), pp. 70–75.

19 חָיוֹת (*ḥāyôt*, "vigorous" or "robust") may well be the Egyptian expression *ʿnḥ.t*, a collective used for the speed and ease with which sheep and goats deliver.

22 כָּל־הַבֵּן הַיִּלּוֹד (*kol-habbēn hayyillôd*, "every boy that is born") seems universal and might also apply to the Egyptians, but the context restricts the reference to Hebrew males.

הַיְאֹר (*hayʾōr*, lit., "the river"), which usually refers to "the Nile" (NIV) in its sixty-six occurrences in the OT, is an Egyptian common name for the Nile (*ʾiwr* or *ʾitrw*). The sacred name for the Nile in the Pyramid Texts was *ḥʿpi* (from *ḥp*, "to flow, run").

Morton Cogan ("A Technical Term for Exposure," JNES 27 [1968]: 133–35) argues that תַּשְׁלִיכֻהוּ (*tašlîḵuhû*, lit., "you must throw him") is better translated: "Every boy that is born you *shall expose* upon the Nile" (as does Brevard S. Childs, "The Birth of Moses," JBL 84 [1965]: 110–18). Cogan finds this sense of abandonment in Ps 71:9; Jer 38:6, 9; and Ezek 16:5 (parallel to *ʿāzaḇ*, "to forsake"). Moses' mother had something else in mind than Pharaoh did when she "placed" the child on the river. Presumably, for Pharaoh, such exposure removed the involvement with blood guilt that drowning would have left. But both senses of "throwing and abandoning" (= exposing) are well attested for this Hebrew verb. It is doubtful, however, that the Egyptian monarch worried about blood guiltiness after the pogroms of such enormity had already been attempted, even if they had been somewhat secretive in nature.

B. *Preparations for Deliverance (2:1–4:26)*

1. *Preparing a leader*

2:1–10

1 Now a man of the house of Levi married a Levite woman, 2 and she became pregnant and gave birth to a son. When she saw that he was a fine child, she hid him for three months. 3 But when she could hide him no longer, she got a papyrus basket for him and coated it with tar and pitch. Then she placed the child in it and put it among the reeds along the bank of the Nile. 4 His sister stood at a distance to see what would happen to him.

5 Then Pharaoh's daughter went down to the Nile to bathe, and her attendants were walking along the river bank. She saw the basket among the reeds and sent her slave girl to get it. 6 She opened it and saw the baby. He was crying, and she felt sorry for him. "This is one of the Hebrew babies," she said.

7 Then his sister asked Pharaoh's daughter, "Shall I go and get one of the Hebrew women to nurse the baby for you?"

8 "Yes, go," she answered. And the girl went and got the baby's mother. 9 Pharaoh's daughter said to her, "Take this baby and nurse him for me, and I will pay you." So the woman took the baby and nursed him.
10 When the child grew older, she took him to Pharaoh's daughter and he became her son. She named him Moses, saying, "I drew him out of the water."

1–4 An unnamed couple from the family of Levi became the parents of Moses. Since Levi's son Kohath was born before the family moved to Egypt (Gen 46:11) where they stayed for 430 years of bondage (Exod 12:40–41), and since Moses was eighty years old at the Exodus (7:7), he was born some 350 years after Kohath's time. Therefore, if Amram was Kohath's "son" (6:18) and Jochebed was Levi's "daughter" (Num 26:59), the meaning of these terms must be in the permissible Oriental sense of "ancestor" or lineal descendant; otherwise the narrative becomes increasingly awkward. For example, Moses' "grandfather" during Moses' lifetime fathered 8,600 males (not counting females) of which 2,750 were between the ages of thirty and fifty years old—all this up to the time of one year after the Exodus (cf. Num 3:19, 27–28)! It is best, then, in conformity with usual biblical reckoning and methods of recording genealogies (cf. William Henry Green, "Primaeval Chronology," *Classical Evangelical Essays in Old Testament Interpretation*, ed. Walter C. Kaiser, Jr. [Grand Rapids: Baker, 1973], pp. 13–28), to allow for several gaps in the four generations that spanned the almost 400 years from Joseph to Moses (cf. *NIV Study Bible*, note on 6:20; Gispen, p. 77, n. 10).

Neither was Moses the firstborn, as the story may seem to imply; for his brother Aaron was three years older and his sister Miriam was a young girl already. The fact that he was a "fine child" (v.2) may relate to his physical appearance (cf. Gen 39:6) as well as to the qualities of his heart (cf. Acts 7:20, *asteios tō theō*, "fair in the sight of God," NIV mg.; and Heb 11:23, *asteion*, "fair" or "proper"; NIV, "ordinary").

When Moses' mother could hide him no longer, she fashioned a basketlike boat from papyrus reeds and caulked it with pitch to make it watertight (v.3; see the Egyptian background for these terms in the Notes). Many scholars have been impressed by a similar story about another Semite, Sargon of Akkad from the second half of the third millennium B.C. He, too, was placed in a basket of rushes coated with pitch and cast on a river only to be found by Akki the gardener who rescued him and raised him as his son (Pritchard, ANET, p. 119). But to argue that the story was borrowed from Sargon and later attached to Moses to give him greater credibility in light of his later accomplishments (so in part, Beegle, p. 53) is to impose categories on the text rather than to discover them evidentially.

Clearly, Moses' mother had something else in mind beside child abandonment or exposure, for each individual action denoted love and hope for deliverance. The intricate detail is a "beautiful illustration of the connection which should always exist between the diligent use of means and a pious trust in providence. Instead of sitting down in sullen despair, or passive dependence on divine interposition to do all the work, everything is done which can be done by human agency" (Bush, *Exodus*, 1:25).

5 Egyptologists generally (e.g., Montet, p. 80) are skeptical about such women of rank as Pharaoh's daughter going down to the Nile to bathe; however, the text does not say the royal party went "into" (*b*e) the river (as did Naaman in 2 Kings 5:14), but they were "at" or "by" (*'al*) the river—presumably a branch of the Nile such as the Tanitic, where crocodiles are not usually found. Cook notices that currently crocodiles seldom are found below Elephantine (Aswan), but that in the ancient empire they were found as far north as Memphis. This indicates that the delta was relatively free of their invasions. But even if the women were not there to bathe in the river (a suggestion John Gardiner Wilkinson, *Manners and Customs of the Ancient Egyptians* [London: J. Murray, 1878], 3:389, defends as being most consistent with actual practice), Strabo, Pliny, and Aelian are quoted by Cook (p. 255) and Rawlinson (1:24) to the effect that the waters of the Nile were regarded as sacred, and such washing was more of an ablution with its health-giving and fructifying effects.

6–9 The princess discovered the reed basket and opened it to find a beautiful Hebrew baby boy, crying (v.6). Her heart was immediately moved with compassion. Miriam emerged from her hiding place and perhaps acted as if she were just casually passing by (v.7). If her words were not according to the careful plan and instruction of her mother, then her inward prompting must have come from God—not a moment too soon or too late, with not a word too many or too few! Not only was the child returned to his own mother, but she was paid wages for nursing the child she feared she might never see alive again (v.9). It was during those days that Moses' mother and father had their only opportunity to teach him all they knew about the God of his fathers.

10 "The child grew," and if the phrase is to be compared with the full expression in Genesis 21:8, then we may add "and was weaned" (see Notes). Moses was then brought to Pharaoh's daughter who adopted him and named him Moses. The name *Mōšeh* ("Moses") is generally considered to be Egyptian in origin, but the attached phrase points to a Hebrew origin: "I drew him out of the water." However, since the Egyptian princess is credited with naming him, and since there is an old perfective form of the Egyptian verb *ms* found in such names as Ptaḥmose, Thutmose, Ahmose, and Ramose meaning "(such and such a god) is born," it is now universally regarded as Egyptian. The Hebrew root "to draw out" (*māšah*) is used, no doubt, because of the assonance it shared with the Egyptian name. In the explanation that follows his name, it is difficult to determine whether the princess meant to give a *reason* for her choice of names, which involved a pun made for her Hebrew audience, or whether she meant to declare her right to assign Moses his name since she had pulled him out of the water (see Notes).

Notes

1 וַיֵּלֶךְ . . . וַיִּקַּח (*wayyēleḵ . . . wayyiqqaḥ*, "married," or lit., "he went . . . and he took") is best rendered by a pluperfect, "he had married," i.e., before Pharaoh's murderous edict. The verb "to go" marked the idea of entering, beginning, or undertaking some action, while the verb "to take" includes in such contexts the concept of getting married (cf. Hos 1:2). Such telescoping of the narrative for its own immediate purpose happens in 2 Sam 12:24–25, where Bathsheba's three children born prior to Solomon are not mentioned (cf. 2 Sam 5:14; 1 Chron 3:5).

3 The word for "papyrus basket," תֵּבַת גֹּמֶא (*tēḇaṯ gōmē'*), is used only here and for Noah's ark. *Tēḇeṯ* ("basket") may well reflect the Egyptian *tb*, and *gōmē'* probably represents the Egyptian *ḳmyt* ("gum," "resin") or *ḳm* ("papyrus").

The basket was coated with חֵמָר וּבַזָּפֶת (*ḥēmar ûḇazzāp̄eṯ*, "tar and pitch"). The Egyptian words (with metathesis) are *mrḥ* ("pitch") and *sft* ("tar"), the latter being very common in Egyptian but only occurring in the OT twice.

סוּף (*sûp̄*, "reeds") is most certainly derived from the Egyptian *ṯwf*. The Hebrew word for these tall grasses is the same that occurs in the name of the "Red" or "Reed" Sea. Notice that the *Yam Suph* may indicate as well the saltwater areas of the Gulf of Aqabah in 1 Kings 9:26 (NIV mg.). See the commentary on 13:17–18 for more details.

5 "Pharaoh's daughter" may have been the very famous Eighteenth-Dynasty princess and queen Hatshepsut. Eusebius records the tradition that her name was Merris (*Praeparatio Evangelica* 9.27). Josephus calls her Thermuthis (Antiq. II, 224 [ix.5]); but others claimed her name was Tharmuth (Jub 47:5), Bityah, or Bithiah (Talmud, B. Meg. 74, 91; B. Ber. 41; cf. 1 Chron 4:18, "Pharaoh's daughter Bithiah") who married Mered of Judah (cf. Midrash Rabbah on Exod 2:10).

The princess was escorted by נַעֲרֹתֶה (*na'ᵃrōṯeh*, "her attendants") who stayed on the riverbank to guard her privacy, no doubt, while אֲמָתָהּ (*'ᵃmāṯāh*, "her slave girl") accompanied her into the water. On the princess's orders, her personal slave girl went out to fetch the improvised floating cradle for the princess's inspection.

7 The Hebrew technical term for a "wet nurse" is אִשָּׁה מֵינֶקֶת (*'iššāh mêneqeṯ*, lit., "a woman, a nursing one"). The equivalent Akkadian term from the same Semitic verb, "to suckle," is *mušēniqtum*.

8 Miriam is called הָעַלְמָה (*hā'almāh*, "girl"). The term is the same as "the virgin" of Isa 7:14.

9 הֵילִיכִי (*hêlîḵî*, "take . . . for me") is pointed in the MT as if it were a verb beginning with an initial yod. Childs ("Birth," p. 113, n. 23) notices that Ehrlich rejects the Hiphil of *hlk* (which "is normally used of that which can move itself" [ibid.]) and accepts the Syrian and Rashi's reading of הא לך (*h' lḵ*, "Here, it's yours!"). Joüon (cited in Childs, "Birth," p. 113) suggests קחי לך (*qḥy lḵ*, "take for yourself"). Childs (ibid.) even wonders whether a technical adoption formula parallel to an Akkadian formula is not involved here: "take the child, he is your child" (*ta-ab-li zu-ḫu-ra-am lu-ú ma-ru-ki*).

10 There is no need to emend the verb וַיִּגְדַּל (*wayyigdal*, "when [the child] grew") to וַיִּגָּמֵל (*wayyiggāmal*, "when he was weaned"). Greenberg (*Exodus*, p. 42) correctly points out that *wayyigdal* alone can mean that an infant has reached boyhood or even manhood (cf. Gen 25:27; Judg 13:24; 2 Kings 4:18).

Moses should have been called מָשׁוּי (*māšûy*), pronounced *mashuey* (passive participle, "drawn out [of the water]"), if his name were to fully fit the explanation. Instead, he was called מֹשֶׁה (*mōšeh*, "One who draws out [of the water]"), almost as if it prophetically pointed to his future work (cf. Isa 63:11). The name is of Egyptian origin, *ms(w)*, a hypocoristicon from a theophoric name-type meaning "to bear, give birth to, beget." See J. Griffiths, "The Egyptian Derivation of the Name Moses," JNES 12 (1952): 225–31. The name Rameses, or Ramesses, uses the same verb *ms*, only it uses the active perfect participle (instead of the Egyptian old perfective form as in Moses), meaning "Re is he who has borne him."

2. *Extending the time of preparation*

2:11–22

11 One day, after Moses had grown up, he went out to where his own
people were and watched them at their hard labor. He saw an Egyptian
beating a Hebrew, one of his own people. 12 Glancing this way and that
and seeing no one, he killed the Egyptian and hid him in the sand. 13 The
next day he went out and saw two Hebrews fighting. He asked the one in
the wrong, "Why are you hitting your fellow Hebrew?"
14 The man said, "Who made you ruler and judge over us? Are you
thinking of killing me as you killed the Egyptian?" Then Moses was
afraid and thought, "What I did must have become known."
15 When Pharaoh heard of this, he tried to kill Moses, but Moses fled
from Pharaoh and went to live in Midian, where he sat down by a well.
16 Now a priest of Midian had seven daughters, and they came to draw
water and fill the troughs to water their father's flock. 17 Some
shepherds came along and drove them away, but Moses got up and
came to their rescue and watered their flock.
18 When the girls returned to Reuel their father, he asked them, "Why
have you returned so early today?"
19 They answered, "An Egyptian rescued us from the shepherds. He
even drew water for us and watered the flock."
20 "And where is he?" he asked his daughters. "Why did you leave
him? Invite him to have something to eat."
21 Moses agreed to stay with the man, who gave his daughter Zipporah
to Moses in marriage. 22 Zipporah gave birth to a son, and Moses named
him Gershom, saying, "I have become an alien in a foreign land."

11–12 Somewhere along the line Moses became aware of his Hebrew descent. When he was forty years old (Acts 7:23; cf. Heb 11:24–25; Jub 48:1 says he was forty-two), he struck and killed an Egyptian for beating a fellow Hebrew (v.11). It was his impetuosity that was wrong, not his sense of justice, nor his defense of the downtrodden. This cost him another forty years of education before he was ready for the task of delivering Israel. Calvin thought Moses acted by the Spirit of God, but Augustine was surely correct when he stressed that Moses had no legal authority to do what he did. His own conscience likewise agreed, for he first looked "this way and that" (v.12) and then buried the corpse in the sand. But the very impulse that led Moses to avenge wrongdoing apart from due process of law was developed to do the work of God when God finished seasoning him through the experiences of life!

13–14 The champion of the oppressed and underdogs went forth the next day—this time to settle a dispute between two of his own people (v.13). But Moses was thoroughly rebuffed and his motives impugned by the one who ought to have been practicing neighborly love (v.14). He thoroughly disarmed Moses by announcing that he knew what Moses had done on the previous day—he was a murderer, and now he was meddling in someone else's business! Moses surmised that it must have become public information, and he wisely decided to leave Egypt as quickly as possible.

15–19 Moses fled to the land of Midian (v.15), in the Arabian Peninsula along the eastern shore of the Gulf of Aqabah, only to be aroused by another scene of injustice. Hebrews 11:27 affirms that "by faith [Moses] left Egypt, not fearing the king's anger"; but that is no real discrepancy with our passage since the NT writer was referring to his final departure from Egypt at the time of the Exodus (so Bush, *Exodus,* 1:32).

Pharaoh's wrath was not so much to avenge the death of an Egyptian as it was to deal with his discovery that Moses was acting as a friend and possible champion of his sworn enemy, the oppressed Israelites. Moses' sole route of safety lay in fleeing Egypt; so he went to Midian.

The seven daughters of a Midianite priest named Reuel were being harassed and chased from watering their flocks at the troughs by unscrupulous shepherds, but Moses saw to that (vv.16–17). Since Moses still had his Egyptian clothing on, they judged him to be Egyptian in nationality (v.19).

20–22 The offer of hospitality (v.20) led to Moses' marriage to Reuel's daughter Zipporah (v.21). Subsequently she gave birth to a son (v.22). Moses betrayed his loneliness by naming his son Gershom; for he explained, "I have become an alien in a foreign land" (v.22; see Notes).

Notes

11 וַיַּרְא בְּסִבְלֹתָם (*wayyarᵉʾ bᵉsiḇlōṯām,* lit., "he watched [them] at their hard labor") is to "look on" with sympathy and real emotional involvement, the opposite of turning one's back on them. Compare 1:11: "forced labor," where the same Hebrew word *bᵉḇālāh* occurs.

11–12 Moses spied an Egyptian מַכֶּה (*makkeh,* "beating") a Hebrew; so he וַיַּךְ (*wayyaḵ,* "killed") him. Both verbs are from the same root in Hebrew, *nkh* ("to beat, smite, kill"). Bush (*Exodus,* 1:30) quotes a law from Diodorus Siculus that obligated an Egyptian to take just such action if he saw a fellow creature being violently assaulted. But was this not a daily occurrence in the slave camps of Egypt? Bush's further appeal to Moses' divine inner call was offered as a parallel to that of Phinehas (Num 25:7, 13), Ehud (Judg 3:21), and Gideon (Judg 6:27), as well as proving why a temporary concealment of the corpse was necessary since, the call had not yet been made public. But the cases are not parallel since no call or specific order preceded Moses' act. Simply stated, minds capable of great virtue are subject to great vice when that God-given asset is turned into a liability through haste, pride, or stubbornness.

14 שַׂר וְשֹׁפֵט (*śar wᵉšōp̱ēṭ,* "ruler and judge") is a figure of speech called hendiadys in which both words form a single idea. The point of the question would be very close to the modern snarl: "Who died and left you *boss*?" Likewise, in Ugaritic *zbl ṯpṭ* ("prince-judge") are used as a hendiadys for the ruling person.

15 Midian derived its name from the fourth son of Abraham by his second wife, Keturah (Gen 25:2). It is not improbable that many of the main doctrines taught by Abraham were retained and transmitted—even if with a mixture of error—to his descendants. Josephus (Antiq. II, 257 [xi.1]) locates Midian on the coast of the Gulf of Aqabah. The older geographer Ptolemy (6.7.27) and Eusebius (*Onomasticon* 136:31) mention a Madiana or Modiana that may be modern el-Bed, twenty-six miles east of the Gulf of Aqabah.

16 The כֹּהֵן מִדְיָן (*kōhēn Miḏyān,* "priest of Midian"), or with the Chaldean "prince of Midian," may have held the same dual office as the prince-king of Salem in Gen 14 (see later comments on Exod 18). Notice that 2 Sam 8:18 called David's sons "priests" (*kōhᵃnîm,* NIV mg.), but 1 Chron 18:17 made them "chief officials" (*riʾšōnîm*).

17 וַיְגָרְשׁוּם (*wayᵉgārᵉšûm,* "[they] drove *them* away," emphasis mine) has a masculine plural suffix as does "*their* flock" (emphasis mine), while "[he] came to *their* rescue" (emphasis mine) has a feminine plural suffix. Therefore, the text indicates that the daughters were accompanied by menservants who worked under their direction. Cassuto disagrees; for him the feminine nun ending is used simply to avoid confusion with the *nun paragogicum.*

18 רְעוּאֵל (*rᵉʿûʾēl*, "Reuel") means "friend or shepherd of God" (cf. 2:18; 3:1; Num 10:29; Judg 4:11 NIV mg.). W.F. Albright first proposed that Reuel is actually a clan name (Num 10:29 and LXX of Gen 25:3; and as an Edomite clan in Gen 36:4 and 1 Chron 1:35, 37) and then that Exod 2:18 be emended to read, "And they came to [Jethro, son of] Reuel, their father" ("Jethro, Hobab and Reuel in Early Hebrew Tradition," CBQ 25 [1963]: 4–9). But no MSS support such an emendation. A better solution is to note that dual names for the same person are well known from South Arabic sources. Exodus 2:21 and 3:1 treat Reuel as if he were the same person as Jethro. Josephus argued that Reuel was his proper name and Jethro his official designation (cf. Antiq. II, 258 [xi.2]). In the LXX his name is spelled Raguel because the Greek cannot represent the Hebrew guttural ע (ʿ), but it is the identical Hebrew spelling in all instances.

21 צִפֹּרָה (*ṣippōrāh*, "Zipporah") means "bird" (feminine), or as we would say, Moses married "Lady Bird."

22 גֵּרְשֹׁם (*gēršōm*, "Gershom") means "stranger" (*gēr*) "there" (*šām*). If *šōm* is an adjective from the root *šmm* ("to be desolate"), then it means "lonely stranger." The Vulgate and LXX borrow a text from 18:4 and add it here for the sake of completeness: "And she conceived again and gave birth to a second son. And he called his name Eliezer, saying, 'For the God of my fathers is my helper, and he has delivered me from the hand of Pharaoh' " (cf. Acts 7:29).

---

3. *Preparing a people for deliverance*

2:23–25

> [23]During that long period, the king of Egypt died. The Israelites groaned in their slavery and cried out, and their cry for help because of their slavery went up to God. [24]God heard their groaning and he remembered his covenant with Abraham, with Isaac and with Jacob. [25]So God looked on the Israelites and was concerned about them.

23 The king of Egypt who died was probably the same one who sought Moses' life for murdering an Egyptian (2:15; 4:19). The only pharaohs who ruled for more than thirty years in the Eighteenth and Nineteenth Dynasties were Thutmose III (1483–1450 B.C.), Amenhotep III (1410–1372 B.C.), Haremhab (1349–1315 B.C.), and Rameses II (1301–1234 B.C.). Thutmost III is probably the Pharaoh of the oppression who had gained control after the death of his aunt-stepmother-mother-in-law (cf. Rea, "Time of the Oppression," pp. 63–64, for arguments disqualifying the others).

Misery finally found a voice, and so the pain of Israel's bodily senses preceded her recognition of the poverty of her spiritual condition. Thus God prepared the audience and people who would be delivered while he prepared the deliverer himself. No longer did Egypt symbolize delightful foods, wealth, and fatness; instead, it now meant slave-masters, forced labor, and bondage. So Israel cried out to God.

24–25 God was pleased to respond to even those first lisps of faith, but he was also moved by his own word that he had promised to the patriarchs Abraham, Isaac, and Jacob (Gen 17:7, 19; 35:11–12 *passim*). It was a remembrance that was more than a mental act; it also included a performance of his word just as it did in Genesis 8:1 and 1 Samuel 1:19. In four consecutive verbs, the divine action is charted: God heard, God remembered, God looked (= considered), and God knew (= was concerned).

Notes

23 בַּיָּמִים הָרַבִּים הָהֵם (*bayyāmîm hārabbîm hāhēm*, "During that long period") is literally "in those many days." It is not necessary to conclude with Rawlinson (1:36, 50) that only Rameses II's sixty-seven-year reign would fit Moses' eighty years of life to this point, for both Thutmose III's thirty-four-year reign and Amenhotep III's thirty-eight-year reign qualify.

25 וַיֵּדַע (*wayyēḏa'*, "he was concerned about [them]") is literally "he knew." It stands without an object (so Gen 18:21) and means to take note of with a view to caring. The LXX reverses the meaning in an obvious harmonistic reading by making *yd'* a Niphal with a passive idea of "he [God] made himself known to them" so as to fit the continuation of the narrative in 6:2–8.

---

4. *Calling a deliverer*

3:1–10

[1]Now Moses was tending the flock of Jethro his father-in-law, the priest of Midian,and he led the flock to the far side of the desert and came to Horeb, the mountain of God. [2]There the angel of the Lord appeared to him in flames of fire from within a bush. Moses saw that though the bush was on fire it did not burn up. [3]So Moses thought, "I will go over and see this strange sight—why the bush does not burn up."

[4]When the Lord saw that he had gone over to look, God called to him from within the bush, "Moses! Moses!"

And Moses said, "Here I am."

[5]"Do not come any closer," God said. "Take off your sandals, for the place where you are standing is holy ground." [6]Then he said, "I am the God of your father, the God of Abraham, the God of Isaac and the God of Jacob." At this, Moses hid his face, because he was afraid to look at God.

[7]The Lord said, "I have indeed seen the misery of my people in Egypt. I have heard them crying out because of their slave drivers, and I am concerned about their suffering. [8]So I have come down to rescue them from the hand of the Egyptians and to bring them up out of that land into a good and spacious land, a land flowing with milk and honey—the home of the Canaanites, Hittites, Amorites, Perizzites, Hivites and Jebusites. [9]And now the cry of the Israelites has reached me, and I have seen the way the Egyptians are oppressing them. [10]So now, go. I am sending you to Pharaoh to bring my people the Israelites out of Egypt."

While Moses was actively engaged at one task, God called him to another—the very one Moses had felt himself so eminently qualified for forty years previously when he had struck out with such impetuosity against the abuses of power he had witnessed in Egypt. The Hebrew text begins in such a matter of fact way, as if to say, "Here now is Moses, shepherding his father-in-law's flock of sheep and goats in Horeb."

All sense of routine and dullness suddenly yielded to an appearance (Niphal form of the verb "to see") of the angel of the Lord. The current practice of most biblical scholars is to begin isolating the various sources for this call in an atomistic way by dividing "mountain of God" from "Horeb" and by separating "to appear," the Niphal form of the verb, from its active form, "to see." But as Jonathan Magonet ("The Bush That Never Burnt: Narrative Techniques in Exodus 3 and 6," *Heythrop Journal* 16

[1975]: 304–11) pointed out, this method overlooks the integrative function of such features in the text. The two different forms of the verb reflect the experience of Moses: from an objective point of view, God *appeared* (Niphal) as Yahweh (= LORD), but from a subjective perspective, he *saw* (Qal form) God (= Elohim). Only coldly dictated literary conventions would freeze each alleged source (usually said to be J and E) to a one-sided perspective when the narrative claimed to be two-sided.

Magonet relates a second organizing principle in this section in the use of narrative pegs to serve as introductions for three stereotyped phrases that each occur twice, viz., "The God of Abraham, . . . of Isaac . . . of Jacob" (vv.6, 15); "A land flowing with milk and honey" (vv.8, 17); and "The home/land of the Canaanites, Hittites . . . " (vv.8, 17). Rather than viewing these repetitions as evidences for some alleged literary sources, they function as devices for emphasis and as a way of combining terms that elaborate on one another to help fix the meaning. Thus "my people" of v.7 becomes "Israelites" in v.9 with both incorporated in v.10.

1–4 The valley of er-Raha, two miles long and one-third to two-thirds of a mile wide, lay between the three summits traditionally identified with the "mountain of God" (so named in retrospect because God had appeared there). There the Lord appeared in "*the* bush" (emphasis mine; the definite article probably being used here because Moses had referred to the bush so frequently in oral references before writing it down). There the Lord appeared "in the form of [see Notes] a flame of fire." What took place was a "strange sight" (v.3) to Moses. Therefore, to explain what happened here as a temporary mirage of reflected sunlight on some red leaves or a campfire of some Bedouin or even the phenomenon of Saint Elmo's fire is to substitute *our* experience for Moses' forty years in that area and his estimate that it was indeed unusual. The burning bush was not consumed; that was the miracle. Notice how miracle is used here, as it so typically is in Scripture, to accredit God's message (or messenger). Miracles are not circus side shows intended to entertain; rather they accredit the Word of God given to his special messengers.

The significance of God's work is not necessarily that the bush pictures the despised and oppressed people of God (KD [1:438] appeals to Judg 9:15, where the thornbush represents God's humiliated people vis-à-vis the lofty trees), for it was "from within a/the bush" (vv.2, 4) itself that the Lord called to Moses. Instead, its meaning is to be found in the fact that God chose the small and the despised burning bush as his medium of revelation, and he waited to see how sensitive Moses was toward the insignificant and small things of life before he invested him with larger tasks. Indeed, the God of glory could well have set the whole of Sinai aglow with light and fire, had he wished, but he wanted to use this bush for a lesson to make an impression on Moses. The fire, then, symbolized God's powerful, consuming, and preserving presence (cf. 19:18; 24:17; Judg 13:20; 2 Chron 7:1–3; Ezek 1:4–28; Dan 7:9–10; Heb 12:29). When Moses went over to inspect this unusual sight, God issued his call by repeating Moses' name to express the urgency of the message (cf. 1 Sam 3:10 for this same type of urgent summons).

5–6 The presence of God demanded a holistic preparation of the one who would aspire to enter his presence. Therefore, to teach Moses this lesson, God set up admittedly arbitrary boundaries—"Do not come any closer"—and commanded that he should also remove his sandals (v.5). This was to prevent him from rashly intruding into the presence of God and to teach him that God was separate and distinct from mortal men (cf. 19:10–13; 2 Peter 1:18). Because God was present, what had been ordinary became "holy ground" and consequently "set apart" for a distinct use. The place where sheep and goats had traveled just a short time ago was transformed into "holy ground" by God's presence. As Bush observed (*Exodus*, 1:44), it is not an intrinsic holiness due to the nature of the ground itself but relative only to and based on the divine appointment that remains true as long as God ordains it so. This also is the first occurrence of the noun "holy" in Scripture (cf. Gen 2:3 for the verb form).

When the condition for meeting God had been satisfied, he revealed himself. He identified himself as the "God of your father" (v.6; collective singular—see Gen 26:24; 31:5, 42, 53; 43:23; 46:1, 3; 49:25; 50:17; Exod 15:2; 18:4 for a similar formula). Of course, the plural form "God of your fathers" appears more frequently (cf. also Stephen's use of our passage in Acts 7:32 in the plural), but the collective singular also had a special point in that it was through the *one* man of promise that the *many* were to receive the blessing of God. Thus God assured Moses that the God of his father had not forsaken his repeated word of promise (Gen 15:1–21; 26:2–5; 35:1–12) or his people, and he would certainly be with Moses in the commission he was about to receive. (On Moses' fear of "looking" at God, see the comment on 24:9–10.)

7–10 The anthropomorphisms (i.e., the descriptions of God's actions and attributes in words usually associated with mankind) in vv.7–8 of God's "seeing," "hearing," "knowing" (= "be concerned about"), and "coming down" became graphic ways to describe divine realities for which no description existed except for partially analogous situations in the human realm. But these do not imply that God has corporeal and spatial limitations; rather, he is a living person who can and does follow the stream of human events and who can and does at times directly intervene in human affairs.

Three times v.8 mentions the land. The often-repeated promise to the patriarchs was about to become a reality after waiting for its fulfillment for over half a millennium! Two facts described the land: it was a good and a spacious land (cf. Deut 8:7–9). It was good because it was a "land flowing with milk and honey," and it was spacious because six nations (or in some parallel lists, ten; see Notes) were living there; but Israel would possess it all. It was a "land flowing with milk and honey" in that the sheep and goats gave the milk while the nectar of the vine and the work of the bees added more delectables, and those in abundance. The phrase took on proverbial status (3:17; 13:5; 33:3; Num 13:27; Deut 26:9, 15; 31:20; Jer 11:5; 32:22; Ezek 20:6) and, in short, meant a land of plenty.

The call of Moses comes to a double conclusion in vv.9–10 with the phrase "And/so now" (see Notes). Verse 9 essentially repeats v.7 by summarizing the preceding speech and by restating the grounds on which this divine call is issued: viz., Israel's present need and God's solution. Verse 10, however, is the bottom line to the whole incident of the burning bush: it is the formal commissioning of Moses as God's emissary to lead Israel out of Egypt.

Notes

---

1 חֹרֵב (*ḥōrēḇ*, "Horeb") is a Semitic name that means "desert," "desolation," and an alternate name for Sinai (meaning unknown). Usually it is identified with Jebel el-Musa (7,363 feet, on the southeast side of the valley) or less often with Jebel es-Safsaf (6,540 feet, on the northwest side) or Jebel Katarin (about 9,000 feet, on the southwest side). Compare Mount Hermon with its alternate name of Sirion in Deut 3:9; Ps 29:6.

חֹתְנוֹ (*ḥōṯenô*, "father-in-law") has the Arabic root *ḥatana* ("to circumcise"); in Akkadian the noun form is *hatanu*, which means "relative by marriage" (CAD, 6:148). T.C. Mitchell ("The Meaning of the Noun *ḤTN* in the Old Testament," VetTest 19 [1969]: 93–112) concluded that the OT term *ḥtn* is likewise a kinship term that means something like "relation by marriage." Notice, however, that when the Masoretes wished to distinguish between *ḥōtēn* ("father-in-law") and *ḥātān* ("brother-in-law"), they did so by the vowels.

Moses led Jethro's sheep to the אַחַר הַמִּדְבָּר (*'aḥar hammiḏbār*, "far side of the desert"). Since the orientation of the Midianites was to face east, the *'aḥar* (lit., "back") would be the west.

2 The easy movement from the title מַלְאַךְ יהוה (*mal'aḵ yhwh*, "messenger [or 'angel'] of the LORD") to LORD and Elohim in v.4 shows that this person was a real being who was at once *identified* with God yet also was sent by him and was therefore *distinct* from the father (cf. E.J. Young, "The Call of Moses," WTJ 30 [1967–68]: 3–6).

לַבַּת (*labbaṯ*) in בְּלַבַּת־אֵשׁ (*belabbaṯ-'ēš*, "in flames of fire") is probably a contracted form of לֶהָבָה (*lahbaṯ*, "flame"; cf. Ps 29:7). The beth of *belabbaṯ* may be, as Childs (*Exodus*, p. 50) suggested, the *beth essentiae* (GKC, sec. 119.i, and BDB, p. 88, s.v. ב, 7). This construction would then be exactly like Exod 6:3 and would be translated "the LORD appeared to him *as/in the form* of flames of fire" (italics marking the force of the *beth essentiae*).

2–3 The difficulty in translating בֹּעֵר . . . לֹא־יְבֻעָר (*bō'ēr . . . lō'-yiḇ'ar*, "was on fire . . . does not burn up") is to capture the shift of the tenses and the separate nuances of meaning for the same verb. The Hebrew text has both an active participle and the Hebrew imperfect form of the verb along with two slightly different meanings of the same verb, *b'r* ("to burn, blaze, or burn up"). David Noel Freedman ("The Burning Bush," *Biblia* 50 [1969]: 245–46) argued that the *lō'* was emphatic and not negative; thus v.3 would read: "Why indeed the bush continues to burn," even though the concluding words of v.2, "(but) the bush does not burn up," are not repeated but understood.

6 Beginning with Albrecht Alt ("The God of the Fathers," *Essays in Old Testament History and Religion*, tr. R.A. Wilson [Garden City, N.Y.: Doubleday, 1968]), scholars have alleged that each patriarch originally had his own separate clan-god. For a refutation of this thesis, see E.J. Young, "The God of the Fathers," WTS 3 (1940–41); Thomas E. McComiskey, "The Religion of the Patriarchs," *The Law and the Prophets*, ed. John H. Skilton (Nutley, N.J.: Presbyterian and Reformed, 1974), pp. 195–206; and W.C. Kaiser, Jr., *Toward an Old Testament Theology* (Grand Rapids: Zondervan, 1978), pp. 58, 60.

7 Israel was no longer a family; she was now a people and a nation. But they were so internally linked to Yahweh that he called them עַמִּי (*'ammî*, "my people").

8 Such anthropomorphic terminology as וָאֵרֵד (*wa'ērēḏ*, "So I have come down"; cf. Gen 11:5, 7; 18:21) should not be used to build a case for an alleged ancient view of a triple-decker universe. It is only a figurative way of communicating the reality of the intervention of God in the stream of human affairs.

לְהַצִּילוֹ (*lehaṣṣîlô*, "to rescue them") is literally the collective singular "to rescue him." This interchange of the one and the many is so frequent in Scripture that it usually calls for little notice. But it does explain why Israel faced little difficulty understanding how one individual (e.g., "seed" or "servant") could embody the whole group and that the God of their fathers was that man of promise who ultimately pointed to the Messiah but who also embodied all believers of all ages in that same collective singular.

The list of the Canaanite nations varies from five names in Num 13:29 to the fullest list of ten in Gen 15:19–21. Other enumerations are found in Gen 10:15–17; Deut 7:1; Josh 3:10; 11:3; 24:11 et al. The name Canaanite (the eponymous son of Ham, Gen 10:6) seems to overlap with the name Amorite, "Westerner" (see Gen 10:15–16, where Canaan's sons include the Amorites; also cf. Gen 15:18–21 with Gen 15:16). Perizzite appears to mean "villager" (*pᵉ rāzî,* "unwalled village" or "dweller in an unwalled place"; cf. Hyatt, p. 74). The Hittites (cf. Gen 23:10–20; 2 Sam 11–12) do not seem to be the Indo-Europeans of present-day Turkey; perhaps they are immigrants from the Old Hittite Empire (Cole, p. 67). The Hivities may be a corruption of the name Horite, for Gen 36:2 speaks of "Zibeon the Hivite" but calls his father a "Horite" in 36:20 (a switch to *ḥry* from *ḥwy,* Hyatt, p. 74). The Jebusites were the owners of Jerusalem prior to David's capture of that city (2 Sam 5:6–8) and probably were Hurrians as Aruna's name shows.

9–10 וְעַתָּה (*wᵉʿattāh,* "And/so now") appears twice, its repetition a common device in biblical narrative; accordingly Magonet ("The Bush," p. 309) points to Gen 44:30–33; 1 Sam 24:21–22; 2 Sam 7:28–29; 1 Kings 8:25–26. Greenberg (*Exodus,* pp. 73–74) has an extensive comparison of this feature with 2 Sam 7:28–29, showing that the first "and now" restates the previous grounds while the second "and now" gives the conclusion that will call for some response.

---

5. *Answering inadequate objections (3:11–4:17)*

a. *Who am I to go to Pharaoh?*

3:11–12

11 But Moses said to God, "Who am I, that I should go to Pharaoh and bring the Israelites out of Egypt?"

12 And God said, "I will be with you. And this will be the sign to you that it is I who have sent you: When you have brought the people out of Egypt, you will worship God on this mountain."

The first of five protests against accepting God's commission reflects the great change that had come over Moses after forty sobering years of reflection and development. He had been only too eager to offer himself as a self-styled deliverer prior to this extended training in Midian, but at this point Moses presented a different problem to the Lord. Moses was now timid, unsure of himself, and shrank back from any self-assertiveness that his divine commission demanded of him.

It is strange that Moses did not raise another, larger issue: the feasibility of organizing, equipping, and sustaining such a massive escape. Apparently that problem was settled by the burning bush, for to preserve one entity (the bush) was no greater than to preserve another (Israel). But Moses had serious doubts about his own qualifications. Once again God was about to use a person who was keenly aware of his own defects and who sought no advantage or position over others.

11 Moses first repeated the twofold divine commission of v.10: that he should personally go to Pharaoh and that he should bring Israel out of Egypt. Then he asked in the familiar idiom of the Near East that stresses the magnitude of the inequity between the agent and the mission, "Who am I?" (cf. 6:12; 1 Sam 18:18; Isa 6:5; Jer 1:6; 2 Cor 2:16).

12 God's response to Moses' alleged inadequacy was twofold: he would personally accompany him (which expands and strengthens the "I have come down" in v.8), and he would give him a sign. As God had promised fourteen times to be "with" (*'ēṯ* or *'im,* see Notes) the patriarchs Isaac and Jacob, he now assured Moses that he would be actively present as he continued to fulfill his promised word of blessing. He gave this assurance in a form that soon became proverbial, a first-person fixed formula of self-introduction: "I will be with you" (cf. Gen 26:3, 24; 31:3; and later Exod 4:12, 15; Deut 31:23; Josh 1:5; 3:7; Judg 6:16 et al.).

This "sign" (see Notes) given to Moses has been variously interpreted. Some refer "this" back to the burning bush or to the preceding clause, while the majority of interpreters understand "this" to look forward to the following clause. Others like Noth (p. 42) argue that something has dropped out of the text. We agree with the majority, for the "sign" here is confirmatory and appeals to faith rather than to immediate evidence or to the presence of the miraculous. This sign is not the same as Gideon's in Judges 6:17; for Gideon requested the sign; Moses did not. Therefore, Moses' sign belongs in the same class as these signs about the future: 1 Samuel 2:34 (a sign that Eli's sons would die in the near future); 1 Samuel 10:2 (a sign that Saul would meet two men), v.3 (or later, three men), and v.5 (or even a band of prophets); 2 Kings 19:29 (the sign of future crop production); Isaiah 7:14 (the sign of the future birth of Messiah); and Jeremiah 44:29–30 (the sign that Pharaoh Hophra would shortly be delivered into the hands of his enemies). Thus while God gave "signs" as "proofs" to the people (Exod 4:1–9), interestingly enough he gave no such "signs" to Moses himself but asked for belief and trust in his word and promised to be present (this parallels our Lord's promise to his disciples).

There was also more than a hint in this sign that the mission of Moses went beyond a mere deliverance of a nation from bondage; Israel was to be set free to "worship" God. Divine worship called for more than sacrifice; it was basically a calling on God's name in adoration and petition (as the patriarchs had already understood, KD, p. 441). In fact, Israel would soon enter into covenant with God on this very mountain (ch. 24) and present their gifts and offerings as part of their worship in order to build the tabernacle (36:1–7; Num 7).

Notes

---

12 In the statement אֶהְיֶה עִמָּךְ (*'ehyeh 'immāk*, "I will be with you"), *'ehyeh* is the first-person form of the name of Yahweh (= LORD) rather than its familiar third-person form, Yahweh (see next section for fuller treatment). In effect, then, God pledged his very person and being as signified by his name; he would be dynamically and powerfully present for Moses and thus for all the people. See the excellent study on "with" by Horst D. Preuss, "*'et; 'im*," TDOT, 1:449–63, esp. pp. 454–58.

On וְזֶה־לְּךָ הָאוֹת (*wezeh llekā hā'ôt*, lit., "This [will be] to you a sign"), see the discussion by F.J. Helfmeyer, "*'ôt*," TDOT, 1:183–85 especially.

The verb root of תַּעַבְדוּן (*ta'abedûn*, "You [pl.] will worship," lit., "serve") does not mean primarily "to sacrifice" as in the Vulgate and Luther. It is much broader and involves all Israel. As Greenberg observes (*Exodus*, pp. 77–78), it is "an adumbration of the great theophany to come," a stating of a totally new goal of "serving God" instead of Pharaoh.

---

b. *What if they ask what your name is?*

3:13–22

[13]Moses said to God, "Suppose I go to the Israelites and say to them, 'The God of your fathers has sent me to you,' and they ask me, 'What is his name?' Then what shall I tell them?"

14 God said to Moses, "I AM WHO I AM. This is what you are to say to the
Israelites: 'I AM has sent me to you.' "
15 God also said to Moses, "Say to the Israelites, 'The LORD, the God of
your fathers—the God of Abraham, the God of Isaac and the God of
Jacob—has sent me to you.' This is my name forever, the name by
which I am to be remembered from generation to generation.
16 "Go, assemble the elders of Israel and say to them, 'The LORD, the
God of your fathers—the God of Abraham, Isaac and Jacob—appeared
to me and said: I have watched over you and have seen what has been
done to you in Egypt. 17 And I have promised to bring you up out of your
misery in Egypt into the land of the Canaanites, Hittites, Amorites,
Perizzites, Hivites and Jebusites—a land flowing with milk and honey.'
18 "The elders of Israel will listen to you. Then you and the elders are
to go to the king of Egypt and say to him, 'The LORD, the God of the
Hebrews, has met with us. Let us take a three-day journey into the desert
to offer sacrifices to the LORD our God.' 19 But I know that the king of
Egypt will not let you go unless a mighty hand compels him. 20 So I will
stretch out my hand and strike the Egyptians with all the wonders that I
will perform among them. After that, he will let you go.
21 "And I will make the Egyptians favorably disposed toward this
people, so that when you leave you will not go empty-handed. 22 Every
woman is to ask her neighbor and any woman living in her house for
articles of silver and gold and for clothing, which you will put on your
sons and daughters. And so you will plunder the Egyptians."

Moses had another objection to God's call. He worried that the people would ask him this difficult question: "What is there in the name of God that will help us in circumstances like these?" Patiently and without rebuke, God provided him first with the answer (vv.14–15) and then with two speeches: one for the elders of Israel (vv.16–18a) and the other for Pharaoh (v.18b).

13 Moses did not anticipate being asked, "By what name is this deity called?" Rather, he feared that if he announced that the God of their fathers, the patriarchs, had sent him to them, they would bluntly ask him, "What is his name?" The point of their question was not the same as "Who is this God?" That question would have been answered: "He is called Yahweh." But as Buber has argued (pp. 48–55), the Hebrew *māh* ("What?") seeks the significance, character, quality, and interpretation of the name. Therefore, as it is implied, the name of Yahweh (= LORD) was already known to Moses and Israel (Genesis gives abundant evidence to support the presence of the name Yahweh already in patriarchal times); what they needed to know was "What does that name *mean* or *signify* in circumstances such as we are in?"

14–15 Elohim gave *two* answers (one in v.14, one in v.15) to the problem posed by Moses, and not three as some scholars allege (who then go on to determine which of the three, if any, was the original reply in the account, e.g., Noth, p. 93; Hyatt, p. 77). The structure of v.14 is aptly described by Cassuto (cf. pp. 37–38): (1) to give the exact quotation that answers the question and (2) to give an explanation of the inner meaning of the quotation. Both phrases are introduced with "And he said . . . and he said"—a frequent Hebraism already seen in Genesis. The second answer in v.15 (Notice: "And God *also* said" [emphasis mine]) builds on the basic explanation of the meaning of Yahweh's name in v.14 and links that name with previous and all future generations (see Childs, *Exodus*, pp. 61–62, for all previous proposals on the relationship of vv.13–15).

As Childs concluded (*Exodus,* p. 61), "Few verses in the entire Old Testament have evoked such heated controversy and such widely divergent interpretation." If little agreement exists on the inner relationship of vv.13–15, still less exists on the meaning of "I AM." Perhaps the most natural explanation that does fullest justice to the fact that this name is connected with some form of the verb *hāyāh* ("to be") and to its own context given our present canonical shape of the text is to see it as expressing the nature, character, and essence of the promise in v.12: "I will be with you" (*'ehyeh 'immāk*).

What, then, was his name? The answer was: "[My name in its inner significance is] I am, for I am/will be [present]." The answer was (1) not an evasion ("I am called what I am called"), (2) not a reluctance to disclose his name (as if he said, "My name really is not the point!"), (3) not a cutting Moses short (as if to say, "One thing at a time, I'm in charge here!"), and (4) not a primitive shout of invocation ("O He!"). Each of these attempts to explain the meaning violates some explicit aspect of the context: (1) and (2) instead of evading Moses or being reluctant, God takes the initiative in supplying his name (v.14a), its meaning (v.14b), and its past and future connections (v.15); or (3) instead of interrupting Moses, God patiently responds directly to four repeated objections that Moses made; and (4) instead of the shout originating with men, it emanates from an unfolding of the character and being of God. (On the form and etymology of the name Yahweh, see the Notes.)

The formula used in v.14 is the Hebrew syntactical construction known as *idem per idem,* where the same root with the same sense is repeated both in the principal clause and also in what is here the dependent relative clause. Some parallel Hebrew expressions are "Send, I pray, by the hand of whom you will send" (cf. 4:13 KJV); "Bake what you want to bake," and "Boil what you want to boil" (16:23); "I will have mercy on whom I will have mercy" and "I will show compassion on whom I will have compassion" (33:19); "They went wherever they went" (cf. 1 Sam 23:13 KJV); "I will go where I will go" (cf. 2 Sam 15:20 KJV); "Sojourn where you can sojourn" (cf. 2 Kings 8:1 KJV) et al. While it may sound to the Occidental ear that God was deliberately trying to avoid disclosing his name, the context shows that he was actually doing the opposite; therefore the formula is positive. Often this construction is used to express a totality, intensity, or emphasis to the form so highlighted by repetition, as in 33:19, viz., "I certainly am he who is gracious and shows mercy" (as contrasted with prima facie impressions of arbitrariness; cf. also Ezek 12:25; 36:20 [cf. NAB]). Therefore, the formula of self-introduction in Exodus 3:14a (along with its explanation in v.14b) means "I am truly he who exists and who will be dynamically present then and there in the situation to which I am sending you."

This was no new God to Israel; for it was the same God of Abraham, Isaac, and Jacob who was sending Moses. His name was Yahweh (= LORD in KJV, NIV, NASB et al.). For the first time God used the standard third-person form of the verb "to be" with the famous four consonants YHWH, instead of the first-person form of *'ehyeh* as previously in vv.12–14. This was to be his "name" forever. His "name" was his person, his character, his authority, his power, and his reputation (see W.C. Kaiser, Jr., "Name," ZPEB, 4:360–70).

So linked was the person of Yahweh and his name that both were often used interchangeably (e.g., Deut 28:58; Ps 18:49). This name was to be a "memorial" (*zēker*); that is, it was to be for the act of uttering the mighty deeds of God throughout all generations (there are twenty-eight instances of this concept in the OT, Cassuto, p. 39). Strictly speaking the noun used here (NIV translates it as a verb to fit an

English idiom—"to be remembered") is not a simple "recollection" or "remembrance." Brevard S. Childs (*Memory and Tradition in Israel* [London: SCM, 1962], pp. 70–73) demonstrates that the parallelism of Psalm 6:5 ("No one remembers [*zik̲rek̲ā*] you when he is dead./ Who praises you from the grave?") shows that the problem with the dead is not their inability to remember Yahweh but their inability to share in the praise of Yahweh (cf. Ps 135:13; Hos 12:5). So here in v.15 the joy of Israel's worship will be to share in the praise of the essence, power, and significance of "I am he who is, was, and will be [present]" when I said I would be there.

16–18a The "elders of Israel" (v.16) were the heads of various families (6:14–15, 25; 12:21; Num 2) or tribes, each having one or more to preside or rule. Moses was to deliver God's message to this body of men and to get them to accompany him when he went to Pharaoh. The message came in the name of the LORD, who was the same as the God of the patriarchs. It began with a repetition of the words used by Joseph on his death bed: literally, "I have surely visited you" (NIV, "I have watched over you"), and "I have promised to bring you up out of your misery in Egypt" (v.17). Joseph had prophesied the very deliverance announced by Moses (see Gen 50:24). Thus the repetition here was equivalent to saying that the Lord would complete and fulfill what he had begun to do as spoken by Joseph (Rawlinson, 1:57). In fact, the very word used for misery (*ʿanî*) in v.17 was used in the original promise to Abraham in Genesis 15:13 that the Egyptians would "mistreat [*ʿinnû*]" them four hundred years (Bush, *Exodus*, 1:52). Moses was assured of a sympathetic hearing from the elders, for the hearts of men are in the hands of God.

18b–20 Moses and the elders were instructed first to make only a moderate and limited request of Pharaoh for a temporary leave of three days' absence in order to offer sacrifices to Yahweh their God (v.18b). This was not an example of a part truth (Bush) or a ruse and an attempt to deceive Pharaoh. The appeal to Psalm 18:26—"To the crooked [Rashi glosses 'with Pharaoh'] you [God] show yourself shrewd"—as a policy statement (Greenberg, *Exodus*, p. 85) misses the point that a divine judgment never came until Pharaoh had repeatedly rejected all divine aids to acquiesce to God's plan. The matter is as Augustine and that fifteenth-century Spanish exegete Abarbanel put it: God deliberately graded his requests of Pharaoh from easier (a three-day journey with an understood obligation to return) to more difficult (the total release of the enslaved people) in order to give Pharaoh every possible aid in making an admittedly most difficult political and economic decision. Had Pharaoh complied, Israel could not have exceeded the bounds of this permission but would have then presented another, presumably more difficult, request. Nevertheless, God certainly knew this king of Egypt well enough to know what his reactions would be. Accordingly, he warned Moses just as the principle of Amos 3:7 states: "Surely the Sovereign LORD does nothing without revealing his plan [*sôd̲*] to his servants the prophets." Not even "a mighty hand" (v.19), in this case the plagues (see Notes on 4:21 on "wonders"), would budge his obduracy and recalcitrance. Thereby Moses was cautioned not to misconstrue any rejection he received as a sign that God had not called him or that God was not with him—all to no avail; for Moses later raised those very complaints (5:22–23).

21–22 God had promised Abram that after Israel had served for four hundred years, they would "come out with great possessions" (Gen 15:14). Thus the early chapters of

Exodus systematically record the fulfillment of one patriarchal promise after another to make the connection beyond any trivial objection. The so-called spoiling of the Egyptians was to be explained by a simple request (refer to the comments and Notes on 11:1–2; cf. 12:35 and Ps 105:37; *šā'al* means "to ask," not "to borrow") and by granting divine favor to the Israelites' request. Israel herself was to live by this same principle of providing a present to the slave who was to be released every seven years (Deut 15:13; Greenberg [*Exodus*, p. 86] notes the striking similarity even in wording). Charges of fraud, deception, deceit, and villainy against Israel are all misplaced. The fact is that the ignominy of their slavery is reversed in this sign of the recovery of their personhood—why even the children were to be decked in the jewels and the gifts of clothing!

Notes

13 מָה (*māh*, "What?") is to be distinguished from מִי (*mî*, "Who?"). The latter asks only the identity, ancestry, or some external feature of a person (cf. Gen 33:8; Exod 3:11; 2 Chron 2:6; Mic 1:5), but *māh* inquires into the character, quality, or essence of a person or event (cf. Gen 31:26 [*meh*]; 32:27; Exod 13:14; Josh 4:21; Prov 30:4; Zech 1:9; 5:6). See Motyer, pp. 17–24.

15 The pronunciation "Jehovah" for יְהֹוָה (*yᵉhōwāh*, "The LORD") was provided by the Masoretes who read the vowels of *'ᵃdōnay* ("my Lord") into יהוה (*yhwh*). The more accurate pronunciation is Yahweh, based on its derivation from the verb הָיָה (*hāyāh*, "to be," v.14) and on analogy with such Amorite names as *Yahwi-ila*, *Yawi-Dagan*.

On the etymology and meaning of the name Yahweh, there is almost no agreement. The bibliography in the last century alone would fill a whole book, and there seems to be no end in sight. There are several major schools of opinion.

1. The name Yahweh has an Egyptian etymology coming from two Egyptian words, *Yah* ("moon") and *we3* ("one"). This view, however, is now totally rejected. (For this and much of what follows, see Roland de Vaux, "Revelation of the Divine Name YHWH," *Proclamation and Presence: Essays in Honour of G.H. Davies* [London: SCM, 1970], pp. 48–75.) A more tenable Egyptian parallel is *p3 nty wn.w.f* ("The one who is who he is"; cf. Cyrus H. Gordon, "He Is Who He Is," *Berytus* 23 [1974]: 27–28).

2. It has an Arabic etymology from *Ya-huwa* ("O He!"), a dervish cry (Buber, pp. 49–50); but this name would then emanate from men.

3. It is a Northwest Semitic root of *hwy* ("to be") in such names as *Yawi-ila*. De Vaux ("Proclamation and Presence"), however, points out that the common root meaning "to be" in Amorite and Ugaritic is *kwn*.

4. It is a Hebrew verbal root from *hāwāy* ("to fall") and thus has the substantive meaning "destruction"; hence Yahweh is the god of storms and thunder. But Exodus does not appeal to this verb. Furthermore, it is only used once in the OT (Job 37:6).

5. Yahweh derives from the Hebrew pronoun *hû'* ("he"), as in Isa 43:10: "I am he," and Ps 102:27(MT 28): "You remain the same [*hû'*]" (S. Mowinckel, "The Name of the God of Moses," HUCA 32 [1961]: 121–33, and Hans Kosmala, "The Name of God [YHWH and HU']," *Annual of the Swedish Theological Institute* 2 [1965]: 103–6).

6. It is a causative Hebrew verbal root of a *yaqṭil/yiqṭol* type meaning "he causes to be" or "he is the Creator," but this solution requires a correction in the explanation given in 3:14 in addition to having some philological problems such as distinguishing between the basic and causative forms of verbs with a weak third radical.

The most likely etymology and meaning for the name Yahweh is that it is the imperfect form of the root *hwh*/*hyh*, meaning "he is/will be." The grammatical problem of moving from a first person *'ehyeh* to the third person of *hāyāh* (whose present vocalization has been modified due to the habit of refraining from pronouncing the ineffable name of God, lest one swear inadvertently) may be more apparent than real because (1) the demands of the sentence structure necessitated switching from first to third person in the context, and (2) the initial aleph can interchange with an initial yod. Gordon ("He is," *Berytus*, pp. 27–28) gives these illustrations of this interchange: Ugaritic *aḥd* and *yḥd*; Ugaritic *ytn*, which equals Hebrew *'itnn* ("gift"), or even within Ugaritic where *aṣḥ* and *yṣḥ* both mean "he shouts." (Also see Young, "Call of Moses," pp. 15–23, for a case for seeing God's aseity, i.e., his being rather than his activism and dynamism, in the name "I am.")

18 The plural suffix on נִקְרָה עָלֵינוּ (*niqrāh 'ālênû*, "he [God] has met with us [Moses and the elders]") again witnesses to Israel's concept of collective or corporate solidarity—but not corporate personality! Moses alone met God at the burning bush; but since Moses was the new leader of the people, God had thereby met with them also. Some versions read *qr'* ("call") instead of *qrh* ("to meet") and thus avoid the difficulty treated above.

22 כְּלֵי־כֶסֶף וּכְלֵי זָהָב (*kᵉlê-ḵesep̱ ûḵᵉlê zāhāḇ*, "articles of silver and gold") appears in all three texts of Exodus (here; 11:2; 12:35), but Ps 105:37 drops the *kᵉlê* ("vessels" or "articles") prefix. The women did not request such objects of value as weapons, armor, cattle, or food supplies for the house, table, or future sacrifices but only jewels and clothes. Therefore, *kᵉlê* should not be translated as a third group of things, viz., "vessels." See the Notes on 11:1.

שְׂמָלֹת (*śᵉmālōṯ*, "clothing") does not refer to festive garments but to daily apparel, as in 22:26; Deut 22:5; Josh 7:6 (so G.W. Coats, "Despoiling the Egyptians," VetTest 18 [1968]: 452), which opposes the elaborate theory of Julian Morgenstern ("The Despoiling of the Egyptians," JBL 68 [1949]: 1–28). Morgenstern has Israel's unmarried girls borrowing wedding garments and jewels as they are about to play the role of brides! But he misunderstands the text and deletes as spurious those elements in the text that refute his theory.

נִצַּלְתֶּם (*niṣṣaltem*, "you will plunder"), the Piel form of the verb *nṣl* (cf. 12:36), does not mean nor suggest the ideas of stealing, taking away secretly, or purloining private property that belongs to another. As in 2 Chron 20:25 (where it is combined with another verb and rendered "take away"), it means to plunder, but not by fraud, deceit, or cunning devices. E.W. Hengstenberg ("The Alleged Purloining. . . ," *The Genuineness of the Pentateuch*, tr. J.E. Ryland [Edinburgh: T. & T. Clark, 1847], 2:417–32) has one of the best surveys of the charges and answers to this problem. *Nāṣal*, he argues, often meant taking away by force but never by fraud. This military metaphor is used to describe the generous gifts of Egyptian jewels and clothing to the Israelites. Since the articles were "asked for" and not loaned (as is so frequently insisted due to the influence of the bad translations in a day when Hebrew was unknown or, as it is now, due to rationalistic prejudice), and since Israel did so on specific orders from God who would shortly affirm, "You shall not steal" (20:15), and not out of any so-called primitive code of ethics, the spoiling or plundering of the Egyptians involved no deception, lying, stealing, or appeal to higher laws with special (albeit temporary) exemptions. The text is too clear for each of these false alternatives (so Hengstenberg).

---

c. *What if they will not believe me?*

4:1–9

1 Moses answered, "What if they do not believe me or listen to me and
say, 'The LORD did not appear to you'?"
2 Then the LORD said to him, "What is that in your hand?"
"A staff," he replied.
3 The LORD said, "Throw it on the ground."

Moses threw it on the ground and it became a snake, and he ran from
it. 4 Then the LORD said to him, "Reach out your hand and take it by the
tail." So Moses reached out and took hold of the snake and it turned
back into a staff in his hand. 5 "This," said the LORD, "is so that they may
believe that the LORD, the God of their fathers—the God of Abraham, the
God of Isaac and the God of Jacob—has appeared to you."
6 Then the LORD said, "Put your hand inside your cloak." So Moses put
his hand into his cloak, and when he took it out, it was leprous, like
snow.
7 "Now put it back into your cloak," he said. So Moses put his hand
back into his cloak, and when he took it out, it was restored, like the rest
of his flesh.
8 Then the LORD said, "If they do not believe you or pay attention to the
first miraculous sign, they may believe the second. 9 But if they do not
believe these two signs or listen to you, take some water from the Nile
and pour it on the dry ground. The water you take from the river will
become blood on the ground."

God had not appeared to any man, as far as we know, in over four hundred years. Therefore, Moses felt he had to raise yet another objection to the Lord's commission if he was to announce a claim. It should have been enough for Moses to have had the divine assurance of 3:18: "The elders of Israel will listen to you," but Moses wanted to play the "what-if game." Graciously, God put into Moses' hands three signs to be used as credentials with the people of Israel.

1 Moses did not flatly contradict God's assurance in 3:17 as if he had said, "Look, they will not believe me or listen to me." Both the Hebrew *w^ehēn* ("what if") and the LXX *ean* ("if") make this a hypothetical situation and not an absolute affirmative (Bush, *Exodus*, 1:55, points to a similar use of *hēn* in Jer 3:1). Thus Moses was by no means a shining model of faith and trust in God, but it is unfair to charge him with being blunt and dictatorial. However, neither could he have been so certain as to know exactly what would be the response of his brethren in Egypt. His object was to stall for time. This he did by posing further nuances to what he had already been told—all of which exhibits a certain lack of confidence in God. But how gracious God is in responding to questions that men may consider to be real and legitimate roadblocks to faith, even though there is enough basis for action in the Word of God alone! Similarly, Jesus in essence said, "Believe me for my word's sake or [for the more tough-minded who must see, feel, and touch in order to believe] believe me for my work's sake" (cf. John 14:10–11).

2–5 *The first sign.* God's prophets were accredited by "signs and wonders" (cf. Deut 13:1–3) with the sole purpose of validating the messenger and the message—that both were truly from God. Accordingly, Moses was given a "sign" to perform "so that [*l^ema'an*] they may believe that the LORD . . . has appeared to you" (v.5). There was to be no hint of the theatrical or circus mentality; this was to be no stunt or caper aimed at entertaining or building a personal following. The principle behind the miracles was to operate just as it did for the Zarephathite woman when Elijah raised her son from the dead in 1 Kings 17:24: "Now I know that you are a man of God [= prophet] and that the word of the LORD [spoken] from your mouth is the truth."

Moses needed first to observe that the staff in his hand was ordinary and unspectacular (see the Notes). But when it was thrown on the ground as God commanded, it became a snake. It is perhaps too much to directly connect this snake with either the uraeus (or cobra, so Cook, p. 265) worn on the headdress of Pharaoh (as if Moses had, so to speak, Egypt's king by the tail) or with the Serpent of Genesis 3:1 (so KD, p. 448), i.e., Satan and his henchman who exercised evil and brutality. However, the side reference could hardly have escaped anyone of that day. Moses called the "serpent" *nāḥāš* in this passage, in Genesis 3:14, and in Exodus 7:15; but in Exodus 7:9–10, when Aaron performed this same miracle before Pharaoh, the staff became a "serpent," and the Hebrew word is *tannîn* (cf. v.12, however). *Tannîn* was probably an Israelite nickname for Egypt and its king (Deut 32:33; Ps 74:13; Ezek 29:3): "you great monster" (perhaps as represented by the crocodile). As if to underscore its supernatural nature, Moses was instructed to grasp the serpent by its tail to further prove the divine source of this miracle; for one would normally pick up a serpent by the neck.

6–7 *The second sign.* The Hebrew word for leprosy covered a number of assorted diseases much as our word "cancer" currently does. Actually, leprosy, or Hansen's disease, was known in antiquity. But leprosy in the Bible apparently also covered cases of psoriasis, vitiligo, ringworm, syphilis, mildew, and the rot—all affecting garments and houses as well as people in some cases (Beegle, pp. 78–79). Which was involved here is uncertain, but the condition of the skin was such that its color resembled snow. Any small or ordinary skin annoyance would hardly be of any "sign" value for Moses to show to the people. It had to pose a greater threat to the life and health of Moses if the instantaneous cure was also to reflect the greatness and majesty of God's power. The significance of this power to take away the health of the body and then to restore it again so that the affected part was "like the rest of his flesh" (*ki<u>b</u>ᵉśārô*) was to warn Pharaoh that this God who had sent Moses had the power to inflict or to save what he would with just a word or a gesture from his ambassador.

8–9 *The third sign.* The Lord next seized the initiative by using in vv.8 and 9 almost identical terms to those used by Moses in v.1: "If they do not believe you or pay attention to the first miraculous sign or, . . . these two signs." What was not being heeded in each case was literally "the voice" (*qôl*) of these two signs (v.8 *bis*, v.9 [the English cannot smoothly include this in the translation]). But their "voices" would leave Israel just as accountable as the "voice" of the words of Moses (v.1). No wonder Scripture teaches that there is a natural revelation in the day, night, heavens, and things on the earth (Ps 19:1–6; Rom 1:19–25). Israel was to be confronted by God through the "voice" of his word and the "voice" of his miracles. This indicates that there would be an appropriate significance that would attach itself to each sign.

In this third sign Moses was to take some water *from* the river (the first plague would later be performed *in* the Nile) and turn it into blood. The Nile (see Notes on 1:22), which flowed with the blood of innocent Hebrew victims, would itself witness to its involuntary carnage with this miracle. Would the point of the "sign" be wasted on any Hebrew—or Egyptian? Like Abel's blood that cried out from the ground, so would the infants' whose lives had been demanded by Pharaoh (1:22). Egypt's mighty god, the Nile, was dominated by the Lord God of Abraham, Isaac, and Jacob.

Notes

1 וְהֵן לֹא (*wᵉhēn lō'*, "What if [they do] not") is echoed by God in vv.8 and 9 as אִם־לֹא (*'im-lō'*, "if [they do] not"), thus verifying the stance taken in the commentary on v.1. The text does not say whether these signs were actually demanded by the people, but Moses and Aaron did show them these signs in v.30. The first sign was also performed before Pharaoh in 7:8–13.

2 מַזֶּה (*mazzeh*, "what?"), from מָה זֶה (*māh zeh*, "What is this?"), is perhaps deliberately used as a wordplay on *maṭṭeh* ("staff").

מַטֶּה (*maṭṭeh*, "staff") must have been Moses' shepherding (cf. v.17) crook (cf. Gen 38:18; Ps 23:4; Mic 7:14), even though the Egyptians had an adversion to this occupation (Gen 46:34). However, the parallelism of Isa 10:24 and 26 shows that the "staff" Moses employed to bring the plagues had more than passing similarities to the "rod" of affliction used by the Egyptian slave masters. In v.20 it is called "the staff of God," and in 7:9 it belongs to Aaron. This is no basis for dividing the narrative into a J tradition (shepherd's staff in Moses' hand), an alleged E source (the miraculous "staff of God"), and a P document (the priestly use of the staff by Aaron); it only differentiates the ultimate source of its power as being from God and its authorized users as Moses and Aaron. Thus by Semitic usage it may be said to belong to all three without always stopping to distinguish between primary and secondary causes and users.

5 Some believe this sentence is incomplete since the verse begins with לְמַעַן (*lᵉma'an*), literally, "that [they may believe]" (Bush, *Exodus*, 1:57). But Cassuto (p. 47) correctly argues that this verse continues the Lord's words from v.4 while the intervening words in v.4 ("So Moses reached out . . . ") describe Moses' action during the time God was still speaking.

The root for יַאֲמִינוּ (*ya'ᵃmînû*, "that they may believe") appears to be thoroughly Hebrew and as yet unattested in related Semitic languages (Alfred Jepsen, TDOT, 1:292)! The Hiphil form with *lᵉ* (Exod 4:1, 8 [bis], 9) means "to have confidence in a messenger, to believe a message" (Jepsen, p. 302) and is always connected with *lō* ("not"; Jepsen, p. 302). Verse 5 uses the verb with *kî* ("so that"), and this usage seems closest to Abraham's believing in the word about the Man of Promise to come (Gen 15:5–6) or the Ninevites' believing God (Jonah 3:5), i.e., the word about God preached by Jonah. Thus belief may center on God's word or God's works of signs and wonders (cf. 14:31; Num 14:11; Ps 106:12). Later, in 14:31; 19:9, *he'ᵉmîn* appears with *bᵉ* ("in") with the meaning of "to put trust in." In this sense it is "an endorsement of man's character, not just some of his statements" (Gordon Wenham, *Faith in the Old Testament* [Leicester, England: Theological Students Fellowship, 1976], p. 3).

8 אֹת (*'ōṯ*, "sign") is used as an authenticator of the call of God to Moses (cf. Gideon, Judg 6:17; Saul, 1 Sam 10:1, 7, 9; and possibly Rahab, Josh 2:12, 18). In 3:12 the sign was a corroboration and a promise to Moses; here it is to be a basis for trust and belief from the people (see F.J. Helfmeyer, TDOT, 1:167–88).

8–9 יִשְׁמְעוּ לְקֹל (*yišmᵉ'û lᵉqōl*, lit., "[if] they will listen to ['pay attention to'] your voice"), used here with *lᵉqōl* (cf. *bᵉqōl* in v.1), makes plain that just as Moses' "voice" in v.1 was a sign to be believed, so the three miracles likewise had "voices" that also spoke to the people if they would hear them. George Bush (*Notes on Genesis*, 2 vols., reprint [Minneapolis: James and Klock, 1976], 1:358) argues that "voice" in this context is equivalent to a "meaning," "drift," or "purport"; thus it is the significance of the sign that cries out to the people for a believing and affirming response.

---

d. *What about my slow tongue?*

4:10–12

[10] Moses said to the LORD, "O Lord, I have never been eloquent, neither in the past nor since you have spoken to your servant. I am slow of speech and tongue."

11 The LORD said to him, "Who gave man his mouth? Who makes him deaf or mute? Who gives him sight or makes him blind? Is it not I, the LORD? 12 Now go; I will help you speak and will teach you what to say."

10 "O Lord," began Moses with yet another objection, thereby adding a note of deprecation and supplication (Rawlinson [1:86] compares the Hebrew *bî* also in Gen 43:20; 44:18; Num 12:11; Josh 7:8), "I have never been eloquent" (lit., "a man of words"). (Bush [*Exodus*, 1:59] recalls Job 11:2, lit., "a man of lips" = "a talker"; Job 22:8, lit., "a man of arm" = "a powerful man"; Ps 140:11, lit., "a man of tongue" = "a slanderer or prattler.")

Then in a truly Oriental phrase, Moses added, literally, "not since yesterday and not since the third day," which adds up to "neither yesterday or any day before"—or simply "never before" (NIV, "neither in the past nor since"). The Hebrew idiom for the future and time to come is "today and tomorrow." Not even the experience at the bush had remedied this problem, observed Moses in a backhanded reproach aimed at almighty God ("since you have spoken to your servant"). Moses summed it all up: he was "slow of speech and tongue" (lit., "heavy/slow of mouth and heavy/slow of tongue"). Scarcely could this imply that he had a natural speech impediment or that he was a stammerer, for Stephen declared that Moses was "powerful in speech and action" (Acts 7:22). Thus Moses' complaint was not in a defective articulation,but in his inability to take command of Hebrew and Egyptian (cf. Ezek 3:5, where "heavy of tongue" = difficulty with a foreign language [NIV, "difficult language"]) with a ready and copious supply of words and thoughts to beat back all objections from his brethren and Pharaoh—though he does quite well with God! The Egyptian "Tale of the Eloquent Peasant" underscores the importance of eloquence in the Egyptian culture.

11–12 Surprisingly, God again answered Moses; this time with a question (v.11) that takes on the proverbial status of a wisdom saying to be repeated in Israel later on (Ps 94:9; Childs [*Exodus*, p. 78] recalls such use of wisdom sayings in the prophets' use of disputational speech). The gifts of speech, sight, and hearing are from the same Lord who was sending this hesitant leader. While God was not to be blamed for directly creating any defects, his wise providence in allowing these deprivations as well as his goodness in bestowing their ordinary functions mirrors his ability to meet any emergency Moses might have suggested. So God announced, "I will help you speak" (lit., "I will be with you," adding "with your mouth"; cf. Jer 1:9; Matt 10:19–20; Luke 21:14–15) "and will teach you what to say."

Notes

10 גַּם מִתְּמוֹל גַּם מִשִּׁלְשֹׁם גַּם מֵאָז (*gam mittᵉmôl gam miššilšōm gam mē'āz*) is a Hebraism that literally means "Also from/since yesterday, also from/since the third day, also from/since [you spoke . . .]" (see Bush, *Genesis*, 2:139), which the NIV smoothly renders, "neither in the past nor since."

11 The verbs translated "gives" or "makes" in this verse are from the same Hebrew verb שִׂים (*śîm*), which means "to place or put" in its root meaning.

12 On "Now" see the Notes on 3:9–10. Enough evidence is again in hand for Moses to come to a conclusion.

וְהוֹרֵיתִיךָ (*w^{e}hôrêṯîḵā,* "I will teach you") is related to the noun "torah" ("law") and means "to instruct" or "to point and show [the way]."

---

e. *Why can you not find someone else?* 4:13–17

[13]But Moses said, "O Lord, please send someone else to do it."
[14]Then the LORD's anger burned against Moses and he said, "What about your brother, Aaron the Levite? I know he can speak well. He is already on his way to meet you, and his heart will be glad when he sees you. [15]You shall speak to him and put words in his mouth; I will help both of you speak and will teach you what to do. [16]He will speak to the people for you, and it will be as if he were your mouth and as if you were God to him. [17]But take this staff in your hand so you can perform miraculous signs with it."

13–14a Moses' groundless opposition angered God (v.14a). Moses could think of no more good objections, for God had met every one point by point. So God's unwilling servant revealed the true nature of his heart: literally he said, "Send, I beg you, by the hand [of whom] you will send," which is another delightful Hebraism for "choose any other man, not me!" (NIV, "please send someone else," v.13).

14b–17 Nevertheless, God mercifully decided still to use his reluctant servant by sending his brother, Aaron, to supply any deficiency Moses might have felt. However, Moses had a price to pay for his intransigence: Aaron would receive the honor of leading the priesthood. At least that appears to be the only reason for including this reference to "the Levite" (v.14b) in the divine announcement—it is a hint about things to come in the future service of Aaron and his sons (cf. 1 Chron 23:13). There is a risk in declining the call of God; it may be a forfeiture of divine blessing even though there is grace and mercy for the obstinate (so Bush, *Exodus,* 1:60).

Once more the omniscience of God is seen in that Aaron was "already on his way to meet [Moses]," having begun at the special prompting of God (v.27)—as perfect a blend of divine sovereignty and human freedom as we will see in the hardening of Pharaoh's heart. Whether Aaron came with the news that the king who sought Moses' life was dead (2:15) or for some other reason is not known.

The arrangement was that Moses was literally "to become [see Notes] God" to Aaron, and Aaron was to become Moses' mouth (or "prophet" according to 7:1). Nothing defines more accurately the intimate relationship between God and his prophet than 4:16 and 7:1. There were to be no more excuses or discussions: "You shall speak to him and put words in his mouth" (v.15). Further, God would teach both of them ("you" pl.) what they were to do. As for action and deeds, it would be the very humble staff in Moses' hand that God would use to perform the miracles he already had begun to speak about (3:20) and to show to Moses (4:2–8).

Notes

---

13 Hebrew often uses the word יָד (*yāḏ,* "hand") when it wishes to stress instrumentality or agency. Here the phrase "send someone else" is literally "by the hand of [whom] you will send." (Compare 9:35: "The LORD had said through [lit., 'spoken by the hand of'] Moses," or 2 Kings 17:13: "The LORD warned Israel and Judah through [lit., 'by the hand of'] all his prophets.")

15 וְאָנֹכִי אֶהְיֶה עִם־פִּיךָ וְעִם פִּיהוּ (*weʾānōkî ʾehyeh ʿim-pîkā weʿim pîhû,* "I will help both of you speak") is literally, "I, I will be with your mouth and with his mouth." The emphatic form "I" and the *ʾehyeh* strongly suggest the presence and meaning of the Lord's name (cf. Notes on 3:12, 15).

16 "As if" attempts to bring into English the Hebrew verb הָיָה (*hāyāh,* "to be") followed by the preposition ל (*l,* lamed), which is best rendered, in most cases, "to become" (so argues Young, "Call of Moses," p. 19).

The LXX and Vulgate soften the last phrase of v.16: "you shall be to him in things pertaining to God"—the very phraseology used in Heb 5:1 for the high priest: "Every high priest is selected from among men . . . in matters related to God."

---

6. *Preparing a leader's family*

4:18–26

18 Then Moses went back to Jethro his father-in-law and said to him, "Let me go back to my own people in Egypt to see if any of them are still alive."

Jethro said, "Go, and I wish you well."

19 Now the LORD had said to Moses in Midian, "Go back to Egypt, for all the men who wanted to kill you are dead." 20 So Moses took his wife and sons, put them on a donkey and started back to Egypt. And he took the staff of God in his hand.

21 The LORD said to Moses, "When you return to Egypt, see that you perform before Pharaoh all the wonders I have given you the power to do. But I will harden his heart so that he will not let the people go. 22 Then say to Pharaoh, 'This is what the LORD says: Israel is my firstborn son, 23 and I told you, "Let my son go, so he may worship me." But you refused to let him go; so I will kill your firstborn son.' "

24 At a lodging place on the way, the LORD met Moses and was about to kill him. 25 But Zipporah took a flint knife, cut off her son's foreskin and touched Moses's feet with it. "Surely you are a bridegroom of blood to me," she said. 26 So the LORD let him alone. (At that time she said "bridegroom of blood," referring to circumcision.)

18 Moses left the region of Sinai and went to Midian to ask Jethro permission to return to Egypt. Even the call of God did not erase the need for human courtesy and respect for one's father-in-law. Interestingly, Moses did not seem to have shared the real reason for his desire to return to Egypt. Whether he was motivated by modesty, as the medieval Jewish commentators explained, or male reluctance to talk about spiritual things with other men, as Calvin would have it, is outside the information we possess. The reason Moses gave was "to see if any of [my own people] are still alive," i.e., "to know how they are getting along" (see Cassuto [p. 53] on a similar expression used by Joseph in Gen 45:3: "Is my father still living?" i.e., "How is his health?" after Joseph had just been told that his father was still alive in Gen 44). So Jethro granted Moses permission to go and wished him well.

19–20 This short section informs us that Moses' conversion took place in Midian, and not in Sinai where God had appeared to him, and that Moses had made his decision to return before he heard that the Pharaoh who had sought his life had already died.

Therefore, in spite of all the various improbable attempts to reject or to relocate these verses, an English pluperfect solves the problem best: "Now the LORD *had* said to Moses" (v.19, emphasis mine). It would also follow that none of his previous objections to the call of God were motivated by fears for his personal safety. This recent news may have influenced him to decide to take along his wife, Zipporah, and their two sons.

Up till now only one son, Gershom, has been mentioned (2:22). Eliezer, though unmentioned in this text, probably had been born (18:4); thus the plural is correct here (see Notes on v.20). Moses' family is not mentioned again until Jethro's visit with Moses and the Israelites camped at Sinai (ch. 18). The fact that Moses "had sent away his wife . . . and her two sons" (18:2–3) does not necessarily mean that they failed to witness the Exodus from Egypt. More probably Moses urged his wife, after they had returned to Sinai with the delivered nation, to take her two sons and go down to Midian to tell her father all that God had done (see on 18:1). After this report Jethro followed his daughter and grandchildren back to the mountain of God where he rejoiced to see all that the Lord had done through his son-in-law.

So Moses took the "staff of God" (v.20). What had once been ordinary became extraordinary by virtue of its use in the service of God. So equipped, Moses prepared to return to Egypt.

21–23 By way of summary, the Lord rehearsed the key features of his previous directives to Moses: (1) you will perform miracles before Pharaoh; (2) Pharaoh will harden his heart and not release the people; (3) You are to inform him that since Israel is "my firstborn son," the Israelites must be set free so that they might worship me; and (4) Pharaoh's refusal will lead to the death of his firstborn son.

The expression "I will harden [Pharaoh's] heart so that he will not let the people go" is used here for the first time. In all there are ten places where "hardening" of Pharaoh is ascribed to God (4:21; 7:3; 9:12; 10:1, 20, 27; 11:10; 14:4, 8, 17). But it must be stated just as firmly that Pharaoh hardened his own heart in another ten passages (7:13, 14, 22; 8:15, 19, 32; 9:7, 34, 35; 13:15). Thus the hardening was as much Pharaoh's own act as it was the work of God. Even more significant is the fact that Pharaoh alone was the agent of the hardening in the first sign and in all the first five plagues. Not until the sixth plague, as KD (1:453–55) carefully point out, was it stated that God actually moved in and hardened Pharaoh's heart (9:12), as he had warned Moses in Midian that he would have to do (v.21).

The announcement that Israel was God's "son," yes, even his "firstborn" (v.22), may have stunned Pharaoh; for he was accustomed to regarding himself alone as the "son of the gods." But for a whole people to be a "son" of the deity was a little surprising. Once again the collective singular for all God's seed is evident (see comments on 3:6 and Notes on 1:5; 3:18; cf. Hos 11:1; Matt 2:15). Added to this filial relationship was the declaration that Israel was God's "firstborn" (*b*ᵉ*k̲ôr*), which does not mean "first" in chronological order, because Jacob (renamed Israel) was actually born *after* his twin, Esau. Here God meant "first in rank," firstborn by way of *preeminence*, with all the rights, privileges, and responsibilities of a "firstborn." Thus what had previously rested on natural rights of primogeniture now rested on grace. With it went the privilege given by God to the seed of Abraham, viz., that by means of this "firstborn" all the nations of the earth should be blessed. Accordingly, God declared David and each of his sons in the line of Messiah to be "my firstborn" (Ps 89:26–27; also cf. Jer 31:9); and later Christ himself is call the "firstborn" (Rom 8:29;

Col 1:15, 18; Heb 1:6). Revelation 1:5, and most convincingly Hebrews 12:23, includes all believers in God's "firstborn" (*prōtotokoi*). Israel was to be set free; for they were sons of God, the LORD, who graciously had adopted them as his special inheritance and had set them apart from the nations to be his instrument for bringing blessing to all the nations of the earth. (See KD, 1:457–58, for the distinction between sonship and election.)

The penalty that Pharaoh would ultimately pay for his refusal to acknowledge Israel as Yahweh's son and firstborn would be aimed at his own firstborn. Just as 3:12 had included an adumbration of Moses' return to Sinai, so vv.21–23 intend to show the future work of God beginning with the "wonders" of the plagues and ending climactically with a threat to Pharaoh's firstborn. The change in person between v.22 and v.23 ("Then [*you*] say . . . and I told you") is remarkable and probably due to the fact that in v.22 we are being given the first and earliest words that Moses was to use as the signs began. In v.23, however, Moses would address Pharaoh more directly after it was clear that his obduracy was fixed and unchangeable and that no amount of divine miracles or prophetic pleading would persuade him to let God's people go.

24–26 Due to its brevity, the abruptness of its introduction, the enigmatic nature of some of its cryptic expressions, and the difficulty of establishing exact antecedents for several of its personal pronouns, this paragraph has continued to baffle interpreters. The place to begin to solve these problems is with the explanation given in the text itself, in v.26b. Childs (*Exodus*, pp. 95–101) convincingly argues that the adverb *'āz* ("at that time") is nowhere in the OT used to introduce etiological material (= a Greek word, *aitia*, "cause"; an attempt to explain why certain things function or mean what they do); therefore, most contemporary critical explanations are missing the writer's intention for including this narrative at this point. Nor is v.26b a tautology or merely an older variant and alternative version for the final words of v.25; for J. DeGroot ("The Story of the Bloody Husband," OTS 2 [1943]: 13–14) points to a similar double ending in 1 Samuel 4:21 and 4:22. Verse 26b explains that this whole episode—what Zipporah did, what she said, and on whom she operated—all have reference to the rite of circumcision.

But then, what was the link with the context in which this paragraph is now located? It cannot be, as Cassuto (p. 59) suggests, Pharaoh's seeking Moses' life (v.19) and the Lord doing the same in v.24; neither is it to be found in the identical verbs "met" with different subjects in vv.24 and 27. It must rather revolve around Pharaoh's "son," his "firstborn" (v.23), and Moses' "son," *perhaps* also his "firstborn" (v.22), along with the fact that all Israel was God's son, his firstborn (v.22) (so in part Hans Kosmala, "The 'Bloody Husband,'" VetTest 12 [1962]: 22).

With the two textual clues, the rite of circumcision as the explanation of the whole episode and "my firstborn son" as the connection between the sections, the rest of the passage yields this explanation. The Lord had attacked Moses as he was enroute to accomplish the mission of God in Egypt. The nature of this nearly fatal experience is not known to us; therefore, it does not figure in the interpretation. That Moses was the object of the divine action is clear from the fact that the otherwise unspecified son in v.25 would need to be identified as belonging to someone other than Moses. The sudden introduction of Zipporah's action leads us to believe that she instinctively connected her husband's peril (a malady so great that it left only her hands free to act, for presumably his were not able to help) with their failure to circumcise their son. This she immediately proceeded to do. But her words of reproach—"Surely you are a bridegroom of blood to me"—indicate that the root of the problem was in her revulsion and disgust with this rite of circumcision.

The narrative was included at this point, then, to demonstrate that there was an additional factor in the preparation of God's commissioned servant: the preparation of his family. In Genesis 17:10–14 God had commanded Abraham to circumcise every male on the eighth day as a sign of the covenant; any uncircumcised male was to be cut off from his people, for he had broken God's covenant. However, in this case the father was suffering for his refusal to circumcise his son. It can only be a matter of conjecture to decide: Which son was this? How long had Moses been married during his forty-year stay in Midian? When was their eldest son, Gershom, born? Or did this episode have reference to the newly born Eliezer?

Thus for one small neglect, apparently out of deference for his wife's wishes, or perhaps to keep peace in the home, Moses almost forfeited his opportunity to serve God and wasted eighty years of preparation and training! To further underscore this connection between Moses' grave condition and the circumcision of his son, Zipporah took the excised prepuce and touched Moses' feet (this need not be as many commentators argue a euphemism for his genitals, for this is not a puberty rite here). The Lord let Moses go, and the grip of death was lifted.

Notes

18 The spelling יֶתֶר (*yeṯer,* "Jethro") is found side by side with יִתְרוֹ (*yiṯrô*) in the same verse. Several commentators point to Neh 6 where the same person, called Gashmu in v.6 (cf. NIV mg.), is called Geshem in vv.1–2 and in 2:19. The orthographic variation in Jethro is only in the retention of the ancient case ending *o.*

19 Our insistence on the pluperfect for וַיֹּאמֶר (*wayyō'mer*) here as the way to solve the otherwise awkward flow of the materials is not accepted by many, though Greenberg (*Exodus,* in loc.) admits that S.R. Driver (*A Treatise on the Use of Tenses in Hebrew* [Oxford: 1892], sec. 76) does show the imperfect consecutive with this meaning, though in very rare instances.

In the NIV נַפְשֶׁךָ (*napšeḵā,* lit., "your soul," "your life") is simply rendered by "you," viz., "wanted to kill you." This use of the Hebrew word *nep̱eš* ("soul") to stand for the whole person is very frequent in the OT and illustrates the phenomenon of the use of a part of a thing to represent its entirety.

20 Many argue that the vowels on בָּנָיו (*bānāyw,* "his sons") have been deliberately altered to make a supposed original singular noun (*b^e^nô,* "his son") plural to fit the facts of chapter 18. But this conjecture is without any support from the versions or the Hebrew MSS.

Moses put his wife and his sons on הַחֲמֹר (*haḥ^a^mōr,* "the donkey"), but the reference need not mean all of them rode on a single donkey at one time. Bush (*Exodus,* 1:63) tries to argue that the singular is put for the plural; thus he sat "each on his own donkey," but Bush gives no evidence for this view. No doubt Moses' humble circumstances are intended by this picture of a single donkey.

21 The word מוֹפֵת (*môp̱ēṯ,* "wonder"; cf. Gr. *teras*) is used thirty-six times in the OT to describe that which is extraordinary and a portent of the divine presence, but nineteen of these instances refer to the plagues in Egypt. The most frequent word (seventy-nine examples in the OT) for the miracles connected with the Exodus is אוֹת (*'ôṯ,* "sign"; cf. Gr. *sēmeion*), which directs attention away from its unusual nature to the meaning and the significance it points to (cf. already 3:12; 4:8–9). Here twenty-five of the seventy-nine instances of this word refer to the plagues of Egypt. The third word, פֶּלֶא (*pele',* "wonder" or "marvel"; or with fifty-one examples of Niphal fem. pl. participle alone—*niplā'ôṯ*) has already been used of the Exodus events in 3:20 and stressed the awesome and breath-taking nature of God's acts in delivering Israel. The noun form of this verb, *pele'*, supplies a part of one of the names for the Messiah in Isa 9:6: "*Wonderful* Counselor." (For a discussion of these three terms, see H. Wheeler Robinson, "The Nature Miracles of the Old Testament," JTS 45 [1944]: 1–12.)

On the distinction between the three Hebrew words used for hardening, see Walter C. Kaiser, Jr., *Toward Old Testament Ethics* (Grand Rapids: Zondervan, 1983), pp. 252–56. The verb used here is חָזַק (*ḥāzaq*, "to strengthen, confirm"). Bush (*Exodus*, 1:65) argued that "the language implies simply [and he cites usage that agrees in Judg 9:24; 2 Chron 26:8; Isa 35:3; 41:7; and Jer 23:14] that the course of events should be so ordered that, without any *positive divine influence* exerted upon him, the haughty king should take occasion to *confirm himself* in the disregard of the counsels of the Most High. . . . This God is said to *have done* because he *permitted it to be done*" (emphasis his).

24 מָלוֹן (*mālôn*, "lodging place") was a stopping place, perhaps near a well, where travelers in those parts were accustomed to spend the night.

25 Stone instruments like the צֹר (*ṣōr*, "flint knife"; cf. Josh 5:2) were retained for ritual purposes long after the introduction of metal implements.

Some argue that there is a wordplay in חֲתַן־דָּמִים אַתָּה לִי (*ḥᵃṯan-dāmîm 'attāh lî*, "You are a bridegroom of blood to me"); for on the basis of the Arabic *ḫatana* ("to circumcise," though this is a secondary sense derived from circumcising the groom prior to the wedding and otherwise unattested to the OT) and *ḥᵃṯan* ("bridegroom" or "husband"), the words would then mean "you are a bloody circumciser" (P. Middlekoop, "The Significance of the Story of the 'Bloody Husband,'" *Southeast Asia Journal of Theology* 8 [1966]: 36; Mitchell, "The Noun ḤTN," pp. 98–99). The Vaticanus codex of the LXX has *dioti eipen estē to haima tēs peritomēs tou paidiou mou* ("because she said: 'The blood of the circumcision of my son are you'"), while the Targum has "Through this blood of circumcision the bridegroom has been restored to us" (see William Dumbrell, "Exodus 4:24–26; A Textual Reexamination," HTR 65 [1972]: 285–90; Julian Morgenstern, "The 'Bloody Husband' (?) (Exodus 4:24–26) Once Again," HUCA 34 [1963]: 35–70). But none of these suggestions are conclusive because (1) there is also an Akkadian verb *ḫatānum* ("to protect"); (2) Hebrew did have available a separate word for "circumcision," מוּלָה (*mûlāh*); and, at any rate, (3) most of the alternative renderings for *ḥᵃṯan* merely bring out the wordplay behind this castigation of her husband as "bloody."

26 On the use of lamed meaning "with reference to" in לַמּוּלֹת (*lammûlōṯ*, "referring to circumcision"), see GKC, sec. 119u. The plural ending on "circumcision" does not seem to suggest that Zipporah circumcised both her sons but appears to be an abstract plural; the word is a *hapax legomenon*.

C. *First Steps in Leadership (4:27–7:5)*

1. *Reinforced by a brother*

4:27–31

27 The Lord said to Aaron, "Go into the desert to meet Moses." So he met Moses at the mountain of God and kissed him. 28 Then Moses told Aaron everything the Lord had sent him to say, and also about all the miraculous signs he had commanded him to perform.

29 Moses and Aaron brought together all the elders of the Israelites, 30 and Aaron told them everything the Lord had said to Moses. He also performed the signs before the people, 31 and they believed. And when they heard that the Lord was concerned about them and had seen their misery, they bowed down and worshiped.

27–28 At God's command (see comment on v.14b) Aaron, now eighty-three years of age, was to meet Moses midway enroute to Egypt at the "mountain of God" (i.e., Horeb, v.27; see on 3:1). As predicted in v.14 ("his heart will be glad when he sees you"), Aaron "kissed" Moses. The men had much to share as to what had happened during the forty years they were apart, but Moses' words about God's liberating directives and miraculous signs were most prominent (v.28).

29–31 Immediately the narrative jumps ahead in time to that meeting with the elders (v.29; see comment on 3:16), which Moses had been instructed to convene when he arrived in Egypt. Evidently God wished to see duly constituted authority respected; therefore an appeal needed to be made to Israel's existing leadership and their consent obtained before initiating any requests of Pharaoh. Aaron, as designated in vv.13–16, acted as chief spokesman in relaying all that God had said to Moses (v.30). Bush asserts (*Exodus,* 1:71) that "the pronoun 'he' . . . indicate[s] that Moses, and not Aaron is the true subject of the verb [performed the signs]." The truth was, however, that though Moses had been told (v.17) to perform the signs God had given in vv.1–9, both Moses and Aaron performed the miracles (note the plural "you will do" in v.15 [NIV, "you what to do"]; see below, 7:19; 8:5, 16).

Since the elders represented the people and subsequently reported to them what they had heard and seen from Moses and Aaron, the text quickly compressed each of these steps in v.30 by saying all this was done "before" (lit., "in the sight of") the people. The response was just as had been predicted in 3:18—"they believed" (v.31; see Notes on v.5). The pressure of physical hardship had made this people more receptive than would be their custom in later years. Whether the signs were needed, as Moses had feared in v.1, the text has no comment. Especially heartening was the fact that God cared about them and their misery. Their response was immediately to worship the Lord, for he was the One who had "visited" (KJV; NIV, "was concerned about") them and "had seen" their trouble (v.31).

Notes

31 פָּקַד (*pāqad*, "was concerned about," lit., "to visit") is used both positively—"to show concern for"—and negatively—"to punish," "to judge."

2. *Rebuffed by the enemy*

5:1–14

[1] Afterward Moses and Aaron went to Pharaoh and said, "This is what the LORD, the God of Israel, says: 'Let my people go, so that they may hold a festival to me in the desert.' "

[2] Pharaoh said, "Who is the LORD, that I should obey him and let Israel go? I do not know the LORD and I will not let Israel go."

[3] Then they said, "The God of the Hebrews has met with us. Now let us take a three-day journey into the desert to offer sacrifices to the LORD our God, or he may strike us with plagues or with the sword."

[4] But the king of Egypt said, "Moses and Aaron, why are you taking the people away from their labor? Get back to your work!" [5] Then Pharaoh

said, "Look, the people of the land are now numerous, and you are stopping them from working."
6 That same day Pharaoh gave this order to the slave drivers and
foremen in charge of the people: 7 "You are no longer to supply the people with straw for making bricks; let them go and gather their own
straw. 8 But require them to make the same number of bricks as before; don't reduce the quota. They are lazy; that is why they are crying out,
'Let us go and sacrifice to our God.' 9 Make the work harder for the men
so that they keep working and pay no attention to lies."
10 Then the slave drivers and the foremen went out and said to the people, "This is what Pharaoh says: 'I will not give you any more straw.
11 Go and get your own straw wherever you can find it, but your work will
not be reduced at all.' " 12 So the people scattered all over Egypt to
gather stubble to use for straw. 13 The slave drivers kept pressing them, saying, "Complete the work required of you for each day, just as when
you had straw." 14 The Israelite foremen appointed by Pharaoh's slave drivers were beaten and were asked, "Why didn't you meet your quota of bricks yesterday or today, as before?"

1–2 After an undefined interval of time (*we'aḥar*, "afterward"), Moses and Aaron, perhaps accompanied by the elders (cf. 3:18), went to Pharaoh and boldly demanded that he release the people (v.1). They wished to celebrate a festival to this God in whose name the demand was being made, viz., "the LORD [Yahweh], the God of Israel." Pharaoh's retort to this affront to his sole right to command these slaves was crisp and cynical: "Who [*mî*, cf. Notes on 3:13] is the LORD?" (v.2). Indeed, if God chose to identify himself with such a hapless and hopeless lot of slaves, and if he was so powerless to effect their deliverance, why should Pharaoh fear him or obey his voice? Pharaoh's answer was clear: "No!"

3 Perhaps stunned by Pharaoh's insolence and arrogance, Moses and Aaron recast their request in somewhat milder terms. Acting now as representatives of the people (rather than ambassadors as the messenger formula "this is what the LORD . . . says" of v.1 would imply) and in language given at the burning bush in 3:18, the demand is changed to a humble request: "Let us take (please) [*nēlᵃḵāh nā'*] a three-day journey into the desert to offer sacrifices to the LORD." (The rationale for sacrificing outside Egypt is given in 8:26. On the request for only a three-day journey, see comment on 3:18b.)

God's servants warned Pharaoh that should he disallow this temporary release, he could suffer untold losses; for this God might allow all sorts of pestilence to break out, or he might even send an invader across the eastern frontier where Israel lived in vulnerable exposure.

4–14 Pharaoh was unmoved by any of these requests or threats. In his judgment the people were much too lazy or too idle, and Moses and Aaron were disturbers of the peace at best and plotters of sedition against the throne at worst. His question to them was in essence, "Why are you encouraging this?" Pharaoh's inner meaning of his words in v.4 are introduced by "said" in v.5 (Cassuto, p. 67). There were already too many people (another witness to God's covenantal faithfulness, see 1:7), and should he give them rest from their labors to further increase their numbers? (See the first pogrom of 1:8–14 and the translation of this verse in the Vulgate.) Alternatively, some understand Pharaoh's question as "Should I lose so large a percentage of my work force just for this little outing?"

The Egyptian slave drivers (see comment and Notes on 1:11) were to instruct the Israelite "foremen" (*šōṭ^erîm,* not necessarily "scribes"; cf. 2 Chron 26:11 and 34:13, where "scribes" are distinguished from *šōṭ^erîm*; see Exod 5:14–16 on their method of appointment and their functions) that no longer would straw be provided for the bricks Israel had to produce (vv.6–7). From then on Israel was to rummage the countryside for what stubble and straw they could find without decreasing their daily quota of bricks (v.8). Brick quotas are abundantly documented in Egypt (see the article cited in Notes on v.7).

Chopped straw was mixed in with the clay to make the bricks more pliable and stronger by first binding the clay together and then by decaying and releasing a humic acid similar to glutamic or gallotanic acid (cf. C.F. Nims, "Bricks Without Straw?" BA 13 [1950]: 22–28). So the people were scattered all over Egypt (v.12) while the slave drivers kept beating the Israelite foremen and pressuring them to meet their daily quota of bricks (vv.13–14).

Notes

---

1 The word וְיָחֹגּוּ (*w^eyāḥōggû,* "so that they may hold a festival") indicates that this was to be a pilgrimage festival. Compare the Islamic cognate *hadji,* a person who has taken the pilgrimage; also the proper name Haggai.

3 נִקְרָא (*niqrā',* "[he] has met [with us]") is, literally, "he has called on us"; but since this exact phrase occurs in 3:18 and is spelled נִקְרָה (*niqrāh,* "[he] has met"), it is probably no more than a spelling variant often seen in some lamed-he verbs where the aleph and the he interchange.

7 On ancient brick making, see the fifteenth-century B.C. Thebes tomb painting of Rekh-mi-Re depicting brick-making (J.B. Pritchard, *The Ancient Near East in Pictures* [Princeton, N.J.: Princeton University Press, 1969], #115; see comment on 1:11). See also the definitive article and bibliography by Kitchen, "Brickfields," pp. 137–47.

7–8, 14 The expressions for time in these verses are כִּתְמֹל שִׁלְשֹׁם (*kiṯmōl šilšōm,* "no longer"); תְּמוֹל שִׁלְשֹׁם (*t^emôl šilšōm,* "as before"); כִּתְמֹל שִׁלְשֹׁם גַּם־תְּמוֹל גַּם־הַיּוֹם (*kiṯmōl šilšōm gam-t^emôl gam-hayyôm,* "yesterday or today [see Notes on 4:10], as before"). All are Oriental modes of speech in which the numerical "three" (*šilšōm*) is used for the day after the one nearest the present day, either in the past or in the future.

9 יִשְׁעוּ (*yiš'û,* "they pay [no] attention to") actually means to have respect for a person or thing when used with the prepositions *'el, 'al,* or *l^e*; cf. Gen 4:4: "God looked with favor on Abel," but when used with the preposition *b^e*, as here, it meant "to meditate, to ponder orally [on a thing]" as in Ps 119:117 (Bush, *Exodus,* 1:77). The play on the word יַעֲשׂוּ (*ya'^aśû*) also with the *b^e* ("so that they keep working") is obvious.

בְּדִבְרֵי־שָׁקֶר (*b^eḏiḇrê-šāqer,* "lies") is literally "words of lying" (RSV, "pack of lies"). Pharaoh labeled such illusory dreams about Israel being suddenly released from their bondage false and presumptuous.

---

3. *Rebuffed by the enslaved*

5:15–21

15 Then the Israelite foremen went and appealed to Pharaoh: "Why have you treated your servants this way? 16 Your servants are given no

> straw, yet we are told, 'Make bricks!' Your servants are being beaten, but the fault is with your own people."
>
> 17 Pharaoh said, "Lazy, that's what you are—lazy! That is why you keep saying, 'Let us go and sacrifice to the LORD.' 18 Now get to work. You will not be given any straw, yet you must produce your full quota of bricks."
>
> 19 The Israelite foremen realized they were in trouble when they were told, "You are not to reduce the number of bricks required of you for each day." 20 When they left Pharaoh, they found Moses and Aaron waiting to meet them, 21 and they said, "May the LORD look upon you and judge you! You have made us a stench to Pharaoh and his officials and have put a sword in their hand to kill us."

It is one thing to receive opposition from the expected quarter of the enemy, but it is another thing to be rebuffed by the very friends you are trying to deliver.

15–16 The Hebrew foremen, unaware of the total deterioration of their position due to Moses and Aaron's request of Pharaoh, personally appealed the "No straw policy" laid on them by the slave drivers. In a courteous but bitter complaint, they asked, "Why have you treated your servants this way?" (v.15). We are given no straw; we are constantly pressed to keep making bricks; we are beaten—and the fault, sir, lies with your own people (v.16). This last charge seems to deferentially use the words "your people" in a circumlocution for Pharaoh himself. But whether it was a thinly veiled complaint out of respect and fear for the man and his power or because the foremen actually believed the slave drivers were exceeding their authority cannot be determined from this context.

17–18 Pharaoh's analysis of the situation has been reduced to a single word: "lazy" (*nirpîm*); that is what Israel was (v.17). He repeated the word for emphasis (v.17; cf. v.8). If their request was "Let us go . . . now" (v.17), then he was ready to render his conclusion: "Get to work" (v.18; see Notes on 3:9–10). No straw would be supplied, and no falling behind in quotas would be allowed either.

19–21 Only now did the real untenability of their position begin to come home to the foremen (v.19). Moses and Aaron had deliberately "stationed" (*niṣṣāḇîm*; NIV, "waiting," v.20) themselves so as apparently to be the first to debrief the men as they emerged from their meeting with Pharaoh, for they had had a fairly good idea what would be the outcome from the foremen's audience with the king of Egypt. What they may not have expected was the full venting of the foremen's anger when they "found" (see Notes) them.

Instead of earning the respect from these Hebrew foremen for all their labors to alleviate their brutal condition, Moses and Aaron felt, in no uncertain terms, the heat of the foremen's anger. Almost like the prayer voiced by two men who hardly trusted one another ("May the LORD watch between you and me," in the Mizpah benediction of Gen 31:49), they asked God to look and judge these two troublemakers; for they had made Israel's reputation to stink (v.21). The words of vv.20–21 reflect those of v.3. Instead of a plague "striking" Israel and a "sword" coming, Moses and Aaron, not an enemy, had put a sword in Pharaoh's hands. So it happened that they "struck," or as we would say, "happened to bump into," Moses and Aaron.

Notes

15 וַיִּצְעֲקוּ (*wayyiṣ'ᵃqû*, "They appealed," lit., "cried out") in the shrill voice of complaint.

16 The root *ḥṭ'* in the expression וְחָטָאת עַמֶּךָ (*wᵉḥāṭā'ṯ 'ammeḵā*, "but the fault [is with] your [own] people") may be a verb (third person sing., perfect tense) or a noun with a feminine ending. But the form, Cassuto argues (p. 71), is so strange as to suggest that the foremen almost began to say, וְחָטָאתָ אַתָּה (*wᵉḥāṭā'tā 'attāh*, "but [it is] you who are at fault") and then somewhat clumsily changed it out of deference (before completing the first word) for Pharaoh and weakly added "your people."

20 "They found" (or "met") is a softened translation for וַיִּפְגְּעוּ (*wayyipgᵉ'û*), which may also be translated to indicate "they attacked." The meeting was anything but friendly. The normal word for "to meet" is יִפְגֹּשׁ (*yipgᵉš*).

4. *Revisited by old objections*

5:22–23

[22]Moses returned to the LORD and said, "O Lord, why have you brought trouble upon this people? Is this why you sent me? [23]Ever since I went to Pharaoh to speak in your name, he has brought trouble upon this people, and you have not rescued your people at all."

22–23 Even though Moses had been forewarned right from the start that Pharaoh would not accede to God's requests or demands (see comment on 3:19–20), he was not prepared for the effect this refusal would have on his own brethren. Filled with an "I told you so" attitude, it was Moses' turn to ask, "Why?" (v.22; cf. Pharaoh in v.4, the foremen in v.15): "Why have you brought trouble upon this people?" "Why did you ever send me [in the first place]?" (lit. tr.). Fortunately, Moses did not vent his wrath on the foremen, but he did pour out to God the keenness of his resentment. Moses did not charge God directly with authoring this evil, for the idiom only means that God allowed and permitted such trouble as Pharaoh had thus spawned.

The clincher for Moses was v.23. His prayer (in essence) was, "O Lord, why is all this happening? Why did you ever send me?" And then he concluded: "Besides, you haven't done what you said you would anyway—deliver them! I've done nothing but bring/make trouble since I arrived here!"

Obviously, Moses was again wrestling with some of his old objections (cf. 3:11–4:17). In his estimation things were moving too slowly, and the suffering was intensifying rather than letting up—he was once more his old, impetuous self.

5. *Reinforced by the Name of God*

6:1–8

[1]Then the LORD said to Moses, "Now you will see what I will do to Pharaoh: Because of my mighty hand he will let them go; because of my mighty hand he will drive them out of his country."

[2]God also said to Moses, "I am the LORD. [3]I appeared to Abraham, to Isaac and to Jacob as God Almighty, but by my name the LORD I did not make myself known to them. [4]I also established my covenant with them to give them the land of Canaan, where they lived as aliens. [5]Moreover, I have heard the groaning of the Israelites, whom the Egyptians are enslaving, and I have remembered my covenant.

> [6]"Therefore, say to the Israelites: 'I am the LORD, and I will bring you out from under the yoke of the Egyptians. I will free you from being slaves to them, and I will redeem you with an outstretched arm and with mighty acts of judgment. [7]I will take you as my own people, and I will be your God. Then you will know that I am the LORD your God, who brought you out from under the yoke of the Egyptians. [8]And I will bring you to the land I swore with uplifted hand to give to Abraham, to Isaac and to Jacob. I will give it to you as a possession. I am the LORD.' "

1 There were no direct answers to Moses' questions, for these were to be gathered from his experience as their leader (cf. KD, in loc.). But Moses' complaint about the time could now be answered, for God announced his "now"—he would delay no longer. The promised show of God's power would commence immediately with a show of his "mighty hand" (cf. 3:19). Whether God was also the subject of the second "mighty hand" in v.1 may be debated since 12:33 uses the same root in a verb form ("the Egyptians *urged* the people to hurry and leave") and in a similar context.

2 The heart of God's response to Moses and the people was a fresh revelation of God's character and nature. One phrase stands out above all the other promises: "I am the LORD" (*'ᵃnî Yahweh*). In fact, this declaration appears four times: (1) to open the message (v.2); (2) to open the set of three promises based on the evidence of vv.2–5 and to affirm the first three verb clauses declaring that God will redeem them (v.6); (3) to underscore two more verb clauses declaring that God will adopt them (v.7); and (4) to validate and confirm the dependability of two more first-person verbs promising that God would endow them with the land of Canaan and to sign his name, as it were, to the whole message (v.8). Notice how similar the function of this formula is to another formula ("declares the LORD [*nᵉ'um Yahweh*]") in Jeremiah 31:31–34. In this new covenant passage, it also occurs four times: "Twice in the first section: at its beginning (v.31a), at its end (v.32b) and twice in the second section: at the beginning (v.33a) and at the end (v.34b)" (Bernhard W. Anderson, "The New Covenant and the Old," *The Old Testament and Christian Faith,* ed. B.W. Anderson [New York: Harper and Row, 1963], p. 230, n. 11). There the particle *kî* is also used and not *gam* as here.

3–5 Once again God reminded Moses that he was the God who had promised the land of Canaan to the patriarchs and that he had also seen the affliction of his chosen people (vv.3–5). Moreover, whereas in the past the patriarchs, Abraham, Isaac, and Jacob, had known him in the character and in his capacity as El Shaddai (see Notes on the *beth essentiae* in *bᵉ'ēl šadday*), the name that disclosed his power to impart life, to increase the goods of life, and to deal with all unrighteousness, now he would be known as Yahweh. The name El Shaddai appears six times in the patriarchal narrative: Genesis 17:1; 28:3; 35:11; 43:14; 48:3; and in part in 49:3. In Job it is used thirty times. Whether Shaddai reflects the Hebrew *šḏ* ("breast") or the Ugaritic *ṯdy* ("mountain") is not clear; hence we cannot say for certain whether El Shaddai is "God the Nourisher" or "God of the Mountain." But it is certain that the name does reflect the might and power of God to work miracles. The LXX rendered El Shaddai in Job as *ho pantokratōr* ("the All-Ruler" or "Almighty"; see Kaiser, *Theology,* pp. 97–99, 101, 106).

Moses and Israel (and even the Egyptians later) would shortly know what "I am the LORD" means. This would not be the first instance of the use of that name, for already it had occurred some 162 times in Genesis, with 34 of those examples on the lips of speakers in Genesis. Significantly, men "began to call on the name of the LORD [Yahweh]" as early as Genesis 4:26; and the place where he almost sacrificed Isaac, Abraham named "The LORD Will Provide [Yahweh-Yireh]" (Gen 22:14). Similarly, the names Jochebed and Joshua are theophoric, i.e., have Yahweh elements in them. It is difficult to claim these all are later modernizations for the older name of God.

Yahweh is the God who would personally, dynamically, and faithfully *be present* to fulfill the covenant he had made with Abraham, Isaac, and Jacob. The patriarchs had only the promises, not *the things* promised. The fullness of time had come when God was to be known in the capacity and character of his name Yahweh/Jehovah as he fulfilled what he had promised and did what he had decreed. These deeds may now be further enumerated and spelled out in the following seven promises of vv.6–8: "Therefore, say."

6–8 The contents of God's ancient promises are brought together and arranged so as to explain what "I am the LORD" means.

1. There were three first-person verbs with his *promise of redemption* (v.6):

I will bring you out
I will free you
I will redeem you

Each of these verbs (and the four that follow) are in the Hebrew past (i.e., perfect) tense instead of the future tense, for so certain was God of their accomplishment that they were viewed as having been completed. In English, however, they are best rendered in the future (the so-called Hebrew prophetic perfect). God will "redeem" (see Notes) Israel with the same "mighty acts of judgment" he had alluded to in 3:20 and 4:23 and had predicted long ago to Abraham in Genesis 15:14. The plagues were to be judgments for crimes as well as spectacular wonders to instill faith.

2. Two more first-person verbs detailed God's *promise to adopt Israel* as his own people (v.7):

I will take you as my own people
I will be your God

These two promises will serve as two parts of the tripartite formula to be repeated in the Old and New Testaments almost fifty times: "I will be your God, you shall be my people and I will dwell in the midst of you" (cf. Gen 17:7–8; 28:21; Exod 29:45–46; Lev 11:45 et al.).

3. The last two promises focused on God's *promise of the land* (v.8):

I will bring you to the land
I will give it to you

This he pledged with the oath of his uplifted hand (cf. Gen 22:16; 26:3) so that by two immutable things—(1) his word of promise and (2) his oath—Israel (and *all* subsequent believers according to Heb 6:17–18) might have a strong encouragement and a solid confidence in the future. Then as if to remind Israel once again, God concluded with his signature: "I am the LORD."

Notes

---

1 יָד חֲזָקָה (*yāḏ ḥᵃzāqāh*, "my mighty hand") was possibly used as a polemic against New Kingdom pharaohs who routinely had *nb ḫpš* ("lord" or "possessor of [mighty] arm") as part of their titulary (cf. James K. Hoffmeier, "The Arm of God Versus the Arm of Pharaoh in the Exodus Narratives," *Biblica* 67 [1986]: 378–87).

2 Most literary critics complain that Exod 6:2–7:7 (along with 11:1–13:22) evidences such a shift in vocabulary and retrogression in the narrative that it can only be considered as a doublet of chapters 1–4 (see Beegle, pp. 117–18; Dennis McCarthy, "Plagues and Sea of Reeds: Exodus 5–14," JBL 85 [1966]: 142, 158). An appeal is made to the unique appearance of the noun "divisions" (6:26; 7:4; 12:17, 41, 51), where elsewhere Israel is just "people"; "the mighty acts of judgment" (6:6; 7:4; 12:12), and the verb "to bring out" (*yṣ'*, e.g., 6:26; 7:4; and in chs. 11–13) instead of the more frequent verb "to let [the people] go" (*šlḥ*) in 7:8–10:27. But these distinctions fail to observe the accuracy of the standpoint of the speaker and the situation of the people. See further the Notes on vv.6, 26.

3 The beth before El in בְּאֵל שַׁדָּי (*bᵉ'ēl šadday*, "as El Shaddai") is the *beth essentiae* (cf. 3:2; cf. GKC, sec 119i; BDB, pp. 88f., 908). The force of this beth carries over to the וּשְׁמִי יהוה (*ûšᵉmî yhwh*, "but [by] my name, the LORD"). In both instances it is the character or capacity of that name that is in view, not the bare knowledge of the name as the label for his person. Likewise, the "name" also stood for his reputation, character, and accomplishments in doctrine and deeds (see W.C. Kaiser, Jr., "Name," ZPEB, 4:360–70; Motyer, pp. 3–31; Robert Dick Wilson, "Yahweh [Jehovah] and Exodus 6:3," in *Classical Evangelical Essays in OT Interpretation*, ed. W.C. Kaiser, Jr. [Grand Rapids: Baker, 1972], pp. 29–40; C.E.B. MacLaurin, "Shaddai," *Abr N* 3 [1961–62]: 99–118).

לֹא נוֹדַעְתִּי (*lō' nôḏa'tî*, "I did not make myself known") is Niphal, not the Hiphil form *hôḏa'tî* ("I did not let them know my name"). The meaning of this verb "to know" as related to the LORD (it appears twenty-six times in the OT) should have been evident from its repetition to the Egyptians in the Ten Plagues—"that they might know the LORD" (cf. 7:5). If identity were the sole object, that would have been clear long before the tenth plague; but if acquaintance with the *character* of that name was the object, then the Ten Plagues would also have an evangelistic purpose.

However, there is also the matter of the *lō'* ("not"). Why have nonevangelical scholars insisted on an absolute negative here instead of a comparative negative (e.g., as also in Jer 7:22–23)—and in a most literal way—even if they missed the import of the *beth essentiae* and the meaning of "to know"? W.J. Martin (*Stylistic Criteria and the Analysis of the Pentateuch* [London: Tyndale, 1955], p. 17), taking another approach, argued that this *lō'* was an orthographic error for the original *lu'* ("indeed"); but there is no evidence or need for that solution in this passage. Neither is the sentence an implied question without the somewhat customary interrogative *hē'* (ibid, p. 18; cf. L.A. Herrboth, "Exodus 6:3b: Was God Known to the Patriarchs as Jehovah?" *Concordia Theological Monthly* 4 [1931]: 345–49; F.C. Smith, "Observations on the Use of the Names and Titles of God in Genesis," EQ 40 [1968]: 103–9).

4–5 וְגַם (*wᵉgam*, "also," "moreover") is used to emphasize, not to add (C.J. Labuschagne, "The Emphasizing Particle *gam*," *Studia Biblica et Semitica* [Wageninger, 1966], pp. 193–203).

6 On וּבִשְׁפָטִים גְּדֹלִים (*ûḇišpāṭîm gᵉḏōlîm*, "And with mighty acts of judgment"), see also 7:4 and 12:12. It is a frequent plural phrase in Ezekiel (5:10, 15; 11:9 et al.). These acts will include deliverance (for Israel) and judgment (for Egypt) just as the unusual plural of *ṣdq* ("righteous acts") in Mic 6:5 and 1 Sam 12:7 imply.

Out of the 277 times הוֹצִיא (*hôṣî'*, "to bring out") occurs in the OT, 83 use the formula וְהוֹצֵאתִי (*wᵉhôṣē'ṯî*, "and I will bring [you] out") for the Exodus event. J. Wijngaards ("הוציא and העלה: A Twofold Approach to the Exodus," VetTest 15 [1965]: 91–102) argues that the הוציא ("will bring you out") formula is reserved for the miraculous crossing of the Reed Sea whereas the העלה ("I brought you up") formula (41 examples) is connected with the giving of the land. The former emanates from the Sinaitic pact while the latter reflects the northern sanctuaries of Bethel and Dan. We find these geographical assignments unsubstantiated. העלה is used very frequently in Exodus (see Solomon Mandelkern, *Veteris Testamenti Concordantiae* [Tel Aviv: Schocken, 1969], p. 873), and the claim that the הוציא formula was a late introduction in the Exodus tradition cannot be proven. Wijngaards himself notices the הוציא formula was joined with land giving in what scholars acclaim to be ancient credos of Deut 6:20–23; 26:5–9. Any isolation of tradition or documents based on an analysis of these two words will have to build into the evidence what it "finds" in the results, for God "will bring them out" even though Pharaoh "will not send them out." The difference in the verbs is the difference in perspective, not sources. The reason "bring out" is used in connection with Egypt and the Red Sea is that the perspective is different. When viewed from Egypt, the Exodus was a "bringing out"; but as soon as the sights were set on Canaan, the familiar topographical note was in vogue: they were "made to go up," i.e., to go up to the hill country, as indeed Canaan was.

The verb גָּאַל (*gā'al,* "to redeem") was used to describe Boaz's redemption of his close kin Ruth, when he married her and redeemed her property as well (Ruth 3:12–13; 4:1–12). Here God performs the same service—וְגָאַלְתִּי (*wᵉg̱ā'altî,* "and I will redeem [you]")—for his close kin Israel, by freeing them from slavery and redeeming their promised property in Canaan (cf. Lev 25:25, 47–55; 27:13; Deut 19:6 ["avenger"]; Isa 43:1 et al.).

---

6. *Reminders of Moses' lowly origins*

6:9–7:5

9 Moses reported this to the Israelites, but they did not listen to him because of their discouragement and cruel bondage.

10 Then the LORD said to Moses, 11 "Go, tell Pharaoh king of Egypt to let the Israelites go out of his country."

12 But Moses said to the LORD, "If the Israelites will not listen to me,why would Pharaoh listen to me, since I speak with faltering lips?"

13 Now the LORD spoke to Moses and Aaron about the Israelites and Pharaoh king of Egypt, and he commanded them to bring the Israelites out of Egypt.

14 These were the heads of their families:

The sons of Reuben the firstborn son of Israel were Hanoch and Pallu, Hezron and Carmi. These were the clans of Reuben.

15 The sons of Simeon were Jemuel, Jamin, Ohad, Jakin, Zohar and Shaul the son of a Canaanite woman. These were the clans of Simeon.

16 These were the names of the sons of Levi according to their records: Gershon, Kohath and Merari. Levi lived 137 years.

17 The sons of Gershon, by clans, were Libni and Shimei.

18 The sons of Kohath were Amram, Izhar, Hebron and Uzziel. Kohath lived 133 years.

19 The sons of Merari were Mahli and Mushi.
These were the clans of Levi according to their records.

20 Amram married his father's sister Jochebed, who bore him Aaron and Moses. Amram lived 137 years.

21 The sons of Izhar were Korah, Nepheg and Zicri.

22 The sons of Uzziel were Mishael, Elzaphan and Sithri.

23 Aaron married Elisheba, daughter of Amminadab and sister of Nahshon, and she bore him Nadab and Abihu, Eleazar and Ithamar.

> 24The sons of Korah were Assir, Elkanah and Abiasaph. These were the Korahite clans.
>
> 25Eleazar son of Aaron married one of the daughters of Putiel, and she bore him Phinehas.
>
> These were the heads of the Levite families, clan by clan.
>
> 26It was this same Aaron and Moses to whom the LORD said, "Bring the Israelites out of Egypt by their divisions." 27They were the ones who spoke to Pharaoh king of Egypt about bringing the Israelites out of Egypt. It was the same Moses and Aaron.
>
> 28Now when the LORD spoke to Moses in Egypt, 29he said to him, "I am the LORD. Tell Pharaoh king of Egypt everything I tell you."
>
> 30But Moses said to the LORD, "Since I speak with faltering lips, why would Pharaoh listen to me?"
>
> 7:1Then the LORD said to Moses, "See, I have made you like God to Pharaoh, and your brother Aaron will be your prophet. 2You are to say everything I command you, and your brother Aaron is to tell Pharaoh to let the Israelites go out of his country. 3But I will harden Pharaoh's heart, and though I multiply my miraculous signs and wonders in Egypt, 4he will not listen to you. Then I will lay my hand on Egypt and with mighty acts of judgment I will bring out my divisions, my people the Israelites. 5And the Egyptians will know that I am the LORD when I stretch out my hand against Egypt and bring the Israelites out of it."

9–12 In spite of the grandeur of what "I am the LORD" meant for Israel in the current situation, the people did not listen "for shortness of breath" (*miqqōṣer rûaḥ*). The NIV weakly translates "their discouragement" (v.9); but it was the inward pressure caused by deep anguish that prevented proper breathing—like children sobbing and gasping for their breath. This made such an impact on Moses that he had another attack of self-distrust and despondency. How could he persuade Pharaoh when he failed so miserably to impress his own countrymen who presumably would have had a naturally deep interest in what he had to say, given their circumstances (vv.11–12a). Anyway, his lips were "faltering" (v.12b; NIV mg., "uncircumcised") for the job they had been given to do (cf. the "uncircumcised" ears of Jer 6:10; "uncircumcised" heart of Jer 9:26). Thus Moses had returned to his fourth objection as stated in 4:10.

13–30 Many regard this section as an "interruption" of the narrative. But the narrative itself is at a turning point. The stage has been set in 1:1–6:12, and now the main action begins. However, before that action begins, it is important that the author once again remind his readers just who were that "Aaron and Moses to whom the LORD" had spoken (v.26). In fact, the whole genealogy of vv.14–25 is surrounded and framed by the near verbatim repetition of vv.10–13 in vv.26–30 and v.14a in v.25b. Therefore, the genealogical list serves no priestly (or even an alleged P document's) liturgical predilections. Rather, it concentrates on two men and how it was that they happened to be at this precise and momentous juncture in the history of men and nations.

Everything in the list suggests that God's choosing Moses had nothing to do with natural advantage or ability. The list stops after naming only three of Jacob's sons—Reuben, Simeon, and Levi—for its object had been reached. Moses and Aaron sprang, not from the "firstborn," Reuben, but from Levi, Jacob's third son, and not even then from Levi's oldest son; but Kohath, his second son (vv.16–19); and Moses was not even the oldest son of his father, for Aaron was older. Moses' calling and election of God were a gift of grace and not based on rights and privileges of birth. Nor was his pedigree that noble from a moral standpoint, for the mere mention of each of these names was enough to remind contemporaries of an "informing theology" that rattled ethical skeletons in his past—Reuben committed incest with his father's concubine (Gen 35:22), while Simeon and Levi were guilty of unwarranted outrage against Shechem (Gen 34:25–31).

So wicked were the three older sons of Jacob that they each inherited a curse: Reuben lost his birthright as "firstborn" (Gen 49:3–4), and Simeon and Levi were denied an inheritance with the tribes and were scattered instead (vv.5–8). But this was not done in any fatalistic way; for while Reuben's and Simeon's descendants did morally follow in their fathers' footsteps, Levi's descendants, with devotion to God, turned what was a curse into a blessing and used their dispersion through the tribes as an avenue of blessing to all through the priesthood and service at the sanctuary of God. This honor did not prevent Levi's descendant Korah (vv.21–24) from destroying himself by his own rebellion (Num 16); yet his descendants were not thereby forever adversely determined for evil, for they later rose to a place of high position in leading Israel in songs of praise in the temple and in composing Psalms 42–49, 84–85, and 87. So the *making* of "this same Moses and Aaron," as well as the *uses* they were put to after they were made, was totally the work of God. There was nothing left for them to claim or boast about in their pedigree. Nevertheless, the record also made plain that there was a congruity between the experiences and all the endowments that had accrued to Moses during these eighty years of life; thus election worked in the natural realm as well as the spiritual.

The text returns to repeat the words of vv.10–13 in vv.26–30 as if to say, "Look who is talking back to God! A man of few credentials except those given him in the providence and grace of God!" But never mind that, v.28 seems to affirm; it is now a whole new game. The style of the Hebrew grammar (see Notes) declares, "I am the LORD." The hour had come, and the name of the LORD would be all the equipment Moses would need.

7:1–5 While the LORD had made Moses as "God" to Aaron and Aaron in turn as his "prophet" to the people, Moses was also ordained (*nāṯan*) as "God" to Pharaoh in that he would speak and act with authority and power from above and Aaron would be Moses' "prophet" addressing Pharaoh (v.1; cf. 4:15–16). But again this team was warned that Pharaoh's heart would be "hardened" (*qšh*, v.3; see on 4:21) even though God would graciously provide him with supporting evidence by way of signs and wonders (see on 4:21). Nevertheless, after God had judged Egypt with his "mighty acts of judgment" (v.4; see Notes on 6:6), Israel would come out by its "divisions" (see Notes on 6:26).

Not only would Israel know what was meant by the name Yahweh, but so would the Egyptians. It would be as Jeremiah 16:21 described what it was to know the LORD: "Then they will know that my name is the LORD." In addition to understanding the significance of the tetragrammaton (YHWH), these miracles would also be an invitation for the Egyptians to personally believe in this LORD. Thus the invitation was pressed repeatedly in 7:5; 8:10, 22; 9:14, 16, 29; 14:4, 18—and some apparently did believe, for there was "a mixed multitude" (12:38 KJV) that left Egypt with Israel.

Notes

13 Whether this verse is a summary of chs. 3–5 (Rawlinson, 1:155) or an anticipation of Aaron's active involvement in 7:1–5 is debatable, but it seems best to understand it as a renewal of the orders received at the bush just as a new start begins in 7:1.

14 רָאשֵׁי בֵית־אֲבֹתָם (*rā'šê bêṯ-'ᵃḇōṯām,* "heads of their families") is literally "heads of their father's houses" (cf. Gen 12:1; 20:13; Exod 1:1; Num 1:4). The word "house" came to mean "household" and thus "family."

The list for Reuben's sons is identical to Gen 46:9 and 1 Chron 5:3.

15 The list for the sons of Simeon is the same as Gen 46:10, but it differs from Num 26:12 and 1 Chron 4:24. In the later two lists Jemuel is Nemuel, Zohar is Zerah, and Ohad is missing, perhaps because he subsequently died or for some other unknown reason. In 1 Chron 4:24 Jakin appears as Jarib.

20 "Amram" mentioned here is probably not the "man of the house of Levi" in 2:1 except in a removed sense (see comment on 2:1). The verb וַתֵּלֶד (*wattēleḏ,* "and she bore") can be used of an ancestor removed by several generations as "bearing" her great-grandchildren, even as Jacob's two wives also "bore" the children their handmaids gave to Jacob (Gen 46:18, 25).

26; 7:4 The term צְבָאוֹת (*ṣᵉḇā'ôṯ,* "divisions" or "armies") had not previously been used of the people of Israel. Later this term with the name of Yahweh would become one of the most frequent names for God: "LORD of hosts" (NIV, "LORD Almighty"), e.g., as David was reassured as he went to meet Goliath in 1 Sam 17:45.

28 וַיְהִי בְּיוֹם דִּבֶּר (*wayᵉhî ḇᵉyyôm dibber,* "Now when the Lord spoke") is literally, "And it came to pass in the day of [Yahweh's] speaking [to Moses]." The unusual Hebrew grammatical form has a noun "day" in the construct with the verb "he spoke" (cf. Gen 2:3; Hos 1:2 et al.). This construction highlights the fact that a new day had dawned.

D. *Judgment and Salvation Through the Plagues (7:6–11:10)*

1. *Presenting the signs of divine authority*

7:6–13

6 Moses and Aaron did just as the LORD commanded them. 7 Moses was
eighty years old and Aaron eighty-three when they spoke to Pharaoh.
8 The LORD said to Moses and Aaron, 9 "When Pharaoh says to you,
'Perform a miracle,' then say to Aaron, 'Take your staff and throw it
down before Pharaoh,' and it will become a snake."
10 So Moses and Aaron went to Pharaoh and did just as the LORD
commanded. Aaron threw his staff down in front of Pharaoh and his
officials, and it became a snake. 11 Pharaoh then summoned wise men
and sorcerers, and the Egyptian magicians also did the same things by
their secret arts: 12 Each one threw down his staff and it became a
snake. But Aaron's staff swallowed up their staffs. 13 Yet Pharaoh's heart
became hard and he would not listen to them, just as the LORD had said.

6–9 After eighty years of preparation, Moses began his life work (v.6). He and Aaron were directed to reappear before Pharaoh who in turn would request them to perform a miracle, presumably to assure him that they were messengers of Israel's God (vv.7–9). Undoubtedly his tone was supercilious and his expectation was that there would be no miracle; for he judged Moses and Aaron to be nothing but opportunists and insurrectionists.

Significantly, Scripture judges Pharaoh's demand for validation of such claims as reasonable. The Lord informed Moses to use the first of the three signs he had drawn on to convince Israel that he was indeed an accredited messenger of God (v.9; see 4:2-9, 30-31). However, in this instance Aaron's staff (it was the same as Moses' staff or the staff of God; cf. 4:17; 7:15, 17, 19-20) when cast down became a *tannîn* ("great serpent," "dragon," or "crocodile"; see Notes). (In 4:3-4 it became a *nāḥāš*, "snake.") The connection of the name *tannîn* with the symbol of Egypt is clear from Psalm 74:13 and Ezekiel 29:3.

10-13 Moses and Aaron did exactly as God instructed them—only to learn that Pharaoh's wise men, sorcerers, and magicians (see Notes) were able to imitate the same feat by their magical arts (vv.10-11; see Notes). The use of magic in Egypt is well documented in the Westcar Papyrus where magicians are credited with changing wax crocodiles into real ones only to be turned back to wax again after seizing their tails. Montet (pp. 92-94, fig. 17) also refers to several Egyptian scarabs that depict a snake charmer holding a serpent made stiff as a staff up in the air before some observing deities (cf. ANET, p. 326, with a spell on a "spotted" knife [representing a snake?] that "goes forth against its like" and devours it).

The relation between Aaron's miracle and the magical act of the magicians, whom Paul knew by the names of Jannes and Jambres in 2 Timothy 3:8, is hard to define. Possibly by the use of illusion and deceptive appearances they were able to cast spells over what appeared to be their staffs but which actually were serpents rendered immobile (catalepsy) by pressure on the nape of their necks and by the use of magical spells. Or perhaps it was by demonic power. (For a fuller treatment of this difficult subject, see KD, 1:475-77.) However, as evidence of God's greater power, Pharaoh's magicians lost their "staffs" when Aaron's "swallowed up" theirs. But Pharaoh was unaffected. His heart "became hard" (v.13; there is no reflexive or passive idea to the verb *yeḥezaq*, as so many translations render it).

Notes

9 תַּנִּין (*tannîn*, "snake," "serpent") is usually used for larger reptiles (Gen 1:21; Deut 32:33) such as crocodiles (Ezek 29:3) or a sea monster and leviathan (Job 7:12; Isa 27:1; 51:9; Jer 51:34). It also often is used metaphorically as a symbol of national empires and power (e.g., Deut 32:33; Ps 74:13; Ezek 29:3).

11 חֲכָמִים (*ḥᵃḵāmîm*, "wise men") were the learned and schooled men of that day.

מְכַשְּׁפִים (*mᵉḵaššᵉpîm*, "sorcerers," "magicians") is the intensive participle of the verb *kšp* ("to pray, offer prayers"; cf. BDB, s.v.). It is used in the OT only in the sense of sorcery.

חַרְטֻמִּים (*ḥarṭummîm*, "magicians") is always plural in the OT except in Dan 2:10 (cf. Gen 41:8, 24; Exod 7:22; 8:7, 18-19; 9:11; Dan 1:20; 2:2). It derives from an Egyptian loan word, *ḥry-ḥbt*, later shortened to *ḥry-tp* ("the chief of the priests"). In a seventh-century B.C. Assyrian document, it appears as *ḥar-ṭibi* (A.H. Gardiner, "The House of Life," *Journal of Egyptian Archaeology* 24 [1938]: 164-65; J. Vergote, *Joseph en Egypte* [Louvaine: Publications Universitaires, 1959], pp. 66-73, 206; D.B. Redford, *A Study of the Biblical Story of Joseph* [Leiden: Brill, 1970], pp. 203-4).

בְּלַהֲטֵיהֶם (*bᵉlahᵃṭêhem*, "by their secret arts") is from the root לוּט (*lûṭ*, "to enwrap"; spelled here with an infixed he but without it in 7:22), hence the meaning "mysterious" or "secret." The Egyptian word for magic is *hike'*.

Excursus: Introduction to the Plagues

The plague accounts exhibit a clear and unified structure. The unitary character of the plagues has long been noticed, especially by Isaac Abravanel (1437–1508), Rabbi Samuel ben Meir (d. 1158), and Bahya ben Asher in his thirteenth century commentary (see Ziony Zevit, "The Priestly Redaction and Interpretation of the Plague Narrative in Exodus," JQR 66 [1976]: 194, nn. 6–7).

It has been pointed out that the first nine plagues are arranged in three groups of three plagues each. The first plague in each group (viz., nos. 1, 4, 7) was introduced by a warning delivered to Pharaoh early in the morning as he went out to the Nile (7:15; 8:20; 9:13 [though this last one does not specify the Nile]). The second plague in each group (nos. 2, 5, 8) was also introduced by a warning, but it was delivered to Pharaoh at his palace (8:1; 9:1; 10:1). The last plague in each group (nos. 3, 6, 9) commenced without any warning (8:16; 9:8; 10:21).

When these same nine plagues are considered sequentially, however, they may likewise be viewed in another arrangement of three sets of triplets in an ascending order of severity: the first three (nos. 1, 2, 3) introduced irritations, the second set (nos. 4, 5, 6) destructions, and the final set (nos. 7, 8, 9) death. Again, each in the first set were brought on with the use of Aaron's staff (7:19; 8:5, 16); the first two plagues in the second set (nos. 4, 5) were the work of the Lord directly while the last one (no. 6) was the result of Moses' word (8:24; 9:3, 6 and 10); and the last set of three (nos. 7, 8, 9) were all brought on by Moses with his outstretched hand and staff (9:22–23; 10:12–13, 21–22).

Other attempts to find the structure and meaning of the plagues are less convincing. Cassuto (pp. 92–93) suggests that all ten plagues be broken down sequentially into sets of two according to the nature of the things affected: the Nile (nos. 1, 2); then two similar plagues (of lice and flies; nos. 3, 4); animals and humans were next affected (nos. 5, 6); then crops were damaged (nos. 7, 8); followed by darkness of days and darkness of death (nos. 9, 10). There is insufficient evidence from the text to justify this arrangement, and the logic is missing in some (nos. 3, 4) or is forced in others (nos. 9, 10).

Dennis McCarthy ("Moses' Dealings With Pharaoh," CBQ 27 [1965]: 341–43) finds a concentric scheme that begins with the miracle of the staff turned into a snake numbered first and continues through the nine plagues by dividing the miracle and nine plagues into two groups of five so that the second set of five is matched with the first set in such a way that episode one is paired off with episode ten, two with nine, and so forth. But this chiastic arrangement is highly selective and artificial. Admittedly, it is dependent on certain key phrases and on the observation of the alternation of long and short units, but it neglects to account for some of these same key phrases in other units and includes the snake-staff miracle as number one. Most damaging is its failure to account for the real purpose and aim of these plagues by this arrangement.

Only the triplet grouping brings out the aim of the plagues and their sequence as recorded here. The initial plague in each triplet (nos. 1, 4, 7) has a purpose clause in which God sets forth for Moses his rationale and aim in bringing the hardships in that set:

The first set (7:17): "By this you [Pharaoh] will know that I am the LORD" (repeated in 8:10 and in effect in 8:19), meaning Pharaoh would come to know just who Yahweh was and what the dynamic presence of his name signified;

The second set (8:22): "That you will know that I, the LORD, am in this land," meaning God's overseeing providence and guidance of the world;

The third set (9:14): "So you may know that there is no one like me in all the earth," meaning the scope and force of God's power (cf. 9:16, 29–30; 10:1) were beyond anything known to man in all the earth (see C.J. Labuschagne, *The Incomparability of Yahweh in the OT* [Leiden: Brill, 1966], pp. 74–75, 92–94). In fact, this overall purpose for the plagues had already been announced in 7:4–5. This display of "power" and "signs" pointing to his person are also part of the psalmist's appeal to these plagues in Psalms 78:42–51 and 105:28–38.

2. *First plague: water turned to blood*

7:14–24

14Then the LORD said to Moses, "Pharaoh's heart is unyielding; he refuses to let the people go. 15Go to Pharaoh in the morning as he goes out to the water. Wait on the bank of the Nile to meet him, and take in your hand the staff that was changed into a snake. 16Then say to him, 'The LORD, the God of the Hebrews, has sent me to say to you: Let my people go, so that they may worship me in the desert. But until now you have not listened. 17This is what the LORD says: By this you will know that I am the LORD: With the staff that is in my hand I will strike the water of the Nile, and it will be changed into blood. 18The fish in the Nile will die, and the river will stink; the Egyptians will not be able to drink its water.' "

19The LORD said to Moses, "Tell Aaron, 'Take your staff and stretch out your hand over the waters of Egypt—over the streams and canals, over the ponds and all the reservoirs'—and they will turn to blood. Blood will be everywhere in Egypt, even in the wooden buckets and stone jars."

20Moses and Aaron did just as the LORD had commanded. He raised his staff in the presence of Pharaoh and his officials and struck the water of the Nile, and all the water was changed into blood. 21The fish in the Nile died, and the river smelled so bad that the Egyptians could not drink its water. Blood was everywhere in Egypt.

22But the Egyptian magicians did the same things by their secret arts, and Pharaoh's heart became hard; he would not listen to Moses and Aaron, just as the LORD had said. 23Instead, he turned and went into his palace, and did not take even this to heart. 24And all the Egyptians dug along the Nile to get drinking water, because they could not drink the water of the river.

14–18 Moses was instructed by God to go early (so in 8:20) in the morning with his brother, Aaron, to intercept Pharaoh and his officials as they went out to the Nile (v.15; cf. v.20). Pharaoh's purpose for going to the Nile accompanied by his officials remains unknown. One might hazard the guess that he was there to worship the Nile River god, Hapi. Moses and Aaron, however, were there to remind Pharaoh that "the LORD, the God of the Hebrews" (v.16) had sent them (5:1); yet the king of Egypt remained resolute in his defiance of this Lord. Therefore, God would help Pharaoh "know" who he was (v.17)—Pharaoh had protested in 5:2, "I do not know the LORD." God would change the water of the Nile River into blood when Moses struck the Nile with his staff (v.17).

It is clear that v.17 and later 17:5 make Moses alone the user of the staff against the Nile River, but 7:19 has God instructing Moses to tell Aaron to stretch out his hand over all the waters in all Egypt so that they would be changed into blood. This hardly seems to be two different events of action by the two men. Verses 20–21 treat it as a single event; and it is not a clumsily overlooked inconsistency that leaves the trail of the divergent sources from which the material came. Instead, it is as Bush noted (*Exodus*, 1:96), an "example of the phraseology by which an agent is said to do that which he commands or procures to be done" (cf. Hos 8:1).

19–21 When Aaron stretched out his staff and struck what the Egyptians regarded as sacred, the Nile and the water all over Egypt turned to blood (vv.20–21). What was the "blood"? W.M. Flinders Petrie (*Egypt and Israel* [London: Society for Promoting Christian Knowledge; New York: E.S. Gorsham et al., 1911], pp. 25–36) was the first to suggest that the sequence of the plagues followed a natural cycle and all happened in one year. More recently Greta Hort ("The Plagues of Egypt," ZAW 69 [1957]: 84–103; id., 70 [1958]: 48–59) traced this connected sequence by beginning with an unusually high Nile flood in July and August. The sources for the Nile's inundation are the equatorial rains that fill the White Nile, which originates in east-central Africa (present-day Uganda) and flows sluggishly through swamps in eastern Sudan; and the Blue Nile and the Atbara River, which both fill with melting snow from the mountains and become raging torrents filled with tons of red soil from the basins of both these rivers. The higher the inundation, the deeper the color of the red waters. In addition to this discoloration, a type of algae, known as flagellates, comes from the Sudan swamps and Lake Tana along the White Nile, which produces the stench and the deadly fluctuation in the oxygen level of the river that proves to be so fatal to the fish. Such a process, at the command of God, seems to be the case for this first plague rather than any chemical change of the water into red and white corpuscles (cf. Joel 2:31: "the moon [will be changed] to blood," or 2 Kings 3:22, where, however, the water looked "like blood," *kaddām*).

Unlike other plagues and in agreement with this natural phenomenon, this plague did not stop suddenly. This explanation was accepted already by such conservatives as Keil (1864; KD, 1:478–79), Lange (1876; p. 20), and more recently Kenneth Kitchen (NBD, pp. 1000–1002). This change affected the "streams" (= seven [in Herodotus] branches of the Nile), the canals (to fertilize the fields), the ponds (left from the overflowing Nile), and the reservoirs (artificially made to store water for later use).

22–24 Once again Pharaoh's magicians applied their "secret arts" and imitated the miracle sufficiently to blunt the force of it on Pharaoh's conscience (v.22). The question, where they found any unblemished water if the fourfold water system in "all Egypt" (vv.19, 21) was affected, is answered in v.24—from subterranean water from freshly dug wells. The expression "all" or "every" must not be pressed in this case on the analogy of 9:6, 11, and 25 (cf. the obvious hyperbole of 10:5; Gen 41:57: "*All* the countries came to Egypt to buy grain"; Matt 3:5: "*All* Judea and the *whole region* of the Jordan" [emphases mine]). Bush (*Exodus*, 1:78) chides, "If they had had any confidence in their own art, they would rather have attempted to turn the blood into water than . . . to ape the miracle of Moses, . . . though there is no evidence of their succeeding even in this." But Pharaoh remained unmoved and merely returned to his palace from the bloody river's edge: his heart grew rigid and hard in spite of this evidence (v.23).

Notes

---

19 וּבָעֵצִים וּבָאֲבָנִים (*ûḇā'ēṣîm ûḇā'ᵃḇānîm*) is literally "and in wooden [things] and in stone [things]." The NIV's "In the wooden buckets and stone jars" is doubtful since vessels of wood and stone were not common in Egypt. Hyatt (p. 106) is most certainly incorrect—"even the sap in the trees and the springs . . . in stony places"—as is Cassuto (p. 99) when he conjectures that the water used to wash the *idols of* wood and stone also turned to blood (the preposition *ḇ* he interpreted as "on"). Rawlinson (1:172) had a better suggestion: "in the wooden and stone settlement tanks," which were used for storing the Nile River water so that the sediment would sink before the water was used. Egypt often received no rain and never more than ten inches rainfall per year in the delta.

23 וְלֹא־שָׁת לִבּוֹ (*w^{e}lō' šāṯ libbô*, "and [he] did not take even this to heart") is an expression widely used in the OT (e.g., 9:21; cf. Hag 1:5, 7; 2:15, 18 with the verb *śîm*). It simply means "pay attention."

---

2. *Second plague: frogs*

7:25–8:15

25 Seven days passed after the LORD struck the Nile.
8:1 Then the LORD said to Moses, "Go to Pharaoh and say to him, 'This
is what the LORD says: Let my people go, so that they may worship me.
2 If you refuse to let them go, I will plague your whole country with frogs.
3 The Nile will teem with frogs. They will come up into your palace and
your bedroom and onto your bed, into the houses of your officials and
on your people, and into your ovens and kneading troughs. 4 The frogs
will go up on you and your people and all your officials.' "
5 Then the LORD said to Moses, "Tell Aaron, 'Stretch out your hand with
your staff over the streams and canals and ponds, and make frogs come
up on the land of Egypt.' "
6 So Aaron stretched out his hand over the waters of Egypt, and the
frogs came up and covered the land. 7 But the magicians did the same
things by their secret arts; they also made frogs come up on the land of
Egypt.
8 Pharaoh summoned Moses and Aaron and said, "Pray to the LORD to
take the frogs away from me and my people, and I will let your people go
to offer sacrifices to the LORD."
9 Moses said to Pharaoh, "I leave to you the honor of setting the time
for me to pray for you and your officials and your people that you and
your houses may be rid of the frogs, except for those that remain in the
Nile."
10 "Tomorrow," Pharaoh said.
Moses replied, "It will be as you say, so that you may know there is no
one like the LORD our God. 11 The frogs will leave you and your houses,
your officials and your people; they will remain only in the Nile."
12 After Moses and Aaron left Pharaoh, Moses cried out to the LORD
about the frogs he had brought on Pharaoh. 13 And the LORD did what
Moses asked. The frogs died in the houses, in the courtyards and in the
fields. 14 They were piled into heaps, and the land reeked of them. 15 But
when Pharaoh saw that there was relief, he hardened his heart and
would not listen to Moses and Aaron, just as the LORD had said.

25–8:5 Seven days after the first plague had begun, Moses and Aaron were instructed by God to take their demands to the king's palace (7:25–8:1). If he would refuse to grant their repeated request to go to the desert to worship the Lord, they were to announce in the set formula, "I will plague your whole country with frogs" (v.2). This was not to be a "sign" but a "plague" only (See Notes). In comparison with what was to come, this was only a trivial annoyance.

6–7 On Aaron's signal the frogs emerged from the water and "covered" the land, says the text with legitimate hyperbole (v.6). These pesty creatures, though regarded as sacred to the Egyptians, were God's scourge to whip men into facing the living God. The intensification of the nuisance by Pharaoh's magicians was totally ignored by him (v.7). The fact was that tons of croaking, crawling, creeping intruders were everywhere.

8–15 Why should the frogs so suddenly abandon their natural habitat in August during a high Nile and invade the homes, bedrooms, ovens, kneading troughs, and even the palace itself? And why should they likewise die off so suddenly? Hort ("Plagues," pp. 95–98) found the connection to be in the dead fish that had been killed by flagellates. The frogs abandoned all the polluted and overflowing waterways (cf. 7:19) and sought cover from the sun on dry land in homes where possibly the presence of some unadulterated water attracted them. However, since they had already been exposed to spores of *bacillus anthracis* from the death spread along the waterways, the frogs also suddenly collapsed and died.

Pharaoh had finally been forced to acknowledge the power of Yahweh, not by the armies of men, but by squadrons of loathsome little frogs. Now he knew who this "LORD" was (cf. 5:2), and he acceded to Moses and Aaron's request (v.8)—only to renege later on (v.15).

Moses' response to Pharaoh's desperate or, as some think, cynical plea was to dare Pharaoh to test his prophetic credentials (v.9) and, more importantly, the power of God (v.10) by setting the time when he wished to be rid of this plague. Pharaoh's quick response of "tomorrow" led Moses to enter into some intensely earnest prayer (v.12). (The whole scene reoccurs with Elijah in a similar daring contest of prayer with the prophets of Baal in 1 Kings 18:36–37.) Moses' freedom to negotiate on his own terms and then to have, as it were, God back him up is remarkable. The frogs dropped dead all over the place—in the houses, fields, and open courtyards (v.13). Frogs were piled up in heaps, and there was a firm reminder to aid Pharaoh's wavering memory—the stench of dead frogs (v.14). Nevertheless, that faded and so did Pharaoh's permission. This "relief" (*hārwāḥāh*, v.15) was worse than the plague for this proud king. Men do not often learn the righteousness of God when he grants them his mercy and his favor (Ps 78:34–42; Isa 26:10).

Notes

---

1 (7:26 MT) Bush (*Exodus*, in loc.) points out that the rendering of the waw conjunction to introduce a purpose clause agrees with usage here in וְיַעַבְדֻנִי (*w^e ya'abdunî*, "so that they may worship me") and in 7:11–12; 8:7–8.

2 (27 MT) Surprisingly few Hebrew terms are used for the plagues in this narrative. Actually, only in 9:14 is the word מַגֵּפֹת (*maggēpōt*, "plagues") used. Here it is נֹגֵף (*nōgēp*, "plague"). In 12:13 it is נֶגֶף (*negēp*, "a hit" or "pestilence"); in 11:1, נֶגַע (*nega'*, "stroke"); and in 9:3, 15, דֶּבֶר (*deber*, "pestilence"). The NIV uniformly renders them "plague."

צְפַרְדְּעִים (*ṣ^e pard^e'îm*, "frogs") may be the Hebrew equivalent of the Egyptian Arabic name *dofda* or, as Cole suggests (p. 91), an onomatopoeic form that attempts to imitate the cacophony of their incessant croaks. Frogs were associated with the froghead goddess Heqet who assisted women at childbirth. The scientific name for these frogs, which are similar to our toads, is *Rama Mosaica*. Frogs are only mentioned in the OT in connection with this plague: Pss 78:45; 105:30. Notice in v.6 "the frog [sing., Heb.] came up" is again used for the collective (NIV, "frogs").

7 (8:3 MT) On "secret arts" see Notes on 7:11.

9 (5 MT) הִתְפָּאֵר עָלַי (*hiṯpā'ēr 'ālay*) is a difficult phrase. The LXX has "appoint for me," but more literally it is "glorify yourself over me." This is more than an ordinary courtesy; it is an invitation to actually give Pharaoh the upper hand for the moment. The NIV translates it "I leave to you the honor of."

10 (6 MT) לְמָחָר (*lemāḥār*, "tomorrow"; lit., "For tomorrow") was Pharaoh's answer to Moses' question: "*For* when" or "*For* what date shall I ask in prayer to God?" (v.9, lit. tr.).

12 (8 MT) וַיִּצְעַק (*wayyiṣ'aq*, "and [Moses] cried out") is a strong expression to denote the earnestness and intensity of the prayer.

---

4. *Third plague: gnats*

8:16–19

16 Then the LORD said to Moses, "Tell Aaron, 'Stretch out your staff and strike the dust of the ground,' and throughout the land of Egypt the dust will become gnats." 17 They did this, and when Aaron stretched out his hand with the staff and struck the dust of the ground, gnats came upon men and animals. All the dust throughout the land of Egypt became gnats. 18 But when the magicians tried to produce gnats by their secret arts, they could not. And the gnats were on men and animals.

19 The magicians said to Pharaoh, "This is the finger of God." But Pharaoh's heart was hard and he would not listen, just as the LORD had said.

16–17 The third plague began without warning to Pharaoh or his magicians. God again used the outstretched staff in the hand of Aaron to initiate this plague. Aaron struck the dust of the ground, just as he had struck the Nile in the first plague (7:20), and "*all* the dust throughout the land of Egypt became gnats" (8:17, emphasis mine)—another hyperbole to stress the tremendous extent and intensity of this pestilence (cf. 7:19, 21; 9:6, 19, 25; 10:5).

The word "gnats" (*kinnîm*) occurs five times in this passage and nowhere else except in the parallel passage of Psalm 105:31 (unless another reading is verified in Isa 51:6). It is debatable whether this word means "lice," as in the KJV, Peshitta, Josephus, the Targum of Onkelos, or "gnats," "mosquitoes," as we favor with most interpreters, especially the LXX translators (who had firsthand acquaintance with Egypt [Gk. *skniphes*]), Philo, Origen, Gesenius, Keil, and others.

18–19 On their fourth attempt to duplicate the miracles of Moses and Aaron, the Egyptian magicians admitted defeat (v.18). Interestingly enough, as Cassuto (pp. 105–6) remarks, the sentence literally reads, "And the magicians did so by their secret arts to bring forth gnats, but they could not." Since the identical expression, as it appears in the first half of that statement, had been used in the previous three contests with these magicians, Cassuto argues that the phrase only meant in those cases also that they attempted to do their trick by their magic and not that they actually worked any miracles. This seems an odd use of language. However, in spite of what success they did or did not experience in the previous three encounters (and it could well have been through slight of hand—given the advance notice of the nature of the plague or sign in those cases, or perhaps it was just plain demonic, supernatural empowerment to mimic God's power), they now realized that the plague of the gnats was the "finger of God" (v.19), i.e., the result of his power (see Notes). But Pharaoh was not so persuaded in his heart and mind—he remained adamant and opposed to any Israelite demands.

Notes

---

16 (12 MT) כִּנִּם (*kinnîm*, "gnats") appears in vv.17–18 (vv.13–14 MT) as a feminine collective (*hakkinnām*) since it is governed by the third person singular verb תְּהִי (*tᵉhî*, lit., "she came").

19 (15 MT) אֶצְבַּע אֱלֹהִים (*'eṣba' 'ᵉlōhîm*, "finger of God") is a figure of speech called synecdoche, where a portion (here of the divine Person) is used to denote the totality (of his power). See "finger of God" in Exod 31:18; Ps 8:3; Luke 11:20, or "hand of God" in 1 Sam 6:9; Ps 109:27. Cook (p. 281) argues that the expression is rather thoroughly Egyptian. It either attributes this act of God as being hostile to one of their protecting gods (e.g., the god of the earth, Set); or it equates Aaron's wooden rod with the finger of a specific deity, as it does, for example, in ch. 153 of the Egyptian *Book of the Dead*. Synecdoche is the preferable explanation, because the magicians' attitude is contrasted with Pharaoh's hard-heartedness.

---

5. *Fourth plague: flies*

8:20–32

20 Then the LORD said to Moses, "Get up early in the morning and
confront Pharaoh as he goes to the water and say to him, 'This is what
the LORD says: Let my people go, so that they may worship me. 21 If you
do not let my people go, I will send swarms of flies on you and your
officials, on your people and into your houses. The houses of the
Egyptians will be full of flies, and even the ground where they are.
22 " 'But on that day I will deal differently with the land of Goshen,
where my people live; no swarms of flies will be there, so that you will
know that I, the LORD, am in this land. 23 I will make a distinction between
my people and your people. This miraculous sign will occur tomorrow.' "
24 And the LORD did this. Dense swarms of flies poured into Pharaoh's
palace and into the houses of his officials, and throughout Egypt the
land was ruined by the flies.
25 Then Pharaoh summoned Moses and Aaron and said, "Go, sacrifice
to your God here in the land."
26 But Moses said, "That would not be right. The sacrifices we offer
the LORD our God would be detestable to the Egyptians. And if we offer
sacrifices that are detestable in their eyes, will they not stone us? 27 We
must take a three-day journey into the desert to offer sacrifices to the
LORD our God, as he commands us."
28 Pharaoh said, "I will let you go to offer sacrifices to the LORD your
God in the desert, but you must not go very far. Now pray for me."
29 Moses answered, "As soon as I leave you, I will pray to the LORD, and
tomorrow the flies will leave Pharaoh and his officials and his people.
Only be sure that Pharaoh does not act deceitfully again by not letting
the people go to offer sacrifices to the LORD."

30 Then Moses left Pharaoh and prayed to the LORD, 31 and the LORD did what Moses asked: The flies left Pharaoh and his officials and his people; not a fly remained. 32 But this time also Pharaoh hardened his heart and would not let the people go.

20–21 As in the first plague, Moses was to intercept Pharaoh again as he went down to the Nile early in the morning. Cook (p. 281) postulated that the occasion for this royal procession was to open the solemn festival held 120 days after the first rising of the Nile, i.e., about the end of October or the beginning of November. This time Pharaoh and all his people and their houses were threatened with a plague of "flies" (*heʿārōḇ*). The modern attempts to identify these creatures include (1) beasts, reptiles, and insects, supposing the word represents an Arabic root meaning "unmixed" (cf. that meaning in 12:38; NIV, "other people"); (2) the LXX rendering *kynomuia* ("dog fly"), a bloodsucking gadfly that, however, appears in the spring of the year and not the fall, when this plague is found; (3) the ordinary housefly, which is found in Isaiah 7:18 as a symbol for Egypt, but the Hebrew word there is *zeḇûḇ*; and (4) the beetle *blatta orientalis*, which gnaws clothes, furniture, plants, man, and beast, arriving in late November, and bearing a close resemblance to the Hebrew *ʿārōb* in an Egyptian word retained in Coptic, *Abeb* (Cook, p. 490; Knight, pp. 63–64, compares it to the scarab beetle).

It seems best to follow Hort ("Plagues," pp. 99, 102) and say that the fly *Stomoxys calcitrans* best fulfills all the conditions of the text. This fly multiplies rapidly in tropical or subtropical regions (hence the delta with its Mediterranean climate would be exempt) in the fall by laying its six hundred to eight hundred eggs in dung or rotting plant debris. When it is full grown, the fly prefers to infest houses and stables, and it bites both men and animals, usually in the lower extremities. Thus it becomes the principal transmitter of skin anthrax (see plague six), which it contracts by crawling over the carcasses of animals that have died of internal anthrax.

22–24 God would aid those hardened Egyptian hearts who suspect nothing more than chance or difficult times had been involved in the preceding three plagues by inaugurating a "distinction" (see Notes) between Moses' people and Pharaoh's people. This distinction is found in the fourth, fifth, seventh, ninth, and tenth plagues (v.23; 9:4, 6, 26; 10:23; 11:7). The purpose of this preferential treatment to Israel was to teach Pharaoh and the Egyptians that the Lord God of Israel was in the midst of this land doing these works; it was not one of their local deities. Gods were thought by ancient Near Easterners to possess no power except on their own home ground. But not so here! The innocent were being delivered and the guilty afflicted because this God was in their midst. He would again do a "miraculous sign" designed to evoke faith in him from the Egyptians and the release of Israel (see Notes on 4:8).

In another innovative feature Moses announced in advance when the plague was due to strike, giving the Egyptians time to repent. This advance notice is found in the fourth, fifth, sixth, eighth, and tenth plagues (v.21; 9:5, 18; 10:4; 11:4). Moreover, Pharaoh and his court were again singled out as the first victims of this plague because of the heavy responsibility they bore for their intransigence (vv.21, 24).

25–32 Moses' claim—that if Israel sacrificed animals in Egypt, it would be extremely offensive to the Egyptians (v.26)—has been challenged by some commentators as a clever ruse on Moses' part. Yet Rylaarsdam (p. 901) was able to document a violent

Egyptian reaction to Jewish sacrifices in the fifth-century B.C. colony at Elephantine (A.E. Cowley, *Aramaic Papyri of the Fifth Century B.C.* [Oxford: Clarendon], 1923, pp. 108–22). Thus Moses rejected Pharaoh's counteroffer to allow Israel to sacrifice in Egypt (v.25).

Finally, Pharaoh conceded the long-denied permission. With a note of self-importance he pontificated, "*I* [*'ānōḵî*] will let you go . . . but [*raq*] you must not go very far" (v.28). And as if to show what his real thoughts were all along, he quickly added, "Now pray for me."

Moses was not to be put down, for his mission likewise had dignity; so he, too, began with the pronoun "I" (*'ānōḵî*): "*I* am leaving you, and *I* will pray" (v.29, lit. tr.). Moses, with an obvious rebuke, said, in effect, "Don't you 'however' me when you are in such a poor bargaining position." But then on a courteous note, with a switch to the third-person form of address, he continued, "Only [*raq*] be sure that Pharaoh does not act deceitfully again."

The plague was removed through Moses' prayer (cf. Elijah, 1 Kings 18:42; Amos, Amos 7:2, 5). So effective was the power of prayer and the evidence that God was in their midst that "not a fly remained" (v.31). But Pharaoh once again (cf. second plague, 8:15) returned to his hard-nosed stand once he obtained the physical relief he desired.

Notes

---

21 (17 MT) אֲשֶׁר . . . עָלֶיהָ (*'ašer . . . 'āleyhā,* "where . . . are") is literally "on which, where." "Even the ground where they [i.e., the Egyptians] are" is sharply contrasted with v.22's *'āleyhā* ("Where [my people live]").

22 (18 MT) The LXX renders וְהִפְלֵיתִי (*wehiplêṯî,* "I will deal differently") as "I will marvelously glorify," misunderstanding it as from פָּלָא (*pālā'*). The term occurs again in 33:16: "What else will distinguish me and your people from all the other people on . . . earth." Also see 9:4 and 11:7.

גֹּשֶׁן (*gōšen,* "Goshen") was the eastern delta region. About fifty miles northeast of modern Cairo is the Wadi Tumilat, a valley five or six miles wide and thirty miles long, ending in Lake Timsah, now part of the present-day Suez Canal. The name Goshen, in an Egyptian name, is spelled like the other two delta names with a word beginning with a bull, *ka* = Hebrew first syllable *Go*.

23 (19 MT) פְּדֻת (*peḏuṯ,* "a distinction") is correct here even though *peḏuṯ* generally is rendered "redemption" or "deliverance" (a concept used of the impending Exodus in 6:6: cf. *gā'al,* "to redeem [as a kinsman]"). To emend the text to read *pelûṯ* ("separation") is unwarranted since that noun form would be a *hapax legomenon.* Likewise, to posit on the basis of an Arabic root an otherwise unattested Hebrew root of *pdd* meaning "was/became apart," as does A.A. Macintosh ("Exodus VII 19, Distinct Redemption and the Hebrew Roots PDH and PDD," VetTest 21 [1971]: 548–55), is difficult since the spelling, meaning, and ending of *t* instead of *h* for feminine absolute nouns from double ayin verbs are all problematical. Therefore, I agree with G.I. Davies ("The Hebrew Text of Exodus VIII 19 [EVV 23]: An Emendation," VetTest 24 [1974]: 489–92), that the letter *d* was omitted by haplography from the text that originally read *prdt* from the verb *prd,* "to separate" in the Hiphil, which is used three times in the OT with *bên* ("between"; Ruth 1:17; 2 Kings 2:11; Prov 18:18).

24 (20 MT) אֶרֶץ . . . תִּשָּׁחֵת (*'ereṣ . . . tiššāḥēṯ,* "the land was ruined") contrasts with Ps 78:45, which says the flies "devoured them" (*wayyo'ḵelēm*), i.e., the Egyptians themselves, while it was the frogs that "devastated [= ruined] them" (*wattašḥîṯēm*). Apparently both plagues had devastating effects.

---

6. *Fifth plague: cattle murrain*

9:1–7

[1]Then the LORD said to Moses, "Go to Pharaoh and say to him, 'This is what the LORD, the God of the Hebrews, says: "Let my people go, so that they may worship me." [2]If you refuse to let them go and continue to hold them back, [3]the hand of the LORD will bring a terrible plague on your livestock in the field—on your horses and donkeys and camels and on your cattle and sheep and goats. [4]But the LORD will make a distinction between the livestock of Israel and that of Egypt, so that no animal belonging to the Israelites will die.' "

[5]The LORD set a time and said, "Tomorrow the LORD will do this in the land." [6]And the next day the LORD did it: All the livestock of the Egyptians died, but not one animal belonging to the Israelites died. [7]Pharaoh sent men to investigate and found that not even one of the animals of the Israelites had died. Yet his heart was unyielding and he would not let the people go.

1–4 The fifth plague was patterned after the second: Moses was to go to Pharaoh's palace and announce the next pestilence (v.1). A "terrible plague" (v.3) would be brought, not by God's "finger," as the Egyptian magicians had put it in 8:19, but by his "hand" (v.3). It would fall on all the cattle in the field. There is no need to press the expression "all the livestock" (v.6) to mean each and every one and then find there are no Egyptian cattle left for the seventh plague (vv.19, 25), for it is already plain in v.3 that the plague affected only those cattle "in the field." Normally the Egyptian cattle were stabled from May to December inclusive, during the flood and the drying-off periods when the pastures were waterlogged. Thus some of the cattle were already being turned out to pasture down south; so it must have been sometime in the month of January. These cattle were then affected when they came into contact with the heaps of dead frogs left from the second plague and died of *bacillus anthracis,* the hoof and mouth disease.

The Israelite cattle were exempted from the plague possibly because the delta would have been slower in recovering from the effects of the flood, which was further downstream. Also, the Israelites' different attitude toward corpses—they took precautions to deal with the heaps of dead carcasses—may have spared their own cattle. Rawlinson (1:199) suggested that the miraculous nature of this plague could be seen in (1) the announcement and timing of the pestilence (vv.3–6), (2) the severity of its effect (v.6), and (3) the selectivity of its impact on the Egyptians' cattle only (v.7). This was the second plague where God placed a distinction between the Egyptians and the Israelites.

5–7 The interval between the announcement and the morrow (v.5), when the fifth plague was to take effect, was to allow time for a believing response from Pharaoh and the Egyptians. Presumably some believed and attempted to rescue their animals by bringing them in from the fields. Others purposely delayed turning their cattle out to pasture.

When Pharaoh heard that all the Israelite cattle had miraculously escaped the cattle plague, he sent envoys to Goshen to investigate (v.7). The rumor was true: "Not one animal belonging to the Israelites died" (v.6). Pharaoh must have had his own explanations and rationalizations, for his position and heart again became resolute and unyielding. Meanwhile, another part of Egypt's wide array of gods was hard hit: the Apis, or sacred bull Ptah; the calf god Ra; the cows of Hathor; the jackal-headed god Anubis; and the bull Bakis of the god Mentu. The evidence was too strong to be mere coincidence: (1) the time was set by Yahweh, the God of the Hebrews (v.5); (2) a "distinction" was made between the cattle of the two peoples (v.4); and (3) the results were total: all Egyptian cattle "in the field" (v.3) died; not one head of Israelite livestock perished.

Notes

3 G.S. Ogden ("Notes on the Use of הויה in Exodus IX. 3," VetTest 17 [1967]: 483–84) asks why the participle of *hyh* occurs here—הוֹיָה (*hôyāh*, "[The hand of the LORD] will bring")—and no other time in the OT when one would expect an imperfect or a nominal clause without a verb. His totally satisfactory answer is (1) the use of the participle plus *hinnēh* lends itself to denoting an impending divine action, and (2) it conforms to a pattern where the participle is used five times in Moses and Aaron's petition for an Israelite pilgrimage, when they threatened Pharaoh with what God would do should Pharaoh fail to comply (7:17; 8:2; 9:3, 14; 10:4). Thus the participial form was "manufactured" to conform to this pattern.

See Notes on 8:2 for דֶּבֶר (*deb̲er*, "plague" or "pestilence"). The word occurs in some fifty places either of the Lord's judgment on a people (Lev 26:25; Num 14:12; 2 Sam 24:13–15 et al.) or as that from which the Lord is able to save his own (Ps 91:3).

Ever since W.F. Albright's remark (*Archaeology and the Religion of Israel* [Baltimore: Johns Hopkins, 1942], p. 96) that it was only in "the eleventh century [B.C.] that camel-riding nomads first appear in our documentary sources," it has been customary to regard verses like Gen 12:16 (Abraham's camels in Egypt), Gen 37:25 (an Ishmaelite camel caravan headed for Egypt), and here—בַּגְּמַלִּים (*baggᵉmallîm*, "on the camels")—as being anachronistic, i.e., they are misplaced in time and space. Cassuto (p. 111), however, affirms that domesticated camels were in Egypt during Moses' time even though no scholarly agreement exists on the time of their original domestication. See also Kenneth Kitchen, "Camel," NBD, pp. 181–83.

4 On וְהִפְלָה (*wᵉhip̲lāh*, "a distinction"), see Notes on 8:22 and 8:23.

7. *Sixth plague: boils*

9:8–12

8 Then the LORD said to Moses and Aaron, "Take handfuls of soot from
a furnace and have Moses toss it into the air in the presence of Pharaoh.
9 It will become fine dust over the whole land of Egypt, and festering
boils will break out on men and animals throughout the land."
10 So they took soot from a furnace and stood before Pharaoh. Moses
tossed it into the air, and festering boils broke out on men and animals.
11 The magicians could not stand before Moses because of the boils that
were on them and on all the Egyptians. 12 But the LORD hardened
Pharaoh's heart and he would not listen to Moses and Aaron, just as the
LORD had said to Moses.

8–9 Like the third plague, this one, which completes the second cycle, was sent unannounced. For the first time the lives of humans are attacked and endangered, and thus it was a foreshadowing of the tenth and most dreadful of all the plagues. With a touch of divine irony and poetic justice, Moses and Aaron were each to take two handfuls (the form is dual) of soot from a limekiln or brick-making furnace, the symbol of Israel's bondage (v.8; see 1:14; 5:7–19). The soot must have been placed in a container and carried to Pharaoh's presence, where Moses then tossed it into the air. The act was to be a symbolic action much like those of the latter prophets (e.g., Jeremiah's smashing the pottery jar in Jer 19 or Ezekiel's siege preparations and prophetically symbolic actions in Ezek 4–5). There was also a logical connection between the soot created by the sweat of God's enslaved people and the judgment that was to afflict the bodies of the enslavers.

10–12 When the soot was tossed skyward, festering boils broke out on all the Egyptians and their animals (vv.9–10). Attempts to identify this malady have produced various results (see Notes).

In a humorous aside, v.11 notes that the magicians (who bowed out in plague three and are unnoticed, though possibly present, in plagues four and five) literally (and vocationally) "could not stand" before Moses. The same could be said for all the Egyptians. Here for the first time God hardened Pharaoh's heart (v.12)—a seconding, as it were, of his own motion made in each of the preceding five plagues.

Notes

---

8 פִּיחַ (*pîaḥ*) is "soot," not "ashes" taken from sacrifices, which are called אֵפֶר (*'ēp̄er*; cf. Num 19:10). This *hapax legomenon* is from the verb פּוּחַ (*pûaḥ*, "to breathe, blow").

כִּבְשָׁן (*kib̄šān*, "furnace") appears four times in the Bible: Gen 19:28 as a simile for the destruction of Sodom and Gomorrah, Exod 19:18 as a simile for the theophany on Mount Sinai, and here in vv.8 and 10. Cook (p. 490) lists an Egyptian and Coptic word *kabusa* meaning "anthrax" or "carbo." Four other Hebrew words were used elsewhere in the OT for ovens or furnaces. That these kilns were used to make bricks along with the more usual sun-dried bricks is attested in the New Kingdom period.

9–10 שְׁחִין (*šeḥîn*, "boils") has an Arabic cognate that means "to be hot." This sickness was associated with Job (2:7–8) and Hezekiah (2 Kings 20:7; Isa 38:21) and with various skin diseases (Lev 13:18–23).

אֲבַעְבֻּעֹת (*'ab̄a'bu'ōṯ*, "blisters," "pustules"; NIV, "festering") is from an assumed verb *bu'* ("to swell up"); but Cook (p. 490) points to the Egyptian *b'b'* ("to drink"), which in Coptic means "to overflow." The initial aleph in the Hebrew spelling is no special problem. Notice the slight difference in the expressions between v.9 and v.10 (lit. tr.): "Boils breaking out in pustules" (v.9) and "boils of pustules breaking out" (v.10).

Various suggestions for the malady are (1) small pox (Cassuto), (2) Nile-blisters similar to scarlet fever (KD), (3) skin anthrax (Leyrer in *Herzog's Cyclopaedia*; Hort, "Plagues," pp. 101–3), and (4) inflammations or blains that become malignant ulcers (Bush, Greenberg). We side with Leyrer and Hort since Deut 28:35 limits this plague principally to the lower extremities of the body—on the knees and legs. Furthermore, the black soot is especially suited, for anthrax (cf. anthracite coal) is a sort of black, burning abscess often occurring with cattle murrain.

The flies of the fourth plague (*Stomoxys calcitrans*) have generally been blamed as the carriers of the anthrax spores, but they were totally removed at the conclusion of that plague. Presumably this was another generation of flies (depending on the temperature, another batch can come in twenty-seven to thirty-seven days). After animals or humans are bitten on the legs by these flies, a small bluish-red pustule with a central depression in the middle of the swelling appears after two or three days. The center of the boil dries up only to have new boils swell up, and the skin festers as if it had been burnt and then peels off (Hort, "Plagues," p. 101).

---

8. *Seventh plague: hail*

9:13–35

[13]Then the LORD said to Moses, "Get up early in the morning, confront
Pharaoh and say to him, 'This is what the LORD, the God of the Hebrews,
says: Let my people go, so that they may worship me, [14]or this time I will
send the full force of my plagues against you and against your officials
and your people, so you may know that there is no one like me in all the
earth. [15]For by now I could have stretched out my hand and struck you
and your people with a plague that would have wiped you off the earth.
[16]But I have raised you up for this very purpose, that I might show you
my power and that my name might be proclaimed in all the earth. [17]You
still set yourself against my people and will not let them go. [18]Therefore,
at this time tomorrow I will send the worst hailstorm that has ever fallen
on Egypt, from the day it was founded till now. [19]Give an order now to
bring your livestock and everything you have in the field to a place of
shelter, because the hail will fall on every man and animal that has not
been brought in and is still out in the field, and they will die.' "

[20]Those officials of Pharaoh who feared the word of the LORD hurried
to bring their slaves and their livestock inside. [21]But those who ignored
the word of the LORD left their slaves and livestock in the field.

[22]Then the LORD said to Moses, "Stretch out your hand toward the sky
so that hail will fall all over Egypt—on men and animals and on
everything growing in the fields of Egypt." [23]When Moses stretched out
his staff toward the sky, the LORD sent thunder and hail, and lightning
flashed down to the ground. So the LORD rained hail on the land of
Egypt; [24]hail fell and lightning flashed back and forth. It was the worst
storm in all the land of Egypt since it had become a nation.
[25]Throughout Egypt hail struck everything in the fields—both men and
animals; it beat down everything growing in the fields and stripped
every tree. [26]The only place it did not hail was the land of Goshen, where
the Israelites were.

[27]Then Pharaoh summoned Moses and Aaron. "This time I have
sinned," he said to them. "The LORD is in the right, and I and my people
are in the wrong. [28]Pray to the LORD, for we have had enough thunder
and hail. I will let you go; you don't have to stay any longer."

[29]Moses replied, "When I have gone out of the city, I will spread out
my hands in prayer to the LORD. The thunder will stop and there will be
no more hail, so you may know that the earth is the LORD's. [30]But I know
that you and your officials still do not fear the LORD God."

[31](The flax and barley were destroyed, since the barley had headed
and the flax was in bloom. [32]The wheat and spelt, however, were not
destroyed, because they ripen later.)

[33]Then Moses left Pharaoh and went out of the city. He spread out his
hands toward the LORD; the thunder and hail stopped, and the rain no
longer poured down on the land. [34]When Pharaoh saw that the rain and
hail and thunder had stopped, he sinned again: He and his officials

hardened their hearts. 35 So Pharaoh's heart was hard and he would not let the Israelites go, just as the LORD had said through Moses.

13–19 As in the first (7:15) and the fourth (8:20) plagues, Moses was to begin this third cycle of plagues by rising early in the morning to confront Pharaoh with the Lord's message (v.13). From these early days in February until the time of the tenth and climactical plague, Pharaoh would spend approximately eight of the most dreadful weeks he had ever known.

To further underscore the theological significance of these weeks and their events, Moses was prompted by God to preface his latest announcement of divine judgment with a long message filled with doctrinal instruction (vv.13b–19). This unprecedented message was calculated to move Pharaoh and his subjects from rebellion to belief in the God of the Hebrews. Its ominous contents included the following:

1. An announcement that God would vent the "full force" (v.14; i.e., "all the remaining plagues"; cf. 29:12 with Greenberg, *Exodus*, p. 160) of his plagues on Egypt so that no one would doubt that there was anyone like this God in all the earth.

2. A reminder that previous pestilences and plagues might well have swept both king and people off the face of the earth had not God deliberately and purposely spared them for one very important reason: that God's power and name would be heralded throughout the earth by means of Pharaoh's stupidity (vv.15–16).

3. A declaration that, in denying the release of Israel, Pharaoh had acted as an obstructionist against almighty God himself (v.17).

4. A threat that Egypt would experience the worst hailstorm it had ever seen in its history (v.18).

5. An extraordinary feature that provided for those Egyptians who believed Moses' words were a means of escape from the effects of the storm (v.19).

The seventh plague was to be judgment with the expectation that it might result in the blessing of belief and trust. Had not Abraham been given this mission to be a means of blessing to "all peoples on earth" (Gen 12:3)? And has not the theme "that the Egyptians might know that I am the LORD" (or slight variations) appeared frequently in the midst of these plagues (7:5; 8:10; 9:14, 16, 29–30; and later in 14:4, 18)? Moses would sigh of Israel (Num 14:11): "How long will these people treat me with contempt? How long will they refuse to believe in me, in spite of all the miraculous signs I have performed among them?" The same words could apply just as well to Egypt.

The months of leniency were about over. Now the full blast of the ensuing plagues would penetrate directly to Pharaoh's "heart" (v.14; NIV, "against you"). The "heart" (*lēḇ*) does not signify "his person," as *nep̱eš* can (KD, 1:489), but rather his inner being, nature, and seared conscience. His pride and arrogance would be tossed to the wind as the terrors of these new plagues forced him in perplexed and desperate sorrow of soul to literally beg that the Israelites leave his presence immediately. Yet Pharaoh was no mere pawn to be toyed with at will, for the object was that he too might come to experience personally and believe ("know") the incomparability of God's person and greatness. The very superlative rating of his deeds(untr. in NIV)—none "like it" (*kāmōhû,* of the hailstorm in vv.18, 24; of the locusts in 10:6)—should have led the king and his people to the identical rating of God's person (*no one* "like you," *kāmōkāh,* in 15:11, and *kāmōnî,* "like me," in 9:14).

20–26 Rainfall comes so occasionally in Upper Egypt that the prediction of a severe hailstorm accompanied by a violent electrical storm must have been greeted with much skepticism. Only the delta receives on the average about ten inches of rainfall per year while Upper Egypt has one inch or, more often, none. But there were some who "feared the word of the LORD" (v.20) and acted accordingly. This is belief as it should be, resulting in appropriate action based on confidence in the word of the Lord. Some Egyptians must have received Moses' words as being from God himself; for they became a part of that mixed company of Gentile believers who left Egypt with Israel (see 12:38).

In the three plagues of the third cycle (9:10; 10:13, 20), Moses apparently lost his shyness and diffidence; for he was the one who now stretched forth his staff and his hand (v.22; cf. Aaron's leading role previously in the first three plagues: 7:19–20; 8:6, 17). Hail joined by unannounced thunder and balls of fire (see Notes) that ran along the ground (v.23) provided Egypt with the most spectacular display in her history (see Notes on vv.18, 23, 24). The destruction was devastating. Five times in vv. 24–25 the word *kol* ("all," "everything") is used; yet it is used hyperbolically and not literally because the first two *kol*s ("in all Egypt," vv.24–25a; NIV, "throughout Egypt") are immediately qualified in v.26 to exempt the land of Goshen where Israel lived. Nevertheless, even though the storm did not take every single tree, herb, or creature in the field, it was tragic enough to impress the most callous individual.

27–30 Pharaoh, obviously shaken, conceded the point: "I have sinned," he allowed, though he included the face-saving qualifier "this time." The question is, however, what made this plague any different than the rest—except its severity. Only when the Lord began to hurt Pharaoh did he (momentarily) seek him (cf. Ps 78:34). Like Jeremiah (Jer 12:1), Pharaoh declared that Yahweh (not Elohim!) was in the right and that he and his people were in the wrong! Indeed! But had not Pharaoh been reduced to plea bargaining with Moses and Aaron twice before (8:8, 25–28)?

Moses' reply was simple, confident, and noble. He would spread out his hands in prayer (a gesture of request and appeal to God) once he was back out in the country with his own people, and the hail and thunder would stop—to prove once again (in this repeated apologetic and evangelistic refrain) that the whole earth belongs to the LORD. "But," Moses added, "I know that you and your officials still do not fear the LORD God" (v.30; an unusual combination of divine names [Yahweh-Elohim] seen only here and in seven other places in the OT besides in Gen 2 and 3; see D.F. Kidner, "Distribution of Divine Names in Jonah," *Tyndale Bulletin* 21 [1970]: 126–28, for its use in another Gentile context, viz., Jonah 4:6).

31–35 Even though most commentators complain about either the location of this parenthetical note in vv.31–32 (most would have preferred it to appear after v.25) or its alleged artless midrashic attempt to explain and harmonize later plagues with the extent of the destruction here, we find it most conveniently located. The integrity of the seasonal observation confirms the order in this text if the narrative is taken on its own terms and allowed to be innocent until proven to be factually guilty. Accordingly, before Moses prayed for the hail to cease, he had sufficient time to tell the reader just how extensive the damage was. Furthermore, since in Egypt flax is usually sown in the beginning of January and is in flower three weeks later while barley is sown in August and is harvested in February, both would be exceedingly vulnerable if this plague occurred in the beginning or middle of February (probably a little later than usual with a high Nile year). Wheat and spelt (see Notes) were also sown in August but were not ready for harvest until the end of March.

That Goshen was unaffected by this storm matches the agricultural observations; for the Mediterranean temperate zone has these storms only in late spring and early autumn but not from November to March (Hort, "Plagues," pp. 48–49). Flax, of which there were several kinds, was used for linen garments. The vicinity of Tanis was ideal for producing it. Barley was used in the manufacture of beer (a common Egyptian drink), as horse feed, and by the poorer classes for bread.

After Moses' prayer was answered, Pharaoh once again rescinded his offer and forgot all about his confession of sin and wrong.

Notes

13–14 More than wordplay is to be found in the divine demand "*Release* my people . . . or I will *release* all my plagues [on you]" (NIV, "Let my people go . . . or . . . I will send"). In both instances the verb is שׁלח (*šlḥ*).

14 For כָּל־מַגֵּפֹתַי (*kol-maggēp̄ōṯay*, lit., "all my plagues"), the NIV has "the full force of my plagues." See Notes on 8:2.

אֶל־לִבְּךָ (*'el-libbᵉḵā*, "against you") is literally "at [or] into your heart." There is no need to emend the text to אֵלֶּה בְּךָ (*'ēlleh bᵉḵā*, "all these . . . on you") with Hyatt (p. 118) and S.R. Driver, for as Childs (*Exodus*, p.129) says, "The MT is clear enough." The NEB renders it "[I will] strike home."

17 מִסְתּוֹלֵל (*mistôlēl*) is a Hithpael participle from the root *sālal*, which means "to raise up a mound or bank," "to obstruct"; hence the reflexive idea of the stem is "to elevate oneself" so as "to be an obstructionist" (NIV, "set yourself").

For an illustration of beth used in the sense of "against," as here—בְּעַמִּי (*bᵉʻammî*, "against my people")—Cassuto points to Mic 7:6.

18 הִוָּסְדָה (*hiwwāsᵉḏāh*, "[from the day Egypt] was founded") is a rare form of the Niphal perfect. B. Couroyer ("Un égyptianisme biblique: 'depuis la fondation de l'Egypte,' " RB 67 [1960]: 42–48) finds evidence for declaring that this phrase is a common Egyptian expression (as Cassuto, p. 117), though the Hebrew *yāsaḏ* ("to found") would correspond to the Egyptian *grg*.

21 לֹא־שָׂם לִבּוֹ (*lō'-śām libbô*, "[those who] ignored [the word]") is literally "did not set his heart [to the word]." See Notes on 7:23. Observe the singular again.

23 נָתַן קֹלֹת (*nāṯan qōlōṯ*, "give voice") is the frequent Hebrew expression for the idea "to thunder." It is also called the "voices of God" in v.28; cf. 19:16; 20:18; 2 Sam 22:14; Job 28:26; 38:25; Ps 29:3–9 et al. The same idiom appears in Ugaritic.

Notice the figure of speech called *zeugma*, where two objects "voice [= 'thunder'] and hail" are linked to the one Hebrew verb "give" (= "sent"), but only the first goes naturally with the verb.

וַתִּהֲלַךְ אֵשׁ אָרְצָה (*wattihᵃlaḵ 'ēš 'ārᵉṣāh*, lit., "and fire ran along the ground") is rendered by the NIV, "lightning flashed down to the ground," which is weaker. Notice the archaic form of the verb for the usual *wattēlēḵ*.

24 אֵשׁ מִתְלַקַּחַת (*'ēš miṯlaqqaḥaṯ*, lit., "fire taking hold of itself," i.e., zigzagging back and forth as if it were trying to grab itself) is clearly retranslated by the NIV as "the lightning flashed back and forth." See the exact phrase in Ezek 1:4, which also describes a storm.

26 On Goshen see Notes on 8:22; cf. also Gen 45:10–47:6.

32 The word כֻּסֶּמֶת (*kussemeṯ*, "spelt" [?]) occurs only here, in Isa 28:25, and in Ezek 4:9. This may be emmer, which is known from Egyptian tombs while spelt is not. See Cook (p. 490) for Egyptian *smw* ("herbs") used in the Coptic version of v.25 and for a kind of Egyptian grain spelled *kmtt, kmdt,* or *kwt.* Rawlinson (p. 220) calls it *doora,* a crop sown in late autumn as an after-crop, which ripens about the time of wheat.

---

9. *Eighth plague: locusts*

10:1–20

1 Then the LORD said to Moses, "Go to Pharaoh, for I have hardened his
heart and the hearts of his officials so that I may perform these
miraculous signs of mine among them 2 that you may tell your children
and grandchildren how I dealt harshly with the Egyptians and how I
performed my signs among them, and that you may know that I am the
LORD."
3 So Moses and Aaron went to Pharaoh and said to him, "This is what
the LORD, the God of the Hebrews, says: 'How long will you refuse to
humble yourself before me? Let my people go, so that they may worship
me. 4 If you refuse to let them go, I will bring locusts into your country
tomorrow. 5 They will cover the face of the ground so that it cannot be
seen. They will devour what little you have left after the hail, including
every tree that is growing in your fields. 6 They will fill your houses and
those of all your officials and all the Egyptians—something neither your
fathers nor your forefathers have ever seen from the day they settled in
this land till now.' " Then Moses turned and left Pharaoh.
7 Pharaoh's officials said to him, "How long will this man be a snare to
us? Let the people go, so that they may worship the LORD their God. Do
you not yet realize that Egypt is ruined?"
8 Then Moses and Aaron were brought back to Pharaoh. "Go, worship
the LORD your God," he said. "But just who will be going?"
9 Moses answered, "We will go with our young and old, with our sons
and daughters, and with our flocks and herds, because we are to
celebrate a festival to the LORD."
10 Pharaoh said, "The LORD be with you—if I let you go, along with
your women and children! Clearly you are bent on evil. 11 No! Have only
the men go; and worship the LORD, since that's what you have been
asking for." Then Moses and Aaron were driven out of Pharaoh's
presence.
12 And the LORD said to Moses, "Stretch out your hand over Egypt so
that locusts will swarm over the land and devour everything growing in
the fields, everything left by the hail."
13 So Moses stretched out his staff over Egypt, and the LORD made an
east wind blow across the land all that day and all that night. By
morning the wind had brought the locusts; 14 they invaded all Egypt and
settled down in every area of the country in great numbers. Never before
had there been such a plague of locusts, nor will there ever be again.
15 They covered all the ground until it was black. They devoured all that
was left after the hail—everything growing in the fields and the fruit on
the trees. Nothing green remained on tree or plant in all the land of
Egypt.
16 Pharaoh quickly summoned Moses and Aaron and said, "I have
sinned against the LORD your God and against you. 17 Now forgive my sin
once more and pray to the LORD your God to take this deadly plague
away from me."
18 Moses then left Pharaoh and prayed to the LORD. 19 And the LORD
changed the wind to a very strong west wind, which caught up the
locusts and carried them into the Red Sea. Not a locust was left

anywhere in Egypt. [20]But the LORD hardened Pharaoh's heart, and he would not let the Israelites go.

1–2 For the first time we are told that Egypt's officials were also as obstinate as Pharaoh; therefore the Lord (the pronoun "I" is repeated in Hebrew for emphasis) had hardened them all (v.1). But Moses was to find a lesson in this divine work of hardening. There follows, then, another theological preface to the eighth plague (vv.1–2), just as Pharaoh had been served in 9:14–16 with a similar lesson prior to the seventh plague. The lesson for Israel was to be twofold: (1) to educate succeeding generations in how the Lord "made sport" (see Notes) of the Egyptians and performed his miracles in their land and (2) to thereby bring Israel to faith in the Lord. Evidence for this recital of their miraculous deliverance from Egypt can be seen in Psalms 77:11–20; 78:43–53; 105:26–38; 106:7–12; 114:1–3; 135:8–9; 136:10–15, as well as reminders such as Deuteronomy 4:9.

3–6 Moses proceeded to the palace, as was his custom in the second plague of each of the three cycles, and announced to Pharaoh the next plague (vv.3–4). The Samaritan Pentateuch, Greenberg notes (*Exodus,* p. 163), mechanically fills in the MT's omission of God's message to Moses prior to his announcement, but the Samaritan style here does not have an authentic ring to it. The message began with a question: "How long will you refuse to humble yourself before the Lord?" His act of self-condemnation and abject humility in 9:27 was just that—an act. But here was the consummate question of all questions that God finally raised against all obstinate sinners: "How long?"

The demand for Israel's release was again laid down along with a time lag providing ample opportunity for reflection and repentance: "tomorrow" (v.4; cf. 8:10, 15, 21; 9:5, 6, 18). Moses informed Pharaoh that God would "bring locusts into your country." Joel 2:25 calls locusts God's "great army." They would finish off every living green thing, leaving destruction in their wake (v.5). It would exceed any locust invasion Egypt had ever known in the past (v.6). With that Moses and Aaron turned their backs on Pharaoh (an amazing gesture for normal protocol) and stalked out.

7–11 Pharaoh's officials, heretofore silent observers in this contest of wills, picked up Moses' "How long?" (v.3) with a "How long?" of their own: "How long will this man [*zeh,* 'this (man),' not *zō'ṯ,* 'this (situation)'] be a snare to us?" (v.7). Out of loyalty to their king and country, they blamed Moses; but it was obvious that they were beginning to become impatient with Pharaoh's intransigence. Could Pharaoh not see the "snare" this man was setting for them, and did Pharaoh not realize that Egypt was about ruined? How long, indeed, could all this continue? Someone had to give in. They urged Pharaoh to yield: "Let the people [*hā'ᵃnāšîm,* 'the men' in the generic sense] go."

In another first Pharaoh had Moses and Aaron return to the palace for some negotiations related to the imminent pestilence (v.8). Clearly as a sop to his frightened officials, Pharaoh half-heartedly gave Moses his permission to take Israel to sacrifice in the desert. However, he coyly asked (as if he did not remember Moses' original request or the advice just given him by his own officials), "Just who will be going [on this religious trip]?" Moses responded out of a position of strength: "We all are going to celebrate this festival to the LORD" (cf. v.9). "Oh no you are not," was Pharaoh's decisive rejoinder (cf. v.10). You take only your "men" (*haggᵉḇārîm,* lit., "strong men," v.11); that would be enough for religious purposes. It is true, of course, that later Israel required only her males to attend these three yearly festivals (23:17; 34:23; Deut 16:16), but the artificiality of this limitation at this time is evident from Herodotus's note (2.60) that the women accompanied the men at Egyptian religious festivals.

The contempt Pharaoh felt for Moses' request and for Yahweh himself can be seen in his biting sarcasm and veiled threat of v.10: "The LORD be with you [i.e., 'May God help you']—if I let you go, along with your women and children!" To Pharaoh it was plain that Moses and his people were up to no good. Cassuto (p. 125) believes all this talk about a three-day journey was just so much diplomatic bargaining in which each side knew what the other wanted without ever explicitly declaring it. Pharaoh did not yield to this moderate first-step request for fear of what was to be (though unknown at the time to him) the ultimate request (see comment on 3:18b). Moses and Aaron were then insulted by being chased from the premises—another in a string of wicked firsts.

12–15 So the plague was ordered to begin as Moses again (see comment on 9:22) stretched out his hand and staff over Egypt (v.12). Swarms of locusts (see Hort, "Plague," pp. 48–52) from the bumper crop produced due to the exceedingly wet summer in Ethiopia (which also had caused the unusually high Nile) were swept away from natural breeding grounds around Port Susa and Jidda (on the west side of the Red Sea across from the Arabian Peninsula) by an east wind that blew all day and all night (v.13; cf. 14:21). Thus these locusts (now ready to migrate in February or March after hatching during the winter from the eggs laid in September) were driven into Egypt by a sirocco (a hot wind) from the Arabian Peninsula, instead of into Canaan, had the winds been from the southwest. They came in droves (v.14, lit., "exceedingly heavy," as in 9:3, 18). They finished off everything the hail had left (v.15).

16–20 Hastily Pharaoh summoned Moses and Aaron and, without any qualifications as in 9:27–28, confessed his sin against Yahweh their God and against these men (v.16). But he still insisted on having the upper hand. "Now," he added, as if to organize Moses' conclusion, "forgive [*śā'*, sing.] my sin once more [*'aḵ happa'am*, i.e., this one more time]" (v.17). He pretended that this was it. No more would he change his mind, no more tricks! Just ask your God, he pled, "(only) [*raq*, untr. in NIV] to take this deadly plague away from me."

Once again God graciously answered Moses' prayer (v.18). He sent a strong "sea breeze" (*rûªḥ yām*), which for people living in Canaan would have been a "west wind," but for those in Egypt it was a wind from the north or northwest, which drove the locusts into the Reed Sea. Hort ("Plagues," pp. 51–52) emends *yām sûp̱* ("Red or Reed Sea"; see Notes on 2:3) to *yāmin* ("right hand" or "south"), but there is no need to do so. The results at the palace, however, were the same.

Notes

2 הִתְעַלַּלְתִּי (*hiṯ'allaltî*, "I dealt harshly") describes an action that brings shame and disgrace on its object. It is used anthropomorphically of Yahweh's treatment of the Egyptians where he

"made toys of" them or even "made fools out of them" (pers. tr.; cf. 1 Sam 6:6). These negative connotations are brought out with Balaam in Num 22:29, the Levite's concubine in Judg 19:25, and Saul's fear of the Philistines' final action in 1 Sam 31:4.

4 אַרְבֶּה (*'arbeh,* "locusts") is from the root *rāḇāh* ("to be numerous, many, multiplied"). The use of the collective singular for the plural is again noteworthy. For other names for locusts, see Joel 1:4. The species intended here is either the *Acridium peregrinum* or the *Oedipoda migratoria*—both no strangers to Arabia, Egypt, and Canaan.

5 עֵין הָאָרֶץ (*'ên hā'āreṣ,* lit., "the eye of the ground") is rendered "face of the ground" by the NIV. "Surface of the ground" would destroy the figure of speech called metonymy, where a faculty is put for an object, i.e., the sight or visibility of the ground would be hidden by the prodigious numbers of locusts (Bush, *Exodus,* 1:122).

6 On מִיּוֹם הֱיוֹתָם (*miyyôm hᵉyôṯām,* "from the day they settled"), see the Notes on 9:18. On the idiom "till now" (עַד הַיּוֹם [*'aḏ hayyôm,* lit., "until the day"]), see B.S. Childs, "A Study of the Formula, 'Until this Day,' " JBL 82 (1963): 279.

8 מִי וָמִי הַהֹלְכִים (*mî wāmî hahōlᵉḵîm,* "just who will be going?") is literally, "Who and who [are] the ones going?" The repetition of the pronouns may be for emphasis, but the expression appears idiomatic, though it occurs only here.

10 On טַף (*ṭāp̱,* "women and children"), see the Notes on 10:24.

14 On כָּמֹהוּ . . . כֵּן (*kēn . . . kāmōhû,* lit., "such [a plague of locusts] as it"), see on 9:14 and 18. See Labuschagne, *Incomparability of Yahweh,* p. 14, for formulas of incomparability.

15 The repeated "all"s in this passage may be similar to those in 9:24–25; see comment there.

---

10. *Ninth plague: darkness*

10:21–29

[21]Then the LORD said to Moses, "Stretch out your hand toward the sky so that darkness will spread over Egypt—darkness that can be felt." [22]So Moses stretched out his hand toward the sky, and total darkness covered all Egypt for three days. [23]No one could see anyone else or leave his place for three days. Yet all the Israelites had light in the places where they lived.

[24]Then Pharaoh summoned Moses and said, "Go, worship the LORD. Even your women and children may go with you; only leave your flocks and herds behind."

[25]But Moses said, "You must allow us to have sacrifices and burnt offerings to present to the LORD our God. [26]Our livestock too must go with us; not a hoof is to be left behind. We have to use some of them in worshiping the LORD our God, and until we get there we will not know what we are to use to worship the LORD."

[27]But the LORD hardened Pharaoh's heart, and he was not willing to let them go. [28]Pharaoh said to Moses, "Get out of my sight! Make sure you do not appear before me again! The day you see my face you will die."

[29]"Just as you say," Moses replied, "I will never appear before you again."

21–23 Unannounced, like the third and sixth plagues, the ninth plague came in the month of March as Moses once again stretched out his hand (v.21; cf. 9:22; 10:12). No doubt God used the yearly phenomenon known as the *Khamsin,* meaning the "fifty"-day wind that blows off the Sahara Desert from the south and southwest usually about the time of the vernal equinox. During two or three of those days, it blows with great force, picking up sand and dust. Given the unusually high Nile with the red dirt it had spilled over everything and the fields now barren and baked after the hail and locusts had destroyed all the vegetation that would hold the soil in its place, this was no ordinary *Khamsin.* The polluted air got so thick—"no one could see anyone" (v.23)—that the sun itself was blotted out for "three days" (v.22). Israel meanwhile was somewhat protected by the hills on the south side of the Wadi Tumilat and by the fact that the red silt would not have dried out as much since their fields were later in clearing the effects of the flood (Hort, "Plagues," pp. 52–54).

24–29 Pharaoh decided to compromise further: Israel could take their families to this festival celebration, but they must leave their flocks and herds (v.24). But Moses yielded nothing. "Not a hoof is to be left," he affirmed in a fine hyperbole rising to proverbial status, for we need them in worshiping God (vv.25–26). The festival was brand new, and it was as yet unannounced, explained Moses. But Pharaoh had had enough. Rudely he demanded they leave and never darken his presence again on penalty of death. But did he think that would prevent further disasters? Had not plagues three, six, and nine come without warning? Was it not strange for him to be threatening Moses with death when the smell of death was all over his court and Egypt? As Bush said (*Exodus,* 1:30), "It is a sad farewell when God, in the persons of his servants, refuses anymore to see the face of the wicked."

Notes

21 וְיָמֵשׁ (*w^{e}yāmēš,* "can be felt") is from the root *mûš,* which means "to feel, grasp" with the hands (Ps 115:7). It is used of Samson's hands on the pillars in Judg 16:26. Here the darkness was so great that it could be touched.

22 חֹשֶׁךְ־אֲפֵלָה (*ḥōšeḵ-'^{a}pēlāh,* "total darkness") is an intensive expression that literally means "darkness of obscurity." The LXX strung three Greek words together: two for "darkness" (*skotos gnophos*) and a third (*thuella*) for "storm"; therefore Hyatt (p. 127) conjectures that the LXX translator may have been the first commentator to associate this darkness with the *Khamsin.*

24 טַפְּכֶם (*ṭapp^{e}ḵem*) is "your women and children." *Ṭap̱* (lit., "little ones") means only the children when women are mentioned separately (Gen 34:29; 45:19; 46:5), but at other times it means "women and children" (Gen 43:8; 47:12; Exod 10:10).

24–26 To Pharaoh's generous גַּם (*gam,* "even, also"), allowing the children to accompany the worshipers, Moses had two *gams* of his own in vv.25 and 26. In the phrase גַּם־אַתָּה תִּתֵּן בְּיָדֵנוּ (*gam-'attāh tittēn b^{e}yāḏēnû,* "You must allow us [to have sacrifices]"), many commentators think that Moses made a new impudent request that Pharaoh donate his animals for this sacrifice, but this makes no sense contextually. Neither did Moses specify their animals. The phrase is either as the NIV has it: "You must allow us," or as Hyatt (p. 127) paraphrases it: "*You* would have to provide us with sacrifices . . . if we did not take along our own livestock." See 3:18; 5:1–3; 8:25–28.

11. *Tenth plague: death of the firstborn*

11:1–10

1 Now the LORD had said to Moses, "I will bring one more plague on
Pharaoh and on Egypt. After that, he will let you go from here, and when
he does, he will drive you out completely. 2 Tell the people that men and
women alike are to ask their neighbors for articles of silver and gold."
3 (The LORD made the Egyptians favorably disposed toward the people,

and Moses himself was highly regarded in Egypt by Pharaoh's officials and by the people.)

4 So Moses said, "This is what the LORD says: 'About midnight I will go throughout Egypt. 5 Every firstborn son in Egypt will die, from the firstborn son of Pharaoh, who sits on the throne, to the firstborn son of the slave girl, who is at her hand mill, and all the firstborn of the cattle as well. 6 There will be loud wailing throughout Egypt—worse than there has ever been or ever will be again. 7 But among the Israelites not a dog will bark at any man or animal.' Then you will know that the LORD makes a distinction between Egypt and Israel. 8 All these officials of yours will come to me, bowing down before me and saying, 'Go, you and all the people who follow you!' After that I will leave." Then Moses, hot with anger, left Pharaoh.

9 The LORD had said to Moses, "Pharaoh will refuse to listen to you—so that my wonders may be multiplied in Egypt." 10 Moses and Aaron performed all these wonders before Pharaoh, but the LORD hardened Pharaoh's heart, and he would not let the Israelites go out of his country.

1–3 These verses are parenthetical; for Moses had one last message to communicate to Pharaoh before he left his presence after the ninth plague in 10:29, and thus he knew that Pharaoh had "spoken correctly" (cf. 10:28) in halting any further audiences. Even though Hebrew does not have a pluperfect tense, its penchant for simply placing side by side events that we would have subordinated in time (KD, 1:87, 499; cf. Gen 2:19; Judg 2:6; 1 Kings 7:13) suggests that it is best to translate v.1 thus: "Now the Lord *had* said" (*wayyō'mer*), as in the NIV. Thus God had informed Moses before he went in to see Pharaoh concerning the ninth plague that this contest was about to end abruptly. One more plague and he would send Israel away, "in the manner of [*k*ᵉ] one's sending away a slavegirl who had been promised to be one's daughter-in-law" (*kāllāh*, see Notes), i.e., filled with gifts on her release from slavery. This interpretation leads easily and naturally into their requests of the Egyptians for gold and silver articles (v.2; see comment on 3:22).

The reasons for the extraordinary generosity of the Egyptians are (1) the LORD made them "favorably disposed" (*nāṯan hēn*, lit., "gave grace") toward Israel (cf. Ps 106:46), and (2) "Moses himself [*hā'îš Mōšeh*, lit., 'the man Moses'] was highly regarded [*gāḏôl m*ᵉ*'ōḏ*]." There is no need to regard this second reason as an interpolation, a post-Mosaic addition (as perhaps Num 12:3), or as a piece of prideful indulgence in self-glorification. The greatness of the man was not because of his personal qualifications but because of the esteem he had accumulated from the magicians (8:18–19), the court officials (9:20; 10:7), and Pharaoh himself (9:27; 10:16).

4–8 Moses' speech to Pharaoh continues the remarks he began in 10:29. Unlike all the other plagues, this time the LORD himself (notice the emphatic repetition of the pronoun—*'ᵃnî yôṣē'*, "I, I will go out") would march (*yāṣā'* is often used in military contexts) through the land of Egypt (v.4). There would be no secondary causes or utilizing instruments such as a strong east wind. The firstborn of all Egyptian families—slaves and cattle (v.5)—would die at midnight (the exact day was not specified). An unprecedented outpouring of grief would follow, but among the Israelites there would be such tranquility on that evening that not a dog would have occasion to bark (vv.6–7)!

A possible historical reminiscence of this event has been uncovered by Mordechai Gilula ("The Smiting of the Firstborn: An Egyptian Myth?" *Tel Aviv*, 4 [1977]: 94–

95). In the Pre-Mosaic Pyramid Texts (par. 339 a–b), there is a reference to "that day of slaying the firstborn" spelled *smsw* in Egyptian. Likewise, the Pre-Mosaic Coffin Texts (VI:178) refer to "that night of slaying the firstborn," while another coffin text has both "that night . . . that day of slaying the firstborn" (II:163 b–c). In the Coffin Texts the Egyptian word for "firstborn" is *wr* or *wrw*, meaning "great" or "eldest." Interestingly the firstborn in the Coffin Texts are gods, while the Pyramid Texts do not say.

Moses' final word was that the Egyptians on bent knee would beg the Israelites to please leave those parts immediately (v.8). Moses said, "After that I will leave" (*'ēṣē'*, "go out"—reechoing the Lord's "going out" in v.4). But the stupidity and waste of all those lives just because of stubborn sinfulness made Moses exceedingly angry. To be in the presence of evil and not be angry is a dreadful spiritual and moral malady.

9–10 Therefore, as a recapitulation of all Moses' negotiations beginning in 7:8, readers are reminded that all had taken place as God had predicted it. No amount of evidence had persuaded Pharaoh's hard heart, and Israel was still enslaved.

Notes

1 On נֶגַע (*nega'*, "plague"), see the Notes on 8:2.

The NIV's "And when he does" for כְּשַׁלְּחוֹ כָּלָה (*kešalleḥô kālāh*) is probably incorrect. The difficulty of this passage was felt already by the LXX, which paraphrased it, "And whenever he sends you forth with everything." *Syn panti* ("with everything") is inserted because the verb is transitive. Onkelos and most modern translations render *kālāh* adverbially (Gen 18:21) by "completely" or "altogether." This, however, requires adding an unwarranted "you": "when he sends *you* away altogether," and it yields little sense in the context. Childs (*Exodus*, p. 130, for documentation) refers to a more recent minor emendation *kešilleḥû kallāh* ("as one sends away a bride"). But I believe the best solution is offered by Reuven Yaron ("On Divorce in Old Testament Times," *Revue Internationale des Droits de l'Antiquite* 6 [1957]: 122–24). His solution is to treat *ke* as referring to mode, "in the manner" (not to time, "when"), and the third-person singular possessive pronoun "his" affixed to "sending" to denote an indefinite person, viz., "one's sending." For *kālāh* he would read *kallāh*, a cognate with the Babylonian *kâllatum* (cf. Hammurabi Code 155, 156; Nuzi Tablet 25 in AASOR X and 30 in AASOR XVI). A Hebrew *kāllāh* with a compound meaning of a "slave-girl" brought to be married as one's "daughter-in-law" would be a *hapax legomenon*, but the Babylonian parallels and the improved meaning of vv.1–3 give it serious weight. Thus the text should be translated: "After that, he will let you go from here, in the manner of one's sending away a *kāllāh* [a slave purchased to be one's daughter-in-law]."

2 On וְיִשְׁאֲלוּ (*weyiš'alû*, "[and they] are to ask"), see the comment and Notes on 3:22.

7 On לֹא יֶחֱרַץ־כֶּלֶב לְשֹׁנוֹ (*lō' yeḥeraṣ-keleb lešōnô*, "not a dog will bark"), see F.C. Fensham, "Remarks on *Keret* 114b-136a," *Journal of Northwest Semitic Languages* 11 (1983): 75, who relates this to the Egyptian *klb ṣpr* ("watch dog").

On יַפְלֶה (*yapleh*, "a distinction"), see the comment and Notes on 8:22; cf. Notes on 8:23.

9–10 On מֹפְתִים (*mōpetîm*, "wonders"), see the comment on 4:21.

E. *The Passover (12:1–28)*

1. *Preparations for the Passover*

12:1–13

1 The LORD said to Moses and Aaron in Egypt, 2 "This month is to be for
you the first month, the first month of your year. 3 Tell the whole
community of Israel that on the tenth day of this month each man is to
take a lamb for his family, one for each household. 4 If any household is
too small for a whole lamb, they must share one with their nearest
neighbor, having taken into account the number of people there are.
You are to determine the amount of lamb needed in accordance with
what each person will eat. 5 The animals you choose must be year-old
males without defect, and you may take them from the sheep or the
goats. 6 Take care of them until the fourteenth day of the month, when
all the people of the community of Israel must slaughter them at twilight.
7 Then they are to take some of the blood and put it on the sides and
tops of the doorframes of the houses where they eat the lambs. 8 That
same night they are to eat the meat roasted over the fire, along with
bitter herbs, and bread made without yeast. 9 Do not eat the meat raw or
cooked in water, but roast it over the fire—head, legs and inner parts.
10 Do not leave any of it till morning; if some is left till morning, you must
burn it. 11 This is how you are to eat it: with your cloak tucked into your
belt, your sandals on your feet and your staff in your hand. Eat it in
haste; it is the LORD's Passover.
12 "On that same night I will pass through Egypt and strike down every
firstborn—both men and animals—and I will bring judgment on all the
gods of Egypt. I am the LORD. 13 The blood will be a sign for you on the
houses where you are; and when I see the blood, I will pass over you. No
destructive plague will touch you when I strike Egypt.

1–2 The instructions for the Passover and the Unleavened Bread feasts were the only regulations given while Israel was still in Egypt. Thus it seems evident from the phrase "in Egypt" (lit., "in the land of Egypt") that the least one can say is that the contents of this chapter were written sometime after the Exodus. This event was so significant that henceforth the religious or ecclesiastical year was to begin (v.2) in the month of Abib (13:4), the month when "the barley had headed" (*'āḇîḇ*, the Canaanite name for the month; cf. also 23:15; 34:18; Deut 16:1—this was part of an early agricultural menology not unlike the Gezer calendar). Later the Babylonian month name of Nisan was substituted (Esth 3:7), matching our present calendar name of late March to the beginning of April (Neh 2:1).

3–11 The following instructions, communicated through the elders (see v.21), were given to the "whole community of Israel" (v.3; see Notes).

1. Preparations were to begin on the tenth day of the month of Abib (v.3).
2. The head of each household was to select a *śeh* ("lamb" or "kid," see v.5) according to the number of people who would be present (v.4).
3. The animal was to be a year old, a male without any defects (v.5; cf. later Lev 22:20–25; Mal 1:8, 14).
4. Each animal was to be slaughtered at twilight (see Notes) on the fourteenth day (v.6).
5. The blood from the animals was to be applied to the doorframe (see Notes) of each house (v.7).

6. That night each family was to eat the roasted lamb or kid along with bitter herbs and unleavened bread (v.8).

7. The meat was to be roasted whole with the head and legs intact and the washed internals left inside; it was not to be eaten raw or boiled in water (v.9).

8. All leftovers were to be burnt; nothing was to be allowed to become profane by putrification or superstitious abuse (v.10, i.e., before daybreak according to 23:18; 34:25; Deut 16:4).

9. The meal was to be eaten with an air of haste and expectancy. Therefore, the people's long robes were to be tucked in their belts, their sandals were to be worn, and their staffs were to be ready and on hand (v.11; Deut 16:3).

Thus the whole nation was to be a nation of priests, as Moses later announced in 19:5–6 (cf. 1 Peter 2:5; Rev 1:6 of the NT believers). The apparent intervention of the Levites in 2 Chronicles 30:17–18 and 35:5–6 was contrary at least to the original design of the Passover. Here there was no priests, no altar, no tabernacle; families were communing in the presence of God and around the sacrificial lamb that was the substitute for each member of that family. The lamb was to be a year-old male because it was taking the place of Israel's firstborn males who were young and fresh with the vigor of life. The bitter herbs (lettuce and endive are indigenous to Egypt) were to recall the bitter years of servitude (1:14), and the unleavened bread was to reflect this event's haste on that first night. This was the Lord's Passover (see Notes), and this was how Israel was to eat it (v.11).

12–13 On that same night, the fifteenth of Abib, the Lord would pass through Egypt and strike down the firstborn of all men and animals whose household had not been believingly placed under the blood of the sacrificial substitute (v.12). This blood was to be a "sign" (*'ôṯ*, v.13). Like the other "signs" or "miracles" Pharaoh had seen, this one also was to be a pledge of God's mercy. The Lord would "pass over" (the verb *pāsaḥ* is the same as the noun *pesaḥ*, "Passover" in v.11) these homes, and no destructive "plague" (*negeḇ*) would affect or touch them. Indeed, even "all the gods of Egypt" (v.12) would be judged by this final plague of God. Obviously, those deities whose representatives were linked with beasts were dealt direct blows—the bulls, cows, goats, jackals, lions, baboons, rams, etc. With the sudden death of these sacred representatives, there could be little doubt that it would be interpreted as a direct blow to the gods of Egypt themselves.

Notes

3 This is the first occurrence of עֵדָת (*'ᵃḏaṯ*, "community," "congregation") in over one hundred usages in the Bible of what becomes a technical term for the "people" of God gathered together to worship God or to be instructed in spiritual things. *Qāhāl* ("congregation"), a parallel term preferred by Deuteronomy and many prophetical books, is often associated in meaning with the NT Greek *ekklēsia* ("assembly," "church").

5 בֶּן־שָׁנָה (*ben-šānāh*, "year old") is literally "son of a year." Rabbinical interpretation took this to mean a year old or less. KD and Lange correctly argue that it must mean a "yearling" since other expressions were available to cover anything prior to that (e.g., Gen 21:4, "son of eight days" or Lev 27:6, "son of a month").

6 Again the collective singular—viz., אתו (*'ōṯô*, lit., "it"; NIV, "[slaughter] them")—is used for the plural. See also the same pronoun in vv.7, 11(bis).

בֵּין הָעַרְבָּיִם (*bên hā'arbāyim*, lit., "between the two evenings"; NIV, "at twilight") has given rise to a much discussed question that is explained in two ways: (1) between sunset and dark (Aben-Ezer, Qaraites, Samaritans, KD) or (2) between the decline of the sun (three to five o'clock) and sunset (Josephus, Mishna, and modern practice). Deuteronomy 16:6 fixes the time at "when the sun goes down," the same time set for the lighting of the lamps in the tabernacle (30:8) and the offering of the daily evening sacrifice (29:39). Latter custom necessitated moving this time up to allow the Levites to help everyone with their sacrifice.

7 הַמְּזוּזֹת (*hamm^ezûzōṯ*, "the sides [of the doorframe]") are easily identified, but הַמַּשְׁקוֹף (*hammašqôp̱*, "the tops of [the doorframes]") perhaps may not be the lintel or top of the doorframe since it is derived from a root meaning to "look out." It may be the latticed window traditionally placed over the doorway in Egyptian houses and also represented in the façades of tombs. See also vv.22–23. "Lintel" seems best, however, until better evidence for the Egyptian model described here is available.

8 מְרֹרִים (*m^erōrîm*, "bitter herbs") were wild lettuce or endive. The Mishnah adds four others that may be used: chicory, pepperroot, snakeroot, and dandelion.

9 Meat that was מְבֻשָּׁל בַּמָּיִם (*m^eḇuššāl bammāyim*, "cooked in water" or "boiled") was forbidden. Deuteronomy 16:7 may appear to contradict Exod 12:9, but 2 Chron 35:13 shows that the verb *biššēl* can mean to "cook" or "bake" as well as "boil"—that is why Moses added here "in water." Justin Martyr, in a poor example of spiritualizing exegesis, said that two wooden spits were placed at right angles to each other, thus placing the victim on a type of cross.

11 בְּחִפָּזוֹן (*b^eḥippāzôn*, "in haste") is literally "in anxious haste" (cf. Deut 16:3 and Isa 52:12).

The etymology of פֶּסַח (*pesaḥ*, "Passover") is disputed and uncertain. Various suggestions include the following: (1) Hebrew *pāsaḥ*, "to leap, limp, hobble," as Jonathan's lame son, in 2 Sam 4:4; between two opinions, in 1 Kings 18:21; as in dancing, in 1 Kings 18:26; or as a parallel "to protect, save," in Isa 31:5; (2) Akkadian *paššāḫu*, "to appease, make soft, placate"; (3) Egyptian *p3 sh̬3*, "the commemoration," or *p3 3sh̬*, "the harvest," or *p3 śḥ*, "the blow, plague." See Segal (pp. 95–100) for elaborate documentation and analysis. But the context (v.13) explains it as a "passing over" the houses of those under the sign of the blood. We cannot address ourselves here to the long discussion on the prehistory (see ibid., pp. 42–46) of this festival; but whatever it may have been, it is here entirely associated with an event in Israel's history.

---

2. *Preparations for the Unleavened Bread*

12:14–20

14 "This is a day you are to commemorate; for the generations to come you shall celebrate it as a festival to the LORD—a lasting ordinance. 15 For seven days you are to eat bread made without yeast. On the first day remove the yeast from your houses, for whoever eats anything with yeast in it from the first day through the seventh must be cut off from Israel. 16 On the first day hold a sacred assembly, and another one on the seventh day. Do no work at all on these days, except to prepare food for everyone to eat—that is all you may do.

17 "Celebrate the Feast of Unleavened Bread, because it was on this very day that I brought your divisions out of Egypt. Celebrate this day as a lasting ordinance for the generations to come. 18 In the first month you are to eat bread made without yeast, from the evening of the fourteenth day until the evening of the twenty-first day. 19 For seven days no yeast is to be found in your houses. And whoever eats anything with yeast in it must be cut off from the community of Israel, whether he is an alien or

native-born. [20] Eat nothing made with yeast. Wherever you live, you must eat unleavened bread."

14–16 The connection between the Passover and the Feast of Unleavened Bread is close yet distinct. The OT uses both names to refer to the same feast: "Passover Feast" in Exodus 34:25; Ezekiel 45:21; and "Feast of Unleavened Bread" in Deuteronomy 16:16; 2 Chronicles 30:13, 21; Ezra 6:22. Yet the two rites are treated separately, even if in sequence, in Leviticus 23:5–6; Numbers 28:16–17; 2 Chronicles 35:1, 17; Ezra 6; Ezekiel 45:21 (likewise the NT uses this twofold designation for the same feast: *pascha* in John 2:13, 23; 6:4; 11:55 et al., while *azymos* is used in Matt 26:17; Luke 22:1, 7; cf. Mark 14:12).

"This day" (*hayyôm hazzeh*) of v.14 refers to the same day in view in vv.1–13. The slaying of the paschal lamb "between the evenings" (a lit. Heb. expression) that divide the 14 and 15 of Abib (= Nisan) looks forward to the festive celebration that night, the day of the Exodus (= the night of the Passover), 15 Abib. The Israelites were to "commemorate" (*lᵉzikkārôn*, i.e., make it a memorial; see 3:15 above) that day as a "festival" (*ḥag̱*) and a "lasting [i.e., perpetual] ordinance" (*ḥuqqat̲ ʿôlām*).

For seven days they were to eat *maṣṣôt̲* ("unleavened cakes," i.e. "bread made without yeast," v.15), to remember Israel's haste in leaving Egypt (v.39) and to again underscore the conviction that impurity and corruption (which leaven sometimes symbolizes) disqualified persons from religious services (see comment on 3:5–6). The whole household needed to be pure and clean of heart; therefore all yeast was to be removed from the entire house (v.19). The first and the seventh days of that week beginning with the celebration of the Passover were to be holy convocations (v.16).

17–20 "I *brought* your divisions out" (emphasis mine; on "divisions" see Notes on 6:26) reflects a post-Exodus stance. Thus (as KD and Rawlinson argue) the words of vv.17–20 may not be the verbatim words of revelation. Instead, they are either a recasting of the original revelation to incorporate the proper time perspective and the institutional nature of the ordinance now given or a new extension of the original use of unleavened bread in the Passover to a new seven-day festival.

Verse 19 is not an empty repetition of v.15 but adds the important notice that Gentiles may be celebrants along with Israel even as was contemplated in the Abrahamic covenant of Genesis 12:3: "all peoples of the earth will be blessed through you." The "alien" (*gēr*) must have included the "mixed multitude" (v.38, KJV; NIV, "many other people") who left Egypt with Israel, the Kenites who joined them in the desert (Num 10:29–31; Judg 1:16), and those who were converted later like Rahab's family (Josh 2:10–14). Rawlinson (1:262) notes how the whole law is filled with references to this class of persons beginning in 20:10; 23:12 et al. Those "native-born" were, no doubt, Abraham's descendants who are here regarded as the true natives to the land of Canaan since it was assigned them by God some six hundred years prior to the Exodus.

Notes

---

15 The exact etymology of מַצּוֹת (*maṣṣôt̲*, "bread [or 'cakes,' notice the pl.] made without yeast") is unknown. Several suggestions are as follows: (1) *mṣṣ*, "to squeeze, press," thus flat cakes;

(2) *yṣ'* ("to go out"), as the Aramaic *paṭṭira* ("unleavened bread") may be related to the Syriac *pṭr* ("depart") or even the Akkadian *pṭr* ("ransom"); (3) the Egyptian *ms.t* or *msw.t* ("food," "cake") or *msw.t* ("evening meal"); or (4) the Greek *maza* ("barley bread") instead of the Greek *artos* ("wheat bread"). Each suggestion has problems according to Segal (p. 107).

15, 19 Two distinct words are used for "yeast" or "leaven"; שְׂאֹר (*śe'ōr*), perhaps the "old leaven" hidden and secret (Luke 12:1) that Paul urged believers to "get rid of" in 1 Cor 5:7 (Bush, *Exodus*, p. 142); and חָמֵץ (*ḥāmēṣ*, perhaps related to *ḥô* + *mēṣ*, "vinegar"), emphasizing "sourness" and open malice and a putrifying form (cf. Pss 71:4 and 73:21 with Bush).

וְנִכְרְתָה (*wenikretāh*, lit., "that soul [fem., 'she'] shall be cut off [from Israel]") probably refers to expulsion from the community of Israel with the possibility that it might prove fatal to the person. A few argue that it is the death penalty; others assure us that it is merely excommunication from the community. See Donald Wold, "The Meaning of the Biblical Penalty *Kareth*" (Ph.D. dissertation, University of California, Berkeley, 1978).

16 מִקְרָא־קֹדֶשׁ (*miqrā'-qōdeš*) is a called or convened gathering for sacred purposes, a "sacred assembly."

---

3. *Celebration of the Passover*

12:21–28

21 Then Moses summoned all the elders of Israel and said to them, "Go at once and select the animals for your families and slaughter the Passover lamb. 22 Take a bunch of hyssop, dip it into the blood in the basin and put some of the blood on the top and on both sides of the doorframe. Not one of you shall go out the door of his house until morning. 23 When the LORD goes through the land to strike down the Egyptians, he will see the blood on the top and sides of the doorframe and will pass over that doorway, and he will not permit the destroyer to enter your houses and strike you down.

24 "Obey these instructions as a lasting ordinance for you and your descendants. 25 When you enter the land that the LORD will give you as he promised, observe this ceremony. 26 And when your children ask you, 'What does this ceremony mean to you?' 27 then tell them, 'It is the Passover sacrifice to the LORD, who passed over the houses of the Israelites in Egypt and spared our homes when he struck down the Egyptians.' " Then the people bowed down and worshiped. 28 The Israelites did just what the LORD commanded Moses and Aaron.

21–23 When the instructions for the preparation of the Passover (and the topically connected but subsequent enlargement of the Passover in the Feast of Unleavened Bread) had been completed, the elders were briefed on what each Israelite family was to do (v.21). Two new items are included here: (1) blood was to be applied to each doorframe by a "bunch of hyssop" dipped into a basin of blood, and (2) no one was to leave the house "until morning" (v.22). This cannot be used to prove that these instructions were not part of God's original revelation to Moses or that these verses preserve a different tradition of the Passover; for, as Cassuto argues (p. 143), there is no need to repeat all the details of vv.1–20, nor is there any literary law that says additional particulars may not come out in subsequent rehearsing of the same material.

The lamb or kid to be slaughtered by each family is called (by the figure of speech known as metonymy: the exchange of one noun for a related noun) "the Passover" (*happāsaḥ*) itself (the NIV attempts to aid the reader by rendering it "the Passover lamb," v.21). Blood from this animal was placed in a basin and with "a bunch of hyssop" (v.22, see Notes) was "slapped" (the verb *ngʿ* is cognate with one of the words for "plague," *negaʿ*, in 11:1) on the doorframe. Israel would know the grounds and means of their deliverance and redemption: a sacrificed substitute and the blood of atonement in which the paschal animal died *in place of* the firstborn of all who took shelter from the stroke of the destroyer.

"The destroyer" of v.23 (see Notes) was not a demonic power that rivaled God but was probably an angel of the Lord who expedited his will. In Psalm 78:49, however, where God lets loose on the Egyptians four different words for his anger, this wrath is collectively called "a band of destroying angels" (*mišlaḥaṯ malʾᵃḵê rāʿîm*). Thus whether an angel was the mediating agent or the term was a figurative personification of the final judgment of God on Egypt, it was still God's direct work. The NT will remember this "destroyer" (*ho olothreuōn*) in Hebrews 11:28. His work in bringing the plague on Israel for Korah, Dathan, and Abiram's rebellion in Numbers 16:41–49 and the serpents in Numbers 21:5–6 will also be labeled the work of "the destroying angel" in 1 Corinthians 10:9–10 (see Notes).

24–28 Once again provision was made for the annual observance of this ceremony and for the parental obligation to instruct children in the meaning and significance of this reenactment (v.24). The section closes with one of those rare notices in Israel's history: they did exactly what the Lord had commanded (v.28)—and well they might after witnessing what had happened to the obstinate king and people of Egypt! (See also Hag 1:12, where the people obeyed the Lord.)

Notes

22 אֵזוֹב (*ʾēzôḇ*, "hyssop") occurs ten times in the OT. ("Hyssop appears twice in the NT: in John 19:29, as the instrument for lifting the vinegar to Jesus' lips when he was on the cross, and in Heb 9:19–20, where the people and the book are sprinkled with blood, though that is probably a different plant.) Seven of the OT references are found in two rituals: cleansing a leper (Lev 14:4, 6, 49, 51, 52) and cleansing those defiled through contact with the dead (Num 19:6, 18). The other three references are Exod 12:22; 1 Kings 4:33; and Ps 51:7. Most identify *ʾēzôḇ* with *Origanum Maru L.*, the Syrian marjoram (Arabic *ṣaʿtur* and Akkadian *zūpu*) or *Origanum Aegyptiacum* from Egypt. It is an aromatic herb in the mint family with a straight stalk, somewhat woody at the base, and forming a dwarf bush with opposite deciduous leaves decreasing in size as they go up the stalk. This plant is found in the Sinai desert—it grew on the walls of Jerusalem (1 Kings 4:33)—and has white flowers tinged with red on the outside. See L. Baldensperger and G.M. Crowfoot, "Hyssop," PEQ 63 [1931]: 89–98.

The LXX, Vulgate, and other passages translate סַף (*sap̄*, "basin") as "threshold." Rylaarsdam (p. 923) reports that Armenian miniatures depict the slaying of the lamb on the threshold and the blood spilled in a hollow place, perhaps especially made for this purpose.

23 The substantive הַמַּשְׁחִית (*hammašḥîṯ*, "the destroyer") appears thirty-five times in the OT, but only here does it seem to be a technical term (cf., however, v.13: לְמַשְׁחִית [*lᵉmašḥîṯ*, "destructive (plague)"]). See especially 2 Sam 24:16 and Isa 37:36. The most recent discussion is B.N. Wambacq, "Les origines de la Pesaḥ israélite," *Bib* 57 [1976]: 207–12.

F. *The Exodus From Egypt (12:29–51)*

1. *Death at midnight*

12:29–32

[29]At midnight the LORD struck down all the firstborn in Egypt, from the firstborn of Pharaoh, who sat on the throne, to the firstborn of the prisoner, who was in the dungeon, and the firstborn of all the livestock as well. [30]Pharaoh and all his officials and all the Egyptians got up during the night, and there was loud wailing in Egypt, for there was not a house without someone dead.

[31]During the night Pharaoh summoned Moses and Aaron and said, "Up! Leave my people, you and the Israelites! Go, worship the LORD as you have requested. [32]Take your flocks and herds, as you have said, and go. And also bless me."

29–30 The final stroke came at midnight of Abib 15. While the previous plagues may have utilized some of the natural and secondary agencies of nature, vv.23 and 29 attribute this tenth plague solely to the LORD. Yahweh went through the land of Egypt, and death touched every "family" (*bayiṯ*, "house," v.30)—from Pharaoh to the prisoner (v.29; cf. 11:5, from Pharaoh to the slave girl working the hand mill).

The "all" (*kol*), or "every," once again must be understood comparatively and not absolutely (cf. comment on 9:24–25), for it would apply only to those households that had firstborn among its members or livestock. Bush (*Exodus*, p. 146) notes that such universal negatives or affirmatives ("none," "all") leave the exceptions unstated when such are so few that they hardly deserve mention when compared to the overwhelming number of cases being considered. (He mentions 1 Sam 25:1: "All Israel assembled and mourned for [Saul]," i.e., with few exceptions, there was a tremendous outpouring of national feeling; Ps 53:3: "There is no one who does good" = scarcely anyone; and John 12:19: "The whole world has gone after [Jesus]," but that too was hyperbolic. Such hyperboles tended to be idiomatic in Semitic languages.)

31–32 How Pharaoh "summoned" (*qr' lᵉ*) Moses and Aaron is unknown. Whether the king retracted his rash oath never to see these two men again (10:28) and recalled them one more time or used ambassadors to convene his unconditional release cannot be determined—the verb is used in both senses. If it were the latter, however, then it was a striking fulfillment of 11:8.

The release granted Israel was for more than a three-day journey to worship the Lord. Previously when Pharaoh had given permission to leave (only to immediately rescind it or place unacceptable restrictions on it), he had said: "Go, worship the LORD your God" (10:8, 24), or "Go, sacrifice to your God" (8:25); but now it was: "Up! Leave my people!" (v.31). As KD argue (2:25), this "cannot mean anything else than 'depart altogether.'" In fact, God had predicted that the effect of this tenth blow would be so hard that Pharaoh would "drive [them] out completely" (11:1). They were to take everything Moses ever bargained for ("as you have said," v.32); yes, their flocks and herds included.

As Moses was taking leave of the king and Egypt, Pharaoh had one more request as a final gesture. "Bless me," he begged. Pharaoh, the god of Egypt, entreated Moses' God to bless him! Israel was both blessed and a means of blessing others even though in this case that blessing fell on an unrepentant heart, as 14:5–9 shows.

Notes

29 הַבּוֹר (*habbôr,* "dungeon") is usually a "well" or "cistern" but by extension is used of "those [= the dead] who go down to the pit."

2. *Preparations for the Exodus*

12:33–36

[33]The Egyptians urged the people to hurry and leave the country. "For otherwise," they said, "we will all die!" [34]So the people took their dough before the yeast was added, and carried it on their shoulders in kneading troughs wrapped in clothing. [35]The Israelites did as Moses instructed and asked the Egyptians for articles of silver and gold and for clothing. [36]The LORD had made the Egyptians favorably disposed toward the people, and they gave them what they asked for; so they plundered the Egyptians.

33 The Egyptians urged the people most vehemently (*watteḥᵉzaq;* cf. the same root *ḥāzaq* for Pharaoh hardening his heart) that they should leave immediately, for soon no Egyptians would be left if things kept up as they were going.

34 The Israelites wrapped the unleavened lumps of dough in sacks made from their outer garments or mantles and slung them over their shoulders along with their kneading troughs (see Notes) and whatever other incidentals they planned to take with them.

35–36 On the spoiling of the Egyptians, see the comments on 3:21–22 and 11:2–3.

Notes

34 On יֶחְמָץ (*yeḥmāṣ,*"[before] the yeast was added"), see Notes on 12:15, 19.

מִשְׁאֲרֹת (*miš'ᵃrōṯ,* "kneading troughs") occurs also in 8:3 (7:28 MT) and Deut 28:5, 17. They were probably something like the old Egyptian kneading trough, portable and wooden (cf. Pritchard, *Ancient Pictures,* No. 152).

3. *The Exodus and the mixed multitude*

12:37–51

[37]The Israelites journeyed from Rameses to Succoth. There were about six hundred thousand men on foot, besides women and children. [38]Many other people went up with them, as well as large droves of livestock, both flocks and herds. [39]With the dough they had brought from Egypt, they baked cakes of unleavened bread. The dough was without yeast because they had been driven out of Egypt and did not have time to prepare food for themselves.

40 Now the length of time the Israelite people lived in Egypt was 430 years. 41 At the end of the 430 years, to the very day, all the LORD's divisions left Egypt. 42 Because the LORD kept vigil that night to bring them out of Egypt, on this night all the Israelites are to keep vigil to honor the LORD for the generations to come.

43 The LORD said to Moses and Aaron, "These are the regulations for the Passover:

"No foreigner is to eat of it. 44 Any slave you have bought may eat of it after you have circumcised him, 45 but a temporary resident and a hired worker may not eat of it.

46 "It must be eaten inside one house; take none of the meat outside the house. Do not break any of the bones. 47 The whole community of Israel must celebrate it.

48 "An alien living among you who wants to celebrate the LORD's Passover must have all the males in his household circumcised; then he may take part like one born in the land. No uncircumcised male may eat of it. 49 The same law applies to the native-born and to the alien living among you."

50 All the Israelites did just what the LORD had commanded Moses and Aaron. 51 And on that very day the LORD brought the Israelites out of Egypt by their divisions.

37 The wilderness itinerary actually begins in this verse. George W. Coats ("The Wilderness Itinerary," CBQ 34 [1972]: 135–52) has collected the itinerary formulas to examine their unity and special function. Usually they consist of two elements: (1) the departure place name with a *mem* ("from") and the verb *nāsa'* ("to journey"; 12:37; 13:20; 16:1; 17:1; 19:2) and (2) the arrival location with *b*[e] ("at"; 13:20; 17:1; 19:2), *'el* ("to"; 15:22; 16:1), *'al* ("to"; 14:2; 15:27), and various verbs such as *ḥānan* ("to camp"; 13:20; 15:27; 17:1; 19:2), *bô'* ("to come"; 15:23, 27; 16:1; 19:2), and *yāṣā'* ("to lead"; 15:22).

"Rameses" is best identified with Qantir instead of the remoter but more popular Tanis (seventeen miles northeast) since Qantir was situated near the water, as the Egyptian documents observed, on the "Waters of Ra," the Bubastite-Pelusiac eastern arm of the Nile River (see comment on 1:11; cf. the Introduction: Route of the Exodus and the map). Succoth is now generally identified with Tell el Maskhuta in the Wadi Tumilat near modern Ismailia. Edward Naville (*The Store-City of Pithom and the Route of the Exodus* [London, 1885], p. 23) argued that Succoth was a district and not a city, the region of *Tkw* near Tell el Maskhuta. Thus Israel pitched their tents in *the land* of Succoth, only a few miles from the store-city of Pithom, where many had labored for years.

With the number of fighting men at 600,000, the total number of Israelites could well be around 2 million. All attempts to explain *'elep̱* ("thousand") as "clan" or "tribe" (George E. Mendenhall, "The Census Lists of Numbers 1 and 26," JBL 77 [1958]: 52–66) in this context (cf., however, Judg 6:15) fail to meet the test of inconsistency in other contexts (e.g., see below on 38:25–26; see Ronald Allen's Introduction to the Book of Numbers, this vol.).

38 The "many other people" (*'ēreḇ raḇ;* KJV, "mixed multitude"; cf. the "swarms" of flies in 8:21 [17 MT], *'ārōḇ*) were composed of Egyptians (some "feared the word of the LORD" in 9:20), perhaps some of the old Semitic population left from the Hyksos era and slaves native to other countries. Some of this group must be part of the "rabble" (*hā'sap̱sup̱,* lit., "a collection") mentioned later in Numbers 11:4. Thus the promise to Abraham in Genesis 12:3, of a blessing to "all peoples on the earth," received another fulfillment in this swarm of foreigners who were impressed enough by the power of God to leave Egypt with Israel after all the plagues had been performed. Another aspect of God's display of his power was so that the Egyptians could, if they only would, be evangelized (7:5; 8:10, 19; 9:14, 16, 29–30; 14:4, 18).

39 As the Lord had predicted in 11:1, the Israelites "had been driven out [*grš*] of Egypt." Indeed, they left so quickly that they had no time to prepare anything, much less set the yeast in the dough; so they left with unleavened bread and made unleavened cakes during those early days (see comment and Notes on v.34).

40–42 Appropriately, now that the Exodus had begun, the narrator took a moment to reflect on the total Egyptian experience. Twice he commented that it had been 430 years, "to the very day" (*beʿeṣem hayyôm hazzeh,* v.41; notice the same expression in vv.17, 51). The LXX and Samaritan texts added the words "and in the land of Canaan" to the Hebrew text, thus making the total sojourn in Egypt only 215 years, a figure also allegedly supported by the genealogy of Moses and Aaron in Exodus 6:16–20 and the Pauline statement in Galatians 3:17. But it is a mistake to suppose that the genealogy of Moses was intended to be complete (see comment on 2:1–4 for evidence to the contrary). One need only consult the genealogy of Joshua (1 Chron 7:22–27) to see that there were many deliberate omissions of generations in Moses and Aaron's genealogy, for Joshua's genealogy has ten generations covering the same time span as Moses' four generations!

With respect to Paul's 430 years, it is important to notice that "the law" came "430 years later" (Gal 3:17) as "an addition" (cf. v.19) to "the promises . . . spoken to Abraham *and to his seed*" (v.16, emphasis mine). The *terminus a quo* for the 430 years in Paul's thinking would seem to be when Jacob received the last of those repeated patriarchal promises (Gen 46:2; 47:27) as he arrived in Egypt. The 430 years accord also with the 400 years predicted in Genesis 15:13–16, when a nation [Egypt] whom they would "serve" could "mistreat" them, at the end of which time that nation would be "judged."

That night was to be observed by all future generations as a "Watchnight Service" (Cole, p. 113), for on that night the Lord "preserved" or "kept" the destroyer from touching them (v.42). There is a clear play on the word *šāmar* ("watch," "preserve," "keep vigil"); as Yahweh watched over Israel that night, so Israel was to watch for Yahweh by keeping this feast perpetually (cf. v.17).

43-49 With the mention of that night and the requirement that it be remembered by all future generations, it did bring to mind, especially in this context, the question of the "mixed multitude" who came out of Egypt with Israel and all such persons who might join them from time to time. Were they to keep the Passover also? Thus arose the necessity for repeating and elaborating on instructions already given in two preceding sections.

No one was allowed to participate in that meal unless he was circumcised and thus a member of the community of faith (v.44; however, notice the requirement in Gen 17:13–14 to be part of the Israelite community). This excluded temporary residents, hired workers, aliens, and all foreigners. Furthermore, each lamb was to remain in one house (as implied in vv.3–10). Its parts were not to be divided and eaten in separate homes; it was to be the basis of a fellowship meal stressing the unity and joy of the participants. In addition to that, no bones of the paschal lamb were to be broken (cf. Ps 34:20 and John 19:33–36 for the same teaching about the antitype). This was the LORD's Passover (*pesaḥ layhwh,* v.48) and not the table of Israel; therefore, the same requirement was made of all, whether native-born (see Notes) or alien (v.49).

50–51 The concluding notice is that Israel "did just what the LORD had commanded" (v.50; cf. v.28); and "on that very day" (v.51; cf. vv.17, 41) the much-delayed Exodus finally took place as the LORD brought Israel out by their "divisions" (see Notes on 6:26). Surprisingly, the desert journey began on the Sabbath!

Notes

37 וַיִּסְעוּ (*wayyis'û,* "[Israelites] journeyed") comes from a verb meaning "to pull up or out," i.e., the stakes or pins holding the tent.

On טַף (*ṭāp̱,* "women and children"), see Notes on 10:24.

39 לְהִתְמַהְמֵהַּ (*lᵉhiṯmahmēᵃh*) is a Hithpilpel infinitive construct of *mhh* ("to tarry"; NIV, "[not] have time").

49 On לָאֶזְרָח (*lā'ezrāḥ,* "native-born," an aborigine), see Albright, *Archaeology and the Religion of Israel,* pp. 127, 210, on the Gentilic form of the word in the titles of Pss 88 and 89 and in 1 Kings 4:31 (LXX, 1 Kings 5:11); however, see O.T. Allis, *The Old Testament: Its Claims and Its Critics* (Philadelphia: Presbyterian and Reformed, 1968), pp. 308–9.

G. *The Consecration of the Firstborn*

13:1–16

1The LORD said to Moses, 2"Consecrate to me every firstborn male.
The first offspring of every womb among the Israelites belongs to me,
whether man or animal."
3Then Moses said to the people, "Commemorate this day, the day you
came out of Egypt, out of the land of slavery, because the LORD brought
you out of it with a mighty hand. Eat nothing containing yeast. 4Today,
in the month of Abib, you are leaving. 5When the LORD brings you into
the land of the Canaanites, Hittites, Amorites, Hivites and Jebusites—
the land he swore to your forefathers to give you, a land flowing with
milk and honey—you are to observe this ceremony in this month: 6For
seven days eat bread made without yeast and on the seventh day hold a
festival to the LORD. 7Eat unleavened bread during those seven days;
nothing with yeast in it is to be seen among you, nor shall any yeast be
seen anywhere within your borders. 8On that day tell your son, 'I do this
because of what the LORD did for me when I came out of Egypt.' 9This
observance will be for you like a sign on your hand and a reminder on
your forehead that the law of the LORD is to be on your lips. For the LORD
brought you out of Egypt with his mighty hand. 10You must keep this
ordinance at the appointed time year after year.
11"After the LORD brings you into the land of the Canaanites and gives
it to you, as he promised on oath to you and your forefathers, 12you are
to give over to the LORD the first offspring of every womb. All the
firstborn males of your livestock belong to the LORD. 13Redeem with a
lamb every firstborn donkey, but if you do not redeem it, break its neck.
Redeem every firstborn among your sons.

> [14]"In days to come, when your son asks you, 'What does this mean?' say to him, 'With a mighty hand the LORD brought us out of Egypt, out of the land of slavery. [15]When Pharaoh stubbornly refused to let us go, the LORD killed every firstborn in Egypt, both man and animal. This is why I sacrifice to the LORD the first male offspring of every womb and redeem each of my firstborn sons.' [16]And it will be like a sign on your hand and a symbol on your forehead that the LORD brought us out of Egypt with his mighty hand."

1–2 Closely linked with the account of Israel's release from Egypt and the Passover was the consecration of all the firstborn in Israel. The connection of v.1 with the preceding events is secured by comparing the repeated reference to "that very day" (12:41, 51) with "this day" (13:3) and "today, in the month of Abib, you are leaving" (v.4). Therefore, the sanctification of all firstborn was commanded by God probably at Succoth, the first stopping place after the Exodus (12:37); and it fell within the seven days set aside for the Feast of Unleavened Bread (12:15).

The general principle is set forth in v.2: every "firstborn" (*bekôr*) male of both man and beast (as explained in vv.12–13), i.e., the first "offspring" (*peṭer*, "that which opens [the womb]") belongs to the Lord and is therefore "to be set apart" (*qādaš*) from common usage for holy purposes. Thus God set aside the seventh day, the tabernacle, the tribe of Levi—and here all firstborn. The basis for God's claim was not connected here with his lordship over all creation (Ps 24:1 et al.); but as KD point out (2:33) from Numbers 3:13 and 8:17, it was based on the fact that God had already set apart to himself the firstborn in Israel on the day he smote all the firstborn of Egypt. Their sanctification did not rest on their deliverance from the tenth plague, but rather God's adoption of Israel as his "firstborn" (see on 4:22) led to his delivering them. From that time onward, that spared nation would dedicate the firstborn of its men and beasts in the way detailed in vv.12–16 in commemoration of God's acts of love and his deeds that night.

3–10 Further directions are given relating this consecration of the firstborn to the Feast of Unleavened Bread. When Israel possessed the land promised to her, this ceremony (see Notes on v.5) was to be observed annually. The Israelites were to explain to their children (v.8) that they ate unleavened bread and set apart the firstborn to the Lord because of what he had done personally for each subsequent Israelite (and believer)—"for me" (*lî*)—when he brought Israel out of Egypt. Likewise, in v.16 subsequent generations would be taught that he brought "us" out of Egypt (cf. Ps 66:6: "There [at the Red Sea] *we* rejoiced in him" [pers. tr., emphasis mine]; or Hos 12:4: "There [at Bethel when God spoke to Jacob a thousand years earlier] he spoke with *us*" [lit. tr., emphasis mine]; more examples of past events being used to speak to those in the present are Matt 15:7; 22:31; Mark 7:6; Acts 4:11; Rom 4:23–25; 15:4; 1 Cor 10:11; 2 Cor 9:8–11; Heb 6:18; 10:15; 12:15–17).

This festival and consecration were to be a "sign" (see comment on 3:12) on the people's hands and a "reminder" or "memorial" (see comment on 3:15) between their eyes (v.9). No doubt this injunction was a figurative and proverbial mode of speech (cf. Prov 3:3: "Bind them around your neck,/ write them on . . . your heart"; also Prov 6:21; 7:3; S of Songs 8:6), for the law of the Lord was "to be on [their] lips" (v.9).

The Jewish practice of writing Exodus 13:1–16 out on two of the four strips of parchment (along with Deut 6:4–9 and 11:13–21 on the other two) and placing them in two cubical leather boxes (*tepillîn*; cf. "phylacteries," Matt 23:5) that were strapped on to the forehead and left arm seems to have originated in the Babylonian captivity. These were worn especially at daily morning prayers. This was, however, to exchange the intended inner reality for an external ritualism. The word was to activate their lips, hearts, and hands, not to be trapped in a box.

11–16 As Israel "passed over" (*'br*) the Red Sea and the destroyer "passed over" their firstborn, so now they were "to cause to pass over" or "give over" (*'br*) to the LORD all their firstborn when they entered the land (v.12). (Notice also the connection between the "Passover" and the "pass[ing] over" of the death angel in the comment on 12:13.) Only two slight modifications (v.13) were made to this principle: (1) all firstborn male humans (firstborn females were exempted) were to be redeemed (*pādāh*) or "bought back at a price" (fixed at five shekels per male in the fuller description in Num 18:16; cf. also Num 3:46–47), and (2) donkeys were to be "bought back" or "ransomed" (*pādāh*) by a lamb or kid since donkeys were unclean animals and therefore unfit for sacrifice (at Mari, however, the Amorites did use the donkey as a sacrificial animal). To prevent any refusal to follow this command to ransom their animals, the Israelites were to kill them by breaking their necks.

The obligation of the firstborn to serve the LORD in some nonpriestly work around the sanctuary was later transferred to the Levites who became God's authorized substitutes for each firstborn boy or man (Num 3). When the number of Levites was exhausted, additional males could be ransomed or redeemed at the price of five shekels apiece. Verses 15–16 again reiterate the explanation: the firstborn were owned by the LORD; for he dramatically spared them in the tenth plague, *and* he had previously called them to be his firstborn in 4:22.

Notes

2 פֶּטֶר כָּל־רֶחֶם (*peṭer kol-reḥem*, "the first offspring of every womb") makes explicit what "firstborn" (*bᵉḵôr*) means here. *Peṭer* is "that which opens [the womb]."

3–4 The interchange of plural second-person pronouns in vv.3 and 4 with second-person singular pronouns in vv.2 and 5ff. is just another extension of the collective singular phenomenon seen before and another illustration of Israel's corporate solidarity. (See William Kesecker, "A Study of the Literary Phenomenon of the Second Person Interchange in Deuteronomy 1–11," Master's Thesis, Trinity Evangelical Divinity School, 1977.)

3 מִבֵּית עֲבָדִים (*mibbêṯ 'ᵃḇāḏîm*, "land of slavery") is literally "from a house of slaveries" (also 20:2; Deut 5:6; 6:12). Bush reminds us (*Exodus*, 1:155) of Egypt being called "the iron-smelting furnace" in Deut 4:20; 1 Kings 8:51; and Jer 11:4.

5 On the list of Canaanite nations, see Notes on 3:8.

On the land "flowing with milk and honey," see comment on 3:8.

Although הָעֲבֹדָה (*hā'ᵃḇōḏāh*) is rendered "ceremony" here and also in 12:25–26, it was "slavery" and "work" in 2:23 and 5:9; but it is a "work [or service of the Lord]" in 35:24; 36:5; 39:42. Thus Israel was saved *from* "slavery" *into* "service" for God as *remembered by* a "ceremony"! A veritable theology in a single word!

10 מִיָּמִים יָמִימָה (*miyyāmîm yāmîmāh*, "year after year") is literally "from days to days" and is an example of the frequent use of "days" for the concept "years" (Bush, *Exodus*, 1:157).

12 שֶׁגֶר (*šeger*, "livestock") is literally "that which is brought forth [cf. Aram. *šᵉgar*, 'to throw,, 'to drop,' hence 'dropped one'] by cattle." Cassuto (p. 153) says "a beast's *reḥem* ['womb'] is apparently also called שֶׁגֶר."

16 וּלְטוֹטָפֹת (*ûlᵉṭôṭāp̄ōṯ;* NIV, "a symbol") is literally "as frontlets" or "bands about the forehead"; cf. v.9 above and see Deut 6:8; 11:18. Rawlinson (1:300) believes that Moses borrowed and reinterpreted the Egyptian practice of wearing as amulets "forms of words written on folds of papyrus tightly rolled up and sewn in linen."

H. *Journey to the Red Sea (13:17–15:21)*

1. *Into the wilderness*

13:17–22

17 When Pharaoh let the people go, God did not lead them on the road through the Philistine country, though that was shorter. For God said, "If they face war, they might change their minds and return to Egypt."
18 So God led the people around by the desert road toward the Red Sea. The Israelites went up out of Egypt armed for battle.
19 Moses took the bones of Joseph with him because Joseph had made the sons of Israel swear an oath. He had said, "God will surely come to your aid, and then you must carry my bones up with you from this place."
20 After leaving Succoth they camped at Etham on the edge of the
desert. 21 By day the LORD went ahead of them in a pillar of cloud to guide them on their way and by night in a pillar of fire to give them light,
so that they could travel by day or night. 22 Neither the pillar of cloud by
day nor the pillar of fire by night left its place in front of the people.

17–18 There were three possible routes of escape: (1) a northeast route going to Qantara through the land of the Philistines to Gaza and Canaan; (2) a middle route heading across the Negeb to Beersheba, which incorrectly assumes Mount Sinai is Ǧebel Halal near Kadesh-Barnea; and (3) a southeast route leading from the wilderness east of modern Ismailia to the southern extremities of the Sinai Peninsula. Israel was warned not to take the shorter route through Philistia, for the prospects of fighting the bellicose Philistines (see Notes) would so demoralize Israel that they would change their minds (see Notes) and return to the servitude in Egypt (v.17). This judgment was proven correct when Israel was threatened with war in Numbers 14:4.

Thus God led Israel around by the "desert road" or the "way of the wilderness" (*dereḵ hammiḏbār*) toward the "Red Sea" or, better, "Sea of Reeds" (*yam-sûp̄*; or Egyptian *p3 ṯ[w]f*, pronounced *pa tjuf*, meaning "papyrus" or "papyrus marshes"). Kenneth Kitchen (ZPEB, 5:46–49) associates this body of water with Lake Menzaleh or Lake Ballah. (The connection of Heb. *sûp̄* with Arabic *ṣuf*, "weeds" or "seaweed," is extremely unlikely because the interchange of these sibilants is unattested.) Kitchen does note that *Yam Suph* (NIV mg.) may also be connected with the Gulf of Suez. Israel camped on the west coast of the Sinai Peninsula by *Yam Suph* on their way to Horeb/Sinai (Num 33:10–11), and later on *Yam Suph* is also used to refer to the salt waters of the Gulf of Aqabah (Deut 1:1; 1 Kings 9:26 et al.; see Notes on 2:3). Thus nothing prevents our linking *Yam Suph* with the Red Sea. (The Red Sea of that day did not include the Gulf of Suez modern extension of the Red Sea.)

19 The records in this verse are a verbatim report of Joseph's words in Genesis 50:25 except for the additional words "with you." God's promise of the land is never far from sight in any of these passages.

20 The exact location of Etham (*'ēṯām*) is unknown. Many associate it with the Egyptian city of *Khetem* (spelled *ḥtm*, meaning "fort"), but the Hebrew aleph sound hardly equals the strong Egyptian guttural *ḫ*sound. Naville (*Pithom and the Route of the Exodus*, p. 24) suggests the region of Atuma, a desert that begins at Lake Timsah and extends west and south of it, where Asiatic Bedouin from the land of Atuma grazed their flocks (Papyrus Anastasi IV.55, ANET, p. 259; Egyptian *'idm*).

Etham is described as a region in Numbers 33:6 and appears to be equated with the Desert of Shur (Exod 15:22). Kitchen (ZPEB, 2:430) locates the wilderness of Shur/Etham from Lake Timsah (near Ismailia) north to the Mediterranean Sea and east of the present Suez Canal, perhaps to El-Arish and the "Brook of Egypt." Rawlinson (1:xxix), noting that Etham was "on the edge of the desert" (13:20), placed Etham at El-Qantara, on the line of the Suez Canal and eleven to twelve miles due east of Tel Defneh (ancient Daphnae). Everyone is guessing!

21–22 How God led the Israelites (v.17) is now explained. This single "pillar" (14:24), which was a cloud by day and a fire by night, whose width at the base was sufficiently large to provide cover for Israel from the intense heat (Ps 105:39), was a visible symbol of the presence of Yahweh in their midst. The pillar of the cloud and fire was but another name for "the angel of God," for Exodus 14:19 equates the two as does 23:20–23. In fact, God's Name was "in" this angel who went before them to bring them into Canaan (23:20–23). He was the "angel of his presence" (Isa 63:8–9). Malachi 3:1 calls this angel the "messenger of the covenant," who is equated with the Lord, the owner of the temple. Obviously, then, the Christ of the NT is the shekinah glory or Yahweh of the OT. Through this cloudy pillar the Lord would speak to Moses (33:9–11) and to the people (Ps 99:6–7). Such easy movement from the pillar of cloud and fire to the angel and back to the Lord himself has already been met in the same interchange between the burning bush, the angel, and the Lord in chapter 3 (see Notes on 3:2).

Notes

17 All references to the Philistines before the twelfth century B.C., it is alleged, are anachronistic since they only arrived on the scene around that time, along with the various waves of other sea peoples. Yet already at the turn of our century, Flinders Petrie had argued that there was substantial evidence for Philistine presence as early as the patriarchal era if but for no other reason than to raise crops to be transported back to their homeland on Caphtor/Crete (see Ed Hindson, *The Philistines and the Old Testament* [Grand Rapids: Baker, 1970], pp. 39, 59).

יִנָּחֵם (*yinnāḥēm*, "[lest the people] change [their] minds") is from the famous root *nḥm* ("to repent") and illustrates its meaning in a nontheologically sensitive passage.

18 The MT has וַחֲמֻשִׁים (*waḥᵃmušîm*, "armed for battle"; so Gesenius, Rashi, Vulgate). The LXX has "the fifth generation"; and Ewald opts for "in five divisions," viz., vanguard, center, rearguard, and two flanking wings, from *ḥāmēš* ("five"). See also Josh 1:14; 4:12; and Judg 7:11 for its other usages.

21 George E. Mendenhall (*Tenth Generation* [Baltimore: Johns Hopkins Press, 1973], pp. 32–66) attempts to locate the roots of the symbolism of בְּעַמּוּד עָנָן (*bᵉʿamûḏ ʿānān*, "pillar of cloud") in the ancient Near East and to define it as the manifestation of the divine sovereignty in the world.

2. *At the Red Sea*

14:1–14

[1]Then the LORD said to Moses, [2]"Tell the Israelites to turn back and
encamp near Pi Hahiroth, between Migdol and the sea. They are to
encamp by the sea, directly opposite Baal Zephon. [3]Pharaoh will think,
'The Israelites are wandering around the land in confusion, hemmed in
by the desert.' [4]And I will harden Pharaoh's heart, and he will pursue
them. But I will gain glory for myself through Pharaoh and all his army,
and the Egyptians will know that I am the LORD." So the Israelites did
this.

[5]When the king of Egypt was told that the people had fled, Pharaoh
and his officials changed their minds about them and said, "What have
we done? We have let the Israelites go and have lost their services!" [6]So
he had his chariot made ready and took his army with him. [7]He took six
hundred of the best chariots, along with all the other chariots of Egypt,
with officers over all of them. [8]The LORD hardened the heart of Pharaoh
king of Egypt, so that he pursued the Israelites, who were marching out
boldly. [9]The Egyptians—all Pharaoh's horses and chariots, horsemen
and troops—pursued the Israelites and overtook them as they camped
by the sea near Pi Hahiroth, opposite Baal Zephon.

[10]As Pharaoh approached, the Israelites looked up, and there were
the Egyptians, marching after them. They were terrified and cried out to
the LORD. [11]They said to Moses, "Was it because there were no graves in
Egypt that you brought us to the desert to die? What have you done to
us by bringing us out of Egypt? [12]Didn't we say to you in Egypt, 'Leave
us alone; let us serve the Egyptians'? It would have been better for us to
serve the Egyptians than to die in the desert!"

[13]Moses answered the people, "Do not be afraid. Stand firm and you
will see the deliverance the LORD will bring you today. The Egyptians you
see today you will never see again. [14]The LORD will fight for you; you
need only to be still."

1–4 The command "to turn back" (*šûḇ*, v.2) meant a change in direction and perhaps even a temporary setback for Israel, but which way did they go? Finegan (p. 85) has Israel turn back to the west and then turn south to get around the bulging upper part of the large Bitter Lake. Then they went southeastward between the mountain range of Jebel Jenefel and the large and small Bitter Lakes—all connected by water with the Gulf of Suez as the Pharaonic Canal, which ran through the Wadi Tumilat (also argued by Bourdon in "La Route de l'Exode," pp. 378–90). Kitchen (ZPEB, 2:430) rejected this reasoning and had Israel go north-northwest, then north toward Qantara. But this northern retreat would take them back to the centers of Egyptian power and toward the divinely forbidden coastal route.

"Pi Hahiroth" (v.2) was opposite Baal Zephon (see Notes) and between Migdol and the sea according to Numbers 33:7. This site of Pi Hahiroth has not been identified as yet (see Notes). A possible location for Migdol ("tower," Egyp. *Mktr*) is either Migdol near Succoth, mentioned in a papyrus of Seti I's time, or the ruins of a square tower on a height known as Jebel Abu Hasan overlooking the southern part of the small Bitter Lake. The latter was discovered by Jean Clédat and contained carvings and texts, some with the names of Seti I and Rameses II (see Finegan, p. 86).

Pharaoh assumed that Israel's divine help had run out and that they were hopelessly entangled on a dead-end trail since the desert, the sea, and marshes barred their way out of this trap. God, however, had commanded Moses (v.3: "Pharaoh will think") to take this impossible route to show the Egyptians once more that he was God (v.4; see 7:17; 9:14) and to show Israel his great power (vv.30–31). Nevertheless, God would receive glory from Pharaoh and his army. That glory would have come to God whether Pharaoh had yielded (cf. much later Cyrus in the exact situation) or had rebelled and said in effect, "Those Hebrews will leave this place over my dead body!"

5–9 For those who reject the fact that Israel numbered somewhere around two million and decide instead that they were about five thousand, the number of chariots and the size of the army must surely be an extreme case of overkill (v.7). Shortly after Israel left, Pharaoh and his officials quickly put aside the terrors of that awful night when they lost their firstborn and decided to go after Israel as they marched out of Egypt "boldly" (v.8; see Notes).

10–12 When they saw the Egyptian troops, the Israelites cried out in despair to the Lord (v.10), but not for long. Moses was a much more immediate target than the Lord; so they complained to him (v.11). Were there "no graves at all [double negative: *mibbᵉlî 'ên*] in Egypt?" They mocked in the most satirical tone possible (since Egypt specialized in graves and had about three-fourths of its land area available for grave sites). Then followed the crepe-hanging with its "I-told-you-so" pseudoprophets (v.12). Suddenly the hardships of their Egyptian bondage were forgotten.

13–14 The former quick-tempered Moses patiently answered the people's hasty accusation with three directives to meet this emergency: (1) "Do not be afraid" (v.13; cf. the word to the patriarchs, Gen 15:1; 26:24; and to Israel as they possessed the land, Josh 1:9; 8:1); (2) "Stand firm" and see the salvation, i.e., the "deliverance of the LORD," for "the LORD will fight for you" (v.14; see Neh 4:20; Ps 35:1); and (3) "Be still," i.e., stop all action and become inactive, for I the Lord will act by myself on your behalf (cf. Gen 34:5; 2 Kings 19:11; Pss 5:3; 83:1).

Notes

2 פִּי הַחִירֹת (*pî haḥîrōṯ*, "Pi Hahiroth") has been explained from the Hebrew as meaning "the mouth of the canals." But the name is probably Egyptian, from *Pi-Ḥrt*, "temple of [the Syrian goddess] *Ḥrt*" (C. DeWit, *The Date and Route of the Exodus* [London: Tyndale, 1959], p. 17), or *Pa-Ḥir*, "The Ḥir-waters [of a canal or lake]" (K. Kitchen, ZPEB, 2:430), or *Pi(r) Ḥwt-Ḥr*, "The dwelling of Hathor" (Montet, p. 64).

K. Kitchen (ZPEB, 2:430) suggests that בַּעַל צְפֹן (*ba'al ṣᵉp̄ōn*, "Baal Zephon") be equated with the later Tahpanhes, Greek Daphnai at Tell Defenneh, eight and one-half miles from Qantara, since a later Phoenician papyrus has "Baal-Zephon and all the gods of Tahpanhes." Montet (p. 63) cites two stelae found by Clédat at Gebel Shaduf (*Kêmi* 7 [1938]: pl. XX), where on one stela Rameses II is perhaps honoring Baal Zephon and on the other he is paying homage to Soped, Lord of the East (Goshen).

6 עַמּוֹ (*'ammô*, "his army") is the usual word for "his people." In this context it is a wordplay on *'immô* ("with him"). See v.17, *ḥêlô* ("his army"), or v.19, *mahᵃnēh* ("army"), for the more usual words.

7 Etymologically the term שָׁלִשִׁם (*šālišim*, "officers") means something like "three-man [chariots]," presumably a driver, a shield-bearer, and a warrior. This practice, however, was known among only the Hittites and Assyrians, not the Egyptians, whose chariots only had two occupants as far as we know. A.E. Cowley ("A Hittite Word in Hebrew," JTS 21 [1920]: 326) plausibly claimed that the word was related to the Hittite *šal-li-iš*, a military title indicating high rank. The Ugaritic parallel *tlṯm sswm mrkbt* ("three horses and a chariot") points to a different solution. P.C. Craigie ("An Egyptian Expression in the Song of the Sea: Exodus XV.4," VetTest 20 [1970]: 85) may have the best solution: *šlš* is Egyptian *srs*, "to have command of [a corps]." See comment on 15.4.

In the expression וְכֹל רֶכֶב (*w^ek̲ōl rek̲eb̲*, "with all [the other] chariots"), the word "all" is probably to be understood in the general sense described in our comments on 9:6 and 9:24–25 and not in a strict mathematical sense.

8 יֹצְאִים בְּיָד רָמָה (*yōṣ^e'îm b^eyād̲ rāmāh*, "marching out boldly") is literally "going out with a high hand" (cf. also Num 33:3). In Num 15:30 "high hand" (NIV, "defiantly") is used for the sin of blaspheming God, i.e., an attempt to personally take on God in deliberate and demonstrative rebellion.

---

3. *Across the Red Sea*

14:15–31

15 Then the LORD said to Moses, "Why are you crying out to me? Tell
the Israelites to move on. 16 Raise your staff and stretch out your hand
over the sea to divide the water so that the Israelites can go through the
sea on dry ground. 17 I will harden the hearts of the Egyptians so that
they will go in after them. And I will gain glory through Pharaoh and all
his army, through his chariots and his horsemen. 18 The Egyptians will
know that I am the LORD when I gain glory through Pharaoh, his chariots
and his horsemen."

19 Then the angel of God, who had been traveling in front of Israel's
army, withdrew and went behind them. The pillar of cloud also moved
from in front and stood behind them, 20 coming between the armies of
Egypt and Israel. Throughout the night the cloud brought darkness to
the one side and light to the other side; so neither went near the other
all night long.

21 Then Moses stretched out his hand over the sea, and all that night
the LORD drove the sea back with a strong east wind and turned it into
dry land. The waters were divided, 22 and the Israelites went through the
sea on dry ground, with a wall of water on their right and on their left.

23 The Egyptians pursued them, and all Pharaoh's horses and chariots
and horsemen followed them into the sea. 24 During the last watch of the
night the LORD looked down from the pillar of fire and cloud at the
Egyptian army and threw it into confusion. 25 He made the wheels of
their chariots come off so that they had difficulty driving. And the
Egyptians said, "Let's get away from the Israelites! The LORD is fighting
for them against Egypt."

26 Then the LORD said to Moses, "Stretch out your hand over the sea so
that the waters may flow back over the Egyptians and their chariots and
horsemen." 27 Moses stretched out his hand over the sea, and at
daybreak the sea went back to its place. The Egyptians were fleeing
toward it, and the LORD swept them into the sea. 28 The water flowed
back and covered the chariots and horsemen—the entire army of
Pharaoh that had followed the Israelites into the sea. Not one of them
survived.

29 But the Israelites went through the sea on dry ground, with a wall of
water on their right and on their left. 30 That day the LORD saved Israel
from the hands of the Egyptians, and Israel saw the Egyptians lying
dead on the shore. 31 And when the Israelites saw the great power the
LORD displayed against the Egyptians, the people feared the LORD and
put their trust in him and in Moses his servant.

15–18 If God had promised to bring Israel out of Egypt and to give them the land of Canaan, then Moses and Israel had best stop their crying (*ṣʿq*) to high heaven and begin moving on (*nsʿ*) (v.15). The contrast between v.16 and v.17 is clear: "You" (*'attāh*), Moses (emphatic position), use the staff in your hand to "divide" or "form a valley" (*bqʿ*) so that Israel may go through the sea "on dry ground" (*bayyābbāšāh*); "I" (*'ᵃnî*, v.17, again in the emphatic position as "you" in v.16), the Lord, will harden the hearts of the (pursuing) Egyptians—this is the first and only time (but cf. 9:12). Verses 17–18 repeat with slight expansions the promises of vv.3–4.

19–20 The identity of the angel of God is clarified in the second part of v.19: the pillar of cloud and fire (see comment on 13:22). The reality of God's promised presence may be stated in the symbol of his presence (the pillar of cloud and fire), in his messenger (the angel of the Lord), or as the Lord himself who "went ahead of them" (13:21; cf. 14:24). But when the presence of God "withdrew" (*nsʿ*), he went behind them to protect Israel's rear guard. What was light for Israel became darkness for the Egyptians (v.20). Thus the double nature of the glory of God in salvation and judgment, which later appears so frequently in Scripture, could not have been more graphically depicted.

21–22 With the single gesture of Moses' upraised hand over the sea, the Lord "drove . . . back" (*yôlek̲*, v.21) the sea by means of a "strong east wind all that night" (lit. tr.; cf. 15:8). The exact location of this "Reed Sea" crossing is unknown; but it would seem best to place it somewhere between the southern end of the Bitter Lakes and the Gulf of Suez or even in the northern tip of the Gulf of Suez itself (Finegan and Bourdon, see above on v.2), rather than in Lake Ballaḥ (cf. Kitchen, ZPEB, 2:430) or south of Lake Timsaḥ (Naville, "Pithom and the Route of the Exodus," p. 26) on the southern end of Lake Menzaleh, with its possible equation of Baal Zephon with Daphnae (Hyatt, p. 159), or even the extreme suggestion of the sandy strip of land that separates Lake Sirbonis (modern Lake Bardawil) from the Mediterranean Sea. Even the width of this separation of the waters must have been somewhere around one-half mile wide (on this conjecture, see KD, 2:47) to allow two million people to pass over in one night before the wind died down during the "last watch" (v.24), i.e., approximately between 2:00 A.M. and 6:00 A.M. (sunrise).

Meanwhile the waters formed a "wall" (*ḥōmāh*, v.22) on the right and on the left. They were piled up like a "heap" (*nēd̲*, 15:8; Ps 78:13 [NIV, "wall"]). It is true that the last two references are found in poems; therefore the language could be poetical and not literal "walls." But the prose text of chapter 14 is so explicit that an attempt to read this as a metaphor poses more problems than it solves. One must then ask, Of what is it a metaphor? Certainly it does not convey the idea of hardness or solidity. If it is a metaphor for protection, would not the sweeping of the waves back in one direction also convey the same message? No, the event, while incorporating the natural elements of the wind, has the element of the exceptional (cf. Deut 4:32, 34) accompanying it, as did the previous plagues. Thus it strongly suggests the presence of God in the event.

23–28 Sometime during the morning watch (NIV, "last watch," v.24), the Lord "looked down" (*šqp*; cf. Deut 26:15; Pss 14:2; 53:2; 102:19; for this anthropomorphism, see comments on 3:7–10). This look is never just ocular but a demonstration of some wrath or mercy (Bush, *Exodus*, 1:181). From the pillar of fire and cloud, the Lord looked down at the Egyptian army as they began to pursue Israel across the recently formed valley in the sea and "threw it into confusion" (*hmm,* a verb used to describe the panic and disarray of an army before a superior challenger, especially when God enters the battle as in 23:27; Josh 10:10; Judg 4:15; 1 Sam 7:10; Ps 18:14). This "look" of God took on concrete proportions, for the pillar of fire must have suddenly lit up the sky with such a flash in the darkness that the chariots careened against one another.

Meanwhile there also was unleashed such a spectacular display of thunder, lightning, rain, and earthquake that the boldest and most arrogant of Egypt's charioteers were struck with terror. So we would understand from Psalm 77:16–20. By this time the thoroughly distracted Egyptians had another problem: God made the chariot wheels "come off" (NIV) or "jam" (cf. NIV mg.) against one another (*yāsar,* from the root *sûr,* "to turn"; see Notes on v.25) so that the Egyptians had difficulty driving. They had enough and were willing to forget about Israel altogether, but it was too late. The Lord had begun his fight against Egypt as was promised in v.14; described in vv.27, 31; and celebrated in the song of 15:3: "The LORD is a warrior;/ the LORD is his name." Israel had only to stand still and watch the victory won on their behalf; for with the upraised hand of Moses, the walls of water cascaded toward each other to resume their usual place just as dawn broke.

Pharaoh lost all the men and chariots he had committed to that engagement. The text never says that Pharaoh himself died here even though Psalm 136:15 records that God "swept Pharaoh and his army into the Red Sea." This may be the figure of hendiadys (i.e., two expressions for one concept) for "Pharaoh's army." Furthermore, "swept" is not necessarily "death" (so argued Rawlinson, 1:345). Even the destruction of the "entire army of Pharaoh" is qualified by the clause "that had followed the Israelites into the sea" (v.28; see discussion of *kōl,* "all," "entire," in 9:24–25). But all involved in the chase certainly perished: "Not one of them survived" (v.28).

29–31 The Lord had "saved" (*yš'*) Israel that day, for Israel saw the corpses of the Egyptians (the Hebrew simply has "Egypt," the entire nation being seen as one individual corpse!) floating by (v.30). Josephus (Antiq. II, 349 [xvi.6]) assures us (without any biblical warrant) that the wind turned around and blew the bodies of the drowned corpses to the eastern shore so that Moses could obtain the weapons and armor for many of his men. Above all, Israel saw with what great powers (*yad,* lit., "hand") the Lord had delivered them, and they feared (*yr';* see comment and Notes on 1:17) him and believed (*'mn;* see Notes on 4:5) him and his servant Moses. Their response was back to where it was in 4:31 (see comment there) and the goal stated in 9:29–30: "that you [in this case, Egyptians] might know that the earth is the LORD's . . . [and] fear [him]." The fear of the Lord (v.31) was the signal of a responsive attitude of submission and love equivalent to putting one's whole trust in him.

Notes

25 For וַיָּסַר (*wayyāsar,* "he made [the wheels of their chariots] come off" or "jam" one another), the LXX (with *synedēse,* "bound"), the Samaritan Pentateuch, and the Syriac read the root as *'sr* ("to bind"), instead of the MT's *sûr* ("to turn aside, depart"); and so the Egyptians' wheels were "bound" (together?), "jammed" (with mud?), or "bogged down" (in mud or quicksand?). This may have caused them to "come off."

וַיְנַהֲגֵהוּ בִּכְבֵדֻת (*wayᵉnahᵃgēhû bikbēdut*) is rendered "so that they had difficulty driving." The verb *nhg* is used for driving a chariot (cf. Jehu's infamous driving habits in 2 Kings 9:20). The word for "difficulty" seems to echo the "severity" (*kābēd mᵉʾōd*, "very heavy") of God's previous warnings in 9:3, 18, 24; 10:14; and 12:38.

27 לְאֵיתָנוֹ (*lᵉʾêtānô*, "to its place") describes the course of the sea after the passing of Israel. The word *ʾêtān* is used in Ps 74:15 and Amos 5:24 of "ever flowing" rivers. Thus the waters were not a temporary high tide, but they had a normal position and depth where Israel had crossed.

If the translation of לִקְרָאתוֹ (*liqrāʾtô*, "toward [or 'from'] meeting it") is "toward," then the picture is of the Egyptians fleeing back to the west side (cf. 15:10) of the sea as the winds swung around to close off their retreat with the walls of water cascading in on them. If it is "from," then their line of retreat is governed by the point where the waters first began to close in on them!

Commenting on וַיְנַעֵר (*wayᵉnaʿēr*, "and [the LORD] swept them [into the sea]"), Bush (*Exodus*, 1:182) paints the vivid picture of the Lord "shaking off" the Egyptians as Nehemiah "shook out" his lap (Neh 5:13). Accordingly, God will "shake out" the disobedient as he "shakes" the wicked out of the earth (Job 38:13; Ps 136:15).

---

4. *Song at the sea*

15:1–21

1 Then Moses and the Israelites sang this song to the LORD:

"I will sing to the LORD,
  for he is highly exalted.
The horse and its rider
  he has hurled into the sea.
2 The LORD is my strength and my song;
  he has become my salvation.
He is my God, and I will praise him,
  my father's God, and I will exalt him.
3 The LORD is a warrior;
  the LORD is his name.
4 Pharaoh's chariots and his army
  he has hurled into the sea.
The best of Pharaoh's officers
  are drowned in the Red Sea.
5 The deep waters have covered them;
  they sank to the depths like a stone.

6 "Your right hand, O LORD,
  was majestic in power.
Your right hand, O LORD,
  shattered the enemy.
7 In the greatness of your majesty
  you threw down those who opposed you.
You unleashed your burning anger;
  it consumed them like stubble.
8 By the blast of your nostrils
  the waters piled up.
The surging waters stood firm like a wall;
  the deep waters congealed in the heart of the sea.

9 "The enemy boasted,
  'I will pursue, I will overtake them.

I will divide the spoils;
  I will gorge myself on them.
I will draw my sword
  and my hand will destroy them.'
10 But you blew with your breath,
  and the sea covered them.
They sank like lead
  in the mighty waters.

11 "Who among the gods is like you, O LORD?
  Who is like you—
    majestic in holiness,
    awesome in glory,
    working wonders?
12 You stretched out your right hand
  and the earth swallowed them.

13 "In your unfailing love you will lead
  the people you have redeemed.
In your strength you will guide them
  to your holy dwelling.
14 The nations will hear and tremble;
  anguish will grip the people of Philistia.
15 The chiefs of Edom will be terrified,
  the leaders of Moab will be seized with trembling,
the people of Canaan will melt away;
16 terror and dread will fall upon them.
By the power of your arm
  they will be as still as a stone—
until your people pass by, O LORD,
  until the people you bought pass by.
17 You will bring them in and plant them
  on the mountain of your inheritance—
the place, O LORD, you made for your dwelling,
  the sanctuary, O Lord, your hands established.
18 The LORD will reign
  for ever and ever."

19 When Pharaoh's horses, chariots and horsemen went into the sea,
the LORD brought the waters of the sea back over them, but the Israelites
walked through the sea on dry ground. 20 Then Miriam the prophetess,
Aaron's sister, took a tambourine in her hand, and all the women
followed her, with tambourines and dancing. 21 Miriam sang to them:

"Sing to the LORD,
  for he is highly exalted.
The horse and its rider
  he has hurled into the sea."

The song in vv.16–18 is one of three composed by Moses (see also Deut 31:22; Ps 90). It is a victory ode that hymns the spectacular power and unrivaled supremacy of God over Pharaoh's chariots when God delivered Israel. The focus of the song is on Yahweh himself. (The divine name appears ten times). The general outline of the song is divided between two themes: vv.1b–12, a retrospective description of the overthrow of the Egyptian forces; vv.13–18, a prospective prediction of Israel's entrance into the Promised Land. There is little agreement, however, on the length and division of the strophes.

Certainly the study by James Muilenberg ("A Liturgy on the Triumphs of Yahweh," *Studia Biblica et Semitica*, eds. W.C. van Unnik and A.S. van der Wonde [Wageningen: H. Veenman & Zonen, 1966], pp. 233–51) has supplied some strong clues for dividing off the strophic structure of this song on the basis of repeated expressions or refrains that acted as dividers between strophes. Thus the two most important refrains are the three similes, "like a stone" (v.5b), "like lead" (v.10b), "as a stone" (v.16a), and the repetitive or staircase Hebrew parallelisms where normally the first two elements of each colon are repeated but the third element is different: "Your right hand, O LORD, . . . Your right hand, O LORD" (v.6); "Who . . . is like you, . . . who is like you" (v.11); and "until your people pass by, . . . until the people . . . pass by" (v.16b).

Muilenberg's divisions were accepted by David Noel Freedman ("Strophe and Meter in Exodus 15," *A Light Unto My Path,* eds. H.N. Bream, R.D. Heim, and C.A. Moore [Philadelphia: Temple University Press, 1974], pp. 163–203), and vv.6, 11, and 16b were considered "hymnic responses" that concluded each strophe. But this allowed scholars to leave vv.17–18 to dangle as a late intrusion. Furthermore, it failed to keep the pattern of v.1b, where Moses and all Israel sang the "hymnic introit" together. Therefore, we would urge that the similes of vv.5b, 10b, and 16a mark the conclusion of each strophe and that the repetitive parallelism of vv.6, 11, and 16b mark the hymnic introduction to the next strophe as it does in v.1b. Accordingly, there are four strophes: (I) vv.1b–5; (II) vv.6–10; (III) vv.11–16a; (IV) vv.16b–18. The first two are retrospective and the last two prospective in nature. Each strophe is then divided into three parts: Part A: an exordium (v.1, which also serves as an introit, as do vv.6, 11, 16b also); Part B: a confession (vv.2–3, 7–8, 12–13, 17); and Part C: the narration (first two strophes—vv.4–5, 9–10) or the anticipation (last two strophes—vv.14–16a, 18) of the work of God in judgment or salvation. Scholars are almost unanimous in labeling this song as being very old based on such archaic features as the *mô* ending in vv.7, 9, 12, 15, 17; the archaic relative particle *zû* in vv.13, 16; and certain technical Egyptological terms in v.4.

Exodus 15: Victory at Sea

Strophe I v.1b–5
- Part A: Introit—v.1b: "I will sing to the LORD"
- Part B: Confession—vv.2–3
- Part C: Narration—vv.4–5

Strophe II vv.6–10
- Part A: Introit—v.6: "Your right hand, O LORD"
- Part B: Confession—vv.7–8
- Part C: Narration—vv.9–10
- Concluding simile: "like lead," v.10b

Strophe III vv.11–16a
- Part A: Introit—v.11: "Who . . . is like you, O LORD?"
- Part B: Confession—vv.12–13
- Part C: Anticipation—vv.14–16a
- Concluding simile: "as a stone," v.16a

Strophe IV vv.16b–18
- Part A: Introit—v.16b: "Until your people pass by, O LORD"
- Part B: Confession—v.17
- Part C: Anticipation—v.18

1 Part A: Hymnic introit. The first person—"I will sing"—is not unusual for such invocations (cf. Judg 5:3; Pss 89:1; 101:1; 108:1) when the whole community praises God as *one* collective person; yet each also makes such praise-confession personally his own. The motivating reason is given immediately: "for [*kî*] he is [lit.] gloriously glorious" in that "the horse and its rider [see Notes] he has hurled into the sea."

2–3 Part B: Confession. The two themes of the introit's two bicola are now treated in sequence: (1) the Lord (in vv.2–3) and (2) the overthrown enemy (the narration in vv.4–5). In this confession five attributes of Yah (a shortened form of Yahweh) are given—all in the first person: "my strength," "my song" (see Notes), "my salvation," "my God," and "my father's God" (on this last one, see the Notes on 3:6). Then v.3 continues in the third person: "The LORD is a warrior;/ the LORD is his name" (on "Name," see on 3:15).

The title in v.3 has caused many Christians to ask, "How can this 'man of war' [also in Isa 42:13] be related to the God and Father of our Lord Jesus Christ?" In Craigie's view ("Man of Wars," pp. 183–88), God must be involved with the world as it is; otherwise his only contact with the world would be through the miraculous. The fact that he acts at all in wars speaks only to the point of his immanence and presence in the fabric of life, but it does not tell us anymore about the moral character of God than "the LORD is our rock" or "stone" or "high tower" does. The phrase, then, is another anthropomorphism. (See also Labuschagne, *Incomparability of Yahweh*, pp. 97–104; Frank M. Cross, "The Divine Warrior in Israel's Early Cult," *Biblical Motifs*, ed. A. Altman [Cambridge: University Press, 1966], pp. 11–30.)

4–5 Part C: The narration of the work of God. The concern shifts to the enemy, and the four key words focus on the water: "sea" (*yām*), "Red Sea" (*yam-sûp̱*), the "deep waters" (*tᵉhōmōṯ*), and the "depths" (*mᵉṣôlōṯ*). Just as the verbs of the confession in Part B were parallel ideas—"I will praise him," "I will exalt him" (cf. the introit: "I will sing"), so here they are synonymous: "he has hurled into the sea. . . . are drowned. . . . The deep waters have covered them; . . . they sank." Then the strophe ends with a simile: "they sank to the depths like a stone." Three expressions in v.4 remind us of the strong Egyptological influence still felt on Israel's culture. The "Red Sea" or "Sea of Reeds" has been discussed above on 13:18. Craigie pointed to A.S. Yahuda's equation of "the best" (*miḇḥar*) with the Egyptian *śtp.w* ("the choicest"). Craigie then added another possible Egyptian root of his own, viz., Hebrew *šlš* ("officers") may come from an Eighteenth-Dynasty Egyptian word *srs* ("to have command of a corps"; see Notes on 14:7 for further discussion and documentation).

6 Strophe II: Part A: Exordium. With repeated use of "Your right hand, O LORD," the song announces the beginning of the second strophe using a descriptive metaphor for the omnipotence of God (cf. Moses' song at Deut 33:2 and numerous Pss.). In this strophe more details and the mode of the enemy's destruction are given.

7–8 Part B: Confession. The first line of four bicola recalls the phrase "highly exalted" of the introit (*gā'ōh gā'āh*, v.1). In the "greatness of your majesty" (*ûḇᵉrōḇ gᵉ'ônᵉḵā*), you "pulled them down" (*hāras* [NIV, "threw down"]; usually of demolishing buildings), those "risers up against you" (*qāmeyḵā* [NIV, "opposed you"]; here of those who wanted to destroy the building of God [KD, 2:52]). God, with the burning heat of his wrath and a fiery look from the pillar of cloud, "consumed them like stubble"—a simile also found in the Egyptian war lore (Cook, p. 311). The "strong east wind" of 14:21 is here represented in theological terms as "the blast of your nostrils" (*b^erû^aḥ 'appeyḵā*; cf. Ps 18:15), thus confirming the divine agency behind the wind. The result was that the "waters piled up" and the "running, surging, flowing ones" stood "like a heap" (*nēḏ;* cf. Ps 78:13). (Later on the Jordan River will also "heap" up [Josh 3:13, 16].) Meanwhile the waves "congealed" (*qāp^e'û*), as if turned to solid ice. This was the power of God that Israel confessed.

9–10 Part C: The narration of the work of God. Five bicola narrate in dramatic form the staccato phrases that almost simulate the heavy, breathless heaving of the Egyptians as, with what reserve of strength is left, they vow: "I will pursue," "I will overtake," "I will divide the spoils," "I will gorge myself," "I will draw my sword," and "my hand will destroy [lit. and ironically, 'dispossess,' *tôrîšēmô*] them." But v.10 changes all that; with a mere gust of God's "breath" or "wind" (*rû^aḥ* ; cf. v.8a), "the sea covered them," and they "sank" (*ṣāl^alû*; cf. the noun in v.5; perhaps an onomatopoeia that sounds like the gurgle of water as it spins into a whirlpool and is sucked inward; Cole, p. 124). The word, however, is a *hapax legomenon* and is usually connected with the Akkadian *ṣalālu* ("to sink down"), hence, "to sleep" (see F.M. Cross and D.N. Freedman, "The Song of Miriam," JNES 14 [1955]: 247). Like the first strophe (v.5), the second strophe ends with a simile: "They sank like lead in the mighty waters" (v.10b).

11 Strophe III: Part A: Exordium. The song now turns to the theological interpretation and the significance of all that was done. Using the formula for incomparability—"Who is like you" (*mî-ḵāmōḵāh*; cf. Pss 35:10; 71:19; 77:13; 89:6; 113:5; Mic 7:18; and Labuschagne, *Incomparability of Yahweh*, pp. 22, 66–77, 94–97)—Israel proclaims that God's exclusive uniqueness had been demonstrated and "proven powerful by his [NIV, 'majestic in'] holiness" (*qōḏeš*) and his "awesome" (*nôrā'*) "wonders" or "miracles" (*pele'*; see Notes on 4:21). No other "gods" (*'ēlîm*, whose reality is neither affirmed nor denied at this point; cf. 12:12) could do what the Lord had done.

12–13 Part B: Confession. The second-person address of these verses matches vv.7–8 and v.17; therefore, these verses belong together and mark the three great works of God in three bicola: the victory at sea, guidance in the wilderness, and the destination of God's "holy dwelling" (v.13) in Canaan. Thus the heroic deeds at the sea were a pledge that God would fulfill his promise of giving the land. The "earth" (*'ereṣ*) may here signify Sheol, the grave (cf. 1 Sam 28:13; Isa 29:4), for it was actually the sea that "swallowed them" (*bāla'*). But it was God's "grace" or "unfailing love" (*ḥeseḏ*) that would lead those who had been "redeemed" (*gā'al*; see comment and Notes on 6:6). The alliterative sequence of the verbs *nāṭîṯā* ("you stretched out"), *nāḥîṯā* ("you will lead"), and *nēhaltā* ("you will guide") add to the majesty of the form and unity of the thought.

"Your holy dwelling" (*n^ewēh qoḏšeḵā*; lit., "your holy pasture or encampment") cannot refer to Sinai since the nations in vv.14–15 would not have been affected by that mountain. Nor is Canaan alone meant; but v.17 clearly indicates that Moses had in mind that place in Canaan where God had promised him he would "put his Name" (Deut 12:5, 11, 21; 14:23–24; 16:2, 6, 11; 26:2) in a place he had chosen (Deut 12:14, 18, 26; 14:25; 16:7, 15–16; 17:8, 10; 18:6; 31:11), i.e., his temple on Mount Zion.

14–16a Part C: Anticipation of the work of God. Once again the song shifts from the second person to the third person (cf. vv.4 and 9). A summary statement in v.14a precedes vv.14b–15, where four of Israel's future enemies are listed: Philistia, Edom, Moab, and Canaan. Thus the "nations" (*'ammîm*) of v.14a may be the Egyptian designation for the "Asiatics" (*'Aamu*) who occupied southern Palestine (see T.H. Gaster, "Notes on the 'Song of the Sea,'" ET 48 [1936–37]: 45). That news of Israel's sensational deliverance from the Egyptian army got around is clearly attested by Rahab (Josh 2:10–11). Canaan is here named by its residents along the southwestern coastal strip (see Notes on 13:17 for the false charge of an anachronism). The "chiefs" or "princes" (*'allûp̱ê*) of Edom introduces another piece of Mosaic identification, for the term is useful in the proto-dynastic era of Edom (cf. Gen 36:15–16), as is the local term of "leaders" or "rams" (*'êlê*) of Moab. But all these peoples and leaders shared one thing in common: fear. Seven expressions for fear are climaxed with the strophe concluding with a simile for "stone"-cold "silence" (see Nahum Waldman, "A Comparative Note on Exodus 15:14–16," JQR 66 [1975–76]: 189–92).

16b Strophe IV: Part A: Exordium. Once more the repetitive parallelism introduces the past and the climactic word—this time the outcome of God's great work at the sea: "Until your people pass by" or "cross over" into Canaan (or perhaps the Jordan), even the people who had been "bought" (*qānāh*; see Notes).

17 Part B: Confession. Based on God's parallel handling of Pharaoh and the nations that would oppose their entrance into Canaan, Israel may now anticipate the fulfillment of the patriarchal promise that they would be given—in that future day when the Lord would reign forever—the land of Canaan as an inheritance (on the figure of "planting," *nāṭa'*, see Pss 44:2; 80:8–16). The text moves from the "mountain of [his] inheritance" to a "place" (*māḵôn*) "for [his] dwelling," even the "sanctuary" (*miqqᵉḏāš*) his "hands established" (see v.13 above).

18 Part C: Anticipation of the work of God. In one final burst of unbounded joy, Moses and Israel rejoice in the prospect of God's universal rule and reign lasting forever. How temporary in comparison were the reigns of such hardened rulers as Pharaoh and the leaders of state in Canaan and its environs (cf. with Cole, p. 126, two other Pentateuchal references to Yahweh's kingship prior to the offer to Gideon and to Saul, Num 23:21 and Deut 33:5)!

19–21 A narrative interlude separates the Song of Moses from Miriam's song in v.21. Miriam is called a "prophetess" (*nᵉḇî'āh*; cf. also Num 12:2) and a "sister" of Aaron, even though she was also Moses' sister (v.20). But apparently, as KD suggest (2:56), Miriam ranked only with Aaron and not with Moses. There would be other prophetesses in Israel (Deborah in Judg 4:4; Huldah in 2 Kings 22:14; Noadiah in Neh 6:14; Isaiah's wife in Isa 8:3; and Anna in Luke 2:36). As a prophetess and a leader in Israel (Mic 6:4), Miriam led the women perhaps in an antiphonal response, repeating the song at the conclusion of each part or strophe, accompanied by timbrels and dancing (see Notes). Thus all attempts to identify Miriam's song as the older and the more original for an alleged expansion in vv.1–18 are unnecessary and without evidence.

Notes

1 Recent scholars argue that Egypt did not use a cavalry at this time. Therefore, רֹכְבוֹ (*rōkᵉḇô*, "its rider") should be translated "charioteer"; yet 14:9, 17, 18, 23, 26, 28; 15:19 refer to "horsemen" (*pārāš*)—unless these also are to be rendered "charioteers"!

2 On זִמְרָת (*zimrāṯ*, "my song"), the pronoun "my" is from the double-duty suffix '*zy* ("my strength"), but the meaning of *zmrt* is hotly contested. Most scholars posit a *dmr/zmr*, meaning "protect" (Cross and Freedman, "Song of Miriam," p. 243, n.b; Simon B. Parker, "Exodus xv.2. Again," VetTest 21 [1971]: 373–79). Parker protests against S.E. Loewenstamm (VetTest 19 [1969]: 464–70) and E.M. Good (VetTest [1970]: 358–59), finding that *zmrt* means "glory." We concur with the idea of "protection" and agree with D.N. Freedman's conclusion ("Strophe and Meter in Exodus 15," p. 176) that the two words "my strength and my protection" are a hendiadys: "Yah is my mighty fortress" or the like.

5 יְכַסְיֻמוּ (*yᵉḵasᵉyumû*, "[the deep waters] covered them") involves a triple archaic form. It preserves the final yod of the root, uses the archaic suffix—*mû* = *mô*—for the third masculine plural pronominal suffix (also see vv.7, 9, 10, 12, 15, 17), and uses the imperfect that in reality must be an archaic preterite like the Akkadian *iprus* (see other imperfect verbs that are translated as past tenses in vv.6, 7, and 12). Since these features are virtually unmixed in this song, they are indications of archaic forms and not deliberate archaizing as Cross and Freedman concluded ("Song of Miriam," p. 245).

6 According to Cross and Freedman ("Song of Miriam," p. 245; cf. v.11), נֶאְדָּרִי (*ne'dorî*, "majestic") is an archaic infinitive with the old ending *î* used as "a surrogate for the finite verb" meaning "awesome" (cf. Akkad. *adāru*, "to fear").

11 בַּקֹּדֶשׁ (*baqqōḏeš*, "in holiness") is usually repointed to read *qᵉḏōšîm* ("holy ones") with the LXX, Syro-hexaplar, and the Hebrew parallelism to the "gods" in the first part of v.11. But this reasoning fails to account for the preposition and the other two adjectival phrases it parallels.

16 קָנִיתָ (*qānîṯā*, "you bought") is correctly translated here even though it is also attested in Deut 32:6 and Prov 8:22 as "your Creator" and "you brought me forth." Also see "maker" or "creator" in Gen 14:19, 22, and Eve's name for Cain in Gen 4:1. This concept of purchase fits well with Israel's "redemption" (*gā'al*; Exod 6:6–7). As Ps 74:2 pleads, "Remember the people you purchased [*qānîṯā*] of old." Deut 32:6 may well contain the same idea.

20 On מְחֹלֹת (*mᵉḥōlōṯ*, "dancing"), see John H. Eaton, "Dancing in the Old Testament," ET 86 (1974–75): 136–40.

I. Journey to Sinai (15:22–18:27)

1. The waters of Marah

15:22–27

²²Then Moses led Israel from the Red Sea and they went into the Desert of Shur. For three days they traveled in the desert without finding water. ²³When they came to Marah, they could not drink its water because it was bitter. (That is why the place is called Marah.) ²⁴So the people grumbled against Moses, saying, "What are we to drink?"

²⁵Then Moses cried out to the LORD, and the LORD showed him a piece of wood. He threw it into the water, and the water became sweet.

There the LORD made a decree and a law for them, and there he tested them. ²⁶He said, "If you listen carefully to the voice of the LORD your God and do what is right in his eyes, if you pay attention to his commands and keep all his decrees, I will not bring on you any of the diseases I brought on the Egyptians, for I am the LORD, who heals you."

27 Then they came to Elim, where there were twelve springs and seventy palm trees, and they camped there near the water.

The wilderness itinerary began in 12:37 and continued in 13:20; 14:2; and 15:22. See the Notes for structural characteristics in the long chain of formulas. Abruptly the narrative starts the journey from the Red Sea to Sinai. One of the most persistent features of this whole section is the "grumbling" theme (*lûn*, or "to murmur"). Except for Joshua 9:18 (a reference to Israel's displeasure with Joshua's handling of the Gibeonite lie) and Psalm 59:15, every other occurrence of "grumbling" in the OT is found in six chapters of the Pentateuch: Exodus 15, 16, 17; Numbers 14, 16, and 17.

22–23 There is general agreement on the locality of these first stops made by Israel. The "Desert of Shur" (v.22) is the whole district ranging from Egypt's northeastern frontier eastward into the northwestern quarter of the Sinai Desert and extending southward to the mountains of Sinai. Shur, meaning "wall," is a place mentioned several times in Genesis (16:7; 20:1; 25:18). In Numbers 33:8, however, this area is called the "Desert of Etham." Perhaps, as Montet contends (p. 62), Etham reflects the old Egyptian word for "fort" (*ḫetem*). It would not have been unusual for a Near Eastern place to have two different names, especially since the meaning of the "wall" may have referred to the defensive line of "forts" along the Egyptian border.

Israel's first stop is traditionally placed by the local Arabs at Ain Musa, the "Springs of Moses," a site not mentioned in any biblical text. It was a source of sweet water about sixteen to eighteen hours' journey north of the site connected with Marah ("bitter"), Israel's first-mentioned stop. This traditional site for crossing the Red Sea is about ten miles south of the northern end of the Red Sea and about one-half mile inland from the coast. The journey from Ain Musa to Marah was about forty miles.

At first the Israelites contended with a stoney desert, bounded by the deep blue waters of the Gulf of Suez on their right and the mountain chains of El Ruhat at some distance from the shore on their left. After nine more miles, they came into the desert plain called el Ati, a white, glaring stretch of sand that turned into hilly country with sand dunes rolling out to the coast. But water was nowhere to be found.

Marah is usually identified with Ain Hawarah, a site several miles inland from the Gulf. Ain Hawarah's waters are notoriously salty and brackish. Describing its well, Edward Robinson (*Biblical Researches in Palestine*, 3 vols. [Boston: Crocker and Brewster, 1857–60], 2:96) says: "The basin is six or eight feet in diameter, and the water about two feet deep. Its taste is unpleasant, saltish, and somewhat bitter . . . The Arabs . . . consider it as the worst water in all these regions."

24 The people's grumbling is strong evidence of the historical truthfulness of the wanderings narrative. As a general pattern the grumblings that preceded the golden calf incident are raised by genuine need, but those that follow are mainly illegitimate forms of murmuring (so argues Childs, *Exodus*, pp. 257–64). The unpalatable waters at Marah made a strong enough impression so as to obliterate all the miracles of Egypt and the parting of the Red Sea—or so it appeared.

25a The Lord *showed* Moses a tree. The verb "showed" is from the root that in the causative conjugation means "to teach" or "instruct" and is the same root from which we derive the word "Torah" ("instruction," "law"). Cassuto (p. 184) believed this expression pointed to the purpose of the narrative, for Israel was to learn that the *instruction* they needed, after being freed from Egypt, would come from heaven. This, in turn, would prepare them for the reception of the precept of the laws.

Ferdinand de Lessups, builder of the Suez Canal, was told by Arab chiefs that they put a thorn bush into some types of water to make it palatable. Others have suggested that certain aromatic plants were used to disguise the bad taste of the water, but the text is clear that God gave Moses special instructions in response to the despair of the people. The tree may have had little more to do with the actual temporary healing of the waters than did the salt in Elisha's healing of the Jericho spring in 2 Kings 2:19–22. In both cases it may only be the power of God and a test of obedience that are present.

25b–27 This miracle was connected with a promise; viz., from now on obedience to commands and statutes would bring healing, both physically and morally. God allowed Israel to go three days without water to "test" (*nāsāh,* v.25b; cf. the same root as "Massah" in 17:7) them. God later tested Israel at Meribah (17:1–7), at Sinai (20:20), at Taberah (Num 11:3; 13:26–33), and elsewhere; but it was "to humble [them] and to test [them] in order to know what was in [their] heart[s]" (Deut 8:2). However, the "diseases" (v.26) God "brought on" or "put on" the Egyptians would afflict Israel if they disobeyed and rebelled against God (Deut 28:27). Even though Herodotus (2.77) declared that the Egyptians were the healthiest of the nations of antiquity, their defiance of God made their diseases and plagues legendary.

Israel journeyed to "Elim" (v.27), located in the large and beautiful valley of Gharandel, about seven miles south of Ain Hawarah. This tract of land lies between the wilderness of Shur and the wilderness of Sin and contains two other wadis besides the Wadi Gharandel, viz., Useit and Tayibeh. In the rainy season there is a constant torrent of water running down to the Red Sea that slows down in the dry season. The grass is thick and high, and there are many tamarisk, acacias, and palm trees in the Wadi Gharandel.

Notes

---

22 The wilderness itinerary has a stereotyped formula that appears in 12:37; 13:20; 15:22, 27; 16:1; 17:1; 19:2; Num 11:35; 12:16; 20:1, 22; 21:4, 10, 11, 12, 13, 16, 18, 19, 20; 22:1. Usually there are two principal elements in each formula according to Coats ("Wilderness Itinerary," pp. 135–52): a departure location and an arrival location. The first element most commonly employs the verb *nāsa'* in the third masculine plural imperfect with a waw consecutive and a place name with a *mem* ("from"); the second element has wider variations, but the most common verb is *ḥānan* with *bô',* *yāṣa',* *hāyāh,* and *yāšaḇ* being used along with *beṯ,* *'el,* *nēgeḏ,* *'al,* or *lip̱nê* (see comment on 12:37).

23 מָרָתָה . . . מִמָּרָה (*mārāṯāh . . . mimmārāh,* "Marah . . . bitter") is a wordplay that brings out the association of the bitter water with the name given to that place. Notice the passive construction implying that this name had already been associated with this place.

24 וַיִּלֹּנוּ (*wayyillōnû,* "they grumbled") represents the negative theme of Israel's apostasy in the wilderness (as seen in Neh 9:13–18; Ps 106:13–33; Ezek 20:13), which is often contrasted with the positive theme of the wilderness as the time of Israel's honeymoon with Yahweh (Deut 32:10–14; Jer 2:2–3; Hos 2:14 [16 EV]; 11:1, 3–4). But these two themes are no more antithetical to each other than the prophets' combined word of judgment and hope.

On the word לון (*lûn*, "to grumble, murmur"), see the fine discussion by Coats, *Rebellion in the Wilderness*, pp. 21–28.

26 On כָּל־הַמַּחֲלָה (*kol-hammah^{a}lāh*, "any of the diseases"), see McMillen's *None of These Diseases.*

---

2. *The manna and the quail*

16:1–36

[1]The whole Israelite community set out from Elim and came to the
Desert of Sin, which is between Elim and Sinai, on the fifteenth day of
the second month after they had come out of Egypt. [2]In the desert the
whole community grumbled against Moses and Aaron. [3]The Israelites
said to them, "If only we had died by the LORD's hand in Egypt! There we
sat around pots of meat and ate all the food we wanted, but you have
brought us out into this desert to starve this entire assembly to death."
[4]Then the LORD said to Moses, "I will rain down bread from heaven for
you. The people are to go out each day and gather enough for that day.
In this way I will test them and see whether they will follow my
instructions. [5]On the sixth day they are to prepare what they bring in,
and that is to be twice as much as they gather on the other days."
[6]So Moses and Aaron said to all the Israelites, "In the evening you will
know that it was the LORD who brought you out of Egypt, [7]and in the
morning you will see the glory of the LORD, because he has heard your
grumbling against him. Who are we, that you should grumble against
us?" [8]Moses also said, "You will know that it was the LORD when he
gives you meat to eat in the evening and all the bread you want in the
morning, because he has heard your grumbling against him. Who are
we? You are not grumbling against us, but against the LORD."
[9]Then Moses told Aaron, "Say to the entire Israelite community,
'Come before the LORD, for he has heard your grumbling.' "
[10]While Aaron was speaking to the whole Israelite community, they
looked toward the desert, and there was the glory of the LORD appearing
in the cloud.
[11]The LORD said to Moses, [12]"I have heard the grumbling of the
Israelites. Tell them, 'At twilight you will eat meat, and in the morning
you will be filled with bread. Then you will know that I am the LORD your
God.' "
[13]That evening quail came and covered the camp, and in the morning
there was a layer of dew around the camp. [14] When the dew was gone,
thin flakes like frost on the ground appeared on the desert floor. [15]
When the Israelites saw it, they said to each other, "What is it?" For they
did not know what it was.
Moses said to them, "It is the bread the LORD has given you to eat.
[16]This is what the LORD has commanded: 'Each one is to gather as much
as he needs. Take an omer for each person you have in your tent.' "
[17]The Israelites did as they were told; some gathered much, some
little. [18]And when they measured it by the omer, he who gathered much
did not have too much, and he who gathered little did not have too little.
Each one gathered as much as he needed.
[19]Then Moses said to them, "No one is to keep any of it until
morning."
[20]However, some of them paid no attention to Moses; they kept part of
it until morning, but it was full of maggots and began to smell. So Moses
was angry with them.
[21]Each morning everyone gathered as much as he needed, and when
the sun grew hot, it melted away. [22]On the sixth day, they gathered twice

as much—two omers for each person—and the leaders of the community came and reported this to Moses. [23]He said to them, "This is what the LORD commanded: 'Tomorrow is to be a day of rest, a holy Sabbath to the LORD. So bake what you want to bake and boil what you want to boil. Save whatever is left and keep it until morning.' "

[24]So they saved it until morning, as Moses commanded, and it did not stink or get maggots in it. [25]"Eat it today," Moses said, "because today is a Sabbath to the LORD. You will not find any of it on the ground today. [26]Six days you are to gather it, but on the seventh day, the Sabbath, there will not be any."

[27]Nevertheless, some of the people went out on the seventh day to gather it, but they found none. [28]Then the LORD said to Moses, "How long will you refuse to keep my commands and my instructions? [29]Bear in mind that the LORD has given you the Sabbath; that is why on the sixth day he gives you bread for two days. Everyone is to stay where he is on the seventh day; no one is to go out." [30]So the people rested on the seventh day.

[31]The people of Israel called the bread manna. It was white like coriander seed and tasted like wafers made with honey. [32]Moses said, "This is what the LORD has commanded: 'Take an omer of manna and keep it for the generations to come, so they can see the bread I gave you to eat in the desert when I brought you out of Egypt.' "

[33]So Moses said to Aaron, "Take a jar and put an omer of manna in it. Then place it before the LORD to be kept for the generations to come."

[34]As the LORD commanded Moses, Aaron put the manna in front of the Testimony, that it might be kept. [35]The Israelites ate manna forty years, until they came to a land that was settled; they ate manna until they reached the border of Canaan.

[36](An omer is one tenth of an ephah.)

1–3 The "fifteenth day of the second month" (v.1) was exactly one month after Israel had left Egypt (12:6, 31). Since Numbers 33:5–11 mentions only seven places of encampment and only one journey of three days' duration (Exod 15:22), it is evident that either Israel stayed at several of these places for a number of days or that they camped in a number of other unmentioned places or areas without distinctive names. Cook (p. 316) notes the peculiarity of the Hebrew text in v.1, which is literally: "They set out from Elim and the whole Israelite community came to the Desert of Sin." This implies that they may have left Elim in various detachments and finally assembled as a complete group when they all reached the Desert of Sin.

The location of the Desert of Sin is problematic. Numbers 33:12 lists Dophkah ("smeltery") as the next stop after the Desert of Sin. Dophkah probably refers to the Egyptian turquoise and copper mining center at Serabit el-Khadim in the Eighteenth and Twentieth Dynasties, thus placing the Desert of Sin south and east of Elim. So the Desert of Sin may be placed either (1) along the coastal plain, el Markha (a site favorable to avoiding the Egyptian miners' settlements, to the descent of the quail near the shore of the Gulf, and to certain details in ch. 18) or (2) the inland Debbet er Ramleh, which forms a crescent between Serabit el-Khadim and the et-Tih plateau (a site favorable by being in direct line between Elim and Sinai, by being a better-watered area, and by being called the desert of et Tih, a name similar in sound to the Hebrew Desert of Sin). The second location is preferred by most scholars today.

This time the people "grumbled" (v.2) about the amount of food and the lack of meat (v.3). Suddenly Egypt seemed all peaches and cream (actually pots of meat and all you could eat—in their idiom) rather than bondage and slave drivers. With a twisted piety and a condescending reference to Yahweh's name, the Israelites pretended that they would have preferred being victims at God's hand in Egypt to being the recipients of so many miracles—and all this hardship. The provisions from Egypt may have lasted these thirty days, but their supplies were undoubtedly exhausted.

4–5 God would graciously answer the Israelites' grumbling by raining down on them "bread from heaven" (v.4; cf. Neh 9:15; Ps 78:24; John 6:31–51). But there was to be a "test" (the root is *nāsāh*) to see whether Israel would obey and trust God by faith.

Already prior to the giving of the Ten Commandments, the seventh day was to be set apart to the Lord because of its establishment in the Creation ordinances in Genesis 2:2–3. On the sixth day, the people were to gather twice the daily amount (v.5). It was not to be left or eaten in the form they gathered it; instead, it was to be prepared by milling and baking (cf. Num 11:8).

6–8 It is not necessary to argue that this paragraph is out of place or that it originally followed vv.9–12. Cassuto (p. 192) observes that when the words (lit. tr.) "And said" (v.6) "and said" (v.8) are repeated with reference to the same subject, then the second "and said" explains the inner significance of the words cited in the first "and said." The first part of v.8 explains that Israel's lapse of memory would be restored that very evening (vv.6–7a), when God sent them food in a way yet to be announced; then they would *know* (here is that evangelistic word from the plagues) that it was the Lord! The second part of v.8 elaborates on the inner meaning of the words in v.7b: your grumbling is not directed at your leaders, but ultimately your complaint is against God. Hence, we have the theology and abiding principles to be gained from Israel's appreciation (and ours!); for what God did here is placed in front of the actual narration of the events.

9–12 Moses instructed Aaron to summon the congregation. They were to "come [near] before the LORD" (v.9; see Notes). After the Sinai legislation this instruction would mean that Israel was to gather before the tabernacle; but this text antedates those times. Consequently, v.10 explains that they were to look toward the desert where the Lord appeared in the cloud (on this cloud, see comment and Notes on 13:21–22). The meaning of this symbol of the real presence of God connected with the splendor of this cloud and fire will be clarified in 24:15–17. Once again, as in vv.6 and 8, Israel "will know that I am the LORD your God" (see comment on 7:4–5).

13–18 The events describing the gift of quail is similar in form but separate in time from the narrative in Numbers 11:4–22, 31–33 (that event took place in the second year of the wanderings, Num 10:11). Quail (not locusts or flying fish, but "feathered fowls" as Ps 78:27–31 makes clear) are a well-known migratory bird (*Coturnix Vulgeris*). They usually fly in vast numbers in the spring to the northern regions and return in the fall. Because of their prolonged flight over the Red Sea, they landed exhausted on the shore of the Sinai Peninsula.

Not only did the quail "come up" (see Notes on v.13) from the horizon, but so did the dew "come up." When the dew evaporated, beneath it appeared "thin flakes like frost on the ground, . . . on the desert floor" (v.14). Bodenheimer (pp. 2–6) contended that this substance was really the honeydew excretion of two types of insects or aphids that live on the numerous tamarisk trees in the region. It is a sweet, sugary, transparent substance that turns white, brown, or yellow and that is rich in carbohydrates but poor in nitrogen (also see Marston Bates, "Insects in the Diet," *American Scholar* 29 [1959–60]: 46–48). Another suggestion for the natural origination of this material is to equate it with the lichen *Leanora esculenta* that grows on rocks about the size of a pea and is light enough to be blown about by the wind.

Both of the above suggestions run into trouble: Bodenheimer could not account for the stinking decay or the melting (he promptly relegated these textual features to a misinterpretation or an interpolation in the text). Furthermore, the manna continued to provide food for the Israelites for almost forty years, not just for the three to six weeks in July and August as Bodenheimer's suggestion would necessitate. It was also produced in quantities far exceeding what either of these methods could possibly deliver. Thus we agree with Rawlinson (2:40): Manna "must be regarded as a peculiar substance, miraculously created for a special purpose, but similar in certain respects to certain known substances which are still produced in the Sinai region." On Israel's question, "What is it?" (v.15), see the Notes.

Each family unit was to gather "an omer," about two quarts or one-tenth of a bushel (v.36), for each person in their tent (v.16). Verse 18 was used by the apostle Paul as an illustration for Christians to share with one another just as Israel had pooled the manna everyone had collected (2 Cor 8:15).

19–21 In spite of his warning that God was testing (v.4) the people by ordering them not to leave any manna until the next morning, "some . . . paid no attention to Moses" (vv.19–20). This test was to remind Israel that they did not live by bread alone but by "every word that comes from the mouth of the LORD" (Deut 8:3). Furthermore, it taught Israel that even their daily bread was a gift from God; therefore, they were to live in daily dependence on him.

22–30 The day of rest, a holy Sabbath to the Lord, did not originate with the Sinaitic legislation; for even in 20:8–11 it was grounded in the ordinances of Creation (Gen 2:2–3). Genesis 29:27 knows of a bridal "week" of seven days in Jacob's time (though a heptad symbolic of seven years). Many compare this ordinance to the Babylonian *šapattu*. But no one has been able to demonstrate that Israel borrowed her concept of the Sabbath from Babylon: the correspondences are just too weak. On the contrary, this pattern of six days for gathering and one day of rest had been ordered by God (v.5). The seventh day was to be a "day of" cessation or "rest" (v.23); therefore, food preparations for the morrow were to be made on the sixth day. But when some failed to obey (v.27), the Lord groaned, "How long [*'aḏ-'ānāh*, v.28; cf. Ps 13:1] will you [plural] refuse to keep my commands and my instructions?" Only then did the people "rest" (lit., "stop," "cease") on the seventh day (v.30).

31 The name and description of manna is given also in Numbers 11:6–9. Coriander seed is a small lobular grain that is white or yellowish gray and is used for seasoning (cf. our use today of caraway and sesame seeds). Numbers 11:7 adds that it "looked like resin" and, according to the older versions, that it had the color of "bdellium" (KJV; = pearl?). Its taste was like wafers made of honey or "something made with olive oil" (Num 11:8); and it could be ground in a mill, crushed in a mortar, cooked in a pot, or made into cakes (Num 11:8).

32–36 At some subsequent time, Moses ordered that this giving of the manna be memorialized by placing some of it into the ark of the testimony. The ark had not been revealed, much less constructed, at this time; therefore v.32 is best put: "this is what the Lord *had* commanded." In support of this position is the historical note in v.35, which describes the eating of manna over the next forty years; therefore, these verses were written by Moses at the end of the wanderings.

Notes

1 On כָּל־עֲדַת (*kol-ʿ^a^dat*, "whole community"), see the Notes on 12:3.

In מִדְבַּר־סִין (*midbar-sîn*, "Desert of Sin"), Sin may be derived from the Hebrew סְנֶה (*s^e^neh*, "thorn bush"). It is mentioned elsewhere in 17:1 and Num 33:11–12. This must not be confused with the Desert of Zin (צִן, *ṣin*), which is directly south of Judah near Kadesh Barnea, far to the north of Sinai, and is spelled with a different Hebrew consonant.

4 אֲנַסֶּנּוּ (*ʾ^a^nassennû*, "I will test them") is a cognate term to the place name in 17:7: מַסָּה (*massāh*, "Massah"). There Israel נַסֹּתָם (*nassōtām*, "tested") the Lord!

This reference to God's law—בְּתוֹרָתִי (*b^e^tôrātî*, "my instructions" or "my law")—is not a later interpolation, as some claim, but is a clear reference to the fact that God held men accountable to his law even before its fuller revelation at Sinai (cf. Gen 2:2–3; 39:9; see also Exod 18:20).

7 The כְּבוֹד יהוה (*k^e^bôd yhwh*, "glory of the LORD") was the sheer weight, gravity (*kābēd*, "to be heavy," then "to glorify") of his divine presence. The presence of the Lord is so central and significant in the Mosaic era that there are four other forms used to speak of it besides the glory of the Lord: the face (*pānîm*) of the Lord, the angel (*malʾak*) of the Lord, the name (*šēm*) of the Lord, and the tabernacle in which God will dwell (*šākan*) among them.

On the repeated references to grumbling, see the commentary and Notes on 15:24. Some have suggested a double ayin root, *lnn*, or even an interchange of the lamed and resh to give *rnn* ("to cry aloud"); but no evidence exists for these reconstructions or for Köhler-Baumgartner's connecting it with the Arabic *l(y)n* ("to blame") (s.v.). The verb לוּן (*lûn*), whether in the Niphal or Hiphil form, means "to express resentment, dissatisfaction, anger, or complaint by grumbling in half-muted tones of hostile opposition." Here it is against God or his appointed leaders.

9 קִרְבוּ לִפְנֵי יהוה (*qirbû lipnê yhwh*, "Come before the LORD") illustrates one of the most important words in the theology of worship, "to draw near" or "to come." For some like Felix Asensio ("Una faceta biblica del 'acercamiento' humanodivino en el A. Testamento," *Estudios Biblicos* 36 [1977]: 5–19), it almost serves as an integrating theme for all theology. As a verb *qārab* is approaching God for service to him; as an adjective *qarōb* states the goal achieved: a spiritual state of sensing the closeness of his presence; and as a noun *qirbāh* is nearness to God on a spiritual plane. Ferris (p. 196) argues that since Lev 9:5 and 16:1 use *lipnê yhwh* in connection with sacrifice, why could it not have such a covenantal meaning here?

13 וַתַּעַל (*wattaʿal*, "came," or lit., "came up" [from the horizon]) matches the same verb in v.14: "the dew *was* gone" or "went up."

הַשְּׂלָו (*haśś^e^lāw*, "the quail") has the article since their appearance was a usual occurrence and was something fairly familiar to the Israelites.

14 מְחֻסְפָּס (*m^e^ḥuspās*, "flakes" or "round") is found only here in the OT. The Ugaritic verb *ḥsp*, like the Hebrew *ḥāsap*, means "to uncover." The meaning of this noun is uncertain.

15 מָן הוּא . . . מַה־הוּא (*mān hûʾ . . . mah-hûʾ*, "What is it?" . . . "What it was") shows why Israel called this bread from heaven מָן (*mān*, v.31) or "manna." But some object that the Hebrew word for "what?" is *mah*, not *mān*. The solution is that there is an old Semitic article *mān* (meaning "what?") that appears as *manna* in the Palestinian Amarna Letters. Therefore, the etymology of *mān* must not be attributed to late Aramaic forms. The LXX translation of this verse is *ti estin touto* ("What is this?").

16 עֹמֶר (*'ōmer*, "an omer") is a dry measure consisting of one-tenth of an ephah (v.36) or a bushel. That would be a little more than 2 quarts or 2.3 liters.

אִישׁ לְפִי אָכְלוֹ (*'îš lᵉpî 'oklô*, "as much as he needs") is literally "each according to his eating." The identical Hebrew expression appears in 12:4.

21 וְנָמָס (*wᵉnāmās*) translated as "it melted away" is to be preferred over Cassuto's (p. 197) "loathsome" or "rejected" on the analogy of *nāmēs* in 1 Sam 15:9 (where it is rendered "weak"). Bodenheimer regards the melting as a late and mistaken interpolation, but this is because it does not fit his theory.

23 The form שַׁבָּתוֹן (*šabbāṯôn*, "day of rest") of the Hebrew Shabbath or Sabbath (שַׁבָּת, *šabbaṯ*) is reflected in the Greek of Heb 4:9 as *sabbatismos*, meaning "rest." The shorter form is reflected in the Greek *sabbaton* in Matt 12:5, 8.

34 The later instruction לִפְנֵי הָעֵדֻת (*lip̄nê hā'ēḏuṯ*, "in front of the Testimony"), which came after the tabernacle had been built, refers to the "ark of the Testimony," by way of an ellipsis, simply as "the Testimony" (see also 30:36; Num 17:4–10). See the comments on 25:10–22.

---

3. *The waters of Meribah*

17:1–7

[1]The whole Israelite community set out from the Desert of Sin, traveling from place to place as the LORD commanded. They camped at Rephidim, but there was no water for the people to drink. [2]So they quarreled with Moses and said, "Give us water to drink."

Moses replied, "Why do you quarrel with me? Why do you put the LORD to the test?"

[3]But the people were thirsty for water there, and they grumbled against Moses. They said, "Why did you bring us up out of Egypt to make us and our children and livestock die of thirst?"

[4]Then Moses cried out to the LORD, "What am I to do with these people? They are almost ready to stone me."

[5]The LORD answered Moses, "Walk on ahead of the people. Take with you some of the elders of Israel and take in your hand the staff with which you struck the Nile, and go. [6]I will stand there before you by the rock at Horeb. Strike the rock, and water will come out of it for the people to drink." So Moses did this in the sight of the elders of Israel. [7]And he called the place Massah and Meribah because the Israelites quarreled and because they tested the LORD saying, "Is the LORD among us or not?"

1–2 Before Israel came to Rephidim (v.1), the people rested at Dophkah and Alush (Num 33:12–14). Rephidim, however, is best identified as the large Wadi Refayid, in southwest Sinai, instead of Wadi Feiran. They had hoped to find water, but the wadi was already dry. This situation presents us with a third narrative on the Lord's provision for Israel's needs in the desert.

As a result of this disappointment, the people "quarreled" (see Notes) with Moses, demanding: "Give [plural form] us water to drink" (v.2). The verb "to quarrel" (from the root *rîḇ*) is the key word in the passage and explains one of the names for this place, "Meribah" (v.7), which means "quarrel," "strife," or "argument." What had been a gracious gift of God through Moses' hands was demanded as a magical solution to their problem: "Give it to us."

Significantly, Israel had traveled to Rephidim specifically "as the Lord commanded" (lit., "at the mouth of Yahweh"). Thus God in his wisdom had directed his people to move from the Desert of Sin (where they hungered but afterwards were satisfied) to Rephidim (where they thirsted).

Instead of submitting to the *tests* God was conducting for them (15:25; 16:4; see comments there), Israel began to *test* the Lord (Pss 78:56; 106:7, 14, 25, 29)! God's people tempt or test their Lord when they distrust his kindness and providential care of them and grumble against him and/or his leaders. Moses would later warn (Deut 6:16) that men were not to put God to the test as they did at Massah. Even Isaiah 7:11–12 does not change this rule, for Ahaz's pious disclaimer was not for religious but political reasons. Furthermore, Ahaz had been invited by God to ask for a sign from heaven or earth.

3 This narrative, and in particular this verse, hardly reflects another recension of the same incident, as some critics assume. Biblical narrative often leads off the story with a general statement (here, v.2); and then by means of a coordinate clause (where Western style would have preferred a subordinate clause), it explains in more detail the theme announced in the previous verse(s). Accordingly, it might be better to translate v.3: "Since the people were thirsty for water."

4–7 One of Moses' most characteristic and praiseworthy traits was that he took his difficulties to the Lord (v.4; 15:25; 32:30; 33:8; Num 11:2, 11; 12:13; 14:13–19 et al.). In his exasperation he pled, "What am I to do with these [*hazzeh,* lit., 'this'] people?" The demonstrative pronoun *this* has the same undertone of alienation and distance that is found in God's word in Haggai 1:2: "This [*hazzeh*] people say." Thus they were ready to stone Moses—an angry mob's solution to an irritating problem.

The Lord's response was not to take sides in this exchange but to move directly to sending relief. Moses, along with a few of the elders, was to go out in front of the people—presumably farther down the wadi (v.5). There, where the pillar of the cloud stood, the symbol of God's own presence and ever-present source of power, Moses was to "strike" (*hikkîṯā*) "[on] the rock" (*baṣṣûr*) just as he had "struck" (*hikkîṯā*) the Nile River. Striking the Nile (7:17, 20) in the first plague, however, signaled an interruption in that nation's water supply, whereas this striking would signal the commencement of the flow of waters (v.6). Just as it was in 14:19–20, so here: What was darkness or death to Egypt was light or life to Israel because of the grace of God.

This incident is not to be confused with a similar episode that comes near the conclusion of Israel's forty years of journeying in Numbers 20:1–13. In this later account, the glory of the Lord is not present; and Moses is explicitly instructed that he is *not* to strike the rock but only *to speak* to it. This shows that the only connection between Israel's need and God's supply was the divine Word. True, they also named that place "the waters of Meribah" (Num 20:13), but the symmetry and naming may indeed be deliberate to emphasize the purpose in allowing the incidents and in directing that they be recorded as Scripture. God's people are prone to grumbling at the first hint of adversity no matter how abundant and spectacular may be the evidence of his power and presence.

Thus the dual name brought out both the people's testing of God (*Massah,* "test") and quarreling (*Meribah,* "contention," "strife"; NIV mg., "quarreling") (v.7). In less than six months they had witnessed ten plagues, the pillar of cloud and fire, the opening and shutting of the Red Sea, the miraculous sweetening of the water, and the sending of food and meat from heaven; yet their real question came down to this: "Is the LORD among us [*b^eqirbēnû*] or not?"

Notes

2 וַיָּרֶב (*wayyāreḇ,* "So they quarreled") can be in strife, contention, or even litigation in words or, more infrequently, in deeds (Gen 49:23; Exod 21:18). This is a dominant word in the prophets' vocabulary to describe God's litigation and case against his people.

Although מַה (*māh*) means "what?" in most contexts, in this adverbial usage here it means "why?" as it does in 14:15; 2 Kings 6:33; 7:3; Ps 42:5 (6 MT); and S of Songs 8:4.

3 אֹתִי . . . בָּנַי . . . מִקְנַי (*'ōṯî . . . bānay . . . miqnay*) is literally "[to make] me, [and] my children, [and] my livestock." The singular possessive pronoun follows the plural "us" ("bring *us*") to stress the collective and individual aspects of suffering simultaneously.

6 Ironically, at the very moment Israel was asking whether the Lord really was in their midst or not (v.7), he said, הִנְנִי עֹמֵד לְפָנֶיךָ שָּׁם (*hinnî 'ōmēḏ l^epāneyḵā šām,* "Behold, I will stand before you there"). He would be standing (*'ōmēḏ,* active participle with durative action) there on the rock, apparently having moved his shekinah glory from in front of them in the desert to on top of the rock alongside Moses and the elders. This christophany enabled Paul to accurately refer to Christ as being present here as *the* Rock (cf. 1 Cor 10:4 with Deut 32:30–31, 37).

Even though Horeb is an alternate name for Sinai (e.g., 3:1), עַל־הַצּוּר בְּחֹרֵב (*'al haṣṣûr b^eḥōrēḇ,* "by the rock at Horeb") definitely treats Horeb as the whole region in that it speaks of "at" or "in Horeb." Notice the writer speaks of the rock (*ṣûr*), not the mountain (*har*).

---

4. *The war with Amalek*

17:8–16

[8]The Amalekites came and attacked the Israelites at Rephidim. [9] Moses said to Joshua, "Choose some of our men and go out to fight the Amalekites. Tomorrow I will stand on top of the hill with the staff of God in my hands."

[10]So Joshua fought the Amalekites as Moses had ordered, and Moses, Aaron and Hur went to the top of the hill. [11]As long as Moses held up his hands, the Israelites were winning, but whenever he lowered his hands, the Amalekites were winning. [12]When Moses' hands grew tired, they took a stone and put it under him and he sat on it. Aaron and Hur held his hands up—one on one side, one on the other—so that his hands remained steady till sunset. [13]So Joshua overcame the Amalekite army with the sword.

[14]Then the LORD said to Moses, "Write this on a scroll as something to be remembered and make sure that Joshua hears it, because I will completely blot out the memory of Amalek from under heaven."

[15]Moses built an altar and called it The LORD is my Banner. [16]He said, "For hands were lifted up to the throne of the LORD. The LORD will be at war against the Amalekites from generation to generation."

8 The Amalekites lived in the desert, south of Canaan around Kadesh (Gen 14:7), otherwise known as the northern part of the Negev (Num 13:29; 14:25, 43). Amalek was the son of Eliphaz (Esau's eldest boy) by a concubine named Timna (Gen 36:12) and became a "clan" or "chief" in the tribe of Esau (Gen 36:15). Thus the Amalekites were distant cousins to the Israelites. There is every possibility that they had known about the promise of the land of Canaan that had been given to Esau's twin brother, Jacob; therefore, they should not have felt any threat to their interests in the Negev had this promise been remembered and taken seriously. After all, the promise was to be a means of blessing Amalek along with all the other nations (Gen 12:3) if only they, like Abraham, would have believed. Instead they "came" (*wayyāḇō'*) and attacked Israel at Rephidim—some distance south of the north-central district of the Sinai where they lived.

Amalek's assault on Israel drew the anger of God on two counts: (1) they failed to recognize the hand and plan of God in Israel's life and destiny (even the farther-removed Canaanites of Jericho had been given plenty to think about when they heard about the Exodus—Josh 2:10); and (2) the first targets of their warfare were the sick, aged, and tired of Israel who lagged behind the line of march (Deut 25:17–19). Thus Amalek became the "first among the nations" (Num 24:20)—in this case, to attack Israel. They are placed in juxtaposition with another group of Gentiles in the next chapter (Jethro's Midianites) who believed in Israel's God. These two chapters illustrate two kingdoms and two responses to the grace of God from the Gentile world.

9 To direct the battle against the Amalekites, Moses commissioned a young man (perhaps about forty-five years old) from the tribe of Ephraim (Joseph's son) named Hoshea (Num 13:8) the son of Nun (1 Chron 7:27), who later was renamed Joshua (see Notes). He was to muster an army to fight against the Amalekites while Moses, with the staff of God in his hand, would stand on top of one of the nearby hills overlooking the plain. Both elements were to be operating: (1) the sword in Joshua's hand and (2) the staff (symbol of divine intervention) in Moses' hand. Once again divine sovereignty and human responsibility were linked in carrying out the will of God.

10–13 Aaron and Hur went with Moses to the top of the Hill. Hur, here mentioned for the first time, is again mentioned with Aaron in 24:14, where Moses placed both of them in charge of the camp while he and Joshua went up into the mountain of God. Whether this is the same Hur who descended from Judah through Caleb (1 Chron 2:18–20) and whose grandson Bezalel built the tabernacle (Exod 31:2) is difficult to say. Josephus (Antiq. III, 54 [ii.4]) preserves a Jewish tradition that Hur was the husband of Moses' sister, Miriam.

"As long as" (see Notes on v.11) Moses held up his hands (presumably with staff alternately in one or the other), Joshua and his men were victorious. However, "whenever he lowered his hands" through weariness, the Amalekites forged ahead in the battle. This gesture was not merely for psychological effect to inspire the troops every time they glanced up the hill (S.R. Hirsch, *The Pentateuch: Exodus,* 2d ed. [Gateshead, Eng.: Judaica, 1973], 2:233). Nor does the text specifically claim that Moses prayed while his hands were raised (the more traditional explanation). Rather, Moses' outstretched arms primarily symbolized his appeal to God. He had commanded Moses on previous occasions, "Stretch out your hand" (*neṭēh 'eṯ-yāḏeḵā*) with the staff (9:22–23; 10:12–13; 14:16). Yet in 10:21–22 only the hand was stretched out.

This staff was no magic wand. Like all OT institutions, the external and visible symbol meant nothing unless (1) it was divinely appointed and (2) the obedient use of the external form was accompanied by the internal and invisible motions of the heart and spirit of a man. Thus the prophetic-symbolic action of the constantly upraised hands did signal the fervent prayers of the heart of Moses as he witnessed the battle. As Bush (*Exodus,* 2:220) aptly remarks, "The whole narrative . . . conclusively shows that God designed to teach Israel that the hand of Moses, with whom [Israel] had just been chiding, contributed more to their safety than their own hands; his rod more than their weapons." Finally the lengthy battle came to an end, with Joshua as victor.

14 The account of this battle, in which the powerful presence of the Lord played an important role, was to be written down on a scroll (*sēp̱er*) and continually reiterated for Joshua's benefit.

There are five notices in the Pentateuch where Moses wrote down something at the LORD's command: here; 24:4, 7; 34:27; Numbers 33:1–2; and Deuteronomy 31:9, 24. Not too long ago some OT scholars disbelieved these notices by alleging that writing was not invented until after Moses' day. It has since become apparent from archaeological evidence that men had already been writing in Moses' day for over a millennium and a half!

Amalek would pay dearly for its awful deed. The psalmist (Ps 83:4, 7) links Amalek's motives with those of other nations: " 'Come,' they say, 'let us destroy them as a nation, that the name of Israel be remembered no more.' " But it would be measured out to them as they had threatened to do to Israel. Elsewhere in the OT this judgment would be called a *ḥērem* ("a ban"), or an involuntary dedication of a total people for destruction after they had steadfastly resisted the goodness of God for generations. This sentence of total extinction was not carried out until Saul's day (1 Sam 15), but Saul failed to do what God had said. David continued the action (2 Sam 1:1–8:12); and it may still have been going on in Esther's day, if Haman indeed is proven to have been an Amalekite.

15–16 Whether "The LORD is my Banner" (*yhwh nissî,* "Yahweh Nissi") is the name of the altar (cf. Jacob in Gen 33:20) or a title for God himself cannot be known for certain. The result is the same in either case. The word for "banner" (*nēs*) reflects the root "to be high," "raised," or "conspicuous." The allusion would be to lifting up the staff as a standard and a testimony to his power. The victory, then, was the LORD's, just as the war had been his. There was no such thing as a "holy war" in the OT, but there were "wars of Yahweh."

The true interpretation of v.16 is most difficult because of the unusual spelling for the word "throne" (*kēs*). Most scholars emend the text (following the seventeenth-century commentator J. Clericus) to read *nēs* ("banner"). Cassuto (p. 207) supposes the meaning "plan" for *kēs* (from the root *kāsas,* "to count, reckon"). The problem is that some (e.g., the Samar., Syr., Vul., Onkelos, Pseudo-Jonathan, Neofiti I, and medieval Jewish commentators) read "throne," even though it should have been spelled *kissē*'; and the grammar of the present text does not fit easily. The best solution (taking the more difficult textual reading) is to see *kēsyāh* as a shortened form of *kissē'-yāh* ("throne of Yah[weh]"). The text would then read "truly [*kî*], the hand is towards [*'al*] the throne of the Lord," i.e., in a supplicating position. An alternate rendering would be "because [*kî*] a hand is against [*'al*] the throne of the LORD." This latter reading fits the context of v.14 better.

Notes

9 יְהוֹשֻׁעַ (*y*^{e}*hôšu*^{a}*ʿ*, "Joshua") is הוֹשֵׁעַ (*hôšē*^{a}*ʿ*) in Num 13:8. The Greek form, Ἰησους (*Iēsous*), is the same name as Jesus; see Acts 7:45; Heb 4:8. The form "Joshua" was given to him by Moses when he was sent out as one of the spies (Num 13:16). Exodus 17:9, then, either reflects the fact that Moses wrote this narrative later in his life, after sending out the spies, or reflects a later textual modernization of this name.

11 Both the verbs "to hold up" and "to lower" are introduced by the perfect וְהָיָה (*w*^{e}*hāyāh*, "As long as") with the waw, and both are preceded by כַּאֲשֶׁר (*ka'*^{a}*šer*, lit., "as that"). Continued or frequentative action is clearly denoted.

12 כְּבֵדִים (*k*^{e}*b̲ēd̲îm*, lit., "tired ones"; NIV, "grew tired") uses a masculine plural even though "hands" is feminine in Hebrew. This may be an archaic form for the usual dual ending, *k*^{e}*b̲ēdayim* (Cassuto, p. 205). The word יָד (*yād̲*, "hand") occurs in vv.9–16 seven times.

אֱמוּנָה (*'*^{e}*mûnāh*, "remained steady") is the usual word for "faithfulness," but this passage affords a great word-picture of what is involved. It is steadfastness and patience under severe trials.

13 וַיַּחֲלֹשׁ (*wayyaḥ*^{a}*lōš*, "overcame") is a rare Hebrew form that on the basis of Aramaic usage can be translated "mowed down," "disabled," or "prostrated."

14 מָחֹה אֶמְחֶה (*māḥōh '*^{e}*mḥeh*, "completely erase") is literally "wiping, I will wipe." The sentence is emphatic with a ring of paronomasia to help the condemned remember it all the better.

The presence of the definite article with בַּסֵּפֶר (*bassēp̄er*, "on the scroll") expresses a special or well-known scroll with similar information collected at God's direction.

---

5. *The wisdom of Jethro*

18:1–27

1 Now Jethro, the priest of Midian and father-in-law of Moses, heard of everything God had done for Moses and for his people Israel, and how the LORD had brought Israel out of Egypt.

2 After Moses had sent away his wife Zipporah, his father-in-law Jethro received her 3 and her two sons. One son was named Gershom, for Moses said, "I have become an alien in a foreign land"; 4 and the other was named Eliezer, for he said, "My father's God was my helper; he saved me from the sword of Pharaoh."

5 Jethro, Moses' father-in-law, together with Moses' sons and wife, came to him in the desert, where he was camped near the mountain of God. 6 Jethro had sent word to him, "I, your father-in-law Jethro, am coming to you with your wife and her two sons."

7 So Moses went out to meet his father-in-law and bowed down and kissed him. They greeted each other and then went into the tent. 8 Moses told his father-in-law about everything the LORD had done to Pharaoh and the Egyptians for Israel's sake and about all the hardships they had met along the way and how the LORD had saved them.

9 Jethro was delighted to hear about all the good things the LORD had done for Israel in rescuing them from the hand of the Egyptians. 10 He said, "Praise be to the LORD, who rescued you from the hand of the Egyptians and of Pharaoh, and who rescued the people from the hand of the Egyptians. 11 Now I know that the LORD is greater than all other gods, for he did this to those who had treated Israel arrogantly." 12 Then Jethro, Moses' father-in-law, brought a burnt offering and other sacrifices to God, and Aaron came with all the elders of Israel to eat bread with Moses' father-in-law in the presence of God.

[13]The next day Moses took his seat to serve as judge for the people, and they stood around him from morning till evening. [14]When his father-in-law saw all that Moses was doing for the people, he said, "What is this you are doing for the people? Why do you alone sit as judge, while all these people stand around you from morning till evening?"

[15]Moses answered him, "Because the people come to me to seek God's will. [16]Whenever they have a dispute, it is brought to me, and I decide between the parties and inform them of God's decrees and laws."

[17]Moses' father-in-law replied, "What you are doing is not good. [18]You and these people who come to you will only wear yourselves out. The work is too heavy for you; you cannot handle it alone. [19]Listen now to me and I will give you some advice, and may God be with you. You must be the people's representative before God and bring their disputes to him. [20]Teach them the decrees and laws, and show them the way to live and the duties they are to perform. [21]But select capable men from all the people—men who fear God, trustworthy men who hate dishonest gain—and appoint them as officials over thousands, hundreds, fifties and tens. [22]Have them serve as judges for the people at all times, but have them bring every difficult case to you; the simple cases they can decide themselves. That will make your load lighter, because they will share it with you. [23]If you do this and God so commands, you will be able to stand the strain, and all these people will go home satisfied."

[24]Moses listened to his father-in-law and did everything he said. [25]He chose capable men from all Israel and made them leaders of the people, officials over thousands, hundreds, fifties and tens. [26]They served as judges for the people at all times. The difficult cases they brought to Moses, but the simple ones they decided themselves.

[27]Then Moses sent his father-in-law on his way, and Jethro returned to his own country.

1–5 Lightfoot and several other commentators wanted to place Jethro's visit to Moses between v.10 and v.11 in Numbers 10 for three reasons: (1) the law on burnt offerings and sacrifices had not been given as yet (cf. v.12); (2) the statutes and laws mentioned in vv.13 and 16 had not yet been revealed; and (3) the judges and rulers appointed in vv.21–26 do not appear to have been appointed until Israel left Sinai according to Deuteronomy 1:9–15. Thus the present arrangement and relationship of the materials in Exodus 18 was topically, not chronologically, motivated. While we have no special objections to this argument in principle, nevertheless we cannot agree with the three reasons cited here. In fact, we have already seen that portions of the law were already known before they were formalized at Sinai (see Notes on 16:4; and notice the loose wording of Deut 1:9–15, along with the presence of sacrifices almost from the beginning of the human race in Gen 4:3–4 and later in 8:20–21). The chapter, then, is in its proper chronological order.

Jethro, Moses' father-in-law, met Moses and the Israelites in the desert at the "mountain of God" (v.5; identified as Horeb or Sinai in 3:1; see comment there). Moses must have sent his wife and children on ahead to Midian to bring Jethro back to Sinai for a visit (v.2). Most commentators feel that Zipporah, Gershom, and Eliezer had been sent back to Midian after the family dispute in 4:20–26, but there is no solid evidence for this view. It would have been most important for Eliezer as the next high priest to be a firsthand witness of all that God had done for Israel in the Exodus.

6–8 Jethro announced his arrival by means of a messenger (v.6 begins, literally, "and he said"), and Moses went out to meet him (cf. Gen 18:2; 19:1; 32:6; 33:1) and to exchange the usual Oriental greetings (v.7). Moses then recounted "all" (*kōl*, see comment on 9:24–25 for hyperbolic usage of *kōl*) that Yahweh (notice the clear reference to the personal and covenantal name of God in deference to the generic name Elohim, which depicts God's relationship to all creation) had done. As the psalmist exhorted (Ps 145:5–7, 12), so Moses acted, recounting the awesome work and abundant goodness of Yahweh both in Israel's rescue from Egypt and in their subsequent "hardships" (v.8) along the way: the Red Sea, thirst, lack of meat, and the war with Amalek.

9–12 The news evoked an instinctive "Praise Yahweh" from Jethro (v.10), thereby showing either that he had continued believing in the God of his fathers (since he, too, was a descendant of Abraham through Midian, Gen 25:2) or that he had spiritually benefited from Moses' forty-year stay in his house. Jethro continued, "Now I know that the Lord [Yahweh] is greater than all other gods" (v.11). This confession formula—"Now I know"—is used by two other Gentile believers: the widow at Zarephath (1 Kings 17:24), and Naaman, commander of the Syrian army (2 Kings 5:15). It is a clear statement to Yahweh's incomparable greatness above all the gods of Egypt (not necessarily Jethro's past or present penchant for polytheism).

Too frequently in the past, textbooks on the religion of Israel have tended to read too much (polytheism) or too little (genuine piety) into such statements as this one and make them normative for all true Israelite religion (e.g., Judg 11:24; 2 Kings 5:17–18). However, if v.11b, with its unspecified subject of the verb ("treat arrogantly"), is a reference to all the gods of Egypt that were smitten in the plagues and not an alleged statement of past competition between Yahweh and polytheistic forms of worship, then Jethro was a true believer and no polytheist. Cassuto would translate the second half of v.11: "Excelling them [the gods] in the very things to which they laid claims" (see Notes).

Jethro then "took" or "brought" (*wayyiqqaḥ*) a burnt offering (*'ōlāh*) and fellowship offerings (*zeḇāḥîm*; NIV, "other sacrifices") to "Elohim" (v.12). "Brought" is the customary word for proffering or providing an animal for sacrifice; it is never used in the OT in the sense of "to offer" (see Bubar, p. 141; see the Notes for further discussion). It is the very same verb used in 25:2 and Leviticus 12:8. Accordingly, those scholars are wrong who wish to see the Midianite priest officiating here: he did not "offer" these sacrifices, but he did worship and fellowship with Moses and Aaron "in the presence of God."

We had expected Yahweh's name in this last phrase, but the generic name for God (Elohim) is used perhaps because God was relating to the Gentile and the Jewish world simultaneously. Yet Cassuto (p. 217) makes a very strong point: Never is any other name for God used in the Torah with any of the sacrifices except Yahweh's name; this is the one exception. Clearly Jethro was an outsider, an alien (a *gēr*, like the name Moses gave to his son—*Ger*shom), even though he had made a strong declaration of faith in vv.10–11. It should be remembered also that "in the presence of God" may simply reflect the phrase "the glory of God," and thus we may have a covenant meal eaten in the presence of the God who dwells in the midst of his people.

13–16 Jethro is depicted as an efficiency expert who wisely suggests a modification in Israel's leadership structure (cf. vv.17–23), which Moses then adopted with divine permission. Previous to this the people came to Moses for two things: (1) instruction (v.15) and (2) judicial settlements (v.16).

17–23 Jethro's solution to this lengthy process, which was wearing out both people and leader (v.18), was to give Moses that portion of the work that involved a twofold office: (1) an advocate on behalf of the people (v.19) and (2) an interpreter on behalf of God to teach the people (v.20). Jethro warned that his plan needed to be executed only if God was pleased with this advice ("and may God be with you," v.19, and "If you do this and God so commands," v.23).

Moses' work was to be supplemented with additional help. He was to "select capable men" (v.21). While it may seem from this passage that Moses autocratically chose his own staff, the actual election was the work of all the people as Deuteronomy 1:9, 13 affirms. Their leadership course (v.20) was to include instruction in (1) "decrees" (*haḥuqqîm,* i.e., specific enactments), (2) "laws" (*hattôrōṯ,* i.e., general enactments, (3) the "way to live" (*ḥaddereḵ yēlᵉḵû,* i.e., "life style and the path of duty"), and (4) the "duties" (*hamma'ᵃśeh,* or "jobs") each was to perform.

The qualifications for these men (v.21) were that they should be (1) "capable men" (i.e., men with a native aptitude for judging), (2) "men who fear [in reverence and belief] God," (3) men of truth (i.e., "trustworthy"), and (4) men who hated all "dishonest gain." These were to be arranged in a decimal system of a graduated series of groups in multiples of ten, with Moses being the court of final appeal (vv.22, 26).

Amazingly enough, Moses listened to his father-in-law. Bush (*Exodus,* 1:230) remarks, "The great Jehovah did not disdain to permit his prophet to be taught by the wisdom and intelligence of a good man, though he was not of the commonwealth of Israel. It is not a little remarkable that the very first rudiments of the Jewish polity were thus suggested by a stranger and a Midianite."

Notes

1 Jethro is called כֹּהֵן מִדְיָן (*kōhēn Miḏyān,* "the priest of Midian"). See also Exod 2:16. In this regard he was much like "Melchizedek king of Salem" and "priest of God Most High" (Gen 14:18). See Albright, "Jethro," pp. 4–9.

4 אֱלִיעֶזֶר (*'ᵉlî'ezer,* "Eliezer") means "my God is [or 'was'] a helper."

The "sword of Pharaoh" Moses was delivered from may refer to the past incident when he slew an Egyptian and fled Egypt (2:11–15). Bush (*Exodus,* 1:225) prefers to translate וַיַּצִּלֵנִי (*wayyaṣṣilēnî,* "he saved me") as a future: "he *will* save me." However, this is an unlikely suggestion for a waw conversive with the imperfect, which is always translated as a past narrative tense.

11 On כִּי בַדָּבָר אֲשֶׁר זָדוּ עֲלֵיהֶם (*kî baddāḇār 'ᵃšer zāḏû 'ᵃlêhem,* lit., "because of the matter when they were arrogant to them"; NIV, "for he did this to those who had treated Israel arrogantly"), Cassuto (p. 216) suggests that the word "gods," which appears in v.11a, is the subject of the verb *zāḏû*; hence, "the gods acted proudly or boasted." The full sense of the verse would be thus: "Now I know that the LORD is greater than all other gods, precisely [*kî,* this is its meaning in 32:29] with respect to those things that [*baddāḇār 'ᵃšer*] the gods [of Egypt] claimed they excelled."

12 Instead of "Then [Jethro] . . . brought" for וַיִּקַּח (*wayyiqqaḥ*), the RSV follows the Syriac, Targum, and Vulgate in reading "offered." These versions did not have another Hebrew text but were probably interpreting the one we presently have. However, Aelred Cody ("Exodus 18, 12: Jethro Accepts a Covenant With the Israelites," *Biblica* 49 [1968]: 159–61) argues that if the Syriac and other versions read *wayyiqqah* as *wᵉqarreḇ* ("and he drew near [in order to offer a sacrifice]"), why did they not use the word meaning precisely that: *hiqrîḇ, hēbî', he'ᵉlâ* with its cognate accusative *'ōlāh,* or some form of *zḇḥ* with its cognate accusative *zᵉḇāḥîm*? Cody wants to take *lāqaḥ* in its more particular sense, "to accept" (BDB, p. 543, s.v. *lāqaḥ*, Qal, 4.f). The point is that Jethro himself did not offer the burnt offering.

It is most unusual to see an עֹלָה (*ʿōlāh*, "burnt offering"; later revealed in Lev 1) coming from this Gentile, unless Jethro, too, was a believer who was willing to dedicate himself totally to Yahweh as this offering symbolized.

15 לִדְרֹשׁ אֱלֹהִים (*lidrōš ʾᵉlōhîm*, "to seek God's will") is literally "to inquire of God." This phrase usually means to secure an answer to a specific question from God (Hyatt [p. 193] calls attention to Gen 25:22–23; 1 Sam 9:9; 1 Kings 22:8; 2 Kings 3:11; 8:8; 22:13, 18). Also notice Moses' practice of entering the tabernacle, where the Lord would speak to him (33:7–11).

21 תֶחֱזֶה (*teḥᵉzeh*, "select") is literally "you will see." Cassuto (p. 220) shows how "seeing" is used for "choosing" in both Hebrew and Ugaritic: e.g., in Gen 41:33: "And now let Pharaoh look for [or 'choose'] a discerning and wise man."

אַנְשֵׁי־חַיִל (*ʾanšê-ḥayil*, "capable men" or "men of worth") possess qualities of character, leadership, and success (cf. the "wife of noble character" in Prov 31:10–31). Notice that some of the same qualities are expected of leaders in the church (Acts 6:3; 1 Tim 3:2–12; Titus 1:7–9).

II. Divine Morality (19:1–24:18)

Israel's deliverance from Egypt partially fulfilled the Abrahamic covenant (Gen 15:13–16; Exod 2:24–25; 6:4–8). But this environment of God's gracious act of deliverance also laid the basis for the revelation of his law, as it reflected his character and/or his word. This law served as a continuation of his promise with the patriarchs and also was decisively important in the history of Israel and of humanity as a whole. Thus the Mosaic covenant with its law is not all that distant and unrelated to the Abrahamic covenant. Given the gracious promises of the Abrahamic covenant and the deliverance from Egypt under Moses, the grace of the Abrahamic promise fits the laws of Moses in the same way that Romans is related to James. In one year's time, some fifty-eight chapters of Scripture (Exod 19–40; Lev 1–27; Num 1–10) were given here at Sinai.

A. *The Eagles' Wings Speech*

19:1–8

1 In the third month after the Israelites left Egypt—on the very day—
they came to the Desert of Sinai. 2 After they set out from Rephidim, they
entered the Desert of Sinai, and Israel camped there in the desert in
front of the mountain.

3 Then Moses went up to God, and the LORD called to him from the
mountain and said, "This is what you are to say to the house of Jacob
and what you are to tell the people of Israel: 4 'You yourselves have seen
what I did to Egypt, and how I carried you on eagles' wings and brought
you to myself. 5 Now if you obey me fully and keep my covenant, then out
of all nations you will be my treasured possession. Although the whole
earth is mine, 6 you will be for me a kingdom of priests and a holy
nation.' These are the words you are to speak to the Israelites."

7 So Moses went back and summoned the elders of the people and set
before them all the words the LORD had commanded him to speak. 8 The
people all responded together, "We will do everything the LORD has
said." So Moses brought their answer back to the LORD.

1–2 In the third month, later known as Sivan (our late May or early June), Israel left Rephidim (see 17:1, 8) and came to the Desert of Sinai (v.1). Thus the last two weeks of what later generations would name the month of Nisan and four weeks of I[y]yar had passed, and it was in the seventh week. "The desert in front of the mountain" (v.2) is called er-Raha (meaning "the palm [of a hand]") in that it is a flat plain about five thousand feet above sea level and stretches over four hundred acres almost like an amphitheater with additional areas in adjoining valleys.

Several mountains have been associated with Sinai: Gebel Musa, Ras eṣ-ṣafṣafeh, Gabel Serbāl, and a mountain near Al-Hrob. The Al-Hrob location makes it impossible to make sense of the route of the Exodus, since it is a volcanic mountain to the east of the Gulf of Aqabah. Gebel Serbāl does not have a wilderness at its base; therefore, the choice is between Gebel Musa (7,363 feet elevation at the southern end of er-Raha) and Ras eṣ-ṣafṣafeh (6,540 feet high at the northern edge of the plain). Most scholars prefer to identify Sinai with Gebel Musa because of its relation to the plain (20:18: "they stayed at a distance") and because of its imposing granite formations.

3–6 The "sign" given to Moses in 3:12 is fulfilled here (v.3): he has returned to the "mountain of God" (3:1). When Moses "went up" (see Notes) the mountain, Yahweh delivered his "eagles' wings speech." A twofold title is used for the people of God (v.3): "house of Jacob" (a reminder of their humble beginnings; cf. Gen 28:13; 35:11; 49:7) and "the people of Israel" (a statement as to what they had become: a nation).

The metaphor of the eagles' wings could refer to one of the eight species of eagles (*n^e^šārîm*) found in Syria, Palestine, and Arabia in addition to the Palestinian vulture. Here it is probably the latter one. This metaphor is developed most extensively in Deuteronomy 32:11, where the loving compassion, protection, strength, and watchfulness of God is compared to the majestic bird's attributes. As the young eagles were carried on the adult wings and brought out of their nests and taught to fly, so Yahweh had lovingly carried and safely delivered Israel.

This covenant (first given to the patriarchs), however, which was unconditional in its transmission and bestowal, was indeed conditioned with regard to its enjoyment and personal participation (see Kaiser, *Old Testament Theology*, pp. 93–94, 111, 130, 156–57). The presence of the "if" (*'im*) in v.5 did not pave the way for Israel's declension from grace into law anymore than an alleged presence of a condition paved an identical fall for the patriarchs (Gen 22:16–18; 26:5) or for David (2 Sam 7:14–15; 1 Kings 2:4; 8:25; 9:4–5; Pss 89:30–37; 132:11–12).

The six verses (vv.3–8) of this eagles' wings speech and its response are cast in the familiar Near Eastern suzerainty treaty form. Mendenhall ("Covenant Forms") has demonstrated that the Hittites in the middle second millennium used a literary pattern to write their treaties imposed by strong kings on their vassals that was similar to the literary pattern found in these six verses and in Exodus 20. This pattern is:

Preamble—v.3b, a summons by God
Historical prologue—v.4
Stipulations—v.5a
Blessings—vv.5b–6a
Acceptance in a solemn assembly—vv.7–8
[see Richard J. Sklba, "The Redeemer of Israel," CBQ, 34 (1972): 3–4]

Three titles summarize the divine blessings that an obedient and covenant-keeping Israel will experience: they would be a "treasured possession" (v.5), "a kingdom of priests and a holy nation" (v.6; see Notes). The first signified that Israel would be God's valuable property and distinct treasure (Deut 7:6; 14:2; 26:18; Ps 135:4; Mal 3:17; cf. Titus 2:14; 1 Peter 2:9) set aside for a marked purpose (see Notes). Furthermore, they were to be at once priest-kings and royal-priests (Isa 61:6; cf. 1 Peter 2:5, 9; Rev 1:6; 5:10; 20:6)—*everyone* in the whole nation. This expression was not a parallel phrase or a synonym for a "holy nation"; it was a separate entity. The whole nation was to act as mediators of God's grace to the nations of the earth, even as Abraham had been promised that through him and his seed all the nations of the earth would be blessed (Gen 12:3). The last title designated Israel as a separate and distinct nation because her God was holy, separate, and distinct, as were his purposes and plans (Deut 7:6; 14:2, 21; 26:19; Isa 62:12; cf. 1 Peter 2:9).

This whole synopsis of God's suzerainty treaty with his vassal Israel is remarkably personal. It begins in v.3 addressed "to the sons of Israel" (*lib̲ᵉnê yiśrā'ēl*) and concludes with an inclusion in v.6 "to the sons of Israel" (*'el-bᵉnê yiśrā'ēl*). Its first and last clauses are introduced by an emphatic "you" (*'attem,* vv.4, 6) along with two other references to "you" in v.4 (*'e̲tk̲em*).

7–8 The people responded, "We will do everything the LORD has said" (v.8). Some commentators have criticized Israel for speaking rashly by agreeing to do all that God said; for they went off promise, so it is alleged, and onto a law standard. On the contrary, the Lord approved of their response in glowing terms: "Everything they said was good. Oh, that their hearts would be inclined to fear me and keep all my commandments always" (Deut 5:28–29).

Notes

---

1 Grammatically the expression בַּיּוֹם הַזֶּה (*bayyôm hazzeh,* "on the very day") can be taken indefinitely: "at this time." It need not be the very first day of the third month. Later Jewish tradition assigned the giving of the law to Pentecost, i.e., the fiftieth day since Passover and the night of the Exodus. This connection between the Feast of Weeks and the giving of the law may go back as far as the time of King Asa in 2 Chron 15:10–15.

3 One of the alleged marks that this passage is a mixture of sources is the fact that Moses עָלָה (*'ālāh,* "went up") the mountain seven times (19:3, 20; 24:9, 13, 15, 18; and 34:4; also he "went back to the LORD" in 32:31); yet he only "went/came down" four times (19:14, 25; 32:15; 34:29). Indeed, Moses did make several trips up the mountain, perhaps as many as three or four. The major difficulty is in Exod 24 (see comment there); but there is no reason why multiple sources or authorship should be set forth as the best solution.

5 On סְגֻלָּה (*sᵉgullāh,* "treasured possession"), see Moshe Greenberg, "Hebrew *sᵉgûllā*: Akkadian *sik̲iltu*," JAOS 71 (1951): 172ff. The basic root of this term was *sakālu* ("to set aside a thing or a property"). While real property (e.g., real estate) could not be removed, this property could. It usually was regarded as extremely valuable property. So God valued his people Israel.

6 There are four defensible Hebrew renderings of מַמְלֶכֶת כֹּהֲנִים (*mamleke̱ṯ kōhᵃnîm*, "kingdom of priests"): (1) *mamleke̱ṯ* as an absolute in apposition to *kōhᵃnîm*, viz., "kings, i.e., priests"; (2) *mamleke̱ṯ* as a construct with the *nomen regens* expressing an attribute of the *nomen rectum*, "royal priesthood"; (3) *mamleke̱ṯ* as a construct with opposite term being the *nomen regens*, "priestly kingdom" (as in Prov 21:20: *kᵉsîl 'āḏām*, "a fool of a man," i.e., "a foolish man," or Ps 2:6: *har-qāḏᵉšî*, "hill of my holiness," i.e., "my holy hill"); or (4) an unexpressed "and" must be read here: "kings (and) priests." The emphasis here is not on the individual but on the whole nation (19:3, 6); and the expression is more a compound noun than it is construct. (See R.B.Y. Scott, "A Kingdom of Priests (Exodus xix.6)," *Oudtestamentische Studiën* 8 [1950]: 213–19; William L. Moran, "A Kingdom of Priests," *The Bible in Current Catholic Thought*, John L. McKenzie, ed. [New York: Herder and Herder, 1962], pp. 7–20; Kaiser, *Old Testament Theology*, pp. 107–10). Israel was to be kings and priests to God on behalf of the nations; they were to be mediators of the gospel as missionaries to the nations ("in your seed shall all the nations of the earth be blessed," Gen 12:3b), and they were to be partakers in the present aspects and coming reality of the "kingdom of God."

B. The Advent of God on Sinai

19:9–25

9 The LORD said to Moses, "I am going to come to you in a dense cloud,
so that the people will hear me speaking with you and will always put
their trust in you." Then Moses told the LORD what the people had said.
10 And the LORD said to Moses, "Go to the people and consecrate them
today and tomorrow. Have them wash their clothes 11 and be ready by
the third day, because on that day the LORD will come down on Mount
Sinai in the sight of all the people. 12 Put limits for the people around the
mountain and tell them, 'Be careful that you do not go up the mountain
or touch the foot of it. Whoever touches the mountain shall surely be put
to death. 13 He shall surely be stoned or shot with arrows; not a hand is
to be laid on him. Whether man or animal, he shall not be permitted to
live.' Only when the ram's horn sounds a long blast may they go up to
the mountain."
14 After Moses had gone down the mountain to the people, he
consecrated them, and they washed their clothes. 15 Then he said to the
people, "Prepare yourselves for the third day. Abstain from sexual
relations."
16 On the morning of the third day there was thunder and lightning,
with a thick cloud over the mountain, and a very loud trumpet blast.
Everyone in the camp trembled. 17 Then Moses led the people out of the
camp to meet with God, and they stood at the foot of the mountain.
18 Mount Sinai was covered with smoke, because the LORD descended on
it in fire. The smoke billowed up from it like smoke from a furnace, the
whole mountain trembled violently, 19 and the sound of the trumpet
grew louder and louder. Then Moses spoke and the voice of God
answered him.
20 The LORD descended to the top of Mount Sinai and called Moses to
the top of the mountain. So Moses went up 21 and the LORD said to him,
"Go down and warn the people so they do not force their way through
to see the LORD and many of them perish. 22 Even the priests, who
approach the LORD, must consecrate themselves, or the LORD will break
out against them."
23 Moses said to the LORD, "The people cannot come up Mount Sinai,
because you yourself warned us, 'Put limits around the mountain and
set it apart as holy.' "

24The LORD replied, "Go down and bring Aaron up with you. But the
priests and the people must not force their way through to come up to
the LORD, or he will break out against them."
25So Moses went down to the people and told them.

9 To forestall all future pretext for saying that the law Moses was about to give to Israel was of his own devising, God conferred on Moses the highest possible honor and deference ever given to mortal man. The "you" in this verse is singular, but the event of the advent or coming of God in a dense, dark cloud was public. Ordinarily God dwelt with his people in a pillar of cloud and fire; but here it turned dense and pitch black, perhaps with a roar of thunder and the flash of lightning as God's voice pierced his creation. The voice of God speaking to Moses (cf. Deut 4:32–33) would be audible in the camp so that Israel and all her true descendants would trust in Moses' words both then and for all time.

10–15 As a token of their inward preparation for meeting with God on the third day, the people were to wash their clothes, stay off the mountain, and abstain from sexual relations with their mates. The theology of this passage, then, is fitness for meeting with God and preparation for the worship of God (see comment on 3:5). What is required to approach the God of gods, King of kings, and Lord of lords is both decorum and a wholistic sanctification of our *bodies* as well as our inner persons. This is not to say that there was intrinsic virtue in the mere act of washing clothes or abstaining from marital relations, but the outward act was to signal that the inner work of sanctification had also been sought.

Sealing off the mountain (v.12) was as much a temporary and arbitrary boundary as it was in 3:5, but it was introduced as an aid for the proper worship of a holy God. Likewise Paul allowed Christian couples a temporary abstinence from sexual relations so that they may devote themselves to prayer (1 Cor 7:5; also cf. 1 Sam 21:4–5). The penalty for intruding on such a holy scene was death since anyone who dared to transgress so explicit a divine precept was already a profane and sacrilegious man whose presence would pollute the rest of the worshiping community. This was tantamount to what Numbers 15:30–31 calls "sinning defiantly" or what the NT regards as blasphemy against the Holy Spirit (Heb 10:26–31).

After the "ram's horn" (see Notes) sounded a long, drawn-out blast, the people could once again ascend the mountain (v.13b). Moses did not rescind this privilege and charge them anew to prevent their ascending the mountain in vv.21–25; but, as Calvin suggested, all the verbs should be translated as pluperfects.

16–19 The advent of God took place amid a most impressive display of cosmic disruptions: thunder and lightning (v.16; cf. Ps 77:18; Heb 12:18–19; Rev 4:5; 8:5; 11:19), an exceedingly loud trumpet blast (cf. Rev 1:10; 4:1), and a thick cloud (Exod 19:9; 2 Chron 5:14). A deep moral impression was made on the people, for they were in the presence of the glorious majesty of the Holy God who was about to reveal his person and character in his law. This magnificent event will be unexcelled until the Lord Jesus returns again in blazing fire (2 Thess 1:7–12).

20–25 If the verbs are translated as pluperfects, then v.20 is parenthetical since we have been told that the Lord had already descended in v.18; but we have not as yet been informed that Moses had been called to the top of the mount. Moses' reaction to this awesome sight is not given here, but in Hebrews 12:21 his response is, "I am trembling with fear." God's response came in v.21. Moses was to warn the people not to intrude rashly on the presence of God. The triple emphasis (vv.12–13, 21–22, 25) is a standard literary practice when the text wants us to notice an important subject. Thus the boundary between the human and the divine was not to be taken lightly by mortals.

"Even" (*w^e^gam*) the priests who approached the Lord were to consecrate themselves (v.22). Certainly this was not the Aaronic priesthood that had not been established as yet. It must be a reference to the "firstborn" of every family who were dedicated and consecrated to God (13:2). Only later was the tribe of Levi substituted for each firstborn male (Num 3:45). In the meantime the "young Israelite men . . . offered burnt offerings and sacrificed young bulls as fellowship offerings" (24:5). Should they fail to observe this request, the Lord would "break out against them" (v.22). The verb to "break out" (*yip̱rōṣ*) is the same one that is preserved in the name given in 2 Samuel 5:20 (Baal-Perazim) and 2 Samuel 6:8 (Perez Uzzah).

Notes

13 הַיֹּבֵל (*hayyōḇēl*, "ram's horn") is literally "trumpet." From *yōḇēl* came the Latin *jubilum* and the English "jubilee." The ancient name שֹׁפָר (*šōp̱ār*, "trumpet") is used in 19:16, 19; 20:18. In this case the sustained blast accompanied the presence of Yahweh; elsewhere it signaled the alarm for war or the summons for assembly or worship (Lev 25:9; 2 Chron 15:14; Pss 47:5; 81:3; Isa 27:13).

17 לִקְרַאת הָאֱלֹהִים (*liqra'ṯ hā'^e^lōhîm*) is rendered "to meet with God." Although the verb *qārā'* is usually used for people meeting each other (4:14, 27; 18:7), it became another word in Israel's worship vocabulary.

20 וַיֵּרֶד (*wayyēreḏ*, "descended") is the same anthropomorphism used of God elsewhere (e.g., Gen 11:5; 18:21).

22, 24 Besides calling the whole nation of Israel a "kingdom of priests" or, better, "kings and priests" (Exod 19:6; Isa 61:6); Melchizedek a priest-king (Gen 14:18; Ps 110:4), and Jethro a priest of Midian (Exod 2:16; 3:1; 18:1); these two verses in Exodus 19 stand alone except for the same title—הַכֹּהֲנִים (*hakkōh^a^nîm*, "priests")—being given to David's sons (2 Sam 8:18), his grandson (1 Kings 4:5), and Ira the Jairite (2 Sam 20:26). See the discussion by Carl Armerding, "Were David's Sons Really Priests?" *Current Issues in Biblical and Patristic Interpretation*, ed. Gerald Hawthorne (Grand Rapids: Eerdmans, 1975), pp. 75–86.

25 Some translate the verb in וַיֹּאמֶר אֲלֵהֶם (*wayyō'mer '^a^lēhem*, "told them") as if it were *wayy^e^dabbēr* ("and he spoke"), i.e., as if chapter 20 were the object of the verb. However, the object is to be supplied from all that was contained in the *previous* verses.

C. *The Decalogue*

20:1–17

1 And God spoke all these words:

2 "I am the LORD your God, who brought you out of Egypt, out of the land of slavery.

3 "You shall have no other gods before me.

4 "You shall not make for yourself an idol in the form of anything in heaven above or on the earth beneath or in the waters below.

5You shall not bow down to them or worship them; for I, the LORD your God, am a jealous God, punishing the children for the sin of the fathers to the third and fourth generation of those who hate me, 6but showing love to a thousands of those who love me and keep my commandments.
7"You shall not misuse the name of the LORD your God, for the LORD will not hold anyone guiltless who misuses his name.
8"Remember the Sabbath day by keeping it holy. 9Six days you shall labor and do all your work, 10but the seventh day is a Sabbath to the LORD your God. On it you shall not do any work, neither you, nor your son or daughter, nor your manservant or maidservant, nor your animals, nor the alien within your gates. 11For in six days the LORD made the heavens and the earth, the sea, and all that is in them, but he rested on the seventh day. Therefore the LORD blessed the Sabbath day and made it holy.
12"Honor your father and your mother, so that you may live long in the land the LORD your God is giving you.
13"You shall not murder.
14"You shall not commit adultery.
15"You shall not steal.
16 "You shall not give false testimony against your neighbor.
17"You shall not covet your neighbor's house. You shall not covet your neighbor's wife, or his manservant or maidservant, his ox or donkey, or anything that belongs to your neighbor."

Excursus: Introduction to the Law

The term "decalogue" can be traced to Exodus 34:28: "he wrote on the tablets the words of the covenant—the Ten Commandments," and Deuteronomy 4:13: "he declared to you his covenant, the Ten Commandments." These "ten words" were distinguished from the rest of the law of God in that they were audibly delivered to Moses by God himself and later written by God on two tables of stone. The laws, however, are not numbered; accordingly, Roman Catholic and Lutheran communions make but one commandment of what the Greek Orthodox and Reformed call the first two. Therefore, to keep the total number to ten, the tenth must be divided into two commandments by Roman Catholics and Lutherans, making the first sentence of the tenth commandment the ninth and the rest the tenth. But this measure presents problems when 20:17 is compared with the repetition of the Ten Commandments in Deuteronomy 5:6–21. In Exodus 20:17 the coveting of a "house" occurs *before* the coveting of a wife; whereas the order is reversed in Deuteronomy 5:21. Thus the content of the ninth commandment is confused. There is also a collocation of the sixth and seventh commandments; for the LXX, Philo, Mark 10:19, and Luke 18:20 place the prohibition on adultery (seventh commandment) *before* that of killing (sixth commandment) (NIV follows the Heb. order). Nevertheless, the LXX of Deuteronomy 5:17–18 and Matthew 19:18 preserve the usual Hebrew order of the text.

The purpose of the law of God was to show (1) man's awful sinfulness in his moral distance from God, (2) man's need for a mediator if he ever was to approach God (which mediatorial work Israel promptly assigned to Moses, but which became the occasion for God to give the promise about "that prophet" who was to come in Deut 18:15–19), and (3) man how to live more abundantly by using the unchangeable perfections of the nature of God as revealed in the moral law as his guide. However, the warning had to be sounded again and again: "By observing the [works of] the law no one will be justified" (Gal 2:16).

The substantive form of the law can be assessed in the following seven points:

1. Although the law has a loving spirit for its opening, and this spirit is not absent in the body of the law, it is mainly stringent and imperative in *form*. One course of action ought to or must be taken, because that course best reflects the character and nature of God.

2. It makes no difference whether the law is stated negatively or positively, for the moral law is always doublesided. It commands and prohibits, for every moral act is at the same time also a refraining from a contrary mode of action that should have been taken.

3. If the mere omitting to do a thing forbidden was all that is commanded, there would be nothing moral in the matter—the command would be fulfilled just by inactivity, which in the moral sphere is but another name for death.

4. When an evil is forbidden in one of the commandments, its opposite good must be understood as being encouraged.

5. When a command is stated, everything contrary is virtually forbidden. For example, Calvin said that "Thou shalt not kill" is not fulfilled merely by abstaining from all injury or wish to inflict injury; it means in addition that we are to aid our neighbor's life by all that is in our power. God forbids us to injure and hurt our brother, for he would have us hold his life to be dear and valuable to us. So when he forbids, he also at the same time demands all avenues of love that can contribute to the life of our neighbor.

6. Our Lord asked, "Which is lawful on the Sabbath: to do good or to do evil, to save life or to destroy it?" (Luke 6:9). We conclude that to reject virtue is to choose vice. In the moral realm mere negatives do have the force of positives.

7. It is easier to state in few words what a believer cannot do. One's freedom to obey God opens up more possibilities than the reverse; hence the law can be stated negatively more succinctly. The negative form also strives to meet the strong current of evil in the human heart.

1–2 God's commandments are simply labeled "all these words" (v.1). The title "Ten Commandments" (*ʿᵃśereṯ haddᵉḇārîm*) comes from Exodus 34:28 and Deuteronomy 4:13, while Hebrews 12:19 speaks of "a voice speaking words." God himself is the speaker and source of these commandments (cf. the emphasis given to this in Deut 5:12–13, 32–33).

The grammatical form of these commandments needs some comment. There are only three positive statements in vv.2–17—all without a finite verb: v.2: "I [am] the LORD your God"; v.8: "Remember [*zāḵôr*] the Sabbath day"; and v.12: "Honor" [*kabbēḏ*, a Piel infinitive absolute by analogy with v.8, though in form it could also be a Piel infinitive construct or a second masculine singular Piel imperative] your father and your mother." John J. Owens ("Law and Love in Deuteronomy," *Review and Expositor* 61 [1964]: 274–83) suggests that these three phrases might divide up vv.2–17 into three sections and govern the other seven commands (notice that Deut 5:6–21 connects commandments 6 to 10 by conjunctions, suggesting that they are governed by the fifth commandment). These phrases might be rendered thus:

1. "I, *being* the LORD your God . . . "
   [Therefore observe commandments one to three]
2. "*Remembering* the Sabbath day . . . "
   [Therefore do vv.9–11]
3. "*Honoring* your father and your mother . . . "
   [Therefore observe commandments six to ten]

The resulting outline would be as follows: (1) Right Relations With God (vv.2–7), (2) Right Relations in the Worship of God (vv.8–11), and (3) Right Relations With Society (vv.12–17).

The lawgiver places his law in the environment of grace, for it was his gracious act of redemption and deliverance from Egypt that revealed his name Yahweh. The "I" (*'ānōḵî*) is both emphatic and the subject; Yahweh is the predicate (so also the LXX and Vul.). Part of this phrase occurred in 15:26 and is repeated here in vv.5, 7, 10, 12, and 23:19. It appears over two hundred times in Deuteronomy but never again in Exodus or Numbers. Indeed, the introduction of Yahweh's name at this point brackets both ends of the Exodus event: In Exodus 3:14 and 6:2, God tied the promise of his deliverance of Israel from Egypt with his name Yahweh. Once that promise became reality, he proclaimed his name once again. All that Yahweh is, says, and does is embodied in this one affirmation: "I am Yahweh." The rest of the statement will become one of the great formulas of Scripture, used 125 times to describe the character and graciousness of Yahweh: "who brought you out of Egypt, out of the land of slavery."

Most scholars point to the similarity between this historical prologue (followed by its stipulations, witnesses, and provisions for succession) and the great suzerain-vassal treaty forms of the ancient Near East. It is especially noteworthy that the second-millennium Hittite suzerain-vassal treaties exhibit the same five parts as the Mosaic Decalogue and the whole Book of Deuteronomy, which conservatives also wish to date in the second millennium, whereas the first-millennium suzerain-vassal treaties of the Assyrians typically left out one or two of these parts.

3 In the first commandment, there is only one difficult expression. It is the phrase *'al-pānāya* ("before/besides me"). Nowhere does this Hebrew phrase mean "except me." Such phrases do exist in Isaiah's vocabulary: "There is no God apart from me [*mibbal'āḏay*] . . . there is none" (*'ayin zûlāṯî*, Isa 45:21) and "none besides me" (*'ên 'ôḏ*, Isa 45:6). But none of these were chosen for use here. The Hebrew preposition *'al* has such a wide use that no one translation can be affirmed to the exclusion of the others. Once in awhile the words carry a hostile undertone (e.g., of Ishmael: "he will live *over against* [NIV, 'in hostility toward'] all his kinsmen," Gen 16:12, pers. tr.; cf. also Gen 25:18; Exod 20:20; Deut 21:16). Thus W.F. Albright (*From Stone Age to Christianity*, 2d ed. [New York: Doubleday, 1957], p. 297, n. 29) translated it, "Thou shalt not prefer other gods to me." The result, however, is the same: "I will not give my glory to another" (Isa 42:8).

4–6 The second commandment discusses the *mode* rather than the *object* of worship (which the first dealt with). It has two parts: the precept (vv.4–5a) and the penalty (vv.5b–6).

The OT is replete with synonyms and words (there are fourteen) for idols and images. Verse 23 explains the proscribed idols as "gods of silver or gods of gold." It also includes images carved from stone or wood and later those made from metal. Since *pesel* ("idol," v.4) refers to statuary, the word *t^emûnāh* ("resemblance" or "form") applies to real or imagined pictorial representations (see Notes). None of these are to be made *with the intention to worship them*. This word was not meant to stifle artistic talent but only to avoid *improper* substitutes that, like the idols of Canaan, would steal hearts away from the true worship of God. One need only to consider the tabernacle with its ornate appointments—all under divine instruction—to see that making representations is not absolutely forbidden.

"You shall not bow down to them or worship them" (v.5) is a figure of speech called hendiadys, where two expressions are used to convey a single idea, viz., "to offer religious worship." This expression is only used with respect to giving worship to foreign deities forbidden to Israel (see Stamm and Andrew, p. 86).

The sanctions attached to this command begin with the majestic reminder that "I, the LORD [Yahweh] your God, am a jealous God." The term "jealous" or "zealous" God must not be understood in such popular misconceptions as God is naturally suspicious, distrustful, or wrongly envious of the success of others. When used of God it denotes (1) that attribute that demands exclusive devotion (Exod 34:14; Deut 4:24; 5:9; 6:15), (2) that attitude of anger directed against all who oppose him (Num 25:11; Deut 29:20; Ps 79:5; Ezek 5:13; 16:38, 42; 25:11; Zeph 1:18), and (3) that energy he expended on vindicating his people (2 Kings 19:31; Isa 9:7; 37:32; Joel 2:18; Zech 1:14; 8:2). Thus all idolatry, which Scripture labels elsewhere as spiritual adultery, that raises up competitors or brooks any kind of rivalry to the honor, glory, and esteem due to the Lord will excite his zealousness for the consistency of his own character and being. Every form of substitution, neglect, or contempt, both public and private, for the worship of God is rejected in this commandment.

Children who repeat the sins of their fathers evidence it in personally hating God; hence they too are punished like their fathers. Moses made it plain in Deuteronomy 24:16: "Fathers shall not be put to death for their children, nor children put to death for their fathers; each is to die for his own sin." The effects of disobedience last for some time, but the effects of loving God are far more extensive: "to a thousand [generations]" (v.6).

7 The third commandment deals, not with internal worship (first commandment) or external worship (second word), but with the profession of the mouth in true adoration of God.

The "name" (*šēm*) of God stands for so much more than the mere pronouncing of his title of address. It includes (1) his nature, being, and very person (Ps 20:1; Luke 24:47; John 1:12; cf. Rev 3:4 [Gk.]), (2) his teaching or doctrine (Ps 22:22; John 17:6, 26), and (3) his moral and ethical teaching (Mic 4:5) (see W.C. Kaiser, Jr., "Name," ZPEB, 4:360–66).

To "take up" (*niśśā'*) the name of the Lord on one's lips "in vain" (*laššāw'*) meant to "misuse" it, i.e., to use it for no purpose (note Jeremiah's adverbial use of this phrase where it precedes the verb: Jer 2:30; 4:30; 6:29; 18:15; 46:11—a usage pointed out by Childs, *Exodus*, p. 411). Some vain uses of God's name on the lips of his people (1) express mild surprise, (2) fill in the gaps in speeches or prayers, and (3) confirm something that is false. If God's name is used lightly, how shall the righteous survive in times of distress (Prov 18:10)? Notice that this commandment does not exclude legitimate oaths, for they appear frequently (e.g., Deut 6:13; Ps 63:11; Isa 45:23; Jer 4:2; 12:16; Rom 1:9; 9:1; 1 Cor 15:31; Phil 1:8; Rev 10:5–6).

8–11 The fourth commandment invokes the remembrance of the Sabbath. The term "Sabbath" is derived from the Hebrew verb "to rest or cease from work." While many have tried to derive the Sabbath from the Babylonian *šapattu/šabattu* (where the first, seventh, fifteenth, and twenty-eighth days were regarded as days of special sacrifice), it has not resulted in any certainty. But the Hebrews were to set aside each seventh day as belonging to the Lord their God.

The command to remember the Sabbath is *moral* insofar as it requires of a person a due portion of his or her time dedicated to the worship and service of God, but it is *ceremonial* in that it prescribes the seventh day. The Christian church is required to observe the morality of *time* by setting aside one day in seven to the LORD, but it has chosen to change that *ceremonialization* of that day from the seventh to the first (cf. the early church's use of "the Lord's Day," i.e., a day belonging to the Lord [Rev 1:10] or "On the first day of every week" [1 Cor 16:2]). The sanctity of the first day in honor of God's new deliverance, which the Lord Jesus accomplished in his death and finally in his resurrection, was already signaled in the symbolism of the feasts in Leviticus 23—"the day after the Sabbath" (v.15); "on the first day hold a sacred assembly" (v.7); "the first day is a sacred assembly . . . on the eighth" (vv.35–36). Indeed, these were the very feasts that pointed forward to the very same events that Christians now celebrate on Sunday!

The reason for memorializing this day rested on two works of God: one retrospective (v.11 links it with the Creation), which pointed to the new Rest of God in the end times; the other prospective in the plan of redemptive history (Deut 5:15 links it with the Exodus from Egypt), which pointed to a new Exodus in the final day. This interpretation is borne out by the fact that the Sabbath was another "sign" of the covenant (see comment on 31:12–17). As Childs points out (*Exodus*, p. 417), in neither case did Israel's memory of either the Creation or the Exodus act as the motivation for observing the Sabbath. Rather, it was the reverse: Israel observed the Sabbath to remember God's work of Creation and the Exodus.

12 The fifth commandment, to "honor" one's parents, involves (1) prizing them highly (cf. Prov 4:8; i.e., wisdom, when sought above everything else and prized more highly than all else, will bring honor to its seekers); (2) caring, showing affection for them (Ps 91:15; i.e., God's honoring of individuals is shown by his care for them in being with them and delivering them from trouble); and (3) showing respect, fear, or revering them (Lev 19:3). When Ephesians 6:1 says, "Obey your parents," it immediately and necessarily qualifies it with "in the Lord." Parents are to be shown honor (v.2), but nowhere is their word to rival or be a substitute for God's Word.

The promise in Ephesians 6:2–3 attached to this commandment to revere one's parents is unique even though there is a sense in which the promise of life stands over all the commandments (Deut 4:1; 8:1; 16:20; 30:15–16). The promise of a long life in the land refers primarily to the land of Canaan and the people of Israel. The national character of this language can be confirmed by referring to Deuteronomy 4:26, 33, 40; 32:46–47. The captivity of Israel would be caused, in part, by a failure to honor their parents (Ezek 22:7, 15). This commandment possesses what we might call a ceremonial or a national promise, but it does have present-day individual application in the same way that all the commandments were meant to give a new quality of life (without creating a merit system to gain eternal life).

13 The sixth commandment forbids murder. The ethical theology that lies behind this prohibition is the fact that all men and women have been created in the image of God (Gen 1:26–27; 9:6). While Hebrew possesses seven words for killing, the word used here—*rāṣaḥ*—appears only forty-seven times in the OT. If any one of the seven words could signify "murder," where the factors of premeditation and intentionality are present, this is the verb. Recently, however, some have complained (see Childs, *Exodus*, p. 420, for the bibliography and argument) that many of the instances of this verb relate to blood vengeance and the role of the avenger (*gô'ēl* in Num 35; Deut 4:41–43; 19:1–13; Josh 20:3). Without exception, however, in the later periods (e.g., Ps 94:6; Prov 22:13; Isa 1:21; Hos 4:2; 6:9; Jer 7:9) it carries the idea of murder with intentional violence. Every one of these instances stresses the act or allegation of premeditation and deliberateness—and that is at the heart of this verb. Thus this prohibition does not apply to beasts (Gen 9:3), to defending one's home from nighttime burglars (Exod 22:2), to accidental killings (Deut 19:5), to the execution of murderers by the state (Gen 9:6), or to involvement with one's nation in certain types of war as illustrated by Israel's history. It does apply, however, to self-murder (i.e., suicide), to all accessories to murder (2 Sam 12:9), and to those who have authority but fail to use it to punish known murderers (1 Kings 21:19).

14 The seventh commandment forbids adultery. The verb "to commit adultery" (*nā'ap̱*) can be used of either men or women. Since the punishment for adultery is death (Deut 22:22) while the penalty for the seduction of a virgin is an offer of marriage or money (Exod 22:16–17; Deut 22:23–29), adultery is distinguished from fornication in the OT.

The sin of adultery is not just a question of violating another person's property; it is also a moral question (see Gen 20:9, Abimelech's narrow escape from "such great guilt" [lit., "sin"], and Gen 39:9, a "sin against God" as well as against Potiphar). Otto Procksch observed (cited in Stamm and Andrew, p. 100) that a "man can commit adultery against a marriage other than his own, the woman only against her own." One of the best allegories on marital fidelity is found in Proverbs 5:15–21.

15 The eighth commandment prohibits stealing (*gānaḇ*) from either a person or an object. Albrecht Alt (in Childs, *Exodus*, p. 423) thought this command originally was alone directed solely against kidnapping and that it had been previously tied into the tenth commandment. But his distinctions cannot be sustained. This commandment recognizes that the Lord owns everything in heaven and earth (as Pss 24:1; 115:16 also claim), and only he can give it or take it away. Therefore no man must despotically enslave or kidnap his fellow man or usurp the rights to property he has not owned or been given.

16 The ninth commandment calls for sanctity of truth in all areas of life, even though the vocabulary primarily reflects the legal process in Israel (*'ēḏ šāqer* here or *'ēḏ šāw'* in Deut 5:18, and *'ānāh*, "to answer" or "give" in response to legal questions posed at a trial). To despise the truth was to despise God whose very being and character are truth. Certainly the reference to "lying" (*kaḥēš*) in Hosea 4:2 demonstrates that this commandment had a broad application.

17 The tenth commandment disallows covetousness. The general idea of the root *ḥāmaḏ* is "to desire earnestly," "to long after," or "to covet." In the parallel passage in Deuteronomy 5:21, it is paralleled by *tiṯ'awweh* ("to set one's desire" on something).

This commandment deals with man's inner heart and shows that none of the previous nine commandments could be observed merely from an external or formal act. Every inner instinct that led up to the act itself was also included. The point is as Paul later told Timothy, "Godliness with contentment is great gain" (1 Tim 6:6). Jesus also commented, "For out of the heart come evil thoughts, murder, adultery, sexual immorality, theft, false testimony, slander" (Matt 15:19). See also Romans 7:7–8 for the importance of the tenth commandment in the apostle Paul's grappling with identifying sin by means of the law.

Notes

4 The LXX translates תְּמוּנָה (*temûnāh*, "form") seven times by *homoiōma* ("likeness"), twice by *doxa* ("glory"), and only once by *morphē* ("form"). The point is that it does not refer to its shape but only to an imagined resemblance. The word is theologically sensitive when used in Num 12:8: "the *form* of the LORD."

בַּמַּיִם מִתַּחַת לָאָרֶץ (*bammayim mittaḥat lā'āreṣ*, "waters below") is literally "in the waters under the earth." Some have pressed this expression and others in a wooden manner to derive an alleged three-tier or triple-decker universe: (1) heavens above, (2) earth beneath, (3) waters under the earth. But the whole picture is of Western fabrication. Simply put, this is the Hebrew idiom for the shoreline. Deuteronomy 4:18 places the fish in these "waters under the earth." If they are believed to be in the netherworld, then the fishermen will need very good sinkers to retrieve these fish!

5 What is the antecedent for these plural suffixes in v.5? It cannot refer to *pesel* ("idol") or *temûnāh* ("form"), since they both are singular—unless both words may be taken *ad sensum* as plural idols. Zimmerli (quoted by Childs, *Exodus*, p. 405) says that these plural suffixes must refer to "other gods" in v.3. If this is so, then some linking of these commandments, such as we have argued for in the introduction to this section, is necessary.

6 Actually חֶסֶד (*ḥesed*), which is rendered "love" here, is one of the best words in the OT for the grace of God. It appears over 250 times. A most recent discussion of *ḥesed* is by Katharine D. Sakenfield, *The Meaning of Ḥesed in the Hebrew Bible*, Harvard Semitic Monographs 17 (Missoula, Mont.: Scholars, 1978).

D. *The Reaction of the People to the Theophany*

20:18–21

18 When the people saw the thunder and lightning and heard the trumpet and saw the mountain in smoke, they trembled with fear. They stayed at a distance 19 and said to Moses, "Speak to us yourself and we will listen. But do not have God speak to us or we will die."

20 Moses said to the people, "Do not be afraid. God has come to test you, so that the fear of God will be with you to keep you from sinning."

21 The people remained at a distance, while Moses approached the thick darkness where God was.

18 The awe-inspiring phenomena that heralded the theophany (= appearance of God) terrified the people. What had been depicted in 19:16–19 is here restated anew from the perspective of the people's reactions (see Notes on the Hebrew order of the subject and predicate) to this same phenomena. Deuteronomy 5:23 explains why the "mountain [was] in smoke"; it was "ablaze with fire."

19 The laity suddenly had no desire to approach God's holy presence (cf. Heb 12:19). They instinctively sensed their need for a mediating priesthood or representative person who would dare to approach God on their behalf. Out of this realized need, one of the greatest revelations in the long line of OT promises of the Messiah came. He would be a "prophet" like Moses who would speak God's word to them (notice the identical setting for Deut 18:15–22; cf. also Deut 5:24–25). As a result of this arrangement, the people "stayed at a distance," and Moses delivered God's word to them.

20–21 "Do not be afraid," Moses told the people (v.20; cf 14:13); for God had not come to kill Israel (cf. Deut 5:24–25) but to test (*nāsāh*) her. This verse contrasts two types of "fear": tormenting fear (which comes from conscious guilt or unwarranted alarm and leads to bondage) or salutary fear (which promotes and demonstrates the presence of an attitude of complete trust and belief in God; cf. the "fear of the LORD God" beginning in Gen 22:12). This second type of fear will keep us from sinning and is at the heart of the OT's wisdom books (cf. Prov 1:7; Eccl 12:13 et al.).

Israel's newly appointed mediator "drew near" or "approached" (*niggaš*) the thick darkness where God was and received the directives contained in the book of the covenant (v.21).

Notes

18 Normally in Hebrew the predicate appears first in the sentence, but the subject—e.g., וְכָל־הָעָם (*wekol-hā'ām*, "when the people")—precedes the verb to express antithesis to the subject of the preceding clause (cf. 9:20–21; 19:3, 18; 20:21) or in consecutive narrative to show that an action so described took place simultaneously with, not subsequently to, the events described above (Cassuto, p. 252).

רֹאִים (*rō'îm*, "saw") means to see with all the senses, like our word "perceiving." It is also an example of the figure of speech called zeugma, for the verb "heard" (v.18) must be inserted by the translators since the one verb "saw" yokes together two objects: one that exactly suits it and the other that does not.

The root *nû'* of וַיָּנֻעוּ (*wayyānu'û*, "they trembled with fear") conveys the ideas of being physically swayed and experiencing great mental agitation and trembling emotionally.

E. *The Book of the Covenant (20:22–23:33)*

The title for this section, "Book of the Covenant," derives from 24:7. The laws may be arranged into two basic types following Albrecht Alt's analysis (*Essays on Old Testament History and Religion* [Oxford: University Press, 1966], pp. 81–132). The conditional form, where the main condition is introduced by "if" or "when" (*kî*) and additional subheadings are introduced by "if" (*'im*), is called the casuistic or case law (i.e., laws based on actual precedents usually beginning with "if a person . . ." or "when a person . . .") formulations. The second type takes a categorical, unconditional form and is in the second person (most frequently the singular), often with a negative command or prohibition. This is the form used for most of the Ten Commandments and called the apodictic (i.e., expressing what is always true) formulation.

Some scholars would isolate a third group of laws from within the category that Alt labeled apodictic. These laws are located in 21:12, 15–17; 22:19–20. They usually are very brief (around five short words), carry the death penalty, and all begin with a Hebrew participle. They are called the "Hebrew participial laws," but actually they are unconditional and apodictic in function. We may speak, then, of three basic types of law in the covenant code.

Every indication, from similar law codes discovered in the ancient Near East, is that the Book of the Covenant is very early. Thus there is no reason for doubting their Mosaic environment and claim. Yet they also markedly differ from these other collections of laws in that they include apodictic laws combined with motive clauses.

The most comprehensive commentary on the covenant code by S.M. Paul ("Studies in the Book of the Covenant in Light of Cuneiform and Biblical Law," VetTest Suppl. 18 [1970]: 101–2) dates these laws to the time just before the settlement of the tribes in Canaan and refuses, to the consternation of scholars who value the results of modern literary criticism, to accept that the casuistic laws were taken over directly from the Canaanites. We agree with him on both accounts. The most complete discussion of the modern relevance of these laws can be found in James B. Jordan's *The Law of the Covenant: An Exposition of Exodus 21–23.*

1. *The prologue*

20:22–26

22 Then the LORD said to Moses, "Tell the Israelites this: 'You have seen for yourselves that I have spoken to you from heaven: 23 Do not make any gods to be alongside me; do not make for yourselves gods of silver or gods of gold.

24 " 'Make an altar of earth for me and sacrifice on it your burnt offerings and fellowship offerings, your sheep and goats and your cattle. Wherever I cause my name to be honored, I will come to you and bless you. 25 If you make an altar of stones for me, do not build it with dressed stones, for you will defile it if you use a tool on it. 26 And do not go up to my altar on steps, lest your nakedness be exposed on it.'

22–23 A fuller account of these verses appears in Deuteronomy 4:14–16. The connection, then, is this: since all of you witnessed the Lord's speaking from heaven even though you saw no visible shape, form, or representation (v.22); therefore, totally abandon any thought of ever trying to embody me in a material image (v.23). First and foremost, then, the worship of God must be without idols (see the second commandment, 20:4–6).

24–26 This passage has played a major role in critical scholarship. The claim has been that the Deuteronomic legislation, requiring one central sanctuary (e.g., Deut 12:5, 11, 14, 18, 21), is a clear advance over this Sinaitic legislation that allows sacrifices at numerous places that the Divine Presence has sanctified. This view cannot be endorsed for many reasons. Just to state one: Deuteronomy 27:1–8 enjoins Israel to build an altar on Mount Ebal (not in Jerusalem!), in the very words of Exodus 20:24, which Deuteronomy was supposed to have revoked (see Kaiser, *Old Testament Theology,* pp. 131–33).

These modest earthen altars were temporary in form and after awhile occasional in usage (see the patriarchs' altars in Gen 12:7; 13:18; 22:9). Stone altars were not to be hewn with a "tool" (*ḥereḇ,* usually translated elsewhere as "sword"), possibly so that no one could turn it into an image or some other fetish. Likewise, steps were not to be built up to the altars. The reason is that the long garment would trail behind the worshiper on the steps as he descended and thus possibly expose his nakedness. Later on, when altars with steps were allowed to be built (Lev 9:22; Ezek 43:13–17), the priests were instructed to wear linen undershorts (28:40–42; Ezek 44:18).

Notes

---

23 Since the sequence תַּעֲשׂוּן אִתִּי (*ta'ªśûn 'ittî,* "make . . . to be alongside me") usually demands an object, NIV has supplied "any gods." Most translations disregard the MT accentuation and place "gods of silver" with the first half of the sentence. Neither solution is totally satisfactory. The NIV faces the problem that the verb *'āśāh* means "to make" and not "to place."

24 In אַזְכִּיר אֶת־שְׁמִי (*'azkîr 'et̲-šᵉmî,* "I cause my name to be honored"), the Hiphil of *zkr* may reflect a denominative usage: "to proclaim [the name]" (Childs, *Exodus*, p. 447). On the "Name," see the comment on 3:13.

---

2. *Laws on slaves*

21:1–11

[1]"These are the laws you are to set before them:
[2]"If you buy a Hebrew servant, he is to serve you for six years. But in
the seventh year, he shall go free, without paying anything. [3]If he comes
alone, he is to go free alone; but if he has a wife when he comes, she is
to go with him. [4]If his master gives him a wife and she bears him sons or
daughters, the woman and her children shall belong to her master, and
only the man shall go free.
[5]"But if the servant declares, 'I love my master and my wife and
children and do not want to go free,' [6]then his master must take him
before the judges. He shall take him to the door or the doorpost and
pierce his ear with an awl. Then he will be his servant for life.
[7]"If a man sells his daughter as a servant, she is not to go free as
menservants do. [8]If she does not please the master who has selected
her for himself, he must let her be redeemed. He has no right to sell her
to foreigners, because he has broken faith with her. [9]If he selects her for
his son, he must grant her the rights of a daughter. [10]If he marries
another woman, he must not deprive the first one of her food, clothing
and marital rights. [11]If he does not provide her with these three things,
she is to go free, without any payment of money.

1 It is strange that the title (for v.1 appears to be such) comes after the section on the altar law (20:22–26). Even so it is not certain that this title was intended to describe the rest of the covenant code, up to 23:19. Since 22:18–23:19 consists mainly of moral and sapiential exhortations along with the ritual calendar in an appendixlike fashion, it is best to regard the title as referring to 21:2–22:17. These "laws," or, better, "judgments" (*mišpāṭîm*), are given as precedents to guide Israel's civil magistrates in cases of civil dispute. While these "judgments" deal mainly with temporal matters, they nevertheless are based on one or another express commandment in the Decalogue. It is most appropriate, therefore, that these judicial and political regulations, given by God to Moses when "Moses approached the thick darkness where God was" (20:21), should be set alongside the Decalogue. The two belong together in time as well as in interpretation.

2–4 Laws on the Hebrew slave are mentioned only in 21:1–11; Leviticus 25:39–43; Deuteronomy 15:12–18; and Jeremiah 34:8–22. But there are differences in these laws. In Deuteronomy 15:12 the Hebrew slave, male or female, is sold, while in Leviticus 25:39 he sells himself, and the servitude is determined by the year of Jubilee. In Exodus 21:2 and Deuteronomy 15:12, the servitude is for six years (Hammurabi Law Code 117 limits bondage to three years). In Exodus 21:6 and Deuteronomy 15:17 it is for life when the slave desires it. Whether "Hebrew" (*'iḇrî*, v.2) is equivalent to the ethnic name or has the more general sociological meaning of "outlaw" or member of a particular class of the population, *ḫabiru* is still a matter of scholarly debate (see Notes). Certainly in 2:11 (and in some thirty other occurrences in the Pentateuch) the word *'iḇrî* is regarded as an ethnic name ("he saw an Egyptian beating a Hebrew, one of his own people"), even though there may be a certain scornful connotation about it (cf. later usage, 1 Sam 14:11; 29:3; Jonah 1:9). The word "buy" (*tiqneh*) in judicial terms means to acquire as one's own property (see Paul, "Book of the Covenant," p. 46, n. 7).

After six years of service, the slave is to go out "free" (*ḥāp̱šî*). As early as 1926, J. Pedersen ("Note on Hebrew *ḥofši*," *Journal of the Palestinian Oriental Society* 6 [1926]: 103–5) saw a connection between the Hebrew *ḥāp̱šî* and the social class *ḫupšu* found in Rib-Addi correspondence from Byblos (see I. Mendelsohn, "New Light on the *Ḫupšu*," BASOR 139 [1955]: 9–11). The term seems to mean a "freeman" in the sense that he was a citizen once again after the emancipation.

The terms for coming (*bô'*) and going (*yāṣā'*) (v.3), or entering and leaving slave status, are similar to those used in the Akkadian Nuzi texts. A slave left his master either single or married depending on what he was when he entered. Where a wife had been given to a slave, that wife and any children that resulted from that union belonged to the master. An exact parallel to v.4 exists at Nuzi (Paul, "Book of the Covenant," p. 48, n. 5).

5–6 "I love my master . . . wife and children" (v.5) has legal rather than romantic overtones (cf. the juridical aspect of its antonym in Deut 21:15–17: "does not love," i.e., "hates"). The "judges" (see Notes on v.6) changed the slave's status from temporary to permanent by a ceremony at the doorpost of the master's house. The perforation of the ear (v.6) is used as humiliating punishment in the Middle Assyrian Laws (A 40:84–86, 101–3; 44:45). Some also believe Psalm 40:6 alludes to this law.

7–11 This pericope pertains to a girl who is sold by her father, not for slavery, but for marriage. Nonetheless, she is designated a "servant" (*'āmāh*, v.7). Should the terms of marriage not be fulfilled, it is to be considered a breach of contract, and the purchaser must allow the girl to be redeemed; she must not be sold outside that family (v.8). Always she must be treated as a daughter or a free-born woman, or the forfeiture clause will be invoked. On the issue of slavery and the Christian, see Kaiser, *Old Testament Ethics*, pp. 288–90, and Willard M. Swartley, *Slavery, Sabbath, War and Women* (Scottdale, Pa.: Herald, 1983), pp. 31–64.

Notes

2 On the question of עִבְרִי (*'ibrî*, "Hebrew") or, according to some, *ḫāpiru*, see Greenberg, *The Hab/piru*; and M.P. Gray, "The *Ḫabirū*-Hebrew Problem," HUCA 29 (1958): 135–202. It is difficult, on the basis of our present knowledge, to determine whether *'ibrî* is (1) a gentilic (Greenberg), (2) a fellow Israelite (Hyatt, p. 228), or (3) an appellative denoting a member of a class (mercenaries) of the population (Cassuto, pp. 265–66; Gray, "*Ḫabirū*-Hebrew Problem," pp. 173–74).

Besides the articles by Pedersen and Mendelsohn cited in the commentary, see N.P. Lemche, "The Hebrew Slave," VetTest 25 (1975): 139–42. He translates לַחָפְשִׁי (*laḥāpši*, "free") as "a dependent on a city-state or on a citizen of the same" (p. 144). In n. 63 he conjectures that *ḥpšu* may be a West Semitic word for the Akkadian *muškēnum*, who also were a client class.

3–4 The etymology of בְּגַפּוֹ (*beḡappô*, "alone") is unclear, but in context it is taken to mean "single, by himself."

6 On הָאֱלֹהִים (*hā'elōhîm*, "the judges"), see Cyrus H. Gordon, "אלהים in Its Reputed Meaning of Rulers, Judges," JBL 54 (1935): 134–44, and A.E. Draffkorn, "Ilāni/Elohim," JBL 76 (1957): 216–24. The background for the Hebrew use of this word to mean "judges" reflects the quasi-juridical function of the *ilāni* ("house gods") at Nuzi. A person would have been required in societies like Nuzi to swear before the house gods, the idols who were protectors of the family estate. The expression thus became a stereotype or stock formulation to signify the court of justice or those before whom witnesses appeared in that court. See the objections to this view in J.R. Vannoy, "The Use of the Word *hā'elōhîm* in Exodus 21:6 and 22:7, 8," in *The Law and the Prophets*, edited by J.H. Skilton (Nutley, N.J.: Presbyterian and Reformed, 1974), pp. 225–41. F. Charles Fensham ("New Light on Exodus 21:7 and 22:7 From the Laws of Eshnunna," JBL 78 [1959]: 160–61) and Vannoy unconvincingly argued that *hā'elōhîm* referred to Yahweh, God of Israel, and a ceremony performed at the door of the sanctuary.

9 כְּמִשְׁפַּט הַבָּנוֹת (*kemišpaṭ habbānôṯ*, "the rights of a daughter") is literally "according to the manner of daughters." Paul ("Book of the Covenant," p. 55, n. 3) finds a similar provision in a Nuzi law on slavery: "She shall treat her as a daughter of Arraphar" (*ša ki mārat Arrábhi ipušašši*), "she shall not return her to [the status of] a slave girl"; and in an Assyrian document Paul found: "(the adopting father) must treat her as his own daughter, an Assyrian" (*ki mārtišuma Aššurayae úpaussi*).

10 The meaning of this third element owed the first wife—עֹנָתָהּ (*'ōnāṯāh*, "her marital rights")—is uncertain. Paul ("Book of the Covenant," pp. 56–61) suggests that the *hapax legomenon* should be translated "oil" or "ointments," since many Sumerian and Akkadian texts list the three items of "food, clothing, and oil" as the basic necessities of life. (See also S.M. Paul, "Exodus 21:10; A Threefold Maintenance Clause," JNES 28 [1969]: 48–53.) Cassuto (p. 269) disputes the later traditional rendering of "times of cohabitation" (see the Gk. *tēn homilian autēs*, "her cohabitation") and conjectured instead "the conditions of her abode." Notice, on the other hand, the apostle Paul's use in 1 Cor 7:3 of *opheilēn* ("marital duty," i.e., the obligation or one's due of conjugal duties).

---

3. Laws on homicide

21:12–17

¹²"Anyone who strikes a man and kills him shall surely be put to death. ¹³However, if he does not do it intentionally, but God lets it happen, he is to flee to a place I will designate. ¹⁴But if a man schemes

and kills another man deliberately, take him away from my altar and put him to death.

15 "Anyone who attacks his father or his mother must be put to death.

16 "Anyone who kidnaps another and either sells him or still has him when he is caught must be put to death.

17 "Anyone who curses his father or mother must be put to death.

12–14 This is a list of offenses that demand the death penalty: murder, striking one's parents, kidnapping, or cursing one's parents. Homicide contravenes the divine order established in Genesis 9:6. Since men and women are made in the image of God, no money or property settlement can atone for the sinful and premeditated destruction of people and the image of God in them. Accidental death is distinguished from intentional murder in vv.13–14, which was an act of God (see Notes). Additional expressions of unintentionality are found in Numbers 35:22–23: "unintentionally" (*beelō' ṣediyyāh,* lit., "without design"); "without seeing" (*belō' re'ôṯ,* "inadvertently"); "[since he was] not his enemy" (*lō'-'ôyēḇ*); and in Deuteronomy 19:4–5: "unintentionally" (*biḇlî-ḏa'aṯ,* "without knowledge").

In the case of accidental death, a place of asylum was to be provided (later there were cities of refuge: Num 35:6–34; Deut 19:1–13). But no sanctuary—even at the altar itself (cf. 1 Kings 1:51; 2:28)—was to be given to the deliberate murderer. Notice the unusual first-person references to God: "I will designate" (v.13) and "my altar" (v.14). According to Paul ("Book of the Covenant," p. 64), these are the only examples of direct address in the biblical corpus of law except for 21:1–2.

15–17 Parental authority is so highly valued in biblical law that striking and cursing parents was a criminal and capital offense. Verses 15 and 17 are illustrations of the fifth commandment. Notice that the father and mother are mentioned together, thereby stressing their basic equality.

Kidnapping (v.16) is not a property offense since no property offense draws a capital punishment, and this law is not listed under property laws. Instead, it is the theft of a human being (cf. Code of Hammurabi 14).

Notes

13 וְהָאֱלֹהִים אִנָּה לְיָדוֹ (*wehā'elōhîm 'innāh leyāḏô,* "but God lets it happen") is an event beyond human control ("an act of God"). Similar expressions of acts of providence occur in the Hammurabi Law Code 249:38–39; 266:77.

4. *Laws on bodily injuries*

21:18–32

18 "If men quarrel and one hits the other with a stone or with his fist and he does not die but is confined to bed, 19 the one who struck the blow will not be held responsible if the other gets up and walks around outside with his staff; however, he must pay the injured man for the loss of his time and see that he is completely healed.

[20]"If a man beats his male or female slave with a rod and the slave dies as a direct result, he must be punished, [21]but he is not to be punished if the slave gets up after a day or two, since the slave is his property.

[22]"If men who are fighting hit a pregnant woman and she gives birth prematurely but there is no serious injury, the offender must be fined whatever the woman's husband demands and the court allows. [23]But if there is serious injury, you are to take life for life, [24]eye for eye, tooth for tooth, hand for hand, foot for foot, [25]burn for burn, wound for wound, bruise for bruise.

[26]"If a man hits a manservant or maidservant in the eye and destroys it, he must let the servant go free to compensate for the eye. [27]And if he knocks out the tooth of a manservant or maidservant, he must let the servant go free to compensate for the tooth.

[28]"If a bull gores a man or a woman to death, the bull must be stoned to death, and its meat must not be eaten. But the owner of the bull will not be held responsible. [29]If, however, the bull has had the habit of goring and the owner has been warned but has not kept it penned up and it kills a man or woman, the bull must be stoned and the owner also must be put to death. [30]However, if payment is demanded of him, he may redeem his life by paying whatever is demanded. [31]This law also applies if the bull gores a son or daughter. [32]If the bull gores a male or female slave, the owner must pay thirty shekels of silver to the master of the slave, and the bull must be stoned.

Following five cases that could involve the death penalty, we have five cases involving assault and bodily injury.

18–19 In the first example, a dispute between two men resulted in one being injured to the extent that he was bedridden and then recovered sufficiently to be able to walk outdoors with the help of a cane or crutches. This injury will not carry the talionic punishment (cf. vv.23–25), but the assailant must indemnify the injured for his "loss of time" (*šiḇtô*, lit., "his sitting" or "his cessation"), loss of income, and all medical expenses. The Code of Hammurabi (206) requires the same action: he must pay the cost of the physician if he swears, "I did not strike him deliberately," i.e., with premeditated malice. The Hittite Laws (10) also prescribe that the assailant is to care for the injured man until he recovers and then pay him six (later edition, "ten") shekels of silver as well as pay for the physician's fee.

20–21 The second case involved a master striking his slave, male or female. Since the slave did not die immediately as a result of this act of using the rod (not a lethal weapon, however) but tarried for "a day or two" (v.21), the master was given the benefit of the doubt; he was judged to have struck the slave with disciplinary and not homicidal intentions. This law is unprecedented in the ancient world where a master could treat his slave as he pleased. When this law is considered alongside the law in vv.26–27, which acted to control brutality against slaves at the point where it hurt the master, viz., his pocketbook (see Notes), a whole new statement of the value and worth of the personhood of the slave is introduced. Thus if the master struck a slave severely enough only to injure one of his members, he lost his total investment immediately in that the slave won total freedom; or if he struck severely enough to kill the slave immediately, he was tried for capital punishment (vv.18–19). The aim of this law was not to place the slave at the master's mercy but to restrict the master's power over him (cf. similar laws in the Code of Hammurabi 196–97, 200).

22–25 The third situation describes men who are fighting, and one of them somehow unintentionally strikes a pregnant woman (perhaps a concerned wife who tried to intervene on her husband's behalf) so that her labor was immediately induced. This law envisions two alternatives: (1) "she gives birth prematurely [*w^{e}yāṣ^e'û y^{e}lāḏeyhā*, lit., "her children came out"; notice the use of the plural to reflect how many and either sex] but there is no serious injury," and (2) "if there is serious injury."

This law may not be classified with the numerous cases of miscarriage in such law codes as Sumerian Laws 1–2; Lipit Ishtar (?) Laws iii, 2'–13'; Hammurabi Laws 209–14; Middle Assyrian Laws A 21, 50–52; and Hittite Law Code 17–18. Rather, it is written principally as an assault case where no real damage (see Notes) came to either the mother's or the baby's life. If this were not so, this case would have appeared in the homicide laws (vv.12–17).

For the accidental assault, the offender must still pay some compensation, even though both mother and child survived (as in vv.18–19). The fee would be set by the woman's husband and approved by a decision of the court. Should the pregnant woman or her child die, the principle of *talio* is invoked, demanding "life for life" (v.23). But why should this principle be invoked if it were an accidental fatality when v.13 exempted such a person from the death penalty? The answer is found in two facts: (1) the *talion* principle (vv.23–25) is a stereotype formula that states simply that the punishment must match, but not exceed, the damage done; and (2) Numbers 35:31 permits a substitute to ransom all capital offenses in the OT except in the one case of willful and premeditated murder. Thus we conclude that the defendant must surrender to the deceased child's father or wife's husband the monetary value of each life (note v.30) if either or both were harmed. The *lex talionis* of vv.23b–25 does impose a strict limit on the amount of damages anyone could collect; in modern terms it would read: car bumper for car bumper and car fender for car fender. No one was to try to get rich quick off such situations. Notice also that this was to be a rule of thumb for the judges, not an authorization of personal vendetta or private retaliation (cf. Lev 24:19–20; Deut 19:21).

26–27 Any slave who suffered a permanent injury from his owner won his freedom immediately (cf. vv.20–21, however, for authorized discipline by the master). Thus a slave was not to be treated with caprice as if he were mere chattel. The economic sanctions against the owner were designed so that the owner would be given plenty of reason to resist any abusive tactics for the sake of his financial investment even if he totally disregarded the slave's dignity and worth as a human being.

28–32 A fifth example of bodily injury involved goring oxen. Men were responsible for the injuries their oxen caused to other people. These laws are closely paralleled by the Code of Hammurabi (250–52) and the Eshnunna Law Code (54–55). The biblical version of these laws, which obviously sprang from the same culture, times, and background, was very different from Hammurabi's or Eshnunna's versions in that the Bible's concern was not economic but moral and religious. The ox, in the case of v.28, and the ox and his owner, in the case of vv.29–30, were guilty of taking another person's life. Notice that Genesis 9:5–6 requires that the life of a beast that killed a man as well as that of a manslayer be taken, because man is made in the image of God. It made no difference what the age, social status, or gender of the person was (vv.31–32); boys and girls, men and women, male and female slaves are all created in the image of God.

Notes

21 כִּי כַסְפּוֹ הוּא (*kî kaspô hû'*, "since [the slave] is his property") is literally "because he is his money." The point is not that men are mere chattel (which the NIV rendering tends to suggest) but that the owner has an investment in this slave that he stands to lose either by death (not to mention capital punishment as well) or by emancipation (vv.27–28).

22–23 אָסוֹן (*'āsôn*, "serious injury") also means "mischief" or "harm" (cf. Gen 42:4, 38; 44:29). Paul ("Book of the Covenant," p. 72, n. 3) quotes the statement on Gen 42:38 in the *Mechilta:* "אסון here means only death."

22 Paul ("Book of the Covenant," p. 72) translates בִּפְלִלִים (*bip̱lilîm*, "the court [allows]") as "the payment to be based on reckoning" with the reckoning to be the estimated age of the embryo. The root *pll* means "to estimate, assess, calculate" according to Ephraim Speiser ("The Stem PLL in Hebrew," JBL 82 [1963]: 301–6, esp. p. 303). The LXX must have taken a similar tact when it distinguished in these verses between a fetus not fully formed (*exeikonismenon*) and one that is. Cazelles (cited in Speiser, ibid.) refers *bip̱lilîm* to a third party who arbitrates a settlement. We believe this is closer to the idea of "assessment" or even "court" or "judge" (cf. Deut 32:31; Job 31:11).

30 For his criminal neglect, a man could פִּדְיֹן נַפְשׁוֹ (*piḏyōn nap̱šô*, "redeem his life") if the slain one's family allowed him to substitute כֹּפֶר (*kōp̱er*, "a [substitute] payment"). That sum is not to indemnify the victim's family but to ransom the man's life (cf. Num 35:31).

5. *Laws on property damages*

21:33–22:15

33 "If a man uncovers a pit or digs one and fails to cover it and an ox or a donkey falls into it, 34 the owner of the pit must pay for the loss; he must pay its owner, and the dead animal will be his.

35 "If a man's bull injures the bull of another and it dies, they are to sell the live one and divide both the money and the dead animal equally. 36 However, if it was known that the bull had the habit of goring, yet the owner did not keep it penned up, the owner must pay, animal for animal, and the dead animal will be his.

22:1 "If a man steals an ox or a sheep and slaughters it or sells it, he must pay back five head of cattle for the ox and four sheep for the sheep.

2 "If a thief is caught breaking in and is struck so that he dies, the defender is not guilty of bloodshed; 3 but if it happens after sunrise, he is guilty of bloodshed.

"A thief must certainly make restitution, but if he has nothing, he must be sold to pay for his theft.

4 "If the stolen animal is found alive in his possession—whether ox or donkey or sheep—he must pay back double.

5 "If a man grazes his livestock in a field or vineyard and lets them stray and they graze in another man's field, he must make restitution from the best of his own field or vineyard.

6 "If a fire breaks out and spreads into thornbushes so that it burns shocks of grain or standing grain or the whole field, the one who started the fire must make restitution.

7 "If a man gives his neighbor silver or goods for safekeeping and they are stolen from the neighbor's house, the thief, if he is caught, must pay back double. 8 But if the thief is not found, the owner of the house must appear before the judges to determine whether he has laid his hands on the other man's property. 9 In all cases of illegal possession of an ox, a

donkey, a sheep, a garment, or any other lost property about which somebody says, 'This is mine,' both parties are to bring their cases before the judges. The one whom the judges declare guilty must pay back double to his neighbor.

10 "If a man gives a donkey, an ox, a sheep or any other animal to his neighbor for safekeeping and it dies or is injured or is taken away while no one is looking, 11 the issue between them will be settled by the taking of an oath before the LORD that the neighbor did not lay hands on the other person's property. The owner is to accept this, and no restitution is required. 12 But if the animal was stolen from the neighbor, he must make restitution to the owner. 13 If it was torn to pieces by a wild animal, he shall bring in the remains as evidence and he will not be required to pay for the torn animal.

14 "If a man borrows an animal from his neighbor and it is injured or dies while the owner is not present, he must make restitution. 15 But if the owner is with the animal, the borrower will not have to pay. If the animal was hired, the money paid for the hire covers the loss.

33–34 Culpable negligence (such as leaving a pit uncovered) that results in loss or damage to the property of another demands full restitution to the person who suffered the loss. The dead animal becomes the property of the person who is negligent and who is to pay to replace that animal.

35–36 A second property damage case concerned a cattle fight, where one animal killed a neighbor's animal. In this case they were to kill the surviving animal, sell its meat, and divide the price as well as the dead animal. But if the animal that survived had a reputation for goring, then its owner must take total responsibility for the animal. This law parallels Eshnunna's Law 53 exactly: "If an ox gores to death another ox, both owners shall divide the price of the live ox and the flesh of the dead ox."

22:1–22:4 This third example of property damage, which also illustrates the morality of the eighth commandment, contains a group of five cases like many of the other paragraphs in the covenant code. The subject is introduced by *kî* ("if") and continues with four special instances prefaced by the word *'im* ("if"). In cases of theft the penalty is much greater than those of negligence involving another person's property. The man is directly guilty and stands to benefit from his theft (Paul, "Book of the Covenant," p. 85).

The reason for the fivefold penalty in the case of stealing an ox is probably because one man stole the means of another man's livelihood. The principle would extend to taking any of the man's plowing or cultivating implements. Bush (*Exodus,* 2:26) notes that Proverbs 6:31 speaks of a "sevenfold" restoration; but this no doubt is an expression for a full, complete, or abundant repayment (cf. Gen 4:24; Pss 12:6; 79:12).

Breaking (see Notes) and entering (vv.2–3) a home in the night could expose the intruder to the loss of his life (justifiable homicide), in which case the householder would not be held responsible (cf. Jer 2:34 for its use as a metaphor). Such invasion during the daylight hours would be a different situation since there would be witnesses and the scope of the intruder's intentions (whether just to steal or also to kill) could be assessed. Eshnunna Law 13 makes this same distinction between nighttime and daylight intrusions.

When the goods have been sold or consumed and the thief has nothing with which to repay his crime, then he must be sold into servitude—presumably until he has repaid the debt. But if the stolen goods are still in his possession, then there is hope of repentance and voluntary restitution. At least the original owner can be reunited with his own animal, and the penalty would be that the thief must provide a similar animal. When the thief voluntarily confessed, Leviticus 6:4–5 required that he add only one-fifth to the theft (cf. Num 5:6–7).

5–6 A fourth type of property damage involved (1) letting livestock graze in another man's field (v.5) and (2) letting a fire get out of control so that it burns over a neighbor's field (v.6). The identical situations appear, only in reverse order, in Hittite Laws 105–7. Notice that both v.5 and v.6 begin with *kî* ("if"), meaning that they are treated as separate laws. Thus men are held responsible, not only for the harm they *do,* but also for the harm they *occasion* (Bush, *Exodus,* 2:26), even though they may not have purposely designed the damage that ensued. The restitution will be the top yield that field has ever produced if the whole field was ruined, or, if not, the choicest sections left will be the standard for the whole field.

7–15 The last section on property damage treats four classes of goods entrusted to other persons for their custody or use.

The first case involved leaving valuable (*kesep̱*; sometimes translated as "money," but coined "money" as we know it was not minted till the seventh century B.C.) articles (vv.7–9) or stuff (*kēlîm*) for safekeeping only to discover a thief stealing them. The thief is to make a double restitution as v.4 specified. Compare a similar twofold penalty for the dishonest bailee in Hammurabi laws 120, 124, 126, and in a case of theft, 125. But unlike the biblical laws, Hammurabi demanded the death penalty for the apprehended thief (laws 6–11). The same situation appears in vv.8–9, only the identity of the thief is not known, and thus there is a suspicion that the keeper may have embezzled these securities. The bailee must appear before "the judges" (*hā'ᵉlōhîm,* as in 21:6 [see Notes in loc.]; 22:8–9 [7–8 MT], 28 mg. [27 MT]; 1 Sam 2:25 [NIV mg.]; Pss 58:1; 82:1, 6), where a deposition of innocence is taken as an oath before God in court. Though this text does not specifically mention an oath, the phrase *'im lô'* (lit., "whether not") is used elsewhere so frequently as the oath formula that we cannot take it as anything else here (the oath is mentioned explicitly in v.11). Verse 8 is the general rule, and v.9 specifies charges of misappropriation or breach of trust.

The second case (vv.10–11) dealt with animals entrusted to another that were mutilated in the pasture, injured themselves, or were driven off by robbers. The same oath in court was required since there were no witnesses and only God could finally decide the keeper's culpability. Interestingly enough the name of Yahweh is used in the oath in v.11 rather than "the Elohim" as in vv.8–9. This is hardly a sufficient basis for detecting two literary sources for this material since Elohim is being used here in the specialized sense of "judges."

In the third case (vv.12–13), the animal given for safekeeping was stolen. Since the bailee was negligent in guarding the animal, he must make restitution by giving the owner an animal for the one stolen. But if the animal given for safekeeping was torn to pieces by wild animals, he would only need to produce the evidence of this fact, and no payment was required. Hammurabi Laws 266–67 were similar but dealt with an outbreak of infections, calling them "the stroke of a god," and also exempted the keeper. (For other laws on livestock being devoured by wild beasts in Mesopotamian law, see Sumerian Law 8, New Sumerian fragments iii, 9'–11', and Hammurabi Laws 75 and 244.)

The last case (vv.14–15) treats the problem of a hired beast being injured or dying while the owner was not present. Since neglect is presumed, a full replacement is required. However, if the owner was present, the wages agreed on were regarded as sufficient to offset the hazard run by the owner in renting out his property; and his firsthand witness to the deed would take away all suspicion of negligence.

Notes

22:1 (21:37 MT) The maximum restitution in Exodus is חֲמִשָּׁה (*ḥᵃmiššāh*, "five"). The Hittite Laws (57–59) went as high as thirtyfold, which later was reduced to fifteenfold. The Hammurabi Code (8) also has thirtyfold.

2 (1 MT) בַּמַּחְתֶּרֶת (*bammaḥtereṯ*, "breaking in") is literally "digging through" the walls since the homes were frequently made of thick, dried mud walls (cf. Job 24:16; Ezek 8:8; and the Greek word in Matt 24:43 for "be broken into").

אֵין לוֹ דָּמִים (*'ên lô dāmîm*, "he is not guilty of bloodshed") is literally "not to him blood." The blood, or value of that life (Gen 9:6), is not placed on him.

5 (4 MT) In יַבְעֶר ... בְּעִירֹה וּבִעֵר (*yaḇ'er* ... *bᵉ'îrōh ûḇi'ēr*, "grazes his livestock ... and they graze"), the verbs *yaḇ'er* and *bi'ēr* are denominative verbs from *bᵉ'îrōh* ("livestock"). There may be some wordplay here since the word *b'r* means "to burn" as well as "to graze"; cf. the next verse: הַמַּבְעִיר (*hammaḇ'îr*, "the one who started the fire").

8 (7 MT) The oath formula אִם־לֹא (*'im-lō'*) is unusual here in אִם־לֹא שָׁלַח יָדוֹ (*'im-lō' šālaḥ yāḏô*, "to determine whether he has laid his hands [on another man's property]"), unless it be taken simply as "whether" (cf. P. Humbert, "Entendre la main," VetTest 12 [1962]: 383–95).

10 (9 MT) The use of the verb נִשְׁבַּר (*nišbar*, "injured") for animals can be seen in Lev 22:22; 1 Kings 13:28; Ezek 34:4, 16; Zech 11:16. This verb has the same meaning in the Nuzi tablets.

14 (13 MT) "Borrows" for יִשְׁאַל (*yiš'al*) is the same meaning we gave the verb *š'l* ("to ask" or "to borrow") in the contexts of 3:22 and 11:2.

Paul ("Book of the Covenant," p. 94) regards וְנִשְׁבַּר אוֹ־מֵת (*wᵉnišbar 'ô-mēṯ*, "it is injured or dies") as a hendiadys similar to the Akkadian Nuzi phrase *ul-te-eb-ir-šu ù im-tu-ut* ("injuries that lead to an animal's death"; lit., "he injured it so that it died"). See the new JPS Torah translation.

6. *Laws on society*

22:16–31

> ¹⁶"If a man seduces a virgin who is not pledged to be married and sleeps with her, he must pay the bride-price, and she shall be his wife. ¹⁷If her father absolutely refuses to give her to him, he must still pay the bride-price for virgins.
> ¹⁸"Do not allow a sorceress to live.
> ¹⁹"Anyone who has sexual relations with an animal must be put to death.
> ²⁰"Whoever sacrifices to any god other than the LORD must be destroyed.
> ²¹"Do not mistreat an alien or oppress him, for you were aliens in Egypt.

[22]"Do not take advantage of a widow or an orphan. [23]If you do and they cry out to me, I will certainly hear their cry. [24]My anger will be aroused, and I will kill you with the sword; your wives will become widows and your children fatherless.

[25]"If you lend money to one of my people among you who is needy, do not be like a moneylender; charge him no interest. [26]If you take your neighbor's cloak as a pledge, return it to him by sunset, [27]because his cloak is the only covering he has for his body. What else will he sleep in? When he cries out to me, I will hear, for I am compassionate.

[28]"Do not blaspheme God or curse the ruler of your people.

[29]"Do not hold back offerings from your granaries or your vats.

"You must give me the firstborn of your sons. [30]Do the same with your cattle and your sheep. Let them stay with their mothers for seven days, but give them to me on the eighth day.

[31]"You are to be my holy people. So do not eat the meat of an animal torn by wild beasts; throw it to the dogs.

16–17 The law on the seduction of a maiden not yet engaged is different from that dealing with the seduction of the betrothed girl in Deuteronomy 22:23, where violence was also involved. The penalty here is that the seducer must pay the bride-price (see Notes) and agree to marry her. Should this offer of marriage be rejected by the girl's father, the man must still pay the bride-price. As Bush (*Exodus,* 2:30) remarks, this payment and offer did not clear the guilt of sin committed here, for cleansing was needed by repentance. Middle Assyrian Law 56 treated the same case and required the seducer to pay one-third the bride-price, and the father was permitted to do as he wished.

18 Childs (*Exodus,* in loc.) notes that the expression "not allow . . . to live" (*lō' ṯeḥayyeh*) is a technical term for placing something under the ban (Num 31:15; Deut 20:16; 1 Sam 27:9–11). On "sorceress" see the Notes.

Sorcery was punished in the Hammurabi Code (2) by drowning in a river. Middle Assyrian Law A, 47 prescribed death for all making magical preparations, and Hittite Laws 9–10 required the one who bewitched another to make a cash settlement with him and to pay for his physician if he were ill.

19 This law, which is written in a participial form like 21:12, 15–17, and 22:20, forbids bestiality, as does Leviticus 18:23; 20:15–16; and Deuteronomy 27:21. The Hittite Laws (187–88, 199:16–18) proscribed this evil involving a sheep, cow, or pig, with the threat of a sentence of death unless pardoned by the king, but 199:20–22 and 200:23–25 does not apply bestiality to sexual relations with a horse or mule as the Bible does (Cassuto, pp. 290–91; Hyatt, p. 241). This offensive sex act apparently was prevalent among the Canaanites.

20 All who sacrifice to any god other than Yahweh "will be dedicated for destruction" (pers. tr.; see Notes). Notice Deuteronomy 17:2–5 for a parallel law.

21–27 These verses treat various forms of oppression against the poor, the widow, the orphan, and the alien. Since these people have few or no natural protectors in the society, they were to be shielded in their vulnerable estate. There are two shifts in these verses: (1) a shift to the first person, which placed God himself as the special protector and advocate of these underprivileged people, and (2) a shift to second-person plural in vv.22–24, which some regard as being more Deuteronomic in origin, but no proof exists beyond this observation on style.

Like the sojourner or resident alien in v.21, so widows and orphans (vv.22–24) were to be protected (see 23:11; Lev 19:9–10; Deut 14:21; 16:11, 14; 24:19–21; 26:12–13; Ps 94:6; Isa 1:23; 10:2; Jer 7:3–6; 22:3; Zech 7:10; Mal 3:5; Matt 23:14 [NIV mg.]). There are many other verses in the wisdom books of the OT, but it was the prophets who chided Israel for their neglect in this area of oppressing the poor and the weak. The cry of the weak will come directly up to God (cf. Jacob in Gen 31:42).

The laws dealing with interest on loaned money are dealt with in vv.25–27 and more fully in Leviticus 25:35–37 and Deuteronomy 15:7; 23:19–20. The negative stance on usury can also be gathered from Job 24:9; Proverbs 28:8; Ezekiel 18:13; 22:12; and Nehemiah 5:6–12. In fact, the righteous man may be defined as the one "who lends his money without usury [*nešek*]" in Psalm 15:5 and "does not lend at usury [*nešek*] or take excessive interest [*tarbît*]" in Ezekiel 18:8 (cf. vv.13, 17). On the other hand, Deuteronomy 23:20 declares, "You may charge a foreigner interest [*nešek*], but not a brother Israelite." This law is not dealing with "usury" in our modern sense of the word, i.e., exorbitant or illegal interest, but interest of any kind to a fellow Israelite. The main problem was that charging interest of one's brother was a way of avoiding responsibility to the poor and to one's fellow man (see Notes).

Retaining one's outer garment (used as temporary collateral) overnight was strictly forbidden, for even an interest-free loan apparently required some type of pledge or security (vv.26–27). But this cloak or poncho, which doubled as a blanket at night, was needed when evening came; otherwise the cold would be as vexing as the requiring of interest. Compare Hammurabi Laws 114–16 and Middle Assyrian Laws A, 39, 44, and 48.

28 Any word or deed that detracts from the glory of God is a reviling or cursing of his name (see the commentary on 20:7). Similarly care must be taken not to curse any who are in authority, for the penalty for cursing God and the king is death (1 Kings 21:10; for cursing God alone, Lev 24:15–16; for cursing the king alone, 2 Sam 16:9; 1 Kings 2:8–9). On the term for "ruler," see the Notes. "God" (*Elohim*) cannot mean "judges"in this context since it usually has the article when it is used in that sense; see, however, v.9b(8b MT).

29–30 The law of the firstfruits required that the following firstfruits be offered to God: (1) "the fullness of your harvest and the outflow [lit., 'the tear'] of your presses" (lit. tr. of v.29), (2) the firstborn of their children (v.29b), and (3) the firstborn of the cattle (v.30). The children were to be redeemed by a money payment or by the substituted service of one Levite for each firstborn (13:13; Num 3:46–48). They were not to "hold back" or "delay" to do these things, even though the text seems to be aware of a natural reluctance on the part of men. Notice the theological significance of this request in our discussion on 4:22–23. On the seven days that the young firstborn were allowed to stay with their mother, see Leviticus 22:27. Rawlinson (2:192) is no doubt correct when he explains that the main purpose was to give natural relief to the dam by suckling its offspring.

31 Underlining all these instructions on societal relations was this call to service: "You are to be my holy people." Such a noble calling as Yahweh's firstborn son (4:22) or his "treasured possession. . . . kingdom of priests and a holy nation" (19:5–6) demanded noble living. Animals killed by another were unclean for two reasons: (1) the carnivorous beasts that tore it were unclean, and (2) the blood of such a slain animal would remain in its tissues, leaving it unclean. Instead, the people were to toss that meat to the dogs. "Men of holiness" (lit. tr. of *'anšê-qōḏeš*) were to be separate in inward principle and outward practice—one of which was illustrated here.

Notes

17 (16 MT) A בְּתוּלָה (*beṯûlāh*, "virgin"), like the Akkadian *batūltu*, was an unmarried girl who was always presumed to be a virgin. This is not the same word found in Isa 7:14.

On מֹהַר (*mōhar*, "bride-price"), see TWOT, # 1153; cf. S. Loewenstamm, "מהר," *Encyclopaedia Biblica* (Jerusalem, 1962), 4:702–6.

18 (17 MT) מְכַשֵּׁפָה (*meḵaššēp̄āh*, "sorceress") is the feminine form of *meḵaššēp̄* ("magician" or "sorcerer"), which some allege comes from the root *kāšap̄*, meaning "to cut," like the Arabic *kasapha*. Hence, as Bush (*Exodus*, 2:31–32) continues, the eclipses of the moon are a cutting, *kusuph* in Arabic. Presumably a sorcerer would be a person who occasions solar or lunar eclipses. But this etymology cannot be verified as Bush acknowledges. The Piel form of this verb is to use incantations, magic, sorcery, or the arts of witchcraft. Our English "witch" is alleged to have come from "to wit," i.e., "to know," in the adjectival *wittigh* or *wittich*, contracted to witch. The Greeks rendered our word by *pharmakos* ("poisoners"), since sorcerers dealt in drugs and pharmaceutical potions.

20 (19 MT) יָחֳרָם (*yāḥorām*) means "[he] must be destroyed." *Ḥerem* is something devoted to God; however, it is not a voluntary but an involuntary dedication. It is now set apart to be banned from the earth and will totally come back to God. Thus a wall, as it were (cf. the king's wives, or harem, who were walled off from others), isolates the anathematized person, place, or thing from anyone touching, using, or benefiting from it ever again. Compare Achan's sin of taking the "devoted" items set apart for destruction in Josh 7:13.

Notice the use of the lamed with the qameṣ in לָאֱלֹהִים (*lā'elōhîm*, "to the gods" or "to any god"). Only in one other passage is *'elōhîm* used as a common noun with a prepositional prefix and a qameṣ, viz., Ps 86:8.

25 (24 MT) נֶשֶׁךְ (*nešeḵ*, "interest") usually occurs with another word, *m/tarbîṯ*, which also means "interest" (Lev 25:36–37; Prov 28:8; Ezek 18:8, 13, 17). *Nešeḵ* appears alone in this passage and in Deut 23:20 and Ps 15:5. The Talmud's *Baba Mesia* 60b and D.H. Müller (*Semitica: Sprach und rechtsvergleichende Studien*, Part 1 Akademie der wissenschaften in Wien, Philosophisch–historische Klasse [1906]: 13–19) came to the conclusion that both words meant approximately the same thing: "interest." Müller even suggested that the two terms were a hendiadys, but others felt that they had two separate meanings.

One school of thought, represented by S. Loewenstamm ("Neshek and M/Tarbit," JBL 88 [1961]: 78–80), made the distinction over the *substance* of the thing loaned: *nešeḵ* referred to a loan of money and *m/tarbîṯ* referred to the loan of food stuffs. Another school made the distinction over the *method* by which compensation for the loan was computed: *nešeḵ* was "a long term, year recurring form of interest," and *tarbîṯ* was a "fixed rate of interest for a small loan of money or grain to be paid together with the capital after the harvest" (S. Stein, "Interest Taken by Jews From Gentiles," JSS 1 [1956]: 163). S. Stein ("The Laws on Interest in the Old Testament," JTS 4 [1953]) and Edward Neufeld ("The Prohibition Against Loans at Interest in Ancient Hebrew Laws," HUCA 26 [1955]) both espouse the widely held view that *nešeḵ* was derived from a Hebrew root meaning "to bite"; hence the "interest" was that which was "bitten off" or deducted before the loan was advanced. *Tarbîṯ*, on the other hand, meant "increase" and referred to the additional sum above the principal. But the debate is not easily settled. Loewenstamm's argument is the most convincing solution, but his theory fails to account for Deut 23:20–21.

The best sense spoken on this whole topic is from Hillel Gamoran ("The Biblical Law Against Loans on Interest," JNES 30 [1971]: 127–34). On p. 131 he says: "The prohibition against interest was written with the poor in mind. Commercial loans were not explicitly banned because they were not considered. Out of sixteen biblical passages dealing with loans (but not with interest), not one deals with a commercial loan. Commercial loans simply did not come under the biblical purview." (The sixteen passages are as follows: Deut 15:1–11; 24:10–13; 28:12; 1 Sam 22:2; 2 Kings 4:1; Neh 5:4; 10:31; Pss 37:21–26; 109:11; 112:5; Prov 19:17; 22:7, 26; Isa 24:2; 50:1; Jer 15:10.)

28 (27 MT) The precise meaning of נָשִׂיא (*nāśî'*, "ruler") is debated. For Noth (in loc.), the *nāśî'* was a tribal representative in the premonarchical amphictyony (cf. Num 1:5–16; 13:1–15; 34:17–28; Hyatt, p. 244). E. Speiser and J. van der Ploeg more convincingly argued that *nāśî'* designated a single overall ruler, a king (in Childs, *Exodus*, p. 479).

---

7. *Laws on justice and neighborliness*

23:1–9

1 "Do not spread false reports. Do not help a wicked man by being a malicious witness.

2 "Do not follow the crowd in doing wrong. When you give testimony in a lawsuit, do not pervert justice by siding with the crowd, 3 and do not show favoritism to a poor man in his lawsuit.

4 "If you come across your enemy's ox or donkey wandering off, be sure to take it back to him. 5 If you see the donkey of someone who hates you fallen down under its load, do not leave it there; be sure you help him with it.

6 "Do not deny justice to your poor people in their lawsuits. 7 Have nothing to do with a false charge and do not put an innocent or honest person to death, for I will not acquit the guilty.

8 "Do not accept a bribe, for a bribe blinds those who see and twists the words of the righteous.

9 "Do not oppress an alien; you yourselves know how it feels to be aliens, because you were aliens in Egypt.

Most of the regulations in this section are apodictic laws (using the second-person singular form) on court cases. Whereas most of the previous sections of the covenant code have stressed love and compassion toward the weak, the poor, and the alien, this section exhorts Israel to practice another virtue: justice. The attempt of J.W. McKay ("Exodus XXIII 1–3, 6–8: A Decalogue for Administration of Justice in the City Gate," VetTest 21 [1971]: 311–25) to organize vv.1–3 and 6–8 into another decalogue of laws is not convincing in that it uses emendation and deletion without any evidential warrant.

1 This prohibition against slander (whether in court or not) is an amplification of the ninth commandment. Compare the injunction of Leviticus 19:16 and the cases of Deuteronomy 22:13–19 and 1 Kings 21:10–13. The clause "Do not help a wicked man" is the NIV's rendering of "set your hand with" (*'al-tāšeṯ yāḏᵉḵā*).

2–3 Justice demands impartiality rather than unwarranted compliance with the "many" (v.2, *rabbîm;* NIV, "crowd") or favoritism to the poor (v.3; cf. Lev 19:15). In late Hebrew *rabbîm* meant "the mighty," giving an excellent contrast with the "poor man" or "the humble" (*dāl*). However, as Childs argues (*Exodus*, p. 481), the original sense is probably "the many," and the verb "follow after" fits this meaning as it does in 1 Kings 16:21.

4–5 Deuteronomy 22:1–3 gives fuller details on a man's responsibility to his brother in the matter of restoring a lost animal or helping one in difficulty. This act of compassion was owed to one another regardless whether the man was an enemy (v.4) or one who hated him (v.5). Kindness to one's enemy is commanded in Job 31:29 and Proverbs 25:21–22. Never does the OT command, "Hate your enemy," as the oral tradition of Jesus' day enjoined (Matt 5:43).

6–8 Cassuto (p. 298) argues that *'ebyōnekā* ("your poor people") is better understood here as "your opponent, adversary" (a synonym for "your enemy," v.4, and "the one hating you," v.5). Thus the suffix "your" is more easily understood and the meaning would be thus: When called to testify or to adjudicate between your enemy and someone else, do not pervert the judgment against your enemy just because he is your enemy.

Verse 7 warns against the very thing Jezebel would later do to Naboth (1 Kings 21:10–13). Justice demands that men distance themselves from any false charges (cf. v.1). God will not hold such men or judges guiltless.

Verse 8 is repeated almost verbatim in Deuteronomy 16:19. Bribery must have been a common temptation, for numerous passages warn against it.

9 This verse is similar in wording and the motivation to 22:21, but it is placed here because this should be one of the great motivators for all Israelites to exercise justice: Remember how you felt when you were aliens (and all that implies) in Egypt.

Notes

5 Cassuto (p. 297) and later W.F. Albright (*Yahweh and the Gods of Canaan* [Garden City, N.Y.: Doubleday, 1968], p. 104, n. 130) take the verb *'zb* in עָזֹב תַּעֲזֹב עִמּוֹ (*'azōb ta'azōb 'immô*, "be sure you help him with it") to be the same as the Ugaritic *'db* ("to arrange, adjust"). Hence the rendering would be "You shall adjust its load."

8. *Laws on sacred seasons*

23:10–19

10 "For six years you are to sow your fields and harvest the crops, 11 but during the seventh year let the land lie unplowed and unused. Then the poor among your people may get food from it, and the wild animals may eat what they leave. Do the same with your vineyard and your olive grove.

12 "Six days do your work, but on the seventh day do not work, so that your ox and your donkey may rest and the slave born in your household, and the alien as well, may be refreshed.

13 "Be careful to do everything I have said to you. Do not invoke the names of other gods; do not let them be heard on your lips.

14 "Three times a year you are to celebrate a festival to me.
15 "Celebrate the Feast of Unleavened Bread; for seven days eat bread made without yeast, as I commanded you. Do this at the appointed time in the month of Abib, for in that month you came out of Egypt.
"No one is to appear before me empty-handed.
16 "Celebrate the Feast of Harvest with the firstfruits of the crops you sow in your field.
"Celebrate the Feast of Ingathering at the end of the year, when you gather in your crops from the field.
17 "Three times a year all the men are to appear before the Sovereign LORD.
18 "Do not offer the blood of a sacrifice to me along with anything containing yeast.
"The fat of my festival offerings must not be kept until morning.
19 "Bring the best of the firstfruits of your soil to the house of the LORD your God.
"Do not cook a young goat in its mother's milk.

The text turns to commandments that apply to seasons and days that are to be set aside to the service of God.

10–12 The laws on the Sabbath year and the Sabbath day begin this section. Every seventh year was to be a "Sabbath of sabbaths to the land, a sabbath to the LORD" (cf. Lev 25:4). The land was to lie fallow and to rest: the two verbs in v.11 are *šmṭ* ("to let drop," "to remit") and *nṭš* ("to leave," "to abandon). The motivation for this legislation is given in v.11; it was to favor the poor and the wild animals. In Leviticus 25:1–7, 18–22, the reasons are more theological than civil: "a sabbath to the LORD" (25:4).

Verse 12 repeats the fourth commandment so that no one would gain the impression that once the sabbatical year was observed, all ordinary observances of the regular Sabbath would no longer be required. This repetition of 20:8–9 adds an additional reason for its observance: so that man and beast alike might "be refreshed" (*yinnāp̄ēš*). Bush (*Exodus*, 2:46) compares the LXX translation with the same Greek word rendered in Acts 3:19 as "(times of) refreshing" (cf. the same humanitarian reason given in Deut 5:14; see also Exod 16:27–30).

13 The caution against idolatry here appears to summarize all the divine precepts given above: literally, "in all things that I have said to you." "Do not let them be heard on your lips" is paralleled by "you shall not cause [all these things] to be remembered" (*lō' ṯazkîrû*, NIV, "do not invoke"). The Hiphil form of *zkr* ("to remember") has the meaning "to invoke" in the Psalms; so also here. There would come a "day" when God would cut off the names of the idols out of the land, and they would "be remembered" no more (Hos 2:17; Zech 13:2). This was the practice of David in Psalm 16:4 (note Exod 20:3; Josh 23:7).

14–17 This section (vv.14–19) deals with the three great annual pilgrimage feasts: the Feast of Unleavened Bread at the beginning of the barley harvest in the spring, commemorating the Exodus (v.15); the Feast of Harvest (also called the Feast of Weeks in 34:22) at the end of the spring harvest of grain, commemorating the giving of the law (v.16a); and the Feast of Ingathering of the summer crops of olives and grapes in early autumn, commemorating the wilderness wanderings (v.16b). Most of this material is found again in 34:18–26 and expanded in Leviticus 23. All three feasts were at once agricultural, historical, and required annual attendance of all men (v.17). On the Unleavened Bread Feast, see 12:34 and Leviticus 23:5–8, 10–14. This feast began with Passover and lasted seven days with a holy convocation on the first and last days. The rule for all the feasts was "No one is to appear before me empty-handed" (v.15).

Fifty days after the offering of the barley sheaf as the "firstfruits" of the harvest, the Feast of Harvest, known later as Pentecost, was to be celebrated (v.16; cf. Lev 23:15–22 and Deut 16:9–11 for this one-day festival).

The Feast of Ingathering or Tabernacles (v.16; cf. Lev 23:33–36; Deut 16:13; 31:10; John 7:2) was a kind of thanksgiving festival. It was grossly neglected for many periods of Israel's history (Neh 8:17).

18 The first part of this verse has nothing to do with eating anything leavened. Rather it means that individual Israelites were not to kill the Passover lamb while leaven was still in their houses. The second half of the verse makes no reference to fat as such; but as the parallel verse in 34:25b says, the "sacrifice from the Passover Feast" (here lit., "sacrifice of my feast") shall not "remain until morning" (cf. 12:10). If the word "fat" is retained over the parallel text in 34:25b, which would make "fat of my feast" parallel to "sacrifice of my feast," then the householders are being told to destroy the intestinal fat by morning. But the first explanation (i.e., the presence of leaven) is preferred. (For this interpretation see Norman Snaith, "Exodus 23:18 and 34:25," JTS 20 [1969]: 533–34.)

19 The law of firstfruits and its theology have already been discussed in 4:22; 11:5; and 12:29. This was to be brought into the house of God yet to be described.

The prohibition of cooking a young goat in its mother's milk (see also 34:26; Deut 14:21b) has been explained since 1933 by a reference in a broken passage of a thirteenth-century B.C. Ugaritic text called "The Birth of the Gods Pleasant and Beautiful" (text 52, line 14). It is generally agreed that the reference is to a fertility rite that entails boiling a kid in milk; but there is no sure reference to the milk of its mother in the broken Ugaritic text. Calum M. Carmichael ("On Separating Life and Death: An Explanation of Some Biblical Laws," HTR 69 [1976]: 1–7, esp. p. 2) concludes: "The crux of the matter is simply, that the young dead kid is being cooked in the very milk that was its life-giving sustenance." See Jacob Migrom, "You Shall Not Boil a Kid in Its Mother's Milk," *Bible Review* 1, no. 3 (1985): 48–55, and Robert J. Ratner and Bruce Zuckerman, "In Rereading the 'Kid in Milk' Inscriptions," *Bible Review* 1, no. 3 (1985): 56–58.

Notes

---

10 The waw that begins this verse is both antithetic, "but," and an example of *casus pendens*, "but in regard to the seventh year" (Cassuto, p. 300).

14 Literally, רְגָלִים (*regālîm*, "times") is "feet"; perhaps "three foot-journeys" are required each year. Notice v.17 uses the more regular *pe'āmîm* ("times").

9. *Epilogue*

23:20–33

20"See, I am sending an angel ahead of you to guard you along the way and to bring you to the place I have prepared. 21Pay attention to him and listen to what he says. Do not rebel against him; he will not forgive your rebellion, since my Name is in him. 22If you listen carefully to what he says and do all that I say, I will be an enemy to your enemies and will oppose those who oppose you. 23My angel will go ahead of you and bring you into the land of the Amorites, Hittites, Perizzites, Canaanites, Hivites and Jebusites, and I will wipe them out. 24Do not bow down before their gods or worship them or follow their practices. You must demolish them and break their sacred stones to pieces. 25Worship the LORD your God, and his blessing will be on your food and water. I will take away sickness from among you, 26and none will miscarry or be barren in your land. I will give you a full life span.

27"I will send my terror ahead of you and throw into confusion every nation you encounter. I will make all your enemies turn their backs and run. 28I will send the hornet ahead of you to drive the Hivites, Canaanites and Hittites out of your way. 29But I will not drive them out in a single year, because the land would become desolate and the wild animals too numerous for you. 30Little by little I will drive them out before you, until you have increased enough to take possession of the land.

31"I will establish your borders from the Red Sea to the Sea of the Philistines, and from the desert to the River. I will hand over to you the people who live in the land and you will drive them out before you. 32Do not make a covenant with them or with their gods. 33Do not let them live in your land, or they will cause you to sin against me, because the worship of their gods will certainly be a snare to you."

An epilogue concludes the Covenant Code. Israel is promised the angel of God, every protection, and success, provided they remain faithful to the covenant. Similar conditional promises are found in 33:1–3; 34:11–16; Leviticus 26:3–11; and Deuteronomy 7:13–15; 28:1–14.

20–22 The angel mentioned here cannot be Moses, God's messenger, or an ordinary angel; for the expressions are too high for any of these: "he will not forgive your rebellion" (who can forgive sin but God alone?) and "my Name is in him" (v.22). This must be the Angel of the Covenant (cf. Isa 63:9; Mal 3:1), the Second Person of the Trinity. (See our discussion in Exod 33 and in *Old Testament Theology*, p. 120, for four forms of Yahweh's divine presence.) Just as Yahweh's name resided in his temple (Deut 12:5, 11; 1 Kings 8:29), so this Angel with the authority and prestige of the name of God was evidence enough that God himself was present in his Son. Obedience to the Angel would result in all of the blessings listed in the text. Israel was commanded: "Do not rebel against him" (v.21); yet they did just that (Num 14:11; Ps 78:17, 40, 56).

23–26 On the nations listed here, see the comment on 3:8. All these nations God's Angel would "wipe . . . out" (v.23), i.e., remove from their national, not necessarily personal, existence; for surely David had Hittites in his army (2 Sam 23:39) and was friendly with a Jebusite (2 Sam 24:18–24). It was the worship and practices of the gods of these nations that were strictly forbidden. Instead, Israel was to demolish these gods and smash their "sacred stones" (v.24). These *maṣṣēḇôṯ* apparently were free-standing stones that were associated with the veneration of deities, particularly the male deity. Examples of these stones have been found at Gezer, Byblos, Ras Shamra, and especially Hazor, where one was found with an offering at its base by the entrance to an important building in the Canaanite citadel (Y. Yadin, "The Fourth Season of Excavation at Hazor," BA 22 [1959]: 14, fig. 12).

The worship of God would affect the Israelites' water and food (v.25). No wonder the prophets connected a series of agricultural reverses with the judgment of God on a particular culture (e.g., Hag 1:5–11). Moreover, unlike the wicked who fail to live out half their days (Ps 55:23), the worshiping obedient will have full life spans (v.26).

27–30 God would also (in addition to his Angel in vv.20, 23) send panic and confusion to every nation Israel would face (v.27). He would also send "the hornet" (*haṣṣir'āh*, always singular), a word that occurs only here in v.28, in Deuteronomy 7:20, and in Joshua 24:12. It is unnecessary to revocalize the text to translate it as "leprosy" or "discouragement" (see Hyatt, p. 252). Perhaps "the hornet" is a symbol of Egypt, just as Isaiah 7:18 uses the "fly" and the "bee" as symbols of Egypt and Assyria, respectively.

The speed of the conquest is stated differently in several texts. Judges 2:20–3:4 also argued for gradual progress in conquering the land; yet Deuteronomy 9:3 promised that it would be done "quickly." The answer lies in noting that the general sweep of the land and its conquest in principle was accomplished speedily. Because of mopping-up operations, however, and the need to have people settle in the areas rid of Canaanite influence and the threat of wild animals infesting them (cf. 2 Kings 17:25), the completion of that task would designedly be slow.

31–33 The borders God would establish would be from *Yam Suph* (here an eastern boundary), the Gulf of Aqabah with its port city of Elath; to the "Sea of the Philistines," the Mediterranean Sea on the west; from the desert in the south, the Negeb; to "the River" (*hannāhār*) in the north. But is the River Euphrates to be equated with "the River" up north? Rather than equating these two terms, it would appear to be better to equate "the River" with a river that preserves the same name in Arabic today, located in a valley north of the Lebanon mountains, currently serving as the boundary between Lebanon and Syria. The Arabic name is *Nahr el Kebir* ("The Great River"; cf. the same name in Heb.: Gen 15:18; Deut 1:7; Josh 1:4). This description traces out limits already given to Abraham in Genesis 15:18 and comes close to matching the extent of the united kingdom under David and Solomon (2 Sam 8:3–14; 10:6–19; 1 Kings 4:21, 24; 2 Chron 9:26).

No covenant was to be made with these people (though the Gibeonites did succeed in making one, Josh 9:3–15). The potential snare of their gods, practices, and worship was too great; thus there was to be no peaceful coexistence between these nations and Israel in Canaan.

Notes

31 On הַנָּהָר (*hannāhār*, "the River"), see the excellent discussion and argument for our Lebanese identification in George W. Buchanan, *The Consequences of the Covenant* (Leiden: E.J. Brill, 1970), pp. 91–109, and J. Simons, *Geographical and Topographical*

Texts (Leiden: E.J. Brill, 1959), pp. 94–105. See also W.C. Kaiser, Jr., "The Promised Land: A Biblical-Historical View," BS 138 (1981): 303–5.

F. *Ratification of the Covenant*

24:1–18

1 Then he said to Moses, "Come up to the LORD, you and Aaron, Nadab and Abihu, and seventy of the elders of Israel. You are to worship at a distance, 2 but Moses alone is to approach the LORD; the others must not come near. And the people may not come up with him."

3 When Moses went and told the people all the LORD's words and laws, they responded with one voice, "Everything the LORD has said we will do." 4 Moses then wrote down everything the LORD had said.

He got up early the next morning and built an altar at the foot of the mountain and set up twelve stone pillars representing the twelve tribes of Israel. 5 Then he sent young Israelite men, and they offered burnt offerings and sacrificed young bulls as fellowship offerings to the LORD. 6 Moses took half of the blood and put it in bowls, and the other half he sprinkled on the altar. 7 Then he took the Book of the Covenant and read it to the people. They responded, "We will do everything the LORD has said; we will obey."

8 Moses then took the blood, sprinkled it on the people and said, "This is the blood of the covenant that the LORD has made with you in accordance with all these words."

9 Moses and Aaron, Nadab and Abihu, and the seventy elders of Israel went up 10 and saw the God of Israel. Under his feet was something like a pavement made of sapphire, clear as the sky itself. 11 But God did not raise his hand against these leaders of the Israelites; they saw God, and they ate and drank.

12 The LORD said to Moses, "Come up to me on the mountain and stay here, and I will give you the tablets of stone, with the law and commands I have written for their instruction."

13 Then Moses set out with Joshua his aide, and Moses went up on the mountain of God. 14 He said to the elders, "Wait here for us until we come back to you. Aaron and Hur are with you, and anyone involved in a dispute can go to them."

15 When Moses went up on the mountain, the cloud covered it, 16 and the glory of the LORD settled on Mount Sinai. For six days the cloud covered the mountain, and on the seventh day the LORD called to Moses from within the cloud. 17 To the Israelites the glory of the LORD looked like a consuming fire on top of the mountain. 18 Then Moses entered the cloud as he went on up the mountain. And he stayed on the mountain forty days and forty nights.

The narrative, which was temporarily interrupted for the contents of the "Book of the Covenant" (20:22–23:33), is resumed from 20:21. Moses and his aides were to ascend ("Come up," v.1) the mountain *after* the actions mentioned in vv.3–8 were completed.

1 "Nadab and Abihu," Aaron's two eldest sons, would have been the next high priests in the line. They died, however, under God's judgment (Num 3:4) because of their perverse deed (Lev 10:1–2; Num 3:4). The official "seventy elders" of Numbers 11:16 had not been formally appointed yet. They were selected here to represent the Twelve Tribes, perhaps representing Jacob's seventy descendants.

2 Moses alone was to function as the mediator between God and the Israelites, just as Christ is designated the second Moses in Hebrews 3:1–6 and thus is the Mediator of the new covenant (Heb 12:24).

3 When the people promised to obey and to observe all that the Lord had said, they did not exchange the blessings of promise for the law. The keeping of the "LORD's words and laws" was to be based on the prior provision of sacrificial blood. The blood cleansed men and women so that "doing" and "obeying" became possible for them. This was not "doing" to merit favor or salvation (see on 19:8).

4 This passage testifies to Moses' direct involvement in the composition of the Book of Exodus. That "Moses then wrote down everything" agrees with his recording the account of the war on Amalek (17:14) and the writing of the Ten Commandments by the "finger of God" (31:18). See the comment on 17:14.

The "twelve stone pillars" represented the Twelve Tribes (Josh 4:5, 20; 1 Kings 18:31). Contrast the evil of "sacred stones" in 23:24, attested in excavations like those at Gezer.

5 The "young Israelite men" were the firstborn, who officiated until the Levites were appointed in their place in Numbers 3:41 (see comment and Notes on 19:22, 24).

6 Both the altar and the people were sprinkled with half of the blood, each in an act of dedication or consecration. Hebrews 9:19 does not mention the altar but speaks of the "book" or "scroll" of the covenant as also being sprinkled with blood. It is probably not correct to speak, as some do, of the altar as representing the Lord on the basis of Genesis 15:9–10, 17. This is a rite of purification (not the water, scarlet wool, and hyssop of Lev 14:6–7 and Heb 9:19–20). The division of the blood points to the twofold aspect of the blood of the covenant: The blood on the altar symbolizes God's forgiveness and acceptance of the offering; the blood on the people points to a blood oath that binds them in obedience. In other words, the keeping of the words and laws was made possible by the sacrificial blood of the altar.

7 The Book of the Covenant includes in its narrowest meaning in scholarly use today words from 20:22 to 23:33 but more fully, here, the contents of chapter 19, the Decalogue of chapter 20, and the case laws of 20:22 to 23:33.

8 The blood by which the covenant was ratified and sealed was the basis for the union between Yahweh and the people. This phrase becomes most important in the NT in its reappearance in the Lord's Supper (Matt 26:28; Mark 14:24; Luke 22:20; 1 Cor 11:25; Heb 9:20; 10:29; also Heb 12:24; 13:20; 1 Peter 1:2).

9–10 That Moses and his company "saw the God of Israel" at first appears to contradict 33:20; John 1:18; and 1 Timothy 6:16; but what they saw was a "form ['similitude'] of the LORD" (Num 12:8), just as Ezekiel (Ezek 1:26) and Isaiah (Isa 6:1) saw an approximation, a faint resemblance and a sensible adumbration of the incarnate Christ who was to come. There is a deliberate obscurity in the form and details of the one who produced such a splendid, dazzling effect on these observers of God's presence.

Under God's feet was a "pavement made of sapphire," (v.10), a deep blue or, more accurately, lapis lazuli of Mesopotamia, an opaque blue precious stone speckled with a golden yellow-colored pyrite. True sapphire, the transparent crystalline of corundum, was unknown in Egypt around 1400 B.C. It symbolizes the heavens (cf. Ezek 1:22).

11 "God did not raise his hand against [lit., 'stretch out his hand'; cf. 9:15] these leaders" who saw him. "Leaders" probably comes from the verb "to be deeply rooted," hence, "eminent ones," "nobles," or "chief men." See the Notes.

In one of the most amazing texts in the Bible, these men saw God. Verse 11 uses another word than v.10; here it stresses inward, spiritual, or prophetic vision.

"They ate and drank" describes a covenant meal celebrating the sealing of the covenant described in vv.3–8. There is, however, no mention of God's participating in the eating or drinking as a human partner!

12 Once again Moses was told to "come up" (cf. v.1). This is the first mention of the "tablets of stone."

13–14 In response to the call of God to Moses, Joshua accompanied him as they went farther up the mountain (v.13). "Aaron and Hur" (v.14), appointed as Moses' deputies in 17:10 and apparently as judges in 18:22, were left in charge. It is noteworthy that Hur does not appear in the golden calf incident (ch. 32). See comment on 17:10.

15–16 As Moses ascended the mountain, all he could see was a cloud (v.15). When the glory of God "settled" on the mountain, the same word (*šāḵan*) is used as the "shekinah" glory (cf. John 1:14, the Word "tabernacling" among us).

17 On "the glory of the LORD looked like a consuming fire," see the comment on 16:10. The three symbols of God's glory, i.e., of his presence, are (1) the cloud, (2) the fire, and (3) the voice of God. The radiance of his presence is like a fiery furnace (cf. Heb 12:18, 29).

18 Once Moses entered the "cloud," he would not be seen again for "forty days and forty nights" (cf. Jesus' fast in Matt 4:2). During this time Moses received all the instructions on the tabernacle and its furnishings in chapters 25–31. Not until chapter 32 do Moses and Joshua come down to face Israel's apostasy.

Notes

7 The name "Book of the Covenant" occurs elsewhere only in 2 Kings 23:2, 21 (2 Chron 34:30), where it designates the whole book of the law found in Josiah's time in the temple. Whether this name has reference only to the covenant code (Exod 21–23), to the Ten Commandments (cf. 34:28: "the words of the covenant—the Ten Commandments"), or even to most of the book of the law cannot be determined with certainty.

9–11 Vriezen ("Exegesis of Exodus XXIV, 9–11," p. 101) calls these verses "some of the most astonishing and inexplicable verses of the O.T." (cf. G. Henton Davis, p. 193).

The antianthropomorphic trend of the LXX can be seen in v.10, which adds, "the place where he stood" to "they saw the God of Israel" (*ton topon hou histēkei ekei*); and in v.11b the LXX adds: "they appeared in the place of God" (*kai ōphthēsan en tō topō tou theou*). The LXX even avoids referring to the "hand" of God in v.11a by substituting "nobody was missing (perished)" (cf. James Barr, "Theophany and Anthropomorphism in the Old Testament," VetTest Suppl. 7 [1959]: 31–33). Even though v.10 says the leaders "saw the God of Israel," it does not describe him any more than Isaiah did when he saw Adonai in Isaiah 6 (Isaiah chose to describe his train and the seraphim around him) or Ezekiel did in Ezekiel 1 (Ezekiel described the likeness, *d^emûṯ*, but not the reality or person himself).

See also E.W. Nicholson, "The Interpretation of Exodus XXIV 9–11," VetTest 24 (1974): 77–97; id., "The Antiquity of the Tradition in Exodus XXIV 9–11," VetTest 25 (1975): 69–79; and Walter A. Maier, "The Analysis of Exodus 24 According to Modern Literary Form and Redactional Critical Methodology," *Springfielder* 37 (1973): 35–52.

11 אֲצִיל (*'āṣîl*, "leaders") is a *qatîl* noun form derived from verbs often used to designate a special class or function such as *nāḇî'*, *nāḡîḏ*, or *nāśî'*. This noun may reflect the verb from the same root found in Num 11:17–25 (a passage analogous to this one where the seventy elders receive the Spirit of God), meaning "those who are taken away [from others]," hence, "distinguished men." The Hebrew noun is a *hapax legomenon*, unique to this passage. Vriezen ("Exodus XXIV 9–11," p. 110) and Nicholson ("Interpretation," p. 83) consider *'āṣîl* as being used figuratively here, meaning "side" or "corner," on the analogy of *pinnāh* ("corner" for "leaders") in Judg 20:2 and 1 Sam 14:38.

III. Divine Worship (25:1–40:38)

The final sixteen chapters of Exodus center on the theology of the worship of God. The only interruption of this theme is the episode of the golden calf (chs. 32–34). But this section only contrasts the divinely appointed worship established in connection with the tabernacle with humanly devised worship that adores the work of human hands and leads to debauchery.

The sheer amount of text devoted to the topic of worship ought to demonstrate its importance. To be sure, some doubt the historicity of the tabernacle itself. The standard view of the hypothetical source theory is that the oldest tradition referred only to a simple tent of the congregation in 33:7–11, which was attributed to an alleged "E" source (= Elohim; northern tradition, first written down c. 750 B.C.). The hypothetical "P" (= Priestly source, first written down after the Exile c. 450 B.C.) source then developed the ideal design of 33:7–11, aided by the (already destroyed) temple of Solomon and the (unbuilt) temple of Ezekiel's vision (Ezek 40–48). However, contrary to the claims of the hypothetical source theory, the text presents Exodus 25–40 as being historical. The source hypothesis fails to see that the tent of 33:7–11 is different from the tabernacle and was only a temporary structure. See comments on 33:7–11.

The most important question about the tabernacle deals with its significance. Some claim (e.g., Philo, Josephus) that the tabernacle represents the *universe* (the court = earth, the tabernacle itself = heaven, the lampstand = the seven planets, the bread of presence = the twelve months). Others (e.g., Cocceius) would have the tabernacle represent the church (the court = the external visible church, the tent = the true invisible church, the Holy Place = the church militant, the Most Holy Place = the church triumphant). Keil (2:166–67), on the other hand, held that the tabernacle embodied the kingdom of God established in Israel, especially since the text stresses forms, numbers, and measurements. This kingdom of God will one day come to completion and encompass the entire world, just as the Most Holy Place is a cube, which points to the completion of the kingdom of God (cf. Rev 21–22).

My view is closest to Keil's kingdom-of-God meaning. The tabernacle, however, primarily embodies the theology of worship. It thereby assumes that God is the Great King who reigns and is therefore worthy of our praise and adoration. Even more specifically, the meaning of the tabernacle is that God has come "to dwell," "to tabernacle" in the midst of Israel, as he would one day come in the Incarnation (John 1:14) and will come in the Second Advent (Rev 21:3). The Lord who dwelt in his visible glory in his sanctuary among his people (Exod 25:8) will one day come and dwell in all his glory among his saints forever.

A. *The Tabernacle (25:1–31:18)*

1. *Collection of materials*

25:1–9

1 The LORD said to Moses, 2 "Tell the Israelites to bring me an offering. You are to receive the offering for me from each man whose heart prompts him to give. 3 These are the offerings you are to receive from them: gold, silver and bronze; 4 blue, purple and scarlet yarn and fine linen; goat hair; 5 ram skins dyed red and hides of sea cows; acacia wood; 6 olive oil for the light; spices for the anointing oil and for the fragrant incense; 7 and onyx stones and other gems to be mounted on the ephod and breastpiece.

8 "Then have them make a sanctuary for me, and I will dwell among them. 9 Make this tabernacle and all its furnishings exactly like the pattern I will show you.

1–2 The "offering" (= contribution) mentioned here (v.2) is not a "heave offering" (KJV, ASV mg.) but one separated for a sacred purpose as a gift to be consecrated to the Lord. See the translation of "special gift" in Deuteronomy 12:6, 11, 17. It was also a voluntary gift as v.2b stresses. Notice that "you" is plural and therefore refers to perhaps Moses and all the people, or it may be another example of Hebrew using the plural pronoun to refer to an individual.

3–7 The fourteen components or materials that went into the tabernacle are listed. They include (1) gold, (2) silver, and (3) bronze. Then follow three colors of yarn.

(4) "Blue" (*tᵉkēleṯ*, v.4) is a color derived from a dye of a shellfish, variously described as sky blue, deep dark blue, blue-purple, or bright violet. Its significance is not stated. Some say it is the "heavenly character of Christ," but scriptural support for this assertion is lacking.

(5) The color "purple" (*'argāmān*, v.4) is derived from the secretion of a gland of the murex snail and was supplied primarily by the Phoenicians. It is a purple-red. Although its significance is not stated, perhaps it speaks of royalty.

(6) The color "scarlet" (*tôla'aṯ*, v.4), or crimson, is derived from the eggs and bodies of the worm *coccus ilicis*, which attaches itself to the leaves of the holly plant. Their maggots are collected, dried, and pulverized; and the powder produces a bright red (or yellow-red) dye. It is a part of the heave offering. Its significance is not stated. Some say it is the "earthly aspect of the Son of Man."

(7) "Fine linen" (*šēš*, v.4) translates an Egyptian loan word in Hebrew. Some linen found in Egyptian tombs has 152 threads per inch in the warp as compared to only 86

threads per inch in the most finely woven modern techniques. It is usually white. Its significance is not stated. Perhaps it represents purity and righteousness.

(8) The "goat hair" (*'izzîm,* v.4) came from long-haired goats and most likely was black in color. It was a coarse material that often was used to weave tents. Felt would be a modern equivalent.

(9) The "ram skins" (*'ōrōṯ 'êlîm,* v.5) were skins that had all the wool removed and then were dyed red; it was like our morocco leather.

(10) The "hides of sea cows" (*'ōrōṯ tᵉḥāšîm,* v.5) no doubt came from the East African sea cows ("porpoise" or "dolphin"), found in the Red Sea.

(11) "Acacia wood" (*'ᵃṣê šiṭṭîm,* v.5) is a species of the mimosa (*mimosa nilotica*) whose wood is darker and harder than oak and therefore avoided by wood-eating insects. It is common in the Sinai Peninsula.

(12) There was also "olive oil" (v.6), made from crushing the olives, for light.

(13) The word for "spices" (*bᵉśāmîm,* v.6) is derived from *bāsam* ("to have a good smell," "to be fragrant"). The four best species for anointing oil are identified in 30:22–25 as "myrrh" (sap of a balsam bush), "cinnamon" (bark of the cinnamon tree, a species of laurel bush), "cane" or sweet calamus (a pink-colored pith from the root of a reed plant), and "cassia" (from the dried flowers of the cinnamon tree). The four species for incense are identified in 30:34–38 as "gum resin" or "stacte" (KJV; a powder taken from the middle of the hardened drops of the myrrh bush, rare and very valuable), "onycha" (from the shell of a type of clam [mollusks] similar to the purple murex snail and found deep in the Red Sea), "galbanum" (a rubbery resin of thick milky juice from the roots of a flowering plant thriving in Syria and Persia), and "frankincense" (a resin from the bark of *boswellia carteri* growing in southern Arabia). The *boswellia carteri* resin dripped spontaneously from the plant in the fall and was "pure," without any foreign matter—pure "white"—hence its Hebrew name "whiteness."

(14) The "onyx stones" (*'aḇnê šōham,* v.7) cannot be positively identified. The LXX translates it as "beryl," mostly a sea-green color. Another suggestion is a chrysoprase quartz ranging in color from blue-green to yellow-green and apple-green. The Egyptians knew chrysoprase. For other gems mounted in the ephod and breastplate, see 28:6–25.

8 The "sanctuary" (*miqdāš*) means "holy" place or "the place set apart." Everything about the tabernacle was holy. The same word in 1 and 2 Chronicles refers to the temple. Hebrews 9:1 calls the sanctuary "the sanctuary of this world" (NIV, "earthly sanctuary").

9 The most important word about the sanctuary was that it was to be built according to the "pattern" God would show Moses. The word "pattern" (*taḇnîṯ*) comes from the verb *bānāh* ("to build"). This word signals the fact that typology is present, for this is only a "model" or "pattern" of the real thing (see v.40).

The word "tabernacle" (*miškān*) appears for the first time here of its 139 OT occurrences. It is from the word "to dwell" (*šāḵan*) and is the place where God dwells among his people (cf. 29:42–46; Lev 26:9–12; Ezek 37:26–28; and in the NT, Rev 21:2–3).

Notes

2 תְּרוּמָה (*t^e^rûmāh*, "offering" or "contribution") can include sacrifices (29:27), money (30:13–15), produce (Num 15:19–21), or land (Ezek 45).

5 תְּחָשִׁים (*t^e^ḥāšîm*, "sea cows") is used in Ezek 16:10 for the "leather" of women's sandals. Most accept the Arabic cognate that means "dolphins" (see Childs, *Exodus*, p. 523). This "leather" then would be waterproof and suitable for the outer covering of the tabernacle.

2. *Ark and mercy seat*

25:10–22

10 "Have them make a chest of acacia wood—two and a half cubits long, a cubit and a half wide, and a cubit and a half high. 11 Overlay it with pure gold, both inside and out, and make a gold molding around it. 12 Cast four gold rings for it and fasten them to its four feet, with two rings on one side and two rings on the other. 13 Then make poles of acacia wood and overlay them with gold. 14 Insert the poles into the rings on the sides of the chest to carry it. 15 The poles are to remain in the rings of this ark; they are not to be removed. 16 Then put in the ark the Testimony, which I will give you.

17 "Make an atonement cover of pure gold—two and a half cubits long and a cubit and a half wide. 18 And make two cherubim out of hammered gold at the ends of the cover. 19 Make one cherub on one end and the second cherub on the other; make the cherubim of one piece with the cover, at the two ends. 20 The cherubim are to have their wings spread upward, overshadowing the cover with them. The cherubim are to face each other, looking toward the cover. 21 Place the cover on top of the ark and put in the ark the Testimony, which I will give you. 22 There, above the cover between the two cherubim that are over the ark of the Testimony, I will meet with you and give you all my commands for the Israelites.

The first item in Moses' list of instructions in the tabernacle was the ark of God with its *kappōreṯ* ("atonement cover") above it. Tyndale was the first to render this word as "mercy seat," followed in 1534 by Luther's translation. However, the ark was the place of atonement or propitiation, hence the place where God was rendered favorable to his people. Here we are taken immediately to the heart of the theology of the tabernacle and its purpose in Israel and now in the life of the church.

10a The "chest" or "ark" (from the Lat. *arca*) is mentioned 180 times, thereby stressing its importance. It is called "the ark [of] the Testimony" (v.15), "the ark of the covenant of the LORD of all the earth" (Josh 3:11), "the sacred ark" (2 Chron 35:3), and "the ark of your might" (Ps 132:8). It is the throne of God. Notice that God begins at the heart of things rather than working from the outside in (cf. also Heb 9:4; also H.J. Zobel, TDOT, 1:363–74).

10b–17 The dimensions of the ark were 3¾ feet long by 2¼ feet wide and high (v.10b mg.). The ark was to be overlaid with "pure gold" (v.11), from which silver and other impurities had been removed. It had a type of "molding" or "collar" (*zēr*) around it; the exact meaning and purpose of the *zēr* is conjectural.

The meaning of *pa^ca^mōṯāyw* is uncertain, but "its . . . [artificial] feet" probably is closest to its basic meaning (v.12; cf. Judg 5:28); the LXX renders it "corner" (cf. 1 Kings 7:30). See also Psalm 57:6; Proverbs 29:5; and Isaiah 26:6. Whatever it was, the four gold rings were attached there. The "acacia wood" poles were slid through the rings for transporting the chest (vv.13–14), and they were not to be removed from the rings (v.15). On the "Testimony" (v.16), see the Notes.

The verb that lies behind the noun "atonement" in the expression "atonement cover" (v.17) means "to ransom or deliver by means of a substitute." (There is no word for "lid" or "cover" here.) The expression is mentioned twenty-seven times. The LXX has "propitiatory covering" or "mercy seat," as does Hebrews 9:5 (NIV mg.). This place of expiating the sins of mankind is an adumbration of Christ's propitiatory work (Rom 3:25; Heb 9:23–24; 1 John 2:2) and is at the heart of our worship of the one who died for us.

18–22 A cherub (pl. "cherubim") is usually depicted as a composite creature with wings, a human head, and a body combining elements of an ox, a lion, or an eagle (cf. Gen 3:24; Ezek 1; Rev 4). In Egypt the sphinx was prevalent. In Assyria the same root word was used to describe one who functioned as a temple guardian. In some manner the two cherubim were to be made from the cover itself and as part of it (v.19). These were hardly made in relief, since they were "looking toward the cover" (v.20; cf. 1 Peter 1:12).

Verse 22 gives the theological relevance of the ark and cherubim, indeed, of all our worship of God: "There . . . I will meet with you." God is continually present in his tabernacle and walks among his people there (Lev 26:11–12). One of the primary intentions of worship is our meeting with the living God. It was from his throne above the cherubim that he spoke and met with his people (cf. 1 Sam 4:4).

Notes

---

16 עֵדֻת (*'ēḏuṯ*) means "Testimony" or "laws" of the Ten Commandments that were placed inside the ark. In Egypt, Babylonia, and the Hittite Empire, important documents were deposited in the sanctuary "at the feet" of the deity.

17 כַּפֹּרֶת (*kappōreṯ*, "atonement") is rendered in the LXX as *hilastērion* ("propitiatory") and in the Vulgate as *propitiatorium*. The basic root of the word *kpr* means "to make an atonement," which in the verbal idea is "to ransom or deliver by offering a substitute" (see Kaiser, *Old Testament Theology*, p. 117; G.L. Archer, TWOT, #1023).

---

3. *Table of the bread of the Presence*

25:23–30

23 "Make a table of acacia wood—two cubits long, a cubit wide and a cubit and a half high. 24 Overlay it with pure gold and make a gold molding around it. 25 Also make around it a rim a handbreadth wide and put a gold molding on the rim. 26 Make four gold rings for the table and fasten them to the four corners, where the four legs are. 27 The rings are to be close to the rim to hold the poles used in carrying the table. 28 Make the poles of acacia wood, overlay them with gold and carry the table with them. 29 And make its plates and dishes of pure gold, as well

as its pitchers and bowls for the pouring out of offerings. 30 Put the
bread of the Presence on this table to be before me at all times.

The table of the Presence was one of three pieces of furniture in the Holy Place. It was made of acacia wood overlaid with gold on which twelve loaves of bread were placed. The table with its bread presented two sides of the same truth: a godward side and a human side. First, it stood before God, reminding Israel that they were ever open to the all-seeing eye and protection of God. Next, it was the place where the priests served and found their bread. That bread pointed to him who was that Bread that would come down from heaven and give to men and women that everlasting bread (cf. John 6).

23–28 The "table" (v.23) measured three feet long by on and a half feet wide by twenty-seven inches high. The table taken from the second temple by Antiochus Epiphanes is depicted on the Arch of Titus among the items the Romans took back to Rome in A.D. 70. (See the description of the table in Josephus, Antiq. III, 139–41 [vi.6].) The description of the table is similar to the ark, overlaid with gold (v.24), with a molding or encircling rim (v.25) and four gold rings (v.26) to hold the transporting poles (vv.27–28).

29 "Its plates and dishes . . . its pitchers and bowls" were not for the purpose of serving God food as in pagan nations. Even the sacrifices set apart for God were not to be boiled or roasted; they were to come up before him in vapors and odors, not in substance or as food. Of course, some of the offerings were to be shared with the priests, and the fellowship offerings were shared in part with the people.

30 "The bread of the Presence" is referred to here and also in 1 Samuel 21:6 and 1 Kings 7:48. In this phrase "presence" (lit., "faces") stands for the Divine Person himself, just as the "angel of his presence" (lit., "face[s]") in Isaiah 63:9, or in Exodus 33:14–15, "my Presence [lit., 'my face'] shall go with you," is an OT designation of Christ. The twelve loaves symbolize the twelve tribes of Israel as constantly being under the scrutiny, care, and preservation of God (cf. John 6:32–38). Just as that bread also supplied the needs of priests on the Sabbath in the Holy Place (see Lev 24:5–9), so Jesus also meets the needs of his children in this generation (John 6:32–35).

Notes

25 The table on the Arch of Titus shows on two sides cross-stays that brace the legs about halfway up from the bottom of the legs to the table top. These cross-stays may be what is meant by מִסְגֶּרֶת (*misgeret*, "rim" or "frame").

29 The shape of many of the utensils mentioned here have had light thrown on them by modern archaeological excavations (e.g., W.F. Albright, *Annual of the American Schools of Oriental Research* [New Haven: Yale University Press], 12 [1933]; 13 [1934]).

4. *Golden lampstand*

25:31–40

[31] "Make a lampstand of pure gold and hammer it out, base and shaft; its flowerlike cups, buds and blossoms shall be of one piece with it. [32] Six branches are to extend from the sides of the lampstand—three on one side and three on the other. [33] Three cups shaped like almond flowers with buds and blossoms are to be on one branch, three on the next branch, and the same for all six branches extending from the lampstand. [34] And on the lampstand there are to be four cups shaped like almond flowers with buds and blossoms. [35] One bud shall be under the first pair of branches extending from the lampstand, a second bud under the second pair, and a third bud under the third pair—six branches in all. [36] The buds and branches shall all be of one piece with the lampstand, hammered out of pure gold.

[37] "Then make its seven lamps and set them up on it so that they light the space in front of it. [38] Its wick trimmers and trays are to be of pure gold. [39] A talent of pure gold is to be used for the lampstand and all these accessories. [40] See that you make them according to the pattern shown you on the mountain.

The third article in the Holy Place was the golden lampstand. The continuing use of the "lampstand" can be found in Zechariah 4 and Revelation 1:12, 20. Central to the teaching of the tabernacle is the One who is the Light of the world. Thus where God dwells, there is light.

31 "A lampstand [*m*ᵉ*nōrāh,* 'menorah'] of pure gold" was to be fashioned all in one piece. It was placed on the south or left side of the Holy Place. The word "candlestick" (KJV) is anachronistic since candles were not invented until Roman times.

The lampstand's design—"flowerlike cups, buds and blossoms"—was patterned after an almond (*amygdalus*) tree (v.33), the first tree of spring in the Near East, awakening as early as mid-December and decking itself in radiant white blossoms before leafing. The triad of its parts cannot be identified with final certainty. The "cups" were either the calyx (outer covering of the flower; cf. the same word translated "cup" in Gen 44:2) or the almond nut whose medical and cosmetic properties are described as perfect. The "bud" (so the Vul., LXX) is also rendered as the knop or bulb, the round object on the branch (same word as the capitals or chapiters on the pillars in Solomon's temple, 1 Kings 7:18). The "blossoms" of the almond tree render the same word as in Numbers 17:8, reported in connection with Aaron's almond rod budding and blossoming.

The expression "hammer it out" (*miqšāh*) is difficult. Josephus (Antiq. III, 144 [vi.6]) claims it was "cast gold [and] hollow," made in a mold. The verb is used of fashioning the cherubim (v.18), the lampstand (vv.31, 36; 37:17, 22; Num 8:4), and the two silver trumpets (Num 10:2). A.R.S. Kennedy (HDB, s.v. "Tabernacle") thinks this is *repousse,* or ornamentation on the reverse side, to get the design, while Unger (UBD, p. 1043) thinks it was hammered into sheets first. The verbal root means only "to be hard." The Greek word merely renders it "golden-turned work."

32–36 The total number of ornaments—i.e., "six branches . . . three cups . . . on the lampstand . . . four cups . . . one bud," etc.—would be 69 (6 branches times 3 sets times 3 figures plus 1 branch times 4 sets times 3 figures plus 3 buds under each set of branches equals 69). Josephus (Antiq. III, 145 [vi.7]) added 1 to make the number an even 70; the lampstand on the Arch of Titus has 42 ornaments while the Talmud (*Men* 28b) has only 30.

37–39 The ancient lamp was a kind of small, round (clay) saucer with the rim pinched together to form a spout from which protruded the top of the wick dipped in the oil of the saucer. Examples of seven-pinched-rim lamps come from the age of Moses (Late Bronze). Beth shan and Meggiddo have supplied examples of metal pedestals designed to carry a lamp, consisting of an upright three-foot-long shaft dividing into three feet and joined in a ring to be placed on the ground on top of which is a ledge for the lamp. "A talent of pure gold" (v.39) was about seventy-five pounds.

40 "According to the pattern" is once again a key word warning Moses and all subsequent readers that what he was really building was only a model, not the real, or the archetype, which lay behind the model. Therefore, it was "only a shadow of the good things that are coming—not the realities themselves" (Heb 10:1). Thus there was a built-in obsolescence in this revelation and the models exhibited in the whole tabernacle and its service as contained in Exodus 25–Leviticus 9. The archetype remained with God while these earthly models merely pictured what was yet to come.

Notes

31 The Arch of Titus depiction of the seven-branched menorah is still the standard for this piece of tabernacle furniture. See E. Goodenough, "The Menorah Among the Jews of the Roman World," HUCA 23 (1950–51): 449–92.

גְּבִיעֶיהָ (*g^e^b̲îʿeyhā*, "its flowerlike cups") is the plural of the word for "cup" used in Gen 44:2, 12, 16. כַּפְתֹּרֶיהָ (*kap̲tōreyhā*, "its buds") is also used in Amos 9:1 and Zeph 2:14, but there it is translated as "columns" or "pillars."

5. *Curtains, framework, veil, and screen (26:1–37)*

a. *The tabernacle's curtains*

26:1–14

[1] "Make the tabernacle with ten curtains of finely twisted linen and blue, purple and scarlet yarn, with cherubim worked into them by a skilled craftsman. [2] All the curtains are to be the same size—twenty-eight cubits long and four cubits wide. [3] Join five of the curtains together, and do the same with the other five. [4] Make loops of blue material along the edge of the end curtain in one set, and do the same with the end curtain in the other set. [5] Make fifty loops on one curtain and fifty loops on the end curtain of the other set, with the loops opposite each other. [6] Then make fifty gold clasps and use them to fasten the curtains together so that the tabernacle is a unit.

[7] "Make curtains of goat hair for the tent over the tabernacle—eleven altogether. [8] All eleven curtains are to be the same size—thirty cubits long and four cubits wide. [9] Join five of the curtains together into one set and the other six into another set. Fold the sixth curtain double at the front of the tent. [10] Make fifty loops along the edge of the end curtain in

one set and also along the edge of the end curtain in the other set.
[11]Then make fifty bronze clasps and put them in the loops to fasten the tent together as a unit. [12]As for the additional length of the tent curtains, the half curtain that is left over is to hang down at the rear of the tabernacle. [13]The tent curtains will be a cubit longer on both sides; what is left will hang over the sides of the tabernacle so as to cover it. [14]Make for the tent a covering of ram skins dyed red, and over that a covering of hides of sea cows.

There are two sets of coverings and two sets of curtains. The coverings were an outer one of hides of sea cows and an inner one of ram skins dyed red. The two sets of curtains were an outer set of goat hair and an inner set of fine linen with blue, purple, and scarlet yarn. Notice once again that the text moves from the inside to the outside because this is ever God's order. We may approach the sanctuary from the outside, but our Lord plans from within the sanctuary.

Within the sanctuary, moving from the inside out, the curtains of fine linen were visible only to the priests who served in the presence of him who is purity and righteousness itself. The curtains of goats' hair were reminders of the daily sin offering that was a kid from the goats (Num 28:15) and of our cleansing from sin (Lev 16). The covering of rams' skins also recalled the sacrifice used in consecrating the priesthood (Lev 8); and it was deliberately dyed red, showing that the priesthood was set apart by blood. Finally, the protective coating of the sea cows' hides marked a protective separation between the dwelling place of God and the world.

1–3 On the "linen" see the comment on 25:4. Each of the "ten curtains of finely twisted linen" was about forty-two feet long and six feet wide (v.2 mg.). They were sewn together in two sets of five (v.3). Notice that the curtains were more important than the tabernacle's frame, for they are described first, thus setting up the same priority we saw in the ordering of the description of all the tabernacle's parts.

4–6 After stitching each five-sectioned curtain together, two curtains were coupled together by fifty loops on one side and fifty loops on the other side (vv.4–5). These were then to be joined by fifty golden clasps or hooks (v.6; cf. v.11). The beauty of these white, fine linen curtains with blue, purple, and scarlet yarn (see comment on 25:4) was enhanced with cherubim (see comment on 25:18) embroidered on them.

7–13 Of the eleven "curtains of goat hair" (vv.7–8), six were sewed in one portion and five in another (v.9), and again the fifty loops on one side were joined to the fifty loops on the other by fifty clasps (vv. 10–11). Goat hair in the Eastern world is black, not white (cf. S of Songs 1:5; cf. comment on 25:4). Since the "tent curtains" (vv.12–13) were larger than the curtains of the tabernacle (vv. 1–6), there would be material left on the end and on either side to "hang down the rear" (v.12) and to "hang over the sides of the tabernacle so as to cover it" (v.13).

14 On the "ram skins dyed red," the first of the two outer coverings placed over the two inner coverings of linen and goat hair, and the "covering of hides of sea cows," see the comment on 25:5.

b. *The tabernacle's framework*

26:15–30

15 “Make upright frames of acacia wood for the tabernacle. 16 Each
frame is to be ten cubits long and a cubit and a half wide, 17 with two
projections set parallel to each other. Make all the frames of the
tabernacle in this way. 18 Make twenty frames for the south side of the
tabernacle 19 and make forty silver bases to go under them—two bases
for each frame, one under each projection. 20 For the other side, the
north side of the tabernacle, make twenty frames 21 and forty silver
bases—two under each frame. 22 Make six frames for the far end, that is,
the west end of the tabernacle, 23 and make two frames for the corners
at the far end. 24 At these two corners they must be double from the
bottom all the way to the top, and fitted into a single ring; both shall be
like that. 25 So there will be eight frames and sixteen silver bases—two
under each frame.

26 “Also make crossbars of acacia wood: five for the frames on one
side of the tabernacle, 27 five for those on the other side, and five for the
frames on the west, at the far end of the tabernacle. 28 The center
crossbar is to extend from end to end at the middle of the frames.
29 Overlay the frames with gold and make gold rings to hold the
crossbars. Also overlay the crossbars with gold.

30 “Set up the tabernacle according to the plan shown you on the
mountain.

15–25 On “acacia wood” see the comment on 25:5. The command to “make upright frames” (v.15; cf. vv.19, 26) introduces the three elements that made up the “walls.” The traditional rendering “boards” has led many to the idea that the walls were solid; but if this were so, it would have obscured the inner linen curtains from sight (Kennedy, “Tabernacle,” 4:660. The LXX translates *qᵉrāšîm* as *stylous,* “pillars”). These frames formed a trellislike structure over which the four curtains were draped.

Each frame was to be fifteen feet long by two and a quarter feet wide (v.16 mg.). The framework of the tabernacle consisted of twenty boards each on the north and south sides (vv. 18–20) with six on the western end with a post at each of the two corners (vv.22–23). The “two projections” (lit., “hands”) are probably the two tenons at the bottom of each frame to be inserted into the bases. The frames were fitted into a foundation of “forty silver bases” (v.19) or sockets on each side. Israel contributed one hundred talents of silver for these bases (38:25–28), which was described as atonement money (30:11–16). Thus it may be said that the foundation of the tabernacle rested on a ransom or redemption, just as the church was “bought with his own blood” (Acts 20:28).

The Hebrew word for “corner” (*miqṣôaʿ*) apparently means “angle.” Thus one frame was cut down the center on a miter, and the two pieces would form the “corner” or “angle” frame on the two sides of the corner.

26–29 Fifteen “crossbars” (v.26) were to be fitted on the outside of the structure to strengthen the trellis framework: five on each of the two sides (north and south) and five on the back (west). One of the five was full length down the middle of the wall (v.28), the other four extended only half the length of the wall, making three rows of bars on the outside of the frame. The “gold rings” (v.29) were to serve as holders (lit., “houses”) for the bars (cf. 25:26–27).

30 Once more we are reminded of the typological nature of this material, for all was to be done "according to plan" (cf. comment on 25:40; cf. also 25:9; 27:8; Acts 7:44). Hebrews 8:5 comments that since the tabernacle was intended to be a "copy and shadow of what is in heaven. . . . Moses was warned when he was about to build the tabernacle: 'See to it that you make everything according to the pattern shown you on the mountain.' "

Notes

15 There is still open debate as to whether הַקְּרָשִׁים (*haqqᵉrāšîm,* "the frames") were open framework, allowing the design on the curtains to be seen (Kennedy, "Tabernacle," 4:563–68; and RSV), or solid boards (Kurt Galling, *Biblisches Reallexition* [Tübingen: J.C.B. Mohr, 1937], cols. 150ff.). See also M. Haran, "The Priestly Image of the Tabernacle," HUCA 36 (1965): 192, and Cross, "The Tabernacle." Note also Baruch A. Levine, "The Description of the Tabernacle Texts of the Pentateuch," JAOS 85 (1965): 307–18, and J. Morgenstern, "The Ark, the Ephod and the Tent," HUCA 17 (1942–43): 153–265; 18 (1943–44): 1–52.

19 The שְׁתֵּי יָדוֹת (*šᵉttê yāḏôṯ,* "two projections"; NIV, "each projection") may have been the two pins at the lower end of each frame that held the frame in the mortises of the bases. Kennedy (HDB, 4:563–68) takes them instead to be the two upright arms that formed two sides of each frame in addition to the three crossbars, one each at the top, the bottom, and the middle (see v.28).

b. *The tabernacle's veil*

26:31–35

31 "Make a curtain of blue, purple and scarlet yarn and finely twisted linen, with cherubim worked into it by a skilled craftsman. 32 Hang it with gold hooks on four posts of acacia wood overlaid with gold and standing on four silver bases. 33 Hang the curtain from the clasps and place the ark of the Testimony behind the curtain. The curtain will separate the Holy Place from the Most Holy Place. 34 Put the atonement cover on the ark of the Testimony in the Most Holy Place. 35 Place the table outside the curtain on the north side of the tabernacle and put the lampstand opposite it on the south side.

31–35 The inner veil (NIV, "curtain," v.31), which was to separate the Most Holy Place from the Holy Place (v.33), was to be made of the same material and design as the inner curtain and supported on four gold-covered acacia wood pillars (v.32). The "veil" is called the "veil of covering" or "shielding curtain" in 39:34; 40:21; and Numbers 4:5, or the "curtain [or 'veil'] that is in front of the Testimony" in Exodus 27:21. Some say the word "curtain" comes from an unattested verb meaning "to break" or "to separate." At the death of Christ, this inner curtain of the temple was torn in two, thereby giving the believer permanent access to the presence of God (Matt 27:51; Mark 15:38; Luke 23:45; Heb 6:19; 9:3; 10:19–22).

d. *The tabernacle's screen*

26:36–37

[36] "For the entrance to the tent make a curtain of blue, purple and scarlet yarn and finely twisted linen—the work of an embroiderer. [37] Make gold hooks for this curtain and five posts of acacia wood overlaid with gold. And cast five bronze bases for them.

36 "The entrance . . . curtain" was like the curtain dividing the two inner rooms (v.33) of the tabernacle and the inner curtain of v.1. The same Hebrew word (*māsāḵ*, "screen," "curtain") is used for the curtain at the entrance to the courtyard (27:16) as the screen for the entrance to the tent (here).

37 Since this curtain went to the outside and to the corners of the wall, it had "five posts of acacia wood overlaid with gold" instead of just four (v.32).

6. *Altar of burnt offering*

27:1–8

[1] "Build an altar of acacia wood, three cubits high; it is to be square, five cubits long and five cubits wide. [2] Make a horn at each of the four corners, so that the horns and the altar are of one piece, and overlay the altar with bronze. [3] Make all its utensils of bronze—its pots to remove the ashes, and its shovels, sprinkling bowls, meat forks and firepans. [4] Make a grating for it, a bronze network, and make a bronze ring at each of the four corners of the network. [5] Put it under the ledge of the altar so that it is halfway up the altar. [6] Make poles of acacia wood for the altar and overlay them with bronze. [7] The poles are to be inserted into the rings so they will be on two sides of the altar when it is carried. [8] Make the altar hollow, out of boards. It is to be made just as you were shown on the mountain.

The first and largest piece of equipment that a worshiper would meet on entering the court of the tabernacle was the bronze altar. On it sacrifices were to be burned to meet and satisfy the claims of a holy God. Its position just inside the gate made it easily accessible, unavoidable, and unmistakable.

1–2 The "altar" (v.1) is called the altar of burnt offering in Leviticus 4:7, 10, 18. It was made of acacia wood (see comment on 25:5) and measured seven and one-half feet square by four and one-half feet high. It was overlaid with bronze (v.2). There was but one altar just as there is but one way of salvation, and this Jesus fulfilled (see John 1:29; Heb 9:13–14, 22–28). The "horns," i.e., "a horn at each of the four corners," were projections of the four corner posts but of one piece with the altar. They symbolized power, help, and sanctuary (cf. 1 Sam 2:1, 10; 2 Sam 22:3; 1 Kings 1:50; 2:28; Pss 89:17; 112:9). The reason the horns symbolized the atoning power of the altar was that in the atonement ritual some of the blood was put on the horns before the rest was poured out at the base of the altar (29:12; Lev 4:7, 18, 25, 30, 34; 8:15; 9:9; 16:18).

3 The "pots" (or pans) were to hold the fat-soaked ashes when they were removed from the hearth by the "shovels." The "sprinkling bowls" (or basins) were to catch the blood of the animals slain beside the altar to be sprinkled on the altar's base later on.

The "meat forks" (fleshhooks) were three-pronged forks for arranging the sacrifice or retracting the priests' portion (1 Sam 2:13). The "fire pans" (or possibly "censers") probably were for carrying fire from the altar of incense inside the Holy Place (Lev 10:1; 16:12; 1 Kings 7:50).

4–8 A "grating" was placed midway between the top and the bottom of the boxlike structure. This grating divided the altar into a lower and an upper part, a division necessitated by the sprinkling of the blood. Since any fire built inside the upper half would have eventually destroyed the altar from the intense heat, most conjecture that the altar box was designed to be filled with earth when it was in use; but the text does not mention this. Perhaps this is why it was to be made "hollow" (v.8).

"A bronze ring at each of the four corners" (v.4) was attached to the bronze grating through which the acacia wood staves (v.6) were placed when the altar had to be moved (v.7). The "ledge" (v.5) was a projection or a collar around the altar halfway up its side.

7. *Court of the tabernacle*

27:9–19

9 "Make a courtyard for the tabernacle. The south side shall be a hundred cubits long and is to have curtains of finely twisted linen, 10 with twenty posts and twenty bronze bases and with silver hooks and bands on the posts. 11 The north side shall also be a hundred cubits long and is to have curtains, with twenty posts and twenty bronze bases and with silver hooks and bands on the posts.

12 "The west end of the courtyard shall be fifty cubits wide and have curtains, with ten posts and ten bases. 13 On the east end, toward the sunrise, the courtyard shall also be fifty cubits wide. 14 Curtains fifteen cubits long are to be on one side of the entrance, with three posts and three bases, 15 and curtains fifteen cubits long are to be on the other side, with three posts and three bases.

16 "For the entrance to the courtyard, provide a curtain twenty cubits long, of blue, purple and scarlet yarn and finely twisted linen—the work of an embroiderer—with four posts and four bases. 17 All the posts around the courtyard are to have silver bands and hooks, and bronze bases. 18 The courtyard shall be a hundred cubits long and fifty cubits wide, with curtains of finely twisted linen five cubits high, and with bronze bases. 19 All the other articles used in the service of the tabernacle, whatever their function, including all the tent pegs for it and those for the courtyard, are to be of bronze.

9–11 The "courtyard for the tabernacle" was a perfect oblong, twice as long as its breadth: 150 feet long by 75 feet wide (vv.9, 12, 13, 18 mg.). Its purposes were fourfold: (1) it was a barrier in that it prevented unlawful approach; (2) it was a protection, keeping out all wild animals; (3) it was a positive line of demarcation between the world and the holy presence of God; and (4) with its single gate, it was a way of approach to God.

The courtyard was to be shielded by a curtain made of the same fabric and colors (v.16) as the entrance, dividing, and inner curtains of the tabernacle (26:31–33, 36–37). It was to be high enough (seven and one-half feet, v.18) to block the view of all persons. Each long side was to have "twenty posts and twenty bronze bases" (vv.10–11). In all there would be sixty posts (or fifty-six if the corner posts were counted twice as belonging to each side from an observer's point of view). The posts were spaced seven and one-half feet apart, with a frame or rod going through the top of the silver capitals or "bands" (v.17) providing a frame or guy rod to give stability to the posts. They were also anchored by guy ropes and pegs.

12–19 The courtyard was divided in half. The tabernacle occupied the central position in the west half, and the altar and laver were probably somewhat centered in the eastern half (vv. 12–13; see NIV Study Bible, p. 124). The entrance was invitingly wide; "curtains fifteen cubits long" were to flank the entrance, which would be twenty cubits (about thirty feet) wide (vv.14–16; cf. 26:36–37). The entrance, too, marked a division between the world and the dwelling place of God. All the poles surrounding the courtyard had silver fillets or "bands" (v.17), which apparently were narrow strips of binding metal used as decoration (so Childs, *Exodus*, p. 526) and not as connecting rods.

8. *Priesthood*

27:20–28:5

[20]"Command the Israelites to bring you clear oil of pressed olives for the light so that the lamps may be kept burning. [21]In the Tent of Meeting, outside the curtain that is in front of the Testimony, Aaron and his sons are to keep the lamps burning before the LORD from evening till morning. This is to be a lasting ordinance among the Israelites for the generations to come.

[28:1]"Have Aaron your brother brought to you from among the Israelites, along with his sons Nadab and Abihu, Eleazar and Ithamar, so they may serve me as priests. [2]Make sacred garments for your brother Aaron, to give him dignity and honor. [3]Tell all the skilled men to whom I have given wisdom in such matters that they are to make garments for Aaron, for his consecration, so he may serve me as priest. [4]These are the garments they are to make: a breastpiece, an ephod, a robe, a woven tunic, a turban and a sash. They are to make these sacred garments for your brother Aaron and his sons, so they may serve me as priests. [5]Have them use gold, and blue, purple and scarlet yarn, and fine linen.

Only Aaron and his four sons were to serve as priests in standing before God. The priest was the indispensable mediator in the life of fellowship with God.

20–21 The "clear oil of pressed olives" (v.20) was extracted from unripened olives that were beaten and pounded in a mortar rather than crushed in a mill. The pulpy mass was then placed in a basket; and the oil, without any mixture of other parts of the olive, dripped through the basket, giving a clear, pure oil that burned with little or no smoke.

Josephus (Antiq. III, 199 [viii.3]) contends that three lamps were kept burning "throughout the day." Verse 21, however, says the lamps were to be kept burning "from evening till morning." Other verses show that all the lamps were lit every evening (30:8) and extinguished in the morning (1 Sam 3:3). Significantly, the people were to provide this oil continuously; otherwise there would be darkness in the dwelling place of God.

1 "Nadab and Abihu" were two of Aaron's four sons who later offered unauthorized fire before the Lord and were consumed (Lev 10:1–2), leaving only Eleazer and

Ithamar. Aaron and his sons were to "serve . . . as priests." They were to stand before the Lord (applied to *all* Levites in Deut 10:8) "to offer gifts and sacrifices for sins" and "to deal gently with those who are ignorant and are going astray" (Heb 5:1–2). They were to teach the people (Neh 8:2, 9) and serve as intercessors for them.

2–5 The garments of the high priest were "to give him dignity and honor" (v.2), i.e., they were to exalt the office and function of the high priest as well as beautify the worship of God. "The skilled men" (v.3) were to make priestly garments for Aaron. Eight garments are mentioned: the four inner garments worn by all priests—tunics, linen undergarments or breeches, girdles or sashes, and headbands (vv.39–42). The four overgarments that were to be especially worn by Aaron were the breastpiece, ephod, robe, and turban (mitre) (v.4).

Notes

---

21 Some wish to view the word וּבָנָיו (*ûḇānāyw*, "and his sons") as a gloss since they are not present in Lev 24:1–4. However, Levine ("Tabernacle Texts," pp. 311–12) would retain the reading, noting this same phenomenon in several comparisons between Exodus and Leviticus.

28:2 בִּגְדֵי־קֹדֶשׁ (*bigḏê-qōḏeš*, "holy or sacred garments") shows that the priests had some type of dress distinguishable from the laity, thereby indicating that their task and mission set them apart to the Lord. It also indicated that they served a holy King (cf. comment on 3:5–6).

---

9. *Garments of the priests*

28:6–43

6"Make the ephod of gold, and of blue, purple and scarlet yarn, and of
finely twisted linen—the work of a skilled craftsman. 7It is to have two
shoulder pieces attached to two of its corners, so it can be fastened. 8Its
skillfully woven waistband is to be like it—of one piece with the ephod
and made with gold, and with blue, purple and scarlet yarn, and with
finely twisted linen.
9"Take two onyx stones and engrave on them the names of the sons
of Israel 10in the order of their birth—six names on one stone and the
remaining six on the other. 11Engrave the names of the sons of Israel on
the two stones the way a gem cutter engraves a seal. Then mount the
stones in gold filigree settings 12and fasten them on the shoulder pieces
of the ephod as memorial stones for the sons of Israel. Aaron is to bear
the names on his shoulders as a memorial before the LORD. 13Make gold
filigree settings 14and two braided chains of pure gold, like a rope, and
attach the chains to the settings.
15"Fashion a breastpiece for making decisions—the work of a skilled
craftsman. Make it like the ephod: of gold, and of blue, purple and
scarlet yarn, and of finely twisted linen. 16It is to be square—a span long
and a span wide—and folded double. 17Then mount four rows of
precious stones on it. In the first row there shall be a ruby, a topaz and a
beryl; 18in the second row a turquoise, a sapphire and an emerald; 19in
the third row a jacinth, an agate and an amethyst; 20in the fourth row a
chrysolite, an onyx and a jasper. Mount them in gold filigree settings.
21There are to be twelve stones, one for each of the names of the sons

of Israel, each engraved like a seal with the name of one of the twelve
tribes.
22 "For the breastpiece make braided chains of pure gold, like a rope.
23 Make two gold rings for it and fasten them to two corners of the
breastpiece. 24 Fasten the two gold chains to the rings at the corners of
the breastpiece, 25 and the other ends of the chains to the two settings,
attaching them to the shoulder pieces of the ephod at the front. 26 Make
two gold rings and attach them to the other two corners of the
breastpiece on the inside edge next to the ephod. 27 Make two more gold
rings and attach them to the bottom of the shoulder pieces on the front
of the ephod, close to the seam just above the waistband of the ephod.
28 The rings of the breastpiece are to be tied to the rings of the ephod
with blue cord, connecting it to the waistband, so that the breastpiece
will not swing out from the ephod.
29 "Whenever Aaron enters the Holy Place, he will bear the names of
the sons of Israel over his heart on the breastpiece of decision as a
continuing memorial before the LORD. 30 Also put the Urim and the
Thummim in the breastpiece, so they may be over Aaron's heart
whenever he enters the presence of the LORD. Thus Aaron will always
bear the means of making decisions for the Israelites over his heart
before the LORD.
31 "Make the robe of the ephod entirely of blue cloth, 32 with an
opening for the head in its center. There shall be a woven edge like a
collar around this opening, so that it will not tear. 33 Make pomegranates
of blue, purple and scarlet yarn around the hem of the robe, with gold
bells between them. 34 The gold bells and the pomegranates are to
alternate around the hem of the robe. 35 Aaron must wear it when he
ministers. The sound of the bells will be heard when he enters the Holy
Place before the LORD and when he comes out, so that he will not die.
36 "Make a plate of pure gold and engrave on it as on a seal: HOLY TO THE
LORD. 37 Fasten a blue cord to it to attach it to the turban; it is to be on
the front of the turban. 38 It will be on Aaron's forehead, and he will bear
the guilt involved in the sacred gifts the Israelites consecrate, whatever
their gifts may be. It will be on Aaron's forehead continually so that they
will be acceptable to the LORD.
39 "Weave the tunic of fine linen and make the turban of fine linen. The
sash is to be the work of an embroiderer. 40 Make tunics, sashes and
headbands for Aaron's sons, to give them dignity and honor. 41 After you
put these clothes on your brother Aaron and his sons, anoint and ordain
them. Consecrate them so they may serve me as priests.
42 "Make linen undergarments as a covering for the body, reaching
from the waist to the thigh. 43 Aaron and his sons must wear them
whenever they enter the Tent of Meeting or approach the altar to
minister in the Holy Place, so that they will not incur guilt and die.
"This is to be a lasting ordinance for Aaron and his descendants.

6–14 The ephod probably was a high priestly waistcoat woven of blue, purple, scarlet, and white linen thread—all entwined with gold thread. Instead of having sleeves or being joined at the sides, it was hung from the shoulders by straps on which one onyx stone was mounted on each strap on top of a golden clasp with the names of the six younger sons of Israel engraved on one stone and the six elder sons engraved on the other stone (vv.9–10). The LXX makes the onyx "emeralds," while Josephus (Antiq. III, 165 [vii.5]) makes them "sardonyx," the best variety of onyx. The purpose of the names is to symbolize the fact that the high priest represented all Israel when he ministered in the tabernacle (v.12). A "waistband" (v.8) made of the same material and style as the ephod held the front and back of the ephod to the priest's body. It had no significance of its own.

15–30 The "breastpiece" (v.15), a square piece of cloth made the same way as the ephod, was folded in half upward to form a sort of pouch in a nine-inch-by-nine-inch square (v.16). Two rings at the inside lower corners attached the breastpiece to the rings of the ephod with a blue cord (v.28). Two golden rings on the top of the breastpiece fastened it to the shoulder pieces of the ephod with two golden chains (vv.22–28). Twelve stones, one for each tribe, were set in four rows of three stones: the name of each son of Jacob was engraved on its respective stone in the proper birth order of the sons (vv.17–21). Thus the nation was doubly represented before the Lord (v.29).

On the identity of the stones, see A. Paul Davis and E.L. Gilmore (*Lapidary Journal* [Dec. 1968]: 1124–28; 1130–34). The stones remind us of the value God sets on each individual made in his image and particularly on the sons of Israel.

The "Urim and the Thummim" (v.30; lit., "lights and perfection") often were used in times of crisis to determine the will of God (Num 27:21), but just how they functioned and what they looked like is unknown. Perhaps they only symbolized the special revelation open to the high priest rather than being the necessary means of achieving that information. See also Leviticus 8:8; Numbers 27:21; Deuteronomy 33:8; 1 Samuel 28:6; Ezra 2:63; and Nehemiah 7:65.

31–35 Under the ephod was a long, sleeveless blue "robe," woven without a seam (v.31), which reached a little below the knees. It had slits for the arms and a hole for the head to pass through (v.32). Along the hem were blue, purple, and scarlet alternating pomegranates and golden bells (vv.33–34). The bells, which jingled as the high priest served in the tabernacle, assured all who listened that he had not died in the Holy Place and that he continued to minister on their behalf (v.35).

36–39 The most conspicuous and important feature of the "turban" (mitre) was the golden plate with the engraving "HOLY TO THE LORD" (v.36). The golden plate stretched over the forehead from ear to ear and was attached with a blue band going through two holes at the ends of the plate and then over the top of the head to a hole in the center of the golden plate (vv.37–38). On the high priest's headdress of a white linen caplike turban, see Josephus (Antiq. III, 157–58 [vii.3]).

The "tunic of fine linen" (v.39) no doubt referred to a long white linen coat worn over the linen drawers or breeches (v.42), which, according to Josephus (Antiq. III, 153–55 [vii.2]), reached down to the ankles and was close-fitted to the body as were the sleeves.

40–43 The attire for the ordinary priests is described next. Its purpose was to give "dignity and honor" (v.40; lit., "glory and beauty") to them in their office. Verse 41 forms a transition to chapter 29, which speaks of the ordination of the priests. On the linen garments (vv.42–43), see on comment 20:26.

Notes

6 The אֵפֹד (*'ēp̱ōḏ*, "ephod") was sometimes a garment such as Samuel (1 Sam 2:18) and David (2 Sam 6:14) wore. Sometimes it was a solid object like an image of a god (Judg 8:27; 17:5;

18:14–17); at other times it was an object used to inquire of the Lord (1 Sam 14:3, 18[the LXX has "ephod"]–19, 36–42). This later usage may reflect the ephod's association with the Urim and Thummim. It may also be that the word "ephod" is used to describe two different objects or that it is a garment also placed on an idol as well as worn by a priest. Some view the garment as a waistcoat and others as an apron or a garment worn over the lower part of the body.

7 Concerning the "two shoulder pieces," Hyatt (p. 282) points to a Sixth-Dynasty Egyptian tomb inscription that shows male dancers with two shoulder pieces holding up a loinclothlike garment (Pritchard, *Ancient Pictures*, p. 210).

---

10. *Ordination of the priests*

29:1–46

[1]"This is what you are to do to consecrate them, so they may serve me
as priests: Take a young bull and two rams without defect. [2]And from
fine wheat flour, without yeast, make bread, and cakes mixed with oil,
and wafers spread with oil. [3]Put them in a basket and present them in
it—along with the bull and the two rams. [4]Then bring Aaron and his
sons to the entrance to the Tent of Meeting and wash them with water.
[5]Take the garments and dress Aaron with the tunic, the robe of the
ephod, the ephod itself and the breastpiece. Fasten the ephod on him by
its skillfully woven waistband. [6]Put the turban on his head and attach
the sacred diadem to the turban. [7]Take the anointing oil and anoint him
by pouring it on his head. [8]Bring his sons and dress them in tunics [9]and
put headbands on them. Then tie sashes on Aaron and his sons. The
priesthood is theirs by a lasting ordinance. In this way you shall ordain
Aaron and his sons.

[10]"Bring the bull to the front of the Tent of Meeting, and Aaron and
his sons shall lay their hands on its head. [11]Slaughter it in the LORD's
presence at the entrance to the Tent of Meeting. [12]Take some of the
bull's blood and put it on the horns of the altar with your finger, and
pour out the rest of it at the base of the altar. [13]Then take all the fat
around the inner parts, the covering of the liver, and both kidneys with
the fat around them, and burn them on the altar. [14]But burn the bull's
flesh and its hide and its offal outside the camp. It is a sin offering.

[15]"Take one of the rams, and Aaron and his sons shall lay their hands
on its head. [16]Slaughter it and take the blood and sprinkle it against the
altar on all sides. [17]Cut the ram into pieces and wash the inner parts and
the legs, putting them with the head and the other pieces. [18]Then burn
the entire ram on the altar. It is a burnt offering to the LORD, a pleasing
aroma, an offering made to the LORD by fire.

[19]"Take the other ram, and Aaron and his sons shall lay their hands
on its head. [20]Slaughter it, take some of its blood and put it on the lobes
of the right ears of Aaron and his sons, on the thumbs of their right
hands, and on the big toes of their right feet. Then sprinkle blood
against the altar on all sides. [21]And take some of the blood on the altar
and some of the anointing oil and sprinkle it on Aaron and his garments
and on his sons and their garments. Then he and his sons and their
garments will be consecrated.

[22]"Take from this ram the fat, the fat tail, the fat around the inner
parts, the covering of the liver, both kidneys with the fat around them,
and the right thigh. (This is the ram for the ordination.) [23]From the
basket of bread made without yeast, which is before the LORD, take a
loaf, and a cake made with oil, and a wafer. [24]Put all these in the hands
of Aaron and his sons and wave them before the LORD as a wave
offering. [25]Then take them from their hands and burn them on the altar

along with the burnt offering for a pleasing aroma to the LORD, an offering made to the LORD by fire. [26]After you take the breast of the ram for Aaron's ordination, wave it before the LORD as a wave offering, and it will be your share.

[27]"Consecrate those parts of the ordination ram that belong to Aaron and his sons: the breast that was waved and the thigh that was presented. [28]This is always to be the regular share from the Israelites for Aaron and his sons. It is the contribution the Israelites are to make to the LORD from their fellowship offerings.

[29]"Aaron's sacred garments will belong to his descendants so that they can be anointed and ordained in them. [30]The son who succeeds him as priest and comes to the Tent of Meeting to minister in the Holy Place is to wear them seven days.

[31]"Take the ram for the ordination and cook the meat in a sacred place. [32]At the entrance to the Tent of Meeting, Aaron and his sons are to eat the meat of the ram and the bread that is in the basket. [33]They are to eat these offerings by which atonement was made for their ordination and consecration. But no one else may eat them, because they are sacred. [34]And if any of the meat of the ordination ram or any bread is left over till morning, burn it up. It must not be eaten, because it is sacred.

[35]"Do for Aaron and his sons everything I have commanded you, taking seven days to ordain them. [36]Sacrifice a bull each day as a sin offering to make atonement. Purify the altar by making atonement for it, and anoint it to consecrate it. [37]For seven days make atonement for the altar and consecrate it. Then the altar will be most holy, and whatever touches it will be holy.

[38]"This is what you are to offer on the altar regularly each day: two lambs a year old. [39]Offer one in the morning and the other at twilight. [40]With the first lamb offer a tenth of an ephah of fine flour mixed with a quarter of a hin of oil from pressed olives, and a quarter of a hin of wine as a drink offering. [41]Sacrifice the other lamb at twilight with the same grain offering and its drink offering as in the morning—a pleasing aroma, an offering made to the LORD by fire.

[42]"For the generations to come this burnt offering is to be made regularly at the entrance to the Tent of Meeting before the LORD. There I will meet you and speak to you; [43]there also I will meet with the Israelites, and the place will be consecrated by my glory.

[44]"So I will consecrate the Tent of Meeting and the altar and will consecrate Aaron and his sons to serve me as priests. [45]Then I will dwell among the Israelites and be their God. [46]They will know that I am the LORD their God, who brought them out of Egypt so that I might dwell among them. I am the LORD their God.

The instructions given to Moses in 28:41 are here elaborated in greater detail and are implemented in Leviticus 8. The consecration of Aaron and his sons in an act of ordination only stressed the seriousness and central mission they had been given in the whole act of worship of our holy God.

1–9 Aaron and his sons were installed as high priest and ministering priests, respectively. This service of consecration uniquely marked them for the service of the tabernacle. The sacrifices for this occasion were to be "without defect" (v.1; cf. comment on 12:5). Similarly, the consecrating sacrifice must be "without yeast" (v.2; cf. comment on 12:15). Then Aaron and his sons were to be washed (v.4). The investiture of the high priest involved nine acts (Lev 8:7–9), but for ordinary priests it involved only three (vv.8–9). Washing with water symbolized the removal of uncleanness resulting from sin (v.4; cf. 40:12–13; Lev 8:6–9; notice its significance in Heb 10:22).

Aaron and his sons were next dressed in the clothes described in chapter 28 and then anointed. The manner in which Aaron, the high priest, was anointed was different than that of his sons (v.7; cf. v.21; cf. also Lev 21:10). For the composition of the anointing oil, see 30:22–25. Notice the connection of the verb *māšaḥ* ("anoint") with the noun *māšîaḥ* ("anointed one," viz., "Messiah"; cf. TWOT, #1255).

10–12 A bull was brought as a sin offering to atone for Aaron and his sons' past sins. This was accomplished in symbol by laying their hands on the bull's head, in effect transferring their sins to the sin-bearer (cf. the sin offering of Lev 4:1–5:13 and the clear parallel of the Day of Atonement in Lev 16:11, 15, 21). The bull was next slaughtered in the presence of the Lord as an act of appeasement (v.11). Applying blood to the horns of the altar and the base of the altar sanctified the offering place as well as the offering (v.12).

13–14 After the sacrifice was killed, the choicest parts were burned on the altar, the enveloping fat adding fuel to the fire (v.13; cf. Lev 3:4–5, 16; 7:23–25). The "flesh and its hide and its offal," however, were thought of as being permeated with sin and were thus burned outside the camp (v.14). Similarly, Christ our Sacrifice offered up his spirit to the heavenly Father, but his flesh went into the tomb, outside the "camp" (cf. Heb 13:11–13).

15–18 As with the bull, Aaron and his sons were to identify with one of the rams by laying on their hands (v.15). This ram was completely offered to the Lord (v.18). Entire and wholehearted dedication of everything they were or hoped to be to God was called for. This constituted the "pleasing aroma" to the Lord (v.18; cf. Lev 1:9).

19–21 The second ram was also to be identified with, but it was to be used to consecrate Aaron and his sons (v.19). After slaughtering the ram, they were to "take some of its blood" and consecrate "the lobes of their [right] ears" (v.20), the organ that hears the Word of God. Next blood was to be applied to "the thumbs of their right hands," organs by which the mediatorial work was to be performed on behalf of the people. Then Aaron and his sons were to apply blood to the "big toes of their right feet," so that the sanctified walk of the priests would be examples to the people. Lastly, some of the blood of the altar was to be mixed with the anointing oil and sprinkled on Aaron and his sons and their clothes (v.21). This represented the full consecration of the priests.

22–26 The second ram was called "the ram for the ordination" (v.22), which is literally "the ram of filling." The choice parts of this ram along with the unleavened bread, oiled cake, and wafer (v.23) were to "fill" the hands of Aaron and his sons and to be used as a "wave offering" (v.24). The waving was not from side to side but toward the altar and back, showing that the sacrifice was given to God and then received back by the priest for his use (cf. Lev 7:30; 23:20). Everything that had been waved except the "breast of the ram" (v.26) was then to be burned on the altar (v.25).

27–28 "The breast that was waved and the thigh that was presented" (v.27) of every animal given as a fellowship offering were henceforth given to the priests.

29–30 The ordination garments of Aaron and his sons were to be passed down for future ordinations (v.29). The priest who would follow Aaron as high priest would wear these garments for seven days (v.30), perhaps symbolizing the completeness of his consecration.

31–34 The "ram for the ordination" (v.31; i.e., the breast and thigh, v.27) was to be cooked in a "sacred place," viz., in the tabernacle courtyard. Then Aaron and his sons were to partake of the various foodstuffs in a type of communion meal (v.32). This was a closed communion (v.33), and all leftovers were to be burned and not passed on (v.34).

35–37 Again obedience is emphasized (v.35). The full consecration of the altar required the sacrifice of a bull for seven days running (v.36). After seven days of consecration, the altar would be "most holy," which is explained to mean that whatever touched it would likewise be made holy (v.37; cf. Matt 23:19).

38–41 Next Moses was instructed as to the nature of the daily offerings (v.38). Two yearling lambs a day were to be sacrificed, one in the morning and the other at evening (v.39; cf. Num 28:3–8; cf. also 2 Kings 16:15; Ezek 46:13–15, for the morning burnt offering and the evening cereal offering). The morning and the evening sacrifices were accompanied by a mixture of about two quarts of flour and one quarter of a hin of olive oil and a drink offering of a quart of wine (vv.40–41). Once again the Lord reminded Moses that the offering was a pleasing aroma for him.

42–43 The Lord gave Moses a prophetic glimpse into Israel's future by referring to the obligation "for the generations to come" (v.42). He promised to meet with the priests and Israel as regularly as the sacrifices were made. The Hebrew for "the place will be consecrated" (v.43) is literally "it will be consecrated." This may refer to the place, but it is better to assume "Israel" would be sanctified, since fellowship was based on atonement. The LXX, Syriac, and Targums read the first person: "and I shall consecrate myself by my glory," but this change in text is unnecessary.

44–46 After the Lord has consecrated the priests and paraphernalia (v.44), he "will dwell among the Israelites and be their God" (v.45). In fact, the divine side of the Exodus was so that God "might dwell among" his people (v.46). The real significance of the tabernacle theology is explicitly stated as God's "tabernacling" or "dwelling" among people so that they could recognize that he indeed was God.

Notes

9 וּמִלֵּאתָ יַד־אַהֲרֹן (*ûmillē'ṯā yaḏ-'ahărōn*, "in this way you shall ordain Aaron") is literally, "so you shall fill the hand of Aaron." The origin of the idiom is unknown, but the idea of "filling" (*millu'îm*) came to mean "ordination."

22 אֵיל מִלֻּאִים (*'êl millu'îm*, "the ram for the ordination") is "the ram of filling," in this case, the hands with a ministry.

39 בֵּין הָעַרְבָּיִם (*bên hā'arbāyim*, "twilight") is "between the two evenings."

11. *Altar of incense (30:1–10)*

a. *Building instructions*

30:1–6

[1]"Make an altar of acacia wood for burning incense. [2]It is to be square, a cubit long and a cubit wide, and two cubits high—its horns of one piece with it. [3]Overlay the top and all the sides and the horns with pure gold, and make a gold molding around it. [4]Make two gold rings for the altar below the molding—two on opposite sides—to hold the poles used to carry it. [5]Make the poles of acacia wood and overlay them with gold. [6]Put the altar in front of the curtain that is before the ark of the Testimony—before the atonement cover that is over the Testimony—where I will meet with you.

The altar of incense also stood in the Holy Place. Whereas the altar inside the gate to the court was overlaid with bronze and was the place of continual bloodshed, this altar was overlaid with gold and had perpetual incense on it to symbolize continual intercession to God.

1–6 The altar was to be made of "acacia wood" (v.1). "Acacia" (*šiṭṭîm*) is variously translated "shittim wood" (KJV; cf. ZPEB, 1:31). This square structure with horns on each corner (v.2) was considerably smaller than the altar of burnt offering (cf. 27:1). The incense altar was to be overlaid with gold (v.3). The altar had the usual rings (v.4) for the transporting poles (v.5). The altar was to be located directly in front of the curtain that shielded the "ark of the Testimony" from view (v.6).

Notes

1 On the use of incense in the OT, cf. M. Haran, "The Uses of Incense in Ancient Israel Ritual," VetTest 10 (1960): 113–15; Nelson Glueck, "Incense Altars," in *Translating and Understanding the Old Testament*, edd. H.T. Frank and W.L. Reed (Nashville: Abingdon, 1970), pp. 325–29; and K. Galling, "Incense Altar," IDB, 2:699–700. For illustrations of such altars, see Pritchard, *Ancient Pictures*, ## 575, 579, 581, 583.

b. *Operating instructions*

30:7–10

[7]"Aaron must burn fragrant incense on the altar every morning when he tends the lamps. [8]He must burn incense again when he lights the lamps at twilight so incense will burn regularly before the LORD for the generations to come. [9]Do not offer on this altar any other incense or any burnt offering or grain offering, and do not pour a drink offering on it. [10]Once a year Aaron shall make atonement on its horns. This annual atonement must be made with the blood of the atoning sin offering for the generations to come. It is most holy to the LORD."

7–10 The effective use of anything depends on following correct procedures. The incense that was to be burned every morning and evening symbolized the prayers of the saints and communion with God (vv.7–8; cf. Ps 141:2; Luke 1:10; Rev 5:8; 8:3–4).

What was not to be used on the altar of incense is explicitly pointed out (v.9). Failure to follow this would result in the desecration of the altar. Also, it was necessary that once a year the altar be cleansed with blood from the atoning offering (v.10).

Notes

---

10 On כִּפֶּר (*kipper*, "to make atonement"), J. Herrmann (TDNT, 3:310) concludes, "It would be useless to deny that the idea of substitution is present to some degree." See also Leon Morris, *The Apostolic Preaching of the Cross* (Grand Rapids: Eerdmans, 1955), pp. 160–78.

---

12. *Census tax*

30:11–16

11Then the LORD said to Moses, 12"When you take a census of the Israelites to count them, each one must pay the LORD a ransom for his life at the time he is counted. Then no plague will come on them when you number them. 13Each one who crosses over to those already counted is to give a half shekel, according to the sanctuary shekel, which weighs twenty gerahs. This half shekel is an offering to the LORD. 14All who cross over, those twenty years old or more, are to give an offering to the LORD. 15The rich are not to give more than a half shekel and the poor are not to give less when you make the offering to the LORD to atone for your lives. 16Receive the atonement money from the Israelites and use it for the service of the Tent of Meeting. It will be a memorial for the Israelites before the LORD, making atonement for your lives."

11–16 The precise reason for taking a census is not given. Perhaps it was to obtain a register of citizens for public duties in the Lord's service. Previously 13:13 stated that the firstborn son belonged to God and had to be redeemed by a sacrifice. Likewise all firstborn belonged to God, and he accepted the tribe of Levi in lieu of all the firstborn (4:22; Num 3:12). Verse 12 extends the principle. The word for "ransom" or "atonement" (*kōp̱er*) signifies "to deliver or redeem by a substitute." In this case the substitute was money by taking a census. Usually a census was equivalent to mustering troops; that is why it was so dangerous in David's case (2 Sam 24). It is clear, however, that those who were numbered under the proper circumstances would be under divine protection.

The "shekel" was mentioned in 21:32. A "half shekel" (v.13) would be about one-fifth of an ounce. This tax was to be paid by adults of military age (v.14). The fact that the rich were to give the same amount as the poor shows that it was not how much one had that obtained atonement for his life (v.15). The proceeds from the census tax were to be used by the Levites in their service for the Lord and were also to serve as a memorial for the Israelites (v.16).

13. *Bronze basin, anointing oil, and incense*

30:17–38

[17]Then the LORD said to Moses, [18]"Make a bronze basin, with its bronze stand, for washing. Place it between the Tent of Meeting and the altar, and put water in it. [19]Aaron and his sons are to wash their hands and feet with water from it. [20]Whenever they enter the Tent of Meeting, they shall wash with water so that they will not die. Also, when they approach the altar to minister by presenting an offering made to the LORD by fire, [21]they shall wash their hands and feet so that they will not die. This is to be a lasting ordinance for Aaron and his descendants for the generations to come."

[22]Then the LORD said to Moses, [23]"Take the following fine spices: 500 shekels of liquid myrrh, half as much (that is, 250 shekels) of fragrant cinnamon, 250 shekels of fragrant cane, [24]500 shekels of cassia—all according to the sanctuary shekel—and a hin of olive oil. [25]Make these into a sacred anointing oil, a fragrant blend, the work of a perfumer. It will be the sacred anointing oil. [26]Then use it to anoint the Tent of Meeting, the ark of the Testimony, [27]the table and all its articles, the lampstand and its accessories, the altar of incense, [28]the altar of burnt offering and all its utensils, and the basin with its stand. [29]You shall consecrate them so they will be most holy, and whatever touches them will be holy.

[30]"Anoint Aaron and his sons and consecrate them so they may serve me as priests. [31]Say to the Israelites, 'This is to be my sacred anointing oil for the generations to come. [32]Do not pour it on men's bodies and do not make any oil with the same formula. It is sacred, and you are to consider it sacred. [33]Whoever makes perfume like it and whoever puts it on anyone other than a priest must be cut off from his people.' "

[34]Then the LORD said to Moses, "Take fragrant spices—gum resin, onycha and galbanum—and pure frankincense, all in equal amounts, [35]and make a fragrant blend of incense, the work of a perfumer. It is to be salted and pure and sacred. [36]Grind some of it to powder and place it in front of the Testimony in the Tent of Meeting, where I will meet with you. It shall be most holy to you. [37]Do not make any incense with this formula for yourselves; consider it holy to the LORD. [38]Whoever makes any like it to enjoy its fragrance must be cut off from his people."

17–21 The "bronze basin" (v.18) was made from the bronze mirrors of the women (38:8) given as a freewill offering. Its exact shape is uncertain, but Keil (2:213) surmises that the "stand" was separate since it is always mentioned separately (cf. 31:9; 35:16; 39:39; 40:11; Lev 8:11). It was vital that the priests washed their hands and feet (v.19) whenever they entered the "Tent of Meeting" (v.20) and when they approached the altar to make an offering to the Lord by fire. Performing service to God in the tabernacle in a state of ritual impurity risks death (vv.20–21; cf. Lev 10:1–2).

22–38 On the spices and anointing oils, see the comment on 25:6. The anointing of the various furniture and accouterments served to consecrate them to the Lord's service (vv.26–29). The "sacred anointing oil" (v.31) was to be unique, in both its makeup and its use. To merchandise it or duplicate it without proper authorization would result in excommunication from the nation (vv.31–33). The incense was likewise to be unique and considered most sacred (vv.34–37). Failure to properly consider it would similarly result in excommunication from the nation (v.38). On the fragrant incense, see the comment on 25:6.

Notes

35 Leviticus 2:13 says that all cereal offerings were to be seasoned with salt. Numbers 18:19 and 2 Chron 13:5 both mention a "covenant of salt."

14. *Appointment of craftsmen*

31:1–11

[1]Then the LORD said to Moses, [2]"See, I have chosen Bezalel son of Uri, the son of Hur, of the tribe of Judah, [3]and I have filled him with the Spirit of God, with skill, ability and knowledge in all kinds of crafts—[4]to make artistic designs for work in gold, silver and bronze, [5]to cut and set stones, to work in wood, and to engage in all kinds of craftsmanship. [6]Moreover, I have appointed Oholiab son of Ahisamach, of the tribe of Dan, to help him. Also I have given skill to all the craftsmen to make everything I have commanded you: [7]the Tent of Meeting, the ark of the Testimony with the atonement cover on it, and all the other furnishings of the tent—[8]the table and its articles, the pure gold lampstand and all its accessories, the altar of incense, [9]the altar of burnt offering and all its utensils, the basin with its stand—[10]and also the woven garments, both the sacred garments for Aaron the priest and the garments for his sons when they serve as priests, [11]and the anointing oil and fragrant incense for the Holy Place. They are to make them just as I commanded you."

1–11 "Bezalel" (v.2) means "in the shadow of God's [protection]." First Chronicles 2:19 describes him as a descendant of Caleb. His ability to work in the arts and his skills as a craftsman were gifts of the Holy Spirit (vv.3–5). "Oholiab" (v.6), Bezalel's assistant, was from the tribe of Dan. His name means "tent of the father" or "the (divine) father is my tent" (cf. the Phoenician name "Baal is tent"; the Sabean name "El is tent"; or the Edomite Oholibamah [Gen 36:2, 41], Esau's wife, whose name means "the high place is my tent").

These two skilled craftsmen were responsible for the construction of all that pertained to the tabernacle and its service, though they themselves possibly only supervised in the construction of the various items (vv.7–11).

15. *Sabbath rest*

31:12–17

[12]Then the LORD said to Moses, [13]"Say to the Israelites, 'You must observe my Sabbaths. This will be a sign between me and you for the generations to come, so you may know that I am the LORD, who makes you holy.

[14]" 'Observe the Sabbath, because it is holy to you. Anyone who desecrates it must be put to death; whoever does any work on that day must be cut off from his people. [15]For six days, work is to be done, but the seventh day is a Sabbath of rest, holy to the LORD. Whoever does any work on the Sabbath day must be put to death. [16]The Israelites are to observe the Sabbath, celebrating it for the generations to come as a lasting covenant. [17]It will be a sign between me and the Israelites forever, for in six days the LORD made the heavens and the earth, and on the seventh day he abstained from work and rested.' "

12–17 Even though the construction of the tabernacle and its furnishings was a sacred work, the workmen were not to overlook the sacred institution of the Sabbath. "You must observe my Sabbaths" is emphatic (v.13). To violate the Sabbath even for the sake of working on the tabernacle would result in death (vv.14–15). "Desecrates" contrasts sharply with "makes you holy" in v.13. As God's covenant people, the Israelites were to carefully observe the sign of that covenant (vv.16–17). The Sabbath was the sign of "a lasting covenant" (*b^erîṯ ʿôlām,* "a perpetual covenant"), as were the rainbow (Gen 9:16), circumcision (Gen 17:7, 13, 19), and the table of the bread of the Presence (Lev 24:8). The Sabbath was thus a gift to Israel signifying that they were a separate people.

Notes

13 Often in the OT, אוֹת (*'ôṯ,* "sign") is a miracle (4:8–9) or a memorial (Josh 4:6). But here it is a pledge of the covenant relationship as was the rainbow after the Flood (Gen 9:12–17) and as circumcision was for the covenant (Gen 17:11). Here, as in Ezek 20:12, 20, the Sabbath is a sign of the Mosaic covenant.

16. *Conclusion to the instructions*

31:18

18 When the LORD finished speaking to Moses on Mount Sinai, he gave him the two tablets of the Testimony, the tablets of stone inscribed by the finger of God.

18 This verse is transitional to the golden calf scene. The forty days (see comment on 24:18) had come to an end. The "two tablets of the Testimony" contained the Ten Commandments (cf. 32:15–16; 34:28; Deut 4:13; 5:22; 10:4). On the "finger of God," see the comment and Notes on 8:19.

B. *False Worship of the Golden Calf (32:1–34:35)*

1. *Golden calf*

32:1–29

1 When the people saw that Moses was so long in coming down from
the mountain, they gathered around Aaron and said, "Come, make us
gods who will go before us. As for this fellow Moses who brought us up
out of Egypt, we don't know what has happened to him."
2 Aaron answered them, "Take off the gold earrings that your wives,
your sons and your daughters are wearing, and bring them to me." 3 So
all the people took off their earrings and brought them to Aaron. 4 He
took what they handed him and made it into an idol cast in the shape of
a calf, fashioning it with a tool. Then they said, "These are your gods, O
Israel, who brought you up out of Egypt."
5 When Aaron saw this, he built an altar in front of the calf and
announced, "Tomorrow there will be a festival to the LORD." 6 So the next
day the people rose early and sacrificed burnt offerings and presented

fellowship offerings. Afterward they sat down to eat and drink and got
up to indulge in revelry.
7 Then the LORD said to Moses, "Go down, because your people, whom
you brought up out of Egypt, have become corrupt. 8 They have been
quick to turn away from what I commanded them and have made
themselves an idol cast in the shape of a calf. They have bowed down to
it and sacrificed to it and have said, 'These are your gods, O Israel, who
brought you up out of Egypt.'
9 "I have seen these people," the LORD said to Moses, "and they are a
stiff-necked people. 10 Now leave me alone so that my anger may burn
against them and that I may destroy them. Then I will make you into a
great nation."
11 But Moses sought the favor of the LORD his God. "O LORD," he said,
"why should your anger burn against your people, whom you brought
out of Egypt with great power and a mighty hand? 12 Why should the
Egyptians say, 'It was with evil intent that he brought them out, to kill
them in the mountains and to wipe them off the face of the earth'? Turn
from your fierce anger; relent and do not bring disaster on your people.
13 Remember your servants Abraham, Isaac and Israel, to whom you
swore by your own self: 'I will make your descendants as numerous as
the stars in the sky and I will give your descendants all this land I
promised them, and it will be their inheritance forever.' " 14 Then the
LORD relented and did not bring on his people the disaster he had
threatened.
15 Moses turned and went down the mountain with the two tablets of
the Testimony in his hands. They were inscribed on both sides, front
and back. 16 The tablets were the work of God; the writing was the
writing of God, engraved on the tablets.
17 When Joshua heard the noise of the people shouting, he said to
Moses, "There is the sound of war in the camp."
18 Moses replied:

"It is not the sound of victory,
  it is not the sound of defeat;
  it is the sound of singing that I hear."

19 When Moses approached the camp and saw the calf and the
dancing, his anger burned and he threw the tablets out of his hands,
breaking them to pieces at the foot of the mountain. 20 And he took the
calf they had made and burned it in the fire; then he ground it to
powder, scattered it on the water and made the Israelites drink it.
21 He said to Aaron, "What did these people do to you, that you led
them into such great sin?"
22 "Do not be angry, my lord," Aaron answered. "You know how prone
these people are to evil. 23 They said to me, 'Make us gods who will go
before us. As for this fellow Moses who brought us up out of Egypt, we
don't know what has happened to him.' 24 So I told them, 'Whoever has
any gold jewelry, take it off.' Then they gave me the gold, and I threw it
into the fire, and out came this calf!"
25 Moses saw that the people were running wild and that Aaron had let
them get out of control and so become a laughingstock to their
enemies. 26 So he stood at the entrance to the camp and said, "Whoever
is for the LORD, come to me." And all the Levites rallied to him.
27 Then he said to them, "This is what the LORD, the God of Israel, says:
'Each man strap a sword to his side. Go back and forth through the
camp from one end to the other, each killing his brother and friend and
neighbor.' " 28 The Levites did as Moses commanded, and that day about
three thousand of the people died. 29 Then Moses said, "You have been
set apart to the LORD today, for you were against your own sons and
brothers, and he has blessed you this day."

While chapters 32–34 continue the narrative interrupted after 24:18, their appearance at this point in the text deliberately contrasts the authorized worship of God set forth in the tabernacle instructions with the fabricated human worship of the golden calf. One could hardly conceive of two greater opposites. There is another contrast between what is taking place on the mountain and what is happening on the desert floor; it is the contrast of the presence of God versus the insidious force of sin (cf. Deut 9:8–21; Neh 9:18; Ps 106:19–23). Therefore, chapters 32–34 form a terrible and ignominious interlude between the instructions on Israel's worship and their implementation.

1 Without proper visible leadership, people fail. Sometimes even the holiest of men, as Aaron, can be persuaded to do things contrary to their testimony. The people's cry, "Come, make us gods who will go before us," revealed their inadequate faith in a time of waiting. The clause "as for this fellow Moses who brought us up out of Egypt" is deliberately cast in coarse language, thus revealing the attitude of the people who had relegated God's works to a mere mortal.

2–4 Aaron instructed the people to "take off" (*pāraq*, lit., "tear off"; contrast *lāqaḥ* ["take"] in 35:5) their "gold earrings." No doubt these were part of the booty-gifts brought from Egypt (see on 3:21–22; 11:2–3; 12:35–36). Aaron then "cast [them] in the shape of a calf" (v.4), probably by applying gold leaf over a wooden form (so KD), which thus could be burned (v.20). Or he may have rough cast it in solid gold and then shaped it by hand. The idol was a calf, i.e., a young bull, the symbol of virile power. On completion Aaron—and probably his sons—had the audacity to proclaim to Israel, "These are your gods," a direct violation of the second commandment, which was so recently given to them. Jeroboam borrowed this statement when he installed the two golden calves at the division of the kingdom in 931 B.C. (1 Kings 12:28).

5 Instead of "he built an altar," the Peshitta changed the vowels and read, "Then Aaron became afraid and built an altar." The idea fits the context even if it is unattested. It is as if the altar built (of field stones and earth as in 20:24–25) in front of the calf were to act as sops for Aaron's conscience and the feast billed as one to honor the true God in this syncretistic confusion.

6 After making an attempt to honor the Lord with their offerings, the people satisfied their own desires and proceeded to "indulge in revelry." The verb *ṣāḥaq* signifies drunken, immoral orgies and sexual play ("conjugal caresses," BDB, p. 850; cf. Gen 26:8; 39:14, 17).

7–10 In response to Israel's behavior, God charged Moses, "Your people whom you have brought up . . . have become corrupt" (v.7). God deliberately changed the possessive pronoun, thereby indicating that he was disowning Israel (contrast "my people" of 3:10 et al.). "Have become corrupt" (*šiḥēṯ*, from *šāḥaṯ*) renders the same verb found in Genesis 6:12 for the apostasy or corruption in Noah's day. It means "to go to ruin or destruction" (cf. Deut 9:6; 10:16; Ps 75:5; Jer 17:23; Acts 7:51). The fact that they were "quick to turn away" (v.8) shows Israel had apostatized from the revealed truth in word and events they had witnessed. The "stiff-necked people" (v.9) would not bow under God's authority (cf. Jer 27:11–12), even though they had readily "bowed down" to the calf and worshiped it (v.8).

God was very angry with the people (v.10). The God who seemed unmerciful, however, is the same God who had mercifully prepared Moses for just such an occasion as this. So God said, by way of testing Moses, "Leave me alone." But God would allow himself to be bound, as it were, by prepared persons doing prepared work in God's way.

11–14 In his role as divinely raised-up mediator, Moses appealed to the Lord (v.11). First, he reminded the Lord of his special covenantal relationship with his people, which he manifested in the Exodus. Then, he appealed to God's need to keep his name holy and trustworthy (v.12). Finally, he referred to the great patriarchal promises (v.13).

As Moses championed the Lord's cause, "the LORD relented" (v.14). In only two of the thirty-eight instances in the OT is this word used of men repenting. God's repentance or "relenting" is an anthropomorphism (a description of God in human forms) that aims at showing us that he can and does change in his actions and emotions to men when given proper grounds for doing so, and thereby he does not change in his basic integrity or character (cf. Pss 99:6; 106:45; Jer 18:8; Amos 7:3, 6; Jonah 3:10; James 5:16). The grounds for the Lord's repenting are three: (1) intercession (cf. Amos 7:1–6); (2) repentance of the people (Jer 18:3–11; Jonah 3:9–10); and (3) compassion (Deut 32:36; Judg 2:18; 2 Sam 24:16).

15–16 This is the only passage that informs us that the "two tablets of the Testimony" were inscribed "on both sides" (v.15). That "the tablets were the work of God" (v.16) emphasizes their divine origin. In 31:18 they are said to be "inscribed by the finger of God," but 34:28 says that "Moses . . . wrote on the tablets the words of the covenant—the Ten Commandments."

17–18 According to 24:13, Joshua had ascended the mountain with Moses, perhaps halfway up. Joshua mistook the "noise of the people shouting" for war cries (v.17). Moses, however, discerned otherwise. The phrase "sound of" is literally "the sound of answering" in all three lines (v.18). There is a play on the word "answer" used in two senses: it was not the "shout" of the victor with its corresponding racket of the vanquished, but it was the antiphonal song of singers.

19–20 The wickedness of the people he had just pled to the Lord to preserve angered Moses when "he saw the calf and the dancing" (v.19). Not only were the stone tablets broken, symbolizing the breaking of God's covenant by the people, but Moses quickly broke up the calf and the festivities, bringing an end to the people's covenant with carnality. Moses took the calf and "burned it," "ground it to powder," and "scattered it on the water and made the Israelites drink it" (v.20), a fitting conclusion for a shameful act. Jeroboam's altar at Bethel was to suffer a similar fate (2 Kings 23:15).

22–24 Aaron had to do some quick thinking to extricate himself from guilt as an accomplice in the people's reveling. He tried four excuses: (1) "you know how prone these people are to evil" (v.22); (2) "they said to me" (v.23); and (3) "we don't know what has happened to [Moses]." The flimsiest excuse came last: (4) "out came this calf!" (v.24). Was Aaron trying to say that a miracle had occurred?

25–26 The people had cast off all restraint; "they were running wild and . . . out of control" (v.25). The exact word used twice in this verse (*pr'*) is found in the warning of Proverbs 29:18: "Where there is no revelation [i.e., message from or attention to the Word of God], the people cast off all moral restraints [i.e., they become ungovernable]" (pers. tr.). The idea of the verb "to cast off all restraints" is that of loosening or uncovering. It would appear that there was a type of religious prostitution connected with the people's worship of the golden calf. Moses realized that decisive action was required. So he challenged the people: "Whoever is for the LORD, come to me" (v.26) The Hebrew literally is "Whoever [is] for the LORD—to me!" (cf. Josh 24:14–15; 1 Kings 18:21; Matt 6:24). "All" in "all the Levites" is undoubtedly a generalization, since Deuteronomy 33:9 implies that some of the Levites also were slain in the action that followed (v.28).

27–29 The Levites who chose to follow God (v.26) were commanded to arm themselves and "go back and forth . . . killing" (v.27). This was not the command of a prophet but of a holy God. Compare the demand for absolute holiness in Matthew 10:37 and Luke 14:26 (cf. 19:6). No small number of people had to pay the consequences for their stiff-neckedness (v.28; cf. Acts 2:41). Following God then as now sometimes requires denying one's family and being cut off from them (v.29; cf. Luke 12:51–53; 14:26). A necessary part of consecration is being obedient to the Lord's command, which always results in his blessings (v.29). The Levites wholeheartedly followed God (Josh 14:8) and counted other ties of kinship as nothing in comparison (Deut 33:9), just as Phinehas was "as zealous as I am for my honor among them" (Num 25:11; cf. Ps 139:21).

Notes

---

1 The plural אֱלֹהִים (*'elōhîm*, "gods") is demanded by the plural verb יֵלְכוּ (*yēlekû*, "who will go [pl.] before us") even though Elohim might legitimately be translated "God" in a plural of majesty where a singular verb form is used (cf. Neh 9:18; Acts 7:40).

4 וַיָּצַר (*wayyāṣar*, "he made") can either be a Qal form of צור (*ṣwr*) or a Hiphil of צרר (*ṣrr*). But the verb יצר (*yṣr*) means "to form," not the hollow or reduplicated verb forms. However, the verb *ṣwr*, with the meaning "to cast out of metal," is used in 1 Kings 7:15 (so Childs, *Exodus*, pp. 555–56).

On the basis of Isa 8:1, חֶרֶט (*ḥereṭ*, "a tool") traditionally has been interpreted as an engraving tool for working metal. How this tool was used with a calf made by pouring molten metal into a form is not known.

29 The NIV follows the LXX, Vulgate, and Targum and renders מִלְאוּ (*mil'û*, "you have been set apart") as a past tense (the KJV makes it an imperative: "Consecrate"). The origin of the idiom may be in the custom described in 29:22–24 and Lev 8:22–29, a gesture of presentation inasmuch as the animal is called the "ram for the ordination" (lit., "the ram of filling").

---

2. *Mediation of Moses*

32:30–35

30 The next day Moses said to the people, "You have committed a great sin. But now I will go up to the LORD; perhaps I can make atonement for your sin."

[31]So Moses went back to the LORD and said, "Oh, what a great sin
these people have committed! They have made themselves gods of
gold. [32]But now, please forgive their sin—but if not, then blot me out of
the book you have written."
[33]The LORD replied to Moses, "Whoever has sinned against me I will
blot out of my book. [34]Now go, lead the people to the place I spoke of,
and my angel will go before you. However, when the time comes for me
to punish, I will punish them for their sin."
[35]And the LORD struck the people with a plague because of what they
did with the calf Aaron had made.

30 Even though the people had repented, atonement for sin was still needed. Moses would attempt (in the basic meaning of "to make atonement") to ransom or deliver the people from the certain judgment of their sin by offering a substitute—himself.

31–32 Moses ascended the mountain once again and proceeded to intercede in prayer on Israel's behalf a second time (v.31). The sincerity of Moses' devotion to his people is seen in his request: "Blot me out of the book" (v.32; cf. Rom 9:1–3). The "book" or "scroll" is called the "book of the living" in Psalm 69:28 and is referred to in Isaiah 4:3: "recorded among the living" (cf. Ezek 13:9; Dan 12:1; Mal 3:16; cf. the roll of those inheriting eternal life in Phil 4:3; Rev 3:5; 20:12, 15; 21:27).

33–34 Moses' offer was refused by the Lord, who replied, "Whoever has sinned . . . I will blot out of my book" (v.33; cf. Pss 9:5; 51:1). Thus the OT principle is reaffirmed: the person who sins is accountable for his own sin (cf. Deut 24:16; Ezek 18:4, 13, 17). Whereas in the past the Lord had led (12:42, 51; 13:17; 15:13; 20:2) and Moses was only his servant, from then on Moses and an angel were to lead (v.34). "The time comes for me to punish" is literally "in the day of my visitation." Perhaps this is the beginning of the Day-of-the-Lord warnings in the later prophets.

35 The order of events is probably not in strict chronological sequence; hence the plague may well be the slaughter of the three thousand mentioned in v.28. The plague came on the people because they caused the calf to be made or asked for it. Frequently in Scripture events may be directly attributed to people when they only occasioned them since the one could implicate the many as a member of a community, just as today one traitor could compromise a whole army or nation. Judas is said to have purchased the field that actually the priests purchased, since it was Judas's returned money that occasioned it (Acts 1:18).

3. *Threatened separation and Moses' prayer*

33:1–23

[1]Then the LORD said to Moses, "Leave this place, you and the people
you brought up out of Egypt, and go up to the land I promised on oath
to Abraham, Isaac and Jacob, saying, 'I will give it to your descendants.'
[2]I will send an angel before you and drive out the Canaanites, Amorites,
Hittites, Perizzites, Hivites and Jebusites. [3]Go up to the land flowing
with milk and honey. But I will not go with you, because you are a stiff-
necked people and I might destroy you on the way."
[4]When the people heard these distressing words, they began to
mourn and no one put on any ornaments. [5]For the LORD had said to
Moses, "Tell the Israelites, 'You are a stiff-necked people. If I were to go

with you even for a moment, I might destroy you. Now take off your
ornaments and I will decide what to do with you.' " 6So the Israelites
stripped off their ornaments at Mount Horeb.
7Now Moses used to take a tent and pitch it outside the camp some
distance away, calling it the "tent of meeting." Anyone inquiring of the
LORD would go to the tent of meeting outside the camp. 8And whenever
Moses went out to the tent, all the people rose and stood at the
entrances to their tents, watching Moses until he entered the tent. 9As
Moses went into the tent, the pillar of cloud would come down and stay
at the entrance, while the LORD spoke with Moses. 10Whenever the
people saw the pillar of cloud standing at the entrance to the tent, they
all stood and worshiped, each at the entrance to his tent. 11The LORD
would speak to Moses face to face, as a man speaks with his friend.
Then Moses would return to the camp, but his young aide Joshua son of
Nun did not leave the tent.
12Moses said to the LORD, "You have been telling me, 'Lead these
people,' but you have not let me know whom you will send with me. You
have said, 'I know you by name and you have found favor with me.' 13If
you are pleased with me, teach me your ways so I may know you and
continue to find favor with you. Remember that this nation is your
people."
14The LORD replied, "My Presence will go with you, and I will give you
rest."
15Then Moses said to him, "If your Presence does not go with us, do
not send us up from here. 16How will anyone know that you are pleased
with me and with your people unless you go with us? What else will
distinguish me and your people from all the other people on the face of
the earth?"
17And the LORD said to Moses, "I will do the very thing you have asked,
because I am pleased with you and I know you by name."
18Then Moses said, "Now show me your glory."
19And the LORD said, "I will cause all my goodness to pass in front of
you, and I will proclaim my name, the LORD, in your presence. I will have
mercy on whom I will have mercy, and I will have compassion on whom I
will have compassion. 20But," he said, "you cannot see my face, for no
one may see me and live."
21Then the LORD said, "There is a place near me where you may stand
on a rock. 22When my glory passes by, I will put you in a cleft in the rock
and cover you with my hand until I have passed by. 23Then I will remove
my hand and you will see my back; but my face must not be seen."

1–3 The Lord issued the command to move on (v.1), promising to "send an angel" before them (v.2; cf. 23:20, 23; 32:34). The angel promised here is altogether different from "the angel of his presence" in Isaiah 63:9, since God declared that his "Name is in him" (23:21). Thus this angel was a christophany, an appearance of Christ in the OT. Although the Lord promised to send his personal representative, he himself would "not go with [them]" (v.3). This withdrawal of the divine presence assured in 23:20–23 was because of the presence of sin.

4–6 The people would rather risk the danger of divine chastisement than be deprived of the divine presence; hence "they began to mourn" and desisted from putting on any further ornaments (v.4). Reminded once more of their stubbornness, the people were asked to "take off [their] ornaments" (v.5), i.e., the ones they were already wearing, as a test of their repentance. Akin to putting on sackcloth and ashes, the people "stripped off their ornaments" as a sign of mourning for their sin (v.6; cf. Gen 35:4; Ezek 26:16).

7–11 The "tent . . . outside the camp" (v.7) was different than the tabernacle or "Tent of Meeting" with its ark and other furniture where the Lord permanently dwelt. This "tent of the meeting" was outside the camp and a temporary structure used until the more permanent shelter was constructed (cf. 27:21 et al.). The verbs in v.7 show that Moses customarily erected this tent. Moses visited this tent whenever he desired a meeting with the Lord (v.8). When Moses entered it, "the pillar of cloud would come down" (v.9), an indication that the Lord was communicating with Moses "as a man speaks with his friend" (v.11; cf. Num 12:8; Deut 34:10). A similar descent would later cap the completion of the tabernacle (40:33–34; see comment on 13:21). The presence of the pillar of the cloud at the tent entrance evoked a spirit of worship from the people (v.10).

12–14 As the time approached for Moses to take up the lead of the Israelites, he became concerned as to the identity of the companion God had promised him (32:34; 33:2). He believed that a mere angel was no substitute for the presence of God. "I know you by name" (v.12) is tantamount to saying, "I have singled you out" or "I have chosen/selected you." There are six uses of the verb *yāḏa'* ("to know"; "teach" in v.13) in five verses (vv.12–17). Moses asked the Lord for a demonstration of his love so that he might know and serve him better (v.13). The Lord responded by promising, "My Presence [lit., 'my face'] will go with you" (v.14). With this new word, the Lord reinstated the angel of his presence in whom he invested his "Name" (23:20–21) as the leader of Israel's way to Canaan.

15–18 Moses beseeched God not to send the people out without his "Presence" to lead them (v.15). Moses knew that God's presence was essential to Israel's testimony before the world (v.16). Without it they would be indistinguishable from the rest of the world. That was the response the Lord was waiting for; so he told Moses that it would be as he requested (v.17). But Moses sought one further thing: he desired to see God's "glory" (v.18).

19–20 In response to Moses' request to see God's "glory," God said that he would "cause all [his] goodness to pass" before Moses (v.19). By his "goodness" is meant his whole character and nature. In a later theophany the Lord passed by what may have been the same cleft of the rock (cave) for the discouraged prophet Elijah (1 Kings 19:11).

A further aspect of the revelation of God's glory was the proclamation of his name. The name of God includes his nature, character, person (Ps 20:1; Luke 24:47; John 1:12), doctrine (Ps 22:22; John 17:6, 26), and standards of living (Mic 4:5). In this context his name includes his "mercy" (i.e., his "grace") and his "compassion" (*raḥam*; lit., "womb," "bowels," i.e., deep-seated feelings). Romans 9:15 quotes this verse and applies it to the sovereignty of God. The one restriction that the Lord gave was that Moses would not be permitted to see the Lord's face (v.20). In fact, "no one may see me and live" (v.20; see John 1:18; 6:46; 1 Tim 1:17; 1 John 4:12).

21–23 To see God's glory Moses was to stand on a "rock" (v.21; cf. Matt 7:24–27). When the glory passed by, Moses would be hid in the "cleft in the rock" and covered by the Lord's hand (v.22). Then the hand of God would be removed so that Moses might see God's back (v.23). "Hand" and "back" are anthropomorphisms (i.e., descriptions of the reality of God in terms or analogies understandable to men). (See the comment on the "finger of God" in 8:19 and 31:18 and cf. Ps 8:3; Luke 11:20; cf. likewise the "hand of God" in 1 Sam 6:9; Ps 109:27.)

Notes

23 אַחֹרָי (*’^{a}ḥōrāy,* "my back") is used of the "back" of the tabernacle (26:12), the "backs" of the twelve bronze oxen holding the molten sea in the temple courtyard (1 Kings 7:25), and of the "backs" of men worshiping in the temple in Ezekiel's day (Ezek 8:16). But since God is Spirit and has no form, and since no one can see him and live (v.20), the word *’^{a}ḥōrāy* could just as well and more accurately be rendered "the after-effects" of his radiant glory, which had just passed by.

4. *Renewal of the covenant*

34:1–35

1 The LORD said to Moses, "Chisel out two stone tablets like the first
ones, and I will write on them the words that were on the first tablets,
which you broke. 2 Be ready in the morning, and then come up on Mount
Sinai. Present yourself to me there on top of the mountain. 3 No one is to
come with you or be seen anywhere on the mountain; not even the
flocks and herds may graze in front of the mountain."
4 So Moses chiseled out two stone tablets like the first ones and went
up Mount Sinai early in the morning, as the LORD had commanded him;
and he carried the two stone tablets in his hands. 5 Then the LORD came
down in the cloud and stood there with him and proclaimed his name,
the LORD. 6 And he passed in front of Moses, proclaiming, "The LORD, the
LORD, the compassionate and gracious God, slow to anger, abounding in
love and faithfulness, 7 maintaining love to thousands, and forgiving
wickedness, rebellion and sin. Yet he does not leave the guilty
unpunished; he punishes the children and their children for the sin of
the fathers to the third and fourth generation."
8 Moses bowed to the ground at once and worshiped. 9 "O Lord, if I
have found favor in your eyes," he said, "then let the Lord go with us.
Although this is a stiff-necked people, forgive our wickedness and our
sin, and take us as your inheritance."
10 Then the LORD said: "I am making a covenant with you. Before all
your people I will do wonders never before done in any nation in all the
world. The people you live among will see how awesome is the work that
I, the LORD, will do for you. 11 Obey what I command you today. I will drive
out before you the Amorites, Canaanites, Hittites, Perizzites, Hivites and
Jebusites. 12 Be careful not to make a treaty with those who live in the
land where you are going, or they will be a snare among you. 13 Break
down their altars, smash their sacred stones and cut down their Asherah
poles. 14 Do not worship any other god, for the LORD, whose name is
Jealous, is a jealous God.
15 "Be careful not to make a treaty with those who live in the land; for
when they prostitute themselves to their gods and sacrifice to them,
they will invite you and you will eat their sacrifices. 16 And when you
choose some of their daughters as wives for your sons and those

daughters prostitute themselves to their gods, they will lead your sons
to do the same.
[17]"Do not make cast idols.
[18]"Celebrate the Feast of Unleavened Bread. For seven days eat bread
made without yeast, as I commanded you. Do this at the appointed time
in the month of Abib, for in that month you came out of Egypt.
[19]"The first offspring of every womb belongs to me, including all the
firstborn males of your livestock, whether from herd or flock. [20]Redeem
the firstborn donkey with a lamb, but if you do not redeem it, break its
neck. Redeem all your firstborn sons.
"No one is to appear before me empty-handed.
[21]"Six days you shall labor, but on the seventh day you shall rest;
even during the plowing season and harvest you must rest.
[22]"Celebrate the Feast of Weeks with the firstfruits of the wheat
harvest, and the Feast of Ingathering at the turn of the year. [23]Three
times a year all your men are to appear before the Sovereign LORD, the
God of Israel. [24]I will drive out nations before you and enlarge your
territory, and no one will covet your land when you go up three times
each year to appear before the LORD your God.
[25]"Do not offer the blood of a sacrifice to me along with anything
containing yeast, and do not let any of the sacrifice from the Passover
Feast remain until morning.
[26]"Bring the best of the firstfruits of your soil to the house of the LORD
your God.
"Do not cook a young goat in its mother's milk."
[27]Then the LORD said to Moses, "Write down these words, for in
accordance with these words I have made a covenant with you and with
Israel." [28]Moses was there with the LORD forty days and forty nights
without eating bread or drinking water. And he wrote on the tablets the
words of the covenant—the Ten Commandments.
[29]When Moses came down from Mount Sinai with the two tablets of
the Testimony in his hands, he was not aware that his face was radiant
because he had spoken with the LORD. [30]When Aaron and all the
Israelites saw Moses, his face was radiant, and they were afraid to come
near him. [31]But Moses called to them; so Aaron and all the leaders of
the community came back to him, and he spoke to them. [32]Afterward all
the Israelites came near him, and he gave them all the commands the
LORD had given him on Mount Sinai.
[33]When Moses finished speaking to them, he put a veil over his face.
[34]But whenever he entered the LORD's presence to speak with him, he
removed the veil until he came out. And when he came out and told the
Israelites what he had been commanded, [35]they saw that his face was
radiant. Then Moses would put the veil back over his face until he went
in to speak with the LORD.

1–3 Since Moses had broken the former tablets (32:19), which "were the work of God" (32:16), it was appropriate that he "chisel out two stone tablets like the first ones" (v.1). No contradiction exists between God's statement that he "will write on them the words that were on the first tablets" and vv.27–28, where Moses did the actual writing. Apparently these are alternate ways of saying the same thing: What Moses said, God said, and vice versa. The law is the direct expression of the mind and will of God. Some make v.27 a pluperfect: "the LORD had said to Moses, 'Write down these words,'" referring thereby to 24:3–8, where Moses was directly responsible for the contents of the covenant code of chapters 21–23.

4–7 Moses obediently followed the Lord's directions and prepared two new stone tablets and then early the next morning brought them to him on top of Mount Sinai (v.4). The Lord once more appeared before Moses and proclaimed his name: "the LORD" (v.5; see comment on 33:19 and God's declaration of his identity in 20:2). Then the Lord "passed in front of Moses" (v.6; see on 33:19). The Lord's self-disclosure is prefaced by the repetition of his name: "The LORD, the LORD," repeated perhaps to emphasize his unchangeableness (the LXX does not repeat the name; see also the comments on 3:14–15; 6:2–3).

Verses 6b–7 are essentially repeated in Numbers 14:18; 2 Chronicles 30:9; Nehemiah 9:17; Psalms 86:15; 103:8; 111:4; 112:4; 116:5; 145:8; Joel 2:13; Jonah 4:2; and Nahum 1:3. On "compassionate" see the comment on 33:19. The "gracious God" bestows his unmerited favor on those who have no claim whatsoever on it. His graciousness is explicated by "slow to anger, abounding in love and faithfulness, maintaining love to thousands, and forgiving wickedness, rebellion and sin." But his grace is balanced, for "he does not leave the guilty unpunished." The other side of our merciful and loving God is his justice and righteouness. Woe to them who reject God's grace! His chastisement will be felt to the "third and fourth generation." The full formula (see 20:5) includes the important qualifier "of those who hate me."

8–9 The revelation of God's person and character humbled Moses (v.8) and caused him to once more plead for his grace to be given to his people, stiff-necked and wicked though they be (v.9).

10–14 The Lord's statement "I am making a covenant with you" (v.10) is not to be understood as the instituting of a second covenant in vv.10–27 but is best seen as a renewing of the same covenant after the events of chapter 33. The word "wonders" (*nip̱lā'ōṯ*) is used of the plagues sent on Egypt (3:20). The wonders would be so outstanding that the people would be awestruck. For Israel to benefit from God's miraculous display, however, they needed to be obedient to his commands (v.11). On the Amorites, Canaanites et al., see the comment and Notes on 3:8.

The Lord further warned the Israelites not to become involved in unholy alliances (v.12; cf. 2 Cor 6:14). More than that, they were to take the initiative and eliminate the pagan "altars, . . . sacred stones and . . . Asherah poles" (v.13). The Asherah were probably sacred trees or wooden poles placed alongside Baal's altar (Judg 6:25; 1 Kings 15:13; 2 Kings 21:7). With the pagan religious objects removed, there would be less temptation to "worship any other god" (v.14). The word "jealous" (*qannā'*) is mentioned twice for emphasis (see comment on 20:5). This particular word is used only of God, occurring but five times in the OT, and illustrates the parallel between idolatry and adultery. As a husband had the right to put to death an unfaithful wife and her paramour (Deut 22:22), "so God relates to his people" (TWOT, 2:803).

15–16 Once more the warning against unholy alliances is sounded (v.15). This time some of the "snares" (cf. v.12) are given: (1) "they will invite you and you will eat their sacrifices," and (2) "you [will] choose . . . their daughters as wives" (v.16). Both actions lead to idolatry.

17 The prohibition against making "cast idols" is most relevant, given the experience of chapter 32 (see also comment on 20:4–6).

18–26 For these verses see the comments on 23:14–19. The way of obedience balances prohibitions with admonitions: "Celebrate the Feast of Unleavened Bread" (see on 12:14–20). For "the first offspring . . . belongs to me" (v.19), see on 13:11–16. See the comment on 20:8–11 for laboring six days and resting one. In 23:16 the "Feast of Weeks" (v.22) is called the "Feast of Harvest."

The Lord added a special promise for the pilgrim to the three annual feasts that required his presence (vv.23–24). The Lord would protect the pilgrim's land from his ungodly neighbor who might move the boundary markers or steal from the land while the pilgrim was absent. The statement "when you go up three times each year" (v.24) looks forward to when the people are settled in the land and need not imply that this verse was written later (cf. Deut 16:16). On v.25 see the comment on 23:18. For the law and theology of "firstfruits," see comment 23:19 (cf. 4:22; 11:5; 12:29).

27–28 For the Lord's commanding Moses to "write down these words" (v.27), see the comment on v.1. For "forty days and forty nights" (v.28), see on 24:18. That Moses was able to go for this length of time without food or water was a miracle requiring the Lord's supernatural care (cf. Deut 9:9, 18; Matt 4:2).

29–32 Spending an extended period of time in the Lord's presence had a telling effect on Moses: "his face was radiant" (v.29). The verb *qāran* (lit., "he radiated") is related to the noun *qeren* ("horn"). The Vulgate confused these two, which thus led to the representation in European medieval art of Moses wearing two horns! Moses' radiant countenance is referred to three times (vv.29, 30, 35; cf. W.F. Albright, "The Natural Face of Moses in Light of Ugaritic," BASOR 94 [1944]: 32–35; J. Morgenstern, "Moses With the Shining Face," HUCA 2 [1925]: 1:27).

The manifestation of the divine countenance struck fear in the Israelites (v.30). A word from Moses, however, encouraged Aaron, the leaders, and all the Israelites to approach him; and he thus delivered the word of the Lord to them (vv.31–32).

33–35 Moses' radiance was only visible to the people when he was acting as the oracle of God (v.33). At other times he kept his face veiled. This was not a priest's mask as in the Canaanite culture, for Moses left the veil off when speaking to the people as God's messenger or when he was alone in the presence of God (v.34).

Paul's use of this text in 2 Corinthians 3:7–18 is *not* an example of rabbinic exegesis or allegorization of an OT passage. He did not assign two different motives to Moses for wearing the veil: viz., (1) because the people were (unnecessarily) frightened and (2) to prevent the people from seeing the end of what was fading away. There was no danger of the termination that was just beginning, but there was the danger (in Moses' symbolic, prophetic action) of the people's iniquities blocking their vision of the "ultimate significance" of that word of God just revealed. "Whenever he entered . . . he removed the veil" indicates the customary action of Moses' practice (in 2 Cor 3:7, 13, Paul used iterative imperfects to the same end).

Notes

1 The statement "the first tablets, which you broke" has led some to argue that "these words were added, probably by the redactor who joined J and E" (Hyatt, p. 322), but evidence is totally lacking for such a claim.

18–26 For a different view of these verses, which are paralleled by 13:12–13; 23:12, 14–19, see H. Kosmala, "The So-Called Ritual Decalogue," *Annual of the Swedish Theological Institute* 1 (1962): 31–61.

33 Many attempt to link מַסְוֶה (*masweh*, "veil") with the "mask" sometimes worn by priests in Egypt and the pottery masks discovered at Hazor and Gezer from the Late Bronze Age, masks possibly used by Canaanite priests. But these practices are unattested in the OT.

C. *Building the Tabernacle (35:1–40:38)*

1. *Summons to build*

35:1–19

1 Moses assembled the whole Israelite community and said to them,
"These are the things the LORD has commanded you to do: 2 For six days,
work is to be done, but the seventh day shall be your holy day, a
Sabbath of rest to the LORD. Whoever does any work on it must be put to
death. 3 Do not light a fire in any of your dwellings on the Sabbath day."
4 Moses said to the whole Israelite community, "This is what the LORD
has commanded: 5 From what you have, take an offering for the LORD.
Everyone who is willing is to bring to the LORD an offering of gold, silver
and bronze; 6 blue, purple and scarlet yarn and fine linen; goat hair;
7 ram skins dyed red and hides of sea cows; acacia wood; 8 olive oil for
the light; spices for the anointing oil and for the fragrant incense; 9 and
onyx stones and other gems to be mounted on the ephod and
breastpiece.
10 "All who are skilled among you are to come and make everything
the LORD has commanded: 11 the tabernacle with its tent and its
covering, clasps, frames, crossbars, posts and bases; 12 the ark with its
poles and the atonement cover and the curtain that shields it; 13 the
table with its poles and all its articles and the bread of the Presence;
14 the lampstand that is for light with its accessories, lamps and oil for
the light; 15 the altar of incense with its poles, the anointing oil and the
fragrant incense; the curtain for the doorway at the entrance to the
tabernacle; 16 the altar of burnt offering with its bronze grating, its poles
and all its utensils; the bronze basin with its stand; 17 the curtains of the
courtyard with its posts and bases, and the curtain for the entrance to
the courtyard; 18 the tent pegs for the tabernacle and for the courtyard,
and their ropes; 19 the woven garments worn for ministering in the
sanctuary—both the sacred garments for Aaron the priest and the
garments for his sons when they serve as priests."

1–3 After he had gathered the Israelites together, Moses relayed to them the commands of the Lord (v.1). The Sabbath, the sign of the covenant, was mentioned first (v.2), an indication of its importance. On "a Sabbath of rest," see on 20:8–11 and 31:12–17. Although the prohibition against lighting a fire on the Sabbath (v.3) is not mentioned elsewhere, it is implied in part in 16:23.

4 Almost every item in 25:1–30:10 is repeated in 35:4–40:38 in identical or similar words except the verbs are mainly in the past tense instead of the future tense as previously. Some, surprised by such lengthy repetitions, though unnecessarily so, conclude that these are additions by a later writer; but such theorists are unaware of how such matters are reported in the ancient Near East. It is customary to repeat the instructions by a literal repetition of the terms except for change in verb forms, e.g., in the Ugaritic epic of Keret from this same era (thirteenth to fourteenth cent. B.C.), some ninety lines are repeated.

"This is what the LORD has commanded" repeats v.1 to revert back to the primary theme after the prefatory words about observing the Sabbath (cf. Lev 23:2, 4).

5–9 See the comments on 25:3–7. The differences are negligible except for the introductory words in 25:3, which would have been out of place here.

10–19 See comments on 25:1–28:43; 30:1–10, 17–38; cf. 31:7–11.

2. *Voluntary gifts*

35:20–29

20 Then the whole Israelite community withdrew from Moses' presence, 21 and everyone who was willing and whose heart moved him came and brought an offering to the LORD for the work on the Tent of Meeting, for all its service, and for the sacred garments. 22 All who were willing, men and women alike, came and brought gold jewelry of all kinds: brooches, earrings, rings and ornaments. They all presented their gold as a wave offering to the LORD. 23 Everyone who had blue, purple or scarlet yarn or fine linen, or goat hair, ram skins dyed red or hides of sea cows brought them. 24 Those presenting an offering of silver or bronze brought it as an offering to the LORD, and everyone who had acacia wood for any part of the work brought it. 25 Every skilled woman spun with her hands and brought what she had spun—blue, purple or scarlet yarn or fine linen. 26 And all the women who were willing and had the skill spun the goat hair. 27 The leaders brought onyx stones and other gems to be mounted on the ephod and breastpiece. 28 They also brought spices and olive oil for the light and for the anointing oil and for the fragrant incense. 29 All the Israelite men and women who were willing brought to the LORD freewill offerings for all the work the LORD through Moses had commanded them to do.

20–29 After Moses' instructions, the people left to set about doing their tasks (v.20). Those whose hearts were moved, however, brought offerings for the the tabernacle and its related service (v.21). The willingness of the people is mentioned repeatedly (vv.21, 22, 26, 29; 36:2). "Men and women alike" (v.22) are specifically mentioned to avoid the misapprehension that "everyone" (vv.21, 23) excluded women even though vv. 25–26 mention women in another connection. On the various gifts of the people, see on 25:1–7.

3. *Bezalel and his artisans*

35:30–36:7

30 Then Moses said to the Israelites, "See, the LORD has chosen Bezalel son of Uri, the son of Hur, of the tribe of Judah, 31 and he has filled him with the Spirit of God, with skill, ability and knowledge in all kinds of crafts—32 to make artistic designs for work in gold, silver and bronze, 33 to cut and set stones, to work in wood and to engage in all kinds of artistic craftsmanship. 34 And he has given both him and Oholiab son of Ahisamach, of the tribe of Dan, the ability to teach others. 35 He has filled them with skill to do all kinds of work as craftsmen, designers, embroiderers in blue, purple and scarlet yarn and fine linen, and weavers—all of them master craftsmen and designers.

36:1 So Bezalel, Oholiab and every skilled person to whom the LORD has
given skill and ability to know how to carry out all the work of
constructing the sanctuary are to do the work just as the LORD has
commanded."
2 Then Moses summoned Bezalel and Oholiab and every skilled
person to whom the LORD had given ability and who was willing to come
and do the work. 3 They received from Moses all the offerings the
Israelites had brought to carry out the work of constructing the
sanctuary. And the people continued to bring freewill offerings morning
after morning. 4 So all the skilled craftsmen who were doing all the work
on the sanctuary left their work 5 and said to Moses, "The people are
bringing more than enough for doing the work the LORD commanded to
be done."
6 Then Moses gave an order and they sent this word throughout the
camp: "No man or woman is to make anything else as an offering for the
sanctuary." And so the people were restrained from bringing more,
7 because what they already had was more than enough to do all the
work.

For these verses see the comments on 31:2–6.

30–35 God's selection and equipping of Bezalel (vv.30–31) was so that he could "engage in all kinds of artistic craftsmanship" (v.32; lit., "engage in every work of thought"). This would include implementing the plan or thought previously given for the project (cf. 31:4–5). Verse 34 adds that Bezalel was given "the ability to teach others," a capability of training and guiding assistants who would work with these two artificers. Verse 35 is almost all new.

36:1–7 The chapter division here is unfortunate, for no break is signified by the verb, as though the account now turns to the execution of the work by these craftsmen. The willingness of the people exceeded the requirements of the craftsmen; so the order was given to the people to make no further offerings for the sanctuary (vv.4–7). This is a noteworthy illustration of generosity for the Lord's work.

4. *Progress of the work and Moses' blessing*

36:8–39:43

8 All the skilled men among the workmen made the tabernacle with ten
curtains of finely twisted linen and blue, purple and scarlet yarn, with
cherubim worked into them by a skilled craftsman. 9 All the curtains
were the same size—twenty-eight cubits long and four cubits wide.
10 They joined five of the curtains together and did the same with the
other five. 11 Then they made loops of blue material along the edge of
the end curtain in one set, and the same was done with the end curtain
in the other set. 12 They also made fifty loops on one curtain and fifty
loops on the end curtain of the other set, with the loops opposite each
other. 13 Then they made fifty gold clasps and used them to fasten the
two sets of curtains together so that the tabernacle was a unit.
14 They made curtains of goat hair for the tent over the tabernacle—
eleven altogether. 15 All eleven curtains were the same size—thirty
cubits long and four cubits wide. 16 They joined five of the curtains into
one set and the other six into another set. 17 Then they made fifty loops
along the edge of the end curtain in one set and also along the edge of
the end curtain in the other set. 18 They made fifty bronze clasps to
fasten the tent together as a unit. 19 Then they made for the tent a

covering of ram skins dyed red, and over that a covering of hides of sea
cows.
20They made upright frames of acacia wood for the tabernacle.
21Each frame was ten cubits long and a cubit and a half wide, 22with two
projections set parallel to each other. They made all the frames of the
tabernacle in this way. 23They made twenty frames for the south side of
the tabernacle 24and made forty silver bases to go under them—two
bases for each frame, one under each projection. 25For the other side,
the north side of the tabernacle, they made twenty frames 26and forty
silver bases—two under each frame. 27They made six frames for the far
end, that is, the west end of the tabernacle, 28and two frames were made
for the corners of the tabernacle at the far end. 29At these two corners
the frames were double from the bottom all the way to the top and fitted
into a single ring; both were made alike. 30So there were eight frames
and sixteen silver bases—two under each frame.
31They also made crossbars of acacia wood: five for the frames on
one side of the tabernacle, 32five for those on the other side, and five for
the frames on the west, at the far end of the tabernacle. 33They made the
center crossbar so that it extended from end to end at the middle of the
frames. 34They overlaid the frames with gold and made gold rings to
hold the crossbars. They also overlaid the crossbars with gold.
35They made the curtain of blue, purple and scarlet yarn and finely
twisted linen, with cherubim worked into it by a skilled craftsman.
36They made four posts of acacia wood for it and overlaid them with
gold. They made gold hooks for them and cast their four silver bases.
37For the entrance to the tent they made a curtain of blue, purple and
scarlet yarn and finely twisted linen—the work of an embroiderer; 38and
they made five posts with hooks for them. They overlaid the tops of the
posts and their bands with gold and made their five bases of bronze.
37:1Bezalel made the ark of acacia wood—two and a half cubits long, a
cubit and a half wide, and a cubit and a half high. 2He overlaid it with
pure gold, both inside and out, and made a gold molding around it. 3He
cast four gold rings for it and fastened them to its four feet, with two
rings on one side and two rings on the other. 4Then he made poles of
acacia wood and overlaid them with gold. 5And he inserted the poles
into the rings on the sides of the ark to carry it.
6He made the atonement cover of pure gold—two and a half cubits
long and a cubit and a half wide. 7Then he made two cherubim out of
hammered gold at the ends of the cover. 8He made one cherub on one
end and the second cherub on the other; at the two ends he made them
of one piece with the cover. 9The cherubim had their wings spread
upward, overshadowing the cover with them. The cherubim faced each
other, looking toward the cover.
10They made the table of acacia wood—two cubits long, a cubit wide,
and a cubit and a half high. 11Then they overlaid it with pure gold and
made a gold molding around it. 12They also made around it a rim a
handbreadth wide and put a gold molding on the rim. 13They cast four
gold rings for the table and fastened them to the four corners, where the
four legs were. 14The rings were put close to the rim to hold the poles
used in carrying the table. 15The poles for carrying the table were made
of acacia wood and were overlaid with gold. 16And they made from pure
gold the articles for the table—its plates and dishes and bowls and its
pitchers for the pouring out of drink offerings.
17They made the lampstand of pure gold and hammered it out, base
and shaft; its flowerlike cups, buds and blossoms were of one piece with
it. 18Six branches extended from the sides of the lampstand—three on
one side and three on the other. 19Three cups shaped like almond
flowers with buds and blossoms were on one branch, three on the next
branch and the same for all six branches extending from the lampstand.

[20]And on the lampstand were four cups shaped like almond flowers with
buds and blossoms. [21]One bud was under the first pair of branches
extending from the lampstand, a second bud under the second pair, and
a third bud under the third pair—six branches in all. [22]The buds and the
branches were all of one piece with the lampstand, hammered out of
pure gold.

[23]They made its seven lamps, as well as its wick trimmers and trays, of
pure gold. [24]They made the lampstand and all its accessories from one
talent of pure gold.

[25]They made the altar of incense out of acacia wood. It was square, a
cubit long and a cubit wide, and two cubits high—its horns of one piece
with it. [26]They overlaid the top and all the sides and the horns with pure
gold, and made a gold molding around it. [27]They made two gold rings
below the molding—two on opposite sides—to hold the poles used to
carry it. [28]They made the poles of acacia wood and overlaid them with
gold.

[29]They also made the sacred anointing oil and the pure, fragrant
incense—the work of a perfumer.

[38:1]They built the altar of burnt offering of acacia wood, three cubits
high; it was square, five cubits long and five cubits wide. [2]They made a
horn at each of the four corners, so that the horns and the altar were of
one piece, and they overlaid the altar with bronze. [3]They made all its
utensils of bronze—its pots, shovels, sprinkling bowls, meat forks and
firepans. [4]They made a grating for the altar, a bronze network, to be
under its ledge, halfway up the altar. [5]They cast bronze rings to hold the
poles for the four corners of the bronze grating. [6]They made the poles
of acacia wood and overlaid them with bronze. [7]They inserted the poles
into the rings so they would be on the sides of the altar for carrying it.
They made it hollow, out of boards.

[8]They made the bronze basin and its bronze stand from the mirrors of
the women who served at the entrance to the Tent of Meeting.

[9]Next they made the courtyard. The south side was a hundred cubits
long and had curtains of finely twisted linen, [10]with twenty posts and
twenty bronze bases, and with silver hooks and bands on the posts.
[11]The north side was also a hundred cubits long and had twenty posts
and twenty bronze bases, with silver hooks and bands on the posts.

[12]The west end was fifty cubits wide and had curtains, with ten posts
and ten bases, with silver hooks and bands on the posts. [13]The east end,
toward the sunrise, was also fifty cubits wide. [14]Curtains fifteen cubits
long were on one side of the entrance, with three posts and three bases,
[15]and curtains fifteen cubits long were on the other side of the entrance
to the courtyard, with three posts and three bases. [16]All the curtains
around the courtyard were of finely twisted linen. [17]The bases for the
posts were bronze. The hooks and bands on the posts were silver, and
their tops were overlaid with silver; so all the posts of the courtyard had
silver bands.

[18]The curtain for the entrance to the courtyard was of blue, purple
and scarlet yarn and finely twisted linen—the work of an embroiderer. It
was twenty cubits long and, like the curtains of the courtyard, five cubits
high, [19]with four posts and four bronze bases. Their hooks and bands
were silver, and their tops were overlaid with silver. [20]All the tent pegs of
the tabernacle and of the surrounding courtyard were bronze.

[21]These are the amounts of the materials used for the tabernacle, the
tabernacle of the Testimony, which were recorded at Moses' command
by the Levites under the direction of Ithamar son of Aaron, the priest.
[22](Bezalel son of Uri, the son of Hur, of the tribe of Judah, made
everything the LORD commanded Moses; [23]with him was Oholiab son of
Ahisamach, of the tribe of Dan—a craftsman and designer, and an
embroiderer in blue, purple and scarlet yarn and fine linen.) [24]The total

amount of the gold from the wave offering used for all the work on the
sanctuary was 29 talents and 730 shekels, according to the sanctuary
shekel.

[25]The silver obtained from those of the community who were counted
in the census was 100 talents and 1,775 shekels, according to the
sanctuary shekel—[26]one beka per person, that is, half a shekel,
according to the sanctuary shekel, from everyone who had crossed over
to those counted, twenty years old or more, a total of 603,550 men.
[27]The 100 talents of silver were used to cast the bases for the sanctuary
and for the curtain—100 bases from the 100 talents, one talent for each
base. [28]They used the 1,775 shekels to make the hooks for the posts, to
overlay the tops of the posts, and to make their bands.

[29]The bronze from the wave offering was 70 talents and 2,400 shekels.
[30]They used it to make the bases for the entrance to the Tent of Meeting,
the bronze altar with its bronze grating and all its utensils, [31]the bases
for the surrounding courtyard and those for its entrance and all the tent
pegs for the tabernacle and those for the surrounding courtyard.

[39:1]From the blue, purple and scarlet yarn they made woven garments
for ministering in the sanctuary. They also made sacred garments for
Aaron, as the LORD commanded Moses.

[2]They made the ephod of gold, and of blue, purple and scarlet yarn,
and of finely twisted linen. [3]They hammered out thin sheets of gold and
cut strands to be worked into the blue, purple and scarlet yarn and fine
linen—the work of a skilled craftsman. [4]They made shoulder pieces for
the ephod, which were attached to two of its corners, so it could be
fastened. [5]Its skillfully woven waistband was like it—of one piece with
the ephod and made with gold, and with blue, purple and scarlet yarn,
and with finely twisted linen, as the LORD commanded Moses.

[6]They mounted the onyx stones in gold filigree settings and engraved
them like a seal with the names of the sons of Israel. [7]Then they
fastened them on the shoulder pieces of the ephod as memorial stones
for the sons of Israel, as the LORD commanded Moses.

[8]They fashioned the breastpiece—the work of a skilled craftsman.
They made it like the ephod: of gold, and of blue, purple and scarlet
yarn, and of finely twisted linen. [9]It was square—a span long and a span
wide—and folded double. [10]Then they mounted four rows of precious
stones on it. In the first row there was a ruby, a topaz and a beryl; [11]in
the second row a turquoise, a sapphire and an emerald; [12]in the third
row a jacinth, an agate and an amethyst; [13]in the fourth row a chrysolite,
an onyx and a jasper. They were mounted in gold filigree settings.
[14]There were twelve stones, one for each of the names of the sons of
Israel, each engraved like a seal with the name of one of the twelve
tribes.

[15]For the breastpiece they made braided chains of pure gold, like a
rope. [16]They made two gold filigree settings and two gold rings, and
fastened the rings to two of the corners of the breastpiece. [17]They
fastened the two gold chains to the rings at the corners of the
breastpiece, [18]and the other ends of the chains to the two settings,
attaching them to the shoulder pieces of the ephod at the front. [19]They
made two gold rings and attached them to the other two corners of the
breastpiece on the inside edge next to the ephod. [20]Then they made two
more gold rings and attached them to the bottom of the shoulder pieces
on the front of the ephod, close to the seam just above the waistband of
the ephod. [21]They tied the rings of the breastpiece to the rings of the
ephod with blue cord, connecting it to the waistband so that the
breastpiece would not swing out from the ephod—as the LORD
commanded Moses.

[22]They made the robe of the ephod entirely of blue cloth—the work of
a weaver—[23]with an opening in the center of the robe like the opening

of a collar, and a band around this opening, so that it would not tear.
24 They made pomegranates of blue, purple and scarlet yarn and finely
twisted linen around the hem of the robe. 25 And they made bells of pure
gold and attached them around the hem between the pomegranates.
26 The bells and pomegranates alternated around the hem of the robe to
be worn for ministering, as the LORD commanded Moses.
27 For Aaron and his sons, they made tunics of fine linen—the work of
a weaver—28 and the turban of fine linen, the linen headbands and the
undergarments of finely twisted linen. 29 The sash was of finely twisted
linen and blue, purple and scarlet yarn—the work of an embroiderer—
as the LORD commanded Moses.
30 They made the plate, the sacred diadem, out of pure gold and
engraved on it, like an inscription on a seal: HOLY TO THE LORD. 31 Then they
fastened a blue cord to it to attach it to the turban, as the LORD
commanded Moses.
32 So all the work on the tabernacle, the Tent of Meeting, was
completed. The Israelites did everything just as the LORD commanded
Moses. 33 Then they brought the tabernacle to Moses: the tent and all its
furnishings, its clasps, frames, crossbars, posts and bases; 34 the
covering of ram skins dyed red, the covering of hides of sea cows and
the shielding curtain; 35 the ark of the Testimony with its poles and the
atonement cover; 36 the table with all its articles and the bread of the
Presence; 37 the pure gold lampstand with its row of lamps and all its
accessories, and the oil for the light; 38 the gold altar, the anointing oil,
the fragrant incense, and the curtain for the entrance to the tent; 39 the
bronze altar with its bronze grating, its poles and all its utensils; the
basin with its stand; 40 the curtains of the courtyard with its posts and
bases, and the curtain for the entrance to the courtyard; the ropes and
tent pegs for the courtyard; all the furnishings for the tabernacle, the
Tent of Meeting; 41 and the woven garments worn for ministering in the
sanctuary, both the sacred garments for Aaron the priest and the
garments for his sons when serving as priests.
42 The Israelites had done all the work just as the LORD had commanded Moses. 43 Moses inspected the work and saw that they had
done it just as the LORD had commanded. So Moses blessed them.

8–19 The start of the actual work on the tabernacle begins here. The order is different from the order of the instructions. The work of the curtains repeats 26:1–13; see comments in loc.

20–34 On the frames and crossbars, see comments on 26:15–30.

35–38 The inner curtain is commented on in 26:31–35.

37:1–9 On the ark, see the comments on 25:10–22. Bezalel is specifically mentioned with the work of the holiest of tabernacle objects.

10–16 On the table of the bread of the Presence, see comments on 25:23–30.

17–24 On the lampstand, see comment on 25:31–40.

25–29 On the altar of incense, see comment on 30:1–6. On the "sacred anointing oil," see comment on 25:6.

38:1–7 On the altar of burnt offering, see comment on 27:1–8.

8 On the bronze basin, see comment on 30:17–21.

9–20 On the tabernacle courtyard, see comment on 27:9–19.

21–39:1 These verses are an inventory of the tabernacle materials. Verses 25–26 give an insight into the population of Israel at this time. There are 3,000 shekels to a talent; therefore 3,000 times 100 equals 300,000 plus 1,775 equals 301,775. Since each man (from twenty years and older) was valued at a half shekel, the total number of men able to bear arms was over 600,000 (301,775 times 2 equals 603,550), a number very much like a later count of Numbers 1:46 (603,550) or Numbers 26:51 (601,730). Such a tally for the army would more than justify estimates of 2 million for the total population.

"As the LORD commanded Moses" is the emphasis of chapters 39–40. The clause occurs nine times in chapter 39 and seven times in chapter 40.

2–31 See the comments on 28:6–43. "The sacred diadem" (v.30) is a new designation here, not found in 28:36–37.

32–41 The statement "so all the work . . . was completed" (v.32) is reminiscent of Genesis 2:1–2, the concluding words of the Creation account. This section emphasizes that the Israelites completed their work "just as the LORD commanded." The workmen, on behalf of all the people, "brought the tabernacle to Moses" (v.33). Once again the list of articles is repeated (cf. 35:11–19; a shortened form occurs in 31:7–11). "With its row of lamps" is a new term for the lamps set in order on the lampstand (v.37).

42–43 "Moses . . . saw that they had done it just as the LORD had commanded" (v.43) is again parallel to the expression in Genesis 1:31. The conclusion was "So Moses blessed them" (cf. Gen 1:22, 28; 2:3).

5. *Erection of the tabernacle*

40:1–33

1 Then the LORD said to Moses: 2 "Set up the tabernacle, the Tent of
Meeting, on the first day of the first month. 3 Place the ark of the
Testimony in it and shield the ark with the curtain. 4 Bring in the table
and set out what belongs on it. Then bring in the lampstand and set up
its lamps. 5 Place the gold altar of incense in front of the ark of the
Testimony and put the curtain at the entrance to the tabernacle.
6 "Place the altar of burnt offering in front of the entrance to the
tabernacle, the Tent of Meeting; 7 place the basin between the Tent of
Meeting and the altar and put water in it. 8 Set up the courtyard around it
and put the curtain at the entrance to the courtyard.
9 "Take the anointing oil and anoint the tabernacle and everything in
it; consecrate it and all its furnishings, and it will be holy. 10 Then anoint
the altar of burnt offering and all its utensils; consecrate the altar, and it
will be most holy. 11 Anoint the basin and its stand and consecrate them.
12 "Bring Aaron and his sons to the entrance to the Tent of Meeting
and wash them with water. 13 Then dress Aaron in the sacred garments,
anoint him and consecrate him so he may serve me as priest. 14 Bring his
sons and dress them in tunics. 15 Anoint them just as you anointed their
father, so they may serve me as priests. Their anointing will be to a

priesthood that will continue for all generations to come." 16Moses did
everything just as the LORD commanded him.
17So the tabernacle was set up on the first day of the first month in the
second year. 18When Moses set up the tabernacle, he put the bases in
place, erected the frames, inserted the crossbars and set up the posts.
19Then he spread the tent over the tabernacle and put the covering over
the tent, as the LORD commanded him.
20He took the Testimony and placed it in the ark, attached the poles to
the ark and put the atonement cover over it. 21Then he brought the ark
into the tabernacle and hung the shielding curtain and shielded the ark
of the Testimony, as the LORD commanded him.
22Moses placed the table in the Tent of Meeting on the north side of
the tabernacle outside the curtain 23and set out the bread on it before
the LORD, as the LORD commanded him.
24He placed the lampstand in the Tent of Meeting opposite the table
on the south side of the tabernacle 25and set up the lamps before the
LORD, as the LORD commanded him.
26Moses placed the gold altar in the Tent of Meeting in front of the
curtain 27and burned fragrant incense on it, as the LORD commanded
him. 28Then he put up the curtain at the entrance to the tabernacle.
29He set the altar of burnt offering near the entrance to the tabernacle,
the Tent of Meeting, and offered on it burnt offerings and grain
offerings, as the LORD commanded him.
30He placed the basin between the Tent of Meeting and the altar and
put water in it for washing, 31and Moses and Aaron and his sons used it
to wash their hands and feet. 32They washed whenever they entered the
Tent of Meeting or approached the altar, as the LORD commanded
Moses.
33Then Moses set up the courtyard around the tabernacle and altar
and put up the curtain at the entrance to the courtyard. And so Moses
finished the work.

1–5 The tabernacle was erected on the "first day of the first month" (v.2). Verse 17 adds that this was the beginning of the "second year" of the wilderness wanderings. Since Israel entered the Sinai Desert in the third month after the Exodus (19:1) and Moses was on Mount Sinai for two forty-day periods (24:18; 34:28) plus the events covered in 19:1–24:11 and chapters 32–33, the building of the tabernacle took less than six months.

Once again, as in 25:10–22, the ark, the most prominent object in the tabernacle, is first to be mentioned (v.3). This was God's throne in the midst of Israel. The "curtain" and how it shielded the ark is further described in v.21 (cf. also 26:31–35; 36:35–38).

On the "table" (v.4), see comment on 25:23–30; 37:10–16; on the "lampstand," see 25:31–40; 37:17–24; on the "gold altar of incense" (v.5), see comment on 30:1–10, 34–38; 37:25–29.

6–8 On the "altar of burnt offering" (v.6), see comments on 27:1–8; 38:1–7; on the "basin" (v.7), see comment on 30:17–21; 38:8; on the "courtyard" (v.8), see 27:9–19; 38:9–20.

9–11 On the "anointing oil," see comments on 25:6; 30:22–33. These instructions were carried out in Leviticus 8:10–12. "Consecrate it" is literally "sanctify it" in the sense of setting it apart for the service of the Lord.

12–16 The anointing and consecrating of the priesthood included Aaron and his sons (v.15). The institution of the priesthood was "for all generations to come" (cf. 12:24; 27:21). Even though the hereditary priestly office of the Aaronic line ended, Christ would carry it out perpetually.

17–33 Verse 17 parallels v.2 in almost every detail. Verses 18–33 contain seven subsections each concluding with the formula "as the LORD commanded him/Moses."

1. "Moses set up the tabernacle" (v.18).
2. "He took the Testimony and placed it in the ark" (v.20; see 25:14, 16, 21).
3. "Moses placed the table" (v.22; 26:35; 40:4).
4. "He placed the lampstand" (v.24; 26:35; 40:4).
5. "Moses placed the gold altar" (v.26; 30:6; 40:5).
6. "He put up the curtain" (v.28) and "he set the altar of burnt offering" (v.29).
7. "He placed the basin" (v.30; 30:18; 40:7).

6. *Dedication of the tabernacle*

40:34–38

34 Then the cloud covered the Tent of Meeting, and the glory of the LORD filled the tabernacle. 35 Moses could not enter the Tent of Meeting because the cloud had settled upon it, and the glory of the LORD filled the tabernacle.

36 In all the travels of the Israelites, whenever the cloud lifted from above the tabernacle, they would set out; 37 but if the cloud did not lift, they did not set out—until the day it lifted. 38 So the cloud of the LORD was over the tabernacle by day, and fire was in the cloud by night, in the sight of all the house of Israel during all their travels.

34–38 The tabernacle had been constructed and set in order as the Lord had commanded Moses; yet something was lacking. Form must be invested with divine life; so "the glory of the LORD filled the tabernacle" (vv.34–35). On the Lord's glory, see 16:7, 10; 24:16–17; 33:18, 22. With the arrival of the glory of the Lord, the nation of Israel was ready to move on. The promise of the divine messenger to lead the people was fulfilled (23:20, 23; 32:34; 33:2). "The Lord now dwelled in their midst as their Leader, their King, and until they reached Canaan the Lord, by means of the cloud, determined whether Israel stayed or moved on" (Gispen, p. 335). The signal to journey was "whenever the cloud lifted" (v.36; cf. comment on 13:21; see also 17:1; 25:22).

LEVITICUS

R. Laird Harris

LEVITICUS

Introduction

1. Historical Background
2. Date and Authorship

   a. The documentary hypothesis
   b. The views of Martin Noth
   c. The Swedish school
   d. Other views
   e. Study by Robert Polzin

3. Literary Form and Classification
4. Theology

   a. Sacrifice
   b. Sin
   c. Cleanness

5. Bibliography
6. Outline

1. Historical Background

Leviticus is the middle book of the Pentateuch. In a sense it also occupies the middle of the Pentateuchal story, for it is largely limited to material revealed at Sinai after the Exodus and before the wilderness wandering. Genesis gives the patriarchal background of the people of Israel. They were molded into a nation, however, at the time of the Exodus by Moses, the great lawgiver. The Israelites left Egypt in the spring on the fourteenth of Nisan,[1] the month that begins the spring season. This was a datum point, the "first month of your year" (Exod 12:2). On the fifteenth of the second month, they came to the Desert of Sin (Exod 16:1). In the third month (Exod 19:1), they arrived at Sinai and encamped before the mount. There they stayed for about one year. The second Passover was celebrated at Sinai (Num 9:5).

The people were "numbered" (i.e., mustered and enrolled for the expected invasion of Canaan) on the "first day of the second month of the second year" after leaving Egypt (Num 1:1). On the twentieth day of the second month of the second year, the Israelites marched on from Sinai toward Kadesh Barnea, the southern gateway to the Promised Land (Num 10:11).

The Israelites thus encamped before Mount Zion just short of a year. During that time Moses spent eighty days on the mountain with God. Then the people of Israel, at

[1] This is the Babylonian name used in the books of Esther and Nehemiah. None of the Babylonian names of the months are used in the Pentateuch—only in Ezra, Nehemiah, Esther, and Zechariah.

Moses' instruction, built the wilderness tabernacle. During this year Moses organized the nation, built up the army, established courts and laws, and ordered formal worship. It was a busy year. Although most of the laws—both secular and profane—that Moses drew up at that time are found in Exodus and Numbers, Leviticus is the law book *par excellence*. Its laws, however, mainly emphasize Israel's worship of God and the instructions for the priests. For this reason, doubtless, the LXX called the book *Levitikōn* ("pertaining to the Levites"). Leviticus therefore does not include numerous prescriptions for secular court procedures and penalties. Such laws are concentrated more in Exodus 20–23. Deuteronomy, being a summary of both history and law, repeats some of the laws of both Exodus and Leviticus and gives other details. The Hebrews customarily named their books after the first word of the text; therefore they called Leviticus *wayyiqrā'* ("and he called").

The Book of Leviticus, presuming the construction of the tabernacle as detailed in Exodus 25–31; 35–40, begins with a description of the offerings for the great brazen altar (chs. 1–7) and continues with the consecration of the first priests and the start of the tabernacle worship (chs. 8–10). The chapters that follow largely set forth those laws for the conduct of the people that were administered by the priests. It is difficult to generalize, however, because the priests were concerned with instruction for and regulation of many aspects of Israel's life, not just the sacerdotal—for instance, chapters 18 and 20 cover laws of incest. The laws of cleanliness come in chapters 11–15, followed by the law of the great national sin offering on the Day of Atonement in chapter 16. The next section (chs. 17–26) is sometimes called the Holiness Code because it emphasizes God's moral standards for his people. Included is a description of the other annual feasts of Israel (ch. 23) and further miscellaneous regulations touching the sabbatical year and laws of land inheritance (ch. 25). The next to last chapter (26) includes extensive warnings of punishment if Israel departs from her God, and the book ends (ch. 27) with regulations concerning property given to the Lord's work. The divisions of the book will be given later in outline form.

2. Date and Authorship

The view taken of the date and authorship of Leviticus depends largely on one's view of the Pentateuch. This, in turn, will usually be greatly influenced by one's view of the rest of the OT.

a. *The documentary hypothesis*

The critical school associated with the name of Wellhausen in the nineteenth century reconstructed Israel's history in an evolutionary vein and postdated most of the OT books. Rationalism was the order of the day. All miracles were thought to be untrustworthy legends, and all prophecies were held to be written after the events prophesied had occurred. Such a priori arguments cannot decide the questions of date for those who do not accept their rationalistic bases.

Before World War I, the Wellhausen critical formulations largely held the field. Wellhausenists believed that the Pentateuch (actually extended to the Hexateuch or Heptateuch) was composed of four strands of material written long after Moses. The variation of the divine names "Jahweh" and "Elohim" and other imagined indications of style, parallel stories, and allegedly contradictory material were explained by assuming composite authorship. They argued that there was a J document written about 850 B.C., an E document from 750 B.C., a D document (largely Deuteronomy) written in 621 B.C., and a P document (giving priestly material) from 450 B.C. This JEDP hypothesis supposed that these documents were interwoven by various redactors and became a unit after 450 B.C. This hypothesis also theorized that the Psalms were postexilic; Isaiah was in two, three, or more parts; Job and Proverbs were postexilic; Chronicles was written quite late (250 B.C.) and was very untrustworthy; and Daniel was written in Maccabean times (168 B.C.). For a fuller explanation, see R.K. Harrison, "Historical and Literary Criticism of the Old Testament," EBC, 1:239ff.

The main argument for the above view was a rationalistic-evolutionary approach. Its exponents almost exclusively denied the miracles of the NT and the full deity and authority of Jesus Christ. Of course, all typical and doctrinal value of the Levitical sacrificial system was also lost. The study of the OT became a study in the history of religions and seemed to gain in fascination as it lost in value. Tomes were devoted to the critical analysis of documents and the minutia of division of verses.

A post-World War I reaction has been caused by many factors, and present OT scholars are much divided in opinion. As Bentzen remarks, "A clear picture of the present situation is not easily given."[2]

Archaeological discoveries especially have piled up numerous arguments against the JEDP hypothesis. Scholars have given up the older picture that early Israel's history was too primitive for advanced legal, religious, or cultural attainments. For instance, Speiser (p. 543) says, "It was not very long ago that critics doubted the possibility of a complex legislation in the Mosaic age on the ground that those times were too primitive and that the knowledge of writing was as yet unequal to the task. Indeed our perspective has changed radically within the past few decades."

The discovery in 1929 of tablets from Nuzi, which gave the legal and cultural background of the Hurrian peoples of Mesopotamia about 1500 B.C., raised a new argument against the JEDP theory. The parallels with the family customs of the patriarchs were amazing, and the conclusion has been widely adopted that the patriarchal narratives in Genesis are not legends to explain later happenings but are historically valid. Conversely, the family laws and customs as given in the Mosaic times are quite different. Presumably, therefore, Genesis tells the story of pre-Mosaic times, and Exodus to Deuteronomy reflect the usage of a later day.[3]

Ugaritic texts also discovered in 1929 brought another argument against Wellhausen's view. These tablets contain examples of early Canaanite religious poetry and have helped to establish an early date for many of the Psalms and other poetic passages. As noted above, a late date of the Pentateuchal documents involves a late date of the Psalms and other writings. Since so many of the Psalms presume the

---

[2]Aage Bentzen, *Introduction to the Old Testament*, 4th ed. (Copenhagen: G.E.C. Gad, 1958), 2:18.

[3]John Van Seters, *Abraham in History and Tradition* (New Haven: Yale University Press, 1976), challenges some of the reconstructions of the Speiser and Albright school concerning the patriarchal religion and culture. His excessive criticism and his own reconstruction at a much later period have been successfully challenged by A.R. Millard and D.J. Wiseman, edd., *Essays on Patriarchal Narratives* (Leicester: Inter-Varsity, 1980). It is now held by a number that the more recently found Ebla Tablets further answer Van Seters's skeptism—although the Ebla material has not yet been fully evaluated. See E. Merrill, "Ebla and Biblical Historical Inerrancy," BS 140, no. 560 (1983): 305. It is of note that the peculiar patriarchal customs that Van Seters argued could have been borrowed from Mesopotamia at any time are not, as a matter of fact, reflected in the laws found in Exodus to Deuteronomy nor in the customs of later Israel.

religion, ritual, and history of the Pentateuch, an earlier dating of the Psalms involves reconsideration of the older critical theories.

Furthermore, the Ugaritic material bears directly on the priestly ritual of Leviticus. A comparable book of priestly ritual from Ugarit has not yet been found, but the technical words of sacrifice appearing in the Canaanite language here come from about Moses' time. Archer, in his valuable discussion of the whole argument (SOTIrev., p. 159), lists the words *'iššeh* ("burnt offering"), *kālîl* ("whole burnt offering"), *š^e^lāmîm* ("fellowship offerings"), and probably *'āšām* ("guilt offering"). As Archer notes (ibid.), these were terms "branded by Wellhausen as Exilic."

Finally, the discovery of the DSS in 1947 has altered the picture somewhat. The oldest scroll is from about 250–225 B.C. and thus not early enough to bear directly on critical questions. The general trend of the discovery, however, has been toward conservative positions. Scribal copying has been shown to be careful and conscientious also in the pre-Christian centuries. The date of Chronicles has been pushed back generally to around 400 B.C.,[4] and some other dates also have been revised backward. If Chronicles is dated to about 400 B.C., it is extremely difficult to suppose that the whole priestly liturgy that it regularly ascribes to Moses was written down only about 450 B.C. The Wellhausen view in its original form is widely being abandoned because of these newly discovered facts.[5] Yet scholars like Bentzen, while allowing that adjustments must be made, declare that the documentary theory of Wellhausen is "still held by a majority of scholars" and names Hölscher (1942), Robert Pfeiffer (1941), Eissfeldt, and Smend.[6] Sellin,[7] Noth,[8] and others also could be mentioned. Bentzen gives little attention to the recent archaeological discoveries.

Bentzen still divides the P document into the P^o stratum (^{o} for German *Opfer*, "offerings") of Leviticus 1–6; the P^h stratum, the code of holiness, Leviticus 17–26; P^g (^{g} for German *Geschichte*, "history"), the historical outline found in P; and P^s, the supplemental parts. He declares that P shows a later view of God and thus avoids anthropomorphisms. P attributes the whole cultus to Moses (wrongly, he thinks). He follows Driver in identifying P's peculiar vocabulary and style, with no reference to the Ugaritic linguistic material. He concludes that P "may be dated to the period between Zerubbabel and Malachi."[9]

b. *The views of Martin Noth*

Since Martin Noth's views typify the more recent critical approach to the Pentateuch, an extensive analysis of them would be of value, though it is beyond the purpose of this introduction. Briefly, however, his remarks in his small treatment (*Leviticus: A Commentary*, pp. 10–17) may be used to illustrate the methodology of the critical approach. Failing factual data, it assumes canons of composition and then builds one supposition on another until the unity of the book is dissolved and its various parts dated long after the data given in the book.

Noth (p. 10) divides the book into its obvious sections: the offerings (chs. 1–7); the

---

[4] F.L. Cross, *The Ancient Library of Qumran* (Garden City, N.Y.: Doubleday-Anchor, 1961), p. 189.

[5] W.F. Albright ("The Bible After Twenty Years of Archaeology," in *Religion in Life* 21 [1952]: 545) speaks of "the total breakdown of Wellhausenism under the impact of our new knowledge of antiquity."

[6] Bentzen, *Introduction*, p. 32.

[7] E. Sellin and G. Fohrer, *Introduction to the Old Testament* (Nashville: Abingdon, 1968), pp. 191–92.

[8] *A History of Pentateuchal Traditions.*

[9] Bentzen, *Introduction*, p. 70.

consecration of priests (chs. 8–10), which he calls "the narrative portion" (p. 11); cultic cleanness (chs. 11–15); the law of " 'making atonement for' the holy place (i.e., the day of atonement)" (p. 11); the "Law of Holiness" (chs. 17–16); and the appended chapter on dedicatory gifts (ch. 27). He notes that there is a "monotonous framework" (p. 10) in which most sections begin "The LORD said to Moses, 'Speak to the Israelites' " or similar phraseology. He remarks that this is varied in the narrative portion (8:1) where the Lord speaks to Moses, commanding him to do something (p. 10). In view of the contents being largely regulations so promulgated, he says that the book from the viewpoint of arrangement has "little coherence" (p. 10). Why this follows is not clear. He apparently feels that narration brings coherence but the assembling of divine instructions does not. However, he says on analysis of the content, there is a "clear inner articulation of the whole." The first seven chapters (on sacrifices) "form a whole relatively separate from the general theme" (p. 11).

After this and after further discussion, it is surprising to read that "Leviticus can hardly have been written down in one draft, despite the unity of the historical situation described and despite the strong concentration on predominantly cultic instructions and operation. It is rather a book that has come into existence in successive stages" (p. 12). There is no proof of Noth's statement. Basing his appeal on the larger questions of the Pentateuch, he says that it is a narrative work and that reference is made in Leviticus to a stage in that narration, the time of Sinai; so the book did not exist alone. Granted. But then he says that the narrative chapters 8–10 "must from the literary point of view be judged primary" (p. 12).

Noth apparently assumes that a narrative work must be exclusively narration. One would think that a history of a nation could well include legal material and descriptions of the circumstances when these were promulgated. Certainly Leviticus 8–10, which records the consecration of the priests, follows beautifully on Exodus 29, which gives in very similar wording instructions for consecrating the priests. We remember that Exodus 25–30 gives instructions for building the tabernacle and that Exodus 35–40 gives the actual construction in very similar wording. The parallel of Exodus 29 and Leviticus 8–9 is instructive. The sin of the golden calf, however, intervenes between chapters 25–30 and chapters 35–40 of Exodus. It therefore seems not at all intrusive to have Leviticus 1–7, in similar fashion, intervene between Exodus 29 (instructions for consecration of the priests) and Leviticus 8–10 (the actual consecration of the priests). Leviticus 1–7 specifies the types of sacrifices the priests are to offer and the ritual for the offering.

There is no apparent reason why chapters 1–7 could not have been written by the same hand that wrote Leviticus 8–10 and Exodus 29–40, except that Noth feels "it can hardly have been" (p. 12). He feels that chapter 10 also is secondary, for it is "obviously linked on to the secondary last verse [24] of the preceding chapter" (p. 13). Now Leviticus 9:23 is not obviously secondary to those who believe that the Lord does on momentous occasions reveal his glory. Actually, Leviticus 9:23–24 picks up and describes again Exodus 40:34–35, which follows the building of the tabernacle and the preparation for the beginning of worship that is then prescribed in Leviticus 1–7 and narrated in Leviticus 8–9. Chapter 10 is a further narration of the priestly service and its history, perhaps not telling of events immediately after chapter 9; but there is no reason to suppose a much later stage in the narrative.

Another secondary stratum, according to Noth, is chapter 8: "Only the story of the first great sacrifice in ch. 9 belongs to the original P-narrative, whilst the account of the carrying out of the priests' institution to office in ch. 8 is clearly secondary P material, both as such, and as an appendix to the instructions—themselves added as a later supplement—for this particular institution in Ex. 29" (p. 13). This is the situation: Noth knows by some second sense that originally there were no instructions for the consecration of priests. Then someone concocted Exodus 29, and someone else decided that the command required a report of the execution. Noth does not explain why an original author could not think this was helpful but that an editor would.

Noth's treatment of Leviticus 11–17 must be considered more briefly. Chapter 16, he says, originally followed on chapter 10 (cf. 16:1, which refers to the incident). "However, the collection of 'cleanness' precepts . . . was worked in before the great cleansing ritual of chapter 16 because it provided, in its aspect of 'cleansing' a bridge" (p. 14). Exactly so, Leviticus 11–15 does fit adequately as a bridge between chapter 10 and chapter 16. Noth thinks so. The alleged redactor thought so. Perhaps the original author also thought so! Then it was perhaps not secondary. There certainly is no proof that it was.

As to the Law of Holiness (Lev 17–26), Noth (p. 15) remarks, "Cultic and ritual regulations usually remain fairly constant; they are relatively independent of the ups and downs of political and historical events." This is an amazing statement. It certainly was not true at the time of the Reformation or the Fall of Jerusalem or the Exile. Actually, we just do not have extrabiblical evidence for the cultic history of ancient Israel, and Noth rearranges the biblical data that we do possess. All we can say is that his statement is not based on evidence and carries only the weight of opinion.

Noth goes on to say that the place of origin of cultic traditions is as important as their date. He argues (in the commentary section, p. 15) that "the sacrificial instructions in chs. 1–7 and probably, too, the purification regulations in chs. 11–15 belong to the Jerusalem tradition (cf., 'the anointed priest' of 4:3ff)." Here is a nest of assumptions. In the whole Pentateuch Jerusalem is mentioned only in connection with Melchizedek in Genesis 14 (if Salem is Jerusalem). The "Tent of Meeting" repeatedly mentioned in these chapters was eventually set up in Shiloh, apparently was destroyed there by the Philistines, and never got to Jerusalem except in bits and pieces. There is nothing in the ritual of Leviticus 1–7 that could not fit the tabernacle at Sinai, Shechem, or Shiloh.

It is pure assumption that the cleanness regulations of chapters 11–15 belong to the Jerusalem tradition. True, some of them (a minor part) are repeated in Deuteronomy 14. DeWette (c. 1805), however, alleged that Deuteronomy was written to support Josiah's centralization of worship at Jerusalem. It is odd, then, that Deuteronomy does not mention Jerusalem nor the great temple of Solomon clearly in existence in Josiah's day; nor does it mention the musical liturgy of the temple that used the Psalms (many of which are now admitted to be of the time of the monarchy). Yet, with some exceptions, it is an item of critical faith that Deuteronomy in its present form is "of the Jerusalem circle" (p. 15). Building another assumption on that assumption, Noth holds that the phrase "anointed priest" refers to the Jerusalem priesthood and cannot refer to Aaron or his successors, whose anointing is mentioned in Leviticus 8:30.

Noth (p. 15) also holds that Leviticus 17:7 and 20:2–5 refer to "local cults in the Jerusalem territory." The mention of "goat idols" in 17:7 and the cult of Molech (20:2), however, has no reference to Jerusalem; nor were these cults at all limited to Jerusalem. The Molech cult spread more from Phoenicia. The assumptions are made, however, because Jerusalem fits Noth's theories.

Of more value is Noth's remark (p. 15) that the Law of Holiness has "many points of contact with the Book of Ezekiel, the background to which is the Jerusalem priestly tradition." Indeed, Ezekiel 20 three times quotes Leviticus 18:5. Further, Noth (ibid.) says, "In point of time the final form of the non-narrative portions of Leviticus, as far as there is any possibility of dating them, belong fairly clearly to the period around the end of the Jewish state and the beginning of the so-called [*sic*] exile." Thus he dates the "non-narrative portions" after Deuteronomy (620 B.C.—the alleged date) and before the Exile, which is dated archaeologically and by contemporary documents to 598 and 586 B.C. This period is only about thirty-four years—rather exact dating for material that has no real chronological tags to indicate any date except the repeated assertions that Moses gave it at Sinai.

Noth does not here give any weight to the studies of Speiser (pp. 138, 142), in which Speiser shows that four passages in scattered areas of the book are best explained by legal parallels with second-millennium Mesopotamia. This cannot of course date the whole of Leviticus, but no such passages point to a late date.

Ezekiel is indeed from the Jerusalem priestly circle, as Noth says. Recent commentators (Zimmerli et al.) show that the temple gates in Ezekiel 40 are close copies of gates built by Solomon in Hazor, Megiddo, Gezer, and surely also Jerusalem, where Ezekiel doubtless saw them in his youth. No such gates were built after Solomon. The implication is that Ezekiel also saw the Solomonic temple, which Ezekiel's symbolic temple closely approximates. This was indeed the center of the Jerusalem priestly circle—and for the whole period of the monarchy. The temple sacrifices parallel those of Leviticus as far as they are described. The picture of Leviticus and Exodus with the Tent of Meeting, smaller altar, single lampstand, etc., however, much more logically represents what it claims to represent—the premonarchical situation, indeed the wilderness situation claimed throughout the book.

c. *The Swedish school*

A chief critical alternative to the views of Bentzen, Noth, and others is the Swedish school of oral tradition. Men like Engnell, Nielsen et al. point out that archaeology forces us to hold that there is old and valid historical material in all the documents. Elements in the P document are older than the J document. Elements in the D document fit the midsecond millennium B.C. Both J and E reflect accurately the patriarchal age (as does the P part of Genesis). These facts must be accounted for: "Indeed the youngest source has an element which is older than the present form of the oldest source. . . . Source criticism indisputably loses it charm, the charm which it possessed when literary critics were fully convinced that source distinction clarified the development of the Israelite religion in the times of the monarchy and the exile."[10]

The obvious response to this argument would be to deny the documentary hypothesis altogether, to recognize the possibilities of harmonizing the alleged discrepancies and contradictions, and to believe the account of God's supernatural revelation. The Swedish view instead is to posit various circles of oral tradition that with marvelous accuracy preserved some ancient history yet were written down in postexilic times. Parallels are found for this in Icelandic legends. For full consider-

[10] E. Nielsen, *Oral Tradition* (London: SCM, 1954), p. 97.

ation of such views, reference must be made to the work of Archer and others cited above.[11]

It seems in passing strange, however, to refer the history, laws, and religious poetry of Israel to oral tradition, when nations all around were writing extensively in just these categories. The Ugaritic tablets have numerous examples of religious poetry. Hammurabi's Laws come from 1700 B.C. The chronicles of the kings of Mesopotamia are extensive and give just such a year-by-year account as we would expect to find in the chronicles of the kings of Israel and Judah, so often referred to as the source of 1 and 2 Kings. Not much Israelite writing has been preserved, it is true; but this is surely because they wrote on papyrus or skins, which perished rapidly in the rainy seasons in Palestine. To argue from silence in this matter is a great error.

Wellhausen argued that the P document was postexilic because the laws of Leviticus were unknown to Ezekiel in his description of the temple worship of the future. Of course, an exception must be made for P^h (the so-called Holiness Code, Lev 17–26) because this section of Leviticus is actually quoted in Ezekiel 20:11, 13, and 21. The rest of P, however, must be late because Ezekiel knew nothing of the P document. This is an argument from silence. It was never very convincing. Ezekiel 48 also draws a very schematic picture of the settlement of the tribes like nothing in Joshua or any other history. Does this prove that all of Joshua–2 Kings was written after Ezekiel? And what of this argument now since old material has been found in P? The oral tradition theory holds that P was being passed on, presumably in priestly circles, by oral tradition for centuries. Surely Ezekiel, a priest, knew something of this oral tradition. Yet Ezekiel was silent with respect to this material. It appears that Ezekiel may well have known all about the alleged P document but was silent for other reasons. Ezekiel's reconstructed temple worship was schematic and typical and varies from P only in unimportant details. It was a reconstruction of the Solomonic temple worship anyhow and had in any case no direct relation to the wilderness tabernacle. Surely the argument from the silence of Ezekiel is unjustified and tells us nothing of the date of P.

d. *Other views*

It is true that other arguments are also advanced against the unity of Leviticus. As to P^g (the historical narrative part of the P document), not much of it is found in the Book of Leviticus (most of chs. 8–10:7; 16, according to Noth [*Leviticus: A Commentary*, p. 18]). The claim is that the tone of the P document is set in Genesis 1 where the formulaic, nonanthropomorphic tone is combined with the use of the divine name Elohim. In the following chapters of Genesis, the "historical" P document becomes very heavily a record of the births, deaths, and longevity of the various characters. It is to be noted that this division involves a circular argument. After designating formulaic sections as P, P is seen to be largely formulaic.

There is nothing in Leviticus of these births, deaths, and chronology given in Genesis simply because the material in Leviticus is legal rather than historical. Furthermore, the divine names in Leviticus are mixed. "The LORD" (YHWH) is the common name used, but the expression "your God" or "the LORD your God" is also much used. This usage of "LORD" is not held to be against the identification as P

[11] Cf. also O.T. Allis, *The Old Testament, Its Claims and Its Critics* (Nutley, N.J.: Presbyterian and Reformed, 1972), esp. pp. 243–45.

because of the long-claimed interpretation of Exodus 6:3. It is said that Exodus 6:3 is a statement by the P author that the name LORD is suitable only for Mosaic times and after. Therefore Leviticus (P) often uses the name "LORD," but the pre-Mosaic parts of P have artfully avoided this name.

This argument has been much discussed, but in any case it seems to give the presumed author of P a good bit of credit for consistency and extreme care in his use of materials. Also, the contrast of Exodus 6:3 is between "God Almighty" (El Shaddai) and "LORD" (YHWH); so it would seem that in the pre-Mosaic literature the P document ought to use "God Almighty," which it does only four times (Gen 17:1; 28:3; 35:11; 48:3). Furthermore, the name "God" (Elohim) would hardly be expected in the P parts of Genesis, where it occurs much more often than El Shaddai. Other inconsistencies of the critical argument are often noted. Even the very interpretation of Exodus 6:3 by critics can be challenged. O.T. Allis claims that the verse only means to emphasize the new revelation of the power and care of God.[12] After Exodus 6:3, the P document uses a mixture of Elohim (God) and YHWH (LORD) with the mixture apparently due merely to the desire for variation. Then why cannot Genesis be credited to one author using different divine names merely because of the desire for variation?

In short there is no need to depart from the time-honored position. We must insist that P^g, P^h, P^o, P^s, and all the rest were included in the judgments, commandments, and ordinances given as a unit to Israel. The view that Leviticus is a unified whole given by Moses can be traced back to the Chronicler, now widely admitted to be as early as 400 B.C.[13] The tradition of Israel with one voice declares that the ritual laws of Leviticus—and the other Pentateuchal material as well—were given by God through Moses.

e. *Study by Robert Polzin*

In addition to the above critical studies based on style, we should give some attention to a recent study by Robert Polzin that claims to show by detailed analysis of linguistic features that the P document can be placed chronologically after the work of the "Deuteronomist" (which he dates about 600 B.C.) and before the Chronicler.[14] Happily he assigns the Chronicler the date orthodox scholars have long held—about 400 B.C. (rather than the older critical date of 250 B.C.). This date is advanced by Cross and others because the type of text in the MT of Chronicles shows similarities to the LXX text of Samuel-Kings, which in turn is held to be early because of DSS MSS.[15] It may be wondered whether the P document can be so positively placed in this postexilic period when the fifth-century witness of Chronicles-Ezra-Nehemiah so definitely ascribes it to Moses. Notice that the Chronicler does not do this uncritically. The Psalms and temple choirs he ascribes to David, but the Pentateuchal laws and ritual he repeatedly ascribes to Moses. His oral tradition on this point must have been very faulty if as a matter of fact the P document was written recently and in the idiom of the Chronicler's time while the rest of the Pentateuch was in an archaic dialect.

Polzin, with considerable care and great industry, analyzes the Chronicler's diction

[12] *The Five Books of Moses* (Nutley, N.J.: Presbyterian and Reformed, 1943), pp. 26–32.

[13] See note 3 above.

[14] Robert Polzin, *Late Biblical Hebrew: Toward an Historical Typology of Biblical Hebrew Prose* (Missoula, Mont.: Scholars, 1976).

[15] See note 3 above.

and finds, in the passages not parallel to Samuel-Kings, twelve distinct linguistic elements. Then he argues that these are not found so extensively in the older literature (which he calls Classical Hebrew) of JE or in the court history of the first part of Samuel or even so much in Deuteronomy. Then he investigates the basic history of P (P^g) and the supplementary parts of P (P^s) and finds the majority of the same elements there as in Chronicles-Ezra and the Memoirs of Nehemiah (Neh 1:1–7:5 and 12:27–13:31). He concludes that the proof of P's lateness is rather solid.

Polzin has done his work with care and discernment and doubtless is correct in his data. We may notice in passing that none of his data indicates a late date for the latter part (or parts) of Isaiah! It may be held, however, that he has counted the evidences more than weighing them. We would suggest several points as a warning.

1. Polzin is comparing the style of various biblical books without any adequate external controls. We wish we had several authors of the days of Moses, of David, of Jeremiah, and of the Chronicler to give us objective standards of comparison, but we do not. We just do not know what differences of dialect there may have been between Samuel in Shiloh and Amos in Tekoa and between the international court of Solomon and the wilderness prophet Elijah. As a consequence we should be wary of using *hapax legomena* to indicate dating. A word may be used once or twice in our whole OT and yet have been a common word in other connections. The Ugaritic texts give us many words familiar from the OT but also many other Canaanite words never seen before. Yet Polzin in his chapter (4) on lexicographic features gives us seven allegedly late words characteristic of the P document. None of these seven words occurs in more than five passages of the OT.

2. Polzin does not adequately consider the influence of scribal editing of grammatical features of old MSS. He does admit that the lengthened first singular imperfect (i.e., with *āh*) that occurs regularly in the Ezra Memoirs and only once in Chronicles but variously in the Nehemiah Memoirs may be due to "a plurality of scribal traditions."[16] If scribes did this to Ezra-Nehemiah (or to Chronicles?), quite possibly they changed the old treatment of collectives as singulars to a more up-to-date treatment of collectives as plurals. The change would often merely be adding a final waw (*w*) to a verb. These scribal changes would be impossible to evaluate. Which scribal hand worked on which book in which century was never recorded. We do know that the two major Dead Sea MSS of Isaiah differ greatly in the use of vowel letters. The late spelling *darmeseq* for Damascus is found seven times in 1QIsa[a]. This also occurs elsewhere in the MT, but only in Chronicles. If the "r" were in the MT of Isaiah, Polzin would call it late Hebrew. As it is, it is clearly scribal in 1QIsa[a]. Perhaps it is scribal also in the MT of Chronicles. Many of Polzin's examples would be undercut if this area of ignorance were observed.

3. Polzin has not adequately considered the consequences for style of the type of material he is concerned with. That the style of Chronicles differs from that of its sister books (Sam-Kings) has long been recognized. It is noteworthy that a lot of the material peculiar to 1 and 2 Chronicles (the 1,026 verses that Polzin works with) is of a specialized nature. Almost nine chapters (296 verses) are nothing but names. Not many infinite absolutes here! Also, the last eight chapters of 1 Chronicles (228 verses) concern David's preparation in music and materials for the temple that Solomon would build. These special materials constitute 84 percent of the material Polzin studies in 1 Chronicles. Second Chronicles also has its special features in the

[16] *Late Biblical Hebrew*, p. 55.

religious revivals narrated extensively in Hezekiah's and Josiah's reigns. The alleged P document is heavily laced with genealogies, data on births and deaths, and, after Genesis, ritual matters. In Genesis his P sections include 268 verses. This material includes nine sections of some length, of which 83 verses concern genealogical material and 148 are miscellaneous (Creation, Flood, circumcision, etc.). Forty-five more verses come from scattered notices, mostly concerning births, deaths, and ages. None of these sections is longer than five verses. The P document was isolated by critics who assigned to it genealogies, numbers, and ritual matters—especially formulaic things. These matters should be kept in mind in comparing the P document to Chronicles.

4. Polzin has isolated thirteen items characteristic of Chronicles. In seven of these P^g is like the classical Hebrew (J, E, early Sam, and Deut). In four it is like Chronicles, and in two it is like neither. He finds the allegedly supplementary P sections (P^s) even further toward Chronicles. It goes with classical Hebrew in only two items and sides with Chronicles in nine.[17] Three remarks may be made. First, these figures are not all that compelling when we remember the questions raised above about the material concerned, the possibility of scribal adjustment, etc. Second, each feature should be considered at length. We can take only one: his No. 2, the increased use of *'et* before a nominative, the *'et* emphatic.

Polzin agrees that *'et* before the subject of passive verbs occurs frequently and in various periods, but he finds thirty-nine cases in the OT of the *'et* before a nominative noun.[18] There are nine in Chronicles and Nehemiah; one in Daniel; five in Numbers (P); ten in the prophets Jeremiah, Ezekiel, Haggai, and Zechariah; and thirteen in the "Deuteronomic history."[19] That this feature occurs only three times in Qumran is explained as due to the archaizing tendencies at work in Qumran.[20] This explanation seems odd when we remember that of the thirty-nine cases, seventeen are in the Pentateuch, Joshua, Judges, Samuel, and Kings. Now Polzin may agree with Noth that these are in P and in a "secondary insertion" into Deuteronomy.[21] We may wonder, however, whether the Qumran archaizers had read Noth and Driver! If almost half the instances were in books ostensibly before the Exile, why would the archaizers avoid the feature? Why not just admit that different authors use different styles for different reasons?

5. We wonder whether Polzin has chosen the right linguistic features to test Chronicles and the P document? There is an interesting linguistic feature of biblical Hebrew that is slightly changed in biblical Aramaic and is a feature of the Gospels as well. It is the expression "answered and said," where often no answer is involved. The phrase is used sometimes in the first person but very often in the third-person singular, with the verb *'ānāh* ("answer") followed by the verb *'āmar* ("say").

The phrase "answered and said" is used eleven times in Genesis but never in the P document, either in Genesis or Exodus-Numbers. It is used extensively in Samuel-Kings (some forty times) but only three times in Chronicles. One might at first conclude that the phrase is nearly absent in late Hebrew and that P is late. But notice that of the three times the phrase is used in Chronicles, one is in a parallel to Kings

[17] Ibid., pp. 96–112.
[18] Ibid., p. 36.
[19] Ibid., pp. 32–35.
[20] Ibid., p. 78, n. 12.
[21] Ibid., p. 35.

(2 Chron 34:15 and 2 Kings 22:8), and Chronicles has the phrase where Kings does not. Also notice that it occurs three times in Haggai, eleven times in Zechariah (1–6), two times in Ezra, two times in Esther, and twenty-eight times in Job—always in the introductory lines and never in the poetry. In Daniel the phrase is found in the Aramaic sections thirty times (in the participial form) but never in the Hebrew sections. In Ezra the Hebrew sections have it two times as noted above, but the Aramaic does not have it at all. A similar phrase, using the infinitive of "to say," occurs three times in the P document of Genesis, once in Numbers (32:31, the E document), and not at all in Chronicles.

What does this mean? Probably nothing except that some types of material, like historical dialogue, are more apt to show the phrase than others. It suggests also that not only a few linguistic items should be selected for study; a broad spectrum may give other results! It is of interest, on the side, that the phrase "he answered and said" becomes a frequent Semitism in the Gospels.

In a final chapter Polzin discusses "Lexicographical Features." He has saved himself by stating early on that lexicographical features are less dependable criteria.[22] It could be argued, however, that scribal modernization of endings and word order is more likely to be expected than modernization of words. Some vocabulary items may be quite significant.

Polzin himself emphasizes a good bit the argument from the first-person pronoun *'ᵃnî* versus *'ānōḵî*.[23] It can no longer be said that *'ᵃnî* is a late word, for it occurs in Ugaritic. Polzin claims, however, that the long form is increasingly scarce and that this is significant. It is not found in Lamentations, Song of Songs, Haggai, Zechariah (1–8), Ezra, Esther, or Ecclesiastes; it is found only once in Ezekiel, Nehemiah, Daniel, and Chronicles. However P uses the short form 130 times and *'ānōḵî* only once. This compares with Ezekiel's 138 to 1 ratio. Is this not remarkable, and does this not prove P's lateness?

Two remarks come to mind. First, the P document is the result of critical choice. Critics segmented out the P document. In Genesis this was done first on the basis of divine names. In subsequent books that criterion failed (after Exod 6:3), and general criteria were applied. One prominent criterion used was that P passages have *'ᵃnî* and non-P use *'ānōḵî*. In the days of Driver et al., it was thought that *'ᵃnî* was a late word. Since this was one important criterion for the selection of P sections, it is not surprising that in P *'ᵃnî* predominates.

Second, again counting is not enough. Sometimes set phrases determine word choice. In the P passages of Genesis, *'ᵃnî* occurs five times, *'ānōḵî* once. In two of the five the phrase is "I am El Shaddai" (Gen 17:1; 35:11). In Leviticus throughout the Holiness Code (not included in Polzin's analysis), the expression "I am the LORD" or a similar one occurs forty-five times. Every time in the phrase *'ᵃnî* is used just as we would expect in a set phrase. After Exodus 7:1–13, however, which is P and uses *'ᵃnî* twice (in v.3 for emphasis and in v.5 in the phrase "I am the LORD"), there is a short section of J (vv.14–18). In v.17 in the phrase "I am the LORD," *'ᵃnî* is used; but immediately afterward "I will strike" uses *'ānōḵî* in a participial construction. One conclusion is that context and phraseology determined the use of these synonyms, and critical selection loaded the witness of the documents that were separated out.

Of Polzin's list of eighty-four words in Chronicles alleged to be late, perhaps a

---

[22] Ibid., p. 16.

[23] Ibid., pp. 126–27.

dozen are actually loan words, chiefly from Persian. Curiously, none of these occur in the P document and, of course, not in other early literature. His other seventy-two words also do not occur in the P document. He finds no late words in his P^g and only six in P^s.[24]

For instance, *ḥ^a^nukkāh* ("dedication") occurs in P^s at Numbers 7:10–11, 84, 88, and otherwise only at 2 Chronicles 7:9 and Nehemiah 12:27. Naturally! These three places record the dedication of the tabernacle, the temple, and the rebuilt walls!

The word *ṭāwāh* ("to spin") occurs in P^s at Exodus 35:25–26—and only here in the Bible. However, it appears in the Mishna, and so Polzin calls it late. Classical Hebrew has a different root—*šzr*—for "spin"; but must we assume that the Israelites used only one word for one item? His other examples are no more impressive.

Against this is the fact that the P document in the Pentateuch (or Tetrateuch) does not have Persian words, Aramaic administrative words, or even the Babylonian month names. These are found only in the exilic books. It does not even mention Jerusalem or the temple. It has none of the clear marks of lateness. And Polzin's efforts to prove its lateness are far from convincing.

C.S. Lewis has something to say concerning all these attempts to analyze and date the Bible's style, motifs, unity, etc. He points out that his own writings have been so analyzed by critics who presume to know the source of his motifs and the origin of his figures and characters. He speaks with regard to NT criticism, but his remarks apply as well to the OT. He declares that the critics (who, he admits, might be right in their estimation of value) were uniformly wrong in their analysis of his own work. Translating this to the biblical field, he argues that it is impossible now at this late date to determine ancient sources, criticize connections, analyze motifs, etc. He says:

> The Biblical critics will have to be almost superhuman . . . to offset the fact that they are everywhere faced with customs, language, racial characteristics, class characteristics, a religious background, habits of composition and basic assumptions which no scholarship will ever enable any man now alive to know as surely and instinctively as the reviewers can know mine, and for the same reason, remember, the Biblical critics, whatever reconstruction they devise, can never be crudely proved wrong. St. Mark is dead. When they meet St. Peter, there will be more pressing matters to discuss.[25]

3. Literary Form and Classification

An insight into any ancient culture is greatly enhanced by consideration of its laws. In the case of Israel, study of its laws is especially important; for not only the mind of the nation, but also the will of God is found in them. These laws are also instructive to us. The laws of Israel must be studied with care, however, because obviously they all do not apply to the Christian today. "When there is a change of the priesthood, there must also be a change of the law" (Heb 7:12). Some of the laws of Israel (e.g., the Ten Commandments) carry over into the present age and are repeated in the NT (Rom 13:9); some of the laws are abrogated (Acts 10:14–15). It is important to know which

---

[24] Ibid., p. 151.

[25] "Modern Theology and Biblical Criticism," *Christian Reflections* (Grand Rapids: Eerdmans, 1967), p. 161.

laws are which and why, and to know what lessons can be learned from all the laws of Israel.

The nation of Israel was unique in that it was a theocracy. God was the Head of the nation. He had chosen Israel and had promised in that period to channel his saving grace particularly through that nation. He has not given such a promise to any nation today. To Israel he gave his revelation through the prophets. To Israel he gave the order of true worship at the tabernacle and temple. God dwelt in the midst of Israel and at last became incarnate as a Jew of Nazareth. Therefore, in Israel things that we call sacred and profane were mingled together. Before the monarchy much of the secular administration was in the hands of the priests. There was no separation of church and state such as the NT requires. There were, therefore, physical penalties—even capital punishment—for religious offenses. The nation as a whole was promised a blessing and threatened with a curse according to its obedience. The nation of Israel was to be isolated and was to make no treaties with the heathen nations round about.

In the present age there have been nations with state churches set up by men, but none has been successful. Such state churches lead to religious wars and religious persecution and result in the dilution of the church's witness, as well as other abuses. God has not chosen any other nation as he did Israel. In this age the church crosses national lines. Christians live under the law of their own government in civil matters and under the laws of God in morals and faith (Matt 22:21). Nonetheless, all the laws of ancient Israel are instructive to the Christian in various ways.

Israel's laws have customarily been classified as moral, civil, and ceremonial—the commandments, judgments, and ordinances. Examples of each would be as follows: a commandment—you shall not murder; a judgment—a person guilty of manslaughter may flee to a city of refuge; and an ordinance—the prescribing of a sin offering for any repentant sinner. Such a classification usually involves the idea that the ceremonial legislation is done away in Christ, the civil legislation changes with the civil government, and the moral legislation continues ever in binding force.

The writer would like to suggest an alternative classification into two divisions of law: the area of our relation to God and the area of our relation to our fellow beings. These laws can be further divided into the eternal principles and their temporary manifestations. Thus the first four commandments give the eternal principles of divine worship. Other laws also stress God's holiness, his hatred of sin, and his love issuing in redemption. These eternal principles were manifested in ancient Israel in the temporary laws of worship that occupy so much of Leviticus. They typify the holiness of God, the uncleanness of man, the necessity of blood redemption, and the restoration of fellowship with God. Of course, they are typical of Christ, the Lamb of God who would come to take away the sins of the world. In the present age the same eternal principles find other temporary manifestations in baptism, the Lord's Supper, and other items of Christian worship.

Similarly, the last six commandments express God's eternal will for our relations with our fellow beings in the world that God has created. Those eternal principles find their temporary manifestation in civil law. In ancient Israel this involved such things as building a protective wall around the edge of the flat-roofed houses so that no one would fall off (Deut 22:8). Today this principle forbids driving a car with bad brakes. The civil laws of modern states reflect in more or less commendable fashion the eternal principles that God has implanted in the consciences of men and has spelled out in the pages of his Word.

There is a third classification of Israel's laws that has lately come into prominence, a classification from the angle of their form and expression. Since the work of Albrecht Alt,[26] Israel's laws have been classified into case laws and categorical laws. Alt's terms are casuistic and apodictic legislation. The case laws apply to a particular situation and are in the following general form: "If a man does such and such, then you shall punish him in such and such a way." The categorical or apodictic laws are in the following general form: "You shall not . . ." or "Whoever does such and such shall surely suffer." This distinction in form between the two types of law is clear and probably significant.

Alt further remarked that the two types of law also differ markedly in their context.[27] In general, he said, the apodictic laws deal with what is considered most sacred in religion; the casuistic law is of a secular nature. He further argued that the case law was derived from Canaanite legal practices, and its adoption was the consequence of the fusion of cultures that occurred when the Israelite tribes pressed into Palestine from the desert. The apodictic laws were more the inheritance of the native Israelite background, in particular, Israel's worship. He believed that the apodictic law arose as a series of short, solemn commandments recited every seven years at the Feast of Tabernacles (cf. Deut 31:9–13).[28]

Much of what Alt has written is instructive, and he has drawn attention to important data. The data may also be interpreted in other ways, however. First of all, the case laws of Israel may not have been derived from Canaanite legal practice but from general Near Eastern law codes. Actually, we do not possess any collections of Canaanite laws; so on the face of it, Alt's theory is unprovable.[29] On the other hand, we have long possessed the Laws of Hammurabi from about 1700 B.C. and have also a Hittite code and much other legal information. There are general parallels between some of the Israelite laws and the legal material of the surrounding nations.

The difference in form between case law and categorical law does not seem to be too significant in Leviticus. Chapter 18 is largely categorical law; chapter 20 repeats many of these items in case law formulation, but the laws in chapter 20 include a penalty. This difference—the mention of a penalty in case laws—may be of more consequence than Alt's claim of different origins of the two formulations.

It is especially interesting that practically all the laws of the surrounding cultures were of the case-law type. For instance, Hammurabi's famous stele has about three hundred laws, all of them casuistic. The parallels to the laws of Moses are interesting but not at all exact. There is doubtless no direct borrowing involved, but perhaps Moses was acquainted with the general common law of the East. Hammurabi's law #22 demands a severer penalty than Moses': "If a citizen has committed a robbery and is caught, that man shall die."[30] Moses specified restitution (Exod 22:1–4).

Speiser (p. 539) draws attention to the fact that Hammurabi's Laws do not form a complete code. Following Miles, he calls them "a series of amendments to the common law of Babylon."[31] It seems that the judge in ancient times did not compare the crime with the law book and give a decision as our judges and juries do. Rather he

---

[26] *Essays on Old Testament History and Religion*, tr. by R.A. Wilson (Garden City, N.Y.: Doubleday-Anchor, 1968), pp. 112ff., 133ff.

[27] Ibid., p. 141.

[28] Ibid., pp. 164ff.

[29] "We have at present no original sources for the study of Canaanite law" (ibid., p. 126).

[30] ANET, p. 167.

[31] Quoted from G.R. Driver and J.C. Miles, *The Babylonian Laws*, vol. 1, Legal Commentary (Oxford: University Press, 1952), p. 41.

considered a crime in the light of the current standards of rectitude and his own common sense. The collections of laws may have given him broad principles and key precedents, but much was left to the wisdom of the judge. It may be remarked that this is also the case in the Pentateuch. The Pentateuchal legislation does not cover all cases, but it covers enough; and the judges on whom God placed his spirit were competent enough to handle all other cases on these principles. We therefore need not speak of Israel obtaining its case law from the Canaanites or even from Mesopotamia. Moses, a learned man, was well acquainted with the common law of the East. God had providentially given him training in the royal academies of Egypt—such as they may have had. And God used Moses to give the Israelites such precedents and case laws as were necessary and helpful in establishing the infant nation.

Incidentally, there apparently were no collections of laws in Egypt. Speiser (p. 539) draws attention to this fact and explains it by the circumstance that in Egypt the Pharaoh was a god in the flesh, and the law was his word: "In Egypt the result was authoritarianism. In Mesopotamia the trend was towards democracy" (p. 549). In Israel, as we have said, there was a theocracy where Moses was giving God's will to the nation. Part of Israel's hatred of Egypt, Speiser has suggested, was based on its hatred of the authoritarianism of Egypt in which the king could do no wrong and actually was to be worshiped as a god. In Israel, on the contrary, God alone was to be worshiped; and all kings, prophets, and priests were subject to his divine Word. Israel's law was different.

The apodictic law of Israel, which appears scattered from Exodus 20 to the end of Deuteronomy, did indeed come with direct divine sanction. It usually concerned sacred relationships of worship and morality. Curiously, the surrounding cultures show few or no instances of such apodictic legislation. In the Bible "you shall not . . ." is a direct expression of the will and nature of God.

There is no need to find, with Alt, an origin of this type of law in Israel's wilderness life with its simpler moral categories. We have no information on what laws may have been in vogue then among wilderness Bedouin. It is far simpler and more satisfying to accept the biblical declaration that God gave these laws by revelation to Moses on the mount and during Moses' later ministry. It is true that some of the principles of this apodictic law were not new with Moses. Cain was aware that murder was a sin. The Egyptian Book of the Dead has a negative confession in which the king claimed that he was innocent of various crimes that partly were covered by the Ten Commandments.[32] Wherever men listen to the voice of conscience, there are parallels to the second table of the law. The particular theological emphases and even the formulation of the apodictic law, however, seem to be unique to Moses.

Since Alt's time there has been much interest in the Hittite and other treaties with special regard to their stipulations. These stipulations follow a historical prelude as the Ten Commandments follow the historical statement of Exodus 20:1. They are couched in the apodictic form: "you shall . . . , you shall not."

Much has been written on these treaty forms, but here space forbids extensive treatment, especially since the discussion primarily concerns Exodus, Deuteronomy, and Joshua.

Mendenhall was one of the early authors to note the similarities of some of the great

[32] Cf. the remarks of W.F. Albright, *Yahweh and the Gods of Canaan* (Garden City, N.Y.: Doubleday, 1968), p. 173.

covenant formulations of the Bible to the treaties established between Hittite kings and their vassals.[33] Some of the OT covenants showing this general format were said to be the giving of the Ten Commandments, the addresses of Deuteronomy (esp. chs. 4–28), and Joshua's final message to Israel (ch. 24). Meredith G. Kline has done a real service in his studies in Deuteronomy,[34] in which he shows that the structure in Deuteronomy argues for a Mosaic date in line with the treaties made by the Hittites of the second-millennium B.C. Hittite practices changed in later times. Kline's views have been questioned, but they are supported by Kitchen, who clearly gives the data.[35]

A major source for these discussions is McCarthy's *Treaty and Covenant,* which gives a translation of the major nonbiblical treaties together with extensive discussion of the ancient treaty forms. On p. 28 he gives the usual analysis of the form of Hittite treaties. They have (1) the title of the king, (2) a historical section, (3) stipulations, (4) a tablet clause requiring the preservation and rereading of the document, (5) a list of gods as witnesses, and (6) a section of curses and blessings. But McCarthy's analysis (p. 80) shows considerable departure from the standard, though he affirms an underlying unity. This basic common form of both Hittite and later treaties is (1) the stipulations, (2) the god lists or invocations, and (3) the curse formula. (Kitchen points out, however, that in the first-millennium treaties the witnesses precede the stipulations.)

The significance of the treaty pattern may be questioned if it is reduced so drastically to bare essentials. Even the apodictic "you shall" of the stipulations is not invariable. For instance, McCarthy (*Treaty and Covenant,* pp. 191–93) points out that the extensive Sfire Stele has mostly casuistic formulations in its stipulations, with only some apodictic commands. Also, the historical section is usually missing in the later treaties. McCarthy argues (p. 104), however, for a basic unity and on these grounds questions whether details of treaty forms can be used to date treaty documents at all. He says this partly because he believes that it is an accident of discovery that, while our Hittite treaties are before the fall of the kingdom in 1200 B.C., the Syrian-Mesopotamian treaties are largely later.

Others, such as Kitchen,[36] support Kline's conclusion that the data we have do show that the covenants in the Pentateuch and Job are in line with the earlier Hittite practice rather than the later Eastern treaties or agreements. His citation of the data is impressive. So far as parallels go, the biblical material relates to the second-millennium treaties, not the first.

When McCarthy considers the OT itself, he finds the true covenant pattern present only in what he regards as the core of Deuteronomy (4:41–28:68). He questions other sections regarded by some as of covenant form. Concerning Sinai he says, "We can only conclude that the form of the Sinai story in Exod 19–24 which is reflected in the text without later additions does not bear out the contention that the story reflects an organization according to the covenant form" (*Treaty and Covenant,* p. 163). He claims that there are aspects of the treaties in Exodus 19–24 but that the emphasis is on ritual and theophany. Likewise, 1 Samuel 12 and Joshua 24 have traces of the covenant form, but in Samuel there is "the application of the covenant structure to a

[33] G.E. Mendenhall, "Covenant Forms in Israelite Traditions," BA 17, pt. 3 (1954): 50–76.

[34] M.G. Kline, *Treaty of the Great King* (Grand Rapids: Eerdmans, 1967).

[35] K. Kitchen, *The Bible in Its World* (Exeter: Paternoster, 1977), pp. 79–85.

[36] *The Bible in Its World,* p. 85. His conclusion is quite emphatic.

special end, a warning about the dangers of monarchy in Israel" (p. 143). In Joshua we have "not so much a covenant as a prophetic theme. Or, more accurately, perhaps it is a prophetic development on the idea of a covenant" (p. 150). He does not think that Deuteronomy 1:1–4:40 is a treaty (p. 132). Of chapter 4 by itself, he says that there are elements of the covenant structure; but they "have been expanded and linked together in a rhetorical manner." Instead of a contract or a record of an agreement, we have an exhortation to fidelity. He does not even consider Leviticus 26 as a part of an ancient covenant formulation.

McCarthy's treatment of the central portion of Deuteronomy has merit but would be more convincing if he did not, in critical vein, frequently subtract or rearrange certain sections of the text. Even so, he concludes that this section of Deuteronomy "has been molded into the covenant form. . . . But in Dt. this more objective point of view has been covered over by the desire to persuade. . . . In the Dtic use of the covenant the desire to produce an internal consent, a conviction which will move one to obedience, has been given an exceptionally important place" (*Treaty and Covenant*, pp. 129–30).

Of the Hittite treaties McCarthy remarks further: "How are the stipulations formulated? Here there is great variation. The stipulation may take the form of the precative, it may be an imperative, it may simply be in the indicative. . . . By far the most common form is the conditional statement. . . . In other words, case law" (ibid., p. 34). This is an interesting admission inasmuch as the original emphasis on treaty formulations grew out of a desire to find a parallel for the apodictic laws, the "you shall nots" of Exodus, Leviticus, and Deuteronomy.

Kitchen also remarks that in the Pentateuch we have "a record of the acts of giving and receiving the covenant . . . not the actual formal covenant-document."[37] So we need not overemphasize the treaty formulations in the Bible, even though it seems apparent that what formulations there were at Sinai exhibit the literary practices of Moses' time, not of later days.

We may conclude that the Bible may reflect to a degree treaty formulations; but the purpose of Moses and the prophets was not to bind by treaty but to exhort to obedience through faith and trust in Almighty God. This surely is the purpose of Leviticus 26, the only chapter in the book with possible treaty-form connections.

To return to the casuistic and apodictic legislation, there is no need to find separate sources for these laws. To separate them so distinctly, Alt finds it necessary to alter the passages and assume later intrusions into the text in a very subjective way. There is no good reason why the usual view cannot be held, that Moses from time to time stated the great principles of God's righteous will and then added in appropriate places various legal interpretations and case studies that would guide judges in their day-to-day work. It may be held, indeed, that the case law was not all given at Sinai. Moses served as chief justice of Israel for forty years, and many cases came before him for judgment. He was knowledgeable on legal principles, and the important cases were collected at his direction and under the Spirit's inspiration during these forty years and were given for the guidance of the nation ever after.

There is a category of Israel's law that does not come under Alt's twofold classification: ceremonial legislation. This instruction for divine worship is found especially in Leviticus, though Leviticus also has the other types of legislation. Where did ceremonial legislation come from? Older critical students believed that the Hebrew religion developed from crude animistic ideas to the organized ritual of a

[37] *The Bible in Its World*, p. 83.

later date. Today students are not so sure of such an evolutionary development. Albright, with becoming reserve, remarks that not much parallel material has survived from the religions of antiquity.[38] Albright hoped for more material as further tablets from Ugarit were published.

There is no evidence that Israel's ritual law was of natural origin. Eighteen of the chapters in Leviticus begin with the words "The LORD said to Moses." Israel's worship, like Israel's theology, was of divine origin; and the prescriptions for ritual were God-given.

It does not follow that Moses invented sacrifices. The Bible makes it plain that the sacrificial system of the OT began as soon as man had sinned. The specialized institutions of national worship, however, were given by God through Moses at Sinai. These prescriptions include some very practical items. For instance, the poor were allowed to bring less costly offerings—which would be equally acceptable (Lev 5:7). At the same time the prescriptions of sacrifice and worship included elements typical of God's redemption by the sacrifice of his Son. The nonpractical is often easiest recognized as the typical.

It is, of course, true that Israel's sacrificial system was not given in a cultural vacuum. Other nations also sacrificed in various ways. The laws of Leviticus doubtless included parallels to those sacrifices and also included differences. In general sacrifices were partly eaten by the worshipers and therefore consisted of edible animals. Sheep, goats, and cows were in common use for sacrifice in the Orient; but in Mesopotamia the ass was also sacrificed. In Egypt the cat (never mentioned in the OT) was considered sacred. In Greece in later times milk was used as a libation offering. Probably the most famous example of a pointed difference from the Canaanite culture is the law not to cook a kid in its mother's milk (Exod 23:19; Deut 14:21). There is a text in Ugaritic (UT 52:14) that seems to specify that a kid shall be cooked in milk, though the text is slightly uncertain (see discussion on p. 621). It is quite possible that the biblical law was a warning against taking part in some heathen rite that is not now fully understood.

We may not be sure of the origin of heathen sacrifice. Did it arise from a natural desire to placate the deity or to give offerings of thanksgiving? Perhaps both ideas were involved. Or was it a remembered remnant of ancient true sacrifices such as those offered by Noah? Perhaps this figured in the picture also. In any case, the sacrifices of the surrounding cultures were significantly different, as we shall see, and were an integral part of very different religious systems. The religion and sacrificial system of Israel were unique.

To summarize, God revealed his laws for the nation to Moses. Some of these laws were revealed on Mount Sinai; some may have been revealed during the course of Israel's wilderness wandering. God used Moses' extensive legal background and knowledge of the common law of the East, and thus some of the laws are of the familiar case-law type. Other types of law dealing with more basic matters make the divine imperative more solemn. These laws embody eternal principles even when some of them are couched in temporary forms of worship that were to be done away with in Christ. Therefore, we can learn principles of atonement, prayer, faith, and grace from Israel's ceremonies and principles of justice in business, honor in home life, truth in speech, and so forth, from Israel's civil legislation.

---

[38] "Nearly all pertinent evidence is extremely fragmentary and elusive because of our lack of knowledge of substantive data" (*Yahweh*, p. 183).

4. Theology

a. *Sacrifice*

The first and perhaps most important matter taken up in the Book of Leviticus is the sacrificial system of ancient Israel. Five major sacrifices are described; then the regulations for the offering of these sacrifices are added. This first section takes up one-fourth of the book. Later parts of the book also bear on the subject—the ordination of the priests (chs. 8–9) and especially the detailed directions for the celebration of the Day of Atonement in chapter 16. None of these places sets forth in formal fashion the meaning of sacrifice, but many things are said that give us considerable guidance. Naturally the Book of Leviticus should be read against the background of all Israel's teaching and experience. However, for reasons of space, we must give most attention to Leviticus itself.

The historic view of the OT sacrificial system is that the death of the sacrificial victim is the God-given type of the death of Christ and that Christ by his death paid the penalty for our sins. The sacrifices were in type and symbol substitutionary. Life was for life, and the one who trusted in God's substitute for sin was freed from penalty. This is most clearly expressed in the Book of Hebrews. It says in sum: "By one sacrifice he [Christ] has made perfect forever those who are being made holy" (10:14); "we have confidence to enter the Most Holy Place by the blood of Jesus, by a new and living way opened for us through the curtain, that is, his body" (vv.19–20). Romans is equally explicit: "God presented him [Christ] as a sacrifice of atonement, through faith in his blood. He did this to demonstrate his justice, . . . so as to be just and the one who justifies those who have faith in Jesus" (3:25–26). It is of some interest that both of these classic passages are directly dependent on the ritual of the Day of Atonement as outlined in Leviticus.

This doctrine of the typological blood of the sacrifices and the efficacious blood of Christ, however, is not limited to Leviticus and Paul. It has often been called the scarlet line of redemption that begins in Abel's sacrifice in Genesis and climaxes in the blood of the Lamb slain from the creation of the world in Revelation (13:8). Jesus said it plainly, "I lay down my life for the sheep" (John 10:15).

There have been, of course, other views of atonement both ancient and modern. Some are quite curious, such as the one expressed in some of the church fathers, that Christ was the bait that caught the Devil.[39] It is not clear whether the Fathers meant this as a considered theory of atonement or more as a homiletical attention-getter. The idea that Christ was bait seems to have been rare. More common was the idea that Christ's death was a ransom paid to the Devil. This view probably arose from a misuse of such verses as Hebrews 2:14–15. In recent time important variations of the OT doctrine have been presented especially by critical scholars.

The names of Wellhausen, Robertson Smith, and George Buchanan Gray are of significance. Wellhausen, who recast the history of Israel's religion to suit his Hegelian theories of progress, held that the root idea of OT sacrifice, like that of the Canaanites round about, was giving to the deity. The worshiper gave his god a gift of thanks for bounteous harvests, recovery from sickness, or other good fortune. Wellhausen, of course, held that Leviticus was part of the P document and was written

[39] See, for example, Charles Hodge, *Systematic Theology*, Reprint ed. (Grand Rapids: Eerdmans, 1975), 2:564–66.

quite late, around 450 B.C. What Wellhausen knew about the religion of the surrounding Canaanites either in 450 B.C. or in Moses' day was precious little. In 1875 archaeology was barely beginning, and very few ancient tablets had come to light. General considerations and comparative religion, however, were enough for his theory.

Robertson Smith in 1899 was not much better off as far as extrabiblical information from ancient times was concerned. Like Wellhausen he was not greatly restricted by the biblical data, which he divided, redated, and reinterpreted in the critical fashion of the day. He said that the basic idea of sacrifice was communion through blood rites. He held that in early times meat was not eaten much. Later on the eating of animals was a rite of blood brotherhood. The worshiper celebrated the kinship of his friends and their kinship with the deity. Smith's studies are much referred to, but his views do not fit the biblical data or the more modern reconstructions.

Today the relation of the Israelite worshiper to his God is said to be more covenantal than genealogical; so the blood brotherhood idea is questionable. It hardly seems to fit the treatment of blood in the OT. The blood was never eaten in a common meal. It was sprinkled before the Lord. The texts that mention the significance of blood point to it as the life, or at least the symbol of life, of the animal (Gen 9:4–6; Lev 17:11–12; Deut 12:23). The animal dies when the worshiper deserves to.

G.B. Gray has returned to the emphasis of the sacrifice as a gift to the deity. In the newer covenantal formulation, the sacrifice is like a gift of a vassal to a suzerain. We need not deny that some sacrifices include the element of thanks. And every worshiper sometimes is moved by a feeling of thanks to express his devotion by a gift. The freewill offerings and vows of Israel witness to this.

This view, however, does not adequately account for the considerable emphasis on the blood of the victim and its treatment. If the animal is given, it need not be killed. And many things—clean, unclean, living, and lifeless—could have served as gifts. Indeed, when the second temple fell, the rabbis, denied an altar in Jerusalem, came to the conclusion that gifts and prayers were as acceptable as animal sacrifice. They espoused the gift theory. Pitifully, when the Romans attacked, the rabbis sacrificed animals until the last animal in Jerusalem was gone while the people starved.

Some studies argue that the use of blood was magical, not primarily ritual.[40] The blood libation warded off the wrath of the deity, and its expiatory use appeased demonic powers that then withdrew. These views may perhaps be supported by reference to various pagan views today. Certainly they cannot be based on Leviticus or other biblical passages (on an alleged demonic power, Azazel, see the comments on ch. 16). It is of real interest that comparative studies of ancient religions find no such treatment of blood in their sacrifices.[41] Evidently blood theology was exclusively Israelite. We should therefore restrict ourselves to the biblical texts in elucidating the meaning of these sacrifices so largely associated with the blood of the victim.

---

[40] See B.A. Levine in the prolegomenon of G.B. Gray, pp. xxivff. Levine outlines the earlier views referred to above.

[41] Daly (p. 30) says, "Comparative religion has been unable to find a highly illuminating parallel for the OT blood rites." McCarthy ("Blood Sacrifice") holds that an extrabiblical survey of the Semitic and Greek areas does not show a general belief outside Israel in blood as a divine element that served as the basic reason or explanation for sacrifice. See also the defense of blood shed as a symbol of the death of the victim in Morris, pp. 110–11, 122–24.

b. *Sin*

In considering the biblical doctrine of atonement, it is logical to begin with the problem for which atonement is the cure—sin. It is natural to avoid this question. To err is human; to deny responsibility is as old as our first parents. Adam blamed Eve; Eve blamed the serpent. Today we blame society or our parents' upbringing or our economic condition. It is popular to allow sin for such extreme cases as Hitler and Stalin. That puts the responsibility far off. But few find the view of C.S. Lewis palatable. Screwtape says to his junior tempter, "The only thing that matters is the extent to which you separate the man from the Enemy. It does not matter how small the sins are, provided that their cumulative effect is to edge the man away from the Light and out into the Nothing. Murder is no better than cards if cards can do the trick. Indeed the safest road to Hell is the gradual one."[42] A prominent psychologist entitled one of his books *Whatever Became of Sin?*[43] Sin is not pleasant to face, especially if we are urged to take it personally. It takes a David to say, "I have sinned against the LORD" (2 Sam 12:13).

The God of the Bible punished sin (Exod 34:7). The immediate example of God's judgment was Israel's sin of idolatry (Exod 32:30–33). In Leviticus 18 are the laws of incest, etc., which are said in v.25 to be like the sin (*'āwōn*) of Canaan. Chapter 19 includes practically every item mentioned in the Ten Commandments. Adultery with a slave girl is specifically called a sin, and a guilt offering to make an atonement is prescribed (vv.20–22). In the chapter of warnings and curses (ch. 26), God adjures Israel to keep his commands, decrees, and laws (v.14). If they do not, he will punish them seven times over for their sins. Their possible sins are mentioned ten times. These sins are lumped together as disobeying God's laws, refusing to listen to God, and being hostile to him (*hōlēk . . . qerî,* "going counter to," v.21). It seems clear that Leviticus calls sin a violation of God's laws—surely all of God's laws: moral, ceremonial, and civil. The emphasis, however, of the so-called Holiness Code is on the moral and ethical.

If then sin is a violation of God's commands, atonement to be valid must provide for forgiveness. Sin is not a matter of irregular ritual. It is not even a matter of stepping outside a cherished covenant relation. It is a violation of God's law. The Ten Commandments are now sometimes looked on as stipulations under which God would keep covenant with a most favored nation. But they are more than that. They are the eternal moral principles set by a holy God. He did not claim covenant relation with the Canaanites; but when the Canaanites indulged in excess of idolatry, adultery, violence, and deceit, this was called sin. Their cup of iniquity (*'āwōn*) was full, and they were judged. Sin was not mere faithlessness to a favored relation. It was (and is) violation of God's holy law.

The atoning significance of the sacrifices is seen best of all in the ritual of the Day of Atonement that Hebrews and Romans refer to as noted above. The verb "atone" (*kipper*) has been much discussed. It has been derived from a root that in Arabic means "cover" (cf. BDB, s.v.). Therefore it has been said by some that God's face is "covered," i.e., placated by the sacrifice. Others have said that the OT sins were not forgiven but only "covered" until the sacrifice of Christ was made. Neither of these views take into account the fact that the verb is Piel, most naturally taken as a

[42] *The Screwtape Letters* (London: Geoffrey Bles, 1942), pp. 64–65.
[43] Karl Menninger (New York: Bantam, 1978).

denominative from the noun *kōp̱er* ("a ransom"). The verb, therefore, should mean "pay a ransom."[44]

The derived noun *kappōreṯ*, the name for the lid of the ark, is of special interest. In the KJV this lid is called the "mercy seat." The NIV more accurately renders it "atonement cover." The LXX calls it the *hilastērion*, a word applied to Christ in his atoning work in Romans 3:25. The significance of the name is that on the solemn Day of Atonement, the blood of the sin offerings for the high priest and for the nation was sprinkled here within the veil as the high point of the ritual. The animal that was the sin offering was to be presented before the Lord and slain. The bull was to make atonement for—*ba'aḏ* (lit., "on behalf of")—the high priest and his family (Lev 16:11). The goat likewise was to make atonement "on behalf of" (*ba'aḏ*) the whole community of Israel (vv.17, 24).

It is not enough to see here merely a ritual of purification for the tabernacle and its furniture. That is referred to (though not with the preposition *ba'aḏ*, "on behalf of"). The tabernacle's uncleanness is "because of" (*min*) the uncleanness and rebellion of the Israelites (Lev 16:16, also v.19: "to consecrate it from [or because of] the uncleanness of the Israelites"). The sin offering was for sin. On the Day of Atonement a general sin offering was made for all the sins of all the people. It symbolized most solemnly the principle that sin demands a penalty in order to be forgiven and that God in grace arranged for that penalty.

The Day of Atonement also involved the unusual ritual of the "scapegoat" (or, better, "escape goat"). More will be said in the comments on chapter 16 about the Hebrew word *'ᵃzā'zēl*. For now, the symbolism is very instructive. This goat, like the sin offering (Lev 4:24), was presented before the Lord, and hands were laid on its head. This was a usual part of the sacrificial ritual (Lev 1:4 et al.), but in Leviticus 16:21 it is explained: the priest is to confess over the animal the sins of the people and put them on the goat's head. There could hardly be a clearer expression of the transfer of sins to the sacrifice. In the sin offering the sins are symbolically judged and the penalty paid. In the ritual of the escape goat, the sins are in the symbol removed far away, and the work of atonement is complete.

The conclusion is natural from the above considerations. To make atonement for sin is to have the penalty paid and the guilt removed. Here lies the significance and the glory of the OT sacrifices, albeit they were not in themselves efficacious. They were only types and shadows (Heb 8:5) and therefore were repeated regularly and often, until the Great High Priest should come who would in a new priesthood offer a final sacrifice to effect atonement for his people.

This is not to say that the various sacrifices do not include other meanings—just as the work of Christ not only atones but also brings the believer near to God in communion, worship, and service. The blood ritual is basic to the whole sacrificial system, and atonement from sin is its foundation.

The question further arises, What did the worshiper of Moses' day understand about this ritual? The answer is not easy, because our information is sketchy. The OT is a very short book in comparison to its extensive subject matter—history, laws, ritual, theology, ethics, exhortation, praise, etc. It does not tell us everything. Some Bible students say the ancient worshiper was told by God to sacrifice. He believed God, obeyed God, and got a blessing. His faith was implicit. He did not know that the

[44]See also Morris, p. 143, and his very helpful discussion of the usage of the verb and noun, pp. 142–52.

sacrifices pointed forward to a Redeemer. Many fine Bible students hold this view.[45] However, it appears that Isaiah, at least, knew and taught something more. In Isaiah 53:10 the Servant is called a "guilt offering." This one who died (v.8) and was buried (v.9) was the righteous one (v.11) who bore our iniquity (v.6). Generations of Christians, following the explicit lead of the NT, have seen here a description of the sacrifice of Christ. But notice that his sacrifice is identified with the sin offerings of Israel. It is attractive to find in Isaiah 55:3 a further identification of the atoning Servant with the promised Davidic Messiah. Indeed, the Targum to Isaiah at the head of this section (Isa 52:13) reads: "Behold my servant, the Messiah." This seems clearly to have been a prominent pre-Christian Jewish view (cf. a similar remark in the Targum to Mic 5:2 [5:1 MT]).

There are earlier references that are less clear. The famous words of Abraham—"God himself will provide the lamb for the burnt offering, my son" (Gen 22:8)—are enigmatic. Did he only intend to allay Isaac's suspicions? Shortly Isaac was persuaded to suffer the knife. He could easily have run away from the old man! Abraham could well have realized what common sense teaches, that the blood of bulls and goats cannot take away sin. Other nations practiced human sacrifice, actually recognizing that at times only a supreme sacrifice will do.[46] Abraham may have thought that somehow his son would be God's great sacrifice and that the promised Seed would then be returned to him by resurrection (cf. Heb 11:19). We may not know how clear was Abraham's conception, but we believe that he was looking forward to a promised Seed who would have a ministry of salvation; and he evidently recognized that the sacrifice of animals was not enough. Christ gave Abraham more credit than we sometimes do (John 8:56). The real problem was that the sacrifice of Isaac was not enough either (Ps 44:7–8). Nor was Moses' offer of himself any better (Exod 32:30–32; cf. Paul in Rom 9:3). God himself is the Redeemer of Israel (cf. Notes to 20:2). As revelation progressed, however, the promised Savior who would strike the Serpent's head was identified with the Davidic King to come who was recognized as divine (Ps 45:6; Isa 9:6) and also was portrayed as a sacrifice suffering unto death (Ps 22:15; Isa 53:12). To what extent the ancient worshiper held these items and held them in tension without understanding them we do not know. When even the angels do not understand these mysteries (1 Peter 1:12), we need not solve all problems. It seems probable, however, that at least the elements of the NT faith were dimly understood by the ancient worthies (Heb 11:13–16).

c. *Cleanness*

Details of the laws of cleanness are given later in the commentary, but the principles should be considered as a whole, especially as they occasionally include reference to other OT passages. There are two main things to consider: the concept of ethical holiness as separation from sin, and the concept of ritual holiness as separation from various defilements. God's holiness involves both the ethical and the ritual.

The construction of the tabernacle is detailed in Exodus and assumed in Leviticus. The ordination of the priests in Leviticus 8 is a point-by-point repetition carrying out in fact the instructions given ahead of time by Moses in Exodus 29. We, therefore, are

---

[45] It is defended capably by Hobart E. Freeman, "The Problem of Efficacy of OT Sacrifices," JETS 5 (1962): 73–79. He distinguishes a "worshiper's standpoint" of implicit faith resulting in assurance of forgiveness and a "hidden purpose" of God centering in Christ's sacrifice.

[46] Cf. the discussion by Albright (*Yahweh*, pp. 233–44).

justified in turning to the tabernacle of Exodus and its meaning to shed light on the material in Leviticus. It seems obvious that the dark, inaccessible inner shrine called the Most Holy Place, where God could be approached but once a year, emphatically symbolized the separateness of God from the camp of Israel. How different was this shrine from the idols of the heathen! The idols were multiplied, sold, manipulated, and then were supposed to be honored.

Israel's God was different. He was ethically different. Above sexuality, self-consistent, thoroughly reliable in his word and promises, personal and beneficent, he was the living and true God. His ethical standards, summarized in the Ten Commandments, are still the guiding light of men. They are paralleled, but not negated, by the sermon given on another mount by one greater than Moses. God is holy.

As mentioned above, the so-called Holiness Code of Leviticus 17–25 expresses in some detail these ethical commands. Emphasized are sexual purity and holy family relations, regard for a neighbor's property, life, welfare, and good name. God's law—"Do not hate your brother in your heart" (19:17)—is at once an answer to Cain's anger and to the legalist's casuistry. The law of justice for the poor and rich alike (19:15) long anticipates the one-man one-vote principle of our day. It says that before a holy God all men are equal.

Further, these laws express God's will that his character is to be recognized in worship. His name is to be honored. The Lord must be worshiped by sinners only in the way he has provided—by a holy priesthood and worthy sacrifices.

The concept of ethical holiness enters here. Why are sacrifices and ritual necessary to cleanse the personnel of the temple, its furniture, and its worshipers? The rather obvious answer is that God is holy and man is sinful. A holy God judges sin; but a God of grace opens a way of access to himself through the sacrifices. These sacrifices were informal in the early days of the race. Abraham and the other patriarchs had no temple nor variety of sacrifices. When Israel became a nation of considerable size, however, God instituted the formalized worship and the diversified sacrificial system to instruct the people in their faith and worship and to preserve his holy name in the midst of an elect but still sinful nation.

So the priesthood, acting for the people before God, must be cleansed by sacrifice. The priests must maintain their distinctive position before God and the people. The office was hereditary; so they could not marry just anybody. The ritual was significant; so they could not do just as they pleased: they dared not be drunk on duty—as Nadab and Abihu probably were. Not just anybody could eat the sacred offerings. The prescribed ritual had meaning, and violations of it were sometimes severely judged. Imperfect animals could not be used: they would be a poor type indeed of the Perfect One. Sick or incompetent priests could not serve. Unconsecrated persons could not officiate. Any use of wrong animals, persons, or ritual was an uncleanness. It reflected on the main thrust—a holy God could receive sinful men only through the God-ordained sacrifices and the other worship of the tabernacle. It was a ritual and a worship that was typical of a perfect redemption.

There was another kind of uncleanness Leviticus speaks of at length, uncleanness that concerned Israel's diet, health, and habits. What was the reason for this? Some writers liken these laws to various taboos. At birth and at death, they say, mysterious powers are at work that are frightening to the primitive mind; thus taboos arose. This is a naturalistic explanation. There are such taboos today in some cultures, but the ancient codes so far discovered by archaeologists have nothing parallel with Leviticus

11–15. There is no hint that death was feared more then than now (cf. Gen 49:33–50:1) or that demonic powers were feared at childbirth (cf. Gen 38:27–30). We get the impression from the recorded births that it was a time of joy, or that if the mother died in childbirth, no malevolent powers were blamed (cf. 1 Sam 4:19–22).

It should also be mentioned that some of the present taboos have a basis in fact. Navaho Indians will not inhabit a hogan someone has died in, for fear of harm by evil spirits. However, there is a good reason apart from demonism—many fatal sicknesses are contagious. The OT ritual protected against the contagion by regulations for uncleanness, but there is not the slightest hint of demonism in the record. After all, in Moses' day the culture of the Near East was not in the primitive stage that Wellhausen had imagined.

Another view is that the state of cleanness is the normal state, which can be raised to holiness or degraded to pollution.[47] There are some problems here. It is hard to see why "fishes with scales and fins are clean, but those without these normal aids to propulsion are unclean" (Wenham, p. 20). Why is a finned fish's propulsion more normal than a catfish's? Why is a pigeon more normal than a crow? The "normal" Israelite could never become a holy priest. Moreover most animals are unclean; so how can cleanness be normal?

The views of Mary Douglas have been advanced as a new approach to the nature of holiness, cleanness, pollution, etc. She approaches the subject as an anthropologist and sociologist and brings illustrations from many tribal cultures of today. The Levitical laws are compared with these current tribal customs—she has no ancient parallels.

In Douglas's chapter on "The Abominations of Leviticus," she refers to other views, first the allegorical-ethical interpretation that is as old as Philo. He said that pig meat is delicious but was forbidden to avoid gluttony. Second, she quotes N. Micklem and S.R. Driver as holding that the cleanness rules are arbitrary, irrational, primitive, and unexplainable. A third view she considers is that they are rituals that distinguish the Israelites from their pagan neighbors. This she rejects because she can quote S. Hooke and others that "the Israelite took over some Canaanite styles of worship" (p. 49), and she asks why they took some items and refused others. The hygienic view, which we will argue for shortly, she notes, was advanced by Maimonides; but in a previous chapter (ch. 2) she had given it short shrift. She had said that the texts do not claim that health is a factor, though possibly hygiene was a by-product.

M. Douglas (p. 49) remarks, "The only sound approach is to forget hygiene, aesthetics, morals and instinctive revulsion, even to forget the Canaanites and the Zoroastrian Magi, and start with the texts." Her treatment of the texts begins with the concept of "holiness" that is indeed common in Leviticus, though the verb *qāḏaš* ("be holy") and its derived nouns are used only in three verses (11:44–45; 14:13) in the laws of cleanness (chs. 11–15). She proceeds to connect God's holiness with his blessing that creates order and withdrawn blessing that unleashes the curse. Conforming to God's holiness brings prosperity, and deviation spells danger (p. 50). She says that the "holy" is "evidently not goodness in the sense of an all-embracing humane kindness. Justice and moral goodness may well illustrate holiness and form part of it, but holiness embraces other ideas as well. Granted that its root means separateness, the next idea that emerges is of the Holy as wholeness and completeness" (p. 51).

---

[47]This is advanced by Wenham (pp. 18–25), following Mary Douglas's *Purity and Danger.*

M. Douglas proceeds to cite the perfection of sacrificial animals, priests, warriors, etc. The reason she feels that bodily discharges (all of which she claims defile) violate completeness and wholeness is that "the idea of holiness was given an external physical expression in the wholeness of the body seen as a perfect container" (pp. 51–52). This idea of the body as a container is a rather surprising extension of the idea of separation—an idea that does not appear in the text at all.

Later M. Douglas makes much of the wholeness of species with "hybrids and other confusions" as abominable (p. 53). The bestiality of Leviticus 18:23 is by "a significant mistranslation" (ibid.) called a perversion. It is really wrong because it is a mixing, as "the rare Hebrew word implies" (ibid.). Now the word *teḇel* occurs only in 18:23 and in 20:12, where it is used of incest. Only by heavy dependence on etymological derivation can she be so sure it does not mean "perversion." In chapter 20 it occurs in a series of sexual sins including various types of incest and adultery. The emphasis is on moral matters, not matters of abnormal usage. Not being very sure of what morality is, however, she claims that "holiness requires that different classes of things shall not be confused . . . all the rules of sexual morality exemplify the holy. Incest and adultery (Lev XVIII 6–20) are against holiness, in the simple sense of right order" (p. 53).

A protest might be lodged that Douglas is herself confusing the section, chapters 18–20 of the Holiness Code, which chiefly concerns matters commonly called moral, with the laws of uncleanness in chapters 11–15, which have practically no explicit mention of holiness. Douglas (p. 53) cites in further support of her position the law against mixtures in Leviticus 19:19 (cf. Deut 22:9–11). This law, however, is quite subordinate in the Levitical legislation and is subject to other interpretations. The law against breeding different kinds of animals probably does not refer to hybridization of horses and asses because the noun is not used for these animals, and because mules were freely used in Israel (see the comment on 19:19). The attempt to mate different species of other animals is so unusual that the law can hardly refer to that. It may possibly refer to the desirability of preserving a good strain of Egyptian cattle or sheep. The two kinds of seed are prohibited perhaps because that would interfere with harvesting, or it may even refer to keeping seed free from weeds. The weaving of two kinds of material (wool and linen in Deut 22:11) may be a rule that would prevent loss by unequal shrinkage.

An interesting suggestion has been made lately by Milgrom that the mixture forbidden in clothing is the use of costly blue-dyed wool with white linen (which did not dye well).[48] This use of "royal blue," he suggests, was for the priests' clothing; and the present verse with its parallel in Deuteronomy forbids its use by laymen. In any case these mixtures are not said to violate either laws of cleanness or laws of holiness. They have no emphasis and may refer to practical matters in that culture whose details and reasons escape us. The injunction "Be holy, because I am holy" (11:44–45) does not specifically precede these laws as Douglas implies.

M. Douglas's approach to unclean meats is the same: "Holiness is unity, integrity, perfection of the individual and of the kind. The dietary rules merely develop the metaphor of holiness on the same lines" (p. 54). She follows S.R. Driver in saying that the Israelites' diet customs came first and the rules came later. In early times they just did not have pigs; so later the rules forbade them. She thinks that possibly the Israelites did not relish wild game—though Deuteronomy 14:5 specifically allows

[48] J. Milgrom, "Of Hems and Tassels," BAR 9 (1983): 65.

seven kinds. Her theory does not explain why the camel was not allowed. Nor does she attempt much comment on the birds that are difficult to identify in detail. She just says, "Those species are unclean which are imperfect members of their class, or whose class itself confounds the general scheme of the world" (p. 55). This is a peculiar statement. The bird names are indeed obscure in detail, but they seem clearly to consist of the hawks, etc., which eat carrion—meat or fish. Why these are more imperfect than pigeons or violate the general scheme of the world is not apparent.

In considering fish M. Douglas cites the threefold creation scheme of the earth, the waters, and the firmament. "Leviticus takes up the scheme and allots to each element its proper kind of animal life. In the firmament two-legged fowls fly with wings [including hawks, owls, and vultures!]. In the water, scaly fish swim with fins. On the earth four-legged animals hop, jump or walk. Any class of creatures which is not equipped for the right kind of locomotion in its element is contrary to holiness" (p. 55). Surely her theories lead her to strange lengths in her definition of holiness. Do not sharks and eels have the right kind of locomotion in water? or camels and pigs on land? or owls and ospreys in the air? There must be some better principle.

M. Douglas's treatment of issues and pollutions springs naturally from her basic premises: "The body . . . provides a basic scheme for all symbolism. There is hardly any pollution which does not have some primary physiological reference" (pp. 163–64). Her theory that the body is symbolic of society as a whole is interesting. It is, however, purely a subjective idea with no basis whatever in the Bible. In the NT the representation of the church as the body of Christ is a totally different thing. She further holds, as cited above, that the body was viewed as a perfect container considered as full, so that any fluids escaping from its orifices would be unclean. Of course, there is no hint of this idea in Leviticus. And she is in error in several significant points. Spittle is not called unclean unless from an unclean person (15:8). Blood is not unclean and does not render one who touches it unclean except for menstrual blood. Tears are not unclean. She nowhere refers to milk from a mother's breasts, which, far from being unclean, was a necessity for infant life. Douglas quotes M. Eliade who argues that water is clean because it dissolves away irregular forms and restores to pristine conditions (p. 194). This is also purely subjective. The Bible just says that water is refreshing as a beverage and that it washes off dirt.

A further point is that the touching of unclean animals does not make a person unclean as is often stated. It is only touching the dead carcasses of unclean animals that causes uncleanness—and for that there is a good hygienic reason as we shall argue later.

Of course, it is correct to say that uncleanness has some physiological reference. This is the basis of the hygienic theory of uncleanness as defended in the commentary section. The text indeed does not say that these rules are hygienic; but it does say that the health of God's people is his concern and that he would defend them from the diseases of Egypt (Exod 15:26; Deut 7:15). He did that in ways the Israelites did not understand, but his reason was good. The health of the Jews in the ghettos of Europe was remarked on by people of the Middle Ages. The hygienic theory adequately explains the dietary laws, the laws covering disease, and the laws covering housing and sanitation. It is an old view worth defending.

A few things further can be noted. First, there is no problem in hygienic laws being tied to the sacrificial system. Sickness and death are ultimately the result of sin. God's redemption of his people and his gathering them to Canaan had a meaning for their total well being. Public health was God's promise. Rules that would promote that health would naturally be given the religious sanctions requiring sacrifices and other ritual for their enforcement. As noted earlier, in the theocracy of Israel state law and church laws were intermingled. For sickness to require sacrifices and what led to sickness to be prohibited is really what we should expect.

Furthermore, most of the laws can be clearly seen to tend toward hygiene and public health. They have been so defended often. Remarks by Albright add to the picture.[49] He points out that the dietary laws are certainly beneficial. In areas where parasites were a continuing problem, pigs, mud-burrowing fish, snails (a source of serious disease in Egypt until recently), carrion-eating birds, etc., were all prohibited. It is true that pork is safe if well cooked, and pigs are no problem if people wear shoes. In former days in the southern United States, where bare feet were common, trichinosis was a serious disease caused by worms carried by pigs.

The rule of thumb—a split hoof and a ruminant animal—gave positive protection under all usual circumstances. It worked well. As with all such rules, however, some things were prohibited that could have been accepted without danger. The horse and the camel, for instance, were not to be eaten. This was no hardship. The horse, not being a ruminant, cannot digest cellulose and so needs grain in its diet. This made it an impractical animal to raise for meat; Israel had little grain to spare. The camel is a wonderful animal and is a ruminant, but it takes seventeen years to reach full growth—it lives forty years. In ancient times the camel probably was considered more valuable for work than food.

It is often forgotten that the uncleanness of some animals affected more than food. True, a live unclean animal was no problem: a horse or a camel, for instance, could be handled without contracting uncleanness. A dead unclean animal, however, could not be touched. It was to be buried, and everything it had touched was unclean. This was not so hygienically important for a horse—except that a large carcass was not left to putrify. The law, however, did help protect against bubonic plague, that scourge of early times. A dead rat was a tragedy. The logical thing was to keep a clean house and street and not attract rats. Cockroaches and bugs of all kinds likewise were not wanted in a Hebrew house. A dead one could spoil a whole sack of precious meal. The laws of uncleanness helped protect against vermin.

The laws of "leprosy" protected against contagious diseases. Leprosy was a sad and frightening disease.[50] Yet other diseases were far more dangerous. Bubonic plague could kill half a town in a week. Measles, scarlet fever, smallpox, etc., took their toll. Most of these diseases have skin rashes and thus could be diagnosed by the priest who was made the public health officer. In ancient times they had no penicillin, gamma globulin, or vaccination. The one thing they did have was quarantine, and this Levitical provision surely saved many lives.

The laws on childbirth also were wise and beneficial. They were not due to superstition. A woman at childbirth was unclean for seven days for a boy (who was circumcised on the eighth day) and fourteen days for a girl. The natural result was that contact was reduced between a woman in childbirth and other mothers or other people. In Austria in a famous hospital in the nineteenth century, the death rate from

---

[49] See the commentary on chs. 11–15.

[50] It is held by many, including the NIV, that the diseases described in Lev 13 included more than true leprosy (Hansen's disease). The progress of these diseases is faster, the symptoms are somewhat different, and the term *ṣāraʿaṯ* is applied to mildew in clothing and house walls. See the discussion in the commentary in loc.

"childbed fever" was gruesome. Doctors went straight from examining cadavers to the work of delivering new babies. A young doctor, Ignace Semmelweiss, noticed that if he washed his hands in lime water between examinations, the deaths were greatly reduced. He had approached the idea of antisepsis. The OT had long anticipated his findings.

Some claim that the uncleanness of discharges from bodily orifices was due to superstition. Actually such discharges are often due to disease, and hygiene calls for precautions to prevent the spread of disease. Deuteronomy 23:12–14 provides that Israel's soldiers should, in effect, use a latrine outside the camp. This is explained as due to God's presence in the camp. Actually God was in the camp, and this was his provision for the health of his soldiers. Even the provisions to get rid of mildew in houses and on garments tended to assure healthy living conditions in an age when the reason for all this was totally unknown.

When all these arrangements can be so beautifully explained as God's care for the health of his people, it seems unfortunate to look to fears of demonic attack or other unsupportable theories to justify such helpful hygienic provisions.

It may be asked, If these laws embodied God's provisions for public health in ancient Israel, why, then, are they not continued in the NT? It is commonly said that the NT abrogates these laws. Actually, though this is probably the right conclusion, the NT evidence is not so clear as is usually supposed. In Matthew 15:1–20 and Mark 7:1–23, the question is not whether one should obey the OT laws but whether the niceties of Pharisaic tradition were obligatory. Jesus answered that the OT laws were not wrong—indeed, that the Pharisees' traditions were wrong. The NIV of Mark 7:19 quotes Jesus as going further and declaring "all foods clean." This may be right, but it is debatable. The KJV rendering is still possible: that it is the process of digestion that purges all foods. On this view Jesus does not speak directly to the subject. He implies that no food is unclean because the heart is what makes one unclean. Strict interpretation might set Jesus against the OT law, but the view that Jesus' contrast is a comparative negative is much better. The heart attitude is more important than the food.

In Acts 10 the question at issue again is not the OT laws but whether Peter should fraternize with Gentiles. The Pharisees forbade this lest a person be defiled with unclean foods and practices, but the OT did not forbid such contact. True, in the vision Peter is called to eat unclean things; and the conclusion is natural, though not absolutely necessary: the laws intended to separate Jews from Gentiles—whom God wanted the Christians to evangelize—were now actually to be done away with.

In any case, if the laws were public health laws, they would not be applicable in the new church age. Like any civil legislation, these laws were applicable to and helpful for a unified society where all obeyed them. But in a pluralistic society such as obtains in the time of the NT church, quarantine, for instance, was of no value to a family when none of the neighbors quarantined. Also, to eat pork or handle rabbits would not help if the neighbors' backyards were infested with worms or if their children had tularemia, etc. Actually, the Jews of the Middle Ages did obey these laws (to the Pharisaic extreme!) and were seen to be more healthy than others; but this was because they were often restricted to ghettos and not living in a pluralistic society as the church is supposed to do.

5. Bibliography

Commentaries

Allis, O.T. "Leviticus." *New Bible Commentary.* Grand Rapids: Eerdmans, 1970.
Bertholet, A. "Leviticus." *Kurzer Handkommentar zum Alten Testament.* Tübingen: Mohr, 1901.
Bonar, Andrew A. *A Commentary on Leviticus.* 1861. Reprint. London: Banner of Truth, 1966.
Calvin, John. *Commentaries on the Four Last Books of Moses.* Reprint. 1852 Translation. Grand Rapids: Eerdmans, n.d.
Clements, R.E. "Leviticus." *Broadman Bible Commentary.* Vol. 2. Nashville: Broadman, 1969–72.
Coleman, R.O. "Leviticus." *Wycliffe Bible Commentary.* Chicago: Moody, 1962.
Douglas, J.D. "Leviticus." *New Bible Dictionary.* Grand Rapids: Eerdmans, 1962.
Eerdman, C.R. *The Book of Leviticus.* New York: Revell, 1951.
Faley, F.J. "Leviticus." *Jerome Bible Commentary.* Englewood Cliffs, N.J.: Prentice Hall, 1968.
Ginsburg, Christian D. "Leviticus." *Ellicott's Commentary.* Reprint. Grand Rapids: Baker, 1954.
Harrison, R.K. *Leviticus: An Introduction and Commentary.* Tyndale Old Testament Commentaries. Downers Grove, Ill.: Inter-Varsity, 1980.
Hertz, J.H. *Leviticus.* The Pentateuch and Haftorahs. London: Oxford, 1932.
Keil, C.F. *The Pentateuch.* Vol. 2. Reprint. Grand Rapids: Eerdmans, 1951.
Kellogg, Samuel. *Leviticus.* The Expositor's Bible. New York: Funk & Wagnalls, 1900.
Kinlaw, D. *Leviticus.* Beacon Bible Commentary. Kansas City: Beacon Hill, 1969.
Lange, J.P., and Gardiner, F. *Leviticus.* Reprint. Grand Rapids: Zondervan, n.d.
Micklem, N. *Leviticus.* The Interpreter's Bible. Edited by G.A. Buttrick. New York: Abingdon, 1953.
Noth, Martin. *Leviticus: A Commentary.* Philadelphia: Westminster and London: SCM, 1965.
Payne, J. Barton. "Leviticus." *The Biblical Expositor.* Vol. 1. Edited by C.F.H. Henry. London: Pickering & Inglis, 1960.
Peisker, A.D. *Leviticus.* Wesleyan Bible Commentary. Grand Rapids: Eerdmans, 1967.
Porter, J.R. *Leviticus.* Cambridge Bible Commentary. Cambridge: University Press, 1976.
Rashi. *Pentateuch with Rashi's Commentary.* Translated by M. Rosenbaum and A.M. Silbermann. New York: Hebrew Publishing Co. London: Shapiro, Valentine, 1929.
Saydon, P. *Leviticus.* New Catholic Commentary on Holy Scripture. 1953. New and revised. Nashville: Thomas Nelson, 1969.
Snaith, N. *Leviticus and Numbers.* New Century Bible. London: Nelson, 1967.
Wenham, G.J. *The Book of Leviticus.* The International Commentary on the Old Testament. Grand Rapids: Eerdmans, 1979.

Special Studies

Albright, W.F. *Yahweh and the Gods of Canaan.* Garden City, N.Y.: Doubleday, 1968.
Bare, G. *Plants and Animals of the Bible.* London and New York: United Bible Societies, 1969.
Baxter, W.L. *Sanctuary and Sacrifice: A Reply to Wellhausen.* London: Eyre and Spottiswood, 1896.
Browne, S.G. *Leprosy in the Bible.* London: Christian Medical Fellowship, 1970.
Cansdale, G.S. *Animals of Bible Lands.* Exeter: Paternoster, 1970.
Childs, Brevard S. *Introduction to the Old Testament as Scripture.* Philadelphia: Fortress, 1979.
Daly, R.J. *The Origins of the Christian Doctrine of Sacrifice.* Philadelphia: Fortress, 1978.
Douglas, Mary. *Purity and Danger.* London: Routledge, Kegan and Paul, 1975.
Eissfeldt, Otto. *The Old Testament, an Introduction.* New York: Harper, 1965.
Fairbairn, Patrick. *The Typology of Scripture.* 2 vols. Edinburgh: T. & T. Clark, 1864.
Gelin, Albert. *Sin in the Bible.* Paris and New York: Desclee, 1964.

Gray, George Buchanan. *Sacrifice in the Old Testament.* Reprint with Prolegomenon by B.A. Levine. New York: Ktav, 1971.
Grunfeld, D.I. *The Jewish Dietary Laws.* London: Soncino, 1972.
Haldeman, I.M. *The Tabernacle, Priesthood and Offerings.* New York: Revell, 1925.
Harris, R.L. *Man—God's Eternal Creation.* Chicago: Moody, 1971.
Heijkoop, H.L. *Die Opfer.* Postfach 303,5830. Schwelm, West Germany, 1973.
Heinisch, P., and Heidt, W. *Theology of the Old Testament.* Collegeville: Liturgical, 1950.
Hooke, S.H. *Babylonian and Assyrian Religion.* London: Hutchinson, 1953.
Hyatt, J.P., ed. *The Bible in Modern Scholarship.* Nashville: Abingdon, 1965.
James, E.O. *The Origins of Sacrifice.* 1933. Reprint. Port Washington, N.Y.: Kennikat, 1971.
Jocz, J. "Clean." *Zondervan Pictorial Encyclopedia of the Bible.* 5 vols. Edited by M.C. Tenney. Grand Rapids: Zondervan, 1975–76, 1:884–87.
Jukes, Andrew. *The Law of the Offerings.* London: James Nisbet, 1847.
Kaiser, Walter C., Jr. *Toward an Old Testament Theology.* Grand Rapids: Zondervan, 1978.
———. *Toward Old Testament Ethics.* Grand Rapids: Zondervan, 1983.
Kaufman, Y. *The Religion of Israel.* Translated and abridged by M. Greenberg. Chicago: University of Chicago, 1960.
Kidner, Derek F. *Sacrifice in the Old Testament.* London: Tyndale, 1952.
Kitchen, Kenneth A. *Ancient Orient and Old Testament.* London: Tyndale, 1966.
Kraus, Hans-Joachim. *Worship in Israel.* Atlanta: John Knox, 1966.
Külling, S.R. *Zur Datierung der "Genesis-P-Stücke."* Kampen: Kok, 1964.
Kurtz, J.H. *Sacrificial Worship of the Old Testament.* Edinburgh: T. & T. Clark, 1863.
McCarthy, D.J. *Treaty and Covenant.* Rome: Pontifical Biblical Institute, 1963.
McEveneu, S.E. *The Narrative Style of the Priestly Writers.* Rome: Pontifical Biblical Institute, 1971.
Milgrom, J. *Studies in Levitical Terminology.* Berkeley: University of California, 1970.
Morris, Leon. *The Apostolic Preaching of the Cross.* Grand Rapids: Eerdmans, 1956.
Nash, Roland H. *Freedom, Justice and the State.* Lanham, Md.: University Press of America, 1980.
North, R. *Sociology of the Biblical Jubilee.* Rome: Pontifical Biblical Institute, 1954.
Noth, Martin. *Laws in the Pentateuch.* Edinburgh: Oliver and Boyd, 1966.
———. *A History of the Pentateuchal Traditions.* Translated by B.W. Anderson. Englewood Cliffs: Prentice Hall, 1972.
Oehler, G.F. *Theology of the Old Testament.* Translated by G.E. Day. New York: Funk & Wagnalls, 1883.
Oesterley, W.O.E. *Sacrifices in Ancient Israel.* London: Hodder & Stoughton, 1937.
Pfeiffer, R.H. *Introduction to the Old Testament.* New York: Harper, 1941.
Pedersen, John. *Israel, Its Life and Culture.* Vols. 3 and 4. London: Oxford University Press, 1953.
Porubcan, Stefan. *Sin in the Old Testament.* New York: Herder, 1963.
Rainey, A.F. "Sacrifice and Offerings." *Zondervan Pictorial Encyclopedia of the Bible.* 5 vols. Edited by M.C. Tenney. Grand Rapids: Zondervan, 1975–76, 5:194–211.
Ringgren, H. *Sacrifice in the Bible.* New York: Association, 1963.
Robertson, O. Palmer. *The Christ of the Covenants.* Grand Rapids: Baker, 1980.
Smith, W.R. *Lectures on the Religion of the Semites.* 1897. Reprint. New York: KTAV, 1969.
Speiser, E.A. *Oriental and Biblical Studies.* Philadelphia: University of Pennsylvania Press, 1967.
Vannoy, J. Robert. *Covenant Renewal at Gilgal.* Cherry Hill, N.J.: Mack, 1978.
Vaux, R. de. *Studies in Old Testament Sacrifice.* Cardiff: University of Wales Press, 1964.
Vos, G. *Biblical Theology of the Old Testament and the New Testament.* Grand Rapids: Eerdmans, 1971.
Young, E.J. *Introduction to the Old Testament.* Grand Rapids: Eerdmans, 1949.

Periodicals

Auerbach, E. "Die Feste im alten Israel." *Vetus Testamentum* 8 (1958): 1–18.

Brueggemann, W. "The Kerygma of the Priestly Writers." *Zeitschrift für die alttestamentliche Wissenschaft* 84 (1972): 377–414.

Cross, F.M., Jr. "The Oldest Manuscripts from Qumran." *Journal of Biblical Literature* 74 (1955): 147–72.

Davies, Douglas. "An Interpretation of Sacrifice in Leviticus." *Zeitschrift für die alttestamentliche Wissenschaft* 89 (1977): 387–99.

Elliott-Binns, L.E. "Some Problems of the Holiness Code." *Zeitschrift für die alttestamentliche Wissenschaft* 67 (1955): 26–40.

Feinberg, Charles. "The Scapegoat of Leviticus 16." *Bibliotheca Sacra* 115 (1958): 320–33.

Fretheim, T.E. "The Priestly Document: anti-Temple?" *Vetus Testamentum* 18 (1968): 313–29.

Gispen, W.H. "The Distinction Between Clean and Unclean." *Oudtestamentische Studien* 5 (1948): 190–96.

Gray, John. "Cultic Affinities Between Israel and Ras Shamra." *Zeitschrift für die alttestamentliche Wissenschaft* 62 (1950): 207–20.

Guglielmo, A. "Sacrifice in the Ugaritic Texts." *Catholic Biblical Quarterly* 17 (1955): 196–216.

Kinghorn, K. "Biblical Concepts of Sin." *Wesleyan Theological Journal* 1 (1966): 21–26.

Kitchen, K.A. "The Old Testament in Its Context, 2, From Exodus to Joshua." *Theological Study Fellowship Bulletin* 60 (1971): 3–11.

Laughlin, John C.H. "The 'Strange Fire' of Nadab and Abihu." *Journal of Biblical Literature* 95 (1976): 559–65.

Levine, B.A. "Kippurim." *Eretz-Israel* 9 (1969): 88–95.

McCarthy, D.J. "The Symbolism of Blood Sacrifice." *Journal of Biblical Literature* 88 (1969): 167–76.

Milgrom, J. "The Biblical Diet Laws as an Ethical System." *Interpretation* 17 (1963): 288–301.

———. "The Cultic *šᵉgāgāh* and Its Influence in Psalms and Job." *Jewish Quarterly Review* 58 (1967): 115–25.

———. "A Prolegomenon to Leviticus 17:11." *Journal of Biblical Literature* 90 (1971): 149–56.

———. "The Alleged Wave-Offerings in Israel and in the Ancient Near East." *Israel Exploration Journal* 22 (1972): 33–38.

———. "Two Kinds of *ḥaṭṭā't*," *Vetus Testamentum* 26 (1976): 333–37.

Morris, Leon. "The Biblical Use of the Term 'Blood'." *Journal of Theological Studies* 3, New Series (1952): 216–27.

———. "*'āshām*," *Evangelical Quarterly* 30 (1958): 196–210.

Rainey, A.F. "The Order of Sacrifices in Old Testament Ritual Texts." *Biblica* 51 (1970): 485–98.

Rowley, H.H. "The Meaning of Sacrifice in the Old Testament." *Bulletin of John Rylands Library* 33 (Sept. 1950): 95–100.

Saydon, P. "Sin-offering and Trespass-offering." *Catholic Biblical Quarterly* 8 (1946): 393–98.

Snaith, N.H. "Sacrifices in the Old Testament." *Vetus Testamentum* 7 (1957): 308–17.

———. "The Sin Offering and the Guilt Offering." *Vetus Testamentum* 15 (1965): 73–80.

Unger, Merrill F. "The Old Testament Revelation of the Beginning of Sin." *Bibliotheca Sacra* 114 (1957): 326–33.

———. "The Significance of the Sabbath." *Bibliotheca Sacra* 123 (1966): 51–59.

Vinck, J.G. "The Date and Origin of the Priestly Code in the Old Testament." *Old Testament Studies* 15 (1969): 1–144.

Wagner, V. "Zur Existenz des sogenannten Heiligkeitgesetzes." *Zeitschrift für die alttestamentliche Wissenschaft* 86 (1974): 307–16.

Zink, J.K. "Uncleanness and Sin." *Vetus Testamentum* 17 (1967): 354–61.

6. Outline

I. Description of the Five Major Offerings (1:1–6:7)
   A. Burnt Offering (1:1–17)
   B. Grain Offering (2:1–16)
   C. Fellowship Offering (3:1–17)
   D. Sin Offering (4:1–5:13)
   E. Guilt Offering (5:14–6:7)

II. Directions for the Priests in Their Service (6:8–7:38)
   A. Burnt Offering (6:8–13)
   B. Grain Offering (6:14–23)
   C. Sin Offering (6:24–30)
   D. Guilt Offering (7:1–10)
   E. Fellowship Offering (7:11–38)

III. The Beginning of the Tabernacle Worship (8:1–10:20)
   A. Consecration of Aaron and His Sons (8:1–36)
   B. Divine Acceptance of the First Worship (9:1–24)
   C. Nadab and Abihu's Profanation (10:1–7)
   D. Explicit Instructions for the Priests (10:8–20)

IV. Laws of Cleanness (11:1–15:33)
   A. Clean and Unclean Food (11:1–47)
   B. Purification After Childbirth (12:1–8)
   C. Cleanness and Skin Diseases (13:1–46)
   D. Mildew (13:47–59)
   E. Cleansing From Skin Diseases (14:1–32)
   F. Cleansing Houses From Mildew (14:33–57)
   G. Uncleanness From Emissions (15:1–33)

V. The Annual Sin Offering of the Day of Atonement (16:1–34)

VI. Laws of Personal Holiness (17:1–22:33)
   A. One Place of Sacrifice (17:1–9)
   B. The Sanctity of Blood (17:10–16)
   C. Laws Against Incest (18:1–18)
   D. Sexual Purity (18:19–30)
   E. Miscellaneous Laws (19:1–37)
      1. Parents, Sabbaths, and idols (19:1–4)
      2. Fellowship offerings (19:5–8)
      3. Help of the unfortunate (19:9–14)
      4. Fairness and neighborly love (19:15–18)
      5. Forbidden mixtures (19:19)
      6. Protection of slave girls (19:20–22)
      7. Fallow fruit trees (19:23–25)
      8. Against heathen practices (19:26–31)
      9. Protection for the old, the stranger, and the poor (19:32–37)
   F. Punishments for Various Sins (20:1–27)
      1. Against the Molech cult (20:1–5)
      2. Various sexual sins (20:6–21)
      3. Exhortations to holiness (20:22–27)
   G. Special Holiness for Priests (21:1–22:16)
   H. Perfection Required in Sacrifices (22:17–33)

- VII. The Feasts and Worship of the Lord (23:1–24:9)
  - A. Introduction (23:1–2)
  - B. The Sabbath (23:3)
  - C. The Passover and Firstfruits (23:4–14)
  - D. The Feast of Weeks (23:15–22)
  - E. The Feast of Trumpets (23:23–25)
  - F. The Day of Atonement (23:26–32)
  - G. The Feast of Tabernacles (23:33–44)
  - H. The Care of the Lampstand (24:1–4)
  - I. The Bread of the Presence (24:5–9)
- VIII. Identical Laws for the Stranger and the Israelite (24:10–23)
- IX. Laws of Land Use (25:1–55)
  - A. The Sabbatical Year (25:1–7)
  - B. The Jubilee (25:8–34)
  - C. Protection of the Poor (25:35–55)
- X. Warnings Against Apostasy (26:1–46)
  - A. Conditions of Blessing (26:1–13)
  - B. Threatened Punishments (26:14–39)
  - C. God's Perpetual Covenant (26:40–46)
- XI. Laws Concerning Gifts and Endowments (27:1–34)

Text and Exposition

I. Description of the Five Major Offerings (1:1–6:7)

God had prescribed offerings from the time of Abel. After the Flood, Noah offered burnt offerings (Gen 8:20). So did Abraham (Gen 22:9). Jacob offered sacrifices to his father's God in Beersheba (Gen 46:1). Moses asked Pharaoh to let Israel worship the Lord with sacrifices and burnt offerings (Exod 10:25). Moses' father-in-law offered the same (Exod 18:12). We have little information as to how these sacrifices were made except that clean animals were used and that they were burned, at least in part, on an altar. Various types of sacrifices probably were used.

When Moses organized the nation of Israel and its worship, he was commanded by God to establish this worship in more formal patterns. Instead of each man building an altar wherever convenient, there was to be a tabernacle where all would worship. Certain set types of sacrifice were prescribed for the people, the nation, and the priests themselves. A father of a family could no longer act as his own priest. That was legitimate in earlier circumstances, but the worship and instruction of a great people called for a certain amount of order and regulation.

The need for various sacrifices arises from the varied needs of a people's worship. The NT makes clear that all the sacrifices of Israel were symbolic and typical of Christ's sacrifice. Hebrews 5–10 is the special NT commentary on Leviticus. It emphasizes the priesthood of Christ and his atoning death. All sacrifices portray this essential truth. This is the implication of Hebrews 10:8–10. No one offering, however, can typify Christ's many-sided work, which includes propitiation, atonement, communion, consecration, worship, and much more. A full directory of worship for Israel thus would be expected to include different types of sacrifices. The main types expected from the people are outlined in Leviticus 1:1–6:7 in enough detail to be self-explanatory to the people of that time, and they are described sufficiently to direct the priests in their service.

A. *Burnt Offering*

1:1–17

1 The LORD called to Moses and spoke to him from the Tent of Meeting.
He said, 2 "Speak to the Israelites and say to them: 'When any of you
brings an offering to the LORD, bring as your offering an animal from
either the herd or the flock.

3 " 'If the offering is a burnt offering from the herd, he is to offer a male
without defect. He must present it at the entrance to the Tent of Meeting
so that it will be acceptable to the LORD. 4 He is to lay his hand on the
head of the burnt offering, and it will be accepted on his behalf to make
atonement for him. 5 He is to slaughter the young bull before the LORD,
and then Aaron's sons the priests shall bring the blood and sprinkle it
against the altar on all sides at the entrance to the Tent of Meeting. 6 He
is to skin the burnt offering and cut it into pieces. 7 The sons of Aaron
the priest are to put fire on the altar and arrange wood on the fire. 8 Then
Aaron's sons the priests shall arrange the pieces, including the head
and the fat, on the burning wood that is on the altar. 9 He is to wash the
inner parts and the legs with water, and the priest is to burn all of it on
the altar. It is a burnt offering, an offering made by fire, an aroma
pleasing to the LORD.

[10] " 'If the offering is a burnt offering from the flock, from either the sheep or the goats, he is to offer a male without defect. [11] He is to slaughter it at the north side of the altar before the LORD, and Aaron's sons the priests shall sprinkle its blood against the altar on all sides. [12] He is to cut it into pieces, and the priest shall arrange them, including the head and the fat, on the burning wood that is on the altar. [13] He is to wash the inner parts and the legs with water, and the priest is to bring all of it and burn it on the altar. It is a burnt offering, an offering made by fire, an aroma pleasing to the LORD.

[14] " 'If the offering to the LORD is a burnt offering of birds, he is to offer a dove or a young pigeon. [15] The priest shall bring it to the altar, wring off the head and burn it on the altar; its blood shall be drained out on the side of the altar. [16] He is to remove the crop with its contents and throw it to the east side of the altar, where the ashes are. [17] He shall tear it open by the wings, not severing it completely, and then the priest shall burn it on the wood that is on the fire on the altar. It is a burnt offering, an offering made by fire, an aroma pleasing to the LORD.

1 Notice that these directions for sacrifice were not given to Moses while he was on Mount Sinai but in the course of his work in arranging for Israel's worship (cf. Introduction, p. 519).

The "Tent of Meeting" is the usual name of the movable tabernacle constructed by Moses at Sinai and set up by him on the first day of the first month of the second year after Israel left Egypt (Exod 40:2). It seems probable that this tent is not in view here, but the reference is to a temporary tent of worship set up during the time at Sinai. We know very little of this temporary tabernacle, but it is mentioned in Exodus 33:7–10 and possibly at Exodus 38:8. It is natural to expect that God did not leave Israel for a year without a place of worship.

2 The "herd" would be cattle. The "flock" would include both sheep and goats. Israel was a nomadic people; but, as Albright has emphasized (*Yahweh,* pp. 70–73), Israel did not live like the Arab Bedouins of today (see comment on 11:4). Their life revolves around their camels. Israel's mainstay was her cows, sheep, and goats. There were many cows in Egypt, and surely the Israelites took some along. It is probable that during the extended wilderness wandering, however, the cows, which needed more pasture, were reduced in number; and the people kept the hardier sheep and goats. The ruminant animals digest cellulose. Goats, especially, can live on dried grass, stalks, and bushes. The directions for sacrifice included all the animals that might be offered both in the wilderness and later in the settled country.

3–17 In brief, the burnt offering was to be made of a clean animal (v.3); and all of it was to be burnt on the altar, except the feathers and crop of a bird (v.16, NIV mg.) and the hide of an animal. The hide was for the priest (7:8). The hand of the offerer was to be placed on the animal's head in symbolic acknowledgment of the substitution of the animal for the worshiper (v.4). This is specified in the burnt offering and also in the fellowship offering (3:2, 8, 13) and the sin offering (4:4, 15, 24, 29, 33). The ritual seems to be self-explanatory but is interpreted clearly in connection with the Day of Atonement (16:21). When hands are laid on the animal and sins are confessed, the sins are in symbol transferred to the animal. In the case of the scapegoat, it carried the sins off into the wilderness, signifying their total removal. In other cases the animal was slaughtered, signifying the substitution of the sacrifice in judgment on sin.

The blood was to be sprinkled on the altar (v.5) to emphasize the fact of substitution by death (for the blood is the life, 17:14). Various animals were used in the ritual depending on the choice and ability of the worshiper. The rich would bring a young bull, the poor a bird, the average person a sheep or a goat (vv.2–3, 10, 14).

Burnt offerings were not the most common type of sacrifice. When thousands of sacrifices were offered, they were usually not burnt offerings but fellowship offerings, which were partly eaten. The burnt offering, which is sometimes called a holocaust offering, was totally consumed on the altar.

The special meaning of the burnt offering is nowhere explicitly given. As remarked above, it included atonement by the giving of life for life, as did the other sacrifices, also. Indeed, v.4 specifically says that it is "to make atonement." It seems probable that the additional meaning of the burnt offering was worship, symbolized by the ascending smoke. Keil (p. 269) claims it symbolized surrender and strangely denies that its meaning of satisfaction was present in pre-Mosaic days. This is surely a poor argument from silence. The idea of substitution is clearly present in Genesis 22. It is, however, also legitimate to see the idea of surrender in the burnt offering.

A burnt offering was given for all Israel every morning and again in the evening. On the Sabbath the burnt offerings were double (Num 28:9), and there were extra offerings on the various feast days. The directions of this chapter refer especially to voluntary burnt offerings that any Israelite might be led to offer in special worship to God.

Notes

3 The NIV's marginal reading—"Or *he*"—seems preferable to the word "it" in "that it will be acceptable to the LORD." Even though the closer antecedent to the pronoun is the offering, namely "it" in the phrase "must present it," the Hebrew construction, using an infinitive of רָצָן (*rāṣan*, "be acceptable") with a pronoun suffix as its subject, may suggest that the suffix subject of the infinitive refers to the subject of the main verb—"he must present"—rather than to the nearer antecedent. In any case, it seems more logical to say that by coming to the tabernacle the offerer, not the offering, is made acceptable. The offerer brings the offering because he feels the need to be accepted before God.

4 The word כִּפֶּר (*kipper*, "to make atonement") is used almost fifty times in Leviticus, each time in a similar context. It is used about fifty times more in the rest of the OT. In most cases there is also reference to the priest making atonement through a sacrifice. Exceptions are Gen 32:20; Prov 16:14; Isa 28:18. The word is never used in the OT in the literal sense of "cover." Once in Gen 6:14 a verb with the same consonants but probably a different root (and used in the Qal stem) is used to mean "smear with pitch." Standard Hebrew lexicons say the word means "cover," and the view is then sometimes given that the OT sacrifices covered sins temporarily until the actual atonement of Christ. This theology may still be held by some, but the meaning "cover" for this verb is very questionable. It is derived from a similar Arabic root that need not be related to the Hebrew.

Actually, it is better Hebrew grammar to derive this verb from the noun of the same letters meaning "a ransom" (Num 35:31; Isa 43:3). The verb derived from this noun is used only in the Piel stem, which is another reason to consider it as a denominative verb; it therefore means "to give a ransom" or "atone by substitution."

A further noun—"a place of atonement"—is derived from the verb and is used for the lid of the ark in the Most Holy Place, the so-called mercy seat (NIV, "atonement cover"; cf. TWOT, #1023). Of course, the OT atonement was only typical of Christ's work yet to come.

The blood of bulls and goats did not itself atone (Heb 10:4). See Morris (*Apostolic Preaching*, pp. 136–56) for a valuable discussion of this root, considering also its Greek translations in the LXX and NT.

5 The NIV translates שָׁחַט (*šāḥaṭ*) as "he is to slaughter," indicating that the worshiper does the killing. The same verb and context appear in the description of the following sacrifices (fellowship and sin offerings). In every case the LXX interprets the verb as plural, indicating that the priests did the killing. The difference often is merely one of vocalization, and we need not suppose that the LXX witnesses to a different text. The third masculine singular verb may be used impersonally—one shall slaughter. The Samaritan Pentateuch, however, has a clear plural. It may not be possible to decide between the two interpretations, but something can be said for the idea of the priests doing the slaughtering. Presumably they did it in the third century B.C., if the LXX reflects this interpretation. Notice that in the case of the sacrifice of birds, the priest is specifically said to do the killing (v.15).

As to the sprinkling of blood against the altar (cf. also v.11), it may be difficult to be sure exactly how the blood was handled at the sacrifice. There was a considerable amount of blood involved. The phrase is almost invariable: "sprinkle [or 'throw,' 'pour'] the blood against [or 'upon'] the altar." The verb used here—זָרַק (*zāraq*)—is different from the verb used when a liquid is sprinkled—נָזָה (*nāzāh*, 14:7)—with the finger or with a bunch of hyssop. Therefore, the RSV uses "throw against." The KJV uses "sprinkle upon," the NIV "sprinkle against." In Num 19:20–21, however, both verbs are used, apparently as synonyms. And the "sprinkling" of blood on the people (*zāraq*, Exod 24:8) is referred to as sprinkling in Heb 9:19.

Actually, the two actions are similar except in the amount of liquid used. More important is the question of whether the blood was thrown *against* the altar round about, i.e., on its four sides (NIV), or sprinkled *on* the altar round about (KJV). The Hebrew preposition עַל (*'al*) has both meanings but is more often "upon." A reasonable interpretation would be that the blood was sprinkled on the altar where the wood and sacrifices were burning. In the case of the sin offering and probably the guilt offering, the remaining blood was poured out at the base of the altar where the ashes were (4:7 et al.). Because the fire was sometimes quite hot, it would be necessary to sprinkle the blood or throw it on the altar from a little distance. To throw the blood against the altar would require frequent cleansing, to say the least.

9 נִיחֹחַ (*nîḥôaḥ*, "pleasing") basically means "rest." The point is that the sacrifice gives an aroma of tranquility by bringing peace between God and the worshiper. The word is used forty-three times in the OT and only in this phrase. This is, of course, an anthropomorphic expression picturing the aroma of the sacrifice (not necessarily pleasant) as being smelled by God in acceptance of the offering. Incidentally, the alleged P document, which used this phrase most frequently, is supposed to minimize anthropomorphisms. It is altogether possible that this was a stock phrase of the language and had no more reference to God's smelling than our common phrase "the sun went under a cloud" has reference to the position of clouds and the sun.

14 The תּוֹר (*tôr*, "dove"; KJV, "turtledove") is mentioned as a bird of sacrifice eleven times and always with a young pigeon. The three nonsacrificial usages are Ps 74:19, figuratively, for the psalmist; S of Songs 2:12, as a sign of spring; and Jer 8:7, as one of the migratory birds. It was, of course, a clean bird and was doubtless used for food.

יוֹנָה (*yônāh*, "pigeon") is translated "dove" in several other places. Its mournful note is referred to in Isa 38:14; Nah 2:7 et al. According to Isa 60:8, a dove was somewhat domesticated and therefore would be a normal item for food and sacrifice.

15 It is again difficult to picture the action (cf. v.5). In this case there is only a little blood to be disposed of. The prepositional phrase עַל קִיר (*'al qîr*) could be translated "on the side of" or "against the side of." It is of interest that the next verse uses a different preposition—אֵצֶל (*'ēṣel*)—specifically saying that the place of the ashes was "beside" the altar. Perhaps the blood of the bird was drained just over the edge of the altar. For a bird the fire would not have to be large. If a sheep or a young bull werr being burnt, the fire would be too hot to get very near. The altar was about seven and a half feet square and four and a half feet high. A roaring fire on it would give off a great deal of heat.

16 מֻרְאָה (*mur'āh,* "crop") is only used here, but the word indicates that it has something to do with food. It may mean all the internal organs. The bird was to be plucked and cleaned, then the carcass burned.

נוֹצָה (*nôṣāh,* "contents") also is uncertain. The NIV margin indicates it might mean "feathers," coming from נָצָה (*nāṣāh,* "to fly"). But it may come from a homonymous root meaning "struggle," "grind"(?); then the pair would mean "the internal organs with the crop." At least the general meaning is clear.

17 שִׁסַּע (šissa', "tear open") refers to some violent tearing like that of Samson tearing a lion (Judg 14:6). Perhaps the priest was to break open the bird so that it would burn better. He was not to divide it in two. Notice that in Abraham's sacrifice in Gen 15 he cut the larger animals in two but did not divide the birds.

B. *Grain Offering*

2:1–16

1 " 'When someone brings a grain offering to the LORD, his offering is
to be of fine flour. He is to pour oil on it, put incense on it 2 and take it to
Aaron's sons the priests. The priest shall take a handful of the fine flour
and oil, together with all the incense, and burn this as a memorial
portion on the altar, an offering made by fire, an aroma pleasing to the
LORD. 3 The rest of the grain offering belongs to Aaron and his sons; it is
a most holy part of the offerings made to the LORD by fire.

4 " 'If you bring a grain offering baked in an oven, it is to consist of fine
flour: cakes made without yeast and mixed with oil, or wafers made
without yeast and spread with oil. 5 If your grain offering is prepared on a
griddle, it is to be made of fine flour mixed with oil, and without yeast.
6 Crumble it and pour oil on it; it is a grain offering. 7 If your grain
offering is cooked in a pan, it is to be made of fine flour and oil. 8 Bring
the grain offering made of these things to the LORD; present it to the
priest, who shall take it to the altar. 9 He shall take out the memorial
portion from the grain offering and burn it on the altar as an offering
made by fire, an aroma pleasing to the LORD. 10 The rest of the grain
offering belongs to Aaron and his sons; it is a most holy part of the
offerings made to the LORD by fire.

11 " 'Every grain offering you bring to the LORD must be made without
yeast, for you are not to burn any yeast or honey in an offering made to
the LORD by fire. 12 You may bring them to the LORD as an offering of the
firstfruits, but they are not to be offered on the altar as a pleasing aroma.
13 Season all your grain offerings with salt. Do not leave the salt of the
covenant of your God out of your grain offerings; add salt to all your
offerings.

14 " 'If you bring a grain offering of firstfruits to the LORD, offer crushed
heads of new grain roasted in the fire. 15 Put oil and incense on it; it is a
grain offering. 16 The priest shall burn the memorial portion of the
crushed grain and the oil, together with all the incense, as an offering
made to the LORD by fire.

1–16 The "grain offering" (v.1) is called the meat offering in the KJV in the old English sense of "meat," i.e., "food." It is sometimes called a meal offering or cereal offering, for it consisted of flour or baked goods. Four kinds of grain offering are specified in Leviticus 2: uncooked flour (v.1), bread baked in an oven (v.4), bread prepared on a griddle (v.5), and bread cooked in a pan (v.7).

The meaning of the grain offering is not explicitly given. It has a practical value in that a "memorial portion" (v.2) of the offering was burnt on the altar (cf. Notes) and the rest was given to the priests for their food (v.3; cf. 1 Cor 9:13). Only males who were priests could eat it in the Holy Place (6:16–18). The rest of the priest's family would eat ordinary yeast bread. Apart from the practical value that this offering gave the priests bread to eat with their meat, the symbolism of the grain offering possibly emphasizes thanksgiving. Aside from its ritual use, the word means "gift" or "tribute" (e.g., Gen 32:13; 2 Sam 8:6). A grain offering was specified to accompany other various types of offerings on the altar (23:13–20; Exod 29:40; Num 28–29 et al.).

The drink offering or libation, which was also to accompany various sacrifices, is not mentioned in this section. "Drink offering" is somewhat of a misnomer. The wine was poured over the sacrifice or poured out in the Holy Place; it was not drunk (Num 28:7–15). For a lamb about a pint and a half was used.

The size of the grain offering is not given here. Elsewhere various amounts are specified—the smallest is one-tenth measure of flour (about two quarts if a "measure" is an ephah) with one-fourth hin of oil (about a pint and a half; cf. Num 28:11–14).

The grain offering was to be accompanied with oil and incense (v.1) and salt (v.13). The familiar olive oil was much used in Hebrew cooking as a shortening and was also used as an ointment, as an ingredient in perfume, etc. Only a portion of the flour was to be burnt (v.2), but all the incense was consumed on the altar. The proscription of yeast with the sacrifices that are burnt on the altar is frequent (vv.4–5, 7, 11 et al.). The law against honey appears only here (v.11). The reason for forbidding yeast with the Passover meal was that when Israel left Egypt, there was no time to use yeast to make the bread rise. This incident may have determined the symbolic meaning in other sacrifices. Yeast and honey were indeed edible and were a suitable gift as an offering of firstfruits for the priests' food, but they were not to be burned on the altar (vv.11–12).

Yeast, because it was forbidden on the altar, is sometimes used in the NT as a type of evil. Christ's words are often quoted: "Be on your guard against the yeast of the Pharisees and Sadducees" (Matt 16:6). Some have felt that yeast is always a type of evil and have interpreted the parable of the yeast as involving the spread of evil in the kingdom of heaven (Matt 13:33–43). It seems, however, that yeast is not exclusively considered evil, because it is used in the firstfruits offering. Yeast may also have been avoided on the altar because of use in heathen worship, but evidence for this is lacking so far. Yeast, though useful in bread making, apparently was recognized as an element associated with corruption. Yeast unchecked will sour dough.

The reason for the prohibition of honey is more obscure. Honey under some circumstances will also ferment, and this may have been a factor.

Notes

1 לְבֹנָה (*l^eḇōnāh*, "incense") is often translated "frankincense" (this English word originally meant "pure incense"). The incense tree grew only in South Arabia and on the nearby coast of Africa. Incense was much prized for the pleasant smell given off when it was burned. The tree was gashed and the exuding sap collected in amber-colored drops (cf. G.W. Van Beek, "Frankincense and Myrrh," BA 23 [1960]: 70–95). Incense is bitter and nauseous to the taste and thus not fit for food.

2 The idea of the translation "memorial portion" for אַזְכָּרָה (*'azkārāh*) apparently is that in the part burned on the altar, the offerer is particularly remembered. Some feel that Pss 38 and 70 were to be recited with this memorial offering, hence the translation "a memorial offering" in the RSV of the titles of those psalms. The same word, however, is used in 1 Chron 16:4 of David's liturgical directions and is translated by the NIV as "to make petition." This translation comes from an Akkadian usage that is not the usual one in Hebrew. Actually, however, this usage may be the true one, not only for 1 Chron 16:4 and for the two psalms' titles (NIV, "a petition"), but also for the memorial offering. It may be an offering of invocation or petition. If this is the case, the meaning of "tribute" or "gift fulfilling a covenant" suggested by Wenham (in loc.)—based on certain usages of the noun מִנְחָה (*minḥāh*) in connection with "gifts" to conquering kings (2 Sam 8:6 et al.)—may be misleading. It should be noted that this offering and the drink offering were the only offerings of Israel not associated with blood. Even in these offerings, however, the blood atonement is emphasized, for they were placed on the great altar with its burning sacrifices.

4 Many ovens are found in excavations in Palestine. They are small depressions in the house floor with clay sides reinforced with pieces of pottery. They would be heated with a small fire, then the dough would be placed on the coals or hot stones, and the oven would be sealed with a lid. Very similar ovens are used in the poorer houses in Arab Palestine today.

חַלּוֹת (*ḥallôṯ*, "cake") seems to be related to the word for "pierce" and may have reference to the form of the cake.

מַצּוֹת (*maṣṣōṯ*) is rendered "without yeast"; the word is familiar from the unleavened crackers (matzos) still used by Jews at Passover time.

5 מַחֲבַת (*maḥᵃḇaṯ*, "griddle") is used for a sheet of iron in Ezek 4:3. Presumably these would be some kind of fried cakes.

7 Unfortunately here, too, the details of Hebrew cooking escape us. The word מַרְחֶשֶׁת (*marḥešeṯ*, "pan") may be related to the word for "stir"; therefore, these cakes may have been deep fried or even boiled, dumpling style. These sacred cakes were made in the regular ways well known to the Hebrew housewife, if not to us.

13 In many places in antiquity, salt was a precious item of commerce, valuable for its seasoning qualities. Palestine had an unlimited supply in the Dead Sea area, but some of this includes bitter bromides that make it unsafe for food. Salt is necessary in the diet and was a necessary ingredient in all the offerings. It became a symbol of God's covenant (v.13) and is so used in his covenant with the priests in which he gave them their portion of the peace offering (Num 18:19). It is referred to again in connection with the Davidic covenant (2 Chron 13:5). Whether this use in the offerings determined the use to seal covenants or that use determined the use in the offerings is uncertain.

Salt is used to bind covenants among the Arabs and Greeks, but it is not clear whether this practice goes back to OT times. Salt is not mentioned in the ancient treaty covenants. Wenham (in loc.) quotes Hertz: "'Salt prevents putrefaction while leaven and honey produce it,'" adding the wise words, "True as this observation is, there is little evidence that it was the symbolism intended here."

Contrary to general opinion, there is no place in the Bible where the preserving qualities of salt are expressly mentioned. They are read into Matt 5:13, but this verse can more strictly be interpreted to say that as salt can become worthless by adulteration, etc., so the Christian can become worthless if he does not closely follow Christ. Perhaps it is safer simply to conclude that salt was specified for the offerings because it was a necessary item of food.

14 A firstfruits offering could be given in baked goods (23:17). If still green grain was used, however, it could not be ground into flour easily. It had to be crushed or diced or even cooked. Green wheat, crushed and prepared as a kind of salad, is still used today in Palestine.

C. *Fellowship Offering*

3:1–17

1" 'If someone's offering is a fellowship offering, and he offers an
animal from the herd, whether male or female, he is to present before
the LORD an animal without defect. 2He is to lay his hand on the head of
his offering and slaughter it at the entrance to the Tent of Meeting. Then
Aaron's sons the priests shall sprinkle the blood against the altar on all
sides. 3From the fellowship offering he is to bring a sacrifice made to
the LORD by fire: all the fat that covers the inner parts or is connected to
them, 4both kidneys with the fat around them near the loins, and the
covering of the liver, which he will remove with the kidneys. 5Then
Aaron's sons are to burn it on the altar on top of the burnt offering that
is on the burning wood, as an offering made by fire, an aroma pleasing
to the LORD.

6" 'If he offers an animal from the flock as a fellowship offering to the
LORD, he is to offer a male or female without defect. 7If he offers a lamb,
he is to present it before the LORD. 8He is to lay his hand on the head of
his offering and slaughter it in front of the Tent of Meeting. Then
Aaron's sons shall sprinkle its blood against the altar on all sides. 9From
the fellowship offering he is to bring a sacrifice made to the LORD by fire:
its fat, the entire fat tail cut off close to the backbone, all the fat that
covers the inner parts or is connected to them, 10both kidneys with the
fat around them near the loins, and the covering of the liver, which he
will remove with the kidneys. 11The priest shall burn them on the altar as
food, an offering made to the LORD by fire.

12" 'If his offering is a goat, he is to present it before the LORD. 13He is
to lay his hand on its head and slaughter it in front of the Tent of
Meeting. Then Aaron's sons shall sprinkle its blood against the altar on
all sides. 14From what he offers he is to make this offering to the LORD by
fire: all the fat that covers the inner parts or is connected to them,
15both kidneys with the fat on them near the loins, and the covering of
the liver, which he will remove with the kidneys. 16The priest shall burn
them on the altar as food, an offering made by fire, a pleasing aroma. All
the fat is the LORD's.

17" 'This is a lasting ordinance for the generations to come, wherever
you live: You must not eat any fat or any blood.' "

1–17 In the phrase "fellowship offering" (vv.1, 6), the word translated "fellowship" (*šelāmîm*) includes the ideas of health, wholeness, welfare, and peace. It is reflected in the common Jewish greeting "Shalom!" The question is, Does this offering symbolize internal peace or peace with God? The answer is probably to be found in the fact that here the worshiper joins in the sacred meal. The peace offering—male or female cow, sheep, or goat—is brought to the priest. As was usual in the other offerings, the worshiper laid his hand on the head of the animal in symbolic identification and transfer of guilt (vv.2, 8, 13), then the priest dressed it, handling the blood in the same way as was done for the burnt offering. In this case, however, only the fat and kidneys were burned on the altar (vv.3–5, 9–11, 14–16). Elsewhere it is specified that the priest is to be given the right breast and the right thigh as his portion (see at 7:34). The balance was for the worshiper and his family to eat.

Since the peace offering, or fellowship offering, involved the sacred meal, it seems that the symbolism involves especially communion and therefore peace between God and the worshiper. Of course, the handling of the blood and the burning of the fat on the altar show that the basis of communion is atonement; but with the atonement goes "peace with God through our Lord Jesus Christ" (Rom 5:1).

A fellowship offering could be voluntary as a special offering of thanks to God or could be given as the result of a vow or as a freewill offering (7:12–26). This offering was given by the thousands whenever Israel congregated for a special celebration. At the dedication of his temple, Solomon himself offered 22,000 cattle and 120,000 sheep (1 Kings 8:63). The large numbers are indicative of the large crowds. It was a vast barbecue! Of course, Solomon did not himself act as priest or slaughter all those animals. They were given out of the royal bounty. Many of the people probably brought their own sacrifices, and many ate of the king's largess. Hezekiah's festival was similar but smaller—2,000 bulls and 17,000 sheep (2 Chron 30:24). These were fellowship offerings given in the continuing feast after the Passover was over. The fellowship offerings do not include birds, which would be too small for such feasting. If a man was too poor to bring a voluntary fellowship offering, he would probably be given a share in the offerings of others.

Neither fat nor blood was to be eaten. The prohibition of blood to the Jew is well known and is explained at 17:10–14. The life is in the blood. This is the basis of sacrificial symbolism. Life is given for life. Blood is obviously and intimately associated with life. Other words are also used for "life." The text need not imply any materialistic belief that the blood is equated with life. The meaning is that blood is taken as the obvious symbol of life and therefore to be specifically treated in token of the sacredness of human life (cf. Gen 9:4–6; cf. Introduction, p. 521).

It generally is not realized that eating the fat was also prohibited. The reason for this is given in 7:22–25. The fat was the special part of the animal that was offered to the Lord. It was therefore sacred and not to be eaten. At first sight it might seem that 7:25 limits the prohibition to an animal that is sacrificed. In view of the flat statement in 3:17, however, it is better to take the prohibition of fat as general: because animals that are sacrificed have fat burned on the altar, therefore no fat at all is to be eaten.

Notes

---

1 Since the purpose of the peace offering included the holy feast, any animal good for food, male or female, was allowed. Normally a farmer first kills his male animals for meat, but in some cases the female also would be butchered. For similar reasons there are no provisions regarding the age of the animals. The animal may be a cow (vv.1–5), a sheep (vv.6–11), or a goat (vv.12–16).

תָּמִים (*tāmîm*) means "perfect," "whole," here aptly translated "without defect." Inasmuch as every sacrifice was typical of Christ to come, it need to be perfect in token of his similar perfection. Thus the sins of the people of Malachi's day involved not only ingratitude to God but also unbelief in the perfection of Christ's person and work (Mal 1:8, 13–14).

2 See the discussion of the ritual of laying on of hands and of sprinkling the blood in connection with the burnt offering in ch. 1.

3 The חֵלֶב (*ḥēleḇ*, "fat") of the animal was the representative portion that was burned on the altar. The major deposits of abdominal fat are listed. In the case of the sheep, the fat tail is also specified (v.9). Fat-tailed sheep are raised in Palestine still today. The animal has the fat reservoir in case of a food shortage. Such a deposit of fat was also to be burned. The large amount of fat from the peace offering would result in quite a saving of fuel for the consumption of the other carcasses, as fat burns readily. The fat also would have burned without odor.

4 It is difficult to identify the יֹתֶרֶת עַל־הַכָּבֵד (*yōṯereṯ ʿal-hakkōḇēḏ*, "covering of the liver"). The KJV translates it "The caul that is above the liver." BDB (s.v.) suggests that it is a fatty mass between the liver and kidneys. The word *yōṯereṯ* is only used in this phrase and in this connection. The NIV translation has as good support as any. The etymology from יָתַר (*yāṯar*, "to be left over") may be fallacious. The idea that it is a lobe of the liver (NEB) does not explain why just one part of the organ so famous in hepatoscopy (taking omens by livers) was burned on the altar. It is of interest that the Hebrews did not give the livers of their sacrifices preferential treatment. In Babylon the liver was much observed and used in taking omens for future events. Clay models of livers with instructions for forecasting are found in Mesopotamia in abundance. Only once does the Bible refer to such a practice, and then it refers to divination by the Babylonian king (Ezek 21:21).

D. *Sin Offering*

4:1–5:13 (cf. Num 15:22–31)

[1]The LORD said to Moses, [2]"Say to the Israelites: 'When anyone sins
unintentionally and does what is forbidden in any of the LORD's
commands—
[3]" 'If the anointed priest sins, bringing guilt on the people, he must
bring to the LORD a young bull without defect as a sin offering for the sin
he has committed. [4]He is to present the bull at the entrance to the Tent
of Meeting before the LORD. He is to lay his hand on its head and
slaughter it before the LORD. [5]Then the anointed priest shall take some
of the bull's blood and carry it into the Tent of Meeting. [6]He is to dip his
finger into the blood and sprinkle some of it seven times before the
LORD, in front of the curtain of the sanctuary. [7]The priest shall then put
some of the blood on the horns of the altar of fragrant incense that is
before the LORD in the Tent of Meeting. The rest of the bull's blood he
shall pour out at the base of the altar of burnt offering at the entrance to
the Tent of Meeting. [8]He shall remove all the fat from the bull of the sin
offering—the fat that covers the inner parts or is connected to them,
[9]both kidneys with the fat on them near the loins, and the covering of
the liver, which he will remove with the kidneys—[10]just as the fat is
removed from the cow sacrificed as a fellowship offering. Then the
priest shall burn them on the altar of burnt offering. [11]But the hide of the
bull and all its flesh, as well as the head and legs, the inner parts and
offal—[12]that is, all the rest of the bull—he must take outside the camp
to a place ceremonially clean, where the ashes are thrown, and burn it in
a wood fire on the ash heap.
[13]" 'If the whole Israelite community sins unintentionally and does
what is forbidden in any of the LORD's commands, even though the
community is unaware of the matter, they are guilty. [14]When they
become aware of the sin they committed, the assembly must bring a
young bull as a sin offering and present it before the Tent of Meeting.
[15]The elders of the community are to lay their hands on the bull's head
before the LORD, and the bull shall be slaughtered before the LORD.
[16]Then the anointed priest is to take some of the bull's blood into the
Tent of Meeting. [17]He shall dip his finger into the blood and sprinkle it
before the LORD seven times in front of the curtain. [18]He is to put some
of the blood on the horns of the altar that is before the LORD in the Tent
of Meeting. The rest of the blood he shall pour out at the base of the
altar of burnt offering at the entrance to the Tent of Meeting. [19]He shall
remove all the fat from it and burn it on the altar, [20]and do with this bull
just as he did with the bull for the sin offering. In this way the priest will
make atonement for them, and they will be forgiven. [21]Then he shall

take the bull outside the camp and burn it as he burned the first bull.
This is the sin offering for the community.
22“ ‘When a leader sins unintentionally and does what is forbidden in
any of the commands of the LORD his God, he is guilty. 23When he is
made aware of the sin he committed, he must bring as his offering a
male goat without defect. 24He is to lay his hand on the goat's head and
slaughter it at the place where the burnt offering is slaughtered before
the LORD. It is a sin offering. 25Then the priest shall take some of the
blood of the sin offering with his finger and put it on the horns of the
altar of burnt offering and pour out the rest of the blood at the base of
the altar. 26He shall burn all the fat on the altar as he burned the fat of
the fellowship offering. In this way the priest will make atonement for
the man's sin, and he will be forgiven.
27“ ‘If a member of the community sins unintentionally and does what
is forbidden in any of the LORD's commands, he is guilty. 28When he is
made aware of the sin he committed, he must bring as his offering for
the sin he committed a female goat without defect. 29He is to lay his
hand on the head of the sin offering and slaughter it at the place of the
burnt offering. 30Then the priest is to take some of the blood with his
finger and put it on the horns of the altar of burnt offering and pour out
the rest of the blood at the base of the altar. 31He shall remove all the fat,
just as the fat is removed from the fellowship offering, and the priest
shall burn it on the altar as an aroma pleasing to the LORD. In this way
the priest will make atonement for him, and he will be forgiven.
32“ ‘If he brings a lamb as his sin offering, he is to bring a female
without defect. 33He is to lay his hand on its head and slaughter it for a
sin offering at the place where the burnt offering is slaughtered. 34Then
the priest shall take some of the blood of the sin offering with his finger
and put it on the horns of the altar of burnt offering and pour out the
rest of the blood at the base of the altar. 35He shall remove all the fat,
just as the fat is removed from the lamb of the fellowship offering, and
the priest shall burn it on the altar on top of the offerings made to the
LORD by fire. In this way the priest will make atonement for him for the
sin he has committed, and he will be forgiven.
5:1“ ‘If a person sins because he does not speak up when he hears a
public charge to testify regarding something he has seen or learned
about, he will be held responsible.
2“ ‘Or if a person touches anything ceremonially unclean—whether
the carcasses of unclean wild animals or of unclean livestock or of
unclean creatures that move along the ground—even though he is
unaware of it, he has become unclean and is guilty.
3“ ‘Or if he touches human uncleanness—anything that would make
him unclean—even though he is unaware of it, when he learns of it he
will be guilty.
4“ ‘Or if a person thoughtlessly takes an oath to do anything, whether
good or evil—in any matter one might carelessly swear about—even
though he is unaware of it, in any case when he learns of it he will be
guilty.
5“ ‘When anyone is guilty in any of these ways, he must confess in
what way he has sinned 6and, as a penalty for the sin he has committed,
he must bring to the LORD a female lamb or goat from the flock as a sin
offering; and the priest shall make atonement for him for his sin.
7“ ‘If he cannot afford a lamb, he is to bring two doves or two young
pigeons to the LORD as a penalty for his sin—one for a sin offering and
the other for a burnt offering. 8He is to bring them to the priest, who
shall first offer the one for the sin offering. He is to wring its head from
its neck, not severing it completely, 9and is to sprinkle some of the
blood of the sin offering against the side of the altar; the rest of the
blood must be drained out at the base of the altar. It is a sin offering.

10 The priest shall then offer the other as a burnt offering in the prescribed way and make atonement for him for the sin he has committed, and he will be forgiven.

11 " 'If, however, he cannot afford two doves or two young pigeons, he is to bring as an offering for his sin a tenth of an ephah of fine flour for a sin offering. He must not put oil or incense on it, because it is a sin offering. 12 He is to bring it to the priest, who shall take a handful of it as a memorial portion and burn it on the altar on top of the offerings made to the LORD by fire. It is a sin offering. 13 In this way the priest will make atonement for him for any of these sins he has committed, and he will be forgiven. The rest of the offering will belong to the priest, as in the case of the grain offering.' "

4:1–35 The sin offering (*ḥaṭṭā'ṯ*) and the guilt offering (*'āšām*; KJV, "trespass offering") are very similar. Indeed, 7:7 says, "The same law applies to both the sin offering and the guilt offering." They are offered in a somewhat similar way, but different animals are specified; and the blood was handled somewhat differently.

The purpose of the sin offering was to give a specific for the penitent sinner who was convicted of sin and wished for full restoration of fellowship with God. It was both a confession of his sin and an assurance of pardon. There were representative sin offerings prescribed for leaders of the people as well as offerings for the individual. A type of sin offering was available for the poorest sinner in the land (5:7, 11).

The difference between the sin offering and the guilt offering was in the nature of the sin. The former was for what might be called general sins; the latter for sins that injured other people or detracted from the sacred worship. The guilt offering thus involved not only a sacrifice but also restitution plus a fine of 20 percent (6:5 [5:24 MT]). The sins for which the sin offering was prescribed are called "unintentional sins" (4:2), or those done "through ignorance" (KJV). The same expression is used in connection with the guilt offering (5:15). The sins concerned are not so strictly limited, however.

The expression "to sin unintentionally" (*ḥāṭā' ḇiše gāgāh*) in v.2 calls for some comment. The NIV reading may give the impression that there was no sacrifice for intentional sins. This would be a problem, for many of our sins are more or less intentional though not necessarily deliberate. The word *šāgaḡ* and its by-form *šāgāh* and their cognates basically seem to mean "to err," "go astray," "wander," "stagger." The nouns mean "error," "mistake." Outside the Pentateuchal legislation, the NIV always translates these words with such expressions (about twenty-five times). The idea of intent is not basic to the word and ought not to be imported.

The usual sins we fall into are covered by the sin offering and the guilt offering. For instance, lying, stealing, cheating, and false swearing are surely intentional; yet they are specifically covered by the guilt offering (6:2–3). Milgrom ("The Cultic *se gāgāh*") argues that the phrase refers to inadvertent sins—conscious acts but sinful because of negligence of the law. He is right that the sins are conscious, but lying about lost property (6:3) can hardly be due to negligence or ignorance of the law.

There is one place where these words seem at first to refer to unintentional sins (Num 15:22–31). There the "unintentional" sin is contrasted with sinning "defiantly" (NIV) or, as the Hebrew expresses it, "with a high hand" (*be yaḏ rāmāh*). Here the NIV has correctly caught the sense of the unpardonable sin—not one done intentionally, but one done "defiantly," i.e., in rebellion, sinning against light (cf. Matt 12:31–32).

The sense of the verb *šāḡāḡ* will be adequately caught if in all the verses concerned here in Leviticus 4–5, the phrase "sins unintentionally" is rendered by "goes astray in sin" or "does wrong" or the like. In Numbers 15:22–29 the translation "wrong" or "wrongly" or "in error" will better replace "unintentional" or "unintentionally." Indeed, the NIV translates *šᵉgaḡāh* by "wrong" in Numbers 15:25 (second instance) and in Leviticus 5:18. "Unintentional" seems better to fit *šāgag* and its cognates only in the manslaughter passages (Num 35:11–22; Josh 20:3–5), and even there "inadvertently" or "by mistake" would actually fit better.

In the case of the sin offering, there was special emphasis on substitutionary atonement. For the sin of a prominent person—e.g., an anointed priest (4:3)—or the whole congregation (v.13), an expensive offering was demanded, viz., "a young bull." Substitution was typified by laying hands on the offering just prior to its being slain (vv.4, 15; cf. v.24). Some of the young bull's blood was to be taken into the Holy Place and sprinkled seven times before the veil and also put on the horns of the altar of incense (vv.5–7a, 16–18a). The rest of the blood was poured out at the base of the brazen altar (vv.7b, 18b, 25), presumably on the ashes. In such cases the fat was to be burned on the brazen altar (vv.8–10, 19–20, 26) and the carcass burned outside the camp in the place of ashes (vv.11–12, 21; cf. Heb 13:11).

In the case of an offering for the sin of an ordinary individual (v.27), blood was applied to the four horns of the brazen altar and the rest of the blood poured out as in the previous cases (vv.30, 34). The fat also was to be burned on the altar (vv.31, 35), but the meat was to be eaten by the priests in the sacred precincts (7:22–27).

There were special sin offerings for the congregation ordained for particular feast days (Num 28–29). Particular solemnity attached to the Day of Atonement in the autumn, when the ritual centered around the goat for a sin offering and the scapegoat (see on Lev 16). All the offerings of the tabernacle included the idea of atonement by blood. The sin and guilt offerings symbolized this basic idea most emphatically.

5:1–13 Verses 1–4 give examples of sins that required a sin offering. Far from the modern idea, it was the duty of a witness to come forward and give his testimony in the interest of truth and justice (v.1). In Israel all the people were to be involved in seeing that justice was done. Not to witness was a sin.

The laws of cleanness (vv.2–3) were partly for public health (cf. chs. 11–15), but they were given sanction in the tabernacle. The priests were the public health officers. Uncleanness demanded ritual cleansing.

An unlawful oath should not be made and should not be kept (v.4). Jesus' teaching on oaths emphasized that a man's word is sacred. Jesus himself went on oath before the high priest (Matt 26:63–64). In certain circumstances an oath is not wrong, but an oath should not be necessary. A Christian's word should be as good as his bond.

One must not suppose that every Israelite who ever sinned intentionally was cut off from the congregation or that no sacrifice availed for him. David at least did not think so (Ps 51:19). The sin offering was available for any tender soul convicted of his wrong (5:5–13). Compassionate provision was made for the poor. Atonement is without money and without price. It is true, however, that there were sins recognized under the old covenant as unpardonable because they were defiant, just as in the NT (see Kaiser, *OT Theology*, pp. 117–18).

When a pigeon or chicken has its neck wrung (i.e., rapidly twisted), the neck is broken and the bird killed; but the head is not necessarily severed (v.8). A somewhat similar procedure is given in 1:17 in connection with the burnt offering, where it is said specifically that the priest should not divide (*bāḏal*—the same word as "sever" here) the bird. The NIV reads as if the sin-offering bird has its head still attached though its blood is to be drained out. The other bird, used as a burnt offering (v.10), is said specifically (1:15–17) to have the head wrung off and burned first, then the blood sprinkled and the carcass cleaned but not "divided" (*bāḏal*) and then burned. Although the details are not clear, it would seem more probable that the two birds were handled alike and that chapter 5 has not repeated the details of the cleaning and opening of the carcass. The priest would presumably have the bird of the sin offering to eat (cf. v.13). The other bird would be put on the altar as a burnt offering.

An "ephah" (v.11) seems to have been about three-fifths of a bushel (twenty-two liters), though there is some uncertainty. Jars marked as containing one bath (= one ephah) have been found; but they are in pieces, and the total capacity is not known. Apparently a tenth of an ephah would be about two quarts. This would be an offering that even the poor should be able to give. It was distinguished from the fellowship offering in that it should have no oil or frankincense and was not to be cooked. Presumably, in accordance with 2:11–13, it also was to have no yeast or honey but would have salt added. Though it was a bloodless offering, a portion of it was burned on the altar and thus associated with the sacrifices offered with blood (v.12). The balance of the flour was for the priest (v.13).

Notes

4:2 The root of שְׁגָגָה (*šᵉg̱āg̱āh*, "unintentionally") basically means "to err" or "to go astray." See above for a discussion and brief word study.

3 The phrase הַכֹּהֵן הַמָּשִׁיחַ (*hakkōhēn hammāšîaḥ*, "the anointed priest") doubtless means the high priest who represented the nation. The phrase is used of Aaron's successor in 6:22 (15 MT).

4, 15, 24 The ritual of laying hands on the head of the bull is interpreted in 16:21, where, on the Day of Atonement, Aaron laid his hands on the head of one of the goats of the sin offering and confessed over it the sins of Israel: "and put them on the goat's head." The same ritual is specified for the burnt offering (1:4) and the fellowship offering (3:2).

6, 17 Only the blood of the major sin offerings was brought into the Holy Place and sprinkled in front of the inner curtain. On the solemn Day of Atonement, the blood of the sin offering was carried within the veil into the Most Holy Place to be sprinkled before the atonement cover (KJV, "mercy seat"). "It is the blood that makes atonement for one's life" (Lev 17:11). "Without the shedding of blood there is no forgiveness" (Heb 9:22).

7 The blood of the sin offering was disposed of differently from that of the burnt and peace offerings, which was sprinkled against or on the altar (see comment on 1:5). This blood already had been used symbolically on the horns of the altar of incense in the Holy Place and sprinkled before the veil or, in some cases, put on the horns of the altar of burnt offering. Therefore, the remaining blood is counted as refuse and poured out at the base of the altar, presumably on the ashes.

8–9 The fat, kidneys, and the "covering of the liver" were to be burned on the altar just as in the case of the fellowship offering (q.v.). A representative part thus was burned on the great altar.

12 Sin offerings that had their blood sprinkled in the Holy Place were to have their carcasses burned outside the camp. The sin offerings of individuals had their blood applied to the horns of the brazen altar, and in this case the priests ate the meat (cf. 6:29–30). There is a practical point here. No one was himself to profit by the giving of a sin offering. If the priest gave it, he would not eat of it. If an ordinary Israelite gave it, the priest could eat it, but not the worshiper. The result was that a sin offering would be presented for conscience's sake alone. There is the further symbolism that the sin offering for the nation was cast out as refuse after the blood was sprinkled and the fat burned. Thus in Christ's case, too, the emphasis was on his blood shed for many. He, too, was cast out—crucified outside the gate.

13–15 In this instance the sin offering was for the whole congregation. The nation had sinned. The representatives of the nation were to confess that sin and transfer it symbolically to the substitute.

22 The leader who sinned was not considered as representing the people. The high priest who sinned involved the whole congregation in his representative capacity (v.3). We are reminded that our High Priest who now represents us in heaven is without sin (Heb 4:15). The leader's sacrifice was a male goat, and the blood was not taken into the Holy Place. In this respect the leader was more like the people than the priest.

28 It is not entirely clear why the ordinary worshiper brought a female goat or lamb. It may be to distinguish what might be called the private sin offering from those public sin offerings given at the set feasts and New Moons. These were always made with a male goat (Num 28:15–29:38). The ewe lamb might be a cheaper offering; at least it took a smaller cereal offering and drink offering to accompany it (Num 28:12–14).

5:1 The NIV is probably correct in translating קוֹל אָלָה (*qōl 'ālāh*) as "a public charge" to testify (KJV, "the voice of swearing"); i.e., when put on oath, a witness is bound to testify.

4 The Hebrew word יְבַטֵּא (*yᵉḇaṭṭē'*, "unaware") is unusual. It is interpreted in Num 30:6, 8 as "rash promise" (cf. "rash words" in Ps 106:33).

6 The word "penalty" is אָשָׁם (*'āšām*). It is translated by RSV and others as "guilt offering." The NIV's "penalty" makes the distinction clearer between the sin offering (חַטָּאת, *ḥaṭṭā'ṯ*) of 4:1–5:13 and the guilt offering (אָשָׁם, *'āšām*) of 5:14–6:7.

E. *Guilt Offering*

5:14–6:7

14 The LORD said to Moses: 15 "When a person commits a violation and sins unintentionally in regard to any of the LORD's holy things, he is to bring to the LORD as a penalty a ram from the flock, one without defect and of the proper value in silver, according to the sanctuary shekel. It is a guilt offering. 16 He must make restitution for what he has failed to do in regard to the holy things, add a fifth of the value to that and give it all to the priest, who will make atonement for him with the ram as a guilt offering, and he will be forgiven.

17 "If a person sins and does what is forbidden in any of the LORD's commands, even though he does not know it, he is guilty and will be held responsible. 18 He is to bring to the priest as a guilt offering a ram from the flock, one without defect and of the proper value. In this way the priest will make atonement for him for the wrong he has committed unintentionally, and he will be forgiven. 19 It is a guilt offering; he has been guilty of wrongdoing against the LORD."

6:1 The LORD said to Moses: 2 "If anyone sins and is unfaithful to the LORD by deceiving his neighbor about something entrusted to him or left in his care or stolen, or if he cheats him, 3 or if he finds lost property and lies about it, or if he swears falsely, or if he commits any such sin that people may do—4 when he thus sins and becomes guilty, he must return what he has stolen or taken by extortion, or what was entrusted to him, or the lost property he found, 5 or whatever it was he swore falsely about. He must make restitution in full, add a fifth of the value to it and give it all to the owner on the day he presents his guilt offering. 6 And as a penalty he must bring to the priest, that is, to the LORD, his guilt offering, a ram from the flock, one without defect and of the proper value. 7 In this way the priest will make atonement for him before the LORD, and he will be forgiven for any of these things he did that made him guilty."

5:14–6:7 As explained above, the guilt offering and the sin offering were very similar in both ritual and meaning. Even the names sometimes interchange. The guilt offering had more reference to sins that had done definite damage to the tabernacle service or to a neighbor. This offering required repair of the damage and a penalty of 20 percent in addition (5:16, 6:5). It is not entirely clear what sort of damage to the tabernacle is referred to. Probably it could include withholding tithes or firstfruits or other required offerings.

The guilt offering required without exception a male sheep plus restitution plus a 20 percent fine. Like the fines for stealing given in the civil law of Exodus 22, there was no remission of fines for the poor. Presumably, as in Exodus 22:3, the poor man had to get the money or be sold into bondage. There is a distinction between the sins mentioned as examples in Leviticus 6:1–5 and outright stealing. These sins are more on the edge of dishonesty. They concern things obtained by false representation, keeping a lost-and-found article, etc. These things also are sins but are not so easily established in court. If a man was guilty of such things and his conscience convicted him, however, he needed to confess and bring his guilt offering and the penalty, too. For cases of outright lawbreaking, such as those given in Exodus, the fines would vary according to the circumstance and as assessed by the judge. A repentant lawbreaker, however, would also presumably offer his guilt offering.

The expression "sins unintentionally" (v.14) is also used at 4:2, 13, 22, 27, and at Numbers 15:25, 27, 28. In the latter passage the contrast is between such sins of error, weakness, or ignorance and sins done "defiantly" (Num 15:30; lit., "with a high hand," i.e., deliberately). The deliberate sin, like the NT unpardonable sin, is against light and results in separation from the people of God. No sacrifice is specified for it. See the comments introducing chapter 4 for a brief study of the words concerned. The meaning "inadvertent" or "in error" was there suggested and is preferable to "unintentional" also in this section.

Guilt in the biblical sense is not just a feeling but a condition. There may be known transgressions that bring feelings of guilt, but there is also the condition of guilt before God, caused by sins known or unknown. Sometimes a hardened sinner has few feelings of guilt when he is the most guilty. Any sinner must bear the guilt of his transgression.

The guilt offering differed from the sin offering in that blood was never sprinkled in the Holy Place. Rather the blood was sprinkled on the altar of burnt offering in the manner of the burnt and peace offerings. The fat parts were to be burned on the altar and the meat to be eaten by the priests as in the case of the ordinary sin offering. This offering is one of those specified for the cleansing of a "leper" in Leviticus 14:12–28. It was a special sacrifice also for a Nazirite who had accidently become unclean during his period of consecration (Num 6:9–12).

In the great prophecy of Isaiah, the predicted Servant is said to suffer and die as a "guilt offering" (Isa 53:10; RSV and KJV, an "offering for sin"). In this significant verse the messianic hope of Israel is associated with the sacrificial system. The Lamb that God would supply for the sacrifice was the coming Messiah. It is worth adding that in the context of Isaiah 53, the glorious results of the suffering and death of the Servant are given in chapter 54, climaxing in the Davidic covenant (55:3): "I will make an everlasting covenant with you, my faithful love promised to David" (KJV, "the sure mercies of David"). In this central portion of Isaiah, the sacrificial system; the suffering, dying Servant to come; and the promised Son of David are in close association. These lines of prophecy and typology thus interpret one another. The

Christ was both to suffer and to die as a sin offering and yet reign as great David's greater Son.

Notes

15 The phrase בְּעֶרְכְּךָ (*bᵉʿerkᵉkā*, "proper value") has been studied by Speiser (pp. 124–28) in the light of Akkadian parallels. He holds that the pronoun ending *kā* ("by you") has become a fossilized part of the word and should not be translated. He says that the whole phrase is old legal terminology referring to a specially solemn payment that envisaged a standard animal of a set valuation, i.e., standard value. This use of the term of "equivalent value" is found also in connection with vows in Lev 27:2ff. and in Num 18:16. Speiser adds, incidentally, that such accurate use of old technical terms argues for an early date of this legislation in Leviticus (cf. the comments on 25:35–55).

16 The restitution required is not specified but could be calculated readily according to the standard values. If a man failed to fulfill a vow or brought less than his tithe, etc., the priest would calculate the damages and then add 20 percent. As remarked above, this restitution with a one-fifth penalty is what distinguishes the guilt offering from the sin offering.

The expression וְנִסְלַח (*wᵉnislaḥ*, "and he will be forgiven"), so common in this section of Leviticus, is a reminder that the believers in Moses' time had, like ourselves, the blessed experience of peace with God and reconciliation through the blood atonement of the Lamb of God yet to come, whose work was typified in the sacrifice.

19 Three times in this verse the root אָשָׁם (*'āšam*) is used: "It is a guilt offering" (*'āšām*); "he has been guilty of wrongdoing [אָשֹׁם אָשַׁם, *'āšōm 'āšam*] against the LORD." The last expression is a Hebrew infinitive plus a finite verb, which expresses emphasis: "He has really done wrong." Since the root can refer to the offering as well as to the offense, the NIV margin is equally possible: "he has made full expiation for his wrongdoing." Perhaps at the end of this paragraph explaining the guilt offering, the margin reading is preferable.

6:2 (5:21 MT) The Hebrew word for "be unfaithful"—מָעֲלָה מַעַל (*mā'ᵃlāh ma'al*)—is widely used and usually translated "break faith" or "act treacherously" in the RSV. The KJV usually renders it "transgress" or "commit a transgression." The expression is used of marital infidelity (Num 5:27) and of Achan in his sin at Jericho (Josh 7:1). The great majority of instances refer to a sin against God. These transgressions are sometimes general, as in the days of Rehoboam (2 Chron 12:2), and sometimes specific, as when Uzziah burned incense in the temple (2 Chron 26:16). Ezekiel uses the verb concerning the apostasy of a righteous man who must therefore die for his sin (Ezek 18:24). It appears to be a general word for sin and transgression. To "deal treacherously" or "break faith" is too weak. In the present verse the sin against God is specified as injuring one's neighbor especially in financial matters.

The word פִּקָּדוֹן (*piqqāḏôn*, "entrusted") is used elsewhere only in Gen 41:36, of the grain on deposit against the famine. The root, however, is common and means "to oversee." Genesis 41:35 makes the meaning clear. The phrase "left in his care" also is rare, being used only here. But again the root שׂוּם (*śûm*) is common and means "put" or "place." The phrase refers to something placed in someone's hand for safekeeping.

3 (5:22 MT) The OT law was not "finders keepers" but that lost property was to be returned to its owner (Exod 22:9; 23:4; Deut 22:1–3). The sin mentioned here is twofold; it includes the failure to restore the lost item plus the lie regarding it.

4 (5:23 MT) The words "become guilty"—אָשֵׁם (*'āšēm*)—are also governed by the "thus": "he thus sins and becomes guilty." He does not become guilty later after the sin is known. The guilt is before God when the sin is committed.

5 (5:24 MT) In any kind of sin involving damage, full restoration must be made. Forgiveness does not allow us just to forget the damage done but requires us in repentance and with

confession to make right as far as possible the wrong done. That forgiveness is free does not mean that it is free of obligation. And there is also a 20 percent penalty. Apparently the fine was given to the person wronged along with the full payment of damage done.

7 (5:26 MT) Confession, restitution, and the added penalty preceded the offering to God and the atonement and forgiveness. The order is the same in Matt 5:23–24.

II. Directions for the Priests in Their Service (6:8–7:38)

A. *Burnt Offering*

6:8–13

> 8 The LORD said to Moses: 9 "Give Aaron and his sons this command: 'These are the regulations for the burnt offering: The burnt offering is to remain on the altar hearth throughout the night, till morning, and the fire must be kept burning on the altar. 10 The priest shall then put on his linen clothes, with linen undergarments next to his body, and shall remove the ashes of the burnt offering that the fire has consumed on the altar and place them beside the altar. 11 Then he is to take off these clothes and put on others, and carry the ashes outside the camp to a place that is ceremonially clean. 12 The fire on the altar must be kept burning; it must not go out. Every morning the priest is to add firewood and arrange the burnt offering on the fire and burn the fat of the fellowship offerings on it. 13 The fire must be kept burning on the altar continuously; it must not go out.

It should be remembered that the Bible does not tell us all the details of the methods of sacrificing. There was no need to tell an ancient priest how to skin a sheep. Enough was given to be self-explanatory to the Israelites and to give us the general outline and meaning of the ritual. There are a few points where our curiosity need not be satisfied. The section on the prescribed ritual of the five major offerings gives mainly instructions for the officiating priests. Leviticus was a directory for worship for the priests from which they in turn were to instruct the people.

8–13 There is an emphasis here on the perpetual fire on the brazen altar (vv.9, 13). Actually, the sacrifices required not a little work. Wood must be secured and cut (v.12). A good bit of wood was needed to get the roaring fire that would burn the sacrifices completely and carry the odor skyward so as not to be offensive. The care of the ashes is detailed in vv.10–11. Leviticus 1:16 says that the place of the ashes was east of the altar, viz., toward the front of the tabernacle court (cf. Exod 27:13–15; Num 3:38). The sacrifices were killed on the north side, viz., to the right as the worshiper would face the tabernacle. It was helpful that the prevailing winds came from the west.

Notes

---

10 (3 MT) The reason for the use of linen is given in Ezek 44:18. No garment "that makes them perspire" was to be worn by the priest while officiating. The alternative materials for clothing would be wool or leather. Linen made a fine cloth, easily washed and comfortable. Flax was grown in Palestine (Josh 2:6), but this linen was doubtless some of the precious material the Israelite women had brought with them from Egypt. The linen garments were to be kept clean. For disposing ashes outside the camp, ordinary clothes were to be worn.

B. *Grain Offering*

6:14–23

14" 'These are the regulations for the grain offering: Aaron's sons are
to bring it before the LORD, in front of the altar. 15The priest is to take a
handful of fine flour and oil, together with all the incense on the grain
offering, and burn the memorial portion on the altar as an aroma
pleasing to the LORD. 16Aaron and his sons shall eat the rest of it, but it is
to be eaten without yeast in a holy place; they are to eat it in the
courtyard of the Tent of Meeting. 17It must not be baked with yeast; I
have given it as their share of the offerings made to me by fire. Like the
sin offering and the guilt offering, it is most holy. 18Any male descendant of Aaron may eat it. It is his regular share of the offerings made to
the LORD by fire for the generations to come. Whatever touches it will
become holy.' "

19The LORD also said to Moses, 20"This is the offering Aaron and his
sons are to bring to the LORD on the day he is anointed: a tenth of an
ephah of fine flour as a regular grain offering, half of it in the morning
and half in the evening. 21Prepare it with oil on a griddle; bring it well-
mixed and present the grain offering broken in pieces as an aroma
pleasing to the LORD. 22The son who is to succeed him as anointed priest
shall prepare it. It is the LORD's regular share and is to be burned
completely. 23Every grain offering of a priest shall be burned completely; it must not be eaten."

14–23 Much of this section repeats material already given in chapter 2 (q.v.). The additional directions concern the grain offering to be given by the priests themselves (vv.19–23). This offering differs from the usual in that it was to be entirely burnt (v.23). It was given every morning and was to accompany the burnt offering (Num 28:5) and the fellowship offerings (Lev 7:12). It required the thanksgiving of the priests and, through them, all Israel.

Notes

---

18 (11 MT) The statement that the grain offering and the sin offering (v.27) make clean anything they touch seems to contradict 7:19–20, which implies that clean meat that touches an unclean thing is itself made unclean (cf. Hag 2:12–13). The statement "Whatever touches them will become holy" (cf. v.27) is a problem. A possible alternative more in line with the principles of 7:19–20 would be: "Whoever touches it must be holy." Verse 27 would read similarly: "Whoever touches any of the flesh must be holy" (cf. NIV mg.). Notice that v.27 says that any garment spattered by the blood must be washed in a holy place; the holy blood must not be defiled.

21 (14 MT) The words מֻרְבֶּכֶת (*murbeḵeṯ,* "well-mixed") and תֻּפִינֵי (*tup̱înê,* "broken") are unusual and difficult in detail, but the general meaning is clear. The LXX translates, "kneaded and in rolls, an offering of fragments." The word "well-mixed" or "kneaded" is fairly clear. The word "broken" (NIV), "baken" (KJV), or "in rolls" (LXX) occurs only here. The noun may come from the root אָפָה (*'āp̱āh,* "bake") or with slight changes in the vowels from the root תֹּף (*tōp̱*, "drum") and refer to the shape of the cakes. Fortunately, it makes little difference. The interpretation of the NIV is as satisfactory as anything until new information is forthcoming.

C. *Sin Offering*

6:24–30

[24]The LORD said to Moses, [25]"Say to Aaron and his sons: 'These are the regulations for the sin offering: The sin offering is to be slaughtered before the LORD in the place the burnt offering is slaughtered; it is most holy. [26]The priest who offers it shall eat it; it is to be eaten in a holy place, in the courtyard of the Tent of Meeting. [27]Whatever touches any of the flesh will become holy, and if any of the blood is spattered on a garment, you must wash it in a holy place. [28]The clay pot the meat is cooked in must be broken; but if it is cooked in a bronze pot, the pot is to be scoured and rinsed with water. [29]Any male in a priest's family may eat it; it is most holy. [30]But any sin offering whose blood is brought into the Tent of Meeting to make atonement in the Holy Place must not be eaten; it must be burned.

24–30 The description of this section adds little to the previous treatment at 4:1–5:13 except to emphasize the holiness of the offering. Offerings whose blood was not taken into the tabernacle could be eaten by the officiating priest, but only by him and the males of his family (vv.26, 29). It was to be eaten in the sacred precincts, and the vessels it was cooked in were to be broken or scoured (v.28). It was apparently the most solemn sacrifice of Israel and was thus an especially fitting type of Christ's atoning death (Heb 13:12).

Notes

---

27 (20 MT) See remarks on v.18.

28 (21 MT) "Broken . . . scoured" was a frequent direction of the law. Vessels that were unclean by vermin were similarly treated (11:32–33). Metal vessels, of course, would be thoroughly cleansed. The coarse, earthen pottery would not clean easily and was to be broken if it were rendered especially holy or defiled. Here, apparently, the remnants left by cooking were not to touch ordinary food; fortunately, pottery was cheap. This is why in excavation today in Palestine hundreds of thousands of fragments of pottery may be uncovered in an ordinary season of excavation.

D. *Guilt Offering*

7:1–10

[1]" 'These are the regulations for the guilt offering, which is most holy: [2]The guilt offering is to be slaughtered in the place where the burnt offering is slaughtered, and its blood is to be sprinkled against the altar on all sides. [3]All its fat shall be offered: the fat tail and the fat that covers the inner parts, [4]both kidneys with the fat around them near the loins, and the covering of the liver, which is to be removed with the kidneys.

[5]The priest shall burn them on the altar as an offering made to the LORD
by fire. It is a guilt offering. [6]Any male in a priest's family may eat it, but it
must be eaten in a holy place; it is most holy.
[7]" 'The same law applies to both the sin offering and the guilt offering:
They belong to the priest who makes atonement with them. [8]The priest
who offers a burnt offering for anyone may keep its hide for himself.
[9]Every grain offering baked in an oven or cooked in a pan or on a
griddle belongs to the priest who offers it, [10]and every grain offering,
whether mixed with oil or dry, belongs equally to all the sons of Aaron.

1–10 As v.7 says, the guilt offering was very similar to the sin offering described above, especially as regards ritual. The main difference was that the blood of the guilt offering was treated like that of the burnt and peace offerings rather than like the sin offering.

Notes

---

4 See the note on 3:4.

8 In sort of a footnote, the share of the officiating priest is stated also for the burnt offering (the skin) and for the cereal offerings (vv.8–10).

9 A difference is made between the cooked and uncooked grain offerings. The former belonged to the officiating priest. The latter, because it was in flour that could be preserved, was distributed among the priests.

E. *Fellowship Offering*

7:11–38

[11]" 'These are the regulations for the fellowship offering a person may
present to the LORD:
[12]" 'If he offers it as an expression of thankfulness, then along with
this sacrifice of thanksgiving he is to offer cakes of bread made without
yeast and mixed with oil, wafers made without yeast and spread with oil,
and cakes of fine flour well-kneaded and mixed with oil. [13]Along with his
fellowship offering of thanksgiving he is to present an offering with
cakes of bread made with yeast. [14]He is to bring one of each kind as an
offering, a contribution to the LORD; it belongs to the priest who
sprinkles the blood of the fellowship offerings. [15]The meat of his
fellowship offering of thanksgiving must be eaten on the day it is
offered; he must leave none of it till morning.
[16]" 'If, however, his offering is the result of a vow or is a freewill
offering, the sacrifice shall be eaten on the day he offers it, but anything
left over may be eaten on the next day. [17]Any meat of the sacrifice left
over till the third day must be burned up. [18]If any meat of the fellowship
offering is eaten on the third day, it will not be accepted. It will not be
credited to the one who offered it, for it is impure; the person who eats
any of it will be held responsible.
[19]" 'Meat that touches anything ceremonially unclean must not be
eaten; it must be burned up. As for other meat, anyone ceremonially
clean may eat it. [20]But if anyone who is unclean eats any meat of the
fellowship offering belonging to the LORD, that person must be cut off
from his people. [21]If anyone touches something unclean—whether
human uncleanness or an unclean animal or any unclean, detestable

thing—and then eats any of the meat of the fellowship offering
belonging to the LORD, that person must be cut off from his people.' "
22 The LORD said to Moses, 23 "Say to the Israelites: 'Do not eat any of
the fat of cattle, sheep or goats. 24 The fat of an animal found dead or
torn by wild animals may be used for any other purpose, but you must
not eat it. 25 Anyone who eats the fat of an animal from which an offering
by fire may be made to the LORD must be cut off from his people. 26 And
wherever you live, you must not eat the blood of any bird or animal. 27 If
anyone eats blood, that person must be cut off from his people.' "
28 The LORD said to Moses, 29 "Say to the Israelites: 'Anyone who brings
a fellowship offering to the LORD is to bring part of it as his sacrifice to
the LORD. 30 With his own hands he is to bring the offering made to the
LORD by fire; he is to bring the fat, together with the breast, and wave the
breast before the LORD as a wave offering. 31 The priest shall burn the fat
on the altar, but the breast belongs to Aaron and his sons. 32 You are to
give the right thigh of your fellowship offerings to the priest as a
contribution. 33 The son of Aaron who offers the blood and the fat of the
fellowship offering shall have the right thigh as his share. 34 From the
fellowship offerings of the Israelites, I have taken the breast that is
waved and the thigh that is presented and have given them to Aaron the
priest and his sons as their regular share from the Israelites.' "
35 This is the portion of the offerings made to the LORD by fire that were
allotted to Aaron and his sons on the day they were presented to serve
the LORD as priests. 36 On the day they were anointed, the LORD
commanded that the Israelites give this to them as their regular share
for the generations to come.
37 These, then, are the regulations for the burnt offering, the grain
offering, the sin offering, the guilt offering, the ordination offering and
the fellowship offering, 38 which the LORD gave Moses on Mount Sinai on
the day he commanded the Israelites to bring their offerings to the LORD,
in the Desert of Sinai.

Several other instructions were given for this most common sacrifice. There were two varieties of the fellowship offerings. The first expressed thanksgiving for God's general benefits (vv.12–15). The second served as a fulfillment of a vow or as a freewill offering (vv.16–18). Slight differences were made in the eating of the remainder from these varieties of offerings. Since, of the sacrifices of the tabernacle, only fellowship offerings might be eaten by the laymen, special warnings are given here with regard to cleanness on the part of those who should eat them (vv.19–21). The prohibition of fat and blood is repeated (vv.22–27; cf. 3:17), and details are given as to the portion of the animals that were given to the priests for food (vv.28–36). The section concludes with a summarizing statement (vv.37–38). On these verses see the remarks on 3:1–17.

11–18 The standard cereal offering is specified to accompany the burnt offering and the meat of the fellowship offering. The description of the cereal offering repeats the term of 2:4 and 6:14. A "memorial portion" (or "offering of the invocation"; see note on 2:2) was burned on the altar.

A second kind of breadstuff is specified, an offering of yeast bread (v.13). This was not burned on the altar. A portion was given the priest, who would present it before the Lord as an "offering" and then eat it. The rest of the bread, like the rest of the meat, was for the worshiper.

As Allis (in loc.) observes, all of the thanksgiving offering was to be eaten on the same day to encourage sharing it with the poor (v.15). The other types of peace offering could be eaten on the second day, but by the third day it was prohibited as unsafe. The same law is given in 19:5–8 and, briefly, in 22:30.

19–21 As mentioned above, only the fellowship offerings were eaten by laymen. Rules for guarding their sacredness were therefore needed (v.19). They must be kept clean. An unclean person must absolutely not eat of the sacred meal (v.20). This point may illustrate the NT warning for the Lord's Supper: "A man ought to examine himself" (1 Cor 11:28).

The phrase "cut off from his people" (vv.20–21) is used over twenty-five times, usually with regard to some ceremonial violation. It is clearly associated with capital crimes only three times (17:14; 18:29; Exod 31:14). Similar phraseology is used repeatedly of cutting off enemies. Lexicons suggest that the phrase means that one who violates these laws of cleanness will pay the extreme penalty. It seems difficult to prove this. It is safer to say that the phrase may have been used variously and often meant only some kind of excommunication from the people of the Lord.

22–27 The carcass of an unclean animal was not to be touched; but a sheep or goat that died a natural death or was killed by a wild beast could be used—only not for food. Its hide and wool, presumably, were usable. Its fat also was usable (v.24), but for what? Presumably the people had not yet learned to make soap from fats. Did they use fat for grease for carts, etc.? Perhaps its chief use would have been for fuel.

28–34 The priest's portion of every fellowship offering was the right breast and the right thigh (v.34). The breast was "waved" (v.30) before the Lord, i.e., presented and then taken by the priest. Similarly, the thigh, being heavier, was lifted up before the Lord (v.32) as a *t*ᵉ*rûmāh* ("contribution"; KJV, "heave offering") and then taken by the priest and his family (Lev 10:14). The translation "heave offering" comes from the root *rûm* ("to lift up"). Whether or not the etymology is decisive, at least the offering was presented before the Lord as a contribution regardless of any gesture that may have been used.

For "the right thigh" the KJV has "the right shoulder." It is difficult to know whether the hind or forequarter is meant. The KJV reading follows the Latin Vulgate and the LXX; but the word *šûq* when applied to humans always means the leg, not the arm. If the Hebrews observed their comparative anatomy, the hind quarter would be intended. Also, the hind quarter is much better meat than the fore quarter, and it is probable that the choicer portion was given to the priests; the rest was for the worshipers.

35–38 These offerings were allocated to the priests from "the day they were presented to serve" (v.35) and onward. There need be no problem between the statement "on Mount Sinai" (v.38) and 1:1, which says God spoke to Moses from "the Tent of Meeting." The preposition *b* is a general one and can mean "in," "on," "at," etc. Or the phrase "Mount Sinai" may have included more than the mountaintop itself. And some of these regulations may indeed have been given to Moses during his two periods on the mount while others may have been added during the year of establishing the worship of Israel.

III. The Beginning of the Tabernacle Worship (8:1–10:20)

Chapter 8 shows in a very interesting way the relationship of Leviticus to Exodus. They are parts of a unified whole. The consecration of the priests here is the fulfillment of the commands in Exodus 29 (cf. vv.1–37).

The last part of Exodus consists largely of the directions for setting up Israel's worship (Exod 25–28, 30) followed by the record that the worship was set up in just that way (Exod 37–39). There is much repetition, with a difference only in tenses. For instance, the instructions for building the ark in Exodus 25:10–21 are repeated almost verbatim in the past tense in Exodus 37:1–9.

In the same way, the directions for the consecration of the priests in Exodus 29:4–20, 22–26, and 31 are very closely paralleled by the record of the consecration in Leviticus 8:6–9, 12–19, and 31. It is rather obvious that Leviticus is a continuation of Exodus. Exodus ends with the setting up of the tabernacle. Leviticus proceeds with the directions for the offerings. Then Leviticus tells how the priests began their ministry using the terms of the directions already given in Exodus.

Moses first acted as priest to consecrate the tabernacle, the altar, and Aaron and his sons. It is hard to overemphasize the work of Moses, the man of God. As the greatest of the OT prophets, he was a type of Christ to come (Deut 18:15–19; John 7:40). As the first priest who instituted Israel's worship, Moses is a type of Christ the Great High Priest. Moses, the great lawgiver, received God's revelations face to face and was faithful in all God's house (Num 12:7–8). Yet even he was but a type and a shadow, far inferior to Christ the High Priest and Son over the house (Heb 3:1–6).

A. *Consecration of Aaron and His Sons*

8:1–36 (cf. Exod 29:1–37)

1 The LORD said to Moses, 2 "Bring Aaron and his sons, their garments,
the anointing oil, the bull for the sin offering, the two rams and the
basket containing bread made without yeast, 3 and gather the entire
assembly at the entrance to the Tent of Meeting." 4 Moses did as the
LORD commanded him, and the assembly gathered at the entrance to the
Tent of Meeting.

5 Moses said to the assembly, "This is what the LORD has commanded
to be done." 6 Then Moses brought Aaron and his sons forward and
washed them with water. 7 He put the tunic on Aaron, tied the sash
around him, clothed him with the robe and put the ephod on him. He
also tied the ephod to him by its skillfully woven waistband; so it was
fastened on him. 8 He placed the breastpiece on him and put the Urim
and Thummim in the breastpiece. 9 Then he placed the turban on
Aaron's head and set the gold plate, the sacred diadem, on the front of
it, as the LORD commanded Moses.

10 Then Moses took the anointing oil and anointed the tabernacle and
everything in it, and so consecrated them. 11 He sprinkled some of the oil
on the altar seven times, anointing the altar and all its utensils and the
basin with its stand, to consecrate them. 12 He poured some of the
anointing oil on Aaron's head and anointed him to consecrate him.
13 Then he brought Aaron's sons forward, put tunics on them, tied
sashes around them and put headbands on them, as the LORD commanded Moses.

14 He then presented the bull for the sin offering, and Aaron and his
sons laid their hands on its head. 15 Moses slaughtered the bull and took
some of the blood, and with his finger he put it on all the horns of the

altar to purify the altar. He poured out the rest of the blood at the base of
the altar. So he consecrated it to make atonement for it. [16]Moses also
took all the fat around the inner parts, the covering of the liver, and both
kidneys and their fat, and burned it on the altar. [17]But the bull with its
hide and its flesh and its offal he burned up outside the camp, as the
LORD commanded Moses.
[18]He then presented the ram for the burnt offering, and Aaron and his
sons laid their hands on its head. [19]Then Moses slaughtered the ram
and sprinkled the blood against the altar on all sides. [20]He cut the ram
into pieces and burned the head, the pieces and the fat. [21]He washed
the inner parts and the legs with water and burned the whole ram on the
altar as a burnt offering, a pleasing aroma, an offering made to the LORD
by fire, as the LORD commanded Moses.
[22]He then presented the other ram, the ram for the ordination, and
Aaron and his sons laid their hands on its head. [23]Moses slaughtered
the ram and took some of its blood and put it on the lobe of Aaron's
right ear, on the thumb of his right hand and on the big toe of his right
foot. [24]Moses also brought Aaron's sons forward and put some of the
blood on the lobes of their right ears, on the thumbs of their right hands
and on the big toes of their right feet. Then he sprinkled blood against
the altar on all sides. [25]He took the fat, the fat tail, all the fat around the
inner parts, the covering of the liver, both kidneys and their fat and the
right thigh. [26]Then from the basket of bread made without yeast, which
was before the LORD, he took a cake of bread, and one made with oil,
and a wafer; he put these on the fat portions and on the right thigh. [27]He
put all these in the hands of Aaron and his sons and waved them before
the LORD as a wave offering. [28]Then Moses took them from their hands
and burned them on the altar on top of the burnt offering as an
ordination offering, a pleasing aroma, an offering made to the LORD by
fire. [29]He also took the breast—Moses' share of the ordination ram—
and waved it before the LORD as a wave offering, as the LORD
commanded Moses.
[30]Then Moses took some of the anointing oil and some of the blood
from the altar and sprinkled them on Aaron and his garments and on his
sons and their garments. So he consecrated Aaron and his garments
and his sons and their garments.
[31]Moses then said to Aaron and his sons, "Cook the meat at the
entrance to the Tent of Meeting and eat it there with the bread from the
basket of ordination offerings, as I commanded, saying, 'Aaron and his
sons are to eat it.' [32]Then burn up the rest of the meat and the bread.
[33]Do not leave the entrance to the Tent of Meeting for seven days, until
the days of your ordination are completed, for your ordination will last
seven days. [34]What has been done today was commanded by the LORD
to make atonement for you. [35]You must stay at the entrance to the Tent
of Meeting day and night for seven days and do what the LORD requires,
so you will not die; for that is what I have been commanded." [36]So
Aaron and his sons did everything the LORD commanded through Moses.

1–13 The service of consecration was carried on according to the Lord's command and was done in the presence of the congregation (vv.2–3). The people had given to the building of the tabernacle, and many had worked on it. Now it and its ministers were ready for the consecration of the priests and the dedication of the house of God.

The steps of the consecration of Aaron and his sons were solemn and meaningful. Aaron first was washed and clothed anew with the holy garments (vv.6–9). He wore the ephod, the breastplate with its twelve-jeweled symbols of the tribes, the Urim and Thummim, and the priest's turban with the golden plate and its inscription "HOLY TO THE LORD" (Exod 28:36; 39:30). Then he, his sons, the altar, and its accouterments were anointed with oil (vv.10–13, 30). This was a special perfumed oil described in Exodus 30:23–25. Psalm 133 says the oil ran down to the skirts of Aaron's garments.

It is generally agreed that the anointing oil typifies the Holy Spirit. When kings were anointed, the Holy Spirit came on them (1 Sam 10:1–6; 16:13). The word "messiah" comes from the Hebrew word for "anoint," and the work of Christ began with such an anointing of the Holy Spirit. In the NT water also typifies the Holy Spirit (Mark 1:8–12). There is no statement in the OT as to why oil typified the Holy Spirit. Oil was widely used in lamps. As the lamp burned, the oil seemed to vanish into the air. Such a connection of oil and air possibly may have made the typology natural in the Hebrew culture. The Hebrew word *rûaḥ* means either "spirit" or "wind, air, breath." The seven-branched lampstand, perpetually fed with oil, is called a symbol of the Spirit in the OT (Zech 4:2–6).

14–30 After being anointed, Aaron and his sons offered first for themselves (Heb 7:27) and then to consecrate the altar (vv.14–17). Then came a burnt offering of worship and consecration (vv.18–21). Next they offered a ram of "ordination" (vv.22–29). This is an unusual name (*millu'îm*), derived from the Piel of the word *mālē'* ("to fill"), used idiomatically in the sense of "filling the hand" of a priest, i.e., installing him in his office or ordaining him (cf. v.33).

The ram was sacrificed as a fellowship offering with special application of the blood to the priests' right ears, right thumbs, and right great toes (vv.23–24). This doubtless symbolized their new total obedience and service, a lesson for Christians who claim the priesthood of all believers.

31–36 The ram of ordination was then eaten at the door of the tabernacle in a new communion with God (vv.31–32). So for seven days Aaron and his sons stayed at the tabernacle in contrition, worship, consecration, and fellowship (vv.33–35). Curiously, we know nothing of the prayers that were offered during that time. The whole OT ritual is given without any prescribed prayers except the Aaronic benediction of Numbers 6:24–26. It would seem that in those days also God wished his people to pray spontaneously from the heart.

Notes

6 No one can say that the OT did not emphasize personal cleanliness. Hebrews speaks of "various ceremonial washings" (Heb 9:10), some of which had the positive effect of washing away dirt that breeds disease (e.g., Lev 14:8–9); the other washings typified cleansing from the defilement of sin.

7 The details of the ephod and its use escape us. The word is used some forty-five times, and half of these are in Exod 28, 39, where Aaron's garments are described. It is hardly possible to say more than that it was a rich garment made of linen with inwrought gold, blue, purple, and scarlet. It had two shoulder pieces set with onyx stones engraved with the names of the tribes as ancient stamp seals were usually engraved. The ephod was bound around the waist with a colored sash. Fixed to the ephod was the breastpiece (KJV, breastplate). It is not clear whether the ephod was coat length or reached to the ankles. The priest also wore a coat and pants of fine linen. It is possible that the coat or tunic was long and the ephod was waist length or hip length and was worn over the tunic.

The ephod is mentioned elsewhere in somewhat different connections. Other priests wore the ephod. Samuel wore one as a child (1 Sam 2:18). Eighty-five priests killed by Doeg wore linen ephods (1 Sam 22:18). David's priest Abiathar came to him with an ephod, but in this case he may have come as high priest since all his family was killed (1 Sam 23:6). Michal reproached David after his dance for having uncovered himself (2 Sam 6:14). This still does not tell us much, for the uncovering may have consisted in laying aside his royal robes. The ephod David wore could still have been a long or shorter garment.

Goliath's sword was wrapped in a cloth behind the ephod (1 Sam 21:9). This could mean that some piece of furniture or image was called an ephod, but it may mean only that there was an ephod coat hanging on the wall with Goliath's sword behind it.

Gideon made an ephod that became a snare to Israel (Judg 8:27). Since it was made from the gold ornaments, it was apparently a round object and either was or was used as an idol. Micah the Ephraimite also made an ephod for idolatrous worship, but it is not clear whether the ephod was itself an idol or only a robe for an officiating priest (Judg 18:14–20). In Hosea 3:4 there is a prophecy that Israel would be deprived of king, prince, sacrifice, pillar, ephod, and teraphim. Again, it is not clear whether the ephod is an idolatrous image or only clothing for the officiating priest.

Nonbiblical literature mentions the ephod. Albright (*Yahweh*, pp. 200–203), in summarizing the material, says that the term is obscure. He cites early Assyrian for the meaning "plaid robe." From Ugaritic he suggests that the robe was wound around like the sari used in India. Albright suggests that it was first an idol, then the robe of the idol, then the robe of the officiating priest. This may have been the situation in the surrounding pagan cultures, and Gideon apparently compromised with such practices. In Israel's official worship, the ephod was merely the liturgical garment of the priest, and a special ephod was worn by the high priest.

The priests' ephod did not represent deity as Albright thinks. Rather it represented the people before the deity. The engraved onyx stones on the shoulders of the ephod carried the names of the tribes, and the breastpiece laced to the ephod did the same. It is unclear how the ephod was used in prediction in 1 Sam 23:9 and 30:7–8. Perhaps the officiating priest determined the will of God by the Urim and Thummim somehow associated with the ephod.

8 The breastpiece, mentioned only here and in Exodus, was part of the vestments of the high priest. Since it was made of gold with twelve semiprecious stones each engraved with the insignia of a tribe of Israel, it would have been quite costly. It is not unlikely that it was taken by enemy raiders and not always replaced. Symbolically the breastpiece reminded the high priest that in his ministry he represented the twelve tribes of Israel before God. Typically it pictures Christ who on our behalf has entered into the heavenly sanctuary and appears in the presence of God (Heb 9:24).

The "Urim and Thummim" are mentioned in Exod 28:30, but no details are given. It does not say they were stones or that they were engraved. They were somehow kept in the breastpiece and were used for determining the will of God. The few instances of their use do not help much. They were used by Saul according to the LXX of 1 Sam 14:41, but at last they failed Saul (1 Sam 28:6). They are mentioned in Ezra 2:63 (Neh 7:65) as something to be hoped for. If the use of the ephod by David involved the use of Urim and Thummim, then it seems that they gave basically a yes or no answer to some questions. They could not have been just dice, for sometimes they did not give any answer at all (1 Sam 28:6).

The meanings of the terms are not clear. Urim is said by some to mean "lights" and Thummim "perfections." This is possible but not proved. J.A. Motyer ("Urim and Thummim," NBD, p. 1306) suggests "cursings" and "perfections" ("completeness" or "blessings"?), which is more logical. He derives the word "Urim," not as usual from אוֹר (*'ôr*, "light"), but from אָרַר (*'ārar*, "to curse"). Interestingly "Urim" starts with the first letter and "Thummim" with the last letter of the Hebrew alphabet. De Vaux (AIs, pp. 352–53) argues that the stones were like our "heads and tails" in which neither stone had an invariable meaning. Actually the details are unknown. They were objects in the ephod used in determining the Lord's will, probably a kind of sacred lot, and their value derived from the providential behavior of the lots when God's priest used them (Prov 16:33).

9 The Hebrew root צָנַף (*ṣānap̱*) implies a winding, and therefore modern versions prefer "turban" (KJV, "mitre," which may have been influenced by the English episcopal headdress). It is also called a holy crown (NIV, "sacred diadem"), which is all right if it be remembered that ancient crowns did not all resemble recent ones. On the turban was the "golden plate" engraved with the words "HOLY TO THE LORD" (Exod 39:30). This plate was fastened to the turban by a blue lace. De Vaux (AIs, p. 465) points out that the word translated "diadem" is from the same root as "Nazirite" and suggests that it should be translated "sign of consecration."

10 The same oil that consecrated Aaron consecrated also the tabernacle and its furnishings. There, too, the Spirit of God was to reign. The formula for this sacred oil is given in Exod 30:23–25. It was not to be used for secular purposes.

15 Since the bull was burned outside the camp, its blood was put on the horns of the altar of incense, as was usual for certain types of sin offering (4:7; cf. 6:30). This was the more solemn type of sin offering, required for atonement for a priest or for the sins of the whole congregation (4:3, 13). In this case the comment is made that this is "to purify" the altar. The verb is חִטֵּא (*ḥiṭṭē'*), which means "to de-sin" or "cleanse from sin." Some commentators argue that the ritual of the Day of Atonement (ch. 16) is basically to cleanse the tabernacle (see Wenham, in loc.), but see the comments on ch. 16. There is a sense in which the tabernacle and its furnishings, made by a sinful people, needed to be cleansed from sin; but the moral concern of the sacrifices was to make atonement for the people themselves.

18 Every feast day of Israel's calendar included a burnt offering (see Num 28–29). Every day began and ended with a burnt offering. The Sabbath had double the usual. If the meaning of the burnt offering was basically atonement—or even if it was worship probably including atonement as argued at ch. 1—it was very suitable that at the start of the tabernacle worship the burnt offering would follow the sin offering.

22 The ram for the ordination was discussed above. It was a type of fellowship offering. The usual fellowship offering was given by a layman. The priest received the breast and right thigh after they were presented to the Lord, and the fat, etc., was burned on the altar; the balance was eaten by the worshiper. In this case the priests ate the balance of the meat (v.31), Moses received the breast (v.29), and the right thigh was burned (v.26).

Thus the major offerings were represented at the beginning of the tabernacle worship. The burnt offering (v.18) involved a grain offering (Num 28:4–5); and the sin offering (v.14) was considered as including the guilt offering, which was of a similar nature except that it involved restitution, which was not applicable in this case.

23 The right ear, right thumb, and right big toe are mentioned again in 14:14, 17, 25, 28 in connection with the cleansing of a person recovered from an infectious skin disease. As mentioned above, these prominent parts symbolize the cleansing or consecration of the whole person's being.

29 Usually the wave breast was the priests' portion from the worshiper. In this case Moses acted as the receiving priest to consecrate Aaron and his sons.

35 Moses was acting under instruction: "what I have been commanded." He could no more initiate the worship than could Aaron. God calls his servants and prescribes their work and message.

B. *Divine Acceptance of the First Worship*

9:1–24

1 On the eighth day Moses summoned Aaron and his sons and the
elders of Israel. 2 He said to Aaron, "Take a bull calf for your sin offering
and a ram for your burnt offering, both without defect, and present them

before the LORD. 3 Then say to the Israelites: 'Take a male goat for a sin
offering, a calf and a lamb—both a year old and without defect—for a
burnt offering, 4 and an cow and a ram for a fellowship offering to
sacrifice before the LORD, together with a grain offering mixed with oil.
For today the LORD will appear to you.' "

5 They took the things Moses commanded to the front of the Tent of
Meeting, and the entire assembly came near and stood before the LORD.
6 Then Moses said, "This is what the LORD has commanded you to do, so
that the glory of the LORD may appear to you."

7 Moses said to Aaron, "Come to the altar and sacrifice your sin
offering and your burnt offering and make atonement for yourself and
the people; sacrifice the offering that is for the people and make
atonement for them, as the LORD has commanded."

8 So Aaron came to the altar and slaughtered the calf as a sin offering
for himself. 9 His sons brought the blood to him, and he dipped his finger
into the blood and put it on the horns of the altar; the rest of the blood
he poured out at the base of the altar. 10 On the altar he burned the fat,
the kidneys and the covering of the liver from the sin offering, as the
LORD commanded Moses; 11 the flesh and the hide he burned up outside
the camp.

12 Then he slaughtered the burnt offering. His sons handed him the
blood, and he sprinkled it against the altar on all sides. 13 They handed
him the burnt offering piece by piece, including the head, and he
burned them on the altar. 14 He washed the inner parts and the legs and
burned them on top of the burnt offering on the altar.

15 Aaron then brought the offering that was for the people. He took the
goat for the people's sin offering and slaughtered it and offered it for a
sin offering as he did with the first one.

16 He brought the burnt offering and offered it in the prescribed way.
17 He also brought the grain offering, took a handful of it and burned it
on the altar in addition to the morning's burnt offering.

18 He slaughtered the cow and the ram as the fellowship offering for
the people. His sons handed him the blood, and he sprinkled it against
the altar on all sides. 19 But the fat portions of the cow and the ram—the
fat tail, the layer of fat, the kidneys and the covering of the liver—
20 these they laid on the breasts, and then Aaron burned the fat on the
altar. 21 Aaron waved the breasts and the right thigh before the LORD as a
wave offering, as Moses commanded.

22 Then Aaron lifted his hands toward the people and blessed them.
And having sacrificed the sin offering, the burnt offering and the
fellowship offering, he stepped down.

23 Moses and Aaron then went into the Tent of Meeting. When they
came out, they blessed the people; and the glory of the LORD appeared
to all the people. 24 Fire came out from the presence of the LORD and
consumed the burnt offering and the fat portions on the altar. And when
all the people saw it, they shouted for joy and fell facedown.

1–5 After one week of ordination service, Aaron and his sons had fulfilled the complete ritual of consecration and were then ready to begin their priestly service. This chapter tells of a sin offering, burnt offerings, peace offerings, and a grain offering for the priests and the people.

5–6 It seems at first sight that this promised manifestation (which occurred at v.23) was a second one, different from that recorded in Exodus 40:34 (so Allis, in loc.). However, it is difficult to see why, if God had already accepted the tabernacle then, the priests here would have to consecrate it with offerings and anointings (see Notes).

7–14 These verses give the details of Aaron's offering for himself the sacrifices mentioned in v.2. As mentioned in 8:15, the blood of the sin offering of the priest was put on the horns of the golden incense altar in the Holy Place; the rest of the blood was poured out at the base of the large bronze altar of burnt offering.

15–21 The details of Aaron's sacrifice of the offering of the people mentioned in vv.3–4 are given here. Notice that in v.21 Aaron presented the wave breast and the right thigh to the Lord but then took them for food for himself and his sons. The people's sin offering (v.15), however, being a sin offering for the congregation, was burned outside the camp (4:13–21).

22–24 After the offerings had been duly made, Aaron lifted up his hands in benediction and blessed the people (v.22). As suggested above, this was probably the prescribed benediction of Numbers 6:24–27. The material in this section need not be strictly chronological. The symbolic presence of God was evidenced by the reality of his glory (v.23). There had been fire on the altar during the week of the priests' consecration. But miraculous fire came from the Lord to consume the offerings and to show the divine acceptance (v.24). That this was miraculous fire could easily be distinguished by its suddenness, intensity, etc. It emphasized the fact that when the sacrifices were burned year after year, God himself accepted them and blessed accordingly. The fire was sacred and was not to be allowed to go out.

The immediate response of the people—"they shouted for joy and fell facedown" (v.24)—was gladness at God's acceptance. Mingled therewith, however, was awe at the presence of the supernatural manifestation of the holy Lord who had promised to dwell with them, to be their God, and to take them for his people.

Notes

6 The verses following Exod 40:34 give a description of the continuing presence of the glory of the Lord on the wilderness journey. Also, the manifestation of God's glory in Exod 40:34 was preceded by burnt offerings and grain offerings (v.29), which implies that it happened after the ritual detailed in Lev 8–9. Probably, therefore, the Exodus passage should be understood as referring to the initial manifestation of the glory of God after the tabernacle was set up and the worship had begun, i.e., that it refers to the same event as Lev 9:6 and 23.

C. *Nadab and Abihu's Profanation*

10:1–7

1 Aaron's sons Nadab and Abihu took their censers, put fire in them
and added incense; and they offered unauthorized fire before the LORD,
contrary to his command. 2 So fire came out from the presence of the
LORD and consumed them, and they died before the LORD. 3 Moses then
said to Aaron, "This is what the LORD spoke of when he said:

" 'Among those who approach me
I will show myself holy;
in the sight of all the people
I will be honored.' "

Aaron remained silent.
4 Moses summoned Mishael and Elzaphan, sons of Aaron's uncle Uzziel, and said to them, "Come here; carry your cousins outside the camp, away from the front of the sanctuary."
5 So they came and carried them, still in their tunics, outside the camp, as Moses ordered.
6 Then Moses said to Aaron and his sons Eleazar and Ithamar, "Do not let your hair become unkempt, and do not tear your clothes, or you will die and the LORD will be angry with the whole community. But your relatives, all the house of Israel, may mourn for those the LORD has destroyed by fire.
7 Do not leave the entrance to the Tent of Meeting or you will die, because the LORD's anointing oil is on you." So they did as Moses said.

1–7 Unfortunately men are feeble and frail, and no amount of oil outside will necessarily change the heart. Two of Aaron's own sons, Nadab and Abihu, profaned the sanctuary with strange fire and died before the Lord (vv.1–3). Judgment was harsh for these two men, but no more so than it was for Ananias and Sapphira when the Christian church was just beginning (Acts 5). To whom more is given, more is required; and Aaron and the congregation needed to know that God was real and that the priests were not playing at religion.

Notes

1 This is the first mention of a censer—מַחְתָּה (*maḥtāh,* "incense burner")—in the NIV. The Hebrew word is also used for the various firepans of the altar (Exod 27:3; 38:3 et al.). Since making a fire was rather a chore in former times, all fire was preserved carefully, and coals were carried about to start other fires. The fire on the incense altar, however, was not perpetual. It could hardly be, without constant attention, for the altar was only a foot and a half square in a confined place. The censers or firepans of Nadab and Abihu should have been lit from the great brazen altar in the court. The men carelessly took coals from a convenient hearth, laid incense on the coals, and went into the tabernacle heedlessly. Possibly they went into the Most Holy Place (cf. 16:12–14). They did not come out alive (cf. the sin of Korah, Dathan, and Abiram in Num 16:6–40).

3 The thought of this verse—"I will show myself holy"—is reiterated in Isa 52:11: "Be pure you who carry the vessels of the LORD."

4 Mishael and Elzaphan are named in the genealogy of Exod 6:22. The genealogy there is incomplete, however, and they may not have been first cousins of Aaron. At least they were near relatives who could care decently for the dead men. Aaron was not to mourn, for his responsibility in his sacred office transcended the human ties. God had done what was right, and Aaron was to acquiesce. Leviticus 21:1–12 gives the rules that allow an ordinary priest to mourn for his immediate family but the high priest for no one at all.

5 The mention of the tunics may indicate that the cousins avoided touching the dead bodies so that they would not contact defilement.

D. *Explicit Instructions for the Priests*

10:8–20

8 Then the LORD said to Aaron,
9 "You and your sons are not to drink wine or other fermented drink whenever you go into the Tent of

Meeting, or you will die. This is a lasting ordinance for the generations
to come. 10 You must distinguish between the holy and the profane,
between the unclean and the clean, 11 and you must teach the Israelites
all the decrees the LORD has given them through Moses."
12 Moses said to Aaron and his remaining sons, Eleazar and Ithamar,
"Take the grain offering left over from the offerings made to the LORD by
fire and eat it prepared without yeast beside the altar, for it is most holy.
13 Eat it in a holy place, because it is your share and your sons' share of
the offerings made to the LORD by fire; for so I have been commanded.
14 But you and your sons and your daughters may eat the breast that was
waved and the thigh that was presented. Eat them in a ceremonially
clean place; they have been given to you and your children as your
share of the Israelites' fellowship offerings. 15 The thigh that was
presented and the breast that was waved must be brought with the fat
portions of the offerings made by fire, to be waved before the LORD as a
wave offering. This will be the regular share for you and your children,
as the LORD has commanded."
16 When Moses inquired about the goat of the sin offering and found
that it had been burned up, he was angry with Eleazar and Ithamar,
Aaron's remaining sons, and asked, 17 "Why didn't you eat the sin
offering in the sanctuary area? It is most holy; it was given to you to take
away the guilt of the community by making atonement for them before
the LORD. 18 Since its blood was not taken into the Holy Place, you should
have eaten the goat in the sanctuary area, as I commanded."
19 Aaron replied to Moses, "Today they sacrificed their sin offering
and their burnt offering before the LORD, but such things as this have
happened to me. Would the LORD have been pleased if I had eaten the
sin offering today?" 20 When Moses heard this, he was satisfied.

8–11 There is more than a hint that Nadab and Abihu profaned the Lord's house because they were drunk. At least immediately there was given a prohibition of drink while serving in the Lord's house (vv.8–11). This was not the last tragedy caused by the bottle.

There is at least one danger of drink and drugs. They rob a man of his reason, and under their influence a man will do things he otherwise would never do. For a man to abdicate his reason for drink or drugs is too grave a risk. From here on the priest entering the tabernacle was to drink no alcohol.

12–20 It appears that Nadab and Abihu were the elder sons of Aaron. When Moses was on the mountain, God invited Aaron, Nadab, Abihu, and seventy elders to come part way to meet the Lord (Exod 24:1–2). It may be guessed that possibly Eleazer and Ithamar were under the canonical age of thirty (Num 4:3, 23, 30). As Aaron, however, was about eighty years old at this point and had been married about forty years, his youngest sons may indeed have been over thirty. The text does not say whether all four sons had been consecrated at the same time. They may have been.

After the death of Aaron's older sons, Moses found that Aaron and his two remaining sons had not eaten the meat of the sin offering as was normal. But Aaron replied that though he was forbidden to mourn, he could not eat in good conscience that day. With that Moses was content; for Aaron had acted, not in negligence nor mechanically, but in responsible sincerity. It is noteworthy that in the OT, also, the heart attitude is more important than the mechanics of all the sacrifices (1 Sam 15:22; 2 Chron 30:19).

"The goat of the sin offering" was not the people's sin offering mentioned in 9:15. When such an offering was made with a male goat, the blood was sprinkled in the

Holy Place, and the meat was not to be eaten by the priests (4:13–21). In the present instance there had been further offerings. Individuals had apparently also brought sin offerings whose blood was not sprinkled in the Holy Place and whose flesh could be eaten by the priest. Aaron, however, had directed the flesh of this sin offering also to be burned outside the camp, as was prescribed for a young bull whose blood had been sprinkled in the Holy Place.

Notes

9 יַיִן (*yayin*, "wine") and שֵׁכָר (*šēḵār*, "fermented drink") go in pairs many times in the OT. The NIV has avoided the translation wine and strong drink (KJV et al.). Israel had no strong drink in the modern sense. Distillation of alcohol was invented by the Arabs in medieval times. Before that only natural drinks were available. The most common natural drinks were light wines and beer. Beer was a common product in antiquity. Grain is largely starch and will not ferment unless the starch is first converted to sugar by enzyme action, the most common being accomplished by sprouting the grain. The Egyptians' converting process left a mixture that needed to be strained. Clay strainers were found in Palestine, especially in Philistine strata. It is a very natural conclusion that the two words should be translated "light wine or beer" (cf. Prov 20:1; Isa 28:7; Mic 2:11). At least *šēḵār* includes beer, though it may include other fermented drinks, like date wine, as well.

12 "Eleazer and Ithamar" were heads of the priestly families thereafter. Eli was of the line of Eleazer. Samuel was evidently considered as adopted by Eli, for he was of the line of Aaron's uncle Izhar (cf. 1 Chron 6:33–38).

14 The explicit mention of the women—"and your daughters"—shows that 7:31–34 is not exclusive in promising the breast and right thigh of the peace offering to Aaron and his sons. It was given to them for the use of their families. The grain offering, however, after a handful was burned on the altar, was exclusively for the priests and was to be eaten in the holy precincts (v.12).

19 The irregularity was not careless, nor was it a violation of the spirit of the law. Aaron was forbidden to desecrate his office by the ordinary signs of mourning, such as rending garments, cutting hair, etc. But to fast on this day of his grief was proper enough. And Moses was satisfied that the Lord's law had not been further broken.

IV. Laws of Cleanness (11:1–15:33)

As mentioned in the Introduction, the Levitical laws of cleanness have no known extensive parallel in the surrounding cultures. It is indeed claimed that they are part of very primitive taboos, but this view is even stranger when surrounding cultures exhibit little of this sort of law. Also, surely this was not the Mosaic meaning. C.L. Feinberg ("Clean and Unclean," NBD, p. 240) lists the spiritual, the hygienic, the psychological, the dualistic, and the national reasons and the rationalistic idea of taboo. The view of wholeness and normality as held by Wenham has already been mentioned in the Introduction, p. 526). The laws were symbolic of spiritual cleansing and served to set Israel apart from the surrounding nations. J. Jocz ("Clean," ZPEB, 1:884) discusses the basis for the cleanness distinction and emphasizes that the Levitical code prohibited the idolatrous practices of the surrounding nations. There is truth in this. Exodus 23:19; 34:26; and Deuteronomy 14:21 possibly were given to avoid a Ugaritic ritual. Some of Jocz's examples, however, are too distant in time and space to be convincing.

The spiritual and the hygienic reasons for the laws may still be affirmed. They are remarkably valuable in the area of public health. Maimonides already in the Middle Ages gave this explanation among others. It would be in line with God's promised blessing that "none of these diseases" of Egypt would be visited on Israel, for "I am the LORD your Healer" (cf. Exod 15:26).

The view that these laws were public health regulations in Israel will be discussed in detail below. In general it can be said that the laws protected Israel from bad diet, dangerous vermin, and communicable diseases. Only in very recent days have better laws of health been possible with the advance of medicine. These were rule-of-thumb laws that God gave in his wisdom to a people who could not know the reason for the provision.

First, the laws protected Israel's diet. Some of the food forbidden was good some of the time, but not unless it was properly prepared. Pigs spread trichinosis; rabbits spread tularemia. Albright (*Yahweh*, pp. 178–81) pointed out that the fish classified as clean are "normally free-swimming, whereas fish without scales and fins, such as eels, are usually mud-burrowers and therefore hosts to a great many more parasites than free-swimming fish." Cows, goats, and sheep are safe to eat under all ordinary circumstances and are economical to raise. The horse and camel were too uneconomical to use for meat (see Introduction, p. 529).

The Hebrew was not only to avoid eating unclean animals; he was not to touch their dead carcasses. Thus the laws automatically helped control vermin. Common unclean animals would be spiders, flies, bugs, rats, and mice. A dead rat in a Hebrew house was not overlooked. It was carefully taken out and buried. In an effort to avoid such problems, the Hebrew housewife would normally keep a clean house.

It is becoming more generally recognized that the "leprosy" mentioned in chapters 13–14 includes several other diseases showing a skin rash. Such illnesses as measles, smallpox, and scarlet fever were not understood in ancient times but were often deadly scourges. For any such disease showing a skin rash, there was a quarantine period with weekly examination until the patient was well. Likewise, the laws on sexual uncleanness would tend to protect Israel from the spread of any venereal diseases and from childbed fever.

It is, of course, true that some cultures have adopted similar rules out of sad experience. The OT did not get its taboos from surrounding cultures, but some other cultures in later times adopted by experience some of these taboos—usually along with many other wrong ones. The OT gives no explanation of these laws of cleanness. No reference is made to demons or spirits, but the laws were wonderfully fashioned by God for the general health of the nation.

A. *Clean and Unclean Food*

11:1–47 (cf. Deut 14:4–21)

1 The LORD said to Moses and Aaron, 2 "Say to the Israelites: 'Of all the
animals that live on land, these are the ones you may eat: 3 You may eat
any animal that has a split hoof completely divided and that chews the
cud.

4 " 'There are some that only chew the cud or only have a split hoof,
but you must not eat them. The camel, though it chews the cud, does
not have a split hoof; it is ceremonially unclean for you. 5 The coney,

though it chews the cud, does not have a split hoof; it is unclean for
you. 6The rabbit, though it chews the cud, does not have a split hoof; it
is unclean for you. 7And the pig, though it has a split hoof completely
divided, does not chew the cud; it is unclean for you. 8You must not eat
their meat or touch their carcasses; they are unclean for you.

9" 'Of all the creatures living in the water of the seas and the streams,
you may eat any that have fins and scales. 10But all creatures in the seas
or streams that do not have fins and scales—whether among all the
swarming things or among all the other living creatures in the water—
you are to detest. 11And since you are to detest them, you must not eat
their meat and you must detest their carcasses. 12Anything living in the
water that does not have fins and scales is to be detestable to you.

13" 'These are the birds you are to detest and not eat because they are
detestable: the eagle, the vulture, the black vulture, 14the red kite, any
kind of black kite, 15any kind of raven, 16the horned owl, the screech
owl, the gull, any kind of hawk, 17the little owl, the cormorant, the great
owl, 18the white owl, the desert owl, the osprey, 19the stork, any kind of
heron, the hoopoe and the bat.

20" 'All flying insects that walk on all fours are to be detestable to you.
21There are, however, some winged creatures that walk on all fours that
you may eat: those that have jointed legs for hopping on the ground.
22Of these you may eat any kind of locust, katydid, cricket or grass-
hopper. 23But all other winged creatures that have four legs you are to
detest.

24" 'You will make yourselves unclean by these; whoever touches
their carcasses will be unclean till evening. 25Whoever picks up one of
their carcasses must wash his clothes, and he will be unclean till
evening.

26" 'Every animal that has a split hoof not completely divided or that
does not chew the cud is unclean for you; whoever touches the carcass
of any of them will be unclean. 27Of all the animals that walk on all fours,
those that walk on their paws are unclean for you; whoever touches
their carcasses will be unclean till evening. 28Anyone who picks up their
carcasses must wash his clothes, and he will be unclean till evening.
They are unclean for you.

29" 'Of the animals that move about on the ground, these are unclean
for you: the weasel, the rat, any kind of great lizard, 30the gecko, the
monitor lizard, the wall lizard, the skink and the chameleon. 31Of all
those that move along the ground, these are unclean for you. Whoever
touches them when they are dead will be unclean till evening. 32When
one of them dies and falls on something, that article, whatever its use,
will be unclean, whether it is made of wood, cloth, hide or sackcloth. Put
it in water; it will be unclean till evening, and then it will be clean. 33If
one of them falls into a clay pot, everything in it will be unclean, and you
must break the pot. 34Any food that could be eaten but has water on it
from such a pot is unclean, and any liquid that could be drunk from it is
unclean. 35Anything that one of their carcasses falls on becomes
unclean; an oven or cooking pot must be broken up. They are unclean,
and you are to regard them as unclean. 36A spring, however, or a cistern
for collecting water remains clean, but anyone who touches one of
these carcasses is unclean. 37If a carcass falls on any seeds that are to
be planted, they remain clean. 38But if water has been put on the seed
and a carcass falls on it, it is unclean for you.

39" 'If an animal that you are allowed to eat dies, anyone who touches
the carcass will be unclean till evening. 40Anyone who eats some of the
carcass must wash his clothes, and he will be unclean till evening.
Anyone who picks up the carcass must wash his clothes, and he will be
unclean till evening.

41" 'Every creature that moves about on the ground is detestable; it is not to be eaten. 42You are not to eat any creature that moves about on the ground, whether it moves on its belly or walks on all fours or on many feet; it is detestable. 43Do not defile yourselves by any of these creatures. Do not make yourselves unclean by means of them or be made unclean by them. 44I am the LORD your God; consecrate yourselves and be holy, because I am holy. Do not make yourselves unclean by any creature that moves about on the ground. 45I am the LORD who brought you up out of Egypt to be your God; therefore be holy, because I am holy.

46" 'These are the regulations concerning animals, birds, every living thing that moves in the water and every creature that moves about on the ground. 47You must distinguish between the unclean and the clean, between living creatures that may be eaten and those that may not be eaten.' "

1–8 Deuteronomy 14:6–19 is almost a verbatim copy of Leviticus 11:3–20. The difference between clean and unclean food is clearly as old as the time of Noah. It was to some extent tied in with sacrifice, for parts of some of the sacrifices were eaten. Noah's purpose in taking extra pairs of the clean animals aboard the ark was to have meat available for his family. There is no reference to clean and unclean items in the history between Noah and Moses, though Job, whose date is uncertain, does frequently mention the difference. Abrahamic sacrifices were of clean animals as far as they are specified (Gen 15:9). The need for extensive laws on these matters concerning public health would only arise when Israel became a nation under Moses.

The phrase "a split hoof completely divided" (v.3) is obscure. It seems to be repetitive in the Hebrew: "A split hoof and splitting a split in the hoofs." The precise meaning of the terminology is not sure, but the emphasis of the NIV surely represents the meaning adequately.

The clean animals are further limited to those that "chew the cud." The ruminants are peculiar in that they can exist on a rough diet. Cows, sheep, goats, and camels actually digest cellulose such as found in straw, leaves, twigs, bushes, etc. Horses and pigs require more nourishing food. Deuteronomy 14:4–5 names nine animals that are clean, including the wild deer and the antelope.

Contrary to general opinion, the use of the camel was not characteristic of ancient Israel. Camels are mentioned twenty-four times in connection with the patriarchs who traveled widely along the caravan routes. The rest of the Pentateuch mentions them only three times. From Moses to the Exile, the use of camels by the Israelites is only mentioned twice. They were more a desert animal; apparently the life of Israel did not nearly so much revolve around the camel as does life for the Arab today. Albright (*Yahweh*, pp. 70–73) argued that camels were not domesticated in the days of the patriarchs. Others, however, have answered this contention adequately (see G.S. Cansdale, ZPEB, 1:695–99; Kitchen, *Ancient Orient*, p. 79), though it may still be true that the Israelites of Moses' day did not use camels extensively.

Neither the "coney" (v.5; NIV mg., "hyrax or rock badger") nor the "rabbit" (v.6) is a ruminant. The coney is a vegetarian and an ungulate (i.e., has hoofs). Though small like a rabbit, it is related to the elephant. Both the coney and the rabbit wiggle their noses in a chewing action that resembles the chewing of a cud. The description is not scientifically precise but one of practical appearances. Some indeed have argued that rabbits do chew the cud because they reingest some special type of their feces (see *Countryside and Small Stock Journal* [June 1976]: 49–50). Even if we admit this, it hardly seems to help. Would this unusual action properly be called "chewing the cud"? And would Israelites be expected to observe this odd, usually nocturnal habit? The practical result of outlawing the rabbit was to protect the nation from tularemia.

9–12 Fish that have fins and scales are free swimming and, in general, are free of parasites. Scaleless fish are more likely carriers of parasites since they are scavengers and mud-bottom dwellers. Clams in current times have carried hepatitis—though this may be due to modern pollution problems. Crabs are scavengers, and some of their meat is said not to be good. Snail fever from infested waters has been a curse in Egypt. The free-swimming fish were always good.

13–19 There was no easy rule of thumb for clean birds. A negative list is given that in cases is difficult to translate with certainty. The different modern versions vary in detail. In general carrion-eating and fish-eating birds were forbidden, just as they are not used for food today. Chickens are not mentioned in the OT. The eating of bird eggs and the mother bird together is forbidden in Deuteronomy 22:6, apparently for conservation reasons. If the eggs are taken, the mother bird will lay more; but if the mother bird is taken, there will be no more eggs! Doves, their eggs, and their young were eaten.

20–23 "Flying insects that walk on all fours" include such pests as cockroaches, flies, or even mosquitoes. Verses 21–22 allow the locust/grasshopper family as food. The distinction is that they have strong hind legs for springing. Evidently in the category of insects, the hind pair of legs was not counted; so these insects are described as creeping on all fours.

The "locust" (v.22) is not the cicada or seventeen-year locust but a large grasshopper-type of insect. These locusts were great pests in antiquity also. A plague of locusts could eat every green thing in a field in a very short time. Travelers in the Near East tell of having seen the sun obscured by clouds of locusts. When they are present in more normal numbers, they are used as food to this day. Only the muscular portion is used and when fried is said to be a delicacy. John the Baptist ate locusts and wild honey. No one in the OT is mentioned as eating locusts, but this silence does not prove that they were not eaten. Modern locust plagues and their control are interestingly described by R.A.M. Conley ("Locusts, Teeth of the Wind," *National Geographic* 136 [Aug. 1969]: 202–26).

24–43 The words for "weasel," "great lizard," "gecko," "monitor lizard," "wall lizard," and "skink" occur only in these verses in Leviticus. It is impossible to be sure of their identification. Some of these names of animals have parallels in later Arabic or Aramaic literature. Fortunately the details are not important.

The basic meaning of the word "moves about" (*šāraṣ*) is to multiply. The little animals like mice, lizards, etc., multiply rapidly if they are not controlled. The word is used again in vv.41–42 to refer to snakes, lizards, centipedes, etc. The word also is used in Genesis 1:21 to refer to animals that multiply in the water and in Genesis 9:7 in the command to people after the Flood to multiply and fill the earth. The small animals mentioned in this verse are characterized by both their movement and their rapid reproduction.

The laws of cleanness had as much to do with touching the carcasses of vermin as with eating them. Even a part of the carcass of an unclean animal was defiled. This was not true of the carcass of a clean animal killed for food. Dead vermin therefore were a problem in the Hebrew house. Dead bugs in an earthen pot meant the pot was to be broken (v.33). Food contaminated by dead bugs or mice was to be thrown out. A carcass on dry seed was all right but on damp seed was contaminating (vv.37–38). Even the carcass of a clean animal that had died a natural death (i.e., by a disease) was unclean (vv.39–40). Such laws resulted in prompt burial of carrion and certainly promoted public health. The Hebrew housewife no doubt took a dim view of bugs.

44–47 The phrase "be holy, because I am holy" is interesting because it is like the words of 19:2, which are said to be characteristic of the Holiness Code (chs. 17–26). Actually the words are characteristic of the laws of holy conduct wherever found. The use of the phrase here unifies stylistically the laws of cleanness and the laws of holiness.

Notes

14 The expression לְמִין (*l^emîn*, "any kind of") is used nine times in this chapter. It is used also in the accounts of Creation (Gen 1:11–12, 21–25) and the Flood (Gen 6–7). The phrase appears to mean "the various kinds of falcon, raven, etc." In the Flood account the word is quite broad: "the various kinds of fowl, cattle, etc." In the Creation account also it designates rather broad categories of life. Variation within the "kinds" is not ruled out, but the stability and continuity of the "kinds" seems to be in view.

B. *Purification After Childbirth*

12:1–8

1The LORD said to Moses, 2"Say to the Israelites: 'A woman who becomes pregnant and gives birth to a son will be ceremonially unclean for seven days, just as she is unclean during her monthly period. 3On the eighth day the boy is to be circumcised. 4Then the woman must wait thirty-three days to be purified from her bleeding. She must not touch anything sacred or go to the sanctuary until the days of her purification are over. 5If she gives birth to a daughter, for two weeks the woman will be unclean, as in her period. Then she must wait sixty-six days to be purified from her bleeding.

6" 'When the days of her purification for a son or daughter are over, she is to bring to the priest at the entrance to the Tent of Meeting a year-old lamb for a burnt offering and a young pigeon or a dove for a sin offering. 7He shall offer them before the LORD to make atonement for her, and then she will be ceremonially clean from her flow of blood.
" 'These are the regulations for the woman who gives birth to a boy or a girl.

8If she cannot afford a lamb, she is to bring two doves or two young pigeons, one for a burnt offering and the other for a sin offering. In this way the priest will make atonement for her, and she will be clean.' "

1–8 Fuller details with regard to sexual impurity are given in chapter 13. Childbirth, like menstruation, rendered the mother unclean. The period was seven days for a boy, twice that for a girl (vv.2, 5). There may be more reasons than one for such a law. First, it would put the mother in sufficient isolation to assist in bringing her back to normal health. Being unclean she could not do the cooking or keep the house. Also, it is possible that such a provision would help prevent the spread of childbed fever, which in former days took so many lives. If the mother was unclean, presumably any midwife would have to wash in water and be unclean until the evening, which might help prevent the direct transmission of this disease.

Circumcision was instituted by God in the family of Abraham (v.3). It distinguished his descendants from all others. Some scholars have questioned the force of this distinction because circumcision was widely practiced in antiquity even as it is today among the Arabs and in some African tribes. But there was a difference. Egyptian pictures of surgeons performing the operation show that the subject was a grown young man. Arabic and African circumcision also are puberty circumcisions associated with entering manhood and sometimes associated with licentiousness. As far as the author can learn, infant circumcision in antiquity was peculiar to Israel. It had one extra virtue. It precluded any licentious puberty circumcision rites that other nations may have observed. That circumcision also had a spiritual import is clear from such verses as Deuteronomy 10:16; Jeremiah 4:4; and Romans 2:29.

There was a further period of semiisolation during which a newly delivered mother could not yet make the journey to the sanctuary for her offering. Travel in ancient days was more strenuous than now. It would be a physical blessing for a mother to wait for about a month. Breast feeding was then a must as now it still is a desideratum. It was a natural and wise provision for a mother to have time at home with her baby until the child was stronger and her milk established.

It is not at all clear why the time of uncleanness and seclusion is doubled for a female child (v.5). There may be the symbolism of the uncleanness that the daughter would eventually suffer in her turn. Or it may be that circumcising the male child at the end of one week was considered symbolically to reduce the attendant uncleanness. There is no statement that the baby is ceremonially unclean. That the child is also a sinner is plain in the OT—else why the ritual of circumcision that is said to be symbolic of circumcision of the heart? David puts it succinctly in Psalm 58:3: "Even from birth the wicked go astray;/ from the womb they are wayward and speak lies."

There may have been good reasons in that culture why the journey to the temple was delayed for a baby girl. Girls are usually smaller at birth. More girls are born than boys, but even now the mortality rate is greater for girls so that the sexes are soon numerically even. To allow a longer time to let a baby girl grow and get established would be a good thing! There may have been cultural influences. In many countries girls are less desired than boys. Thoughtless husbands might have taken better care of baby boys and their mothers; so a longer time at home might have been a positive help for a mother with a baby girl. There is no difference made in the temple ritual between the birth of a boy or a girl. The only difference is in the periods of uncleanness and seclusion.

The prescribed offering for the new mother was a burnt offering and a sin offering that was normal for a woman with any unnatural discharge (15:30). The OT does not state that conception and birth are sinful; but all who conceive and bear are sinners, and the end of all such uncleanness was accomplished by ritual laws of cleansing. The laws were for public health, but there was also the religious sanction. Doubtless the physical uncleanness was typical of spiritual uncleanness as well.

Notes

3 Clarence Vos (*Women in Old Testament Worship* [Amsterdam: Free University Press, 1968], p. 53) argues that in Egypt circumcision was administered only to privileged or elite groups, such as priests. In one of the sources he quotes, however, the subject says, "I was a commoner of repute who lived on his own property" (ANET, p. 326).

8 The mother of Jesus brought the offering of the poor (cf. Luke 2:24, which quotes this verse).

C. *Cleanness and Skin Diseases*

13:1–46

1 The LORD said to Moses and Aaron, 2 "When anyone has a swelling or
a rash or a bright spot on his skin that may become an infectious skin
disease, he must be brought to Aaron the priest or to one of his sons
who is a priest. 3 The priest is to examine the sore on his skin, and if the
hair in the sore has turned white and the sore appears to be more than
skin deep, it is an infectious skin disease. When the priest examines
him, he shall pronounce him ceremonially unclean. 4 If the spot on his
skin is white but does not appear to be more than skin deep and the hair
in it has not turned white, the priest is to put the infected person in
isolation for seven days. 5 On the seventh day the priest is to examine
him, and if he sees that the sore is unchanged and has not spread in the
skin, he is to keep him in isolation another seven days. 6 On the seventh
day the priest is to examine him again, and if the sore has faded and has
not spread in the skin, the priest shall pronounce him clean; it is only a
rash. The man must wash his clothes, and he will be clean. 7 But if the
rash does spread in his skin after he has shown himself to the priest to
be pronounced clean, he must appear before the priest again. 8 The
priest is to examine him, and if the rash has spread in the skin, he shall
pronounce him unclean; it is an infectious disease.

9 "When anyone has an infectious skin disease, he must be brought to
the priest. 10 The priest is to examine him, and if there is a white swelling
in the skin that has turned the hair white and if there is raw flesh in the
swelling, 11 it is a chronic skin disease and the priest shall pronounce
him unclean. He is not to put him in isolation, because he is already
unclean.

12 "If the disease breaks out all over his skin and, so far as the priest
can see, it covers all the skin of the infected person from head to foot,
13 the priest is to examine him, and if the disease has covered his whole
body, he shall pronounce that person clean. Since it has all turned
white, he is clean. 14 But whenever raw flesh appears on him, he will be
unclean. 15 When the priest sees the raw flesh, he shall pronounce him
unclean. The raw flesh is unclean; he has an infectious disease.
16 Should the raw flesh change and turn white, he must go to the priest.
17 The priest is to examine him, and if the sores have turned white, the
priest shall pronounce the infected person clean; then he will be clean.

18 "When someone has a boil on his skin and it heals, 19 and in the
place where the boil was, a white swelling or reddish-white spot
appears, he must present himself to the priest. 20 The priest is to
examine it, and if it appears to be more than skin deep and the hair in it
has turned white, the priest shall pronounce him unclean. It is an
infectious skin disease that has broken out where the boil was. 21 But if,
when the priest examines it, there is no white hair in it and it is not more
than skin deep and has faded, then the priest is to put him in isolation
for seven days. 22 If it is spreading in the skin, the priest shall pronounce

him unclean; it is infectious. [23]But if the spot is unchanged and has not
spread, it is only a scar from the boil, and the priest shall pronounce him
clean.
[24]"When someone has a burn on his skin and a reddish-white or white
spot appears in the raw flesh of the burn, [25]the priest is to examine the
spot, and if the hair in it has turned white, and it appears to be more
than skin deep, it is an infectious disease that has broken out in the
burn. The priest shall pronounce him unclean; it is an infectious skin
disease. [26]But if the priest examines it and there is no white hair in the
spot and if it is not more than skin deep and has faded, then the priest is
to put him in isolation for seven days. [27]On the seventh day the priest is
to examine him, and if it is spreading in the skin, the priest shall
pronounce him unclean; it is an infectious skin disease. [28]If, however,
the spot is unchanged and has not spread in the skin but has faded, it is
a swelling from the burn, and the priest shall pronounce him clean; it is
only a scar from the burn.
[29]"If a man or woman has a sore on the head or on the chin, [30]the
priest is to examine the sore, and if it appears to be more than skin deep
and the hair in it is yellow and thin, the priest shall pronounce that
person unclean; it is an itch, an infectious disease of the head or chin.
[31]But if, when the priest examines this kind of sore, it does not seem to
be more than skin deep and there is no black hair in it, then the priest is
to put the infected person in isolation for seven days. [32]On the seventh
day the priest is to examine the sore, and if the itch has not spread and
there is no yellow hair in it and it does not appear to be more than skin
deep, [33]he must be shaved except for the diseased area, and the priest
is to keep him in isolation another seven days. [34]On the seventh day the
priest is to examine the itch, and if it has not spread in the skin and
appears to be no more than skin deep, the priest shall pronounce him
clean. He must wash his clothes, and he will be clean. [35]But if the itch
does spread in the skin after he is pronounced clean, [36]the priest is to
examine him, and if the itch has spread in the skin, the priest does not
need to look for yellow hair; the person is unclean. [37]If, however, in his
judgment it is unchanged and black hair has grown in it, the itch is
healed. He is clean, and the priest shall pronounce him clean.
[38]"When a man or woman has white spots on the skin, [39]the priest is
to examine them, and if the spots are dull white, it is a harmless rash
that has broken out on the skin; that person is clean.
[40]"When a man has lost his hair and is bald, he is clean. [41]If he has
lost his hair from the front of his scalp and has a bald forehead, he is
clean. [42]But if he has a reddish-white sore on his bald head or forehead,
it is an infectious disease breaking out on his head or forehead. [43]The
priest is to examine him, and if the swollen sore on his head or forehead
is reddish-white like an infectious skin disease, [44]the man is diseased
and is unclean. The priest shall pronounce him unclean because of the
sore on his head.
[45]"The person with such an infectious disease must wear torn
clothes, let his hair be unkempt, cover the lower part of his face and cry
out, 'Unclean! Unclean!' [46]As long as he has the infection he remains
unclean. He must live alone; he must live outside the camp.

Clearly chapters 13–14 are not limited to what is now termed leprosy or Hansen's disease. The Hebrew word *ṣārāʿaṯ* is used only in connection with sickness and mildew, and its use elsewhere gives no great light on the identification. The word is used in connection with the miracles of Moses' hand (Exod 4:6), Miriam's plague (Num 12:10), and Naaman's healing and Gehazi's plague (2 Kings 5:1–27). These all refer to the whiteness of skin and thus would be true leprosy. Uzziah's curse, being a continuing disease (2 Kings 15:5; 2 Chron 26:21), also could be true leprosy. The other references are general and do not add to the picture (22:4; Num 5:2; Deut 24:8; 2 Sam 3:29).

The symptoms listed in chapter 13 are more applicable to the communicable diseases characterized by skin rash, such as measles, smallpox, scarlet fever, etc. The word used in the Greek translation also was more inclusive than just leprosy. Hansen's disease does not change the hair color but causes loss of hair. It makes no pocks in the skin. The different symptoms listed in the chapter are hard to follow in detail; but the main consideration is whether the sore is virulent, spreading, and deeper than the skin. Such a disease would be watched for seven days and if necessary seven days more. By that time, if the disease were serious, the man would likely be either well or dead. Hansen's disease is slow in onset and does not improve in seven days. Of course, the references to *ṣārā'at* in a garment or in a house (vv.47–49; 14:33–53) cannot apply to Hansen's disease. (For a fuller discussion, see "Diseases in the Bible," ZPEB, 2:138–39; cf. S.G. Browne, *Leprosy in the Bible* [London: Christian Medical Fellowship, 1970].)

No medication is prescribed because in those days there was nothing appropriate. The only weapon the people had to prevent the spread of disease was quarantine, and this was applied as sensibly as it could be in those times. No other ancient law code has these quarantine prescriptions or even approaches the questions of public health.

Some damage may have been done by the translation "leprosy." Some of the diseases here referred to are highly communicable. Leprosy is not easily communicable; but partly because of these biblical references, leprosy cases, even in modern days, have been more isolated than necessary. It is true that leprosy is more communicable among children. With modern treatment, however, it can be controlled without the strict quarantine that has usually added to the pitiable state of the victims. Such unfortunate hardships were perhaps overbalanced by the beneficial results of an ancient quarantine for measles, smallpox, scarlet fever, and other such communicable diseases.

1–11 The translation of the words "swelling," "rash," and "bright spot" is uncertain (see Notes). That the victim "must be brought" indicates that he would be too sick to walk and would be carried. Leprosy in its incipient stages does not incapacitate a person. No details are given about the type of "isolation" (v.4) required. The sick person was probably not confined at home, and no quarters were available around the tabernacle. His family would probably avoid him. He would stay outside the camp (see v.46). The implication is that a "rash" (*sappaḥaṯ*) was a temporary thing (v.6). At least there was no serious disease. He was to wash and be clean. True leprosy does not change enough in fourteen days to be recognized by such an examination. Some other affliction is intended.

The details of these symptoms and the examinations by the priest escape us. It appears that the main questions were, Is the sore more than skin deep? Is there raw flesh? Is the infection spreading? A temporary disease meant quarantine; a chronic disease meant segregation (v.11); an abated disease meant cure—the man was clean.

12–17 Any disease that would leave the whole body white after a couple of weeks would not be serious (vv.12–13). Apparently it means that the rash had gone, leaving the skin white. Perhaps the whiteness would refer to new skin, not as sun-bronzed as usual. However, if raw flesh appeared (vv.14-15), the man was unclean.

18–23 The word "boil" (*šᵉḥîn*) is used of Job's affliction, and boils were one of the ten plagues of Egypt. The similar Arabic word refers to inflammation. That the person is pronounced "unclean" (v.20) means that the boil has not healed. The test is, Is the infection more than skin deep? Again, leprosy is too specific for the disease.

24–28 The case of a "burn" is more clear. This sore is caused by fire (*mik̲wat̲-'ēš*, lit., "an accident of the fire"). Burns are not contagious, but they can become infected; in that case, for his own good as well as for others, the infected person would be quarantined. Again the key questions are, Is it deep? Is the hair dead? Is it spreading?

29–37 The "itch" is possibly a scab that is complicated by the hair of the head or the beard. The derivation is from the verb *nāt̲ēq* ("to pull off"). The patient is to shave the hair around the sore and watch it. Such open sores were not allowed to fester without care. And the person with the sore was not to spread the infection.

38–46 The dull white spot, it must be remembered, is against the background of the darker skin of the tanned Jew of Palestine. The spots are not active, raw, or deep. They are a "harmless rash" (*bōḥaq*), a word used only here (v.39) and without clear derivation, possibly a scar. From the context, at least, it was harmless.

The word for "unkempt" (v.45) is difficult. *Pārûa'* may come from a word referring to long hair such as a Nazirite had (Num 6:5) or from a word meaning "a bit loose," "untied" (a turban). In 21:10 the priest was forbidden thus to take off his turban (or let his hair grow long) as a sign of mourning. The unclean man was to do what a priest was forbidden to do.

The quarantined person in Israel was not quarantined in his house; that would endanger the family. He was to warn others of his illness by dress and action and was to stay outside the camp. He probably got little care except from a mother who was willing to share his uncleanness. Till relatively recent years many a country town had a pest house where victims of communicable diseases were put. The author's grandfather once nursed a relative in such a pest house. Mortality was high; but it would also have been high at home, and the well people were preserved. It is hard for moderns to imagine the severity of ancient epidemics. The black death (bubonic plague) killed a quarter of Europe's people in about 1350. Whole villages would move away from those stricken with the disease. Quarantine was the only available relief. The OT specified such quarantine already in the days of Moses.

Notes

---

2 שְׂאֵת (*śᵉ'ēt̲*) comes from נָשָׂא (*nāśā'*, "to lift up") and is very likely "a swelling" or "an eruption."

סַפַּחַת (*sappahat̲*, "rash") is used only here and in 14:56. Its derivation is uncertain.

בַּהֶרֶת (*baheret̲*, "bright spot") is used only in this section of Leviticus. Its derivation suggests something bright, possibly the bright red of inflammation.

11 Such a chronic disease—נוֹשֶׁנֶת (*nôšenet̲*, "old")—indicated a continued quarantine until the man was well.

D. *Mildew*

13:47–59

[47]"If any clothing is contaminated with mildew—any woolen or linen clothing, [48]any woven or knitted material of linen or wool, any leather or anything made of leather—[49]and if the contamination in the clothing, or leather, or woven or knitted material, or any leather article, is greenish or reddish, it is a spreading mildew and must be shown to the priest. [50]The priest is to examine the mildew and isolate the affected article for seven days. [51]On the seventh day he is to examine it, and if the mildew has spread in the clothing, or the woven or knitted material, or the leather, whatever its use, it is a destructive mildew; the article is unclean. [52]He must burn up the clothing, or the woven or knitted material of wool or linen, or any leather article that has the contamination in it, because the mildew is destructive; the article must be burned up.

[53]"But if, when the priest examines it, the mildew has not spread in the clothing, or the woven or knitted material, or the leather article, [54]he shall order that the contaminated article be washed. Then he is to isolate it for another seven days. [55]After the affected article has been washed, the priest is to examine it, and if the mildew has not changed its appearance, even though it has not spread, it is unclean. Burn it with fire, whether the mildew has affected one side or the other. [56]If, when the priest examines it, the mildew has faded after the article has been washed, he is to tear the contaminated part out of the clothing, or the leather, or the woven or knitted material. [57]But if it reappears in the clothing, or in the woven or knitted material, or in the leather article, it is spreading, and whatever has the mildew must be burned with fire. [58]The clothing, or the woven or knitted material, or any leather article that has been washed and is rid of the mildew, must be washed again, and it will be clean."

[59]These are the regulations concerning contamination by mildew in woolen or linen clothing, woven or knitted material, or any leather article, for pronouncing them clean or unclean.

47–59 Obviously the word *ṣārāʿa͟t* here refers, not to leprosy, but to some kind of rot, fungus, or "mildew" (NIV), just as it does in 14:33–53. Harrison (*Leviticus*, p. 146) suggests that the mildew was called by the same name as the various diseases (KJV, "leprosy") because of the rough appearance and the irregular surfaces that swell, flake, or peel off. This may be. It is clear, at least, that *ṣārāʿa͟t* is not a technical term for leprosy (Hansen's disease).

Palestine has a winter rainy season that could generate mildew. One unfortunate aspect of this fact is that we have few remnants of the writings of ancient Israel. If the Israelites had written on clay tablets, we might have had an abundance; but except for those found in the dry, hot Jordan valley, the leather and papyrus copies have perished.

Leather was used for clothing, as these verses point out (cf. Heb 11:37); but leather clothing is not often referred to in the OT, being, perhaps, the poor man's clothing. It would seem to be durable but hot and uncomfortable. As v.48 shows, leather was also used for other objects: belts (2 Kings 1:8), skins for liquids (Josh 9:4), etc. Leather was cheap and versatile but subject to decay. Linen and woolen objects likewise would mildew if stored in a damp place. Such mildew could be irritating to the lungs and certainly would be damaging to the articles. The law that declared such objects unclean was good for both hygiene and economics.

The ancient housewife could not spray the item with a disinfectant or bleach. The Lord did not instruct Moses in the biology of fungi. He did prescribe, however, practical public health measures to be administered under what Harrison (*Leviticus*, p. 140) calls the priest-physician. The article was to be shown to the priest who isolated it for seven days; then if the fungus had not spread, the article was to be washed and watched for another week. If the fungus was gone, the garment was safe to wear; if not, the spot was to be cut out or the whole article was to be burned up. If the mildew was caused by storage in a damp place, the transfer to the priests' quarters would probably fix an ordinary problem (v.50). Probably a housewife would go over stored clothes rather often to prevent such trouble and loss. If the garments were frequently inspected and aired, that alone would be a good thing. The principle of quarantine was a practical means to control mildew in clothes or houses as well as to control sickness.

Some add to these data the idea that mildew here and sickness elsewhere render a person or thing unclean because it is a type of sin. It is indeed an interesting illustration, but as Harrison (*Leviticus,* p. 152) observes, "Nowhere in the Bible is *ṣārāʿa̱t* regarded as symbolic of sin." As he further points out, the biblical symbols of sin are blindness, hardness of heart, and stiff-neckedness.

To wash the item was a logical treatment (v.54). If washing did not fix the trouble, nothing more could be done in those days—better to burn it and keep any problem from spreading (v.55). Much was left to the priests' judgment. If washing helped, cutting out the spot would cure (v.56). Then watch it again, wash it again, and the garment was safe to wear (v.58).

Verse 59 summarizes the matter of mildew only. Similar summaries for other regulations appear in 11:46–47; 14:57; and 15:32. At 13:59, Wenham (p. 203), in keeping with his opinion that hygiene is not in view in these chapters, says: "If a man looked bad, he was declared unclean. It was not that the disease as such was thought to be infectious or would result in his death, but the symptoms were incompatible with full membership of the covenant people. . . . Holiness in Leviticus is characterized by wholeness." But cripples, though they could not officiate as priests, were never called unclean—indeed, they were allowed to eat the holy food (Lev 21:22). Even defective animals, though not fit for sacrifice, were clean and fit for food (Deut 15:21–22). Evidently wholeness is not necessary for holiness.

Notes

---

48 The words שְׁתִי (*šᵉṯî*, "woven") and עֵרֶב (*ʿēreḇ*, "knitted") are only found in this section in Leviticus and nowhere else in the Bible. It is impossible to be sure of their meaning. The NIV's "knitted" for the latter word may be an anachronism, for knitting apparently was an invention of the Middle Ages. Most translate these words "warp and woof" (KJV, RSV, NASB). Wenham (p. 202) suggests the yarn of the warp and of the woof before it was used for weaving because this phrase follows mention of woven cloth (so also Keil, p. 383). Better, perhaps, is Harrison's view (*Leviticus*, p. 146), that it is a summary expression for "the totality of a woven garment."

51 The word מַמְאֶרֶת (*mam'ereṯ*, "spreading"), a Hiphil participle from מָאַר (*mā'ar*), is used only of mildew in articles and houses (Lev 13:51–52; 14:44) and of briers in Ezek 28:24

("painful"). The precise sense is not clear, but "spreading" or "dangerous" is very close. "Malignancy" (NASB) and "malignant" (RSV) may have unnecessary overtones.

55 The word פְּחֶתֶת (*p^{e}ḥeṯeṯ*, "affected") is used only here but seems clearly to be related to פַּחַת (*paḥaṯ*, "pit"). The translation "affected" is a little light. "Whether the mildew has eaten into one side or the other" is better.

E. *Cleansing From Skin Diseases*

14:1–32

[1]The LORD said to Moses, [2]"These are the regulations for the diseased
person at the time of his ceremonial cleansing, when he is brought to
the priest: [3]The priest is to go outside the camp and examine him. If the
person has been healed of his infectious skin disease, [4]the priest shall
order that two live clean birds and some cedar wood, scarlet yarn and
hyssop be brought for the one to be cleansed. [5]Then the priest shall
order that one of the birds be killed over fresh water in a clay pot. [6]He is
then to take the live bird and dip it, together with the cedar wood, the
scarlet yarn and the hyssop, into the blood of the bird that was killed
over the fresh water. [7]Seven times he shall sprinkle the one to be
cleansed of the infectious disease and pronounce him clean. Then he is
to release the live bird in the open fields.

[8]"The person to be cleansed must wash his clothes, shave off all his
hair and bathe with water; then he will be ceremonially clean. After this
he may come into the camp, but he must stay outside his tent for seven
days. [9]On the seventh day he must shave off all his hair; he must shave
his head, his beard, his eyebrows and the rest of his hair. He must wash
his clothes and bathe himself with water, and he will be clean.

[10]"On the eighth day he must bring two male lambs and one ewe lamb
a year old, each without defect, along with three-tenths of an ephah of
fine flour mixed with oil for a grain offering, and one log of oil. [11]The
priest who pronounces him clean shall present both the one to be
cleansed and his offerings before the LORD at the entrance to the Tent of
Meeting.

[12]"Then the priest is to take one of the male lambs and offer it as a
guilt offering, along with the log of oil; he shall wave them before the
LORD as a wave offering. [13]He is to slaughter the lamb in the holy place
where the sin offering and the burnt offering are slaughtered. Like the
sin offering, the guilt offering belongs to the priest; it is most holy. [14]The
priest is to take some of the blood of the guilt offering and put it on the
lobe of the right ear of the one to be cleansed, on the thumb of his right
hand and on the big toe of his right foot. [15]The priest shall then take
some of the log of oil, pour it in the palm of his own left hand, [16]dip his
right forefinger into the oil in his palm, and with his finger sprinkle some
of it before the LORD seven times. [17]The priest is to put some of the oil
remaining in his palm on the lobe of the right ear of the one to be
cleansed, on the thumb of his right hand and on the big toe of his right
foot, on top of the blood of the guilt offering. [18]The rest of the oil in his
palm the priest shall put on the head of the one to be cleansed and
make atonement for him before the LORD.

[19]"Then the priest is to sacrifice the sin offering and make atonement
for the one to be cleansed from his uncleanness. After that, the priest
shall slaughter the burnt offering [20]and offer it on the altar, together
with the grain offering, and make atonement for him, and he will be
clean.

[21]"If, however, he is poor and cannot afford these, he must take one
male lamb as a guilt offering to be waved to make atonement for him,

together with a tenth of an ephah of fine flour mixed with oil for a grain
offering, a log of oil, [22]and two doves or two young pigeons, which he
can afford, one for a sin offering and the other for a burnt offering.
[23]"On the eighth day he must bring them for his cleansing to the
priest at the entrance to the Tent of Meeting, before the LORD. [24]The
priest is to take the lamb for the guilt offering, together with the log of
oil, and wave them before the LORD as a wave offering. [25]He shall
slaughter the lamb for the guilt offering and take some of its blood and
put it on the lobe of the right ear of the one to be cleansed, on the
thumb of his right hand and on the big toe of his right foot. [26]The priest
is to pour some of the oil into the palm of his own left hand, [27]and with
his right forefinger sprinkle some of the oil from his palm seven times
before the LORD. [28]Some of the oil in his palm he is to put on the same
places he put the blood of the guilt offering—on the lobe of the right
ear of the one to be cleansed, on the thumb of his right hand and on the
big toe of his right foot. [29]The rest of the oil in his palm the priest shall
put on the head of the one to be cleansed, to make atonement for him
before the LORD. [30]Then he shall sacrifice the doves or the young
pigeons, which the person can afford, [31]one as a sin offering and the
other as a burnt offering, together with the grain offering. In this way the
priest will make atonement before the LORD on behalf of the one to be
cleansed."
[32]These are the regulations for anyone who has an infectious skin
disease and who cannot afford the regular offerings for his cleansing.

1–7 The priests were the public health officers, but they served in their priestly capacity. Israel was a holy nation, and even her cleansing from sickness was done with religious ceremony. Sickness was symbolic of sin, and even now it should not be forgotten that sickness and death are part of God's curse on the sin of Adam and his race. Therefore, cleansing the diseased person required sacrifices (cf. Luke 5:12–15).

It is difficult to see in detail the symbolism of the two live birds in vv.4–7. The ritual of cleansing a house in vv.49–53 is so similar to the cleansing of a diseased person that the latter passage may be used to explain the former. Verse 52 makes it quite explicit that the fresh water was mingled with the small amount of blood of the slaughtered bird and used in the cleansing. When the bird was killed over the fresh water, its blood dripped into the water. The wording of vv.51 and 53 on both sides of v.52 is so similar to that of vv.6–7 that we may use v.52 to interpret the action of the earlier verses to include the fresh water also in the sprinkling. The live bird was identified with the blood of the dead bird so that both penalty for and removal of sin are symbolized (cf. the ritual of the scapegoat at 16:21–28). The scarlet yarn, hyssop, and cedar wood were presumably used in the sprinkling. How, we do not know, except that hyssop is a plant that can be used like a paint brush; and the wood may have served as a handle around which to wrap the yarn. There is no warrant for de Vaux's remark (AIs, p. 463) that red was the color used to scare away demons.

8–20 The rather unusual practice of shaving was a real help in cleansing the body and showing up any remaining scabs (v.8). After seven days of semiisolation and a final bath, the man was clean and must offer his sacrifice (v.9). The order of the offerings was first a guilt offering (v.12), then a sin offering (v.13), then the burnt offering (v.19). The cereal offering was three-tenths of an ephah, indicating that one-tenth should be offered with each sacrifice. Allis (p. 147) suggests that the man was absent from tabernacle worship for a time and thus needed to give the guilt offering. It may also be that a guilt offering was due the priests for their work and trouble in his case.

The same extremities are touched with blood and oil that were consecrated with blood at a priest's ordination (Exod 29:20). The ear, thumb, and great toe stand for the whole man who is cleansed and anointed with the "log of oil" (v.15)—a little over one cup of olive oil.

21–32 As usual in the case of a necessary offering, there is provision for the poor, but the principles of the offering are maintained. Verses 24–31 are almost a duplicate of the regulations of vv.12–18 with the changes of the two doves instead of two lambs. Like many other repetitive passages in Leviticus, this illustrates the usual Hebrew style that loves duplication. The practice can be illustrated also from the poetry of Ugarit from the fourteenth century B.C. It is unfortunate that critics have sometimes used the similarity of parallel accounts to argue for different authorship of the doublet.

F. *Cleansing Houses From Mildew*

14:33–57

33 The LORD said to Moses and Aaron, 34 "When you enter the land of
Canaan, which I am giving you as your possession, and I put a spreading
mildew in a house in that land, 35 the owner of the house must go and
tell the priest, 'I have seen something that looks like mildew in my
house.' 36 The priest is to order the house to be emptied before he goes
in to examine the mildew, so that nothing in the house will be
pronounced unclean. After this the priest is to go in and inspect the
house. 37 He is to examine the mildew on the walls, and if it has greenish
or reddish depressions that appear to be deeper than the surface of the
wall, 38 the priest shall go out of the house and at the entrance close up
the house for seven days. 39 On the seventh day the priest shall return to
inspect the house. If the mildew has spread on the walls, 40 he is to order
that the contaminated stones be torn out and thrown into an unclean
place outside the town. 41 He must have all the inside walls of the house
scraped and the material that is scraped off dumped into an unclean
place outside the town. 42 Then they are to take other stones to replace
these and take new clay and plaster the house.

43 "If the mildew reappears in the house after the stones have been
torn out and the house scraped and plastered, 44 the priest is to go and
examine it and, if the mildew has spread in the house, it is a destructive
mildew; the house is unclean. 45 It must be torn down—its stones,
timbers and all the plaster—and taken out of the town to an unclean
place.

46 "Anyone who goes into the house while it is closed up will be
unclean till evening. 47 Anyone who sleeps or eats in the house must
wash his clothes.

48 "But if the priest comes to examine it and the mildew has not
spread after the house has been plastered, he shall pronounce the
house clean, because the mildew is gone. 49 To purify the house he is to
take two birds and some cedar wood, scarlet yarn and hyssop. 50 He
shall kill one of the birds over fresh water in a clay pot. 51 Then he is to
take the cedar wood, the hyssop, the scarlet yarn and the live bird, dip
them into the blood of the dead bird and the fresh water, and sprinkle
the house seven times. 52 He shall purify the house with the bird's blood,
the fresh water, the live bird, the cedar wood, the hyssop and the scarlet
yarn. 53 Then he is to release the live bird in the open fields outside the
town. In this way he will make atonement for the house, and it will be
clean."

54These are the regulations for any infectious skin disease, for an itch,
55for mildew in clothing or in a house, 56and for a swelling, a rash or a
bright spot, 57to determine when something is clean or unclean.
These are the regulations for infectious skin diseases and mildew.

33–57 As remarked above, the use of the word *ṣārāʿaṯ* for infection in houses as well as infection of skin proves that its meaning is not restricted to leprosy. In this section the translation of the NIV ("mildew") surely is preferable. Verse 34 shows that the Israelites had the expectation of being in Canaan within the year. This law of mildew in a house was obviously not for the wilderness journey. It is equally obvious, however, that God did not expect Israel to live forever in tents.

In dealing with this problem, the house was first to be emptied of furniture and materials because it was suspect and may be pronounced unclean (v.36). For all the contents to be pronounced unclean unnecessarily would be quite a loss. As would be expected in such a context, the symptoms of "greenish or reddish depressions" (v.37) are not very clear. The words for the colors are used elsewhere, but the word "depressions" (*šeqaʿarûrōṯ*) is used only here. It may mean "hollow," "crack," "spot," etc. The main thing is that it is not a surface stain.

The procedure for dealing with the mildew in the house is again isolation (v.38). If the house is emptied of its contents and the mildew continues or spreads, the affected stones must be removed and the area scraped and replastered. If the mildew persists, the house must be condemned (v.45). If the mildew is cured, the house is clean (v.48). We see once more a useful procedure for public health. A house with such mildew conditions would normally not be a healthy place to live because of dampness, allergies, etc.

The procedure for purifying the house is similar to that of cleansing persons (vv.2–7). This time it is clear that fresh water was used in the cleansing, mixed with the blood that had dripped into it. The symbolism of blood atonement and removal of defilement is maintained, but no further guilt, sin, or burnt offering was required. The problem of the house's mildew was impersonal.

G. *Uncleanness From Emissions*

15:1–33

1The LORD said to Moses and Aaron, 2"Speak to the Israelites and say
to them: 'When any man has a bodily discharge, the discharge is
unclean. 3Whether it continues flowing from his body or is blocked, it
will make him unclean. This is how his discharge will bring about
uncleanness:
4" 'Any bed the man with a discharge lies on will be unclean, and
anything he sits on will be unclean. 5Anyone who touches his bed must
wash his clothes and bathe with water, and he will be unclean till
evening. 6Whoever sits on anything that the man with a discharge sat on
must wash his clothes and bathe with water, and he will be unclean till
evening.
7" 'Whoever touches the man who has a discharge must wash his
clothes and bathe with water, and he will be unclean till evening.
8" 'If the man with the discharge spits on someone who is clean, that
person must wash his clothes and bathe with water, and he will be
unclean till evening.
9" 'Everything the man sits on when riding will be unclean, 10and
whoever touches any of the things that were under him will be unclean

till evening; whoever picks up those things must wash his clothes and bathe with water, and he will be unclean till evening.

11" 'Anyone the man with a discharge touches without rinsing his hands with water must wash his clothes and bathe with water, and he will be unclean till evening.

12" 'A clay pot that the man touches must be broken, and any wooden article is to be rinsed with water.

13" 'When a man is cleansed from his discharge, he is to count off seven days for his ceremonial cleansing; he must wash his clothes and bathe himself with fresh water, and he will be clean. 14On the eighth day he must take two doves or two young pigeons and come before the LORD to the entrance to the Tent of Meeting and give them to the priest. 15The priest is to sacrifice them, the one for a sin offering and the other for a burnt offering. In this way he will make atonement before the LORD for the man because of his discharge.

16" 'When a man has an emission of semen, he must bathe his whole body with water, and he will be unclean till evening. 17Any clothing or leather that has semen on it must be washed with water, and it will be unclean till evening. 18When a man lies with a woman and there is an emission of semen, both must bathe with water, and they will be unclean till evening.

19" 'When a woman has her regular flow of blood, the impurity of her monthly period will last seven days, and anyone who touches her will be unclean till evening.

20" 'Anything she lies on during her period will be unclean, and anything she sits on will be unclean. 21Whoever touches her bed must wash his clothes and bathe with water, and he will be unclean till evening. 22Whoever touches anything she sits on must wash his clothes and bathe with water, and he will be unclean till evening. 23Whether it is the bed or anything she was sitting on, when anyone touches it, he will be unclean till evening.

24" 'If a man lies with her and her monthly flow touches him, he will be unclean for seven days; any bed he lies on will be unclean.

25" 'When a woman has a discharge of blood for many days at a time other than her monthly period or has a discharge that continues beyond her period, she will be unclean as long as she has the discharge, just as in the days of her period. 26Any bed she lies on while her discharge continues will be unclean, as is her bed during her monthly period, and anything she sits on will be unclean, as during her period. 27Whoever touches them will be unclean; he must wash his clothes and bathe with water, and he will be unclean till evening.

28" 'When she is cleansed from her discharge, she must count off seven days, and after that she will be ceremonially clean. 29On the eighth day she must take two doves or two young pigeons and bring them to the priest at the entrance to the Tent of Meeting. 30The priest is to sacrifice one for a sin offering and the other for a burnt offering. In this way he will make atonement for her before the LORD for the uncleanness of her discharge.

31" 'You must keep the Israelites separate from things that make them unclean, so they will not die in their uncleanness for defiling my dwelling place, which is among them.' "

32These are the regulations for a man with a discharge, for anyone made unclean by an emission of semen, 33for a woman in her monthly period, for a man or a woman with a discharge, and for a man who lies with a woman who is ceremonially unclean.

Various matters are taken up in this chapter: defilement from normal sexual activity, abnormal sexual discharge, and, probably, diarrhea (cf. Deut 23:9–14). The disease of the male is considered first (vv.1–15), then normal emissions (vv.16–18), next normal female impurity (vv.19–24), and lastly abnormal female flow (vv.25–32).

1–3 BDB (p. 264) suggests that the expression "bodily discharge" (v.2), or "flow from his flesh" (*zāḇ mibbeśārô*), is an euphemism for "flow from his genital organ." There is no definite proof of this, and the word *bāśār* in the context (vv.13, 16) just means "body." The words "any man" (*'îš 'îš*, lit., "a man, a man") may indicate that the first section (vv.2–15) applies to both men and women. The question, of course, involves the nature of the "bodily discharge." This is not the normal male emission that is specifically mentioned in vv.16–18 and that involves only washing and temporary uncleanness. This discharge, like a woman's unnatural discharge of blood (vv.25–30), requires a sacrifice. It may therefore be a virulent male discharge such as in the case of gonorrhea. Or it may not be a sexual discharge at all. Diarrhea is common still in the Near East and is sometimes a symptom of many serious diseases. It is perhaps safest to say that this section is all-inclusive, and both diarrhea and any unnatural male discharge are covered.

4–12 The regulations covering the uncleanness of a person in this case are very stringent. Anything he touches is unclean, and anyone who touches anything he touches is unclean. It might be observed that these prohibitions better fit diarrhea. For instance, the scourge of cholera is very serious. It involves diarrhea and is very contagious. Venereal diseases, on the other hand, are almost always transmitted by sexual contact rather than by infected clothes, beds, chairs, etc.

13–15 Examination by the priest was not required because there were no external symptoms such as 13:1–44 mentions. A waiting period of seven days, however, was required in this case also, then a bath, and then offerings. The offerings specified are only the sin offering and burnt offering, and only doves or pigeons are required, not lambs. After all, diarrhea may sometimes be a serious symptom, but it may also be common and not at all serious.

16–18 Normal sexual activity resulted in temporary uncleanness requiring washing, but no guilt was attached and no offering required. The Bible says a good bit about sex. It heavily condemns extramarital and perverted sex. Marriage, however, is plainly said to be honorable (Heb 13:4). A Christian perhaps may not speak much of sex, not because it is shameful, but because it is intimate, wonderful, and holy when God's governing laws are followed.

19–24 Notice the emphasis on washing (vv.21–22), which is good hygiene. No offering is prescribed for cleansing after a woman's regular period. The natural result of the stipulation in v.24 is to protect a woman with cramps and some weakness from the unwelcome advances of an unfeeling husband. The penalty is not severe; the situation is probably different from 20:18, which should be compared.

25–33 The ancient law distinguishes between normal flow and abnormalities causing a discharge possibly due to disease (v.25). The net effect of the quarantine imposed would be to prevent contagion and to give the woman a real rest from housework, marital relations, and family care. A person perpetually unclean could hardly prepare the food and do the housework. Pity the poor woman of Matthew 9:20 who had been so afflicted for twelve years. She probably was not a unique case.

The offering prescribed for a woman's trouble was exactly the same as that for a man's (cf. vv.13–15, 28–30).

V. The Annual Sin Offering of the Day of Atonement

16:1–34 (cf. Lev 23:27–32; Num 29:7–11)

1 The LORD spoke to Moses after the death of the two sons of Aaron
who died when they approached the LORD. 2 The LORD said to Moses:
"Tell your brother Aaron not to come whenever he chooses into the
Most Holy Place behind the curtain in front of the atonement cover on
the ark, or else he will die, because I appear in the cloud over the
atonement cover.
3 "This is how Aaron is to enter the sanctuary area: with a young bull
for a sin offering and a ram for a burnt offering. 4 He is to put on the
sacred linen tunic, with linen undergarments next to his body; he is to
tie the linen sash around him and put on the linen turban. These are
sacred garments; so he must bathe himself with water before he puts
them on. 5 From the Israelite community he is to take two male goats for
a sin offering and a ram for a burnt offering.
6 "Aaron is to offer the bull for his own sin offering to make atonement
for himself and his household. 7 Then he is to take the two goats and
present them before the LORD at the entrance to the Tent of Meeting. 8 He
is to cast lots for the two goats—one lot for the LORD and the other for
the scapegoat. 9 Aaron shall bring the goat whose lot falls to the LORD
and sacrifice it for a sin offering. 10 But the goat chosen by lot as the
scapegoat shall be presented alive before the LORD to be used for
making atonement by sending it into the desert as a scapegoat.
11 "Aaron shall bring the bull for his own sin offering to make
atonement for himself and his household, and he is to slaughter the bull
for his own sin offering. 12 He is to take a censer full of burning coals
from the altar before the LORD and two handfuls of finely ground fragrant
incense and take them behind the curtain. 13 He is to put the incense on
the fire before the LORD, and the smoke of the incense will conceal the
atonement cover above the Testimony, so that he will not die. 14 He is to
take some of the bull's blood and with his finger sprinkle it on the front
of the atonement cover; then he shall sprinkle some of it with his finger
seven times before the atonement cover.
15 "He shall then slaughter the goat for the sin offering for the people
and take its blood behind the curtain and do with it as he did with the
bull's blood: He shall sprinkle it on the atonement cover and in front of
it. 16 In this way he will make atonement for the Most Holy Place because
of the uncleanness and rebellion of the Israelites, whatever their sins
have been. He is to do the same for the Tent of Meeting, which is among
them in the midst of their uncleanness. 17 No one is to be in the Tent of
Meeting from the time Aaron goes in to make atonement in the Most
Holy Place until he comes out, having made atonement for himself, his
household and the whole community of Israel.
18 "Then he shall come out to the altar that is before the LORD and
make atonement for it. He shall take some of the bull's blood and some
of the goat's blood and put it on all the horns of the altar. 19 He shall
sprinkle some of the blood on it with his finger seven times to cleanse it
and to consecrate it from the uncleanness of the Israelites.
20 "When Aaron has finished making atonement for the Most Holy
Place, the Tent of Meeting and the altar, he shall bring forward the live
goat. 21 He is to lay both hands on the head of the live goat and confess

over it all the wickedness and rebellion of the Israelites—all their sins—and put them on the goat's head. He shall send the goat away into the desert in the care of a man appointed for the task. 22The goat will carry on itself all their sins to a solitary place; and the man shall release it in the desert.

23"Then Aaron is to go into the Tent of Meeting and take off the linen garments he put on before he entered the Most Holy Place, and he is to leave them there. 24He shall bathe himself with water in a holy place and put on his regular garments. Then he shall come out and sacrifice the burnt offering for himself and the burnt offering for the people, to make atonement for himself and for the people. 25He shall also burn the fat of the sin offering on the altar.

26"The man who releases the goat as a scapegoat must wash his clothes and bathe himself with water; afterward he may come into the camp. 27The bull and the goat for the sin offerings, whose blood was brought into the Most Holy Place to make atonement, must be taken outside the camp; their hides, flesh and offal are to be burned up. 28The man who burns them must wash his clothes and bathe himself with water; afterward he may come into the camp.

29"This is to be a lasting ordinance for you: On the tenth day of the seventh month you must deny yourselves and not do any work—whether native-born or an alien living among you—30because on this day atonement will be made for you, to cleanse you. Then, before the LORD, you will be clean from all your sins. 31It is a sabbath of rest, and you must deny yourselves; it is a lasting ordinance. 32The priest who is anointed and ordained to succeed his father as high priest is to make atonement. He is to put on the sacred linen garments 33and make atonement for the Most Holy Place, for the Tent of Meeting and the altar, and for the priests and all the people of the community.

34"This is to be a lasting ordinance for you: Atonement is to be made once a year for all the sins of the Israelites."

And it was done, as the LORD commanded Moses.

The Day of Atonement is not mentioned in Exodus 23:14–17 and 34:18–23. Nor does it appear in Deuteronomy 16:1–16. These places mention only the three so-called pilgrimage festivals when the males of all Israel were to assemble before the tabernacle. The Day of Atonement was not such a pilgrimage festival. The ordinary Israelite remained at home, and the priests carried out the ritual. It was the only day of fasting enjoined on Israel—"you must deny yourselves [NIV mg., 'fast']" (vv.29, 31)—and was to be a special Sabbath of rest and solemnity. It was a time of special contrition, special sin offerings, and atonement. It is kept to this day by the Jews and is called Yom Kippur ("Day of Atonement"). The biblical term is plural, viz., "Day of Atonements."

This day had a special symbolism. Two goats were taken to bear the people's sins. One was killed as a sin offering; the other was sent off into the desert to bear away the sins of the people into an uninhabited place. The two goats thus symbolized both propitiation for sins by death and complete removal of the sins for which atonement was made. Many a person today who suffers from what is called a guilt complex could profit by a study of this ritual for the atonement and removal of sin. The theological expression of this glad release is in David's psalm of praise (Ps 103:12): "As far as the east is from the west,/ so far has he removed our transgressions from us" (cf. Mic 7:19). The goat sent into the desert is called in the RV and RSV "the goat of Azazel." In the KJV it is the scape (i.e., escape) goat.

Clearly the Day of Atonement was to symbolize for Israel every year the substitutionary atonement God provided for their sins and the total removal of their guilt. This major picture is somewhat obscured for Wenham (pp. 19–20) by his emphasis on the uncleanness of things being a state of abnormality that God cannot bear: "Cleanness is a state intermediate between holiness and uncleanness. Cleanness is the normal condition of most things and persons. Sanctification can elevate the clean into the holy, while pollution degrades the clean into the unclean. The unclean and the holy are two states which must never come in contact with each other."

Wenham's formulation blurs the basic dichotomy of holiness versus sinfulness. God hates sin. Uncleanness is a defilement typical of and in many cases due to sin. Wenham has it that "the main purpose of the day of atonement ceremonies is to cleanse the sanctuary from the pollution introduced into it by the unclean worshippers" (p. 228). But 16:6 says that Aaron was to sacrifice his sin offering "for" (*ba'aḏ*, lit., "on behalf of") "himself and his household." Also, he made atonement "for" (*ba'aḏ*) the people (v.24). In symbol he put the sins of the people on the head of the scapegoat (v.21) that they might be carried far away.

Aaron did indeed make atonement "for" (*'al*, "concerning"[?]) the Most Holy Place "because of" (*min*, "by reason of"[?]) the uncleanness *and* rebellion and sins of the Israelites (v.16). The sins of Israel defiled the courts of the Lord, and these sacred precincts were sprinkled with blood to cleanse them from such uncleanness (v.17). The basic problem, however, was sin; and this was atoned for by substitutionary sacrifice, a beautiful type of Christ's atoning death as Hebrews 9:7 makes clear. See further remarks at p. 526 on the idea of Wenham that cleanness is basically normalcy.

1–10 The mention of the death of the two sons of Aaron shows that chronologically this law of the Day of Atonement was not given until near the end of the stay at Sinai, which is one good reason why it is not found in Exodus. The occasion of the institution was the necessity to protect the priests in their ministry. It appears probable that Nadab and Abihu had entered the Most Holy Place. This privilege and duty was now limited to the high priest who "entered the inner room, and that only once a year, and never without blood, which he offered for himself and for the sins the people had committed in ignorance" (Heb 9:7). Christ, as Hebrews emphasizes, has entered heaven itself once for all with his own blood, "having obtained eternal redemption" (Heb 9:12).

The "Most Holy Place" behind the curtain is often called the "Holy of Holies" (KJV). It was the inner shrine where the ark was kept. The golden lid of the sacred chest, the "atonement cover" (v.2), is called the "mercy seat" in the KJV. As mentioned in the Introduction (pp. 522–23), this perhaps can better be translated "the atonement place" than the "mercy seat." The emphasis of the root *kipper* ("to cover"), from which the noun *kappōreṯ* ("atonement place") is derived, is on the atonement rather than on the mercy lying behind the atonement. In the symbolism of the tabernacle, this inner shrine was the dwelling of God; and the place above the ark was the place where he would meet with men. But the holiness of God was so awesome that for sinful man to approach him carelessly and without an atoning sacrifice could be fatal—as it was for Nadab and Abihu. Today also God cannot be approached by sinful man unless he comes through Christ's atoning blood (John 14:6).

A young bull was the sin offering specified for a priest (4:3). The sin offering was to be followed by a burnt offering. These offerings were for Aaron himself, that he might be cleansed and consecrated afresh before acting as priest for the people. Hebrews

7:27 declares that Christ had no need of this first cleansing sacrifice. Christ is the perfect Priest. Aaron was but a human type.

Some have suggested that the garments mentioned here (v.4) are unadorned and are a symbol of humiliation, typical of the humiliation of Christ. The description, however, is similar to that of the garments used for the priest as he served and are described in 8:7 and Exodus 28. The emphasis in this verse is rather on their special sacredness. It would seem that they were regular priestly garments reserved for this special occasion. The high priest would never enter the Most Holy Place without these garments.

What is the "scapegoat" (v.8)? The Hebrew word *ʿ^{a}zāʾzēl* is used in the Bible only in this chapter. In later Jewish theology the Book of Enoch uses the word as a name for one of the fallen angels, Azazel. Enoch's extensive demonology is demonstrably late (c. 200 B.C.). It often uses late Aramaic forms for names of the demons, which suggests that they were of postbiblical invention. Enoch is dependent on Leviticus 16 rather than vice versa and is no guide to the interpretation of Leviticus.

Many modern scholars insist that Azazel is a name because it is used with the preposition "for" in exact parallel to the "lot for the LORD" (v.8). This seems to press grammatical parallel too far. De Vaux (AIs, pp. 508–9) argues for this view and compares a ritual in the Babylonian New Year ceremony in which a sheep was decapitated in the temple, then carried away and thrown in a river. But there is no need to hold any relation between the Babylonian and Hebrew rituals, except that the Babylonian ritual may well also indicate that the human heart cries out for the removal of its sin. It will be remembered that one bird was let free in the ritual for cleansing a diseased person (14:7). There is no hint of demonology there or that the use of the Hebrew word "Azazel" as a proper noun is an erroneous and dangerous concession to the idea that Israel's religion shared the heathen demonology and other superstitious views of the surrounding nations.

A much simpler view is that of the KJV, followed by the NIV and NASB, going back to the LXX of 200 B.C. The first part (*ʿaz*) can mean "goat" and the last part (*ʾāzēl*) is from a verb that means "go away." Compound nouns like this are rare in ancient Hebrew, but new evidence for them is turning up in Ugaritic. It is simply the designation of the goat to be taken away, the escape goat. In Numbers 29:11 the escape goat is called "the sin offering for atonement" (see further TWOT, #1593).

11–14 The formula for the "fragrant incense" (v.12) is given in Exodus 30:34–38. It was not to be used for private perfume. It was holy. This incense was not burned on the altar of incense in the Holy Place but in the censer that Aaron was to carry into the Most Holy Place. The smoke of the incense in the dark shrine would add to the awesomeness of Aaron's work in the annual blanket atonement for Israel's sins.

The "Testimony" (v.13) was the tablets of the Ten Commandments (Exod 25:16; 31:18); thus the tent is called the tabernacle of the Testimony. The phrase "ark of the Testimony" is used eleven times in Exodus, twice in Numbers, and once in Joshua. The more usual name is the "ark of the covenant," used twice in Numbers, four times in Deuteronomy, and often in the later histories, Joshua–2 Chronicles. It is clear that the tables of the law are also called the "testimony" and the "covenant," and this is the reason also for the phrase "ark of the covenant" (2 Chron 6:11). Studies of ancient treaties draw attention to this nature of the Ten Commandments as sharing parts of the treaty form of early times (see Notes).

In this most solemn act of worship in the inner shrine (v.14), the blood sprinkled before God symbolizes the substitutionary atonement. "Without the shedding of blood there is no forgiveness" (Heb 9:22).

15–19 The same ritual is now repeated by Aaron for the people. The newly cleansed priest representatively bears the nation before God for atonement. The shrine, the whole tent, and the brazen altar must be cleansed by the sin offering because these things dwell among an unclean people (see remarks at v.2). It is clear that the ritual cleansing of the temple furniture was not due to their physical uncleanness. Rather, it stemmed from the Israelites whose sin and rebellion defiled the tabernacle when they worshiped.

20–28 Attention has already been called to this part of the ritual for sacrifice wherein the symbolism of transfer of sins is prominent (v.21; cf. 1:4 et al.). In this special case the symbolism is quite clear. The priest confesses Israel's sins over the goat, putting them on the goat, who then bears them away. Of course, this was only symbolic. The NT antitype is our union with Christ (Rom 6:5) in virtue of which "he himself bore our sins in his body on the tree" (1 Peter 2:24). The divine order set forth here is, first, sins must be dealt with; then comes worship and consecration. Aaron's own burnt offering was delayed until the sin offerings were all completed; then both Aaron's and the people's burnt offerings were acceptable. The sin offering for a priest and the sin offering for the nation were to have the carcass burned outside the camp (v.27; cf. 4:12, 21). Hebrews 13:11–12 applied this principle to the death of Christ who suffered outside the gate as a sin offering.

29–34 A series of holy days cluster in the fall in the Jewish calendar (see Notes). The phrase "deny yourselves" in vv.29, 31 probably signifies fasting (NIV mg.). It is used in conjunction with fasting in Psalm 35:13 and in parallel with fasting in Isaiah 58:3 (where in both instances it is referred to as humbling). But as the context in Isaiah 58 shows, God's injunction was not for mere external fasting but for fasting as an accompaniment of true repentance and new obedience (cf. Kaiser, *OT Theology*, p. 117). The title "high priest" (v.32) is not common in the OT, but this verse shows that a hereditary succession is in view. (On the whole matter of the high priest, see D.A. Hubbard, "Priests and Levites," NBDrev, pp. 966–72.) Notice that the conclusion to the whole chapter does not mention the cleansing of tabernacle furniture but specifies that atonement was thus "made once a year for all the sins of the Israelites" (v.34).

Notes

---

8 A. Noordtzij (*Leviticus*, Bible Students' Commentary [Grand Rapids: Zondervan, 1982], p. 162) attempts (without success) to admit the demon reference but ascribe it to antipathy to demonism. He calls Azazel "a desert demon that was capable of feeding on an animal that was laden with the sins of the entire nation of Israel." He calls the ritual an expression of contempt for Moses' contemporaries who gave offerings to desert demons. But there is no evidence for belief in such a demon Azazel in Moses' day. See further the excellent study by C.L. Feinberg, "The Scapegoat of Leviticus Sixteen," BS 115 (1958): 320–33.

13 The Greek word in the LXX ἱλαστήριον (*hilastērion*) renders the Hebrew word כַּפֹּרֶת (*kappōreṯ*, "atonement cover") and is applied to Christ in Rom 3:25 (KJV, "propitiation"). The NIV rendering in Rom 3:25 ("sacrifice of atonement") is equivalent to the more technical word "propitiation" and quite properly connects the teaching of Romans with the Hebrew name of the lid of the ark and its background of the atoning sacrifice on the great Day of Atonement (see Introduction, pp. 522–23).

Kitchen (*The Bible in Its World,* pp. 79–85) compares Exodus-Leviticus, Deuteronomy, and Joshua 24 with treaty forms of various periods and shows that their closest parallels are with fourteenth-thirteenth century types of treaties (see also Introduction, pp. 516–18).

29 The first day of the seventh month is the Feast of Trumpets, called by Jews today Rosh Hashanah. The tenth is the Day of Atonement, Yom Kippur. From the fifteenth to the twenty-first is the Feast of Booths, Sukkoth. There is a tendency at present to compare Israel's festival of Rosh Hashanah with the Babylonian New Year festival, at which time the Babylonian king was humiliated, bore the bad luck of the year, then was reenthroned amid general rejoicing. It is even said by a misuse of 2 Sam 8:18 (cf. 2 Chron 18:17) that the kings of Israel were priests and that Israel's king was considered divine! It should be noted that the rituals of these fall festivals bear no relation to the royal humiliation and reenthronement of Babylonian kings. For that matter, no known ritual in Israel really resembles the Babylonian festivals. On the Day of Atonement, it may be added, the priest bears no sin and suffers no humiliation. The sacrifices bear the sin, and the priest is merely a representative of the people in the worship. See the discussion at 23:26–32.

VI. Laws of Personal Holiness (17:1–22:33)

As mentioned in the Introduction, this section (with chs. 23–26) is called in critical circles the Holiness Code. The section is not as distinctive as some scholars imagine; but it is characterized by moral and ethical instruction (with one chapter on the annual feasts), and it does base moral obligation in the nature of God. This last point is not unique, however. The Ten Commandments are prefaced by the statement "I am the LORD your God" (Exod 20:2), and a typical "Holiness Code" phrase has already been pointed out in Leviticus 11:44.

The details of the terminology are not as impressive as the title "Holiness Code" would suggest. Actually, the expression "I am the LORD who makes you holy" or "You shall be holy, for I the LORD am holy" or variants of these are found only about ten times in these ten chapters (19:1; 20:8, 26; 21:8, 15, 23; 22:2, 9, 16, 32). Much more common (over thirty times beginning with 18:1) is the expression "I am the LORD" or "I am the LORD your God." The two types of expression are not the same. The second grounds ethical obligation in the authority, sovereignty, and proprietorship of God. Repeatedly the phrase "I am the LORD your God" is associated with his deliverance of Israel from Egypt and is a repetition of the thought of Exodus 20:2. It is not an adequate basis for the title "Holiness Code." Indeed, the setting off of chapters 17–26 as a unit is somewhat arbitrary. Chapter 17 could as easily be classed with the preceding directions for priests, and chapters 21–26 are quite diverse. The critical school has catalogued chapters 17–26 together, but they by no means call it a unit. The study by E. Sellin and G. Fohrer (*Introduction to the Old Testament,* tr. by D.E. Green [Abingdon: Nashville, 1968], pp. 117–43) supposes that the section consists of about twenty original pieces reworked then combined in various stages to make what we have now. There is not a shred of evidence in this whole argument—only the usual critical, subjective preconceptions.

Rather, it is more logical to see in the first part of Leviticus a manual of instructions for priests, both in their sacrificial and in their public health roles. The second part of the book refers more to the conduct of the general public, that is, the matters of eating blood (ch. 17), of incest (chs. 18, 20), and of personal justice and conduct (ch. 19). Then come matters for the priests, not about their ritual, but about their conduct and that of their families (chs. 21–22). These have most of the expressions emphasizing holiness. Next follow chapters addressed to Israel on feasts (ch. 23), then on the supply of oil and bread for the tabernacle (ch. 24), on the jubilee year (ch. 25), and on rewards and punishments (ch. 26).

Thus this latter section of Leviticus is of quite varied content. Its terminology fits its material and is hardly a basis for finding different authorship. One reason—a poor one—for isolating this section and calling it earlier than the balance of the book is the quotation of 18:5 in Ezekiel 20:11, 13, 21. This is no problem for the historic view of the unity and Mosaic authorship of Leviticus.

A. *One Place of Sacrifice*

17:1–9 (cf. Deut 12:1–27)

[1]The LORD said to Moses, [2]"Speak to Aaron and his sons and to all the
Israelites and say to them: 'This is what the LORD has commanded: [3]Any
Israelite who sacrifices a cow, a lamb or a goat in the camp or outside of
it [4]instead of bringing it to the entrance to the Tent of Meeting to
present it as an offering to the LORD in front of the tabernacle of the
LORD—that man shall be considered guilty of bloodshed; he has shed
blood and must be cut off from his people. [5]This is so the Israelites will
bring to the LORD the sacrifices they are now making in the open fields.
They must bring them to the priest, that is, to the LORD, at the entrance
to the Tent of Meeting and sacrifice them as fellowship offerings. [6]The
priest is to sprinkle the blood against the altar of the LORD at the
entrance to the Tent of Meeting and burn the fat as an aroma pleasing to
the LORD. [7]They must no longer offer any of their sacrifices to the goat
idols to whom they prostitute themselves. This is to be a lasting
ordinance for them and for the generations to come.'

[8]"Say to them: 'Any Israelite or any alien living among them who
offers a burnt offering or sacrifice [9]and does not bring it to the entrance
to the Tent of Meeting to sacrifice it to the LORD—that man must be cut
off from his people.

1–2 As noted above, chapter 17 does not have the expressions thought to characterize the "Holiness Code." Wenham (p. 241) aptly calls it a hinge chapter between the public and private regulations. At least it deals with the requirement for central sacrifice, as does Deuteronomy 12:1–27, and likewise forbids eating blood. These matters concerned the general public (v.2).

3–7 The KJV and the RSV use the word "kill" here in v.3; the NASB has "slaughter." There are several Hebrew words for "kill." The one used here (*šāḥaṭ*) practically always is used for killing animals for sacrifice, except that it also refers to the slaughter of people. The NIV's "Any Israelite who sacrifices" can be defended (see also TWOT, #2362). As Deuteronomy 12:15 makes plain, people could kill animals at home but not for sacrifice. Animals sacrificed elsewhere would not have God's blessing, and blood guilt would be imputed to the offerer (v.4). Wenham and others (cf. other tr.) argue that vv.3–7 forbid *any* killing of domestic animals at home. Many assume a contradiction between Leviticus and Deuteronomy. Wenham (in loc.) assumes that Deuteronomy 12:20–25 applied to Israel only after the settlement and Leviticus 17:3–7 only to the wilderness situation. The texts do not make this distinction, and it does not follow the uniform word usage of Leviticus and the most common usage of the words elsewhere. It is unnecessary to hold that *butchering* was not done at home. The alleged contradiction of Leviticus 17:3–5 and Deuteronomy 12:15 disappears if "sacrifice," the usual meaning of *zāḇaḥ*, is adopted in Leviticus 17:3–5 (see the Notes on v.3). On the "goat idols" (v.7), see the Notes.

8–9 The prohibition against sacrificing away from the central tabernacle (vv.8–9) is a repeat of the law at v.3, except that it adds mention of the major kind of sacrifice—the burnt offering. Repetition is not surprising in Hebrew; indeed, it is characteristic (see Notes). A double prohibition also is given in Deuteronomy 12:4–6 and 13–14, which is probably dependent on the earlier command in Leviticus, giving, however, a few extra details—the mention of wild animals as examples of legitimate butchering at home (v.15). Deuteronomy 14:23–26 takes up the further question of converting tithes into money if the central sanctuary is too far away to carry gifts to it.

The expression "must be cut off from his people" (v.9; cf. v.4) is not easy to identify. It usually refers to ceremonial offenses (Passover, Exod 12:15, 19; Num 9:13), uncircumcision (Gen 17:14), eating of unclean foods, or failing to be cleansed after defilement (Lev 17:4, 9, 10, 14; Num 19:13, 20 et al.). The times when it may refer to judgment on moral matters are Leviticus 18:29, where it refers to all the previous matters of incest; Numbers 15:30, the unpardonable sin; Exodus 31:14, Sabbath desecration; and Leviticus 20:3, 5–6, idolatry and spiritualism. It is hard to think that all these instances involve capital punishment—though some may. Another view is that they involve excommunication. Wenham (p. 242) may be right in saying that it involves divine rejection, which was tragic indeed, but which might be averted by repentance.

Notes

1 Much critical discussion has revolved around the subject of "one place of sacrifice" as given here and in Deut 12:1–16. Wellhausen following DeWette claimed that Israel worshiped anywhere until Josiah's reform. Then the "D document" was "discovered" in the temple and, following the instructions of Deut 12, worship was centralized. The present passage in Leviticus is in the alleged P document and shows, he thought, a developed form of the law of the central sanctuary. But there are problems with this view.

It is clear from 2 Kings 18:22 that already Hezekiah had centralized the worship in Jerusalem (even Sennacherib cited Hezekiah's activity in the matter [2 Kings 19:22]). Indeed, one can hardly imagine Solomon building his great temple to be merely one place among many shrines. It is true that Samuel, David, and also Solomon in his early days worshiped in various places; but this was because the tabernacle at Shiloh had been destroyed and the temple not yet built. Neither Deut 12 nor Lev 17 speak of Jerusalem as the place of valid worship. Actually, Jerusalem is not named in the entire Pentateuch. This would be strange indeed if Deuteronomy were written to support a program of centralizing worship at Jerusalem! Some scholars are now dating Deuteronomy at other than the usual critical date of 621 B.C. because they question whether chapter 12 is an integral part of the original book. The critical view on these matters largely rests on assumptions. Surely Deut 27:4–5 (cf. Josh 8:30–35) does not fit a reform of Josiah centralizing worship in Jerusalem.

It is an interesting exercise to read the Book of Jeremiah with the idea of discovering the theological situation of the days of Josiah and his successors who reigned over the next twenty-two years. Surely Jeremiah gives no hint that one of the problems of his day was altars to the true Lord scattered over the country instead of being centralized in Jerusalem. Jeremiah is most emphatic that Israel's sins consisted of pagan worship at the shrine of Baal, the queen of heaven, etc., in Jerusalem. The critical estimate of Josiah's reforms flies in the face of such biblical evidence as we possess—and we have practically no nonbiblical evidence.

It is far better to accept the documents as they stand, allowing the centralization of Israel's worship from Sinai on, but recognizing that there were exceptions for good reasons—and some exceptions for poor reasons.

7 The word שָׂעִיר (*śā'îr*) is identical with the word for he-goat; but as it obviously refers to idolatry, it is translated "goat idol." Some think this points to what the Greeks called satyrs—mythical creatures in half-human, half-goat form. But the LXX translation is "vanities," a name for idols, and the word is used in 2 Chron 11:15 clearly in a context of idolatry—with mention of Jeroboam's golden calves. As far as is known, satyrs were creatures of Greek mythology, not of Semitic idolatry. There is no hint that these idols were half-human. It is easiest to see here just an idol in goat form similar to the more common one in calf or bull form.

8 Where English would say, "He struck a blow," Hebrew says, "He struck a strike." The repetition in Hebrew of a verb in the infinitive absolute for emphasis is another example of the Hebrew love of repetition. The repetition involving the death of Sisera in the old poem of Judg 5 (v.27) is typical. Hebrew poetry in general is given to repetition. Far from indicating different authors or redactors, much of the repetition is just characteristic Hebrew style.

B. *The Sanctity of Blood*

17:10–16

10 " 'Any Israelite or any alien living among them who eats any blood—
I will set my face against that person who eats blood and will cut him off
from his people. 11 For the life of a creature is in the blood, and I have
given it to you to make atonement for yourselves on the altar; it is the
blood that makes atonement for one's life. 12 Therefore I say to the
Israelites, "None of you may eat blood, nor may an alien living among
you eat blood."

13 " 'Any Israelite or any alien living among you who hunts any animal
or bird that may be eaten must drain out the blood and cover it with
earth, 14 because the life of every creature is its blood. That is why I have
said to the Israelites, "You must not eat the blood of any creature,
because the life of every creature is its blood; anyone who eats it must
be cut off."

15 " 'Anyone, whether native-born or alien, who eats anything found
dead or torn by wild animals must wash his clothes and bathe with
water, and he will be unclean till evening; then he will be clean. 16 But if
he does not wash his clothes and bathe himself, he will be held
responsible.' "

10–16 The sanctity of blood is found in the fact that it stands for the life of the creature (v.11a). Blood, so obviously necessary to life, plays the major role in the sacrificial system (v.11b) and did so from the first sacrifice of Abel. God told Noah that man's blood was sacred, for it stands for the life of man made in God's image (Gen 9:4–6). That animal blood was forbidden as food further emphasizes this fact. The additional reason for its sacrificial meaning is given in the present passage (cf. Deut 12:23).

Notes

13 As this verse refers to animals of the hunt, it reinforces the idea that v.3 does not forbid killing animals for food at home or in the field. The prohibition was against *sacrificing* away from the central altar. Blood of ordinary butchering was to be disposed of by pouring it out and covering it.

15–16 Compare the similar legislation in 11:39–40

C. *Laws Against Incest*

18:1–18

1 The LORD said to Moses, 2 "Speak to the Israelites and say to them: 'I
am the LORD your God. 3 You must not do as they do in Egypt, where you
used to live, and you must not do as they do in the land of Canaan,
where I am bringing you. Do not follow their practices. 4 You must obey
my laws and be careful to follow my decrees. I am the LORD your God.
5 Keep my decrees and laws, for the man who obeys them will live by
them. I am the LORD.

6 " 'No one is to approach any close relative to have sexual relations. I am the LORD.

7 " 'Do not dishonor your father by having sexual relations with your mother. She is your mother; do not have relations with her.

8 " 'Do not have sexual relations with your father's wife; that would dishonor your father.

9 " 'Do not have sexual relations with your sister, either your father's daughter or your mother's daughter, whether she was born in the same home or elsewhere.

10 " 'Do not have sexual relations with your son's daughter or your daughter's daughter; that would dishonor you.

11 " 'Do not have sexual relations with the daughter of your father's wife, born to your father; she is your sister.

12 " 'Do not have sexual relations with your father's sister; she is your father's close relative.

13 " 'Do not have sexual relations with your mother's sister, because she is your mother's close relative.

14 " 'Do not dishonor your father's brother by approaching his wife to have sexual relations; she is your aunt.

15 " 'Do not have sexual relations with your daughter-in-law. She is your son's wife; do not have relations with her.

16 " 'Do not have sexual relations with your brother's wife; that would dishonor your brother.

17 " 'Do not have sexual relations with both a woman and her daughter. Do not have sexual relations with either her son's daughter or her daughter's daughter; they are her close relatives. That is wickedness.

18 " 'Do not take your wife's sister as a rival wife and have sexual relations with her while your wife is living.

The laws of chapter 18 and much of chapter 20 are not against indecent exposure as the KJV phrase "You shall not uncover the nakedness of" might suggest. The phrase is a euphemism for sexual relations, and the chapter forbids all such incestuous connections. Chapter 20 covers much the same ground giving the penalties for such actions. As mentioned in connection with chapter 17, the ground for these laws is found in the lordship of God (ch. 18) and his holiness (ch. 20). The Lord had brought the Israelites out of Egypt where such practices were common. In their new land they were to avoid these common sins of pagan society.

1–5 A frequent emphasis of critics is that Israel borrowed her religion from her neighbors. Doubtless some faithless Israelites did borrow, but the constant emphasis of the Law and Prophets was for Israel's faith to be kept unique (v.4). It was to be different from the practices of Egypt and Canaan (v.3). Its greatest distinction was expressed in the refrain "I am the LORD your God."

Excursus

Verse 5 is quoted three times in Ezekiel (20:11, 13, 21), once in Nehemiah (9:29), and three times in the NT (Luke 10:28; Rom 10:5; Gal 3:12). There is some difference of opinion how it should be taken. Ezekiel and Nehemiah use the verse to condemn Israel. She had violated God's ordinances and was exiled. Christ told the questioning lawyer to keep the commandments, and he would live. It is sometimes said that Christ here allowed a hypothetical salvation by works. But he then told the parable of the Good Samaritan in order to search out the lawyer's sin and bring conviction.

There are two main views of this verse and similar passages. These can only be summarized since the subject is so large. The first view, represented by the 1917 edition of the Scofield Bible, is that the OT offered salvation by law (to be fair, we must insist that in the Scofield context this meant the entire law including sacrifices), but that this has been superseded by the dispensation of pure grace. Much has been made of the Scofield footnote on page 20 (n. 1), which says that at Sinai Israel "rashly" accepted the new dispensation of law. This view sets the Pauline teaching of grace in some opposition to the OT giving of the law.

The second main view, and the common one since the Reformation, is that Paul did not oppose the OT law as such but declared that the commandments only condemn. They are not a way of salvation (except hypothetically for a perfect person), but by their impossible demands they drive the sinner to Christ. The references to "law" according to this view are mainly to the moral law. The "works of the law" (KJV) are not a way of salvation but are the results of salvation. Salvation is by grace alone in both the NT and the OT. Even here it must be said that Paul never said that the "works of the law" are good. The results of salvation are called good works or fruit of the Spirit, not "works of the law." This latter phrase is always negative.

W.C. Kaiser, Jr. ("Leviticus 18:5 and Paul: 'Do this and you Shall Live' [Eternally?]," JETS 14 [1971]: 19–28), addresses this problem, particularly the NT quotation of Lev 18:5 at Rom 10:5. He concludes that the true interpretation is that the law people live (eternally) by is a law that points to Christ, as do the verses following the quotation (Rom 10:6–7). This may be correct theology, but it is not exegetically obvious from Lev 18:5 and the NT quotations at Rom 10:5 and Gal 3:12 (which he does not discuss). In Gal 3:12 the contrast between law (quoting Lev 18:5) and faith (quoting Hab 2:4) is quite sharp. Paul says of Lev 18:5, "The law is not based on faith."

There is another possibility, which the author expects to elaborate elsewhere. Often Paul castigated the Judaizers just as Christ did the Pharisees. These Judaizers enforced the law (including the ceremonial law—circumcision, etc.) as a way of salvation and made it, Paul said, an unbearable yoke (Gal 5:1) that can justify no one (Gal 2:16). Notice that the problems addressed in Galatians, Romans, and other Pauline epistles are not merely matters of the moral law but the ceremonial law also—even especially. Evidently his opponents thought and taught that external keeping of the moral and ceremonial law—they did not distinguish—would save them. But Paul had gone that route in his former life and knew that it had not saved him.

It is possible to synthesize these many verses by saying that Paul in Gal 3:12 (et al.) is referring to the OT as the Judaizers misinterpreted it. This false interpretation of the law led to death. It could save no one but rather was a yoke of bondage. It said, "Do this and live." Paul quoted Lev 18:5 as the Judaizers used it, but he answered the misinterpretation with abundant quotations of the OT giving the true interpretation of the law. He would agree with Kaiser and most others that Lev 18:5 promises a good life here and eternal life hereafter in the whole OT context of faith in God and trust in his promises, including those given in the symbolism and typology of the sacrifices detailed in this very Book of Leviticus.

No, Lev 18:5 does not teach salvation by works. It teaches that the OT believers who trusted God and obeyed him from the heart received life abundant both here and hereafter. Actually, Paul was saying, "The Pharisees and the Judaizers teach that the law offers salvation by works, but that is a misuse of the law that cannot contradict the promise of grace" (cf. Gal 3:12, 17).

Regardless of various applications of v.5, it would seem that the things here required to be done include all the laws of God—including keeping the laws of morality and the rituals of atonement and worship in the tabernacle. Observance of these laws in an attitude of faith resulted in spiritual life and power for the godly Israelite. But, as Lev 19:17 and other verses show, the Lord required more than mere external obedience and ritual. The Lord desired a circumcised heart (Deut 30:6). Therefore it is best to take Lev 18:5 as a command to keep all God's laws by faith and thus attain a full spiritual life.

This full spiritual life of the OT saint is not just for this life. M. Dahood (*Psalms III*, AB, pp. XLII–LII) has argued that the word *ḥayyîm* in the Psalms and Proverbs should be translated "eternal life." He shows that Prov 12:28 has a close parallel in Ugaritic literature where the word "life" clearly refers to eternal life. The material is considered and reinforced by E.B. Smick (TWOT, #644; cf. also id., "The Bearing of the New Philological Data on the Subjects of Resurrection and Immorality in the Old Testament," WTJ 31 [Nov. 1968]: 12–21). This conclusion should surprise no one who gives attention to Jesus' view of the OT teaching (Matt 22:31–32) and the declaration in Heb 11:16.

The problem of finding immortality in the OT has been that, in several passages in the OT, Sheol is pictured as a shadowy, cheerless place (e.g., Ps 88:3–21), whereas in other passages the righteous are said to go there (Gen 37:35). This has led many to hold that the hope of heaven was very faint or nonexistent in the OT. This is not a necessary conclusion. The writer has argued elsewhere (TWOT, #2302c; also id., "The Meaning of the Word Sheol as Shown by Parallels in Poetic Texts," BETS 2 [Dec. 1961]: 129–35) that "Sheol" is not the place of departed spirits. It could hardly be, for both righteous and wicked go there. Rather, the word usually refers to the grave, and that is why it is said that all mankind goes there. More cannot be said here for lack of space, but it must be remembered that in the OT man began with eternal life. Sin entered into the world and death by sin, but the OT salvation would naturally be thought of as a salvation that restored man at last to his pristine state of eternal life with God.

6–18 The forbidden degrees of relationship (see comment in the introduction to this section) are father, mother, stepmother, half-sister, sister, perhaps including (as born "elsewhere") the sisters by a parent's previous marriage, the granddaughter born of either a son or a daughter, own sister, paternal aunt, maternal aunt, paternal uncle's wife, daughter-in-law (Mohammed claimed a special revelation to allow that!), sister-in-law, a woman and her daughter or daughter-in-law or her granddaughter (i.e., those by a previous marriage), and a woman and her sister while both were alive. Some of these provisions seem unnecessary because the marriage is impossible anyway (i.e., with a daughter-in-law, she being already married), but the law would be in point if the person were widowed or divorced.

Two items call for special mention: v.16, marriage with a brother's wife, and v.18, with a wife's sister. The problem with v.16 is that it seems to forbid the levirate marriage of Deuteronomy 25:5. It is usually supposed that levirate marriage was an old and acknowledged exception (Gen 38:6–11). It was in force only if the widow was childless. Was it also required only if the surviving brother was single (Deut 25:5, if brothers were living together)? As to v.18, at the very least it forbids this special case of polygamy. This does not mean that polygamy in general is approved—only that its excesses are curbed.

The reason for forbidding these relationships is probably twofold. Extensive intermarriage results in tragic abnormalities and also destroys the freedom of the family that should be able to have normal love and intimacy without sexual overtones. In a polygamous society such rules were the more necessary. And incest was common in antiquity under certain circumstances. For three generations just prior to Moses, the kings of Egypt had married their half-sisters to maintain the kingship in the royal family. The laws of incest as given in this chapter are those recognized in civilized society. Notice that marriage with first cousins is not forbidden.

Notes

---

6 Euphemisms are often used in matters of sex, birth, and death; the words לְגַלּוֹת עֶרְוָה (*l^e^gallôṯ ʿerwāh*) are doubtless a euphemism with a deeper meaning than "uncover the nakedness" (KJV), as suggested by the NIV's "have sexual relations." In v.8 the phrase is used of a man's father's wife—"that would dishonor your father." The same situation is found in 20:11, which says, "If a man sleeps with his father's wife, he has dishonored his father." Notice

Deut 27:20, 22–23, where also the euphemism is not used. Clearly the phrase in question is a euphemism for intercourse. These particular sexual relations are forbidden because, in most cases, of near relation. The laws are therefore against incest. By the side, it may be mentioned that the recognition of the meaning of this phrase may bring further light on Gen 9:22. Ham's sin may have been homosexuality.

D. *Sexual Purity*

18:19–30

19" 'Do not approach a woman to have sexual relations during the uncleanness of her monthly period.

20" 'Do not have intercourse with your neighbor's wife and defile yourself with her.

21" 'Do not give any of your children to be sacrificed to Molech, for you must not profane the name of your God. I am the LORD.

22" 'Do not lie with a man as one lies with a woman; that is detestable.

23" 'Do not have sexual relations with an animal and defile yourself with it. A woman must not present herself to an animal to have sexual relations with it; that is a perversion.

24" 'Do not defile yourselves in any of these ways, because this is how
the nations that I am going to drive out before you became defiled.
25Even the land was defiled; so I punished it for its sin, and the land
vomited out its inhabitants. 26But you must keep my decrees and my
laws. The native-born and the aliens living among you must not do any
of these detestable things, 27for all these things were done by the
people who lived in the land before you, and the land became defiled.
28And if you defile the land, it will vomit you out as it vomited out the
nations that were before you.

29" 'Everyone who does any of these detestable things—such persons
must be cut off from their people. 30Keep my requirements and do not
follow any of the detestable customs that were practiced before you
came and do not defile yourselves with them. I am the LORD your God.' "

Mostly these are further laws against sinful sexual relations. Some have been covered before. The prohibitions are (1) intercourse during menstruation (v.19; cf. 15:24); (2) adultery (v.20; cf. Exod 20:14; Deut 22:22); (3) infant sacrifice to Molech (v.21; of unwanted or illegitimate children?); (4) homosexuality (v.22); and (5) bestiality (v.23; Exod 22:19; Deut 27:21).

19 As argued at 15:24, the restriction of this verse is a general protection for a woman against an inconsiderate husband's approach. The penalty in 15:24 is a seven-day period of uncleanness. In view of that regulation, it seems that here to "be cut off from their people" (v.29) does not involve death but perhaps excommunication, perhaps divine displeasure.

20 This verse defines adultery as specifically forbidden in the seventh commandment. Other sexual aberrations are mentioned and various penalties given. Intercourse with a single girl simply required marriage (Deut 22:28–29). But violation of another man's wife broke the marriage bond and destroyed the home. Men lightly call it "cheating" today, but in God's sight it is a capital offense.

21 "Sacrificed to Molech" (*lᵉhaʿᵃḇîr lammōleḵ*) is literally "to cross over, or through, to Molech." It seems to be an abbreviation of the phrase used elsewhere (2 Kings 23:10), "to make one's child pass through the fire to Molech." On Molech see further at 20:1–8.

22 Homosexual acts are clearly denounced here as hateful to God. The penalty given at 20:13 is capital punishment. They are denounced also in Romans 1:26–27. The sin of homosexuality was well known in Canaan—witness Sodom (Gen 19:5) and Gibeah (Judg 19:22)—but it was no less wicked in God's sight. It is hard to understand how "gay churches," where homosexuality is rampant, can exist. Clearly it is possible only where people have cast off biblical authority and teaching.

23 Bestiality is likewise a perversion punishable by death (20:15–16; Exod 22:19 [18 MT]; Deut 27:21). In contrast, the gods of Ugarit, by their example, led their devotees in this sin (cf. ANET, pp. 139, 142; also Kaiser, *OT Ethics*, pp. 117–19, 195–96). So wicked a perversion of the holy sexual relationship given mankind for marriage and the home shows how deeply the human race has fallen!

24 Men forget that God judges nations when iniquity runs rampant. The Canaanites had no covenant relation to God. Yet for their excess of abominations God punished them, and the land vomited out its inhabitants. There comes a day when the patience of God runs out. Evil brings its own reward, though not immediately or infallibly in this life. But at last when the cup of iniquity is full, evil brings God's judgment. This eternal principle of justice applied also to Israel, as she found out in the days of the judges.

Notes

19 There may be, however, a question whether the situation at 15:24 is actually the same as here and at 20:18. The terms are slightly different, and the context and the penalties are considerably different. At 20:18 (not 15:24) the phrase גִּלָּה אֶת־עֶרְוָתָהּ (*gillāh 'eṯ-'erwāṯāh*, KJV, "uncover her nakedness") is used. This is obviously a euphemism for sexual intercourse in some degree and is translated by the NIV as "have sexual relations." It is also used in Ezek 16 and 23 in regard to the spiritual prostitution of Judah. It is used in Lev 18 and 20 of various incestuous connections but never of normal marital relations. It is possible that 18:19 and 20:18 refer to some kind of prostitution complicated by menstrual impurity. The penalty, as previously mentioned, is probably excommunication.

R.J. Rushdoony (*The Institutes of Biblical Law* [San Antonio, Calif.: Craig, 1973], pp. 428–29), in discussing 20:18, goes far afield. He confuses מָקוֹר (*māqôr*, "fountain"; NIV, "source [of her flow]") with עַיִן (*'ayin*, "fountain," sometimes "eye"). Then he concludes that God is our ultimate source, and therefore each person has his own private "springs"—areas inviolate to spouse, state, or other agency. This is a good bit to allege on the basis of an obscure sexual euphemism.

E. *Miscellaneous Laws* (19:1–37)

These laws of varied content show how intimately the moral and ceremonial legislation was mixed in ancient Israel. A number of these laws have parallels elsewhere (see Notes). Such parallels are cited by critics as proof of different documents. But in view of the general Semitic love of repetition, it is questionable whether these scholars are not applying our criteria of literary unity to ancient documents instead of observing Semitic criteria. In the Ugaritic poems the dream of King Keret is told three times and repetitions are the rule rather than the exception.

It is difficult to classify the laws of this chapter and perhaps unnecessary to try. Ancient law codes do not always follow the arrangement we think of as logical. After the introduction (vv.1–2), the material (vv.3–37) may be conveniently treated under nine subjects, though other arrangements are possible.

1. *Parents, Sabbaths, and idols*

19:1–4 (cf. Deut 27:15–16)

1 The LORD said to Moses, 2 "Speak to the entire assembly of Israel and say to them: 'Be holy because I, the LORD your God, am holy.

3 " 'Each of you must respect his mother and father, and you must observe my Sabbaths. I am the LORD your God.

4 " 'Do not turn to idols or make gods of cast metal for yourselves. I am the LORD your God.

1–3a Verse 2 was alluded to by Christ (Matt 5:33) and quoted in 1 Peter 1:16 (cf. Lev 11:44; 20:7). The character of God is behind all his commandments. Among the sensual and foolish deities of antiquity, no god could ground all moral duty in his divine character; only the God of Israel could. The word "respect" (*yārē'*, v.3) is frequently used of the fear of God. The principle is the same as the fifth commandment (Exod 20:12) and is stated negatively in the curse ritual at Deuteronomy 27:16.

3b References to the Sabbath occur fifteen times in Exodus, twenty-four in Leviticus, three in Numbers, three in Deuteronomy, and sixty-one times in the books that follow. The word refers to the annual feasts and the sabbatical years as well as the weekly Sabbaths. All parts of the Bible emphasize the Sabbaths. Attempts to explain away the Jewish Sabbath without reference to revelation are unsatisfactory. No other nation of antiquity observed a seven-day week. Efforts are made to derive the Sabbath from Assyrian unlucky days and from the phases of the moon, but the twenty-nine and a half days of the lunar month are not so divisible.

4 The word "cast" (*massēḵāh*) means "poured out" and refers to the casting process—an ancient invention. The proscription of idolatry is pervasive in the OT. This matter also is emphasized in the Ten Commandments and in the curse ritual at Deuteronomy 27:15. The basis for the prohibition is given *in extensu* in Deuteronomy 4:15–19. God has no form or likeness. To represent the Deity by any material object is to represent the Creator by an item of his creation—and thus to limit him. In the words of Christ, God is spirit. Again, such teaching is unique in antiquity. It has often been pointed out that in all the excavations of Palestine no idol of Israel's God has been found.

Notes

---

3 Whether the Sabbath is for Christians has been much debated. There are three main views.

1. Some say the Sabbath law is part of the moral law and must be kept today. But these (e.g., the Seventh Day Adventists) do not keep the day as the OT believers did, resting at home. And the NT emphasizes the Lord's Day, the first day of the week, as did the early church.

2. Others say that the Sabbath was wholly ceremonial and is done away in Christ. These also seem to neglect some NT data and the witness of the early church.

3. Most Christians, with varying emphases, hold that the Sabbath day, the various feasts called Sabbaths, and the sabbatical years were part of Israel's worship. However, they are based on eternal principles of rest. And they are ceremonial also in that they refer to the OT forms of worship. The spiritual significance of the OT law is kept in the NT by its setting apart of the Lord's Day. The ceremonial part of the law specifying the seventh day and certain feast days and sabbatical years is done away (cf. Gal 4:10 et al.). It should be noted that the OT ceremonies were not exactly "done away" in Christ. They were fulfilled and their principles continue to be represented in the simpler NT ceremonies.

---

2. *Fellowship offerings*

19:5–8 (cf. Deut 24:19–22; 27:18)

5 " 'When you sacrifice a fellowship offering to the LORD, sacrifice it in such a way that it will be accepted on your behalf. 6 It shall be eaten on the day you sacrifice it or on the next day; anything left over until the third day must be burned up. 7 If any of it is eaten on the third day, it is impure and will not be accepted. 8 Whoever eats it will be held responsible because he has desecrated what is holy to the LORD; that person must be cut off from his people.

5–8 This is really a rule about eating the fellowship offering. The same thing is said in more detail in 7:15–18 (q.v.). There it requires a thanksgiving fellowship offering to be eaten on the same day and allows other fellowship offerings to be eaten on the second day. That passage is a rubric for priests especially. The reason is clear. Meat quickly spoils without refrigeration. Meat that could not be eaten was to be promptly shared with others or else burned up.

3. *Help of the unfortunate*

19:9–14

9 " 'When you reap the harvest of your land, do not reap to the very edges of your field or gather the gleanings of your harvest. 10 Do not go over your vineyard a second time or pick up the grapes that have fallen. Leave them for the poor and the alien. I am the LORD your God.

11 " 'Do not steal.

" 'Do not lie.

" 'Do not deceive one another.

12 " 'Do not swear falsely by my name and so profane the name of your God. I am the LORD.

13 " 'Do not defraud your neighbor or rob him.

" 'Do not hold back the wages of a hired man overnight.

14 " 'Do not curse the deaf or put a stumbling block in front of the blind, but fear your God. I am the LORD.

9–10 These verses are almost identical with 23:22. Chapter 19 has an added phrase referring to vineyards. Deuteronomy 24:19–22 gives the same law in other words.

Deuteronomy 23:24–25 adds a further thought that a person may eat his fill in a neighbor's vineyard or field but must not carry anything away in a vessel. This last law, incidentally, is still followed among the Arabs of Palestine and, I am told, in the orchards of Germany.

11 "Steal. . . . lie. . . . deceive" are standard ethical prohibitions given in the Ten Commandments and elsewhere. In this particular setting they may have special reference to defrauding the poor. The word "another" (*'āmît*) is used only a dozen times—eleven in Leviticus and once in Zechariah 13:7. It is translated twice in the KJV as "another," once as "fellow," and nine times as "neighbor." It is handled similarly in the NIV, except "countryman" is used at 25:14–15.

12 Verse 12 probably sheds light on the third commandment, though the wording there is slightly different. To take the name of God in vain (KJV) is not merely to use it as a curse word but to invoke the name of God to support an oath that is not going to be kept. A false oath profanes the name of God as does idolatry (20:3) or violation of God's commands for worship (22:32).

13 Evidently hired servants, at least the poor, were paid daily (cf. Jesus' parable of the laborers in the vineyard, Matt 20:1–8). To keep their wages until later would work a hardship. Deuteronomy 24:15 gives the explanation that the laborer is poor and needs his pay daily.

14 To curse the deaf might have been fine sport, for they could not hear the cursing! But God would hear, and he is the Protector of the unfortunate. Likewise, such a callous attitude toward the blind—and there was much blindness in antiquity—comes under God's condemnation. Again there is a parallel to the curse ritual of Deuteronomy 27:18.

Notes

9 The reason for this law also is the lordship of our God. The Westminster Shorter Catechism says of the preface to the Ten Commandments: "Because God is the Lord and our God and Redeemer, therefore we are bound to keep all his commandments." It is not natural to let gleanings in one's field "go to waste." But Deut 24:19 promises that this kind of giving to the poor brother should be done "so that the LORD your God may bless you in all the work of your hands." The early church took good care of its poor, its widows, and its orphans. In our affluent society we feel the need less and leave it all to the government. But the church should be careful to care for its own (Gal 2:10). Kaiser (*OT Ethics*, p. 120) finds here in vv.9–18 five sections with five precepts each and each section ending with the emphatic "I am the LORD."

11 The word עָמִית (*'āmît*, "another") is presumably derived from the verb *'āmāh*, which may be a by-form of the common root *'āmam*, from which is derived the word *'am*, which means "people." It may support the idea that a special regard for the poor Israelite is expressed here.

4. *Fairness and neighborly love*

19:15–18

15 " 'Do not pervert justice; do not show partiality to the poor or favoritism to the great, but judge your neighbor fairly.
16 " 'Do not go about spreading slander among your people.
" 'Do not do anything that endangers your neighbor's life. I am the LORD.
17 " 'Do not hate your brother in your heart. Rebuke your neighbor frankly so you will not share in his guilt.
18 " 'Do not seek revenge or bear a grudge against one of your people, but love your neighbor as yourself. I am the LORD.

15 Justice is not justice unless the scales of the balance swing even. King Jehoshaphat's instruction for his judges rather closely parallels this verse (2 Chron 19:7). Deuteronomy 27:19 also treats this subject, recognizing, however, that it is usually the "alien, the fatherless or the widow" who gets the small end of justice. Nonetheless, partiality for the poor is also not justice. Nash (pp. 73–74) draws the distinction nicely between social justice, justice, and love. Exodus 23:3 parallels our verse. Exodus 23:6 shows what Nash calls "remedial justice."

16 The word "slander" (*rāḵîl*) is used also in Proverbs 11:13 and 20:19, where it is translated "gossip." The translation "slander" is preferable in each case (cf. Jer 6:28; 9:4 [3 MT]; Ezek 22:9, where slander and murder are again connected). The wording is similar in the Proverbs passages, and they may allude to the Leviticus text (see TWOT, #2165b, and the author's comment on Proverbs in WBC, p. 573, n. on 20:19).

17 This significant verse shows that the OT law did not concern itself only with outward obedience. Jesus in the Sermon on the Mount was not giving a new spiritual meaning to the law as is often supposed. It already had the spiritual meaning. He was protesting against the Pharisaic interpretation of the law that limited it to externals. (See the author's discussion on Matt 5:43 in *Inspiration and Canonicity of the Bible*, rev. ed. [Grand Rapids: Zondervan, 1969], pp. 48–56.)

18 Verse 18 is quoted often in the NT (Matt 5:43; 19:19; 22:39; Mark 12:31; Luke 10:27; Rom 13:9; Gal 5:14). From the passage in Luke, it seems that Jesus was not the first or only one to couple this verse with Deuteronomy 6:5 as the greatest commandments. The error of the lawyer who tempted Jesus was not that he did not know the law but that he did not apply it to himself. The law is plain and gives a noble teaching. As Paul says, it sums up the commandments of our duty to our fellow man. Notice that the same law is given requiring love for aliens in v.34.

The great parable on this verse is the story of the Good Samaritan (Luke 10:30–37). Its usual interpretation is that to love your neighbor is to help the unfortunate as the Good Samaritan did. This is somewhat more limited than the Levitical law that forbids revenge and anger against any "one of your people." The view of J. Gresham Machen on the parable of Luke 10 is also noteworthy (from class notes): Obviously the Good Samaritan is the hero of the story. Jesus asked who became neighbor *to the wounded man.* The obvious answer is the Samaritan. The natural teaching is, then, love the Samaritan your neighbor. And this was exactly the sin of the expert in the law. He hated Samaritans. Jesus knew this and placed his finger on the man's deep sin. He prided himself on keeping the law; yet the lawyer really did not keep it in this vital point. The parable is more against justice than specifically in favor of helping the poor.

5. *Forbidden mixtures*

19:19 (cf. Deut 22:9–11)

19 " 'Keep my decrees.
" 'Do not mate different kinds of animals.
" 'Do not plant your field with two kinds of seed.
" 'Do not wear clothing woven of two kinds of material.

19 The reason for these provisions is not clear. Allis (p. 153) argues that the first forbids the breeding of mules. But the reason is not given. The noun *behēmāh* refers to horses in only one passage (Neh 2:12–14). The term could refer to keeping pure a superior breed of cattle brought from Egypt, but details are unknown. The reference to mixed seeds or cloth is difficult to understand without more background. It might be an effort to reduce adulteration of a good product. Mixing wheat and barley would make harvest difficult because of different times of ripening. Or possibly the prohibition is against using good seed mixed with weed seed. See the discussion of mixtures in the Introduction (p. 527).

Similar laws are given in Deuteronomy 22:9–11. In Deuteronomy the clothing mixtures are specified as wool and linen. Why these should not be mixed is not clear. Flax and wool are spun differently. Whether weaving them together was difficult for people of antiquity we cannot say. Or perhaps different threads in warp and woof would cause difficulties in washing—surely they would shrink differently. They also take dyes differently.

These three prohibitions of mixtures closely parallel those in Deuteronomy 22:9–11. There the first (v.9) about mixed seeds is parallel with the second of Leviticus. The third of Deuteronomy, mixed cloth materials (v.11), is parallel with the third of Leviticus. One would expect the second of Deuteronomy ("Do not plow with an ox and a donkey yoked together," v.10) to be parallel with the first of Leviticus ("Do not mate different kinds of animals"). The trouble is that Deuteronomy seems to speak of mismatching animals, Leviticus of mismating them.

Is Leviticus, however, so clear? Different kinds of animals just do not mate. The only exception is the horse and donkey, which produce the sterile mule. The mule (*pered*) was not forbidden in Israel. Mules are mentioned seventeen times in the OT, often in a favorable context (e.g., "the king's mule," 1 Kings 1:44). This law can hardly forbid mules. Either the Leviticus law refers to keeping breeds of cattle pure, or the usual translation is faulty. I would argue the latter.

"Do not mate different kinds of animals" is the NIV rendering. The KJV, NASB, and RSV are similar. But the word "mate" is *rāba'* ("lie down"; cf. Ps 139:3). It is only used elsewhere in Leviticus 18:23 and 20:16, where it refers to bestial relations. The word is an Aramaic cognate to the common Hebrew *rābaṣ,* which many times means "to lie down to rest." Once the word is used for a donkey fallen down under a burden (Exod 23:5). It is never used for copulation.

Is it possible that the figure in Leviticus 19:19 is not sexual at all? More naturally it would forbid causing different animals to bear a load in such a way that it would be an unequal load under which they would fall. If this interpretation is adopted, the law would fit beautifully its parallel in Deuteronomy. Indeed, the LXX on Leviticus 19:19 can be read thus: "You shall not hold down your animals with an unequal yoke." The word "hold down" is rare and is translated here sexually by some, but its derivatives usually refer to "restraint" in general. The word *heterozeugos* ("unequal yoke") is used in the LXX only here and is probably alluded to by Paul in 2 Corinthians 6:14. We would suggest for Leviticus 19:19, therefore, something like, "Do not make your animals fall down with an unequal yoke."

6. *Protection of slave girls*

19:20–22

20" 'If a man sleeps with a woman who is a slave girl promised to another man but who has not been ransomed or given her freedom, there must be due punishment. Yet they are not to be put to death, because she had not been freed. 21The man, however, must bring a ram to the entrance to the Tent of Meeting for a guilt offering to the LORD. 22With the ram of the guilt offering the priest is to make atonement for him before the LORD for the sin he has committed, and his sin will be forgiven.

20–22 The expression "due punishment" (*biqqōreṯ,* v.20) is troublesome. The KJV reads "she shall be scourged." Speiser (pp. 128–31) has clarified the matter remarkably by comparison with Mesopotamian law. He reconstructs the situation thus: a slave woman is *betrothed* to a man, i.e., is assigned in advance, but not yet given her freedom (the man presumably was a free man); and then a different man sleeps with her. In such a case normally the penalty was death. But the slave girl was presumed to be not free to resist or not so guarded by a father. So the penalty was not death, but she is not marriageable to the original man. Therefore, the original suitor must be reimbursed; the damages would be a fine (NIV, "due punishment") paid to the original suitor or slave owner. Then the moral offense would be dealt with by the sacrifice, and presumably the slave girl, after being freed, would be married to the second man (vv.21–22). Here again (cf. 5:15–16) Speiser (ibid.) calls attention to the great antiquity of the legislation.

7. *Fallow fruit trees*

19:23–25

23" 'When you enter the land and plant any kind of fruit tree, regard its fruit as forbidden. For three years you are to consider it forbidden; it must not be eaten. 24In the fourth year all its fruit will be holy, an offering of praise to the LORD. 25But in the fifth year you may eat its fruit. In this way your harvest will be increased. I am the LORD your God.

23–25 The common fruit trees of Palestine were the olive, fig, and date palm. The details of Israelite horticulture are unknown. Does this verse mean that fruit may be eaten in the fifth year of the tree or in the fifth year of its fruit bearing? Probably the latter. Olives are slow-growing trees. Date palms reach full maturity in thirty years but last for nearly two hundred years. The main idea, probably, is that the first three crops are light and that the firstfruits given to the Lord should be a good crop such as would be borne in the fourth year.

8. *Against heathen practices*

19:26–31 (cf. Exod 22:18; Deut 18:9–13)

26 " 'Do not eat any meat with the blood still in it.
" 'Do not practice divination or sorcery.
27 " 'Do not cut the hair at the sides of your head or clip off the edges of your beard.
28 " 'Do not cut your bodies for the dead or put tattoo marks on yourselves. I am the LORD.
29 " 'Do not degrade your daughter by making her a prostitute, or the land will turn to prostitution and be filled with wickedness.
30 " 'Observe my Sabbaths and have reverence for my sanctuary. I am the LORD.
31 " 'Do not turn to mediums or seek out spiritists, for you will be defiled by them. I am the LORD your God.

26 The emphasis and frequent prohibition of blood suggests that in this context (v.26) eating blood or the flesh with the blood was a common heathen practice. Albright (*Yahweh,* pp. 131–32) quotes a Ugaritic text in which the goddess Anat drank the blood of her brother Baal.

The words for practicing divination and sorcery (*nāḥaš* and *'ānan*—see TWOT, ##1348, 1656) and other words sometimes used all involved heathen worship. To engage in such practices, therefore, was a capital offense (see comment on v.31; cf. Exod 22:18; Deut 18:9–13). The errors of the English and the New England witch trials were multiple. The definition of witchery was wrong, the court procedure—exhorting confession by torture—was poor, and, in any case, the state should have been kept separate from the church so that there would not have been civil trials for religious offenses. But in ancient Israel as a theocracy, false religion was not to be tolerated. Those who apostatized were free to leave. But those who were Israelites remained bound to Israel's religion.

The difference between Israel as a theocracy and the church-states of the Middle Ages and later was that God promised his Holy Spirit and grace to Israel in a special way and demanded a special response. Today in a worldwide pluralistic situation, he has purposed for weeds and wheat to grow together in the world (Matt 13:37–43). The church today, like the nation of Israel, is supposed to be a community of believers in the midst of a godless world.

27–28 There was nothing morally wrong with cutting the hair or the beard or with tatooing. But these practices then, and also now in some places, were parts of heathen ritual. The translation is doubtless correct in understanding the word *nep̱eš* as a corpse (NIV, "dead"). It is so used elsewhere (21:1, 11).

29 Probably in the context to degrade a daughter by making her a prostitute means to make her a religious harlot, a devotee of a heathen shrine (v.29).

30 The command to "observe my Sabbaths" (v.30) is identical with 26:2 (q.v.).

31 "Mediums" (*'ōḇōṯ*; cf. TWOT, #37a) and "spiritists" (*yidd^e'ōnîm*; cf. TWOT, #848d) were common and very degrading in the surrounding religions (see comment on v.26).

9. *Protection for the old, the stranger, and the poor*

19:32–37 (cf. Deut 25:13–26)

> 32 " 'Rise in the presence of the aged, show respect for the elderly and revere your God. I am the LORD.
> 33 " 'When an alien lives with you in your land, do not mistreat him. 34 The alien living with you must be treated as one of your native-born. Love him as yourself, for you were aliens in Egypt. I am the LORD your God.
> 35 " 'Do not use dishonest standards when measuring length, weight or quantity. 36 Use honest scales and honest weights, an honest ephah and an honest hin. I am the LORD your God, who brought you out of Egypt.
> 37 " 'Keep all my decrees and all my laws and follow them. I am the LORD.' "

32–34 Verse 32 seems to be unique in the Pentateuch, though it is implied in the fifth commandment that honor be given to parents. Proverbs 20:29 and 16:31 give similar thoughts. Verse 34 is a complement to v.18. The neighbor is not to be treated differently from the alien. Both are to be loved as ourselves because God is the LORD who loved Israel when she was a stranger in Egypt and who loved us while we were yet sinners. The lawyer who asked Christ, "Who is my neighbor?" did not need to ask the question.

35–37 There are more ways to steal than by thievery (vv.35–36). And the poor are usually the defenseless ones who suffer most. The emphasis on just weights and measures is given again in Deuteronomy 25:13–16 and finds an echo in Proverbs 11:1; 16:11; 20:10, 23. Without a central bureau of weights and measures, it was all too easy to cheat the poor. Exodus 30:13, 24 et al. show that the priests served to some extent as such a bureau of weights and measures. In Egypt we find examples of a "royal cubit." There the king established the standard. Genesis 23:16 appeals to common, well-known standards. God here reminds them of his constant presence and concern: "Keep . . . all my laws . . . I am the LORD."

F. *Punishments for Various Sins (20:1–27)*

1. *Against the Molech cult*

20:1–5

> 1 The LORD said to Moses, 2 "Say to the Israelites: 'Any Israelite or any alien living in Israel who gives any of his children to Molech must be put to death. The people of the community are to stone him. 3 I will set my face against that man and I will cut him off from his people; for by giving his children to Molech, he has defiled my sanctuary and profaned my holy name. 4 If the people of the community close their eyes when that man gives one of his children to Molech and they fail to put him to death, 5 I will set my face against that man and his family and will cut off from their people both him and all who follow him in prostituting themselves to Molech.

1–5 The giving of children to Molech seems clearly to be human sacrifice and is strictly forbidden. It is mentioned in the OT in 2 Kings 23:10; Jeremiah 32:35 (in the days of Josiah and Jeremiah); and 1 Kings 11:7 (which, however, may be *Milcom* as in v.5 [cf. NIV mg.]). In the past it was supposed that the name was a false vocalization for *meleḵ* ("king"), i.e., a divine king-idol, and that the consonants were mixed with the vowels for "shameful thing," which were written in by a later pious Jewish scribe. The deity Molech was equated with *Melkar* ("Melech of the city"), a deity of Tyre. The cult came into northern Israel in force with Queen Jezebel.

Evidently the sacrifice of children was a dreadful reality among Israel's neighbors and a danger to Israel herself. Albright's argument (see Notes) may be correct that the verses in Leviticus refer to burning children in *mōleḵ* sacrifices rather than in sacrifice to a deity Molech. The net result, of course, is similar. Notice that a bystander is also guilty if he fails to inform on a neighbor performing this monstrous sacrifice (v.4).

Notes

2 Albright (*Yahweh*, pp. 234–44), following the work of Eissfeldt and others, claims that there is a reference to מֹלֶךְ (*mōleḵ*) sacrifice in a Ugaritic text, and he finds allusion to it in Amos 2:1 (reading the line "king of Edom" with different vowels as "*mōleḵ* of men"). He argues that a *mōleḵ* sacrifice has no relation to a deity Molech or Melek but refers to a kingly sacrifice (considering *mōleḵ* as an abstract noun from *meleḵ*), i.e., the highest type of sacrifice, a human sacrifice. Such human sacrifices are mentioned elsewhere in the Bible (2 Kings 3:27; 17:31; 23:10; Ps 106:37; Jer 7:31; 19:5). Jeremiah 19:5 speaks of burning children in sacrifice to Baal, not to Molech, which would strengthen Albright's argument. Excavations in Carthage, a daughter city of Phoenicia, show "Tophet pits" and burial urns of cremated children.

If Albright is correct that a human sacrifice is considered the most heroic and most effective, what is wrong with it? Three things: first, it is to a false god; second, it is a horrible example of misplaced heroism—it doesn't work; third (and Abraham had to learn this), no mere man is good enough to be a sacrifice for others—not Moses (Exod 32:32) or Micah (Mic 6:7) or Isaac (Gen 22:8) (see the Introduction, p. 524).

2. *Various sexual sins*

20:6–21 (cf. Exod 21:17; 22:19; Deut 22:30; 27:20)

6 " 'I will set my face against the person who turns to mediums and
spiritists to prostitute himself by following them, and I will cut him off
from his people.

7 " 'Consecrate yourselves and be holy, because I am the LORD your
God. 8 Keep my decrees and follow them. I am the LORD, who makes you
holy.

9 " 'If anyone curses his father or mother, he must be put to death. He
has cursed his father or his mother, and his blood will be on his own
head.

10 " 'If a man commits adultery with another man's wife—with the wife
of his neighbor—both the adulterer and the adulteress must be put to
death.

11 " 'If a man sleeps with his father's wife, he has dishonored his
father. Both the man and the woman must be put to death; their blood
will be on their own heads.

12" 'If a man sleeps with his daughter-in-law, both of them must be put to death. What they have done is a perversion; their blood will be on their own heads.

13" 'If a man lies with a man as one lies with a woman, both of them have done what is detestable. They must be put to death; their blood will be on their own heads.

14" 'If a man marries both a woman and her mother, it is wicked. Both he and they must be burned in the fire, so that no wickedness will be among you.

15" 'If a man has sexual relations with an animal, he must be put to death, and you must kill the animal.

16" 'If a woman approaches an animal to have sexual relations with it, kill both the woman and the animal. They must be put to death; their blood will be on their own heads.

17" 'If a man marries his sister, the daughter of either his father or his mother, and they have sexual relations, it is a disgrace. They must be cut off before the eyes of their people. He has dishonored his sister and will be held responsible.

18" 'If a man lies with a woman during her monthly period and has sexual relations with her, he has exposed the source of her flow, and she has also uncovered it. Both of them must be cut off from their people.

19" 'Do not have sexual relations with the sister of either your mother or your father, for that would dishonor a close relative; both of you would be held responsible.

20" 'If a man sleeps with his aunt, he has dishonored his uncle. They will be held responsible; they will die childless.

21" 'If a man marries his brother's wife, it is an act of impurity; he has dishonored his brother. They will be childless.

The section, in addition to repeating much that is given in chapter 18, specifies the penalties for the various forms of incest and perversion. The form of the laws in this section is what Alt would call "case law or casuistic law" rather than "apodictic law" such as appears in chapter 18 (see Introduction, pp. 514–15).

6 "Mediums and spiritists" are the same evil pair mentioned in 19:31; 20:27; and elsewhere. Verse 27 implies that the persons are inhabited by these evil spirits: *yihyeh b̲āhem* '*ôb̲* (lit., "in whom shall be a medium"). Isaiah 8:19 and the report of the witch of Endor (1 Sam 28:3–11) show that these people claimed contact with the dead. Of course, this was common in the heathen religions. For the author's view of demon possession, see "One View of Demon Possession" (*His* 35 [Mar. 1975]: 9–10).

7–8 Following the call to consecration (v.7), v.8 nicely associates the ideas of human responsibility—"Keep my decrees"—and divine grace—"I am the LORD, who makes you holy."

9 This verse is quoted in Matthew 15:4 and Mark 7:10. Cursing one's parents was a capital offense (so also in Exod 21:17; cf. Prov 20:20). Also, striking one's parents was a capital crime (Exod 21:15); and a "stubborn and rebellious son," "a profligate and a drunkard," was to be stoned (Deut 21:18–21). This appears to be very severe punishment. What parent would wish to have his son stoned to death for being "stubborn and rebellious"? It is probable that there is more to these verses than meets the eye.

In any language there are words relating to sin that gather a connotation with usage.

In colloquial English a "square" is not a four-sided man; a "loose woman" is a woman loose in morals, etc. So in ancient Hebrew the connotation of to "curse" father and mother or to be "stubborn and rebellious" is of importance in understanding the passages. Unfortunately, after the lapse of so many centuries, the connotation of the words is hard to discover. In such a case it is wise to be guided by the context and general situation.

The phrase "stubborn and rebellious" is applied to wayward sons in Deuteronomy 21:18. It is applied to Israel's apostasy from God in Psalm 78:8 and Jeremiah 5:23. From this we may surmise that the connotation of the phrases included apostasy and idolatry. As to the duty of parents to accuse such a son, the implication is that parents should not shield even their own children who descend to apostasy and black magic (cf. Deut 13:6–11).

Likewise, cursing father and mother here surely does not refer to the angry response that a child might give in a fit of temper. The word is widely used. It includes blaspheming the name of God (24:11–16). Shimei cursed David in open rebellion (2 Sam 16:5–13). Gaal, the son of Ebed, cursed Abimelech (Judg 9:27). Cursing in ancient times sometimes involved a malevolent operation of magic against the person cursed. The modern equivalent is to put a hex on someone. It could thus include an appeal to false religion. Such cursing of parents (or anyone in authority, Exod 22:28), if it were a determined and aggravated offense, was punishable by death. The place of this sin at the head of a list of sexual crimes may or may not be significant; we do not know. Many times the laws recorded in the Pentateuch are not according to a system we would expect. It may be that the law has closer affinity with the law forbidding "mediums and spiritists" in v.6.

In vv.9–16 death is specified as the penalty. The method of execution was usually by stoning. This was the penalty for idolatry (Deut 13:10; 17:5; Lev 20:2, 27), adultery (Deut 22:21, 24), blasphemy (Lev 24:13–16), profligacy (Deut 21:21), and Sabbath breaking (Num 15:35). Often the method of execution is not named. Burning (v.14; Gen 38:24) was apparently rare.

10 On v.10 compare 18:20. The law of Israel took very seriously the sacredness of marriage. Both parties who broke that bond were judged guilty of death. In Deuteronomy this law is put in connection with the one in Exodus 22:16–17 on forcible rape of a betrothed or married woman. In such a case only the man was guilty and had to die.

11–12 On these verses compare 18:8, 15 (cf. also Exod 22:19; Deut 22:30; 27:20). These more serious cases of incest received the death penalty. At first glance it seems that adultery would also be involved, and it may have been. More likely this refers to marriage after the death of the woman's husband.

13 On this verse compare 18:22. Homosexuality was quite common among the Greeks of a later time. The Bible is quite emphatic that it is a serious sin. Here the death penalty is specified. The NT condemns homosexual acts as shameless perversion (Rom 1:27). Notice that the legal format is apodictic in chapter 18 and casuistic here.

14 On v.14 compare 18:17. The Hebrew phrasing shows that marriage is under consideration, and this would be impossible with a wife and her mother unless the mother were widowed or divorced. Theoretically in a polygamous society such a marriage would be possible, but it was strictly forbidden as was also marriage with two sisters (18:18). As mentioned above, the reason for such prohibitions is reinforced by the necessity to keep the areas of family love and affection among children in the house from the overtones of possible sexual attraction that could lead to incest and weird promiscuity.

"Burned in the fire" is a peculiar provision. The method of execution is mentioned only two other times (Gen 38:24; Lev 21:9). In both cases it is punishment of especially grave harlotry. Evidently this type of incest was regarded as especially reprehensible.

15–16 Bestiality is mentioned also in 18:23. There it is forbidden; here it has the death penalty attached. Also in Exodus 22:19 it is listed among capital offenses; and in Deuteronomy 27:21 it is included among the curses at Mount Ebal. The stories of the gods and goddesses of Ugarit frequently exhibit such practices. Israel's pagan neighbors probably followed their gods in these revolting practices.

17 On this verse compare 18:9. This incest with a full or half-sister was forbidden but apparently did not receive the death penalty.

18 The prohibition of intercourse during menstruation was given earlier (15:19; 18:19). See the discussion on 18:19. It seems probable that here the phrase "cut off from their people" does not refer to execution.

19–21 These verses cite various cases of incest, all of which were covered in chapter 18. The penalties here added are minor and apparently are to be executed by divine providence. "They will be held responsible" (vv.19–20). "They will be childless" (v.21). Interestingly, v.21 was appealed to by Henry VIII of England in his divorce of Catherine, his first wife. She had been married to Henry's older brother who had died while still quite young. Catherine declared that the first marriage had not been consummated, but Henry's marriage produced no heir; so he went ahead with the famous divorce that had such far-reaching consequences for the church in England and for the royal succession. See the discussion of levirate marriage on 18:16.

3. *Exhortations to holiness*

20:22–27

22" 'Keep all my decrees and laws and follow them, so that the land where I am bringing you to live may not vomit you out. 23You must not live according to the customs of the nations I am going to drive out before you. Because they did all these things, I abhorred them. 24But I said to you, "You will possess their land; I will give it to you as an inheritance, a land flowing with milk and honey." I am the LORD your God, who has set you apart from the nations.

25" 'You must therefore make a distinction between clean and unclean animals and between unclean and clean birds. Do not defile yourselves by any animal or bird or anything that moves along the ground—those which I have set apart as unclean for you. 26You are to be holy to me because I, the LORD, am holy, and I have set you apart from the nations to be my own.

27" 'A man or woman who is a medium or spiritist among you must be
put to death. You are to stone them; their blood will be on their own
heads.' "

The strong emphasis on holiness in these verses and this whole section of Leviticus is noteworthy. In the midst of an immoral age and in an era of false religion, the demands of Israel's God stood out in bright light.

22–23 To dwell securely in the Promised Land, it was necessary for the Israelites to shun "the customs of the nations" (v.23). The word for "customs" is literally "statutes" (*ḥuqqōṯ*). The morals and worship of the surrounding nations were low. Therefore, the Lord required Israel to be separated and different from the nations. He had cast out the Canaanites because they did all "these things," i.e., the incest, perversions, and immoralities referred to in the previous chapters. Israel was to be holy because the Lord is holy (v.26).

24 The expression "flowing with milk and honey" is used fourteen times in the Pentateuch and five times in the rest of the OT. It is, of course, symbolic of the agricultural plenty of Palestine. Palestine today is far from attractive, agriculturally speaking; the rainfall is seasonal, and the summers are dry. It is probable that a similar climate obtained in Moses' day, though the subject is debated. A little more rain would have made a great difference. At present Palestine is deforested and badly eroded. Even if the climate was similar in ancient days, a cover of trees would have better conserved the winter rains; and careful irrigation would have made the hills and western slopes of the mountains quite productive. The mention of honey is perhaps lost to modern ears. To us honey is a dispensable condiment. Then it was the only sweetner at hand.

25–26 In the midst of moral prescriptions and warnings on false religion, there is an emphasis again on the laws of cleanness (v.25). There is here a reminder that all God's laws for Israel were intertwined and all had a religious sanction. It is convenient to divide the laws into moral, ceremonial, and civil; but the Bible itself makes no such distinction. They were all God's laws and were given in wisdom for the regulation of the life and worship of his people. For the principles involved, see the Introduction: Laws of Cleanness, and the comments on chapter 11.

27 The two words "medium" and "spiritist" usually go together (see v.6). In the Pentateuch they are forbidden in Leviticus 19:26, 31; 20:6, here; and in Deuteronomy 18:11. The latter verse is the inclusive one and should be compared for discussion of the terms. Only in the present verse is the penalty assigned. Since all such practices involved pagan worship, the penalty naturally was death. See further on 19:26.

G. *Special Holiness for Priests*

21:1–22:16

1The LORD said to Moses, "Speak to the priests, the sons of Aaron, and
say to them: 'A priest must not make himself ceremonially unclean for
any of his people who die, 2except for a close relative, such as his
mother or father, his son or daughter, his brother, 3or an unmarried
sister who is dependent on him since she has no husband—for her he

may make himself unclean. 4 He must not make himself unclean for
people related to him by marriage, and so defile himself.
5 " 'Priests must not shave their heads or shave off the edges of their
beards or cut their bodies. 6 They must be holy to their God and must not
profane the name of their God. Because they present the offerings made
to the LORD by fire, the food of their God, they are to be holy.
7 " 'They must not marry women defiled by prostitution or divorced
from their husbands, because priests are holy to their God. 8 Regard
them as holy, because they offer up the food of your God. Consider
them holy, because I the LORD, who makes you holy, am holy.
9 " 'If a priest's daughter defiles herself by becoming a prostitute, she
disgraces her father; she must be burned in the fire.
10 " 'The high priest, the one among his brothers who has had the
anointing oil poured on his head and who has been ordained to wear
the priestly garments, must not let his hair become unkempt or tear his
clothes. 11 He must not enter a place where there is a dead body. He
must not make himself unclean, even for his father or mother, 12 nor
leave the sanctuary of his God or desecrate it, because he has been
dedicated by the anointing oil of his God. I am the LORD.
13 " 'The woman he marries must be a virgin. 14 He must not marry a
widow, a divorced woman, or a woman defiled by prostitution, but only
a virgin from his own people, 15 so he will not defile his offspring among
his people. I am the LORD, who makes him holy.' "
16 The LORD said to Moses, 17 "Say to Aaron: 'For the generations to
come none of your descendants who has a defect may come near to
offer the food of his God. 18 No man who has any defect may come near:
no man who is blind or lame, disfigured or deformed; 19 no man with a
crippled foot or hand, 20 or who is hunchbacked or dwarfed, or who has
any eye defect, or who has festering or running sores or damaged
testicles. 21 No descendant of Aaron the priest who has any defect is to
come near to present the offerings made to the LORD by fire. He has a
defect; he must not come near to offer the food of his God. 22 He may eat
the most holy food of his God, as well as the holy food; 23 yet because of
his defect, he must not go near the curtain or approach the altar, and so
desecrate my sanctuary. I am the LORD, who makes them holy.' "
24 So Moses told this to Aaron and his sons and to all the Israelites.
22:1 The LORD said to Moses, 2 "Tell Aaron and his sons to treat with
respect the sacred offerings the Israelites consecrate to me, so they will
not profane my holy name. I am the LORD.
3 "Say to them: 'For the generations to come, if any of your
descendants is ceremonially unclean and yet comes near the sacred
offerings that the Israelites consecrate to the LORD, that person must be
cut off from my presence. I am the LORD.
4 " 'If a descendant of Aaron has an infectious skin disease or a bodily
discharge, he may not eat the sacred offerings until he is cleansed. He
will also be unclean if he touches something defiled by a corpse or by
anyone who has an emission of semen, 5 or if he touches any crawling
thing that makes him unclean, or any person who makes him unclean,
whatever the uncleanness may be. 6 The one who touches any such
thing will be unclean till evening. He must not eat any of the sacred
offerings unless he has bathed himself with water. 7 When the sun goes
down, he will be clean, and after that he may eat the sacred offerings,
for they are his food. 8 He must not eat anything found dead or torn by
wild animals, and so become unclean through it. I am the LORD.
9 " 'The priests are to keep my requirements so that they do not
become guilty and die for treating them with contempt. I am the LORD,
who makes them holy.
10 " 'No one outside a priest's family may eat the sacred offering, nor
may the guest of a priest or his hired worker eat it. 11 But if a priest buys

a slave with money, or if a slave is born in his household, that slave may eat his food. [12]If a priest's daughter marries anyone other than a priest, she may not eat any of the sacred contributions. [13]But if a priest's daughter becomes a widow or is divorced, yet has no children, and she returns to live in her father's house as in her youth, she may eat of her father's food. No unauthorized person, however, may eat any of it.

[14]" 'If anyone eats a sacred offering by mistake, he must make restitution to the priest for the offering and add a fifth of the value to it. [15]The priests must not desecrate the sacred offerings the Israelites present to the LORD [16]by allowing them to eat the sacred offerings and so bring upon them guilt requiring payment. I am the LORD, who makes them holy.' "

The thrust of this section is twofold: the office of a priest is holy, and the office is above the man. A priest must be holy in body, upright in conduct, and ceremonially clean; for he is the representative of God. The OT priest was a type of Christ. We see this from the priest's work of mediation, which was nevertheless not perfect or final (cf. Heb 9). We see this also from the priest's official character: he was to be cleansed and more holy than other men. His perfection pointed to a perfect priesthood. We see the priesthood as a type of Christ especially from the references to a Melchizedekian priesthood in Psalm 110 and to a king-priest to come mentioned in Psalm 110 and Zechariah 6:11–14.

1–4 To touch a dead body brought uncleanness for seven days (Num 19:11). The prohibitions in this chapter include more than just touching the dead body of a friend. They also refer to visible signs of mourning. Aaron was not to tear his clothes in mourning even for his two sons (10:6). The case there, however, was somewhat different; for they had died under the judgment of God, and Aaron was the high priest (cf. v.11). The verses here allow mourning by an ordinary priest for death in the immediate family. Ezekiel 44:25 gives the same law for the Restoration temple. The description of Ezekiel is thought by many (including the author) to refer to the millennial period. In any case that future period is described in terms of the OT economy.

Curiously, the priest's wife is omitted in vv.2–3! Surely this omission is insignificant, and the wife is implied (see Notes on v.4). The Hebrew word "relative" (*šᵉʾēr*) means flesh-and-blood kin, and the degree of this relationship is here specified.

5–6 The practices of self-disfigurement (v.5) were forbidden all Israelites (19:27–28). They were apparently heathen signs of grief. What heathen superstition or religion they implied, we can only guess. At least they were forbidden to Israel and especially to Israel's priests. In the Ugaritic story of Baal and Anat, the god Baal is killed and the other gods, his friends, cut their cheeks and chins and lacerate their forearms, chests, and backs (ANET, p. 139, vi.).

7–8 One special reason for the prohibition in v.7 is that there should be no question of paternity about the next generation of priests. For the same reason the high priest must marry a "virgin from his own people" (v.14). Josephus (Antiq. XIII, 291–92 [x.5]) tells of a high priest in the Hasmonean house who was accused of doubtful paternity because his mother had been a slave (and therefore not able to resist illegitimate union).

9 On "burned in the fire," see the remarks on 20:14. As the priest is to be holy, his family also is to be holy. Sin is more heinous on the part of those chosen by God for special service.

10–15 The phrase "the anointing oil poured on his head" (v.10) designates the high priest and his sons who were called to a special sanctity of service. The anointing is commanded for Aaron in Exodus 30:30, and the anointing of Aaron as high priest is recorded at Leviticus 8:12. There are not many references to the high priest (Heb.: "great priest") in the OT; Aaron is called simply "the priest" (Exod 31:10; Num 25:11), as well as "chief priest" (or "high priest"; Num 35:25, 28).

In v.10 and at Numbers 35:25, the phrase "high priest" is explained as the anointed priest, which is the term used in Leviticus 4:3, 5; 6:22, and 16:32. The latter verse further qualifies this anointed priest as the high priest. In Numbers 20:28 and Deuteronomy 10:6, the high priesthood is transferred from Aaron to his son Eleazer and in Numbers 25:11 to Phinehas. Deuteronomy 26:3 refers to the "priest in office." Outside the Pentateuch the office is referred to using various terms; and prominent men like Eli, Jehoiada, and Hilkiah occupied it. The office gathered importance after the Exile, when the high priest eventually assumed governmental functions. Some critics have doubted that the high priesthood was ancient, but to do so they have had to treat the references to Aaron and his office with unwarranted selectivity (cf. discussion in Archer, SOTIrev., pp. 157–59).

The curious provision that the priest must not "leave the sanctuary" (v.12) is not clear. There were no living quarters in the tabernacle or its court. Actually the phrase is more general. It forbids the high priest from going away from the tabernacle on any business. It was a twenty-four hour job! Numbers 3:38 says that Moses, Aaron, and his sons should encamp in front of the tabernacle to the east. After the temple was built, the officiating priests lived in the rooms built in three stories against the outside walls of the temple.

As explained above, a priest's children also were to be holy and above reproach (v.15). If the high priest married only a virgin from his own people, the legitimacy of his successor to the holy office could not be questioned.

16–24 It is difficult to translate some of the terms of these verses with certainty, but it is clear that the priest was to be physically perfect (v.17). This is an understandable provision for priests who stood in a public relation; but as remarked earlier, it carries out the typology of Christ the perfect Priest.

Blindness (v.18) was common in antiquity. With improper setting of broken bones as well as no way to correct birth defects, lameness was also common. The word *ḥāram* is used only here and is uncertain. It may be related to a word for "network," but this would only suggest "disfigured" (NIV; KJV, "a flat nose") The Greek LXX translated it "stumpnosed"—perhaps referring to the disfigurement of a hare lip. Similarly the word *śārûaʿ* ("deformed") is used only two other times (22:23; Isa 28:20 ["to stretch out"]) and may refer to an extralong arm or leg, but this is quite rare. The LXX has "his ears cut off," which is a famous interpretation. Josephus (Antiq. XIV, 366 [xiii.10]) informs us that when the high priest Hyrcanus II was captured by his nephew Antigonus in 40 B.C., the nephew did not kill him but cut off his ears, "thus taking care that the high priesthood should never come to him another time, because he was now mutilated, and the law requires that this office should belong only to those who are sound of body."

"A crippled foot or hand" (v.19) surely refers to common deformities when broken bones would have been poorly set. The word *gibbēn* is used only here, but its derivation and the LXX make "hunchback" probable (v.20). The word *daq* means "thing" or "small" and could refer to a "dwarf" (NIV), though the evidence is scanty. "Eye defect" is literally "blurred or spotted in his eye," but what kind of defect is intended is beyond our information. "Festering . . . sore" is used only here and in similar contexts in 22:22 and Deuteronomy 28:27. Surely it refers to some long-continuing disease or scab. The Greek has "a malignant ulcer." "Running sore" is used only here and at 22:22. The exact meaning is unsure.

The term *merôaḥ 'āšek̲* ("damaged testicles") is used only here (v.20), and the precise meaning is uncertain, though the word for "testicle" is clear from Ugaritic and Akkadian. If this is the correct reading, why was the ordinary word for eunuch not used? Perhaps because that word (*sārîs*) was not specific enough and was also applied to high court officials who were not eunuchs. Could a eunuch officiate as a priest? Clearly not. Deuteronomy 23:1 is translated similarly but has totally different Hebrew words and is subject to some obscurities. Leviticus 22:24 rejects castrated animals as offerings.

The unfortunate cripple in the priest's family could not serve in office but received his regular food like others of the family (v.22). He could even eat the most holy things, which shows that there was no superstitious or callous attitude inculcated toward the cripple.

22:1–3 Chapter 22 continues the directions for sanctity and cleanliness that govern the priesthood. The translation "treat with respect" fits the context better than "separate themselves" (KJV) or "keep away" (RSV). It is the verb (*nāzar*) from which the word "Nazirite" is derived. A Nazirite not only kept away from certain things, he kept himself holy in respect to those things. The word *nēzer* has the double meaning of "separated" and "consecrated." William Holladay (*A Concise Hebrew and Aramaic Lexicon of the Old Testament* [Grand Rapids: Eerdmans, 1971], p. 232) says that with the preposition "*min*" it means "to treat with awe."

The dual meaning is natural, for the Nazirite kept himself separate from sin and uncleanness and consecrated himself to the Lord. In v.2, however, it seems that the priests were not to separate themselves from the sacrifices—which, after all, they were to offer—but were to consecrate those sacrifices, to treat them with respect. As the following verses explain, the priest was to keep the holy things inviolate when he himself had some uncleanness.

4–8 The standard causes of uncleanness listed in vv.4–5 have been given before. The emphasis is further given that an unclean priest not only must not minister but also must not eat of the holy offerings. The unclean priest should bathe and be unclean the rest of the day. He would again be clean "when the sun goes down" (v.7). The Hebrew day then as now began at sundown. This was usual in the Orient. It was so among the Sumerians, Babylonians, and Greeks. Modern Arabs also use this system. The Romans began the day at midnight (see Notes).

9 It was no small matter to be a priest of God. The institution was divine and not to be trifled with. The judgment on Nadab and Abihu was supernatural as it later was on Korah and his company. On the other hand, the judgment on Eli's sons was providential. Many a faithless priest escaped catastrophe in his lifetime, but the threat of judgment was always there.

10–13 The definition of an "outsider" (v.10) is interesting. He was a temporary visitor or workman. The slave was considered family. The principle is that an outsider should not eat of the holy things (vv.12–13). A married daughter with a nonpriest husband was no longer in the priest's family. A widow or divorced daughter with children might bring a stranger's children into the family. This was not allowed. But a priest's daughter without children would revert to her childhood status.

14–16 To "eat a sacred offering by mistake" (v.14) would be one of the sins that required the guilt (or "trespass," KJV) offering. There, too, a 20 percent penalty was specified (5:16).

Verses 15–16 are somewhat obscure. The meaning chosen by the NIV is that these verses oblige the priests to enforce the rules against the practice of the sacred portions being eaten by the people who offered them. This interpretation unites vv.15–16 with the preceding verses. The KJV seems to take v.15 to require the priests to maintain their sanctity, and v.16 requires the priests to preserve the people from profaning the holy things. The NIV reading seems to fit the context better.

Notes

21:4 The NIV margin for v.4 reads "as a leader among his people" (cf. KJV). The significant Hebrew word here is בַּעַל (*ba'al*). It is used for the god Baal and also means "lord," "husband," "chief." The question is, Does the verse emphasize the priest's position *as* a chief man (NIV mg.; KJV), or does it refer to his not defiling himself for a relationship by marriage (NIV)? Another good possibility is the Vulgate's "not make himself unclean for a leader among his people." Neither the "as" or "for" is expressed. The NIV takes *ba'al* to mean "husband" and assumes a preposition: "like a husband," i.e., as a husband would do for his wife's relatives.

22:7 Claudius Ptolemy, the astronomer (second cent. A.D.), in line with earlier Greco-Roman practice, chose for his calculations the beginning of the day at midnight and used high noon as his reference point rather than sunrise. This made his calculations independent of the seasons. This reckoning seems to be used in John's gospel (1:39; 4:6; 19:14). The Ptolemaic system of a round earth with the sun going around it was the standard until Copernicus. Our A.M. and P.M. preserve the old Latin nomenclature for morning and afternoon, with the meridian (noon) as the reference point.

H. *Perfection Required in Sacrifices* 22:17–33

17 The LORD said to Moses, 18 "Speak to Aaron and his sons and to all
the Israelites and say to them: 'If any of you—either an Israelite or an
alien living in Israel—presents a gift for a burnt offering to the LORD,
either to fulfill a vow or as a freewill offering, 19 you must present a male
without defect from the cattle, sheep or goats in order that it may be
accepted on your behalf. 20 Do not bring anything with a defect, because
it will not be accepted on your behalf. 21 When anyone brings from the

herd or flock a fellowship offering to the LORD to fulfill a special vow or
as a freewill offering, it must be without defect or blemish to be
acceptable. 22 Do not offer to the LORD the blind, the injured or the
maimed, or anything with warts or festering or running sores. Do not
place any of these on the altar as an offering made to the LORD by fire.
23 You may, however, present as a freewill offering a cow or a sheep that
is deformed or stunted, but it will not be accepted in fulfillment of a vow.
24 You must not offer to the LORD an animal whose testicles are bruised,
crushed, torn or cut. You must not do this in your own land, 25 and you
must not accept such animals from the hand of a foreigner and offer
them as the food of your God. They will not be accepted on your behalf,
because they are deformed and have defects.' "
26 The LORD said to Moses, 27 "When a calf, a sheep or a goat is born, it
is to remain with its mother for seven days. From the eighth day on, it
will be acceptable as an offering made to the LORD by fire. 28 Do not
slaughter a cow or a sheep and its young on the same day.
29 "When you sacrifice an offering of thanksgiving to the LORD,
sacrifice it in such a way that it will be accepted on your behalf. 30 It must
be eaten that same day; leave none of it till morning. I am the LORD.
31 "Keep my commands and follow them. I am the LORD. 32 Do not
profane my holy name. I must be acknowledged as holy by the Israelites.
I am the LORD, who makes you holy 33 and who brought you out of Egypt
to be your God. I am the LORD."

The principle of a perfect sacrifice has been already stated at Leviticus 1:3. It is emphasized here with details. Other laws on the subject are in Deuteronomy 15:21 and 17:1. Malachi reproached the people after the Exile for offering their worthless and blemished animals (though the words he used are somewhat different). He complained that Israel offered to the Lord animals that would not be acceptable for taxes and that "the Lord," the "great king, . . . the LORD Almighty," was displeased (Mal 1:14).

17–25 Numbers 15:14–15 says that if an alien wishes to join in worship, he must do so in the same way as the Israelite. The "alien" (*gēr*) was probably not just a visitor (v.18). He was a foreigner living temporarily in Israel without full rights (cf. TWOT, #330a). Abraham was a sojourner (alien) among the Canaanites. He has been likened to a man having taken out first papers for citizenship. Doubtless the legal status of a sojourner varied over the centuries.

The word "defect" (v.20) is the same one used in 21:18. It is defined in the context as well as by common sense. If the offering was to mean anything, it should be an offering of perfection. As the priesthood symbolized Christ the Perfect Priest, so the offering symbolized Christ the Perfect Sacrifice.

As at 21:18, the words "blind, the injured or the maimed" (v.22) are sometimes obscure. The words "blind" and "injured" are obvious. The word "maimed" probably means "cut." The word "warts" is used only here, but similar words suggest a running sore. The KJV has a "wen" and the RSV "discharge" (cf. TWOT, # 835f). On "festering" or "running sores," see the comment on 21:20.

At 7:15–16 the fellowship offerings are divided into thanksgiving, votive, and voluntary or "freewill offerings" (v.23). Here it is explained that a stunted or overgrown animal (if not diseased or blemished) can be used for a freewill offering regardless of its market value. However, an offering made in consequence of a vow would require the standard market value of a standard animal. The words "deformed" and "stunted" (v.23) are uncertain, but the general sense is clear. These animals are not normal in growth, but neither are they diseased. They are all right for some purposes.

There is no word here in the Hebrew for "testicles" (v.24). There may be truth in the translation, however, that would forbid the offering of an emasculated animal. The Greek translation takes it so. Wenham (in loc.) takes the phrase "you must not do this in your own land" to mean to forbid castration of animals for any purpose. But the previous context refers to animals for sacrifice, and the contrast in v.25 with animals bought from a foreigner for sacrifice strengthens the idea that the prohibition is for sacrificial animals only.

Animals purchased from a foreigner were apparently not forbidden as sacrifice, but such purchased animals as were defective were unacceptable. Deuteronomy 15:21–22 explains that defective animals may be eaten for food at home but must not be offered to the Lord.

26–33 The reason for the law in v.27 is not entirely clear. But even today newborn calves are not usually slaughtered. The meat improves with age. Also, it probably is better for the mother that the calf not be taken at once. We might add that to transport a calf under a week old for some distance to the tabernacle or temple would likely in some cases kill the calf.

Similar provisions to v.28 are found in the thrice-repeated law "You shall not boil a kid in its mother's milk" (Exod 23:19; 34:26; Deut 14:21) and also in the law not to kill a mother bird with her young (Deut 22:6–7). The provisions are curious. Allis suggests that the Israelites were to emphasize mother love even in the area of humane treatment of animals. However, there may be other reasons. To boil a kid in its mother's milk is probably a Canaanite ritual referred to in the Ugaritic literature (UT, p. 175, 52.14), though the tablet is slightly broken; and this heathen practice was therefore to be avoided. The first-attempted reading of the damaged Ugaritic tablet was "cook a kid in milk, a lamb in butter" (C. Gordon, UT, p. 59). More recently R. Ratner and B. Zuckermann have declared that reexamination of the tablet shows that the third letter of *ṭbḥ* ("cook") is not there (HUCA 57 [1986]: 15–60). The parallel with Ugaritic is therefore uncertain, though the reference in the tablet to "a kid in milk" seems probable, and the context is one of fire and offerings.

It is barely possible that Deuteronomy 22:6–7 gives the key to the present verse (v.28). Those verses forbid the killing of the mother bird when the young are taken. The mother bird is easily caught with her fledglings, but then the goose that lays the golden egg is killed. The mother must be preserved so that the species will not become extinct. Possibly the thrust of the phrase "on the same day" is general and means "at the same time." The mother cow especially should not be slaughtered just when she "comes in fresh" with plenty of milk.

"That same day" (v.30) is slightly different from the phrase in v.28. This repeats the law of 7:15. Leviticus 19:5 gives the general law of the fellowship offerings that are of three types as the discussion on 22:23 explains. Repeatedly in this section the character of God is given as the basis of his will for Israel. Verse 33 (as Exod 20:1) also gives the basis of God's saving work in bringing Israel out of Egypt. Because he has redeemed us, and because he is the holy God, therefore we are bound to keep his commandments.

VII. The Feasts and Worship of the Lord (23:1–24:9)

A. *Introduction*

23:1–2 (cf. Exod 23:10–17; 34:18–23; Num 28:9–29:39; Deut 15:1–16:17)

1 The LORD said to Moses, 2 "Speak to the Israelites and say to them: 'These are my appointed feasts, the appointed feasts of the LORD, which you are to proclaim as sacred assemblies.

1–2 A directory for Israel's worship would not be complete without a catalog of the annual feasts. Leviticus has so far given the rules for offerings, ordination of priests, public health, and personal holiness. Now the religious ceremonial seasons are given. The emphasis is on the things the general public would need to know. Numbers 28–29 is more technical and for the use of the priests. The major feasts are also cataloged in Exodus 23:12–17; 34:21–24; Numbers 28:9–29:39; and Deuteromony 16:1–17. There are two feasts celebrated by Jews today that do not appear in these Pentateuchal lists because their origin was much later—Purim, which was established in Esther's day, and Hanukkah, which celebrates the rededication of the temple in 165 B.C., after it had been desecrated by the Syrian invaders. Of the five major feasts, three required the presence of all grown men at the tabernacle, later at the temple (Exod 23:17; 34:23 et al.). These are often called the pilgrimage festivals. They were the special times when offerings would be brought in great numbers.

Notes

2 The word "assembly" is from the same root—קָרָא (*qārā'*)—as "proclaim." The word "assembly" in the sense of a gathering is not suitable to several of these feasts, for no gathering was held on them. Perhaps the words could better be rendered as "holy proclamations" or "holy announcements."

The word "feasts" also is misleading. The Sabbath, for instance, was not a day of feasting. The word מוֹעֵד (*mô'ēḏ*) means "appointed time." The phrase "set celebrations" might be better.

B. *The Sabbath*

23:3

3 " 'There are six days when you may work, but the seventh day is a Sabbath of rest, a day of sacred assembly. You are not to do any work; wherever you live, it is a Sabbath to the LORD.

3 All the festivals are properly called Sabbaths, but the weekly Sabbath gains great emphasis in the Pentateuch and many other places in Israel's instruction and history (cf. Exod 20:8–11; 23:12; 31:12–17; 34:21; 35:2; Num 15:32–36; 28:9–10; Deut 5:12–15). An attempt has been made by S. Langdon (*Babylonian Menologies and the Semitic Calendars* [London: Oxford University Press, 1935], p. 54) to derive the Jewish Sabbath from the Assyrian and Babylonian unlucky days associated with the phases of the moon. Seventh-century tablets declare that work is unlucky on the seventh, fourteenth, nineteenth, twenty-first, and twenty-eighth days. The nineteenth day is of interest, for it is the seventh seven after the first Sabbath of the previous month. Langdon holds that the principle of unlucky days was borrowed by the Hebrews as a weekly Sabbath found in the P document, which he holds to be late.

It is, of course, interesting to notice that there was some emphasis on seven-day periods in antiquity. Langdon says that the tablets available are copies of older tablets going back to the days of Hammurabi. There is therefore no need to argue that the arrangement is late. However, the Hebrew sources nowhere make any mention of the relation of the weekly Sabbath to the moon's phases. Indeed, the moon's phases are not even mentioned in the OT except for the new moon that began every month (and a moon month lasts twenty-nine and a half days, not twenty-eight). The basis for the Sabbath is God's Creation activity. It might indeed be that God ordained the weekly Sabbath on the basis of Creation to protect the Israelite from the pagan unlucky days associated with moon worship in the surrounding cultures. At least the Sabbath is never called unlucky or sinister as in the Assyrian tablets. It is a "holy convocation" (KJV) or day of "sacred assembly." See the comment on 19:3 as to the Christian and the Sabbath.

Notes

3 There is an emphasis here that the Israelite rested at home. There were special offerings given in the tabernacle (e.g., a double burnt offering), but the ordinary Israelite and his whole family rested. Presumably here was an opportunity for family worship and instruction in the law of God, but this is not specifically enjoined. What a boon a weekly rest must have been to the ancient laborer and farmer in his weary round of toil! The Sabbath was a great blessing.

C. *The Passover and Firstfruits*

23:4–14

4" 'These are the LORD's appointed feasts, the sacred assemblies you
are to proclaim at their appointed times: 5The LORD's Passover begins at
twilight on the fourteenth day of the first month. 6On the fifteenth day of
that month the LORD's Feast of Unleavened Bread begins; for seven days
you must eat bread made without yeast. 7On the first day hold a sacred
assembly and do no regular work. 8For seven days present an offering
made to the LORD by fire. And on the seventh day hold a sacred assembly
and do no regular work.' "

9The LORD said to Moses, 10"Speak to the Israelites and say to them:
'When you enter the land I am going to give you and you reap its
harvest, bring to the priest a sheaf of the first grain you harvest. 11He is
to wave the sheaf before the LORD so it will be accepted on your behalf;
the priest is to wave it on the day after the Sabbath. 12On the day you
wave the sheaf, you must sacrifice as a burnt offering to the LORD a lamb
a year old without defect, 13together with its grain offering of two-tenths
of an ephah of fine flour mixed with oil—an offering made to the LORD
by fire, a pleasing aroma—and its drink offering of a fourth of a hin of
wine. 14You must not eat any bread, or roasted or new grain, until the

very day you bring this offering to your God. This is to be a lasting ordinance for the generations to come, wherever you live.

4–5 The Passover was probably the greatest feast of the year, commemorating as it did the deliverance from Egyptian bondage (cf. Exod 12:14–20; 43–49; 23:14–15; 34:18; Num 9:1–14; 28:16–25; Deut 16:1–8). In type it represents Christ our Passover sacrificed for us (1 Cor 5:7). The Jews today, because of the destruction of the temple in A.D. 70, celebrate the Passover using only a dry bone instead of the paschal lamb. The ancient Passover ritual, like most all the other sacrifices, emphasizes redemption through the blood of the slain lamb. It was against this background that John the Baptist proclaimed Christ as "the Lamb of God, who takes away the sin of the world!" (John 1:29). Members of the Samaritan sect, which was relatively untouched by the Fall of Jerusalem in A.D. 70, still celebrate the Passover by the slaughter of a lamb, which is roasted and eaten at midnight much like the biblical prescriptions. The Jews today celebrate the Passover far differently from the OT regulations. Jesus, of course, celebrated the Passover in the OT manner. The Jewish liturgy changed greatly at A.D. 70, but there were probably other changes that we do not know about before and after this time.

For "at twilight" (v.5) the Hebrew has *bên hā'arbāyim* ("between the evenings"). This curious phrase is explained, however, in Deuteronomy 16:6 as "in the evening, when the sun goes down." Some Arabs today distinguish two evenings—one when the sun sets, the other when it is dark. The author once observed a Samaritan Passover. The lambs were killed at sundown, the blood was sprinkled on the tent doors, and the carcasses were cleaned and hung in roasting pits until the midnight meal. See the comment and note on 22:7.

6–8 More details on the Feast of Unleavened Bread are given elsewhere (cf. esp. Exod 12; Deut 16). In the latter passage unleavened bread is called the "bread of affliction" (Deut 16:3). It commemorated the fact that the Israelites left Egypt in haste with no time to let their dough rise. The Passover and the time of Unleavened Bread were so closely intertwined that in the NT the whole week is called the Passover (Acts 12:3–4; cf. John 19:14). Directions for the special sacrifices to be offered on this and on the other feast days are given in Numbers 28–29.

9–14 Allied to Passover and Unleavened Bread was the Feast of Firstfruits celebrated at the same time. The firstfruits at Passover would be barley, which ripens in the warmer areas as early as March (see Notes).

Critical students in general believe that the spring festival was originally agricultural, a firstfruits feast. Later, when the tradition (or "legend"!) of the deliverance from Egypt became prominent, that event was attached to the spring festival as the "Exodus event" was "historicized," i.e., as the "legend" of the Exodus became treated as real. There is no evidence for this reconstruction. It was natural for God to arrange for the Exodus to be in the spring—the best season to travel with sheep in Sinai! That the two festivals should be combined from the beginning is just as possible.

The presentation of the sheaf "on the day after the Sabbath" (v.11) symbolized the dedication of the whole year's crop; and until this was done, none of the new grain was to be eaten (v.14). There is some question about the date of waving the sheaf. If "the Sabbath" refers to the regular Saturday Sabbath, then the sheaf was always waved on a Sunday regardless of the date of the Passover (which could be any day of the week). If "the Sabbath" refers to the Passover Day, then the sheaf was waved on Nisan fifteenth. The former usage seems more likely because the Feast of Weeks comes fifty days later, also on the day after a Sabbath (v.16).

At Numbers 28:27 there are other offerings specified for this day; but as the context shows, they are the standard offerings for every day of Unleavened Bread. This "burnt offering" (v.12) is an extra one for the firstfruits ceremony.

An "ephah" (v.13) was about three-fifths of a bushel. Two-tenths would be about four quarts (dry measure). See the comment on 5:11. The value of the "hin" is not sure, but a prominent estimate is about one gallon (see F.B. Huey, "Weights and Measures," ZPEB, 5:916). A "quarter of a hin" would then be about a quart. The name "drink offering" is a misnomer. The Hebrew word refers to pouring. The drink offering was never drunk but was poured out over the sacrifice at a holy place (Gen 35:14; Num 28:7; 2 Kings 16:15).

Notes

10 H. Wolf (ZPEB, 3:36) says that the barley harvest begins at the coast in mid-April and about a month later in high areas. Shewell-Cooper (ZPEB, 2:568) says the wheat harvest begins about four weeks later. If the first month began at the new moon following the spring equinox, the earliest Passover would be fourteen days after March twenty-first; the latest would be twenty-nine days after that. See also H. and A. Moldenke, *Plants of the Bible* (New York: Ronald, 1952), p. 112.

D. *The Feast of Weeks*

23:15–22

15 " 'From the day after the Sabbath, the day you brought the sheaf of the wave offering, count off seven full weeks. 16 Count off fifty days up to the day after the seventh Sabbath, and then present an offering of new grain to the LORD. 17 From wherever you live, bring two loaves made of two-tenths of an ephah of fine flour, baked with yeast, as a wave offering of firstfruits to the LORD. 18 Present with this bread seven male lambs, each a year old and without defect, one young bull and two rams. They will be a burnt offering to the LORD, together with their grain offerings and drink offerings—an offering made by fire, an aroma pleasing to the LORD. 19 Then sacrifice one male goat for a sin offering and two lambs, each a year old, for a fellowship offering. 20 The priest is to wave the two lambs before the LORD as a wave offering, together with the bread of the firstfruits. They are a sacred offering to the LORD for the priest. 21 On that same day you are to proclaim a sacred assembly and do no regular work. This is to be a lasting ordinance for the generations to come, wherever you live.

22 " 'When you reap the harvest of your land, do not reap to the very edges of your field or gather the gleanings of your harvest. Leave them for the poor and the alien. I am the LORD your God.' "

15–21 The Feast of Weeks is called the Feast of Harvest in Exodus 23:16 and the "firstfruits of the wheat harvest" in Exodus 34:22 (cf. Num 28:26–31; Deut 16:9–12).

As mentioned in v.10, it always occurred on the first day of the week and would fall seven weeks and one day after the Sabbath after the full moon of the Passover (14 Nisan). From the day after the Passover Sabbath to the day after the Pentecost Sabbath is "fifty days" (v.16) by inclusive reckoning, counting both the first and last days. It would therefore be around the end of May to mid-June. The wheat harvest in Palestine "runs from the end of April to well into June depending on the location, soil and season" (Moldenke, *Plants*, p. 232).

It should be remembered that there is a wide latitude of seasons in Palestine from the seacoast to the mountains to the Jordan Valley. This feast was a dedication of the wheat harvest to the Lord. Special sacrifices were specified (vv.17–20). The fellowship offering was normally prepared without yeast. Here in v.17 it is different. It is the first part of the harvest prepared as a Hebrew housewife would prepare it. The "seven male lambs" and other offerings (vv.18–19) were to sanctify Israel and cleanse her anew for the new season's work and rejoicing.

All the males were to appear at the tabernacle; but, in this time when the harvest was beginning, they would not stay long. The NT antitype is Pentecost, which was, as a consequence, on Sunday, and was the day of the outpouring of the Holy Spirit in a new phase of God's saving work extending the harvest to the Gentiles also (cf. v.2, lines 5–6, of the hymn "O Day of Rest and Gladness," where Sunday is said to commemorate the creation of light, the resurrection of Jesus Christ, and the outpouring of the Holy Spirit).

22 This rule is appropriate for a harvest festival. In all Israel's life, the poor in Israel were helped and protected. Christians should search their hearts to be sure they have a similar attitude toward the unfortunate in our day. There is much talk of the church's duty to the poor. It is obvious that in a time of famine, emergency, or tragedy, no Christian should withhold his means if he is able to help. Still, the NT examples and teaching emphasize the church's duty toward the poor *in the church* (Acts 6:1; 11:29; 24:17; 1 Tim 4:9–10; cf. Notes). The law on gleaning with mention also of the treatment of vineyards is stated in 19:9–10.

Notes

17 The New Scofield Reference Bible (p. 157) notes that these verses suggest that leaven symbolizes evil and that the church to be founded at Pentecost was to include evil. The offerings typical of Christ include no yeast (leaven). Another view is that given by Allis (p. 138), who suggests that the leavened loaves of the firstfruits offering represent the daily food of the Israelites, consecrated to God. This interpretation may be preferred because, among other things, the church is not supposed to include unsaved people any more than Israel was. First Cor 5:9–13 gives the ideal of a true church in an immoral world.

22 Galatians 6:10 is frequently quoted today to teach the church's duty toward relieving poverty, etc., in society in general. But this is not specifically in the context and is not the OT teaching here in Leviticus. "Doing good" in Gal 6:9 is the same as to "do good" in 6:10, which harks back to the "fruits of the Spirit" in 5:22–23 (cf. 6:8). Galatians 6:10 refers to "the manifestation of a kindly temper towards others" (EGT, 3:190).

E. *The Feast of Trumpets*

23:23–25

> 23 The LORD said to Moses, 24 "Say to the Israelites: 'On the first day of
> the seventh month you are to have a day of rest, a sacred assembly
> commemorated with trumpet blasts. 25 Do no regular work, but present
> an offering made to the LORD by fire.' "

It is interesting that this ancient fall feast was not given the extra emphasis that its equivalent, the New Year (Rosh Hashanah), is given among Jews today. Neither was the New Year given the emphasis that it had in Babylon (see Notes on 16:29). In Babylon it was a week-long celebration. The Babylonian creation story was recited; special processions were held. At one point the king laid aside his robes and was humiliated by the Babylonian priest who then punished him for the bad luck of the year. It was a good sign if the blow brought tears! The next morning the king was reenthroned amid general rejoicing (for details, cf. Frankfort, *Kingship*, pp. 313–33).

Much has been made of this New Year ritual by comparative religion scholars in recent years. Their view is conveniently summed up by H. Ringgren (*The Messiah in the Old Testament* [London: Student Christian Movement, 1956]). But the comparisons fail on several counts. The Babylonian New Year was celebrated by the king. Kings in Israel were not priests. Nor were the kings regarded as gods in Israel (and not even in Babylon, despite claims of this theory [Frankfort, *Kingship*, pp. 313–33; ZPEB, 2:524]). In his final chapter, Frankfort rejects the idea of divine kingship in Babylon and questions the parallel with Israel.

Finally, the Jewish fall Feast of Trumpets is given no emphasis in the Pentateuch or in the balance of the OT. It was a one-day celebration with special sacrifices, and that was all. Actually, the phrase Rosh Hashanah occurs only once in the OT (Ezek 40:1), where it is used of the "beginning of the year" (NIV) without reference to what month is in question; and it just as well could be in the spring. The Hebrew year began in the spring (Exod 12:2). The "turn of the year" (*t*^{e}*qûpaṯ haššānāh*) of Exodus 34:22 and the "going out of the year" (*ṣēʾṯ haššānāh*) of Exodus 23:16 need not mean the "end of the year" but only the turn of the season (cf. below).

23–25 Every new moon in Israel began with a special celebration marked by blowing the trumpets (Num 10:10; 28:11; Ps 81:3 et al.) and special sacrifices (Num 28:11–15). It was of some importance for business as well as for religious observances for the new month to be fixed definitely, and this announcement was made by the priests with the blowing of trumpets. Since a lunar month is twenty-nine and a half days long, there is some possibility for variation in the calendar. Probably, as in surrounding nations, the decision to start a new month was arrived at partly by observation, partly by calculation. It is not improbable that the beginnings of the months of Israel were integrated with the dates decided by the surrounding nations, at least in later years. It seems clear that the blowing of trumpets reechoed the signal across the hills of Palestine (cf. Notes on 25:9). It was helpful to know when the seventh month started since it included important religious festivals. The prescribed offering for the Feast of Trumpets is given in Numbers 29:1–6.

F. *The Day of Atonement*

23:26–32

26The LORD said to Moses, 27"The tenth day of this seventh month is the Day of Atonement. Hold a sacred assembly and deny yourselves, and present an offering made to the LORD by fire. 28Do no work on that day, because it is the Day of Atonement, when atonement is made for you before the LORD your God. 29Anyone who does not deny himself on that day must be cut off from his people. 30I will destroy from among his people anyone who does any work on that day. 31You shall do no work at all. This is to be a lasting ordinance for the generations to come, wherever you live. 32It is a sabbath of rest for you, and you must deny yourselves. From the evening of the ninth day of the month until the following evening you are to observe your sabbath."

26–32 The Day of Atonement has been discussed in connection with the ritual prescribed for it at Leviticus 16 (cf. Lev 16:1–34; Num 29:7–11). It was to be a day of fasting. People were to remain in their houses and remember that on this day their high priest was to enter the Most Holy Place bearing the name of their tribe on his breastpiece. Verse 32 underlines the fact that any of the annual feasts could also be called a Sabbath. There seems to be no special reason why the tenth of the month was chosen for this Sabbath. It was a proper and convenient time for repentance and spiritual preparation for the Feast of Tabernacles of the following week.

G. *The Feast of Tabernacles*

23:33–44

33The LORD said to Moses, 34"Say to the Israelites: 'On the fifteenth day of the seventh month the LORD's Feast of Tabernacles begins, and it lasts for seven days. 35The first day is a sacred assembly; do no regular work. 36For seven days present offerings made to the LORD by fire, and on the eighth day hold a sacred assembly and present an offering made to the LORD by fire. It is the closing assembly; do no regular work.

37(" 'These are the LORD's appointed feasts, which you are to proclaim as sacred assemblies for bringing offerings made to the LORD by fire—the burnt offerings and grain offerings, sacrifices and drink offerings required for each day. 38These offerings are in addition to those for the LORD's Sabbaths and in addition to your gifts and whatever you have vowed and all the freewill offerings you give to the LORD.)

39" 'So beginning with the fifteenth day of the seventh month, after you have gathered the crops of the land, celebrate the festival to the LORD for seven days; the first day is a day of rest, and the eighth day also is a day of rest. 40On the first day you are to take choice fruit from the trees, and palm fronds, leafy branches and poplars, and rejoice before the LORD your God for seven days. 41Celebrate this as a festival to the LORD for seven days each year. This is to be a lasting ordinance for the generations to come; celebrate it in the seventh month. 42Live in booths for seven days: All native-born Israelites are to live in booths 43so your descendants will know that I had the Israelites live in booths when I brought them out of Egypt. I am the LORD your God.' "

44So Moses announced to the Israelites the appointed feasts of the LORD.

33–44 The Feast of Tabernacles (or Booths) (cf. Exod 23:16; 34:22; Num 29:12–40; Deut 16:13–17) is called the Feast of Ingathering "at the end [*beṣē'ṯ*, the 'going out'] of the year" (Exod 23:16). As noted above, this does not necessarily mean the end of the calendar year—just as we have other years: school years, fiscal years, etc. The usual expression (*tᵉšûḇaṯ haššānāh,* "turn of the year") always means "spring" (2 Sam 11:1 = 1 Chron 20:1; 1 Kings 20:22, 26; 2 Chron 36:10). The present Jewish new year starts in the fall, but the biblical text nowhere calls this Rosh Hashanah (head of the year). The biblical new year began in the spring. From these references some have concluded that there were two new years in Israel—spring and fall—but the fall new year is probably a later Jewish development.

Like Passover and the Feast of Weeks, Tabernacles was a pilgrimage festival when all the men were to appear at the tabernacle or temple. Of course, in many cases the whole family came. The offerings (vv.36–37) are detailed in Numbers 29. A peculiar feature is that the burnt offering on the first day of the feast includes thirteen bulls and that each subsequent day the number is reduced by one until the last day, when seven bulls are offered (Num 29:13–32). The other offerings stayed the same in number every day.

Fall was a convenient time to bring an offering from the year's harvest. Even the grapes, olives, and dates would have been ripe by then (v.39). The weather would have been mild and clear, ideal for the temporary stay in booths. There is a problem in v.40 in the relation of fruit and branches. It is probable that eating the good fruit of fruit trees was part of the festivities of rejoicing during the eight days. The waving of the palms and branches, perhaps in processions, would be another part of the rejoicing. The branches were used in any case to make the booths (Neh 8:15–17).

The feast was a reminder of the Exodus from Egypt and the long trek to Sinai with the people living in tents. It would in future days be a reminder of the simple desert life when they walked with God at their head. The Hebrew name is Sukkoth, which in modern Hebrew is changed in pronunciation to Sukkos. The word is not the same as the word *'ōhel* ("tent") used for the wilderness tabernacle.

In contrast to the fast and repentance of the Day of Atonement, the Feast of Booths was an occasion of joy—a thanksgiving day. Indeed, it is clear that when the Puritans proclaimed their Thanksgiving Day in New England, they had in mind the OT harvest festival.

H. *The Care of the Lampstand*

24:1–4

1 The LORD said to Moses, 2 "Command the Israelites to bring you clear
oil of pressed olives for the light so that the lamps may be kept burning
continually. 3 Outside the curtain of the Testimony in the Tent of
Meeting, Aaron is to tend the lamps before the LORD from evening till
morning, continually. This is to be a lasting ordinance for the generations to come. 4 The lamps on the pure gold lampstand before the LORD
must be tended continually.

1–4 In a sense this section, like chapter 8, is a complement to the Book of Exodus. Exodus 25:31–40 has the directions for making the seven-branched lampstand. Exodus 37:17–24 records Moses' having made the lampstand. Then Exodus 27:20–21 gives directions for the care of the light. Here in vv.1–4 these directions are to be carried out. The wording of this section (vv.2–4) is almost identical to that in Exodus 27:20–21. This is not surprising if Leviticus is a unit with Exodus in the larger structure of the Pentateuch. Many times in Exodus 35–40 the description of the building of the tabernacle and its furniture is almost word for word the same as the instruction for its building in Exodus 25–29.

The fire on the altar was never to go out. But it seems from the phrase "from evening to morning" (v.3) and the similar one in Exodus 27:21 that the lamps were to burn every night but not through the day. This arrangement may explain the statement in 1 Samuel 3:3: "The lamp of God had not yet gone out," i.e., it was toward morning but still dark. On the meaning of "Testimony," see the comment on 16:13.

I. *The Bread of the Presence*

24:5–9

5 "Take fine flour and bake twelve loaves of bread, using two-tenths of
an ephah for each loaf. 6 Set them in two rows, six in each row, on the
table of pure gold before the LORD. 7 Along each row put some pure
incense as a memorial portion to represent the bread and to be an
offering made to the LORD by fire. 8 This bread is to be set out before the
LORD regularly, Sabbath after Sabbath, on behalf of the Israelites, as a
lasting covenant. 9 It belongs to Aaron and his sons, who are to eat it in a
holy place, because it is a most holy part of their regular share of the
offerings made to the LORD by fire."

5–9 This is the only place where the details of the offering of the bread of the Presence are given (cf. Exod 25:30; 40:23). It was the priests' grain offering. It was set out before the Lord every Sabbath and eaten at the end of the week. Presumably it was hard baked and would not spoil in the interim. On the other hand, the text does not strictly say that the bread would stay on the table a week. It may have been taken off at a convenient time—after the Sabbath was over—and eaten by the priests. This was the background of the famous incident when David ate the consecrated bread (1 Sam 21:6; Matt 12:4).

"Two-tenths of an ephah" (v.5) is about four quarts of flour (the ephah being about twenty quarts), which seems to be an impossibly large amount for each loaf or cake. Actually, the Hebrew says "two-tenths" to each cake. The measure is not specified. Probably some smaller measure like the seah (five quarts) or the omer (four pints) is intended. The flat, round, pancakelike loaf of bread would not take very much flour.

"Along each row put some pure incense" (v.7) is a better translation than KJV's "upon each row." The incense was not eaten. It is not edible. It was burned with the "memorial portion" of the bread. The meaning of the ritual, like the ordinary grain offering, surely includes communion as the bread was eaten before the Lord in the Holy Place.

VIII. Identical Laws for the Stranger and the Israelite

24:10–23

10 Now the son of an Israelite mother and an Egyptian father went out
among the Israelites, and a fight broke out in the camp between him and
an Israelite. 11 The son of the Israelite woman blasphemed the name of
the Lord with a curse; so they brought him to Moses. (His mother's
name was Shelomith, the daughter of Dibri the Danite.) 12 They put him
in custody until the will of the LORD should be made clear to them.

13Then the LORD said to Moses: 14"Take the blasphemer outside the camp. All those who heard him are to lay their hands on his head, and the entire assembly is to stone him. 15Say to the Israelites: 'If anyone curses his God, he will be held responsible; 16anyone who blasphemes the name of the LORD must be put to death. The entire assembly must stone him. Whether an alien or native-born, when he blasphemes the Name, he must be put to death.

17" 'If anyone takes the life of a human being, he must be put to death. 18Anyone who takes the life of someone's animal must make restitution—life for life. 19If anyone injures his neighbor, whatever he has done must be done to him: 20fracture for fracture, eye for eye, tooth for tooth. As he has injured the other, so he is to be injured. 21Whoever kills an animal must make restitution, but whoever kills a man must be put to death. 22You are to have the same law for the alien and the native-born. I am the LORD your God.' "

23Then Moses spoke to the Israelites, and they took the blasphemer outside the camp and stoned him. The Israelites did as the LORD commanded Moses.

10–23 Not much of Leviticus is narration. The whole year's stay at Sinai is told in a few chapters in Exodus and Numbers. But the incident of the son of Shelomith (v.11) gave rise to legislation and therefore finds a place in Leviticus. His offense was plain and called for execution if he had been an Israelite. But his father was one of the mixed multitude who went out with the Israelites (v.10), probably because he had married a woman of the tribe of Dan.

Just what the crime was is hard to say. It may well have been more than thoughtless profanity. The Hebrew does not have the Tetragram (*YHWH*, "LORD") here at v.11 or at the end of v.16. It is, however, at the beginning of v.16. Clearly the sacred Name is intended. The word "curse" (*qālal*, v.11) is used when Balak hired Balaam to curse Israel so that he might conquer her. The man may have engaged in some curse procedure to injure his opponent by a kind of hex in the name of the Lord, or it may have been an angry cursing of the Israelite man and his God. Blasphemy, of course, was strictly forbidden and punishable by death. The man was stoned.

The decision in the case established the principle that one who lived in Israel's company was counted as an adherent of her faith. The sojourner already had been made subject to Israel's laws of offering and cleanliness (17:8–15). Likewise, the sojourner (*gēr*) enjoyed the protection of the law (Exod 23:9). But the sojourner who blasphemed would have to pay the extreme penalty.

The stoning of the blasphemer is taken as the occasion for the summation of the principles of justice. Here again the principle of lex talionis or retaliation (v.20) is stated as a form of justice. The principle similarly appears in Exodus 21:23–25 and Deuteronomy 19:21. It occurs also in the Code of Hammurabi (##196–200). Christ quoted the law in Matthew 5:38–42 and seems to have opposed it. Some would argue that this law was primitive and unworthy of the claim of divine sanction. Others would justify the law as a step in advance from the revenge that would exact two deaths for one death, five teeth for one tooth. Christ's standard is then said to be the higher Christian standard (cf. Notes).

It is another question whether this law was taken literally or is an emphatic statement of the principle that the punishment must fit the crime. Actually, even in Hammurabi's Code the punishment was not always in the same kind. Here also, if a man killed a beast, his own beast was not killed (v.18). There is no example in the OT of a judge exacting literally an eye for an eye. The usual penalties of Hebrew law were capital punishment for a limited number of serious offenses and fines and restitution for the remainder. There were no prisons in the early days, and none are mentioned in the Pentateuchal legislation. Apparently we have both here and in Hammurabi an emphatic legal idiom meaning that the punishment must be commensurate with the offense.

Notes

17–21 The views stated above in the commentary are deficient. Robert O. Coleman ("Leviticus," WBC, p. 105; see also Wenham, p. 312, to the same effect) puts it better when he remarks that Christ "condemned, not the principle of civil law involved here but the spirit of retaliation and revenge which was most likely to be found in association with it." See the author's discussion in connection with Christ's view of the OT (*Inspiration and Canonicity of the Bible,* rev. ed. [Grand Rapids: Zondervan, 1969], pp. 50–52). Christ was not contradicting the OT but was denouncing the Pharisaic use of these verses to justify personal revenge. The three passages where this law is found are all in a context of court justice. They emphasize that justice must be equal to be just. The symbol of justice to this day is a blindfolded lady holding scales that swing level.

IX. Laws of Land Use (25:1–55)

There are three subdivisions to this section: the sabbatical year, the Jubilee, and the laws of indebtedness. The basis of the land laws God gave to Israel is his statement that "the land is mine" (v.23). When Joshua conquered Palestine, the land was divided by sacred lot, not secured by individual military prowess. The people, therefore, could not sell their land. Society was agricultural; and the farms belonged, under God, to the people in perpetuity. The question was, How do you keep such a system working? The constant tendency is for the rich to increase their holdings at the expense of the poor. To obviate this danger the Lord instituted a land reform of return to the old homestead every fifty years. Actually, the Jubilee was one of the first land reforms known in history.

The sabbatical year likewise was a humane and very advanced social program. Imagine all debts forgiven and slaves released every seven years! Ingrained into Israel's laws and faith was a concern for the poor and unfortunate. It is observable in many of the laws already noticed and is made most emphatic in this chapter. It is not by accident that v.10 of this chapter is the motto on the Liberty Bell that hangs in front of Independence Hall in Philadelphia, Pennsylvania.

A. *The Sabbatical Year*

25:1–7

1 The LORD said to Moses on Mount Sinai, 2 "Speak to the Israelites and
say to them: 'When you enter the land I am going to give you, the land
itself must observe a sabbath to the LORD. 3 For six years sow your fields,
and for six years prune your vineyards and gather their crops. 4 But in
the seventh year the land is to have a sabbath of rest, a sabbath to the
LORD. Do not sow your fields or prune your vineyards. 5 Do not reap what

grows of itself or harvest the grapes of your untended vines. The land is to have a year of rest. [6]Whatever the land yields during the sabbath year will be food for you—for yourself, your manservant and maidservant, and the hired worker and temporary resident who live among you, [7]as well as for your livestock and the wild animals in your land. Whatever the land produces may be eaten.

1–7 The sabbatical year (*šabbāṯ*) is mentioned also in Exodus 23:10–11 and Deuteronomy 15:1–18. In the former passage, however, it is described as a year to leave the land fallow (as here in Lev 25) without the year being specifically named. In the Deuteronomy passage the year is called a *šᵉmiṭṭāh* and is described as a year of canceling debts and freeing slaves, not as a year of rest from the tillage of the land. However, the verb *šāmaṭ* is used in Exodus 23:11 and translated by the NIV as "let the land lie unplowed" (cf. TWOT, ##454b, 2408). It appears from the combination of these two ideas that the seventh year was both a fallow year for the land and a year of canceling debts. For the further matter of liberating slaves (*dārar*), see the Jubilee below.

As far as Moses knew, the occupation of Canaan would begin in a few months, and Israel would begin this program of land tenure at once. Though Israel was in the wilderness, she was looking toward a settled condition within a year, similar to what they had known in Egypt—without the slavery! The adoption of such a law does not imply that the legislation is late, long years after the Conquest. Indeed, v.2 says it is a law adopted to cover future circumstances.

The terminology "the land itself must observe a sabbath" (v.2) apparently comes from the weekly Sabbath that was already in force. The emphasis of the Sabbath was the resting. The land "I am going to give you" (notice the proprietorship) will have its rest as well. Presumably no one then knew why this would be good for the land. Principles of crop rotation were not known, and God did not give them such advanced wisdom. But he did give them the idea of the land lying fallow, and he gave it religious sanction. It does not seem that any other nation had any custom like this.

Verse 5 seems at first to contradict v.4. The solution seems to be that there is to be no normal work of harvest or grape-gathering that would involve servants and include storage. It was all right to eat and gather directly from the fields (v.11), but regular harvest work was forbidden. The idea was twofold. First, the produce of the sixth year would be so abundant because of the Lord's blessing that there would be a surplus. Second, the natural produce of the land would feed the poor (Exod 23:11). It would even give wildlife a chance to repopulate itself. The natural crop would be public property. There is an additional reason for the sabbatical year that does not appear in this chapter. In the Feast of Booths of the sabbatical year, the law was to be read to the people. The whole nation was to have a short-term Bible institute (Deut 31:10–13). There would be opportunities for other instruction during the rest of this vacation year.

B. *The Jubilee*

25:8–34

[8]" 'Count off seven sabbaths of years—seven times seven years—so that the seven sabbaths of years amount to a period of forty-nine years.
[9]Then have the trumpet sounded everywhere on the tenth day of the seventh month; on the Day of Atonement sound the trumpet throughout your land. [10]Consecrate the fiftieth year and proclaim liberty throughout

the land to all its inhabitants. It shall be a jubilee for you; each one of
you is to return to his family property and each to his own clan. 11 The
fiftieth year shall be a jubilee for you; do not sow and do not reap what
grows of itself or harvest the untended vines. 12 For it is a jubilee and is
to be holy for you; eat only what is taken directly from the fields.
13 " 'In this Year of Jubilee everyone is to return to his own property.
14 " 'If you sell land to one of your countrymen or buy any from him, do
not take advantage of each other. 15 You are to buy from your
countryman on the basis of the number of years since the Jubilee. And
he is to sell to you on the basis of the number of years left for harvesting
crops. 16 When the years are many, you are to increase the price, and
when the years are few, you are to decrease the price, because what he
is really selling you is the number of crops. 17 Do not take advantage of
each other, but fear your God. I am the LORD your God.
18 " 'Follow my decrees and be careful to obey my laws, and you will
live safely in the land. 19 Then the land will yield its fruit, and you will eat
your fill and live there in safety. 20 You may ask, "What will we eat in the
seventh year if we do not plant or harvest our crops?" 21 I will send you
such a blessing in the sixth year that the land will yield enough for three
years. 22 While you plant during the eighth year, you will eat from the old
crop and will continue to eat from it until the harvest of the ninth year
comes in.
23 " 'The land must not be sold permanently, because the land is mine
and you are but aliens and my tenants. 24 Throughout the country that
you hold as a possession, you must provide for the redemption of the
land.
25 " 'If one of your countrymen becomes poor and sells some of his
property, his nearest relative is to come and redeem what his countryman has sold. 26 If, however, a man has no one to redeem it for him but
he himself prospers and acquires sufficient means to redeem it, 27 he is
to determine the value for the years since he sold it and refund the
balance to the man to whom he sold it; he can then go back to his own
property. 28 But if he does not acquire the means to repay him, what he
sold will remain in the possession of the buyer until the Year of Jubilee.
It will be returned in the Jubilee, and he can then go back to his
property.
29 " 'If a man sells a house in a walled city, he retains the right of
redemption a full year after its sale. During that time he may redeem it.
30 If it is not redeemed before a full year has passed, the house in the
walled city shall belong permanently to the buyer and his descendants.
It is not to be returned in the Jubilee. 31 But houses in villages without
walls around them are to be considered as open country. They can be
redeemed, and they are to be returned in the Jubilee.
32 " 'The Levites always have the right to redeem their houses in the
Levitical towns, which they possess. 33 So the property of the Levites is
redeemable—that is, a house sold in any town they hold—and is to be
returned in the Jubilee, because the houses in the towns of the Levites
are their property among the Israelites. 34 But the pastureland belonging
to their towns must not be sold; it is their permanent possession.

8–12 The word "Jubilee" means "blowing the ram's horn," which was done in announcing the year. Thus the root occurs also in the name Jubal, the father of musicians (Gen 4:21). The identifying name Jubilee occurs only in Leviticus and in Numbers 36:4. But the idea of release of those enslaved for debt (*d^{e}rôr*) occurs, not only at v.10, but also at Isaiah 61:1; Jeremiah 34:8, 15, 17; and Ezekiel 46:17. From this word the idea of celebration has come into English, especially the celebration of a fiftieth anniversary.

In v.8 the Hebrew is "seven sabbaths" of years, not "seventy sevens" as it is in Daniel's prophecy of the Seventy Weeks (Dan 9:24–27, though there, too, and clearly in the pseudepigraphal Book of Jubilees the word "seven" is used for a sabbatical year period). Probably it was well that the announcement came "on the Day of Atonement" (v.9), that solemn day of contrition. Otherwise many a hard-hearted, rich Israelite would have refused the obligations of the release. Indeed, the Jubilee and sabbaticals were not always observed (2 Chron 36:21). It was suggested above that the new moon trumpet reechoed through the land as others took up the signal of the start of a new moon. Here, clearly, there was such an arrangement for the word to get around.

It seems rather impractical to have had two fallow years in succession, viz., the forty-ninth and the fiftieth, though, of course, God could have simply compounded the blessing for the forty-eighth year. A suggestion to relieve the problem comes from the Book of Jubilees. This book, written perhaps about 200 B.C., is a reworking of Genesis with every event dated. The dates are counted from Creation and are given in terms of jubilees, sabbaticals, years, months, and days. But the Jubilees are only forty-nine years long. This may have been a mistake on the part of the author of Jubilees. Or it may give a clue to a better translation of v.10. Just as seven weeks from Sunday to Sunday is called fifty days by inclusive reckoning in 23:15–16, so in the present sense the last of the forty-nine years might be called the fiftieth year by inclusive reckoning.

Perhaps the difference is inconsequential, but at least one ancient interpretation of this verse was that the seventh sabbatical was the Jubilee. The LXX gives no additional light. It simply translates the Hebrew verbatim. Wenham (p. 319) escapes the difficulty by seeing in v.8 a reference to a short year of forty-nine days to serve as the Jubilee. But such an intercalary period is nowhere else referred to, and his translation of v.8 appears forced. From a different standpoint, S.B. Hoenig ("Sabbatical Years and the Year of Jubilee," JQR 59 [1969]: 222–36) also concluded that the Jubilee was not a fiftieth year.

"To proclaim liberty" (v.10) for the slaves was characteristic of every sabbatical year. The return to the family homestead was a special feature of the Jubilee. The word for "liberty" (*d*[e]*rôr*) is used at Jeremiah 34:8–17 of the freeing of slaves in the sabbatical year. The inference is as suggested above, that the seventh sabbatical year was the Jubilee.

13–17 In the Jubilee the land was not absolutely entailed as it was in Nuzi in Mesopotamia. According to the Nuzi tablets, the Hurrian law forbade the sale of land. An interesting legal fiction arose by which a man who wanted to sell his land would adopt (for a price) the man who wanted to buy it. These sale-adoptions were ancient ways to get around the law. Other Nuzi adoption customs and family laws are reflected in the families of the patriarchs in Genesis who came from Mesopotamia; but the Mosaic legislation on land had no parallel with those land laws. There was no way to get around the law except by Jezebel's simple expedient of murder (1 Kings 21).

The arrangement for buying or selling considering the number of years since the Jubilee was simple (v.15). A field that could be possessed forty years before the Jubilee was worth more than one that would be possessed only ten years. A man might speculate in land for temporary advantage, but no family could be permanently disadvantaged. In all this social legislation, successful operation really must proceed on the basis of the cooperation of the citizens (v.17). And Israel's regard for the poor was supported by the knowledge that the Lord is God and that he has respect for the poor: "When he cries out to me, I will hear, for I am compassionate" (Exod 22:27).

In a sense Israel had a kind of communism. The wealth was partially redivided every few years. But it is unfair to call this communism, just as it is inaccurate to call the communal living of the early church communism. This was the communal sharing that works well in a family where all have the strongest ties of love and interest. Even in families the system breaks down if the common bond is not there. Israel, like the early church, was a community of people united in worship of the true God and sanctified in him. In times of revival, at least, the bulk of Israel's citizens would have been God-fearing men and women earnest in obeying God's law.

During the present age of pluriformity, with the church a separated body gathered out of the world, there is no exact parallel to the nation of Israel. No rule of the saints, such as the Puritans envisaged, long endures today. Even Israel's land reforms probably would not be tolerated today by a self-seeking citizenry. These land laws cannot be duplicated in our day, but they can teach us the importance of curbing the tendency to increase wealth in the hands of the few. The poor had better be protected in any society, or revolts will follow as wealth accumulates and people decay.

18–28 The success of laws such as these depended on the people's obedience; but the system still would not work except for the special blessing of God, who owned the land and also the people and had his sovereign purposes for both (vv.18–19). Verse 21 underlines the importance of the providential blessing of God. It was doubtless good for the land to lie fallow one year. God would bless an obedient nation with rains, and pests would cease under his hand. Unfortunately the nation turned to other gods, and God vacated the land until it had "enjoyed its sabbath rests" (2 Chron 36:21).

Verses 23–24 spell out the details of the Jubilee. There are certain exceptions and special regulations. The NIV's "must not be sold permanently" is a better translation than the KJV's "not be sold forever," which is ambiguous. This law of land reform is perpetual, but the land when sold was to be sold for a limited time only, not permanently, which is just what the Hebrew means.

Not only was the land to return to its original family in the Jubilee, but a man who had been forced to sell his land out of necessity could buy it back at any time he could raise the money (v.24). If his near kin could do it, he should. If the man's fortunes increased, he could do it himself. The best example of this law's working is in the Book of Ruth in the family of Naomi. The family was poor and sold their possessions. On Naomi's return a near kinsman was at first willing to buy back her land for her. It appears that he was willing because she had no heirs, and he thought the fields would revert to him. When he learned that he must also marry Ruth, the widow, and raise up an heir who would get the property, he refused and gave way to Boaz, the next kinsman in line.

To "refund the balance" (v.27) is to pay back the price of the field at the later day, which would be less than the price at the earlier date. The translation "balance" is more accurate than the RSV's "overpayment" or KJV's "overplus."

The city is different from the country (v.29). To live in a walled city was a privilege, not a right. Real estate in the walled city was at a premium. Its value was not just its land but the improvements in terms of house and fortifications. A man temporarily in need could sell the house and redeem it in a year, but after that time the buyer was protected. As explained in v.16, when a man sold his farm, he was selling so many crops until the Jubilee. In contrast to walled cities, the villages, which were unrestricted in extent, counted in with their respective fields (v.31). They were released in the Jubilee.

32–34 The point of v.32 is that many, if not all, of the Levitical cities listed in Joshua 21 were walled, where normally the right of redemption was limited to one year. Levites usually did not have any property outside these cities. Thus, except for this provision, the Levites eventually could have lost their cities and, therefore, all their holdings. But in these cities the Levites could redeem their property at any time.

The Hebrew of v.33 is somewhat involved, but the total meaning is clear. Any Levitical house cannot be bought in perpetuity. It will go out in the Jubilee. The Hebrew seems literally to say, "the house that was sold, and the city of his possession" (KJV). But although the KJV reads "and," it is not possible, for whole cities were not sold. The LXX, feeling the difficulty, omits the Hebrew conjunction completely. The problem can now be reduced by admitting that the Hebrew conjunction, when emphatic, can be used on a word placed later in the sentence (M. Dahood, *Psalms I,* AB, p. 24). With this new information gathered from Ugaritic and other studies, the words can be satisfactorily translated as in the NIV: "a house sold in any town." In a sense the lands of the Levites were like lands of the church in the Middle Ages. To this day in Arab Palestine, lands dedicated for religious purposes are held in perpetuity.

Notes

17 Kaiser (*OT Ethics,* pp. 219–20) very rightly objects to liberation theology, which proposes land reform and forcible redistribution of wealth on the basis of Lev 25. But, as he says, liberation theology leaves untouched the whole ministration of the saving grace of God on which Lev 25 is based. Consideration of what is now called social justice could lead us far afield. Significant work basic to the discussion has been given by Nash (*Freedom*). He distinguishes nicely between justice and charity. Obviously we need more of both!

As to the teaching of Leviticus, we would argue that this is a piece of civil legislation for the nation like the "parapet around your roof" in Deut 22:8. This civil legislation was good and proper for Israel in her situation, but it was no longer applicable to Israel after she became mingled among the nations. Christians can, however, gather from these laws principles of good government that we can strive to have adopted today. Good laws are based on good principles of ethics and morality that are ingrained in the human heart but are found more completely in the Word of God.

For instance, cities today usually require fences to be built around swimming pools. Also today governments have a duty toward the poor. It is a duty of mercy and justice both. The poor need more than land in Central America or money in a city ghetto. They need care, advice, support, and also restraint and punishment for crime. A good government should deal effectively with these problems. Christian citizens should also be concerned in these areas as city missions have been for years in a small way. Christians can add, in addition to physical help, the basic ingredient of God's saving grace, which the government cannot directly offer.

C. *Protection of the Poor*

25:35–55

35 " 'If one of your countrymen becomes poor and is unable to support himself among you, help him as you would an alien or a temporary

resident, so he can continue to live among you. 36 Do not take interest of
any kind from him, but fear your God, so that your countryman may
continue to live among you. 37 You must not lend him money at interest
or sell him food at a profit. 38 I am the LORD your God, who brought you
out of Egypt to give you the land of Canaan and to be your God.
39 " 'If one of your countrymen becomes poor among you and sells
himself to you, do not make him work as a slave. 40 He is to be treated as
a hired worker or a temporary resident among you; he is to work for you
until the Year of Jubilee. 41 Then he and his children are to be released,
and he will go back to his own clan and to the property of his
forefathers. 42 Because the Israelites are my servants, whom I brought
out of Egypt, they must not be sold as slaves. 43 Do not rule over them
ruthlessly, but fear your God.
44 " 'Your male and female slaves are to come from the nations around
you; from them you may buy slaves. 45 You may also buy some of the
temporary residents living among you and members of their clans born
in your country, and they will become your property. 46 You can will
them to your children as inherited property and can make them slaves
for life, but you must not rule over your fellow Israelites ruthlessly.
47 " 'If an alien or a temporary resident among you becomes rich and
one of your countrymen becomes poor and sells himself to the alien
living among you or to a member of the alien's clan, 48 he retains the
right of redemption after he has sold himself. One of his relatives may
redeem him: 49 An uncle or a cousin or any blood relative in his clan may
redeem him. Or if he prospers, he may redeem himself. 50 He and his
buyer are to count the time from the year he sold himself up to the Year
of Jubilee. The price for his release is to be based on the rate paid to a
hired man for that number of years. 51 If many years remain, he must pay
for his redemption a larger share of the price paid for him. 52 If only a few
years remain until the Year of Jubilee, he is to compute that and pay for
his redemption accordingly. 53 He is to be treated as a man hired from
year to year; you must see to it that his owner does not rule over him
ruthlessly.
54 " 'Even if he is not redeemed in any of these ways, he and his
children are to be released in the Year of Jubilee, 55 for the Israelites
belong to me as servants. They are my servants, whom I brought out of
Egypt. I am the LORD your God.

In this section there are three cases that are covered by the Mosaic law on loans (cf. Exod 22:25; Deut 23:19–20). Usually they have been treated as (1) loans without interest, (2) indentured servitude for debt, and (3) indentured servitude to an alien. New studies have been made on this section by Speiser (pp. 131–42; see Notes), who sheds much light on the passage from close parallels he discovered in documents from Alalakh and Nuzi. Speiser argues very convincingly that the three cases differ only in degree. He remarks that in Mesopotamia all loans were discounted in advance. If a man would borrow a hundred shekels, the interest (Akkad. *ḫubullū*; Heb. *nešek*) would be deducted in advance. If the loan was not repaid on time, extra interest (Akkad. *ṣiptu*; Heb. *tarbîṯ* or *marbîṯ*) was charged. Seldom could a debtor pay this extra interest, and indentured servitude resulted.

According to Speiser (p. 132), case 1 involved a man who could not repay his loan on time. He would be seized by the creditor for an indefinite time of servitude, but no further interest would accrue. Case 2 specifies that a man who saw his plight, perhaps after an extension and a second interest charge, would sell himself into servitude. Such servitude, it was specified, must be humane and, in any case, end at the Jubilee. Case 3 involved debt to a resident alien who could not be trusted to be humane, etc. In such a case the debtor should be redeemed by the next of kin.

Precise parallels are offered by Speiser for all these cases. He goes on to show in an interesting way that the Levitical law here follows ancient pre-Mosaic custom and was totally misunderstood in later Jewish traditional exegesis. He concludes that this and three other passages he treats "bear unmistakable imprint of pre-exilic times" (p. 142). It may be added, also, that they argue for a very careful transmission of the text in that ancient details, misunderstood for centuries, can now be seen to have been quite accurately preserved.

35–38 "Help him" (v.35) is not a fair translation of the Hebrew words *heḥ^{e}zaqtā bô*. The Hebrew says, "you shall seize him" (cf. Speiser, p. 134). The supposition is that a creditor has seized his debtor like a resident alien while he works off the debt. Speiser (p. 141) holds that while the debtor was working off the debt, he himself served as a pledge for its payment, and no further interest or second interest could be charged. That would be "excessive" interest or usury (v.36, NIV mg.). This verse is a conclusion to v.35. If you seize him, you will not make further charges but must treat him like a brother. The implication is that it is wrong to treat him like a resident alien (v.35).

Speiser (p. 140) thinks that originally the distinction between first interest (*nešek̲*) and added interest (profit, *marbît̲*) was maintained. In v.37, however, there may only be a repetition with details of v.36. *Nešek̲* and *marbît̲* are again the forbidden interest in a loan for money or for food. After enslavement no further interest should accrue. Otherwise the poor man could never work off his debt.

Much controversy has revolved around such verses. In the Middle Ages some church leaders frowned on any interest-bearing loan; and, as a result, a large Jewish banking business sprang up especially in the twelfth and thirteenth centuries. The Eastern Orthodox Church never took a position against interest, and trade in the East flourished. The Reformers allowed interest that was not exorbitant (cf. KJV). The word "interest" (*nešek̲*) is from the root "to bite" (*nāšak̲*). The rate of interest mentioned in Nehemiah 5:10–11 is 1 percent—probably 1 percent a month.

Verses 36–37 do not forbid a loan to the poor man, for Exodus 22:25–27 pictures a loan to a poor man with his garment as collateral. (Or was it really not collateral but a token that was taken before witnesses and restored promptly?) The passage in Deuteronomy 24:10–13 on pledges specifies that the creditor could not enter a house to choose the pledge he desired. The pledge chosen by the borrower must be accepted by the creditor, then recorded and restored promptly. In case of default, temporary enslavement would result. It seems strange in such a context to assume, as many have done in the past, that no interest at all could be charged. But in any case, no excessive interest could be charged—interest beyond the usual regulations. The poor were to be protected.

39–46 Speiser (p. 134) holds that the situation in v.39 is similar to that in v.35, only more extreme. True, the two verses begin with exactly the same words. In this instance a man has no credit to obtain a loan. His case is hopeless, and he takes the initiative. But he has his rights; he is not a slave. "A hired worker or a temporary resident" (v.40) is translated by Speiser as "resident laborer" (p. 134), i.e., not a resident alien (cf. comment on v.36).

The notice "until the Year of Jubilee" (v.40) would apply equally well to case 1 of v.35, if that man's debt were not worked off before the Year of Jubilee. The mention of "resident laborers" brings up the contrasting positions of "slaves" (v.44). Hebrews could not be enslaved by their compatriots. Slaves of the nations were permitted, and these were not released in the Jubilee. The most that could be exacted of a brother Israelite was indentured servitude. Of course, slaves, too, had their rights. Indeed, a runaway slave was not to be returned to his master (Deut 23:15). This would tend greatly to affect a master's attitude toward his slaves.

47–55 "An alien or a temporary resident" (v.47) who bought a Hebrew slave did so under the stipulations of Hebrew law. The redemption of such a slave was a kinsman's duty (v.48). Or the slave might grow rich and redeem himself (v.49). This says a good bit about the relative independence of such a slave. His time with his owner was counted like that of a hired servant (v.53). In any event, the slave with his children would be freed at the Jubilee (v.54). Of course, if a man died in slavery, his children would not be slaves forever. They would benefit by the Jubilee.

Verse 55 is remarkably like the thought of Colossians 4:1: "Masters, provide your slaves with what is right and fair, because you know that you also have a Master in heaven." All Israelites were God's servants. They therefore should be compassionate masters—an attitude that Christians should remember even though the institution of physical slavery is happily over.

Notes

Speiser's view is discounted by S.E. Loewenstamm ("נשך and מ/תרבית," JBL 88 [1969]: 78–80) on the grounds that Speiser has confused Assyrian *ḫubullu* with *ḫubuttu.* But Speiser's contention does not rest on the definition of *ḫubullu* and does fit very well with the context of Lev 25—as outlined above. If the situation is as often pictured, that the words *nešek* and *tarbîṯ* refer to interest and not usury, then in Ezek 18:8, 13 et al., and Prov 28:8, any interest for a righteous man is forbidden. Kaiser (*OT Ethics*, pp. 213–17) questions Speiser's view but admits that Christ did not forbid interest in commercial transactions. It may still be held that these Hebrew words can mean a second interest beyond the original discounted interest of the loan and, therefore, amount to usury.

36 The Hebrew for "interest of any kind" is נֶשֶׁךְ (*nešek*) and תַּרְבִּית (*tarbîṯ*), which in my view would be the forbidden extra interest charged after enslavement.

37 In Neh 5:1–11 apparently Nehemiah and his government had ransomed poor Hebrew debtors from the Persians. But rich Hebrew nobles were making new loans to them and enslaving those who defaulted. "The hundreth part" (v.11) is 1 percent per month or 12 percent a year. The word מַשָּׁא (*maššā'*) is, like *nešek*, a rare word hard to define in detail because we do not have the whole picture of loan practices, but probably "usury" is a good translation.

X. Warnings Against Apostasy (26:1–46)

A. *Conditions of Blessing*

26:1–13 (cf. Deut 28:1–14; 30:1–10)

1 " 'Do not make idols or set up an image or a sacred stone for yourselves, and do not place a carved stone in your land to bow down before it. I am the LORD your God.

2 " 'Observe my Sabbaths and have reverence for my sanctuary. I am
the LORD.
3 " 'If you follow my decrees and are careful to obey my commands, 4 I
will send you rain in its season, and the ground will yield its crops and
the trees of the field their fruit. 5 Your threshing will continue until grape
harvest and the grape harvest will continue until planting, and you will
eat all the food you want and live in safety in your land.
6 " 'I will grant peace in the land, and you will lie down and no one will
make you afraid. I will remove savage beasts from the land, and the
sword will not pass through your country. 7 You will pursue your
enemies, and they will fall by the sword before you. 8 Five of you will
chase a hundred, and a hundred of you will chase ten thousand, and
your enemies will fall by the sword before you.
9 " 'I will look on you with favor and make you fruitful and increase
your numbers, and I will keep my covenant with you. 10 You will still be
eating last year's harvest when you will have to move it out to make
room for the new. 11 I will put my dwelling place among you, and I will
not abhor you. 12 I will walk among you and be your God, and you will be
my people. 13 I am the LORD your God, who brought you out of Egypt so
that you would no longer be slaves to the Egyptians; I broke the bars of
your yoke and enabled you to walk with heads held high.

This chapter has strong affinities with Deuteronomy 28–30 (cf. esp. Deut 28:1–14; 30:1–10). It is a solemn reinforcement of the preceding laws with an appeal to Israel to obey God's laws and be blessed rather than to turn away to disaster. The warnings are more extensive than the promises, but the chapters (Deut 28–30) end with a reminder of God's enduring mercy and the ancient covenants he made with the patriarchs.

The conditions given here are only summarized. The things specified are avoiding idols (v.1), keeping the Sabbath (v.2), and revering the sanctuary (v.2). Beyond that the broad statement is "Obey my commands" (v.3). The promises, which are emphatic and detailed, largely concern material blessing; but the crowning spiritual blessing—"I will walk among you and be your God, and you will be my people"—is included (v.12; cf. Jer 30:22; Hos 2:23 et al.)

The physical blessings and curses characterize Israel's establishment as a nation. Even in God's dealings with the patriarchs, the promised material blessings were largely not for the present. Abraham died having seen the promises afar off. He owned only a sepulcher in the Promised Land. Abraham grew rich, but Isaac probably grew poor; and Jacob certainly had a hard life. Material blessings such as favorable rains, health, peace, etc., were appropriate promises for Israel as a nation living in one area with unified culture, laws, and worship. In other situations the people of God shared the common lot of men. God sends his "rain on the righteous and the unrighteous" (Matt 5:45). Today when God punishes a nation with war, the innocent must suffer with the guilty.

Material prosperity is not so much the promise for Christians now, living as they do in a mixed society. Still there are special providences of God that bless his children even today, and the promises of spiritual blessings are always valid. Nevertheless, there is a difference between the material prosperity promised to Israel and the blessing promised to the church. It is hard to generalize as to what material blessings are promised to nations today. God surely holds them accountable for excess of sin as he did the ancient Canaanites. The evils of Hitler brought untold suffering to Germany in the closing days of the war. But the Muslim nations have been blessed (?) with abounding riches in recent decades. America, in general, has honored the true

God and has been blessed abundantly. But the particular discernment of God's providential blessings is difficult. It was a problem to the prophets when a more wicked nation was given supremacy over Israel (Isa 10:5–12; Hab 1:13).

1–5 The ban on idols is sharp and pervasive throughout the OT. The reason is plainly given in Deuteronomy 4:15–19. God has no form and is not a part of his creation. Any material god is less than God. The prohibition of idolatry was so emphatic that ancient Israel made no images of God, at least as far as archaeological evidence goes. The idols that Israel worshiped were of the heathen gods. The word "idols" (*'elîlim*) in v.1 is a word of scorn, viz., "worthless things."

The word for "image" (*pesel*) is a general word for any image constructed or sculptured of wood, stone, metal, etc. The word "sacred stone" (*maṣṣēḇāh*; KJV, "standing image") refers to a monumental stone stele or slab with or without inscription. Some such monuments apparently associated with the temple of Baal Berith in Shechem (Judg 9:6, 46) have been found (cf. C.F. Pfeiffer, ed., *The Biblical World* [Grand Rapids: Baker, 1966], p. 520).

The word for "carved stone" (*'eḇen maśkîṯ*) is less certain but refers to some kind of sculptured figure. It may be added that the absence of idols was wonderful for the advancement of faith, but it is troublesome to the archaeologist. Much can be learned of the surrounding cultures' religion, history, and art by the carved work that often bears inscriptions. Palestine digs are sadly (or happily) lacking in these idolatrous materials.

As mentioned in the comments on ch. 23, the Sabbaths include the set feasts as well as the weekly Sabbath. The word "sanctuary" (v.2; lit., "holy place") is used many times in the OT from Exodus 15:17 on and usually refers to the tabernacle or the later temple. Verse 2 repeats 19:30, but here it serves well as a summary of God's will for his worship. Both instances of this verse are in the so-called Holiness Code, which critical scholars assign to a different author from the rest of the book. Usually their claim is that repetition of similar material in different places is due to assembling of duplicate materials by different editors. A duplicate verse or story usually is said to mean, for example, that one comes from E and the other from the P source. In this case, however, both verses are within the alleged Holiness Code (H or P) source. Apparently ancient authors repeated themselves, and the argument for diverse authorship from duplicate passages is poorly founded. Actually, such duplications are not rare in the Pentateuch or other books. They are especially common in the Psalms, probably for liturgical reasons.

Significantly, the first blessing mentioned is "rain" (v.4). Palestine is water conscious. In those days farmers and housewives, too, were totally dependent on the rain and the perennial springs. Albright and others have remarked that the invention of lime plaster in the thirteenth century B.C. made cisterns practicable to help somewhat in saving water. There are two views of the amount of rainfall in antiquity. The first view, popularized by Ellsworth Huntingdon, argues that the climate in Palestine has greatly changed. The other view argues that it has not (so Albright, Glueck et al.).

The whole question of climate is temperately discussed by Denis Baly (*Geography of the Bible* [New York: Harper and Row, 1957], pp. 70–82). He concludes that there is no evidence for great changes in climate; but many parts of Palestine are marginal, and a little difference would mean a lot. Actually, Jerusalem has about the same average annual rainfall as London. But in Palestine the rain is all concentrated in the months from October to April. If the rains have a good spread, i.e., including early and latter rains, then crops grow well. Also forestation and irrigation can conserve the water for a longer growing season. It was a very small matter for the Lord to give better rains and rains spread out in a better way so as to bless a faithful nation.

It would be quite a harvest that would last from June to September (v.5)! Actually, with ancient methods of harvesting and threshing, this may not have been much hyperbole for a really good year. A similar promise of millennial abundance is given in Amos 9:13: " 'The days are coming,' declares the LORD, 'when the reaper will be overtaken by the plowman and the planter by the one treading grapes.' "

6–8 There is a causal connection as well as a providential connection here. Decent living and decent government to an extent beget peace (v.6). Immoral, reckless government invites wars, both civil and foreign. In the years from the division of the kingdom to the Fall of Samaria, the two kingdoms had a diverse character. The northern kingdom openly encouraged idolatry and in its national life apostatized from the Lord. During those two hundred years, the northern kingdom saw nine different dynasties fight for the throne. In the southern kingdom, which in general maintained the faith, the dynasty of David continued with one small interregnum at the time of Athaliah. God often uses wars as an instrument of punishment (Isa 10:6).

Dangerous animals—"savage beasts" (v.6)—except for snakes and scorpions, have not been much of a problem in Palestine for many years. In biblical times, however, both lions and bears are mentioned repeatedly. There must have been a somewhat different situation (cf. v.4 above). Egyptian pictures show pharaohs hunting lions where now there are only deserts. Such animals require lesser game for food. The lesser game require some grass and woodland. Palestine in ancient times clearly must have been somewhat different from what it is today, for "savage beasts" were a real danger to Israel. In fact, God promised to drive out the Canaanites gradually so that the dangerous animals would not multiply unduly (Exod 23:30).

The same sort of expression as "five of you will chase a hundred" (v.8) is found in Deuteronomy 32:30. Of course, there is hyperbole here, but it is true even today that small things can turn the tide of history. An assassination attempt on Hitler failed by a couple of feet. If the briefcase with its bomb had been placed just a little differently, World War II would have been greatly shortened. In Israel's history Gideon's 300 men defeated 135,000 Midianites; Jonathan and his armor-bearer alone defeated a Philistine force. When David killed Goliath, all the Philistines fled. In ancient warfare, even more than in modern times, a little incident such as the death or prowess of a hero could turn the whole tide of battle. God promised Israel victory if she would remain faithful to him.

9–13 "Will keep my covenant" (v.9) is literally "will cause to rise up [*hēqîm*] my covenant." It is probably legal language. There has been much study in recent years on the concept of a covenant in antiquity (see Introduction, pp. 516–18). In any case, the covenant referred to in the present verse is probably the covenant God made with Israel on Mount Sinai. Verses 1–2 refer to prominent parts of that covenant. However, this chapter should not be pressed into a covenant-treaty mold. There is no historical prelude. The commands or "stipulations" are very brief if they can be found at all. The copies are not specified, as is usual in treaties, etc. The chapter is a logical presentation of the consequences of obedience or disobedience to God's law.

God promised to dwell among his people (v.11) in the tabernacle spiritually, not materially. From the word for "dwelling" (*miškān*) and its root, the later Israelites developed a name for the presence of God in the Most Holy Place—the Shekinah. The expression "I will walk among" (v.12) is not to be literalized in this connection. It is like the NT word translated in the KJV "have your conversation." It refers to life, fellowship, and behavior. Enoch, Abraham, and many others were said to "walk with God." The form of the verb used (Hithpael) is usually said to be reflexive, but the studies of Speiser on a similar Akkadian form emphasize that it can also express continuous action and duration (pp. 508–12). God would continually fellowship with his people if they obeyed his word; he would *live* among them. The thought repeats that of the promised dwelling at v.11. The promise "and be your God" is repeated elsewhere (Jer 30:22; Ezek 11:20; Hos 2:23; Rom 9:26; cf. the study on this promise by O. Palmer Robertson, *The Christ of the Covenants* [Grand Rapids: Baker, 1980], pp. 46–52).

Ten times in Leviticus and over a hundred times in the rest of the OT, God's miraculous deliverance of Israel from Egyptian bondage is emphasized. The event made an indelible impression on the Hebrew mind and record. The expression "enabled you to walk with heads held high" (*qômᵉmîyûṯ*, lit., "upright"; v.13) is an interesting commentary on how the ancient mind regarded slavery—about as we do today.

B. *Threatened Punishments*

26:14–39 (cf. Deut 28:15–68; 29:18–28)

14" 'But if you will not listen to me and carry out all these commands,
15and if you reject my decrees and abhor my laws and fail to carry out all
my commands and so violate my covenant, 16then I will do this to you: I
will bring upon you sudden terror, wasting diseases and fever that will
destroy your sight and drain away your life. You will plant seed in vain,
because your enemies will eat it. 17I will set my face against you so that
you will be defeated by your enemies; those who hate you will rule over
you, and you will flee even when no one is pursuing you.

18" 'If after all this you will not listen to me, I will punish you for your
sins seven times over. 19I will break down your stubborn pride and make
the sky above you like iron and the ground beneath you like bronze.
20Your strength will be spent in vain, because your soil will not yield its
crops, nor will the trees of the land yield their fruit.

21" 'If you remain hostile toward me and refuse to listen to me, I will
multiply your afflictions seven times over, as your sins deserve. 22I will
send wild animals against you, and they will rob you of your children,
destroy your cattle and make you so few in number that your roads will
be deserted.

23" 'If in spite of these things you do not accept my correction but
continue to be hostile toward me, 24I myself will be hostile toward you
and will afflict you for your sins seven times over. 25And I will bring the
sword upon you to avenge the breaking of the covenant. When you
withdraw into your cities, I will send a plague among you, and you will
be given into enemy hands. 26When I cut off your supply of bread, ten
women will be able to bake your bread in one oven, and they will dole
out the bread by weight. You will eat, but you will not be satisfied.

27" 'If in spite of this you still do not listen to me but continue to be
hostile toward me, 28then in my anger I will be hostile toward you, and I
myself will punish you for your sins seven times over. 29You will eat the
flesh of your sons and the flesh of your daughters. 30I will destroy your
high places, cut down your incense altars and pile your dead bodies on

the lifeless forms of your idols, and I will abhor you. [31]I will turn your
cities into ruins and lay waste your sanctuaries, and I will take no delight
in the pleasing aroma of your offerings. [32]I will lay waste the land, so
that your enemies who live there will be appalled. [33]I will scatter you
among the nations and will draw out my sword and pursue you. Your
land will be laid waste, and your cities will lie in ruins. [34]Then the land
will enjoy its sabbath years all the time that it lies desolate and you are in
the country of your enemies; then the land will rest and enjoy its
sabbaths. [35]All the time that it lies desolate, the land will have the rest it
did not have during the sabbaths you lived in it.

[36]" 'As for those of you who are left, I will make their hearts so fearful
in the lands of their enemies that the sound of a windblown leaf will put
them to flight. They will run as though fleeing from the sword, and they
will fall, even though no one is pursuing them. [37]They will stumble over
one another as though fleeing from the sword, even though no one is
pursuing them. So you will not be able to stand before your enemies.
[38]You will perish among the nations; the land of your enemies will
devour you. [39]Those of you who are left will waste away in the lands of
their enemies because of their sins; also because of their fathers' sins
they will waste away.

14–17 A long list of threatened punishments to Israel if she disobeyed God's laws follows (cf. Deut 28:15–68; 29:18–28). These punishments and the preceding blessing sound like the imprecations and benedictions of a Hittite treaty. Yet in this section the whole of a covenant-treaty structure is not easily observable. This should perhaps be a warning against too mechanical an approach to the covenant format. It was not always followed nor slavishly observed, and appropriate parts could be used alone for particular emphasis. The more extensive presentation of imprecations and benedictions is in Deuteronomy 28 and 30.

Very similar words to "but if you will not listen to me" (v.14) introduce the corresponding section at Deuteronomy 28:15, which adds "I am giving you today." Here we do not have the conclusion of a long sermon as Deuteronomy was but a code of laws and rituals. In one sense, all the legislation of Exodus and Leviticus is part of the covenant God ordained at Sinai. The summary was the Ten Commandments that were engraved in stone as a witness and testimony. The sacred chest that contained them was therefore often called the "ark of the covenant" or the "ark of the testimony." The curtain separating the holy shrine where the ark was kept was even called the "curtain of the Testimony" (24:3).

The word "covenant" (v.15) as used in such biblical phrases is somewhat like the word "contract" or "treaty"—only it was a one-sided treaty imposed on the nation chosen for God's blessing. To break the covenant or contract meant not only to forfeit all God's promised blessings but to incur his curse. The word "covenant" as used in these biblical phrases is somewhat different from the theological formulation of "covenant" when the word is used in such contexts as "covenant theology." In such contexts the covenants of works and grace embrace a representative principle that some would and others would not find in God's dealings with his people.

The word "sudden terror" (v.16) does not seem to require the idea of surprise. The root *bāhal* means "to be terrified" or "to be confused." The LXX says "perplexity." The words "wasting diseases and fever" are used only here and at Deuteronomy 28:22. They refer to physical ailments. The Arabic equivalent of "wasting diseases" is the disease formerly called consumption—tuberculosis. Quite likely the words "that will destroy your sight and drain away your life" are not adjectival referring to previous diseases. The normal result of fever is not to "destroy the sight." The words are participles and probably substantival in use: "a destruction of sight" and "a draining away of life."

Palestine was situated on the land bridge between the great powers of antiquity. And there were local enemies, too. The threat of enemy domination was very real. The Midianites of Gideon's day are likened to grasshoppers who devour everything.

Verse 17—"you will flee even when no one is pursuing you"—is picked up by Proverbs 28:1: "The wicked man flees though no one pursues." How different the situation if Israel were obedient (v.8)!

18–26 Verse 18 is a surprisingly rare usage of the number seven. It is apparently restricted to this chapter (vv.21, 24, 28) and is a threat of multiple punishment.

The expression "sky . . . like iron and the ground . . . like bronze," which refers to a rainless sky and dried ground, is used only here and at Deuteronomy 28:23, where the symbols of iron and bronze are reversed! Obviously they are figures of speech. No Israelite thought the heavens were solid metal. The Deuteronomy passage adds further description of the dryness of the ground.

The word "brass" (KJV) is really incorrect throughout the OT. The KJV uses it exclusively for copper and its alloys. The NIV uses "copper" for a few places (e.g., Deut 8:9) referring to the mining of the metal but usually uses "bronze," which is more accurate. Brass is an alloy of copper and zinc with sometimes some other metal in small proportion. Brass was not much used until nearly the time of Christ. Bronze is an alloy of copper and tin and was used early, but how early is hard to tell. The first bronzes were probably accidental, for tin and copper occur together in some minerals. Bronze is a very practical metal. It can be cast and hammered easily and makes good hard tools and weapons. Its properties vary according to the amount of tin used.

Verse 19 is only the second mention of iron in the Bible. The first mention (Gen 4:22) is a special case and perhaps refers to meteoric iron or even an ironlike stone that first received the name. A minor use of iron can be documented at a very early age (see W.C. Kaiser, "The Literary Form of Genesis 1–11," *New Perspectives on the Old Testament,* ed. J. Barton Payne [Waco, Tex.: Word, 1970], p. 55). Nothing in the tabernacle was made of iron. A little iron was found in the tomb of the Pharaoh Tutankhamun (c. 1360 B.C.). Two talents (about 150 lbs.) of iron are mentioned in a Ugaritic inventory tablet (#120). Deuteronomy 3:11 mentions it in connection with Og's bedstead (which was probably a sarcophagus trimmed with iron). But the secret of successful iron-working and tempering into steel did not come into Palestine until about 1180 B.C., when the Philistines introduced iron weapons and implements and brought in the Iron Age generally (1 Sam 13:19–22). This verse only refers to iron as a hard metal and would fit well the pre-Philistine period. The crop failure obviously would be because of a drought so harsh as to affect the trees, too. The roads would not be much traveled because of danger from wild animals and enemies (v.22).

The Hebrew of v.25 is quite emphatic. The sword will "avenge the vengeance" of the covenant. The broken covenant cannot be passed over by God without awful judgment. The Israelites will "withdraw into [their] cities," i.e., in a state of siege. In time of war the surrounding people fled to the cities for protection. In the crowded cities hunger and pestilence took their awful toll. "Ten women will be able to bake your bread" (v.26) indicates that there would be many people but very little bread to go around. Every crumb would be weighed and conserved, and still people would go hungry.

27–34 The horrors of ancient sieges are matched perhaps only by the modern siege of Leningrad in World War II. There also cannibalism occurred (v.29). There are biblical references to these horrors in the sieges of Samaria (2 Kings 6:28–29) and Jerusalem (Lam 4:10). Josephus (*War* VI, 15–32 [3–4]) tells similarly dreadful stories of the siege of Jerusalem by the Romans.

So dreadful would be God's judgments that even the enemies around would be "appalled" (v.32). These references to captivity have been used to argue that this chapter could not have been written until after the Exile. It seems like a strange argument. By the same token, the blessings of vv.4–13 are so wonderful that one might think they could not have been written until after the Millennium! Actually, anyone in antiquity who could write a treaty of the Hittite suzerainty type could write such maledictions. The anguish of famine, conquest, and siege were well enough known in Moses' time.

Verse 34—"enjoy its sabbath years"—is alluded to in 2 Chronicles 36:21, using the same words; and the verse is combined with Jeremiah's prophecy (25:11) that the Captivity would last seventy years. As Allis (p. 160) points out, there is no need to be mechanical and hold that the sabbatical-year provision was neglected for just 490 years. But it was evidently neglected for a long time. "Enjoy" is the regular translation of the Hebrew word *rāṣāh*. It is used again at v.43 (q.v.).

36–39 It may be suggested that v.36 repeats v.17. The words "as though fleeing from the sword, and they will fall" may be parenthetical. The point is that the people will flee at the sound of a driven leaf—when none pursues. The wording is somewhat different from v.17, but the thought is similar. This section ends with an emphasis on their end and the unreasoning panic that God will put in their hearts. Proverbs 28:1 probably alludes to v.37 as well as v.17.

C. *God's Perpetual Covenant*

26:40–46

40" 'But if they will confess their sins and the sins of their fathers—their treachery against me and their hostility toward me, 41which made me hostile toward them so that I sent them into the land of their enemies—then when their uncircumcised hearts are humbled and they pay for their sin, 42I will remember my covenant with Jacob and my covenant with Isaac and my covenant with Abraham, and I will remember the land. 43For the land will be deserted by them and will enjoy its sabbaths while it lies desolate without them. They will pay for their sins because they rejected my laws and abhorred my decrees. 44Yet in spite of this, when they are in the land of their enemies, I will not reject them or abhor them so as to destroy them completely, breaking my covenant with them. I am the LORD their God. 45But for their sake I will remember the covenant with their ancestors whom I brought out of Egypt in the sight of the nations to be their God. I am the LORD.' "

46These are the decrees, the laws and the regulations that the LORD established on Mount Sinai between himself and the Israelites through Moses.

God had promised the land of Palestine to Abraham, Isaac, and Jacob (Gen 15:18) by a covenant. The elements of a Hittite suzerainty covenant are largely absent from that covenant formulation, which is not surprising since such covenants came after Abraham's time. But God's promises are inviolable. God remembered the promise to

Abraham as the people groaned in Egyptian bondage (Exod 3:15–17). The promise of vv.40–46 is quite similar to that in Deuteronomy 30, and there, too, God remembers the word he "swore to . . . Abraham, Isaac and Jacob" (v.20). Two other passages give somewhat similar promises. Solomon prayed that the Lord would hear the people's prayer of repentance in captivity (1 Kings 8:46–53). Nehemiah prayed (Neh 1:8–9) that the Lord would remember his promise to Israel through Moses, probably referring to Leviticus 26 and Deuteronomy 30, that if they returned to God, he would regather them.

The 1 Kings and the Nehemiah passages, however, have an element not found in the Pentateuch. In his prayer Solomon included the idea that the dispersed people should pray toward the holy temple he had just built in Jerusalem. And Nehemiah's prayer assumes that God would regather Israel to the place where God's names dwelled, Jerusalem. Such ideas are proper in the later books, but in Moses' time Jerusalem had not yet been chosen for the sanctuary. It was not even conquered until David's day. This chapter therefore makes no mention of Jerusalem. Indeed, the only possible mention of Jerusalem in the whole Pentateuch is in Genesis 14:18.

40–45 Confession is essential if we would be rid of sin and right with God (v.40). The word in Deuteronomy 30:2 is "return to the LORD . . . with all your heart and with all your soul." The idea of the circumcised heart (v.41) is thought to be characteristic of Deuteronomy and Jeremiah. And it is true that the phrase is found in Deuteronomy 10:16 and 30:6, as well as in Jeremiah 4:4; but the Leviticus passage has the equivalent thought in negative expression and is in fact similar to Jeremiah 9:25, which complains that Israel is uncircumcised in heart like the heathen round about.

Actually, God's law never emphasized the merely external, though there was far more of the external in the OT than in the NT. Proverbs 23:26 expresses the eternal desire of God in the words "My son, give me your heart." Circumcision was not just a physical mark of national origin. Paul says real circumcision is a matter of the heart (Rom 2:29; more lit., "circumcision . . . is of the heart").

In 25:23 God said, "The land is mine," and he would remember his promises to the patriarchs to give them that land. Incidentally, the promises given here to Israel are not limited to the time of the judges or the Babylonian captivity. Paul declares that the promises to Israel and the fathers are "irrevocable" (Rom 11:28–29). But the Jews will not reinherit Palestine in peace and blessing until they return to the Lord.

Verse 36 stated that only some of the people of the Captivity will be left. But God will spare some (v.44) and use their punishments to bring them back to him. A sad commentary on human nature is that in prosperity men tend to forget God from whom all blessings flow, and God must often punish them to bring them back to him. The wise child of God will stay close to God in the first place and rejoice in the blessings without having to get the punishments.

46 The mention of the mutuality of the covenant is interesting, though it is also stated that God "gave" (*nāṯan*) the laws. This verse is really a summary of the material of Leviticus, though some additional material on vows is given before Numbers begins with the order to break camp and move on toward the land of Canaan.

Notes

41 The use of the word רָצָה (*rāṣāh*) to mean "pay for" iniquity is unusual. See the note on v.43.

43 The word רָצָה (*rāṣāh*), the same word as in vv.34, 41, is used in the first half of v.43 in its usual meaning "enjoy" in phraseology very like v.34. The developed meaning "pay for" (v.41) apparently derives from the idea of satisfying a debt. In the first half of v.43 the verb is feminine singular with the subject "the land" that will "enjoy" its Sabbaths. In the last half the subject is masculine plural—"they will pay"—as is the case with the verb "they rejected" my laws. Those who reject God's laws will pay for their iniquity. This double usage adds emphasis.

XI. Laws Concerning Gifts and Endowments

27:1–34

[1]The LORD said to Moses, [2]"Speak to the Israelites and say to them: 'If anyone makes a special vow to dedicate persons to the LORD by giving equivalent values, [3]set the value of a male between the ages of twenty and sixty at fifty shekels of silver, according to the sanctuary shekel; [4]and if it is a female, set her value at thirty shekels. [5]If it is a person between the ages of five and twenty, set the value of a male at twenty shekels and of a female at ten shekels. [6]If it is a person between one month and five years, set the value of a male at five shekels of silver and that of a female at three shekels of silver. [7]If it is a person sixty years old or more, set the value of a male at fifteen shekels and of a female at ten shekels. [8]If anyone making the vow is too poor to pay the specified amount, he is to present the person to the priest, who will set the value for him according to what the man making the vow can afford.

[9]" 'If what he vowed is an animal that is acceptable as an offering to the LORD, such an animal given to the LORD becomes holy. [10]He must not exchange it or substitute a good one for a bad one, or a bad one for a good one; if he should substitute one animal for another, both it and the substitute become holy. [11]If what he vowed is a ceremonially unclean animal—one that is not acceptable as an offering to the LORD—the animal must be presented to the priest, [12]who will judge its quality as good or bad. Whatever value the priest then sets, that is what it will be. [13]If the owner wishes to redeem the animal, he must add a fifth to its value.

[14]" 'If a man dedicates his house as something holy to the LORD, the priest will judge its quality as good or bad. Whatever value the priest then sets, so it will remain. [15]If the man who dedicates his house redeems it, he must add a fifth to its value, and the house will again become his.

[16]" 'If a man dedicates to the LORD part of his family land, its value is to be set according to the amount of seed required for it—fifty shekels of silver to a homer of barley seed. [17]If he dedicates his field during the Year of Jubilee, the value that has been set remains. [18]But if he dedicates his field after the Jubilee, the priest will determine the value according to the number of years that remain until the next Year of Jubilee, and its set value will be reduced. [19]If the man who dedicates the field wishes to redeem it, he must add a fifth to its value, and the field will again become his. [20]If, however, he does not redeem the field, or if he has sold it to someone else, it can never be redeemed. [21]When the field is released in the Jubilee, it will become holy, like a field devoted to the LORD; it will become the property of the priests.

22“ ‘If a man dedicates to the LORD a field he has bought, which is not
part of his family land, 23the priest will determine its value up to the Year
of Jubilee, and the man must pay its value on that day as something holy
to the LORD. 24In the Year of Jubilee the field will revert to the person
from whom he bought it, the one whose land it was. 25Every value is to
be set according to the sanctuary shekel, twenty gerahs to the shekel.
26“ ‘No one, however, may dedicate the firstborn of an animal, since
the firstborn already belongs to the LORD; whether a cow or a sheep, it is
the LORD’s. 27If it is one of the unclean animals, he may buy it back at its
set value, adding a fifth of the value to it. If he does not redeem it, it is to
be sold at its set value.
28“ ‘But nothing that a man owns and devotes to the LORD—whether
man or animal or family land—may be sold or redeemed; everything so
devoted is most holy to the LORD.
29“ ‘No person devoted to destruction may be ransomed; he must be
put to death.
30“ ‘A tithe of everything from the land, whether grain from the soil or
fruit from the trees, belongs to the LORD; it is holy to the LORD. 31If a man
redeems any of his tithe, he must add a fifth of the value to it. 32The
entire tithe of the herd and flock—every tenth animal that passes under
the shepherd’s rod—will be holy to the LORD. 33He must not pick out the
good from the bad or make any substitution. If he does make a
substitution, both the animal and its substitute become holy and cannot
be redeemed.’ ”
34These are the commands the LORD gave Moses on Mount Sinai for
the Israelites.

It is difficult to understand this section fully because we know so little about the details of dedicating things to the Lord in ancient Israel (cf. Exod 34:19–20; Deut 23:21–23). The chapter discusses dedicated persons, clean animals, unclean animals, houses, and lands. Firstborn animals cannot be dedicated because they belong to the Lord already. Then comes an enigmatic paragraph on devoted things and people. These are apparently the spoils of certain types of war that belong absolutely to the Lord. This is followed by a brief section on tithes.

It seems clear that a person normally would dedicate to the Lord some person or thing, not an amount of money. It was not an age of money exchange. Coinage was not yet invented. Things and people were given. But often, if not usually, the person or thing given was redeemed, and its value in silver was given instead. As Allis (p. 160) remarks, “In most cases no actual change in ownership takes place.” The value of a person is interesting. The person given would presumably become a temple slave; so the values are those of a slave. They may be given in tabular form:

Age	*Value of Male*	*Value of Female*
1–5	5 shekels	3 shekels
5–20	20 shekels	10 shekels
20–60	50 shekels	30 shekels
60 plus	15 shekels	10 shekels

We may not conclude from these figures that women are considered of less worth in the OT. It is merely that adult males were more capable of and valuable for the heavy work of the tabernacle. A bride was purchased in ancient Israel; a groom cost nothing! This proves nothing!

The value of a slave, male or female, gored to death by a vicious ox is thirty shekels according to Exodus 21:32. The similar law in Hammurabi's code (##251–52) specifies thirty shekels of silver for a man of citizen class and twenty for a serf.

The devoted things and persons mentioned in vv.28–29 are quite different. These are not things vowed to the Lord by an individual but spoils of war devoted to destruction by the Lord. The best-known examples are the spoils of Jericho (Josh 6:24) and of the Amalekites of Saul's day (1 Sam 15:3–9). Such spoils and captives could not be redeemed, sold, or ransomed.

Numbers 18:14 is in line with this interpretation. At first sight it might seem that the devoted thing there promised to the priests is the firstborn of man or beast mentioned in v.15. But actually there is in this section of Numbers a list of items to be given to the priests. First-ripe fruits are mentioned in v.13. Devoted things under the ban come next as another category (v.14); then come firstborn animals and men (vv.15–16). There is therefore no problem between the Numbers statements and the Leviticus laws that devoted things, animals, or men may not be redeemed (v.29); that firstborn animals may be redeemed (v.27); and that it is obligatory that firstborn men must be redeemed (Exod 13:13; Num 18:15–16). The redemption price of firstborn men is five shekels of silver according to Numbers 18:16, which is the valuation of a male up to five years of age according to Leviticus 27:6.

1–8 The rendering of *pālā'* to mean "special" (v.2) is strange. It is used many times to mean "wonderful" or even "miraculous"; but here and in Numbers 15:3, 8, it is used in the sense of making a vow that is special or particular (KJV, "singular"). Nothing in the contexts of these verses indicates that this type of vow was out of the ordinary. It was just the special reaction of a consecrated heart to the goodness of God. The LXX has "whoever shall vow a vow." The Hebrew word order differs a little from the English: "a special vow in valuation of persons." The presence of the word "valuation" or "equivalent value" in this connection suggests that a common practice was to give the money equivalent, not the person, for the tabernacle service. It was otherwise when Hannah vowed to give her son to the Lord (cf. 1 Sam 1). There was no thought of redemption there.

On the other hand, Jephthah's vow (Judg 11:32–40) was very different and was an evil vow that never should have been made or kept. The KJV softens Jephthah's vow by translating it "Whatsoever cometh forth of the doors of my house . . . I will offer it up as a burnt offering" (Judg 11:31). However, since the reference is to one coming out of the house to meet him, it is probable that Jephthah really intended to sacrifice a person, perhaps a slave. F.F. Bruce ("Judges," NBC^3, p. 250) cites a report of Idomeneus, king of Crete, who made a similar vow that resulted in the offering of his son. It is not impossible that several ancient warriors in dire straits made this vow and that Jephthah knew and feared the possible consequences. But Jephthah's vow is not approved in Scripture. He himself was on the edge of Israel and was not following the laws of God. Neither is his vow called a "special vow."

On "fifty shekels of silver" see the table of values of a dedicated tabernacle slave given above.

Apparently "if a man is too poor" (v.8) refers to a man who wanted to make a vow but was too poor to redeem the person (slave or child?) whom he had vowed. In this case the priest was not to take the one who made the vow as a slave in lieu of the money but was to reduce the evaluation to what the man could afford.

9–13 In the case of clean animals, the vow of an animal was supposed to be final. The case was quite different from the dedication of men. A man might dedicate to the Lord the next male sheep born in his flock. If so, he should give it regardless of whether it looked especially good or bad. And if he tried to exchange it for another animal, both animals would be forfeited (v.10). Allis (p. 160) says that in later times such animals given to the tabernacle sometimes were sold to other worshipers for offerings, and the money was put into the treasury. Possibly so, but the text gives no information as to whether this could or should be done.

The "unclean animal" (v.11) might or might not be given to the tabernacle. There was a need for such animals. Priests used donkeys, too. But such an animal could be redeemed. It is not clear why the animal was valued by the priest if the animal, and not the monetary equivalent, was actually being given. Perhaps the priest's evaluation would be a factor in the worshiper's decision whether or not to add 20 percent and redeem the animal (vv.12–13).

14–15 The law for dedicating a house is similar to that for an unclean animal. Notice that if the man adds 20 percent and redeems the house, "the house will again become his" (v.15). Otherwise the house is the property of the tabernacle. Nothing is said about the house going out in the Jubilee. Probably this case applied to houses in fortified cities that were sold absolutely (25:30).

16–21 The law for other land acquired by purchase is given in vv.22–25. Land values were determined by formula depending on the area of what we would call tillable land. Rock outcropping, ravines, etc., did not count. The area that would normally be sown by a homer of barley (about six bushels) cost fifty shekels. Modern planting calls for about a bushel and a half of seeds per acre, which would mean that land values would be fifty shekels for four acres of arable land—twelve and a half shekels per acre.

A comparison with ancient Nuzi of 1500 B.C. is of some interest. Ordinary land at Nuzi was worth twelve shekels of silver per *imēr*, and the *imēr* was about eighteen thousand square meters (Francis R. Steele, *Nuzi Real Estate Transactions* [New Haven: American Oriental Society, 1943], pp. 39–40). This figures out to be three shekels per acre. These two values seem to agree within the limits of probable error, remembering that Nuzi was earlier and was in the Mesopotamian area. Without fertilizer they surely could not sow their fields so thickly as is now done, which would enlarge the acreage sown by a homer and bring the price per acre down.

"The priest will determine the value" (v.18). For instance, if twenty-five years had passed since the last Jubilee, the value of the land would be reduced by half. If a man had redeemed a field by paying an extra 20 percent, the field would be his (v.19). But if he gave it to the tabernacle without redeeming it, it would be an irrevocable gift. Also, the gift would be irrevocable if he had promised it eventually to the tabernacle but had sold it to another person until the Jubilee (v.20). When it went out in the Jubilee, it would then not revert to the owner but to the tabernacle to which it was promised (v.21). Allis (p. 160) suggests that the owner may have sold it surreptitiously as well as dedicating it. But there is no need to assume trickery. It was just an arrangement like a future bequest made today. Notice that by this method the tabernacle lands could greatly increase over the years. Whether they did or not, we cannot tell. Such increase of church properties was a great problem in late medieval times. Perhaps it was kept within bounds in ancient Israel.

22–25 It was impossible for a man to dedicate perpetually to the Lord a part of some other family's inheritance (v.22). Perhaps his own line of heirs might run out, and he could properly give his own land. But bought land must revert to its owners at the Jubilee (v.24), and even the tabernacle could have no claim on it. "The sanctuary shekel" (v.25) was an established weight. Present-day governments have effective control over weights and measures to keep them standard. Such standardizing in antiquity was difficult. There are many references in the OT to the sin of using false weights and measures.

26–27 The principle that "the firstborn already belongs to the LORD" (v.26) first is stated in Exodus 13:2. God had killed the firstborn of men and animals of the Egyptians but had spared the firstborn of the Israelites. Therefore, he claimed a special ownership of the firstborn. The firstborn of men and animals that could not be offered were to be redeemed (Exod 13:13). All the firstborn of clean animals were to be the Lord's (Exod 13:12). In consequence of this principle, the clean firstling was already the Lord's and obviously could not be given by a vow.

Verse 27 adds another option to Exodus 13:13. There it is said that every firstborn donkey should be redeemed with a lamb. Here it says that the animal may be redeemed with its money value plus 20 percent, or if not redeemed, the priest may take it and sell it. The law in Exodus 13:13 says that if a man does not redeem it, he must break its neck. That is, the owner cannot keep the animal in any case. The law in Leviticus is in full agreement; the animal, if not given to the Lord's work, must be redeemed either by a lamb (Exod) or money (Lev), or it must be killed.

28–34 See the discussion on devoted things at the introduction to this chapter. The word for "devoted thing" (*ḥērem*, v.28) has a curious double usage. It refers to the totally holy and the totally evil. It is used especially of the holy war of conquest of Canaan that put the spoils of war "under the ban," as it is sometimes translated. The spoils of Jericho, for instance, that were perishable were devoted to the flames (Josh 6:17, 21, 24). The spoils that could stand the fire belonged absolutely to the Lord. This principle in the Conquest kept the Israelites from fighting for the sake of the spoils, as was so often done in ancient warfare. The individual got no personal reward for his fighting.

The tithe belonged to the Lord (v.30). It also could not be dedicated by a vow, though that point is not raised here. The tithe of grain and fruit was sufficiently uniform to be redeemed by adding 20 percent (v.31). Perhaps also this provision was used because some fruits were too perishable to transport to the tabernacle.

Some animals are strong and healthy; other are scrawny and poor. An unscrupulous herdsman could easily have given to the Lord the worst, as the priests did later (cf. Mal 1:8). Or an overzealous herdsman could injure his own flock by always giving the best breeders to the tabernacle. The Lord gave a wise provision that every tenth animal regardless of its condition should belong to the Lord (vv.32–33).

Allis (p. 161) remarks that v.34 is less full than 26:46 and probably applies only to chapter 27. This last chapter adds a footnote, as it were, to the main body of laws concluded in chapter 26. There were yet a few more laws to be given at Mount Sinai that were included in the early chapters of Numbers, but this section at least is concluded by the formula that had been used with variation before (7:38; 25:1; 26:46). The opening verses of Numbers, which immediately follow, begin the directions preparing for the march from Sinai to the Promised Land.

Notes

2 Speiser (p. 125; cf. Notes on 5:15) argues that the pronoun ending "your" on the Hebrew noun בְּעֶרְכְּךָ (*beʿerkekā*) has become fossilized and lost its meaning. He translates simply "valuation," as does the NIV substantially, which fits far better the use here of the noun in the construct position before the word "persons."

12 Speiser (pp. 135–37) questions the old translation "good or bad" for טוֹב וּבֵין רָע (*ṭôḇ ûḇên rāʿ*), which does not fit the context very well. He finds parallels in Nuzi for these terms. The point is that in such judgments the decision of the priest must be final with no appeal—as the last words of the verse emphasize. Speiser would translate it "high or low, whatever the priest's assessment, it shall be so."

NUMBERS

Ronald B. Allen

NUMBERS

Introduction

1. Background
2. The Book of Numbers as Scripture
3. The Book of Numbers as Torah
4. Text
5. Historical Background and Purpose
6. Authorship and Date
7. Unity and Organization
8. Theological Themes

   a. The Old and the New
   b. Balaam
   c. Worship
   d. Numbers

9. The Problem of the Large Numbers

   a. Corruption in transmission
   b. Different meanings
   c. Dual meanings
   d. Symbolic meanings

10. The Large Numbers—Toward a Solution

   a. The problem
   b. A suggestion

11. Bibliography
12. Outline

1. Background

Commentators on the Book of Numbers tend to begin with a survey of the problems. We begin where Arnold Goldberg concludes. In summary he asserts the importance of the Book of Numbers to *Heilsgeschichte*, the "salvation history" of the people of God.[1] Going beyond him we contend that the Book of Numbers is sublime. It forms an essential link in that forward-directedness from Adam to Jesus. In the most unusual of ways, it heightens our appreciation of and response to the person of Yahweh. For Christians this book is even more rewarding; for we find ourselves confronting in new

[1] He writes, "For the Christian reader, this book is first of all an epoch of *Heilsgeschichte*, an epoch of that history that moves forward from Adam the fallen man to Jesus" (p. 136).

ways the meaning of our salvation in Jesus Christ. He who is the goal of all history is the goal of the Book of Numbers.[2]

The theme of the Book of Numbers is worship. It is generally known that the book contains important materials for the worship patterns of Israel. Documentary-critical scholars, for example, are convinced that much of the book is the work of priests—so pervasive are "priestly" elements in this book.[3] But it is not just that the Book of Numbers *contains* worship materials such as the famous Aaronic Benediction (Num 6) or instructions on Passover (Num 9). Finally, we discover that the pulse of the book is worship. It *is* the worship of God by Moses and those who align themselves with him. By God's grace it may become a book of worship for us as well.

However, before the Book of Numbers will become a book of worship for us, we will find it to be a book of trouble. The introduction to this book is longer than many in this series because of its special problems.

The Book of Numbers, while presenting unusual problems for the modern interpreter, yields significant rewards for the patient reader. In a day marked by pop art, quick fixes, and fast foods, the Book of Numbers is particularly troublesome. It simply does not appeal to the person who is unwilling to invest time and energy in the study of Scripture. Often the modern reader first will be discouraged just by the name of the book. "Numbers" seems to be a particularly inappropriate title for a part of the revelation of God. The title seems as interesting as a book named, for example, "Telephone Directory" or, perhaps, "Principles of Arithmetic." A suspicion of increasing dullness settles in long before finishing the first chapter. By the fifth chapter the reader may have dropped out altogether. Numbers is not "fast food" literature! Indeed, some wonder whether it is any kind of literature at all.

Once a reader braves these murky waters, he or she will discover that there are four major problems to face in the Book of Numbers: (1) its seeming lack of coherence as a book, (2) the dizzying variety of the contents, (3) the problematic large numbers of the tribes of Israel, and (4) the fascinating but confusing story of Balaam (Num 22–24). These factors combine to arrest even the interest of the most pious readers.[4]

In the nonevangelical, critical study of the Bible—by which I mean the schools of Continental and American biblical scholarship that have pursued "J-E-D-P source" criticism in the Pentateuch, or some of the more recent forms of redaction criticism—the Book of Numbers provides a fruitful source for analysis. The book is something of a "garden of flowers," each to be plucked, then placed in a different vase, and then labeled according to critical ideas of source criticism. Most of the commentaries available on the Book of Numbers attempt to trace several supposed sources in the varied materials in the book. Surprisingly, a recent commentary on the Book of Numbers published by a major evangelical house is one of the most critical of all. Budd's commentary is marked by an aggressive appeal to source criticism and a

---

[2] This is the sentiment of Johann Christian Konrad von Hoffmann (1810–77), the scholar who gave the term *Heilsgeschichte* its classic, precritical definition. See the sympathetic exposition of von Hoffmann's contribution to biblical theology by Hans-Joachim Kraus, *Die biblische Theologie: Ihre Geschichte und Problematik* (Neukirchen-Vluyn: Neukirchener Verlag, 1970), pp. 247–53.

[3] They term the book the work of "P"; more on this later.

[4] The history of the study of the Book of Numbers only exacerbates the problem. For the most part evangelicals have not found a great interest in this book. The comparison is unfair, perhaps; but a check of the card catalog in a theological library will confirm a suspicion that may have arisen in a casual search of a Christian bookstore: there are very few independent works on the Book of Numbers. Most commentaries (including this one) have been published as part of a larger series that covers each of the books of the Bible.

theology that is Unitarian in nature. Budd, for example, is entirely negative concerning the historical value of the Book of Numbers. He writes, "The book appears to lack the kind of information the historian of the second millenium [*sic*] requires" (p. xxvi).

In view of these difficulties, then, it is not surprising that many Bible readers do not come to the Book of Numbers with noticeable enthusiasm.

This commentary seeks to provide a modest reason for a reassessment of the Book of Numbers as an important contribution to the Torah, as an integral part of Holy Scripture, and as a necessary component in the building of a balanced and informed biblical theology. It also endeavors to rescue this book for worshiping believers. We need to rediscover reverence, recital, and reality as elements of our worship today.

2. The Book of Numbers as Scripture

For those who take the concepts of Scripture and canon seriously, the Book of Numbers may take on an increasing significance. Evangelical Christian theologians have long paraded their conviction that the Scriptures are the result of the out-breathing of God, or "inspiration." Indeed, we stand or fall on this conviction. There are churches, denominations, Bible schools, seminaries, and even scholarly societies that hold together on the basic premise of the inspiration of Scripture and its concomitant inerrancy. One of the texts cited repeatedly to buttress this point of view is 2 Timothy 3:16: "All Scripture is God-breathed." Rarely are these grand words taken beyond their bare statement of inspiration. They are used merely as a prooftext for the divine origin of the Bible, not an inconsiderable issue! But these words are not the principal assertion of Paul in this well-known passage. They are the assumption. Paul argues that since Timothy knows that the Scriptures are the out-breathing of God himself, therefore he—and we—should regard them as eminently worthwhile. The Holy Scriptures that have the ability to make one wise to salvation (2 Tim 3:15) and that are the product of the out-breathing of God (v.16a) are profitable for "teaching, rebuking, correcting and training in righteousness" (v.16b). Indeed, they are the means for the full equipping of the Christian for doing every good work of God (v.17).

Furthermore, the "holy Scriptures" (2 Tim 3:15) and "all Scripture" (v.16) these verses directly refer to comprise the Hebrew Scriptures, or what is commonly known today as the "Old Testament." To be sure, these words by extension include the NT writings, but this is not their principal concern. At the time Paul was writing, the NT was not complete; and many believers did not have access to what was written. The Scriptures that Timothy had studied from his earliest youth were not the writings of Paul or the Evangelists. Timothy was a student of Moses, Isaiah, and David—but particularly of Moses. In classical Jewish thought the Scriptures are first the books of Torah and then the Prophets and the Writings (the emphasis on Torah at the expense of the rest of the OT developed in post-Christian Judaism).

Thus the principal teaching of this classic NT passage on inspiration focuses on the place of the Torah in Christian living. Moreover, Paul's familiar command to "Preach the Word" (2 Tim 4:2) really continues the postulate of 2 Timothy 3:16–17 (the chapter division notwithstanding). Interestingly, numerous theologians and preachers who make much of the importance of the inspiration of Scripture from these verses fail to recognize the importance of the Torah as the foundational document of biblical faith.

The logic of the passage may be visualized as follows:

Since the Scriptures make you wise to salvation, . . .
continue in them as you have from your youth.

Since they are the out-breathing of God,
. . . these Scriptures are eminently useful for teaching, rebuking, correcting, and training in righteousness;
. . . indeed, they may equip the person of God for every good work.
. . . So preach the Word, a task that begins with the preaching of Torah.

When one discovers the significance of the Book of Numbers as a creditable unit in the unfolding of the whole of Scripture, then its material becomes essential to building a biblical theology. This commentary proceeds along these lines. Even though the title seems uninspiring, and despite those aspects of the book that the modern reader may consider to be less than scintillating, this book of Torah can make one wise to salvation and is useful for teaching, rebuking, correcting, and training in righteousness. The Book of Numbers is an essential part of the Holy Scriptures of God. God's people dare not ignore its teachings.

3. The Book of Numbers as Torah

The Book of Numbers is not only a part of Scripture and, hence, inspired, inerrant, and relevant for doctrine, guidance, and instruction in righteous living. It is also an essential part of the Torah, the Pentateuch of Moses. While many acknowledge the foundational nature of the Torah to the development of Scripture, there is rarely a serious consideration of its contributions as authoritative and informing Scripture in the practical outworking of evangelical theology.[5] Aside from a few celebrated texts on Creation and the fall of man, selections dealing with the names and ascriptions of deity, and passages presenting the basic ideas of covenant, the Torah is generally neglected. True, passages are chosen from time to time to illustrate truth already affirmed in the NT, but rarely do theologians build theological propositions solidly on Torah truth. Frequently a few passages that are regarded as messianic are selected for study.[6] But the rest of the text seems to be regarded as just "filler." Genesis, understandably, is read more than the rest of the books of the Torah; Numbers, however, is read very little for basic theology.

Yet the Bible only holds together in so far as it is seen as an organic development from the beginning forward. The books of the Torah are like the bud of a rose; all the flower is present, but not all its inner beauty is expressed. Yet everything the flower will become is already present in the full-bud stage. The Prophets and the Writings

[5]Certainly we do not suggest that all have neglected the teachings of the Torah as informing evangelical faith. A number of evangelical scholars have written spirited presentations of numerous biblical themes from the Pentateuch. These writers include, among others, Walter C. Kaiser, Jr., Meredith G. Kline, John H. Sailhamer, Elmer B. Smick, Willem A. VanGemeren, Bruce K. Waltke, and Ronald F. Youngblood. My point is that, these writers and others notwithstanding, the broad teachings of the Torah as important contributions to biblical faith for evangelical churches are still waiting to be discovered by many scholars.

[6]In E.W. Hengstenberg's significant study of messianic texts in *The Christology of the Old Testament and a Commentary on the Messianic Predictions*, abridged ed. (Grand Rapids: Kregel, 1970), he considered only two texts in the Book of Numbers.

are akin to the opening of the rose. They do not present so much new truth as they develop and clarify truth that has been already expressed in the books of the Torah.

In the teaching of Jesus we find the rose of Scripture, as it were, in the full-bloom stage. His words reveal more fully than ever what God has meant from the beginning in his revelation. In a sense we may say that the teaching of Jesus is the full blossom of Torah truth. The Epistles in the NT are akin to the rose in the full-blown stage. In this stage of the flower, the bloom is still intact, but the petals are opened to their fullest extent. In this stage much attention is given to the fine detail of a given petal, but there is a danger in losing a sense of the form and contours of the flower.

To begin a study of Scripture in the Epistles poses the danger of proceeding on the basis of a great deal that is not known. Since the texture of Scripture is so detailed, the balance of teaching the whole of Scripture on a given topic may be lost. This is particularly so among evangelicals who believe that only the Epistles are "church truth" and that the OT is truly "old," connected only with the Hebrews in the past, but not really of value to God's people today. Equally disastrous is to view the Bible as a "flat book" (Walter C. Kaiser, Jr.,'s phrase), devoid of development whatsoever. This view sees the Book of Genesis and the Book of John presenting the same theological ideas with the same precision. These "gospelizers" of the Torah inadvertently make it irrelevant; for if the Torah teaches precisely what the Gospels teach, then the Torah is not needed. It is merely quaintly redundant.

This commentary proceeds on the premise that the Torah is foundational to the entirety of Scripture, that the rest of the Bible cannot be understood correctly apart from a solid basis in Torah. Further, this commentary also proceeds on the theses that the Book of Numbers is truly a "book," that the book has a sense of coherence, and that the problematic use of large numbers in the book is capable of solution. Indeed, the numbers when viewed rightly become its glory!

4. Text

The Hebrew text (the MT) of the Book of Numbers is relatively free of difficulty. Since the Torah was especially revered in ancient times, its transmission seems to be cleaner than most other biblical books. Periodically in the commentary that follows, we will refer to special textual difficulties, particularly in the poetic sections; and comparisons will be made with the Samaritan Pentateuch and the LXX. A few times we will suggest emendations of the MT, new meanings for disputed words, or unusual meanings to more common words. The very large numbers in the two census lists (Num 1–4; 26) do not betray corruption of numbers. Thus those who resort to the solution of the problem of the large numbers by suggesting textual corruption have to assume that such problems are very ancient. The Hebrew text used throughout the commentary is BHS.

5. Historical Background and Purpose

The Book of Numbers, the fourth book of the Pentateuch, is traditionally ascribed to Moses. The name of the book in the EVV comes from the LXX (the Greek translation of the Hebrew Bible), through the Latin, and is based on the census lists that are found in chapters 1–4 and 26. The Greek name for the book, an attempt to describe the prominence of the numerical listings of the tribes of Israel, is *Arithmoi*. The Latin translation in the Vulgate is *Numeri*, the basis for the title in standard English translations. Eusebius mentions that Jewish designations for the book include the Hebrew phrase *sēper misparîm* ("The Book of Numbers"). More commonly, however, we think of two other Hebrew names for the book. One comes from the first word of Numbers 1:1, *wayedabbēr* ("And [Yahweh] spoke [to Moses]"). This term is significant in that it is a characteristic phrasing that marks section after section in this Torah scroll as the revelation of the Lord to Moses. An even more descriptive Hebrew name for the book is taken from the fourth word in v.1, *bemidbar* ("In the Desert"). This generally is regarded as more descriptive of its contents. The book is set in the thirty-eight-year period of Israel's experience in the Desert of Sinai following the exodus from Egypt. Hence "In the Desert" seems to be a particularly apt description of its contents. This term is not only fitting for the experience of Israel in this part of her early history, but it is a metaphor as well for the condition of judgment that fell on the people who refused to enter the land of rest. We will argue below, however, that the word "Numbers" really is the superior title for the book as a whole.

The Book of Numbers contains much material that is similar to the books of Exodus and Leviticus in terms of legislation for the people and particularly material dealing with the rights and regulations of the Levites and the priests. The dramatic narrative of the book is most significant. It is in the Book of Numbers that we read of the murmuring and rebellions of the people of God against his grace and their subsequent judgment. Those whom God had redeemed from slavery in Egypt and to whom he had displayed his grace at Mount Sinai responded with indifference, ingratitude, and repeated acts of rebellion. The community of the redeemed was punished by the Lord by being forbidden to enter the Promised Land. They were made to live out their lives in the Desert of Sinai; only their children would enjoy the promise that was originally to be theirs.

Since the Book of Numbers presents the story of the rebellion of the people of Israel in the Desert of Sinai, there is a sense in which the book stands in the middle of the salvation experience of the people of God. The generation that was delivered from slavery in Egypt did not continue to respond to the Lord with faith and gratitude. Instead, they forfeited their part in the Land of Promise. Only their children would experience the blessing of conquest. The book covers a span of thirty-eight years, from the first day of the first month of the second year of the Exodus (Num 7:1; Exod 40:2, 17; cf. the first day of the second month, Num 1:1) until the first day of the eleventh month of the fortieth year (Deut 1:3). The whole of the desert period is usually called "forty years" (as in Num 14:33).

Provisionally, we may state that the original recipients of the book were the people of Israel in the second generation from the Exodus, awaiting the command of God to cross the Jordan to conquer the land of Canaan. The book describes the affairs of the people of the first generation, but its teaching is for their children who are now mature and are about to enter Canaan.

We may also venture the purpose of the book in this manner: To compel obedience to Yahweh by members of the new community by reminding them of the wrath of God on their parents because of their breach of covenant; to encourage them to trust in the ongoing promises of their Lord as they follow him into their heritage in Canaan; and to provoke them to the worship of God and to the enjoyment of their salvation. Thus the book that describes the "Desert Years" is designed to encourage spiritual confidence on the part of the people who are about to leave the desert. Despite its sorry record of blemish, betrayal, and benighted living, the Book of Numbers as a whole portrays a confident life of faith in the fear of Yahweh. Further, this confident living, this triumphalism, becomes a major element in the worship of Yahweh.

6. Authorship and Date

As noted above, the Book of Numbers, at least in its core, traditionally has been ascribed to Moses, the great prophet of God. This conclusion has much to commend it: (1) the statements concerning the writing activity of Moses found here and elsewhere in the Pentateuch (e.g., Num 33:1–2; Exod 17:14; 24:4; 34:27 et al.); (2) the assumption that the Pentateuch is a unity and comes from one great scribe; (3) the excellent training of Moses in the educational system of Pharaoh in Egypt that would have prepared him for this great literary task (see the report of the Jewish tradition in the preaching of Stephen, Acts 7:22); (4) the involvement of Moses as the principal human protagonist in the record of the deliverance and desert experiences of Israel in its formative years, which makes him the logical choice for the recorder of those events; and (5) the NT citations that speak of Moses as the one who is responsible for the books of the Torah (e.g., Matt 19:8; John 5:46–47; Rom 10:5 et al.).[7]

Many modern Bible scholars proceed from other lines of inquiry to argue that Moses was not the author of the Book of Numbers (either in its final form or basic core) or, for that matter, of any of the books of the Pentateuch. These critical scholars[8]

[7] Standard evangelical introductions to the OT detail these and other points. The reader is encouraged to review these arguments in Merrill F. Unger, *Introductory Guide to the Old Testament* (Grand Rapids: Zondervan, 1951); Gleason L. Archer, *A Survey of Old Testament Introduction*, rev. ed. (Chicago: Moody, 1971); R.K. Harrison, *Introduction to the Old Testament* (Grand Rapids: Eerdmans, 1969); as well as the more recent work of William Sanford LaSor, David Allan Hubbard, and Frederic Wm. Bush, *Old Testament Survey: The Message, Form, and Background of the Old Testament* (Grand Rapids: Eerdmans, 1982), especially pages 54–67, where they conclude: "Although it is unlikely that Moses wrote the Pentateuch *as it exists in its final form*, the connectedness and uniformity of the evidence certainly affirms that he is the originator, instigator, and most important figure in the stream of literary activity that produced it" (p. 63, emphasis theirs). This is the approach taken in the present commentary.

[8] By the term "critical scholars," I refer to those who to some degree follow the "assured results of [higher] criticism" usually associated with the Graf-Kuenen-Wellhausen school of Documentary Hypothesis, or to more modern scholars who follow various schemes of redaction criticism. The phrase "critical scholars," to be sure, is not a very good term; it is far too vague. Numerous critical theories respecting Pentateuchal origins have come into play in the century since Wellhausen. Moreover, not all critical scholars are as "critical" as others. Some display a robust faith in God and interest in the theology of the text, even when they criticize its origin and unity. Numerous conservative scholars are "critical" in the sense that they bring the text under critical purview but with very different results than the standard documentarian. Evangelicals tend to gather all critical scholars in the same pouch and then to dismiss them entirely. Along the way we may even speak in judgment of their faith in God, a judgment we should not make apart from a clear denial on the part of such a scholar. Actually, we all owe a debt of a sort to these critical scholars. They have been marked by a rugged determination to observe details in the text that others tend to ignore; they have forced more conservative writers to think through issues rather than to read the text with a simplistic naïveté; and in our response to some of their more egregious opinions, we may have come nearer truth concerning the origin of Scripture than we might have done had there never been these attacks on the integrity of Scripture. The one common element that marks those whom I designate "critical scholars" is their view of inspiration and its corollary, inerrancy. Critical scholars seem to come to the text with a bias against inspiration and inerrancy; the text comes under their judgment and acumen. The ideal stance of the conservative, evangelical (I suggest, the "reverent") scholar is that while he or she reads the text with attention to detail and is forced to deal with ambiguities, astringencies, and abnormalities, nonetheless such a reader comes to the text from the vantage of

believe that at most only a few seed thoughts of the Pentateuch really go back to the man Moses,[9] that Jewish tradition (uncritically adopted by Christian tradition) oversimplified the matter by ascribing the writing of these books to their ancient hero Moses, and that the process of the writing of the Book of Numbers was exceedingly complex, comprised primarily of Priestly source materials ("P"),[10] as well as some materials from the Yahwist ("J") and the Elohist ("E").

The classic statement on the Book of Numbers in this regard is given by George Buchanan Gray:

> Judged even by itself, Numbers supplies abundant evidence that it is not the work of Moses, or even of a contemporary of the events described. Not only is Moses referred to throughout in the 3rd person, and, in one passage in particular, in terms that have always occasioned difficulties to those who assumed the Mosaic authorship, but the repetitions, the divergent and contradictory accounts of the same matter, the marked differences of style in different parts, the impossible numbers, and many other features of the book, prove clearly that Numbers is not the work of one who was contemporary with the events described, or familiar with the conditions presupposed. (pp. xxix–xxx)

The "one passage in particular" that was so bothersome to Gray—and indeed even to many readers who are more favorably predisposed to Mosaic authorship—is 12:3: "Now Moses was a very humble man, more humble than anyone else on the face of the earth." The presumption of many readers is that this is the last possible thing a truly humble man would write about himself. For many documentary-critical readers, this verse is the last nail in the coffin of the question of the Mosaic authorship of the book.

Gray then turns to 33:2, which seems to be a clear statement of Mosaic authorship: "At the LORD's command Moses recorded the stages in their journey." But even this verse is turned on its head. Gray writes,

> In one passage only (33:2) does the book lay any claim to the authority of Moses for its statements; that passage is closely related to others (P) which are clearly of far later origin than the age of Moses, and consequently the Mosaic *authorship* even of this particular passage cannot be seriously considered. (p. xxx, emphasis his)

---

faith in the inerrancy of the Word of God. Finally, the "reverent scholar" (who may use some critical tools!) stands, not *over* the text, but *under* its authority. Rather than the scholar/reader being critical of the text, the text is critical of him, as it is of all faithful readers.

[9] Actually, the most critical of these scholars cast doubt on the existence of the man Moses. Noordtzij reports that E. Meyer in 1906 argued that the question as to whether Moses was historical or mythological is not meaningful for historical research; that Hölscher in 1922 affirmed Moses was not a historical person; that Wellhausen viewed Moses as a postulate, not a person, and that the man Moses left nothing positive behind; that G. Beer presented Moses as a finder of springs and a snake charmer; that the most R. Kittel could say of the historicity of the man Moses is *ernstlich nahegelegt* but that his existence is only proven on the basis of a historical postulate: the founding of the nation demands an individual playing a key role (p. 9).

[10] Generally the Priestly portions of the Pentateuch ("P") are regarded to be postexilic by critical scholars, following the lead by Wellhausen. He and his followers considered the tabernacle and its traditions to be a projection back into Mosaic times from the latest period in biblical history. More recently there has been a movement, led particularly by Jewish scholars, to date P in preexilic times. See David R. Hildenbrand, "A Summary of Recent Findings in Support of an Early Date for the So-Called Priestly Material of the Pentateuch," JETS 29, 2 (June 1986): 129–38.

The negative-critical assessment of the contribution of the historical Moses to the writing of the Book of Numbers presented with such confidence by Gray near the beginning of our century has been carried on with little waning of enthusiasm by critical scholars throughout our century. Another major figure in modern German critical scholarship, writing in mid-century, was Martin Noth. He minced no words in his negative evaluation of the unity of the Book of Numbers and the role of Moses in its composition:

> There can be no question of the unity of the book of Numbers, nor of its originating from the hand of a single author. This is already clear from the confusion and lack of order in its contents. It is also clear from the juxtaposition of quite varied styles and methods of presentation, as well as from the repeated confrontation of factually contradictory concepts in one and the same situation. It is also clear, finally, from the relationship of secondary dependence which can sometimes be established between one section and another. These facts are so self-evident that the assertion of the disunity of the book does not require exhaustive proof. (p. 4)

Now, near the end of the century, we have yet another only slightly less dogmatic assertion. Budd, for example, states with approval:

> The confidence of these earlier analysts is not often shared by more recent investigators, particularly in matters of detail, but there remains a very wide measure of agreement as to the identity and extent of the priestly material (P). In the book of Numbers there is very general acceptance of a total priestly contribution in the following chapters—1–9, 15, 17–19, 26–31, 33–36—and of a substantial influence in 10, 13–14, 16, 20, 25, 32. The only chapters lacking such influence would appear to be 11–12, 21–24.[11]

Many of the arguments given by these scholars may be countered by evidence from within the Bible and from what we now know concerning patterns of writing in the ancient world that run directly counter to the basic postulates of standard critical theory. But the most telling distinction between nonevangelical scholars and evangelical scholars is one's starting point. When a person begins with the postulate of divine inspiration of Scripture and of its concomitant inerrancy, then the data of Scripture are read quite differently than if one does not begin with a belief in the inspiration, authority, and inerrancy of Scripture.

We believe that it is prudent to make the following points:

1. Gray and others notwithstanding, Moses certainly wrote the travel itinerary of the book (see 33:2). This is an explicit statement of Scripture. Gray's rejection of the statement, based on an appeal to prior late-dating of the so-called Priestly document, is quite simply nothing more than an example of special pleading. He argues that Moses cannot have been the author because the book does not assert his authorship; and in the one verse where the book does assert that Moses wrote a section, Gray dismisses that datum for other reasons. In this manner one can deny just about anything.

2. Moses is portrayed as the central character of the book (with the exception of chs.

[11] Pp. xviii–xix. Budd then states why P must be dated to the exilic or early postexilic periods (p. xix). As to the chapters that escape assignment to P, they are consigned to JE (p. xxii). Further, the classic critical dating of J in about 850 B.C. is now lowered by Budd considerably. He argues that the Yahwist was a member of the court of King Josiah; that is, a contemporary of Jeremiah in the last part of the seventh century B.C. (p. xxiv).

22–24, concerning Balaam). This factor makes it highly probable that Moses was the source of the materials, *if Moses is a historical figure.* The use of the third person allows the writer to use his name repeatedly. The third-person format in the book is a factor that we observe; but this seeming peculiarity may be just a matter of taste and style, not necessarily the betrayal of the hand of another author.

3. Moses is the person the book repeatedly emphasizes as the one who received the words of Yahweh. Among the most characteristic phrases in the book are the statements speaking of the revelation of the Lord to Moses (e.g., 1:1: "The LORD spoke to Moses in the Tent of Meeting"). If another than Moses wrote the Book of Numbers, and if the book relates genuine revelation of God to Moses, then that writer would have had to have been quite dependent on Moses for his material. One may, of course, decide that the relevance of these words to the real person of Moses is inconsequential. Some believe the phrasing "And the LORD said to Moses" serves merely to introduce a new topic but has neither historical, revelatory significance nor any personal reference to the Moses of history. It is suggested that later writers, desiring to present their material as authoritative, would have used these formulaic words as a matter of course.[12] But it is also possible, and is the belief of many, that these words may report Moses' reception of the Word of God.

When one argues for the Mosaic composition of the Book of Numbers, it is not necessary to claim that the book came from his hand complete and finalized. We may style the Book of Numbers "The Memoirs of Moses in the Desert." The varied styles and the seeming inconsistencies of the book may have been produced in part by its occasional nature in the lifetime of Moses. Further, this book may have received some additions following the lifetime of Moses, though this material may have reached back to the time of Moses. Thus some of what we may regard as later insertions may be just as ancient as the larger framework into which these insertions are placed, having been written by a contemporary of Moses. They may have been added to the book as a whole, under the direction of the Holy Spirit at a later time, or the book may have been compiled by another hand using Mosaic material. This would also explain the Balaam story.

Further, if we accept the possibility of insertions and additions to the Book of Numbers or a compilation from a period later than Moses, we would still accept these as a part of the Holy Spirit's ongoing work on his word. We certainly confront instances of this ongoing work in the Book of Psalms. Numerous psalms have later editorial (sometimes musical) additions; and some psalms are later constructions of various parts of earlier poems. Yet the "reverent critical reader" of the Psalms still speaks of the product as the work of the Spirit of God through various hands.[13] The

---

[12] A twist on this issue is presented in the "Temple Scroll" from Qumran (one of the DSS), believed to have been written in the second half of the second century B.C. In this scroll Moses is regarded as the principal means of revelation, but the speaker is generally God in the first person. This is notable where the scroll quotes from Num 30:3–16, for example. In this Scripture that was originally given to Moses, the Temple Scroll cites it as God speaking in the first person. This factor leads Jacob Milgrom to conclude, "There can be no doubt that the Dead Sea sectarians regarded the Temple Scroll as quintessential Tora, the true word of God" ("The Temple Scroll," BA 41, 3 [Sept 1978]: 119).

[13] I refer here to musical notations such as the famous "Selah"; to various notations in the superscriptions; to the clearly editorial addition to Psalm 72 (v.20); to psalms such as 108, which is an anthology of parts of Psalms 57 and 60; and the like. My point is that the work of the Spirit of God did not stop on the frets of the harp of David; the work of the Spirit extended to the singers who shaped the music of earlier times for continuing use in temple worship. Evangelical scholarship has been too long at an impasse; in rejecting critical theories that argue against any unity of a text or authenticity of a unit, we have pressed too strongly for too naïve a view of

additions and insertions from a later time—if that is what they are—are still Scripture. They are a part of the word as we have received it; the additions and insertions also comprise a part of the Hebrew-Christian canon. The proper stance for the reader who has sought to determine these factors is, not in judgment, but in acknowledgment; not in superior knowledge, but in reverent submission.

When we examine the text of Numbers, we conclude that it is highly probable that some portions of the book were additions from later periods of Israel's history.[14] For example, the supposed protestation of the humility of Moses (12:3) would hardly be convincing if it came from his own mouth, as Gray and countless others have observed.[15] An even more likely example of an addition to the book in my judgment is the passage in Numbers 15 describing the incident of the man caught in violation of the Sabbath rest (vv.32–36). This pericope bears the marks of a later addition to that chapter. Notice the way it begins: "While the Israelites were in the desert" (v.32). This is very similar to other biblical accounts that were written long after the events they portray. Compare, for example, the opening words of the Book of Ruth: "In the days when the judges ruled" (Ruth 1:1). The words in Numbers 15:32 take the reader back to an earlier age,[16] and they seem quite surprising in a book whose primary setting is "in the desert."

Equally difficult to determine in the Book of Numbers is the origin of the Balaam story (chs. 22–24). As we note in the commentary, great speculation centers on the possible ways that this story could have come to Israel and have become a part of the Book of Numbers. Since Moses was not a participant in these events—or even an observer of them—their origin as Scripture is somewhat problematic. (Although the pericope is about Balaam and Barak, it is definitely an Israelite document. A good analogy would be the Book of Job, whose author we do not know and whose main characters are people outside the covenant community.) It is not my purpose to list all the passages in the Book of Numbers that may have been later additions, but I am interested in posing the possibility with these three examples.

If we are willing to admit even one sentence (12:3), one pericope (15:32–36), or one section (chs. 22–25) as a possible later addition to the book than the time of Moses, then we should be willing to examine each pericope, perhaps each sentence, with the question as to whether it, too, may be a possible later addition.[17] We will not conclude

---

the composition of certain sections of Hebrew Scriptures based on the (presumed) model of a NT epistle rather than the dynamics that truly seem to have functioned in earlier biblical times. Again, while we cannot follow critical scholarship in its denial of inspiration and inerrancy, neither can we pretend that these scholars and their work do not exist. Even the most critical Bible scholars can motivate the Bible believer to reexamine the text and to refine his own viewpoint.

[14] Noordtzij, for example, is an antagonist of the Wellhausen school and its methods. But he observes, "Like the other parts of the Pentateuch, Numbers does not constitute a literary unit in that its various elements do not date from the same time period." He then proceeds to list a number of texts that he feels come from a later period. His listing may not be correct (perhaps too limited or too broad); but the questions he raises are valid ones. Again, he raises them for different reasons than the standard critical approach suggests; yet it is likely that if the standard critical approach had not brought its assaults on the text, neither would a reverent scholar like Noordtzij have asked his questions. Unlike the critical scholars he brings under critical scrutiny, Noordtzij concludes that "for the most part the contents of Numbers . . . can be explained without any difficulty on the basis of the situation as it existed during Moses' time" (pp. 12–16).

[15] However, see the commentary following for an alternative explanation. The translation of this troubling verse of Moses' vaunted humility may be something quite different. In the commentary I suggest this verse may be read to present no difficulty whatsoever in a view of Mosaic authorship.

[16] Again, see the commentary for more detail.

[17] Perhaps we should add that we should also be willing to face each verse, each pericope, and each section as though it *is* part of the original work of Moses. Bias can work two ways. The critical bias of one scholar may be offset by the conservative bias of another.

with the critical scholar that the entirety of the book came from a later time, but neither should we insist that every word and every verse necessarily came from the pen of Moses. We evangelicals have usually been pressed so hard by documentary-critical scholars who deny any part of the book as coming from Moses that we may have been tempted to claim too much for Moses. Our desire is to be ruggedly, radically biblical, no matter where that leads us.[18]

We may conclude, however, that it is reasonable to assume that the essential content of the book did come from Moses, the servant of the Lord. His name is repeatedly in the book; he is the principal human protagonist in the book; and he is the one with the training, opportunity, motivation, and opportunity to produce the book. It is almost axiomatic to observe that God brings good out of even the most grim, the most dismal situations. We may reckon that one of the good things that came out of the ghastly waste of life and energy of the condemned, rebellious first generation of the Hebrew people was the opportunity the desert experience afforded Moses, prince and prophet of God, to write the books that are associated so strongly with his name.

If Moses was the principal writer of the Book of Numbers, then we may assert that he would have written these accounts over a lengthy period that included the stay of Israel in the Desert of Sinai as well as on their encampments enroute to the plains of Moab. Much of the unevenness of style may be occasioned by the periodic nature of the writing. But the unity of the book overrides its uneven style. The Book of Numbers may be regarded as *The Memoirs of Moses in the Desert Years.*

An interesting use of the principal story line of the Book of Numbers is found in the message of the judge Jephthah to the Ammonites (Judg 11:15–27). The basic plot and many of the details of the Book of Numbers are well known by this Hebrew judge and are used by him with the facility of a Stephen of a much later day. The knowledge of these events during the chaotic period of the judges suggests that at least part of the basic story line of the Book of Numbers was known in his day and that it is not unreasonable to say that the framework of the book was written before the period of the judges—something that is explained in the traditional belief in the Mosaic authorship of the book. The best suggestion for the time when the book reached finished form seems to be during the united monarchy. Much later, against critical thought, the cultural and geographical issues of the book become moot and arcane. So we believe the finished[19] form of the Book of Numbers may have come as early as the time of Samuel, but certainly by the age of Solomon.[20]

7. Unity and Organization

The Book of Numbers is not easy to analyze or to outline to show its inner structure. The contents are remarkably varied, and the arrangement of materials seems problematic. It is difficult to know how to divide the book or even how to argue that the thirty-six chapters really form a "book." Many feel that there is no real independent unity of the Book of Numbers at all. Goldberg, for example, says that the Book of Numbers was never a self-standing literary work. Its existence as a "book"

[18]A point made by LaSor, Hubbard, and Bush, *Old Testament Survey*, p. 62.

[19]I propose "finished form" as preferable to "final form," as the latter may not admit even the smallest of scribal activities.

[20]These are the conservative conclusions of R.K. Harrison (p. 622).

was always as just a part of the larger Pentateuch (p. 11).[21] Rolf Rendtorff begins his discussion of the Book of Numbers in this vein: "Of all the books in the Pentateuch, the Book of Numbers is the hardest to survey. It contains a great deal of material of a very varied kind and gives the impression of being very heterogeneous. It is even difficult to decide how to divide it."[22]

So while it may sound strange when we first say it, many are not sure that the Book of Numbers is really a "book" at all. While we all are aware of the ancient Jewish and Christian designation that speaks of "the Five Books of Moses," or the Pentateuch, there are some scholars who believe that this arrangement is not apt. Of all the books in that section of the Bible, Numbers is felt by many to be the least clearly a "book." We expect a book to have a beginning, a middle, and an ending, as is true of Genesis and Deuteronomy and, perhaps to a lesser sense, Exodus and Leviticus. But in the Book of Numbers many feel there is no real beginning, no clear ending, and only a muddled middle.

Many readers find the opening chapters of the Book of Numbers to be merely a continuation of the situation of Israel in the region of Sinai, beginning in Exodus 19, and including the extensive materials in the Book of Leviticus. The last chapters of Numbers present Israel in the plains of Moab, the staging area for the Book of Deuteronomy. In between are a few connecting passages describing the misadventures of Israel in the region of Kadesh. In all this, many believe, there is not really a book at all, just a miscellany of varied accounts. Indeed, some commentators present the material of the Book of Numbers as a collection of somewhat disconnected parts of other books in the Torah.

An example of the disconnected-collection approach is afforded by Gray (p. xxiv). He suggests that the materials of Exodus, Leviticus, and Numbers would far better be regrouped into the following sections:

1. The Exodus from Egypt to Sinai (Exod 1–18)
2. At Sinai (Exod 19—Num 10:10, including the Book of Leviticus)
3. From Sinai to the Jordan (Num 10:11–36:13)[23]

Noth speaks rather strongly against the literary integrity of the Book of Numbers. He writes: "We can scarcely speak of a special significance peculiar to the book of Numbers. It has its significance within the framework and context of the greater Pentateuch whole."[24]

Thus the "Book" of Numbers may exist merely to allow the (presumably) sacred or mystical number five to be used in the seminal section of the Bible, the Torah, and the arrangement of the material in the book may be rather inadequate. We really have no solid information that the number five had a mystical or sacred sense apart from the fact that the Torah is in five parts. Otto Eissfeldt, for example, suggests that the fivefold division of the books of the Torah is secondary in nature, that it arises from a

[21] We may observe that the issues are complex. We do not know that Numbers ever existed apart from the larger unity of the Pentateuch, but we believe that it does have a compelling literary unity to it that does make it a "self-standing book."

[22] *The Old Testament: An Introduction,* tr. by John Bowden (Philadelphia: Fortress, 1986), p. 147.

[23] Noordtzij is of a similar opinion. He writes, "Therefore the division of the Pentateuch into five books has, where Numbers is concerned, ignored the clear intention of the author, since 1:1–10:10 is a continuation of Leviticus and 33:50–36:13 forms an introduction to Deuteronomy" (p. 5).

[24] *Within* the Pentateuch, however, he affirms that the Book of Numbers is "indispensable," but he sees no independent significance of the "Book" of Numbers (p. 11).

desire to divide the larger complex into five manageable parts of approximately equal size.[25]

Not only does the Book of Numbers seem to lack a literary sense of coherence as a "book," the materials in Numbers seem to present themselves in an amazing, almost incoherent, variety. The book contains numerous lists of names and numbers, involved genealogies, dramatic historical narratives, arcane rites of purification and ritual sacrifice, lists of sites visited in the wanderings of Israel, lovely poetry, the quintessential blessing of the Lord on his people, impassioned personal encounters, rather dull and prosaic documents on priestly duties, engaging flashes of personality conflicts, stories of intrigue and betrayal, accounts of robust heroism and daring faith, tedious descriptions of detail in ritual, some hymn fragments, quotations from other ancient books, exultant praises to God, and—most surprisingly—exalted poetic prophecies providing a blessing of Israel from a pagan mantic prophet who has fallen under the "spell" of the God of Israel. With all this discordant material in view, it is difficult to imagine a biblical category of writing (except, perhaps, apocalyptic, yet see 24:23–24) that does not find some part or other in this book. In all this variety one searches for meaning and coherence. What is it, we wonder, that holds the book together? Or must we concede, with some readers, that this is not really a very successful book at all?

So we turn to the question of the nature of the "Book" of Numbers. The standard approach to the study of a book of the Bible begins with an attempt to discover the author's intended structure. On the basis of this structure, one may develop an outline and begin to see how the parts relate to the whole. Organizing principles of a book of the Bible may be one of several types. Some books are arranged along chronological lines; some along geographical lines; some along thematic lines; some along logical, deductive reasoning lines. Some books present a narrative flow (tell a story); others argue ideas.

The problem with the Book of Numbers is that it does not seem to follow any of these several lines of development. There is some attention to the issues of chronology in the book. But the chapters that have chronological notes are not given in sequence, and some of the chronological notes are only partial. We do not seem to be helped in our quest for a sense of meaning in the Book of Numbers by examining the chronological notices. There are several notices of time, but they are incomplete and are not arranged in a strict order:

1:1	First day of the second month of the second year of the Exodus; this follows the erection of the tabernacle by one month (see Exod 40:2, 17).
7:1	First day of the first month of the second year of the Exodus; the day of the completion of the tabernacle (see Exod 40:2, 17).
9:1	In the first month of the second year of the Exodus; a notice that precedes chapter 1.
9:15	On the day the tabernacle was set up; agrees with 7:1.
10:11	On the twentieth day of the second month of the second year of the Exodus; that is, following the events described in 1:1.
20:1	In the first month. The year is not given, but a comparison of 20:22–29 with 33:38 leads to the conclusion that this date is in the fortieth year of the Exodus; that is, thirty-eight years after the events of the earlier chapters.

[25] *The Old Testament: An Introduction* (Oxford: Blackwell, 1965), pp. 256–57.

We are appreciative of these few dates, for without them we would make several errors in our understanding of the book. But these few dates are scarcely sufficient for rendering a scheme for the order and structure of the book as a whole. In fact, the larger period of Israel's experience in the desert is passed over with scarcely a comment, something strange if chronology were the binding glue for the book. Noordtzij observes:

> The thirty-eight years of Israel's wanderings, punishment for their refusal to enter Canaan from Kadesh (ch. 14), thus fall between the first five and the sixth dates. Of this period we are only told of the rebellion of Korah, Dathan, and Abiram (ch. 16), the budding of Aaron's staff (ch. 17), and Moses' sin (20:7–12). The school of Wellhausen concluded from the paucity of information that the author knew little or nothing about those years; but this ignores the fact that the Old Testament does not give us a history of Israel, but rather a history of God's revelation. Periods during which little or nothing happened that would be important for a knowledge of that history are simply passed over in silence. (p. 6)

The problem we face in attempting to discover a principal framework for the arrangement of the Book of Numbers is exacerbated when we survey the ways that scholars have attempted to arrange the larger sections in a major structural outline. Most scholars tend to look at the book in terms of three large units, based on geographical considerations. The book begins, as we have noted, with Israel encamped in the Desert of Sinai (1:1). A common break comes after 10:10, where the people move from Sinai to make their way to Kadesh (10:11). Third, the people are suddenly in the region of Moab, across from Jericho, some thirty-eight years later in chapter 22. However, the precise division between this second and third section is greatly debated.

Here we may survey some examples of standard outlines of the book to make the issue plain.

Gray's outline of the book (pp. xxvi–xxix) is in three parts:

1. Numbers 1:1–10:10 (plus 10:29–32)
   Scene: The Desert of Sinai
   Period: nineteen days
2. Numbers 10:11–21:9
   Scene: North of Sinai, west of the 'Arabah.
   Period: thirty-seven (or, in round numbers, forty) years
3. Numbers 21:10–36:13
   Scene: East of the 'Arabah (Jordan valley)
   Period: Not more than five months

There are two unusual factors in his outline. The first is the reminder that Moses' invitation to his brother-in-law Hobab to accompany Israel on their journey must have preceded their leaving Sinai (hence the inclusion of 10:29–32 in the first section). The other is his singular marking of the second/third division at 21:9/21:10, which speaks of the Hebrews beginning their journey to Moab.

A more common example of a three-part structure to the Book of Numbers is given by Merrill F. Unger in his popular Bible dictionary:

1. Departure from Sinai (1:1–10:10)
2. From Sinai to Moab (10:11–21:35)
3. Plains of Moab (22:2–36:13)[26]

Rendtorff has a slightly more complex three-part outline:

1. Part of the Sinai pericope, which begins with Exodus 19:21; primarily regulations about the cult (1:1–10:10)
2. The stay of the Israelites in the desert, connected with Exodus 15:22–18:27 (10:11–20:13)
3. The occupation of Transjordan (some make the break only within or at the end of ch. 21). Passages in 33:50–56 and others display a marked Deuteronomistic stamp (20:14–36:13)[27]

Again, Rendtorff's approach has a geographical break in the latter part of the book, but he is not sure where to place it (20:13/14 or somewhere within or at the end of ch. 21).

Here is an outline of the Book of Numbers that has four parts, inserting a subdivision of the initial march of Israel from Sinai to Paran (10:10–12:16):

1. Organization prior to leaving Sinai (1:1–10:10)
2. Israel on the march—Sinai to Paran (10:11–12:16)
3. The murmurings in the Desert of Paran (13:1–21:35)
4. Israel encamped in the plains of Moab (22:1–36:13)[28]

Here is an outline that has five parts, the standard three geographical divisions coupled to two units of journeyings:

1. Israel in the Desert of Sinai (1:1–10:10)
2. From Sinai to Kadesh (10:11–12:16)
3. In the Kadesh area (13:1–20:21)
4. Detour to avoid Edom (20:22–21:35)
5. Israel in the plains of Moab (22:1–36:13)[29]

Finally, here is one of the most satisfactory of the standard, geographically based outlines. The presentation I give shows the subordinate relationship of the journey motifs to the stationary sections:

1. At Sinai: Preparations for departure (1:1–10:10)
   —Journey from Sinai to Kadesh (10:11–12:16)
2. At Kadesh in the Desert of Paran (13:1–20:13)
   —Journey from Kadesh to the plains of Moab (20:14–22:1)

---

[26] *Unger's Bible Dictionary*, 3d. ed. (Chicago: Moody, 1966), p. 799. Notice that 22:1 is curiously omitted; perhaps he intended to include it with the second section. Many writers have their principal break between the second and third major blocks of Numbers at this point.

[27] *The Old Testament: An Introduction*, pp. 147–49.

[28] Owens, pp. 80–82. Earlier in his work (p. 75), Owens suggests a threefold geographical division:
1. At Sinai. Preparations are made for the journey of unknown duration (1:1–10:10)
2. From Sinai to the Desert of Paran (10:11–20:29)
3. The approach east of the Dead Sea (21:1–36:13)

[29] John B. Taylor, "The Five Books," in David and Pat Alexander, edd., *Eerdmans' Handbook to the Bible* (Grand Rapids: Eerdmans, 1973), pp. 185–94.

3. On the plains of Moab (22:2–32:42)
—Miscellaneous matters (33:1–36:13)[30]

This sampling of outlines of the Book of Numbers shows a tendency to group the materials of the book along geographical lines in three broad categories, with occasional resorts to transitional elements. But these outlines also show the difficulty that scholars have in coming to a consensus in this endeavor. While there is a general agreement that the first section ends in 10:10, there seems to be very little agreement on the ending of the second section of the book. Brevard S. Childs writes:

> However, the problem of determining the structure from the geographical indicators appears most clearly in the division of 21:9. From a literary perspective a major division at this point is far from obvious. Moreover, Noth ends his second section at 20:13 before the beginning of the conquest traditions, and de Vaulx [see Bibliography] sets the break at 22:1 when Israel encamped on the plains of Moab beyond the Jordan at Jericho. This disagreement confirms the impression that there are no clear indications within the text of how the editors wished to divide the material at this juncture. For this reason, although geographical features are significant, their importance in establishing a structure should not be exaggerated. The biblical editors seem less concerned with this literary problem than are modern commentators.[31]

All this uncertainty leaves us somewhat uncomfortable. Childs may be correct in suggesting that the ancient biblical editors were not really concerned with structure as we seem to be. But analogies with other biblical writings flies in the face of this too facile an evasion of the difficulty.

There are two principal difficulties with the standard approach of outlining the Book of Numbers geographically. First, as Childs observes, the details of the text are not sufficiently clear (and have not been recognized by scholars) to make these divisions. Second, the threefold division of the book on geographical terms only adds to the sense that the "Book" of Numbers is not really a book at all, only a strange cluster of varied chapters that really belong to the larger unity of the Pentateuch. Again, we hear the words of those scholars from Gray to Budd that suggest that the "Book" of Numbers really has no independent unity or independent significance.

The problem with this general approach to the book is that it leaves it dependent on both Exodus and Deuteronomy and somewhat derivative of both. Some writers are so taken by this that they have developed the idea of a "tri-teuch" instead of a "pentateuch." They assert the independent existence of the Books of Genesis and Deuteronomy but lump Exodus-Leviticus-Numbers together, principally on geographical grounds.

Dennis T. Olson was one of the first to break from this tradition of the geographical approach and to develop the Book of Numbers as an independent book with structural integrity of its own.[32] The book assuredly has its place in the larger Torah, but it is

---

[30] LaSor, Hubbard, and Bush, *Old Testament Survey*, pp. 164–65. The enumerating of the elements and the partial indenting are my own representation of their prose description.

[31] *Introduction to the Old Testament as Scripture* (Philadelphia: Fortress, 1979), p. 195. Perhaps this idea of uncertainty explains the fact that in Maarsingh's recent commentary on the Book of Numbers there is no outline at all. The commentary is based on comments on each of ninety-five sections with no attempt at all to relate these sections to larger units. See the table of contents, pp. iii–v.

[32] Actually, Elmer Smick anticipates Olson in several aspects in his 1962 commentary on Numbers in WBC. Smick's outline has three major sections: (1) Part one: Israel in the desert (1:1–21:35 [+22:1]); (2) Part two:

truly a book in its own merits with a coherent beginning, middle, and ending. He observes, as we have done, that "the central problem in the interpretation of the book of Numbers . . . is the failure to detect a convincing and meaningful structure for the book" (p. 31). The direction of Olson's work is simply stunning. In my reading he is the first to break through the morass of scholarship that treats the "Book" of Numbers as merely a convention and not a true book, a weak sister in the Pentateuch.

The genius of Olson's approach is that once he has stated it, one says, "Of course!" and one wonders why someone has not done something like this before him. Most of the treatments we have surveyed are somewhat at a loss to explain the chronological abnormalities in the book. Why does the book begin "out of order," with the events of the second month of the second year of the Exodus (1:1) rather than with the events of the first month (7:1; 9:1, 15)? Rashi (A.D. 1040–1105) thought this was so the book could begin on a positive note rather than on something that reflected negatively on Israel (Noordtzij, p. 6). Yet there is really nothing negative in the events of chapters 7 and 9. Further, the tendency of many readers is to rush through the numbers to get to the heart of the book. The importance of the "numbers" in Numbers has simply not been understood. Since the Book of Numbers begins with the "numbers," so shall we.

Olson argues that the two census listings in the book are its framing principle; these lists serve as "the overarching literary and theological structure of the book of Numbers" (p. 81). The first census, of course, describes the first generation of the Hebrews who left Egypt in the Exodus. The second census describes the second generation of the Hebrews who left Egypt. The first generation rebelled against the Lord and was consigned to living out their lives in the desert. The second generation was given the opportunity of God to recapture the promises first given to their parents, to move into the Land of Promise, and to receive their proper inheritance. Olson characterizes this pattern as "the death of the old and the birth of the new" (ibid.).

So Olson begins with the census lists in chapters 1 and 26, chapters that some commentators rush by to get to the "meat" of the text. Olson finds these chapters to be essentially important in establishing the correct approach to the book. Indeed, the Book of Numbers is a biped rather than a triped. The first major unit concerns the experiences of the first generation of the Exodus and their failure to act in obedience to the Lord to claim their inheritance in the land of Canaan. Hence the text moves resolutely to a presentation of the word of God for the second generation. The famous division at 10:11 turns out to be subordinate to the principle division markers that center on the numbers of the tribes (chs. 1, 26). The reason for the second census list, of course, is because the first census listing became irrelevant for the new generation. The first listing was of their parents. The new listing was for the people of their own day.

This observation led Olson to propose an outline that has two unequal sections, 1:1–25:18 and 26:1–36:13. In the first section the focus is on the first generation of the people of God in their march in the desert; the second section presents the new generation being prepared to enter the Promised Land. In the first section there are two major subdivisions, the preparation for the march (1:1–10:36), a subsection that presents the hope of conquest in a positive manner, followed by the cycle of rebellion

---

Foreign intrigue against Israel (22:2–25:18); (3) Part three: Preparation for entering the land (26:1–36:13). Smick presents the Balaam story as a hinge between the two larger sections, each which begins with a census. Still, Olson's work stands on its own, not only in the outline he presents, but also in the theology he derives from this outline.

(11:1–25:18), in which there is a mixture of texts of hope and failure. The second section has two "parts" as well, one stated and the other implied. The stated subsection (26:1–36:13) is the preparation for the people to enter the land, a section that roughly parallels the first part of the book and is positive in nature. The book ends in an implied question: Will the new generation be faithful to God, or will they rebel as did their parents?

Here is a modification of Olson's basic structural outline,[33] which we shall follow in our commentary:

I. The Experience of the First Generation in the Desert (1:1–25:18)
  A. The Preparation for the Triumphal March to the Promised Land (1:1–10:36)
    1. Setting apart the people (1:1–10:10)
    2. Setting forth the people (10:11–36)
  B. The Rebellion and Judgment of a Fearful People (11:1–25:18)
    1. A cycle of rebellion and atonement and the record of death (11:1–20:29)
    2. A climax of rebellion and hope and the end of their dying (21:1–25:18)

II. The Prospects for the Second Generation to Enter the Promised Land (26:1–36:13)
  A. The Preparation for the Triumphal March to the Promised Land, the Second Generation (26:1–32:42)
  B. A Review of the First Generation's Journey and Words of Warning and Encouragement to the Second Generation (33:1–56)
  C. An Anticipation of the Promised Land (34:1–36:13)
  [D. The Prospects for the Second Generation Are for Good, but the Warning From the Experience of the First Generation Must Not Be Forgotten]

8. Theological Themes

a. *The Old and the New*

The simplest summary of the theology of the Book of Numbers is found in the slogan of Olson that we have referred to above: "the death of the old and the birth of the new." The Book of Numbers presents the concept of the chastening wrath of God on his own disobedient people. Yet in his wrath Yahweh remembers mercy; a new generation will arise to inherit the land. The association of the Lord's wrath and mercy, his anger and his love—no matter how strange it may seem to us—is a marked feature of the teaching of the Torah and the Prophets.[34]

An entire generation that had formed a holy community; a people related to God by the sovereignty of grace and the cultic rites of the sacrifice of Passover; a nation delivered from their formidable foes by the direct intervention of his powerful right

---

[33] His wording may be superior; see his outline (pp. 118–20) plus his commentary (pp. 120–24).

[34] See S. Erlandsson, "The Wrath of YHWH," *Tyndale Bulletin* 23 (1972): 111–16. He writes, "Anger seems to be an essential element of YHWH's love which is inseparably connected with His holiness and His justice" (p. 115).

hand in the Exodus from Egypt; a community entrusted with his Torah, graced with his word, and allowed to participate in his holy worship—this people lost their right of the enjoyment of the Promised Land, their true heritage in the Lord. Of all the nations of the earth, the word of God had come only to the descendants of Jacob (see Ps 147:19–20). Of all the nations of the earth, the right hand of the Lord had reached out only to them in their deliverance (see Deut 4:32–34). Of all the peoples of the earth, only they were the family of God (see Deut 7:7–10). But even on them his heavy hand came.

Because of their rebellion against God's grace and disbelief in his power to deliver them to the uttermost, the people of Israel were in breach of covenant. Those who were caught in the breach comprised an entire generation (all persons over the age of twenty). These included women and men, mighty and lowly, godly and profane. Miriam and Aaron, yes, and even Moses, the great prophet and servant of the Lord, were not exempt from God's wrath when they disobeyed him or resisted his will (see esp. 20:1–13).

The fourth book of the Pentateuch thus presents a sobering, chilling reality. The God who had entered into covenant with Abraham (Gen 12), who had delivered his people from bondage in the Exodus (Exod 14–15), who had revealed his holiness and the means to approach his grace through celebrative and sacrificial worship (Lev 1–7)—this same Yahweh was also a God of wrath and a consuming fire. His wrath extends to his errant children as well as to the enemy nations of Egypt and Canaan.

God's wrath, as von Rad writes, is *his* wrath, not the supposed wrath of the law. God's wrath is a mark of his sovereignty—and a memorial of his grace:

> Certainly, the Old Testament tells of many judgments which overtook the disobedient nation. But who was their author? Was it the Law? It was God himself acting on Israel, and not a legal system of salvation which worked out according to a prearranged plan. In particular, it was God himself who always remained Lord even over Israel's sin, and whose judgments even the pre-exilic prophets—and their successors even more clearly than they—represented as being at the same time evidence of his faithfulness to his chosen people. None of these judgments brings irrevocable rejection. The Lord never failed to accompany his faithful people, and he always took them back.[35]

That even Moses would come under the wrath of God is stunning! Chapter 20, which records the error of Moses, begins with the notice of the death of Miriam (v.1) and concludes with the record of the death of Aaron (vv.22–29). Here is the passing of the noblest of the leadership of the people, the old guard. Those whom God had used to establish the nation were dying before the nation came into its own. Miriam who had led the joyful singing at the day of redemption (Exod 15) would not live to sing a song of praise to the Lord in Canaan. Aaron who had led the people for a generation in the worship of sacrifice of untold numbers of animals would not be allowed to offer a tiny pigeon in the Promised Land. And Moses, hoary old man that he was—a life that cannot be rivaled in the service of God save only in the life of Jesus—Moses, who spoke the words of God from the holy mount of Sinai, would only see the Promised Land from a promontory in Moab.

No doubt thoughts came to a people who had experienced such greatness at the

---

[35]Gerhard von Rad, *Old Testament Theology: Vol. II, The Theology of Israel's Prophetic Traditions*, tr. D.M.G. Stalker (New York: Harper & Row, 1965), p. 406.

hand of God and now sensed such ignominy: Has God indeed finished with us? Is he done with the nation as a whole? Are the glorious promises God gave to our fathers and mothers just a thing of the past? Have we no hope?

In one of the most remarkable sections of the Bible, the Lord worked providentially and directly to proclaim his continued faithfulness to his people, despite their continuing unfaithfulness. This section is the comic account of Balaam the pagan diviner (Num 22–24). Here the God of laughter brings a smile to his people to encourage them in the prospects of their new hope, even as the older persons among them were still dying: God's promises will still be realized . . . in us!

b. *Balaam*

In Balaam we have the pagan counterpart to Moses the man of God. The recovery of prophetic texts of Balaam in Aramaic from the sixth century at Deir ʿAllah in Jordan shows how very famous this man was in the ancient Near East, even centuries after his death.[36] Balaam was an internationally known prophet, a diviner who was expert in examining the entrails of animals and in watching the movement of birds to divine the will of the gods. He thought that the Lord God of Israel was like any other deity whom he imagined he might manipulate by mantic acts. But from the early part of the narrative, when he first encounters the true God in visions, and in the hilarious narrative of the journey on the donkey (ch. 22), Balaam begins to learn what for him was a strange, bizarre, even incomprehensible lesson: An encounter with the God of reality was fundamentally different from anything he had ever known. But then he had never known Yahweh!

When Balaam finally begins to utter his words of cursing on the nation Israel at the instigation of Balak, king of Moab, the pagan mantic finds his mouth unable to express the least of the contempt he desired to declare. Instead, from his mouth, and at the loss of his honorarium(!), come the most lovely of blessings on Israel and the most ferocious of cursings on the enemies round-about (chs. 23–24). Balak is furious! And Israel, who later hears this account, rollicks joyfully with the laughter of God.

In his seven prophetic oracles, Balaam displays God's great grace for his people, his grace revealed in his blessing: "I have received a command to bless; he has blessed, and I cannot change it" (23:20).

It is the blessing of God on Israel that is the heart of the Book of Numbers and the heart of the Torah. This reminder of the blessing of God in the most unusual circumstances of the oracles of Balaam leads us to the celebrative and joyful aspects of the book. Zdeněk Soušek writes:

> The Balaam pericope is a weighty component of the message concerning the salvation work of Yahweh. The superiority of Yahweh over all his foes is there demonstrated. The incident is a mighty comfort to the threat and quaking in the presence of wicked powers and is an eloquent testimony that no annihilator, no destroyer, no death has the last word, but Yahweh, who intervenes entirely

---

[36] See Jacob Hoftijzer, "The Prophet Balaam in a 6th-Century Aramaic Inscription," BA 39, 1 (March 1976): 11–17. The fact that the prophecy was written on a wall seems to indicate that it was an important historical example of the oracles of this diviner that might be preserved for posterity. Stephen A. Kaufman observes that the texts of these inscriptions "remain enticingly obscure," that perhaps we need the powers of a Balaam to help banish the darkness ("Review Article: The Aramaic Texts from Deir ʿAlla," BASOR 239 [Summer 1980]: 71–74).

> unexpectedly to save his community, to open to it new horizons and to give to it new hope.[37]

Soušek is not the only scholar deeply impressed with the importance of the Balaam story in biblical theology. Moriarty writes:

> Textual difficulties disregarded, few sections in the Pentateuch are more important theologically than this remarkable narrative. In a real sense the Balaam story may be said to summarize the revelation of God's purpose as it was communicated to Moses. (1:95)

God's blessing on Israel rests in his sovereign will. The immediate enjoyment of God's blessing will ever be dependent on the faithfulness of his people. But the ultimate realization of God's blessing is sure—because of the character of God, which is incapable of change:

> "God is not a man, that he should lie,
> nor a son of man, that he should change his mind.
> Does he speak and then not act?
> Does he promise and not fulfill?"
>
> (Num 23:19)

Most remarkably, this untoward, alien man, Balaam—who stands at enmity with Israel and is no friend of God—was given a prophetic vision of the coming of a Victor-King, a Deliverer who is the Promised One, even Messiah Yᵉshua:

> "I see him, but not now;
> I behold him, but not near.
> A star will come out of Jacob;
> a scepter will rise out of Israel.
> He will crush the foreheads of Moab,
> the skulls of all the sons of Sheth."
>
> (Num 24:17)

The story of Balaam the pagan mantic has its sorry side, however. What he was unable to do by means of the negative prophetic word, the curse viewed as a word of power, he did by means of seduction and deception. The events of Numbers 25 are sometimes thought to be just another in the long recital of the sins of Israel against God, followed by yet another outburst of God's anger against his sinning people. In a sense, however, the rebellion in Numbers 25 is the spiritual nadir of the book. And Balaam was at the heart of it, though we do not discover this until chapter 31.

Midianite women, at the instigation of Balaam and Moabite enemies of Israel, seduced leading figures of Israel to join them in the worship of their god, the manifestation of Baal at Peor. The worship of Baal used some of the same terminology as the worship of the Lord. Perhaps some of the people went to the pagan sacrifice feasts in innocence. But the terms meant different things. Instead of a celebration of the wonder of knowing God and being his people of all the peoples of the earth, the worship of Baal moved from feasting and drinking to the most debased of sexual orgies. It is not unlikely, though some have overstated the case, that hallucinogenic drugs were involved. Certainly the rites became a frenzy of sexual activity. As the

---

[37] "Bileam und seine Eselin: Exegetischetheologische Bemerkungen zu Num. 22," *Communio Viatorum* 10 (1967): 185.

people easily succumbed to Egyptian-styled pagan rites at Sinai while Moses was speaking with God (see Exod 32, where the golden calf was similar to the Egyptian bull-god Apis), so now they have their first taste of the seductive religion of Canaan in the sexually oriented worship of Baal and his consorts.

At one unbelievable moment the frenzy broke into the camp of Israel and extended to the very entrance of the tabernacle of God (see commentary in loc.). One prince of Israel brazenly copulated with a woman we believe to be a Midianite priestess of the Baal cult, in boldest daring, in the very proximity of the place for the worship of the Lord. As they gyrated one against the other in their primeval dance in celebration of Baal, a profanation of the holy that is nearly unspeakable, a great hero of faith thrust his knife through both of them. The knife went through the back of the man and into the belly of the woman. And Phinehas, grandson of Aaron, showed himself of all the men present to be a hero. His zeal for Yahweh was like the very zeal of God himself. Phinehas's zeal reminds us of the zeal of the Promised One (Pss 2; 110). Phinehas typifies the strong sword of Jesus (Rev 19:11–16). Moreover, his action stemmed the plague that had broken out in the camp. This was the last plague; it was the end of the dying of the older generation. Now they were all gone.

Two things transpired. First, Yahweh established his covenant of peace with Phinehas. In addition to the great covenant God established with Israel through Moses on Mount Sinai, we are accustomed to think of the covenant of God with Abraham and the covenant of God with David. We also look forward in the Hebrew Scriptures to the establishment of the new covenant. In the Book of Numbers we discover another of God's gracious covenants, his covenant with Phinehas. This covenant with God's priest is as important for true worship as the covenant God established with David is important for the true royal house. Second, through Phinehas's action "atonement was made for Israel" (25:13). The holy relationship of God and people was reestablished.

c. *Worship*

We find that the Book of Numbers has a great deal to contribute to the theology of worship. The NT concept that in worship all should be done in an orderly and fitting manner (1 Cor 14:40) finds its basis in the Book of Numbers. Not only do we learn of order and procedure, we also learn of pageantry and procession, festival and fasting, demanded sacrifices and freewill offerings, restrictions and blessing. Other special features of the book include the provisions for the Nazirite vow (6:1–21), the beauty of the Aaronic Benediction (6:22–27), and the repetitive words of the lengthy record of the dedication offerings of the elders of each tribe (ch. 7)—these lengthy repetitions emphasizing the solemnity of the event and the magnanimity of the people in their gratitude to God the Deliverer. Most of all we learn of blessing. The words God gave to Aaron and to his sons, hence, words that are vouchsafed to Phinehas, are words whereby God shows his desire to bring his blessing on his people; his desire is to have them sense the smile of his face (see the commentary on 6:23–27).

Thus it is in the Book of Numbers that the ongoing purposes of God for his covenant people are reaffirmed. Despite his judgment on the first generation of those he redeemed from Egypt, his murmuring people, God was still determined to bring the new generation into the Land of Promise and realization.

From this it follows that the entire Book of Numbers is a pointing back to failure and an addressing forward of the possibility of success. Yes, the first generation failed; no, the new generation does not have to fail. Yes, there are repeated instances reported of the rebellions of the first generation (chs. 1–25); but as yet there are none, not one, reported of the second generation (chs. 26–33). The first generation was one of the dead and the dying; there is not one death mentioned in the latter section of the book (chs. 26–33).

The fortunes of the people are not the result of time and tide, of chance and happenstance, of the fickle wills of capricious deities. The people can make their own fortune, for the eternal God has given them carte blanche. If they will respond in faithfulness and in wholehearted obedience, there is no promise he has given that will not be fulfilled. If they behave as their parents had done, then there might have to be another forty years of waiting it out in the desert.

God has time! He is not in a hurry. Finally he will have a generation of people like Joshua and Caleb who will focus on him entirely and not be intimidated by walls of cities, by stature of men, or by sniveling words of the weak and the cowardly. The Book of Numbers is the call to a robust faith in the Lord. And for people of such faith, there is no end of blessing.

d. *Numbers*

So then we come to the numbers of the book. What seems to be the most embarrassing element of the book—the numbers that seem impossibly inflated for a small nation at the beginning of its existence—are its crown and glory. These numbers are a mark of God's blessing. They are a fulfillment of his covenant. They anticipate numbers of peoples who will be like the stars of the heavens, the sand of the seashore.

The numbers in each of the census takings, the old and the new, add up to more than 600,000 fighting men, an immense army under the banners of the Lord. These numbers lead us to extrapolate a population that may exceed 3 million persons. But the numbers may also lead us to think in superlatives. They remind us of God's grace, they point to his mercy, and they anticipate his glory. These numbers have a theological meaning. They are used for effect, not simple bombast.

Poor old Balaam thought he had the "number" of the people of Israel. He found that he could not number their dust (see commentary on 23:10)! God has their number! And their number is their destiny. Their number is their full complement. This, too, Balaam saw. He looked down from his height and saw their expanse, and what he saw was only the fringe of their habitation; he saw their dwelling was apart from all nations (23:9).

The number of the people had grown from a small figure to an immense number in an amazingly brief period of time. But their number at present was only a cipher compared to their number in God's future for them. The numbers in the Book of Numbers are also part of its theology. The numbers extol the glory of God in his people.

In the Book of Numbers there are more than numerical listings of the tribes. This book records events of lasting significance for Israel and for the inheritors of blessing in God's church. God does display his wrath even against his errant people; but his grace is renewed as surely as is the dawn.

9. The Problem of the Large Numbers

The exceedingly high numbers of the able-bodied men over the age of twenty conscripted into the armies of Israel, as recorded in chapters 1 and 26, continue to trouble modern scholars. The numbers of soldiers in each listing total in excess of 600,000 (603,550 in 1:46; 601,730 in 26:51). These numbers of men mustered for warfare demand a total population in excess of 2 million. Indeed, perhaps a population of nearly 5 million might be required to supply a conscripted army of 600,000 able-bodied men over twenty years old. Such numbers are exceedingly large for the times, for the locale, for the desert wanderings, and in comparison to the numbers of the inhabitants of the land of Canaan whom the Israelites set out to conquer.

Many faithful readers of the Bible have taken these numbers at face value. Frankly I am sympathetic with them and have written elsewhere in support of this point of view.[38] Some commentators go to considerable length to work out the mathematical possibilities of these numbers in terms of birth-rate statistics, the logistics of crossing the Red Sea in one night, dwelling in the desert, marching in the order of the tribes, massing on the eastern shore of the Jordan, and conquering the Promised Land (see, for example, KD, *Pentateuch,* 2:46–47; 3:4–15). Yet the more the modern reader studies these attempts to make these large numbers manageable in the constraints of the social-geographical context of the Late Bronze Age, the more difficult these issues become. Frankly, we begin to wonder whether we are not engaging in special pleading.

a. *Corruption in transmission*

Various solutions have been suggested to solve the problem of the large numbers. Some have argued that these numbers may have been corrupted in transmission. The general faithfulness of the textual transmission of the Hebrew Bible (and the Greek NT) is truly marvelous. At the same time, in neither testament is this process perfect. We have certain examples of corruption of numbers in parallel passages in the historical literature. An event described in 2 Samuel 10:18 speaks of 700 chariots; but the parallel text in 1 Chronicles 19:18 reads 7,000. 1 Samuel 13:1 lacks the number altogether for the age of Saul: "Saul was . . . years old." The number of people who died in the final plague of Numbers is listed as 24,000 (25:9), but 1 Corinthians 10:8 gives 23,000 for the same event. So it is possible for one to argue that the numbers of the census listings in Numbers 1–4 and 26 have suffered transmission problems. This is possible, but we may observe that the present text does not betray notices of textual difficulties in these numbers. Moreover, if textual transmission error is the explanation for these large numbers, it would not be the isolated addition of a digit here or the dropping of a digit there. For textual transmission difficulties to be of any "help" in coming to terms with these census lists, they would have to be massive in scope. The entire list has to be in error. Again, the textual record does not betray any discussion of such problems. It almost takes more faith to believe in transmissional problems in these lists than it does to work out the logistics of the numbers as they stand.

b. *Different meanings*

Others have felt that the word for "thousand" might have a different meaning here than the usual numerical idea. The word *'elep̱* is a graphic term derived from pastoral language that was used to number herds. As one looks out over many sheep, one may

[38] I refer to the notes to the Book of Numbers in *The NIV Study Bible,* Introduction: Special Problem, and note on 1:46.

speak of an *'elep̱* ("a thousand") sheep. Thus the word "thousands" may be a simple statement of approximation: There were "thousands" of persons in each tribe.

In some biblical passages the Hebrew word for "thousand" (*'elep̱*) is a technical term for a company of men that may or may not equal 1,000 (e.g., Num 31:5; Josh 22:14 ["a family division"]; 1 Sam 23:23 ["clans"]). Thus one might argue that the term *'elep̱* has lost all sense of a specific numerical value and means simply a "troop." Thus each tribe might be composed of 30 to 70 troops, and the total of the fighting men for these troops would number in the hundreds. This would mean that for Reuben there were 46 troops with 500 fighting men; for Simeon 59 troops with 300 fighting men, etc. This would yield a total of 589 troops and some 5,550 fighting men; with each troop having about 9 or 10 men. This is the preferred conclusion of Noth (*Numbers*, pp. 22–23). The problem with this, however, is that the numbers are totaled in such a way as to regard the term *'elep̱* as one more than 999. To regard the word *'elep̱* as a rough approximation only works where approximation is the intent. (See, for example, 1 Sam 4:10, where Israel had 30,000 foot soldiers defeated by the Philistines. Doubtless the number in this passage gives merely an approximation of the number of soldiers who were defeated.)

Others have observed that the term *'elep̱* ("thousand") is very close in spelling to the word *'allûp̱*, a term meaning "chieftain" or "commander" elsewhere in the Bible. In Genesis 36:15–43, this word is used for the chieftains of Edom. Sir Flinders Petrie argued in 1923 that the term *'elep̱* may mean a family unit, living in one tent, perhaps a "clan." One solution for the large numbers in these lists may be found in this confusion of the word for "thousand" and that for "chieftain" or "clan." In this way the figure 53,400 (of Asher in 26:47) might mean "53 units (chiefs, clans) and 400 men." The figure 32,200 (of Manasseh in 1:35) would mean "32 units (chiefs, clans) and 200 men." Such a procedure would give a greatly reduced total for the whole population. But this procedure would also be at variance with the fact that the biblical text adds the "thousands" in the same way that it adds the "hundreds" for the large total. The numbers joined to *'elep̱* and to the hundreds are linked in Hebrew by the simple "and" (waw), which normally suggests that they should be added together. This approach would presuppose that the early meaning of the word *'elep̱* (or *'allûp̱*) as "chief" or "clan" was not understood by later editors, who mistakenly added these words as numbers to the hundreds. Such an approach leads to a greatly reduced number for the fighting men and the total population of Israel than is usually assumed. The totals for the Twelve Tribes in this approach would be 5,550 men and 598 "chiefs." With the additional numbers required for women and children, the population of the community would be more nearly 15,000 to 18,000, rather than the 2 million or more required by the traditional understanding of these numbers.

This sort of speculation, however, has its own difficulties, which may be as hard to solve as the problem of the larger numbers. First, the proportion of "chiefs" to fighting men seems quite top-heavy (46 "chiefs" for 500 men in Reuben; 59 "chiefs" for 300 men in Simeon, etc.) This is a very high percentage of officers to fighting men in any army. Second, the totals in 1:46 and 2:32 do not bear this distinction in the meaning of the term *'elep̱*. The ancients were able to add figures in the same manner we do, and they seem to have added the numbers for the Twelve Tribes without any distinction for the hundreds and the thousands as different types of groupings. They carried the figures for the hundreds into the column for the thousands, as any school child might.

A variation on the above approach is given by Noordtzij, who states that we cannot translate the term *'elep̱* as "thousand" but only by an *X*, as we no longer know how large it was. He concludes that the total complement of the army of Israel in Numbers 1:46 should not be read 603,550, but 603 *X* + 550 men (p. 27).[39]

c. *Dual meanings*

John Wenham has a more complex solution to the problem of these large numbers. He believes that the term *'elep̱* is used in two distinct ways in these lists, one to indicate "armed men" and the other to indicate "thousands." Along the way scribes confused the two meanings and simply added both terms as though they were "thousands." Wenham says the numbers for the tribe of Simeon, given as 59,300 (Num 1:22), were originally intended to mean something like this:

57 armed men and 23 hundreds of units.

But this came to be written:

57 *'lp* and 2 *'lp*, 3 hundreds.

He summarizes:

> Not realizing that *'lp* in one case meant "armed man" and in the other "thousand," this was tidied up to read 59,300. When these figures are carefully decoded, a remarkably clear picture of the whole military organization emerges. The total fighting force is some 18,000 which would probably mean a figure of about 72,000 for the whole migration.[40]

Many would regard this total as a more satisfactory number for the Hebrew population in terms of its former slave status in Egypt, the gravely difficult conditions for provision of a very large population in the desert, and the fright occasioned by the smallness of their numbers against the fortified cities of Canaan. There are some texts in the Torah that suggest the population of the Hebrew nation was quite small. For example, Deuteronomy 7:7 states that the Lord's affection was set on Israel, not because they were more numerous than other peoples, "for you were the fewest of all peoples" (however, see below).

Yet in this case, as in the former, the totals of 1:46 and 2:32 would have to be regarded as errors of understanding by later scribes of an unusual, complex, and otherwise nonattested use of the word *'elep̱*. Inerrantists, those who believe strongly in the reliability of the text of Scripture, have difficulty in approaches such as these, for they suggest the possibility of an error in the text of Scripture, even if the error of a scribe at a later time than the writing of the text and made as a later insertion. There are later insertions in the text of Scripture that most scholars, including inerrantists, regard as mistakes. The "three witnesses" text of 1 John 5:7–8 is a classic example.

---

[39] His translator, Ed van der Maas, observes that Noordtzij does not gain very much by this approach. He runs into trouble along three lines: (1) squaring with the totals that the text presents (1:46; 2:32; 26:51, plus Exod 38:25–28); (2) dealing adequately with the shekels paid as atonement money in Exod 38:25–26, where one-half shekel was paid for each of the Israelites (100 talents and 1,775 shekels; as 1 talent = 3,000 shekels, the 100 talents comprise 300,000 talents; when this sum is added to 1,775, the total is 301,775 shekels, precisely one-half shekel for each of the 603,350 men of the census); and (3) if *'elep̱* is less than 1,000, it cannot be less than 751 (an absurdity!), for the number of the Kohathites was 2 *'elep̱* and 750 (Num 4:36); if the *'elep̱* were less than 750 men, then one could subtract an *'elep̱* and simply add it to the 750 men. If the *'elep̱* is 751, then there is only a 25 percent reduction of the total number, a sum still presenting innumerable problems. See the translator's footnote 1, p. 27.

[40] "The Large Numbers of the Old Testament," in Alexander and Alexander, edd., *Eerdmans Handbook to the Bible*, p. 192. He adds that the figures for the Levites seem to have an extra zero. When that is dropped, the Levites become a standardized tribe of 2,200 males.

Yet the text critical conclusion is also unanimous in asserting that no Greek texts from before the sixteenth century have this reading. There is, however, no known textual suspicion for the integrity of Numbers 1:46. If this is an error in calculation by a later scribe who was unaware of Moses' sophisticated employment of the word *'elep̱* in the census in the desert, we have no record of this.

It may be observed that this type of reduction in the numbers in Numbers 1 and 2 will not solve other problems of "large numbers" in the book but will only compound them. What, for example, are we to do with the totals for the tribe of Levi that are given as 22,000 males from one month old and upward (3:39)? Surely here one could not speak of 21 chiefs and 1,000 men (chiefs from one month old and upward?). Yet if the figure of 22,000 males is maintained for this tribe, it would be unusually lopsided with respect to the revised numbers of a population of 60,000 to 75,000 members. There is in fact a consistency in the totals given in the Bible for the large numbers of Numbers 1:46 (see Exod 12:37; 38:26; Num 2:32; 11:21; 26:51). Suggestions for changes in Numbers 1 and 2 will demand a wholesale revision of numerous other texts and will assume a methodological path of misunderstanding in various points of Scripture.

Further, the use of numbers of peoples who die in various plagues does not accord with a smaller population suggested by modern scholars. One example only is the destruction of 24,000 in the plague at Baal Peor (Num 25:9). Would this number be read 23 chiefs and 1,300 fighting men? Not likely, especially when at least one woman was included among the slain along with the men (see vv.9, 18). Yet 24,000 would be nearly a third of the entire population on the basis of revisionary theories. (However, see the commentary on chapter 25.)

Finally, it may be argued that moderns do not likely appreciate the sheer numbers of men that would be necessary to maintain assaults on the walled cities of Canaan. While it is true that the destruction of the walls of Jericho in Israel's first battle in the land was all the Lord's doing, the fighting against the men of the city was the work of the army. In the cases of the other cities and armies that Israel would encounter, there was a demand for immense numbers of military personnel, which numbers a plain reading of the text affords.

For these reasons we may wish to conclude that despite the clever and interesting suggestions made by some scholars, both liberal or critical and conservative or reverent, to reduce significantly what appear to be impossibly large numbers in these chapters—and despite our own sense of uneasiness about these very large numbers—it appears to be safer and more "biblical" to stay with the large numbers of the census figures of Numbers 1 and 2 rather than to attempt to reduce them for our own reasons, apart from adequate textual warrant. Further, we may understand the words "fewest of all peoples" of Deuteronomy 7:7 to be either an example of the use of hyperbole for effect or perhaps a reference, not to the population of Israel at the time of the Exodus, but at the time of God's choice of her in one man (Abram) and in the subsequent family of seventy that made its way to Egypt at the beginning of the sojourn. (Yet see further on 1:46 for another interpretation.)

We do not mean to imply that the above type of approach necessarily springs from a misbelief in miracles, as is sometimes assumed; for numerous reverent or conservative scholars have been attracted to this or similar positions. The work of God with his people is miraculous throughout the desert experience, no matter how many or how few they might have been. This type of approach is based on an attempt to find what is believed to be a more realistic number for the peoples of Israel at this time.

d. *Symbolic meanings*

We should also give attention to options that regard the numbers as symbolic figures rather than strictly mathematical items. One possibility for the meaning of the large numbers may lie in *gematria*, a rhetorical-symbolical use of numbers for effect. One suggestion has been made that the numerical equivalent for the Hebrew letters of the phrase "people of Israel" (*b^e^nê-yiśrā'ēl*) works out to 603, the number of the thousands of Israel (b = 2 + n = 50 + y = 10 + y = 10 + s = 300 + r = 200 + ' = 1 + l = 30, with a grand total = 603).[41] Less convincing are the attempts to discover the gematria underlying the number 550 (see Budd, p. 7, for development). Nor is there any convincing gematria presented to explain the 601,000 in Israel in the census of Numbers 26 (see Noordtzij, p. 24). Further, there is no pattern alleged to explain the seemingly random numbers for each of the tribes leading to the grand sum of 603,550. The numerical value of the Hebrew letters in the expression *b^e^nê-yiśrā'ēl* ("the sons of Israel," or "the Israelite community," in 1:2) equals 603 (the number of the thousands of the fighting men); the remaining 550 (plus 1 for Moses) might come from the numerical equivalent for the Hebrew letters in the expression "all the men . . . who are able to serve in the army" (1:3). I find the gematria for the 603 to be interesting (and perhaps a fine numerical pun in this text). But gematria alone cannot explain the multiple uses of numbers in this passage.

This symbolic use of numbers is not unknown in the Bible (see Rev 13:8).[42] It is found in the Hebrew Scriptures in the Book of Proverbs. The major section of the Proverbs of Solomon (Prov 10:1–22:16) has precisely 375 proverbs, the numerical equivalent for the name of Solomon in Hebrew. Scholars wonder, however, whether the gematria concept was known as early as the time of Moses. The suggestion of gematria is intriguing but not now capable of proof at this early stage of Israel's experience. One wonders what the gematria would be for the numbers of the second generation of 601,730. If the first number is the full complement of the "sons of Israel" in chapter 1, would one then argue that the lesser number in chapter 26 means fewer than "the sons of Israel"? If so, then the gematria explanation does more harm than good.

One observation many have made about the numbers in these census lists is that while they are rounded off, they appear to be random in nature. Olson has observed, however, that the impression of randomness is not really accurate. Both of the sums approximate 600,000. This is the product of 12 x 50,000. In other words, the Twelve Tribes have an average of 50,000 members in the army. Further, in each listing there are six tribes that have fewer than 50,000 men and six that have greater than 50,000. Moreover, the tribe of Judah has the largest number in both lists, a mark of its superiority (over Reuben!) in the desert experience. Olson nicely concludes that the number, as it presently stands, "appears to express the gracious extent of God's blessing of Israel in multiplying Israel's descendants to such large numbers and strength" (p. 79).

An even more complicated explanation has been advanced where the numerical totals for each tribe are said to be symbolic of the numeric equivalents of certain

[41] We may observe that this formula works only if the sere yod combination that ends the word *b^e^nê* is given the *consonantal* equivalent of "y = 10"; otherwise the total is only 593.

[42] Joseph A. Romero argues for a gematria on the number of fish caught in John 21:11; the precise number 153 is equal to the Hebrew letters forming the words "the children of God" ("Gematria and John 21:11—the Children of God," JBL 97, 2 [1978]: 163–64).

astronomical periods. For example, the number of the men of Benjamin (35,400, Num 1:37) is 100 times a short lunar year (354 days). Other numbers are said to be compounds of the periods of various planets (Mercury, Venus, Mars, Jupiter, Saturn) in differing combinations.[43] This point of view seems to be faulted seriously both by its complexity and its unexpectedness in a literature that seems to bear no clues of this type of hidden significance. It appears to me that comparisons of the tribes of Israel to astral and planetary bodies would be a precarious venture, given the antipathy of the faith of Israel to these ideas. It is possible, of course, that such procedures might be used in a subtle polemic against Babylonian religion, but it would seem that this would only be appropriate in the context of a clash with the Babylonian world. This type of argument might carry more weight for one who argues for an exilic provenance for the Book of Numbers (which, indeed, the propounder of this theory, Barnouin, suggests).

We may observe as a preliminary conclusion that while the problems of the large numbers have not been solved satisfactorily today—or at least that the solutions that have been suggested have not seemed to have won large appeal—the Bible does point to a remarkable increase of the descendants of Jacob within the four centuries of their sojourn in Egypt (see Exod 1:7–12) and that these high numbers, with all their problems, point to the great role of providence and miracle in God's dealings with his people in their period of life in the desert.

10. The Large Numbers—Toward a Solution

a. *The problem*

Still we cannot escape the problem of the large numbers in the Book of Numbers. Perhaps it is the numbers that are the most troubling problem of all, not just the tedium of chapters of names and numbers, though it is true that the modern reader who is not an accountant will have little patience for the long lists of tribes, families, and their numbers in this book. The principal problem is one of believability. To put it bluntly, the numbers of the tribes of Israel stated and implied in this book just seem to be far too large to be historically credible. If the numbers of the men who are mustered for war from the age of twenty and up actually add up to over 600,000, then the total populace would have had to be at least 2 million persons—perhaps considerably more. This does not seem to be an excessively large number for the people of a nation in our own crowded days, but it seems to be nearly an impossibly large sum for the totals of the nation of Israel in ancient times at the very beginning of its existence, a fugitive people fleeing Egypt, crossing the sea bed in one night, gathering at a mountain in the Sinai, then living a generation in the desert before finally entering Canaan.

Perhaps some perspective is in order. The city near where I live is moderately sized

[43]This is the work of M. Barnouin, "Les recensements du Livre des Nombres et l'astronomie babylonienne," VetTest 27 (1977): 280–303; it is discussed by Gordon Wenham (pp. 64–66). Wenham seems to be somewhat open to Barnouin's approach but uses (British?) understatement in evaluating its convincing quality. In another article Barnouin suggests that the original number of the men mustered for war was but 6,000 (the later total of 600,000 being a multiplication by 100) ("Remarques sur les Tableaux Numeriques du Livre des Nombres," RB 76 [1969]: 351–64). I am also open to multiplication (see below) but regard 6,000 to be pitifully few.

by modern standards. The population of the city of Portland, Oregon, as of July 1987 is 419,810. When the surrounding cities and towns that make up the metropolitan area are added, the number increases to 1,159,300. Now this is a lot of people. I look around the area where I live and see wide-ranging territories, massive structures, as well as large areas of single-family homes that are built to house and provide for this populace.[44] But if the numbers of the Bible are correct, I have to imagine a population twice the size of the metropolitan area in which I live and then to view that vast number of people living their lives in the Desert of Sinai for a period of forty years. I know that scholars have attempted to explain exactly how such numbers can be accounted for. Keil, for example, even worked out the mathematics for the crossing of the Red Sea by a population this size. Yet I have to ask if it is reasonable to have to account for these large numbers in this literal a manner.

Here is another comparison. The mid-1988 estimate for the population of the present state of Israel is 4,400,000. The present population of the modern country of Israel is only roughly twice the size of the number of Hebrews who approached from the desert with great fear to conquer the land. The population of Israel is mixed between scattered rural settlements, small towns, and three large cities. As we look at the modern cities with their sprawling size and multistoried buildings, we wonder how the ancient farmlands, towns, and cities might have accommodated such numbers. Since the testimony of the wicked Hebrew spies was an exaggerated report of the size of the cities, their towering walls, and hulking men—all the stuff of fear—the implication at the least is that the Canaanite population was significantly larger and more powerful than the approaching Hebrew populace (see, for example, the refrain of proportion: "to drive out before you nations greater and stronger than you," Deut 4:38; 7:1). The more we think of them, these numbers boggle our minds.

Then we may ask what we know of the population of Canaan in the biblical period. Numerous attempts have been made to estimate populations at various periods. More recent scientific estimations of the population of Canaan during the Iron Age reduce greatly earlier estimates of several million. Israeli archaeologist Yigal Shiloh suggests the combined population of Judah and Israel in the eighth century B.C. to be about 900,000.[45] Since we may presume that the population of Canaan was as least as dense in the eighth century under Hebrew settlement as in the fifteenth century during Canaanite times, it is just not possible to imagine an invading force of Hebrews that might number several millions having any reason to trust in the Lord for the conquest of the land. By sheer numbers they would simply overwhelm the native population.

A well-worn problem in the large numbers of the families of Israel in the Book of Numbers has to do with the growth from seventy persons to more than two million in just four centuries. Again, there have been commentators who have worked out the mathematics of this increase and have stated that such an increase, while grandly dramatic, is not beyond the possibility of human reproduction—particularly when that reproduction capacity is enhanced and blessed by the Lord in fulfillment of his promise to make his people many, though they began with so very few.

We do know that Scripture assures us that the growth of the population of the

[44] I certainly do not mean to suggest that peoples in ancient times lived in similar structures and territories as people in modern, Western cities. But a view of a modern city gives at least a sense of the enormity of what we mean when we say, perhaps a little glibly, that the people of Israel numbered in the millions at the beginning of their history as a nation.

[45] "The Population of Iron Age Palestine in the Light of a Sample Analysis of Urban Plans, Areas, and Population Density," BASOR 239 (Summer 1980): 32.

Hebrew peoples was a dramatic outworking of God's grace, a fulfillment of his promise. The narrative of growth in Exodus 1:7 is emphatic. Three verbs along with complementary adverbs and rhetorical flourish exult in the work of God in their dramatic growth: "but the Israelites were fruitful and multiplied greatly and became exceedingly numerous, so that the land was filled with them." This unprecedented growth of the nation was in fulfillment of numerous promises of God to the fathers (see Gen 17:2, 6; 22:17; 26:4; 28:14; 35:11; 48:4). Moses is able to use the patriarchal phrase of abundance as he recounts his experience as their leader: "The LORD your God has increased your numbers so that today you are as many as the stars in the sky" (Deut 1:10; cf. Exod 32:13).

Yet there are counterindications to this immense size of the population also well known. That we have some answers to these issues may not necessarily mean that we have dealt adequately with them. One points to just two midwives in Exodus 1:15, Shiphrah and Puah—certainly some very overworked women in a nation so large! Another points to the rhetorical underplaying of the size of the nation in Deuteronomy 7:7, where the numbers of the Hebrew peoples are greatly minimized: "for you were the fewest of all peoples." This is a rhetorical use of language, but its effect will be in proportion to the sense of the people, "Yes, we were few compared to other great nations."

Another counterindication has to do with the sheer logistics of 2 million people or more crossing the Red Sea (or Sea of Reeds) in one night and their organization and provision in the desert for a generation. Now all this is possible within the wonder of the work of the Lord, certainly. We have no doubt of the ability of God to provide for 2 million or 2 billion persons, if that is his pleasure. But we still wonder at these large numbers in terms of the lands and cities of the ancient world. Were the cities of ancient Canaan in the Late Bronze Age sufficiently large to be a formidable threat to the millions of Hebrews who were about to descend on them from the desert? Would the ten spies have been so fearful of the residents of the land if they represented a people so very large in numbers? And could the very land of Canaan have absorbed such a huge company in biblical times, right at the beginning of Israel's experience? We do not doubt that the population of Israel under her great kings David and Solomon might have numbered one million. But we pause at the thought of more than twice that many persons right at the beginning of her history.

So there we have it: The numbers of the Book of Numbers are just too large!

b. *A suggestion*

For the above reasons, I suggest for consideration the possibility that the large numbers in the census lists in the Book of Numbers are deliberately and purposefully exaggerated as a rhetorical device to bring glory to God, derision to enemies, and point forward to the fulfillment of God's promise to the fathers that their descendants will be innumerable, as the stars.

It appears to me that the figure given in the two census lists for the army of Israel may possibly be a magnification by a factor of ten. An army of about 60,000 men would fit what we know of the criteria of the region and the times. John Wenham's reduction to 18,000 (see above) seems to be too small a figure and is based on too complex a solution to be convincing. Similarly, Barnouin's reduction by the factor of one hundred and Petrie's and Noth's proposals leave much too small a figure and are based on an extraordinarily complex and alien system. We desire a solution that is both simple in concept and yet provides a sufficiently large population to be the fulfillment of promise but not so large as to be seemingly impossible.

The suggestion of a rhetorical exaggeration by a factor of ten has much to commend it. It is a simple answer that does not demand convolutions in numbers that other suggestions require. It takes into account the "round" number nature of each integer. It fits in nicely with the approximation of 600,000 as a multiple of 50,000 times 12, the number of the tribes. It results in an army in excess of 60,000 men, with a total population of about 250,000 to 300,000. This sum seems to fit the requirements of the social, geographical, and political realities without diminishing at all the sense of the miraculous and providential care of God. An army of 60,000 is not an insignificant force, but it was likely considerably smaller than the combined armies of the city-states of Canaan at the time. In this way the peoples of Israel must have seemed to be a "swarm" as they lived in Egypt, but they were still "the smallest of nations" when ranked with great world powers. This smaller number accords with the large (but not supernatural!) force the Egyptian Pharaoh sent in pursuit of them to the Sea of Reeds. Six hundred chariots (Exod 14:7) is a considerable force and would surely be a death threat against the unorganized people of Israel. This approach also allows for the drama of the conquest of the Book of Judges, where battles were won by the armies of Israel in league with Yahweh their Great Warrior. This smaller number fits as well for the failures to occupy the full land as that book also details. It also accords well with the well-known Mernepthah stele that records Israel as among the peoples of Canaan during his raid, which we may place during the period of the judges. A population of several million would have more of an impression on this pharaoh!

Again, this smaller number does not diminish the miraculous.[46] It enhances it; for we confront now a cluster of miracles that we may embrace readily rather than shun from some sense of embarrassment, as some do! The supernatural increase of the people in Egypt, the crossing of the Red Sea in one night, the gathering of the people at Mount Sinai, their daily provision in the desert, their entry into the Promised Land—all was miracle! Only the Lord could so provide for this vast number of people in this manner; and mark it well, a population of over one-quarter million is indeed vast. But now we can envision a series of miracles that fits the geography, the topography, and the times. The "myth" of the Exodus becomes the history of redemption.

Furthermore, now we can also deal with the large numbers, not as problem words, but as power words. The deliberate exaggeration was not for misrepresentation nor for simple bombast. This rhetorical use of numbers (see above) was a mark of faith in the Lord who had provided great increase to a family of seventy persons and who one day would make his people as the stars in number. One day they would truly be innumerable—except to him, who counts them all and knows their names! These "embarrassing numbers" are not embarrassing at all. These numbers celebrate Yahweh. They are numbers of worship! I envision this text being read in worship celebrations. The studied units, with their formulaic structure and power numbers,

[46] Nonbelieving rationalism undermines the whole notion of the irruption of God in the lives of his people. *Rationalism* as an antitheistic point of view is to be contrasted with the role of *reason* in biblical interpretation. A view that is more reasonable but which does not attempt to diminish the miraculous should not be brashly charged with the ugly notion of rationalism.

would evoke pride of patriotism, sense of belonging, and—most importantly—the celebration of the Lord.[47]

John Wenham may offer a historical parallel that serves as an explanation for this magnification of the numbers by ten, although he applies it only to the tribe of Levi. He writes that there is now a solution to the mystery of Plato's Atlantis. Plato received his information on this civilization from Egyptian priests. What they gave him was a detailed account of the Minoan culture. But they had inflated the population by a factor of ten. Plato could not locate such an immense population in the Mediterranean. Instead he placed it in the Atlantic and removed the date to remote antiquity.[48]

It appears to me that the numbers of the census are real figures. They are treated like real integers; there is no confusion of hundreds and thousands. Here are numbers that are internally consistent and coherent. Yet I propose that they may have been deliberately magnified by a factor of ten for rhetorical reasons. The promise was that the people would number as the stars. Six-hundred thousand must have seemed like an "astronomical" number in these early biblical times. Certainly the "real" number of 60,000 men was very large, particularly for the desert sojourn. But the 60,000 would still not be an overwhelming force for the task ahead of conquering the peoples of the land, who are seven in number and far more numerous than Israel. To have any success in their task, this army would need to have the help of the Lord along every step of their path. From the abortive battle in the first generation with the Amalekites (14:44–45) to their decisive victories a generation later with Arad (21:1–3) and the small kingdoms of Sihon and Og (21:21–31), these numbers fit the situation. Here now is a seasoned army of approximately 60,000 men, ready to march across the (dry bed of the) Jordan and to take the ancient city of Jericho as the firstfruits of conquest in the land—an offering to the Lord.

This number of about 60,000 fits the requirements of both a great (miraculous) growth and a manageable size for the time and place of their habitation. The use of deliberate exaggeration by a factor of ten may be regarded as a *celebration of the work of the Lord*. We have not taken seriously enough the formulaic nature of the chapters that give the numbers of the tribes. Not only does this make "neat" record keeping,

---

[47]The principal objection that may come to the position I advance is the observation that the number 603,550 is in general agreement with the similarly large number in the second census in 26:51 (601,730); and it is in accord with other statements in the Torah of a population of about 600,000 men (see again, Exod 12:37; 38:26). We may observe that the same deliberate rhetorical function occurs in the second census. In fact, it is even more important that the new generation be regarded in the same significance as the first. The words of Balaam (Num 23:10) emphasize the "mystique" of the immense numbers of Israel. But what to him was but "mystique" was to Moses nothing less than the power of God. As to the numbers in Exodus, they must be based on the numbers in the census lists of Num 1:46; that is, the interpretation of the numbers in the Book of Numbers has priority over the interpretation of these same numbers in Exodus. This means that the interpretation we derive in Numbers will work as well for the round figure of 600,000 in Exod 12:37. Exodus 38:26 is more difficult because of the very specific numbers used for weights (vv.25–31). Yet if the pattern of 600,000 (strictly 603,550) is established as the power number for Israel, then the payment of the redemption price would be rhetorically inflated to fit the established number. The "truth" of the passage is that there was the exact payment of one-half shekel for each of the numbered men in the census, whatever that exact number might have been.

The one problem remaining is the payment of the half-shekel in Exod 38:25–26. This 100 talents + 1,775 shekels is the one number that does not easily arise from a purposeful tenfold increase. I suggest, with some temerity, that the numbers in this passage may have been inserted into the text of Exodus on the basis of the census of Num 1–4. The number 603,550 in Exod 38:25 is certainly based on the census total in Num 1:44. That is, once the factor of a tenfold magnification was established in Numbers, then the payment of the redemption price, to be consistent, would be presented in such a way as to agree with this larger number.

[48]"Large Numbers," *Eerdmans Handbook*, p. 192.

there is within these sections a sense of the sublime, of the orderly presentation of an offering of joy to God. These census lists that some moderns find to be frightfully dull may well have been conceived by their author as a joyful offering of praise to God. And may we not think that God takes pleasure in these words still?

This rhetorical use of numbers is also a *prophetic symbol* (a type!) of the numbers yet to come! One day the people of God will be astrallike; they will be innumerable, uncountable to all but him who knows the number and name of every star (Ps 147:4)!

The obvious objection one may bring, that people do not use numbers this way today, is not overwhelming. We know that in ancient times numbers were used with deliberate exaggeration for rhetorical effect. One needs only to think of the ancient Sumerian king list to find an example that long predates the time of Moses. In this list the reigns of kings from remote antiquity were vastly exaggerated. We believe this was for the rhetorical function of indicating their tremendous importance. We may also find rhetorical uses of numbers in the genealogies of Genesis.[49]

An even more common use of rhetorical language is in battle braggadocio and mottoes of heros:

> Saul has slain his thousands,
> and David his tens of thousands.
> (1 Sam 18:7)[50]

I am aware that some may regard the concept of "rhetorical use of numbers" as a departure from "literal interpretation." In fact, it is not. A departure from literal interpretation would be to spiritualize the numbers, to find some mystical significance in them that was never really intended, or to pretend to some bizarre meaning imported from another environment. Without evidence in the text, Barnouin's approach, using Babylonian astrological symbolism, appears to me to be spiritualizing the text.

Literal interpretation of numbers includes understandings that extend from mathematical exactitude, through general approximation, to literary license. The only demand of literal interpretation (better, "normal" interpretation) is that the reader seek to find the use he believes the text itself presents and demands. It is an abuse of literal interpretation to insist that the way we use numbers in our digital and pocket-calculator age is the way that biblical persons ought to have used numbers in their day.

In summary, the Book of Numbers is just that! It is a book that uses numbers to celebrate the work of the Lord! And in these numbers is his praise.

11. Bibliography

Allen, Ronald B. "The Theology of the Balaam Oracles," in *Tradition and Testament: Essays in Honor of Charles Lee Feinberg*. Edited by John S. Feinberg and Paul D. Feinberg. Chicago: Moody, 1981, pp. 79–119.

[49] Dwight Wayne Young has developed several considerations that help explain the immense numbers used in the lives of the antediluvians. He contends that the attribution of extraordinary length of life was a rhetorical device to elevate these thirty patriarchs to an elite circle in the Pentateuch ("The Incredible Life Spans of the Antediluvian Patriarchs," JNES 47 [1988]: 123–29).

[50] Some may ask, "But is not this simply poetic license?" And I would respond, "Of course!" Battle braggadocio is indeed poetic license—a rhetorical use of language. Notice especially Saul's response: " 'They have credited David with tens of thousands,' he thought, 'but me with only thousands' " (v.8). More modern examples of rhetorical numbers are used by politicians and (dare we say it) some evangelists!

Baentsch, Bruno. *Exodus-Leviticus-Numeri. Handkommentar zum Alten Testament.* Edited by W. Nowack. Gottingen: Vandenhoeck and Ruprecht, 1903.

Binns, L. Elliott. *The Book of Numbers.* Westminster Commentaries. Edited by Walter Lock and D.C. Simpson. London: Methuen, 1927.

Budd, Philip J. *Numbers.* The Word Biblical Commentary. Waco: Word, 1984.

Bush, George. *Notes on Numbers.* Reprint of 1856 edition. Minneapolis: James & Klock, 1976.

Dillmann, August. *Die Bücher Numeri, Deuteronomium und Josua.* Kurzgefasstes exegetisches Handbuch zum Alten Testament. 2d ed. Leipzig: Verlag von S. Hirzel, 1886.

Edelkoort, A.H. *Numeri.* Tekst en Uitleg: Praktische Bijbelverklaring. Groningen: Bij J.B. Wolters' Uitgevers-Maatschappij, 1930.

Fisch, S. "The Book of Numbers." *The Soncino Chumash: The Five Books of Moses With Haphtaroth.* Edited by A. Cohen. London: Soncino, 1947.

Goldberg, Arnold M. *Das Buch Numeri.* Die Welt der Bibel. Dusseldorf: Patmos-Verlag, 1970.

Gray, George Buchanan. *A Critical and Exegetical Commentary on Numbers.* The International Critical Commentary. Edinburgh: T. & T. Clark, 1903.

Greenstone, Julius H. *Numbers, With Commentary.* The Holy Scriptures. Philadelphia: The Jewish Publication Society of America, 5699/1939.

Heinisch, Paul. *Das Buch Numeri Ubersetzt und Erklart.* Bonn: Peter Hanstein Verlagsbuchhandlung, 1936.

Hirsch, Samson Raphael. *The Pentateuch Translated and Explained.* Vol. 4. *Numbers.* Translated by Isaac Levy. London: Isaac Levy, 1964.

Holzinger, H. *Numeri.* Kurzer Hand-Commentar zum Alten Testament. Tubingen und Leipzig: Verlag von J.C.B. Mohr (Paul Siebeck), 1903.

Keil, C.F. *Biblical Commentary on the Old Testament: The Pentateuch.* Vol. 3. KD. Translated by James Martin. Grand Rapids: Eerdmans, n.d.

LaSor, William Sanford; Hubbard, David Allan; and Bush, Frederic Wm., *Old Testament Survey: The Message, Form, and Background of the Old Testament.* Grand Rapids: Eerdmans, 1982.

Maarsingh, B. *Numbers: A Practical Commentary.* Translated by John Vriend. Grand Rapids: Eerdmans, 1987.

Mendenhall, George E. "The Census Lists of Numbers 1 and 26." *Journal of Biblical Literature* 77 (1958): 52–66.

Moriarty, Frederick L. "Numbers." *The Jerome Biblical Commentary.* Edited by Raymond E. Brown, Joseph A. Fitzmeyer, and Roland E. Murphey. 2 vols. bound as one. Englewood Cliffs, N.J.: Prentice-Hall, 1968.

Noordtzij, A. *Numbers.* Bible Student's Commentary. Translated by Ed van der Maas. Grand Rapids: Zondervan, 1983.

Noth, Martin. *Numbers: A Commentary.* The Old Testament Library. Translated by James D. Martin. Philadelphia: Westminster, 1968.

Olson, Dennis T. *The Death of the Old and the Birth of the New: The Framework of the Book of Numbers and the Pentateuch.* Brown Judaic Studies. Chico, Calif.: Scholars, 1985.

Owens, John Joseph. "Numbers." *The Broadman Bible Commentary.* Edited by Clifton J. Allen. Nashville: Broadman, 1970.

Smick, Elmer B. "Numbers." *The Wycliffe Bible Commentary.* Edited by C.F. Pfeiffer and E.F. Harrison. Chicago: Moody, 1962.

Snaith, N.H. *Leviticus and Numbers.* The Century Bible. Greenwood, S.C.: Attic, 1967.

Thompson, J.A. "Numbers." *The New Bible Commentary: Revised.* Edited by D. Guthrie and J.A. Motyer. Grand Rapids: Eerdmans, 1970.

Vaulx, J. de. *Les Nombres.* Sources Bibliques. Paris: J. Gabalda, 1972.

Wenham, Gordon J. *Numbers: An Introduction and Commentary.* Downers Grove, Ill., and Leicester, England: InterVarsity Press, 1981.

12. Outline

I. The Experience of the First Generation in the Desert (1:1–25:18)
  A. The Preparation for the Triumphal March to the Promised Land (1:1–10:36)
    1. Setting apart the people (1:1–10:10)
      a. The census of the first generation (1:1–4:49)
        (1) The muster (1:1–54)
          (a) The command of the Lord (1:1–4)
          (b) The names of the men (1:5–16)
          (c) The summary of the census (1:17–19)
          (d) The listings of the census by each tribe (1:20–43)
          (e) The summary of the census (1:44–46)
          (f) The reason for the exclusion of the Levites (1:47–54)
        (2) The placement of the tribes (2:1–34)
          (a) Summary command (2:1–2)
          (b) Details of execution (2:3–33)
            (i) Eastern encampment (2:3–9)
            (ii) Southern encampment (2:10–16)
            (iii) Tent and the Levites (2:17)
            (iv) Western encampment (2:18–24)
            (v) Northern encampment (2:25–31)
            (vi) Summary totals (2:32–33)
          (c) Summary conclusion (2:34)
        (3) The placement and the numbers of the Levites and firstborn of Israel (3:1–51)
          (a) The family of Aaron and Moses (3:1–4)
          (b) The duties for the Levites (3:5–10)
          (c) The separation of the Levites (3:11–13)
          (d) The census of the Levites (3:14–39)
            (i) The principals (3:14–20)
            (ii) Gershon (3:21–26)
            (iii) Kohath (3:27–32)
            (iv) Merari (3:33–37)
            (v) Moses and Aaron (3:38)
            (vi) The sum (3:39)
          (e) The census and redemption of the firstborn (3:40–51)
            (i) The census (3:40–43)
            (ii) The redemption (3:44–51)
        (4) The numbers of the Levites in tabernacle service (4:1–49)
          (a) The command for the census and a description of duties (4:1–33)
            (i) The family of Kohath (4:1–20)
            (ii) The family of Gershon (4:21–28)
            (iii) The family of Merari (4:29–33)
          (b) A description of the census (4:34–45)
            (i) The family of Kohath (4:34–37)
            (ii) The family of Gershon (4:38–41)
            (iii) The family of Merari (4:42–45)

(c) A summary of the census and the work of Moses in the census (4:46–49)

b. Diverse commands and rituals in preparation for the triumphal march (5:1–10:10)

(1) The test for purity and the law of jealousy (5:1–31)

(a) The expulsion of the impure from the camp (5:1–4)

(b) Restitution for personal wrongs (5:5–10)

(c) The law of jealousy (5:11–31)

(i) The seed of jealousy (5:11–15)

(ii) The curse of the oath (5:16–22)

(iii) The bitter waters (5:23–28)

(iv) The summary of the law of jealousy (5:29–31)

(2) The vow of the Nazirite and the Aaronic Benediction (6:1–27)

(a) The vow of the Nazirite (6:1–21)

(i) The basic prohibition against wine (6:1–4)

(ii) Basic prohibitions concerning hair and dead bodies (6:5–8)

(iii) The specific prohibition concerning accidental death (6:9–12)

(iv) The ritual for the completion of the vow (6:13–20)

(v) The summary of the Nazirite vow (6:21)

(b) The Aaronic Benediction (6:22–27)

(3) The offerings at the dedication of the tabernacle (7:1–89)

(a) The presentation of carts and oxen (7:1–3)

(b) The distribution of the carts and oxen (7:4–9)

(c) The plan of the tribal offerings (7:10–11)

(d) The offerings of the Twelve Tribes (7:12–83)

(e) The totals of the offerings (7:84–88)

(f) Moses' conversation with God (7:89)

(4) Setting up the lamps and the separation and age of service of the Levites (8:1–26)

(a) Setting up the lamps (8:1–4)

(b) The separation of the Levites (8:5–22)

(i) Their ceremonial cleansing (8:5–14)

(ii) Their position before the Lord (8:15–19)

(iii) A summary of their separation (8:20–22)

(c) The age of service of the Levites (8:23–26)

(5) The celebration of the Passover (9:1–14)

(a) The command to keep the Passover (9:1–5)

(b) The ceremonially unclean (9:6–8)

(c) Divine permission for a legitimate delay (9:9–13)

(d) The rights of the alien at Passover (9:14)

(6) The covering cloud (9:15–23)

(7) The two silver trumpets (10:1–10)

(a) The command to fashion two silver trumpets (10:1–7)

(b) The ordinance for the silver trumpets (10:8–10)
2. Setting forth the people on the triumphal march (10:11–36)
 a. The march begins (10:11–13)
 b. The grand procession of tribes and Levites (10:14–28)
 c. The request for Hobab to join the march (10:29–32)
 d. The three-day procession behind the ark of the Lord (10:33–36)

B. The Rebellion and Judgment of a Fearful People (11:1–25:18)
1. A cycle of rebellion and atonement and the record of death (11:1–20:29)
 a. The beginning of sorrows (11:1–35)
  (1) A judgment of fire (11:1–3)
  (2) A surfeit of quail (11:4–34)
  (3) A journey note (11:35)
 b. The opposition of Miriam and Aaron (12:1–16)
  (1) The attack on Moses from his family (12:1–3)
  (2) The defense of Moses by the Lord (12:4–9)
  (3) The punishment of Miriam (12:10–15)
  (4) A journey note (12:16)
 c. The twelve spies and the mixed report (13:1–33)
  (1) The command of the Lord (13:1–2)
  (2) The roster of names (13:3–16)
  (3) The instructions of Moses (13:17–20)
  (4) A summary of the reconnaissance (13:21–25)
  (5) The mixed report (13:26–33)
 d. The rebellion of the people and defeat by the Amalekites (14:1–45)
  (1) The final rebellion of the faithless people (14:1–4)
  (2) The words of the faithful warning against rebellion (14:5–9)
  (3) The appearance of the Lord to withstand the rebels (14:10–12)
  (4) The pleading of Moses on behalf of the rebellious people (14:13–19)
  (5) The judgment of the Lord against the rebels (14:20–35)
  (6) The death of the evil spies (14:36–38)
  (7) Defeat by the Amalekites (14:39–45)
 e. Laws on offerings, the Sabbath, and tassels on garments (15:1–41)
  (1) Teaching on special offerings (15:1–16)
  (2) Instructions on the cake offering (15:17–21)
  (3) Instructions on offerings for unintentional sins (15:22–29)
  (4) Instructions for defiant sins (15:30–31)
  (5) A man who violated the Sabbath (15:32–36)
  (6) Instructions for tassels on garments (15:37–41)
 f. The rebellion of Korah and his allies (16:1–50)
  (1) The beginning of revolt (16:1–3)
  (2) Moses' rejoinder (16:4–7)

(3) Moses' warning to the rebels (16:8–11)
(4) Confrontation with Dathan and Abiram (16:12–14)
(5) Judgment on his enemies (16:15–35)
(6) The aftermath of the contest—more distress (16:36–50)
g. The budding of Aaron's staff (17:1–13)
(1) The test for the true priest (17:1–7)
(2) The outcome of the ordeal (17:8–13)
h. The priest and the Levites (18:1–32)
(1) Their general duties (18:1–7)
(2) Their offerings and support (18:8–13)
(3) The firstborn offerings and redemptions (18:14–19)
(4) Aaron's special portion (18:20)
(5) The tithes and the Levites (18:21–24)
(6) The contributions of the Levites (18:25–32)
i. The red heifer and the cleansing water (19:1–22)
(1) The statute of the red heifer (19:1–10)
(2) Application of cleansing waters (19:11–13)
(3) Specifics of uncleanness (19:14–16)
(4) Application of the cleansing waters for uncleanness (19:17–22)
j. The ultimate rebellion in the sin of Moses (20:1–13)
k. The resistance of Edom (20:14–21)
l. The death of Aaron and the succession to Eleazar (20:22–29)
2. A climax of rebellion and hope and the end of their dying (21:1–25:18)
a. The destruction of Arad (21:1–3)
b. The bronze snake (21:4–9)
c. The journey toward Moab and the Song of the Well (21:10–20)
d. The defeat of Sihon of Heshbon (21:21–31)
e. Israel's defeat of Og of Bashan (21:32–22:1)
f. Balak and Balaam (22:2–41)
(1) The "call" of Balaam (22:2–20)
(2) The donkey story (22:21–41)
g. Balaam's seven oracles (23:1–24:25)
(1) Balaam's first oracle (23:1–12)
(a) The setting of the oracle (23:1–6)
(b) The oracle: The blessing of Israel is irrevocable (23:7–10)
(c) The aftermath (23:11–12)
(2) Balaam's second oracle (23:13–26)
(a) The setting of the oracle (23:13–17)
(b) The oracle: the source of Israel's unique blessing (23:18–24)
(c) The aftermath (23:25–26)
(3) Balaam's third oracle (23:27–24:14)
(a) The setting of the oracle (23:27–24:2)

(b) The oracle: the beauty and strength of Israel (24:3–9)
(c) The aftermath (24:10–14)
(4) Balaam's fourth oracle (24:15–19)
(5) Balaam's fifth oracle (24:20)
(6) Balaam's sixth oracle (24:21–22)
(7) Balaam's seventh oracle (24:23–25)
h. Israel's final rebellion with the Baal of Peor and the death of the first generation (25:1–18)
(1) The involvement of Israel in the worship of Baal Peor (25:1–3)
(2) The judgment of the Lord on his errant people (25:4–5)
(3) The zeal of Phinehas (25:6–9)
(4) The Lord's covenant with Phinehas (25:10–13)
(5) The aftermath of the rebellion (25:14–18)

II. The Prospects for the Second Generation to Enter the Promised Land (26:1–36:13)
A. The Preparation for the Triumphal March to the Promised Land, the Second Generation (26:1–32:42)
1. The second census of the new generation that will enter the land (26:1–65)
a. The command of the Lord to take the census (26:1–4)
b. The enumeration of the people by their ancestral tribes and clans (26:5–50)
(1) The tribe of Reuben (26:5–11)
(2) The tribe of Simeon (26:12–14)
(3) The tribe of Gad (26:15–18)
(4) The tribe of Judah (26:19–22)
(5) The tribe of Issachar (26:23–25)
(6) The tribe of Zebulun (26:26–27)
(7) The tribe of Manasseh (26:28–34)
(8) The tribe of Ephraim (26:35–37)
(9) The tribe of Benjamin (26:38–41)
(10) The tribe of Dan (26:42–43)
(11) The tribe of Asher (26:44–47)
(12) The tribe of Naphtali (26:48–50)
c. The grand celebrative number, to the praise of the Lord (26:51)
d. The allotment of the land on the basis of the names of the families of Israel (26:52–56)
e. The families and numbers of the Levites, the holy tribe of Israel (26:57–62)
f. A recapitulation of the point of the census: this is the new generation (26:63–65)
2. The inheritance of women on entering the land (27:1–11)
3. The successor to Moses (27:12–23)
4. Commands for the second generation on regular offerings, festival offerings, and vows (28:1–30:16)

a. Regular offerings (28:1–15)
   (1) The daily offerings (28:1–8)
   (2) The Sabbath offerings (28:9–10)
   (3) The monthly offerings (28:11–15)
b. Festival offerings (28:16–29:40)
   (1) The Passover (28:16–25)
   (2) The Feast of Weeks (28:26–31)
   (3) The Feast of Trumpets (29:1–6)
   (4) The Day of Atonement (29:7–11)
   (5) The Feast of Tabernacles (29:12–38)
   (6) Summary (29:39–40)
c. Vows (30:1–16)
   (1) The issue of vows to the Lord (30:1–2)
   (2) The vows of a woman who lives with her father (30:3–5)
   (3) The vows of a (newly) married woman (30:6–8)
   (4) The vows of a widow or a divorced woman (30:9)
   (5) The vows of a married woman (30:10–15)
   (6) A summary statement (30:16)

5. The reprisal against Midian, Moses' last campaign (31:1–54)
   a. The report of the battle (31:1–24)
      (1) The instructions for the battle (31:1–6)
      (2) The report of the victory (31:7–12)
      (3) The destruction of the women and boys (31:13–18)
      (4) The purification of the soldiers (31:19–20)
      (5) The purifying of the goods (31:21–24)
   b. The division of the spoils (31:25–54)
      (1) The share for the soldiers (31:25–41)
      (2) The share for the people (31:42–47)
      (3) The extra share for the Lord (31:48–54)
6. The settlement of the Transjordan tribes (32:1–42)
   a. The request of Reuben and Gad to settle in Transjordan (32:1–19)
      (1) The original request (32:1–5)
      (2) The angry response of Moses (32:6–15)
      (3) The assurances of Reuben and Gad (32:16–19)
   b. The decision of Moses for their settlement (32:20–30)
   c. The public declaration of the agreement (32:31–32)
   d. The territories of Reuben and Gad (32:33–42)

B. A Review of the First Generation's Journey and Words of Warning and Encouragement to the Second Generation (33:1–56)
   1. The stages of the journey in the desert (33:1–49)
      a. Introduction (33:1–2)
      b. The point of departure (33:3–4)
      c. The stages of the journey from Rameses to Mount Hor (33:5–37)
      d. The events at Mount Hor (33:38–40)
      e. The stages of the journey from Mount Hor to the mountains of Abarim (33:41–47)

f. The encampment in Moab as the staging area for the assault on the land of Canaan (33:48–49)

2. Words of warning and encouragement to the second generation (33:50–56)

C. An Anticipation of the Promised Land (34:1–36:13)

1. A preview of the land (34:1–26)

a. The boundaries (34:1–12)

(1) Introduction (34:1–2)

(2) The southern boundary (34:3–5)

(3) The western boundary (34:6)

(4) The northern boundary (34:7–9)

(5) The eastern boundary (34:10–12a)

(6) Summary (34:12b)

b. The inheritance in Transjordan (34:13–15)

c. The personnel of the inheritance (34:16–29)

2. Levitical cities and cities of refuge (35:1–34)

a. The Levitical cities (35:1–5)

b. The cities of refuge (35:6–33)

(1) The basic concept of the cities of refuge (35:6–8)

(2) Further details on the cities of refuge (35:9–15)

(3) Basic stipulations concerning the taking of life and the cities of refuge (35:16–21)

(4) Cases to be decided concerning the taking of life and the cities of refuge (35:22–32)

(5) The divine perspective on murder and the land (35:33–34)

3. A review of the inheritance of women (36:1–13)

a. Concerns of the Gileadites for the daughters of Zelophehad (36:1–4)

b. The law for the marriages of the women who inherit familial land (36:5–9)

c. The compliance of the daughters of Zelophehad (36:10–12)

d. A summary statement of the law of the Lord (36:13)

[D. The Prospects for the Second Generation Are for Good, but the Warning From the Experience of the First Generation Must Not Be Forgotten]

Text and Exposition

Two types of response are possible for the modern reader who first glances at chapter 1 of the Book of Numbers. One is boredom. First, the reader is told about the command of the Lord for Moses and Aaron to take a military census of Israel. This sounds rather unpromising. Then the reader is assaulted by a list of unfamiliar, compound Hebrew names (1:5–15), names that are a threat to any but the most self-assured Scripture reader. As though this is not enough, the reader then finds twelve two-verse paragraphs that are identical in wording except for the name of the tribe and the sum of its people (1:20–43).

Worse, the paragraphs all center on numbers. The first chapter of the book bristles with numbers; everywhere we turn we read number after number. No wonder the book has come down to us in English with its singularly uninspiring title! Who but a mathematician could rise with joy to a book called "Numbers"?

But these same features may bring another response, especially for the reader who approaches tasks with curiosity. This is the response of intrigue, interest, and even wonderment. Surely the Torah was not written to bore the reader—ancient or modern! The listing of names was never meant to be simply a test of the skills of a reader, nor could the repetitions merely have been designed to test a person's resolve. There must be significance in these names, numbers, and repetition.

Further, we soon discover that the tedious repetition in chapter 1 is not unique to the book. The repetition of chapter 7 similarly seeks to undermine whatever appreciation we might try to muster up for the values underlying such repetitious language.

Thus the expectations of the modern reader in approaching this text are quite irrelevant to a valid evaluation of the purpose and nature of the book. As with any book of Scripture—indeed, any book of intrinsic merit—the Book of Numbers must be read on its own grounds. The Bible sets its own agenda; the materials of Scripture take their own shape. That its interests and methods may be diverse from our own is quite beside the point. If this book is to be received by the modern reader with the integrity and demands of Scripture as a significant part of the divine out-breathing (2 Tim 3:16), the fourth portion of the Torah, the book of Moses—then we need to set bias aside, avoid negative prejudgments, escape first impressions, and come to the book as it is.

The best approach toward any obtuse or "difficult" portion of Scripture is to pepper it with questions. In the case at hand, why would the ancient sages feel it important to include the names of each tribal representative? Why was it believed impressive to list the number of men from each tribe in such a formal manner, requiring the measure of repetition as 1:20–43 presents? What are the values suggested by these repeated paragraphs? Is it possible that in this alien aesthetic these verses of repeated phraseology are not to be regarded as tiresome at all but something of dignity, solemnity, and even beauty? Is there perhaps an impressive nature to these paragraphs that speaks of the pride of each tribe? Indeed, the repetitions are likely instructive as to the power of God and his faithfulness to his promises. That reader who first turned his face away from these pages with disdain may have turned away from something that is intended to bring praise to God and confidence among his people. It becomes our point of view that these numbers, in their highly stylized environments, are a matter of *celebration of the faithfulness of Yahweh to his covenant people.*

So as we come to these numbers and words, let us come to them on their own terms, to see what is impressive in them and what in them is instructive for us.

I. The Experience of the First Generation in the Desert (1:1–25:18)

An explanation is given in the Introduction (Section 7: Unity and Organization) for the unusual outline this commentary presents. Following the lead of Dennis Olson, I see the macrostructure of the Book of Numbers as a bifid of unequal parts. The two censuses (chs. 1–4, 26) are key to understanding the structure of the book. The first census (chs. 1–4) concerns the first generation of the Exodus community; the second census (ch. 26) focuses on the experiences of the second generation, the people for whom this book is primarily directed. The first generation of the redeemed were prepared for triumph but ended in disaster. The second generation has an opportunity for greatness—if only they will learn from the failures of their fathers and mothers the absolute necessity for robust faithfulness to the Lord despite all obstacles.

A. *The Preparation for the Triumphal March to the Promised Land (1:1–10:36)*

The record of the experiences of the first generation is presented in two broad parts. Chapters 1–10 record the story of their preparation for triumph; chapters 11–25 follow with the sorry record of repeated actions of rebellion and unbelief punctuated by bursts of God's wrath and instances of his grace.

1. *Setting apart the people (1:1–10:10)*

As the book as a whole presents itself as a bifid of unequal parts, so chapters 1–10 also form a bifid of unequal sections: 1:1–10:10 records the meticulous preparation of the people for their triumphal march into Canaan; 10:11–36 describes their first steps under the leadership of Moses.

a. *The census of the first generation (1:1–4:49)*

(1) *The muster (1:1–54)*

(a) *The command of the Lord*

1:1–4

1 The LORD spoke to Moses in the Tent of Meeting in the Desert of Sinai on the first day of the second month of the second year after the Israelites came out of Egypt. He said: 2 "Take a census of the whole Israelite community by their clans and families, listing every man by name, one by one. 3 You and Aaron are to number by their divisions all the men in Israel twenty years old or more who are able to serve in the army. 4 One man from each tribe, each the head of his family, is to help you.

1 Each phrase of v.1 is significant for our study; we need to move slowly here. One of the most pervasive emphases in the Book of Numbers is that the Lord spoke to Moses—and through Moses—to Israel. From the opening words of the book (1:1) to the closing words (36:13), this is stated over 150 times and in more than twenty ways. One Hebrew name for the Book of Numbers is *wayᵉḏabbēr* ("And [Yahweh] spoke"), from the first word in the Hebrew text. This has a certain appropriateness, given the strong emphasis on God's revelation to Moses in Numbers.

These opening words really set the stage for the chapter and, indeed, for the entire book. The phraseology "the LORD [Yahweh] spoke to Moses" presents a point of view that will be repeated (and restated) almost to the point of tedium throughout this book. Yet it is just such a phrase that is so important to the self-attestation of the divine origin of the Book of Numbers. Whatever the modern reader may think of this phrase and however it may be interpreted, it stands as the record of a divine disclosure of the eternal God to his servant Moses and from Moses, a faithful transmission to the people of God. This type of phrase does not at all exhaust our curiosity as to how Moses heard the word of God—whether as the articulated words of a man's voice; a mystical inner sensation, perhaps a clearly articulated cluster of words in his mind; or some vague mental image—all this phrase does is to present the source and the reception of communication. Numbers 12:6–8 is the major text describing the Lord's use of Moses as his prophet. This section will indicate something of the special manner of the divine disclosure to Moses; but the phrasing that is most characteristic merely states the most important thing: Yahweh spoke to Moses.

That the subject of the verb "spoke" is Yahweh points to his initiation and, by that measure, to his grace. The fact that God speaks at all to anyone is a mercy, that he continued to speak to Moses throughout his leadership of the people of God is a mystery, and that he spoke to Moses with the intent that others would read these words throughout the centuries is a marvel. The repetition of phrases such as this throughout the Torah is for emphasis. We are to be duly impressed with the fact that the Lord is the Great Communicator, that he has reached out to Moses of his own volition to convey to him his word and to relate through him to the nation his own will. Other gods are mute. Other gods are silent. Other gods are no God at all. But the God of Scripture, the Lord of covenant—Yahweh, God of Israel—speaks! What he desires more than anything else is a people who will hear him, who will take joy in obeying him, and who will bring him pleasure by their response.

The second phrase of v.1 centers in the place of God's speaking to Moses: "in the Tent of Meeting." (Actually, this phrase follows "in the Desert of Sinai" in the Hebrew construction.) There are other terms and phrases used for this tent in Numbers. It is called "the tabernacle" (v.51) and "the tabernacle of the Testimony" (vv.50, 53). The expression "the Tent of Meeting" speaks of the revelatory and communion aspect of the tent. The term "tabernacle" by itself points to the temporary and transitory nature of the tent; it is a moveable and portable shrine, specially designed for the worship of God by a people on the move. The expression "the tabernacle of the Testimony" suggests the covenantal signification of the tent; within are the symbols of the presence of the Lord among his people, his guarantees of continuing relationship. Critical scholarship has sought to confound the issue by suggesting these several terms refer to different tents or are telltale pointers to different strata of composition of the Torah. But this approach is not only unnecessary, it confounds the meanings of the words. It is not just a matter of evangelical reaction to critical writers to balk at this approach. The terms themselves lose signification if they are regarded only as markers of sources. Certainly it seems preferable to read these several terms as correlative, stylistic variants used for effect to describe various realities of the central focus of God's relationship with his people in the desert—the tent of his presence.

The more common Hebrew name for the Book of Numbers is *b^e midbar* ("In the Desert"), the fifth word in the Hebrew text. God spoke to Moses in the Tent of Meeting during that lengthy period Israel spent in the Desert of Sinai. In some ways "In the Desert" is a more preferable term for the book than "Numbers." The book certainly shows a concern for the concept of census, but the desert setting is pervasive. The book begins with the leadership of Israel following faithfully the commands of the Lord and the people being mustered together for war against the cities of Canaan in anticipation of a great conquest of the Land of Promise. But because of the perfidy of the people, that great event of conquest—the realization of the promise of God to the fathers and mothers of Israel—was denied for a generation. Instead, in judgment for doubt and for casting the worst possible motivation to God for their deliverance—that their "wives and children will be taken as plunder" (14:3)—the entire populace over the age of twenty would spend the rest of their natural days in the desert. Only Joshua and Caleb because of their exceptional faith, unswerving in the face of their compatriots, would enter the land. As it turns out, Miriam and Aaron—and even Moses—died in the desert. The expression "in the desert" is not just descriptive of a physical feature of topography. It is a metaphor for the experience of the people of Israel described in this book. One day their descendants would enter the land; but this book is the record of the experience of the people "in the Desert of Sinai."

The first verse also gives a specific time notice for the command of God to take a census of the nation. The historical cast to this narrative is precise and detailed: "on the first day of the second month of the second year after the Israelites came out of Egypt." The Book of Numbers begins thirteen months after the Exodus. Israel had spent the previous year in the region of Mount Sinai receiving the law, erecting the tabernacle, and becoming a people. Now she was to be mustered as a military force and formed into a cohesive nation to provide the basis for an orderly march. The events of Numbers cover a period of thirty-eight years and nine or ten months, i.e., the period of Israel's desert wanderings. The second month in the Hebrew calendar corresponds roughly to our April. Later, when Israel was established in Canaan, this second month would be the month of general harvest between the Harvest of Firstfruits and Pentecost or Weeks, seven weeks following Passover. That Israel was being numbered during a time that later would be associated with harvesting of crops would probably not have been lost on the later readers of this book.

This pattern of dating events from the Exodus signifies the centrality of the Exodus in the experience of the people of God. Time will now be measured from their leaving Egypt. The wording is not unlike Christian reckoning of time as B.C., "Before Christ," and A.D., "Anno Domini," "in the Year of our Lord." Time, for Israel, had its beginning with the Exodus, just as time for the Christian has its beginning and meaning with the salvation provided in the Savior, Jesus. The Exodus was God's great act of deliverance of his people from bondage; the story of the Exodus is the gospel in the OT.

Another example of dating from the Exodus is found in 1 Kings 6:1, where the beginning of the building of the temple of Solomon is dated in the four hundred and eightieth year of Israel's exodus from Egypt. Whether this date is an exact figure, that is, one year more than four hundred and seventy-nine years, or, as is sometimes suggested, a round number suggesting twelve generations (i.e., 12 x 40—the approximation of a generation), the point is still sure: the dating of Israel's experience with God begins with the exodus from Egypt.

Gordon J. Wenham (p. 56) observes that the materials of the Book of Numbers are not arranged strictly in chronological order (also, see Introduction: Unity and Organization). The descriptions of 7:1–9:15 belong to the first two weeks of the first month of the second year of the Exodus (cf. Exod 40:2; Num 9:1); whereas the census and related affairs of Numbers 1–6 begin on the first day of the second month (see, again, v.1). The concern of the writer was thematic rather than strictly chronological, literary rather than pedantic. The issues of the numbering of the people and the ordering of the camp were believed to be foundational to the understanding we need for the stories of offerings, worship, and Passover in chapters 7–9. Moreover, as we argue in the Introduction, the Book of Numbers is a biped, each section beginning with a census (chs. 1–4; 26). The deliberate changing of chronology of the materials of the book is a signal to the reader that chronology is not nearly so important as the fact of the census.

The precise dating of the Exodus itself remains a deeply debated issue among biblical scholars—liberal, moderate, and conservative. Archaeological evidence has been adduced for both an early thirteenth-century date (the "late date view") as well as a mid-fifteenth-century date (the "early date view"). See the introductory article by Gleason L. Archer, Jr., "The Chronology of the Old Testament" (EBC, 1:366–67), for a vigorous defense of the fifteenth-century date for the Exodus. Such a pattern would suggest the events of the Book of Numbers extend thirty-eight years in the second half of the fifteenth century B.C.

2 The Hebrew verbs "take" and "number" (v.3) are in the plural, indicating that Moses and Aaron were to complete this task together (see v.3, "you and Aaron"), but the primary responsibility for the task lay with Moses. The purpose of this census was to form a military roster, not a social, political, or taxing document, as some moderns have suggested. There are other reasons for the census however: (1) to demonstrate to the people the extent of God's faithfulness in fulfilling the provisions of the Abrahamic covenant in multiplying the physical descendants of Abraham (Gen 12:2; 15:5; 17:4–6; 22:17); (2) to provide a clear sense of family and clan identity for the individual; and (3) to provide the means for an orderly march of the people to their new home in Canaan.

There is a remarkable specificity in the numbering process, moving from the broadest groupings to the individual. These Hebrew phrasings are "families," "father's houses," "names," and "every male by their heads." This stylistic device is common in Hebrew prose, moving from the most general to the very specific, giving a sense of the totality of a task and the enormity of carrying it out. We find the same type of thing, for example, in the words that came to Abram describing the associations he must leave as he sets out on his journey of faith with the Lord: "your country," "your people," "your father's household" (Gen 12:1; order as in MT). Similarly, in the story of the binding of Isaac, Abraham is told to take his "son," his "unique son," whom "he loves," "even Isaac" (Gen 22:2; order as in MT).

3 The words of v.3 also point clearly to the principal military purpose of the census: those males who are over the age of twenty and who are able to go forth for war. This type of phrase occurs fourteen times in chapter 1 and again in 26:2.

Those who are bothered by the military nature of the census prefer to view it as an early experiment in sociology. The wording of the MT is so patently military in nature, however, that this escape is simply not possible. The point of the census was to prepare the armies of Israel for their triumphal war of conquest against the peoples of Canaan. In fulfillment of the promise the Lord made to father Abraham (Gen 15:16–21), the descendants of those who went to Egypt would return with great possessions and would then be given the land inhabited by numerous nations and ethnic groups. Those nations and groupings were pervaded with evil; the sins of the Amorites had now reached its full measure (cf. Gen 15:16); the campaign of conquest was soon to begin.

Perhaps the saddest thing to bear in mind in reading this text is the memory we have of the end of the story: all the peoples who are numbered for military duty in this chapter—every one of them save only Joshua and Caleb—died without ever facing the war in which God demanded they become engaged. It is true that some participated in the abortive engagement with the Amalekites following their rebellion against the Lord (14:44–45), but this was not a glorious war of victory. It was an ignoble rout! Victory would come only to their children, a generation removed. Hence this listing that was intended by God to be a roster of soldiers, a table of heroes, a memorial of victors, became instead a memorial of those who were to die in the desert without ever achieving the aim of God in their lives.

There is another mustering of soldiers for war at the end of the desert period (ch. 26). Those mustered for war in that account are entirely different persons than those listed for war in chapter 1. Except for Joshua and Caleb, the total died in the desert between slavery and liberty, between cursing and blessing, between there and here, with hopes dashed and desires never fulfilled. All died in the dry, barren desert when God had intended for them the enjoyment of the good life in the good land and his gracious hand. But in the new roster of Numbers 26 there is a new generation, a new beginning, a new hope. It is "the death of the old and the birth of the new" (Olson; see Introduction, pp. 21–22).

4 By having a representative from each tribe assist Moses and Aaron, not only would the task be made somewhat more manageable, but the resultant count would be regarded as legitimate by all. No tribe would have a reason to suggest it was under or over-represented in the census, since a worthy man from each tribe was a partner with Moses and Aaron in accomplishing the task.

Notes

1 The wording of the first verse of Numbers, when compared with the wording of the last verse (36:13), fits well with the concept that Numbers is an independent "book" within the larger collection of the fivefold book, the Pentateuch. This is a point argued well by Olson (pp. 46–49). He also ties the Book of Numbers to the *tôl*[e]*d̲ôṯ* (toledot) formula of Genesis (cf. Gen 2:4a; 5:1 et al.) and finally provides the overarching structure for the entirety of the Pentateuch (pp. 83–114; cf. commentary on 3:1).

4 The Hebrew expression אִישׁ אִישׁ לַמַּטֶּה (*'îš 'îš lammaṭṭeh;* lit., "man, man for the tribe") is distributive: "one man from each tribe."

(b) *The names of the men*

1:5–16

5These are the names of the men who are to assist you:

from Reuben, Elizur son of Shedeur;
6from Simeon, Shelumiel son of Zurishaddai;
7from Judah, Nahshon son of Amminadab;
8from Issachar, Nethanel son of Zuar;
9from Zebulun, Eliab son of Helon;
10from the sons of Joseph:
from Ephraim, Elishama son of Ammihud;
from Manasseh, Gamaliel son of Pedahzur;
11from Benjamin, Abidan son of Gideoni;
12from Dan, Ahiezer son of Ammishaddai;
13from Asher, Pagiel son of Ocran;
14from Gad, Eliasaph son of Deuel;
15from Naphtali, Ahira son of Enan."

16These were the men appointed from the community, the leaders of their ancestral tribes. They were the heads of the clans of Israel.

5–15 The names of these luminaries occur again in chapters 2, 7, and 10. Most are theophoric, that is, these names are built by compounding one of the designations for God into a name that is a significant banner of faith in the person and work of God. The antiquity of a list of names is revealed by the fact that many are built on the names *El, Shaddai, Ammi, Zur,* and *Ab.* At a later time in Israel's history, we would expect many names to be based on the covenant name *Yahweh.* The paucity of names based on the divine name Yahweh is an argument for the antiquity of this text. Whereas the name Yahweh was available for name building in the pre-Exodus period, it did not come into high use until after the revelation of a new significance of that name in Yahweh's encounter with Moses (Exod 3; 6) and his subsequent teaching of these truths to the populace of Israel.

Here are the names and their probable meanings (in the order of their listing):

Elizur ("[My] God Is a Rock") son of Shedeur ("Shaddai Is a Flame"), chief of Reuben.

Shelumiel ("[My] Peace Is God") son of Zurishaddai ("[My] Rock Is Shaddai"), chief of Simeon.

Nahshon ("Serpentine") son of Amminadab ("[My] Kinsman [God] Is Noble"), chief of Judah.

Nethanel ("God Has Given") son of Zuar ("Little One"), chief of Issachar.

Eliab ("[My] God Is Father") son of Helon ("Rampart-like" [?]), chief of Zebulun.

Elishama ("[My] God Has Heard") son of Ammihud ("[My] Kinsman [God] Is Majesty"), chief of Ephraim.

Gamaliel ("Reward of God") son of Pedahzur ("The Rock [God] Has Ransomed"), chief of Manasseh.

Abidan ("[My] Father [God] Is Judge") son of Gideoni ("My Hewer"), chief of Benjamin.

Ahiezer ("[My] Brother [God] Is Help") son of Ammishaddai ("[My] Kinsman [God] Is Shaddai"), chief of Dan.

Pagiel ("Encountered by God") son of Ocran ("Troubled"), chief of Asher.

Eliasaph ("God Has Added") son of Deuel ("Know God!"), chief of Gad.

Ahira ("My Brother Is Evil") son of Enan ("Seeing"), chief of Naphtali.

Noth (pp. 13–19) assumes the source for this material is the supposed P (late in the fifth century B.C.) because of the schematic nature and orderliness of presentation but that the name lists that P used in his record must have come from a very early period in Israel's experience (at least from a pre-Davidic period). His admission of the antiquity of the names is in fact something that may slightly undermine his approach to the writing of this text.

16 The Hebrew word underlying the phrase "the men appointed" is a technical term for representatives. Verse 16 is legal, formal, and precise in tone. Three phrases are used to give sanction to each of these leaders. Levi is not represented in this listing (see 1:47).

Notes

5 On the problems and precarious nature of attempting to discover the precise meaning of Hebrew names, see the commentary on 13:4–15. The meaning of a biblical name is tenuous, as the word is not determined by context in the same manner as other nouns and verbs.

16 The Hebrew word נָשִׂיא (*nāśî'*, "leader") speaks of one who is "lifted up" or "selected." The noun is derived from the verb *nāśā'* ("to lift up"). The vowel pattern of this noun is the same as that for the word "prophet," *nābî'*. It presents a passive infix.

(c) *The summary of the census*

1:17–19

[17]Moses and Aaron took these men whose names had been given, [18]and they called the whole community together on the first day of the second month. The people indicated their ancestry by their clans and families, and the men twenty years old or more were listed by name, one by one, [19]as the LORD commanded Moses. And so he counted them in the Desert of Sinai:

17 The leadership of Moses and Aaron in the task is indicated by this verse, as is their obedience to the command of the Lord. This chapter is marked by a studied triumphalism. Numbering the tribes and mustering the army are sacred functions that prepare the people for their war of conquest, under the right hand of God, who is their warrior (see Exod 15:3).

18 The expression "twenty years or more" is taken by Gershon Brin to be an indicator of generational identity; i.e., one who was under the age of twenty would still be regarded as a member of his father's house; one over the age of twenty was an individual who was morally and civilly responsible ("The Formulae 'From . . . and Onward/Upward,'" JBL 99, 2 [1980]: 161–71).

19 Hebrew prose often gives a summary statement and then the details that explicate that summary. So here v.19 is the summary statement, and vv.20–43 give the details.

Genesis 1:1 is a similar summary statement; the details are given in the rest of the chapter.

(d) *The listings of the census by each tribe*

1:20–43

[20]From the descendants of Reuben the firstborn son of Israel:
All the men twenty years old or more who were able to serve in the army were listed by name, one by one, according to the records of their clans and families. [21]The number from the tribe of Reuben was 46,500.

[22]From the descendants of Simeon:
All the men twenty years old or more who were able to serve in the army were counted and listed by name, one by one, according to the records of their clans and families. [23]The number from the tribe of Simeon was 59,300.

[24]From the descendants of Gad:
All the men twenty years old or more who were able to serve in the army were listed by name, according to the records of their clans and families. [25]The number from the tribe of Gad was 45,650.

[26]From the descendants of Judah:
All the men twenty years old or more who were able to serve in the army were listed by name, according to the records of their clans and families. [27]The number from the tribe of Judah was 74,600.

[28]From the descendants of Issachar:
All the men twenty years old or more who were able to serve in the army were listed by name, according to the records of their clans and families. [29]The number from the tribe of Issachar was 54,400.

[30]From the descendants of Zebulun:
All the men twenty years old or more who were able to serve in the army were listed by name, according to the records of their clans and families. [31]The number from the tribe of Zebulun was 57,400.

[32]From the sons of Joseph:
From the descendants of Ephraim:
All the men twenty years old or more who were able to serve in the army were listed by name, according to the records of their clans and families. [33]The number from the tribe of Ephraim was 40,500.

[34]From the descendants of Manasseh:
All the men twenty years old or more who were able to serve in the army were listed by name, according to the records of their clans and families. [35]The number from the tribe of Manasseh was 32,200.

[36]From the descendants of Benjamin:
All the men twenty years old or more who were able to serve in the army were listed by name, according to the records of their clans and families. [37]The number from the tribe of Benjamin was 35,400.

[38]From the descendants of Dan:
All the men twenty years old or more who were able to serve in the army were listed by name, according to the records of their clans and families. [39]The number from the tribe of Dan was 62,700.

[40]From the descendants of Asher:
All the men twenty years old or more who were able to serve in the army were listed by name, according to the records of their clans and families. [41]The number from the tribe of Asher was 41,500.

[42]From the descendants of Naphtali:
All the men twenty years old or more who were able to serve in the army were listed by name, according to the records of their clans and families. [43]The number from the tribe of Naphtali was 53,400.

20–43 For each tribe there are two verses in repetitive, formulaic structure giving (1) the name of the tribe, (2) the specifics of those numbered, (3) the name of the tribe restated, and (4) the total enumerated for that tribe.

Certainly one of the most difficult issues in the Book of Numbers concerns the large numbers of these lists. Noth, for example, places the issue darkly:

> The main problem of the section 1.20–46 consists in the figures that are given. Their size, as is generally recognized, lies outside the sphere of what is historically acceptable. In no sense do they bear even a tolerable relationship to what we otherwise know of the strength of military conscription in the ancient East. (p. 21)

More recently Budd concurs, "The central difficulty here is the impossibly large numbers of fighting men recorded. The historical difficulties in accepting the figure as it stands are insuperable" (p. 6).

That the numbers for each of the tribes are round numbers may be seen in that each unit is rounded off to the hundred (but Gad to the 50 [1:25]). A peculiarity in the numbers that leads some to believe that they may be symbolic is that the hundreds are grouped between 200 and 700; there are no hundreds in 000, 100, 800, or 900. Yet whatever we may make of these factors, we may observe that the same numbers are given for each tribe in chapter 2, where there are four triads of tribes with consistent use of numbers, sums, and grand totals. Further, the total might have been rounded off to 600,000 but was not (see 1:46; 2:32).

Since in this chapter the word *'elep̱* seems to have been taken to mean 1,000 for the totals to be achieved, suggestions such as that by Noth demand that the totals arose from a later period in which there was confusion about the unusual meaning of the term *'elep̱* in this section (see the extensive treatment of this term in the Introduction, pp. 681–83).

Because the descendants of Levi were excluded from the census (see on v.47), the descendants of Joseph are listed according to the families of his two sons, Ephraim (vv.32–33) and Manasseh (vv.34–35). In this way (1) the traditional tribal number of twelve is maintained, and (2) Joseph is given the "double portion" of the ranking heir of Jacob (cf. Gen 49:22–26; Deut 33:13–17). Second Kings 2:9 is also to be understood in this manner; Elisha was not asking Elijah that he might have double the power of his master or do double the number of miracles. Rather, of all the sons of the prophets who might wish to be regarded as the proper heir of Elijah, Elisha desired that honor for himself. The phrase "a double portion of your spirit" suggests the honor of the privileged son who would receive a double share of the inheritance of the father.

(e) *The summary of the census*

1:44–46

> 44These were the men counted by Moses and Aaron and the twelve leaders of Israel, each one representing his family. 45All the Israelites twenty years old or more who were able to serve in Israel's army were counted according to their families. 46The total number was 603,550.

44–46 As noted in the Introduction (pp. 680–81), there appears to be no textual difficulty in the Hebrew tradition in the soundness of this large number for the census of the fighting men of Israel. The number 603,550 is the proper sum of the twelve components listed in vv.21–43, with no convincingly unusual meaning suggested for the word "1,000."

The mathematics of these numbers is accurate and complex. It is complex in that the totals are reached in two ways; (1) a linear listing of twelve units (1:20–43), with the total given (1:46); (2) four sets of triads, each with a subtotal, and then the grand total (2:3–32), which equals the total in 1:46. These numbers are also consistent with the figures in Exodus 12:37–38 ("about six hundred thousand men on foot, besides women and children") and in Exodus 38:26 (603,550 men, twenty years old or more). Further they relate well to the figures of the second census in Numbers 26 (601,730 men) at the beginning of the new generation. This large number of men conscripted for the army suggests a population for the entire community in excess (perhaps considerably in excess) of 2 million people.

There are at least three implications we may draw from this immense number: (1) all those numbered, excepting Joshua and Caleb, were to die in the desert because of the unbelief the people had in the power of God and his faithfulness to his promise; (2) Moses was responsible for this immense number of people in the most difficult of circumstances; the management task God gave to Moses was nearly incalculable; and (3) the demands on God's providence (and overt miracle) were immense during the generation of desert sojourn.

Most importantly, the numbers of the people may also be regarded as a fulfillment of the particular blessing of God in the unusual growth of the people of the family of Jacob in Egypt. Exodus 1:7 describes in five Hebrew phrases the stunning growth of the Hebrew people in Egypt during the four centuries of their sojourn. So numerous had the Hebrew peoples become that they were regarded as a grave threat to the security of Egypt (Exod 1:9–10, 20). Israel's numerical growth from the seventy who entered Egypt (Exod 1:5) was an evidence of God's great blessing and his faithfulness to his covenant with Abraham (Gen 12:2; 15:5; 17:4–6; 22:17). The growth of the nation was God's benediction on them. Instead of continually attempting to find the elusive "key" for understanding the large numbers, we should first reflect on this benediction the numbers present and respond to the Lord in wonder.

As we reflect on the Lord's benediction, we are still drawn back to the problems of logistics in these large numbers. It is not necessary in order to praise God to magnify difficulty. And as we return to the difficulty of these numbers, we find ourselves concluding with most critical scholars and many conservative scholars that these numbers cannot be what they first appear to be. Yet because of the manner in which they are added together, we may find ourselves uncomfortable with those suggestions that speak of earlier understandings that the later scribes forgot. To speak of their error in adding hundreds and "thousands" as an understandable error is a troubling expression. Understandable error is still error of the text.

So I return to the position I suggested in the Introduction: The Problem of the Large Numbers (q.v.). We may treat these numbers as "real" numbers, even as the text presents them. The hundreds are added to the thousands as in all such sums. But these real numbers (in terms of their addition) are numbers that are used for effect. I personally believe there is a deliberate exaggeration of the sums for each tribe and hence for the total, as a rhetorical device. By deliberately magnifying these numbers by a common factor (ten, the number of the digits), the writer was able to use them as power words. That is, the ancients who were the recipients of these words knew what we may forget, that numbers can be used for purposes other than merely reporting a given datum. I suggest, as noted in the Introduction, that we should possibly regard these sums as a deliberate exaggeration by the factor of ten, a rhetorical device used to give praise to God and hope to his people.

(f) *The reason for the exclusion of the Levites*

1:47–54

[47]The families of the tribe of Levi, however, were not counted along with the others. [48]The LORD had said to Moses: [49]"You must not count the tribe of Levi or include them in the census of the other Israelites. [50]Instead, appoint the Levites to be in charge of the tabernacle of the Testimony—over all its furnishings and everything belonging to it. They are to carry the tabernacle and all its furnishings; they are to take care of it and encamp around it. [51]Whenever the tabernacle is to move, the Levites are to take it down, and whenever the tabernacle is to be set up, the Levites shall do it. Anyone else who goes near it shall be put to death. [52]The Israelites are to set up their tents by divisions, each man in his own camp under his own standard. [53]The Levites, however, are to set up their tents around the tabernacle of the Testimony so that wrath will not fall on the Israelite community. The Levites are to be responsible for the care of the tabernacle of the Testimony."

[54]The Israelites did all this just as the LORD commanded Moses.

47–49 The Levites, because of their sacral tasks, were excluded from this military listing; they were to be engaged in the ceremonies and maintenance of the tabernacle. Chapter 3 is given over entirely to their families, numbers, and functions.

50 As in Exodus 38:21, the sanctuary is here called "the tabernacle of the Testimony." The Testimony refers to the Ten Words written on stone tablets (Exod 31:18; 32:15; 34:29). These tablets were placed in the ark (Exod 25:16, 21; 40:20), leading to the phrase "the ark of the Testimony" (Exod 25:22; 26:33–34 et al.). In Psalm 19:7 the Hebrew term "testimony" ("statutes" in NIV) is used for the Word of God in a more general sense but still with the background of the Ten Words of Exodus.

51–52 The Hebrew word rendered "anyone else" (v.51) is often translated "stranger," "alien," or "foreigner" (as in Isa 1:7; Hos 7:9). Thus a non-Levite Israelite was considered an alien to the religious duties of the tabernacle (see Exod 29:33; 30:33; Lev 22:12). The punishment of death is reiterated in Numbers 3:10, 38; 18:7, and was enacted by divine fiat in 16:31–33 (see 1 Sam 6:19). The sense of the Divine Presence was both blessing and cursing in the camp: blessing for those who had a proper sense of awe and wonder of the nearness of deity; cursing for those who had no sense of place, no respect for the Divine Presence.

53 The tents of the Levites are detailed in 3:21–38. The encampment of the Levites around the tabernacle was a protective hedge against trespass by the non-Levites to keep them from the wrath of God. The dwelling of the Levites around the central shrine was a measure of God's grace and a reminder of his presence.

54 In view of Israel's great disobedience in the later chapters of Numbers, these words of initial compliance to God's word have a special poignancy. Israel began so well then failed so terribly that her experience remains a potent lesson to all people of faith who follow them. Ending well is the desire. Most racers get off the blocks reasonably well, but the winner is only certified as such at the end of the track.

(2) *The placement of the tribes (2:1–34)*

Chapter 2 has a symmetrically arranged structure (see Introduction: Outline).

The details of this chapter are presented in studied orderliness as a literary exhibit of the physical symmetry expected of the peoples who would be encamped around the central shrine. As in the case of chapter 1, the details of this chapter seem to reflect the joy of the writer in knowing the relation each tribe has to the whole, each individual to the tribe, and the nation to the central shrine—and to the Lord Yahweh. Thus in some manner this chapter is another means of bringing glory to God. The Book of Numbers is *a book of the worship of Yahweh!* There is an element of pride, joy, and expectation in the seemingly routine matters of this chapter. Here is the place of encampment for each tribe in proximity to the Divine Presence; and from these camps the people will set out under the hand of God to enter the Land of Promise and take possession in his power. The chapter should be read with expectation that the Conquest will be as orderly and purposeful as will the place of camping in the desert.

There is a sense in which the orderliness of these early chapters of Numbers is akin to the orderliness of Genesis 1. As God has created the heavens and the earth and all that fills them with order, beauty, purpose, and wonder, so he constitutes his people with order, beauty, purpose, and wonder. And as the heavens and earth may "praise" God in their responses to his commands (Ps 147:13–18), so the peoples of God may praise him in their responses to his commands (Ps 147:19–20). Indeed, his people must praise him.

Critical scholars respond to the orderliness and symmetry of this text in quite another manner. Snaith, for example, regards the whole chapter "as an idealistic reconstruction to fit in with later religious ideas" (p. 186). For writers such as he, the very beauty of the text is its downfall. For more conservative writers, the beauty of the text is its strength and is designed to be reflective of the beauty of the Lord in the midst of his people.

(a) *Summary command*

2:1–2

> [1]The LORD said to Moses and Aaron: [2]"The Israelites are to camp around the Tent of Meeting some distance from it, each man under his standard with the banners of his family."

1 The standard pattern of formal Hebrew prose is followed in this chapter. First there is an announcement of the topic, then come the details of that topic in an orderly presentation, followed, finally, by a summary of the whole. This type of organization must have been very satisfying to the ancient writers, giving a sense of wholeness, direction, and orderliness to an account. As in the case of chapter 1, material of this sort may fail to excite the modern reader. Yet if one pauses to think of the order and structure of the text, then the underlying significance of the passage may be realized more easily. God was about to bring to pass a great marvel with his people, but it will only occur as that people is rightly related to him and to one another.

The relatedness of the people round about the central shrine was the essence of their meaning as a people. Without this pattern, apart from this order, the Hebrews would have remained a mob—large, disorganized, unruly, and bound for disaster. With this pattern, and the discipline and devotion it implied, was the opportunity for grand victory. The order of the chapter is a promise of the fulfillment of the working of God in their midst. That Israel in fact did fail God is the sadder story because he had given to them the means for full success.

This chapter begins with the announcement of the word of the Lord to Moses and Aaron. The more usual phrasing in the Torah is "And Yahweh spoke to Moses, . . . saying," as in 1:1. Here the words "and Aaron" are added, as in 4:1, 17; 14:26; 16:20; 19:1. A similar phrase (with a different Hebrew verb), "And the LORD said to Moses and Aaron," is found in 20:12, 23. The reference to Aaron along with his illustrious brother in this chapter indicates the strong focus on the shrine of God's presence in the center of the camp. Aaron, as will be detailed in chapter 3, has the principal task of maintaining the purity, order, and organization of the work respecting the central shrine.

2 The Hebrew word order of v.2 stresses the role of the individual in the context of the community; each one was to know his exact position within the camp. A more literal translation, following the studied order of the Hebrew original, follows:

> Each by his standard,
>   by the banners of their father's house,
> the Israelites will encamp;
>   in a circuit some way off from the Tent of Meeting
> they will encamp.

The repetition of the verb "will encamp" is for stately stress. Here is the meaning of the individual in Israel, and here is the significance of his family.

The people of Israel were a community that had their essential meaning in relationship to God and to one another. But ever in the community was the continuing stress on the individual to know where he belonged in the larger grouping. Corporate solidarity in ancient Israel was a reality of daily life; but the individual was also very important. The words interplay with one another in these texts: each individual / the people // the people / each individual.

The text stresses, not just the relationship each person and each tribe was to have to the central shrine, but that none was to approach the shrine too casually. The dwelling of the tribes was in a circuit about the shrine but at some distance from it. The Hebrew word *minneged* means "some way off" or "from a distance." These words build on 1:52–53 and the protective grace of God, demanding a sufficient distance to serve as a protective barrier from untoward approach to the shrine of the Divine Presence and the judgment of God such an approach might provoke. Gerhard von Rad writes that all true knowledge of God begins with the assertion of his hiddenness (*Old Testament Theology*, 2:374–78). Too casual an approach betrays too minimal a reverence.

Here we sense anew a recurring theme in the Torah. God's holiness may not be forgotten by his people, but his grace is protective for them. His desire is not to destroy the unwary but to protect such from their own folly—and to demonstrate the wonder of his person in the midst of their camp.

God could have maintained a distance between himself and the people, rendering the warning unnecessary. Then no one would be in danger of harm. The true believer, however, so caught up with the wonder of knowing that the God of all the universe was present in some mysterious way in the midst of the encampment of the people of the new Israel, would seek to learn to live with the mystery of God's awesome presence. The fright of danger is lost in the sense of the proximity of his glory and the nearness of his grace.

Each tribe had its banner and each triad (group of three) of tribes had its standard. Jewish tradition suggests that the tribal banners corresponded in color to the twelve stones in the breastpiece of the high priest (Exod 28:15–21). Further, this tradition holds that the standard of the triad led by Judah had the figure of a lion, that of Reuben the figure of a man, that of Ephraim the figure of an ox, and that of Dan the figure of an eagle (see the four living creatures described by Ezek 1:10; cf. Rev 4:7). These traditions are late, however, and difficult to substantiate historically, as the Torah does not describe the nature or designs of the banners of Numbers 2 (see KD, p. 17).

(b) *Details of execution (2:3–33)*

(i) *Eastern encampment*

2:3–9

3 On the east, toward the sunrise, the divisions of the camp of Judah are to encamp under their standard. The leader of the people of Judah is Nahshon son of Amminadab. 4 His division numbers 74,600.

5 The tribe of Issachar will camp next to them. The leader of the people of Issachar is Nethanel son of Zuar. 6 His division numbers 54,400.

7 The tribe of Zebulun will be next. The leader of the people of Zebulun is Eliab son of Helon. 8 His division numbers 57,400.

9 All the men assigned to the camp of Judah, according to their divisions, number 186,400. They will set out first.

In chapter 1 the nation is mustered, and the genealogical relationships are clarified. In chapter 2 the nation is set in structural order, and the line of march and the place of encampment are established. The numbers of chapter 1 are given in new patterns of arrangement—four sets of triads—but they are the same numbers. The repetition of these grand sums of each tribe is a further reflection of the grace of God in their increase during their sojourn in Egypt. The numbers of chapters 1 and 2 are in agreement; if one wishes to suggest ways to change the seemingly clear sense of the numbers in chapter 1, then that person also has to deal with the repetitions in this chapter as well. The same leaders of chapter 1 figure here again and also in 10:14–28. The listing of their names is a matter of significant honor; it is also a matter of sadness. Their names were not forgotten in Israel, but their lives were lost in the desert, far from the place of God's gracious promise.

3–9 Judah, Issachar, and Zebulun were the fourth, fifth, and sixth of the six sons born to Jacob by Leah. It is somewhat surprising to have these three tribes first in the order of march since Reuben is regularly noted as Jacob's firstborn son (1:20). However, because of the perfidy of the older brothers (Reuben, Simeon, and Levi; see Gen 49:3–7), Judah is ascendant and is granted pride of place among his brothers (Gen 49:8). Judah becomes the royal line in which the Messiah is born (Gen 49:10; Ruth 4:18–21; Matt 1:1–16).

Further, the placement on the east is very significant in Israel's thought. East is the place of the rising of the sun, the source of hope and sustenance. Westward was the sea. Israel's traditional stance was with its back to the ocean and the descent of the sun. The ancient Hebrews were not a sea-faring people like the Phoenicians and the Egyptians. For Israel the place of pride was on the east. Hence there we find the triad of tribes headed by Judah, Jacob's fourth son and father of the royal house that leads to King Messiah.

As observed in the Introduction (pp. 681–84), the numbers in this section are as consistent as the names of the tribal leaders. Those who desire for whatever reason to reduce the large numbers of chapter 1 to more "manageable" units will need to do so throughout the Torah. This is not an insignificant step. It is still a necessary final conclusion for the reasons stated in the Introduction. If we view these large numbers as a deliberate rhetorical exaggeration, however, then we do not need to play some type of mathematical wizardry with them to make them come out right.

(ii) *Southern encampment*

2:10–16

10 On the south will be the divisions of the camp of Reuben under their standard. The leader of the people of Reuben is Elizur son of Shedeur. 11 His division numbers 46,500.

12 The tribe of Simeon will camp next to them. The leader of the people of Simeon is Shelumiel son of Zurishaddai. 13 His division numbers 59,300.

14 The tribe of Gad will be next. The leader of the people of Gad is Eliasaph son of Deuel. 15 His division numbers 45,650.

16 All the men assigned to the camp of Reuben, according to their divisions, number 151,450. They will set out second.

10–16 Reuben, Jacob's firstborn son, leads the second triad, on the south. As one's stance in facing east has the south on the right hand, one senses a secondary honor given to the tribes associated with Reuben. He is joined by Simeon, the second son of Jacob by Leah. Levi, Leah's third son, is not included with the divisions of the congregation but is reserved the special function of the service of the tabernacle and the guarding of the precinct from the untoward actions of the rest of the community (see v.17 and ch. 3). This triad is completed by Gad, the first son of Leah's maidservant Zilpah.

Notes

14 There is a well-known textual difficulty in v.14 respecting the name דְּעוּאֵל (*de'û'ēl*, "Deuel"). The MT actually reads רְעוּאֵל (*re'û'ēl*, "Reuel") in this place but had "Deuel" in 1:14. The Hebrew letters daleth (*d*) and resh (*r*) were easily confused by scribes because of their similarity in form. See the NIV margin on Gen 10:4, where a similar problem is presented by the name Rodanim versus Dodanim. Many other Hebrew MSS, along with the versions, read Deuel here in v.14, which we suspect is the superior reading. A primary rule of textual criticism is that the most difficult reading is to be preferred since copyists tended to "level out" the text to the simpler reading.

(iii) *Tent and the Levites*

2:17

[17]Then the Tent of Meeting and the camp of the Levites will set out in the middle of the camps. They will set out in the same order as they encamp, each in his own place under his standard.

17 The tent in the middle, representative of God's presence within the heart of the camp, is a change from Exodus 33:7–11. Then the tent was without the camp, and Moses would go outside the camp to seek the word of God. Here the tent is within the camp, and all Israel is positioned around the tent. Then God would come from time to time; here he is continually in their midst. There is a sense here of the progressive manifestation of the presence of God in the midst of the people. First he is on the mountain of Sinai; then he comes to the tent without the camp; then he indwells the tent in the midst of the camp. One day he would reveal himself through the Incarnation in the midst of his people (John 1:1–18); and, on a day still to come, there will be the full realization of the presence of the person of God dwelling in the midst of his people in the New Jerusalem (Rev 21:1–4). The story of the Bible is largely the story of the progressive revelation of God among his people and the progressive preparation of a people to be fit to live in his presence.

This verse relates not only to the manner of encampment but especially to the manner of march. On the line of march the Judah and Reuben triads would lead the community; then would come the tabernacle with the attendant protective hedge of Levites (see 1:53); last would come the Ephraim and Dan triads. In this way there was not only the sense of the indwelling presence of God in the midst of the people, there was as well the sense that the peoples in their families and tribes were protecting before and behind the shrine of his presence.

Notes

17 Some critical scholars have made much of the position of the tent within or without the camp as a means of distinguishing putative sources (JE, the tent without the camp as a source of revelation; P, the tent within the camp as a place of worship). Yet James Orr (*The Problem of the Old Testament Considered With Reference to Recent Criticism* [New York: Charles Scribner's Sons, 1906], pp. 165–70) showed long ago that the texts agree that it was God's intention that the regular placement of the tent was to be within the camp, both for revelation and for worship.

(iv) *Western encampment*

2:18–24

[18]On the west will be the divisions of the camp of Ephraim under their standard. The leader of the people of Ephraim is Elishama son of Ammihud. [19]His division numbers 40,500.

[20]The tribe of Manasseh will be next to them. The leader of the people of Manasseh is Gamaliel son of Pedahzur. [21]His division numbers 32,200.

[22]The tribe of Benjamin will be next. The leader of the people of Benjamin is Abidan son of Gideoni. [23]His division numbers 35,400.
[24]All the men assigned to the camp of Ephraim, according to their divisions, number 108,100. They will set out third.

18–24 The Rachel tribes were on the west. Joseph's two sons, Manasseh and Ephraim, received a special blessing from their grandfather Jacob; but in the process the younger son, Ephraim, was given precedence over Manasseh (Gen 48:5–20). Here, true to Jacob's words, Ephraim is ahead of Manasseh. Last comes Benjamin, the last-born son of Jacob, Joseph's younger brother, on whom the aged father doted after the presumed death of Joseph.

(v) *Northern encampment*

2:25–31

[25]On the north will be the divisions of the camp of Dan, under their standard. The leader of the people of Dan is Ahiezer son of Ammishaddai. [26]His division numbers 62,700.
[27]The tribe of Asher will camp next to them. The leader of the people of Asher is Pagiel son of Ocran. [28]His division numbers 41,500.
[29]The tribe of Naphtali will be next. The leader of the people of Naphtali is Ahira son of Enan. [30]His division numbers 53,400.
[31]All the men assigned to the camp of Dan number 157,600. They will set out last, under their standards.

25–31 Dan was the first son of Bilhah, the maidservant of Rachel. Asher was the second son of Zilpah, the maidservant of Leah. Naphtali was the second son of Bilhah. These, then, are secondary tribes and are positioned on the north side of the shrine of the presence, as it were, on the left hand. Here again we need to read these texts with the values of the people who first experienced them. Our orientation tends to be to the north, but Israel's orientation was to the east. It is of interest that in the final settlement of the land, these three tribes situated to the north of the shrine actually settled in the northern sections of the land of Canaan.

(vi) *Summary totals*

2:32–33

[32]These are the Israelites, counted according to their families. All those in the camps, by their divisions, number 603,550. [33]The Levites, however, were not counted along with the other Israelites, as the LORD commanded Moses.

32–33 These verses conform to and summarize 1:44–53. The total number is the same as in 1:46 (see Introduction, p. 683), and the distinction of the Levites is maintained (see comments on 1:47–53). The arrangement of the numbers of the tribes in triads, each with subtotals, and the grand total for the whole suggest the concept of the stability of these large numbers in the text. Suggestions to reduce the numbers to obtain a "more manageable" portrait should be presented with due care for all the citations, not just a few.

(c) *Summary conclusion*

2:34

> 34 So the Israelites did everything the LORD commanded Moses; that is the way they encamped under their standards, and that is the way they set out, each with his clan and family.

34 As in 1:54, these words of absolute compliance contrast with Israel's later folly. This verse also speaks of significant order—a major accomplishment for a people so numerous, so recently enslaved, and more recently a mob in disarray. The text speaks well of the administrative leadership of Moses, God's reluctant prophet, and of the work done by the twelve worthies who were the leaders of each tribe. Certainly the text points to the mercy of God and his blessing on the people. It may have been the beauty of the order of this plan of encampment that led the unlikely prophet Balaam to say, "How beautiful are your tents, O Jacob,/ your dwelling places, O Israel!" (Num 24:5).

Fittingly, Balaam's words—the gasp of an outsider—became among the most treasured in the community. Cyrus Gordon wrote of them, "They have remained the most cherished passages in Scripture throughout Synagogue history" (*Before the Bible: The Common Background of Greek and Hebrew Civilizations* [London: Collins, 1962], p. 41). In soliciting praise from the outsider Balaam, the order and beauty of the camp must continue to stir the heart of the faithful to even more robust praise. For again, the Book of Numbers, despite our initial misgivings, is a book of worship.

Notes

The diagram of the camp (with an eastern orientation!) would look like this:

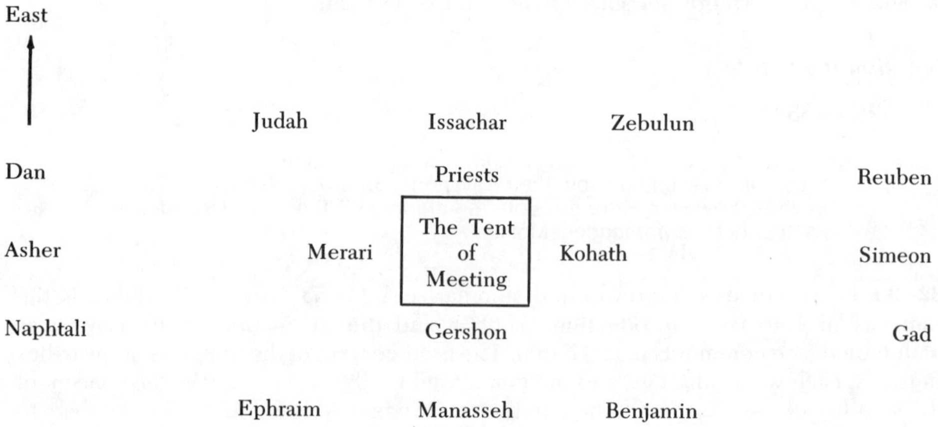

(3) *The placement and the numbers of the Levites and firstborn of Israel (3:1–51)*

The notion of order continues to lace itself unabatedly through this chapter. When the reader slows down to the pace of the text, he or she begins to discover something of the beauty and dignity of these chapters. True, no one would confuse these texts with great literature. There is nothing about these texts of story, of characterization, of emotive depth, of literary finesse. These chapters are neither psalm nor proverb, oracle nor epic.

This is not to say, however, that these early chapters of Numbers are not written well—for indeed they are. They have about them a stately grace, a dignity, and a sense of presence. When the modern reader attempts to envision the magnitude of the task the Lord gave to Moses to bring order to an immense number of people who were so recently slaves and now so newly free, the resulting sensation the reader may feel is one of overwhelming burden. But these chapters do not speak of burden at all. There is about them a sense of calm control—the control of God himself. In these chapters is an implied call to order in our own lives and affairs—a call that may cut some of us deeply who have grown accustomed to the disaster of disorder.

Not only is each chapter marked by order, but so is the placement of these several chapters in the book. The first chapter of Numbers records the organization of the nation of Israel along the lines of family, clan, and tribe, with leaders for each tribe and the totals of the fighting men for each of the tribes. Chapter 2 shows how the various tribes are arranged around the central shrine in their encampments. In the midst of the tribes was the shrine, and about the shrine were the priestly and Levitical families as a protective hedge for the people and as the authorized personnel admitted to handle sacred things on behalf of the people. In chapter 3 we draw closer to the center and observe the families and their numbers who made up these cultic personnel.

(a) *The family of Aaron and Moses*

3:1–4

[1]This is the account of the family of Aaron and Moses at the time the LORD talked with Moses on Mount Sinai.

[2]The names of the sons of Aaron were Nadab the firstborn and Abihu, Eleazar and Ithamar. [3]Those were the names of Aaron's sons, the anointed priests, who were ordained to serve as priests. [4]Nadab and Abihu, however, fell dead before the LORD when they made an offering with unauthorized fire before him in the Desert of Sinai. They had no sons; so only Eleazar and Ithamar served as priests during the lifetime of their father Aaron.

1–2 At first blush the wording "the family of Aaron and Moses" (v.1) seems out of order because of the normal placing of Moses before Aaron. But the emphasis is correct: it is the family of Aaron that is about to be described (see v.2). The genealogy of Exodus 6:16–20 (cf. 1 Chron 6:1–3) suggests that Aaron and Moses were the (direct) sons of Amram and Jochebed. However, it is likely that this listing is incomplete (a common practice among the writers of these lists in the Bible, something that must be kept in mind in reading all genealogies including those of Genesis and Matthew). Amram and his wife-aunt Jochebed were likely more remote ancestors to Aaron and Moses.

At the time of the Exodus, there were numerous descendants of Amram, as we learn in this chapter (v.27). Moses and Aaron's sister, Miriam, was the oldest of the three siblings. It was she who kept watch over the infant Moses when he was placed in his boat in the reeds of the Nile (Exod 2:4). Aaron was three years older than Moses (Exod 7:7). Aaron's wife was Elisheba, the daughter of Amminadab and sister of Nahshon, prince of the tribe of Judah (see Num 1:7; 2:3), and the mother of the four sons noted in this chapter (see Exod 6:23).

Olson has remarked on the singular importance of the Hebrew term *tôl^ed̲ōt̲* ("account") in v.1 (pp. 98–114). He regards the phrase "These are the generations of Aaron and Moses" to be the principal link that ties the books of the Pentateuch together. This use of the word *tôl*[e]*d̲ōt̲* hearkens back to the eleven times it is used in the Book of Genesis (see Notes). He states:

> For the first time after the formative events of the Exodus deliverance and the revelation on Mount Sinai, the people of Israel are organized into a holy people on the march under the leadership of Aaron and Moses with the priests and Levites at the center of the camp. A whole new chapter has opened in the life of the people of Israel, and this new beginning is marked by the toledot formula. (p. 108)

Olson then presents the structure of the Pentateuch based on the term *tôl*[e]*d̲ôt̲* (p. 14):

I. Genesis Prologue—The First Generations of God's People to Whom the Promises Are Made and Given in Each Succeeding Generation up to the Toledot of Jacob

II. Exodus The First Generation of God's People Who Experience the Exodus out of Egypt and God's Revelation at Mount Sinai—The Toledot of Jacob

III. Leviticus Further Instructions to the Generations of the Exodus and Sinai—The Toledot of Jacob Continued

IV. Numbers The Death of the Old Generation and the Birth of the New
   A. The Continuation of the Toledot of Jacob and the Introduction of the Toledot of Aaron and Moses (Num 1–25)
   B. The Continuation of the Toledot of Jacob and the Toledot of Aaron and Moses Into a New Generation (Num 26–36)

3 Exodus 28:41 records God's command to Moses to anoint his brother, Aaron, and his sons as priests of the Lord (see Exod 30:30; Lev 8:30). This solemn act gave recognition of a special consecration to the Lord and a particular knowledge on their part that they were no longer ordinary—they were now special to God. Olive oil was also used to anoint prophets (1 Kings 19:16) and kings (1 Sam 16:13) for special service to God.

Apparently not only olive oil was used for anointing but so was the oil of the ancient persimmon (called balsam by Greek writers). A Herodian jug still containing once-fragrant oil of the type that was used to anoint the kings of Judah was found buried in one of the Qumran caves in 1988 by scholars under the direction of the Hebrew University. In this case the fragrance of the ancient oil came from the (now extinct) ancient persimmon (cf. Joel Brinkley, "Ancient Balm for Anointing Kings Found," *New York Times Service* [16 Feb. 1989]).

Inanimate objects could be anointed as well: e.g., the stone at Bethel (Gen 28:18) and the altar of the tabernacle (Exod 29:36). The general Hebrew term "anointed" (*māšîaḥ*) became in time the specific term for the Messiah (Christ). While many things may be anointed (and be a "messiah"), it is he who is the Messiah, the Anointed One, who fulfills God's covenant promises.

This anointing led naturally to being ordained. The Hebrew idiom "who were ordained" literally means "to fill the hand" (Heb. of Exod 32:29). The act was an investing of authority, a consecration, and a setting apart. The anointeds' "hands were filled" with a sense of the presence of the divine mystery. These were men of moment, servants of God.

4 For earlier reference to Nadab and Abihu, see Leviticus 10:1–2. The accentuation of Numbers 3:2 indicates that Aaron may still have been in grief for his firstborn son, Nadab. The accents lead to the following punctuation: "Now these are the names of the sons of Aaron: the firstborn, Nadab; also Abihu, Eleazar, and Ithamar." Hirsch observes, "It is as if the report pauses painfully over Nadab, then lingers on Abihu and then quickly adds Eleazar and Ithamar" (p. 23). Nadab is given double "honor" in this wording; he is identified as the firstborn, and the accents set his name off from those of his brothers. It is for these reasons that the mysterious report of the sin of Nadab and Abihu is so trenchant to us—and to Aaron!

"Unauthorized fire" translates a Hebrew expression that is seemingly deliberately obscure, as though the narrator finds the very concept to be distasteful. This is not unlike the reserve of the Torah in detailing the nuances of the notorious sin of Genesis 6:1–4. The essential issue here is that Nadab and Abihu were using fire that the Lord had not commanded (Lev 10:1). The pain of the account is strengthened by its brevity and mystery. We are left at a loss to explain their motivation, just as we do not know the precise form of their error. Were they rebellious or presumptuous? Were they careless or ignorant? Or was their sin some combination of these and other things? Because of the prohibition of wine and beer among the priests in their priestly service in Leviticus 10:8–11, it may be inferred that these sons of Aaron had committed their offense against God while in a drunken state.

All the commands for obedience on the part of the priests beginning in Leviticus 8:1 leave us quite unprepared for the rash disobedience of the older sons of Aaron. The story is shocking and is marked by the pathos of a father forbidden to grieve the death of his sons (Lev 10:3–7). The lesson is starkly evident: proximity to the holiness of God placed tremendous demands of righteousness, exactitude, and obedience on his priests. For all time the deaths of Aaron's newly consecrated sons should warn God's ministers of the awesome seriousness of their tasks (but see 1 Sam 2:12–17, 22–25, 27–36; 3:11–14; 4:1–11). Seemingly the most common reports of failure we hear of God's ministers in our own day are of their malfeasance, indolence, greed, lust, and abuse of power. Tragically the lessons of the past are forgotten with frightful ease. The spiritual descendants of Nadab and Abihu continue to occupy the ranks of the "ministers" of God.

Verse 4 states the matter of the death of these errant priests of the Lord succinctly: "[They] fell dead before the LORD." Leviticus 10:2 specifies more fully: "So fire came out from the presence of the LORD and consumed them, and they died before the LORD." This wording suggests a bolt of lightning, as seems to be the case of the fire from the Lord that consumed the offering and the altar of Elijah on Mount Carmel (1 Kings 18:38). In any event, there is a certain sense of poetic justice in the fact that these wicked priests who used unauthorized fire in the worship of the Lord were themselves destroyed by fire from his presence. Nadab and Abihu's fate is made even sadder, from the Hebrew point of view, in that they did not leave sons after them to continue their names among the priestly rolls in Israel. When they died, their story was over. Each time they are mentioned in the Bible, it is with sadness (cf. Num 26:61; 1 Chron 24:2). It is also the mercy of God that Aaron had two other sons who were not involved in the perfidy of their brothers. Hence the Aaronic priestly line is found to extend through the two younger sons Eleazar and Ithamar (see 1 Chron 24:1–4), who continued to minister throughout the lifetime of Aaron.

The reference to Nadab and Abihu serves another purpose: it sets the tone for the seriousness of the priestly and Levitical duties this chapter presents. If a person who had no right to be in the proximity of the central shrine, or near its holy things, happened to come near, that person might die. This warning is given repeatedly (1:51, 53; 2:2, "some distance from it"). A person who came near without authorization is like a stranger, an alien; such has no right to approach and might lose his life in the process. But those who had their proper place in the proximity of holy things and near the holy shrine were themselves under warning. They were also to take care, for their opportunity for sin was enhanced by their familiarity with holy things.

It is ever this way. Preachers tend to tell jokes about the Bible, to use the Lord's name casually, to speak light-heartedly of the institutions of the Lord. Often common people have a higher sense of reverence for the things of God than those whose job it is to handle those things reverently but who merely deal with them routinely.

Notes

1 The Hebrew word תּוֹלְדֹת (*tôl^{e}ḏōt*, "the account of" or "family histories") is used as the organizing principle of the Book of Genesis, where it occurs ten times—at the beginning of each main section (2:4; 5:1; 6:9; 10:1; 11:10, 27; 25:12, 19; 36:1 [with a repetition for emphasis at 36:9]; and 37:2).

(b) *The duties for the Levites*

3:5–10

5 The LORD said to Moses, 6 "Bring the tribe of Levi and present them to
Aaron the priest to assist him. 7 They are to perform duties for him and
for the whole community at the Tent of Meeting by doing the work of the
tabernacle. 8 They are to take care of all the furnishings of the Tent of
Meeting, fulfilling the obligations of the Israelites by doing the work of
the tabernacle. 9 Give the Levites to Aaron and his sons; they are the
Israelites who are to be given wholly to him. 10 Appoint Aaron and his
sons to serve as priests; anyone else who approaches the sanctuary
must be put to death."

5–8 These commands are not followed by a report of obedience as were those in chapters 1 and 2, but further details are given in chapter 8. Clear distinctions are made here between the priestly house (the sons of Aaron) and the Levites. The latter were to be aids to the priests. The Levites serve not only Aaron but the whole nation in the process (vv.7–8). The Levites come out from among the nation; they were a part of the nation but are now distinct.

Interestingly, Moses is addressed in v.5. He is responsible for the nation as a whole and, hence, for the faithful obedience of the Levites in their service of the priestly house of Aaron. Moreover, the tribe of the Levites was to be "brought near" (v.6), terminology for the approach of the Divine Presence. Only Moses had an open invitation to draw near to God in a direct manner. Now he is presented with the task of drawing these other ministers near to their work before the Lord. This work consisted of service to Aaron and the guarding of the ministry relating to him and the whole congregation (v.7). Moreover, they were responsible for the tasks of moving the furnishings of the tabernacle at times when the camp would be on the move (v.8).

The key to the work of the Levites during times when the camp was not on the move may be in the words "perform duties for him" (v.7). The Hebrew phrase has both verb and noun from the same root (*wᵉšomrû 'e*t̲*-mišmartô*), a common form of emphasis in Hebrew rhetorical style. The basic meaning of the Hebrew *šāmar* is "to keep watch," "to guard." Hence, as G.J. Wenham suggests (p. 70), it seems that the Levites had two tasks: one was to guard the holy things from affront of foolish people; the other was to care for the holy things when the people were to be on the move.

9 That the Levites are subsidiary to the priests is made quite clear by the wording of this verse. The Hebrew for this expression is the repetition "given given" (NIV, "wholly given"), an idiom for totality. Despite the textual difficulty of this text, it appears that the issue here is service to Aaron (and through him to the Lord); in 8:16 the service is to the Lord.

10 The warning of the death penalty of 1:51 is repeated. The Hebrew term is literally "stranger" (NIV, "anyone else"), anyone lacking authorization. Service at the tabernacle may be done only at the express command of God. There is a special poignancy in the words of v.10 as they follow the paragraph reminding us of the deaths of Aaron's sons. They were authorized persons and used unauthorized means. If the sons of Aaron were put to death at the commencement of their duties, how dare an unauthorized person even think to trespass (see 3:38; 18:7)! G.J. Wenham's suggestion is that the Levites are those who are authorized to carry out the death penalty, to keep the wrath of God against untoward offenders of his majesty and holiness from breaking out against the entire camp. A splendid example of just this is seen in 25:7–8; but there the protagonist is not a Levite but a priest, Phinehas, son of Eleazar. Perhaps the Levites were so lax on that occasion that Phinehas decided he had to work quickly himself or there would not be time to quell the evil that was right before the tent (see ch. 25).

Notes

9 לוֹ (*lô*, "to him") is the reading in our text, but some MSS of the MT, Samaritan Pentateuch, and LXX read לִי (*lî*, "to me"), as in 8:16. It appears that here in v.9 the issue is service to Aaron; in 8:16 service is respecting the Lord.

(c) *The separation of the Levites*

3:11–13

> [11]The LORD also said to Moses, [12]"I have taken the Levites from among the Israelites in place of the first male offspring of every Israelite woman. The Levites are mine, [13]for all the firstborn are mine. When I struck down all the firstborn in Egypt, I set apart for myself every firstborn in Israel, whether man or animal. They are to be mine. I am the LORD."

11–13 The words "in place of" (v.12) serve as a clear example of substitution in the Hebrew Scriptures (cf. Gen 22:13: "a ram . . . instead of his son"; cf. also Matt 20:28).

The MT emphasizes the word "mine" (*lî*, or "for myself") by using it four times in vv.12–13, by the emphatic "I" at the beginning of v.12, by the concluding "I am the LORD," and by three verbs constructed with the first person pronoun ("I have taken," "I struck down," and "I set apart"). Again we are told that the Levites were from the midst of Israel but are now the exclusive property of the Lord. See Exodus 13:2. The last phrase of this section, "I am Yahweh," is a characteristic punctuation in the legislative portions of the Torah. These words add authority, significance, and weight to the text. "I am the LORD" is a reminder of both what has been revealed about his blessed person and work as well as what he has shown himself to be in relation to his people. The phrase points to him and to his people in relationship to him, but it does so as a divine punctuation of the text.

(d) *The census of the Levites (3:14–39)*

(i) *The principals*

3:14–20

> [14]The LORD said to Moses in the Desert of Sinai, [15]"Count the Levites by their families and clans. Count every male a month old or more." [16]So Moses counted them, as he was commanded by the word of the LORD.
>
> [17]These were the names of the sons of Levi:
> Gershon, Kohath and Merari.
> [18]These were the names of the Gershonite clans:
> Libni and Shimei.
> [19]The Kohathite clans:
> Amram, Izhar, Hebron and Uzziel.
> [20]The Merarite clans:
> Mahli and Mushi.
> These were the Levite clans, according to their families.

14–20 The enumerating of the Levites corresponds to that of the other tribes in chapters 1–2 but is to be done of males from the age of one month rather than from twenty years. The Levites were not being mustered for war but for special service in the sacral precincts of the Lord. The Levites were distinct from the rest of the tribes in several aspects: (1) they had their service in and about the holy things and the holy place of God; (2) they were not numbered among the tribes but were to be distributed among them; (3) they are numbered differently than the other tribes; (4) they are not the fighting men of Israel but her ministers, subject to the leadership of the priests;

and (5) they had certain restrictions of behavior and manner that marked off their office as distinct from the rest of the people.

The obedience of Moses to the commands of God in these early texts of Numbers is explicit and total. These records of his obedience will serve to display the incongruity of his terrible lapse as described in 20:1–13. Also in these verses we have one of many texts in Numbers that speak of the revelation of the word of God to his servant Moses. Those who minimize the role of Moses do so in the face of abundant direct textual assertions to the contrary.

(ii) *Gershon*

3:21–26

[21]To Gershon belonged the clans of the Libnites and Shimeites; these were the Gershonite clans. [22]The number of all the males a month old or more who were counted was 7,500. [23]The Gershonite clans were to camp on the west, behind the tabernacle. [24]The leader of the families of the Gershonites was Eliasaph son of Lael. [25]At the Tent of Meeting the Gershonites were responsible for the care of the tabernacle and tent, its coverings, the curtain at the entrance to the Tent of Meeting, [26]the curtains of the courtyard, the curtain at the entrance to the courtyard surrounding the tabernacle and altar, and the ropes—and everything related to their use.

21–26 The words of 1:53—"their tents around the tabernacle of the Testimony"—are detailed by the four paragraphs in vv.21–38:

Gershon to the west (vv.21–26)
Kohath to the south (vv.27–32)
Merari to the north (vv.33–37)
Moses and Aaron and sons to the east (v.38)

In the secular tribes we began with the most favored:

Judah on the east (2:3)
Reuben on the south (2:10)
Ephraim on the west (2:18)
Dan on the north (2:25)

In the Levitical clans we lead up to the most favored, as noted above. The leaders of the Levitical houses correspond to the leaders of the secular tribes (see 1:5–15). As in the case of the names of the other tribal leaders, these names are theophoric (built on compounds of terms for God):

Eliasaph ("[My] God Has Added") son of Lael ("Belonging to God") (3:24)
Elizaphan ("[My] God Has Protected") son of Uzziel ("My Strength Is God") (3:30)
Zuriel ("My Rock Is God") son of Abihail ("My Father [God] Is Might") (3:35)

Under the leadership of Eliasaph, the clan of Gershon was to camp on the west side of the tabernacle (v.23); i.e., away from its entrance. Their particular charge was the structure itself: the tent, its coverings, and the varied curtains and ropes. This was a significant charge for the people of the house of Gershon, whose male members over the age of one month were 7,500.

There were three curtains or covering screens of the tabernacle: (1) one at the gate of the court (v.26; 4:26); (2) a second at the entrance of the tent (vv.25, 31; 4:25); (3) and a third dividing off the Most Holy Place within the tent (4:5).

(iii) *Kohath*

3:27–32

27 To Kohath belonged the clans of the Amramites, Izharites, Hebronites and Uzzielites; these were the Kohathite clans. 28 The number of all the males a month old or more was 8,600. The Kohathites were responsible for the care of the sanctuary. 29 The Kohathite clans were to camp on the south side of the tabernacle. 30 The leader of the families of the Kohathite clans was Elizaphan son of Uzziel. 31 They were responsible for the care of the ark, the table, the lampstand, the altars, the articles of the sanctuary used in ministering, the curtain, and everything related to their use. 32 The chief leader of the Levites was Eleazar son of Aaron, the priest. He was appointed over those who were responsible for the care of the sanctuary.

27–32 The Kohathites under the leadership of Elizaphan were to encamp on the south side of the sanctuary. This clan, the largest of the Levitical families, had particular concerns for the care of the principal furnishings of the tabernacle, including the ark, the table, the lamps, the altars, along with many implements of their service. Aaron's son Eleazar, "the chief leader" (lit., "the leader of the leaders," v.32), was placed over this group of Levites, probably because of the inordinately sensitive nature of their work.

The term "Amramites" reminds us of the family of Aaron and Moses. Aaron is an Amramite (see Exod 6:20). The presence of the family of the Amramites suggests that Amram was not the direct father of Aaron, Miriam, and Moses but an ancestor. Hence, Aaron and Moses were from the family of Kohath, of the tribe of Levi. The Kohathites were responsible for the care of the most holy things (4:4–18).

The total of Levites given in v.39 is 22,000, which is 300 less than the total of 7,500 Gershonites (v.22), 8,600 Kohathites (v.28), and 6,200 Merarites (v.34) (= 22,300). Many scholars believe that there has been a textual corruption in the number in v.28, that the correct number of the Kohathites is 8,300 (as in the LXX). Because the totals of all other numbers in these chapters of Numbers are consistent, it is reasonable to assume a textual transmission disfunction in this instance. The fact that there is a textual difficulty here with numbers, however, cannot be projected back to the numbers of chapter 1 as a way to evade the problems of the large numbers. Again, for textual corruption to be a factor, it would have to be on a scale unprecedented in the Bible. What we have in this instance is that all the numbers are sound except for one that has gone awry.

(iv) *Merari*

3:33–37

33 To Merari belonged the clans of the Mahlites and the Mushites; these were the Merarite clans. 34 The number of all the males a month old or more who were counted was 6,200. 35 The leader of the families of the Merarite clans was Zuriel son of Abihail; they were to camp on the north side of the tabernacle. 36 The Merarites were appointed to take care of the frames of the tabernacle, its crossbars, posts, bases, all its

equipment, and everything related to their use, [37]as well as the posts of the surrounding courtyard with their bases, tent pegs and ropes.

33–37 The house of Merari, camped on the north of the tabernacle, was led by Zuriel and numbered 6,200 males from the age of one month. Their particular charge was the care of the frames, posts, bases, and crossbars of the tent, as well as all auxiliary materials. It is fitting that this clan of Levites is stationed on the north, as their work is not nearly as glamorous as that of the other two companies of Levites. There is a consistency in that this house of the Levites is on the same side of the tent as the triad of tribes led by Dan.

(v) *Moses and Aaron*

3:38

[38]Moses and Aaron and his sons were to camp to the east of the tabernacle, toward the sunrise, in front of the Tent of Meeting. They were responsible for the care of the sanctuary on behalf of the Israelites. Anyone else who approached the sanctuary was to be put to death.

38 Moses and Aaron had the most honored location, as we would expect. They guarded the entrance to the Tent of Meeting, and they did so facing the sun. There is a sense in which the opening of the tent best faces the east, for this is the direction of the encampment of the people. Later on Solomon was to build the holy temple in Jerusalem. Its entrance also would face east. The morning sun would shine first on the entrance of the Holy Place, as a symbol of the life-giving light of God that illumines the place of his presence.

Moses and Aaron were not placed in the posture of arrogance on the east side of the tabernacle; they were placed there for a representational ministry ("on behalf of the Israelites"). Theirs was an exclusive work but beneficent to the community. Service in the tabernacle was an act of mercy, a means for the people to come before God. Yet it was marked by severity—it had to be done in God's way! Worship to God is acceptable only because of his mercy. The sovereignty of God was evident in his limitations on the means to approach him. The "stranger" (NIV, "anyone else") could be a better man or woman, more pious and devout than a given son of Aaron; he or she would still face death based on presumption. The warning of death to the "stranger" is found four times in the book (see 1:51; 3:10, 38; 18:7).

(vi) *The sum*

3:39

[39]The total number of Levites counted at the LORD's command by Moses and Aaron according to their clans, including every male a month old or more, was 22,000.

39 Concerning the grand sum of 22,000 Levites, we observe that this is a bit small compared with the numbers given for the other tribes in chapter 1. There is a consistency, however, when this number is compared to the 23,000 Levites in the second census (26:62). It is particularly small when we realize that the 22,000 included all males in the tribe of Levi who were over the age of one month rather than over the age of twenty years as in the other tribes. The most single difficult issue in the numbers of the tribes is the lack of relationship of the numbers of Levi to the numbers of the other tribes. This is true however we judge the meaning of these numbers. If we suggest that the numbers of the other tribes are deliberately inflated by a factor of ten (see Introduction, pp. 688–91), then that would make the totals for Reuben to be 4,650 and for Simeon 5,930, from the age of twenty and upward. The smallest of the secular tribes would be Benjamin at 3,400. The largest would be Judah with 7,400. If we assume that the numbers for the tribe of Levi are similarly inflated, then they would number 2,200—again a small number with respect to the other tribes. If we regard the number for the tribe of Levi as the only noninflated figure of the tribes of Israel, then the 20,000 males over the age of one month would suggest a tribe that is very large; indeed, they would become the largest tribe of all. Even with the priestly centeredness of the Book of Numbers, we would be quite surprised to find a number this large in proportion to the whole for the tribe of Levi. The smaller figure, then, of 2,200 seems the more reasonable. John Wenham suggests the number of the tribe of Levi is likely inflated by a factor of ten (see Introduction). This number, too, would have been rhetorically exaggerated as a *power number* (see Introduction, pp. 688–91, for a description of this concept).

Notes

---

39 The word וְאַהֲרֹן (*we'ahᵃrōn*, "and Aaron") has special dots over the word indicating doubt on the part of ancient Jewish authorities as to its integrity in this verse. The presence of these dots over a questionable word the scribes were loath to drop shows the level of care and concern for the minutia of the text by the Jewish scholars through the ages. The word is lacking in numerous Hebrew MSS as well as in the Samaritan Pentateuch and the Syriac version. It may have been added here because of the presence of the name "Aaron" at the beginning of the chapter.

(e) *The census and redemption of the firstborn (3:40–51)*

(i) *The census*

3:40–43

40 The LORD said to Moses, "Count all the firstborn Israelite males who are a month old or more and make a list of their names. 41 Take the Levites for me in place of all the firstborn of the Israelites, and the livestock of the Levites in place of all the firstborn of the livestock of the Israelites. I am the LORD."

42 So Moses counted all the firstborn of the Israelites, as the LORD commanded him. 43 The total number of firstborn males a month old or more, listed by name, was 22,273.

40–43 The basic teaching of this text is that the male Levites over the age of one month were regarded by the Lord as a redemption for the firstborn of the nation. The firstborn of animals were to be sacrificed to the Lord; but God never countenanced the sacrifice of persons on his altars. Hence a substitution was done. A male Levite was regarded as a substitution for the firstborn member of a secular tribe. Notice that the firstborn of the livestock were also included in the substitutionary arrangement; Levite for firstborn of Israel and Levite's livestock for firstborn livestock of Israel.

The command of God seems to be distinct in this text (v.40). Not only was there to be a count of a discrete populace grouping, but the names were to be written down (cf. 1:2). The number of the firstborn of the Israelites came to 22,273 (v.43). This number stands out from all the other numbers we have seen in these three chapters. All other numbers are rounded off, including the number of the Levites, 22,000. Yet this specific number of the firstborn of Israel is related to the rounded number of the Levites, to provide a surplus of 273 firstborn, for whom a redemption price had to be made (v.46).

As the number of firstborn Israelite males exceeds the number of the Levites by 273 (v.43), the remainder have to be redeemed by the payment of five shekels each (v.47), as in Leviticus 27:6. A question presents itself as to why the rounded number of the Levites (22,000) is posed against a specific number of the firstborn of Israel (22,273). Perhaps the rounded number is in accordance with the rounded numbers of the other tribes. This disparity in types of numbers allows the text to bare a significant lesson on redemption.

The number of the firstborn sons of Israel (22,273) seems to be much too small for a population in excess of 2 million. In fact, this number accords very nicely for a population of about 250,000. This number is regularly used as an argument for attempting to find a means of reducing the total number of the people from the high figures suggested in chapter 1. Keil (KD, pp. 7–9) proposes a solution for the seeming disparity: the 22,273 firstborn of Israel were those born since the time of the Exodus; all the firstborn of Israel at the time of the Exodus had already been sanctified to the Lord at the time of the Passover (Exod 12:22–23). But this solution presents its own problem, "since nowhere is that allegedly distinct group assigned any special service of the Lord" (*NIV Study Bible*, note on 3:43). It also presents some special pleading. There is no indication in the text that these firstborn were born after the Exodus. Nor do we think anyone likely would have thought that this number of the firstborn of Israel was restricted to those born since the Exodus—except in an attempt to deal with the impossibly large numbers of the population indicated in chapter 1.

With some temerity I suggest the following possibility. First let me say that I am well aware that there is no indication in the text that this may be the correct point of view. This is a proposal that is suggestive of an alternative way of thinking of numbers. In point of fact, however we approach this passage, we confront two difficulties: one concerns the disparity of a mere 22,273 firstborn in a population of several million; the other concerns the subtraction of a rounded number (22,000) from a specific number (22,273) and then making much of the difference between the two. I venture this proposal as an alternative to that which Keil presented on other grounds (see section above). Keil's proposal was based on the postulate that the numbers of the conscripted troops of Israel were "ordinary numbers" as were these two disputed numbers of 22,273 firstborn and 22,000 Levites of a certain age. Hence he had to deal with the unusually small number of firstborn children of Israel for a population so very large. My own suggestion is that the unexpectedly small number of the firstborn is an impressive clue to the size of the population as a whole and that there may be two different uses of numbers in this passage, specific and rhetorical. Although we normally do not use numbers this way today, that is quite beside the point. Neither would we subtract a rounded number (for 22,000 is certainly that) from a very specific number (and 22,273 is that) and then make a major point of the remainder (273). Yet this is precisely what this passage does.

My proposal, then, is that Moses here presents a comparison of numbers of different sorts. The one number is specific, exacting (22,273); the other is rounded, inflated, rhetorical (22,000). The number of the firstborn of Israel, 22,273, is a specific, concrete number of the firstborn of all the families of Israel in the first generation. This is the surest figure for calculating the numbers of the whole community; the extrapolation of 250,000 is considered fitting for this number of firstborn persons. Against this specific figure (22,273) is pitted a rhetorical figure (22,000, the number of Levites of a certain age) in order to provide an analogy of redemption. The "surplus" of these two discordant types of figures (one specific, concrete; one inflated, rounded off) affords the opportunity to deal with the problem of a surplus. The payment of a redemption price of five sanctuary shekels per individual teaches us that every individual needs to be accounted for, no matter how these numbers are used. That is, there is the possiblity that the point of the passage is not the numbers per se but that which the numbers represent—the importance of paying the redemption price for each individual firstborn person in the young nation, as a symbol of the redemption of each individual in the nation. The theology of the Exodus demands that the nation as a whole was under the blood of the Passover, that the nation as a whole was rescued from Egypt, and that the nation as a whole was a part of the new community in relation to Yahweh. In the attention given to the 273 supernumeraries, there is a focus on the individuals who make up the nation. Certainly we are not interested in making any numerical symbolism of the number 273. The number is not as important as the issue the number represents: corporate solidarity and the importance of the individual are twin realities in the new community of Israel.

Notes

41 The words אֲנִי יהוה (*'anî yhwh,* "I am the LORD") add solemnity and emphasis. It is an intrusive phrase in the original—startling and surprising, having the force: "Listen to ME!" What is being commanded conforms to God's character, as expressed in his covenant name Yahweh.

(ii) *The redemption*

3:44–51

[44]The LORD also said to Moses, [45]"Take the Levites in place of all the firstborn of Israel, and the livestock of the Levites in place of their livestock. The Levites are to be mine. I am the LORD. [46]To redeem the 273 firstborn Israelites who exceed the number of the Levites, [47]collect five shekels for each one, according to the sanctuary shekel, which weighs twenty gerahs. [48]Give the money for the redemption of the additional Israelites to Aaron and his sons."

[49]So Moses collected the redemption money from those who exceeded the number redeemed by the Levites. [50]From the firstborn of the Israelites he collected silver weighing 1,365 shekels, according to

the sanctuary shekel. 51 Moses gave the redemption money to Aaron and
his sons, as he was commanded by the word of the LORD.

44–51 To make up for the number of the firstborn Israelites beyond the number of the Levites, a special tax of five shekels (the price of a slave for a boy under the age of five; see Lev 27:6) was to be paid for each of the 273 supernumeraries. This is the payment of a redemption price, according to the heavier sanctuary shekel. That silver was then paid to Aaron and his sons, as commanded by the Lord so that the full complement of the firstborn sons of the community might all be redeemed together.

The redemption of the firstborn is a marvelous expression of the grace of God. Never since the story of the binding of Isaac (Gen 22) has God demanded the firstborn son of any of his people as a sacrifice to his majesty. Nor does God demand that his people enslave themselves to him (cf. Rom 12:1–2). Nevertheless, the firstborn sons are the special possession of the Lord. God does not demand the life of these sons; such would be abhorrent to the Hebrew faith. God does not demand their enslavement; such would be a slight on his mercy. But he does demand their redemption—and provides the means for bringing that to pass. We suspect the community paid the redemption; it is possible that the families of those judged to be the supernumeraries may have had to pay this tax themselves. The resultant weight of the shekels so collected is given (1,365 shekels, v.50) as a statement of the impressive nature of the transaction and as a witness to its accuracy (5 x 273). The pattern was one Levite for each firstborn, five shekels for each child beyond the number of the Levites. In this way each firstborn was accounted for in God's plan of redemption.

Christians cannot but have their thoughts directed to the NT and the Savior who has brought about the redemption for his people. There it was, not by the payment of silver and gold, but with his own precious blood. And there we have been redeemed.

(4) *The numbers of the Levites in tabernacle service (4:1–49)*

The sense of order and organization already observed in this book comes to its finest point in this chapter. Again, we observe that the standard pattern in Hebrew prose is a movement from the general to the specific, from the broad to the particular. Chapters 1–4 follow this concept nicely. Chapter 1 presents the leaders and the numbers of the soldiers conscripted from each tribe; chapter 2 shows how each of the tribes is related to groupings surrounding the Tent of Meeting; chapter 3 gives the census of the Levite males from one month and older and a listing of the Levites by their families; and chapter 4 presents the census of the Levites from twenty-five to fifty years of age and the work each family was to have. The chapters have moved from the nation as a whole to the particular families of the one tribe that has responsibility to maintain the symbols of Israel's worship of the Lord. Each chapter gets more specific, more narrow in focus, with the central emphasis on the worship of the Lord at the Tent of Meeting.

Another standard feature of Hebrew prose is to give a topic sentence, then to detail the particulars relating to that topic, and then to conclude with a summary of the completion of the intended action. Genesis 1:1–2:3 is written this way: 1:1 gives the topic sentence on creation, 1:2–31 details the creative actions of God, and 2:1–3 (or, better, 2:1–4a) summarizes God's creative work. We find a variation on this same pattern nicely displayed in Numbers 4. In this case there is not a topic sentence but an extended command (vv.1–33) followed by an execution report (vv.34–45) and a summary (vv.46–49).

(a) *The command for the census and a description of duties (4:1–33)*

(i) *The family of Kohath*

4:1–20

[1]The LORD said to Moses and Aaron: [2]"Take a census of the Kohathite branch of the Levites by their clans and families. [3]Count all the men from thirty to fifty years of age who come to serve in the work in the Tent of Meeting.

[4]"This is the work of the Kohathites in the Tent of Meeting: the care of the most holy things. [5]When the camp is to move, Aaron and his sons are to go in and take down the shielding curtain and cover the ark of the Testimony with it. [6]Then they are to cover this with hides of sea cows, spread a cloth of solid blue over that and put the poles in place.

[7]"Over the table of the Presence they are to spread a blue cloth and put on it the plates, dishes and bowls, and the jars for drink offerings; the bread that is continually there is to remain on it. [8]Over these they are to spread a scarlet cloth, cover that with hides of sea cows and put its poles in place.

[9]"They are to take a blue cloth and cover the lampstand that is for light, together with its lamps, its wick trimmers and trays, and all its jars for the oil used to supply it. [10]Then they are to wrap it and all its accessories in a covering of hides of sea cows and put it on a carrying frame.

[11]"Over the gold altar they are to spread a blue cloth and cover that with hides of sea cows and put its poles in place.

[12]"They are to take all the articles used for ministering in the sanctuary, wrap them in a blue cloth, cover that with hides of sea cows and put them on a carrying frame.

[13]"They are to remove the ashes from the bronze altar and spread a purple cloth over it. [14]Then they are to place on it all the utensils used for ministering at the altar, including the firepans, meat forks, shovels and sprinkling bowls. Over it they are to spread a covering of hides of sea cows and put its poles in place.

[15]"After Aaron and his sons have finished covering the holy furnishings and all the holy articles, and when the camp is ready to move, the Kohathites are to come to do the carrying. But they must not touch the holy things or they will die. The Kohathites are to carry those things that are in the Tent of Meeting.

[16]"Eleazar son of Aaron, the priest, is to have charge of the oil for the light, the fragrant incense, the regular grain offering and the anointing oil. He is to be in charge of the entire tabernacle and everything in it, including its holy furnishings and articles."

[17]The LORD said to Moses and Aaron, [18]"See that the Kohathite tribal clans are not cut off from the Levites. [19]So that they may live and not die when they come near the most holy things, do this for them: Aaron and his sons are to go into the sanctuary and assign to each man his work and what he is to carry. [20]But the Kohathites must not go in to look at the holy things, even for a moment, or they will die."

1 When the sons of Levi are mentioned in 3:17, their order is Gershon, Kohath, and Merari; this order also informs the structure of the balance of chapter 3: Gershonites (vv.21–26), Kohathites (vv.27–32), and Merarites (vv.33–37). The same order is given in the family records of Jacob (Gen 46:11), Moses and Aaron (Exod 6:16), and the Levitical families (1 Chron 6:1, 16).

2 The order of the listing of sons in the Bible is not necessarily that of birth order; but the consistent pattern Gershon, Kohath, Merari suggests that birth order is intended in this case. This makes the order of the Levitical families in Numbers 4 somewhat unexpected, as the families of Kohath (the presumed second son) are mentioned first (vv.2–20), then the families of Gershon (vv.21–28), and finally the families of Merari (vv.29–33). The same pattern is recapitulated in the numberings listed at the end of the chapter (vv.34–45).

The reason for this elevation of the second son over his older brother seems to be based on the sovereign selection of the Lord and the favored work he gives this family in proximity to the holiest things. Further, we find here that which reflects a recurring pattern in the MT: the surprising elevation of a lesser son over his older brother. These are examples of the grace of God that reaches out in sovereign selection, bringing blessing to whom he wishes to bring blessing, elevating whom he desires to elevate, for reasons of his own will. The pattern is found repeatedly in the Pentateuch (Isaac over Ishmael, Jacob over Esau, Joseph over Reuben, Moses over Aaron, Saul and David over their respective brothers). It almost would seem that the standard place of ascendancy was to be the second, or the younger, son!

3 The census in this chapter is distinct from that of chapter 3. Here the census is of all males from *thirty to fifty years*. In chapter 3 the census listed all males over the age of one month (v.15). This chapter lists those Levites who were of the age to serve in the tabernacle. Of the 22,000 Levite males mentioned in 3:39, there were 8,580 of service age (v.48). If these numbers are to be reduced by a factor of ten (see comment on 3:39), then the corresponding numbers would be 2,200 and 858. From 8:24 we learn that the beginning age for service was twenty-five; perhaps the first five years were something of an apprenticeship.

Critical scholars seize on precisely "contradictions" such as these as markers of the confusion within the development of the supposed P source. J. Alberto Soggin, for example, cites the contrasting ages for the Levites and differing offerings in similar texts and then concludes, "Even at the heart of P we have contradictions, duplicates and interpolations of compositions which clearly show signs of being of autonomous origin" (*Introduction to the Old Testament*, tr. John Bowden [Philadelphia: Westminster, 1976], p. 140). Yet there are other ways of dealing with the difficulties of these texts.

Along with the negative conclusions that these approaches bring to the text in terms of its veracity are the damaging attitudes these approaches yield with respect to the artistry and beauty of the text. When a writer begins with P and then decides that P is made of numerous conflicting elements, which now become centers of research, the sense of the whole of the text is lost. Variety of expression is not seen as stylistic creativity but as indicators of fracture; disagreements of parallel passages are not amenable to harmonization in the whole but are necessary components of a theory of the discovery of supposed parts. The result is the loss of Scripture—the loss as the authoritative Word of God; the loss as the living sword, sharp and active; and the loss as a beautiful expression of the person of God.

4–5 The paragraphs detailing the work of the Kohathites in their care of the most holy things (v.4) come to the modern reader as truly from another time. The attention to care and detail for holy things is, lamentably, a lost art. Even though the primary care of these holy things was given to the Kohathites, they were forbidden to touch them (v.15)—or even to look on them (v.20)—lest they die. These strictures are stunning. As the holy angels who surround the throne of the Divine Presence shield their faces and feet from his presence (cf. Isa 6:1–3), so the Kohathites were to shield themselves from too familiar an approach to the holiest of things (v.5); for most holy things symbolize the presence of the most holy God.

All the work of the Kohathites was to be strictly supervised by Aaron and his sons, and only the priests themselves were able to touch and look on the unveiled holy things. We presume that even they had to be extremely careful in this regard; the memory of the story of Nadab and Abihu still rings in our ears (see 3:2–4).

Several impressions emerge in the reading of this section:

1. *The sense of planning, order, and execution.* Nothing in the holy things of God was to be left to chance or to improvisation. None of the sacred persons who ministered in his presence was to be unprepared or untaught. All the preparation suggests a rigorous training schedule before actual work would be done by a given priest. This call for preparation may account for the distinction of twenty-five years of age in 8:24 and thirty years in 4:3. That intervening five-year period may have been a time of intense internship.

2. *The sheer quantity and variety of the holy things.* At times we have an impression of a crude, primitive nature of the worship patterns of ancient Israel, especially in the earliest periods. Yet if these texts adequately reflect the times of Moses, as a natural reading suggests, then the worship implements from the time of Moses were many and varied—and, we suspect, quite precious.

3. *The use of color, texture, and layers.* Each of the covering curtains must have been impressive in color, texture, and design; but the variety of the coverings and their several uses speaks of a legitimate enjoyment of luxury in worship and a celebration of the presence of God. The solid blue cloth, the scarlet cloth, the blue cloth, the gold altar, the bronze altar, the purple cloth, plus numerous hides, skins, and other cloths all present a wondrous delight in serving in the presence of God.

4. *The mobility and transportability of the tabernacle.* A further impression is the sense we have that everything is movable. The tent was designed to be set up and taken down; it was a temporary abode.

5. *The sense of hierarchy among the workers, along with an affirmation of the sense of dignity of purpose and the importance of work in one's life.* Each individual was given a task to do (see v.33). Some tasks were more elegant than others, but every task had to be done.

6–15 Translators have had difficulty in identifying the precise nature of the "hides of sea cows" (i.e., the outer covering of the ark) and the other items of holy furniture. The Hebrew word rendered "sea cow" (*taḥaš*) is similar to the Arabic term for the dolphin; hence, porpoise-hide or hide of sea cows seems correct.

The use of dramatic colors in the elements of holy worship in Israel has led to speculation as to the symbolic interpretation each color represents; however, the fact that colors were used may be more significant for the modern reader who tends to have a dour view of worship in Israel and an unimaginative appreciation of color in his own worship tradition.

The manner of the transport of the holy things was by foot, with the six packages of holy things suspended between carriers by poles (see vv.6, 8, 11, 14) or kept on a carrier frame (vv.10, 12). The sad story of Uzzah, who attempted to keep the ark of the covenant from tumbling to the earth when David was having it brought to the city of

Jerusalem (2 Sam 6:6–7), is an unwitting self-test of the profound significance of these words.

16 The special functions of the high priest are specified in this section both as a delimitation and as a mercy to the other sacral persons. The priest had certain duties peculiar to his office that none other might ever do. But the mercy of God was that there was a person who could draw near to the most holy things on behalf of the people. Were the high priest unable to attend to the holy things, there could be no worship from any of the community. Hence, his welfare ought to have been the concern of the people, for theirs was certainly tied to him.

17–20 The final section relating to the Kohathites in this portion concerns their ongoing service before the Lord in the context of the ongoing people of God; but it also presents a significant warning: any improper approach toward, touch of, or glance at the sacred things would mean death.

As in other instances of this sort, we may observe that the underlying reason on God's part may well have been mercy. It was a mercy of God that he had made himself known to anyone; it was the continuing mercy of God that he does not destroy more persons more quickly because of their wickedness; and it is a condescending mercy of God that he presents himself in their midst. The revelation of God's word brings with it demands, some of which seem harsh and difficult. But God is near. Some seem to be so judgmental; yet God has not destroyed all. Some seem to be so threatening; yet God by his mercy allows some sense of his presence to remain known in the camp. His manifestation is based on his mercy; his strictures allow his mercy to continue to be realized.

(ii) *The family of Gershon*

4:21–28

21The LORD said to Moses, 22"Take a census also of the Gershonites
by their families and clans. 23Count all the men from thirty to fifty years
of age who come to serve in the work at the Tent of Meeting.
24"This is the service of the Gershonite clans as they work and carry
burdens: 25They are to carry the curtains of the tabernacle, the Tent of
Meeting, its covering and the outer covering of hides of sea cows, the
curtains for the entrance to the Tent of Meeting, 26the curtains of the
courtyard surrounding the tabernacle and altar, the curtain for the
entrance, the ropes and all the equipment used in its service. The
Gershonites are to do all that needs to be done with these things. 27All
their service, whether carrying or doing other work, is to be done under
the direction of Aaron and his sons. You shall assign to them as their
responsibility all they are to carry. 28This is the service of the Gershonite
clans at the Tent of Meeting. Their duties are to be under the direction
of Ithamar son of Aaron, the priest.

21–28 What we term "typical Hebrew stylistics" is displayed in this chapter, with its repetition and restatement, the very things that classical criticism has gone wrong-headed about. Repetition and restatement in the prose sections of the Bible may have a similar effect on the reader as the use of parallelism in the poetic. We are in an alien aesthetic when we come to passages such as this. Before dismissing them, an arrogant act, we should learn to understand their underlying values. Then we will be better able to appreciate these values.

The Gershonites cared for the outer curtains and hides of the tabernacle. They and the Merarites were permitted to touch the things they were responsible for; the men of Kohath were not even to look at or to touch the things of the Most Holy Place. But the Gershonites and the Merarites were not to do their work alone. Even with them Aaron was to be the chief responsible agent, but he was able to delegate some of that responsibility to his son Ithamar (v.28).

(iii) *The family of Merari*

4:29–33

> 29 "Count the Merarites by their clans and families. 30 Count all the men from thirty to fifty years of age who come to serve in the work at the Tent of Meeting. 31 This is their duty as they perform service at the Tent of Meeting: to carry the frames of the tabernacle, its crossbars, posts and bases, 32 as well as the posts of the surrounding courtyard with their bases, tent pegs, ropes, all their equipment and everything related to their use. Assign to each man the specific things he is to carry. 33 This is the service of the Merarite clans as they work at the Tent of Meeting under the direction of Ithamar son of Aaron, the priest."

29–33 Similar phrasing to the two other family units graces this section, with the instructions that the Merari family was to have their principal with the frames, crossbars, posts, bases, pegs, ropes, and other equipment. Their work was as important as that of any other family group; for without it the more desirable, prestigious work of the tabernacle could not be done. Hence the Merarites could take an interest even in the placing of a post, a peg, or a rope, not because each of these items is a distinct, suitable "type of Christ," but because the worship of God could not proceed—nor could the camp move out—unless these people were doing their holy work.

(b) *A description of the census (4:34–45)*

(i) *The family of Kohath*

4:34–37

> 34 Moses, Aaron and the leaders of the community counted the Kohathites by their clans and families. 35 All the men from thirty to fifty years of age who came to serve in the work in the Tent of Meeting, 36 counted by clans, were 2,750. 37 This was the total of all those in the Kohathite clans who served in the Tent of Meeting. Moses and Aaron counted them according to the LORD's command through Moses.

(ii) *The family of Gershon*

4:38–41

> 38 The Gershonites were counted by their clans and families. 39 All the men from thirty to fifty years of age who came to serve in the work at the Tent of Meeting, 40 counted by their clans and families, were 2,630. 41 This was the total of those in the Gershonite clans who served at the Tent of Meeting. Moses and Aaron counted them according to the LORD's command.

(iii) *The family of Merari*

4:42–45

[42]The Merarites were counted by their clans and families. [43]All the men from thirty to fifty years of age who came to serve in the work at the Tent of Meeting, [44]counted by their clans, were 3,200. [45]This was the total of those in the Merarite clans. Moses and Aaron counted them according to the LORD's command through Moses.

34–45 The most notable thing in the census of the Levitical families in this section is the use of numbers. The numbers still appear to be rounded off; but since the numbers are smaller than the numbers in chapter 1, the rounding off is done to the tens level: 2,750 from Kohath, 2,630 from Gershon, and 3,200 from Merari.

(c) *A summary of the census and the work of Moses in the census*

4:46–49

[46]So Moses, Aaron and the leaders of Israel counted all the Levites by their clans and families. [47]All the men from thirty to fifty years of age who came to do the work of serving and carrying the Tent of Meeting [48]numbered 8,580. [49]At the LORD's command through Moses, each was assigned his work and told what to carry.

Thus they were counted, as the LORD commanded Moses.

46–49 Here we find the seemingly routine use of a summary text in which notice is given of compliance on the part of the leaders. Further, the total number of the men from the three Levitical families from the age of thirty to fifty who worked in and about the Tent of Meeting was 8,580. The addition of the three addends could be displayed as follows: 2,750 + 2,630 + 3,200 = 8,580—the total number of the Levites who are mustered for the service of God in the Tent of Meeting. Again, if the theory of a tenfold inflation of these figures is presumed, then the numbers may be reduced to 275 + 263 + 320 = 858. In either case, the addition is the same.

These summary texts serve to give a sense of completion to the unit. Hebrew style seems to allow the reader to enjoy a sense of "going full-circle." When the summary of actions of obedience is given as here, there is a sense in which the reader may derive satisfaction. When there is no summary, no record of final action, then questions arise: What is the point? Where is the obedience? What is the basic meaning?

b. *Diverse commands and rituals in preparation for the triumphal march (5:1–10:10)*

(1) *The test for purity and the law of jealousy (5:1–31)*

The ordering, numbering, and structuring of the camp was completed at the end of chapter 4. Men of military age have been mustered for service (ch. 1); the secular tribes have been arranged around the central shrine (ch. 2); and the Levites have been numbered, arranged around the inner core of the shrine (ch. 3), and given their appropriate duties in the management of the holy things (ch. 4). The next six and one-half chapters present various commands for ritual purity within the camp, all necessary for the final preparations for the movement of the people through the desert and their journey on to their new home in the land of Canaan. This new stage—the setting forth of the holy people on their triumphal march—begins in 10:11.

The information in chapter 5 is especially interesting and is marked by a symmetry of the chapter and its elements. There are three issues in this chapter: (1) a command of the Lord for expelling from the camp those who are ritually defiled (vv.1–4); (2) a command of the Lord for restitution for offenses against another person within the camp (vv.5–10); and (3) a command of the Lord for a ritual procedure in cases of marital jealousy (vv.11–31). Each section begins in precisely the same way and develops in a similar manner (though of uneven length): (1) an introductory monocolon with the command of the Lord to Moses (see vv.1, 5, 11); (2) a subordinate command for Moses to speak the command to the people (see vv.2a, 6a, 12a); (3) the substance of the command and its application in the life of the people (see vv.2b–3; 6b–8; 12b–28); (4) a concluding section on the command (see vv.4, 10, 29–31).

The introductory commands of the Lord to Moses (vv.1, 5, 11) are not to be read merely as stylistic devices to introduce a new subject, though this is one function of this phrasing. Reverent readers find in the wording "And the LORD spoke to Moses, saying . . . ," a recurring emphasis on the divine origin of these texts and a repeated emphasis that the Lord has taken the initiative in communicating his word to his people through his servant Moses. There are some passages and narratives that are provoked by the inquiry of the people, and the response of the Lord is forthcoming (see, e.g., the story of the daughters of Zelophehad, ch. 27). But the customary thing in the Torah is the initiation of God in his gracious self-disclosure and in the presentation of his will for the good of his people.

Further, the subordinate commands for Moses to relate the word of the Lord to the people (vv.2a, 6a, 12a) present three aspects of the divine communication: (1) Moses is the prophet of Yahweh, the great *nāḇî'*, one who is called by God and who speaks for him; (2) the commands of God were to be disseminated throughout the community, not reserved for Moses or some elite few in an inner circle; and (3) the words of God were to be presented to the people as authoritative commands, not just as divine suggestions ("command the Israelites," v.2a; "speak to the Israelites," v.6a; "speak to the Israelites and say to them," v.12a).

(a) *The expulsion of the impure from the camp*

5:1–4

[1]The LORD said to Moses, [2]"Command the Israelites to send away from the camp anyone who has an infectious skin disease or a discharge of any kind, or who is ceremonially unclean because of a dead body. [3]Send away male and female alike; send them outside the camp so they will not defile their camp, where I dwell among them." [4]The Israelites did this; they sent them outside the camp. They did just as the LORD had instructed Moses.

1–2 In biblical times skin diseases, especially open sores, were among the three prominent factors (along with oozing discharges and contact with dead bodies) that rendered one unclean and hence unfit to be with the community and a possible contaminate to the tabernacle and the pure worship of the Lord. Such ones were to be excluded from the community during the period of their malaise. This brief paragraph uses the verb *šālaḥ* ("to send away," "to expel") no fewer than four times in vv.1–4. The emphasis on this strong verb points to the seriousness of the situation: such ones must be expelled.

The OT concept of "uncleanness" is hard for the modern, Western reader to understand. To be unclean was to be "dirty," unfit in the realm of the purity of the rule of God. Aspects of uncleanness were not left in the abstract or theoretical; the focus was on tangible issues such as clearly evident skin diseases. It is implied that the priests were the agents for dismissal from the congregation of those who were unclean.

The Hebrew word for "skin disease" (v.2, *ṣārûaʿ*; Qal passive participle from *ṣāraʿ*) has traditionally been translated "struck with leprosy." Nonetheless, this word is not used in the Bible to describe what we know of leprosy, today usually termed "Hansen's disease." John Wilkinson has described the biblical data in clinical terms ("Leprosy and Leviticus: The Problem of Description and Identification," SJT 30 [1984]: 153–69). The verb *ṣāraʿ* and the corresponding noun *ṣāraʿaṯ* (used esp. in Lev 13) do not seem to describe one specific disease but a number of complex disorders of the skin, including swellings, eruptions, spots, and itches (see Lev 13:2). These disorders are further described in terms of five secondary features: change of skin color, change of hair color, infiltration of the skin, extension or spread in the skin, and ulceration of the skin.

Some moderns have attempted to give precise identifications of these various diseases. E.V. Hulse ("The Nature of Biblical 'Leprosy' and the Use of Alternative Medical Terms in Modern Translations of the Bible," PEQ 107 [1975]: 87–105) suggests that some of the diseases indicated in Leviticus 13 and Numbers 5 include psoriasis, favus, leucoderma, and various types of eczema. While Hulse is likely correct in his general lines of identification, the issue of these texts is not the precise diagnosis of disease so much as the observation of certain symptoms of disease.

Wilkinson suggests that the priests of the period were not required to identify a specific disease, only a manifestation of a serious disorder. Leviticus 13 gives a diagnostic flow chart in which certain physical manifestations, not the underlying disease, were signs for the priests to rule whether or not a person was ritually unclean and hence not permitted to remain in the camp of Israel during the period of skin inflammation. The issue in skin disease is similar to that of the identification of animals that were clean or unclean in the dietary laws of Israel (see Lev 11). Again, the principal issue in this chapter is not precise identification of genus and phylum but, with reference to the animals, an observation of digestive habits and an examination of the hoof.

Even the translation in the NIV in these passages may be too specific: "an infectious skin disease." It is not clearly indicated that the offending skin diseases be infectious, for some of the diseases that might cause the disorders described in Leviticus 13 (psoriasis [?], for example) are not infectious. A preferable, nonspecific translation of the noun *ṣāraʿaṯ* and the passive forms of the verb *ṣāraʿ* is "[to suffer] a serious skin disorder." Incidentally, the broad range of meaning for the Hebrew term translated "a serious skin disorder" should carry over into the NT (Greek) words as well. "Leprosy" is too specific a translation in either testament and has been misleading for many readers and unfortunate for many who suffer from Hansen's disease today. We may also observe that this text presents the basis in the Book of Numbers for an application in the life of Miriam (see ch. 12).

The second problem rendering a person ritually unclean in v.2 is a discharge of any kind (see Lev 15:2). The Hebrew term *zāḇ* is used in four ways in Scripture: (1) of the flow of water from the rock (Ps 78:20), (2) of the land flowing with milk and honey (Exod 3:8), (3) of one pining away from hunger (Lam 4:9), and (4) of an uncontrolled fluid discharge from a man (Lev 15:2) or a woman (v.25). These discharges were primarily from the sexual organs and were chronic in nature. Again, this was a tangible matter. The people who suffered from these maladies became living object lessons to the whole camp of the necessity for all people to be "clean" in their approach to God.

The third factor rendering a person unclean in ancient Israel, and hence to be excluded from the camp, was contact with a dead body. The ultimate tangible sign of uncleanness in ancient Israel was the corpse. Processes of decay and disease in dead flesh were evident to all. Physical contact with a corpse was a sure mark of uncleanness and quite possibly a source of infection; normal contacts with others in the community of those who had become unclean would have to be curtailed until proper cleansing had been made (see comment on 6:6).

3 The modern reader should be impressed with the fact that these various disorders that render one unclean, and hence to be expelled from the camp, include male and female alike. The concept of clean versus unclean cuts across sexual lines. Women are excluded along with men, and women may be released of exclusion along with men.

The essential issue in all laws of purity in Israel was not magic or health or superstition; the great reality was the presence of Yahweh in the camp; there can be no uncleanness where he dwells. The last words of v.3 are dramatic in their presentation: "I am dwelling in their midst."

4 Verse 4 presents the full compliance of Israel to this law when it was initiated. As in 1:54; 2:34; 3:16, 42, 51; 4:49, this section ends with a report of the obedience of the people and of Moses to the commands of God. It is with sadness we will recall these reports at later times in Israel's experience, when she learned the pattern of failure to obey the Lord's commands.

When we think through the issues of this pericope (vv.1–4), we discover mercy. We may observe, in view of the dramatic phrase "I am dwelling in their midst," that the essential reason for the importance of "uncleanness" in the camp is the indwelling presence of the Lord. His commands that the unclean be expelled from the camp essentially are expressions of his mercy: (1) the polluting presence of the unclean may make others unclean, thus spreading the problem; (2) the continuing presence of the unclean within the camp may demand God's judgment; and (3) the pervasive spread of the unclean in the camp may demand that the Lord withdraw his own presence. It is God's lavish mercy that allows him to abide with his people at all; it is his continuing desire to express that mercy that prompts the expulsion of the unclean from the camp.

For these reasons Christians are impressed with the fact that the Lord Jesus extends the mercy of God dramatically in that he reached out to meet the needs of persons who had become unclean from each of the three stipulations of this text. Further, following the wording of v.3, "male and female alike," we see that Jesus in his ministry reached out both to women and to men who were ritually unclean. In these acts of mercy, the Lord acted as healer and then as priest; he cleansed their diseases and then declared them pure.

(b) *Restitution for personal wrongs*
5:5–10

5The LORD said to Moses, 6"Say to the Israelites: 'When a man or woman wrongs another in any way and so is unfaithful to the LORD, that person is guilty [7]and must confess the sin he has committed. He must make full restitution for his wrong, add one fifth to it and give it all to the person he has wronged. [8]But if that person has no close relative to whom restitution can be made for the wrong, the restitution belongs to the LORD and must be given to the priest, along with the ram with which atonement is made for him. [9]All the sacred contributions the Israelites bring to a priest will belong to him. [10]Each man's sacred gifts are his own, but what he gives to the priest will belong to the priest.' "

Another issue that leads to impurity in the camp is an unresolved personal injury. This type of evil may be harder to diagnose than even the mysterious skin disorders or fluid discharges of the earlier section. While the skin disorders and contact with dead bodies may lead to exclusion from the ritual of the worship of God in the community, social disorders will equally disrupt the cohesion of the people. These are examples of the concept in the MT sometimes described as "corporate solidarity." The health and effectiveness of the whole community depends on the health and effectiveness of the individuals within the community. There is an inner flow of continuity between the concepts of the community and the individual in these texts.

5–7 In this situation a person within the camp wrongs another. The connection of vv.5–10 (personal wrongs) to the first paragraph (ritual uncleanness) may be one of moving from the outward and visible to the inward and more secret faults that mar the purity of the community. Those with evident marks of uncleanness are to be expelled for the duration of their malady. But more insidious are those people who have overtly sinned against others in the community and who think that they may continue to function as though there were no real wrong.

A casual reader of the EVV may notice the consistent use of masculine pronouns and may then assume that this is yet another text dealing with the religious and moral obligations of the male believer under the provisions of Torah. Yet the section clearly begins with the words "when a man or *woman*" [lit. Heb.; emphasis added]. The point is that the worship of God is for women and for men. The obligations of repentance are for men and for women. Women are also sinners. Women are also significant. It is important that the woman reader see herself in these words just as the male reader does.

The particulars of the text demand a procedure for restitution in the case of unspecified personal wrongs. Of first importance is the recognition that such wrongs are not slight offenses between people only but are in fact acts of treachery against Yahweh, the Great Suzerain. The expression "and so is unfaithful to the LORD" may be more strongly rendered "to commit a serious act of treachery against Yahweh." As David was later to confess, his principal sin was not against Uriah or Bathsheba or his family or his nation; he said, "I have sinned against the LORD" (2 Sam 12:13).

The steps in the ritual for restitution include (1) a condition of guilt—that person is guilty (v.6), which excludes that person from active participation in the community as surely as a serious skin disease or contact with a dead body; (2) a public confession of that sin (v.7a)—presumably in the precincts of the sacred shrine, before witnesses and priests; (3) full restitution plus one-fifth to the one wronged (see Lev 22:14; 27:11–13, 31); (4) a sacrifice to the Lord of a ram offering for atonement.

8 Each above step is enumerated in Leviticus 6:1–7 in the initial presentation of the law of defrauding. However, Numbers 5 has an additional provision. What if a person has defrauded another but that person is no longer living and has no living relative to whom restitution might be paid. Verse 8 adds the next proviso: (5) the payment of restitution is to be made to the priest when there is no suitable relative to whom such payment might otherwise be made. In this way the debt is paid fully, no matter who of the injured family has survived.

The term for "close relative" is *gō'ēl*, the protector of the family rights, sometimes translated "kinsman-redeemer" (e.g., Ruth 4:3).

9–10 Finally, a note is added that the offerings presented to the priests truly belong to the priests. The offering is not a sham that is then withdrawn secretly after a public presentation.

Again, the intent of this law on defrauding is clear in the context of this chapter: purity among the people is essential for their successful journey through the desert and their eventual triumph over the inhabitants of the land. Just as the physically impure needed to be expelled from the camp, so those attitudes and jealousies one might have against another of petty or serious nature also need to be dealt with equitably for the camp to remain pure.

(c) *The law of jealousy (5:11–31)*

Yet another element that will lead to impurity within the camp is undetected marital infidelity. The law concerning jealousy is best read in the context and flow of the two earlier laws in this chapter. As a diseased person who is ritually unclean will compromise the entire camp and so must be expelled during the time of his disease (5:1–4), and as an unrequited wrong will bring trouble between people who are within the camp as surely as would be brought by one with disease of the skin (5:5–10), so the unexposed but treacherous act of marital infidelity also brings harm to the camp as a whole. Acts of marital infidelity were not regarded as peccadilloes in Israel; to be unfaithful to one's spouse was to be unfaithful to one's God. The following text has its harsh side; there is also mercy in it, as we shall discover.

(i) *The seed of jealousy*

5:11–15

11 Then the LORD said to Moses, 12 "Speak to the Israelites and say to them: 'If a man's wife goes astray and is unfaithful to him 13 by sleeping with another man, and this is hidden from her husband and her impurity is undetected (since there is no witness against her and she has not been caught in the act), 14 and if feelings of jealousy come over her husband and he suspects his wife and she is impure—or if he is jealous and suspects her even though she is not impure—15 then he is to take his wife to the priest. He must also take an offering of a tenth of an ephah of barley flour on her behalf. He must not pour oil on it or put incense on it, because it is a grain offering for jealousy, a reminder offering to draw attention to guilt.

11–13 Again, the connection with the preceding two paragraphs seems to be from the more open and obvious to the more personal and hidden sins. Issues of purity are established with the physical marks (vv.1–4), expanded to interpersonal relationships (vv.5–10), and then extended into the most intimate of relationships, that of purity of a man and woman in their marriage bed (vv.11–31). A test for marital fidelity is far harder to prove than a test for a skin disorder; hence the larger part of the chapter is given over to this most sensitive of issues.

The provisions of this law have connections (and discontinuities) with other laws in the ancient Near East. The Code of Hammurabi (c. 1727 B.C.) has a pair of laws that we may compare with our text:

> CH 131: If a seignior's wife was accused by her husband, but she was not caught while lying with another man, she shall make affirmation by god and return to her house.
>
> CH 132: If the finger was pointed at the wife of a seignior because of another man, but she has not been caught while lying with the other man, she shall throw herself into the river for the sake of her husband. (ANET, p. 171)

These laws from ancient Babylon deal with two types of accusation. The second law suggests a community knowledge of infidelity, but the woman was not caught "in the act." The presumed unfaithful woman was to undergo the ordeal of trial by death by flinging herself into the sacred Euphrates River. If she were guilty, it was presumed she would drown; if innocent, she would survive the ordeal and would be able to return to her husband with no attachment of guilt (see G.R. Driver and John C. Miles, *The Babylonian Laws,* 2 vols. [Oxford: Clarendon Press, 1952], 2:283–84). The first law is closer to the biblical example in Numbers 5:11–31. In this case the husband has only a private suspicion of his wife's infidelity. She is to present herself in a temple for a solemn oath and may then return to her home. This text has an implied possibility of failure to affirm (or survive the false affirmation of) this oath. The Akkadian text does not say how that failure might be recognized, but the parallel Hebrew text suggests one possibility. We may find in this type of law both an affirmation of the importance of marital fidelity in the ancient world—even in Babylon!—as well as a measure of protection for a woman under false accusation. Without limiting legislation such as this, presumably the husband might have done her physical harm—or even killed her—on the sole basis of private feelings of jealousy, real or imagined. The function of law in the ancient Near East was to limit private acts of vengeance and retribution while maintaining propriety and civil order. The fascinating comparison of this text from the Code of Hammurabi with Numbers 5 is the paucity of information concerning the oath-ceremony in the Babylonian temple compared to the unusual richness of the text in Scripture.

14–15 The husband's "feelings of jealousy" (v.14) may have been provoked on the basis of good cause, and the issue must need to be faced; the concern is not just for the bruised feelings of the husband but is ultimately based on the reality of God's dwelling among his people (v.3). Yet the chapter has a strong and serious thrust to it that is designed to prevent a childish, self-centered charge of unfaithfulness. As in Babylonian law, this text was not to be used as a pretext by a capricious, petty, or malevolent husband to badger a good woman. Everything about the text speaks of seriousness, intention, and the presence of the Lord in the process.

The use of the word "impure" (v.14) shows the subject matter of this chapter is of a piece; the purity of the camp of the people whom God indwells is the burden of the text. Further, the religious nature of the text is seen in the presentation of the woman under accusation to the priest (v.15). The actions presented in this chapter seem to be severe and harsh. Perhaps we should imagine the consequences on a woman rightly or falsely charged with adultery by an angry husband in a context in which there was no provision for her guilt or innocence to be demonstrated. That she was taken to the priest is finally an act of mercy.

This chapter provides abundant insight into the role of ritual in ancient Near Eastern thinking, practices remote to the Western reader but more common in certain Eastern and (especially) African peoples. The text is of special interest to those who search for what they believe to be remnants of primitive rites within the books of Moses. Each element of the ritual is charged with meaning, though we may not understand all the meaning today. Yet we need to take our lead from the text, not from supposed African or even ancient Near Eastern parallels. This passage is not an ordeal of death; the Hebrew woman does not cast herself into the sacred river or drink a magic potion. She presents herself before the Lord and his priest for vindication or condemnation; the results will be seen in the future in her own body (see below).

The gravity of the ritual for a suspected faithless wife shows that the Torah regards marital infidelity most seriously. Such was not just a concern of a jealous husband; the entire community was affected by this breach of faith. Hence the judgment was in the context of the community. Contemporary attitudes that suggest sexual infidelity is a minor, personal matter are far removed from the teaching of Scripture. This celebrated text is subject to much discussion these days in which the issues of women and men continue to be debated within the circle of faith. With respect to women, this text may be viewed constructively and sympathetically or negatively and angrily. The negative, angry approach tends to focus on the obvious inequities inherent in the situation. The husband of a woman may shame her publicly and force her to a rigorous, demeaning religious trial merely on the (unfounded) suspicion of a misdeed on her part of marital faithlessness. She may have presented no evidence whatsoever; merely the thought on the part of the husband is sufficient to bring her to trial. Further, there is no mention whatsoever of the guilt, trial, and judgment of the man this woman is supposed to have been involved with—all the weight of guilt, shame, trial, and judgment rest on the shoulders of the woman under accusation. Again, the accusation is by her husband, a presentation suggestive of intense marital discord.

There is, however, another manner of approach to this and similar passages. The alternative approach, as noted even with reference to the Babylonian law, is to suggest the passage is a limitation on an angry, suspicious husband—a protection of the wife from his abusive hand. Were there not such a provision of this text in a male-dominant culture, we may suppose that an angry, suspicious husband might strike out against his wife without any sure reason for his angry suspicions, harm her physically and mentally, and even take her life. Certainly there have been men throughout history who have behaved in just this manner. But God reaches out through Moses and the gift of the Torah—and with the precedent of ancient Near Eastern law!—and has a means of escape for a woman under suspicion of unfaithfulness by a jealous husband. The trial she is taken to is not a kangaroo court; it is in the precincts of the tabernacle, under the jurisdiction of the priests, in concert with a solemn sacrifice—she places herself under the hand of the Lord.

The woman who has been brought to such a place will not take this issue lightly. Public humiliation, shame, anger with her spouse, and exposure before priests and people were all terrifying prospects. But then neither would her husband take these issues lightly. For he was not just spreading rumors nor digging at his wife in the privacy of their home. He, too, was coming before the Lord, and he, too, might be judged. Hence the better approach to this text is not one of primitive magic or of rampant male dominance. It is another expression of the mercy of God to women who are so often abused by prideful men. Here is a means of escape from suspicion and evasion of punishment. If the woman was indeed guilty of unfaithfulness, then the husband was vindicated. This was important, not just for the pique he might be feeling, but for the sense of the ongoing stability of the family. If a woman was unfaithful to her husband, she might be carrying the child of another man; and the rights of inheritance in a tribe/clan/family setting might become hopelessly enmeshed in the complexities of family relationships that are common in modern society (and soap operas) but unusual in earlier days.

But if the woman was innocent, then her husband would have his reasons for jealousy alleviated. Again, this is a limitation on his jealous nature. Most men, we suspect, would be very careful before pressing the issue. The results could be disastrous for themselves.

(ii) *The curse of the oath*

5:16–22

[16]" 'The priest shall bring her and have her stand before the LORD.
[17]Then he shall take some holy water in a clay jar and put some dust
from the tabernacle floor into the water. [18]After the priest has had the
woman stand before the LORD, he shall loosen her hair and place in her
hands the reminder offering, the grain offering for jealousy, while he
himself holds the bitter water that brings a curse. [19]Then the priest shall
put the woman under oath and say to her, "If no other man has slept
with you and you have not gone astray and become impure while
married to your husband, may this bitter water that brings a curse not
harm you. [20]But if you have gone astray while married to your husband
and you have defiled yourself by sleeping with a man other than your
husband"—[21]here the priest is to put the woman under this curse of the
oath—"may the LORD cause your people to curse and denounce you
when he causes your thigh to waste away and your abdomen to swell.
[22]May this water that brings a curse enter your body so that your
abdomen swells and your thigh wastes away."

" 'Then the woman is to say, "Amen. So be it."

16 The central phrasing of this text is that the priest shall bring the woman to stand before the Lord. The repetition in v.18 is for emphasis. These phrases demand that we distance ourselves from the approach of some interpreters who suggest that this passage is merely an adventure in magic and potions or psychology and manipulation. The biblical phrasing demands a theological understanding of the woman's judgment. Further, that she is brought before the Lord helps again to demonstrate the concept of purity and the proper connection of this law with the two earlier laws of the chapter.

17–18 Admittedly, the wording of v.17 (cf. v.23) seems like what we might imagine a magical rite to be. Taking holy water, adding dust, and then mixing a doubtful drink seems to be a world away from things we understand. Many interpreters assume that the addition of the dust from the floor to the holy water is what makes that water "bitter" (v.18). Yet that seems most unlikely. A small amount of soil from the floor of the tabernacle was not likely to bring about a "bitter" taste to the water. Rather, we should think of the notion of the holiness of the place, hence, the holiness of the ground on which the tabernacle is placed. It is holy dust that is added to holy water, not to change the taste, but to emphasize the holiness of the matter.

In v.18 we learn the woman is made to loosen her hair. This action may be a sign of openness on her part. In the solemn place she found herself, with holy priests and holy drinks, the tendency for this woman might be to shrink away, to cover herself with her garments. She is not to do so, however. She is to be presented in a manner of openness before the Lord. This loosening of the hair would be for the guilty woman an expectation of judgment and mourning (see Lev 13:45; 21:10). For the innocent wife, who had nothing to fear but the glory of the Lord to demonstrate, the loosening of her hair is a strengthening action of feminine personhood in the Holy Place.

The terminology that bitter water brings a curse is problematic. The Hebrew phrase could also be translated "the curse-bringing water of bitterness." It is not just that the water was bitter tasting but that this water had the potential of bearing with it a bitter curse. That this potion was neither simply a tool of magic nor merely a psychological device to determine stress is to be seen in the repeated emphasis on the role of the Lord in the proceedings (vv.16, 18, 21, 25). That is, the verdict of the woman was precipitated by her physiological and psychological responses to the bitter water, but the judgment was from the Lord. The bitterness of the water was potential, not actual; the cursing associated with the water was also potential, not essential. The water was holy, set apart for specific function in the worship of God. But it was not necessarily of a bad taste. Again, the phrase may be rendered in somewhat an expansive manner: "the water that may result in bitterness and provoke a profound curse."

19–20 The priest presents two possibilities. First, the woman is truly innocent (v.19). In this case his specific prayer to the Lord is that the water with the potential of bitterness not harm her. The priest's words to the innocent woman assure her of no harm from the bitter water. If she is truly guilty of the deed that her husband suspects (v.20), then the full onus of the curse-bearing waters will come to her, enter her body, descend through her intestines, and be the physical means the Lord will use to produce a physical change in her body.

21–22 Verse 21 describes the physical change: "your thigh to waste away and your abdomen to swell." The NIV margin has "causes you to have a miscarrying womb and barrenness." The figurative language here (and in vv.22, 27) speaks of the loss of the capacity for childbearing (and, if pregnant at the time of her judgment, the miscarriage of the child); this is demonstrated by giving attention to the opposite case in the determination of the fate of a woman wrongly charged ("she will be cleared of guilt and will be able to have children," v.28). For a woman in the ancient Near East to be denied the ability to bear children was a personal loss of inestimable proportion. It was in bearing children that a woman's worth was realized. This was a grievous punishment indeed!

We reject, then, those interpretations that suggest the woman who was guilty would drop dead following her drinking of the potion. Rather, like the woman in the Babylonian text, she may return to her home to await the outcome of the oath. If she was innocent of infidelity, she should count on progeny. This means, of course, she returns to her husband's embrace. If she was guilty of infidelity but not caught in the act, then she would suffer debilitating physical symptoms that would prohibit successful pregnancies. Again, this also presumes that she returns to the embrace of her husband. She would then bear her guilt in her body and the inner chambers of her heart. In either case the woman was to hear the words of the curse, in the midst of the solemn precincts, and then to bring that potential curse on herself by saying to the

Lord and his priest, "Amen. So be it" (v.22). The double "Amen" (lit. Heb.) is her signal that she understands the issues and is in agreement with the judgment—or escape from judgment—that will come into her body.

(iii) *The bitter waters*

5:23–28

[23] " 'The priest is to write these curses on a scroll and then wash them off into the bitter water. [24] He shall have the woman drink the bitter water that brings a curse, and this water will enter her and cause bitter suffering. [25] The priest is to take from her hands the grain offering for jealousy, wave it before the LORD and bring it to the altar. [26] The priest is then to take a handful of the grain offering as a memorial offering and burn it on the altar; after that, he is to have the woman drink the water. [27] If she has defiled herself and been unfaithful to her husband, then when she is made to drink the water that brings a curse, it will go into her and cause bitter suffering; her abdomen will swell and her thigh waste away, and she will become accursed among her people. [28] If, however, the woman has not defiled herself and is free from impurity, she will be cleared of guilt and will be able to have children.

23–28 The language of this section is somewhat repetitive of the earlier paragraphs. These repetitive and similar phrasings have prompted many critical scholars to posit varied strata in the text, inelegantly pieced together. The tendency today, however, is to view the text as a whole. In this approach the repetitions and similar phrasings are marks of literary purpose and structure (see, e.g., Michael Fishbane, "Accusations of Adultery: A Study of Law and Scribal Practice in Numbers 5:11–31," HUCA 45 [1974]: 25–45; Herbert Chanan Brichto, "The Case of the Sota and a Reconsideration of Biblical 'Law'," HUCA 46 [1975]: 55–70; and esp. Tikva Frymer-Kensky, "The Strange Case of the Suspected Sotah: [Numbers V 11–31]," VetTest 34 [1984]: 11–26).

Verses 23–28 give the final step in the procedure. After the words of the cursing had been announced, the priest would write them on a scroll (or perhaps a wooden tablet) and then blot the letters off into the water. The woman was not only going to hear the words, but in a dramatic, figurative sense she was to drink them. In this way the awful sense of taking the curse into one's own body was realized. The bitterness of the waters, again, was not in their taste but in the potential they bore in their association with the curse attendant to them. The NIV suggests the very drinking of the water would cause suffering: "this water will enter her and cause bitter suffering" (v.24). This phrase may also be read in a more benign manner: "and the waters that cause curses shall enter her for bitterness." The bitterness was not in taste, convulsions, or physical shock but in the latent sense of the potential judgment on her body of childlessness. "Bitterness" is a most appropriate term for just this potential judgment. The innocent woman would not suffer the bitterness of the water, for she was innocent of the curses associated with it.

(iv) *The summary of the law of jealousy*

5:29–31

[29] " 'This, then, is the law of jealousy when a woman goes astray and defiles herself while married to her husband, [30] or when feelings of jealousy come over a man because he suspects his wife. The priest is to

> have her stand before the LORD and is to apply this entire law to her. 31 The husband will be innocent of any wrongdoing, but the woman will bear the consequences of her sin.' "

29–31 The summary statement of this law is stated in terms of the woman who has been rightly accused by her husband. Again, in this summary statement there is repetition and recapitulation of dominant themes from the involved legislation—typical devices of the writers of biblical prose texts. The section ends ominously, as the chapter began. The chapter has a cohesion to it of instances relating to the maintaining of purity within the camp. The importance of marital fidelity in this passage should not be lost on modern readers in a time in which such ideas are quaint but irrelevant. Numerous NT texts may be cited (esp. 1 Cor 5) affirming God's continuing affirmation of the seventh commandment: You are not to commit adultery.

(2) *The vow of the Nazirite and the Aaronic Benediction (6:1–27)*

Numbers 6 continues the theme of the purification of the people of the new nation in two disparate manners. First is the opportunity for an individual to make an extraordinary vow of religious devotion as a distinctive way of showing separation to the Lord for a limited period of time. The chapter then provides the regular manner in which the priests were to invoke the blessing of the Lord on the entire community. The text thus moves from the particular to the general, from the unusual to the regular. In this way the issue of special relationship with God is presented in a comprehensive manner.

(a) *The vow of the Nazirite (6:1–21)*

The special, unusual vow of the Nazirite is the first focus of the chapter.

(i) *The basic prohibition against wine*

6:1–4

> 1 The LORD said to Moses, 2 "Speak to the Israelites and say to them: 'If a man or woman wants to make a special vow, a vow of separation to the LORD as a Nazirite, 3 he must abstain from wine and other fermented drink and must not drink vinegar made from wine or from other fermented drink. He must not drink grape juice or eat grapes or raisins. 4 As long as he is a Nazirite, he must not eat anything that comes from the grapevine, not even the seeds or skins.

1–2 It is not generally recognized that these vows of special devotion to God could be made by a woman as well as a man. Many simply assume that the religious vows of the Nazirite were intended for males alone. However, this text expressly begins, "If a man or woman." Thus women were not precluded from this vow (contra the pronoun renderings in most EVV; cf. 30:1–16, which speaks of the differences between the vows of men and women).

The Hebrew text uses an unusually strong verb in describing the vow of the Nazirite in the phrasing "wants to make a special vow." The verb *pālā'* in the Hiphil means "to make a hard, difficult vow." This verb in the Niphal is used extensively throughout the Bible with God as subject and is often rendered by words of wonder or amazement (cf. Exod 3:20, "the wonders that I will perform"; Ps 118:23, "it is marvelous in our eyes"). In our passage, as in Leviticus 27:2, the Hiphil is used of an extraordinary vow of a devotee of Yahweh. This vow, then, does not describe a routine matter or even an expected act of devotion one might make from time to time. It is an act of unusual devotion to God, based perhaps on an intense desire to demonstrate to the Lord one's utter separation to him.

The term "Nazirite," from the Hebrew *nāzîr,* describes this person who has marked out a special time of separation or consecration for a specific period of unusual devotion to God. This text speaks of a restricted period of time for the Nazirite vow, but there were some persons who took the vow for a lifetime. The word Nazirite is sometimes confused with Nazarene, the word used to describe Jesus in terms of his hometown origin (see Matt 2:23; Mark 14:67; 16:6; Acts 24:5). While these words are based on the same root (*nāzar,* "to vow"), they are distinctive words.

In discussions of the Nazirite, attention is usually given to the prohibitions demanded on the person who takes this vow. Yet more important is the positive "separation to Yahweh" that the vow afforded (vv.2, 8). This is where the text lays its primary stress; the prohibitions were means of achieving the sense of separation. The Nazirite vow was not just an act of superior self-discipline, an achieving of a spiritual machismo; it was to be regarded as a supreme act of total devotion to the person and work of the Lord that would override certain normal and expected patterns of behavior.

The person who made pledges to a particular time of special devotion to the Lord as a *nāzîr* had to face three very demanding limitations: (1) absolute abstinence from all produce of the vine, (2) total forswearing of trimming of the hair, and (3) utter separation from contamination by any contact with a dead body. Thus three areas of life were mandated for the Nazirite during the period of his vow: diet, appearance, and associations. Every Israelite was under regulations in these general areas; for the Nazirite each of these regulations was heightened. Leviticus 11 details the dietary restrictions for the nation as an act of daily holiness (the practice of being distinct, separate). For the Nazirite one major clean food was prohibited during the course of one's vow. This chapter is not a tract against the drinking of wine by spiritual people. Rather, it concerns a specific aspect of the expected (good!) diet that was voluntarily foresworn for a period of time as a physical reminder of the duty of devotion to God. After the period of the consecration was over, wine (and all grape products) was permitted again (v.20). An analogy may be found in the practice of some Christians to forego certain good foods during the period of Lent as prods to spiritual devotion to Christ in the special period of remembrance of his sufferings.

3–4 The first paragraph contains prohibitions concerning the produce of the vine. All intoxicating drinks (the Hebrew words sometimes translated "wine and strong drink" form an hendiadys, meaning "all intoxicants") and everything associated with them were prohibited the Nazirite during this period of vow. The term "fermented drink" (v.3) is the Hebrew *šēḵār,* a word often used in association with "wine" (*yayin*). *Šēḵār* is often found in texts condemning drunkenness (see 1 Sam 1:15; Prov 20:1; Isa 5:11, 22; 28:7; 56:12; Mic 2:11). But this word is also used in other texts describing the normal, moderate drinking (along with wine) that was part of the expected common food of the people of Israel, which they did not have opportunity to enjoy during the desert experience (see Deut 29:6), as well as for sacral meals enhanced with wine and fermented drinks in the true worship of God (see Num 28:7; Deut 14:26). Further, *šēḵār* could be used in the drink offering (Num 28:7) in the worship of the Lord. Since *yayin* is the fermented product of the vine, we may assume that *šēḵār* is the fermented product of the field, i.e., beer (see KB, p. 972). Again, the usual association with this word is drunkenness, but this is not a necessary association. The Nazirite was to abstain from both wine and beer and from everything associated with the wine grape (v.4).

Verse 4 prohibits the Nazirite from partaking of anything that comes from the grapevine, not just the fermented beverages, but even the vinegar that results when such products sour. Moreover, the prohibition included fresh grape juice, grapes either fresh or dried, and even the seed and skin of the grape. It is unclear why the products of the grapevine are specifically forbidden to the Nazirite. It may be that the forbidding of all products of the grapevine is a way of saying that he or she was not to have even a remote association with wine. The Hebrew words translated by the NIV as "seeds and skins" are uncertain in meaning but refer to the most insignificant products of the vine. The prohibition could not have been more inclusive. The Nazirite was not even "to smell the cork," as it were.

Notes

---

2 The Hebrew term נָזִיר (*nāzîr*, "consecrated one," "devotee," "Nazirite") has two other uses in the MT besides the person who takes the special vow intended in this chapter; these other uses help us to understand its special meaning here. Joseph is called a *nāzîr* in the blessings of Jacob on his sons (Gen 49). Joseph was given the chief blessing of his father. He was regarded as a *nāzîr* in the sense of "a prince, a consecrated person": "Let all these [blessings] rest on the head of Joseph,/ on the brow of the prince among his brothers" (Gen 49:26). The word is also used of "untended" vines during the time of the sabbatical year (Lev 25:5, 11). Presumably these vines are termed *nāzîr* because they were not tended or trimmed, just as the Nazirite was not to trim his or her hair during the period of special vow. Thus a *nāzîr* was a person who was specially consecrated to the Lord and who was marked out as distinct by his or her unusual manner of hairstyle.

(ii) *Basic prohibitions concerning hair and dead bodies*

6:5–8

5" 'During the entire period of his vow of separation no razor may be used on his head. He must be holy until the period of his separation to the LORD is over; he must let the hair of his head grow long. 6 Throughout the period of his separation to the LORD he must not go near a dead body. 7 Even if his own father or mother or brother or sister dies, he must not make himself ceremonially unclean on account of them, because the symbol of his separation to God is on his head. 8 Throughout the period of his separation he is consecrated to the LORD.

5 A second voluntary prohibition for the Nazirite was the normal and expected trimming of the hair. During the period of one's Nazirite vow, the hair was not to be trimmed at all (see Judg 13:5 for the account of Samson). The unexpectedly long hair of a Nazirite man was a physical mark of his vow of special "separation" (*nēzer*, from the same root as the term Nazirite) to the Lord; as distinctive, say, as the habit of a monk or a nun. It is misleading to call these persons the "monks and nuns" of Israel, however, as they were not required to be celibate. Since women in most cultures wear their hair longer than men do, we may presume that the Nazirite woman might not only have let her hair grow long but may have allowed it to remain relatively unkempt (compare, again, the use of *nāzîr* of untended vines, Lev 25:5, 11), or perhaps she let it hang loose as opposed to putting it up. Otherwise, it is difficult to see how the (unusually) long hair of a woman would be a distinctive sign of her period of vow. The Nazirite was to be "holy" (v.5); the untrimmed (and perhaps unkempt) hair would be a special mark of one who was so set apart. (Leviticus 21:5 prohibited the priests of Israel from certain types of shaving of the head or the beard, presumably in imitation of pagan mantic practices.) The Nazirite was not to trim his or her hair at all. Compare as well the shaving of the entire body of the Levite at the time of his initial consecration in the service of the Lord in the holy tabernacle (8:7). The paragraph ends with the primary issue of the Nazirite relationship: he was consecrated to the Lord (v.8).

6–8 The third prohibition for the Nazirite concerned physical contact with dead bodies (see comment on 5:2 for general contamination by contact with dead bodies). For the Nazirite the prohibition extended even to the deceased within his own family (v.7). The listing of family members who might die during the time of one's vow makes this text particularly piquant; this text stings the soul. In this way the general commands become intense; here a person faced heart-rending decisions not to do normal things in times of great grief because of a prior decision based on a desire for a time for an intense consecration to the Lord. No one making a Nazirite vow would be able to know for certain what the personal demands might be in this regard. Even a priest was expected to care for the dead body of a close relative (Lev 21:1–3). But the Nazirite could not care for such a body, no matter how beloved the person, or he would bring contamination on himself. The vow of the Nazirite was most serious indeed! Notice, however, that the Nazirite was not prohibited sexual enjoyment, as is commonly assumed.

(iii) *The specific prohibition concerning accidental death*

6:9–12

> 9 " 'If someone dies suddenly in his presence, thus defiling the hair he has dedicated, he must shave his head on the day of his cleansing—the seventh day. 10 Then on the eighth day he must bring two doves or two young pigeons to the priest at the entrance to the Tent of Meeting. 11 The priest is to offer one as a sin offering and the other as a burnt offering to make atonement for him because he sinned by being in the presence of the dead body. That same day he is to consecrate his head. 12 He must dedicate himself to the LORD for the period of his separation and must bring a year-old male lamb as a guilt offering. The previous days do not count, because he became defiled during his separation.

9–12 This paragraph makes the demands of the Nazirite even more severe, as it speaks of the accidental death of a person in the proximity of the person under vow (v.9). In this case the accidental death makes the Nazirite unclean, guilty of sin before the Lord. The basic provisions of the Nazirite vow concerned areas where he was able to make conscious decisions. This section deals with the unexpected and the unplanned events of daily living. The particularity of the hair, the *nēzer* ("dedicated," v.9), is the special focus of the person's contamination. This dedicated hair was to be shaved on the seventh day of the Nazirite's rite of purification. Then, following obligatory offerings of birds (the less expensive offerings) for sin (v.8) and burnt offerings and a lamb (the more expensive) for guilt offerings, the person would rededicate himself to the Lord for the period of time that had originally been planned (v.11); the time spent up to that point would no longer count (v.12) because of the contamination, no matter how inadvertent. No wonder this vow is termed a "hard vow" (*pālā'*, "wants to make a special vow," v.2); no wonder that all vows to the Lord were to be made with great caution (Prov 20:25). The terrible tragedy of the life of Samson was that he never took his vow to God serious until the end of his sorry life.

(iv) *The ritual for the completion of the vow*

6:13–20

13" 'Now this is the law for the Nazirite when the period of his separation is over. He is to be brought to the entrance to the Tent of Meeting. 14There he is to present his offerings to the LORD: a year-old male lamb without defect for a burnt offering, a year-old ewe lamb without defect for a sin offering, a ram without defect for a fellowship offering, 15together with their grain offerings and drink offerings, and a basket of bread made without yeast—cakes made of fine flour mixed with oil, and wafers spread with oil.

16" 'The priest is to present them before the LORD and make the sin offering and the burnt offering. 17He is to present the basket of unleavened bread and is to sacrifice the ram as a fellowship offering to the LORD, together with its grain offering and drink offering.

18" 'Then at the entrance to the Tent of Meeting, the Nazirite must shave off the hair that he dedicated. He is to take the hair and put it in the fire that is under the sacrifice of the fellowship offering.

19" 'After the Nazirite has shaved off the hair of his dedication, the priest is to place in his hands a boiled shoulder of the ram, and a cake and a wafer from the basket, both made without yeast. 20The priest shall then wave them before the LORD as a wave offering; they are holy and belong to the priest, together with the breast that was waved and the thigh that was presented. After that, the Nazirite may drink wine.

13–20 The offerings of the Nazirite at the completion of the period of the vow (v.13) were extensive, expensive, and expressive of the spirit of total commitment to Yahweh during this period of special devotion. In addition to these several offerings (vv.14–17), there was also the presentation for burning of the sign of the vow, the hair (*nēzer*) of the Nazirite. Burning the hair signified the completion of the vow. That it was burned and not kept as a trophy or a memorial demonstrates that the act of the Nazirite was in devotion to the Lord.

The rites described in these verses are very solemn and the prescriptions precise. The three sacrifices were a male lamb for the burnt offering, a ewe lamb for the sin offering, and a ram for the fellowship offering, each with the accompanying grain offerings and libations. These sacrifices were very dear; it was not a trifling thing to take on oneself the vow of a Nazirite.

The libation, or "drink offering" (*nese<u>k</u>*, v.15), is particularly interesting in the context of the Nazirite vow. Since the Nazirite was prohibited any contact whatsoever with wine and vine products during the time of his vow, one might conclude that such things are essentially evil in themselves. However, the wine offering was presented on the altar to the Lord along with the clean animals and the associated grain offerings mixed with olive oil; so such a conclusion is misguided. The *nesek* offering of wine poured out on the altar of the Lord is found from patriarchal times (see Gen 35:14) and became part of the religious system commanded by the Lord to Moses (see Exod 29:40; Lev 23:13, 18, 37; Num 4:7; 15:5, 7; 28:7; 29:6 et al.). The conclusion respecting the significance of the prohibition of wine and beer to the Nazirite during the time of his vow must take into account the use of wine in the Nazirite's rite of vow completion as well as the notice that at the end of the rites of purification the Nazirite was then free to drink wine again (v.20).

The public presentation of the Nazirite by the priest at the Tent of Meeting before the Lord shows that this type of vow was not just a personal, private, and secret thing. Any public rite such as these verses describe suggests that the vow was also a matter of public knowledge. Presumably, the community could be supportive of the person during the time of his vow. But more important in this text than the public aspect is the personal presentation before the Lord at the Tent of Meeting (see vv.13–14, 16–17, 20). This vow, though in a public context, is an intensely personal act of relationship with the Lord, properly entered into only with a profound sense of one's coming into the presence of the Holy One.

(v) *The summary of the Nazirite vow*

6:21

> 21 " 'This is the law of the Nazirite who vows his offering to the LORD in accordance with his separation, in addition to whatever else he can afford. He must fulfill the vow he has made, according to the law of the Nazirite.' "

21 Summary statements such as this serve not only to end a section but to solemnize the contents of the section. This verse also indicates that the previous sacrifices and offerings are the minimal demands and that additional offerings might also be expected. The costs of the Nazirite vow were considerable and varied. In addition to numerous personal and private feelings and discomforts, a significant property outlay was demanded as well. Again, the Nazirite vow was not a demand of God on his people; it was a provision for men or women who voluntarily desired an unusually demanding means of showing their devotion to him.

(b) *The Aaronic Benediction*

6:22–27

> 22 The LORD said to Moses, 23 "Tell Aaron and his sons, 'This is how you are to bless the Israelites. Say to them:
>
> 24 " ' "The LORD bless you
> and keep you;
>
> 25 the LORD make his face shine upon you
> and be gracious to you;
>
> 26 the LORD turn his face toward you
> and give you peace.' "
>
> 27 "So they will put my name on the Israelites, and I will bless them."

In the well-known words of the Aaronic Benediction, we find a broad, national complement to the restrictive words of the Nazirite vow that were so very personal and demanding. These words are expansive and gracious, and they are inclusive of the whole community. They are also a part of the purification of the camp that the Book of Numbers features in these several chapters. The reader is also arrested by the form of these words. Their poetic cast not only makes them more memorable but contributes significantly to the aesthetics of the prayer and draws one in more deeply to its meaning. The function of poetry is to intensify feeling and deepen response.

22–23 The words of the prayer of vv.24–26 are termed the Aaronic Benediction. In some ways these lovely words may be thought of as the Lord's Prayer of the Old Testament (see Matt 6:9). The priests were told here how to pray for God's blessing on the people in the same way that the disciples were instructed how to pray for God's blessing in their lives by the Savior. Perhaps the most impressive aspect of this prayer is that it is a provision for God's desire to bless his people. Blessing is his idea, his purpose. It is not something his people must beg for, but it is the outreaching of his grace.

The supreme beauty of the words of this prayer (evident in translation) and the formulaic words of introduction (vv.22–23) and conclusion (v.27) give ample warrant for the concept of fixed, repeated prayers in spiritual worship. Some people suggest that only spontaneous prayer is "real" prayer; verses such as these show that such sentiment is not correct.

The pattern of the words of this prayer is exquisite; the language is poetic and emotive. There are three lines each with the divine name Yahweh ("LORD"); the repetition of the divine name gives force to the expression of v.27—"So they will put my name on the Israelites"—and is certainly fitting with the (later) Christian revelation of the Three Persons of the Trinity. Each line conveys two elements of benediction, and the lines are progressively longer. In the Hebrew text the first line has three words (in the pattern 2 // 1), the second has five words (in the pattern 4 // 1), and the third has seven words (in the pattern 4 // 3). If one does not count the threefold use of the divine name, there are twelve words to the prayer, which suggest the twelve tribes of Israel.

This prayer has a luminous sense about it. It speaks of the light of the presence of the Lord in a vivid, anthropomorphic manner; but there is a sense that the prayer itself is light-giving. This prayer prayed in faith expects God to respond by drawing near and enfolding one in his grace. In fact, the concluding words promise that he will bless his people. The Hebrew wording is emphatic: "and *I* will bless them" (v.27).

24 The first line literally reads, "May Yahweh bless you and may he keep you." While these words are directed to the entire community, the pronouns are singular. This is characteristic of covenantal language: The Lord blesses the whole by blessing the individuals; he blesses the individuals by blessing the whole. The invocation of the blessing of God reveals that the covenant community knows who they are: they are the people who are particularly blessed of the Lord because of his own choice of the patriarchs, Abraham, Isaac, and Jacob, and because of the solemn relationship he has entered into with the fathers, mothers, and their children. "The LORD bless you and keep you" are words of reminder, words of attestation of promise. These are words whereby the community says, "Yes, Amen!" to God's promise, where they request from his presence the continuity of the blessing that he has already begun. The buttressing words "and keep you" further explain his blessing. God's intention for his people is for their good; he will preserve them to enjoy that good.

25 The words "make his face shine upon you" take us back to the experience of Moses on Mount Sinai. There the theophany of the Lord appeared to Moses (see Exod 34:29–35), and he experienced in a dramatic and direct manner God's presence. As his glory had caused Moses' face to shine, so the LORD desires to make his presence known to all his people. When Moses was on the mountain, it was in the context of terror; all the physical signs of the theophany of God in Exodus 19–20 provoked horror on the part of the people. But God had come down in grace; his revelation was of mercy. Hence we have the splendidly suitable tie of the light of his face and the grace of his presence in the words: "[May] Yahweh make his face shine upon you/ and be gracious to you."

Again, and throughout the prayer, the pronoun "you" is in the singular in the MT; this is a prayer for the community, but its force is to be realized in the life of the individual. Only in the introductory and concluding formulas are the plurals used.

26 The climax of the prayer is: "[May] Yahweh turn ['lift up'] his face toward you/ and give you peace." The Hebrew word *šālôm* (lit., "shalom"; NIV, "peace") is here seen in its most expressive fullness, not just as an absence of war, but as the positive state of rightness and the fullness of well being. This kind of peace comes only from the Lord. The expression "turn his face" suggests pleasure and affection. This terminology has the functional equivalent of the word "smile." Here the people are led to pray that the Lord will turn his face toward them in a gracious smile! (Mayer I. Gruber, "The Many Faces of Hebrew 'lift up the face'," ZAW 95, 2 [1983]: 253). We may thus translate this text: "May Yahweh smile on you, and may he grant you well being!"

The words of this prayer are first introduced by the monocolon "[And] the LORD said to Moses" (v.22), showing both that this is a new section in the book (see 6:1) and that it is a divine communication. The idea of invoking God's blessing, presence, and smile on his people is not a creation of the people or a development of the priests but a gracious provision by God himself. The words of the prayer itself are framed by an introductory formula (v.23) and a conclusion formula (v.27); these framing sections highlight the words of the prayer and provide its proper setting.

The prayer was a priestly function, for the priests were God's gift to the nation to stand between himself and his people. The people might come to God through the agency of the priests, and God would speak to his people through these priests. Further, without these instructions the priests might have sought the mantic acts of their neighbors as a means of seeking the pleasure of the Lord. God's intention is to bring his pleasure to his people; thus he presents the means whereby that may be sought and received.

27 The words of the conclusion formula may be the most surprising of all; for here the Lord says that this prayer is the means of placing his name on his people. Since the name Yahweh is itself a term of blessing whereby the eternal God states his relatedness to his people, these words of blessing could not be more appropriate. The prayer is designed to help the people experience the reality of the blessing of the Lord whose delight is to bring that blessing near; his promise is that he will do just that very thing.

Surely this is a prayer that needs to be recovered by the believing community today.

Christians may read these words and find in them, not only the Lord's special covenantal relationship with Israel at Mount Sinai, but also a reflection of the covenantal relationship God has with his people, the church, through the work of Savior Jesus, in whom we have experienced preeminently the smile of God. The threefold invocation of the name of the Lord is not going to be lost on Christian readers either:

> May the Lord Yahweh as Father, Son, and Spirit
> bless his people and keep them,
> cause them to know his presence and his grace,
> and allow them to sense his smile and his peace.
> Amen!

(3) *The offerings at the dedication of the tabernacle (7:1–89)*

In the stylized organization of the Book of Numbers, the presentation of the concept of the purity of the camp moves from the prayer for the blessing of the Lord on his people to the blessings of the people that are brought to him. Chapter 7 is a text of gifts—monumental gifts—presented with great pageantry and significant pomp. Here is a festival of offerings to the Lord stretching over twelve days. The chapter stands as a monument to the pleasure of God who took enjoyment from the repetition—for these were grand gifts in the good days of his early relationship with his people. These were the honeymoon days of the marital relationship of the Lord and Israel (see Jer 2:2–3). Each of the gifts is relished, as presentations by a lover in the early days of the bliss of marriage.

(a) *The presentation of carts and oxen*

7:1–3

[1]When Moses finished setting up the tabernacle, he anointed it and consecrated it and all its furnishings. He also anointed and consecrated the altar and all its utensils. [2]Then the leaders of Israel, the heads of families who were the tribal leaders in charge of those who were counted, made offerings. [3]They brought as their gifts before the LORD six covered carts and twelve oxen—an ox from each leader and a cart from every two. These they presented before the tabernacle.

1 Exodus 40:1–33 presents the prose description of the setting up of the tabernacle. That chapter ends with the report of the cloud covering and the presence of the Lord filling the tabernacle (v.34). With much repetition of language, chapter 7 records the magnificent (and identical) gifts given to the Lord for tabernacle service by the leaders of each of the Twelve Tribes. It is wonderfully fitting that the record of these gifts in Numbers follows the text of the Aaronic Benediction (vv.24–26): in response to God's solemn promise to bless his people, they bring their blessing to him—magnificent gifts in twelve sequential days of celebrative pageantry.

The terminology of v.1 is significant. First, we observe that this is the first major section of Numbers to begin as a narrative text. Each of the other sections has begun either with the introductory monocolon of divine revelation (e.g., "And Yahweh spoke to Moses"; see 1:1; 2:1; 3:11, 14, 44; 4:1; 5:1, 5, 11; 6:1, 22) or with a statement of background fact (see 3:1, "Now this is the family history of Aaron and Moses"). Chapter 7 begins with a narrative action-sequence pattern: "When Moses finished . . . , he anointed. . . . Then the leaders . . . made offerings." G.J. Wenham has nicely summarized the relationship of the dated events of Numbers 7–9 with the events of Exodus and Leviticus. The following chart of the events of the first two months of the second year of Israel's Exodus is adapted from his book (p. 91):

Date (in second year)	*Event*	*Text*
Day 1, first month	Completion of tabernacle	Exod 40:2; Num 7:1
	Laws for offerings begin	Lev 1:1
	Offerings for altar begin	Num 7:3
	Ordination of priests begins	Lev 8:1
Day 8, first month	Ordination of priests completed	Lev 9:1
Day 12, first month	Offerings for altar completed	Num 7:78
	Appointment of Levites	Num 8:5
Day 14, first month	Second Passover	Num 9:2
Day 1, second month	Census begins	Num 1:1
Day 14, second month	Passover for those unclean	Num 9:11
Day 20, second month	The cloud moves, the camp begins its trek	Num 10:11

The focus in the chapter is on the tabernacle, the "dwelling place of God," and the altar, the point of approach to God's dwelling. After Moses had completed supervising the construction and erection of the sacred tent and its altar, he anointed and consecrated them for the Lord's special services. The verb "anoint" is the same term used for the anointing of special persons (see Notes). The second verb used of the dedication rites is "consecrated." It is a declarative action (see Notes), to be noted by those present that the tabernacle and its furnishings and the altar and its implements were no longer common items but were now marked out as special, distinct, and other. The common was now sacred, the ordinary was now set apart to the worship of God.

2–3 Then the leaders of the tribes, whom we have met already in chapters 1 and 2, come forward with their first gifts. The Hebrew word for their gifts is *qorbān,* a noun related to the verb meaning "to bring near" (*qāraḇ,* in the Hiphil). This type of language is particularly apt, for the leaders were "bringing near" to the symbols of God's presence their own gifts. These gifts were necessary and utilitarian. There were six carts, each drawn by a pair of oxen, for the special use of the priests in transporting the elements of the sacred tent and its furnishings when the people would set out on their march toward Canaan. The Hebrew word for "cart" (*ʿagālāh*) is modified by the noun *ṣāḇ* ("litter"), used only here and in Isaiah 66:20. This phrase has traditionally been understood to describe a covered wagon, though the precise meaning of the wording is debated. Covered wagons would certainly be appropriate for transporting the sacred items. I suspect the pairs of oxen were matched and stately, suitably chosen for their significant work.

Notes

1 מָשַׁח (*māšaḥ*) has the basic meaning of "to smear," "to anoint." It can be used of covering a surface with paint (as in Jer 22:14) but is used especially for the anointing of a person or an object with olive oil in a consecration ritual. When done of persons such as priests, kings, and prophets, oil was poured on the head of the sacral person (e.g., Exod 28:41; 1 Kings 1:45; 19:16). When done of objects, the oil could be poured or smeared over the surface of sacred things. Jacob anointed a sacred pillar before the Lord at Bethel (Gen 31:13), and Moses was commanded to anoint the altar of the tabernacle (Exod 29:36). The oil to be used in these consecrating ceremonies is described in Exod 30:23–25. It was an extraordinary oil, blended with exotic spices in exacting proportions and termed "a sacred anointing oil"—the recipe for which was sacrosanct; unauthorized use or duplication was an affront to the holiness of God and was grounds for being cut off from the people of God (v.33).

וַיְקַדֵּשׁ (*wayeqaddēš*, "and [he] consecrated") is a form of the verb קָדַשׁ (*qādaš*, "to be holy"). The Piel stem used here means "to make holy," "to set apart."

(b) *The distribution of the carts and oxen*

7:4–9

4 The LORD said to Moses, 5 "Accept these from them, that they may be used in the work at the Tent of Meeting. Give them to the Levites as each man's work requires."

6 So Moses took the carts and oxen and gave them to the Levites. 7 He gave two carts and four oxen to the Gershonites, as their work required, 8 and he gave four carts and eight oxen to the Merarites, as their work required. They were all under the direction of Ithamar son of Aaron, the priest. 9 But Moses did not give any to the Kohathites, because they were to carry on their shoulders the holy things, for which they were responsible.

4–9 Following the command of God, Moses took these six covered carts and their pairs of oxen and distributed them to the three Levitical families based on their need and their particular responsibilities. Two of the carts and their four oxen he gave to the families of Gershon for their work in transporting the varied curtains of the tabernacle and the courtyard (see 4:24–28); the other four carts and their pairs of oxen went to the families of Merari for their work in transporting the frames, crossbars, posts, bases, ropes, and pegs of the tabernacle and the courtyard (see 4:29–33). Moses made these divisions of carts and oxen based on the needs that each family had for transporting the material of the tabernacle. The Kohathites, therefore, were not given any carts; they were to carry the holy things on their shoulders, with staves placed through the carrying loops (see 4:4–20; esp. vv.6, 8, 11–12, 14). This prohibition of the use of carts for the holiest objects was not followed by David in the first attempt he made to transport the ark to the city of Jerusalem, following the establishment of his kingdom (see 2 Sam 6:3). This untoward act led to the death of Uzzah, who attempted to stay the ark as it seemed about to tumble from the cart (v.7). The lesson was drastic, but David learned from it. He had the priests carry it the second time (v.13).

(c) *The plan of the tribal offerings*

7:10–11

[10]When the altar was anointed, the leaders brought their offerings for its dedication and presented them before the altar. [11]For the LORD had said to Moses, "Each day one leader is to bring his offering for the dedication of the altar."

10–11 The Hebrew text is emphatic in v.11: "And Yahweh said to Moses, one leader for one day, one leader for one day, let them bring their offering near for the dedication of the altar" (pers. tr.). The repetition "one leader for one day" shows the pacing that God required. Each leader's gift was worth a day's celebration. None of the gifts were to be grouped, none of the leaders bunched. Each leader, and the people he represented, was to have his day in the sun—better, his day of approach with significant gifts to the supernal presence of the Lord.

(d) *The offerings of the Twelve Tribes*

7:12–83

[12]The one who brought his offering on the first day was Nahshon son of Amminadab of the tribe of Judah.

[13]His offering was one silver plate weighing a hundred and thirty shekels, and one silver sprinkling bowl weighing seventy shekels, both according to the sanctuary shekel, each filled with fine flour mixed with oil as a grain offering; [14]one gold dish weighing ten shekels, filled with incense; [15]one young bull, one ram and one male lamb a year old, for a burnt offering; [16]one male goat for a sin offering; [17]and two oxen, five rams, five male goats and five male lambs a year old, to be sacrificed as a fellowship offering. This was the offering of Nahshon son of Amminadab.

[18]On the second day Nethanel son of Zuar, the leader of Issachar, brought his offering.

[19]The offering he brought was one silver plate weighing a hundred and thirty shekels, and one silver sprinkling bowl weighing seventy shekels, both according to the sanctuary shekel, each filled with fine flour mixed with oil as a grain offering; [20]one gold dish weighing ten shekels, filled with incense; [21]one young bull, one ram and one male lamb a year old, for a burnt offering; [22]one male goat for a sin offering; [23]and two oxen, five rams, five male goats and five male lambs a year old, to be sacrificed as a fellowship offering. This was the offering of Nethanel son of Zuar.

[24]On the third day, Eliab son of Helon, the leader of the people of Zebulun, brought his offering.

[25]His offering was one silver plate weighing a hundred and thirty shekels, and one silver sprinkling bowl weighing seventy shekels, both according to the sanctuary shekel, each filled with fine flour mixed with oil as a grain offering; [26]one gold dish weighing ten shekels, filled with incense; [27]one young bull, one ram and one male lamb a year old, for a burnt offering; [28]one male goat for a sin offering; [29]and two oxen, five rams, five male goats and five male lambs a year old, to be sacrificed as a fellowship offering. This was the offering of Eliab son of Helon.

[30]On the fourth day Elizur son of Shedeur, the leader of the people of Reuben, brought his offering.

[31]His offering was one silver plate weighing a hundred and thirty
shekels, and one silver sprinkling bowl weighing seventy shekels,
both according to the sanctuary shekel, each filled with fine flour
mixed with oil as a grain offering; [32]one gold dish weighing ten
shekels, filled with incense; [33]one young bull, one ram and one
male lamb a year old, for a burnt offering; [34]one male goat for a sin
offering; [35]and two oxen, five rams, five male goats and five male
lambs a year old, to be sacrificed as a fellowship offering. This was
the offering of Elizur son of Shedeur.

[36]On the fifth day Shelumiel son of Zurishaddai, the leader of the people
of Simeon, brought his offering.

[37]His offering was one silver plate weighing a hundred and thirty
shekels, and one silver sprinkling bowl weighing seventy shekels,
both according to the sanctuary shekel, each filled with fine flour
mixed with oil as a grain offering; [38]one gold dish weighing ten
shekels, filled with incense; [39]one young bull, one ram and one
male lamb a year old, for a burnt offering; [40]one male goat for a sin
offering; [41]and two oxen, five rams, five male goats and five male
lambs a year old, to be sacrificed as a fellowship offering. This was
the offering of Shelumiel son of Zurishaddai.

[42]On the sixth day Eliasaph son of Deuel, the leader of the people of
Gad, brought his offering.

[43]His offering was one silver plate weighing a hundred and thirty
shekels, and one silver sprinkling bowl weighing seventy shekels,
both according to the sanctuary shekel, each filled with fine flour
mixed with oil as a grain offering; [44]one gold dish weighing ten
shekels, filled with incense; [45]one young bull, one ram and one
male lamb a year old, for a burnt offering; [46]one male goat for a sin
offering; [47]and two oxen, five rams, five male goats and five male
lambs a year old, to be sacrificed as a fellowship offering. This was
the offering of Eliasaph son of Deuel.

[48]On the seventh day Elishama son of Ammihud, the leader of the
people of Ephraim, brought his offering.

[49]His offering was one silver plate weighing a hundred and thirty
shekels, and one silver sprinkling bowl weighing seventy shekels,
both according to the sanctuary shekel, each filled with fine flour
mixed with oil as a grain offering; [50]one gold dish weighing ten
shekels, filled with incense; [51]one young bull, one ram and one
male lamb a year old, for a burnt offering; [52]one male goat for a sin
offering; [53]and two oxen, five rams, five male goats and five male
lambs a year old, to be sacrificed as a fellowship offering. This was
the offering of Elishama son of Ammihud.

[54]On the eighth day Gamaliel son of Pedahzur, the leader of the people
of Manasseh, brought his offering.

[55]His offering was one silver plate weighing a hundred and thirty
shekels, and one silver sprinkling bowl weighing seventy shekels,
both according to the sanctuary shekel, each filled with fine flour
mixed with oil as a grain offering; [56]one gold dish weighing ten
shekels, filled with incense; [57]one young bull, one ram and one
male lamb a year old, for a burnt offering; [58]one male goat for a sin
offering; [59]and two oxen, five rams, five male goats and five male
lambs a year old, to be sacrificed as a fellowship offering. This was
the offering of Gamaliel son of Pedahzur.

[60]On the ninth day Abidan son of Gideoni, the leader of the people of
Benjamin, brought his offering.

[61]His offering was one silver plate weighing a hundred and thirty shekels, and one silver sprinkling bowl weighing seventy shekels, both according to the sanctuary shekel, each filled with fine flour mixed with oil as a grain offering; [62]one gold dish weighing ten shekels, filled with incense; [63]one young bull, one ram and one male lamb a year old, for a burnt offering; [64]one male goat for a sin offering; [65]and two oxen, five rams, five male goats and five male lambs a year old, to be sacrificed as a fellowship offering. This was the offering of Abidan son of Gideoni.

[66]On the tenth day Ahiezer son of Ammishaddai, the leader of the people of Dan, brought his offering.

[67]His offering was one silver plate weighing a hundred and thirty shekels, and one silver sprinkling bowl weighing seventy shekels, both according to the sanctuary shekel, each filled with fine flour mixed with oil as a grain offering; [68]one gold dish weighing ten shekels, filled with incense; [69]one young bull, one ram and one male lamb a year old, for a burnt offering; [70]one male goat for a sin offering; [71]and two oxen, five rams, five male goats and five male lambs a year old, to be sacrificed as a fellowship offering. This was the offering of Ahiezer son of Ammishaddai.

[72]On the eleventh day Pagiel son of Ocran, the leader of the people of Asher, brought his offering.

[73]His offering was one silver plate weighing a hundred and thirty shekels, and one silver sprinkling bowl weighing seventy shekels, both according to the sanctuary shekel, each filled with fine flour mixed with oil as a grain offering; [74]one gold dish weighing ten shekels, filled with incense; [75]one young bull, one ram and one male lamb a year old, for a burnt offering; [76]one male goat for a sin offering; [77]and two oxen, five rams, five male goats and five male lambs a year old, to be sacrificed as a fellowship offering. This was the offering of Pagiel son of Ocran.

[78]On the twelfth day Ahira son of Enan, the leader of the people of Naphtali, brought his offering.

[79]His offering was one silver plate weighing a hundred and thirty shekels, and one silver sprinkling bowl weighing seventy shekels, both according to the sanctuary shekel, each filled with fine flour mixed with oil as a grain offering; [80]one gold dish weighing ten shekels, filled with incense; [81]one young bull, one ram and one male lamb a year old, for a burnt offering; [82]one male goat for a sin offering; [83]and two oxen, five rams, five male goats and five male lambs a year old, to be sacrificed as a fellowship offering. This was the offering of Ahira son of Enan.

12–83 The leaders of the Twelve Tribes have already been named in 1:5–15 and 2:3–32. The order of the presentation of their great offerings to the Lord is the same as the order of march: first the triad of tribes camped to the east of the tabernacle (Judah, Issachar, and Zebulun; 2:3–9; 7:12, 18, 24); then the triad of tribes camped to the south (Reuben, Simeon, and Gad; 2:10–16; 7:30, 36, 42); then the triad on the west (Ephraim, Manasseh, and Benjamin; 2:18–24; 7:48, 54, 60); finally those on the north (Dan, Asher, and Naphtali; 2:25–31; 7:66, 72, 78).

The gifts of each of the twelve worthies were the same:

one silver platter weighing about 1.5 kilograms
one silver sprinkling bowl weighing about 0.8 kilogram
one gold ladle weighing about 110 grams

the plate and bowl contained flour mixed with oil for a grain offering
the ladle was filled with incense
one young bull, one ram, and one male lamb for a burnt offering
one buck goat for a sin offering
two oxen, five rams, five buck goats, and five male lambs for a fellowship offering

These gifts were all to be used in the worship patterns of the temple service. The "silver plate" (v.13) may have been used in association with the bread of the Presence. The sprinkling bowls were for the blood that would be sprinkled on the altar. The gold "dish" (*kap̱*, lit., "palm of the hand," v.14) might have been used for incense, as this is the way it was presented to the Lord. The shekel used to weigh the silver and gold gifts is termed the "sanctuary shekel" (v.13), as against the half-value shekel sometimes used. The MT uses this phrase with the "sprinkling bowl," which the NIV (probably rightly) implies to extend to the weight of the "dish" as well (v.13). The weight of the sanctuary shekel was established in Exodus 30:13 as "twenty gerahs" (= .403 ounce or 11.4 grams; see Gleason L. Archer, Jr., "The Metrology of the Old Testament," EBC, 1:379). Attempts to determine what something was worth in terms of our present economy are futile for at least three reasons: (1) the economy of ancient Israel was not a money-based system, as in our day; (2) the relative values of gold and silver were likely closer to each other than they are in our day; and (3) the abundance or scarcity of silver and gold at any given period is difficult to ascertain. Certainly these gifts were regarded as substantial, particularly so coming from a people so recently slaves. They had despoiled the Egyptians (Exod 12:35–36) to enrich the worship of their God. The incense that filled the dishes was the prescribed, fragrant incense of Exodus 30:34.

Obviously the writer might more easily have said that each of the twelve leaders brought the same magnificent offerings to the Lord on his appointed day during the twelve-day celebrative period. How are we to regard his seeming excess of repetitive detail throughout the long chapter? Is it not possible that in this daily listing we catch a glimpse of the magnificent pomp and ceremony attending these gifts? Do we not see the genuine spirit of worship of each of the successive tribes as their turn came to bring gifts to the Lord? And finally, do we not see the joy of the Lord in his reception of these gifts? This chapter has a stately charm, a leisurely pace, and a studied sense of magnificence as each tribe in its turn was able to make gifts to God that he received with pleasure.

This text gives warrant to the ideas of rite and ritual, of ceremony and tradition. For many Christians in free churches, ritual and ceremony are regarded with suspicion, if not with disdain. Yet ritual and ceremony are deeply imbedded in the Scriptures. This text describes events in which the people took joy and in which they believed there was the corresponding joy of the Lord. As we have noted already, the daily pacing of the gifts was the directive of the Lord; their obedience was his joy (v.11).

Analogies of the repetition found in this chapter may be made with graduation ceremonies. Sometimes when schools are very large, degrees are granted en masse; sometimes this is done on an athletic field. No names are read, no graduates cross the platform for a handshake and the receipt of a diploma. The class is asked to stand, all are pronounced in receipt of their degrees, and word is made that their diplomas will be in the mail. In smaller schools the situation is markedly different. Here each name is read, and each student crosses the platform; each receives a diploma and a handshake and may even hear a few personal words. This latter type of highly personalized situation is reflected in Numbers 7.

(e) *The totals of the offerings*

7:84–88

[84]These were the offerings of the Israelite leaders for the dedication of the altar when it was anointed: twelve silver plates, twelve silver sprinkling bowls and twelve gold dishes. [85]Each silver plate weighed a hundred and thirty shekels, and each sprinkling bowl seventy shekels. Altogether, the silver dishes weighed two thousand four hundred shekels, according to the sanctuary shekel. [86]The twelve gold dishes filled with incense weighed ten shekels each, according to the sanctuary shekel. Altogether, the gold dishes weighed a hundred and twenty shekels. [87]The total number of animals for the burnt offering came to twelve young bulls, twelve rams and twelve male lambs a year old, together with their grain offering. Twelve male goats were used for the sin offering. [88]The total number of animals for the sacrifice of the fellowship offering came to twenty-four oxen, sixty rams, sixty male goats and sixty male lambs a year old. These were the offerings for the dedication of the altar after it was anointed.

84–88 At long last the twelve-day procession of givers and gifts came to its conclusion. Each tribal leader had his moment, each tribe its opportunity, and on each day there was experienced the smile of the Lord. In characteristic Hebrew style, this paragraph gives the sums of the twelve sets of gifts, a further witness to the opulence of the offerings, the festive nature of the ritual of presentation, and the sense of celebration each tribe had in its part. The totals are given in fine mathematical detail. The addition of elements in this type of paragraph shows that numerical precision was possible in ancient Israel and that numbers may be transmitted with care. The ordinary use of numbers in this section is important, as we think of their possible rhetorical use in chapter 1, with its seemingly immense numbers of fighters for each tribe.

(f) *Moses' conversation with God*

7:89

[89]When Moses entered the Tent of Meeting to speak with the LORD, he heard the voice speaking to him from between the two cherubim above the atonement cover on the ark of the Testimony. And he spoke with him.

89 The climax is Moses' hearing the voice of the Lord speaking to him from the central shrine, amid the cherubim and over the atonement cover. Communion is established between the Lord and his prophet; the people have an advocate with the Lord. All the sumptuous gifts of the people through their tribal leaders have their effect. The eternal Yahweh now speaks to Moses and through Moses to the people. Moses may also speak to God for the people. There is access to heaven within this shrine. Here is forgiveness of sin. Here is grace and here is mercy. Here is the voice of God, as promised in Exodus 25:22.

Many scholars have assumed that God is to be pictured as enthroned on the cherubim that were on the mercy seat of the ark. It seems far more likely, however, that the cherubim and the mercy seat of the ark are symbols of the Divine Presence and that the voice of God came to Moses from amid that cluster of symbols. The description for the construction of the ark, the cover of atonement, and the cherubim is given in Exodus 37:1–9. The workmanship must have been exquisite; it was the special work of the Spirit-endowed craftsman Bezalel. But more exquisite than the cherubim of hammered gold or the atonement cover of pure gold was the voice of God, which is beyond computation of value. It was that voice that Moses heard (see ch. 12).

There is something of a play on words in this verse. The verse begins with the activities of Moses: "When Moses entered the Tent of Meeting to speak with the LORD." The verse ends "And he [Yahweh] spoke with him [Moses]."

(4) *Setting up the lamps and the separation and age of service of the Levites (8:1–26)*

Chapter 8 deals with two issues: lamps and Levites. Both the proper setting of the lamps and the distinction of the Levites from the community are further elements in the purification of the nation in preparation for the holy task God had prepared for her. One may wonder, Is there a possible connection intended in the materials of this chapter between the proper positioning of the lamps within the tabernacle and the Levites outside in the camp? May one suggest that as the lamps were to be properly focused on the bread of the Presence, so the Levites were to have their proper stance within the community as well? Lamps that were not properly focused gave poorly diffused light; God's intent was illumination. Levites that were not properly stanced within the community would give a diffused picture; God's intention was that the nation understand who the Levites were and what they presented of the nature of God.

(a) *Setting up the lamps*

8:1–4

> [1]The LORD said to Moses, [2]"Speak to Aaron and say to him, 'When you set up the seven lamps, they are to light the area in front of the lampstand.' "
>
> [3]Aaron did so; he set up the lamps so that they faced forward on the lampstand, just as the LORD commanded Moses. [4]This is how the lampstand was made: It was made of hammered gold—from its base to its blossoms. The lampstand was made exactly like the pattern the LORD had shown Moses.

1 Chapter 8 begins in the characteristic manner of the Book of Numbers, with the formulaic words: "The LORD said to Moses." As noted on other occasions, these words serve a double purpose: they present a new topic and as such may be regarded as a narrator's device. But they are more than just the sign of a new topic; they are the reminder of the divine origin of the words and of the role Moses had as the intermediary between God and man.

2 The seven lamps and the lampstand are described more fully in Exodus 25:31–40. There we find the notations of the exquisite beauty of the lampstand; it was made of hammered pure gold and consisted of a base, a shaft, and seven branches (three on each side of the central shaft) with cups shaped like almond blossoms, along with other decorative buds and blossoms. The lampstand must have been truly elegant, a stunning symbol of God who created light, the first of his works, of the Lord who illuminates, of God who is light. In this chapter the new information concerns the direction of the light: it was to be cast forward from the lampstand. This chapter does not explain what might be significant in this positioning. Only when we think through the relative positioning of the other furnishings of the tabernacle are we able to see the point of the paragraph: the lamps were to be positioned so that they would light the area in front of the lampstand, that is, the area where the bread of the Presence was displayed. In this way there would always be *light* on the *bread;* the twin symbols of life would work together to speak of the life-giving mercies of the Lord, whose attention is ever on his people.

As one enters the Holy Place, the golden lampstand would be on the left side and the table of the bread of the Presence on the right side, with the altar of incense straight ahead. Beyond that altar was the veil leading into the Most Holy Place with the ark, the mercy seat, and the cherubim.

3–4 Aaron is reported to have obeyed the command of God in the proper focusing of the lamps (v.3), and then a reminder of the beauty of the design of the lampstand is given (v.4). The most remarkable aspect of this section is the note that the lampstand was made in exact accordance with the pattern the Lord had given to Moses. The pattern of the lampstand was not regarded just as brilliant human artifice; the plan and design were of God (see Exod 25:40; also cf. Heb 8:5; Rev 1:12–20).

Notes

---

4 The MT has מַרְאֶה (*mar'eh,* "appearance"; NIV, "the pattern"), a noun from the verb רָאָה (*rā'āh,* "to see"), here in the Hiphil, "to show." This is a familiar Hebrew device where the object is from the same root as the verb (a cognate accusative), a device that plays to the eye and the ear and brings emphasis on the object.

(b) *The separation of the Levites (8:5–22)*

A pattern of Numbers is to move from the priests to the Levites (see 4:5–15a, priests; compared with 4:15b, Levites); here the brief paragraph on priestly duties is followed by a more extensive section on the Levites. Another pattern in Numbers is to interweave texts dealing with lay persons and texts dealing with sacral persons. This is a point noted by Victor P. Hamilton (*Handbook on the Pentateuch* [Grand Rapids: Baker, 1982], p. 328). Chapters 1–2 deal with lay persons, 3–4 with sacral persons, 5:1–6:21 with lay persons, 6:22–27 with sacral persons, 7:1–89 with lay persons, and chapter 8 with sacral persons.

Numbers 8 is a significant text on the role and nature of the Levites in ancient Israel; it is also an important reminder of the theology of redemption. The Levites belonged to the Lord in exchange for his deliverance of the firstborn sons of Israel at the time of the tenth plague.

(i) *Their ceremonial cleansing*

8:5–14

5The LORD said to Moses: 6"Take the Levites from among the other Israelites and make them ceremonially clean. 7To purify them, do this: Sprinkle the water of cleansing on them; then have them shave their whole bodies and wash their clothes, and so purify themselves. 8Have them take a young bull with its grain offering of fine flour mixed with oil; then you are to take a second young bull for a sin offering. 9Bring the Levites to the front of the Tent of Meeting and assemble the whole Israelite community. 10You are to bring the Levites before the LORD, and the Israelites are to lay their hands on them. 11Aaron is to present the Levites before the LORD as a wave offering from the Israelites, so that they may be ready to do the work of the LORD.

12"After the Levites lay their hands on the heads of the bulls, use the one for a sin offering to the LORD and the other for a burnt offering, to make atonement for the Levites. 13Have the Levites stand in front of Aaron and his sons and then present them as a wave offering to the LORD. 14In this way you are to set the Levites apart from the other Israelites, and the Levites will be mine.

5–10 This section (vv.5–14) describes the cleansing of the Levites and may be compared with the account detailing the ordination of Aaron and his sons to the priesthood (Lev 8). The Levites are helpers to the priests, and the language describing their consecration is somewhat distinct from that of the priests. The priests were made holy, the Levites clean; the priests were anointed and washed, the Levites sprinkled; the priests were given new garments, the Levites washed theirs; blood was applied to the priests, it was waved over the Levites.

One of the refrains in this section is the idea that the Levites were taken from among (*mittôḵ*, "from the midst of") the people (see vv.6, 14, 16, 19). This reminds us that the Levites were distinct from the other tribes: they were to have no tribal allotment; their places of living would be spread throughout the other tribes, but they were drawn from the tribes to have a special service before the Lord in assisting the priests.

The verb *ṭāhar* in v.6 describes ceremonial cleansing. In the Piel stem it speaks of cleansing, making pure, of cleansing ceremonially. The verb is used, for example, in the cleansing process for the altar of incense by applying blood of a sin offering. The cleansing process of the Levites was to begin with a sprinkling of water on them rather than with a sprinkling of blood. This water is termed *mê ḥaṭṭā'ṯ* (lit., "water of sin," v.7), a phrase taken to mean "water of cleansing" or "purification from sin." A similar phrase is found in 19:9: "the water of cleansing; it is for purification from sin." The phrase "water of sin" may also be compared with the phrase "bitter water" in 5:18, in the rite of the woman suspected of adultery.

The second factor in cleansing the Levites was shaving their entire bodies (v.7). This symbolic act speaks of the fullness of their cleansing, as in the case of the ritual cleansing of one cured of a serious skin disorder (Lev 14:8; see comments on Num 5:2). Shaving the entire body, not just the head, is in some ways a return to innocence and an initiative symbol of purity. It is well known that hair tends to be dirty; bodily hair needs to be cleansed regularly, for the follicles tend to collect and hold dirt. The ancient Egyptians were fastidious about cleanliness; upper-class Egyptians shaved their bodies regularly, then wore wigs. Egyptian priests shaved their whole bodies every other day, according to Herodotus (2.37). The cleansing of the Levites in Israel seems not to be a repeated action but an initial rite of purification. Since Semitic men were characterized generally in the ancient world by wearing beards and by ample bodily hair, shaving these men's bodies must have been regarded as a remarkable act of devotion to God.

The third factor in cleansing the Levites was washing their garments. The verb used for washing is *kāḇas* (a verb meaning "to tread," "to walk," related to the Akkadian *kabusu*, "to tread down," "to wash garments by treading"). The verb pictorially represents the ancient form of washing clothing. The same verb was used to describe the cleansing that had to be done by the whole nation when Moses was about to go to the mountain to meet with the Lord (Exod 19:10, 14). On occasion *kāḇas* is used in parallel with *rāḥaṣ* ("to wash the person"; e.g., Lev 14:8; 15:5).

Following the sprinkling with water of purification, the shaving of their bodies, and the washing of their clothes, the Levites were ready for the next step in their purification: the presentation of offerings and sacrifices to God. They were each to bring two bulls along with the fine flour mixed with oil that constitutes the grain offering. This would then be presented by Moses before the Tent of Meeting, with the nation gathered to witness the event (vv.8–9). The people (their representatives) would then place their hands on the Levites (v.10) as a means of identifying with them. The Levites had come from among the people; now they were standing in their place before the Divine Presence. This was a solemn act, worthy of reflection. The Levites were the substitutes for the nation; by placing hands on them, the people of the nation were dramatically acknowledging this substitutionary act (see 8:16–18).

11–14 Our text makes a subtle move from the placing of the hands of the people on the Levites to the placing of the hands of the Levites on the two bulls. This is a double substitution. The Levites substitute for the people, the bulls substitute for the Levites. The bulls, with this double signification, are then sacrifices of sin offering and burnt offering to provide atonement for the Levites. This double ritual is engaging; persons present for these actions must have had their attention riveted to the ritual, wondering at its meaning.

In v.11 Aaron comes more directly into the picture, as he is to present the Levites as a "wave offering" before the Lord. The notion of "wave offering" is somewhat mysterious to us. We have some concept of the burning of sacrifices, of the pouring of libations, and of the presenting of grain offerings. But the "wave" offering is the most obscure to us. The idea in the wave offering was to hold an object, usually the part of the offering that would be the food for the priests, before the Lord, to wave it back and forth, and then to keep it for one's own use. The presenting of an offering in this manner was unusually symbolic—as indeed is all sacrifice!

In the case of the Levites, we may suspect that Aaron and his sons would place hands on their shoulders and then cause them to move from side to side in a symbolic way to represent the fact that they were a living sacrifice presented before the Lord and that they now belonged to the priests to assist them in their work of service in the tabernacle. In this way the Levites were separated from the rest of the community; they belonged to the Lord, and in turn they would belong to the priests.

(ii) *Their position before the Lord*

8:15–19

15 "After you have purified the Levites and presented them as a wave offering, they are to come to do their work at the Tent of Meeting.

> [16]They are the Israelites who are to be given wholly to me. I have taken them as my own in place of the firstborn, the first male offspring from every Israelite woman. [17]Every firstborn male in Israel, whether man or animal, is mine. When I struck down all the firstborn in Egypt, I set them apart for myself. [18]And I have taken the Levites in place of all the firstborn sons in Israel. [19]Of all the Israelites, I have given the Levites as gifts to Aaron and his sons to do the work at the Tent of Meeting on behalf of the Israelites and to make atonement for them so that no plague will strike the Israelites when they go near the sanctuary."

15–16 The Levites were next acknowledged by the Lord as his particular possession. The Hebrew uses the Qal passive participle *nᵉṯunîm* (meaning "a given one," from *nāṯan*, "to give") and doubles the word: *nᵉṯunîm, nᵉṯunîm:* "given, given," meaning "given wholly" (v.16). The Levites are the substitutes for the firstborn of every mother in Israel. The story line of salvation comes strongly here: Passover! Israel was in Egypt. The tenth plague was imminent. Faithful people had slaughtered a lamb, roasted it, and were eating it along with bitter herbs and matzo bread. When the angel of death was passing over the camp of the people of Israel, the angel looked for blood on the posts and lintel of each home. Where that blood was found, the angel moved on to the next home. No one died. All lived. But in those homes that lacked the prescribed blood, there came blood; instead of the blood of an animal on the door bracing, there was blood in the bed of the oldest child; for the angel of death had extracted the most vicious toll, the death of the firstborn. The firstborn children of the faithful Israelites were not killed. They lived. But for them a price was to be paid, and that price was the Levites. The Levites were to be taken in the service of God (v.15) as a substitute for the loss of life of the firstborn in those homes where the blood was found on post and lintel.

17 The statement "every . . . man or animal" is inclusive. No similar ritual was necessary for the animals, but the focus is on mankind.

18–19 The Levites were the people who were given to the Lord for his exclusive use (v.18; cf. v.14). In v.19 the Lord gives his Levites to the priests as their aids for the work of the ministry in the tabernacle worship. The Levites had three functions: (1) they were servants to the priests in their work at the tabernacle, generally responsible for the heavy work that priestly duties demanded (*laʿᵃḇōḏ ʾeṯ-ʿᵃḇōḏaṯ*, lit., "to do the work of the work"); (2) they were the means of bringing redemption for the firstborn of the nation (*taḥaṯ*, "in place of," vv.16, 18); and (3) they served as a protective hedge, an atonement (*ûlᵉḵappēr*, "and to make atonement," v.19) against unwarranted approach of the holy things, "so that no plague will strike the Israelites." The Levites were a protective hedge for the community against trespass in sacred precincts of the tabernacle (see 1:53). In this language we have portraits of both the wrath and the mercy of the Lord. His wrath will be extended against evil assaults on his holiness; but in his mercy he has a protective hedge to keep such confrontations from being necessary. Throughout these chapters there is the insistence on God's wrath and his mercy and on his holiness and his grace. To hold one of these excellencies out of balance with the other is to distort the biblical portrait of our Father.

(iii) *A summary of their separation* 8:20–22

20Moses, Aaron and the whole Israelite community did with the Levites just as the LORD commanded Moses. 21The Levites purified themselves and washed their clothes. Then Aaron presented them as a wave offering before the LORD and made atonement for them to purify them. 22After that, the Levites came to do their work at the Tent of Meeting under the supervision of Aaron and his sons. They did with the Levites just as the LORD commanded Moses.

20–22 This section serves two functions: it reports the completion of the act of separation as a literary device; it also reports the obedience of the people as a mark of their initial compliance to the will and work of God. Verses of complete obedience to the commands of the Lord occur regularly in the first chapters of Numbers (see 1:54; 2:34; 3:16, 51; 4:49; 5:4; 8:4, 20, 22; 9:5, 23). The implicit obedience of Moses and the people of Israel to the commands of God in the areas of ritual and regimen leave us quite unprepared for their complaints against his loving character and their outrageous breaches of faith in the rebellions that begin in the narrative of chapter 11.

(c) *The age of service of the Levites* 8:23–26

23The LORD said to Moses, 24"This applies to the Levites: Men twenty-five years old or more shall come to take part in the work at the Tent of Meeting, 25but at the age of fifty, they must retire from their regular service and work no longer. 26They may assist their brothers in performing their duties at the Tent of Meeting, but they themselves must not do the work. This, then, is how you are to assign the responsibilities of the Levites."

23–26 At 4:3 the age for the service of the Levite is said to be from thirty to fifty. The present paragraph has the same upper limit but a new lower limit, twenty-five. This is a controverted passage and is not easily solved (see Notes).

After a Levite had reached the mandatory retirement age of fifty, he was still free to assist his younger coworkers as long as he was able to do so (perhaps at the great festivals), but he no longer was to do the hard and difficult work he had done in his prime. Again, in these regulations we sense the holiness and the mercy of God. His holiness demands that his ministers be fully able to do the work that is required for them; to slip or err in holy things would be a most grievous offense. His mercy precluded a man doing the work that was demanded when he might be past his physical prime. There were to be no elderly, doddering Levites stumbling about in the precincts of the Holy Place, carrying poles too heavy for them to carry or doing things they were no longer able to do.

The last words of the chapter, "This, then, is how you are to assign the responsibilities of the Levites," serve as a fine finish for the section that begins "Take the Levites from among the other Israelites" (v.6). This is just another example of the beauty of order in the Book of Numbers. Not only is the camp to be ordered and the work of the cultic personnel to be done in order, so is the written record of these descriptions done in superb order. Finally, the order and organization presented by this chapter further elevate the significance of the Levites. They are treated with dignity and honor, for they hold a special function in the worship of God for the good of the community.

Notes

24 We do know that the age for entering service for the Levites was reduced to twenty by David (1 Chron 23:24, 27), as the circumstances of their work had greatly changed by the time of the monarchy (v.26). Yet it is difficult to imagine a change in circumstances between Num 4:3 and 8:24, as Noordtzij suggests (p. 81), if these texts are regarded as both from Moses and ultimately from God. Critical scholars, of course, seize on such contradictions as indicators of varied sources used in the making of the Pentateuch (Noth calls this "a later correction" [p. 67], and Budd posits a highly complex picture of late editing [pp. 90–92]). Yet one would think that such an obvious "blunder" could have been smoothed over by even a partially aware redactor. The blatant distinction between the ages given in these two chapters (which naturally call for comparison) suggests that there was not necessarily believed to be any real contradiction in these numbers at the time these words were written. For these reasons I believe the rabbinical harmonization of these two texts by indicating a five-year period of apprenticeship seems appropriate. The contrary data in the texts themselves call for harmonization on the part of the reader. This is simply a demand in the careful reading of Scripture by those who are sympathetic to the integrity of the text.

(5) *The celebration of the Passover (9:1–14)*

Numbers 9 begins with instruction and interaction—a dynamic exchange between the Lord and Moses that provides a rare glimpse into how the Lord's instruction for his people could be modified on the basis of new conditions and circumstances. The theological implications of this are enormous, as we shall see. The particular issue addressed in Numbers 9 concerns the command of the Lord for the celebration of the Passover in the second year of Israel's redemption and the request for special treatment prompted by those who were ceremonially unclean at the time and hence excluded from participation in this sacred festival. The first Passover was celebrated in Egypt on the eve of the redemption of the nation from bondage (see Exod 12 for details). Now, a year later, the celebration was to be commemorated by the redeemed populace in the shadow of Mount Sinai.

(a) *The command to keep the Passover*

9:1–5

1 The LORD spoke to Moses in the Desert of Sinai in the first month of
the second year after they came out of Egypt. He said, 2 "Have the
Israelites celebrate the Passover at the appointed time. 3 Celebrate it at
the appointed time, at twilight on the fourteenth day of this month, in
accordance with all its rules and regulations."

4 So Moses told the Israelites to celebrate the Passover, 5 and they did
so in the Desert of Sinai at twilight on the fourteenth day of the first
month. The Israelites did everything just as the LORD commanded
Moses.

1–2 The arrangement of materials in the Book of Numbers is not strictly chronological, as we have observed from time to time. The events of this chapter actually preceded the beginning of the census of 1:2 ("first day of the second month of the second year," 1:1). The first two months of the second year of redemption were an exceedingly busy period of activity (see the Notes for a chronological listing of the events of chs. 1–10). The long stay at the base of Mount Sinai was not a time of inactivity or indolence. It was a time of great activity in celebration of the goodness and mercy of the Lord and in preparation for what was expected to have been the soon triumphal march into the land of Canaan. The chronological discontinuity of the Book of Numbers suggests that the principle of arrangement was not time related (see Introduction: Unity and Organization).

The first Passover was held in Egypt in the midst of the saving works of the Lord (Exod 12); the next one was to be celebrated in the Desert of Sinai in commemoration of his works, even as commanded by him (Exod 12:14: "for the generations to come"). The celebration of Passover had become a commemorative act by the redeemed Hebrew community, just as the celebration of the Lord's Table is the commemorative act by the redeemed community in Christ.

There are two discreet emphases in vv.1–2. The first concerns the appropriate time and the proper regulations for the Passover; the second is found in the verb "to celebrate." Repeatedly in these few verses we find an interchange between the words "appropriate time" and "celebrate." In these two words are compelling complementary ideas. One is the proper focus on the demands, obligations, and rites of worship in Hebrew Scripture. The second is the ability to reach out for the celebrative, enjoyable, and festive nature of that worship. Error may come in omitting either aspect. To lose sight of the regulation is to trespass in presumption. To forget the celebrative is to lose the joy and heart of worship; only to follow the obligation is to slip into the dreary work of "religion." Any approach to God by his people ought to meld these two ideas. Only in that which is appropriate is there really room for celebration; celebration apart from a sense of the appropriate is the bittersweet failure of pseudohappiness.

3–4 The Hebrew term translated "at twilight" (v.3) is literally "between the evenings," speaking of that period just between sunset and true darkness. In traditional Hebrew practice, this period is regarded as the end of one day and the beginning of the next. The official determination of the precise moment of twilight in Jewish tradition became that point where one could no longer distinguish between a white or a black thread when standing outside in the growing darkness.

In addition to the emphasis on the appropriate timing of the Passover, we find ourselves impressed with the necessity for complete obedience to the legislation of the celebration. It is to be celebrated according to all its statutes and judgments. These correlative words speak in hendiadys of complete compliance to detail, a full respect for and obedience to the regulations that God had established. This emphasis on complete obedience in the minute details can lead in two directions: (1) to the obedience of faith that regards the minute details as important and compliance to them as that which will bring the pleasure of the Lord; (2) to legalism that finds itself so preoccupied with the details and the regulations as to lose the primary sense of the meaning God had in the legislation in the first place.

5 Verse 5 is a report of compliance—yet another example of the obedience of Israel to the demands of the Lord in these early chapters of Numbers. Reports such as this assure us that things were as they should have been. Yet these same reports ill-prepare us for the dreadful rebellion of Israel at Kadesh, described in the following chapters.

Notes

1 The chronology of the first two months of the second year after the Exodus is as follows:

1. The setting up of the tabernacle (7:1) was declared to be completed on the first day of the first month of the second year (Exod 40:2). It was on this day that the cloud covered the tabernacle, as we will see later in this chapter (Num 9:15–23). Then, in response to the symbol of God's presence over the completed tabernacle, it was also on that day that the first of the offerings from the twelve leaders of the tribes was given to the Lord (Num 7:3–17). The presentation of the gifts from each tribe extended until the twelfth day of the first month.
2. The setting apart of the Levites (8:26) would have followed immediately after the twelve days of gifts, perhaps on the thirteenth day of the month. It seems unlikely that the setting apart of the Levites would have been on the same day as the last of the tribal gifts; to have another significant action on that day would have minimized the importance of the gifts of Ahira of Naphtali (7:78–83).
3. The second Passover was celebrated on the fourteenth day of the first month (9:5).
4. The census began on the first day of the second month (10:1).
5. Those who were ceremonially unclean at the time of the second Passover were permitted to celebrate it on the fourteenth day of the second month (9:11).
6. Then the cloud lifted and the march from Sinai began on the twentieth day of the second month (10:11).

2 The verb used throughout this section is the common term עָשָׂה (*ʿāśāh*, "to do"). It has an extraordinary range of meaning in biblical usage. The translation "celebrate" for וְיַעֲשׂוּ (*weyaʿaśû*) is appropriate here because of the environment of the festival that Passover suggests.

The word הַפָּסַח (*happāsaḥ*, "the Passover") has three basic usages in the MT: (1) the sacrifice of the Passover, the associated communion meal (as in Exod 12:11, 27); (2) the animal that is sacrificed, the particular lamb (or goat) of Passover (as in Exod 12:21); and (3) the Feast of the Passover, which is the broader use (as in 9:2).

בְּמוֹעֲדוֹ (*bemôʿadô*, "at the appointed time") is from the verb יָעַד (*yāʿad*, "to appoint"). This is the same word used to describe the "Tent of Meeting" (12:4), which could also be called "the tent of the appointed meeting."

(b) *The ceremonially unclean*

9:6–8

6 But some of them could not celebrate the Passover on that day because they were ceremonially unclean on account of a dead body. So they came to Moses and Aaron that same day 7 and said to Moses, "We have become unclean because of a dead body, but why should we be kept from presenting the LORD's offering with the other Israelites at the appointed time?"

[8]Moses answered them, "Wait until I find out what the LORD commands concerning you."

6–7 A crisis developed within the community because of ritual impurity on the part of some; they had come in contact with a dead body. As seen in 5:1, such contact rendered a person ritually unclean and no longer able to participate in the community until rites of purification had been completed (see v.2). Hence a person in a state of ritual impurity would not have been permitted to participate in the celebrative Feast of the Passover. The section points to two issues: (1) the desire of these people to obey God fully in his calls for worship and festivals and (2) the formidable obstacle of participation based on ritual uncleanness.

The concept of ritual impurity is so foreign to modern thinking as to be nearly unintelligible to most readers. The idea of being "unclean" is not simply that of being physically soiled, of course; though that which is dirty is a physical presentment of what is "unclean." The best way to think of the notion of "uncleanness" is as a teaching device to remind the people of Israel of the holiness of God. The idea that any person at all might have the effrontery to dare to approach the presence of the Lord is audacious in itself. Only by his grace may anyone come before him to worship. By developing a concept of ritual purity, an external symbol, the notion of internal purity might be presented. Ever in the Bible the notions of external symbols are representative of internal realities. Only the obdurate miss the point here. In our Lord's confrontation with the Pharisees, the principal battle was not over the essential demands of God but on the tendencies the Pharisees had in focusing on external compliance without due attention to internal meaning. In our passage the recognition of ceremonial uncleanness on the part of some people and their consequent inability to participate in the activities of celebrative worship in the Passover speaks of their high level of compliance to the dictates of Torah and the keen desire they had to worship the Lord in spirit and truth (see John 4:24).

8 Moses' response to the people that he would seek an answer from the Lord to redress their need presents an amazing dynamic in Scripture. In this instance there were two conflicting ideals: the demand of the Lord for the community-wide celebration of Passover was confronted by the ceremonial uncleanness of a part of the community. In a case of such conflict, Moses sought the intervention of the Lord, a new word from glory, as it were. That word would bring a means of maintaining the best of both ideals without compromising either. We may observe as well that Moses' response to the genuine needs of believing people is a mark of his spiritual leadership, his humility before God, and his desire to be the spokesman, not only for the Lord to the people, but for the people back to the Lord. In this scenario we have not only a historical instance but a template of how such decisions should be made. Another dramatic example of this process is found in chapter 27 regarding the problem of the estate of a father who has daughters but no sons.

Notes

6 לְנֶפֶשׁ (*lᵉnep̱eš;* NIV, "on account of a dead body") is the preposition "to" or "for" plus the noun often translated as "soul" or "person."

(c) *Divine permission for a legitimate delay* 9:9–13

> [9]Then the LORD said to Moses, [10]"Tell the Israelites: 'When any of you or your descendants are unclean because of a dead body or are away on a journey, they may still celebrate the LORD's Passover. [11]They are to celebrate it on the fourteenth day of the second month at twilight. They are to eat the lamb, together with unleavened bread and bitter herbs. [12]They must not leave any of it till morning or break any of its bones. When they celebrate the Passover, they must follow all the regulations. [13]But if a man who is ceremonially clean and not on a journey fails to celebrate the Passover, that person must be cut off from his people because he did not present the LORD's offering at the appointed time. That man will bear the consequences of his sin.

9–11 The grace of God is to be seen, not only in the words of his response to Moses, but in that he responded at all. We need to grasp anew the concept of the audacity of faith: by what right, excepting only God's great grace, dare even Moses go before Yahweh, the Creator of the universe, asking for a provision for exception from his demands? All God's actions and words to his people are gracious, undeserved, and unmerited. That he speaks at all, even in demands, is a mark of his condescension; that he speaks favorably in response to the request of Moses is a marvel. Throughout we have the sense of the ongoing wonder of grace.

God's gracious provision for those who were ritually unclean was an alternative opportunity to celebrate the Passover on a day one month later so that they would not be excluded totally from its observance. The text thus presents the reality of the distancing that uncleanness brings between a believer and his participation in the worship acts of the community; it also provides a merciful alternative from the Lord. Further, the answer of the Lord went even beyond the request by adding the alternative of a later celebration for those who might be away on a trip as well as for those who were ritually impure.

This gracious and provident provision of the Lord is not dissimilar to some modern civil legislation. For example, the U.S. tax code emphasizes strongly the notion of an "appointed time" for filing yet does include provisions for late filing due to personal exigency or foreign travel. As in the case of the law of the Lord, these provisions do not nullify the obligation; they only delay it; there is no mercy for one who merely decides not to obey. The text gives no room for indifference (KD, 3:52); God's mercy must never be trampled by the uncaring.

Even when the Passover was celebrated a month later, it was still to be done fully in order. The text emphasizes the essentials of the meal and the essentials of the ritual. In terms of the meal, there was to be the lamb (noted by the word "Passover"), the unleavened bread, and the bitter herbs. In the contemporary, traditional Passover Haggadah ("recitation"), Rabbi Gamaliel, the teacher of Saul (later the apostle Paul; see Acts 22:3 [5:34–39]; see also Acts 21:39; 26:4–5; Gal 1:13–14), is quoted as saying that if anyone does not eat the lamb, the unleavened bread, and the bitter herbs, he has not kept the Passover. He built his words on v.11.

12 The strictures for the Passover include two additional items in this verse: (1) none of the feast is to be left over until morning, and (2) the bones of the sacrificial lamb are not to be broken. Eating the Passover lamb and its attendant foods is to be done entirely in one evening. This provision follows the original command for Passover in

Exodus 12:10 (and v.46, which even insists that the meal be consumed in one house, family by family, and not carried from one house to another), where Moses is commanded to have the people burn any of the meat not eaten the night before. The concept of not leaving sacred foods over until morning also extended to the legislation respecting manna (see Exod 16:19) and the fat of the three annual sacrifices (Exod 23:18). No reasons are given for this part of the legislation, but we surmise these possibilities: (1) the meal of Passover was not to be regarded as an ordinary meal but a great feast that was a sacred occasion between the Lord and his people; (2) hence the food of the Passover was not like ordinary food that could go from one meal until the next with impunity; and (3) secondary to these religious reasons was the implied health aspect that underlies some of the legislation in Torah concerning food: there was, of course, no refrigeration in ancient times, and cooked meats that were exposed to heat and humidity would soon go bad.

The second emphasis in v.12 is in the words "or break any of its bones." This was also a provision of the first legislation of Passover in Exodus 12:46. When the Lord Jesus ("our Passover lamb," 1 Cor 5:7; see also John 1:29) was crucified, it was reported that none of his bones were broken, in fulfillment of the Scripture (John 19:36). The Scriptures John points to included Numbers 9:12 plus Exodus 12:46 and Psalm 34:20. This is one of many concepts from the Hebrew Scriptures that the reader would not expect to be predictive of the Messiah. It may be that there are similar surprises awaiting us with respect to his second coming.

13 Wherever there is grace, there are those who will make presumption. Those who had no reason not to celebrate the Passover and simply failed to do so were to be cut off from the community. God's gracious provision for the distressed to have an alternative time of celebration was not to be license for the careless to ignore the Passover altogether. Such ones by their own neglect show that they are not part of the community and are not deserving of further union with it. The obdurate is to be "cut off," a phrase signifying either death by divine agency or perhaps banishment. In either case the judgment is severe indeed. The NT also gravely warns against the abuse or misuse of the celebration of the Lord's Table (1 Cor 11:28–30).

Notes

10 איש איש (*'îš 'îš*, "man, man") is repetition for distribution, "if any man" or "any of you" (NIV).

(d) *The rights of the alien at Passover*

9:14

[14] " 'An alien living among you who wants to celebrate the LORD's Passover must do so in accordance with its rules and regulations. You must have the same regulations for the alien and the native-born.' "

14 The alien first had to be circumcised before he was able to participate in the Passover celebration (cf. Exod 12:48). But there was an opening for the non-Israelite who had come to faith in the God of Israel to participate fully with the Israelites in holy worship. This is the point of the Abrahamic covenant: "and all peoples on earth/ will be blessed through you" (Gen 12:3). The inclusion of the alien in covenantal legislation such as this reminds us of God's great grace and also of his determined purpose to reach out through his people to all peoples.

(6) *The covering cloud*

9:15–23

[15]On the day the tabernacle, the Tent of the Testimony, was set up, the cloud covered it. From evening till morning the cloud above the tabernacle looked like fire. [16]That is how it continued to be; the cloud covered it, and at night it looked like fire. [17]Whenever the cloud lifted from above the Tent, the Israelites set out; wherever the cloud settled, the Israelites encamped. [18]At the LORD's command the Israelites set out, and at his command they encamped. As long as the cloud stayed over the tabernacle, they remained in camp. [19]When the cloud remained over the tabernacle a long time, the Israelites obeyed the LORD's order and did not set out. [20]Sometimes the cloud was over the tabernacle only a few days; at the LORD's command they would encamp, and then at his command they would set out. [21]Sometimes the cloud stayed only from evening till morning, and when it lifted in the morning, they set out. Whether by day or by night, whenever the cloud lifted, they set out. [22]Whether the cloud stayed over the tabernacle for two days or a month or a year, the Israelites would remain in camp and not set out; but when it lifted, they would set out. [23]At the LORD's command they encamped, and at the LORD's command they set out. They obeyed the LORD's order, in accordance with his command through Moses.

15 The cloud was the dramatic symbol of the presence of the Lord hovering above the tabernacle (cf. Exod 13:21; 40:34). That this was no ordinary cloud is attested not only by its spontaneous appearance at the completion of the setting up of the tabernacle but also by the fact that at night it had the appearance of fire. It was by means of the cloud that the Lord would direct the movements of his people.

16 It must have been an extraordinary sight, this mystic cloud, this fiery heaviness, this enveloping presence. The text suggests the permanent abiding of the cloud over the camp in the words "this is how it continued to be." The Hebrew word *tāmîḏ* has the sense of "continually," "incessantly." The idea of the presence was so impressive that there was a sense of an implied threat if ever this presence was found to be missing. The cloud and fire were both reversals of the expected phenomena of the time. Both the cloud and the fire were striking, unusual, and unexpected. These were symbols one would not, could not ignore. They were awesome and eerie, unnatural and unexpected, comforting and protective. To relieve the heat of the desert sun, there was a cloud by day. To reverse the cold darkness of the desert night, there was the comforting fire overhead. Everything about this paragraph is wrapped in mystery, a mystic sense of the Divine Presence. The passage shimmers with awe and delight.

But there is also about this text something of regret, of a loss. The vantage point of the language of the passage is to describe something that used to be true but was no longer visible. The description is not unlike that of manna in 11:7. The tense of the verbs does not suggest a present reality but a historical experience. In this paragraph in which something from the past is evoked, we sense the possibility of a latter hand adding this description to the text of Numbers. That is, Moses and his original audience were the participants of these events, the ones who observed directly the manifestation of the cloud of the presence. There would be no need for Moses to say to his contemporaries that the cloud reminded them of fire at night or that it gave the signals for encampment or for setting out on the march. All this was a vital part of their personal experience. Only we, the heirs of the text who were not present at the time, need the explanation. The point is not that Moses could not have written this paragraph but that it is not likely he would have written in this past tense form of something he and his contemporaries were experiencing daily.

17 Two significant verbs are used to describe the presence of the cloud as the symbol of God's nearness. One is the verb meaning "to cover" (v.15); the other is the verb meaning "to settle" (v.17). The expression "wherever the cloud settled" contains the significant verb *šā<u>k</u>an*, which gives us the basis for the idea of the "Shekinah glory." The English rendering "shekinah" is built on the verb meaning "to dwell" and the shortened form of the divine name Yahweh. The Hebrew text rings with the sound of *šā<u>k</u>an*, as it is also the basis for the term for "tabernacle," *miškān*. This phrasing symbolizes both God's nearness and his remoteness. He is present as a cloud but hovers above; he is near as a fire, but one cannot draw very close.

18 The words "at the LORD's command" are literally "by the mouth of Yahweh." The cloud was one of the ways in which the Lord spoke to his people. The identification of the lifting and settling of the cloud and the command of the Lord is made sure in this and the following verses. The cloud was the means God used to direct the movements and the resting times of his people Israel.

19–22 The movement of the cloud and its presence were unpredictable, without discernable pattern. This was to impress on the people the sense that it was God who was leading them, not some pattern of creation nor some whim from above. The cloud might linger only a day or so, or it might linger in one spot nearly indefinitely. The wording of these verses indicates a very lengthy stay (v.19), a briefer stay (v.20), or a very short stay (v.21). Whatever it might be, the people were to move or to encamp based on the movement or settling of the cloud.

23 This verse gives a report of compliance: "They obeyed the LORD's order." The repetitious nature of this section (vv.15–23) enhances the expectation of continued complete obedience to the sure direction of the Lord in Israel's movements through the desert. The role of Moses is mentioned for balance: Moses was the agent of the Lord who interpreted the movement of the cloud as signaling the movement of the people. The level of the tragedy of their subsequent disobedience is heightened by this paragraph of great obedience.

The whole section (vv.15–23) is harmonious. There are several repeated phrasings ("by the mouth of," "the cloud," "settling/lifting," and "journeying/encamping"). The perspective seems to be distant from the event. The narrator uses broad strokes of summary, suggesting the ideals of God's direction and the promptness of the people's response. There is no hint of disobedience here.

The emphasis in this section is on God's grace and the people's recognition of his grace, marked by their prompt response. God's grace is seen in his giving them direction at all, that he gave it by clear signs, and that Moses was the interpreter of his meaning (v.23). A passage that speaks in this manner is didactic of how the people should respond to God. The second generation should obey God this well, and future generations (down to our own day!) should take a lesson. God will be directing them also, and they (and we) must attend to his voice.

Finally, we observe the emphasis on the sovereignty of God in this text. The variation from a night's rest, to a camp of a couple of days, to a month-long rest, to a lengthy period of many years was all dependent on the work and will of God. In no case was there an explanation given or needed from God. "Just watch the cloud," one might say, "and we will know what to do." George Bush writes, "In this there is evidently nothing capricious or unstable to be charged upon the people, as their movements were constantly regulated by the divine direction, and this again was undoubtedly governed by reasons of infinite wisdom, though not expressly made known" (p. 132).

Notes

---

15 וּבְיוֹם (*ûḇ^eyôm*, NIV, "on the day") can be translated as "when." The Hebrew expression for "on the day" is more properly וּבַיּוֹם (*ûḇayyôm*, e.g., with the definite article indicated).

16 The versions read the word "by day" in the phrase "the cloud covered it *by day*." The Hebrew word יוֹמָם (*yômām*, "by day") is lacking in the MT but is a likely emendation.

18 עַל־פִּי יהוה (*'al-pî yhwh*, "according to the mouth of Yahweh"; i.e., according to the command of the Lord; NIV, "the LORD's order") is a characteristic phrase of compliance to the word of God in Numbers. The expression is found seven times in vv.18–23 (twice in v.18; twice in v.20; three times in v.23). The repetition of this phrase seven times in this pericope is inescapably emphatic. The phrase is also found in 3:16, 39; 4:37, 41, 45, 49; and 10:13.

---

(7) *The two silver trumpets (10:1–10)*

All seems to be in readiness now for the triumphal march of the people of God. They have been mustered for battle and stationed for encampment. They have been put through numerous paces of purification ritual, celebrated their deliverance from Egypt in the Feast of Passover, worshiped the Lord with sumptuous gifts, responded faithfully to his every word through his prophet Moses, and sensed the awe of his presence through cloud and fire. One thing remains, the fashioning of trumpets and the establishment of the appropriate tattoos that they will signal. Then, let the march begin!

(a) *The command to fashion two silver trumpets*

10:1–7

[1]The LORD said to Moses: [2]"Make two trumpets of hammered silver, and use them for calling the community together and for having the camps set out. [3]When both are sounded, the whole community is to assemble before you at the entrance to the Tent of Meeting. [4]If only one is sounded, the leaders—the heads of the clans of Israel—are to assemble before you. [5]When a trumpet blast is sounded, the tribes camping on the east are to set out. [6]At the sounding of a second blast, the camps on the south are to set out. The blast will be the signal for

setting out. [7]To gather the assembly, blow the trumpets, but not with the same signal.

1 Ordinarily we might expect that the wording in such a verse as this suggests a sequential act, one that follows one event and precedes another. However, it is possible in this case that this introductory sentence may be intended to be read as something that God had said on an earlier occasion; its placement here between the narrative reporting the enveloping cloud (9:15–23) and that describing the beginnings of the march (10:11–35) may not be sequentially significant but topically appropriate. I suspect that considerable time would have been necessary for Moses (and/or his artisans) to make these trumpets of hammered silver. Throughout these early chapters of Numbers, there is a topical presentation rather than a chronological arrangement of the material. God may have instructed Moses to have these trumpets fashioned months before the people actually set out on their triumphant march.

2 While it is possible that the Lord's command to Moses would allow an artisan to work under his direction, the MT has the type of construction that often means the command is to be done by the person addressed. Perhaps Moses himself hammered out these trumpets.

The Bible speaks of two types of trumpets. One is the silver trumpet, such as this chapter presents (see also 31:6; 1 Chron 13:8; 2 Chron 13:12; 29:26; Ps 98:6). The other is the ram's horn trumpet, the shofar, or the *qeren* as in Joshua 6:4. Both instruments are far removed from the modern trumpet, as they are capable of producing notes of only certain intervals such as fourths or fifths. But like all trumpets, these instruments amplify and channel the sound made by the rapid buzzing of pursed lips. They may be compared to the post horn. They were a long, straight, slender metal tube with a flared end. As in the case of the cherubim and the lampstand, the trumpet or clarion was made of hammered metal. Trumpets would be blown for order and discipline; the immense numbers of the people presented an evident need for demonstrating order and discipline among the ranks.

3–7 Two trumpets were blown for assembly of the people (v.3) and one for assembly of the leaders (v.4). Trumpets were also blown for a signal to the people to set out on the line of march (vv.5–6), at times of battle (v.9), and during festivals of worship (v.10). Obviously different tattoos would be used (v.7, "but not with the same signal"); hence, we may presume the development of a guild of priestly musicians was demanded (v.8). These were not casual players who would "jam" from time to time; they were professional players whose making of music was as serious as the work of a soldier on the battlefield and as sacred as any task done by a sacrificing priest in the tabernacle courts.

Notes

2 Language similar to עֲשֵׂה לְךָ (*ʿaśēh lᵉk̲ā*, "make to you"; i.e., "you make!") is used by God in his initial command to Abram (Gen 12:1), "you go!" Alternatively, Hirsch presents a Jewish tradition that the prepositional phrase *lᵉk̲ā* in this text was used to exclude others from using these trumpets after the death of Moses (p. 151).

(b) *The ordinance for the silver trumpets*

10:8–10

8"The sons of Aaron, the priests, are to blow the trumpets. This is to be a lasting ordinance for you and the generations to come. 9When you go into battle in your own land against an enemy who is oppressing you, sound a blast on the trumpets. Then you will be remembered by the LORD your God and rescued from your enemies. 10Also at your times of rejoicing—your appointed feasts and New Moon festivals—you are to sound the trumpets over your burnt offerings and fellowship offerings, and they will be a memorial for you before your God. I am the LORD your God."

8 The role of the sons of Aaron as the sole players of these silver trumpets in ancient Israel further signals the sacral function of this music. These instruments were not just noisemakers; they were like the lampstand and the censures, implements in the worship of God.

9 In times of battle the distinctive Israelite trumpet tattoo for war would be blown so that (1) Israel would be remembered before the Lord and (2) the people might be rescued from their enemies. In this way the trumpet is seen to be analogous to prayer, a means of participation in activating the will of God. God's will will be done whether we pray or not. But by praying we become expectant of his response, and we praise him when he does. Trumpets were another means for participating in the activating of God's will. By blowing the trumpets before the battle, Israel confidently could expect God's active presence in the battle scene. The blowing of these trumpets prepared the people for the presence of God.

10 As in the case of battle, it appears that the blowing of the trumpets was a means of knowing that the people were remembered by the Lord: "They will be a memorial for you before your God." The trumpets were blown, not as an invocation of deity as in pagan societies, but as an introit to prepare the people for an active confrontation with God. Here, then, is one of the OT bases for the use of instrumentation in divine worship.

Trumpets in the worship of God in the tabernacle or the later temple were also used similarly. The blowing of the trumpets was not a charm to summon a deity but an active response to his presence, an appeal to his will, a participation in his work. Trumpets were to be played in times of festive worship, including feasts, New Moon festivals, burnt offerings, and fellowship offerings. They serve as a memorial of the people to God and of him to them. The text ends with the solemn assertion: "I am Yahweh your God." This is a slogan that marks the importance of a text; here it also indicates the completion of a major unit of our book.

Certain biblical words evoke strong associations. Many readers of the Bible think of a trumpet blast as initiating the resurrection of the righteous dead to life imperishable (1 Cor 15:52). Here in the beginning the trumpet blast has more modest but still significant associations.

2. *Setting forth the people on the triumphal march (10:11–36)*

Most commentators divide the Book of Numbers into three parts, with the second major section beginning at 10:11. The approach in this commentary is to treat the

Book of Numbers as a biped of two unequal parts (chs. 1–25; 26–36), structured on the basis of the two census lists (chs. 1–4; 26). In this approach, suggested by Olson (see Introduction: Unity and Organization), 10:11 does not begin the second major unit of the book; it leads instead to the conclusion of the first part of the first major section. Thus 10:11–36 is key to understanding the Book of Numbers. But the function of this section is not to introduce Israel's gradual failure, as is commonly supposed. It presents Israel at last on the move, under the hand of God, faithful to his word, and on the way to victory in Canaan. This is a section of triumphalism of the first generation. Nothing prepares us for the shock of their rebellion as described beginning in chapter 11. The fact that their triumphant march lasts only briefly with Israel still in the desert is a great sadness.

a. *The march begins*

10:11–13

11 On the twentieth day of the second month of the second year, the cloud lifted from above the tabernacle of the Testimony. 12 Then the Israelites set out from the Desert of Sinai and traveled from place to place until the cloud came to rest in the Desert of Paran. 13 They set out, this first time, at the LORD's command through Moses.

11–13 After eleven months in the region of Mount Sinai (see the Notes on 9:1), the people moved out at the first time led by the Lord in his wondrous cloud (v.11). Israel, on the move from the Desert of Sinai (v.12), was on a journey that in a few weeks could lead them into the conquest of the land of Canaan. This was a day not to be forgotten: the second year, the second month, the twentieth day. Generations later, one suspects, this day might have been memorialized. At last the Israelites were on their way to Canaan!

Once again we sense the spirit of the Lord's initiation, of the peoples' compliance, of the role of the cloud of his presence, and of the work of Moses in the guidance of the people. Possibly the command of Moses in v.13 includes the blowing of the trumpets (as described in vv.1–10). The journey that this text describes is not detailed fully here. It is not until 12:16 that the destination of the Desert of Paran is achieved. More specifically, the people settled at Kadesh in the Desert of Zin (20:1). There are at least three stops on this initial journey: Taberah (11:3), Kibroth Hattaavah (11:35), and Hazeroth (11:35).

The Desert of Paran is a large plateau in the northeastern Sinai, south of what later would be called the Negev of Judah, and west of the Arabah. This forms the southernmost portion of the Promised Land, the presumed staging area for the assault on the land itself. The principal lines of assault on the land of Canaan are from the southwest, following the Way of the Sea from Egypt, and from the northwest, following the Way of the Sea from Phoenicia. Israel's staging for attack in the Desert of Paran was a brilliant strategy. In this way they would avoid the fortified routes to the west, presumably under the control of Egypt. This unusual line of attack from the south would stun the inhabitants of the land. They would come like a sirocco blast from the desert, and the land would be theirs, under the hand of God.

Notes

One of the ways that significant events are highlighted in biblical narrative is by a finely crafted structure. This text shows such a structure:

v.11	The time frame
vv.12–13	Introductory summary of the people setting out on their journey
vv.14–17	Setting out of the Judah tribes (see 2:3–9)
vv.18–21	Setting out of the Reuben tribes (see 2:10–16)
vv.22–24	Setting out of the Ephraim tribes (see 2:18–24)
vv.25–27	Setting out of the Dan tribes (see 2:25–31)
v.28	Concluding summary of the line of march

b. *The grand procession of tribes and Levites*

10:14–28

14The divisions of the camp of Judah went first, under their standard.
Nahshon son of Amminadab was in command. 15Nethanel son of Zuar
was over the division of the tribe of Issachar, 16and Eliab son of Helon
was over the division of the tribe of Zebulun. 17Then the tabernacle was
taken down, and the Gershonites and Merarites, who carried it, set out.
18The divisions of the camp of Reuben went next, under their
standard. Elizur son of Shedeur was in command. 19Shelumiel son of
Zurishaddai was over the division of the tribe of Simeon, 20and Eliasaph
son of Deuel was over the division of the tribe of Gad. 21Then the
Kohathites set out, carrying the holy things. The tabernacle was to be
set up before they arrived.
22The divisions of the camp of Ephraim went next, under their
standard. Elishama son of Ammihud was in command. 23Gamaliel son
of Pedahzur was over the division of the tribe of Manasseh, 24and
Abidan son of Gideoni was over the division of the tribe of Benjamin.
25Finally, as the rear guard for all the units, the divisions of the camp
of Dan set out, under their standard. Ahiezer son of Ammishaddai was in
command. 26Pagiel son of Ocran was over the division of the tribe of
Asher, 27and Ahira son of Enan was over the division of the tribe of
Naphtali. 28This was the order of march for the Israelite divisions as they
set out.

14–28 The names of the leaders of the Twelve Tribes are given for the fourth time in the book (see 1:5–15; 2:3–31; 7:12–83); the order for the tribes in the line of march is the same as was presented in chapter 2. The new detail is that the Gershonites and the Merarites bearing the tabernacle followed the triad of the Judah tribes in the line of march (v.17). The Kohathites carrying the holy things followed the triad of the Reuben tribes (v.21). Each of the four triads of tribes had a standard or banner for rallying and organization (cf. 2:3, 10, 18, 25).

It is difficult to read these words without wincing. We know what is coming, for we have already read the story. But there is nothing in these chapters to suggest that the worthies mentioned here for the fourth time will not be the leaders who will make their mark with their tribes, their armies, and their banners in the Promised Land. The stately pageantry of this section is, it turns out, the setup for a terrible fall.

c. *The request for Hobab to join the march*

10:29–32

[29]Now Moses said to Hobab son of Reuel the Midianite, Moses' father-in-law, "We are setting out for the place about which the LORD said, 'I will give it to you.' Come with us and we will treat you well, for the LORD has promised good things to Israel."

[30]He answered, "No, I will not go; I am going back to my own land and my own people."

[31]But Moses said, "Please do not leave us. You know where we should camp in the desert, and you can be our eyes. [32]If you come with us, we will share with you whatever good things the LORD gives us."

29–32 Hobab was Moses' brother-in-law, the son of Reuel (Jethro; see Exod 2:18; 3:1). Reuel had been most helpful to Moses earlier (see Exod 18); now his son, with an expertise in the desert lands of the Sinai, would be a significant aid in locating water and pasturage in regions that were unknown to Moses. It is significant that Moses appeals to Hobab on several lines: one was likely in terms of their relatedness through marriage, a not insignificant bond among peoples of the desert; another is based on the goodness of God that is promised to Israel and in which Hobab may participate; and another is the expertise of Hobab, that is, an appeal to his sense of a special ability. In this latter instance Moses says that Hobab might become the "eyes" of the people (v.31). Moses then reinforces the benefits that will come to Hobab; he will share in the benefits the Lord is about to bring on the nation (v.32).

Hobab refused at first, citing the need to care for his own family in his own land, following the traditional ancient Eastern pattern of adherence to family and place. We recognize that there is also a tie to his family gods involved, though he does not state this clearly. Moses continued to urge Hobab to join Israel. In a sense this is an act of evangelism. Hobab did not come easily. But subsequent biblical texts indicate that he did come. As such, he is like Ruth who joins Naomi en route to the Land of Promise, leaving all behind, with a promise of something ahead that is of more value than anything left at home. Coming with Moses was not just a change of address; it was a radical reorientation of life itself. To come with Moses was to have a new family. To come with Moses was to gain a new land. To come with Moses was to come to believe in a new God.

Judges 1:16 indicates that Hobab acceded to this request from Moses to be "eyes" for the people in the desert (v.31), as his descendants receive a share in the land. But he himself does not share in the land. Presumably, the sadness of Israel's impending rebellion against the Lord included Hobab in the judgment. He experienced the goodness of God in the same way that the rest of the people did: in the providential care that God gave his erring people in the inhospitable desert of their banishment. Hobab must have been an invaluable aid to Moses. The few weeks' journey was to last a lifetime.

d. *The three-day procession behind the ark of the Lord*

10:33–36

[33]So they set out from the mountain of the LORD and traveled for three days. The ark of the covenant of the LORD went before them during those three days to find them a place to rest. [34]The cloud of the LORD was over them by day when they set out from the camp.

35 Whenever the ark set out, Moses said,

"Rise up, O LORD!
May your enemies be scattered;
may your foes flee before you."

36 Whenever it came to rest, he said,

"Return, O LORD,
to the countless thousands of Israel."

33–34 The journey began with a three-day march. Eleven months earlier the people of Israel were a rag-tag group of former slaves, gathered in the desert in the first rush of deliverance, but unorganized and unruly. Now they were prepared for the march, the battle, and the victory. Because of the significant numbers of the people in the tribes of Israel, and since this was their first organized march, it is not likely that the first journey of three days covered much territory. But it was marked by sufficient success to be regarded as a victory march in these verses.

35–36 The sense of a victory march is enhanced by the recording of what we may call the "Battle Cry of Moses" (contrast the "Lament of Moses," 11:11–15). This little poem is potent in its living theology (see Notes); it rests ultimately on the notion of cursing and blessing that goes all the way back to the Abrahamic covenant (Gen 12:2–3). As the cloud of the Lord would arise, and as it would settle for the people to rest, Moses would call out: "Rise up, O Yahweh!" and "Return, O Yahweh!" The words of v.35 are a cursing of the enemies of the Lord and his people; the words of v.36 are a blessing on the people of his promise.

Finally, the wording of the blessing section is significant for the presentation of the idea of the rhetorical use of numbers in the census lists. The Hebrew phrase for "countless thousands" is "myriads of thousands" (v.36). The idea is akin to "untold numbers" or "teeming millions." This deliberative hyperbole (no matter how many peoples the census lists indicate) is perhaps an example of Moses using "power numbers" in his Battle Cry (see the Notes; see also the Introduction: The Problem of Large Numbers; The Large Numbers—Toward a Solution).

Thus in these words of Moses we have a shout of victory based solidly on the faithfulness of the Lord to his covenant promise to the Fathers. The people are on their way to Canaan; soon Canaan will be the land of Israel, or so we might think, based on these words of exuberant confidence in God. Significantly, these words of Moses are used by David in the beginning of his triumphal song in Psalm 68.

Notes

29 Words of familial relationships such as חֹתֵן (*ḥōṯēn*, "father-in-law") are troublesome in Hebrew. The basic idea of the root *ḥtn* seems to be that of an in-law relationship; the precise relationship is sometimes debated. In the case of Hobab, the text of v.29 suggests he is the brother of Zipporah, wife of Moses. He is thus the brother-in-law of Moses. Judges 4:11 complicates the issue; in some translations this verse reads that Hobab is the father-in-law of Moses. Judges 4:11 should be read in the light of Num 10:29, however. Upon the death of his father, Reuel (Jethro), Hobab would become the head of his household. Since he is the one who joins in the fortunes of Israel, he is regarded by later generations as the head of his household. His tie to Moses through marriage makes him particularly memorable.

35–36 The structure of the little poem is as follows:

Introductory prose line: At the time of the departure of the ark (5 words):
A call for Yahweh to rise and to scatter his enemies (Tricolon—2:2:3)
Introductory monocolon: At the time of the resting of the ark (2 words):
A call for Yahweh to return and to bless his people (Bicolon—2:3).

The second and third members of the tricolon, "may your enemies be scattered/ may those who hate you flee before you," form a synonymous pair; the two units are strongly contrasting: Rise/Return; Curse/Bless.

In the MT these verses are braced with an unusual phenomenon, long debated in meaning—inverted נs (*ns*). There is an inverted נ before v.35 and another at the end of v.36. Medieval Jewish tradition suggests that these two verses were not from Moses but from an otherwise suppressed book by Eldad and Medad (see 11:26–27). This view is explained and then critiqued by Sid Z. Leiman, "The Inverted Nuns at Numbers 10:35–36 and the Book of Eldad and Medad," JBL 93, 3 (September 1974): 348–55. His view is that these two verses did not come *from* an independent book but that the nuns suggest that they *form* an independent "book."

36 רִבְבוֹת (*ri<u>b</u>ᵉ<u>b</u>ô<u>t</u>,* "countless") is a term that speaks in grand, rhetorical style of very large numbers. It can mean "ten thousand" in an approximate manner. A more exacting way of saying "ten thousand" in Hebrew would be to use the term "thousand" along with the numeral "ten." More often, however, *ri<u>b</u>ᵉ<u>b</u>ô<u>t</u>* means "myriads," "innumerable," or "countless." This is a significant term to use in the deliberate inflation of numbers as "power words."

B. *The Rebellion and Judgment of a Fearful People (11:1–25:18)*

We now begin an entirely new and unexpected account in the experience of the people of the first generation. They had been prepared by Moses, at the instruction of the Lord, to be a holy people on a march of triumph bound for the Promised Land. But by the third day of the march, the people faltered; the holy people became sullied with contempt for the Lord. Chapters 11–20 present a dismal record of their acts of ingratitude and of God's consequent judgments on his ungrateful people. Within these chapters are innumerable instances of his continuing grace. The reader of these texts goes astray if he or she focuses solely on God's wrath or on the constant provocations to his anger by his meandering people. The more impressive feature in this text is God's continuing mercy against continuing, obdurate rebellion.

Chapters 21–25 bring the narrative to an arresting climax, bringing together the motifs of rebellion and hope. The materials of these chapters do not at all present a complete record of Israel's experiences in the desert. The writing is focused; the choice of stories is selective. The aspect of God's grace is presented arrestingly in the amazing narrative of Balaam, the pagan mantic who failed to destroy Israel by the power of his words, but who nearly destroyed the people by the persuasion of his guile (chs. 22–25). The judgment of God at the final rebellion of the people in chapter 25 ends the record of rebellion of the first generation. The experience of the new generation begins in chapter 26.

1. *A cycle of rebellion and atonement and the record of death (11:1–20:29)*

These ten chapters now balance and contrast with the ten chapters that present the record of Israel's preparation. Barely has the march begun before the rebellion is underway—a rebellion of the spirit of the people that manifests itself in a variety of ways. But always it comes down to this: God's demand of complete obedience and robust faith, a devotion of the whole person, was infrequently found in his people. These chapters call to mind the observation of Gleason L. Archer, Jr., who reacts against the hypothesis of "Israel's genius for religion" as an explanation for the lofty spirituality of the Bible and especially for its grand monotheistic faith. Certain theologians ascribe to Israel a penchant for religion that is akin to the Greeks' love for beauty and the Romans' gift for order. Archer rightly rejoins, "It was not [a] product of the natural Hebrew 'genius for religion' (as is often asserted), for the scripture record witnesses rather to the natural Hebrew genius for irreligion and apostasy" (SOTIrev, p. 145). Such a judgment is not a racial slur, by the way; many of the people of God in all ages seem to display similar traits of irreligion and apostasy. This is why the Book of Numbers is so important for readers today.

a. *The beginning of sorrows (11:1–35)*

(1) *A judgment of fire (11:1–3)*

11:1–3

> 1 Now the people complained about their hardships in the hearing of the LORD, and when he heard them his anger was aroused. Then fire from the LORD burned among them and consumed some of the outskirts of the camp. 2 When the people cried out to Moses, he prayed to the LORD and the fire died down. 3 So that place was called Taberah, because fire from the LORD had burned among them.

There is a cyclical nature to Israel's rebellions against God; obdurate people tend to repeat the sins of the past. The first rebellion of the redeemed people came on the third day of marching toward the Mount of God after their miraculous crossing of the Sea of Reeds (Exod 15:22–24). Now, three days out on their triumphal march to Canaan from Mount Sinai, they fall back into their complaining behavior. The pattern of "three days" in both cases shows both similarity of actions as well as an intemperate, impatient attitude on the part of the people.

1 Instead of "Now the people complained," the MT could also be translated, "Now the people became truly murmurous, an offense to Yahweh's ears." Nothing in the first ten chapters of Numbers has prepared us for this verse; rather these chapters have emphasized repeatedly the complete obedience of Moses and the people to the dictates of the Lord. But only three days into their march, the people had reverted to the disloyal complaining they had expressed a year earlier only three days from their deliverance from the waters of the Red Sea (Exod 15:22–27). In that earlier experience they had vented their subsequent complaints about manna (Exod 16) and a lack of water (Exod 17:1–7). So now the people again reverted to the behavior of ingratitude that marked their early experience in the desert. This attitude of ingratitude was seditious against the covenant and malicious against the person of God. They were actually in breach of covenant, deserving of the Suzerain's wrath.

The narrator of Numbers has arranged his materials so carefully that this sudden outbreak of renewed pettiness against God seems unprecedented, unexpected—unbelievable. How, we wonder, with all the preparation for a holy walk, could there come such stumbling so soon?

The response of the Lord to this outbreak of murmuring was one of wrath. The text says that "fire from the LORD" burned among them. This purging fire was limited to the outskirts of the camp, a mercy of the Lord. He might have cast his fire into the very midst of the camp and killed many more persons than suffered this terrible judgment. The judgment by "fire" is suggestive, not only of judgment, but of refining, of cleansing. Perhaps a burst of fire will not only judge the offenders of God's grace but will serve as well as a symbol of cleansing for the entire camp.

At times the expression "fire from the LORD" may refer to fire ignited by the divine casting of lightning (as seems possible in 1 Kings 18:38, in the encounter of Elijah with the prophets of Baal on Mount Carmel). The imagery of Baal in the nature religion of Canaan often presents him in association with lightning and storm, as the one who casts his bolt, beats the drums of the heavens, then drives the clouds across the sky. The poets of the Bible sometimes build on this imagery but apply it to the Lord. In this way they despoil Baal of his titles, and they ascribe greatness to the Lord. Psalm 68, for example, to which reference was made at 10:35, extols the Lord as the one "who rides on the clouds" (see NIV text and mg., Ps 68:4).

It seems altogether possible that the "fire from the LORD" in this text is judgment in the form of a bolt (or bolts) of lightning that caused terrible fire among the people on the outskirts of the camp. There are other times when it may be that the phrase refers to a flash from the fires of his altars.

2 In the midst of his wrath, the Lord remembers mercy. This is one of the ongoing themes of Scripture and is a particular truism in the Book of Numbers. The people truly deserve God's considerable wrath. But the survivors of this outburst of his anger cry out to Moses for help in their behalf before the Lord. Moses prays, and the fire subsides. The Hebrew verb is *šāqaʿ*, a word meaning "to sink down," a particularly picturesque term for the dying out of a raging fire.

3 The place name "Taberah" comes from a Hebrew noun meaning "burning"; it is mentioned only here and in Deuteronomy 9:22. This name comes in association with the verb "had burned." Because of the raging of the fire of God in their midst, the people named that place of awful memory "Taberah," Burning.

Notes

1 כְּמִתְאֹנְנִים (*kᵉmit̲ʾōnᵉnîm*, "complained") is a Hithpo'el participle from the root אָנַן (*ʾānan*). It may be related to an Akkadian term *enenu*, *unninu*, "to sigh." The Hebrew term is used only here and in Lam 3:39. The problem with the grammatical form is the *k* prefix. It is possible to take this as the preposition and translate, "they have become as those who complain." But it is more likely that the *k* is asseverative, expressing identity (Ronald Williams, *Hebrew Syntax* [Toronto: University Press, 1968], sec. 261). The idea seems to be this: "Now the people became truly murmurous, an offense to the LORD's ears."

The NIV reads רַע (*raʿ*, "evil thing," "an offense") as a prepositional phrase following the participle "they complained," thus rendering it as "hardships." However, the BHS text has a strong disjunctive accent with the participle; the term *raʿ* goes with the following phrase. I suggest the translation: "Now the people became truly murmurous, an offense to the Lord's ears."

(2) *A surfeit of quail*

11:4–34

[4]The rabble with them began to crave other food, and again the
Israelites started wailing and said, "If only we had meat to eat! [5]We
remember the fish we ate in Egypt at no cost—also the cucumbers,
melons, leeks, onions and garlic. [6]But now we have lost our appetite; we
never see anything but this manna!"

[7]The manna was like coriander seed and looked like resin. [8]The
people went around gathering it, and then ground it in a handmill or
crushed it in a mortar. They cooked it in a pot or made it into cakes. And
it tasted like something made with olive oil. [9]When the dew settled on
the camp at night, the manna also came down.

[10]Moses heard the people of every family wailing, each at the
entrance to his tent. The LORD became exceedingly angry, and Moses
was troubled. [11]He asked the LORD, "Why have you brought this trouble
on your servant? What have I done to displease you that you put the
burden of all these people on me? [12]Did I conceive all these people? Did
I give them birth? Why do you tell me to carry them in my arms, as a
nurse carries an infant, to the land you promised on oath to their
forefathers? [13]Where can I get meat for all these people? They keep
wailing to me, 'Give us meat to eat!' [14]I cannot carry all these people by
myself; the burden is too heavy for me. [15]If this is how you are going to
treat me, put me to death right now—if I have found favor in your
eyes—and do not let me face my own ruin."

[16]The LORD said to Moses: "Bring me seventy of Israel's elders who
are known to you as leaders and officials among the people. Have them
come to the Tent of Meeting, that they may stand there with you. [17]I will
come down and speak with you there, and I will take of the Spirit that is
on you and put the Spirit on them. They will help you carry the burden of
the people so that you will not have to carry it alone.

[18]"Tell the people: 'Consecrate yourselves in preparation for tomorrow, when you will eat meat. The LORD heard you when you wailed, "If
only we had meat to eat! We were better off in Egypt!" Now the LORD will
give you meat, and you will eat it. [19]You will not eat it for just one day, or
two days, or five, ten or twenty days, [20]but for a whole month—until it
comes out of your nostrils and you loathe it—because you have
rejected the LORD, who is among you, and have wailed before him,
saying, "Why did we ever leave Egypt?" ' "

[21]But Moses said, "Here I am among six hundred thousand men on
foot, and you say, 'I will give them meat to eat for a whole month!'
[22]Would they have enough if flocks and herds were slaughtered for
them? Would they have enough if all the fish in the sea were caught for
them?"

[23]The LORD answered Moses, "Is the LORD's arm too short? You will
now see whether or not what I say will come true for you."

[24]So Moses went out and told the people what the LORD had said. He
brought together seventy of their elders and had them stand around the
Tent. [25]Then the LORD came down in the cloud and spoke with him, and
he took of the Spirit that was on him and put the Spirit on the seventy
elders. When the Spirit rested on them, they prophesied, but they did
not do so again.

[26]However, two men, whose names were Eldad and Medad, had
remained in the camp. They were listed among the elders, but did not go
out to the Tent. Yet the Spirit also rested on them, and they prophesied
in the camp. [27]A young man ran and told Moses, "Eldad and Medad are
prophesying in the camp."

[28]Joshua son of Nun, who had been Moses' aide since youth, spoke up and said, "Moses, my lord, stop them!"

[29]But Moses replied, "Are you jealous for my sake? I wish that all the LORD's people were prophets and that the LORD would put his Spirit on them!" [30]Then Moses and the elders of Israel returned to the camp.

[31]Now a wind went out from the LORD and drove quail in from the sea. It brought them down all around the camp to about three feet above the ground, as far as a day's walk in any direction. [32]All that day and night and all the next day the people went out and gathered quail. No one gathered less than ten homers. Then they spread them out all around the camp. [33]But while the meat was still between their teeth and before it could be consumed, the anger of the LORD burned against the people, and he struck them with a severe plague. [34]Therefore the place was named Kibroth Hattaavah, because there they buried the people who had craved other food.

Sadly, the memory of the cause of the burning at Taberah seems to have been lost quickly. For it was followed directly by another even more serious attack on God's mercy in the people's rejection of manna, the bread of heaven. It is possible that there was a considerable lapse of time between the provocation of burning (vv.1–3) and the provocation of the plague of quail (vv.4–35), but the placement of these stories in abrupt linking suggests that the time lapse is negligible. It seems this new rebellion transpired on the next stop along the march (see v.34).

There is a symmetry to the narratives of rebellion in the Bible. The scream for "real food" rather than the divine provision of manna takes us back to the initial complaint about food in Exodus 16:1–3, where God initiates his wonder of manna; it also carries us forward to the last rebellion about food near the end of the generation in the desert (21:4–9), where the people spurn manna as detestable, only to have an image of the truly detestable, the snake, be their only means of escape from God's plague.

Indeed, God's provision of food for his people (and their common actions of ingratitude for his mercy) is one of the dominant motifs of biblical faith. The biblical vista of mankind's adventure with God begins in the midst of a garden teeming with all manner of food (Gen 2), and the eating of one forbidden item led to expulsion from Paradise (Gen 3). The Bible ends with the portrait of a glorious day in the future in which there will be no lack of provision for the people of God, and nothing is prohibited (Rev 22:1–5). Along the way on the journey from the paradise of Eden to the coming Garden of Glory, the provision of food is a mark of God's love and care for his people (cf. Ps 111:5).

Further, the provision of food is often a sign of worship of God's wonder and grace (as in the fellowship offerings of the OT and the Lord's Table of the NT). Food is more than "fuel" for the body, more than nutrients for living. The biblical view is that food is sacral; there are no "common meals." Paul attacks the ideas of some in his day who minimized food to the mechanical processes of digestion (see 1 Cor 8:13). There is more to eating than food and stomach. This is why we must bless God especially at meal times. Eating a satisfying meal is for the believer a provocation to the praise of the Lord who gives good gifts (Deut 8:10). Similarly, to attack God for meagerness in food or for a lack of variety may be a cowardly act of impiety. So we learn in the story that follows.

4 This account appropriately begins with the "rabble," an apt term for the non-Israelite mixed group of people who followed the people of Israel from Egypt. This term points to a recurring source of complaints and trouble in the camp. Those who did not know the Lord and his mercies too easily incited those who did know him to rebel against him. But however the murmuring began, it soon spread throughout the camp of Israel. It is likely that familiar texts on separation from people who do not share biblical faith have their first instance in this account (see 1 Cor 6:14–18; see also prohibited mixtures in Torah, Deut 22:10–11).

In any event, as in Exodus 16, the people began to complain concerning their diet, forgetting what God had done for them: "in the desert they gave in to their craving; / in the wasteland they put God to the test" (Ps 106:14). We may suspect that meat was not the common fare of the slaves in Egypt. By romanticizing the past, the people tended to minimize earlier discomforts when in a new type of distress. This is a common human failing.

The verb "to crave" (*'āwāh*, in the Hithpael) leads to the name of the location of the subsequent judgment, Kibroth Hattaavah, "Graves of Craving" (v.34). The verb can be used for positive and proper desires but is especially fitting for feelings of (improper) lusts and bodily appetites. The verb is enhanced by its cognate accusative *ta'āwāh* ("desire"), a word that can be used in good senses (as Pss 10:17; 38:9 [10 MT]; Prov 11:23 et al.) as well as in contexts of covetousness and lusts (Pss 10:3; 112:10; Prov 21:25–26). The wording "they craved a craving" is emphatic in nature; the meaning is something like "they had an intense craving [for meat]."

5–6 The several types of vegetables and fruit mentioned in this verse are suggestive of the varieties of foods available in Egypt, in contrast to the diet solely of manna in the desert (v.6). Further, the poor in Egypt were able to supplement their diet with fish that are found in many canals and waterways (see Gray, p. 103). We may suggest that they were exaggerating the variety and plenty of their diet in Egypt. But the contrast was sure: there are no fish or vegetables to be had in the desert. The focus of faith, however, is that there should have been no food at all in the desert. That there was anything at all to eat was solely by God's mercy. To spurn a regularly occurring, abundant and nutritious food only because it is boring is understandably human—a pitiable mark of our tendency toward ingratitude.

7–9 The description of the manna in terms of its appearance and its taste would be meaningful only to people who lived later than the time of its provision (cf. also Exod 16 for a description of manna). As in the instance of the description of the hovering cloud and fire (9:15–23), the nature and appearance of manna would have been very familiar to the persons of this story. In fact, that is the point: they were sick of it!

These words could have been written by Moses in anticipation of the curiosity of later generations; but conceivably these descriptive words were added considerably later than Moses, based on the memory of the food at a time when it was no longer a part of Israel's experience. (See Introduction: Authorship and Date, for a discussion of post-Mosaic additions to the book.) To speak in this way of the possibility of later additions to the text of Numbers is not to imply that these additions, if that is what they are, are not accurate, are untrustworthy, or are not inspired by God. They are, in fact, an essential part of the text as we have received it. Even though descriptions such as these may come from a time later than Moses, they may still be viewed as the work of the Spirit—i.e., true Scripture. In such a case the concept of inspiration—and its corollary inerrancy—extends to such bona fide additions. The issue of the "autograph" is far more complex in some books of Hebrew Scripture than perhaps in some NT writings.

Many naturalistic explanations have been given to account for the provision of manna by those who have traveled in the Sinai. Some point to a secretion of the tamarisk tree of small, yellow-white balls that have a sweet taste. Others believe this secretion is not the product of the tree but is the excreta of certain scale insects made on the leaves of these trees during June in some areas of the Sinai. But no naturally occurring substance truly fits the data of the text. Several factors suggest that manna was a unique provision from the Lord for the people of Israel in the desert, not just a natural substance given in greater than usual abundance (see Notes).

10 The rejection of his gracious gift of heavenly food (called "bread from heaven" in Exod 16:4) was extremely evil to the Lord. Israel's rejection of his provision was a failure of the test of faith. God had said that the reception of the manna by the people would be a significant test of their obedience (Exod 16:4). The people had allowed themselves to think back to their lives in slavery and to regard that estate as more pleasurable than their present walk with the Lord on their way to the land of his promise. In view of the "good things" that the Lord was to give them (see 10:32), the people were expected to receive each day's supply of manna as a gracious gift of a merciful God and a promise of abundance to come. In their spurning the manna, the people had contemned him. They repeat this grave evil thirty-eight years later (ch. 21). There is a sense that the rebellion of Israel in Numbers begins and ends on the subject of food and a despising of God's provision.

11–15 The reaction of the people to God's mercy in manna was greatly troubling to Moses as well. Instead of turning to the Lord to ask that he understand the substance of their complaint, Moses turned to the Lord to ask why he was given such an ungrateful people to lead. There is a very human touch in all this; Moses is caught off guard, as it were—ill-prepared for the magnitude of the problem he faced in leading this sinful people.

This leads to what we may call "Moses' Lament" (vv.11–15), a studied contrast with the "Battle Cry of Moses" (10:35–36). There are elements in this section that remind one of the lament psalms in the Bible. The layout of the text in the standard MT is presented as prose, as in the NIV. But there is a musical, poetic feel to these words. It is possible to present this section in a poetic format and thus to sense more thoroughly the deep passions that underlie them:

11 And Moses said to Yahweh:
"Why have you brought calamity to your servant?
Why do I still not find grace in your eyes?
[Why have you] placed the burden of all this people on me?
12 "Surely it is not I who conceived all this people?
Did I give birth to them?
"Why should you say to me,
'Hold them to your bosom;
Carry them as a nurse does a nursing child
to the land you promised to their fathers'?
13 "Wherever may I find meat
to give to all this people?
"For they come weeping against me saying,
'Give us meat that we may eat!'
14 "I am unable to do it alone!
I cannot bear all this people;

They are too heavy for me!
15 “If this is what you wish to do to me,
then slay me quickly!
“Do this, if I still have any favor in your sight!
Only let me not see my calamity!”

Viewed in this manner, this lament has a highly poetic cast to it. It is marked by lines of tricola (three elements) and bicola (two elements) in standard parallel structures familiar from other poetry of the Bible. Moreover, the rhetoric is poetic in nature, expressing deep passion in hyperbolic flourishes. The lament is marked by an inclusio, the use of the same or a similar element at the beginning and the end to give a sense of binding and unity. The poem begins with Moses asking God why he has brought calamity on him, using the verbal form *h^{a}rē‘ōṯā* (a Hiphil from the verb *rā‘a‘*, “to treat badly”). The poem ends with Moses begging the Lord not to let him see the full extent of his calamity, using the noun form *b^{e}rā‘āṯî* (the noun *rā‘āh*, “trouble,” “misery,” plus preposition and pronominal suffixes).

Moses brings all this on himself. He would rather die than continue to be so very troubled by this obdurate people. In this deeply moving lament, which I take to be an exquisite poem of great artistry, Moses serves as a mirror of the feelings of God!

The language is impassioned when we hear it from Moses. It is unbearable when we hear it from the Lord. That is where these words drive us. After all, it is the Lord who has conceived this people. It is he who has given them birth. He is their nurse, their mother, their succor in the desert place. He has promised them their land; he will give them their place. The people were screaming out to Moses; but ultimately they were ranting against the Lord. When Moses rhetorically contemplates death as escape, there is the suggestion of unrelieved horror: What if the Lord were to “die” to his people? What if he were to be no more their God? The words of this poem are troubling enough when we hear them from Moses, servant of the Lord. When we realize they mirror the rage of God, in anthropopathic feelings of frustration and incredulity, then this poem is expressive of genuine mystery and wonder!

16–17 The response of the Lord to the great distress of his prophet was twofold—mercy and curse: (1) there was mercy to Moses in that his work load was now to be shared by seventy leaders who will help him to carry the burden of the people in future encounters (vv.16–17); (2) there was a curse on the people that was in kind with their complaint: they asked for meat and would now become sick with meat (vv.18–34).

The blessing of the provision of seventy elders must have been an enormous sense of relief to Moses. It is dangerous, even silly, to attempt to psychoanalyze someone in antiquity. Nonetheless, the language of Moses’ Lament (vv.11–15) suggests deep depression. Moses’ desire to die (v.15) is not unlike the death wish of Elijah following the ultimate failure of his revival at Mount Carmel (1 Kings 19:4; see my article, “Elijah the Broken Prophet,” JETS 22, 3 [September 1979]: 193–202). It is my conviction that the enormous weight of these feelings of depression are the signal elements of understanding the troublesome words of 12:3, the “meekness” of Moses (NIV, “very humble”; see below).

The language used with reference to the Spirit in this section is of high interest. God tells Moses that he will take of the Spirit that is on Moses and put that Spirit on the seventy (v.17). The idea in this strange wording is clear enough: they will share the same Holy Spirit who animates and empowers Moses.

18–20 The people's distress at the lack of variety in the daily manna led them to challenge the goodness of the Lord. Ultimately, it would be such a challenge to his essential goodness that it would lead to their own deaths in the land (chs. 13–14). At present the judgment is partial; the judgment that will come will be all-inclusive. They had screamed for meat. Now they were going to get a surfeit of meat, so much that it would make them physically ill. There is a sardonic humor in this, a sense of comic justice. In effect, God says to them that he will give them all the meat they want and then some! They claimed that manna was a boring diet, that they could not live without variety, without some meat to eat. Now they were going to receive a diet of constant meat, not for a day or so, but for a full month. They will be so filled with meat that it will spew from their nostrils.

The principal issue was not meat at all. The Lord explains to Moses what the real issue is; he says of the people, "You have rejected the LORD" (v.20). The language is emphatic and gripping: "Surely you have rejected Yahweh who is among you!" The idea is one of incredulity. He is near in grace, but they have turned their back on him. He is in their midst, and they wish he were not. He has come down, and they wish he would go away. The issue was not just failure to demonstrate proper gratitude to the Lord who was in their midst and who was their constant source of good; it was turning from him entirely and grudgingly rejecting his many acts of mercy on their behalf. I suspect the only comparable thing for the modern reader would be for one who has made a Christian commitment to say to the Savior, "I wish you had not died for me! Leave me alone!" Only when we put things in these terms may we sense the enormity of the language of this verse.

21–23 The response of Moses in these verses is not to the basic theological issue of the rejection of the Lord by the people. His head is still spinning from the declaration of the Lord that he will provide meat for all the people for a month. Moses reminds God (!) of the numbers involved: six hundred thousand men on foot. The numerics of the men numbered for war are consistent throughout the Book of Numbers, a strong argument, it seems to me, against arbitrary judgments of textual corruption. A marching force of this size suggests a total population of over two million people (or perhaps one-tenth of this total; see the sections on large numbers in the Introduction). Moses' distress at providing meat for this immense number of people (and it is immense, even if the numbers are rhetorically inflated!) is nearly comical—the task is staggering; it is an impossibility. The Christian has an advantage over Moses, knowing already the corresponding works of Jesus in the Gospels of feeding immense populaces from the smallest of provisions.

The familiar level of the dialogue between Moses and the Lord is provocative of the level of trust and relationship that Moses, God's servant, was able to have with his Suzerain. The special nature of Moses' relationship with God, and the level of intimacy in his communication with the Lord and the Lord with him, is detailed in 12:6–8. The response of God is, "Is the LORD's arm too short?" (v.23; actually, the Hebrew idiom is, "Is the hand of Yahweh too short?"). The human impossibility of the task of providing meat for the immense numbers of Israelites is an occasion to demonstrate the wonder of the Lord. Moses also needed an encouragement to his faith. His depression made him like Elijah after Carmel, a prophet in need of a fresh experience of the wonder and presence of Yahweh.

24–25 This chapter interplays several themes: the arrogant lust of the people, the impassioned distress of Moses, the plan of God to bring an answer of judgment to the people, and the purpose of the Lord to bring an answer of grace to his servant. These two verses relate to the subject of the seventy elders, introduced in vv.16–17. The coming near of the Lord in the cloud (v.25) brings us back to 9:15–23, the description of the hovering cloud and fire. But this text advances on it in some way, speaking of the cloud coming down or, better, of the Lord coming down by means of the cloud. Sovereignly, mysteriously, graciously, the Lord apportioned the same Spirit that was on Moses on the seventy elders. Again, the idea is not that the Spirit is divided into smaller units but that it is the very same Spirit of God who empowers Moses that now animates these men. The Christian cannot but think of Pentecost in Acts 2. In a sense what occurred here in the desert is a presentment ahead of time of the bestowal of the Spirit on the believers in the Upper Room following the resurrection of the Lord Jesus. The taking of "some" of the Spirit from Moses suggests the release of some of the burden that he bore. They will share in that work with him. The text states that these elders prophesied, but they did not continue to do so. It seems that the temporary gift of prophecy to these elders was primarily to establish their credentials as Spirit-empowered leaders rather than to make of them ongoing agents of the prophecy of the Spirit. Their principal task will not be revelatory; God still speaks through Moses. The task of the elders will be to help in the administration of the immense population, in its varied needs, especially in the context of the increasing impiety of the people.

26–30 Two of the designated elders did not meet with the others when the Spirit of God came on the group. For some reason they remained in the camp. But they also received the gift of the Spirit, and they also began to prophesy. A young man who was devoted to Moses rushed to his master to inform him of this phenomenon and to beg his master to have them cease. The prophesying of Eldad and Medad in the camp where the common people would see them was perceived as an opportunity for further personal attacks on Moses. If these men had the same gift as Moses, and if they were in the midst of the people making prophetic proclamations, then could they not use their new gifts to bring about further sedition against God's servant?

Here the true spirit of Moses is demonstrated. Rather than being threatened by the public demonstration of the gifts of the Spirit by Eldad and Medad, Moses desired that all the people might have the full gifts of the Spirit. This verse is a suitable introduction to the inexcusable challenge to the leadership of Moses in Numbers 12. Moses' magnanimity compares with that of Jesus in Mark 9:38–41 and Paul in Philippians 1:15–18. His expression of the desire for the falling of the Spirit of God on all the people is anticipative of the promise of God through the prophet Joel (2:28–32) and the experience of the early Christians in Acts 2:5–21.

The "young man" of v.27, so protective of the reputation of Moses, is likely the same as the person named in v.28: Joshua son of Nun. How propitious it is that the first time we read of him it is in association with his service of Moses as an aide from his youth. Perhaps it was this very close association with Moses that emboldened Joshua, along with Caleb, to take his stand with the promise of God rather than with the fears of the people when he withstood the evil report of the majority of the spies (chs. 13–14).

31–34 The sickening feast of the plague of quail ends this chapter of Numbers. The people had begged for meat. In a tragicomic act of miraculous provision, the Lord supplied more quail than the people possibly could eat. The Hebrew text is somewhat ambiguous in the phrasing translated "about three feet above the ground" (lit., "about two cubits," v.31). The NIV suggests that the quail were borne along by the wind of the Lord at the height of about three feet; the birds may have been stupefied by the supernatural wind and hence were low enough to be seized by people quite readily. The Hebrew phrase has also been read to mean that the quail were found in stacks upwards of three feet deep. In any event, the supply of the birds was stupendous. One who did not do very well at the gathering of birds still captured "ten homers" worth (nearly sixty bushels, v.32). The figures here are staggering! In some ways it reminds us of the great provision of the Lord Jesus in the feeding of the five thousand (Matt 14:13–21) and the four thousand (Matt 15:29–39). In those cases the feeding of many from God's plenty was a demonstration of God's grace; in the instance in Numbers it was a manifestation of God's wrath.

The scene must have been similar to a riot: people screaming, birds flapping their wings, everywhere the pell-mell movement of a meat-hungry people in a sea of birds. Dare we picture people ripping at the birds, eating flesh before cooking it, bestial in behavior? They must have been like a sugar-crazed boy in a child's daydream, afloat on a chocolate sandwich cookie raft in a sea of chocolate syrup, nibbling at the cookie before drowning in the dark, sweet sea.

The drama of the text is exquisite: "while the meat was still between their teeth" (v.33), the plague of the Lord struck them down. Before they could swallow, God made them choke. And so this place also took on an odious name: Kibroth Hattaavah (v.34), "Graves of Craving." These graves marked the death camp of those who had turned against the food of the Lord's mercy. What a contrast with the ending of chapter 10! We are in a different world—and certainly not a better one.

Notes

4 The term וְהָאסַפְסֻף (*wᵉhā'sap̱sup̱*, "the rabble") is used only here in the MT, a term to describe the camp followers attending the Hebrews at the Exodus. The aleph is quiescent; the noun is a reduplicative type of the pattern *qetaltul*. The form *'ᵃsap̱sup̱* is augmented from *asûp̱*.

6 הַמָּן (*hammān*, "manna") is made of the particle *mān*, meaning "what?" coupled to the definite article. The idea seems to be quite idiomatic: "What is it?" Thus the very name indicates the unusual nature of the bread from heaven.

The following factors support the idea that manna was indeed from the Lord and not a natural phenomenon.

1. The very Hebrew word manna ("What [is it]?") suggests that it was something unknown by the people at the time (see Exod 16:15).

2. The description of the appearance and taste of the manna (Exod 16:31; Num 11:7) suggests that it was not something experienced by other peoples in other times.

3. The daily abundance of the manna and its regular periodic surge and slump (double amounts on the sixth day but none on the seventh; Exod 16:22, 27) hardly suggest a natural phenomenon.

4. The fact that it was available in ample supply for the entire desert experience, no matter where the people were (Exod 16:35), goes against the idea of a natural substance.

5. The keeping of a sample of the manna in the ark for future generations (Exod 16:33–34) suggests that this was a unique food, a holy provision.

20 In לָמָּה זֶּה (*lāmmāh zzeh,* "why ever?") the demonstrative pronoun *zeh* is enclitic as an undeclined word for emphasis. Compare 1 Sam 10:11, "What in the world?" and 1 Sam 17:28, "Why ever?" The pattern is noted in Williams, *Hebrew Syntax*, sec. 118.

25 וְלֹא יָסָפוּ (*wᵉlō' yāsāpû,* "and did not do so again") is from the root *yāsap* ("to do again," "to repeat"). The standard understanding is that these elders were given a temporary gift of prophecy that served to validate their ministry as the aides of Moses, but they did not continue to prophesy. The NIV margin has "Or *prophesied and continued to do so.*" This is derived from an alternate reading found in the Targumim, presumably based on *wᵉlō' yāsupû,* from *sûp,* "to come to an end," meaning, "and they did not stop." The MT reading is surely preferable here.

---

(3) *A journey note*

11:35

[35]From Kibroth Hattaavah the people traveled to Hazeroth and stayed there.

35 Surely there was a sense that the people could not leave Kibroth Hattaavah quickly enough. "Hazeroth" means "enclosures." This was a location that allowed them a temporary residence on their journey northward. But it also became the locus of yet another place of trouble, the attack on Moses by Miriam and Aaron (12:1–15).

b. *The opposition of Miriam and Aaron (12:1–16)*

If the issues of chapter 11 were troubling, those of chapter 12 are unbearable. The challenges to Moses in the complaints of the people at Taberah (11:1–3) and Kibroth Hattaavah (vv.4–34) drove him to such a state of depression that he asked God to take his life in the stirring poem (so I have argued above) we have called the Lament of Moses (vv.11–15). Moses was well aware that the attacks were not on him exclusively; in a sense he was but a foil for God as the people had rejected their Savior (v.20). Nonetheless, the attacks on his person had affected him deeply. We recall that when God first spoke to Moses, he shrank from the task (cf. Exod 4), believing that he was not capable for the work God wanted him to do. Likely that burlesque of a dialogue came back to him in these days of assault. If there was any compensating factor in the attacks on Moses and the Lord described in chapter 11, it was that the people called the "rabble" (v.4) were prime instigators. These were other escaped slaves or displaced persons who decided for their own reasons, not for spiritual commitment, to attach themselves to the populace of Israel in her adventure in leaving Egypt. In chapter 12 the attacks against Moses come from his sister and his brother. These are the most unkindhearted cuts of all.

(1) *The attack on Moses from his family*

12:1–3

[1]Miriam and Aaron began to talk against Moses because of his Cushite wife, for he had married a Cushite. [2]"Has the LORD spoken only through Moses?" they asked. "Hasn't he also spoken through us?" And the LORD heard this.

3 (Now Moses was a very humble man, more humble than anyone else on the face of the earth.)

1 The attack against Moses in this chapter is filled with surprise. We are stunned to find that the principal in this case is Miriam, Moses' sister. We are quite unprepared for the first salvo, an attack on Moses' wife; and we discover amid these questions the real issue: Why is Moses God's favorite? The story finally becomes a classic example of sibling rivalry—but not among children. These are adults who adopt the tactics of children in the schoolyard.

The feminine singular verb that initiates the chapter (lit., "and she spoke," v.1) and the placement of her name before that of Aaron indicate that Miriam is the principal in the attack against Moses. Aaron apparently joined her at her instigation. Some have read this chapter as an attack on women in general in Scripture and especially an attack on the person of Miriam. It appears to me, however, that this account does not unduly demean Miriam. It rather presents her in a very human, very understandable manner. She is not judged because she is a woman; she is judged for her sin like any other person. Further, although this may seem tortuous to some, her very significance in the history of Israel is assured in a curious manner by the inclusion of this story in the Torah. I suspect that in the very male-oriented culture of the biblical world, thought might have been given to the propriety of a major section included in the Torah that is devoted to the misadventure of a (mere) woman. In the highly selective account of Israel's thirty-eight years in the desert, the story of Miriam's attack on her brother is included because of how very important she really was.

Miriam is grand. She preserved the life of the helpless infant who later became the great Moses, servant of Yahweh (see Exod 1). She made it possible for Moses' true mother to become his nurse when he was adopted into the harem of Pharaoh in Egypt. She led the singing of the first psalm we find recorded in the Scriptures, the Song of Miriam (Exod 15)—the praise of the people of God celebrating their deliverance from the army of Egypt at the Sea of Reeds. Again, it is not because Miriam is a woman that she is presented in this chapter in an unfavorable light; it is precisely because she is such a magnificent person in the history of salvation that her act of rebellion is recorded. One final note, it would be a strange male conspiracy that would later bring even Moses under judgment (see Num 20). Miriam behaves badly in this chapter; yet so does Moses in a text yet to come.

The initial attack on Moses concerns his wife. It is a very human phenomenon, not restricted to women, to present a smoke screen before coming out with the real issue. The marriage of Moses to a Cushite woman is not the issue at all. This is only pretext; the real issue concerns Moses' special relationship with God.

We remain somewhat puzzled by the reference to the "Cushite wife" of Moses. Cush was the first son of Ham, the father of the southernmost peoples known to the Hebrews (Gen 10:6–7), living in the southern Nile valley (Ethiopia). It is possible that Moses' wife, Zipporah, is intended by this phrase (see Exod 2:15–22). If so, then her foreign ancestry is attacked rhetorically by exaggeration. Perhaps her skin was more swarthy than the average person in Israel. Is it possible that the term "Cushite" was a slanderous term stemming from racism? We really do not know, as this text is not sufficiently clear, and we have no other analogies to assist us coming to a conclusion. So it is possible that the term "Cushite" is used by Miriam in contempt of Zipporah's Midianite ancestry.

More likely, however, is the idea that Moses has taken a new wife, perhaps after the death of Zipporah (which is not recorded). The language of 12:1 seems to point to a recent marriage of a Cushite woman (lit., "concerning the issue of the Cushite woman that he had married, for it was a Cushite woman whom he had married"). The repetition of the phrases suggests emphasis as well as the appropriateness of the charge, if not a validation of the attitude that underlies it. So it is not "woman versus woman" or "woman against man" here so much as a basic resentment of race against race. In any event, the attack on the woman was a pretext; the focus of the attack was on the prophetic gift of Moses and his special relationship with the Lord.

2 Miriam and her brother Aaron ask, rhetorically, "Has the LORD spoken only through Moses? Has he not spoken as well through us?" Of course, he had. Micah 6:4 speaks of Moses, Aaron, and Miriam as God's gracious provision for Israel. God speaks through Aaron and Miriam; but his principal spokesman is ever Moses. The prophetic gifting of the seventy elders (11:24–30) seems to have been the immediate provocation for the attack of Miriam and Aaron on their brother.

Verse 2 ends in an ominous manner: "And the LORD heard." The writer is well aware that the Lord "hears" everything. This special notice means that the Lord has heard with an intention of acting, of intervening on behalf of his servant. The phrasing is not unlike that in Exodus 2:23–25, where four verbs are used of the LORD's relatedness to his people: he hears, he remembers, he sees, and he knows.

3 The most difficult line in the chapter, and one of the most difficult verses in the entire book, is v.3. Critical scholars have long (and rightly) observed that it is not likely that a truly humble person would write in such a manner about himself. Some have used this verse as a cudgel against those who believe in the Mosaic authorship of the Torah. The supposition is that this verse, along with the general use of the third person ("Moses said, . . . Moses did . . . "), is regarded by many as clear evidence of later authorship of the book. It is theoretically possible that Moses might have authored such a line under inspiration, just as it is possible that he might have recorded the account of his death and burial by prophetic insight (Deut 34). These things are possible but not likely. It may be observed that our Lord spoke of himself in the words, "I am gentle and humble in heart" (Matt 11:29). But even he (who alone could speak in such a manner!) did not add, "more than all the people on the face of the earth."

Some scholars have argued that the verse began as a gloss, which, through time, slipped into the text of the book. Scribes might have added this note to the margin to help the reader to understand how unfair the attack against Moses was. Later scribes, not realizing this was an explanatory gloss, included the verse in the text proper. Yet there is no evidence that this is the case. Frankly, without textual evidence such a procedure is quite risky, for it might be used by one to evade any clear teaching of Scripture that one finds personally distasteful.

I find myself drawn strongly to the suggestion of Cleon Rogers that the key term in v.3 should be translated "miserable" rather than "meek" ("Moses: Meek or Miserable?" JETS 29, 3 [Sept. 1986]: 257–63; see Notes below). Moses was not really an exceptionally meek man. He was a man given to rage, self-pity, questioning, and debate. He was also a man given to greatness. He is one of the most impressive figures in biblical history, certainly one of the most pivotal. But this verse aside, it is not likely that observers of the story line of the Torah would automatically include "meekness" among the character traits of this significant biblical personage.

The word "miserable" could hardly be more fitting in the context of this chapter. Moses has been under assault from every front. He has found his lot so difficult, his task so unmanageable, his pressure so intense that he has called out to God saying, "It is too much!" (cf. 11:14). With assault now coming from within his family, he passes even beyond that feeling of desperation we observed in the Lament of Moses (11:11–15). At this point he is utterly speechless; he is a broken man. Verse 3, in my judgment, should be translated with confidence in this manner: "Now the man Moses was exceedingly miserable, more than any man on the face of the earth!" Many have felt like this from time to time; none has felt it so deeply as Moses at this nadir of his life. Hence there is nothing in this verse that speaks against the role of Moses as the author of Numbers. It is merely in keeping with the third-person nature of the general recitation.

Notes

1 וַתְּדַבֵּר (*wat^{e}ḏabbēr,* "and she spoke"), the Piel preterit verb that begins the chapter, is feminine singular, which serves to heighten our understanding of Miriam's leadership in the conspiracy against Moses. When a clause has a compound subject ("Then Miriam and Aaron spoke"), the tendency in Hebrew style is to have the verb agree in person, number, and gender with the noun that is nearer the verb. The word order of the Hebrew clause is then-she-spoke, Miriam, and-Aaron, against-Moses. The notion of speaking "against" is captured by the *b* that is prefixed to the name Moses. This is the beth *adversus;* with the verb "to speak," it has the meaning "to speak with hostility" or "to speak against." The same use of *b* is found, for example, in v.8; 21:5, 7; Pss 50:20; 78:19.

2 The interrogative particle הֲ (*h^{a}*) is attached to the adverb רַק (*raq,* "only") resulting in הֲרַק (*h^{a}raq,* "only?"). The placement of this phrase at the beginning of the clause in Hebrew makes it emphatic: "Is it only through Moses that Yahweh has spoken?"

3 Instead of עָנָו (*'ānāw,* "meek"), the Qere reading is עָנָיו (*'ānāyw*), an indication that the last syllable is to be pronounced. Rogers, in the article cited above, presents evidence from etymology and usage that "miserable" is a possible reading and from context that it is the preferable meaning in this text. The basic meaning of the root *'ānāh* is "to be bowed down." One could be bowed down by force (i.e., to be subdued) or bowed down with submissiveness (i.e., to be humble) or bowed down with care and trouble (i.e., to be miserable or afflicted). Among the uses of *'ānāw* in the Prophets and the Wisdom Literature is to describe the socially oppressed and the miserable; similarly, the word can also be used to describe one who has his or her full confidence in God and thus is humble before him. As we have traced the story line of Numbers beginning in 11:1, one thing after another has brought pressure on Moses so that in 11:14 he whimpers to God that he is not able to bear the load any longer. He even asks God that he might die to be relieved of the pressures that are grinding him down. Now with this assault of his sister and brother on his character, it was simply too much. He was now the most miserable man on earth. As Rogers says, "In the complaining of the people heightened by the complaining of his own sister and brother it would be the most natural thing in the world for someone to describe himself as the most miserable person on earth" ("Moses: Meek or Miserable?" pp. 262–63).

(2) *The defense of Moses by the Lord*
12:4–9

4 At once the LORD said to Moses, Aaron and Miriam, "Come out to the Tent of Meeting, all three of you." So the three of them came out.
5 Then

the LORD came down in a pillar of cloud; he stood at the entrance to the
Tent and summoned Aaron and Miriam. When both of them stepped
forward, 6 he said, "Listen to my words:

"When a prophet of the LORD is among you,
I reveal myself to him in visions,
I speak to him in dreams.
7 But this is not true of my servant Moses;
he is faithful in all my house.
8 With him I speak face to face,
clearly and not in riddles;
he sees the form of the LORD.
Why then were you not afraid
to speak against my servant Moses?"

9 The anger of the LORD burned against them, and he left them.

4 The Hebrew adverb *pi<u>t</u>'ōm* ("at once") expresses suddenness, an abrupt response of the Lord that was pregnant with terror (see Job 22:10; Isa 47:11; Jer 4:20). We may observe that ordinarily God is slow to anger and hesitant in judgment, longing for repentance rather than stubbornness, and desiring to forgive rather than to destroy. But the association of the Lord to his servant Moses is so very strong that here suddenly he comes of a sudden to redress the wrong done to his friend. That God speaks to Moses along with Aaron and Miriam suggests that he was present when they were berating Moses so unfairly.

5 When the trio came to the Tent of Meeting, according to the command of the Lord, then he descended to them in the cloud (as in 11:25; see above). The language here is even more dramatic: "Then the LORD came down in a pillar of cloud" (see Exod 13:21 for this expression used to describe the Lord's guidance of his people). Descriptions of the appearances of God in Hebrew Scripture are usually styled "theophanies." The term "epiphany" may be used where there is a dramatic descending of God, as in Psalm 18:7–15. The Hebrew verb *yāra<u>d</u>* ("to come down") is often used in these contexts. In 11:25, the Lord came down in grace; in Genesis 11:5–8, the Lord came down in judgment. It is quite beyond comprehension to reflect on the wonder of the Lord "coming down." Psalm 113 speaks of his incomparable glory, "exalted with respect to sitting" (cf. v.5). Yet it is his indescribably condescending nature to stoop down, as it were, to see and even to come down to meet with man. In a sense, every theophany (appearance of God) and epiphany (descent of God) is a picture and promise of the grand theophany, the great epiphany of the Lord Jesus Christ.

There is a bad side to the good news, however; for God comes down in wrath as well as in grace. When the Lord appeared from the midst of the cloud before the Tent of Meeting, he spoke to Aaron and Miriam. They came forward. What a dramatic moment in the history of salvation! Then he told them to listen. And then he spoke.

6–9 The Oracle of the Lord in vv.6–8 is presented in poetic format. As in the Battle Cry of Moses (10:35–36) and the Lament of Moses (11:11–15), so the Oracle of Yahweh in this paragraph speaks more impressively in poetry than it would in prose. The function of poetry is to make much little; that is, poetry compresses the greatest significance into the fewest words. The overall effect of great poetry is the feeling or experience one receives of the impact of the words.

Here is a personal translation of this poem, with a couple of difficult text-critical decisions included (explained in the Notes):

6 And he said:
"Hear my words:
"If there is one of your prophets
—I am Yahweh!
I may speak to him by means of vision,
or I may talk to him by means of a prophetic dream.
7 But not so with my servant Moses;
in all my household he is reliable.
8 Face to face I speak with him,
in personal presence and not in riddles;
he gazes on the semblance of Yahweh.
Why then are you not terrified,
to speak against my servant, against Moses?"

Some salient features of this poem may be noted. The usual wording "if there is a prophet among you" is likely the correct meaning of the phrase. But the Hebrew word as it stands (see the Notes below) is more usually translated "your prophet." There seems to be a subtle note here. All other prophets are "your prophets." Only Moses is "my" prophet. Second, the poem stresses in an unusual manner the sovereignty of the Lord in the way he deals with prophets and other persons. He decides how he shall speak, to whom, and in what manner. This is why I suggest the interjection "I am Yahweh" is so fitting. Commonly in solemn utterances the words *'ᵃnî yhwh* ("I am Yahweh") will be inserted. This is especially common in the Book of Leviticus.

Third, the poem presents in a powerful manner the distinctiveness of Moses as against all other agents of divine disclosure. The contrasts are in the areas of levels of intimacy. To other prophets God may speak in a variety of ways, some more clearly than others (see Heb 1:1; 1 Peter 1:10–11). But to Moses there is a one-on-one relationship. Only Moses could approach the holy mountain and gaze on the Divine Person. Only his face radiated following these encounters. Others might hear the words; only Moses sees God's person. What we are to make of these words is somewhat uncertain, given the language of mystery in the Hebrew Bible and the denial in the NT that anyone ever saw God at any time (see John 1:18). At the very least, these words speak of an unprecedented level of intimacy between God and Moses.

At the most, it is possible to argue that Moses spoke with the preincarnate Christ; it seems to be the point of John 1:18 that no one has ever seen the Father but that the role of the Son is specifically revelatory of the Father to others. All we can do is to speculate in these matters. The one sure thing in this text is to insist that while God has spoken through Aaron, Miriam, and a host of others, there was none who was on such a familiar ground with God as was Moses (see also Deut 34:10). The expression "my house" refers to the household of the nation.

The reason given for this special relationship is unexpected: Moses' faithfulness is what has set him apart from all others. It is intriguing to associate this idea with the description of Abram in Genesis 15:6. It is also ominous to contrast the faithfulness of Moses as described in this poem with the faithlessness of the people in the story to follow (chs. 13–14).

Finally, the last bicolon of the poem is chilling. In feigned incredulity God asks the potent question: "Why are you not very afraid?" Clearly, the ax of his wrath is about to fall on the block below! Verse 9 speaks of the wrath of God and of his awesome departure. Just reading the text is stunning. To have been present must have been beyond comprehension.

Notes

6 The phrasing of the words נְבִיאֲכֶם יהוה (*nᵉḇîʾᵃḵem yhwh*) is quite difficult. The first word would usually be translated, "your prophet," but it is customary to read this word as though it were two: *nāḇîʾ bāḵem* ("a prophet among you"), as in the versions. More difficult, however, is the relationship of this word to the divine name that follows it. The term *nᵉḇîʾᵃḵem* has a major disjunctive accent that ordinarily would separate it from what follows; further, a noun with a pronominal suffix ("your prophet") would not form a binding unit with a following word. Hence the rendering "a prophet of the LORD among you" in the NIV is only one approximation of the situation. Generally, there are three solutions presented: (1) to transpose the divine name to follow the introductory verb at the beginning of v.6 to read: "And the LORD said, . . ."; (2) to add a preposition "to" to the divine name, as is suggested in the LXX; to leave the divine name where it is, but to ignore the accents, leaving a translation such as the NIV; (3) to presume the loss of the pronoun "I" (*ʾᵃnî*) before the divine name, maintaining the accents as they are, resulting in a new colon: "I am the LORD," the solution of the Syriac (and Targum). This last solution I find to be the most convincing; it is reflected in the translation I give in the text above.

(3) *The punishment of Miriam*

12:10–15

10 When the cloud lifted from above the Tent, there stood Miriam—
leprous, like snow. Aaron turned toward her and saw that she had
leprosy; 11 and he said to Moses, "Please, my lord, do not hold against
us the sin we have so foolishly committed. 12 Do not let her be like a
stillborn infant coming from its mother's womb with its flesh half eaten
away."
13 So Moses cried out to the LORD, "O God, please heal her!"
14 The LORD replied to Moses, "If her father had spit in her face, would
she not have been in disgrace for seven days? Confine her outside the
camp for seven days; after that she can be brought back." 15 So Miriam
was confined outside the camp for seven days, and the people did not
move on till she was brought back.

10 The immediate effect of the wrath of God was seen on the body of Miriam. This is not a man-God wrath against women. The fact that Miriam is "leprous" and Aaron is not is a signal to the reader that the initial impression is correct: Miriam was the principal offender. Now God has spoken out against her; his hand has struck. She has broken out with the type of infectious skin disease that excluded persons from participation in the activities of the community (see 5:1–4). It has long been asserted that the term "leprous" in such contexts is misleading. While modern Hansen's disease may be a subset of the biblical disease, they are not the same illness (see Notes). The result of this judgment was that Miriam, the principal offender against her brother Moses, has become a pariah, an outcast, as she now suffers from the type of infectious skin disease that would exclude her from the community of Israel.

11–13 The repentance of Aaron for the sin of presumption (v.11) is touching both in its intensity and in his concern for their sister. His description of the appearance of Miriam's skin (v.12) is ghastly but effective. Moses then calls out to God to heal her. His prayer is remarkable in its urgency and simplicity (v.13). He screams out, "O God ['*ēl*], please heal her!"

14–15 The response of God is gracious mingled with sobriety. He grants Miriam healing but demands a period of time of public shame. Building on cultural elements of the day, the Lord refers to a public rebuke and the time of shame that would entail (v.14). It would seem that the period of seven days was the briefest of periods of such shame before restoration might be accomplished. A period of seven days was a standard time for uncleanness occasioned by touching or being in contact with a dead body (see 19:11, 14, 16).

Notes

10 R.K. Harrison suggests that the form of skin disease that Miriam suffered—מְצֹרַעַת (*mᵉṣōra'at*, "leprous")—as well as that which Moses suffered as a sign (Exod 4:6) may well have been leucoderma or psoriasis; in both texts the word כַּשָּׁלֶג (*kaššāleg*, "white as snow") describes the form of the skin disorder; yet chronic *ṣāra'at* ("leprosy") was never white. See his article "Leper, Leprosy," ISBErev, 3:103–6.

(4) *A journey note*

12:16

[16]After that, the people left Hazeroth and encamped in the Desert of Paran.

16 At last, the destination of the grand march was achieved (see 10:12 and comments). The Desert of Paran was the staging area for the attack on the land of Canaan. Despite numerous terrible events that marred the dream of the triumphal march, at last the people were at their destination. Now was the time for regrouping, for reconnaissance and evaluation, for placing strategy in place, and for mounting the assault of victory over the Canaanite peoples. Yes, there had been troubled times on the journey. But glory awaits. Or at least that is what should have been the case.

c. *The twelve spies and the mixed report (13:1–33)*

We seem to be at a new beginning when we enter this chapter. The vindication of Moses as the servant of the Lord has been stunning and unforgettable. The presence of the people in the vastness of their numbers here on the plateau of Paran is undeniable. The desire of the people to enter the Land of Promise is unquestionable. The faithfulness of the Lord to his promise and his commitment to his people are sure and unalterable. Given all the experiences that the people have gone through in the previous months of preparation and journey, at last—at long last—it was time to claim God's word, to believe in his power, to march in his name, and to enter his land.

Hence the surprise in the unexpected turn of events we discover in this and the following chapter is even more startling than the surprise we felt as we first read the narrative of the rebellion of the people in chapter 11 after the record of their compliance in chapters 1–10. Chapters 13–14 are the way of sorrows of the Torah. These chapters are a blight on Israel and a warning to all who read the story. That which marked Moses apart from all others was his utter faithfulness to Yahweh (see again 12:7). That which marked the nation as a whole was a fear of their enemies instead of the fear of Yahweh.

(1) *The command of the Lord*

13:1–2

[1]The LORD said to Moses, [2]"Send some men to explore the land of Canaan, which I am giving to the Israelites. From each ancestral tribe send one of its leaders."

1–2 Years after they transpired, Moses reflected on the events of this chapter. As he recounted the story in his homily in Deuteronomy to the sons and daughters of those who lived the account, he filled in some details that this chapter omits. Moses' words to the people were to rise, to go up, to begin the attack, and to seize the land (see Deut 1:21). But the people petitioned him to send forth spies first to discover the best routes for making their assault successful (v.22). This seemed a reasonable idea to Moses; so he selected twelve men, one from each tribe, to reconnoiter (*tûr*, "to explore," v.2, with the special meaning "to reconnoiter" in this text) the land (v.23).

Comparing this longer account in Deuteronomy with Numbers 13:1–2, we see that the command to send spies was from the Lord. It is likely that Deuteronomy 1:21–23 presents the story from the level of the people and that Numbers 13:1–2 presents the same account from the divine perspective. When the people requested that spies be sent, Moses decided, on the basis of the will of God, to accede to their request. Both accounts meld into a whole. What we gain from putting the two accounts together, however, is that the very idea of sending spies to the land was a further example of the grace of God to the people.

The specification of the type of men that were to be selected reminds us that while God is not a respecter of persons with regard to his mercy (see Deut 10:17), he does use select persons for his leadership tasks. Yet ten of the twelve men in this listing turn out to be dismal failures. That they were each leaders of their tribes did not guarantee that they were adequate for the leadership role God desired they would have. The term used to describe them as "leaders" is the same used to describe the tribal leaders in the making of the rosters of the tribes in chapter 1 (*nāśî'*, see 1:16).

Notes

---

2 In שְׁלַח־לְךָ (*šᵉlaḥ-lᵉḵā*, "send to you"), the preposition and pronoun element is the so-called dative of personal reference that emphasizes the active participation on the part of the one who receives the command. It has the force "you send!" (NIV, "send one"). This is the same construction we find in God's command to Abram in Gen 12:1: "You go!"

On the phrase "From each . . . tribe," see the Notes on 9:10.

---

(2) *The roster of names*

13:3–16

3 So at the LORD's command Moses sent them out from the Desert of Paran. All of them were leaders of the Israelites. 4 These are their names:

from the tribe of Reuben, Shammua son of Zaccur;
5 from the tribe of Simeon, Shaphat son of Hori;
6 from the tribe of Judah, Caleb son of Jephunneh;
7 from the tribe of Issachar, Igal son of Joseph;
8 from the tribe of Ephraim, Hoshea son of Nun;
9 from the tribe of Benjamin, Palti son of Raphu;
10 from the tribe of Zebulun, Gaddiel son of Sodi;
11 from the tribe of Manasseh (a tribe of Joseph), Gaddi son of Susi;
12 from the tribe of Dan, Ammiel son of Gemalli;
13 from the tribe of Asher, Sethur son of Michael;
14 from the tribe of Naphtali, Nahbi son of Vophsi;
15 from the tribe of Gad, Geuel son of Maki.

16 These are the names of the men Moses sent to explore the land. (Moses gave Hoshea son of Nun the name Joshua.)

3 As in the records of chapters 1–10, the story begins with the compliance of Moses to the will of God. He does just as God has commanded in selecting one worthy from each tribe to represent his people on the reconnaissance mission. There is a sense in these chapters that when God speaks, then Moses does—thus our terrible shock when even he falters in chapter 20! The names listed in vv.4–15 are different from the tribal leaders given in chapters 1, 2, 7, and 10. Presumably the tribal leaders in these four earlier lists were older men. The task for the spies called for men who were younger and more robust but no less respected by their peers.

There is a symmetry in this chapter, as we have found on other occasions. The whole impression is orderly and straightforward, granting a sense of importance and dignity. There is nothing casual about this text. The travel of the spies begins in the Desert of Paran (v.3); it is to that wilderness they return in v.26. The text comes full circle geographically. But the men who come back are not the same as the men who left. Presumably they left in confidence, with a spirit of divine adventure; but they returned in fear, groveling before men, no longer fearful of God. This factor provides intertwining circles of geography and character development in the chapter.

4–15 The significance of the listing of the names in these verses (cf. 1:5ff.) is multiple: (1) the names add a certain historical verisimilitude; (2) they provide a level of accuracy in the narrative; (3) they should give the occasion for pride of family, clan, and tribe; (4) they become, because of the failure of the majority in this case, markers of sadness, just as the names of places of Israel's judgment (e.g., Taberah and Kibroth Hattaavah); and (5) they, like all lists of names in Scripture, remind us of the significance of names to God (e.g., the Lamb's book of life, Rev 20:12).

The names of the tribal leaders and their respective tribes are listed in vv.4–15.

There are some observations we may make about these names and the meanings that may be suggested for them (see Notes for suggested derivations of names): (1) while few of these names are specifically theophoric (built with a term for deity, such as the names Gaddiel, Ammiel, and Geuel), most of them are implicitly theophoric (e.g., Sethur and Nahbi both likely have the idea of being hidden [in God]); (2) Joseph is mentioned along with Manasseh (v.11) but not with Ephraim (v.8); further, these allied tribes are separated in this listing, an unusual thing in listings such as this; (3) the tribe of Levi is omitted, as is common in such lists of the laic tribes; the omission of Levi allows for the listing of both Ephraim and Manasseh; (4) only the name of the good spy Caleb does not seem to have a moral or theophoric meaning (see Notes).

16 The particular significance of Joshua is noted in v.16. We have already discovered that Joshua was an attendant of Moses from his youth and was particularly concerned about the reputation of his master when it seemed threatened by the independent prophesying of Eldad and Medad (see 11:27–28 and commentary in loc.). Here we learn that Joshua's name was first known as Hoshea, but it was Moses who changed it to Joshua. This parenthetical statement anticipates the later prominence of Joshua. The reader is alerted to the significance of this name among the list of the spies; here is a man of great destiny. The Hebrew word Hoshea means "salvation"; the new form of the name Joshua means "Yahweh saves"; the latter form is the Hebrew spelling for Jesus (*Y'shua*).

Moses' act of changing Hoshea's name to Joshua is a mark of a special relationship between the two men. This change of name, which is slight, something of a play on words, is a fatherly action on Moses' part. It is as though he has adopted his young aide and marked him for greatness. We are reminded of the way that the Lord changed the name of Abram to Abraham (Gen 17). The names are related, but in this changing of name a new relationship results.

It is notable that the two spies who render a report that is faithful to the promise of God come from the two tribes that later will become most prominent in the land. Joshua is from the tribe of Ephraim, the tribe that will become dominant in the north; Caleb is from the tribe of Judah, the dominant tribe in the south. There is something salutary in this as well. At least the two who stand for faithfulness in God come from prominent tribes.

The ancestry of Caleb is particularly intriguing. Verse 6 says that he is Caleb son of Jephunneh (*ben-yᵉp̱unneh*). He is called the Kenizzite in Numbers 32:12; Joshua 14:6, 14. In 1 Chronicles 2:18 he is called son of Hezron (*ben-ḥeṣrôn*). Hezron is the son of Peres, the grandson of Judah. If we put all these data together, we may conclude that Caleb is of the tribe of Judah, the son of Jephunneh, a descendant of Hezron the son of Peres, the son of Judah. It may have been Judah's relationship with Tamar that linked the family with the Kenizzite tribe.

Notes

4–15 The names of the leaders of Israel and their meanings are as follows:

1. Shammua (*šammûaʿ*, related to the verb *šāmaʿ*, "to hear"; perhaps meaning "report [of God]") of Reuben
2. Shaphat (*šāpāṭ*, from the verb *šāpaṭ*, "to judge"; perhaps meaning "he has judged") of Simeon
3. Caleb (*kālēb*, related to *keleb*, "dog") of Judah
4. Igal (*yigʾāl*, from the verb *gāʾal*, "to redeem"; perhaps meaning "he redeems") of Issachar
5. Hoshea (*hôšēaʿ*, from the verb *yāšaʿ*, "to save"; perhaps meaning "salvation") of Ephraim
6. Palti (*palṭî*, perhaps related to the verb *pālaṭ*, "to escape"; perhaps meaning "my escape [is God]") of Benjamin
7. Gaddiel (*gaddîʾēl*, perhaps related to the noun *gād*, "fortune"; perhaps meaning "my fortune is God") of Zebulun
8. Gaddi (*gaddî*, a name with the same meaning as the man of Zebulun, "my fortune [is in God]") of Manasseh
9. Ammiel (*ʿammîʾēl*, a name combining the words "my people" and "God"; perhaps meaning "God is my kinsman") of Dan
10. Sethur (*seṯûr*, a name perhaps related to the verb *sāṯar*, "to hide"; perhaps meaning "sheltered [by God]") of Asher
11. Nahbi (*naḥbî*, a name perhaps related to the verb *ḥābāh*, "to withdraw," "to hide"; perhaps meaning "my hiding [is God]") of Naphtali
12. Geuel (*geʾûʾēl*, a name perhaps relating the verbal root *gāʾāh*, "to rise up [in majesty]" with the word "God"; perhaps meaning "majesty of God") of Gad

As in all attempts to identify the meaning of biblical names, the suggestions here are somewhat tentative. This is of necessity. The attempt to pin down the relationship of names to so-called verbal roots is a precarious adventure, in part due to the multiplicity of homonyms in Hebrew (words with the same spelling but unrelated in meaning; there are four words spelled *ʿānāh*, for example, each with a different etymology). The principal difficulty with the meaning of names, however, is usage. A noun or a verb has its meaning in the context of its use. A name, by its very nature, cannot be identified with precision based on the story in which it is found.

The order of the tribes varies in the several listings. No reason seems to be given for these variations. Here is a comparison of the listings of chapter 1 and of chapter 13:

Num 1:5–16	*Num 1:20–43*	*Num 13:4–15*
1. Reuben	1. Reuben	1. Reuben
2. Simeon	2. Simeon	2. Simeon
3. Judah	3. Gad	3. Judah
4. Issachar	4. Judah	4. Issachar
5. Zebulun	5. Issachar	5. Ephraim
6. Ephraim	6. Zebulun	6. Benjamin
7. Manasseh	7. Ephraim	7. Zebulun
8. Benjamin	8. Manasseh	8. Manasseh
9. Dan	9. Benjamin	9. Dan
10. Asher	10. Dan	10. Asher
11. Gad	11. Asher	11. Naphtali
12. Naphtali	12. Naphtali	12. Gad

These variations raise questions. Why is Gad listed third in 1:24 but last in 13:15? Why is Judah third in 1:7 and 13:6 but fourth in 1:26? The birth order of the sons of Jacob is given piecemeal in Genesis:

1. Reuben (mother Leah, Gen 29:32)
2. Simeon (mother Leah, Gen 29:33)
3. Levi (mother Leah, Gen 29:34)

4. Judah (mother Leah, Gen 29:35)
5. Dan (mother Bilhah, maid of Rachel, Gen 30:6)
6. Naphtali (mother Bilhah, maid of Rachel, Gen 30:8)
7. Gad (mother Zilpah, maid of Leah, Gen 30:10)
8. Asher (mother Zilpah, maid of Leah, Gen 30:13)
9. Issachar (mother Leah, Gen 30:18)
10. Zebulun (mother Leah, Gen 30:20)
11. Joseph (mother Rachel, Gen 30:24)
12. Benjamin (mother Rachel, Gen 35:18)

One daughter, Dinah (mother Leah, Gen 30:21)

Genesis 35:23–36 gives the sons in the order of their mothers. Two other significant listings of the sons of Jacob are found in the blessing of Jacob (Gen 49) and the blessing of Moses (Deut 33). In the blessing of Jacob, Zebulun and Issachar are out of birth order but are grouped with the other sons of their mother, Leah. In the blessing of Moses the tribe of Simeon is missing.

6 כָּלֵב (*kālēḇ*, "Caleb") is the name of the spy from the tribe of Judah. Because of the usual negative associations of the word "dog" in Hebrew culture (*keleḇ*), it appears that the biblical scribes have altered the pronunciation of the name as it is used of various individuals in the Bible. Gerhard F. Hasel ("Caleb," ISBErev., 1:573) surmises that the positive associations of a dog as faithful and humble might have given rise to this name in Israel. We tend to think of these ideas as modern; but at times the ancients must have had some sense of a dog as "man's best friend." So though slightly disguised in pronunciation, the name of this heroic companion of Joshua is indeed a word that means "dog"—but in a positive sense. Perhaps we may term him "a dog of God" in the most honorable sense this phrase may convey.

---

(3) *The instructions of Moses*

13:17–20

> 17 When Moses sent them to explore Canaan, he said, "Go up through the Negev and on into the hill country. 18 See what the land is like and whether the people who live there are strong or weak, few or many. 19 What kind of land do they live in? Is it good or bad? What kind of towns do they live in? Are they unwalled or fortified? 20 How is the soil? Is it fertile or poor? Are there trees on it or not? Do your best to bring back some of the fruit of the land." (It was the season for the first ripe grapes.)

17–20 The instructions of Moses to the twelve spies were comprehensive; a thorough report of the land—its produce, the peoples, and their towns—was required in the reconnaissance mission. The plan of approach was practical, and it shows that Moses had some sense of the lay of the land of Canaan. From their location in the northernmost boundary of the Desert of Paran, the spies were to move into the Negev, the southernmost part of the land of Canaan. Then they were to ascend the hill country and to journey as far as they could through the land. The journey upward was not only geographical; there is a sense in which we may see this upward journey as a symbol of assault, conquest, and victory.

The scouts were to give special attention to the people and the produce of the land, to the cities and towns, to the soil and the presence or absence of forests. Since the journey was at the time of the harvest of grapes, there is a personal note that they should bring back some of the fruit they might discover in the land. They were to show themselves courageous in taking some of the fruit (see Notes), words that would later come to haunt the nation. But the quest for a sampling of fruit is a nice touch; it had been a long time since grapes were seen in the desert community. The principal harvesting of grapes in Palestine comes after the long, hot summer, in September and October. But the first, early grapes may be harvested by mid- or late July. So the journey of the spies would have come in the summer months.

Notes

20 The NIV translation of וְהִתְחַזַּקְתֶּם (*wᵉhiṯḥazzaqtem*) as "Do your best" seems weak for this strong verb, a Hithpael perfect with the waw consecutive, used as a command, from the verb *ḥāzaq*, meaning "show yourselves courageous!" The act of heroism was in fact the bracing for thievery! They were told to take a sample of the fruit of the land, not a purchase from a stand, but the seizure from a field. Since the whole of the land was to be theirs, including cities they had not built, vineyards they had not cultivated, and trees they had not planted (Deut 6:10–11), in a sense the taking of the sample of the fruit of the land is a sampling of that which would all become theirs.

(4) *A summary of the reconnaissance*
13:21–25

[21]So they went up and explored the land from the Desert of Zin as far as Rehob, toward Lebo Hamath. [22]They went up through the Negev and came to Hebron, where Ahiman, Sheshai and Talmai, the descendants of Anak, lived. (Hebron had been built seven years before Zoan in Egypt.) [23]When they reached the Valley of Eshcol, they cut off a branch bearing a single cluster of grapes. Two of them carried it on a pole between them, along with some pomegranates and figs. [24]That place was called the Valley of Eshcol because of the cluster of grapes the Israelites cut off there. [25]At the end of forty days they returned from exploring the land.

21 The journey of the spies began in the southernmost extremity of the land (the Desert of Zin) and took them to the northernmost point (Rehob near Lebo Hamath; see 34:8). This journey of about 250 miles in each direction took them forty days (v.25). This is possibly a round number, similar to saying "a month" in our idiom, when an approximate period of time is intended. Since a month is nearer to thirty days, forty days is regarded as more than a month, a complete cycle, a fullness of time. Nonetheless, the citing of forty days is a number suitably fitting for the sacral nature of their task.

22 The first city the spies came to in the land of Canaan was Hebron. The parenthetical comment about the building of the city seven years before Zoan in Egypt may have been prompted by their amazement at the size and fortification of the city that was so closely associated with the lives of their ancestors four centuries before this time (see Gen 13:14–18; 14:13; 23:1; 25:9; 35:27–29; 50:13). In the stories of the ancestors of their people, Hebron had not been a great city but a dwelling and trading place for shepherds and herdsmen.

What is strange in the spies' interest in the city of Hebron is what they do not mention. This was the burial place of Abraham and Sarah, Isaac and Rebekah, Jacob and Leah. Why would they not have said, "Here we have arrived at the place where our fathers and mothers are buried. Where they lie, soon we shall live"?

Instead of looking to the patriarchs and the promises, the spies noticed sizes of buildings and statures of persons. Moreover, they ignored the clear timetable of God as recorded in Genesis 15. They were in the land at the time of promise. Yet they averted their glance from the tombs of the fathers, and they neglected the promise of God; they were too preoccupied with the sandal sizes of three huge men who lived in Hebron.

The other association with Hebron was the population of Anakites who lived there. Three notables from the descendants of Anak are mentioned as living at Hebron. The Anakites were men of great stature; their physical size became a rallying point for the fear of the people (see vv.32–33). In a later day of faith, Caleb was to drive these giants from their city (Josh 15:14; Judg 1:10). Would that he had been given his chance forty years earlier!

23–25 Due to the size of the grape cluster that they found, the spies named the valley in which it was found "the valley of the cluster" (v.24; cf. NIV mg.). The Valley of Eshcol is near Hebron; presumably the spies cut the cluster of grapes on their return journey, but they may well have marked the location as they passed through this valley on their journey north. The very size of the grape cluster, indicated by the item describing the manner of transporting it to the camp (v.23), was a mark of the goodness of the land that God was giving them. To think of clusters of grapes so large that two men would transport the cluster on a pole—why the people should have thought they had discovered Eden! The grapes they brought back to the camp were wine grapes, of course. Hence they were a symbol of the joy the land would provide for the people. The good land would provide for them the good life. As is well known, the present state of Israel uses the logo of the two spies carrying an immense cluster of grapes on a pole as the symbol of the Department of Tourism. The Bible does not specify which of the men carried the grapes; the modern tourism department supplies the names freely: Caleb and Joshua!

Alas, the size of the cluster these spies brought back to the camp became a provocation of fear for the faithless. Such a large cluster of fruit was intimidating and unnerving to them. It ought to have intoxicated them with joy; instead, it inebriated them with paralyzing terror.

(5) *The mixed report*

13:26–33

26 They came back to Moses and Aaron and the whole Israelite community at Kadesh in the Desert of Paran. There they reported to them and to the whole assembly and showed them the fruit of the land.
27 They gave Moses this account: "We went into the land to which you sent us, and it does flow with milk and honey! Here is its fruit. 28 But the people who live there are powerful, and the cities are fortified and very large. We even saw descendants of Anak there. 29 The Amalekites live in the Negev; the Hittites, Jebusites and Amorites live in the hill country; and the Canaanites live near the sea and along the Jordan."
30 Then Caleb silenced the people before Moses and said, "We should go up and take possession of the land, for we can certainly do it."

[31]But the men who had gone up with him said, "We can't attack those people; they are stronger than we are." [32]And they spread among the Israelites a bad report about the land they had explored. They said, "The land we explored devours those living in it. All the people we saw there are of great size. [33]We saw the Nephilim there (the descendants of Anak come from the Nephilim). We seemed like grasshoppers in our own eyes, and we looked the same to them."

26–29 The first portion of the report of the spies was truthful, if timorous. The clear goodness of the land was offset in their eyes by the many and mighty peoples who dwelt in it. They did give assent to the bounty of the land in the proverbial phrase, a land flowing with milk and honey. This phrase takes us back to Exodus 3:8 and the words of God to Moses at the beginning of his call to return to Egypt to rescue God's people from slavery and to bring them to the good land. This phrase forms a leitmotif of blessing with respect to the land. The biblical intent in this phrase is on productivity and abundance. As Moses heard these words from the spies, his heart must have leaped within. This phrase is given by Moses again to the second generation, after the first generation lost their opportunity to enjoy the land (see Deut 11:9–12).

But immediately after praising the land for its bounty, the spies lamented its people and cities. Verse 28 begins with the limiting phrase *'eḇes kî* ("except that"; NIV, "But"). This reversal of mood was deadly. The size of the grape cluster now became ominous. No longer did it point to plenty but to people, no longer to joy but to fear. The cities were described as being inaccessible, impregnable. The term *b^{e}ṣurôṯ* (NIV, "fortified") is used in 2 Kings 18:13 of inaccessible cities and in Jeremiah 33:3 of inaccessible things. The cities of Canaan were said to be beyond the reach of the people of Israel. The listing of the nations that inhabited the land became a new reason for terror: the Amalekites, the Hittites, the Jebusites, the Amorites, and the Canaanites. Yet in a sense this listing of nations could as well be taken as an indication of the numerous victories that God was going to give his people in fulfillment of his promise to Abraham in the covenant between the parts (see Gen 15).

30 The report of the majority must have caused the people to become very frightened. This is indicated by the words that speak of Caleb's silencing the people. Only Caleb and Hoshea (Joshua) returned a report that was prompted by faith in God. Caleb's words, "We can certainly do it," were not merely bravado; they were the words of one who really believed that the Lord was giving the land to the people. These words were in the spirit of Moses who knew that "the LORD has promised good things to Israel" (10:29). Boldly, confidently Caleb assured the people, "We are most assuredly able to do it" (see Notes).

31–33 But the evil report prevailed. Ten fearful men can out-shout, and certainly out-scare, two brave men. At last they state explicitly what they had implied, "We are unable to do it" (cf. v.31). In this strong denial they not gave a negative caste to the words of faith that Caleb had just spoken; they indeed said that God was not sufficient to bring the task to completion. At this point these men were in a state of denial that included the power and presence of God, the promises and assurances of God, their own resources—indeed, even their own names. Those wonderful names their parents had given them—most of which speak of the blessing of being the people of God—were being denied as they spoke their words of calumny (see Gen 37:2; Jer 20:10).

The Land of Promise was a good land, a gracious gift of the Lord. By speaking evil concerning the land, the faithless spies were speaking evil of him. At this point their words became exaggerations and distortions. The Anakites (who were of large size) were now said to be Nephilim, the race of giants described briefly in the mysterious context of the cohabitation of the sons of God and the daughters of men (Gen 6:4). The use of the term *Nephilim* seems to be deliberately provocative of fear, a term not unlike the concept of bogeymen and hobgoblins. The exaggeration of the faithless led them to their final folly: "We seemed like grasshoppers in our own eyes, and we looked the same to them."

We have noted the possible use of rhetorical exaggeration, hyperbole, in the numbers of the tribes of Israel—power numbers to bring encouragement to the nation in the confidence they must have in the fulfillment of the promises of God (see Introduction, sections on large numbers). In the report of the evil spies, we see that rhetorical exaggeration can work both ways. By describing themselves as mere grasshoppers in the sight of the fabulous Nephilim, they frightened the sandals off the people and led a nation to grievous sin of unbelief against their caring God.

Notes

---

30 The phrase כִּי־יָכוֹל נוּכַל לָהּ (*kî-yāk̲ôl nûk̲al lāh*, lit., "we are most assuredly able to do it!"; NIV, "we can certainly do it") begins with an asseverative *kî*, meaning "surely." Then a Qal passive infinitive absolute is joined to a Qal passive imperfect, both from the same root *yāk̲ōl* ("to be able"). Sadly, we do not have to go far to find a contrast (v.31).

---

d. *The rebellion of the people and defeat by the Amalekites (14:1–45)*

The narrative of this section of Numbers is tied directly to the events of chapter 13; indeed, these two chapters are the most tightly connected of all the narrative sections of the book. This chapter brings to climax and conclusion the story of the central rebellion of the people against the Lord and Moses. The location of the rebellion is Kadesh in the Desert of Zin, in the northernmost reaches of the Desert of Paran. Poised at the base of the Land of Promise, and presumably ready for assault on the land in completion of their divine destiny, the people spurn the land, contemn their Savior, and make plans to return to the slavery of Egypt. Their acts of rebellion on this occasion are so grievous, so outrageous, that God bitterly regrets that he has ever reached out to them.

The Lord threatens to destroy the people utterly and to begin anew with Moses. But Moses implores God to reconsider, to extend anew his mercy, to be again their Savior. The decision of the Lord is one of mitigated judgment. Instead of killing off the rebellious nation at once, he condemns those over the age of twenty to a sentence of a listless existence in the desert. They are like banished peoples, landless and homeless, without place in a period in which having a sense of place was more important than in our own day. Only their children—whom they claimed outrageously that God desired dead—would be able to enter the land. But of the first generation none save the two righteous spies, Caleb and Joshua, would enter the land of God's promise.

The central ideas of this chapter are simply overwhelming. Here was the lost generation. All over the age of twenty were to mark time until they would breathe their last and the sands of Sinai would enwrap their remains. All was to be a waiting game. Throughout the years as parents aged, they would look at their children, living for them; for only through their children's hope of seeing the land could another day in the desert be livable. It is one thing to have a passive impression of the story line of Numbers. But when we really begin to think about the enormity of the sentence of the population, the sense of the text overwhelms us.

(1) *The final rebellion of the faithless people*

14:1–4

> [1] That night all the people of the community raised their voices and wept aloud. [2] All the Israelites grumbled against Moses and Aaron, and the whole assembly said to them, "If only we had died in Egypt! Or in this desert! [3] Why is the LORD bringing us to this land only to let us fall by the sword? Our wives and children will be taken as plunder. Wouldn't it be better for us to go back to Egypt?" [4] And they said to each other, "We should choose a leader and go back to Egypt."

1–2 The malicious report of the ten spies (13:26–33) spread throughout the populace like a vicious virus on rampage. The words of Caleb and Joshua were not heard. Everywhere people heard of walled cities, strong men, giants, and the fabled Nephilim. The giant clusters of grapes were a portent of doom. If clusters of grapes were as great as these, imagine what the people would be like! No one talked about God's grace. None recited his miracles. Forgotten was the act of God where the most powerful nation of their world was stymied at the rushing of waters back to their beds. The thunder of Sinai, the fire of God, that he had spoken and delivered and graced his people beyond imagination—all these things were forgotten in their paroxysm of fear. Fear unchecked becomes its own fuel, a self-propelling force that expands as it expends. The words of a mid-twentieth-century American president, "The only thing we have to fear is fear itself," have their outworking in the self-consumptive absorbtion with terror that raged through the camps that night.

Verses 1–2 emphasize the pervasiveness of the fear and the outrage of the entire populace. The words are "all the people of the community" (v.1), "all the Israelites" (v.2), and "the whole assembly" (v.2). This threefold emphasis on the extent of the rebellion is important; for the judgment of God will extend to the entire community. The entirety of the community was given over to wailing, as only people in the East can do. This was not a scene of passive resignation, of silent ruing. We are to imagine the worst sort of rage, a picture of screaming, rending, throwing, cursing anger—an intoxication of grief.

Moses and Aaron became the principal culprits, the central targets of the anger of the nation. They "grumbled" against Moses and Aaron (v.2), even as they grumbled against the Lord. They were the grumblers of Israel; Scripture accords them their own distinctive verbal expression (see Notes).

As the people gave themselves over to more and more outrageous attitudes, they began to wish that they had already died. It seemed to them that it would have been preferable to have died in Egypt or even in the desert than to come this close to their goal, only to discover that it was unattainable. The irrationality of their words are understandable from the perspective of weakened, sinful humanity. But from the vantage of faith, from the stance of belief in God, these words are intolerable; they are self-destructive, self-fulfilling prophecies. The people who wished to have died in the desert will find that is exactly what they will have to do.

3–4 The more the people wailed, the more excessive their words. The more the people cried, the more they outreached one another in protests of rage. This is the crowd psychology that leads to riots, lynchings, stormings, and rampages. Now they begin to aim their anger more directly at Yahweh himself. Moses and Aaron were the fall guys, but the Lord was the one really to blame; he had delivered them from Egypt. He had brought Pharaoh to his knees, had cast horse and rider into the sea, had led them through a barren land, and had provided bread from heaven and water from a gushing rock. He had spoken, revealing grace and wonder, power and gentleness, direction and Torah. God was the one at fault! And they began to curse him, to contemn his goodness, to reject his grace.

Forgetful of God's power against Egypt, surely a nation stronger than any petty Palestinian city-state, the people worked themselves into such a frenzy of fear that they wished that God had not brought them here at all. Why had he not just left them alone? Slavery began to look good to them. The hovels in Egypt became home again. The memory of a variety of food made the memory of oppressive taskmasters less fearsome.

So it was that the frightening words of the faithless spies led to the mourning of the entire community and to their great rebellion against the Lord. They forgot all the miracles that the Lord had done for them; they contemned his mercies and spurned his might. In their ingratitude they preferred death (v.2). Unfortunately, it was death they deserved and death they were to get. The most reprehensible charge against the grace of God was that concerning their children (see vv.31–33). Only their children would survive. All the rest would die in the desert they had chosen over the Land of Promise.

Notes

1 The syntax of the verse is somewhat abrupt and rough. The word order of the first clause literally reads: "and-they-raised all-the-congregation and-they-gave their-voices." Despite their separation, we expect that the two verbs—"they raised" and "they gave"—work together in hendiadys: "and they gave themselves over completely to wailing." This is buttressed by the last colon of the verse: "and the people wept all that night."

2 The verb לוּן (*lûn*, "to murmur" or "to grumble") is a term of special use for the desert community. It is used only in Exod 15, 16, 17, and in Num 14, 16, 17 (and in Josh 9:18). In the Niphal and Hiphil themes (which are used interchangeably), this verb becomes the marker of a generation of people.

(2) *The words of the faithful warning against rebellion*

14:5–9

5 Then Moses and Aaron fell facedown in front of the whole Israelite assembly gathered there. 6 Joshua son of Nun and Caleb son of

Jephunneh, who were among those who had explored the land, tore
their clothes [7]and said to the entire Israelite assembly, "The land we
passed through and explored is exceedingly good. [8]If the LORD is
pleased with us, he will lead us into that land, a land flowing with milk
and honey, and will give it to us. [9]Only do not rebel against the LORD.
And do not be afraid of the people of the land, because we will swallow
them up. Their protection is gone, but the LORD is with us. Do not be
afraid of them."

5 In the midst of this riot of rebellion, there were a few voices that still spoke of God's grace and remembered his power. This text mentions four such persons: Moses, Aaron, Joshua, and Caleb. These are the only ones mentioned who were not a part of the larger, rebellious community. I suspect that these four are listed because of their prominence in the central story. But I also suspect that they were not in fact the only persons in the entire community who were faithful to God. In any period of great apostasy, we—and Scripture—tend to focus on the pervasiveness of the rebellion and to minimize the numbers of those who are exceptions to the general depravity. Certainly this was the experience of Elijah at Carmel (1 Kings 19:10, 14; cf. v.18).

When we view chapter 14 with its emphasis on the entire community with only four exceptions, and the exceptions are the notables, it is possible that here and there was a mother in Israel who did not capitulate to her husband's rage or a son in the land who raised his doubts against his parents' folly. "All" versus "four" is used to impress on the reader the enormity of the collapse of the nation because of the malicious report of the spies.

Be that as it may, the only voices of reason and faith that we hear in the text are those of Moses, Aaron, Caleb, and Joshua. Their passion for truth in the midst of monumental error caused Moses and Aaron to fling themselves to the ground, prostrate before the enraged leaders of the people. In this posture they symbolized their awareness that the anger of the Lord was likely to burst on the people in a moment.

6–7 Joshua and Caleb tore at their clothing (v.6), a ritual symbolic of mourning. They were mourning, not the loss of parent or loved one, but the loss of faith, the death of hope. Yet even as they mourned, Joshua and Caleb tried to revive the dead. They extolled the land and its virtues with extravagant language. Joshua and Caleb had been there: the land they described to be "exceedingly good" (v.7; see Notes). They reminded the people that the land still flows with milk and honey (see commentary on 13:27).

8 Then these righteous men present the posture of faith. It is still possible to gain the land and to enjoy its fruit. The only thing necessary is that "the LORD is pleased with us." The Hebrew verb *ḥāpēṣ* ("to be pleased with," "to enjoy," "to smile over") is one of the rich verbs expressive of the relationship God desires with his people. The biblical view is not that of an angry deity, smoldering with rage, nastily looking for yet another miserable wretch to zap from on high. Biblical faith believes in the great grace of God, the Lord of mercy, who desires to smile over his people (see again the words of the Aaronic Benediction, 6:24–26, and commentary there). Judgment is God's "strange work." Anger is as alien to his inner nature as it is awful to those who are its target. This is what those four worthies knew. If only the people would listen, would repent, and would believe—then the land could still be theirs and be enjoyed under the smile of heaven.

9 Two things were needful: the people needed to stop their rebellion against the Lord, and they must cease to be afraid of the people of the land. The worthy spies shouted, "Their protection is gone." The word translated "protection" is *ṣēl*, often rendered "shadow" or "shade." In the hot and arid regions of the Middle East, the notion of a shadow or shade is a symbol of grace and mercy, a relief from the searing heat (cf. Ps 91:1). Sometimes the wings of a mother bird form the shadow of protection for her young; in the imagery of the poets of Israel, this mother-hen language is used of the protective care of God (e.g., Ps 17:8). God has served as a protecting shadow for the peoples of the land of Canaan; now that protection is gone. Yahweh is with his people. They can swallow their foes alive!

The depth of the faith of Joshua and Caleb is seen particularly in this vivid expression of the loss of the protective shade in Canaan. There are no walls, no fortification, no factors of size or bearing, and certainly no gods that can withstand the onslaught of the people of God when they know that the Lord is with them. Perhaps these words were based on the covenant language of Genesis 15, which incident came to mind in this crisis. At the covenant between the parts, the Lord had assured Abram that his descendants would return to the land in the fourth generation, at the time when the sins of the Amorites had reached a full measure (Gen 15:15–16).

Notes

---

7 The repetition of the modifier מְאֹד מְאֹד (*m*^{e}*'ōd̲ m*^{e}*'ōd̲*, "exceedingly"), which means "very, very," is used to elaborate on the exceeding goodness of the land. This type of repetition is a way of presenting a heightened sense, a superlative.

---

(3) *The appearance of the Lord to withstand the rebels*

14:10–12

> [10] But the whole assembly talked about stoning them. Then the glory of the LORD appeared at the Tent of Meeting to all the Israelites. [11] The LORD said to Moses, "How long will these people treat me with contempt? How long will they refuse to believe in me, in spite of all the miraculous signs I have performed among them? [12] I will strike them down with a plague and destroy them, but I will make you into a nation greater and stronger than they."

10 Despite the impassioned language of Joshua and Caleb and the portent of the prostrate forms of Moses and Aaron, the people were deaf to mercy, blind to truth. In a grand perversion the people began to shout to one another, "Stone them!" We are reminded of similar attempts to take the life of Jesus. When he spoke truth to an obdurate people, their response was not unlike their distant ancestors in the desert.

Certainly one of the more chilling lines in Scripture is the description of the irruption of the Lord's presence in the middle of v.10. In the midst of the peoples' rage, which was building into a storm that might lead to the stoning of the righteous, the holy God in an awesome display of his wonder burst into their midst at the entrance of the tabernacle.

Moses and Aaron had a foreboding this would happen; likely this is why they were prostrate (v.5). There they lay, grieving and praying; there they lay, waiting, for God was near. The sudden theophany of the Lord at this moment must have been staggering in its abrupt and intense display of his wonder and wrath.

11 When God appears, he does not thunder against the people; but he speaks to his servant Moses about their outrageous behavior. His words have the sense of incredulity: "How long will these people treat me with contempt?" The verb *nā'aṣ* (here and in v.23; cf. 16:30; Ps 10:3, 13; Isa 1:4) is a strong term for utter disregard of a person. As we think of God's promise to bless those who bless Israel and to curse the individual who treats the people with less than a sense of dignity and respect (cf. Gen 12:3), we wonder what must be in store for one who holds God in contempt! This was the central issue. By refusing to believe in the power of the Lord, especially in view of all the wonders they had experienced themselves, the people of Israel were holding him in contempt by their unbelief.

12 The anger of God against his people is at fever pitch. In a moment he would destroy them all. With a word they would cease to afflict him with their arrogance. By a plague the populace could be reduced to a handful. And God could begin again. Moses could be the new paterfamilias; he could be Abraham redivivus. God says, "I will make you into a nation." For the second time since the Exodus, God speaks of starting over with Moses in creating a people faithful to himself (see Exod 32:10).

As we read these words, we are aware of several dynamics at work. One is the very real anger of the Lord, expressed here anthropopathically, that is, in the feelings and frustrations that mirror our own ways of reacting to stress. By using language to describe the "feelings" of God in such palpable terms, God is brought near! Even the expressions of his wrath are manifestations of his grace!

A second dynamic in these words is their effect on Moses. God does not lead his people into temptation, but he does allow them to pass through the tempering fires of stress. He does not do this to break them but for the righteous to have the opportunity to demonstrate what they really believe. The stinging fires lap the dross, but they harden metals that matter. While we hear the words of God, we are anticipating the response of Moses.

A third dynamic in these words is their effect in the lives of those who read them after the fact. The Book of Numbers, as in the case of all Scripture, has a target audience. The primary audience for this book is the second generation, the sons and daughters of these people who behaved so egregiously. The second generation was to learn a lesson that their parents did not learn: God can be provoked only so far. Finally, his wrath is kindled.

A fourth dynamic in these words is their effect in the lives on the more distant readers, including ourselves. Moderns tend to ignore passages that speak of God's wrath, preferring more comfortable passages, texts with "possibilities." Surely the Spirit of God measures our own response to these words. The question they pose is inescapable: Do we or do we not really believe in the judgment of God? And if we do believe that finally he will bring judgment on the wicked, those who hold him in contempt, then what does it matter in our own living?

My point is this: No one dares remain unmoved by these words of the expression of the wrath of God. We remember that this wrath was not against Canaanites or Hittites, not against the Egyptians or the Assyrians, but against his own people. There is a measured, almost dispassionate judgment of remote peoples who pass by the world scene. But when God is forced to rise up in judgment against his own people, we are made to feel what that anger means to him.

(4) *The pleading of Moses on behalf of the rebellious people* 14:13–19

13 Moses said to the LORD, "Then the Egyptians will hear about it! By your power you brought these people up from among them. 14 And they will tell the inhabitants of this land about it. They have already heard that you, O LORD, are with these people and that you, O LORD, have been seen face to face, that your cloud stays over them, and that you go before them in a pillar of cloud by day and a pillar of fire by night. 15 If you put these people to death all at one time, the nations who have heard this report about you will say, 16 'The LORD was not able to bring these people into the land he promised them on oath; so he slaughtered them in the desert.'

17 "Now may the Lord's strength be displayed, just as you have declared: 18 'The LORD is slow to anger, abounding in love and forgiving sin and rebellion. Yet he does not leave the guilty unpunished; he punishes the children for the sin of the fathers to the third and fourth generation.' 19 In accordance with your great love, forgive the sin of these people, just as you have pardoned them from the time they left Egypt until now."

13–16 To the extent that the expression of the wrath of God was a test of the character of Moses, we see in his response one of his grandest moments. Not for a second does he mull the possibility of a new people of God, "the sons of Moses." Instead, zealous for the protection of the perception of the character of God among the nations (who do not know him!), Moses bursts with protest, "But the Egyptians will hear!" (cf. v.13). There is something far more important than his own pride and destiny, something even more important than the people themselves—the reputation of God! Impassioned with zeal for the Lord (see Phinehas's similar reaction [25:11] and the comparison Moses makes in that text between his own zeal for the Lord and that of the young priest), Moses shouts, "No!"

The idea of the reputation of Yahweh among the nations may sound strange to us, but it is a vital concern of Scripture. This idea relates to the manifestation of the glory of God. It also speaks to the "preevangelism" of the nations. There was a marketplace of ideas about gods in the ancient world. But there was no God like Yahweh; never had a deity done for his people what Yahweh had done for his, by sign and wonder and outstretched arm (see Deut 4:32–40). And the nations were watching! A generation later, when Israel finally entered the land of Canaan under Joshua, the nations still remembered what they had heard of Israel's deliverance from Egypt. The sadness is that the nations did not fall captive to the grace of God. But individuals did do so from time to time. One of the most interesting stories concerns a pagan whore who lived at Jericho. But she heard. She remembered. And she believed. And this harlot was transformed. She became a means of deliverance for another group of spies of Israel. Indeed, Rahab became an honored mother in Israel and an ancestress of the Savior! (See Josh 2; Ruth 4:18–22 [Salmon married Rahab]; Matt 1:5; Heb 11:31; James 2:25.)

So the response of Moses is in keeping with his character and is in deference to his desire to maintain the reputation of Yahweh. He shouts, "But the Egyptians will hear!" (v.13). After all the demonstration of the reality of God as against the shallow, hollow, vapid nature of their supposed deities, Moses is aghast at the thought that word would go back to Egypt that God was not able to complete the deliverance of his people. Moses knows that the enemies of God's people will charge Yahweh with an inability to complete his work of their deliverance and will add their own contempt to that of the rebellious people of Israel. To Moses such a prospect was intolerable.

17–19 The second tack that Moses takes is to affirm the splendors of the character of God, particularly his grace. He says, "Now may the LORD's strength be displayed!" (v.17). At this point Moses moves from the reputation of the Lord to the character of the Lord, presenting a composite quotation of his own words of loyal love for and faithful discipline of his people (see Exod 20:6; 34:6–7). These are the basic ideas of the Hebrew Bible in its revelation of the character of God. Moderns who have rejected the message of the OT have often done so on the basis of a "bad rap." They have been taught through popular culture and through misinformed religionists that the "God of the OT" is a god of wrath whereas the God of the NT is all mercy and grace.

But Moses knew God intimately. He knew him as a consuming fire; he also knew his warm embrace. We tend to focus on the flashes of God's wrath. Moses reminds us that while the wrath is real, it is long delayed. The most remarkable thing about the wrath of God is how much provocation he tolerates before he finally acts in righteous judgment. I suspect that there are occasions when we all have wished that God would "zap" this evil or reach out and destroy that evil. But the fact that he has not is a loving reminder that he may extend his patience with us as well.

Notes

19 The phrase כְּגֹדֶל חַסְדֶּךָ (*k^e^g̱ōḏel ḥasdeḵā*, "in accordance with your great love") contains one of the most significant terms in Hebrew Scripture to describe the gracious aspect of the character of God, the word *ḥeseḏ*, best translated "loyal love," as this pairing of words ties together both the mercy and the loyalty aspect this word portrays. In Moses' impassioned plea for God to forgive the people, he heightens the focus on the Lord's loyal love by using the phrase *k^e^g̱ōḏel* ("according to the greatness of").

(5) *The judgment of the Lord against the rebels*

14:20–35

[20]The LORD replied, "I have forgiven them, as you asked. [21]Neverthe-
less, as surely as I live and as surely as the glory of the LORD fills the
whole earth, [22]not one of the men who saw my glory and the miraculous
signs I performed in Egypt and in the desert but who disobeyed me and
tested me ten times—[23]not one of them will ever see the land I
promised on oath to their forefathers. No one who has treated me with
contempt will ever see it. [24]But because my servant Caleb has a different
spirit and follows me wholeheartedly, I will bring him into the land he

went to, and his descendants will inherit it. 25Since the Amalekites and
Canaanites are living in the valleys, turn back tomorrow and set out
toward the desert along the route to the Red Sea."
26The LORD said to Moses and Aaron: 27"How long will this wicked
community grumble against me? I have heard the complaints of these
grumbling Israelites. 28So tell them, 'As surely as I live, declares the
LORD, I will do to you the very things I heard you say: 29In this desert your
bodies will fall—every one of you twenty years old or more who was
counted in the census and who has grumbled against me. 30Not one of
you will enter the land I swore with uplifted hand to make your home,
except Caleb son of Jephunneh and Joshua son of Nun. 31As for your
children that you said would be taken as plunder, I will bring them in to
enjoy the land you have rejected. 32But you—your bodies will fall in this
desert. 33Your children will be shepherds here for forty years, suffering
for your unfaithfulness, until the last of your bodies lies in the desert.
34For forty years—one year for each of the forty days you explored the
land—you will suffer for your sins and know what it is like to have me
against you.' 35I, the LORD, have spoken, and I will surely do these things
to this whole wicked community, which has banded together against
me. They will meet their end in this desert; here they will die."

20–21 Finally God speaks. He is moved by the words of Moses. Think about that; it is another aspect of his grace. In response to Moses' request, "Pardon the iniquity of this people on the basis of the greatness of your loyal love" (cf. v.19), God declares that he has forgiven them (v.20). The verb used in this sentence is *sālaḥ*, a term that basically means "to pardon." There is a sense that this verb may be seen as the antonym to the word "to requite" (*nāqāh*), the word used by Moses to describe God's righteous judgment of the wicked in v.18. But the forgiveness in this case is not complete. The people who have behaved so intolerably will not be put to death, but neither can things go back to the way they were on the day before the rebellion. The words of God in v.21 are forceful and direct; as surely as he lives, as surely as his glory fills the earth, there is a sentence to be paid.

22–23 The judgment is mitigated. The people are not put to death, but neither will they live as God intended. They will not be allowed to see the land (v.23), the prize of his grace for the faithful. As vv.1–2 emphasized the term "all" (see comments above), so vv.22–23 emphasize "not one." Since all the people were in rebellion, not one will escape the mitigated judgment.

The Lord speaks of ten times when the people tested (*nāsāh;* see Notes) him. Quite possibly this use of the number "ten" is a rhetorical way of saying "these many times" (see Notes). Whether the list in the Notes is *the* list of ten or not, for it may be that God was not intending ten in the sense of one more than nine, the listing is still a dismal record. It is as though the people had a penchant for disobedience, a special gifting for murmuring. Yet time after time God forgave them in the midst of his judgment. And that may be the point; the story of the rejecting attitudes and evil actions of the people is not the proper center of Scripture. Rather, we ought to focus on the Lord, watch his actions and reactions, his invitations and his responses.

24 The Lord singles out Caleb, calling him "my servant" and remarking with affection on his "different spirit." It may be that Caleb was the principal spokesman in the defense of the goodness of the land and the sureness of the character of God in vv.7–

9; perhaps Joshua joined in. Caleb's ultimate vindication came forty-five years later (see Josh 14:10; see also comment on 13:22).

25 Here is a verse of sadness. The Lord reminds Moses that there are inhabitants in the land, Amalekites and Canaanites; hence, the people need to turn back to the desert. They had been brought near for the very purpose of confronting these inhabitants of the land in a struggle for possession. But now they were not to fight. They had lost their opportunity; it was back to the sands.

26–35 These verses appear as a second take on the mitigated judgment of God on the nation. Verses 20–25 present a unity of forgiveness and judgment, concluding with a travel notice. Then v.26 seems to take us back to the point we were at in vv.20–21. The observation of such phenomena in the Torah was part of the prompting for many scholars to argue for varied sources for it (the Documentary approach). I confess I am no fan of the "JEDP" approach to the Torah. I find this approach atomizing, splitting the text into smaller and smaller pieces, but with little interest in the whole of Scripture as we have it. Usually the practitioners of this approach proceed in a judgmental rather than reverential manner to Scripture; and rarely is the divine inspiration of Scripture taken seriously in a context that does not credit the text with basic integrity or the authority of God. Nonetheless, some of the features that Documentary scholars have noticed in the text are actually there. This section presents an instance.

Verses 26–35 form a unit of address of the Lord to Moses and Aaron that overlaps in some way with the unit of vv.20–25, where God speaks directly to Moses in response to his plea for the forgiveness of the people. Explanations for this feature do not have to proceed along the classic lines of putative Documentary research. One may suggest that one or the other of these two units was "original" and that the other is a later addition, given to the text to fill it out. But one also may observe that a peculiar feature of Hebrew stylistics is just this very thing: two accounts take on the same issue, each a self-contained unit, but the two together forming a more significant whole. Many of the "doublets" of the Documentary approach may be viewed in this manner. The most obvious example is the pairing of two dissimilar but complementary accounts of Creation (Gen 1 and Gen 2).

I regard vv.26–35 as a distinct entity from vv.20–25. It is possible that these two blocks have had a different history; it is possible that one was added to the Book of Numbers considerably later than the other. But it is also possible that both sprang from the experience of Moses, that both were deliberately used by him, consciously from the beginning. The resultant impression of these two overlapping blocks heightens the mitigated judgment of God on his errant people, just as the dissimilar, overlapping but complementary blocks of God's response to the faithfulness of Abraham on Mount Moriah work together for a greater whole (see Gen 22:11–14, 15–18).

The heart of the second oracle of judgment is one of comic justice. The rash words of the people asking to die in the desert become in a sense the judgment of the Lord. They have brought on themselves their punishment. They had said that they would prefer to die in the desert (v.2) rather than to be led into the land of Canaan to die by the sword. All those who were above the age of twenty, who were counted in the census, were to die in the desert. The only exceptions would be Joshua and Caleb (v.30).

God's sharpest rebuke of his errant people comes in response to their charge that he wanted to kill their children (v.3). The attacks on his grace and the rebuffs of his mercy he will tolerate. The forgetfulness of his power and the ignoring of his acts of deliverance he will set aside. But there is one thing that God simply will not tolerate, the accusation that he had brought the people into the desert with the intent that he might thereby destroy their children, that they would die in the desert or be taken as plunder by victorious enemies. So a further element in the comic justice of this section is the notice that the children, whom the people made such a false charge against the Lord concerning their safety, would be the only ones who actually would come to enjoy the land (v.31). The rest of the people's bodies would "fall in this desert" (v.32).

The forty days of the travels of the spies became the numerical paradigm for the suffering of the people: one year for one day—for forty years they would recount their misjudgment (v.34), and for forty years the people over the age of twenty would be dying (v.35). Thus, when the time is fulfilled, only the young generation might enter the land.

Notes

22 וַיְנַסּוּ (*wayenassû*, "and they tested") is from the verb נָסָה (*nāsāh*), which means "to test" or "to try." This verb can be used with God as the subject with the intent of testing the character of someone; this is its use in Gen 22:1, as God put Abraham to the test of his life. When God is the object of this verb, then the idea is usually one of trying his patience. This is the meaning here and in Exod 17:2, 7; Deut 6:16; Pss 78:18; 95:9; 106:14.

We have seen numerous uses of rhetorical numbers in this book; this may be another one. Yet it may be valuable to attempt to count the times of rebellion, to see whether we can arrive at a listing of ten discrete occurrences. The ten times of the rebellions of the people against the grace of the Lord perhaps may be enumerated as follows:

1. At the Red Sea where it seemed that Pharaoh's army would destroy them (Exod 14:10–12)
2. At Marah where they found bitter water (Exod 15:22–24)
3. In the Desert of Sin as they hungered (Exod 16:1–3)
4. In the Desert of Sin as they paid no attention to Moses concerning the storing of the manna until the morning (Exod 16:19–20)
5. In the Desert of Sin as they disregarded Moses concerning the gathering of the manna on the seventh day (Exod 16:27–30)
6. At Rephidim as they complained for water (Exod 17:1–4)
7. At Mount Sinai as Aaron led the people in making the golden calf (Exod 32:1–35)
8. At Taberah where the people raged against the Lord (Num 11:1–3)
9. At Kibroth Hattaavah in the grumbling provoked by the rabble for quail (Num 11:4–34)
10. At Kadesh in the Desert of Paran when the people refused to receive the good report of Joshua and Caleb but rather wished themselves dead (Num 14:1–3)

27 תְּלֻנּוֹת (*telunnô̱t*, "complaints") is a noun (sing., *telunnāh*) that is related to the verb *lûn* ("to grumble," "to murmur") discussed in the comments on 14:2. As with the verb with which it is associated, this noun is a part of the distinctive language of the Torah to describe the desert community.

(6) *The death of the evil spies*

14:36–38

[36]So the men Moses had sent to explore the land, who returned and made the whole community grumble against him by spreading a bad report about it—[37]these men responsible for spreading the bad report about the land were struck down and died of a plague before the LORD. [38]Of the men who went to explore the land, only Joshua son of Nun and Caleb son of Jephunneh survived.

36–38 The people as a whole receive a commuted sentence, a mitigated judgment. But not the men who were responsible for the attitudes that led to this debacle of doubt! Those responsible for spreading the bad report had to be put to death. The judgment on the ten evil spies was immediate; the generation that they influenced would live out their lives in the desert, but their lives were forfeit. Only Joshua and Caleb were exempt from this judgment. The repeated mention of these two men is deserved; together they withstood a nation.

(7) *Defeat by the Amalekites*

14:39–45

[39]When Moses reported this to all the Israelites, they mourned bitterly. [40]Early the next morning they went up toward the high hill country. "We have sinned," they said. "We will go up to the place the LORD promised."

[41]But Moses said, "Why are you disobeying the LORD's command? This will not succeed! [42]Do not go up, because the LORD is not with you. You will be defeated by your enemies, [43]for the Amalekites and Canaanites will face you there. Because you have turned away from the LORD, he will not be with you and you will fall by the sword."

[44]Nevertheless, in their presumption they went up toward the high hill country, though neither Moses nor the ark of the LORD's covenant moved from the camp. [45]Then the Amalekites and Canaanites who lived in that hill country came down and attacked them and beat them down all the way to Hormah.

39–45 Here is the classic example of too little, too late. Now too late to be in faith, the people determine to go up to the land they had refused. They confessed that they had sinned (v.40), but it is difficult to know what they meant by this confession since it is not elaborated on. But their confession was partial at best, as their actions are rash and foolish, not measured and deliberate. Such a course of action was doomed to failure. Not only was the Lord not with them in this belated act; he was against them (v.41). In fact, he had warned them not to go this way at all but to turn back to the desert (v.25). Their subsequent defeat (v.45) was another judgment the rebellious people brought on their heads. In fact, any soldiers who died in this abortive warfare only hastened their own punishment for the rebellion at Kadesh.

e. *Laws on offerings, the Sabbath, and tassels on garments (15:1–41)*

After reading the dramatic, if depressing, story of the rebellion of Israel at Kadesh and their mitigated judgment by the Lord on the edge of the land (chs. 13–14), it is hard for the reader to move to a priestly text on sacrifice, Sabbath, and tassels. The change of topic is too abrupt; the shift of mood is too distinct; the issue is anticlimactic. In fact, such seeming mismatching of texts leads many scholars to wring their hands over the Book of Numbers (see Introduction: Unity and Organization).

Umberto Cassuto once wrote on this problem from a Jewish perspective (in an essay delivered to the World Congress of Jewish Studies, Jerusalem, 1947), suggesting that the principles for arrangement in the Torah, which at times seem to be so random and arbitrary to ourselves, may have been more meaningful and tangent to the ancients. He suggests, and I paraphrase here, that instead of what we might think of as "logical" ties, there was on occasion an association of words and ideas on a nearly subliminal level that guided the ancient sages in their arrangement of material ("The Sequence and Arrangement of the Biblical Sections," *Biblical and Oriental Studies, Vol. I: Bible* [Jerusalem: The Magnes Press, The Hebrew University, 1973], pp. 1–6). It seems that this is the case in the way that Numbers 15, with its material on spiritual propriety, follows the dramatic narrative of apostasy and rebellion in chapters 13–14.

Here is the possible association. Chapter 14 of Numbers leaves us with a sunken feeling. The people have behaved in such a grossly inappropriate manner to the mercy of God and so arrogantly reacted against his servant Moses that they have been excluded from their inheritance in the land. Only their children would inherit what should have been theirs.

Chapter 15 begins as though nothing has happened! It begins precisely the same way that chapter 1 does. In fact, the opening, with some variation, was found repeatedly through chapters 1–10. Those were the chapters preparing the people for their march to Canaan and their entrance into the land. Chapter 15 is another collection of texts designed to prepare the people for their life in the land. Hence this chapter is one of promise. Though a great deal has happened, and the results are overwhelming for the adult population involved; nonetheless there is a sense in which we may say that nothing has happened. God has pardoned his people (14:20), the second generation will enter the land (14:31), and preparations still need to be made for that period after the Conquest and the achieving of "normalcy" in Canaan.

It seems that the connecting thought between chapters 14 and 15 is the phrase in 15:2: "when you enter the land of your dwelling places that I am giving to you" (pers. tr.). This ties to 14:31: "I will bring them in to enjoy the land you have rejected." The connection is not rubbing salt in the wound; it is the connection of promise. Although much has happened, nothing has happened. The land still awaits the people, but the people must now wait for the land.

Further, the people are to know through both of these verses that the land is the Lord's and that the granting of it to Israel will be his work. Often the question is raised, to whom does the land of Israel belong? The correct answer, both in antiquity and in our own day, is clear: the land is the Lord's. The Canaanite who lived in the land did not own the land. God has the right to give the land to Israel, but he may also take it back again. He holds the title; he grants the use of the land but may withhold it for his own reasons.

Not only is the holiness code material of chapter 15 an abrupt change from the action of the previous chapters, the inner structure of the chapter is difficult to determine. There are three times in the chapter where the same introductory phrasing is used (vv.1, 17, 37), but it seems that there are six discreet sections to the chapter (counting breaks at vv.22, 30, 32). Our analysis follows these lines.

(1) *Teaching on special offerings*

15:1–16

[1]The LORD said to Moses, [2]"Speak to the Israelites and say to them:
'After you enter the land I am giving you as a home [3]and you present to
the LORD offerings made by fire, from the herd or the flock, as an aroma
pleasing to the LORD—whether burnt offerings or sacrifices, for special
vows or freewill offerings or festival offerings—[4]then the one who
brings his offering shall present to the LORD a grain offering of a tenth of
an ephah of fine flour mixed with a quarter of a hin of oil. [5]With each
lamb for the burnt offering or the sacrifice, prepare a quarter of a hin of
wine as a drink offering.
[6]" 'With a ram prepare a grain offering of two-tenths of an ephah of
fine flour mixed with a third of a hin of oil, [7]and a third of a hin of wine
as a drink offering. Offer it as an aroma pleasing to the LORD.
[8]" 'When you prepare a young bull as a burnt offering or sacrifice, for
a special vow or a fellowship offering to the LORD, [9]bring with the bull a
grain offering of three-tenths of an ephah of fine flour mixed with half a
hin of oil. [10]Also bring half a hin of wine as a drink offering. It will be an
offering made by fire, an aroma pleasing to the LORD. [11]Each bull or ram,
each lamb or young goat, is to be prepared in this manner. [12]Do this for
each one, for as many as you prepare.
[13]" 'Everyone who is native-born must do these things in this way
when he brings an offering made by fire as an aroma pleasing to the
LORD. [14]For the generations to come, whenever an alien or anyone else
living among you presents an offering made by fire as an aroma
pleasing to the LORD, he must do exactly as you do. [15]The community is
to have the same rules for you and for the alien living among you; this is
a lasting ordinance for the generations to come. You and the alien shall
be the same before the LORD: [16]The same laws and regulations will apply
both to you and to the alien living among you.' "

1–2 The conjunction of these verses with the sad ending of the narrative of Numbers 14 is dramatic. The sins of the people were manifold; they would be judged. The grace and mercy of the Lord are magnified as he points to the ultimate realization of his ancient promise to Abraham (Gen 12:7) and his continuing promise to the nation that they would indeed enter the land.

3–12 Leviticus 1–7 presents the basic standards of offerings for the community, with a focus on those sacrifices that deal with the issues of sin and guilt. The offerings in Numbers 15 are special; that is, they relate more to the desire of the Hebrew believer for spontaneous, grateful response to the wonder of knowing God. Verse 3 is broad in scope on offerings by fire (*'iššeh;* see Notes). Grain and wine offerings were to accompany the offerings by fire; the grain was to be mixed with oil. We may observe that the grain and wine offerings increased in amounts with the increase of size of the sacrificial animal (vv.6–7; vv.8–12). These passages are the first to indicate that wine offerings, or libations, must accompany all burnt or fellowship offerings.

The provision of "fine flour" (*sōleṯ,* v.4) speaks of luxurious food rather than ordinary flour. This type of flour was used in dainty cooking (Ezek 16:13), at the table of the king (1 Kings 4:22), for honored guests (Gen 18:6), and in the worship of God. Hence, the attitude toward the flour was the same as toward the animals one might bring to the worship of God; only the best was good enough, for the gift was to the Lord. We suspect that the oil and wine used in these offerings were similarly selected from choice, not common, stocks.

The NIV marginal notes aid the modern reader in gauging the ancient measurements used with these sacrifices. The tenth ephah of fine flour (vv.4–5) is about two quarts; the quarter hin of oil or wine is about one quart. The other measurements are proportional to these rough conversions. We may wish to make some mystical meaning of these varied proportions, but my judgment is that the real issue in these proportions is not in some special sense to the numbers; rather, the point of view ought to be in the recognition that God has spoken on how these offerings are to be presented. If God demands one-quarter hin of wine as the drink offering with the sacrifice of a lamb (v.5), then one-quarter hin of the finest wine is what he should get. If he demands one-half hin of wine with the sacrifice of a young bull (v.10), then one-half hin of the finest wine is what he should get.

Verse 4 stresses the concept of approach to the Lord, with all the awe and wonder such a concept should evince. The first three words in the MT are each from the same root (*qāraḇ*, "to make an approach"; see Notes), each speaking of coming near and making an approach to deity. Our modern notions of biblical worship suffer from distaste, distance, and a sense of strangeness. To understand the issues of this chapter, the verb meaning "to come near to God" ought to be stressed in our thinking.

The system of sacrificial worship in ancient Israel was more complex than we may imagine. We tend to focus on those sacrifices that relate directly with the issue of sin and those that typify most clearly the death of Christ. Some of the sacrifices God demanded were presented in the context of a mournful admission of sin, a guilt-laden expression of repentance. But many of the sacrifices in the biblical period were presented in contexts of celebration and a joyful, heartfelt expression of one's delight in knowing the Lord. The tone and texture of this chapter leads us to focus on the celebrative in worship. Even the celebrative and spontaneous were done in a context of method, order, and proportion.

Another element in these worship texts that arrests our attention is the concept of a pleasing aroma to the Lord (vv.7, 10; see also Lev 1:9). The odor of sacrifice, whether the holocaust or the burning of heavy organs and fat, would be heavy, acrid, and pungent. The addition of flour, oil, and fine wine to the fire would add an exotic element to the smells. In pagan nations the production of certain odors was designed to soothe an angry deity. In some cultures odorous gifts are placed near the openings of volcanoes to pacify the demons beneath. But the God of Israel does not need to be soothed. The point of these phrases seems to be the bringing of pleasure to him. Then we ask, would mere smell and smoke make God happy? To ask is to answer: of course not! It is the offerer, not the offering, that brings pleasure to God (see Ps 40:6–8; Mic 6:8–10). But the smells and the smoke, the flesh and the flour are all elements that make the offering "real" by adding substance and action to the feeling of worship. Ultimately the odor of the sacrifice of the Hebrew festivals pointed to the "fragrance" of the offering of the Savior (see Eph 5:2).

13–16 The "native-born" (*hā'ezrāh*, see Notes) and the alien were to complete these regulations in the same manner. As in the case of the celebration of the Passover (see comment on 9:14), the alien had the same regulations as the native-born Israelite. The point in these notes about the alien was to ensure that the commonwealth of Israel would always be open to proselytes. Indeed, the charter of Israel's faith embraces "all peoples on earth" (Gen 12:3). Because the *gēr*, the one who sojourns with Israel, was under the same Torah, he also was able to bring pleasure to the Lord. If the *gēr* continues to be a pleaser of God, soon he might become a part of the community as a whole. In Israel the concept of native and alien was not designed to enforce the distinction forever but to provide a process for assimilation. While still an alien, the proselyte must learn to worship in the same manner as the native populace; and together they needed to learn their worship from the Lord.

In summary of this section (vv.1–16), we make the following observations: (1) the varied offerings, no matter how they are motivated, need to be done in order; (2) the proportion of wine, grain, and oil to the specified animal sacrifice is prescribed; no reasons are given for these ratios, for the issue is simply one of compliance; (3) the rules are the same no matter who the players are; the free citizen and the new-coming alien both follow the same statute.

Notes

---

3 The word אִשֶּׁה (*'iššeh*, "offerings made by fire") is built on the word אֵשׁ (*'ēš*, "fire") and is used chiefly of sacrifices of animals; the word is also used of the *minḥāh* (the "offering" of grain). Grain offerings and wine offerings were also burned on the altar.

The word זֶבַח (*zeḇaḥ*, "sacrifice") is a general term for all sacrifices that culminate in the eating of feasts. The whole burnt offering (*'ōlāh*, "holocaust") was not the only type of animal sacrifice in Israel. Many sacrifices were occasions for festivity, dancing, music, and feasting—a celebration of the wonder of knowing God.

לְפַלֵּא (*lepallē'*, "to make a special offering," "special vow," from the verb *pālā'*, "to be special," "extraordinary," "wondrous") is a verb used of the person and work of God. Here is the presentation of an extraordinary offering (only 15:3, 8, and Lev 22:21), motivated by a heart of gratitude to God.

4 Each of the words וְהִקְרִיב הַמַּקְרִיב קָרְבָּנוֹ (*wehiqrîḇ hammaqrîḇ qorbānô*, lit., "and he offers-the one who offers-his offering"; NIV, "the one who brings his offering shall present") is related to the root *qāraḇ* ("to make an approach," "to offer [to God]").

13 הָאֶזְרָח (*hā'ezrāh*, "the native-born") is a reference that points directly to the time of being settled in the land. At the time of the writing of the Book of Numbers, there were no "native-born" Hebrews; all had been born in a foreign place. This word has led some to believe the whole section is a piece from a later period that has been inserted into the Book of Numbers. This is possible, for one pericope (vv.32–36) is surely from a later time. However, it is still possible to argue that the stance of the chapter is deliberately set by Moses in a future time frame of being settled in the land (see again the wording of v.2, "after you enter the land"; cf. v.18). In this way the function of the chapter is anticipative and encouraging to the people whose lives were lived still in the desert.

---

(2) *Instructions on the cake offering*

15:17–21

17 The LORD said to Moses, 18 "Speak to the Israelites and say to them:
'When you enter the land to which I am taking you 19 and you eat the
food of the land, present a portion as an offering to the LORD. 20 Present
a cake from the first of your ground meal and present it as an offering
from the threshing floor. 21 Throughout the generations to come you are
to give this offering to the LORD from the first of your ground meal.

17–21 This small section begins with the same introductory formula as vv.1–16 (see also v.37), a notice of the source of the instruction being the revelation of the Lord to Moses. This law also looks forward to when the Israelites would be in the land. There is a synergism of sorts in the wording "when you enter" and "I am taking you" (v.18). They must come; yet God will have brought them. The attempt to enter the land on their own ended in disaster (14:44–45). God's actions in bringing them near the land were not effective when they were unwilling to move in at his command (14:4). Since the Book of Numbers presents two generations, we need always to remember who is addressed. The "you" in these verses may have been spoken to the community as a whole, but they are addressed to the children; for only they will actually enter the land. The words of 14:29 are riveting in this regard: every individual who was numbered in the census (chs. 1–4) will perish in the desert; all twenty years of age and over had their prospects for the land forfeited, save Joshua and Caleb.

The first of the threshed grain was to be made into a cake and to be presented to the Lord (v.20). This concept of the firstfruits is a symbol that all blessing is from the Lord and all produce belongs to him. When the people would be blessed to eat of the varied products of the land, this sacred offering was to be presented as a reminder that their food was not just the product of their hands or a gift of "nature"—a foreign notion in biblical times. Each meal is a gift from Yahweh; his people are ever dependent on his largess.

This offering is made of coarse grain (*ʿᵃrisāh*, "ground meal") instead of the fine grain of the previous offerings (see on v.4). The idea seems to be one of immediacy. Right at the time of the threshing of the grain, before the processes of refining for princely flour, a cake is to be made in worship of God and held high from the threshing floor. As v.4 is marked by the verb *qāraḇ* ("to offer"), so v.20 is marked by an elegance in the use of four forms of the word *rûm* ("to raise"). The raising of the first cake of coarse grain is similar to the custom today in small businesses to frame the first dollar. The difference is potent as well; the cake was raised in gratitude to the Lord; such is less common in the framed dollar bill. Verse 21 repeats and extends the teaching on this offering. This is a perpetual ordinance; for the further removed the people become from the events of their salvation, the more likely they will be forgetful of the nature of their salvation. The first generation was not able to remember much longer than three days (11:1–3)!

(3) *Instructions on offerings for unintentional sins*

15:22–29

[22] " 'Now if you unintentionally fail to keep any of these commands the LORD gave Moses—[23]any of the LORD's commands to you through him, from the day the LORD gave them and continuing through the generations to come—[24]and if this is done unintentionally without the community being aware of it, then the whole community is to offer a young bull for a burnt offering as an aroma pleasing to the LORD, along with its prescribed grain offering and drink offering, and a male goat for a sin offering. [25]The priest is to make atonement for the whole Israelite community, and they will be forgiven, for it was not intentional and they have brought to the LORD for their wrong an offering made by fire and a sin offering. [26]The whole Israelite community and the aliens living among them will be forgiven, because all the people were involved in the unintentional wrong.

27 " 'But if just one person sins unintentionally, he must bring a year-old female goat for a sin offering. 28 The priest is to make atonement before the LORD for the one who erred by sinning unintentionally, and when atonement has been made for him, he will be forgiven. 29 One and the same law applies to everyone who sins unintentionally, whether he is a native-born Israelite or an alien.

22–29 These verses comprise a new section, but they do not have the customary introductory formula of their revelatory origin. This new unit deals with the failure to comply with all the commands of the Torah and the provisions of restitution. Verse 22 could be translated, "And *when* you err"; for the expectation is that by acts of omission and commission there will be failures of compliance. The verb *šāg̱āh* focuses on sins of ignorance and inadvertence.

This section reminds us that God's attitude toward his Torah is complex: (1) he is serious about his commands; they are not trivial nor subject to the trifling attitudes of casual people; (2) but he is also gracious; just as man is not made for the Sabbath but the Sabbath for man, so we may aver that man was not made for the Torah but the Torah for man. This suggests that the theological approach that presents the Hebrew law as an impossible standard that was destined to make sinners of its people is in error. God could not justly have commanded impossibilities, for he knows our frame (see Ps 103:13–17; cf. 1 Cor 10:13). God made high demands and expected compliance, but he also provided avenues for redress when one did not comply fully. Therefore we conclude that in the Torah God speaks in grace; in the most exacting law there is mercy, and in all of the Torah the intention is to know him and to relate to him.

Hence sins may be unintentional, but they still need to be covered. See Leviticus 4:2. Such unintentional sins might be done by the people as a whole (Num 15:22–26) or by an individual (vv.27–29). In either case procedures were to be followed for one to be restored to a sense of God's presence and grace. As in the case of other sacrifices, the alien and the citizen have the same demands of compliance.

Notes

---

22 אֶל־מֹשֶׁה (*'el-mōšeh,* "[which the LORD gave] to Moses") is a phrase that compares with the wording of 15:23: בְּיַד־מֹשֶׁה (*b^e yad̲-mōšeh,* "[which the LORD your God commended] by the hand [i.e., by means] of Moses"; NIV, "through him"). These phrases, which are not isolated, suggest that it is a misnomer to speak of "the law of Moses." The Torah is the Lord's; he is the source of the law. It belongs to him. Moses is the means, the agent, the transmitter. See the wording of John 1:17: "the law was given through Moses"; the giver of the Torah is Yahweh.

---

(4) *Instructions for defiant sins*

15:30–31

30 " 'But anyone who sins defiantly, whether native-born or alien, blasphemes the LORD, and that person must be cut off from his people.

[31] Because he has despised the LORD's word and broken his commands, that person must surely be cut off; his guilt remains on him.' "

30–31 Quite another case is presented by defiant sin. The Hebrew idiom is "sins with a high hand," a posture of arrogance, blasphemy, and revolt. Unlike the unintentional sins, for which there are provisions of God's mercy, one who sets his hand defiantly to despise the word of God and to blaspheme his name must be punished. The punishment is one of death, not just banishment or exile. Such a person is gone! Walter C. Kaiser, Jr., compares the "sin of the high hand" of this passage with the NT expression of the offense of blasphemy against the Holy Spirit (Heb 10:26–39). He writes, "As such it becomes an unpardonable sin, since it represents high treason and revolt against God" (*Toward Rediscovering the Old Testament* [Grand Rapids: Zondervan, 1987], p. 132). This verse should not be understood to include all manner of evil actions; for most were subject to forgiveness. The verse deals with outrageous behavior of blasphemy, not mild infractions. However, what the Torah regards as outrageous behavior may be surprising to us, as the illustration in the next paragraph demonstrates. Before we move to that paragraph, however, we may reflect on the application of this unit to the experience of Israel in their rebellion at Kadesh. They deserved to be cut off, utterly destroyed. The grace of God is seen in his commuting their sentence to banishment in the desert (see again, 14:20).

Notes

---

30 The phrase בְּיָד רָמָה (*b^eyā*d̲ *rāmāh,* "with a high hand"; NIV, "defiantly") can be used positively (33:3 and Exod 14:8 ["boldly"]; Deut 32:27 ["our hand has triumphed"]). But here the phrase is used of a person acting in deliberate presumption, pride, and disdain. Moreover, the phrase is modified in v.30 with the words "blasphemes the LORD"! This is why the posture presented in this verse is one of treason, for which there is no provision in the Torah for escaping the results of this sin.

---

(5) *A man who violated the Sabbath*

15:32–36

[32] While the Israelites were in the desert, a man was found gathering wood on the Sabbath day. [33] Those who found him gathering wood brought him to Moses and Aaron and the whole assembly, [34] and they kept him in custody, because it was not clear what should be done to him. [35] Then the LORD said to Moses, "The man must die. The whole assembly must stone him outside the camp." [36] So the assembly took him outside the camp and stoned him to death, as the LORD commanded Moses.

32–36 The introductory phrasing of this pericope suggests that this narrative was inserted into the text of Numbers at a later time, but the experience it relates is from the time of the desert experience of Israel. It is not likely that a story that begins with the phrasing "While the Israelites were in the desert" was an original part of the narrative that has its primary setting in the desert. The phrasing is quite similar to the opening words of the Book of Ruth, also a later reflection of events from long ago.

Whatever its history and origin, this story is something of a cause célèbre of the very thing vv.30–31 describe. The breaking of the Sabbath was not akin to using one-third hin of oil rather than one-quarter or a two-year-old goat instead of a yearling. The point of the story is that Sabbath breaking is the act of a raised fist in defiance of the Lord; the offense strikes at the very center of Israel's responsibility before the Lord. By his action (v.32) this man was thumbing his nose at God.

The brief account is presented in fine narrative style. The ones who discovered the man in Sabbath violation did not know quite what to do. Perhaps they were stunned by his brazenness. They presented him to Moses, Aaron, and the elders to see what must be done (v.33). The answer came from the Lord: "The man must die" (v.35, see Notes). And the sentence was to be carried out by the people, outside the camp. The public participation in his death sentence must have been a chilling event, deeply impressed on the psyche of the nation: "For this thing, I too might die."

The penalty for breaking the Sabbath was death (Exod 31:15; 35:2). As in the case of the willful blasphemer (Lev 24:10–16), the Sabbath breaker was guilty of high-handed rebellion and was judged with death.

By the time of the life of our Lord, observance of Sabbath keeping had become distorted to the point that the regulations concerning the Sabbath were regarded as more important than the genuine needs of people. Our Lord confronted the Pharisees on this issue on several occasions (e.g., Matt 12:1–14). From their point of view, the regulations in vv.32–36 gave the Pharisees their reasons to seek his death (Matt 12:14).

We may add a comment on "Christian sabbath keeping." The Sabbath was the seal of God's covenant with Israel; as a distinctly Israelite institution, we speak in an oxymoron if we describe Sunday, the Lord's Day, as a "Christian sabbath." If we really believed that Sunday is the "Sabbath," then not only would we need to transform it to a day of rest (rather than the frenetic activities that mark most church-going families on this day!); but we would logically have to consider the application of the seriousness of this pericope for infraction. For Sabbath breaking in this story is a blatant revolt against God that is deserving of death!

Notes

35 The verbs מוֹת יוּמַת (*môṯ yûmaṯ*, "must die") are Old Qal passive formations (not Qal and Hophal) of the imperfect and the infinitive of the verb *mûṯ* ("to die"). The meaning is "violent death" (see 35:16; Exod 21:12; 22:19 [18 MT]; Lev 20:2; 24:16). The stoning of Stephen (Acts 7:54–60) is a piece with the stoning of the Sabbath breaker from the vantage point of those who participated. Saul may well have had this text running through his mind when he consented to the death of Stephen. Only later did Saul as Paul realize that it was not blasphemy but praise of the risen Savior that led Stephen to speak as he did.

(6) *Instructions for tassels on garments* 15:37–41

37 The LORD said to Moses, 38 "Speak to the Israelites and say to them: 'Throughout the generations to come you are to make tassels on the

corners of your garments, with a blue cord on each tassel. [39]You will have these tassels to look at and so you will remember all the commands of the LORD, that you may obey them and not prostitute yourselves by going after the lusts of your own hearts and eyes. [40]Then you will remember to obey all my commands and will be consecrated to your God. [41]I am the LORD your God, who brought you out of Egypt to be your God. I am the LORD your God.' "

37–40 As in many of the pericopes of this sort, the connection with the preceding is not at once clear. What has the wearing of tassels to do with the stoning of a Sabbath breaker? Yet there is a connection of sorts. The story of the execution of the high-handed offender is designed to bring fear to all people that they, too, might be led to the breaking of the demands of the Lord in his Torah. Hence, a most practical device is given, the wearing of tassels on one's garment as a perpetual reminder of the demands of God in his Torah. Again, this is a mark of grace—as is all of the Torah.

The reason for the tassels is given in this paragraph. As one would walk along, the tassels would swirl about at the edge of his garment. These would be excellent memory prods to keep faith with the Torah, to obey the commands of God. Each step of the believer was to be encircled by tassels that symbolized the restraints and freedoms of knowing Yahweh (cf. Deut 6:8–9).

The tassels were on the fringes of the garment, with special cords on the corners made of blue (or violet) color (v.38). This passage is the legislation that establishes the wearing of the tallis (or tallith), the traditional prayer shawl of Israel (and which is the pattern for the flag of the state of Israel today).

41 The pericope—and the chapter—ends on a high note of the self-revelation of the Lord and his declaration of purpose for his people. The words "I am the LORD your God" (repeated) have about them the sound of a litany, a recitation of faith. The demands that God made on his people came from his right of redemption. By his act of deliverance, Yahweh speaks with the demands of his character. Further, the chapter begins and concludes with the continuing promise of God to bring his people into the land. He is still at work in the process of completing their redemption from Egypt. The command to turn back to the desert (14:25) is for a lengthy detour, not an abandonment of the journey itself.

This verse is nearly poetry. It can be displayed in this manner:

I am Yahweh your God,
    who is bringing you from the land of Egypt
    to be your God;
I am Yahweh your God!

Notes

41 The words אֲנִי יהוה (*'anî yhwh,* "I am the LORD"), repeated in this verse, are the regular assertion of God at points of singular emphasis of his sovereign grace in the lives of his people. It will be remembered that it is possible that the phrase was intended in the beginning of the poem of the Oracle of the Lord (12:6–8; see comment and note in loc.). Here the language is even more expressive; the full phrasing at the beginning and the ending of this verse is: "I am the LORD your God." This declaration of the Lord should have been especially comforting to the people, coming after their terrible rebellion at Kadesh.

f. *The rebellion of Korah and his allies (16:1–50)*

Earlier there had been a rebellion against the leadership of Moses led by Miriam and Aaron (see ch. 12). This chapter presents an attack on the leadership of Moses and Aaron by Korah and his allies. Korah was descended from Levi through Kohath. As a Kohathite he had high duties in the service of the Lord at the tabernacle (see 4:1–20), but he desired something higher. His passion was to assume the role of priest; he used subterfuge to advance his claim by advancing the false piety of common holiness before the Lord. Korah was joined by the Reubenites Dathan, Abiram, and On and some 250 other leaders of Israel (perhaps from several tribes) who had their own complaints and their own pretensions. Politics and strange bedfellows are not modern phenomena. Their charge was that Moses had "gone too far" in taking the role of spiritual leadership of the people; they asserted that the whole community is equally holy, hence Moses and Aaron had no special privilege with the Lord nor special authority over them. To these scurrilous charges Moses retorts, "You Levites have gone too far!" (v.7) and sets up a trial by fire. The chapter is dramatic in nature and is profound in its basic teaching.

The text does not have a time indicator. We may presume by its placement, however, that it records an event that took place after the debacle at Kadesh. In this manner the rebellion of Miriam and Aaron (ch. 12), which comes before Kadesh, serves to balance this post-Kadesh assault on the character of Moses. The story of Moses' own failure before the Lord (ch. 20) can only be understood with these stories of rebellion against his leadership by trusted people. Finally, even Moses capitulates to rage.

This narrative is one of a few instances where the desert experience following the mitigated judgment of God against the people is detailed for later generations. I suggest that with a few exceptions, such as this story, the reason that Moses passes over most of the experiences of the people in the desert is that these experiences were not properly part of the *Heilsgeschichte* of the people. The movement from Egypt to Kadesh was detailed quite fully. The movement of the people toward Moab is also nicely developed. The intervening years are lost time, the working out of judgment, a waiting for a generation to pass from the scene. Only occasionally, when an event of great import transpires, does Moses break his code of silence and inform the later generation of the event.

(1) *The beginning of revolt*

16:1–3

> 1 Korah son of Izhar, the son of Kohath, the son of Levi, and certain Reubenites—Dathan and Abiram, sons of Eliab, and On son of Peleth—became insolent 2 and rose up against Moses. With them were 250 Israelite men, well-known community leaders who had been appointed members of the council. 3 They came as a group to oppose Moses and Aaron and said to them, "You have gone too far! The whole community is holy, every one of them, and the LORD is with them. Why then do you set yourselves above the LORD's assembly?"

1 This is the second account of a presumptuous, unprincipled rebellion against Moses by leading figures who were not content to continue in subservient positions under his leadership. Given the results of that first rebellion (ch. 12), this account seems to be particularly grievous.

Perhaps there was always some resentment of Moses among leading persons in the community. Petty, insecure people will always rise up against constituted leadership with questions of an unbalanced nature, pushing, pressing to assert their own ends. On the very first occasion when Moses intervened on behalf of righteousness among his people while still a young man in Egypt, he found himself rebuffed by a ruffian who challenged his right to intervene. At that time he was still a privileged scion of the harem of Pharaoh, and he intervened in a fight between two Hebrews (see Exod 2:13–14). Now, long the leader of the nation, Moses still finds himself under terrible attack by others who ought to have been supporters of his leadership. They may have been jealous of his privileged upbringing in the harem of Pharaoh (Exod 2:1–11), resentful of his futile attempt to redress wrong in his rash behavior against the slave master, suspicious of his forty-year absence while they continued to suffer under Pharaoh (vv.15–25), and doubtful of his audacious claim to have been singled out by God as his mediator for the nation (Exod 3:1–15).

It may also be possible that Moses was a difficult person to function under! Since we have discovered that the classic text ascribing meekness or humility to Moses is a misunderstanding (see commentary on 12:3), it may be time to reassess his personal character. Rebellion against persons in authority may spring from a variety of reasons. But when principled people of varied sorts rise against a leader from time to time, it is possible that there is something amiss in that person. Scripture clearly places the blame on others in this case. But Moses may unwittingly have given rise from time to time to opposition to his leadership. This possibility does not dismiss the error of the insurrections, but it may help to explain why they occurred.

The name "Korah" (*qōraḥ,* v.1) may mean "baldness" (see Notes). His paternity is traced through Izhar and Kohath to Levi. As we shall see, his name is later famous for the role his descendants had in the making of music in the time of David and following. The phrase "A son of B son of C" in this instance extends over four hundred years. Levi, son of Jacob, was one of the twelve patriarchs who entered the land of Egypt over four hundred years before the time of the events of this text. Numerous intervening generations are demanded. This may explain, for example, the name Amminadab instead of Izhar between Kohath and Korah in 1 Chronicles 6:22. We might paraphrase today, "Korah was a Levite whose line may be traced through Kohath and Izhar."

Korah's cohorts in this evil plan of insurrection were the Reubenites Dathan (*dāṯān,* "decree," "law") and Abiram (*'ᵃḇîrām,* "the exalted One is my Father"), sons of Eliab (*'ᵉlî'āḇ,* "God is Father"), and On (*'ôn,* "vigor," a man mentioned only here). The father of On is said to be Peleth, but this may be a substitution for the name Pallu (see Gen 46:9; Exod 6:14; 1 Chron 5:3).

2 The principals are joined by another 250 men. These were not rogues, however. They were dignified leaders and are credited with three descriptive phrases in the MT: (1) they were chiefs of the congregation (*nāśî',* "one lifted up as a chief"; NIV, "community leaders," the same term used for the tribal leaders in chs. 1, 2, 7, and 34, and for the spies in ch. 13); (2) they were official representatives of the assembly (*qᵉrî'ê mô'ēḏ,* "the summoned ones of the assembly,"; NIV, "appointed members of the council," an expression found in 1:16); and (3) they were "men of name," that is, men of reputation (untr. in NIV). The text thus draws considerable attention to the fact that this was not a rebellion of rude, impudent ruffians but of creditable leaders, esteemed men of rank. That is even more tragic, since they were not content with the privilege they had received by God's grace. Now they wanted more. Korah was a direct descendant of Levi from an esteemed line. The brothers Dathan and Abiram and their friend On were Reubenites. And the men associated with them were constituted officials, men of name. Together this was a formidable company of nobles who brought their seditious attempt to discredit Moses.

3 Aaron also was under attack. Perhaps Korah's real desire was not only to demean Moses but to make himself priest instead of Aaron. Both Moses and Aaron were (at least) in their eighties at this time. The nation was under a sentence of God's judgment, and these men knew that they were a part of the doomed community. Perhaps they thought that by a forced change of guard they might even reverse the fortunes of the people. The verb translated "they came as a group" suggests an organized, well thought-out conspiracy. This was not just a momentary, casual play of a motley crew. They had not just come up to Moses and Aaron but "against" (NIV, "to oppose") them; the preposition is significant.

The conspirators' words to Moses and Aaron are compressed and impassioned; they are difficult to translate smoothly. Literally they say, "Much to you" (*raḇ-lāḵem*). The idea is that Moses and Aaron arrogated to themselves too much, that they have presumed on their power for self-aggrandizement. Perhaps they are charged as well with not sufficiently sharing their power with these antagonists. The charge was much the same in chapter 12; but on this occasion Aaron was not a coconspirator; he is also charged with the same offense.

When Korah and his cohorts say that the entire congregation is holy, they emphasize the word "all." They also insist that the Lord is in the midst of the whole community, not just residing in the privacy of the Tent of Meeting.

All this is true but distorted. Even though the entire nation was holy, yet there are gradations of holiness in the divine intent. By their words they appear to be arguing for a democratization of the divine privilege. But in fact they merely desired a shift of power—to themselves. The pattern of leadership the Lord established in Israel was *not* an even-handed, ideal democracy. His pattern was theocratic—a rule of God—mediated through a divinely sanctioned regent. The Lord was present with all the people. The leaders have more privilege than the common people, and Moses and Aaron were the most privileged and had the greatest responsibilities. A prudent response of a privileged person is gratitude to God and loyal service to his praise. Only a fool would attack the structure of God's rule based on a mistaken notion of democracy. Fools these worthies became!

Notes

1 קֹרַח (*qōraḥ*, "Korah") is presumably derived from the verbal root *qāraḥ* ("to be bald"). However, there is another word with the same spelling that is the presumed root for the word "frost" or "ice." When the meaning of a name is not commented on in Scripture, suggestions may be precarious.

The verb וַיִּקַּח (*wayyiqqaḥ*, "became insolent"[?]) seems to be the word regularly rendered "and he took," a Qal preterit of the common verb *lāqaḥ* ("to take"). The NIV translation "became insolent" is suggested by comparison with an Arabic word, leading to an as yet otherwise unattested Hebrew root, *yāqaḥ* ("to become insolent," "to act with impudence"). We are attracted to this translation for two reasons: (1) the verb "to take" has no accusative given in the verse; rather the sentence is construed as though the verb is not a transitive word; and (2) the verb "to become impudent" is greatly significant in this context. Other suggestions have been given for this difficulty, but the NIV solution seems convincing.

---

(2) Moses' rejoinder

16:4–7

4 When Moses heard this, he fell facedown. 5 Then he said to Korah and all his followers: "In the morning the LORD will show who belongs to him and who is holy, and he will have that person come near him. The man he chooses he will cause to come near him. 6 You, Korah, and all your followers are to do this: Take censers 7 and tomorrow put fire and incense in them before the LORD. The man the LORD chooses will be the one who is holy. You Levites have gone too far!"

4 The response of Moses is sudden, dramatic, and decisive. He fell to his face on the ground. The baselessness of the attack of Korah and his company is superbly demonstrated by this action. An arrogant man might have lashed out at them. A threatened man might have become defensive. Moses was neither. He fell to his face in obeisance to the Lord, whose regent he was and to whom his sole allegiance belonged. Although Aaron was also under attack, all focus is on Moses. If he stumbles, Aaron stumbles as well. If Aaron stumbles, Moses may still stand.

5 There is no indication of the length of time Moses is lying prone to the earth. But when he rises, he speaks decisively. His words are now the Lord's words. Tomorrow will be "High Noon" in the encampment of Israel. Once and for all the role of Moses in Israel will be defined. One way or another tomorrow will tell. The verb rendered "will show" is likely a jussive and may be translated: "In the morning, let Yahweh make known who belongs to him" (NIV, "will show"). This phrasing may be compared with the words of 2 Timothy 2:19: "The Lord knows those who are his" (see also Nah 1:7; John 10:14). Moses uses language of the prayer of faith commingled with his sense of the certainty of his own position.

Further, Moses' term for the choice one of God is "the holy," perhaps "the holiest" (as the term "holy" with the article may be an example of the article indicating the superlative). The Lord will bring near to himself the one who is the holiest, based on his own choice in that one.

The enemies have asked for a showdown. Moses will give them one, and it will be far more than they bargained for. When Moses rises from his prone position, it is with resolution and a grim determination. Finally, it has come to him that it is not he nor his brother who are under attack; it is the Lord himself. If Moses had indeed arrogantly assumed power that was not properly his, then he would have been in error and Korah would be vindicated. But Moses knew. It was his story. It was Moses who had heard the voice of the Lord from the burning bush. It was Moses who had withstood Pharaoh to his face. It was Moses who had stood on the holy mount to receive the word of God. And it was Moses who had faced a similar challenge from his own sister and brother. Now they would get their chance, but it would be their ruin.

6–7 Only the initial provisions for the test are laid out at this point; more will come later. Moses tells each of those involved to take a censer and fire and incense. This is remarkable since the priests alone were to hold the censers. While Korah was of the house of Levi, he was not a member of the priestly family. The others as Reubenites were not even remote possibilities. But Moses dared them to do as he demanded. Then the Lord would make his choice known to all in a dramatic, vivid manner. Here would be an unforgettable demonstration of the supernal power of God and of his gracious choice in his true servant. In an arresting turn of phrase, Moses shouts to these detractors that it is they who "have gone too far" (v.7), using the same words (*rab̲-lāk̲em,* "much to you!") they had used against him and Aaron (v.3).

(3) *Moses' warning to the rebels*

16:8–11

> 8 Moses also said to Korah, "Now listen, you Levites! 9 Isn't it enough for you that the God of Israel has separated you from the rest of the Israelite community and brought you near himself to do the work at the LORD's tabernacle and to stand before the community and minister to them? 10 He has brought you and all your fellow Levites near himself, but now you are trying to get the priesthood too. 11 It is against the LORD that you and all your followers have banded together. Who is Aaron that you should grumble against him?"

8 Although the text says "Korah," Moses is addressing all the assembled insolent men. The verb "listen" is in the plural and is strengthened by the energic ending, giving special force to his charge. Since the principals along with Korah are Reubenites, it is difficult to know whether Moses' words "you Levites" are inclusive of other Levites who are joined with Korah or are meant to include Dathan, Abiram, and On in a sarcastic manner.

9 "Isn't it enough for you" translates the Hebrew idiom "Is it a little thing from you?" In other words, In your judgment is it nothing that the Lord has marked you out as distinct from the entire community for a special work for his pleasure? They were in a special place in God's economy, but they were not satisfied. They desired more than ever. There is an emphasis in these verses on the grace of God being trampled shamelessly by these arrogant men. Korah is the ringleader, but all in his company are culpable. The issue is gratitude versus pride. A humble, grateful person thanks God for any task and carries it out faithfully. A prideful person like Korah, selfishly desiring a bigger place, a larger slice of the action in God's kingdom, is in fact an enemy of God. Anytime one begins so heavily to emphasize "my ministry," then such a one is in danger of standing in Korah's sandals.

10 That the conspirators were really after the priesthood becomes clear to Moses. It was not that Moses was in error or that Aaron was at fault. It was simply that these wicked men wanted their positions.

11 The phrase "banded together" shows the determination of Korah and his followers. This was not a rag-tag group but a congealed body who were on the make. Moses adds literally, "And Aaron!" after "against the LORD." His language is incredulous, as though to say, "What did he ever do to you that you should strike out against him?"

(4) *Confrontation with Dathan and Abiram*

16:12–14

[12]Then Moses summoned Dathan and Abiram, the sons of Eliab. But they said, "We will not come! [13]Isn't it enough that you have brought us up out of a land flowing with milk and honey to kill us in the desert? And now you also want to lord it over us? [14]Moreover, you haven't brought us into a land flowing with milk and honey or given us an inheritance of fields and vineyards. Will you gouge out the eyes of these men? No, we will not come!"

12–14 It is difficult to believe the level of acrimony that we find in Dathan and Abiram. They are not even willing to come to appear before Moses to face charges. Twice they refuse absolutely (vv.12, 14). The charge of Dathan and Abiram against Moses was to sing again the old song that he had not led them into the Land of Promise. The ludicrous level of their apostasy was given in their absurdity that Moses had in fact led the people from "a land flowing with milk and honey" (v.13). By this strange alchemy, the land of Egypt has changed from prison to paradise; and Moses is some sort of dunce who has been leading them in the wrong direction. Moreover, they charge Moses with play-acting the role of a prince (*śārar* in the Hithpael; NIV, "to lord it"). Their contempt is simply audacious.

The behavior of Dathan and Abiram is, if possible, even more intolerable than that of Korah: (1) they refuse to appear before Moses; (2) they mock his words, using the language of "a little thing" (NIV, "Isn't it enough?" v.13) back on him; (3) they abuse the language of choice for Canaan to describe contemptuously the land of Egypt; (4) they accuse Moses of their plight in the desert, quite forgetting all the events of Kadesh; (5) they mock him as a strutting prince always prancing about; (6) they blame him that they do not possess the fields and vineyards of Canaan; (7) they taunt him with such a misuse of power that he attempts to blind others to his faults; and (8) they repeat their outrage of disobedience, "We will not come!" (v.14). Was there ever such impudence against Moses as comes from these men? Later in Israel's history a poet will write a psalm that will chronicle the experience of Israel from her roots. This poet included the rebellion of Dathan and Abiram but fails even to mention Korah (see Ps 106:17–18).

The expression "to gouge out their eyes" (v.14) is a rhetorical exaggeration. The rebels charge Moses with blinding men to his true intentions. It is as though he were to gouge out their eyes so that they cannot see the wicked things that he is alleged to have been doing to them.

(5) *Judgment on his enemies*

16:15–35

[15]Then Moses became very angry and said to the LORD, "Do not accept their offering. I have not taken so much as a donkey from them, nor have I wronged any of them."

[16]Moses said to Korah, "You and all your followers are to appear before the LORD tomorrow—you and they and Aaron. [17]Each man is to take his censer and put incense in it—250 censers in all—and present it before the LORD. You and Aaron are to present your censers also." [18]So each man took his censer, put fire and incense in it, and stood with Moses and Aaron at the entrance to the Tent of Meeting. [19]When Korah had gathered all his followers in opposition to them at the entrance to

the Tent of Meeting, the glory of the LORD appeared to the entire
assembly. 20 The LORD said to Moses and Aaron, 21 "Separate yourselves
from this assembly so I can put an end to them at once."
22 But Moses and Aaron fell facedown and cried out, "O God, God of
the spirits of all mankind, will you be angry with the entire assembly
when only one man sins?"
23 Then the LORD said to Moses, 24 "Say to the assembly, 'Move away
from the tents of Korah, Dathan and Abiram.' "
25 Moses got up and went to Dathan and Abiram, and the elders of
Israel followed him. 26 He warned the assembly, "Move back from the
tents of these wicked men! Do not touch anything belonging to them, or
you will be swept away because of all their sins." 27 So they moved away
from the tents of Korah, Dathan and Abiram. Dathan and Abiram had
come out and were standing with their wives, children and little ones at
the entrances to their tents.
28 Then Moses said, "This is how you will know that the LORD has sent
me to do all these things and that it was not my idea: 29 If these men die
a natural death and experience only what usually happens to men, then
the LORD has not sent me. 30 But if the LORD brings about something
totally new, and the earth opens its mouth and swallows them, with
everything that belongs to them, and they go down alive into the grave,
then you will know that these men have treated the LORD with
contempt."
31 As soon as he finished saying all this, the ground under them split
apart 32 and the earth opened its mouth and swallowed them, with their
households and all Korah's men and all their possessions. 33 They went
down alive into the grave, with everything they owned; the earth closed
over them, and they perished and were gone from the community. 34 At
their cries, all the Israelites around them fled, shouting, "The earth is
going to swallow us too!"
35 And fire came out from the LORD and consumed the 250 men who
were offering the incense.

15 In Moses' plea of innocence, we sense his humanity. In his pleading for mercy from the Lord for the people (v.22), we sense again his magnanimity. In his wrath Moses asks God not to turn his face with gracious favor on their offering; he proclaims himself innocent of misuse of his office for personal gain; he proclaims himself guiltless of any harm. He has not enriched himself by one donkey nor brought harm to one person.

16 The trial was to be by fire: which men would the Lord accept as his priests in the holy tabernacle? The 250 men allied with Korah came with arrogance to withstand Moses and Aaron at the entrance of the Tent of Meeting. The revelation of the glory of Yahweh was sudden, with words of impending doom for the rebellious people. The punishment was sure and with fitting irony. Those 250 men who dared to present themselves as priests before the Lord with fire in their censers were themselves put to death by fire from the Lord (v.35).

This section is similar to the command Moses gave earlier (vv.5–7), though it has more refinements. Some scholars might regard this restatement as an example of a tortured history of the text. But it is also possible to see statement and refinement such as this as a standard pattern of Hebrew style. The reader is drawn into the experience by not being told exactly what will happen.

17–18 The text emphasizes the participation of the individual by its repeated use of the term *'îš* ("man") in vv.17–18 ("each man," NIV). There also seems to be a focus on Korah versus Aaron, rather than Korah versus Moses. It seems that with Aaron now quite old, Korah wants his position. Even though the "job" is the service of the Lord in his holy precincts, it seems that Korah believes he will be able to wrest that service by force. Somehow he must have decided that the Lord will acquiesce to his demands!

19 But God is not one to capitulate! Suddenly the glory of the Lord bursts into their midst. The "glory of the LORD" speaks of the weight of his presence, the semblance of his majesty. This is a way of referring to God in potent, frightful mystery.

20–21 The Lord speaks again that he has had it with the people. He is about to wipe out the nation again, not just the company of evil, grasping men, but the congregation. Moses and Aaron understand that it was all the people, not just the foolish rebels, whom God was about to destroy.

22 Again we see the character of Moses and Aaron who pray to God to preserve the nation despite yet another outrageous attack. The prayer is unusual in the manner of address: "O God, God of the spirits of all mankind." Perhaps in this unusual phrasing Moses and Aaron were urging God to act in mercy since all life is ultimately dependent on him. They ask whether it is right that the whole nation be destroyed just because one man has sinned (or perhaps, "Shall just a single man sin, and the whole be destroyed?").

23–27 The Lord seems to accede to the reasoning of these words, for he demands that the people move away from the tents of Korah, Dathan, and Abiram. The judgment of the Lord was going to be severe, but he did not wish to have it lash out on the bystanders. It appears that Korah himself had left the 250 priests and was standing with Dathan and Abiram to continue their opposition to Moses. The use of the term for "tent" (*miškān*) is unusual here, as this is the word normally used for the tabernacle of the Lord. We may wonder whether the term is not used sarcastically: the Lord has his *miškān*, and now these false claimants to the priesthood have their *miškān*. It is possible that we find here a dark witticism against the enemies of God.

28–30 Moses wished to assure the people that the judgment that was coming was certainty the direct work of Yahweh and not a happenstance that might be interpreted differently. The opening of the earth to swallow the rebels was a sure and evident sign of the wrath of God and the vindication of Moses and Aaron. It was a new phenomenon (*b^erî'āh;* NIV, "something totally new"), something unmistakably the work of God. The earth is pictured as a ravenous monster whose jaws suddenly open and whose gullet descends to the inner chambers of Sheol. This passage is frightful, a thing of horror. The new phenomenon is that these people will not die and then go into Sheol; they will fall into Sheol alive (v.33). It is the spiritual antithesis of Enoch being caught alive into heaven; they are to descend alive into "hell."

31–34 It happened as soon as Moses finished speaking (v.31); the earth split open and swallowed the rebels, with their households (v.32). Numbers 26:11 explains that the sons of Korah did not die. Apparently they did not join their father in his rash plan.

The households of the other rebels died with them. The men and all with them were under *ḥerem,* the ban (cf. Achan in Josh 7). There is no mercy, no pleading, no help. The children, wives, and even toddlers died with their wicked fathers. It was the wiping out of a family. In this judgment we see that which was immediate, catastrophic, horrible, and complete. Yet there is something in it that is also satisfying: something of the honor of the Lord; of the servants he had named; of the purity of the camp; and, in a sense, of poetic justice.

35 The 250 men were then devoured by fire (perhaps lightning); the smell of their incense would not be able to cover that of their stinking, burning flesh.

After these revolts, the word would be out: those who seek to take the positions of Moses and Aaron may find that God has no more use for them. He took them to the home they chose when they made their choice not to follow him.

The horror of the story is that the punishment included women and children. No easy answer presents itself to deal with this issue in a satisfactory manner. One may speak of a corporate solidarity, of the sense of compliance of the family, of the possibility that the children will grow to be like the fathers. Yet ultimately one has to back away from such problems and simply, humbly admit, we really do not know. But there is one thing that we do know: the God of Israel will do right!

The issue is theodicy. Not just the ego of Moses was at stake here, but the vindication of the work of God, his name, and his glory. Possibly Korah felt with his leadership the nation might overcome the judgment of God, and he and the others might not die in the desert. Perhaps his original intention was a self-deluded attempt to give the nation one more chance. Such a theory provides Korah with a sense of motivation that otherwise seems to be lacking.

We would expect that the line of Korah was obliterated in this text, along with the families of Dathan and Abiram. Yet it turns out that there are survivors of Korah's family who extend all the way to the time of David and beyond. Numbers 26:10–11 tells us that Korah was among those whom the earth swallowed but that his sons did not die with him. His descendants would later become the temple singers, responsible for the crafting of numerous psalms (see headings to Pss 42; 44–49; 84–85; 87–88; cf. Exod 6:21, 24; 1 Chron 6:22–31). In the survival of the house of Korah and their ongoing participation in the worship of God, we find both irony and mercy. The irony is self-evident. The mercy ought to be; that God will allow this family to restore its former prestige—carrying the name of their infamous father—is a remarkable tribute to his grace. At the same time the memory of their father was not lost; it is cited in the NT (Jude 11) as one of the prime exemplars of rebellion and evil in the biblical record.

Notes

30 The word בְּרִיאָה (*b^e^rî'āh,* "a new thing," i.e., "a new phenomenon," "a unique creation"; NIV, "something totally new") comes from the root *bārā'* ("to create"), which has the basic idea of "to fashion anew—a divine act."

(6) *The aftermath of the contest—more distress*

16:36–50

36The LORD said to Moses, 37"Tell Eleazar son of Aaron, the priest, to
take the censers out of the smoldering remains and scatter the coals
some distance away, for the censers are holy—38the censers of the men
who sinned at the cost of their lives. Hammer the censers into sheets to
overlay the altar, for they were presented before the LORD and have
become holy. Let them be a sign to the Israelites."
39So Eleazar the priest collected the bronze censers brought by those
who had been burned up, and he had them hammered out to overlay the
altar, 40as the LORD directed him through Moses. This was to remind the
Israelites that no one except a descendant of Aaron should come to
burn incense before the LORD, or he would become like Korah and his
followers.
41The next day the whole Israelite community grumbled against
Moses and Aaron. "You have killed the LORD's people," they said.
42But when the assembly gathered in opposition to Moses and Aaron
and turned toward the Tent of Meeting, suddenly the cloud covered it
and the glory of the LORD appeared. 43Then Moses and Aaron went to
the front of the Tent of Meeting, 44and the LORD said to Moses, 45"Get
away from this assembly so I can put an end to them at once." And they
fell facedown.
46Then Moses said to Aaron, "Take your censer and put incense in it,
along with fire from the altar, and hurry to the assembly to make
atonement for them. Wrath has come out from the LORD; the plague has
started." 47So Aaron did as Moses said, and ran into the midst of the
assembly. The plague had already started among the people, but Aaron
offered the incense and made atonement for them. 48He stood between
the living and the dead, and the plague stopped. 49But 14,700 people
died from the plague, in addition to those who had died because of
Korah. 50Then Aaron returned to Moses at the entrance to the Tent of
Meeting, for the plague had stopped.

36–40 After the terrible conflagration that had destroyed the 250 rebels who had joined with Korah and his cohorts, Moses receives a new command from the Lord. He is told to have Eleazar son of Aaron take the censers from the midst of the smoldering remains (v.37). Perhaps the most chilling incident in the narrative is the description of the true priests taking the censers of the 250 deceased impostors from their charred remains and employing these holy instruments in hammered bronze sheets for the altar (v.38). Can you imagine the scene? True priests are picking among the bodies, charred flesh, stench, smoke, smoldering embers, and twisted parts. They are to make a count. There were 250 censers; not one is to be lost. Each one is recorded, each one cleansed, each one holy. And the fire is to be scattered yonder. It is strange fire, not worship fire. It is a fire of judgment.

Even with the death of the false priests, the holy things had to be treated as holy things. This is amazing! The men were wicked and had to be destroyed; the implements were holy and needed to be preserved! From that time on the sheet of bronze over the altar would be a memorial of the utter folly of the self-proclaimed priest of the most holy God (v.40). Their families would know. Their neighbors would remember. Every time they would look at the altar or think of it again, they would be forced to remember the folly of their fathers.

Moreover, those who went to pick out the censers became unclean because of their contact with the bodies of their foes. Everything was a lesson in ancient Israel. All was a mix of holy and profane, of clean and unclean, of good and evil.

The censers were hammered together to form the overlay for the altar, to fit the shape and contours of the stones. This metal sheath over the stone, gleaming and resplendent, with a patina, became a thing of beauty, a decoration of loveliness. Yet it was also a reminder of horror, a stab of vengeance. As the pieces were hammered together, the identity of an individual piece was lost. The collective guilt of the troop was identified with the resultant single sheet; no one would be able to approach the altar and say of one section of the bronze sheath, "This part belonged to X."

As we think about the notion of the "holy," we recognize that things are made holy in Scripture, not because people are holy, but because the things are presented to the Lord, who is holy. Since these wicked men presented their censers to the Lord, the censers are holy, despite the men's own wickedness.

A mark of Eleazar's faith is that he does precisely what Moses commands him (v.39). He is thus a strong contrast to Korah and his allies (v.40). Just as the name of God is a memorial of his grace (See Exod 3:15) and as the stones in the Jordan will later make a memorial for Israel on their entry into the land (Josh 4:7), so these censers and the resultant metal plate are a memorial to God's wrath and a witness to his holiness.

God has established his personnel; he will allow none to breach their ranks. The sons of Eliab—Dathan and Abiram—were Reubenites, not Levites (v.1); they were not of the right tribe to serve as priests. Korah was a Levite but not a son of Aaron; hence he was not suited for the priesthood either. Each was a "strange man" (*'îš zār*) to desire to serve at the altars of God.

We suspect that God's desire in the memorial was not to perpetuate his wrath but to prevent further reasons to provoke it. This was a preventative symbolism. If another man was to approach the altar with his censer and he was not of the descendants of Aaron, the sparkling light of the sun dancing on the hammered metal should sparkle in his eyes a threat of doom.

After the smoke clears, it is now certain that Eleazar will follow his father, Aaron the priest, not Korah. And as we conclude this section, we feel that surely things will settle down now before we come to the time to enter Canaan.

41 With all the results of murmuring against Moses and the Lord, one would think that the people would have had their bellies' worth of grumbling. Nevertheless, they were at it again. On the next day following the terrible judgment of God against the apostate nobles, the would-be priests of God, we read that the whole Israelite community grumbled against Moses again. The verb used here and in similar contexts is the Hebrew term *lûn*. The people who had seen the judgment of God in such a remarkable manner still did not interpret things correctly. Again they blasted against Moses, unfairly charging him with the death of "the LORD's people."

The attack on Moses is audacious in its language. The pronoun "you" is emphatic; they say to him, "You are responsible! You have killed the men of Yahweh!" Oblivious to the vindication of Moses and Aaron by the Lord, the frenzied crowd, mad as rabid wolves, presses in on them.

42–43 Verse 42 speaks of the men turning toward the Tent of Meeting. This may merely mean that they looked toward the tent. But it may mean that the crowd was about to take over the territory, to seize the tent as their own holding.

At once, as before, the Glory of the Lord was in the midst of the people—in judgment. Fear must have seized them as a bulldog grabs a pant leg. They must have been wrenched with terror, sickened with self-loathing, ashen faced, trembling, weeping. The Lord had come!

Moses and Aaron are not groveling with fear. They are where they belong—in the presence of the Lord. Calmly, sedately they approach. Only they may; all others would become smoking brands. Moses and Aaron approach the tent, entering into the eerie darkness within the mysterious cloud, with lightning flashing and darkness enveloping—they come to God.

44–45 Again, but for the intervention of Moses and Aaron (see vv.4, 22), the entire nation might have been destroyed by the Lord because of their continued rebellion (v.45). The Lord speaks to them to depart so that he might destroy the nation; instead they fall to the ground, just as they had done in the incident with Korah and his allies (see v.4). There is a sense that v.45 is a reprise of vv.21–22, with slightly different phrasing (see Notes). Again the Lord is about to destroy the nation. Again Moses and Aaron, under unbelievable personal assault, bow down to seek his mercy, to turn away his wrath.

In each of the dialogues of Moses and the Lord, there is a sense in which the Lord uses Moses as a foil. As the words of the Lord evoke responses in Moses, praise comes to the Lord; and the true spirit of Moses is displayed. In each instance the falseness of the attacks on Moses is exposed. The very one the people are attacking is the one praying that they might be spared. There is something in the praying of Moses for his enemies that is a forward-directing thought of the praying of the Savior for his enemies.

46 Moses tells Aaron to take his censer and to begin his work as an atoning priest. This chapter has turned on the account of holy censers being used by unholy men in mock piety. Now Aaron, whose right it was, was to take his censer and do the work of the true priest to stay the plague of the Lord and to bring mercy to the people.

In the former revolt Moses stayed the anger of God by debate; only the guilty died. This time the wrath of God had already burst out in indiscriminate slaughter by means of a virulent, rapidly spreading plague, a supernatural visitation of sickness devoid of natural protection. People who were railing against Moses and Aaron are now screaming in death throes.

Moses and Aaron might have said, "Let them die." Instead, Moses calls to Aaron to act, to take a censer and to do his priestly work. How precious is this text! What poetic justice! The very implement used by the enemies to force God's hand to wrath now has to be used by his true priest to force his hand to mercy.

This presents a conundrum: Is God fickle? Is man the hero? Or does God use these crises to occasion heroic acts among his servants, who then display in palpable terms his mercy and his grace?

We notice that the priest was told to take fire from the altar. He was not to use "strange fire" but fire of propriety. He used only the fire that will be efficacious.

Earlier there were censers with strange fire to attack Moses and Aaron, provoking the wrath of God. Now there is a censer with the proper fire to protect the people against God's wrath.

Moses tells his brother to "hurry" (*m^ehērāh,* in an adverbial use). This is the rush of grace by two old men to protect the people who moments before shouted their virulent hatred of them. Surely in their actions we find God's mercy! Their character mirrors his own. Moses knows the plague has already begun before he has even looked. But Moses also knows that the plague may be stemmed; only they must hurry.

47–50 So Aaron ran (v.47)! This old priest with sacral items runs to save and to heal. He stands in the breach between the dead and the living (v.48). He stops the plague. What drama! And what loss! Thousands died needlessly. The text says 14,700 died (v.49; see Notes), and these were in addition to those who died in the incident of Korah. All these people died needlessly, too soon, before their time—forlorn, forsaken, victims of their own folly.

But at last the plague is stemmed. Moses and Aaron meet again at the entrance to the Tent of Meeting. Verse 50 is a salutary vindication of the role that God had given to these two men. Despite repeated attempts by powerful persons to wrest away from them their special place in the work of God, there they stand, two old men, blessed of the Lord.

We who read this verse, weary with the wickedness of many men and women, finally come to a sense of peace. Surely now, at last, there will be no more offense. Surely now there is a new beginning for the new people, a new generation, a new day. Soon, surely, we will come to Canaan.

Notes

36 (17:1 MT) The EVV have vv.36–50 as a continuation of chapter 16. In the MT these fifteen verses form the first part of chapter 17. This means that verse numbers will present unusual problems in these two chapters.

45 (17:10 MT) הֵרֹמּוּ (*hērōmmû*, "Remove yourselves!"; NIV, "Get away") is a rare word, the Niphal imperative masculine plural of *rāmōm* ("to be removed"). In v.21 the verb used was *hibbāḏᵉlû*, a Niphal imperative masculine plural from *bāḏal* ("to separate self from"). The meaning is nearly the same, but this similar story uses a more unusual word.

49 (17:14 MT) The number of people who died—14,700—because of the arrogance of Korah and his allies is staggering. The number also makes sense only if the community is as large as the census lists of Numbers 2 suggests. That is, the very large number of 2:32 is confirmed by many indicators throughout the text.

g. *The budding of Aaron's staff (17:1–13)*

The connection of this chapter with the narrative of chapter 16 is obvious; indeed, chapters 16 and 17 overlap in versification as we move from the MT to the EVV (see Notes). This text presents the final vindication of the Lord's confidence in his selection of Aaron as the true high priest. It is especially important as Aaron's life is reaching its end that there be no question concerning God's choice in him and in his posterity. Aaron and his wife, Elisheba, daughter of Amminadab and sister of Nahshon, the prince of the tribe of Judah listed in 1:7, had four sons. The first two, Nadab and Abihu, died because of arrogant acts of impiety (see Lev 10). The others, Eleazar and Ithamar, were to become the twin lines of the divine priesthood of Israel throughout their generations. The issues of this chapter insured that this line would continue.

(1) *The test for the true priest*

17:1–7

[1]The LORD said to Moses, [2]"Speak to the Israelites and get twelve staffs from them, one from the leader of each of their ancestral tribes. Write the name of each man on his staff. [3]On the staff of Levi write Aaron's name, for there must be one staff for the head of each ancestral tribe. [4]Place them in the Tent of Meeting in front of the Testimony, where I meet with you. [5]The staff belonging to the man I choose will sprout, and I will rid myself of this constant grumbling against you by the Israelites."

[6]So Moses spoke to the Israelites, and their leaders gave him twelve staffs, one for the leader of each of their ancestral tribes, and Aaron's staff was among them. [7]Moses placed the staffs before the LORD in the Tent of the Testimony.

1 As we have seen so very often, this text is introduced by the standard motto, "The LORD said to Moses." We have noted this before but may assert it anew: If these words are just the mechanical device of a late redactor to introduce a new story that he pieces into the flow of his gradually developing book, then these words really have no more significance than the other stylistic device used in other narrative sections of the Bible: "After these things" or "Some time later" (e.g., Gen 22:1). But if the words in this introductory clause mean what they seem to mean, then we have a constant punctuation throughout the Book of Numbers (in over 150 instances!) that Yahweh has spoken and that he has spoken principally to Moses.

2 God's word to Moses is to collect twelve staffs, one from the leader of each of the tribes of Israel. Each staff was to have the name of its owner written thereon so that the identification would be sure in the test that follows. This story follows on the heels of the account of the divine judgment of Korah (16:1–35) and the narrative of the symbolic use given to the censers of the rebels and its aftermath (vv.36–50). Numbers 17 is thus the third in a series of accounts vindicating the Aaronic priesthood against all opposition. The selection of the twelve staffs, one from each tribe, was for a dramatic symbolic act whereby the divine choice of Aaron would be indicated again.

3 The incidental line concerning writing the name of each staff's owner is significant in terms of the history of writing in Israel. Some scholars in the past regarded this notion as quite anachronistic, believing that the use of writing would not possibly have been known by the Hebrews at this primitive stage of their experience. More modest scholars find this line to be a confirmation of the idea of literacy among the Hebrew peoples from their beginnings, at least among the people who were in leadership positions. It is hard to believe that it was not too many years ago that people denied the Mosaic authorship of the Torah in part because they thought that he would not have known how to write!

The test needed to be unequivocal. In addition to the staffs from each of the other tribes, the staff of the tribe of Levi had to have Aaron's name written clearly on it. The staff of Levi must be chosen over the staffs of the other tribes; this was necessary again because of the transcommunity support given to the rebellion of Korah. The 250 who joined with Korah were from many, perhaps all, the tribes. The name of Aaron on the staff of Levi would limit the choice to him and his descendants; this was necessary to ward off attacks on his leadership similar to that of Korah by others of the tribe of Levi but not of the family of Aaron.

4–5 These several staffs were to be placed "in front of the Testimony" (v.4). This means that the staffs were brought not only to the Tent of Meeting but within the Most Holy Place. I suspect the staffs would have been placed as near the ark as practical. The symbolism is that these staffs were right, as it were, in the "lap" of God. The very issue of bringing these staffs into the Most Holy Place must have been chilling. Moses, who brought these staffs near, must have realized that he was doing a most unusual act. The most immediate placement of the staffs in the presence of God is assured by these words. The intention was to rid the nation from the grumbling (*t^elûnnô<u>t</u>,* from the verb *lûn,* "to murmur," "to grumble"; the verb is used in v.10: "their grumbling against me") concerning the validity of the priests (v.5).

6–7 As we have come to anticipate, Moses complied with God's command without reservation. The Hebrew narrative style, which is deliberately repetitive for clarity and emphasis, rehearses Moses' acts of obedience to the Lord's command (vv.6–7), making certain that the reader is alert to the fact that among the several staffs is the one with Aaron's name on it.

The ordeal, if one can term it that way, was to identify the "right" staff by having it sprout (v.5). Now it was patent in that ancient day, as in our own, that a sprout may arise from a living branch and even from the trunk of a tree that has been felled (see Isa 6:13). But it is clearly not possible for a wooden staff that is long dead to sprout again as though it were still part of a growing tree.

The story demands nothing short of a miracle, an intervention of the power of God in the normal order of things in such a way as to produce wonder and awe. This demonstration of the power of God and his sovereign work was to be wondrous, something for the people to remember throughout all their generations. This was the call for a major demonstration of the power of God. It was to be regarded as truly stunning. It was also to be regarded as absolutely and finally convincing, for the act of God would be impossible for anyone else to duplicate.

Notes

---

1 The EVV have the story of Aaron's staff as a separate chapter (17:1–13). In the MT the first fifteen verses of chapter 17 correspond to 16:36–50, and the English section 17:1–13 appears as 17:16–28. Despite the difficulty of finding corresponding verses that this arrangement presents, both the MT and the translations have the same total number of verses.

5 (17:20 MT) In the MT there is a marginal note that this verse forms the center of the book, by verse numbers.

---

(2) *The outcome of the ordeal*

17:8–13

8 The next day Moses entered the Tent of the Testimony and saw that Aaron's staff, which represented the house of Levi, had not only

sprouted but had budded, blossomed and produced almonds. 9 Then
Moses brought out all the staffs from the LORD's presence to all the
Israelites. They looked at them, and each man took his own staff.
10 The LORD said to Moses, "Put back Aaron's staff in front of the
Testimony, to be kept as a sign to the rebellious. This will put an end to
their grumbling against me, so that they will not die." 11 Moses did just
as the LORD commanded him.
12 The Israelites said to Moses, "We will die! We are lost, we are all
lost! 13 Anyone who even comes near the tabernacle of the LORD will die.
Are we all going to die?"

8 On the next morning Moses entered the Most Holy Place. When he looked at Aaron's rod, he found that it not only had sprouted, it had budded! This is an example of God exceeding the demands of a test so that there might be no uncertainty as to who had done the act or what was intended by it (cf. Elijah on Mount Carmel, where the response of God [1 Kings 18:38] went considerably beyond the specific request [v.24]). It might be regarded as possible, if a fluke, for a staff to have a small sprout, given right conditions. But none would dare say that what had happened to Aaron's rod was by chance: Not only did it sprout, "it budded, blossomed and produced almonds"—all on the next day!

Miracles in the Bible are often of this sort: natural events in unnatural conditions, timing, and placement. For almonds to grow from a branch is normal. It is not normal at all, however, for a dead pole to sprout, flower, and produce its fruit, all in the process of a night. Almond trees are notable for their rapid production of blossoms, but this example is without parallel. This is a stunning miracle!

9 It must have been humbling for the men from the other tribes to take back their staffs. But only those who aspired to an office that was not theirs would feel shame. That Moses had each of the men take back his staff in a sense made them give silent assent to the decision of the miracle of God and the choice of Aaron as his priest.

10–11 Aaron's rod, however, was not returned to him. It was to be a perpetual reminder of the wonder of the night and the choice of God in his priest. Hence, it was to remain in front of the Testimony in perpetuity (v.10). Aaron's rod joined the stone tables of the law of Moses (see Exod 25:16) and the jar of manna (Exod 16:33–34) within the ark of the Lord. This would be a reminder to rebels and malcontents as long as the ark and the Holy Place would stand. The presence of these reminders in the central shrine was designed by God as an act of his mercy: people who were sufficiently warned would escape dying for breach of propriety.

The interesting thing is that these memorials were put in a place where no one would ordinarily see them. They would be told of them in later generations, but they would not be on public display. None, save the high priest, would enter the Holy Place, excepting Moses on rare occasions such as this chapter presents. While the text focuses on the role these symbols have in the memory of the people, the placement of these symbols in the seclusion of the shrine indicates that the one who will ever be reminded is the Lord! These holy symbols were ever before him as memorials of his special works with his people. Should anyone of a later age dare to question the unique and holy place of the Aaronic priests in the service of the Lord, this memorial of God's symbolic choice of Aaron would stand poignantly in opposition to his audacity.

The writer of Hebrews suggests that at some point the staff of Aaron was kept inside the ark (9:4), but it seems not to be inside the ark at the time of the dedication of the temple (1 Kings 8:9).

It is difficult to overestimate the importance of the role of Aaron and his sons in the worship system of Israel. It is impossible to overestimate the role of the Priest who replaced Aaron, the Lord Jesus Christ (Heb 4:14–8:13). The extensive treatment of the priesthood of the Savior is necessary, given the divine validation of the priesthood of Aaron in Numbers 16–17.

12–13 The larger pericope begins with insolent, bragging language of grasping people (v.1). Now it ends with the disconsolate weeping of the people (vv.12–13), all fearful of dying. At last the enormity of the arrogant sin of the people in challenging the role of Aaron hit them. Their remorse was justified; death was deserved. Any untoward approach to the holy tabernacle would result in disaster. But there are appropriate manners of approaching the Lord; these are detailed in the next two chapters. They really do not need to die from trespass against holy things.

Notes

---

13 (17:28 MT) In הַאִם תַּמְנוּ לִגְוֹעַ (*ha'im tamnû ligô*[a]*'*, "Are we all going to die?"), the common verb מות (*mûṯ*, "to die") is paired with the less common גָּוַע (*gāwa'*, "to expire, perish"; also used in v.12, "we will die," where it is paired with אָבַד ['*āḇaḏ* , "to perish, be lost"]).

---

h. *The priests and the Levites (18:1–32)*

The crisis of leadership in the spiritual ministry of the people that the revolt of Korah provoked (ch. 16) leads the Book of Numbers to detail anew the regulations and responsibilities that affect the true priests of God. There is reason, then, to see how the material of chapters 18–19 fits into the larger structure of the Book of Numbers. It is possible that the materials in these chapters constitute later additions to the book, as they do not relate directly to the historical flow of the narrative. But they do form an essential part of its deep theology, and these two chapters are certainly part of the book as we receive God's gift of canon.

The preoccupation with priestly themes has led many scholars to believe that the Book of Numbers is the product largely of the putative P source. Those who reject this source-critical approach to the composition of the Pentateuch may point out that there is sufficient reason inherent within the story line of the Book of Numbers to give such emphasis to priests and Levites in the Hebrew culture. The issue of rightful priests is not just a record of power struggles between competing families, stories that can be paralleled in cultures throughout time. In Israel the issue was more significant because the stakes were higher. In this case it is the worship of Yahweh, the true God, that is at issue and his choice of who shall be serving at his altars.

The house of Aaron has been convincingly validated by the miracle of the budding, blossoming, and fruiting staff (Num 17). Now, as Aaron was growing older and his sons Eleazar and Ithamar were assisting him more and more in his sacred duties, tasks that would be theirs alone on his demise, it is necessary to explain more fully the manner of the priesthood. The inclusion of chapters 18–19 in the story line of the desert experience is not intrusive but compelling.

Nevertheless, the modern reader comes to chapters 18–19 with a sense of foreboding; what, we may wonder, is in these chapters for me? The answer to that question is fivefold:

1. The reader of Scripture needs to have general knowledge about the major institutions of the the biblical period just for Scripture to make sense.

2. Our understanding of the true worship of God begins with the sense that he controls and directs true worship; who the priests are and how they function are first his concerns. This means that worship is not a game where we may make up the rules as we play.

3. A general knowledge of the work of the priests in the Hebrew Bible gives many insights to the modern reader as to the interests of God in our own worship. Often we think of worship in terms of what we like and appreciate. This misses the mark; worship is principally for God's pleasure.

4. A general knowledge of the work of priests in the time of Hebrew worship gives the Christian reader significant insights into the priestly work of the Lord Jesus Christ. The Book of Hebrews has an intense priestly orientation in its presentation of the Lord Jesus Christ, priest of God in the manner of Melchizedek.

5. In contrast with the highly regulated, highly strictured patterns demanded of the priests of the Hebrew economy, the believer in the Lord Jesus Christ today has a direct access to God through the Savior that is nearly unbelievable. We are all priests; we can come near the presence of the Lord without an intermediary. Yet our privilege as believer-priests can only really be appreciated against the background of priests in the biblical period.

Thus it is not just for arcane, antiquarian reasons that we come to this chapter and the one following.

(1) *Their general duties*

18:1–7

> [1]The LORD said to Aaron, "You, your sons and your father's family are to bear the responsibility for offenses against the sanctuary, and you and your sons alone are to bear the responsibility for offenses against the priesthood. [2]Bring your fellow Levites from your ancestral tribe to join you and assist you when you and your sons minister before the Tent of the Testimony. [3]They are to be responsible to you and are to perform all the duties of the Tent, but they must not go near the furnishings of the sanctuary or the altar, or both they and you will die. [4]They are to join you and be responsible for the care of the Tent of Meeting—all the work at the Tent—and no one else may come near where you are.
>
> [5]"You are to be responsible for the care of the sanctuary and the altar, so that wrath will not fall on the Israelites again. [6]I myself have selected your fellow Levites from among the Israelites as a gift to you, dedicated to the LORD to do the work at the Tent of Meeting. [7]But only you and your sons may serve as priests in connection with everything at the altar and inside the curtain. I am giving you the service of the priesthood as a gift. Anyone else who comes near the sanctuary must be put to death."

1–4 The Lord's choice of Aaron and his family as the true priests of holy worship presented an onerous task. The lament of the people in 17:12–13 was a genuine expression of distress; grievous sins against the holy meeting place of the Lord and his people would be judged with death. It was only in the mercy of the Lord in providing a legitimate priesthood that there could be any hope for deliverance from judgment. Modern readers are not always aware that the Lord's provision of the priesthood was an aspect of his grace. Without proper priests doing their work effectively, there would be only death among the sinning community. Psalm 99:6 points to the grace of God in providing priests for his people. The provision of the Great Priest, the Lord Jesus Christ (Heb 4:14), is in line with this work of his grace.

A characteristic phrase, troubling to understand, is the line: "you . . . are to bear the responsibility for offenses against the sanctuary." This NIV rendering is somewhat expansive but is a development of the meaning of the Hebrew term *'ᵃwōn* ("iniquity"). At times it is used to describe the iniquity that one commits or that mars one's life. But in this context *'ᵃwōn* relates to the whole sphere of sin, guilt, and responsibility for offense. The words of the people in 17:13 were based on reality: it is a fearful thing to make an inappropriate approach to the shrine of God's dwelling. The priests, who have their work in the precincts of his dwelling, must realize that they are there at the leave of God. But they cannot forget where they are nor be casual in what they are to do. To act foolishly, brazenly, carelessly in the holy places is to invite disaster. Their priestly ministry puts them in roles of awesome responsibility (see Exod 28:38).

The priests of the line of Aaron were to be assisted in their work by the people of the tribe of Levi (v.2); but the assistants were not to usurp their serving role. Were they to do so, not only would they die, so would the priests who were responsible (v.3). Aaron and his sons were the only true priests of God in the worship of Israel. The Levites were joined (see Notes) to the priests as their assistants. But the Levites were never to be regarded as "priests in training." They had a serious "career ceiling" in their vocation. The sanctity of the Holy Place is not to be underestimated.

Aside from the Levites, who have their limited functions in the worship of God in the sacred places, no other individual may come near at all (v.4). The term "stranger" (*zār;* NIV, "no one else"), which often speaks of a foreign national, is used to describe all other people in the Holy Place. The only people who have a right to work in the shrine are the Levites under the supervision of the priests. All others are "foreigners."

5–7 The frightful obligations of the priests and the Levites and their responsibilities were balanced in the sense of the importance and honor of the work they did in the presence of God (v.5). The divine vantage point is that they should regard their service of the priesthood as a gift—a gift that is priceless (v.6). The gift was to the priests; they of all men were able to approach the Holy Place and minister before the Lord (v.7). The Lord's gift of the priesthood was also to the people; that there was a legitimate priesthood was an act of God's mercy. The priests have a dual identity. On their shoulders rests the protection of the nation before God. The weight of that responsibility must be enormous. But the priests were also the most privileged persons in the community, for they could draw near to God.

Notes

2 וְיִלָּווּ (*wᵉyillāwû,* "to join you") is a wordplay on the word for "Levite," לֵוִי (*lēwî*). The text may be read (woodenly): "the tribe of Levi . . . will 'levi' with you." The presumed root of the word "Levi" is the verb לָוָה (*lāwāh,* meaning "to be joined" in the Niphal).

5 מִשְׁמֶרֶת (*mišmeret*, "service," "charge"; NIV, "to be responsible"), related to the Hebrew verbal root *šāmar* ("to keep"), has the idea of charge and responsibility. The work of the priests was a sacred trust. The fulfillment of the trust provides the peace of the nation with God.

---

(2) *Their offerings and support*

18:8–13

8Then the LORD said to Aaron, "I myself have put you in charge of the offerings presented to me; all the holy offerings the Israelites give me I give to you and your sons as your portion and regular share. 9You are to have the part of the most holy offerings that is kept from the fire. From all the gifts they bring me as most holy offerings, whether grain or sin or guilt offerings, that part belongs to you and your sons. 10Eat it as something most holy; every male shall eat it. You must regard it as holy.

11"This also is yours: whatever is set aside from the gifts of all the wave offerings of the Israelites. I give this to you and your sons and daughters as your regular share. Everyone in your household who is ceremonially clean may eat it.

12"I give you all the finest olive oil and all the finest new wine and grain they give the LORD as the firstfruits of their harvest. 13All the land's firstfruits that they bring to the LORD will be yours. Everyone in your household who is ceremonially clean may eat it.

8 The priests were to be supported, to earn their livelihood, in their work of the ministry of God (see Lev 6:14–7:36). Since the Levites as a whole and the priests in particular had no part in the land that God was going to give to the nation, it was necessary that the means for their provision be spelled out fully. They were not to have a part in the land; their share was the Lord himself (v.20). The language of this chapter is anticipative of the settlement in the land of Canaan. Moses continues to speak about the revelation of God for the new land; for in doing so he assures the fathers and mothers that while they will not enjoy the land because of their sins, their lives have not been valueless: their children will be able to enter the land.

The language of God in v.8 is strongly expressive, with a pronounced emphasis on himself and his work in making Aaron his priest. The priesthood in Israel was not to be regarded as the result of self-aggrandizement; the priests were the choice of God himself. Here is God's gracious provision for the care and maintenance of his priests. The sacral gifts are their provisions. They may enjoy the things they receive without guilt. This provision is from the hand of the Lord.

9–10 Verse 9 helps the priests to know what of the offerings belong to them for their support. The starting point is to know that the offerings that are not put through fire will be given to the priests. And in v.10 we find a helpful use of the concept of the holy. Something was regarded as holy, not because of some mysterious inner quality, but because it has been presented to the Lord for his use. He then transfers the use of some of his holy things to the priests. Among the gifts he gives to the priests is abundant food. But the food is no longer ordinary; it is holy food that must be regarded as such. The basic meaning of the word "holy" (*qōḏeš*) is seen here quite clearly: something is *qōḏeš* when it is set apart for special use in the service of God. These holy foods are specifically restricted to the males and must be eaten only by those who were ritually clean.

11 The wave offerings were for the entire family to eat. Provision was made not only for the priests themselves (v.10) but for their families as well. Only the ceremonially unclean family members were forbidden the eating of the gifts and offerings of the people (cf. v.13). Provisions for cleansing are stated in Leviticus 22:4–8.

12–13 Since the very best items of produce were to be given to the Lord, they became the special foods of the priests and their families: the best oil, the finest wine, and the choicest grains were theirs (v.12). On the basis of the provisions God intended for the priests in the OT, the NT writers argue that those who minister the Word of God in the present period should also be paid suitably for their work (see 1 Cor 9:3–10). The grace of God is manifest in this provision for his servants, but so are the demands of God: the priests and their families are to be in a state of ritual purity when they eat sacred foods (v.13). The foods remain sacred; they may not be profaned by unclean persons.

The concept that God gets "the best of the first" is a constant in the worship texts of the Bible. The oil and the wine mentioned in this verse are not the dregs but the finest of the firstfruits. In giving the first and best to the Lord, believers are affirming with confidence that there will be something left for their own needs. And if not, true believers will still bless the Lord. They do not worship God just because it is a way to a full stomach. But in their worship of God, they then and now expect that the giving of the first and the best to God will often result in more than ever for themselves and for their family.

Perhaps a farmer who practices giving to the Lord is more likely to be a better farmer than one who does not give to the Lord. It may be that the very act of giving makes demands on him for greater diligence in his work. But even if such a farmer does not prosper, he will continue to trust in the Lord—even if no more food is to come at all.

Here is where we tend to fall down. Often we find ourselves giving out of our surplus. When there is no surplus, we are not giving to the Lord. Others find that when they give to God of the first of their best, then they wind up with a surplus they had not even anticipated.

Notes

---

8 תְּרוּמָה (*t^erûmāh,* "contribution," "offering") is a noun built on the verb *rûm* ("to be high," "to be raised"). This is something set apart for or "presented to" (NIV) the priests (see 5:9; Lev 22:12; 2 Chron 31:10, 12, 14; Ezek 44:30).

לְמָשְׁחָה (*l^emošḥāh,* "portion") is a word used only here. It is related to the verb *māšaḥ* ("to anoint"). A similar noun is *mišḥāh* ("anointing [oil]," 4:16).

11 תְּנוּפָה (*t^enûp̱āh*) is from the verb *nûp̱* ("to move to and fro," "to wave"). It can be used in contexts of hostility to God or to wave one's hand in a menacing manner against God (Isa 19:16). Such is similar to the expression "high handed" (see Notes on 15:30). But in the context of worship, this noun is a technical term for the "wave offering." By holding up grain or produce and waving it back and forth in the air in a respectful manner, the offerer was marking out the Lord as the source of his plenty. Since this food was not put to fire, it was then given over to the priests for their own family use.

12 The Hebrew expression for the "finest oil," חֵלֶב יִצְהָר (*ḥēleḇ yiṣhār*)—and likewise for the "finest wine"—is constructed by using the noun *ḥēleḇ* ("fat") as a descriptive term. This use goes back to the offering of Abel in Gen 4:4, where the Hebrew word translated "and of their fat" may refer to "the best of the firstborn" rather than to their "fat portions." In any event, the term is used as a superlative adjective; only the best is good enough for God.

---

(3) *The firstborn offerings and redemptions*

18:14–19

14 "Everything in Israel that is devoted to the LORD is yours. 15 The first
offspring of every womb, both man and animal, that is offered to the
LORD is yours. But you must redeem every firstborn son and every
firstborn male of unclean animals. 16 When they are a month old, you
must redeem them at the redemption price set at five shekels of silver,
according to the sanctuary shekel, which weighs twenty gerahs.
17 "But you must not redeem the firstborn of an ox, a sheep or a goat;
they are holy. Sprinkle their blood on the altar and burn their fat as an
offering made by fire, an aroma pleasing to the LORD. 18 Their meat is to
be yours, just as the breast of the wave offering and the right thigh are
yours. 19 Whatever is set aside from the holy offerings the Israelites
present to the LORD I give to you and your sons and daughters as your
regular share. It is an everlasting covenant of salt before the LORD for
both you and your offspring."

14–16 Whenever there is something under the ban (*ḥērem;* NIV, "devoted," v.14), it belongs to the priests (unless, of course, such things are destroyed, as in the story of Jericho). The firstborn of every womb was to be consecrated to the Lord (Exod 13:2); now we learn that the firstborn were a means of supporting the priests. They would receive the firstborn of animals and man or their redemption price (v.15).

There was to be no sacrifice of man(!) and no sacrifice of unclean animals. These needed to be redeemed (i.e., their owners would pay a price to the priests). The priests were to take the redemption price in exchange for the firstborn of people. The price set for the redemption of the firstborn of women is five shekels, a considerable sum (v.16). The shekel is specified by weight (twenty gerahs—otherwise unknown; NIV mg., "about 2 ounces"), a reminder of the differing standards of weights and measures in the ancient Near East.

Seemingly the reason for paying a redemption price for the firstborn of man and unclean animals and the sacrifice of the firstborn of clean animals was to provide a perpetual reminder that conception, birth, and life are gifts of God. Thus Exodus 22:29–30 reads, "You must give me the firstborn of your sons. Do the same with your cattle and your sheep." As we think of the extent of these rituals throughout the biblical period, we realize that they extend to the life of the Savior. Since Jesus was the firstborn of Mary, he had to be redeemed; then he became the Redeemer of all.

17–19 The firstborn of clean animals were not to be redeemed; they were holy, devoted to the Lord (v.17). They were to be sacrificed in the usual manner (see ch. 15 on offerings by fire), but the meat would belong to the priests (v.18). This was a permanent obligation, symbolized by salt (v.19)—a lasting compound. The precise idea of the salt covenant (see 2 Chron 13:5) remains somewhat obscure. We know that salt was sometimes a medium of trade in the ancient world. Perhaps an exchange of salt was a part of some covenant ceremonies. We also know that salt was used in some of the sacrifices to the Lord (Lev 2:13; Ezek 43:24) and in special incense that was used in the worship of God (Exod 30:35). Moreover, salt was a common table element; its mention here speaks of eating and, hence, of communion (see Gen 31:54; Exod 24:5–11; Ps 50:5).

(4) *Aaron's special portion*

18:20

20 The LORD said to Aaron, "You will have no inheritance in their land, nor will you have any share among them; I am your share and your inheritance among the Israelites.

20 The basic idea of this verse has been stated before (see ch. 3), but this verse presents the issue definitively. A mechanical layout of the verse, representing the word order (emphasis) of the MT, is impressive:

And Yahweh said to Aaron:
"In their land you will not gain possession,
and a portion will not be for you in their midst;
I am your portion
and [I am] your possession
in the midst of the Israelites."

This verse, marked by emphatic repetition and chiasm (see Notes), gives Yahweh's special blessing on Aaron. The second-person pronouns in this verse are singular: This is a remarkable word to Aaron, which, by extension, would continue to be the portion of the true priests of Israel. While Aaron does not have a part in the land that the rest of the people will inherit, he has more—a peculiar relationship to the Lord.

Verse 20 in some way anticipates the possession of the people of God in the church age. Today believers have no land promise but enjoy a special relationship with the Lord. There is a sense in which we enjoy what the high priest in Israel had, along with all priests and Levites—and more.

Notes

20 The idea of chiasm is an inverting of the order of parallel elements; the name comes from the Greek letter chi, which appears something like an *X*. In the somewhat wooden translation I have given, the verb "to take possession" is in the first colon [accentual unit], followed by the noun "portion" in the second; "portion" then precedes the use of the noun form "possession" in the remaining cola. This literary device helps to make the verse more memorable.

(5) *The tithes and the Levites*

18:21–24

21 "I give to the Levites all the tithes in Israel as their inheritance in return for the work they do while serving at the Tent of Meeting. 22 From now on the Israelites must not go near the Tent of Meeting, or they will

bear the consequences of their sin and will die. [23]It is the Levites who are to do the work at the Tent of Meeting and bear the responsibility for offenses against it. This is a lasting ordinance for the generations to come. They will receive no inheritance among the Israelites. [24]Instead, I give to the Levites as their inheritance the tithes that the Israelites present as an offering to the LORD. That is why I said concerning them: 'They will have no inheritance among the Israelites.' "

21–24 Much of the previous section has already been explained in other portions of the Torah. But giving tithes to the Levites is a new development; vv.21–24 form an independent unit. This gift of God was in return for their work of ministry of service in the tabernacle precincts. These verses are marked by considerable emphasis and repetition, all designed to make the deepest impression on the people who read them. There is a sense in which this text presents the "exchange of the Lord"—full reward for full service. Verse 21 uses forms of the word "to serve" (*'āḇaḏ*). The term the NIV translates "in return for" (*ḥēlep̱;* here and v.31 [untr. NIV]) speaks of God's justice in rewarding them for their work. But no longer may any but Levites approach the Tent of Meeting. The precincts were now sacred, fitted only for sacral people. The wrong people who may approach for even a "right" reason will die.

Verses 21–24 form a complete torah, an authoritative instruction, dealing with the rationale for the tithes going to the Levites. The section is highly repetitive. God is in control; it is he who speaks. And in the section we notice that the Levites are cared for very well. The Levites have a double portion: they are related to the Lord in a special way, and they are provided for by him from special sources. The Levites have a special work: only they may do the service of the Tent of Meeting; only they may bear the consequences for their own guilt. They can come and live; others who approach will die. This section does not have the ordinary introduction, "the LORD said to Moses"; but it does represent itself as the voice of God speaking (v.21, "I give").

Possibly this section is a later addition to the Book of Numbers, as seems to be the case of 15:32–34. Chapter 18 is a logical part of the flow of Numbers, as earlier sections were divine addresses to Aaron on priestly duties, responsibilities, and care. But this section both adds to the chapter (tithes as well as meat) as well as overlaps the chapter (no portion in Israel). Hence, it is possible that this unit was inserted here later at what seemed to be a logical point. In any event, the approach we take is that insertions into the Book of Numbers are divinely intended, are inspired Scripture, and are authoritative.

(6) *The contributions of the Levites*

18:25–32

[25]The LORD said to Moses, [26]"Speak to the Levites and say to them: 'When you receive from the Israelites the tithe I give you as your inheritance, you must present a tenth of that tithe as the LORD's offering.
[27]Your offering will be reckoned to you as grain from the threshing floor or juice from the winepress. [28]In this way you also will present an offering to the LORD from all the tithes you receive from the Israelites. From these tithes you must give the LORD's portion to Aaron the priest.
[29]You must present as the LORD's portion the best and holiest part of everything given to you.'

[30]"Say to the Levites: 'When you present the best part, it will be reckoned to you as the product of the threshing floor or the winepress.
[31]You and your households may eat the rest of it anywhere, for it is your

wages for your work at the Tent of Meeting. 32 By presenting the best part of it you will not be guilty in this matter; then you will not defile the holy offerings of the Israelites, and you will not die.' "

25–32 Now we return to a word addressed specifically to Moses; the earlier sections were addressed to Aaron (vv.1, 8, 20), including a specific torah for the Levites (vv.21–24). The instruction of this section, which Moses is to relate to the Levites, is impressive: those who make their living by contributions for the Lord's work shall themselves be responsible for giving to the Lord as well. There is a tendency, then and now, for persons to believe that if their lives are spent in the Lord's work, then they are exempt from contributing to that work. This leads to a concept, lamentably more and more observed in our own day, that payment for ministry is something deserved and is something to be demanded. The last phrase, "a tithe from the tithe" (lit. Heb.; NIV, "a tenth of that tithe") is sharp and pointed (v.26). As others give, so must the Levites give; how can they who live from the contributions of others be less giving than the community? That this was regarded as a most serious matter is seen in the promise that, by keeping faith in these matters, the Levites will escape judicial death (v.32).

The offerings that the Levites would render to the Lord are not themselves fresh. Their grain is not new; neither is their wine. But since they themselves are not doing the harvesting of their own lands to bring their firstfruits to the Lord, the produce of others will be regarded as their own. For those who cannot harvest for themselves, God reckons (*nehšab̲,* Niphal perfect of *ḥāšab̲,* "to be reckoned"; v.27) their gifts as though they are just harvested. As in the case of the people, the Levites are to render to the Lord "the best and holiest part of everything" (v.29). Never is God the happy recipient of shoddy gifts; his demands are of the very best that one has.

Notes

30–32 This small torah repeats and amplifies the preceding section (vv.25–29) and makes its obligation of signal importance: "and you will not die."

The chapter begins with the note that the holy persons in the worship of God serve in an awesomely wondrous ministry, one that is a life-and-death issue. Not only may the lay person who presumes on holy things receive a sentence of death (v.22); neither may those who are in the holy service of God presume on holy things, for they too might die if they do. But the thrust of the text is not just to be a threat: "Do this and you may die." It is to be a gracious provision: "Do this and you will not die." Thus the sovereign grace of the Lord displays itself in ever varied ways in the Torah.

i. *The red heifer and the cleansing water (19:1–22)*

Chapter 18 presents basic instruction on the role, responsibilities, duties, and privileges of the priests and the Levites. This chapter follows with ritual instruction for the purification of people, the laic segment of the population of Israel. Its flavor and intention is priestly, but the chapter does not concern sacral persons so much as common people. The issue is one of ritual cleansing, answering a basic question in ancient, biblical culture: How may a person be ritually "clean" before the Lord? It also is a chapter that presents unusual problems of interpretation and understanding for the modern reader. This is a fascinating text that rewards the patient reader. The subject of the chapter reminds us of other bizarre sections in the Torah, such as the rituals of Numbers 5.

(1) *The statute of the red heifer*

19:1–10

1 The LORD said to Moses and Aaron: 2 "This is a requirement of the law
that the LORD has commanded: Tell the Israelites to bring you a red
heifer without defect or blemish and that has never been under a yoke.
3 Give it to Eleazar the priest; it is to be taken outside the camp and
slaughtered in his presence. 4 Then Eleazar the priest is to take some of
its blood on his finger and sprinkle it seven times toward the front of the
Tent of Meeting. 5 While he watches, the heifer is to be burned—its hide,
flesh, blood and offal. 6 The priest is to take some cedar wood, hyssop
and scarlet wool and throw them onto the burning heifer. 7 After that, the
priest must wash his clothes and bathe himself with water. He may then
come into the camp, but he will be ceremonially unclean till evening.
8 The man who burns it must also wash his clothes and bathe with water,
and he too will be unclean till evening.
9 "A man who is clean shall gather up the ashes of the heifer and put
them in a ceremonially clean place outside the camp. They shall be kept
by the Israelite community for use in the water of cleansing; it is for
purification from sin. 10 The man who gathers up the ashes of the heifer
must also wash his clothes, and he too will be unclean till evening. This
will be a lasting ordinance both for the Israelites and for the aliens living
among them.

1–4 The material of this chapter is not congenial to modern Western readers. Many have no understanding of or appreciation for the concept of ritual, and the slaughter of a magnificent animal for the purpose of burning its flesh for ash is repugnant. For such readers the opening words of this verse should have a special importance. The ritual of the cleansing waters is presented here as a direct requirement of God. For all its strangeness, this chapter too presents the righteous works of the Lord. The chapter is addressed to Moses and Aaron, but Eleazar is the one who is to do the ritual the text demands. This suggests that Eleazar is operating as an associate with his father, proving that the threat to his ascendancy by the rebellion of Korah and his allies (ch. 16) was now a thing of the past.

Verse 2 begins in the NIV, "This is a requirement of the law that the LORD has commanded." Likely the term "law" is a scribal confusion for the word "cow" or "heifer" (see Notes); the words are very close in spelling in Hebrew. I suggest that the verse should begin thus: "This is the statute of the [red] heifer that the LORD has commanded." This, then, would be the proper heading for the section (so Vul.).

The words used to describe the heifer are familiar in the context of sacrificial worship: the heifer was to be perfect, without defect, and unused, i.e., one that has not been used as a draft animal with a yoke about its neck. As in all the legislation respecting the use of animals in worship, God will accept no culls. The tendency of people presented with commands to kill animals in ritual worship would be to use that occasion to get rid of animals that are not worth the demands of their feed and care. But the demands of the Lord are quite specific: only the very finest animals, ones that ordinarily would be used for the improvement of the herd, are acceptable for him.

This means a person had to have sufficient faith to believe that if one used his finest animals for sacrifice, the other animals would still improve the herd and flock—or that it would not matter, because obedience was more important than anything else.

There are many things that are quite unfamiliar to sacrificial ritual in this text. First, the color of the heifer is important. It was to be red, presumably because of the color of blood. In the standard sacrifices of Leviticus 1–9, there is no mention of the color of the animal that is to be offered; the only requirements are in configuration and perfection.

The factor that makes this pericope unique is that the animal involved is not a sacrificial beast. This is a cow, not a bull (contrast Lev 1:3, "a male without defect"). It is to be slaughtered, not sacrificed; and it is to be killed outside the camp, not at the holy altar. In contrast to the blood of sacrificial animals that is sprinkled against the altar on all sides (see Lev 1:5), some of the blood of the heifer is to be sprinkled from the priest's finger seven times toward the front of the Tent of Meeting (v.4).

5–6 Instead of the separation of hide and offal from the meat and fat of the sacrificial victim, as in the case of the sin offering (see Lev 4:3–12), the heifer was to remain intact while it was burned (v.5). The fire of the holocaust was to be augmented with cedar, hyssop, and scarlet stuff (perhaps scarlet-colored wool). These elements were associated in the Hebrew mind with cleansing properties (see Lev 14:4). They help us see the cleansing association that the resultant ashes are to have in the Hebrew consciousness.

It is primarily the ashes of the red heifer (v.9) that are the focus of this act, for they will be used in the ritual of the waters of cleansing. It is striking that the animal is to be burned in its entirety—"hide, flesh, blood and offal" (v.5). The burning of the beast with its blood and offal is unprecedented in the OT. The normal pattern for the sacrifice of the burnt offering is given in Leviticus 1:3–9.

Distinctives from the killing of the red heifer are several: (1) the burnt offering was to be a male; (2) the animal was to be presented at the entrance to the Tent of Meeting; (3) the priest was to place his hand on it in identification of the act of atonement; (4) the animal was to be sacrificed at the altar; (5) the blood was to be sprinkled on the altar, not burned with the animal; (6) the animal was to be skinned and cut in pieces; (7) special attention was to be given to burning the head and the fat; (8) the various parts were to be cleansed and washed before being burned.

In nearly every respect the killing of the red heifer is distinct: this was a female that was taken outside the camp to be killed; the priest had to be present, but there was no identification made with it; a bit of blood was sprinkled from the priest's finger toward the tabernacle seven times; but the rest of the animal was to be burned in its entirety, without the draining of the blood or the cleansing of its offal.

7–8 The priest who officiates at the burning of the heifer is ceremonially unclean for the rest of the day, as is the one who does the actual work at his command; both may be considered clean after washing their bodies and their clothes.

9–10 In a fascinating turn of events, the priest and the worker, since they are unclean, are not to handle the ashes after the fire has died down (v.9). A third person, one who is ritually clean, is designated to gather the ashes and then to place them in a place outside the camp that is ceremonially clean. The ashes cannot be brought into the camp, but they are holy. Only the clean can touch them; but in touching them that person himself becomes unclean (v.10). So the one who subsequently gathers the ashes from the holocaust becomes ritually unclean because of his contact with the dead remains. He too is unclean for the rest of the day and needs to bathe before returning to the camp.

This text gives rise to innumerable questions. We would like to have a precise signification for each of the elements. In fact, a text like this serves as something of a field day for allegorists. But the point of the text is probably best seen in broad strokes, rather than in purported symbolism we might find in the minutia. The minutia are there, but the overall effect is in the recognition that the passage describes a ritual. The major meaning is in the ritual nature of the matter, not the details that comprise the ritual.

The text is like a dance: each move is specified, each step choreographed. There is color and pageantry. There is also drama and death. The senses are assaulted throughout. One hears the mooing of the cow as she is led outside the camp. There is the violent stroke of the knife against the bound animal's neck, likely the severing of the carotid artery, the quickest way to kill an animal by a knife. One hears her muffled bleating as she bleeds from her death wound. There is the priest dipping his finger in the blood and making seven flicks of the dripping finger toward the holy altar. One smells the acrid odor of the fire, the admixture of cedar and hyssop adding their own sweet-awful smells.

The conclusion of the matter is that this is a lasting statute, pertaining to both the native-born and the aliens who live among them (v.10). The importance of the passage is assured by language such as this, but the meaning still escapes us. The next paragraphs illuminate the uses of the ashes of the red heifer. All we know for sure in this section is that the ashes will be used in the water of cleansing (see Notes) as a purification from sin.

Notes

2 The opening phrasing of the verse is awkward and unusual: "This is the statute of the Torah." It seems quite likely that the Hebrew word הַתּוֹרָה (*hattôrāh*, "the Torah" or "law") is a scribal error for the word הַפָּרָה (*happārāh*, "the heifer"), in which case the verse should begin: "This is the statute of the [red] heifer." Compare the wording of 6:13: "This is the Torah for the Nazirite."

9 The term נִדָּה (*niddāh*) is a feminine noun meaning "impurity," likely related to the verb *nāḏaḏ* ("to flee, depart"). The noun is used to describe ceremonial impurity in such cases as a man having sexual congress with a brother's wife (Lev 20:21—a forbidden act) and a woman's uncleanness caused by her menstruation (Lev 12:2). The phrase לְמֵי נִדָּה (*lᵉmê niddāh*, "for waters of purification") thus literally means "waters of defilement" but has the derived meaning "waters that purify from defilement"; hence, "waters of cleansing" as in the NIV.

10 The BHS text has a space following the phrase "till evening." It is as though a new verse number should have been placed before the words beginning "This will be for the Israelites." We have similar problems in verse division from time to time in Numbers; see 26:1.

(2) *Application of cleansing waters*

19:11–13

> [11]"Whoever touches the dead body of anyone will be unclean for seven days. [12]He must purify himself with the water on the third day and on the seventh day; then he will be clean. But if he does not purify himself on the third and seventh days, he will not be clean. [13]Whoever touches the dead body of anyone and fails to purify himself defiles the LORD's tabernacle. That person must be cut off from Israel. Because the water of cleansing has not been sprinkled on him, he is unclean; his uncleanness remains on him.

11–13 This paragraph reveals the nature of the phrase in v.9, "for purification from sin." It is not that the ashes take on a magical property nor that they replace the sacrificial rites that are so very important in the worship of biblical faith. These ashes are to be used in the ritual of cleansing from impurity, particularly in cases of impurity occasioned by contact with dead bodies.

The ashes from the red heifer were kept outside the camp in a ritually pure place. Then a portion of these ashes would be mixed as needed with water to provide for means for the cleansing from contact with dead bodies. The period of uncleanness was to be seven days; acts of purification were to be done on both the third and the seventh days.

Anyone who refused to follow the rites of purification or who was neglectful in this area was said to defile the tabernacle. This means that willful neglect of the provision for cleansing brought not only judgment on the person but a pollution of the tabernacle itself. Willful neglect to avail oneself of the waters of purification would be a most serious matter. The idea of being in a state of cultic uncleanness is found in many contexts: of men (Lev 5:3), of women (Lev 15:25–27), of food (Judg 13:7–14), of things (Ezek 24:11). Zechariah 13:2 speaks of a "spirit of impurity."

Perhaps there are several ideas associated with ritual uncleanness. One has to do with being soiled. The fact that "unclean" is used suggests that, at the very least, this is the place to begin. A woman's menstrual flow, certain mildews and skin diseases, animals that feed on cadavers—these things in some way or other speak of something soiled. But it is difficult to go very far with this notion. Further, the association of a woman's menstrual flow with mildew and mold is an odious one to make; such linkings lead very easily to demeaning views of women as in some manner "dirty."

Since Israel lived long before the discovery of microbiology, it is an error to assume that it was principally concerns for infectious disease that led them to their ideas of clean and unclean. While a certain sense of cause and effect might be granted, nonetheless, we read back into the text our own ideas if we determine that clean and unclean have to do principally with health concerns. Ultimately, the ideas of clean and unclean have to do with appropriateness and inappropriateness for participation in the cultus of Israel. The ideas go all the way back to the time of Noah but are constantly being developed and refined through the biblical period. Finally, the idea of clean and unclean has to do with the basic idea of holiness, which is separation and distinction. Animals are clean and unclean, not because they necessarily will or will not make a person sick if they are used as food; they are clean and unclean primarily because God desired his people to live in a world of discrimination (see esp. Lev 11:44–47). We may look back from a twentieth-century understanding of infection and disease and remark, "How kind it was of God that some of the animals he declared to be unclean to Israel are foods that might be conveyers of disease." But the principal issue is distinction, discrimination, the marking out of that which is different from something else.

In v.13 the basic idea seems to be accidental contact with a corpse because of the death of a person in the proximity of the one affected. This could be a member of one's family in the home or a total stranger in the marketplace.

The idea of contact with the dead causing disease might have been discovered empirically in the ancient world. But the wording of v.13 suggests someone who is recently dead. The risk of bacterial infection would be less in this case. The ancient idea of the uncleanness of a dead body more likely sprang from a sense of the mystery of life. Life is a force; the leaving of life from a body is a terror of the unknown. Yet it is not that the people of Israel were unacquainted with death. The incidents of famine, disease, pestilence, war, and the interminable dying in the desert made death something that the people saw all about them. More likely the context was in some way related to sin; for death—ultimately—is the result of sin.

The Lord is the Great Teacher. He is the one who uses teaching aids. Inadvertent contact with a dead person is a time for a reminder of the ultimate, life and death, sin and forgiveness, cleanness and uncleanness.

There is an issue of responsibility here. The person who was contaminated had to initiate the action. But there is also a sense of consequences. For the community the individual's state of uncleanness will pollute the dwelling place. This means that one person's sinful state may endanger God's continuing presence in the midst of his people. A holy God demands a holy people. The second danger is for himself. Such a one who refuses the provision of cleansing is to be a cast-off. To protect the whole, such a one is to be consigned outside the camp (cf. 1 Cor 5:5).

In this passage we have the ideas of corporate solidarity and individual responsibility seen together. Yahweh condescends to dwell with his people, but he is not constrained to continue to do so in the event of unrestrained contempt for the demands of his presence. See, especially, Ezekiel 8–10 for a portrait of his gradual removal from the people as the symbol of his presence gradually moves from the people who have rejected his glory.

Notes

13 זֹרַק (*zōraq*, "sprinkled") is to be parsed as a Qal passive perfect rather than a Pual (as in BDB, p. 284c). The general rule is this: If a verb is used as the passive of the simple, basic stem and there is no Piel attested, then the supposed Pual is really a passive formation of the simple (Qal) stem. The use of the Qal passive has nearly disappeared, except in the participle; the Masoretes tended to treat them as Puals. See, e.g., "a child will be born" in Isa 9:6 [5 MT], a simple passive (Qal) rather than a Pual (NIV, "a child is born").

(3) *Specifics of uncleanness*

19:14–16

14 "This is the law that applies when a person dies in a tent: Anyone who enters the tent and anyone who is in it will be unclean for seven

days, 15and every open container without a lid fastened on it will be unclean.

16"Anyone out in the open who touches someone who has been killed with a sword or someone who has died a natural death, or anyone who touches a human bone or a grave, will be unclean for seven days.

14–16 These two small paragraphs (vv.14–15 and v.16) and the preceding overlap some, suggestive of a complex process of assimilation of these various Toroth (Sacral Instructions) into the text of Numbers. Yet there is no real conflict between them; they meld together into a coherent whole. The resultant repetition may be used for emphasis. It may be that these two units (vv.14–15 and v.16) came as the result of specific instances of ritual defilement in which petitioners came to Moses asking what they should do in their specific circumstance. When Moses ruled, under the direction of the Spirit, then these became Toroth for cleanness as well.

The point of v.16 seems to be that the cause of death is not the issue, but the fact of death is what renders a corpse unclean. The person might have died in battle from a sword wound or expired of age in a natural death. In either case the result is a corpse that is unclean and that makes all who touch it unclean. If this is the case in v.16, then the situation in vv.14–15 seems to be the result of a question concerning a corpse that is out in the open in a tent or that might be in a container. If the container is open, then the result is uncleanness for persons who are in the room; it is as though the corpse is in the room with them. If the container is fastened, then, presumably, there is no effect on others nearby.

As we think of this text with its restrictions and limitations, we should also reflect on the opportunities it grants for relief from the bondage of uncleanness. There would be many occasions in which a person would become unclean, not because of a deliberate act of contact with a dead body, but just by being in the proximity of one who died. Given the factor of uncleanness, the cleansing water becomes a great gift of grace. Moreover, family members were freed to minister to the bodies of their deceased loved ones, knowing that their ritual impurity could be removed (see Notes).

Notes

16 Touching a dead body was a matter of serious consequence. One would think twice before extending a casual touch, given these laws. These factors heighten our appreciation of those who cared for the body of the Savior Jesus, helped with his burial, and planned for anointing his body after the Passover and Sabbath were completed. These loving disciples were voluntarily placing themselves in a position of ritual uncleanness for seven days. Yet it was something they did without hesitation; such was their love for him.

(4) *Application of the cleansing waters for uncleanness*

19:17–22

17"For the unclean person, put some ashes from the burned purification offering into a jar and pour fresh water over them. 18Then a man who is ceremonially clean is to take some hyssop, dip it in the water and sprinkle the tent and all the furnishings and the people who were there. He must also sprinkle anyone who has touched a human bone or a grave or someone who has been killed or someone who has died a natural death. [19]The man who is clean is to sprinkle the unclean person on the third and seventh days, and on the seventh day he is to purify him. The person being cleansed must wash his clothes and bathe with water, and that evening he will be clean. [20]But if a person who is unclean does not purify himself, he must be cut off from the community, because he has defiled the sanctuary of the LORD. The water of cleansing has not been sprinkled on him, and he is unclean. [21]This is a lasting ordinance for them.

"The man who sprinkles the water of cleansing must also wash his clothes, and anyone who touches the water of cleansing will be unclean till evening. [22]Anything that an unclean person touches becomes unclean, and anyone who touches it becomes unclean till evening."

17–22 The ritual application of the cleansing waters for purification rites is detailed in this section. First is the preparation of the water (v.17). Ashes from the heifer were placed in a clay pot. Then fresh water was added and mixed. This is not magic but ritual. The water is still water, the ashes are still ashes. The resultant swill is ordinary in its components but holy in its designation and divine in its application. The Christian may wish to make comparisons with the "ordinariness" of the substances we use in our own ritual. There is no magic in the baptismal waters, no magic in bread and wine. Ordinary things, however, may be used for extraordinary rites; ordinary items—not magic!—may be used by the Spirit of God to effect any result in which he takes pleasure.

We notice that hyssop, a plant long associated with cleansing in the ancient East (e.g., Exod 12:22) and already associated with the ashes of the heifer (v.6), is used to dip the water and to sprinkle it on all that was unclean, persons and things (v.18). Here the methodology of the cleansing ritual is explained. It took a ceremonially clean person to sprinkle the ceremonially unclean person or thing (v.19). Following the sprinkling the person being cleansed would then bathe and wash all his clothes. Failure to avail oneself of these provisions would result in his being cut off from the community, for his failure affected both himself and the sanctuary (v.20).

The cleansing is twofold. One is the sprinkling with the waters of cleansing. The other is bathing and washing with ordinary water (and soap). David's prayer in Psalm 51:7 takes on special significance in this regard: "Cleanse me with hyssop, and I will be clean;/ wash me, and I will be whiter than snow" (cf. v.2). The parallel members speak of the two washings of the ceremony; in David's case, he requests that the entire cleansing be done by God himself!

The cleansing water of the ashes of the red heifer is specifically related to the cleansing property of the blood of Christ in the NT (Heb 9:13; notice the words "How much more," v.14) and is a portrait of the cleansing of the believer available on confession of sin (1 John 1:7–9).

The Torah of the Cow (!) (see comment on v.2) turns out to be another of the great texts on the grace of God in the Hebrew Scriptures.

Introduction to chapter 20

Numbers 20 is made up of three significant units. The first concerns the rebellion of Moses against God as he strikes the rock to gain the waters of God (vv.1–13); the second concerns an arrogant rebuff by Edom to allow Israel right of passage through their territory (vv.14–21); and the third describes the sad story of the death of Aaron, priest of the Lord (vv.22–29). Nearly unnoticed in all these sad events is the death of Miriam, prophetess of the Lord (v.1); her death, sadly, merits only a line. The resultant chapter has a grim structure to it, with four (!), not just three, sad events:

The death of Miriam, prophetess of the Lord (v.1)
The rebellion of Moses, prophet of the Lord (vv.1–13)
The arrogant inhospitality of Edom (vv.14–21)
The death of Aaron, priest of the Lord (vv.22–29)

The result of these varied events, with the bookend nature of the deaths of Miriam and Aaron (an inclusio), presents a central picture that is most grim indeed: Moses is now a rebel against Yahweh! And a petty power stymies the march of the armies of Israel. This is a chapter of unrelieved gloom. Between the death of Miriam and the death of Aaron are the stories of the waters of Meribah and the borders of Edom.

j. *The ultimate rebellion in the sin of Moses*

20:1–13

1 In the first month the whole Israelite community arrived at the Desert of Zin, and they stayed at Kadesh. There Miriam died and was buried.
2 Now there was no water for the community, and the people gathered in opposition to Moses and Aaron. 3 They quarreled with Moses and said, "If only we had died when our brothers fell dead before the LORD!
4 Why did you bring the LORD's community into this desert, that we and our livestock should die here? 5 Why did you bring us up out of Egypt to this terrible place? It has no grain or figs, grapevines or pomegranates. And there is no water to drink!"
6 Moses and Aaron went from the assembly to the entrance to the Tent of Meeting and fell facedown, and the glory of the LORD appeared to them. 7 The LORD said to Moses, 8 "Take the staff, and you and your brother Aaron gather the assembly together. Speak to that rock before their eyes and it will pour out its water. You will bring water out of the rock for the community so they and their livestock can drink."
9 So Moses took the staff from the LORD's presence, just as he commanded him. 10 He and Aaron gathered the assembly together in front of the rock and Moses said to them, "Listen, you rebels, must we bring you water out of this rock?" 11 Then Moses raised his arm and struck the rock twice with his staff. Water gushed out, and the community and their livestock drank.
12 But the LORD said to Moses and Aaron, "Because you did not trust in me enough to honor me as holy in the sight of the Israelites, you will not bring this community into the land I give them."
13 These were the waters of Meribah, where the Israelites quarreled with the LORD and where he showed himself holy among them.

1 In several ways this is a problematic verse. There are problems with respect to the geographical and chronological issues as well as with the obituary notice. The phrase order in the MT follows along these lines: "Then the entire community of the Israelites entered the Desert of Zin, in the first month, and the people dwelled in Kadesh. And it was there that Miriam died, and there she was buried."

Several suggestions are available to explain what seems to be a redundancy in the first words, describing the arrival of the people in the Desert of Zin (see Notes) and their dwelling at Kadesh (see 13:21, 26).

1. This notice may be read as sequentially chronological; it would thus describe the

return to Zin and Kadesh from a lengthy period of wandering about elsewhere in the Desert of Sinai.

2. The notice may betray its origin in a different source than the earlier record from which chapter 13 was drawn; hence the writer of this section was not aware that earlier mention had been made of Zin and Kadesh (see 13:21, 26).

3. The verb translated "they arrived," although a preterit (see Notes), may be used in a pluperfect sense: "They had arrived . . . and they had dwelled." In this sense the action of the verbs is a throwback to chapter 13.

4. Yet another solution is to understand that this phrase is a narrator's device designed to take us back into the narrative story line by the use of recall. This is my own preference. There have been numerous sections dealing with a wide variety of topics; now it is time to remind the reader of the geographical setting of the main narrative story line. Hence, it is as though the narrator were to say, "Now you will recall that the nation had moved to the Desert of Zin and had dwelled for a lengthy period at Kadesh. It was at Kadesh where Israel had rebelled against the Lord, thus losing the opportunity for the people to enter the land of Canaan for an entire generation. In this way the words "Desert of Zin" and "Kadesh" serve as an ominous cloud over the entire chapter.

We have already observed that the larger part of the sojourn in the desert is left without record. This may be deliberate on Moses' part. It is as though the time of sojourn was time that did not really count in the history of salvation. The *Heilsgeschichte* of the Exodus traditions is one of movement and victory, not stagnation. We are left to ourselves to try to imagine what it was like for the people during this long, dreary time in the desert.

It is often thought that the people were constantly on the move in the Desert of Sinai during the thirty-eight years of their exile. Yet the indication of Deuteronomy 1:46 is that Israel may have made Kadesh their principal base for the long sojourn in the desert: "And so you stayed in Kadesh many days—all the time you spent there." Perhaps the best reconstruction of events is to presume that the people may have sent out parties on a cycle of roving travels, following the slight water sources and the sparse vegetation, supported primarily by the manna, the bread from heaven. But their circuits would bring them back to the central camp at Kadesh, the scene of their great rebellion (Num 13–14). They have now come full circle; the Land of Promise lay before them again.

The chronological notice in v.1 is incomplete. It indicates that this was the "first month" but does not give us the year (cf. 9:1, "the first month of the second year after they came out of Egypt"). BHS raises the question about the possible dropping of the year from this verse. A comparison of 20:22–29 and 33:38 leads us to conclude that this chapter begins in the fortieth year from the Exodus (see Notes on 1:1; 9:1). The larger number of the people over the age of twenty at the time of the rebellion at Kadesh (Num 13–14) already would have died. This is the winding up of the clock of God's program of redemption. *Heilsgeschichte,* long on hold, was about to resume; the Lord's saving work was about to begin again. But not yet! First, there is a sad story of dying and a sadder story of rebellion.

Verse 1 notes the passing of Miriam, sister of Aaron and Moses, prophetess of the Lord. It is at least of interest that her death and burial are mentioned in this record, but it is sad to see that only a clause or two are given to record these events. It seems as though after her challenge of the authority of Moses, along with her brother Aaron (ch. 12), Miriam nearly disappears from the scene. She may never have fully recovered the position of trust and privilege that she had enjoyed before this rebellion. This is not just to be explained by the antiwomen stance of the Torah (see commentary on ch. 12), as some writers aver. It may be a notice that even when a person has been forgiven of enormous sin, the subsequent realm of influence that person has in the work of God may be limited thereafter. In any event, when we read of her death, we grieve. It really is true: all those over the age of twenty at the time of the rebellion will die; even Miriam is buried in the sands of the desert instead of being given the opportunity to enter the Land of Promise.

Centuries later another Miriam, her namesake, would be the happy agent for the birth of the Promised One; we pronounce her name as Mary.

2–8 In the opening words of v.2, "now there was no water," we have a sense of déjà vu. We think back forty years to the incident at Rephadim when the people screamed to Moses to give them water to drink (Exod 17:1–3). Moses was instructed by the Lord to take the staff he had used to strike the Nile in the curse of plague (Exod 7:20) and to strike the rock at Horeb to initiate a flow of the water of blessing. Now, forty years later, at the place of Israel's worst act of rebellion, the story was being rerun. The people of the rebellious nation now desire to die with those who had already passed away in earlier judgments of the Lord (vv.3–4; see 14:22; 16:31–35). It takes an especially desperate people to wish themselves dead by God's judgments. The complaints against the bread of heaven are repeated by the sons even as earlier by their fathers.

The response of Moses and Aaron to this new assault on their persons was similar to that on earlier occasions; they went to the entrance of the Tent of Meeting and fell down in obeisance to the Lord (v.6; see 14:5; 16:4, 22, 45). As in times past, they were prepared for an awesome display of the presence of God and the scourge of his flaming judgment against a people who continually rebel against him, despite repeated acts of mercy and grace.

Then, as they anticipated, there was the appearance of the Lord (v.6). There he was in glory. There he was in wonder. In this case, however, there was no fire. There was no judgment. There was no anger. There was just a gentle word, telling Moses to take his staff and to go with Aaron to bring water from the rock for the thirsting community. The instructions of the Lord were quite clear: "Speak to that rock before their eyes" (v.8). We notice that the staff is not the rod of Aaron that had budded but the same staff that Moses has used to do wonders in Egypt (see Exod 17:5) and in the desert all these years. While he was to take his staff, the symbol of his power through the Lord, he was merely to speak to the rock; and it would give its water for the people.

9–12 This paragraph begins with words that we are accustomed to hear respecting Moses, prophet of Yahweh. He begins by doing exactly as the Lord had instructed him (v.9). He took his staff in hand and went to gather the assembly (see Notes on v.2) before the rock (v.10a).

Then, at long last, Moses exploded! Was he disappointed that the Lord had not burst out against his people, as had happened time after time? Moses burst out against them—and against the rock—to his lasting regret (vv.10b–11). Suddenly the accumulated anger and frustration of forty years bore down on Moses, servant of Yahweh. The death of his sister was the end of an era. Yet nothing had changed; the children were as rebellious as ever. He addresses the assembly in harsh words, "Listen, you rebels" (v.10). In a sense all Moses was saying was what God had said numerous times to the same people and for the same reasons. The term "rebels" (*hammōrîm*, a plural Qal active participle) that Moses uses is very similar to the noun the Lord uses to describe their contentious behavior in 17:10 (17:25 [MT]; *li<u>b</u>nê-merî*, lit., "to [these] rebellious sons").

Moses' words—"must we bring you water out of this rock?"—express the intense level of his exasperation and pain. At this point he reached out with the rod of wonder and struck the rock twice (v.11). In his rage Moses disobeyed the clear instructions of the Lord to speak to the rock (v.8). While the water was released and the people and their livestock were refreshed with its blessing, the rash action of Moses brought a stern rebuke from the Lord.

The nature of Moses' offense is not clearly stated in this text; here are elements we may bring together:

1. In some way the action of Moses was a lack of trust in the Lord. This is part of the charge of the Lord against him (see v.12). It is not clear how Moses failed to trust God in this story. One might suppose that he did not believe a word alone would suffice to bring water from the rock, that he felt a blow against the rock was necessary. However, I believe it is more likely that he was disappointed with the failure of God this time to respond in wrath to the rebellious people as he had in the past. It is almost as though he thought it was necessary to do the work of vengeance himself; thus his harsh, condemnatory words, his sarcasm, and his blows against the rock. In this Moses forgot the basic stipulate of the Torah concerning judgment: "Vengeance is mine, I will repay, says the LORD" (see Deut 32:35–43; Rom 12:19).

2. In some way the holiness of the Lord was assaulted by Moses' rash action (v.12; see also 27:14), for he had not treated with sufficient deference the rock of God's presence. In some manner the rock speaks of God. This was a mysterious symbol of his person, a gracious provision of his presence. In the NT we learn that the rock actually speaks of the person of the Lord Jesus Christ; it is called "Christ" by Paul in 1 Corinthians 10:4. Hence, unwittingly, Moses in his wrath had lashed out against the physical embodiment of God's grace. What an awful moment this is! Had Moses an opportunity to erase one sequence of events in his life, to do the sequence correctly, surely this was it! But Moses, like ourselves, had no erase track. All is forward play; yet the rest of his life he would relive the infamy of this moment.

3. Even the rash words of Moses were an act of rebellion against the Spirit of God. This is the conclusion of the poet in Psalm 106:32–33, who rehearses these events in song:

> By the waters of Meribah they angered the LORD,
> and trouble came to Moses because of them;
> for they rebelled against the Spirit of God,
> and rash words came from Moses' lips.

4. A factor that we easily might have missed is that Moses was not alone in his rash action and his violent words; he was accompanied in word and deed by his brother, Aaron, the aged priest. We learn this from the divine words of judgment on the two of them (v.12: "the LORD said to Moses and Aaron, 'Because you [pl. pronoun] did not trust in me' "). It is an awful example of coming full circle for both of these men. In Numbers 12 Moses was the object of the wrath and jealousy of his sister and brother; in Numbers 16 Aaron was the object of the wrath and jealousy of Korah and his allies. Now both Moses and Aaron, who had behaved so marvelously in these past times, were rebellious against God.

The judgment of God had not flashed out against the people, but now it bursts against his (usually) faithful servants: "You will not bring this community into the land" (v.12). The end result of Moses' action is sure: neither he nor Aaron would enter the Land of Promise; of their contemporaries only Joshua and Caleb would survive to enter the land. The inclusion of Aaron in this verse demonstrates his partnership with his brother in the breach against the holiness of Yahweh.

13 Once again a name of judgment was given to a place of Israel's journey. This time the name is Meribah, a word that means "a place of strife" or "quarreling." The same name was used forty years earlier at the first occasion of bringing water from the rock (Exod 17:7; also called Massah, "testing"). Psalm 95:8 laments the rebellion at Meribah and Massah, and Psalm 114:8 celebrates both occasions of God's grace. For Meribah/Massah is both: a reminder of the rebellion and a symbol of celebration of God's mercy.

Notes

---

1 The spelling of the place name מִדְבַּר־צִן (*midbar-ṣin,* "Desert of Zin") is with the Hebrew sade (*ṣ*) rather than with the zayin (*z*), as is suggested by the English rendering. This very northerly outreach of the Sinai desert area, just south of Judah and west of the southern shore of the Dead Sea, is mentioned in 13:21; 20:1; 27:14; 33:36; 34:3–4; Deut 32:51; Josh 15:1, 3. Often the Desert of Zin is associated with its principal oasis, Kadesh (see 13:26; 20:1, 14, 16, 22; 27:14; 33:36–37; cf. also Deut 1:46; 32:51; Judg 11:16–17; Ps 29:8; Ezek 47:19; 48:28). Kadesh is also known by its longer name, Kadesh Barnea (32:8; 34:4; Deut 1:2, 19; 2:14; 9:23; Josh 10:41; 14:6–7; 15:3).

The tense of וַיָּבֹאוּ . . . וַיֵּשֶׁב (*wayyāḇō'û* . . . *wayyēšeḇ,* "[they] arrived . . . and they stayed") is preterit (termed in some authorities as an imperfect with waw-consecutive); but see Ronald Williams (*Hebrew Syntax,* par. 176) for the preferred terminology. This type of verb is the workhorse of Hebrew narrative prose. It normally speaks of sequential acts: this happened, then this, then this. On occasion the preterit may take on special uses (determined by environment) such as the pluperfect (had done), as in Gen 12:1: "The LORD had said to Abram."

2 וַיִּקָּהֲלוּ (*wayyiqqāhᵃlû,* "[they] gathered") is a play on words on the term "community" (see v.4). The verb is the Niphal of the root *qāhal,* here meaning "to gather together for conflict, rebellion" (see also 16:3, 42). In v.10 the expression *wayyaqhilû* . . . *'eṯ-haqqāhāl* ("[and they] gathered [the Hiphil of *qāhal*] the assembly") speaks of the usual construction, an assembly gathered for a religious purpose.

---

k. *The resistance of Edom*

20:14–21

14 Moses sent messengers from Kadesh to the king of Edom, saying:

"This is what your brother Israel says: You know about all the
hardships that have come upon us. 15 Our forefathers went down
into Egypt, and we lived there many years. The Egyptians mistreated us and our fathers, 16 but when we cried out to the LORD, he
heard our cry and sent an angel and brought us out of Egypt.

"Now we are here at Kadesh, a town on the edge of your territory.
17 Please let us pass through your country. We will not go through
any field or vineyard, or drink water from any well. We will travel
along the king's highway and not turn to the right or to the left until
we have passed through your territory."

18 But Edom answered:

"You may not pass through here; if you try, we will march out and attack you with the sword."

19 The Israelites replied:

"We will go along the main road, and if we or our livestock drink any of your water, we will pay for it. We only want to pass through on foot—nothing else."

20 Again they answered:

"You may not pass through."

Then Edom came out against them with a large and powerful army.
21 Since Edom refused to let them go through their territory, Israel
turned away from them.

14–17 The grief of this chapter is unrelieved. Moses' attempt to pass through the territory of their brother nation Edom on the basis of peaceful negotiation and the payment for services rendered is met by an arrogant rebuff and a show of force that dissuades Israel from taking the most direct route toward their rendezvous with destiny.

The nation is now about to begin their last trek in the desert; they are now ready to begin the march that will lead them to the land. When they came to Kadesh thirty-eight years before, it seemed that their plan of attack was to march northward through the land of Canaan, conquering as they would go. But the events of the evil reports of the spies and the rebellion of the people against the Lord changed all that. This time the plan appears to be one of circumventing the south of the land, traversing southern Transjordan, then bursting into the land from the east. This means the nation planned to take the "king's highway" (v.17), the major north-south highway in Transjordan from Arabia to Damascus. The first nation whose land they would cross to take this route was Edom, a brother nation to Israel, as the people of Edom were descended from Esau, brother of Jacob (see Gen 36:1).

Moses diplomatically sent messengers from his camp at Kadesh to the king of Edom, requesting passage through his land. The message is summarized in vv.14–17, a highly interesting document from the ancient world. In this message Moses uses language and appeals that were designed to bring the most favorable decision: he calls Edom a brother; he rehearses their experience in Egypt and in the desert (a section that sounds almost creedal—a confession of faith); he speaks of the deliverance of the Lord; he states their present condition; and he asks permission to pass through the land of Edom, with a promise that they will not forage along the way nor veer to one side or the other. In all this Moses evinces humility of person and confidence of purpose. He betrays no desire for military aggrandizement; his only request is passage through their land.

18 The response of Edom is unusually hostile. It is an unprovoked stroke of anger with rash threats of war.

19 Moses countered with an elaboration of his purpose. Again he assures Edom that he has no intention of conquest, that there is no desire even to live off the land as they pass through on the major highway, and that, if in fact there would be any need for local water for the people or their flocks, they would pay for it fully. In fact, Israel was forbidden by the Lord to take even a foothold of the land of Edom (Deut 2:4–6).

20 Once more, even more abruptly, Edom refuses. And Edom backs up its haughty behavior with a show of force of their large army in the field.

21 With a sigh, Israel turned away to the east to make a broad circuit of the territory.

As we read this story, we may make some observations:

1. Israel was likely a more numerous people than Edom, the people from whom they requested passage. If the population of Israel is indeed the 2.5 million or more that the numbers of the census of an army of 600,000 would indicate, then they must have been immensely larger as a nation than the population of Edom. The territory of Edom is rather arid, a territory that was populated sparsely in biblical times, as well as today. If the army of Israel numbered 60,000, instead of 600,000 (as we have suggested in the Introduction: The Large Numbers—Toward a Solution), then the story becomes more plausible. It is hard to imagine that an army raised by the people of Edom could be much of a threat to an army of over half a million, even green troops! Yet, if the army of Israel was about 60,000 in number, then they might feel that even though they were a larger force than the army of Edom, they were not ready to take on the seasoned troops of Edom.

2. We may surmise that Israel turned away rather than force the issue and enter a war they might have won for two reasons: (1) they were brother nations, and Israel had no claim at this time on the territorial integrity of Edom; and (2) the first military campaign of Israel should be for reasons of conquest and righteousness rather than spite and pettiness.

3. Moses believes that the experiences of his people were well known to the other nations of the region. He says to the king of Edom through his messengers, "You know" (v.14). This is a part of a significant issue in the story of the Exodus, that the saving work of the Lord was not done in a vacuum or in a hiding place. The nations round about were expected to understand something of what had happened, that it was the Lord who had brought deliverance for his people.

In all of this, however, the people turn away and begin a long circuit around the nation of Edom. The rebuff and its aftermath must have been especially galling to Moses and Aaron; it is another step in their decline.

I. *The death of Aaron and the succession to Eleazar*

20:22–29

> 22The whole Israelite community set out from Kadesh and came to Mount Hor. 23At Mount Hor, near the border of Edom, the LORD said to Moses and Aaron, 24"Aaron will be gathered to his people. He will not enter the land I give the Israelites, because both of you rebelled against my command at the waters of Meribah. 25Get Aaron and his son Eleazar and take them up Mount Hor. 26Remove Aaron's garments and put them on his son Eleazar, for Aaron will be gathered to his people; he will die there."

> [27]Moses did as the LORD commanded: They went up Mount Hor in the sight of the whole community. [28]Moses removed Aaron's garments and put them on his son Eleazar. And Aaron died there on top of the mountain. Then Moses and Eleazar came down from the mountain, [29]and when the whole community learned that Aaron had died, the entire house of Israel mourned for him thirty days.

Finally, we come to the end of this grim chapter. The chapter began with a note of the death of Miriam; the chapter ends with the story of the death of Aaron. And in the midst of these sadnesses is the death of the hope of Moses to enter the land and the end of the opportunity to take the king's highway to mid-Transjordan.

22 At last the people were on the move, north and east from their long stay in the desert near the oasis of Kadesh. They came to Mount Hor, a place that possibly may be identified with Jebel Madurah, a mountain about fifteen miles northeast of Kadesh on the northwest border of Edom. This mountain is on the direct route from Kadesh to Moab and fits the particulars of the story in this section quite well (S. Barabas, "Mount Hor," ZPEB, 3:201).

23–24 As Israel came to the region of Mount Hor on the border of Edom (v.23), the word of the Lord came to Moses and Aaron that Aaron, the aged priest, was now about to die. The reason for his death is stated (v.24), a reminder of the sin of the two brothers at Meribah, as described earlier in this chapter. Yet in this passage there is still a sense of the grace of God. The language is merciful, not vindictive. The interests of Moses and Aaron in the transfer of power are also the interests of God. Even in the death of his servant, the Lord shows his continuing grace.

25–29 Before Aaron died he was to see that his son Eleazar was his sure successor. This must have been the one comfort that came to him as he knew that his days were at an end. In a dramatic symbol of this transfer of power, Moses took the garments from his brother, the insignia of his divine office, and placed them on his dutiful son Eleazar (v.28). At this point Moses did precisely as the Lord commanded (v.27); there is no more rash action on his part, no more flashes of anger.

Three men ascended the mountain; two returned. One, Aaron, died there (v.28). The presumption is that Aaron was buried there by his brother and his son. From the mount there was a sense of looking out to the land to the northwest; this was as close as Aaron would get. Later Moses would have a view of the land from another hill; like his brother, he, too, would see the land only from a distance. Both brothers are associated with mountains on their dying. Their sister is buried near the oasis of Kadesh.

With the death of Aaron, the story of the first generation is quickly winding down. The promise of the next generation is soon to be realized.

Notes

24 The idiom of death, "Aaron will be gathered to his people," is characteristic of the OT narrators, particularly when the death is of a notable person of faith in God (see Gen 25:8, 17; 35:29 et al.). The expression seems to be a double entendre: (1) the laying of the body in the grave is a return to the dust from which man has come (Gen 3:19); (2) but the person will be gathered to his people in the realm of the life beyond death. Although Aaron was about to die and would not enjoy the blessings of the Land of Promise, he would still have his part in the life to come.

Further in this passage we have another notice of the culpability of the two brothers in the rebellion at Meribah. Aaron had joined Moses in rebellion against God (v.12); the impending death of Aaron was a precursor of the death of Moses as well (see Deut 34).

25 A principal issue of this section is that the death of Aaron was not to leave in doubt the question of his successor, any more than the death of Moses was to leave in doubt the one who would succeed him (see Deut 34). While Aaron still lived his garments were to be placed on his son; only then did Aaron die. The mourning of the people (v.29) was not only for the death of the old priest. It was also a mourning as the mark of the end of an era. The old generation was now nearly gone; in forty years there had been almost a complete turnover of the population over the age of twenty.

---

2. *A climax of rebellion and hope and the end of their dying (21:1–25:18)*

If Numbers 20 is a tableau of unrelieved gloom, chapter 21 begins to show some glimmers of light in the dark sea of Israel's desert experience. This is not to say that there would be no more trouble or no more rebellion; such is hardly the case. Indeed, this chapter and chapter 25 present notorious instances of Israel's continued acts of rebellion against the Lord. But this chapter presents as well some victories, victories against hostile enemies as well as victories against the dark side of themselves. Chapter 21 is also the setting for the enormously important set of texts on the dramatic story of Balaam the pagan mantic from Mesopotamia who confronts the power of Yahweh, God of Israel—one of the most amusing, wondrous, and engaging of biblical narratives (chs. 22–24).

Numbers 21 is a bit of a turning in the story of Israel in the desert. It does not present the radical renewal that sometimes comes when a ne'er-do-well suddenly becomes a leading citizen; but then ne'er-do-wells rarely spring ready-made to cleansed living. Israel did not spring to new life either. But at least she began to show that she did not wish to keep dying.

Numbers 21 has five discreet sections to it. Our commentary will proceed along those lines. Then Numbers 22–24 follows immediately with the account of Balaam and Balak, with two major movements. On the heels of this story is the dramatic, unexpected, and frightful aftermath, the seduction of Israel at Baal Peor. Altogether, then, Numbers 21–25 has some eight sectional divisions.

a. *The destruction of Arad*

21:1–3

[1] When the Canaanite king of Arad, who lived in the Negev, heard that Israel was coming along the road to Atharim, he attacked the Israelites and captured some of them. [2] Then Israel made this vow to the LORD: "If you will deliver these people into our hands, we will totally destroy their cities." [3] The LORD listened to Israel's plea and gave the Canaanites over to them. They completely destroyed them and their towns; so the place was named Hormah.

1 The first battle of the new community against the Canaanites was provoked by the king of Arad, perhaps as he was on an incursionary raid. The result was a complete victory for the Israelites, a new day for Israel indeed since their defeat by the Amalekites a generation ago (14:41–45).

Unlike the situation with Edom in chapter 20, Arad was a Canaanite region that was a part of the people and territory under the interdict of the Lord. Here was the first occasion for a military operation by the new generation. The text emphasizes several things: (1) that the king of Arad was a Canaanite (vv.1, 3); (2) that he deliberately provoked an attack on Israel, including the taking of hostages; and (3) that, unlike their rebellious fathers (14:41–45), the people of Israel fought this time under the blessing and empowerment of the Lord (v.3).

The site of biblical Arad is well identified with Tell ʿArad, about twenty miles south of Hebron in the eastern Negev. While the 1962–67 Israeli excavations at Arad have demonstrated a large fortified city of the Early Bronze II period (c. 2900–2700 B.C.), there was no evidence found of a Late or Middle Bronze city on the tell. It is possible that in the time of Moses the term Arad was used for a region of the Negev rather than a city proper or that at that time the name Arad had "floated" to another site nearby. Y. Aharoni ("Arad," ISBErev., 1:229) suggests this possibility, naming Tell el-Milh, eight miles south of Tell ʿArad where strong Hyksos fortifications have been found and which may be mentioned along with Tell ʿArad in the Shishak list (see Notes).

2 The vow of the people to God speaks of their dependence on him for their victory, as well as their determination to fulfill the vow by making a complete destruction of their cities. The verb translated "totally destroy" is the verbal form related to the word *ḥerem*, meaning "to devote to the ban." This ruthless action was determined, not just by the rugged spirit of the age, but from a sense that the people were engaging in holy war, where the extermination, not just the subjugation, of her enemies was the spiritual goal for the people in their conquest of Canaan. The cup of iniquity of the people of the land was now full (see Gen 15:16); Israel was to be the instrument of the Lord's judgment to cleanse the land of the people who had polluted it. All contemporary feelings of revulsion against such "barbarism" need to be evaluated in terms of the later history of Israel. As is well attested in biblical history, the people did not carry out the policy of *ḥerem* to the peoples of the land, except on rare occasions; thus it happened that the peoples who survived became the instruments of Israel's later judgment.

3 The success of the military action against the Canaanite army of the king of Arad was thorough. They named the place "Hormah" (*ḥormāh*), a noun related to the verb *ḥāram* ("to devote to destruction"). Since the name "Hormah" was used in the first (and unsuccessful) battle against the Canaanites and Amalekites of the region (14:45), it is possible that the naming of the region came as a result of this present battle and that the earlier passage uses the name (of what became a well-known place) proleptically. In any event, the association of the victorious battle with Israel's earlier defeat is made certain by the use of this place name. The new generation faces a new day; victory ahead seems assured.

Notes

---

1 עֲרָד (*ʿărāḏ*, "Arad")—Shishak or Sheshonk I—was a Libyan war chief who became the Pharaoh of Egypt (c. 945–924 B.C.). Following the death of Solomon, Shishak invaded Judah and captured many of its cities (see 1 Kings 14:25). The record of his campaign was recorded on a wall of the temple of Amon at Karnak (Thebes). Among the lists of cities are two Arads: "Arad of the House of Yrhm" and "the Great Arad."

---

b. *The bronze snake*

21:4–9

[4]They traveled from Mount Hor along the route to the Red Sea, to go around Edom. But the people grew impatient on the way; [5]they spoke against God and against Moses, and said, "Why have you brought us up out of Egypt to die in the desert? There is no bread! There is no water! And we detest this miserable food!"

[6]Then the LORD sent venomous snakes among them; they bit the people and many Israelites died. [7]The people came to Moses and said, "We sinned when we spoke against the LORD and against you. Pray that the LORD will take the snakes away from us." So Moses prayed for the people.

[8]The LORD said to Moses, "Make a snake and put it up on a pole; anyone who is bitten can look at it and live." [9]So Moses made a bronze snake and put it up on a pole. Then when anyone was bitten by a snake and looked at the bronze snake, he lived.

It is not unusual in Scripture, or in our own lives, to have a story of defeat follow quickly on a story of victory. The author of Numbers places two such contrasting stories side-by-side in this chapter, perhaps to show the reader that while progress was being made toward dependence on the Lord, there was still a long way to go for these desert people! Right on the heels of the story of Israel's great victory over the Canaanites of the Negev, they fall on their own swords on the issue of food again in the rebellion that leads to the story of the bronze serpent.

4 This passage has a geographical and logical connection to the account of the death of Aaron on Mount Hor (20:27–29) and to the rebuff of Edom, not permitting Israel to pass through its territory for any price (20:14–21). There is no real connection indicated with the little pericope of the victory over the Canaanites of Arad (vv.1–3). These are separate accounts, juxtaposed for effect in the Scripture as we have received it.

The people had to detour because of the intransigent attitude of Edom. Each step they made south and east, rather than north and west, seemed to be an unbearable back-tracking. They rejoined the road to the Sea of Reeds to make a broad circuit around Edom. Finally, it got to them again. They had been so very near the land and had even tasted the sweet wine of victory. But now they were wandering again, and in their wanderings they seemed to be as far away from "real" food as ever.

With Moses' determination not to engage Edom in battle (see comment on 20:19), the people became impatient with him and with the direction the Lord was taking them. Flushed with victory, their confidence was in themselves. They forgot that their victory over the army of Arad was a victory granted to them by the Lord in response to their solemn pledge to Yahweh (vv.2–3); now they were ready to rebel again.

5 So the people began to complain, speaking against God and against Moses. Again, as their fathers, they asked why they had not been left back in Egypt and why they should be brought to this awful place to die. They did not deny the miracle but disparaged their deliverance from Egypt. Again they complained about the lack of food and water. But then they went beyond their fathers and mothers. They not only spoke of the monotony of manna, but they described it as "miserable bread" (see Notes). In their styling the "bread of heaven" (see Ps 78:23–24) as something vile and despicable, the people were actually contemning the Lord its giver.

The venom of the people's anger led them to blaspheme the Lord (v.4), to reject his servant Moses, and to contemn the bread of heaven. This is the most vitriolic of their several attacks on the manna (see Notes on 11:6). Just as the attack of Moses on the rock was more than it appeared to be (see comment on 20:11), so the contempt of the people for the heavenly bread was more serious than one might think. The Lord Jesus speaks of the manna as a type of himself, that he is the true Bread from heaven (John 6:32–35, 48–51, 58). A rejection of the heavenly manna is tantamount to one spurning the grace of God in the Savior.

6 Once more God had been rejected by his people; again he brings judgment on their heads. The pattern of rebellion by the people followed by the judgment of God on them is well established in the Book of Numbers. We believe it is possible that the basic trigger that provoked the outrageous actions and words of Moses in his rebellion against the Lord (20:9–11) was precisely because he felt this pattern had been broken at that time. God did not burst out against the people as Moses might have expected in response to their attack on him as described in 20:2–5. So Moses raged against them, and in the process he forgot who is God and who is servant. He confused the holy with the profane. For that moment he seems not to have believed that God would vindicate his own name (see 20:12).

But this time God acted as Moses expected. He brought a new instrument of his judgment on the people. This time it was snakes. The KJV's "fiery serpents" has led children to think of burning snakes (cf. the Heb. phrase *hannᵉḥāšîm haśśᵉrāp̱îm*, "the burning snakes" or, better, "the snakes that produce burning"). The "fire" was in their venom, of course; hence the NIV's "venomous snakes." The poison in these snakebites must have been particularly virulent, leading to horrible, agonizing deaths.

We notice something in these snakes that points to what is common in the miracles of the Bible; naturally occurring phenomena may come in unnatural ways, in exaggerated numbers, or in unusual timings. Manna, as we have argued above (see 11:5), seems to be an exception. Manna is not naturally occurring—it is wholly divine. And the people spurned it.

The people receive something from the desert rather than from heaven. They receive a sting instead of a blessing. They find themselves dying instead of being preserved alive by "that miserable bread." There is something very human about the people in their complaints about their diet. The timing of their renewed complaint is understandable, given the fact that they were backtracking into the wide waste of the desert in order not to provoke Edom. But understandable or not, human or no, they were engaging in outrageous rebellion again, coupled to an almost visceral hatred of God's gift to them in the "bread of angels" (Ps 78:25).

There is a pattern to complaining; it is habit forming. The tendency among people is to go beyond where one left off the last time, to become ever more egregious, ever more outspoken. Rarely does a complaining person become milder in his complaints. Finally, complaining becomes self-destructive.

7 Nonetheless, there is change of sorts in the people as they are described in this chapter. They continue to rebel (and they will rebel again in ch. 25), but now they ask for forgiveness. They were sinners, but they were confessing their wrong. They scream out to Moses, "We sinned when we spoke against the LORD and against you." In this act of repentance, we have the seeds for renewal. In their desire for forgiveness, there is hope for their future.

So Moses prayed for the people as he had prayed before (e.g., 11:2). And God answered, but in a most unusual way. In the case of the fire that flashed from heaven at the beginning of their troubles (11:1–3), the prayer of Moses eventuated in the fire dying out. In this case the snakes did not slither away, nor did they lose their fangs; the fiery serpents continued to plague the people with their horrible bites, and the people continued to grow ill and die.

8 Instead of losing the snakes, the people had to get their fill of them, as they had been forced to stomach quail at another time (11:31–34). Meanwhile, Moses was told to make an image of a snake (see Notes)! As we think about this, we realize several levels of incongruity:

1. The description of the plague seems to be of something that was spreading very quickly; yet Moses had to take the time to fashion, or direct the fashioning of, a metal image of one of the poisonous snakes. Sometimes even in a crisis one needs to move purposefully, surely.

2. Moses had transmitted to Israel God's prohibition against making images of any animal or other life form because of the dangers of idolatry that were so inherent in graphic art in the biblical period; yet now he was asked to make a graven image. This command must have been inordinately surprising, even to Moses.

3. There are few things so intensely disliked and feared the world over as snakes. Herpetologists cannot understand the revulsion seen in the lay opinion of snakes, and they seem to suffer umbrage at what they regard to be terrible misinformation about snakes in popular culture. No matter. Most people simply do not care for snakes; we may presume (from the tenor of this text) that this is a value we share with people thirty-five hundred years ago.

4. More specifically, in biblical culture it was a snake that became associated with the Evil One himself (Gen 3). Satan's first manifestation in the biblical story is serpentine; he is later to be called the primordial serpent, the dragon (see Rev 20:2). There is a sense in biblical thought that snakes are not only detestable in themselves, but they may even be symbolic of the prince of darkness himself.

With all these factors in view, now we think again of the enormity of what Moses was asked to do, of the taboos he was asked to break. This is not unlike Peter being told to kill and eat food that he regarded as unclean (Acts 10). The people had called the bread of heaven detestable. Moses is commanded of God to make an image of something truly detestable in their culture and to hold that high on a pole as their only means of deliverance from disease. Only those who looked at the image of the snake would survive the venom that coursed through their bodies. This is an extraordinary act of cultural shock, an exceptionally daring use of potent symbols. As the people had transformed in their own thinking the gracious bread of heaven into detestable food, so the Lord transforms a symbol of death into a source of life and deliverance. The rejection of God's grace brings a symbol of death. The intervention of God's grace brings a source of life.

9 Some err in their evaluation of the "salvation" that came from looking at this snake. Some contemporary theologians and Bible teachers debate on how intense one's gaze at the bronze serpent had to be for one to be "saved." Discussions rage on the meaning of the verb "to look" (*nāḇaṭ*, in the Hiphil). One party says merely a glance was needed; the other says the text demands a constant, groping stare. The one party says the glance is akin to making a commitment of faith in Christ; the other party says that the gaze is akin to making Christ the Lord of one's life. In this arcane debate these teachers quite miss the point. This text does not speak of eternal salvation or of what a Hebrew person had to do to be saved forever before God. It certainly should not be used as a touch-point for the debate over "lordship salvation." The passage speaks plainly of physical healing from a critical disease. Health, not heaven, is the issue here. The people were redeemed already by blood and covenant and by Passover deliverance; the issue remained for each of them: How long may they continue to live this life? Those over twenty were already on a death course; those under twenty had an opportunity for a long life in the land. Many would die in the desert of the fiery venom of these snakes, but not all had to die. God would keep many alive if they would only do as he demanded.

What is distinctive in this essentially judgment text is the unusual symbol of God's grace that reaches all the way to the Savior. In the earlier judgments there was regularly the demonstration of the wrath of God, the prayer of Moses for help, and the repentance of the people. These acts would then usually lead to some lessening of the pain of the plague until the evil ebbed away. In this plague there is something that is truly different: there is a symbol of hope that is disgusting in nature but has healing properties that are most surprising. Here we find an amazing sense of God's presence in the most unlikely of places, the symbol of evil—a snake.

This was not magic but the dramatic provision of the Lord to demand personal responses from the people. Similar actions demanded of people are found elsewhere in the OT; an example is the story of leprous Naaman who was told to dip seven times in the Jordan to be cleansed (2 Kings 5:10). The healing of the afflicted people of Israel was not in the efficacy of the metal snake any more than the cleansing of Naaman was in the purging waters of the Jordan; the issue was a purposeful and deliberate response of faith in the mercy of the Lord. The improbability of a person being able to survive a deadly snake bite simply by looking at a metal image of a snake held high on a pole is seized on by our Lord to affirm an even greater imponderability: "Just as Moses lifted up the snake in the desert, so the Son of Man must be lifted up, that everyone who believes in him may have eternal life" (John 3:14–15).

The reader of John 3 is impressed with the interplay of judgment and salvation themes. This creative admixture lends itself splendidly to the interplay of serpents and deliverance. By the initiative of God, the curse becomes the basis for salvation. This is a paradox that spans the testaments.

No one reading this can shirk the sense of foreboding the snake conjures in most people. The snake reaches all the way back to the Garden, the unwelcome and cunning intruder (see the pun on "crafty" on Gen 3:1, compared with "naked" in 2:25). Yet it is principally to the Gospel of John that this text drives us.

The contemptible bread—relates to John 6:48–51.

The contemptible snake—relates to John 3:14.

In both there are portraits of the Savior Jesus. In some circles these days, it has fallen out of style to speak of biblical types. The abuse of typology in former generations, where every spiritual lesson one might derive from a text was declared to be a "type," has led to a gradual but sure reaction against typology of any kind. Yet the idea of typology is a factor of the text of Scripture, not an innovation of "creative" interpretation (see John Bright, *The Authority of the Old Testament* [Nashville: Abingdon, 1967], pp. 79–95).

If ever there were a less expected pairing of types, this would be it. The manna was an altogether gracious gift of God, which the people turned against with stomach revulsion. The snakes were an instrument of God's judgment because of the peoples' ingratitude and rebellious spirits; yet it was a metal copy of just such a snake that became the means for their deliverance.

The bread is a picture of Jesus; as the Bread of Heaven he is the proper nourisher of his people. The bronze snake is a picture of Jesus, who became sin for us as he hung on that awful tree. The manna had to be eaten. The snake had to be seen. The commands of Scripture are for doing. The manna was no good if left to rot. The metal snake would not avail if none looked at it. The manna and the snake are twin aspects of the grace of God.

Notes

5 בַּלֶּחֶם הַקְּלֹקֵל (*balleḥem haqqᵉlōqēl,* "contemptible, worthless bread") is rendered "miserable food" in the NIV. The adjective *qᵉlōqēl* is used only here in the Bible. It is derived from the verb *qālal* ("to be slight, trifling," which verb, incidentially, gives us our stem name "Qal"). The verb can refer to something that is light, inconsequential; it may also speak of cursing someone or something in the sense of to treat as of no value. This is the verb used by God in the promise to Abram at the beginning ("whoever curses you," Gen 12:3); now the people were cursing the food God had given.

8 In this verse only the word שָׂרָף (*śārāp̱,* "fiery [i.e., venomous] [serpent]") is used; compare *hannᵉḥāšîm haśśᵉrāp̱îm* ("the venomous snakes") in v.6 and *nᵉḥāš nᵉḥōšeṯ* ("bronze snake," a play on words) in v.9. The term *nāḥāš śārāp̱* is used in Deut 8:15 of the "venomous snakes" (collective) of the desert. G.J. Wenham (pp. 156–57) associates the making of a metal snake with a Midianite shrine near Timna in which a copper snake was found.

c. *The journey toward Moab and the Song of the Well*

21:10–20

10The Israelites moved on and camped at Oboth. 11Then they set out
from Oboth and camped in Iye Abarim, in the desert that faces Moab
toward the sunrise. 12From there they moved on and camped in the
Zered Valley. 13They set out from there and camped alongside the
Arnon, which is in the desert extending into Amorite territory. The Arnon
is the border of Moab, between Moab and the Amorites. 14That is why
the Book of the Wars of the LORD says:

"... Waheb in Suphah and the ravines,
  the Arnon 15and the slopes of the ravines
that lead to the site of Ar
  and lie along the border of Moab."

16From there they continued on to Beer, the well where the LORD said to
Moses, "Gather the people together and I will give them water."
17Then Israel sang this song:

> "Spring up, O well!
> Sing about it,
> 18 about the well that the princes dug,
> that the nobles of the people sank—
> the nobles with scepters and staffs."

Then they went from the desert to Mattanah, 19 from Mattanah to Nahaliel, from Nahaliel to Bamoth, 20 and from Bamoth to the valley in Moab where the top of Pisgah overlooks the wasteland.

10–12 At last the people are on the march; they skirt Edom and make their way to the Arnon (v.13), the wadi that serves as the border between the region of Moab and that of the Amorites; the Arnon flows west into the midpoint of the Dead Sea. Along the way the people make encampments at Oboth (v.10), Iye Abarim (v.11), and Zered Valley (v.12).

13–15 This portion of the itinerary leads to a quotation from a fragment of an ancient book termed "the Book of the Wars of the LORD" (compare the Book of Jashar in Josh 10:13; 2 Sam 1:18), which is mentioned only here in the OT. Not extant, this book was presumably an ancient collection of songs of war in praise of God (see commentary on 10:3 for music in war); the poem fragment attests to the variety of sources used by the author of the book. It also shows how distant we are from those days and the life they represent, for the song fragment is nearly unintelligible to us today. It seems merely to be a simple listing of place names and their relative placement. Some have attempted to emend this text rather drastically in order to produce a "spiritual song" in which the Lord plays a significant role (see Notes). Such reconstructions are intriguing and may be correct. Yet in biblical times one might well use song to set in the memory various places of encampment in the desert. Those who are training for war in the army of the Lord (if that is the intent of the title of this old fragment) might find that their lives would depend on knowing this ancient ditty. The reason for its inclusion here is based on the catchwords "Arnon" and "Moab."

16–18a The "Song of Places," as we may style the fragment in vv.14–15, leads to the "Song of the Well" in vv.17–18. The quest for water had been a constant problem during the desert experience (see Exod 17, Num 20). At this new promise of water from Yahweh, the people burst forth into the triumphant words of the "Song of the Well"—a dramatic departure from their earlier behavior! When the people came to a likely spot, the Lord instructed Moses to have a well dug. The place received the happy name "Beer," meaning "well" in Hebrew (*habbᵉʾēr*). Here come also happy words from the Lord: "Gather the people together and I will give them water" (v.16). Is it possible that this is the first time in the desert period that God has provided water apart from the complaint of the people and their subsequent rebellion? How fitting it is that this is a place of song!

The NIV rendering of the Song of the Well has much energy and enjoyment to it:

> Spring up, O well!
> Sing about it,
> About the well that the princes dug,
> that the nobles of the people sank—
> the nobles with scepters and staffs.

Quite possibly this song came from the same collection as the Song of Places, the Book of the Wars of the LORD (see v.14). It is possible to attempt to make a spiritual lesson from this song as well, particularly since the idea of salvation and wells and springs are so closely connected (see, e.g., Isa 12). But it seems more likely to me that this is a song one might sing in conjunction with the digging of a well! Instead of attempting to make some spiritual lesson from this brief song, it is possible that the song is the nearest we come in the Bible to "popular music." In this song there is a sense of the joy of knowing God even though the name of God is not mentioned. The association of princes and nobles with the digging of a well is likely a use of "power language" to ensure that the well will last a lengthy period.

18b–20 From Beer the people journey ever onward, finally coming to the valley of Moab where Pisgah is such a fine lookout spot to spy out the land of Canaan. Only later (Deut 34:1) do we associate this peak with Moses' final moments.

Notes

---

14 C.L. Christensen ("Num. 21:14–15 and the Book of the Wars of Yahweh," CBQ 36 [1974]: 359–60) translates the poem as follows:

> Yahweh came in a whirlwind;
>   He came to the branch wadis of the Arnon
>   He marched through the wadis;
>   He marched, he turned aside to the seat of Ar.
>   He leaned toward the border of Moab.

This translation involves the following emendations: (1) The term usually translated as a place name, "Waheb" (*wāhēḇ*, v.14), is emended to "Yahweh" (*yhwh*); (2) the definite direct object marker (*'eṯ*) is emended to the verb "he came" (*'āṯāh*) here and in the next colon; (3) the supposed place name "Suphah" (*bᵉsûp̄āh*) is translated as "whirlwind" (as in Ps 83:15; Hos 8:7; Amos 1:14; Nah 1:3 et al.); (4) the term translated "slopes" (*wᵉ'ešeḏ*, v.15) is emended to "he marched" (*'āšar*), as is the relative pronoun "that" (*'ᵃšer*) in the next colon. Christensen's approach is viewed as quite attractive by G.J. Wenham (pp. 159–60) but as undemonstrable because of the numerous conjectures involved. Any perusal of the MT of these two verses, however, shows that this little fragment has presented numerous problems to interpreters through the ages. This fragment is a text-critical minefield.

---

d. *The defeat of Sihon of Heshbon*

21:21–31

[21]Israel sent messengers to say to Sihon king of the Amorites:

[22]"Let us pass through your country. We will not turn aside into
any field or vineyard, or drink water from any well. We will travel
along the king's highway until we have passed through your
territory."

[23]But Sihon would not let Israel pass through his territory. He
mustered his entire army and marched out into the desert against Israel.
When he reached Jahaz, he fought with Israel. [24]Israel, however, put

him to the sword and took over his land from the Arnon to the Jabbok, but only as far as the Ammonites, because their border was fortified.
25 Israel captured all the cities of the Amorites and occupied them, including Heshbon and all its surrounding settlements. 26 Heshbon was the city of Sihon king of the Amorites, who had fought against the former king of Moab and had taken from him all his land as far as the Arnon.
27 That is why the poets say:

"Come to Heshbon and let it be rebuilt;
let Sihon's city be restored.

28 "Fire went out from Heshbon,
a blaze from the city of Sihon.
It consumed Ar of Moab,
the citizens of Arnon's heights.
29 Woe to you, O Moab!
You are destroyed, O people of Chemosh!
He has given up his sons as fugitives
and his daughters as captives
to Sihon king of the Amorites.

30 "But we have overthrown them;
Heshbon is destroyed all the way to Dibon.
We have demolished them as far as Nophah,
which extends to Medeba."

31 So Israel settled in the land of the Amorites.

The victories over Sihon and Og are celebrated throughout Israel's history, even to our own day. These are the true beginning of victories. The defeat of Arad was a nuisance issue. Sihon and Og represented reputable opponents; their land became part of the inheritance of the tribes of Israel. There is a sense in which the area of Transjordan is somewhat touchy; we are ambivalent about these territories. They are a part of the promise; yet they are not the heart of the land. But they were the first of victories, a note of assurance from God that the real victories were still to come (see Notes).

21–23 The Amorites, unlike the Edomites, were not related to the Israelites. But as in the case of their approach to Edom (20:14–19), Israel first requested a right of passage. The language of the request (v.22) is very similar to that Israel had made of Edom. And the response of Sihon, king of the Amorites, was the same as that of Edom—a show of force to block their path (v.23).

24–26 When Sihon tried to meet Israel with a show of force, he suffered an overwhelming defeat (v.24). The land of the Amorites was in Transjordan, extending from the Arnon River at the midpoint of the Dead Sea to the Jabok River (v.24), which flows into the Jordan River some twenty-four miles north of the Dead Sea. Among Israel's conquests were the cities of Heshbon and its dependent settlements (v.25). Heshbon originally had been a Moabite territory (see vv.25–30); Israel, however, had wrested it from Sihon and the Amorite conquerors. It was this victory that cast such a pale of fear into the Moabites (see 22:2–3). The syllogism was clear: Sihon had defeated Moab; Israel now defeated Sihon; Moab was next, and their defeat seemed imminent. Thus Balak king of Moab wished to transfer the battle arena from the field of men to the realm of the gods (see on 22:5–7).

27–30 Numbers 21 is unusual in its inclusion of three short songs. Possibly each of the three (vv.14–15, 17–18, and 27–30) was included in the Book of the Wars of the LORD (see v.14). This third song in the chapter was originally an Amorite taunt song celebrating their earlier victory over Moab (v.29); this is what we may understand to be the meaning of the phrase "why the poets say" (v.27). Heshbon, the capital city of Sihon, had been wrested by the Amorites from a former Moabite king, perhaps Zippor, the father of Balak (see 22:2). A.H. van Zyl (*The Moabites, "Praetoria Oriental Series,"* vol. 3, ed. A. van Selms [Leiden: E.J. Brill, 1960], pp. 7–10) observes that taunt songs were regularly used in warfare. If this was a song originally used by the Amorites against the Moabites, whom they had recently conquered, its reuse by Israel must have been particularly galling to Moab and the principal reason for Moab's call for Balaam.

In any taunt song such as this, there is more at stake than the reputation of the armies or the kings who participate in the battle. Ultimately, the outcome of wars in the ancient Near East was evaluated in terms of victories and defeats of respective gods. We observe, for example, the dramatic story in 1 Kings 20 of the first battle between Ben Hadad of Syria and Ahab of Israel. When Israel was the victor in this battle, the counselors of Ben Hadad instructed him on ways to improve his position for the next year's encounter (1 Kings 20:23–25). Their first line of advice was to fight the next battle in a plain rather than in the hills. It was evident to them that the victory of Israel had been won because "their gods are gods of the hills" (v.23). Presumably, they reasoned, if we move the battle to a turf that Israel's "gods" did not control, then the battle would be won for the Syrians (whose gods are powerful on level plains!).

In the Taunt Song of Heshbon, it was not just the people of Moab who had been defeated by Sihon in the earlier engagement; it was their god Chemosh as well (v.29). But now a new God had come on the scene. His name was Yahweh, and his power was not limited by geography at all!

Since Israel had defeated the nation that had been the victor over Moab, the likelihood was that Moab would fair poorly in battle against Israel. Perhaps this "Song of Heshbon" was also added to the Book of the Wars of the LORD (v.14). The victory of Israel over this nation gave them a new song to sing in irony and triumph. Verse 30 of the Song of Heshbon must have sent Moab reeling (see Notes).

31 The concluding verse of this section is a dramatic mark of accomplishment. After forty years of sojourn in the Desert of Sinai, now, at last, the people had entered the land of the Amorites—the land that would become theirs.

Notes

21 J. van Seters has argued strongly against the historical validity of the account of Israel's conquest of these Transjordan kingdoms in his article "The Conquest of Sihon's Kingdom: A Literary Examination" (JBL 91 [1972]: 182–97). He argues that the editor-redactor of Num 21 has borrowed heavily from the (late) Deuteronomist tradition (see Deut 2:26–37 and Judg 11:19–26). His rather negative assessment is countered by John R. Bartlett in his rejoinder "The Conquest of Sihon's Kingdom: A Literary Re-Examination" (JBL 97 [1978]: 347–51). Bartlett deals with each of Van Seter's points seriatim and concludes that it is more likely that the Deuteronomy passage is dependent on the text of Numbers, "for Deuteronomy removes the inconsistencies and clarifies the point left obscure in Numbers" (p. 351). See also John R. Bartlett, "Sihon and Og, Kings of the Amorites," VetTest 20 (1970): 257–77, for a critical analysis of the biblical representation of these two kings and their kingdoms in the biblical traditions.

30 Critical scholars have suggested numerous other settings for this song, other than that presented in this chapter. Martin Noth, for example, relates the victory song of Num 21 to the events of 32:28–36, the story of Gad's victory in Transjordan (*The Old Testament World*, tr. Victor I. Gruhn [Philadelphia: Fortress, 1966], p. 75). Earlier, Bruno Baentsch (*Exodus-Leviticus-Numeri*, Handkommentar zum Alten Testament, ed. W. Nowack [Göttingen: Vandenhoeck and Ruprecht, 1903], p. 584) held that the song refers to the defeat of Mesha, king of Moab, by Omri, king of Israel.

31 The term "Amorite" is regarded by J. van Seters as an ideological and rhetorical term that was superimposed by Israel's later thought rather than reflecting the historical situation in the land. He states that the term moves in the direction of representing "super-human evil" ("The Terms 'Amorite' and 'Hittite' in the Old Testament," VetTest 22 [1972]: 64–81). Without accepting his very critical evaluation of the historicity of the text of Num 21, it is possible to agree that van Seters points in a constructive direction when he speaks of the connotation of this term. He says, "One must be very skeptical about attributing any historicity to the conquest of the Amorite kingdoms of Sihon and Og in Transjordan. The accounts serve primarily as etiologies legitimizing Israel's territorial claims east of the Jordan" (ibid., p. 81). The "Amorites" were a symbol of evil whom Israel now rightly had come to dispossess.

---

e. *Israel's defeat of Og of Bashan*

21:32–22:1

32 After Moses had sent spies to Jazer, the Israelites captured its surrounding settlements and drove out the Amorites who were there. 33 Then they turned and went up along the road toward Bashan, and Og king of Bashan and his whole army marched out to meet them in battle at Edrei.

34 The LORD said to Moses, "Do not be afraid of him, for I have handed him over to you, with his whole army and his land. Do to him what you did to Sihon king of the Amorites, who reigned in Heshbon."

35 So they struck him down, together with his sons and his whole army, leaving them no survivors. And they took possession of his land.

22:1 Then the Israelites traveled to the plains of Moab and camped along the Jordan across from Jericho.

32–35 The region of this king and his people was east of the Sea of Galilee. By defeating Og, Israel was now victor of Transjordan from the region of Moab to the heights of Bashan in the vicinity of Mount Hermon. The victories over Sihon and Og were matters for singing (Pss 135:11; 136:19–20) and regular parts of the commemoration of the works of the Lord in the Passover celebration.

Significantly, this section begins with a notice that Moses sent spies to scout out the land before he began his attack on the region of Bashan (v.32). These spies must have done as they were instructed, in contrast to the rebellious spies of chapters 13–14. It is also notable that the battle was joined with the army of Og only after the word of the Lord had come to Moses assuring him of a divine victory (vv.33–34). This is to be the pattern of holy war, an obedient people following the sure word of their great God. The victory was complete because God's ways were followed (v.35).

22:1 This section ends in 22:1 with the statement of the journey of Israel to the plains of Moab and their subsequent encampment near the Jordan River across from the city of Jericho. They are now on the lip of the land; Canaan—God's gift—is in view. Soon the land will be theirs. But this verse also sets the stage for one of the most remarkable stories in the Bible: the dramatic encounter of Balaam the pagan mantic with the God of Israel (22:2–24:25).

Thus chapter 21 of Numbers presents a remarkable shift in the fortunes of the people. They are still rebellious (and will continue to rebel—see ch. 25); but they are now on a victory march, not fearful of battle against the people of the land. At least they have learned this lesson from their parents: When God is for us, what can man do against us? (cf. Ps 118:6).

f. *Balak and Balaam (22:2–41)*

One thing the misplaced verse number does at the beginning of chapter 22 is to help us read the story of Balak and Balaam in the context of the emerging power and nascent victories of Israel. The story of Balaam's dramatic encounter with the Lord is of a piece. It stands by itself as a remarkable unit of great writing. Even though Documentary scholars believe these three chapters afford them something of a field day in putative source analysis (see Notes), nonetheless the story reads as a unified whole; and it stands alone on its own merit.

(1) *The "call" of Balaam*

22:2–20

2 Now Balak son of Zippor saw all that Israel had done to the Amorites,
3 and Moab was terrified because there were so many people. Indeed, Moab was filled with dread because of the Israelites.

4 The Moabites said to the elders of Midian, "This horde is going to lick up everything around us, as an ox licks up the grass of the field."

So Balak son of Zippor, who was king of Moab at that time,
5 sent messengers to summon Balaam son of Beor, who was at Pethor, near the River, in his native land. Balak said:

> "A people has come out of Egypt; they cover the face of the land and have settled next to me.
> 6 Now come and put a curse on these people, because they are too powerful for me. Perhaps then I will be able to defeat them and drive them out of the country. For I know that those you bless are blessed, and those you curse are cursed."

7 The elders of Moab and Midian left, taking with them the fee for divination. When they came to Balaam, they told him what Balak had said.

8 "Spend the night here," Balaam said to them, "and I will bring you back the answer the LORD gives me." So the Moabite princes stayed with him.

9 God came to Balaam and asked, "Who are these men with you?"

10 Balaam said to God, "Balak son of Zippor, king of Moab, sent me this message:
11 'A people that has come out of Egypt covers the face of the land. Now come and put a curse on them for me. Perhaps then I will be able to fight them and drive them away.' "

12 But God said to Balaam, "Do not go with them. You must not put a curse on those people, because they are blessed."

[13]The next morning Balaam got up and said to Balak's princes, "Go back to your own country, for the LORD has refused to let me go with you."

[14]So the Moabite princes returned to Balak and said, "Balaam refused to come with us."

[15]Then Balak sent other princes, more numerous and more distinguished than the first. [16]They came to Balaam and said:

> "This is what Balak son of Zippor says: Do not let anything keep you from coming to me, [17]because I will reward you handsomely and do whatever you say. Come and put a curse on these people for me."

[18]But Balaam answered them, "Even if Balak gave me his palace filled with silver and gold, I could not do anything great or small to go beyond the command of the LORD my God. [19]Now stay here tonight as the others did, and I will find out what else the LORD will tell me."

[20]That night God came to Balaam and said, "Since these men have come to summon you, go with them, but do only what I tell you."

2–3 The story of Balaam begins with the gut-wrenching fear of Balak son of Zippor, the king of Moab. With the vast army of Israel now encamped on the edge of his territory, he feared the very worst. The text uses the verb *gûr* to describe his fear ("was terrified," v.3), intensified by the adverb *me'ōḏ* ("very"). This is then brought into even sharper relief by the strong term of fear, *qûṣ* ("to feel a sickening dread"; NIV, "filled with dread"). Rabbi Hirsch explains that this verb is a word that causes such violent emotion within that it may provoke one to vomit: "All that they had became distasteful, despicable, yea repulsive at the thought of the children of Israel" (p. 390; cf. Marcus Jastrow, *A Dictionary of the Targumim, the Talmud Babli and Yerushalmi, and the Midrashic Literature*, 2 vols. [New York: Pardes, 1950], p. 1339).

Balak's fear was intensified because of the victories that Israel had won over his northern enemy neighbors (see Num 21). A new, stronger enemy was now present, before whom Balak and his people seemed to be powerless. Balak was not aware that Israel had no designs on the land of Moab. As the Lord was about to give Canaan to Israel, so the Moabite land was a gift of the Lord to Moab. In fact, the Lord had prohibited Israel any attack on the territorial integrity of Moab in their wars of conquest (Deut 2:9). Israel under God's blessing had divine limits on it. God is sovereign in all of Israel's actions. Yet there was a reason for the fear of Moab: the events of the Exodus salvation of Israel were designed by the Lord to provoke fear in all nations (see Deut 2:25). The defeat of the Amorite kings to the north of Moab, Sihon and Og (21:21–35; cf. Deut 2:26–3:11), put Moab in an especially difficult position. The taunt song of 21:27–30 must have been particularly galling to Moab (see above).

4 The proverbial figure of an ox licking the grass is particularly fitting for a pastoral people. Balak knew how quickly the fragile grasses of the lands of Moab could be eaten by large beasts. The image of Israel as an ox is an emphatic symbol of her strength and power. The association of Moab to the Midianites in this verse is more significant than we might first think. It will be another plot developed by Midianite collusion with Moab that will finally bring great disaster on Israel (ch. 25, the apostasy of Israel at Baal Peor).

5–7 Since Balak believed that there was no military means available to withstand the forces of Israel, he sought to battle Israel on the level of pagan divination. He sent for a diviner with an international reputation, Balaam son of Beor (v.5)—a drastic move to use the supernatural means of the effective curse. This was predicated on the belief in the ancient world of the power in the spoken word. The diviner with the most remarkable reputation of the day was Balaam.

Balaam is the pagan counterpart to Moses the man of God. The recovery of prophetic texts of Balaam in Aramaic from the sixth century at Deir-'Allah in Jordan shows how very famous this man was in the ancient Near East, even centuries after his death. See Jacob Hoftijzer, "The Prophet Balaam in a 6th-Century Aramaic Inscription," BA 39, 1 (March 1976): 11–17. The fact that the prophecy was written on a wall indicates that it was an important historical example of the oracles of this diviner that might be preserved for posterity. Stephen A. Kaufman observes that the texts of these inscriptions "remain enticingly obscure" and that perhaps we need the powers of a Balaam to help banish the darkness ("Review Article: The Aramaic Texts from Deir 'Alla," BASOR 239 [Summer 1980]: 71–74).

Balaam was an internationally known prophet, a diviner expert in examining the entrails of animals and observing natural phenomena to determine the will of the gods. He thought that the Lord God of Israel was like any other deity whom he imagined he might manipulate by mantic acts. But from the early part of the narrative, when he first encounters the true God in visions, and in the humorous narrative of the journey on the donkey, Balaam begins to learn what for him was a strange, bizarre, even incomprehensible lesson: An encounter with the God of reality was fundamentally different than anything he had ever known.

Verse 5 presents several problems of the interpretation of words. The name "Balaam" is an example of a deliberate corruption of names by the Hebrew scribes. As in the case of the name Jezebel, the scribes want us not to know the (presumably) honorable name by which this character was first known but only the dishonorable name they give him as his nickname: Balaam, the "devourer of the people" (see Notes).

The letter of Balak to Balaam indicates the intent he had: to bring a curse on a people who were under a blessing of a god. This story thus takes us into the mysterious world of blessing and cursing in the ancient Near East. It was believed that some men were agents of the gods who could utter curses or blessings that would bind the will of the gods to these declarations. Since Israel seemed to Moab to be too formidable a force to attack on the battlefield, the decision—prompted by Balak's Midianite advisors—was to attack them on a spiritual level. If their blessing could be destroyed, then they would no longer be a threat.

8–11 The language of v.8 and the conversation that Balaam has with the Lord in this section have led many readers to believe that Balaam was a believer in Yahweh, the God of Israel. The most significant phrasing along this line comes in the words of v.18: "the LORD my God." It seems best, however, based on the subsequent narrative, to take Balaam's words as examples of braggadocio. Balaam is universally condemned in the Scripture for moral, ethical, and religious faults (see 31:8, 16; Deut 23:3–6; Josh 13:22; 24:9–10; Judg 11:23–25; Neh 13:1–3; Mic 6:5; 2 Peter 2:15–16; Jude 11; Rev 2:14).

The character of Balaam continues to be a conundrum in biblical study. From the early Fathers to the most recent interpreters, many have argued that he was a good prophet who went bad or a bad prophet who attempted to go right. The classic study of his person by Bishop Joseph Butler concluded: "So that the object we have now before us is the most astonishing in the world: a very wicked man, under a deep sense of God and religion, persisting still in his wickedness, and preferring the wages of unrighteousness, even when he had before him a lively view of death. . . . Good God, what inconsistency, what perplexity is here!" ("Upon the Character of Balaam," 2:80; see Notes).

Rather than see Balaam as a true believer caught up in greed, it is better to understand that he was a sorcerer, more specifically, a *bārû* diviner (see Notes on v.8), for whom the God of Israel was just another deity he might manipulate. Daiches (see bibliography in Notes) argues that the considerable emphasis on magical elements in these chapters is best explained by understanding Balaam as a *bārû* diviner of the Mesopotamian type (see esp. v.7, "the fees for divination"; Josh 13:22 speaks of Balaam as "the soothsayer" [*haqqôsēm;* NIV, "who practiced divination"). He finds of special interest the descriptions in v.41, the preparatory sacrifice; 23:1–2, the offering of seven bulls and seven rams on seven altars; 23:2, the sacrifices brought by both the diviner and the person for whom he divines; 23:3, the expression of Balak as "the owner of the sacrifice," standing by his offering; 23:3, the difficult word *šep̱î*, usually "barren height," may instead be a term describing the manner of his mantic acts, "quietly" or "step by step." Albright regarded the researches of Daiches as valid and impressive in the main ("Oracles," p. 231); they seem to point to the correct view.

Balaam is not a good prophet who went bad or a bad prophet trying to be good. He is altogether outside Israel's prophetic tradition. He is a pagan, foreign national whose mantic acts center on animal divination, including the dissection of animal livers, the movement of animals, and the flight of birds. He believed that he had a way with the gods, a hold on them. To him Yahweh was not the Lord of heaven but just another deity whom he might manipulate. He was in for the surprise of his life.

The narrator of this chapter shows his strong aversion to the pagan prophet Balaam by the interchange of the name for God (Yahweh, "the LORD") in Balaam's mouth (v.8) by the term "God" as the narrator speaks of him (v.9). By this subtle interchange, the narrator demonstrates his distance from Balaam's outrageous claims. That God did speak to Balaam is not to be denied; it is just that Balaam did not yet realize that the God of Israel was not like the supposed deities of his usual machinations.

12–20 The words of v.12 reveal the nature of the crisis. Israel was under the blessing of the Lord as the heritage of the Abrahamic covenant (Gen 12:1–3). Balaam was being sought by Balak to bring Israel under a divine curse; this God would not allow, for Israel was "blessed." Moreover, one who would attempt to curse Israel would bring himself under God's curse (cf. Gen 12:3). The story of Balaam is thus an example of the folly of attempting to destroy the eternal blessing of the people of the Lord.

The first words of God to Balaam are a prohibition for him to accompany the emissaries of Balak (v.12). But when these emissaries returned to Balak, he refused to listen to their report of Balaam's refusal to return with them. He sent grander and nobler representatives, with greater and finer promises of gifts for this mantic to come with them (v.15). Balaam first says that nothing can change his mind (v.18). Then in a dream he is given permission to go with them (v.20).

There appears to be a contradiction in the permission God grants Balaam in v.20 with the prohibition he had given earlier (v.12) and the anger of the Lord that was displayed against Balaam on his journey (v.22). The difficulty is best seen as lying in the contrary character of Balaam rather than in some fickle flaw in the character of God. God first had forbidden him to go to Moab to curse Israel; then God allowed Balaam to go to Moab, but only as he would speak at the direction of the Lord. Balaam's real intentions, however, were known to the Lord, and hence by his severe displeasure he confronted the pagan mantic on the road.

Notes

2 The story of Balaam the pagan mantic has elicited a voluminous literature. A list of some of the more significant articles, essays, and monographs follows. References to these various sources in the following notes will be abbreviated. For further information, see the following:

Ronald B. Allen, "The Theology of the Balaam Oracles," in John S. Feinberg and Paul D. Feinberg, edd., *Tradition and Testament: Essays in Honor of Charles Lee Feinberg* (Chicago: Moody, 1981), pp. 79–119.

William Foxwell Albright, "The Home of Balaam," JAOS 35 (1915): 386–90.

______, "The Oracles of Balaam," JBL 43 (1944): 207–33.

Julius A. Bewer, "The Literary Problems of the Balaam Story in Numbers, Chapters 22–24," AJT 9 (1905): 238–62.

James Black, "A Discharge for Balaam," *Rogues of the Bible* (New York: Harper & Brothers, 1930), pp. 59–79.

Eric Burrows, *The Oracles of Jacob and Balaam*, "The Bellarmine Series," ed. Edmund F. Sutcliffe (London: Burns Otes & Washbourne, 1938).

Joseph Butler, "Upon the Character of Balaam," *The Works of the Right Reverend Father in God Joseph Butler, D.C.L., Late Lord Bishop of Durham*, 2 vols. (Oxford: At the University Press, 1850), 2:74–86.

J. Coppens, "Les oracles de Biléam: Leur origine littéraire et leur portée prophétique," *Mélanges Eugène Tisserant*, vol. 1, *Écriture Sainte-Ancien Orient*, "Studi e Testi," 231 (Città del Vaticano: Biblioteca Apostolica Vaticanna, 1964), pp. 67–80.

Samuel Cox, "Balaam: An Exposition and a Study," Exp 2d series, 5 (1883): 1–21, 120–44, 199–210, 245–58, 341–52, 402–25; 6 (1883): 1–25. Later published in book form (London: Kegan, Paul Trench, & Co., 1884).

______, "Balaam's Ass. Numbers xxii. 28–30," Exp 1st series, 8 (1871): 397–409.

Samuel Daiches, "Balaam—A Babylonian *bārū*," *Assyrische und Archaeologische Studien: H.V. Hilprecht gewidmet* (Leipzig, 1909), pp. 60–70.

H. Eising, "Balaams Eselin," *Bibel und Kirche* 13 (1958): 45–46.

Otto Eissfeldt, "Die Komposition der Bileam-Erzählung," ZAW 57 (1939): 212–41.

______, "Sinai-Erzählung und Bileam-Sprüche," HUCA 32 (1961): 179–90.

F.W. Farrar, "Balaam's Ass," Exp 1st series, 1 (1975): 366–79.

R. Frieling, "Bileam (Stern-Weissagung im Alten Testament)," *Christengemeinschaft* 6 (1930): 299–303.

J. Halévy, "Patrie de Balaam," *Revue Sémitique* 2 (1894): 201–9.

E.W. Hengstenberg, *Die Geschichte Bileams und seine Weissagungen* (Berlin: Ludwig Dehmigte, 1842). Eng. tr. *A Dissertation of the History and Prophecies of Balaam*, tr. J.E. Ryland (Edinburgh: T. & T. Clark, 1848).

A. van Hoonacker, "Quelques observations critiques sur les récits concernant Bileam," *Le Muséon* 7 (1888): 61–76.

René Largement, "Les oracles de Biléam et la mantique suméro-accadienne," *École des Langues Orientales Anciennes de l'Institute Catholique de Paris: Mémorial du Cinquante-*

naire 1914–1964 (Paris: Bloud & Bay, Travaux de l'Institute Catholique de Paris, 1964), pp. 37–50.

Max Löhr, "Bileam, Num. 22, 2–24, 25," *Archiv für Orient-Forschung* 4 (1927): 85–89.

J. Mauchline, "The Balaam-Balak Songs and Saga," *Presentation Volume to William Barron Stevenson,* "Studia Semitica et Orientalia," 2 (Glasgow: Glasgow University Oriental Society, 1945), pp. 73–94.

Sigmund Mowinckel, "Der Ursprung der Bil'amsage," ZAW 48 (1930): 233–71.

Ladislas Martin von Pákozdy, "Theologische Redaktionsarbeit in der Bileam-Perikope (Num 22–24)," *Von Ugarit Nach Qumran,* ed. Otto Eissfeldt (Berlin: Verlag Alfred Töplemann, 1958), pp. 161–76.

Gerhard von Rad, "Die Bileam perikope, 4. Mose 22 bis 24," *Deutches Pfarrenblatt* 40 (1936): 52–53.

R.D.C. Robbins, "The Character and Prophecies of Balaam—Numbers xxii–xxiv," BS 3 (1946): 347–78, 699–743.

Calvin G. Seerveld, *Balaam's Apocalyptic Prophecies: A Study in Reading Scripture* (Toronto: Wedge Publishing Foundation, 1980).

George Adam Smith, "The Experience of Balaam as Symbolic of the Origins of Prophecy," Exp 8th series, 5 (1913): 1–11.

Zdeněk Soušek, "Bileam und seine Eselin: Exegetischtheologische Bemerkungun zu Num. 22," *Communio Viatorum* 10 (1967): 183–86.

D.M. Stanley, "Balaam's Ass; or a Problem in New Testament Hermeneutics," CBQ 20 (1958): 50–56.

Merrill F. Unger, "Balaam—Heathen Diviner or a Prophet of the Lord?" *Our Hope* 41 (1949): 461–66.

Géza Vermes, "Deux Traditions sur Balaam," *Cahiers Sionens* 9 (1955): 289–302.

A.S. Yahuda, "The Name of Balaam's Homeland," JBL 44 (1945): 547–51.

The text of Numbers 22 is used by some critical scholars as a locus to test their approaches to the source analysis of the Bible. Edelkoort, for example, speaks of the Balaam story as the result of "three threads promiscuously twisted" (p. 170); he concludes that the final redaction did not come before the time of 2 Isaiah, after c. 500 B.C. (p. 21). Von Pákozdy remarks on the masterful skill of the final redactor who, "forming so artfully of his ancient and written tradition, and in the spirit of the prophetic religion, was able to create such a unity out of diverse theological concepts" ("Theological Redactionsarbeit," p. 176). Our approach will presume a unified whole in the text as it stands. Questions of the origin of these chapters are highly interesting, but the answers appear to be unusually subjective.

5 Some critical scholars argue that Balaam and Bela (Gen 36:32) are confused in the Scriptures, as they are both called "the son of Beor" (so Mowinckel, "Der Ursprung der Bil'amsage," p. 237). However, it was Albright who argued most strongly that such an association cannot be maintained ("The Oracles of Balaam," p. 231). Albright suggests that the original name of Balaam might have been something such as *Yabil-'ammu* (an Amorite name from the thirteenth-century B.C. made of an imperfect + a divine name), a name indicating "the [divine] uncle brings forth" (ibid., p. 232). But the Hebrew connotation, "The devourer of the people," is an intentional change, not unlike the change of the original name of Jezebel from something like "My divine father is prince" to "un-exalted." The process in this last name involves the dropping of the letter beth; an original *'ᵃḇîzeḇel* became the corrupted form *'îzeḇel* (see Leah Bronner, *The Stories of Elijah and Elisha as Polemics Against Baal Worship* [Leiden: E.J. Brill, 1968], pp. 9–10); the element *'î* is the Phoenician negation.

פְּתוֹרָה (*pᵉṯôrāh,* "at Pethor") is now to be identified as a reference to the city Pitru (Pi-it-ru) of the Assyrian texts, a city located on the river Sagur, near its junction with the Euphrates (indicated by the words "the River" in this verse). Pitru is mentioned by Shalmaneser III (c. 859–824 B.C.) in the annalistic report of 853 B.C. L. Yaure argues that this term should be translated, not as a place name, but as a descriptive nomen agentis, "the interpreter" ("Elymas–Nehelamite–Pethor," JBL 79 [1960]: 297–314).

בְּנֵי־עַמּוֹ (*b^e^nê-ʿammô,* "in his native land") is the most difficult of the phrases to identify in this verse. The NIV has rephrased the traditional understanding, "in the land of the sons of his people" (as in the LXX). Albright, in an article published in 1950 describing an inscription on a statue of King Idrimi of Alalakh (c. 1480–1450 B.C.), believes he found the solution to this phrase as a place name ("Some Important Recent Discoveries: Alphabetic Origins and the Idrimi Statue," BASOR 118 [1950]: 11–20). He finds that this king of Alalakh ruled also over three lands: Mukishkhe, Ni', and ʿAmau, the last being the place intended by our text: the land of ʿAmau, the region of the Sājûr Valley between Aleppo and Carchemish. This translation has been accepted by the NEB, JB, and La Sainte Bible/Segond.

The resultant translation of v.5 would be:

> So he sent messengers to Balaam the son of Beor,
> to Pethor [Pitru], which is near the River [Euphrates]
> in the land of the sons of ʿAmau.

These several data all suggest that Balaam was a North-Syrian from the northern Euphrates valley, near the Haran of the patriarchal stories; this accords remarkably well with the words of his opening bicola (23:7a):

> From Aram Balak has brought me,
> Moab's king from the mountains of the east.

6 Three times in this verse Balak uses forms of the Hebrew verb אָרַר (*'ārar,* "to curse," "to bind with a curse"). This verb is cognate to the Akkadian *'araru* A ("to curse," or in weaker contexts, "to treat with disrespect"; CAD I, "A" Part II, 234–36). One example of this word in an Akkadian text illustrates its foreboding connotation:

> May the great gods of heaven and nether world curse him [*li-ru-ru (su)*], his descendants, his land, his soldiers, his people, and his army with a baleful curse; may Enlil with his unalterable utterance curse him [*li-ru-ur-su-ma*] with these curses so that they speedily affect him. (CAD, I, "A" Part II, 235)

This example has the element of the inflexible nature of a curse once uttered. There is a sense in which the curse may be said to be "bound" on one. The Hebrew cognate *'ārar* seems to be associated with effective force as well. This is certainly true when God is the actor or the subject of the verb (see Gen 3:14, "cursed [*'ārûr*] are you more than all cattle"; Gen 12:3, "I will curse [*'ā'ōr*]").

Paul van Imschoot writes:

> The efficacy of the word is attributed either to the formula itself—this is the case of the magic formulas of all countries and times—or to the power of him who says it; also then it may be considered as capable of constraining the gods and remains in the sphere of magic. . . . In Israel, without doubt, the use of magic formulas has existed at all times among the lower classes, but has been reproved by the official religion (Ex 22:17; Lev 20:6.27; Dt 18:9–13; I Sm 15:23; 28:3; Mi 5:11; Jer 27:9; Ez 13:18–20; Mal 3:5). The efficacy of curses and of blessings is derived from Yahweh (Prv 3:33; Sir 4:6; Gn 12:3; Nm 22:6; 23:8); the curse can be obstructed (Nm 22:22ff.), weakened (Prv 26:2), or changed into a blessing by Yahweh (Dt 23:6); it is ordinarily pronounced in the form of a prayer (Jer 15:15; 18:19–23; Ps 109, etc.). (*Theology of the Old Testament,* tr. Kathryn Sullivan and Fidelis Buck [Tournai: Desclee & Co., 1965], 1:189–90)

U. Cassuto also observes the ancient belief in the power of the spoken curse to effect the will of gods on the lives and destinies of the peoples:

> In the ancient East there was current the belief, based on the concept of the magic power of the spoken word, that blessings and curses, and particularly curses, once uttered, act automatically and are fulfilled of their own accord, as it were, unless

another force opposes and annuls them. (*A Commentary on the Book of Genesis*, tr. Israel Abrahams, 2 vols. [Jerusalem: Magnes Press, The Hebrew University, 1961, 1964], 2:155)

But Cassuto goes on to explain that in the true religion of Israel such ideas are intolerable:

The sublime religion of Israel cannot acquiesce in such a conception. In the view of Israel's Torah, it is impossible to imagine that a man's word should have the power to effect anything without God's will, for only from the Lord do evil and good issue. Human blessings, are, according to the Torah, no more than wishes and prayers that God may be willing to do this or that. So, too, human imprecations, in so far as they are not iniquitous, are, in the ultimate analysis, but prayers that God may act in a given way. (Ibid., 2:156)

8 On the meaning of *bārû,* Noordtzij (p. 199) says:

The *baru* belongs to the priestly class, and his speciality is "seeing" what will happen on the basis of phenomena that escape the common person, but are found e.g., in the liver of a ritually slaughtered animal, or in the configuration of drops of oil on water, or in the stars, or in the shape of the clouds. Such *barus* were believed to be able to influence the will of the gods because of their secret knowledge and mysterious manipulations, and to force the gods to do, or not to do, a given thing.

The most whimsical approach to the complex problem of the character of Balaam was taken by James Black (*Rogues of the Bible*, pp. 59–79). He argued that the good Balaam has been confused by "Jewish prejudice in the Bible" with a wicked man of the same name; one was a true worshiper of the Lord, and the other was a soothsayer or oracle-monger of the Midianites. It is the duty of Christian people "to rehabilitate the true Balaam and to grant him a discharge from the world's calumnies"! Balaam for him was a "great white soul who loved the will of God to his own worldly loss" (p. 79); but Jewish prejudice against seeing a Gentile believer in the Lord led them deliberately to confuse the textual witness to his character.

---

(2) *The donkey story*

22:21–41

21 Balaam got up in the morning, saddled his donkey and went with the princes of Moab. 22 But God was very angry when he went, and the angel of the LORD stood in the road to oppose him. Balaam was riding on his donkey, and his two servants were with him. 23 When the donkey saw the angel of the LORD standing in the road with a drawn sword in his hand, she turned off the road into a field. Balaam beat her to get her back on the road.

24 Then the angel of the LORD stood in a narrow path between two vineyards, with walls on both sides. 25 When the donkey saw the angel of the LORD, she pressed close to the wall, crushing Balaam's foot against it. So he beat her again.

26 Then the angel of the LORD moved on ahead and stood in a narrow place where there was no room to turn, either to the right or to the left. 27 When the donkey saw the angel of the LORD, she lay down under Balaam, and he was angry and beat her with his staff. 28 Then the LORD opened the donkey's mouth, and she said to Balaam, "What have I done to you to make you beat me these three times?"

29 Balaam answered the donkey, "You have made a fool of me! If I had a sword in my hand, I would kill you right now."

30 The donkey said to Balaam, "Am I not your own donkey, which you have always ridden, to this day? Have I been in the habit of doing this to you?"

"No," he said.

> [31]Then the LORD opened Balaam's eyes, and he saw the angel of the LORD standing in the road with his sword drawn. So he bowed low and fell facedown.
>
> [32]The angel of the LORD asked him, "Why have you beaten your donkey these three times? I have come here to oppose you because your path is a reckless one before me. [33]The donkey saw me and turned away from me these three times. If she had not turned away, I would certainly have killed you by now, but I would have spared her."
>
> [34]Balaam said to the angel of the LORD, "I have sinned. I did not realize you were standing in the road to oppose me. Now if you are displeased, I will go back."
>
> [35]The angel of the LORD said to Balaam, "Go with the men, but speak only what I tell you." So Balaam went with the princes of Balak.
>
> [36]When Balak heard that Balaam was coming, he went out to meet him at the Moabite town on the Arnon border, at the edge of his territory. [37]Balak said to Balaam, "Did I not send you an urgent summons? Why didn't you come to me? Am I really not able to reward you?"
>
> [38]"Well, I have come to you now," Balaam replied. "But can I say just anything? I must speak only what God puts in my mouth."
>
> [39]Then Balaam went with Balak to Kiriath Huzoth. [40]Balak sacrificed cattle and sheep, and gave some to Balaam and the princes who were with him. [41]The next morning Balak took Balaam up to Bamoth Baal, and from there he saw part of the people.

21–28 The pagan mantic, the donkey, and the angel of the Lord are brought together in this truly tragicomic scene. The internationally known seer is blind before the angel of the Lord, but his proverbially dumb beast is able to see the spiritual reality of the living God on the path. Balaam as a *bārû* prophet was a specialist in animal divination. Here his animal saw what he was blind to observe.

Against the assertion of many critical scholars who state that the donkey story contributes nothing to the story line, both Mowinckel ("Der Ursprung," p. 260) and von Pákozdy ("Theologische Redaktionsarbeit," pp. 17–72) have noted that the donkey story serves the purpose of slowing the action and heightening the tension of the story. In fact, this is the "best part" of the story (so Goldberg, p. 106). The story is one of studied ridicule. We see the prophet Balaam as a blind seer, seeing less than the dumb animal. In this graphic representation of Balaam pitted against the donkey, we also see a more important contrast, as Goldberg avers, the contrast of Balaam and Moses. The long shadow of Moses falls across the pages of the Balaam story even though Moses is never named once. Moses spoke face to face with God (see ch. 12); Balaam does not even know that God is near—but his donkey does!

This section is the ultimate in polemics against paganism. It is well known that the ass has been depicted from the earliest times as a subject of stupidity and contrariness. Yet here the "stupid" ass sees the angel of the Lord and attempts to protect her rider from God's drawn sword. Three times the hapless Balaam beat his donkey.

Then the donkey spoke (v.28). Some have imagined too much here. The donkey did not give a prophetic oracle; she merely said what a mistreated animal might say to an abusive master if given the chance. There was no preaching from the donkey! Others have stumbled at the improbability of an animal speaking, for such is the stuff of fairy tales. What keeps this story from the genre of legend or fairy tale is the clear factor that the animal did not speak of its own accord but as it was given the power to do so by the Lord. Only an exceedingly limited view of God would deny him the ability to open the mouth of a dumb animal; such an objection should lead one to a rereading of Job 40–41.

Noth observes that the speaking of the ass is not particularly stressed but is an integral part of the story and is attributed to a miracle on the part of the Lord, "which indicates how directly and unusually Yahweh acted in this affair of blessing or curse for Israel" (p. 179). The speaking of the donkey is affirmed by the NT (2 Peter 2:16), a genuine element in the righteous acts of the Lord. It is not that this miracle is the focus of the text; it is not. It is just an amazingly humorous way to humiliate the prophet Balaam. Before the Lord revealed himself to Balaam, he first "got his attention" in this dramatic fashion. Balaam had to learn from a donkey before he could learn from God. This is one of the most amusing stories in the Bible.

29–30 The high camp of the story is furthered by Balaam's words, "If I had a sword in my hand, I would kill you right now" (v.29). The ridiculous picture of the hapless Balaam looking for a sword is precious; there was a sword very near, but the object was not about to be the donkey! (vv.23, 31–33). Again, all the donkey says is what a donkey might who was being so abused. We err in speaking of this text as though God spoke through the donkey. Here is no oracle, no prophecy, no poem; all she says is that she has been a good donkey. We also laugh as we hear Balaam talking with her, as though nothing was out of the ordinary. His rage must have been so heightened that he does not even stumble at the voice that comes from his donkey.

31–33 The wording "Then the LORD opened Balaam's eyes" follows the same structure as in v.28, "Then the LORD opened the donkey's mouth." In some ways the opening of the eyes of the pagan prophet to see the reality of the living God was the greater miracle. The animal was but a brute beast; the prophet was a man bent on trafficking with idolatrous gods.

34–35 The words of Balaam to God, "I have sinned" (v.34), lead us to think that he is truly repentant. Only the later outcome of the story shows this to be false (see chs. 25, 31). There is the confession of error, but it is a confession that falls short of the repentance of saving faith. Doubtless, he spoke with one eye on the sword that menaced from above.

The Lord tells Balaam to continue on his journey but to "speak only what I tell you" (v.35). This is the point of the whole chapter: Balaam the pagan mantic will not be able to speak cursing as he had planned. Instead, he would be the most surprised of all; he would be the most remarkable instrument of God in the blessing of his people, Israel. The one great gain was that Balaam was now more aware of the seriousness of the task before him; he would not be able to change the word that the Lord would give to him (see 23:12, 20, 26).

36–38 Balak's sense of urgency heightens the comic element in this story. He is so anxious to have Balaam begin his curse-work that he goes to some distance to meet him at the border of his land, and then he upbraids his visitor for the delay in his journey. Doubtless Balak would puzzle over the words that Balaam greets him with, "I must speak only what God puts in my mouth" (v.38). Our interpretation is based on the presupposition that ordinarily Balaam believed he could say pretty much what he pleased to say, if the price was right, with the belief that the will of the gods would in some manner correspond with his words. But not this time. Nevertheless, we are led by the narrative into the enemy camp, and we learn of their consternation over the power of God in the camp of Israel.

39–41 Verses 39–41 speak of the propitiatory sacrifices that Balak and Balaam engaged in as they prepared for the mantic acts. It seems unlikely that these were sacrifices to the Lord. The pieces given to Balaam presumably would have included the livers; for as a *bārû* diviner, Balaam was a specialist in liver divination. Numbers 24:1 reports that Balaam subsequently gave up on his acts of sorcery as the power of the word of the Lord came on him. But at the beginning he starts his procedures as he always has. Yet never did he speak as he was about to speak.

g. *Balaam's seven oracles (23:1–24:25)*

Chapters 23–24 of Numbers form a very close unity, based on the oracles of Balaam. Characteristic to Semitic style they come in a set of seven. The first four oracles are more lengthy, the last three are quite brief; nonetheless, each has its own independent nature within the corpus. Each oracle is introduced in the same manner (23:7a, 18a; 24:3a, 15a, 20b, 21b, 23a). Considering the role that the number seven plays in the narrative of our section (see the sevens in 23:1, 14, 29) and in the Torah in general, this can hardly be accidental. The oracles also show a sense of progression and development. There is a repetitive nature to the structure but not static repetition. There is a development, a growing intensity—indeed, a crescendo. Our analysis will follow this line of approach.

(1) *Balaam's first oracle (23:1–12)*

(a) *The setting of the oracle*

23:1–6

1 Balaam said, "Build me seven altars here, and prepare seven bulls and seven rams for me." 2 Balak did as Balaam said, and the two of them offered a bull and a ram on each altar.

3 Then Balaam said to Balak, "Stay here beside your offering while I go aside. Perhaps the LORD will come to meet with me. Whatever he reveals to me I will tell you." Then he went off to a barren height.

4 God met with him, and Balaam said, "I have prepared seven altars, and on each altar I have offered a bull and a ram."

5 The LORD put a message in Balaam's mouth and said, "Go back to Balak and give him this message."

6 So he went back to him and found him standing beside his offering, with all the princes of Moab.

1–6 The elaborate sacrificial actions of Balaam and Balak in these verses are to be contrasted to the sacrificial texts already described in the Book of Numbers. The sacrifices here are not the sacrifices of chapters 15 and 28–29. These are pagan actions that contrast with the true worship of God. The use of the number seven is significant in this section: seven bulls and seven rams on seven altars. These sacrifices were prepared as a part of Balaam's *bārû* actions. The number seven was held in high regard among Semitic peoples in general; the many animals would provide abundant liver and organ materials for the diviner from the east. Balaam is in charge; Balak is now his subordinate.

The most arresting element of the introductory section is in the words "God met with him" (v.4) and "the LORD put a message in Balaam's mouth" (v.5). Despite the pagan and unsavory actions of this ungodly man, the Lord deigns to meet with him and to speak through him. This is utterly remarkable. We often say that God will never use an unclean vessel. This is not quite accurate. God may use whatever vessel he wishes; the issue concerns what happens to an unclean vessel when God has finished using it for his purposes. It appears that such vessels are tossed aside, dashed on the road.

The story is dramatic as Balaam returns to those who had sent for him (v.6). They were standing by the altar, hoping for a word from heaven that would destroy their presumed foe. They received a word from heaven, all right; but it was far from what they expected.

Notes

---

3 שְׂפִי (*šep̱î*, "barren height") is a word that Daiches believes to be a term of pagan mantic actions; see comment on 22:8, describing the manner of Balaam's behavior. More recently Karl Elligen defends the meaning "bare height" ("Der Sinn des hebraischen Wortes שְׂפִי," ZAW 83 [1971]: 317–29).

(b) *The oracle: The blessing of Israel is irrevocable* 23:7–10

7 Then Balaam uttered his oracle:

"Balak brought me from Aram,
the king of Moab from the eastern mountains.
'Come,' he said, 'curse Jacob for me;
come, denounce Israel.'
8 How can I curse
those whom God has not cursed?
How can I denounce
those whom the LORD has not denounced?
9 From the rocky peaks I see them,
from the heights I view them.
I see a people who live apart
and do not consider themselves one of the nations.
10 Who can count the dust of Jacob
or number the fourth part of Israel?
Let me die the death of the righteous,
and may my end be like theirs!"

The theme of this first oracle is centered on the notion of the blessing of Israel. This blessing is unique. It is altogether different than anything Balaam (or Balak) had ever experienced. It is an irrevocable blessing; hence, any attempt to curse Israel is ineffective. Israel is a nation that is distinct from all others. Her uniqueness is to be found in her God.

The oracle may be outlined in this way:

Introductory formula: Balaam takes up his oracle (v.7a).
Exordium: Balaam states his purpose to curse Israel (v.7b).
Blessing:
A. Balaam is unable to curse Israel (v.8).
  1. God has not cursed Israel.
  2. Balaam cannot curse Israel.
B. Balaam blesses Israel as unique among the nations (vv.9–10a).
  1. Balaam views Israel as unique among the nations.
  2. Balaam regards Israel as immune from curses.
C. Balaam expresses a desire to share in Israel's blessing (v.10b).

7 The Hebrew word *māšāl* is more usually translated as "proverb"; here the translation "oracle" is appropriate. By this word the distinctive nature of the prophecies of Balaam is established; none of the prophecies of the true prophets of Israel is described by this term. There are seven poetic oracles in the set: the first four are longer, have introductory narrative bridges, and are in exquisite poetry (23:7–10, 18–24; 24:3–9, 15–19); the last three are brief, are much more difficult to understand, and follow one another in a staccato pattern (24:20, 21–22, 23–24).

The words of the exordium (v.7b) are problematic in terms of their poetic arrangement. The accents suggest an imbalanced pair of bicola with a 4:1 count, with a resultant translation:

> Balak the king of Moab brought me from Aram,
> from the mountains of the east.

But a more natural alignment of the bicolon would be a more balanced pair with a 3:2 count:

> From Aram Balak brought me,
> the king of Moab from the eastern mountains.

The result is a balanced line of what we may call complementary parallelism. The verb gaps the couplet, and the words of the second member explain more fully the meaning of the corresponding words of the first.

This is then followed by the instructions Balak gave to the erstwhile agent of curse:

> Go, curse for me Jacob!
> And Go, execrate Israel!

These words form a balanced bicolon, 3:3 meter, with emphatic verbal forms expressing great urgency with which Balak beseeched Balaam to come. The two verbs are *'ārar* (the verb "to curse" that we saw in 22:6) and *zā'am* ("to speak against with indignation"; see Ps 7:11, "a God who expresses his wrath every day"). The verbs in our couplet work together to give the sense of anger and indignation, to speak of execration. "Jacob" and "Israel" are regularly occurring pairs, of course; they are interchangeable words marking out the people of God's covenant. In these words there is the call, witting or not, for the Lord to break his promise to the fathers.

8 Yet that which Balaam had been hired to do he was unable to do. The blessing of Israel was inviolable; Balaam had no power to attack their blessing. God forbade him to speak in a curse on his people, who were unlike the nations of the world:

> How may I imprecate
>   whom God has not imprecated?

How may I execrate
whom Yahweh has not execrated?

It seems we have an unusual pattern here, with long bicola subdivided into two units: 2/3 : 2/3. The word *māh* is used at the beginning of each of the two units to indicate utter impossibility. The new synonym for curse is *qāḇaḇ,* a word used elsewhere in our corpus (22:11, 17; 23:8, 11, 13, 25, 27; 24:10). Here we also find the word *'ēl* used for "God," and it is found parallel to Yahweh.

9 In v.9 Balaam explains that Israel is unique among the nations:

As I see him from the top of the mountains,
and as I gaze at him from the hills—
Look! A people that dwells alone;
It is not reckoned among the nations.

These two lines of bicola are also nicely balanced with clear parallel terms and concepts. There seems to be a protasis and an apodosis in the respective lines of the bicola. We are brought alongside Balaam, and with him we look down. With him we discover with shock: this people is not like any other; they are alone, not a part of the families of the nations. Their distinction is in their relationship with their God. As he is holy, so they are holy. The first bicolon of the verse has a 3:2 pattern; the second a 3:3 pattern by its accents.

10 Here is Balaam's wistful desire to share in Israel's blessing! He who had come to curse wished himself to be blessed. The words "my end" speak of the glorious future, of life beyond the grave. That Balaam never participated in the death of the righteous is not learned until 31:8, 16.

Who may number the dust of Jacob?
Who can count the dust-cloud of Israel?
O that I might die the death of the upright!
Ah, that my latter end might be like his!

Again we have two nicely balanced lines of bicolon (4:3 and 4:3). The relationship between the two lines is one of exasperation and futility. Just as Balaam cannot "get their number," so he realizes that he is not a part of their destiny. One almost comes to a point of feeling sorry for Balaam at this point. Further, the words concerning "getting the number" of Israel have a double entendre in this book. Balaam wanted to "get the number" in a mantic sense, to have a handle for control. The book has made much of "numbers" as a means of displaying God's great blessing on his people. This is an unexpected confirmation of the idea of rhetorical use of numbers within this text.

Notes

---

7 The principal work on the accents used in the MT is William Wickes, *Two Treatises on the Accentuation of the Old Testament,* The Library of Biblical Studies, ed. Harry M. Orlinsky, reprint ed. (New York: Ktav, 1970). The accents are discussed briefly in GKC (sec. 15, pp. 57–63). See also P. Paul Joüon, *Grammaire de l'Hébreu Biblique* (Rome: Institut Biblique Pontifical, 1947), sec. 15, p. 45; cf. pp. 39–46.

10 Rather than emending וּמִסְפָּר (*ûmispār*, "or number"), as many have done, it seems best to regard this word as an abbreviation for *ûmî sāpar* ("and who may count?"). This yields a nice balance with the first word, "who may number?" See Christian D. Ginsburg, *Introduction to the Massoretico-Critical Edition of the Hebrew Bible*, reprint ed. (New York: Ktav, 1966), p. 168; G.R. Driver, "Abbreviations in the Massoretic Text," *Textus* 1 (1960): 112–31.

רֹבַע (*rōḇaʿ*, "the fourth part") seems to be a rather poor parallel to the word "dust" in the first colon. We accept as probable a solution proposed by many scholars that the word *rbʿ* may be compared with the Akkadian *turbuʾu* ("dust cloud") and the Arabic *rabaʿun* with the same meaning. See H.L. Ginsberg, "Lexicographical Notes. 3. *robaʿ* Dust," ZAW 51 (1933): 309; James Barr, *Comparative Philology and the Text of the Old Testament* (Oxford: At the Clarendon Press, 1968), index; D. Miller, "Animal Names in Ugaritic," UF, II, 184.

(c) *The aftermath*

23:11–12

11 Balak said to Balaam, "What have you done to me? I brought you to curse my enemies, but you have done nothing but bless them!"
12 He answered, "Must I not speak what the Lord puts in my mouth?"

11–12 In the introductory oracle the major elements of the passage are on display. Balaam is unable to curse Israel; Israel is unique because of her blessing from the Lord. Balak is furious—and the Lord is sovereign. The words of consternation of Balak and the response of Balaam are marvelous; we are supposed to chuckle as we witness the work of God among the enemies of his people.

(2) *Balaam's second oracle (23:13–26)*

(a) *The setting of the oracle*

23:13–17

13 Then Balak said to him, "Come with me to another place where you can see them; you will see only a part but not all of them. And from there, curse them for me." 14 So he took him to the field of Zophim on the top of Pisgah, and there he built seven altars and offered a bull and a ram on each altar.
15 Balaam said to Balak, "Stay here beside your offering while I meet with him over there."
16 The Lord met with Balaam and put a message in his mouth and said, "Go back to Balak and give him this message."
17 So he went to him and found him standing beside his offering, with the princes of Moab. Balak asked him, "What did the Lord say?"

13–17 Trying to cover all the angles, Balak attempted to reduce the power of the people by selecting a point where their immense numbers would be obscured. Alas for Balak, the oracle that followed exceeded the first in its blessing on Israel. Again, we sense the idea of numbers in this text. There is a power in numbers in the ancient world. If one is confronted only with a small percentage of the whole, Balak reasoned, then the enormity of the nation will not cause the gods to bless when they were requested to curse Israel. Again, sevens are used in the offerings. These are the uses of magical charms, not true worship. The note of "Pisgah" (v.14; see 21:20) causes the reader to think of Moses, even though he is not mentioned. His long shadow is everywhere present.

The result of all this frenetic activity is the same as the first time. Again the Lord meets Balaam and gives him a new word, to the consternation of Balak who is piously pretending at his pagan altar.

(b) *The oracle: the source of Israel's unique blessing*

23:18–24

18 Then he uttered his oracle:

"Arise, Balak, and listen;
  hear me, son of Zippor.
19 God is not a man, that he should lie,
  nor a son of man, that he should change his mind.
Does he speak and then not act?
  Does he promise and not fulfill?
20 I have received a command to bless;
  he has blessed, and I cannot change it.

21 "No misfortune is seen in Jacob,
  no misery observed in Israel.
The LORD their God is with them;
  the shout of the King is among them.
22 God brought them out of Egypt;
  they have the strength of a wild ox.
23 There is no sorcery against Jacob,
  no divination against Israel.
It will now be said of Jacob
  and of Israel, 'See what God has done!'
24 The people rise like a lioness;
  they rouse themselves like a lion
that does not rest till he devours his prey
  and drinks the blood of his victims."

The theme of this oracle is an extension of the first; now it is more explicit. The uniqueness of Israel is found in her unique relationship to the Lord. The oracle may be outlined as follows:

Introductory formula: Balaam takes up his oracle (v.18a).

Exordium: Balaam demands the attention of his hearer for the stunning oracle he is about to pronounce (v.18b).

Blessing:

A. Israel's unique blessing issues from her unique God (v.19).
  1. He is unlike man in his person.
  2. He is unlike man in his word.

B. Israel's unique blessing is irrevocable in her God (v.20).
  1. Balaam is commanded to bless.
  2. Balaam is powerless to curse.

C. Israel's unique blessing is explained by the presence of her God (vv.21–23).
  1. God permits no cursing of Israel (v.21a).
  2. God is present with Israel (v.21b).
  3. God is the protector of Israel (v.22).
  4. God is the power effective in Israel (v.23).

D. Israel's unique blessing is to be exhibited in her power in battle (v.24).
  1. As a lion she rises for the kill.
  2. As a lion she feasts on the slain.

The introductory formula and exordium (v.18) are characterized by a full use of fixed pairs of parallel words as well as by the use of arresting figures. The person of God as the effective force in Israel permeates the article. God is different from man; his word is different from that of man. God is the source of blessing, not man. God is with his people and is their King. God is the Deliverer from Egypt and is the strength of his people. Because of God his people become victorious.

Here is the introduction:

> And he took up his oracle and said:
> "Rise up, O Balak, and hear!
> Give ear to me, O son of Zippor!"

18 The introductory monocolon is followed by a bicolon of 3:4 meter that is marked by unusual energy. The naming of Balak in the second member as "son of Zippor" is a fine use of parallelism.

19 The words "God is not a man, that he should lie" describe the immutability of the Lord and the integrity of his word. Balaam is himself a foil for God. Balaam is constantly shifting, prevaricating, equivocating, changing—he is himself the prime example of the distinction between God and man.

> God is not a man, that he is able to lie,
> Nor is he human, that he is able to change;
> Has he said, and will he not do it?
> Or has he spoken, and will he not confirm it?

Again, two lines of bicolon mark this verse (4:2 and 4:3 meter), with the pairs enhancing each other. Balaam's view of gods was based on his own human failings. Now he confronts God who is not like man in his failures at all. This is the stunning reality. All others may change; God—even with all his power—cannot change, for he cannot deny himself (cf. 1 Sam 15:29; Ps 89:35–37). God must fulfill his promise, for he has bound his character to his word.

20 The blessing of God is thus irrevocable:

> Look! I have received [orders] to bless;
> Since he has blessed, I am unable to revoke it!

Verse 20 is a bicolon with 3:3 meter that advances the implication of v.19 to the present situation. Since the Lord is unlike fickle people, the command to bless is not subject to change at all.

21 That the first declaration of the kingship of the Lord in the Pentateuch was made by Balaam is a suitable improbability. It is because God is the King that he was able to use Balaam for his own ends—to bless his people in a new and wonderful manner.

> He does not see evil in Jacob,
> Nor does he regard trouble in Israel.
> Yahweh his God is with him.
> And the battle cry of a King is in him.

The negative wording of the first bicolon contrasts with the most positive elements in the second. The meter is 3:3 and 3:3. At first blush the wording of this verse is nearly incredible. The whole course of Israel's experience in the desert was one evil after another, one trouble on another. Yet it is evidently the standing of Israel that is in view here, rather than her state. It is also possible that the words "evil" and "trouble" in this verse are not used to refer to moral issues but to mantic concerns. That is, God does not not look on his people with "an evil eye" or a hostile glance. This interpretation may fit better with the first bicolon of v.23. When Israel is presented in the context of a hostile environment, then it is the blessing of Israel that is maintained. Only in the family is the sinfulness of the people addressed. Since Yahweh the King is in their midst, they are invincible from outside attack.

22 The wild ox (aurochs) of the ancient Near East is a traditional image of power (also 24:8). The KJV "unicorn" was wrong from the beginning; the Hebrew expression speaks of two horns (dual), which the NIV paraphrases as "strength."

> God is bringing them out of Egypt,
> He is their aurochs horns!

This bicolon (3:3) is powerful in its imagery. The verbal form is a participle, describing ongoing action. God is in the process still of bringing his people from Egypt; he will complete his work soon by bringing them into his land. And along the way he is their strength. They are not empowered by magic but by his person, not by potion but by his presence.

23 The reason for Israel's eventual triumph is given in a new way in this verse: there is "no sorcery against Jacob." Balaam speaks here from his frightful experience. He had no means in his bag of tricks to withstand the blessing of Israel. Instead of the tricks of the sorcerer, it will be said of Israel: "See what God has done!"

> For there is no divination against Jacob,
> Neither is there augury against Israel.
> Now it must be said for Jacob,
> And for Israel—"What God has done!"

These two bicola are made of 3:2 and 3:3 meter; the first is complementary and the second is completive. The two lines form a contrastive parallel, the first is negative and the second positive (as in v.19); there is a relationship of cause and effect here. Since there is no possibility of the use of magic either for or against Israel, whatever comes of Israel will truly be regarded as the work of God. This verse forms an insider's key to the whole of Balaam's work. He had come to use magic, but he could not "get their number" (v.10). He had come to bring a curse, but he found them blessed. He had come to bring a divination and an augury, but he found such ineffective. God is in control, and Balaam is his puppet in this Punch and Judy show.

24 Israel was about to arise and devour its foes, as a lioness on the hunt (see 24:9).

> Ah! A people rises as a lioness,
> And as a lion it rouses itself.
> It will not lie down until it devours its prey,
> And drinks the blood of the slain.

At this point the would-be victim of the curse of Balaam and Balak becomes the instrument of the destruction of its own enemies. As a lioness (the huntress), Israel is about to rouse herself and bring her foes down to destruction. She will not rest until the enemy is devoured, its blood lapped clean at the end of the chase. These two bicola are closely connected (3:2 and 4:2), with contrasting verbs of rising and lying down, plus positive and negative contrasts. The effectiveness of the lion image was not lost on Israel. Witness the seal from Megiddo with the figure of the roaring lion, inscribed, "Belonging to Shema/, servant of Jeroboam" (item 276, ANEP). The image hearkens back to the earliest patriarchal period (cf. Gen 49:9). The lion is a way of speaking of Israel's vocation as the warrior of God (see Mic 5:8).

Notes

23 נַחַשׁ (*naḥaš*, "sorcery") is an exceedingly important term in the context of the Balaam oracles. This noun is used here and in 24:1. The verb form is used in the Piel with the meaning "to practice divination," "to observe signs." It may even have the sense of "to cast a spell" or "to utter a magical curse." Key texts include Gen 30:27; 44:5, 15; Lev 19:26; Deut 18:10; 2 Kings 17:17; 21:6; 2 Chron 33:6. Divination in all its forms was prohibited in Israel; here we learn that there is no divination that may be made against Israel. The other word used in this verse is קֶסֶם (*qesem*, "divination," "augury"). This is also a word that is always negative in the viewpoint of normative Yahweh faith. It is prohibited in Israel in Deut 18:10 (along with *naḥaš*). Compare 1 Sam 15:23; Ezek 13:6, 23.

(c) *The aftermath*

23:25–26

[25]Then Balak said to Balaam, "Neither curse them at all nor bless them at all!"

[26]Balaam answered, "Did I not tell you I must do whatever the LORD says?"

25–26 The tragicomic nature of the story is seen in the aftermath. It is as though Balak is incredulous. He gasps, "What have you done to me!" in v.11. Now he says, in essence, "Stop it all together." But Balaam is indefatigable in his mission from the Lord.

(2) *Balaam's third oracle (23:27–24:14)*

(a) *The setting of the oracle*

23:27–24:2

[27]Then Balak said to Balaam, "Come, let me take you to another place. Perhaps it will please God to let you curse them for me from there." [28]And Balak took Balaam to the top of Peor, overlooking the wasteland.

[29]Balaam said, "Build me seven altars here, and prepare seven bulls and seven rams for me." [30]Balak did as Balaam had said, and offered a bull and a ram on each altar.

[24:1]Now when Balaam saw that it pleased the LORD to bless Israel, he did not resort to sorcery as at other times, but turned his face toward the desert. [2]When Balaam looked out and saw Israel encamped tribe by tribe, the Spirit of God came upon him

23:27–24:2 Once more Balak tries another tack. Perhaps a change of place will lead to a change of words (v.27). The mention of Peor (v.28) takes on a horrible association in Numbers 25; it would appear that this was the center in Moab for the worship of the god Baal. Von Pákozdy believes that this section means that Balaam was being asked by Balak to call up his own deity (a demon), one with whom he had some hold ("Theologische Redaktionsarbeit," p. 174).

Again the sevens of altars and sacrifices are prepared (vv.29–30), but this time there is a significant change. Balaam does not go about his normal routine of sorcery (v.1). This time "the Spirit of God came upon him" (v.2). This unexpected language is used to prepare the reader for the heightened revelation that is about to come from the unwitting messenger. The oracles are building in intensity and in their depth of meaning.

(b) *The oracle: the beauty and strength of Israel*

24:3–9

3 and he uttered his oracle:

"The oracle of Balaam son of Beor,
the oracle of one whose eye sees clearly,
4 the oracle of one who hears the words of God,
who sees a vision from the Almighty,
who falls prostrate, and whose eyes are opened:

5 "How beautiful are your tents, O Jacob,
your dwelling places, O Israel!

6 "Like valleys they spread out,
like gardens beside a river,
like aloes planted by the LORD,
like cedars beside the waters.
7 Water will flow from their buckets;
their seed will have abundant water.

"Their king will be greater than Agag;
their kingdom will be exalted.

8 "God brought them out of Egypt;
they have the strength of a wild ox.
They devour hostile nations
and break their bones in pieces;
with their arrows they pierce them.
9 Like a lion they crouch and lie down,
like a lioness—who dares to rouse them?

"May those who bless you be blessed
and those who curse you be cursed!"

Again we may present an outline for this oracle:

Introductory formula: Balaam takes up his oracle (v.3a).

Exordium: Balaam, empowered by the Holy Spirit, speaks in a new way of the source of his revelation.

Blessing:

A. The blessings of Israel will be demonstrated in the land (vv.5–7).
1. Israel's dwellings will be beautiful (v.5).
2. Israel's productivity will be bountiful (v.6).
3. Israel's resources will be plentiful (v.7a).
4. Israel's king and kingdom will be powerful (v.7b).

B. The blessings of Israel are in her God (v.8).
  1. Israel's God is her deliverer (v.8a).
  2. Israel's God is her protector (v.8b).
  3. Israel's God makes her victorious (vv.8c–e).
C. The blessings of Israel are absolute (v.9).
  1. Israel is like a lion, sovereign and grand (v.9a).
  2. Israel's blessing is vouchsafed by the promise of God (v.9b).

3–4 The introduction to this oracle is extensive and descriptive of Balaam's experience in the presence of the Lord. Now Balaam's eyes were opened (see 22:31, where the Lord opened Balaam's eyes to see his presence).

And Balaam took up his oracle and said:

> The utterance of Balaam the son of Beor,
> Even the utterance of the strong man whose eye is opened;
> The utterance of one who hears the words of God,
> Who sees the vision of Shaddai—
> Falling down, but whose eyes are uncovered.

These words are truly remarkable. The use of the term "oracle" (*ne'um*) three times adds significant solemnity to these words, as do the lines descriptive of his own personal experience on the road. As Saul had his experience on the road to Damascus, so Balaam had his experience on the road to Moab. In both cases there was a revelation. In the case of Saul, it was a revelation to grace; in the case of Balaam, it was to judgment. In both there was the protection of the true people of God by those who wished to do them harm.

The introductory monocolon of this verse is followed by a bicolon (4:4) that is self-descriptive of past and present experience. Then there is a tricolon in v.4 (3:4:3), with the first member repeating the word *ne'um* of the previous verse. These words are so expressive of something new in his experience: he has now heard God and seen the vision of him. He lay prone before him, but his eyes were now opened to wonder he had never dreamed. The seer now sees, but the seer Balaam still is not a man of faith; he is not a member of the family (see again 23:10: "Let me").

5 Now Balaam speaks prophetically. He looks down on the tents in which the people are dwelling, but he thinks of their future. He sees the orderliness of the encampments, but he is given a vision of their coming grandeur.

> O how beautiful are your tents, O Jacob,
> Your dwellings places, O Israel.

This verse is one bicolon (3:2 meter) celebrating the astonishment of Balaam as he gazes on the beauty of the encampments of Israel and views their future glory.

6 Balaam speaks here in general but luxuriant terms of the blessings that will fall on the people of Israel as they will settle in their new land. The people will have a sense of Eden in the lushness of their blessing from the Lord.

> As palm trees that stretch themselves out,
> As orchards beside the river,
> As aloes planted by Yahweh,
> As cedars by the waters.

Verse 6 has two lines of bicola with complementary parallelism throughout. The first line has the meter 2:3; the second is 3:2—together an altogether satisfactory line.

The meaning of the first word is problematic, however. The word *nāḥāl* ordinarily means "wadi" (see NIV, "like valleys"). Yet the other words in this verse are terms for trees. It seems that a word meaning a type of tree, or a cluster of trees, is called for by this word. The NEB and the Torah translation have read "palm tree," following a suggestion made already in BDB (p. 636), comparing the Hebrew word with an Arabic term for the date palm. Further, the verb *nāṭāh* seems more fitting with the stretching of the boughs of a tree than with the sprawl of a wadi.

7 This verse speaks of luxuriance of productivity as well as of the majesty of the coming king of Israel. It is prophetic in tone.

> Water flows from his buckets,
> And his seed is by many waters;
> His king is higher than Agag,
> And his kingdom is exalted.

This verse has two lines of bicola (2:3 and 3:2) in an unusual pairing of ideas: water and seed tied to king and kingdom. The ideas of water and seed probably point to a luxuriance in the inhabitation of the land. The words may also be a double entendre for sexual fecundity (see Notes).

The most problematic issue is the reference to "Agag." Because Agag was the opponent of King Saul in the tenth century, the mention of him in a text that is ostensibly from a period hundreds of years earlier leads liberal commentators to take the reference to Agag to be a telltale sign that this oracle, and the others like it, were written in the time of David (or later) and then projected backward into the remote past (see, e.g., Eissfeldt, "Sinai-Erzählung und Bileam-Spräche," p. 188).

It is possible, however, that the reference to Agag is based on a common name among the Amalekite kings (like the names Abimelech in Philistia and Ben-Hadad in Syria). In this case the use of this name here may grow out of the attack on Israel by Amalek (see Exod 17:8–13) and again when Israel first came against Canaan (see Num 14:45).

But it is also possible that here we confront something wondrous: a specific, predictive prophecy of a victory of a king of Israel over a great enemy. In the words "Their king will be greater than Agag," we may have a *heilsgeschichtliche* continuity that begins in the desert with the attacks of Amalek in Israel's recent past, that leads to the future victory of Saul over his nemesis, Agag (1 Sam 15:32–33), and that culminates in the final victory of Israel's greatest King (Y'shua) over all her enemies. This is certainly fitting with the prophecies that follow in the fourth oracle (see v.17). The fact that the Spirit of God fell on Balaam (v.2) gives the reverent reader a sense of expectation for just such a dramatic convergence of ideas.

8 This broad interpretation suggested for v.7 fits with the direction of v.8 as well. It is stunning to hear the central words of Israel's salvation ("God is bringing him out of Egypt") recited by one who was an outsider and a hostile foe (see commentary on 25:1).

> God is bringing him out of Egypt,
> He is his aurochs horns!
> He will devour the nations, his enemies,
> Their bones he will crush,
> And their arrows he will shatter.

The first couplet is repetitive from the second oracle (23:22), a factor that helps tie the corpus together, as well as to emphasize its central importance. The only change is in the pronoun (singular here; plural in 23:22). This bicolon is followed by a tricolon projecting a time of ultimate victory over all enemies (as in v.7, with the reference to Agag). The imagery of victory is in the manner of a lion (as in v.9). Thus there is a tightly woven connection in these verses. The tricolon has the pattern 3:2:2, with complementary parallelism of the strong verbs devouring, crushing, shattering. There is an Akkadian text that speaks of the crushing of bones in battle: "I had his (own) sons crush these bones, the bones of PN, which they had taken to Assyria from GN" (CAD, IV, 342; "PN" stands for "personal name," "GN" for "geographical name"). This is a stark image of complete victory over one's enemy.

9 The theology of blessing and cursing of the Abrahamic covenant (Gen 12:2–3) is now made an explicit part of the oracle of blessing. Perhaps here Balaam was reasserting his wistful desire to be a part of Israel's blessing (see 23:10).

> He couches, he lies down as a lion,
> And as a lion, who dares to rouse him?
> All who bless you are blessed;
> But all who curse you are cursed.

These two lines of bicola have 3:3 and 2:2 meter, giving a sense of balance and conclusion. The idea of the lion is taken from the second oracle (see 23:24). The stunning climax is in the blessing of God on all who bless Israel. This, of course, takes us back to the original promise of God to Abram. The irony cannot be missed by Balaam or by any who hear his words. In his actions he brings a curse on his own head, even as he speaks blessing!

Notes

7 Rembert Sorg (*Ecumenic Psalm 87* [Fifield, Wis.: King of Martyrs Priory, 1969], pp. 36, 46–52) presents an argument that the phrasing of the first part of the verse is to semen virile; he makes similar comments on the words of our Lord in John 7:37–39: "out of his belly shall flow rivers of living water" (KJV). His point is not without problems, but he argues that John 7:37–39 is based on our text.

(c) *The aftermath*

24:10–14

10 Then Balak's anger burned against Balaam. He struck his hands
together and said to him, "I summoned you to curse my enemies, but
you have blessed them these three times. 11 Now leave at once and go
home! I said I would reward you handsomely, but the LORD has kept you
from being rewarded."
12 Balaam answered Balak, "Did I not tell the messengers you sent me,
13 'Even if Balak gave me his palace filled with silver and gold, I could
not do anything of my own accord, good or bad, to go beyond the
command of the LORD—and I must say only what the LORD says'? 14 Now

I am going back to my people, but come, let me warn you of what this
people will do to your people in days to come."

10–14 The oracles could well have ended with the great third word from Balaam. But they do not end; there is one grander yet to come. Balak is beside himself. He rages in anger, strikes his hands, and rants. He observes that at this point Balaam has given three distinct blessings of Israel (v.10). At least Balak has got this right. In his disgust with the failure of Balaam to curse Israel, Balak now dismisses him without pay—the ultimate insult to his greed (2 Peter 2:15).

Balaam is ready to leave; the whole thing must have been very uncomfortable for him as well! But before he goes, he is constrained by the Lord to speak again, his greatest oracle. In the phrase "in days to come" we recognize the signal in biblical literature for the distant future.

(4) *Balaam's fourth oracle*

24:15–19

15 Then he uttered his oracle:

"The oracle of Balaam son of Beor,
the oracle of one whose eye sees clearly,
16 the oracle of one who hears the words of God,
who has knowledge from the Most High,
who sees a vision from the Almighty,
who falls prostrate, and whose eyes are opened:
17 "I see him, but not now;
I behold him, but not near.
A star will come out of Jacob;
a scepter will rise out of Israel.
He will crush the foreheads of Moab,
the skulls of all the sons of Sheth.
18 Edom will be conquered;
Seir, his enemy, will be conquered,
but Israel will grow strong.
19 A ruler will come out of Jacob
and destroy the survivors of the city."

Unlike the preceding oracles, there is no set up for this nor any aftermath. The only importance is the oracle itself. Here is an outline of the fourth oracle:

Introductory formula: Balaam takes up his oracle (v.15a).
Exordium: Balaam about to utter his most important oracle expands the exordium of the preceding section (vv.15b–16).
Blessing:
A. Israel has a coming deliverer (v.17).
1. The deliverer will come in the future (v.17a–b).
2. The deliverer will be like a star and a scepter (v.17c–d).
3. The deliverer will bring victory over his enemies (v.17e–f).
B. Israel has a coming dominion (vv.18–19).
1. Her enemies will be destroyed (v.18).
2. Her people will have dominion (v.19).

15–16 As in the third oracle (vv.3–4), the introduction to the fourth oracle is lengthy (vv.15–16), helping to prepare the reader for the startling words of the prophecy to come.

And he took up his oracle and said:
"The utterance of Balaam the son of Beor,
Even the utterance of the strong man whose eye is opened;
The utterance of one who hears the words of God,
Who knows the knowledge of the Most High,
Who sees the vision of Shaddai—
Falling down, but whose eyes are uncovered."

As we compare this section with 23:3–4, we find one new colon: "Who knows the knowledge of the Most High." This expansion changes the line arrangement of the second verse from a tricolon to two lines of bicola (3:3 and 3:3). The addition of the new colon tends to intensify the anticipation of the blessing that follows; the repetition helps to tie these oracles together, to give us a sense of crescendo and climax.

17 Without question the most debated and the most important verse in the oracle corpus is v.17. The prophecy of the star out of Jacob and the scepter out of Israel is a specific prophecy of the coming messianic Ruler, the Lord Jesus Christ. Israel's future Deliverer will be like a star and a scepter in his royalty and will bring victory over the enemies of his people (see also v.19). That this prophecy was given through the improbable prophet Balaam is remarkable, reminding us of the unexpectedness of the thoughts of God (Isa 55:8).

"I see him, but not now,
I behold him, but not near,
A star shall march out from Jacob,
And a scepter shall rise from Israel—
And shall crush the temples of Moab,
Even the skulls of the sons of Sheth."

The theme of this verse is Israel has a coming deliverer. This keenly debated verse has been debased by some, devalued by others, and allegorized by still others (see Notes). For our part, in agreement with many in the early church and in early Judaism (see Notes), we believe this text speaks unmistakably of the coming of the Messiah. That this prophecy should come from one who was unworthy makes the prophecy all the more dramatic and startling.

Indeed, that Balaam, who was none of God's, could speak of the coming of the Messiah, who is all of God, is a fascinating aspect of the biblical doctrine of inerrancy. The truth of the Scripture could never be dependent on the worthiness of the writer or the personal piety of the speaker. Else we would have gradations in inspiration and shadings in trustworthiness. I say this reverently but strongly; the words of Balaam the pagan mantic, *when he was speaking under the control of the Holy Spirit of God*, were as sure as the words of the Savior Jesus in a red-letter edition of the NT. Balaam was unworthy of the words that passed through his lips, even as others were unworthy of the role they played in the salvation history of the Bible. But the words were not compromised; it was the Spirit who gave him utterance (v.2). It was also the Spirit who directed the process that led to these words being included in the Torah of God (a point I develop more fully in my essay "The Theology of the Balaam Oracles," in the *Feinberg Festschrift*).

The terms "star" and "scepter" certainly may speak of the promise of a king like David, Israel's greatest king in the historical period. But ultimately these words reach beyond him. The setting for the text is "in days to come" (see again v.14), an eschatological notice. The inclusion of these words in the text is for the final victory over the enemies of Israel. The section reaches to the end, because it reaches all the way to the Savior.

The first bicolon has the meter 3:3 in a complementary parallelism that is unusually moving: "but not now," "but not near"—words that stress the futurity of the referent. The second line of bicola has a 3:3 meter, speaking of the marching of the star-scepter as a great victor. These nouns speak of the royalty of the Messiah.

The third bicolon in the verse has a 3:2 meter with complementary parallelism, describing the shattering of the enemies in a complete judgment. Jeremiah 48:45 serves as a very important parallel of our words, helping solve the problem of the word the NIV renders "skulls" (see Notes). The other problematic word in this verse is "Sheth," a word that may refer to early inhabitants of Moab (and so a parallel word to Moab; see Notes). The point of the verse, of course, is that the coming King will be the ultimate victor over all his enemies (cf. Pss 2; 110; Rev 19–20).

18–19 There is a sense in which the modern reader regards these verses as somewhat anticlimactic with what follows. Yet this is not at all unusual in biblical prophecy. One can pick almost any well-known messianic text (Isa 9:6–7; Mic 5:2) and find it to have what appears to be rather humble associations. Yet the wording of these two verses does not present something insignificant; they further the idea of v.17 that the coming Deliverer will have the great victory and will provide a dominion for his people.

And Edom will become a possession,
And Seir, his enemies, will be a possession,
While Israel is demonstrating power.
  One from Jacob will have dominion,
  And shall destroy the remnant of the city.

Verse 18 is made of one line of tricolon with a 3:4:4 meter; the first two cola are complementary, and the third is expansive of these two. Edom and Seir are correlative terms (Gen 32:3; 36:8–9; Deut 1:44; 2:4, 8, 12 et al.). The pairing of these two words may be the key to understanding the pairing of Moab and Sheth in v.17 (see Notes on v.17). In the time of Moses, Edom was a nation that Israel was forbidden to attack. The future projection of the text assumes a time of enmity of Edom against Israel (cf. the Book of Obadiah), for which they finally receive comeuppance for their shabby treatment of Israel when they requested passage (see 20:14–21). David became a victor over Edom (2 Sam 8:14). But after the division of the kingdom, Edom became independent (2 Kings 8:20–22) and remained an implacable foe of Israel, awaiting the final wrath of God (Isa 63:1–6). In the eschaton, words such as Edom and Seir stand for any enemies of the people of God and of their Messiah.

The contrasting words to the ultimate downfall of Edom at the end of v.18 are to be stressed: Israel will grow strong while her enemies languish. This is also the point of v.19: Jacob will provide the ruler who will destroy all survivors of the enemies of the people of God.

Verse 19 forms a bicolon with 2:3 meter. There is no subject for the verb "will come out"; likely the referent is the Star-Scepter of v.17. The Star-Scepter makes Israel triumphant as he gains dominion over the enemies of God's people. Messiah in his kingdom will exercise dominion over all peoples. The theme of this oracle is sustained: Israel's ultimate blessing centers in her Deliverer from all enemies.

Notes

17 John Allegro attempts to join this verse of the star and the scepter to his theory of a pan-phallic and hallucinogenic cult in Israel (*The Sacred Mushroom and the Cross: A Study of the Nature and Origins of Christianity Within the Fertility Cults of the Ancient Near East*, reprint [New York: Bantam Books, 1971]). Even Luther was unable to see this prophecy as speaking of Christ because he regarded Balaam as unworthy of such a sublime subject (see Heinrich Bornkamm, *Luther and the Old Testament*, tr. Eric W. and Ruth C. Gritsch; ed. Victor I. Gruhn [Philadelphia: Fortress, 1969], p. 240, n. 72). Many have allegorized the text, pointing, for example, to the Star of Bethlehem as the fulfillment of the passage (Paul L. Maier, "The Magi and the Star," *Mankind* 3 [Feb. 1972]: 5).

Among the church fathers who interpreted the Star of Num 24:17 to be the Lord Jesus Christ was Justin Martyr (d. 166). His *First Apology* (ch. 32) presents an amalgam of Num 24:17; Isa 11:1; and 51:5: "Isaiah, another prophet, prophesying the same things in other words, said: 'A star shall rise out of Jacob, and a flower will come forth from the root of Jesse, and upon his arm will the nations hope.' The shining star has risen and the flower has grown from the root of Jesse—this is Christ." Another is Athanasius the Great (d. 373); his *On the Incarnation of the Word* (sec. 33) includes the lines of Num 24:17 in a christological section.

In early Judaism, Targum Onkelos reads on this verse: "When a mighty king of Jacob's house will reign, and the Messiah will be magnified"; Targum Jonathan reads on this verse: "When there shall reign a strong king of the house of Jacob, and Messiah shall be anointed, and a strong scepter shall be from Israel." In the Talmud this section is tied to Messiah in *Jerusalem Taanith* (68.4); *Debarim Rabba* (sec. 1); *Pesikta Sotarta* (58.1). Further, the *Damascus Document* (CD:vii.9–20) ties this verse to Amos 9:11, the raising of the fallen booth of the house of David; in the *War Scroll* from Qumran (1QM:VII), the star and scepter passage is tied to the final battle of good and evil. Indeed, the text was a particular favorite among the Qumran covenanters (see F.F. Bruce, *The Teacher of Righteousness in the Qumran Texts* [London: Tyndale, 1956], p. 10).

The word וְקַרְקַר (*weqarqar*, "even tear down") as it stands is a Pilpel infinitive of the rare root meaning "to tear down" (used only elsewhere in Isa 22:5, where it is also in dispute). Many emend to *weqoḏqōḏ*, a word meaning "crown," "head," or "skull" (see Isa 3:17, where this is used in parallel construction to *pē'āh* ["temple"]; cf. also Jer 48:45, where the words of our verse are slightly rephrased).

כָּל־בְּנֵי־שֵׁת (*kol-benê-šēṯ*, "All the sons of Sheth") is apparently a parallel ethnic term for Moab; the Shutu people in ancient Egyptian documents (So Albright, "Oracles," p. 220, n. 89). As v.18 balances "Edom" and "Seir," so we may expect v.17 balances "Moab" and "Sheth."

(5) *Balaam's fifth oracle*

24:20

20Then Balaam saw Amalek and uttered his oracle:

"Amalek was first among the nations,
but he will come to ruin at last."

20 The remaining three oracles seem to spring almost involuntarily from the fourth oracle. They overlap the promise of the victory of Israel over all enemies; hence these oracles are "curse oracles." It may be that these were very similar to the types of oracles that Balaam intended to present against Israel; instead these harsh words lash out against the foes of the covenant community. Here is the final irony: Balak and

Balaam had plotted to bring Israel under a curse, but in their machinations they only assured their own doom.

> And he saw Amalek,
> And he took up his oracle and said:
> "First among the nations was Amalek,
> But its end will be destruction."

The structure of this brief oracle is simple. There is a bicolon that serves as the introduction, then a bicolon of prophetic indictment with a 3:3 pattern.

The first defeat of Israel in the desert was at the hand of the Amalekites, when Israel went against them foolishly without the blessing of God (see 14:44–45). There will come a day of reckoning on Amalek that will be dreadful. The Amalekites were defeated by Saul (1 Sam 14:48; but see 15:1–35) and David (1 Sam 30:18; 2 Sam 8:12). These defeats may be regarded as fulfillments of this prophecy. But there is also the possibility that this verse, as the others in the set, has an extension into the days of the Messiah's final victory over all enemies. The final victory would be couched in the names familiar in the day in which they were given. Later on these names become prototypes for the enemies of Israel in the future.

(6) *Balaam' sixth oracle*

24:21–22

21 Then he saw the Kenites and uttered his oracle:

> "Your dwelling place is secure,
> your nest is set in a rock;
> 22 yet you Kenites will be destroyed
> when Asshur takes you captive."

21–22 The spotlight of judgment turns now from Amalek to the Kenites:

> And he saw the Kenite,
> And he took up his oracle and said:
> "Your dwelling place is enduring,
> And your nest is set in the cliff;
> Nevertheless, the Kenite shall be consumed
> When Asshur takes him captive."

The structure of this little oracle is somewhat similar to the preceding; it begins with a couplet of introduction, then follows with a double bicola in the pattern 2:3 and 4:3.

This oracle is problematic in several respects; it is based on wordplays (the word "nest" [*qēn;* see Jer 49:16; Obad 4; Hab 2:9] is a pun on the word "Kenite" [*qênî*]) and seems to point to the distant day when the seemingly unassailable Kenites will be taken captive by Asshur (Assyria). Why the Kenites come under attack here is not sure, except that it is possible that they became associated with the Midianites who come under the scourge of Israel (Num 31). The mention of Assyria is also a surprise, as its ascendancy to power in the ancient Near East was centuries away from Balaam's day; yet Assyria was known as a powerful city-state even in Abraham's day. This text may be a powerful insight into the way of the prophets—the taking of familiar things and peoples and juxtaposing them in startling ways.

(7) *Balaam's seventh oracle*

24:23–25

[23]Then he uttered his oracle:
"Ah, who can live when God does this?
[24] Ships will come from the shores of Kittim;
they will subdue Asshur and Eber,
but they too will come to ruin."

[25]Then Balaam got up and returned home and Balak went his own way.

23–24 Balaam now presents his last oracle, one that is more difficult than any of the others to interpret. This may be fitting. The relative obscurity of the words compel attention; clarity may come as the time of the oracle is realized.

> And he took up his oracle and said:
> "Woe! Who can live except God establish him?
> For ships will come from the direction of Kittim,
> And they will afflict Asshur and they will afflict Eber,
> And he also will come to destruction."

The first verse has a bicolon with 3:5 meter; the introductory words set a grim stage for the words that follow. The second verse is in the form of a tricolon, with 3:3 meter; yet the text is so corrupt that it presents an assortment of guesses as to meaning and interpretation.

The way we have translated the second colon of v.23 leads one to a sense of utter dependance on the Lord. This is the lesson that is taught throughout the oracles. None is able to live, except God establishes it. In his "Ah!" Balaam realizes the ultimate futility of his vocation.

Verse 24, as it stands, has a mention of Asshur that connects it with the preceding oracle (v.22). The reference to "ships from Kittim" presents unusual difficulties. The identification of Kittim in the early period of Israel's history seems to be Cyprus. But ultimately the word was applied to Rome, as in Qumran (see, e.g., 1QM, VII, "From of old Thou hast announced to us the time appointed for the mighty deed of Thy hand against the Kittim") and perhaps also (prophetically!) in Daniel (e.g., 11:30). The resulting meaning may refer to the final battle between forces of the west (the Kittim) and forces of the east (Asshur and Eber)—a battle in which both will be destroyed, presumably before a greater power then either (the Lord of glory).

The difficulties that we face in precision in our interpretation of this verse does not obscure the general direction: one nation will rise and supplant another, only to face its own doom. In contrast there is the implied ongoing blessing on the people of Israel and their sure promise of a future deliverer who will have the final victory (vv.17–19).

25 With these promises of a future deliverer ringing in their ears, the defeated collaborators Balaam and Barak depart.

Notes

25 We really have no idea how the story of Balaam and his donkey or the oracles of Balaam came into the Torah. That the question was asked from antiquity is evinced by the wording of the tract *Baba Bathra* 14b–15a: "Moses wrote his own book and the section concerning Balaam, and Job." The inclusion of the section on Balaam and Job could only have been provoked by the question, "How did these sections come into the Bible?"

The view of Hengstenberg may be advanced as an attempt to present a credible scenario for the authorship of the section by Moses. He says that when Balaam left Balak, he sought from the Israelites the payment he had been refused by Balak. In return for payment, he offered to relate the whole story to Moses. When Moses refused to give him payment, then in revenge he turned to the Midianites and advanced the plan that led to the debacle of Num 25 (*The History of Balaam*, Eng. ed., p. 513). Another view was given by Keil, who surmises that Balaam would have communicated the events and the prophecies to whomever captured him after the battle with Midian (Num 31), in an attempt to save his life—in which he also failed (KD, 3:203). Cox suggested that Balaam suffered a judicial death (his understanding of Num 31:8); at the trial he would have used the relating of the story and the prophecies as a part of his defense (*Balaam*, pp. 14–15). Allis suggested that the events and the prophecies might have been granted to Moses by a direct revelation of the Holy Spirit (Oswald T. Allis, *The Old Testament: Its Claims and Its Critics* [Philadelphia: Presbyterian and Reformed, 1972], p. 127). Others feel the story and the oracles may not have been added to the Book of Numbers during the life of Moses but may have been added sometime later in Israel's history as a way of finishing the story of Israel's desert account. Harrison, for example, suggests the possibility that the materials may even have come from a Moabite source or through a disciple of Balaam (IOT, pp. 620, 630). In point of fact, we really do not know. All we know for sure is that these chapters form an essential part of the Book of Numbers as the Spirit has had it come to the synagogue and the church. And as Scripture the words of Balaam's prophecies are as true as the Gospel—of which they ultimately form a part.

---

h. *Israel's final rebellion with the Baal of Peor and the death of the first generation (25:1–18)*

Many readers of the Book of Numbers have considered the events of this chapter as just another incident of rebellion and judgment in the long, sorry story of Israel's intransigence in the desert. Norman C. Habel was one of the first to observe that the events of this chapter are something more than that; these events were no mere peccadillo (see his *Yahweh Versus Baal: A Conflict of Religious Cultures: A Study in the Relevance of Ugaritic Materials for the Early Faith of Israel* [New York: Bookman Associates, 1964], pp. 24–25). As Rabbi Hirsch writes, "The sword of no stranger, the curse of no stranger had the power to damage Israel. Only it itself could bring misfortune, by seceding from God and his Torah" (p. 426). This chapter presents a formative encounter with Baal worship, a miniature of the disaster that would one day engulf and destroy the nation. It evokes the images of Genesis 38, when Judah nearly became a "Canaanite." And it projects the end of Israel and of Judah, for this was the result of their becoming like the peoples of Canaan.

So we now come to the ultimate rebellion of Israel in the desert. The time is the end of the forty-year period of their desert experience. The place is the staging area for the conquest of the land of Canaan. The issue is that of apostasy from the Lord by participation in the debased, sexually centered Canaanite religious rites of Baal worship—that which would become the bane of Israel's experience in the land. This chapter is an end and a beginning. It marks the end of the first generation; it also points to the beginning of a whole new series of wicked acts that will finally lead to Israel's punishment (see comments on 33:50–56). All the rebellions up to this point described in the Book of Numbers have centered in murmurings against the Lord and against his servants Moses and Aaron. The people have provoked the anger of the Lord by grumbling about water and food and by refusing to believe that he was able to deliver on his promise to bring them into the land of Canaan. But this chapter is unique in the record of the experience of Israel in their move from Sinai to Moab—it describes their involvement in the worship of another deity.

In a sense this chapter matches the grim account of Israel's involvement in the pagan rites of the worship of the golden calf at the base of Sinai (Exod 32). The apostasy of Israel in their flagrant worship of the golden calf points back to Egypt. The golden calf was a symbol of the Egyptian bull-god Apis, likely referred to in Jeremiah 46:15 (see EBC, 6:652). Apis was the sacred bull in Egypt, the incarnation of Osiris, the principal deity of Egypt. Exodus 32:6 reads, "So the next day the people rose early and sacrificed burnt offerings and presented fellowship offerings. Afterward they sat down to eat and drink and got up to indulge in revelry." The verb translated "to indulge in revelry" (*leṣaḥēq,* Piel infinitive construct of *ṣāḥaq;* meaning "to laugh" in the Qal—the word that forms the base for the name "Isaac") sometimes speaks of sexual involvement. It is a euphemism for "caressing" in sexual play (as in Gen 26:8). So in this chapter Israel engages in sexual acts of the worship of a god of Canaan.

(1) *The involvement of Israel in the worship of Baal Peor*

25:1–3

1 While Israel was staying in Shittim, the men began to indulge in sexual immorality with Moabite women, 2 who invited them to the sacrifices to their gods. The people ate and bowed down before these gods. 3 So Israel joined in worshiping the Baal of Peor. And the LORD's anger burned against them.

1 "Shittim" (see 33:49, "Abel Shittim") is another name for the region of Israel's staging for the conquest of the land; it was in Transjordan, across from the ancient city of Jericho (see Josh 2:1). The story of Numbers 25 has some breaks in it; it is not until 31:8, 16, that we learn that the principal instigator of the apostasy of the people of Israel was Balaam son of Beor (see Notes on 22:5). Failing to destroy Israel by the means of the mantic curse, Balaam then seduced Israel by the Canaanite practices of the sexually centered worship of the god Baal.

The phrase "Moabite women" is the connecting link that ties this chapter to the preceding ones (22–24). What the fathers of Moab could not do, their daughters were able to accomplish, to bring Israel to its knees—sexually, morally, in false worship, and in great judgment. The verb used to describe the action of the men is one normally used to describe the behavior of a loose woman, a harlot. Here the people, as a man, bewhore themselves with foreign, pagan women. Always in the ancient Near Eastern context, references to sexual imagery such as this suggest interconnecting circles of sexual immorality tied to sacral rites of prostitution, essential parts of pagan religious systems of the day.

2 The phrase "to the sacrifices of their gods" reminds us that the true worship of the Lord, which was sacrificial in nature, was easily compromised in the minds of the people because of the sacrificial systems of their neighbors (see Exod 34:15; Deut 32:38; Judg 16:23; 2 Kings 10:19; Isa 57:7; Ezek 20:28; Hos 4:19). Psalm 106:28 terms these pagan acts "sacrifices . . . to lifeless gods" (*ziḇḥê mēṯîm*)—as against the living Lord!

There is nothing in 24:25 to prepare us for the suddenness of 25:1. This chapter is the last word on the old generation. This is the end; the new is coming. The events in this chapter are no mere petty sins on Israel's part. Israel's engagement in the sexually centered worship of Baal was not only the evil of immorality; it was a breach of covenant with the Lord, a worship of the gods of the land (v.3), and a foretaste of the ruin of the people in the unfolding of their history. That this terrible evil followed so closely on the heels of the blessings the Lord pronounced through the improbable prophet Balaam is most lamentable.

The Torah is always hesitant to describe these licentious actions of pagan worship in detail; it refers to these events with considerable restraint. There are at least two reasons for this: (1) the people for whom these texts were first written were well aware of the issues; only we on this side of the vast chasms of time, culture, history, and language have questions; (2) to dwell unduly on the licentious character of the nature religions of the neighbors of Israel could itself become a subtle enticement to draw one in, rather than to repel the reader from the evil itself.

3 Verse 3 is especially telling; the crafting of the verse is powerful. The wording contrasts the actions of Israel with God's evaluation of her:

> And so Israel was yoked to Baal Peor;
> But Yahweh was enraged against Israel.

The verb "to be yoked" (*ṣāmaḏ;* NIV, "joined") is a binding together as oxen are yoked in a common task. In this case Israel was "yoked" to pagan peoples in the worship of their god. The verb speaks of adapting to the worship patterns of a foreign people, an abhorrent concept, such as the false yokings from which Israel was prohibited (see Deut 22:10; cf. 2 Cor 6:14). This passage is the first encounter of Israel with Baal, and it forms the death rattle of the first generation. The term "Peor" describes a mountain in Moab (see 23:28) where the manifestation of Baal was worshiped. In v.18 Peor is used alone of the god (see 31:16; Josh 22:17). Some writers see this as a distinct religion from the Baal worship of Canaan; we agree with Habel (*Yahweh Versus Baal,* p. 25) that the Baal worship at Peor was a part of the same religion as that which was found throughout Canaan.

The wrath of the Lord is a "reddening of his nose" (lit. Heb.), a flashing of his rage. These anthropomorphisms (better, anthropopathisms) are vivid ways to describe what is unimaginable: to be on the receiving end of the wrath of Deity. The point of the Torah is not to show how often God rages or how violent are his judgments. The texts regularly assert how slow he is in coming to rage. But God has his flash point; his rage has a trigger. The rage of the Lord should have been expended against Moab and Balaam because of their effrontery; but here it is directed against Israel. They have deflected his rage from others to themselves by their obdurate folly.

Notes

1 וַיָּחֶל (*wayyāḥel,* "began") may be an example of double entendre. The root *ḥālal* III means "to pollute," "to defile," "to profane" in the Niphal, Piel, and Pual stems. In the Hiphil, as

here, the verb means "to begin." It is used in the same way in other odious contexts (e.g., Gen 6:1; 10:8 ["grew to be"]). In any event, the next verb, לִזְנוֹת (*liznôṯ*, "to play the whore"), leaves nothing to the imagination. The root *zānāh* has the idea of "fornication" in Gen 38:24; Lev 21:9; Deut 22:21; Hos 4:13–14 et al.—all in the case of women engaging in illicite sexual relationships. Here the verb is used of men. They went "whoring" after the women priestesses of the Canaanite religion of Baal. It is a defect of our language that we have numerous words for loose women but few really suitable terms for loose men.

2 The verb וַיִּשְׁתַּחֲווּ (*wayyištaḥᵃwû*, "and [they] bowed down"), now parsed as a Hishtaphel preterit of the root *ḥāwāh* (rather than a Hithpael of the root *šāḥāh*), speaks of "causing oneself to bow down" (the Hishtaphel is causative-reflexive). This is the principal term in the MT for acts of worship, used of the worship of the Lord (see Ps 29:2; cf. Eph 3:14) as well as of pagan gods (as here). It is fitting that the biblical term for worship is physical in nature. See "The Body of the Believer in Worship" (Ronald Allen and Gordon Borror, *Worship: Rediscovering the Missing Jewel* [Portland, Ore.: Multnomah, 1982], pp. 119–35).

---

(2) *The judgment of the Lord on his errant people*
25:4–5

4The LORD said to Moses, "Take all the leaders of these people, kill them and expose them in broad daylight before the LORD, so that the LORD's fierce anger may turn away from Israel."

5So Moses said to Israel's judges, "Each of you must put to death those of your men who have joined in worshiping the Baal of Peor."

4–5 God's rage against his people provoked a terrible judgment: those who were the leaders of the people in this awful act of impiety were to be put to death. The gravity of the sin called not only for death but for a special display of the corpses of the offenders so that those who would survive would be strongly warned of the consequences (v.4). Moses was commanded to execute the offenders (see Notes) and to expose their mutilated bodies before the Lord in "broad daylight." As the animals and birds had been cut in half in the covenant ceremony at the beginnings of Israel's history (Gen 15:10), so the bodies of these rebels were to be dismembered and displayed in an awful symbol of divine judgment. The expression "in broad daylight" (lit., "before the sun") speaks of something done openly, publicly (so 2 Sam 12:12; cf. "before the eyes of the sun" in the MT of v.11). The execution of the leaders was designed to divert his anger from the populace as a whole. The expression *ḥᵃrôn 'aṗ* ("fierce anger") is used elsewhere of the anger of the Lord (32:14; Exod 32:19, 22; Deut 13:17; Josh 7:26; 1 Sam 28:18; 2 Kings 23:26; 2 Chron 28:11; Zeph 2:2; 3:8 et al.); but this anger may be averted, be turned back, once it flashes against its target.

So Moses commanded the judges of Israel to kill those persons who had attached themselves to Baal Peor. The verb "to kill" (v.4) is usually used to speak of ruthless violence, murder (as in Exod 5:21). Here is a rare use, to speak of judicial taking of life by the command of God (so Exod 32:27; Lev 20:15–16; Deut 13:10).

Chapter 25 is the nadir of the Book of Numbers. It is worse even than the sins of chapters 12–14. Here is the great sin at the end of the road. This may be one of the most indelicate texts of Scripture, where Israel's judges are commanded to kill their own people who are engaged in the worship of Baal (v.5). We have trouble at times coming to grips with the commands of Scripture for Israel to kill her enemies. This chapter is harder for us to face; it is the command to kill some of their own people.

But these rebellious persons are like a cancer in the body. If they are not excised, they will soon ruin the whole. So the call is to kill, to execute, and to do it quickly. In chapter 15 was the story of the public execution of one person, a blasphemer. Now the whole populace is in danger.

Notes

4 The NIV translation "kill them and expose them" is a rendering of וְהוֹקַע (*wᵉhôqa'*, "expose [them]"). From v.5 we understand that this verse calls for Moses to take the leaders of the people and to execute them and then to "set them aside" or "expose them" to the Lord in broad daylight. The verb *yāqa'* ("to set aside," "to expose") is used in the Qal stem to describe a bone dislocation (Gen 32:25 [26 MT], of Jacob's thigh). Possibly here the meaning of the Hiphil is "to [kill them and then] expose them with legs and arms broken" (so KB, p. 398c; BDB says, "of some solemn form of execution, but mng. uncertain," p. 429c). Second Sam 21:6, 9 may describe the same type of "exposing" of mutilated bodies (see also the Hophal in 2 Sam 21:13). The Samaritan Pentateuch reads an explanatory line: "And Yahweh said to Moses, 'Let them kill the men who have joined themselves to Baal Peor.' " This seems to be a smoothing of the Hebrew of v.4, based on the words of v.5. It is reading back a clearer idea into a verse where the text is less clear to later readers.

(3) *The zeal of Phinehas*

25:6–9

6 Then an Israelite man brought to his family a Midianite woman right before the eyes of Moses and the whole assembly of Israel while they were weeping at the entrance to the Tent of Meeting. 7 When Phinehas son of Eleazar, the son of Aaron, the priest, saw this, he left the assembly, took a spear in his hand 8 and followed the Israelite into the tent. He drove the spear through both of them—through the Israelite and into the woman's body. Then the plague against the Israelites was stopped; 9 but those who died in the plague numbered 24,000.

6 The wording of v.6 is somewhat problematic. It is possible to take the verse as the NIV has rendered it and to sense in these words that something quite terrible was happening. But I suspect the actions described here were so very shocking that the scribes of Scripture found it to be quite repellent and that the precise nature of the offense was softened somewhat through time. Perhaps the verse is best read this way:

> Then a certain Israelite man brought *the* Midianite woman to *the Tent [of God]* right before the eyes of Moses and the eyes of all the congregation of Israel; *and they were sporting* at the entrance of the Tent of Meeting.

This translation is based on some textual considerations (represented in the emphasized phrases; see Notes) and on an attempt to reconstruct what may have been the most outrageous action of apostate behavior known anywhere in the Torah.

The MT reads in the first instance "to his brother" (*'el- 'eḥāyw*), a phrase the NIV renders "to his family." The LXX translates: "the man brought his brother to the Midianite woman." Yet the mention of "brother" or "family" is not nearly so shocking as the possibility that the phrase should read "to his tent" (reading *'āhᵒlô* instead of *'ehāyw*). Because of what follows, I understand the emended text "his tent" to refer to the Tent of the Lord; i.e., a specific tent is in view. It is most shocking that the tent may be the Tent of Meeting.

This emendation and change of meaning is prompted by the last phrase of the verse, which the NIV renders "while they were weeping at the entrance to the Tent of Meeting." This indicates that it was Moses and the congregation of Israel who were weeping at the entrance to the holy precincts. This is certainly possible; the outrage of the events might have driven Moses and pious persons to weep and to beg God for forgiveness.

It seems likely to me, however, that the subject of the verb "weeping" is not Moses and the congregation but the sinning Israelite and his Midianite partner. The focus of action in the verse is on them, not Moses. What they did was before Moses, in his presence—under his nose! And what they did was to engage in a sexual embrace in the manner of Baal worship—right at the entrance of the holy Tent of God!

The scribes, I suggest, have made a deliberate substitution of an opposite word, "weeping," to connote "caressing," an unusual form of euphemism to stress the heightened enormity of this act. They are not weeping; they are laughing—that is, engaged in delirious love-making (cf. Gen 26:8; Exod 32:6). Just as to say "curse God" is for the godly scribe too much; so "bless God" is stated when "curse God" is intended (see 1 Kings 21:10, 13; Job 1:5, 11; 2:5, 9; Ps 10:3); here, to "cry" in the sacred precincts (as in a cry of remorse) is used to present the antithetical meaning, "to laugh in sexual pleasure"—at the opening of the sacred tent.

The audacious action of this Israelite man is unparalleled and totally unexpected. The contempt for the holy things and the word of the Lord shown by Żimri and his Midianite lover, Cozbi (v.15), is unimaginable. This is a climax to the first section of the Book of Numbers; here is Israel at her very worst. This provides an unhappy justification for the ways of the Lord; it also provides a theodicy of his judgment of the entire first generation.

The man is a blasphemer in the strongest sense. His sin is a deliberate provocateur of the wrath of the Lord, flaunting and taunting holiness in an almost unbelievable crudity. The issue was so blatant, so outrageous, so unspeakable—I suggest—that the ancients had to hide the meaning somewhat in code words. Those who read the text today find between the words that stand (which are awful enough) something that is truly an outrage against Majesty that is nearly unbelievable.

Most of those who saw this happening must have been so shocked that they were motionless. They must have been stunned by audacity, numbed by horror. Someone had to do something; finally, one man did act. Notice that the evil man in this verse is a Hebrew. It would have been bad enough had this been a foreign man with his foreign mate. But it was a prominent man from the congregation. This act, then, is the cause célèbre of v.1, the principal action of "playing the whore" with foreign women. This man's disregard for the sacred (*qōḏeš*) is so outrageous as to shock us even today, in our jaded, secular age.

The point was that in joining the sexual frenzies of the sacrificial feasts of Baal, the man and his priestess-partner now act to transform the worship of the Lord into the type of sexual rites that were the mode of Canaan. Had this outrage not been stopped, there could never have been true worship in the Holy Place again. They were making the place of entrance into a bordello, the entrance of the meeting of God and man into a trysting spot. No wonder the ancients may have been uncomfortable with this text.

That the woman was a Midianitess but the people Moabites reminds us of the complexities of the relationships of the transient peoples of the ancient Near East at this time (compare the Ishmaelites and Midianites in Gen 37:25–36). More importantly, she is identified in the Hebrew of v.6 with the definite article, "the Midianitess." This suggests that this was not just one of the local sacred prostitutes but a person of prominence. I suggest that the article is used to mark her out as a pivotal player. Perhaps she is the high priestess of the religion at Baal Peor. The story when read this way explains the action of Phinehas in the next verses.

We may observe that while priests were always male in Israel, priests could be women in the pagan religions that surrounded Israel. In fact, the sexually centered religions of Canaan would have catered to women in their priesthood. Women priests were so very closely tied to the sexual outrages of Baal and Asherah worship that the very notion of a women priest conjured up images of sexual worship. Perhaps this is the principal reason that Israel had no women priests.

It was the brazenness of the acts of these two that made them not just sinners but an abomination to the Lord. Here is a frontal assault on the true, high, and pure worship of the Lord that the priestly interests in the Book of Numbers stress repeatedly. Only an act of equal force to the nature of the affront will suffice. That powerful act came in the person of Phinehas.

7–8 When Phinehas the son of Eleazar saw what was happening right at the entrance of the tent (v.7), he reached for a "spear" (*rōmaḥ,* v.8) and drove it through the licentious couple. While all saw what was happening, Phinehas not only watched, he also acted. He came from the midst of the people as the protagonist. Possibly the implement he used was a spear that he took from a soldier nearby. It is hard to know what a priest would be doing with a spear (yet see the use of spears by pagan priests in 1 Kings 18:28). It is also just possible that *rōmaḥ* might here mean "knife," as this would be the more expected tool for a priest. It would be suitably ironic for him to have used a tool he normally used to kill animals in sacrifice to the Lord as the weapon to destroy this sinning couple.

Phinehas is a grandson of Aaron (Exod 6:25). His name may be Egyptian in origin; BDB suggests *Pe-nehasi* ("the negro," p. 810), speaking of dark complexion. Phinehas is a "man of the in-between" (*'îš habbēnayim,* 1 Sam 17:4), as Goliath had been to the Philistines, a "champion" (cf. v.23). Phinehas is a *gibbôr ḥāyil,* a mighty man of valor (1 Sam 9:1 [NIV, "man of standing"]; 16:18 ["brave man"]). He is also a true *'eḇeḏ yhwh* ("servant of the LORD"). Ultimately, he is typical of Christ the Victor (see Pss 2; 110; Rev 19). He is an early embodiment of "star" and "scepter" of 24:17, the smiter of Moab. He is the hand of God extended in rage against the profanation of his joy. Phinehas is one of the great heroes of faith in Scripture; though he is quite unknown to most of us, he is never forgotten by God. His zeal is that of one who fears the Lord, who waits on his mercy (Ps 147:11), but who also acts when not to act would be to sin.

Verse 8 says that Phinehas pursued the couple into the "vaulted canopy" (*haqqubbāh;* NIV, "tent"), a word used only here in the Bible. If our conceptualization of this story is correct, it is possible that the term *qubbāh* refers to some canopy at the entrance of the Tent of Meeting. It would not be necessary to imagine that the couple were actually in the Most Holy Place; nor does it seem likely that they were in the man's tent, as is commonly supposed. In any event, there is a grisly pun on the word *haqqubbāh* and the word for "her belly" (*qᵒḇāṯāh*). That Phinehas pierced through the two of them is forcefully stressed: (1) the knife or spear could not have been a little thing but could well have been a narrow, sharp blade; (2) there would have to be tremendous force to plunge the knife or spear through both bodies; (3) the emphasis on "both" stresses that they were oblivious to Phinehas, both caught up in their licentiousness, so that the knife would have gone through his back, out his sternum, and into her abdomen; and (4) with this the plague was stayed, indicating that this couple was not just an outrageous instance of debauchery—likely they were the instigators of the pagan rites!

9 The number of those who died because of the flagrant actions of the people in their worship of the Baal of Peor (24,000; see 1 Cor 10:8 where 23,000 is given; see EBC, 10:249) exceeded even those who died in the rebellion of Korah and his allies (14,700; see 16:49). If the numbers of the two census lists (1:46; cf. 26:51) are taken at face value, then the loss of 24,000 people, while significant, is not overwhelming. If the numbers of the census lists are rhetorically inflated, then we have to ask whether this number is also inflated. It seems quite possible that this number and the number of those who died in Korah's rebellion may be "common numbers" rather than inflated ones. In this case, the enormity of the numbers who died in this plague is truly impressive—nearly 10 percent of the total population of 250,000. The issues of the "numbers in Numbers" continue to intrigue—and to baffle! (See the sections on large numbers in the Introduction.)

(4) *The Lord's covenant with Phinehas*

25:10–13

> [10]The LORD said to Moses, [11]"Phinehas son of Eleazar, the son of Aaron, the priest, has turned my anger away from the Israelites; for he was as zealous as I am for my honor among them, so that in my zeal I did not put an end to them. [12]Therefore tell him I am making my covenant of peace with him. [13]He and his descendants will have a covenant of a lasting priesthood, because he was zealous for the honor of his God and made atonement for the Israelites."

10–11 The words of the Lord to Moses concerning Phinehas (v.10) take us back to the words of the Decalogue (Exod 20:4–6). The zeal of Phinehas for the honor of the Lord became the occasion for the Lord's covenanting with him and his descendants as God's true priests. What a contrast this son of Eleazar is with the casual wickedness of his uncles Nadab and Abihu (see comment on 3:4)!

Standard post-modern criticism regards the present shape of the Book of Numbers to be the work of P, the priestly source, lately designed to elevate the priests in the life of the people and their institutions. Thus not only are chapters such as 15 and 19 significant in their calm presentation of sacrifices, worship, duties, and tithes, but so is this chapter, as the hero of the piece is a priest.

For the more conservative reader, whose understanding does not proceed from the putative P source, the emphasis on priest should still be maintained. Since the hero of our story is a priest, our estimation of priests and priesthood should be enhanced. These men could be noble and brave; they are not just cultic functionaries. Then we remember that Christ is priest. He is noble and brave. The best in priests points to Christ. This is true of Aaron, Eleazar, and Phinehas. The chapter celebrates a great priest, just as it excoriates a terrible evil.

Verse 10 introduces an oracle of the Lord, attached directly to the preceding dramatic narrative. The focus of the oracle is on Phinehas who has acted with the zeal of the Lord. There is almost a sense of pride in the way Phinehas is addressed in this text: "Phinehas son of Eleazar, the son of Aaron, the priest" (v.11). This is the language of celebration. The zeal of Phinehas stayed the rage of Yahweh; the zeal of Phinehas restrained the zeal of the Lord to annihilate the nation. Perhaps in these words we should stand beside his father, Eleazar, and sense his pride in his son.

12 The Lord now institutes his covenant with the priests through Phinehas. We often speak of the Abrahamic, Mosaic, and Davidic covenants. In all probability we should also speak of the Lord's covenant with Phinehas. He was priest by divine right, being descended from the right family in an immediate line. He showed himself to be the rightful priest by his interest in divine righteousness. He is now confirmed priest by the rite of the divine covenant.

13 As in the Lord's covenant with Abram, this covenant is God's doing; it involves his "seed," and it is lasting (*'ôlām*). In the case of Abram, God first chose him; then by Abram's action of faith, the Lord confirmed his covenant with him (see Gen 12, 15, 22). In the case of Phinehas, he was already chosen by God; but in his action, God's covenant with him is confirmed.

Most surprisingly, by the action of Phinehas "atonement" (*wayᵉkappēr*) was made for the people; for the plague was stopped (v.9). This chapter is a pivotal section in the theology of the Torah.

Notes

---

12 The phrase בְּרִיתִי שָׁלוֹם (*bᵉrîṯî šālôm*, "my covenant of peace") is somewhat problematic, as we do not usually find intervening pronoun suffixes in bound constructions. We would have expected בְּרִית שְׁלוֹמִי (*berîṯ šᵉlômî;* cf. *har qoḏšî*, "my holy mountain"). Some have emended the word *šālôm* to *šillûm* ("my covenant of requital").

---

(5) *The aftermath of the rebellion*

25:14–18

> [14]The name of the Israelite who was killed with the Midianite woman was Zimri son of Salu, the leader of a Simeonite family. [15]And the name of the Midianite woman who was put to death was Cozbi daughter of Zur, a tribal chief of a Midianite family.
>
> [16]The LORD said to Moses, [17]"Treat the Midianites as enemies and kill them, [18]because they treated you as enemies when they deceived you in the affair of Peor and their sister Cozbi, the daughter of a Midianite leader, the woman who was killed when the plague came as a result of Peor."

14–18 Only after the role of Phinehas has been suitably celebrated are the names of the antagonists given. The Israelite was a prince of the house of Simeon, Zimri son of Salu (v.14). It is important that we realize this was not an insignificant individual—here was one who should have ennobled himself and his father's house. As the great pride of Eleazar must have swelled over the actions of his son that day, so there must have been extraordinary shame among the members of Zimri's family on realizing what this promising young man had done.

Zimri ("My Remembrance") had been named in praise of God. However, he has come to be forever remembered as the one who nearly destroyed his people in his flagrant, wanton attack on the pure worship of God. With his name turned on its head, he serves as a memorial to destruction. The name of his Midianite partner is given as Cozbi daughter of Zur (v.15). Her name is an example of names deliberately changed by Israel because of their contempt for her (see on the name of Balaam in 22:5). "Cozbi" means "My Lie" or "Deception." She stands forever memorialized as a prime example of the deception of the allure of pagan worship. Verse 18 speaks of her as one who was also from a noble house of her own people. Likely she was a priestess of her religion, a prototype of Jezebel who would later be instrumental in bringing Baal and Asherah worship into the center of the life of Israel.

Because of their active participation in the seduction of the sons of Israel, the Midianites were put under the curse of God and were henceforth to be treated as enemies (v.17). The Midianites had been in league with Balak from the beginning of the confrontation (see on 22:4) and became the objects of a holy war of Israel to declare the glory of the name Yahweh (see ch. 31).

In the MT the words "After the plague" (26:1) form a separate verse at the end of the chapter (25:19). However, this is an exceedingly poor chapter division; the words do not really form a separate verse. They end in an *Athnach* accent, the principal disjunctive punctuation mark within a unit. These words rightly belong to the beginning of v.1 of chapter 26. But they are emphatic; this was the final, definitive plague. The old generation is gone; the new is born.

II. The Prospects for the Second Generation to Enter the Promised Land (26:1–36:13)

Following the lead of Olson (see Introduction: Unity and Structure), I suggest that this chapter begins the second major part of the Book of Numbers. The book is best seen as a bifid based on the two generations that are celebrated in the two census lists. Other approaches to the book use chronological or geographical clues to help establish the relevant portions. However, the chronological notes are too few and piecemeal to be helpful, and the arrangement of the blocks of materials turns out not to be in chronological sequence. Similarly, the geographical issues, which at first seem to be more helpful than the chronological for discovering the author's purpose, do not yield convincing results.

Most who follow the geographical approach are able to agree on the first major division at 10:11, the beginning of the march from Sinai. But there is no consensus as to the beginning of the third movement, the march to or the sojourn in Moab. But more problematic than the issue of which verses should be included in which geographical section (and the lack of the precise indicator in the text of Numbers ought to be regarded as a problem in this approach) is that the geographical approach slights over the most prominent feature of the book, its census lists!

The Book of Numbers is rightly named; its organization is really quite simple. There are two grand sections: (1) the census and preparation for march of the first generation and their subsequent failure and judgment (chs. 1–25); (2) the census and preparation for march of the second generation and the hope that they will not repeat the sins of their fathers and mothers (chs. 26–36).

The unequal nature of the two sections is because the story is fully told of the first generation; they were prepared, but they rebelled and did not inherit the land. The second generation is prepared, but their subsequent success or failure is left for another day.

The first section begins with the preparation of a holy camp and is then followed by the material describing the rebellion of the people, their subsequent judgment, and their return to the desert to await the dying of the rebellious people. The chapters on priesthood, purification, and the like are included in this section as encouragements to the people. Even though the one generation will never be able to participate in the blessings of the land, yet those blessings have not been forgotten by God. The new generation may be making confident preparation for their day in glory. Then the story of Balaam comes as the new generation is about to have its opportunity. The pagan prophet is a foil for the person of Moses, and his attempted cursings of Israel are opportunities for God to renew his promises of blessings and to affirm them to the people. Thus there is in this incident tremendous assurance that despite all the sins, rebellions, and untoward actions of the people on so many occasions and in the most diverse of circumstances, the Lord is not only not finished with his people, he is more ready than ever to bless them and to complete his promise of salvation for them. Yet immediately on the heels of this monumental blessing of the people by their God, they rebel in the most egregious way possible.

Chapter 25 records Israel's bowing to the lust of Baal Peor, the last rebellion of the first generation. And the plague is their last judgment, the final assault of God on wicked persons, the final dying of the people.

Then chapter 26 begins with the idea that after the plague the Lord commanded that Moses do a census of the people. The expression "after the plague" is to be regarded as the turning point from the first generation to the second, the shift from the fathers and mothers to sons and daughters. God was about to begin a new work with a new people. The younger generation would begin to have their day.

The second section of the Book of Numbers presents only the positive, preparatory side of things. It deals with the taking of the new census, a demonstration that God has kept faith with the people in a remarkable manner. Despite innumerable setbacks and plagues that touched many lives, and despite the judgment of God that decreed that everyone over the age of twenty would have to die in the forty years spent in the desert, the total numbers of the people remain nearly precisely the same. This is an enormous miracle, a great demonstration of the power of God to do his will and work even in the most unlikely of places.

But the new generation will also have to face its tests. What those will be are anybody's guess, but they will not likely be easier than those suffered by their parents. The great question, looming like a heavy cloud on the horizon, is being asked all along the way through these last chapters of the Book of Numbers: Is it possible that the new generation will finally be used of God to enter the land, to conquer the inhabitants, to deplace them, and to enjoy the land that is God's great and gracious gift for them? Or is it possible that this new, second generation will be like its predecessors? Will they also come to the lip of the land, send out their spies, and then find that the evil report of these spies will also dissuade them? God forbid! May the new generation be new; may they be faithful to God in all their house even as Moses was for most of his lustrous career. And may they enter the land with joy and delight, praising God for giving them the opportunity that their parents had but which they forswore.

So the Book of Numbers ends with a great, haunting question: What will the children be like? Will they be like their parents? Or will they be like Moses and Aaron, like Joshua and Caleb, like Miriam and others faithful to God? Will they believe in him, obey his commands, and take up their weapons as they march in victory song?

Incidentally, the bifed approach to the Book of Numbers greatly heightens the importance of the subsequent story of the sending out of the spies from Israel's encampment in Transjordan to the city of Jericho (Josh 2). The work of those spies and their report is the accomplishment of daring men of faith. They are like Caleb and Joshua (and, notably, there are just two spies this time). The plan is on. The people will do as God demands.

A. *The Preparation for the Triumphal March to the Promised Land, the Second Generation (26:1–32:42)*

In view of the approach we have suggested, chapters 26–36 match and mirror the basic thrust of chapters 1–10. In each case there is the enumeration of the people in celebration of the Lord's grace to his people, their preparation for a holy march, and the anticipation that soon they shall be in Canaan and Canaan shall become the land of Israel.

1. *The second census of the new generation that will enter the land (26:1–65)*

a. *The command of the Lord to take the census*

26:1–4

> 1 After the plague the LORD said to Moses and Eleazar son of Aaron, the
> priest, 2 "Take a census of the whole Israelite community by families—
> all those twenty years old or more who are able to serve in the army of
> Israel." 3 So on the plains of Moab by the Jordan across from Jericho,
> Moses and Eleazar the priest spoke with them and said, 4 "Take a census
> of the men twenty years old or more, as the LORD commanded Moses."
> These were the Israelites who came out of Egypt:

1–4a The first phrase, "After the plague," is key for understanding this text. The plague of chapter 25 was not just another plague; it was the final judgment of God on the first generation and the opportunity to unleash the blessing of God on the second generation who have now reached their majority.

The first census of the redeemed community had been taken over thirty-eight years earlier. This was a census for conscription to the army of the people, soldiers who were drafted for the war of conquest of the Land of Promise. That first generation of men over the age of twenty had died. It was now time for the new generation to be numbered and mustered for the campaign of conquest that now awaited them. The aged Moses was joined in the task this time by his nephew Eleazar. Aaron was dead (20:28). Miriam was dead (20:1). And Moses was soon to die as well.

How sad it must have been for Moses to realize what might have been! And yet there must have been enormous satisfaction to realize that it still might be—though without him. This was a bittersweet time, one of ruing the past while still anticipating the future. It was the same task: number the able-bodied men over the age of twenty to conscript them for the army of Israel. But it was a different task. The place had changed from Sinai to Moab. The personnel had changed; Moses was assisted now by Eleazar instead of his brother Aaron. More importantly, the people had changed; now it was a new generation.

The passage thus presents a collective sigh. At last we will be at it. We will finally be on the trail again. Yet the passage also evokes a certain sadness. What we are now doing has already been done. What we are about to do should have been done long ago. Our parents should have entered the land, and we should have grown up there rather than here in this desert. The passage is also a warning. Those mustered earlier were disqualified; just being in the roll call of the Lord's army does not mean acquittal in his service.

Eleazar is not the only son that participated this day; they were all sons of fathers who had died. There is a final poignancy in the heart of Moses. The last time he was going as the leader of the people. This time he is involved in their preparation, but he will not be with them in their campaign. This must have eaten away at his inner man as a tourniquet of regret wrenching his heart.

4b These words actually serve as the section heading for the listing of tribe by tribe that follows. How impressive it is that the phrasing is inclusive of the departure from Egypt! This generation is regarded as the Exodus people. It is as though their parents had not lived, as though they had not rebelled. The new generation is the substitute for the first. The story begins anew, as though the people had just left bondage in Egypt.

Notes

1 The first phrase of v.1, וַיְהִי אַחֲרֵי הַמַּגֵּפָה (*wayᵉhî 'aḥᵃrê hammaggēp̄āh*, "after the plague"), is somewhat problematic in that the chapter division is misplaced in the present MT. In BHS these words are called 25:19 (observe that there is no v.19 in the EVV), but they do not form a complete verse. These three words end in an *Athnach* accent, a major disjunctive within a verse, then 26:1 in Hebrew begins with the words "and Yahweh said." There is no *Athnach* within 26:1; it clearly is the same verse begun with the words "After the plague." A further complication is in the inclusion of the Hebrew letter pe as a section marker after this introductory phrase. In this case we may have an example of a chapter number being written inadvertently in the midst of the first verse of the unit; the first part of the verse was then assigned a supernumerary for convenience of citation.

3 עַל־יַרְדֵּן יְרֵחוֹ (*'al-yardēn yᵉrēḥô*, "by the Jordan of Jericho") seems to be an older way of speaking of the region of the Jordan River that is across from the city of Jericho (so NIV; see also v.63; 31:12; 33:48, 50; 35:1; 36:13).

b. *The enumeration of the people by their ancestral tribes and clans (26:5–50)*

(1) *The tribe of Reuben*

26:5–11

5The descendants of Reuben, the firstborn son of Israel, were:

through Hanoch, the Hanochite clan;
through Pallu, the Palluite clan;
6 through Hezron, the Hezronite clan;
through Carmi, the Carmite clan.
7 These were the clans of Reuben; those numbered were 43,730.
8 The son of Pallu was Eliab, 9 and the sons of Eliab were Nemuel,
Dathan and Abiram. The same Dathan and Abiram were the community
officials who rebelled against Moses and Aaron and were among
Korah's followers when they rebelled against the LORD. 10 The earth
opened its mouth and swallowed them along with Korah, whose
followers died when the fire devoured the 250 men. And they served as a
warning sign. 11 The line of Korah, however, did not die out.

5–7 Pride of place is given to Reuben, firstborn of Jacob. These chapters serve as the account of the generations of Jacob (see on 1:17–19). The four clans are descended from his sons Hanoch, Pallu, Hezron, and Carmi (whose names are given first in Gen 46:9). Numbers 26 should be compared with Genesis 46:8–27. Genesis 46 is a full mustering of the fathers' houses as Israel went down to Egypt. Numbers 26 is a full mustering of the fathers' houses as they were about to reenter Canaan. From the seventy persons of Genesis 46:27 to the quarter million (or two and one-half million!) of Numbers 26:51 is an enormous increase, despite the conditions in Egypt for four hundred years, coupled to the experience in the desert for another forty years. Reuben's sons are also mentioned in Exodus 6:14 (the same listing as in Gen 46 and Num 26).

8–11 The listing of the families of Reuben becomes an occasion to remind the reader of the part that certain of their number (esp. Dathan and Abiram) had had in the rebellion of Korah (16:1; On is not mentioned in ch. 26). The tragic memory of the rebellion of Korah is made as well in Jude 11.

This paragraph is impressive. It is something of an intrusion into the ordered format of the tribal listings, clans, and numbers. But it is extremely important that the reader know this list is not just business as usual.

The overwhelming judgment of those who joined Korah in his ill-advised rebellion was to remain a *nēs*, "a warning sign" or "signal flag of warning," to succeeding generations (v.10). They, too, may suffer a similar fate if ever they attempted similar folly.

The wording of v.9 is dramatic: "the very Dathan and Abiram" (*hû' dāṯān wa'ᵃḇîrām*). Further, the verb translated "rebelled" (*nāṣāh*) against Moses and Aaron is rare, signifying a strong contest of wills. But ultimately they found they were struggling, not just with man, but with God. He used heaven (fire) and earth (the sink hole) to destroy them. Take on God and one finds he has a no-holds-barred fight. After all, "The LORD is a warrior" (Exod 15:3).

Some names of infidels and rascals are to be forgotten. They are to be treated as though they never had lived. But others have behaved so shamefully that their names are to be preserved as bywords for future generations, a warning to others not to be like them. These names are like the salten image of the unfortunate wife of Lot, a symbolic barrier to misbehavior.

Names are of interest in the biblical narrative. These men were named for God but became his enemies. As Elimelech in the Book of Ruth, a godly name does not necessarily mean a godly life. Nor is a godly name a device effective to ward off his judgment. A godly name on an ungodly person is in fact a double offense, more deserving ever of God's judgment.

In Sum: The tribe of Reuben numbered 43,730 in the second census, a decrease of 2,770 from the 46,500 of the first census (a loss of about 6 percent). There are four clans. In both lists Reuben is in the first rank. The further history of the Reubenites is found in 1 Chronicles 5:1–10.

Notes

The listing of the clans in the second census calls for special mention. These names would be very important for the nation later in the land as people would wish to be able to trace with certainty their ancestry for purposes of tribal inheritance. The listing of the clans is also a dramatic mark on the part of the narrator; this is the list that will count! We may observe that not all those who were part of Israel were genetically descended from Jacob through his twelve sons. From the beginning there was a joining of destiny with the people of Israel of persons of varied backgrounds. However, to have their part in the land, they had to have a tie with a tribe and a family. Perhaps ritual adoption was the means used to include such persons in the community rosters.

The number of the tribe of Reuben in the second listing is a slight decrease from the first. Several of the tribes increase in number in the second census over the first (Judah, Issachar, Zebulun, Manasseh, Benjamin, Dan, and Asher). Like Reuben, Gad suffers a slight decline; Ephraim and Naphtali a greater decline, and the tribe of Simeon takes a decisive cut.

Possibly the slight reduction of the families of Reuben (46,500 in 1:20; 2:10) was brought about by the judgment on their members during the rebellion of Korah and his Reubenite allies (see comment on 26:9). In the intervening years the family of Reuben had nearly caught up with its former numbers.

Here is a comparison of the numbers of each of the tribes from the first census to the second:

Tribe	*First Census*	*Second Census*
Reuben	46,500	43,730
Simeon	59,300	22,200
Gad	45,650	40,500
Judah	74,600	76,500
Issachar	54,400	64,300
Zebulun	57,400	60,500
Ephraim	40,500	32,500
Manasseh	32,200	52,700
Benjamin	35,400	45,600
Dan	62,700	64,400
Asher	41,500	53,400
Naphtali	53,400	45,400
Total	603,550	601,730

As we observed in the first census listings, there are several interesting factors in these various numbers. First, none of these numbers is brought down to the digit; only two are rounded to the tens (Gad in the first census, 45,650) and Reuben in the second (43,730); all the others are rounded off to the hundreds. In both lists there are six tribes that number over 50,000 men and six that number fewer than 50,000. Twelve units of 50,000 is a convenient way to reach the grand totals of 600,000:

Tribes With More Than 50,000 Men

First Census		Second Census	
Simeon	59,300		
Judah	74,600	Judah	76,500
Issachar	54,400	Issachar	64,300
		Manasseh	52,700
Zebulun	57,400	Zebulun	60,500
Dan	62,700	Dan	64,400
		Asher	53,400
Naphtali	53,400		

Tribes With Fewer Than 50,000 Men

First Census		Second Census	
Reuben	46,500	Reuben	43,730
		Simeon	22,200
Gad	45,650	Gad	40,500
Ephraim	40,500	Ephraim	32,500
Manasseh	32,200		
Benjamin	35,400	Benjamin	45,600
Asher	41,500		
		Naphtali	45,400

7 For a discussion concerning the large numbers in this chapter and in the census lists for the first generation, see the Introduction, the sections on large numbers.

---

(2) *The tribe of Simeon*

26:12–14

12 The descendants of Simeon by their clans were:
through Nemuel, the Nemuelite clan;
through Jamin, the Jaminite clan;
through Jakin, the Jakinite clan;
13 through Zerah, the Zerahite clan;
through Shaul, the Shaulite clan.
14 These were the clans of Simeon; there were 22,200 men.

12–14 The greatest loss was among the tribe of Simeon (down to 22,200 from 59,300). The exceedingly wicked Zimri (see ch. 25) was a prince of the house of Simeon (v.14). Perhaps the larger number of the 24,000 who died in the plague of that time were of the house of Simeon. The judgment was so recent that the tribe had not had time to recover, as had Reuben (see comment on v.7).

Five clans are listed as descended from Simeon in v.12: Nemuel, Jamin, Jakin, Zerah, and Shaul. Nemuel is called Jemuel in Genesis 46:10 and Exodus 6:15. Further Ohad of Genesis 46:10 and Exodus 6:15 is not mentioned in Numbers; perhaps he died childless or for some other reason did not found a bona fide clan of Israel. Genesis 46:10 notes of Shaul that his mother was a Canaanite woman, an interesting note when compared with the story of Judah and Tamar in Genesis 38.

In Sum: The tribe of Simeon numbered 22,200 in the second census, a decrease of 37,100 from the 59,300 of the first census (a decrease of about 63 percent). There are five clans. The tribe of Simeon is in the second rank in both lists. In 1 Chronicles 4:24 the sons of Simeon are listed as Nemuel, Jamin, Jarib, Zerah, and Shaul; 1 Chronicles 4:24–43 develops the later history of the family of Simeon.

(3) *The tribe of Gad*

26:15–18

15The descendants of Gad by their clans were:
through Zephon, the Zephonite clan;
through Haggi, the Haggite clan;
through Shuni, the Shunite clan;
16through Ozni, the Oznite clan;
through Eri, the Erite clan;
17through Arodi, the Arodite clan;
through Areli, the Arelite clan.
18These were the clans of Gad; those numbered were 40,500.

15–18 Here we notice a standard, even stereotypical pattern of the tribal listings. Only in the rebellious tribe of Reuben is there a strong variation. The other listings follow a bookkeeper's tidy pattern, at least in format.

There are several problems in parallel passages with the names of these sons of Gad. Further, when we compare the names of the sons of Gad in Genesis 46:16, we find some variations of names. Zephon of v.15 is Ziphion in Genesis 46:16 (NIV mg.); Ozni of v.16 is Ezbon in Genesis 46:16. The problems with these names in parallel passages could be regarded as an embarrassment to the tenet of inspiration. Yet in a sense the very problems we find in these parallel listings of names may be a strong indicator of the tradition of textual integrity. If the text were not highly regarded by the scribes as the Word of God, then blemishes such as these would have been smoothed over. Spellings would have been agreed on, divergences expunged. Surely we are not the first to read one name in Numbers 26 and another in Genesis 46, one in Numbers 26 and another in 1 Chronicles. The preservation of discordant spellings and even dissimilar names argues for, not against, inspiration. At one time the names were known and were correct. When errors crept in, or when alternate names were used that resulted in some confusion, the scholars of later generations did not disturb the evidence they had. This is not to say that scribes never meddled with names; in fact they did! But the amazing thing is that they did not meddle more, especially in instances such as these. In cases of such "muddled" names, there are several alternative explanations: (1) different spellings for the same name, (2) different names for the same person, (3) confusion of scribes and hence mistakes in the copying of the names.

In Sum: The tribe of Gad numbered 40,500 in the second census, a decrease of 5,150 from the 45,650 of the first census (a decrease of about 11 percent). There are seven clans. The tribe of Gad is in the third rank in both lists. The further history of the tribe of Gad is found in 1 Chronicles 5:11–17.

(4) *The tribe of Judah*

26:19–22

19Er and Onan were sons of Judah, but they died in Canaan.
20The descendants of Judah by their clans were:

through Shelah, the Shelanite clan;
through Perez, the Perezite clan;
through Zerah, the Zerahite clan.
[21]The descendants of Perez were:
through Hezron, the Hezronite clan;
through Hamul, the Hamulite clan.
[22]These were the clans of Judah; those numbered were 76,500.

19–22 Compare v.19 with Genesis 46:12: "The sons of Judah: Er, Onan, Shelah, Perez and Zerah (but Er and Onan died in the land of Canaan). The sons of Perez: Hezron and Hamul." As in the case of the sons of Eliab of Reuben (vv.9–11), the sadnesses of the fathers' families are not glossed over in these lists but are to be remembered for posterity. The family of Judah was unique among the tribes of Israel in that two of the father's sons died childless in Canaan because of their perfidy before their father ever left for Egypt. Now, hundreds of years later, the sordid story of Er and Onan is alluded to, not to titillate, but to warn, to cause the people to remember.

Here we are reminded that Shelah went on to marry and to father a clan. Further, the sons of Judah by his son's wife, Tamar, each fathered a clan. The firstborn twin, Perez, has two subclans, a mark of significance, since most of the grandsons are not mentioned here. It is likely that the listing of these subclans makes up for the loss of the clans that might have been founded by the two deceased older sons. Perez has the double honor; indeed, his is the line that Yahweh selects for his great king David (Ruth 4:18–22) and for David's greater Son, Jesus (Matt 1:3; Luke 3:33). It is fascinating that already in Genesis 46:12 the precedence of Perez was asserted. He alone is noted of the grandsons.

In Sum: The tribe of Judah numbered 76,500 in the second census, an increase of 1,900 from the 74,600 of the first census (a gain of less than 3 percent). There are five clans (two are subclans). The tribe of Judah is in the fourth rank in both lists. The further history of the tribe of Judah is found in 1 Chronicles 2:3–4:23; this includes an extensive listing, not only of sons, but of mothers and daughters, an unusual feature in these lists. Since it is from the tribe of Judah that the kings were traced, the unusual listing is made significant. For obvious reasons Christian readers are aware of the special care of the Spirit of God in these lists.

(5) *The tribe of Issachar*

26:23–25

[23]The descendants of Issachar by their clans were:
through Tola, the Tolaite clan;
through Puah, the Puite clan;
[24]through Jashub, the Jashubite clan;
through Shimron, the Shimronite clan.
[25]These were the clans of Issachar; those numbered were 64,300.

23–25 The clans of Issachar are traced through Tola, Puah, Jashub, and Shimron. Two of these names are problematic; there is difficulty with the spelling of Puah (see Notes on v.23), and the name Job (*yôḇ*, "Iob") is mistakenly written in the MT of Genesis 46:13 for Jashub (*yāšûḇ*). There is also a slight variation in spelling for the name Shimron (*šimrōn* in Num; *šimrôn* in Gen). The point is that we can put these various data together and attempt to harmonize them. The scribes did not, presumably based on their sense of caution of destroying the varied evidence that was before them.

In Sum: The tribe of Issachar numbered 64,300 in the second census, an increase of 9,900 from the 54,400 of the first census (a gain of about 18 percent). There are four clans. The tribe of Issachar is in the fifth rank in both lists. The further history of the tribe of Issachar is found in 1 Chronicles 7:1–5.

Notes

---

23 The name פֻּוָה (*puwāh*, "Puah") is spelled variously in different texts and is represented differently in the versions. Many Hebrew manuscripts read the word as *puwwāh;* the Samaritan Pentateuch, LXX, Syriac, and Vulgate read *pû'āh.* Genesis 46:13 reads *puwwāh;* 1 Chron 7:1 reads *pû'āh.* In each case the same individual is intended, but the spelling variations suggest some confusion. Matters are made more difficult by the name of the judge Tola in Judg 10:1. He is called "a man of Issachar, Tola son of Puah, the son of Dodo." Some scholars suggest that this judge was assigned to an earlier time by the P source in Genesis and Numbers (e.g., BDB, p. 1069a). However, it would not be at all unusual for patronymic names to be used in later generations in alternating sequences; such was common in ancient (and modern) times.

---

(6) *The tribe of Zebulun*

26:26–27

26 The descendants of Zebulun by their clans were:
through Sered, the Seredite clan;
through Elon, the Elonite clan;
through Jahleel, the Jahleelite clan.
27 These were the clans of Zebulun; those numbered were 60,500.

26–27 Sered, Elon, and Jahleel, sons of Zebulun, founded the three clans of this tribe; the names are the same in Genesis 46:14.

In Sum: The tribe of Zebulun numbered 60,500 in the second census, an increase of 3,100 from the 57,400 of the first census (a gain of over 5 percent). There are three clans. The tribe of Zebulun is in the sixth rank in both census lists. Unlike the other tribes, the further history of the tribe of Zebulun is not recorded in 1 Chronicles 2–8; only the name of the tribe is given in 2:1. This is a strange omission (but see on Dan, vv.42–43).

(7) *The tribe of Manasseh*

26:28–34

28 The descendants of Joseph by their clans through Manasseh and Ephraim were:

29 The descendants of Manasseh:
through Makir, the Makirite clan (Makir was the father of Gilead);
through Gilead, the Gileadite clan.
30 These were the descendants of Gilead:

through Iezer, the Iezerite clan;
through Helek, the Helekite clan;
31 through Asriel, the Asrielite clan;
through Shechem, the Shechemite clan;
32 through Shemida, the Shemidaite clan;
through Hepher, the Hepherite clan.
33 (Zelophehad son of Hepher had no sons; he had only daughters, whose names were Mahlah, Noah, Hoglah, Milcah and Tirzah.)
34 These were the clans of Manasseh; those numbered were 52,700.

28–34 There is an inclusio of sorts grouping the tribes of Manasseh and Ephraim. Verse 28 introduces these two tribes as the descendants of Joseph; v.37 ends with a notice that these were the descendants of Joseph. In this way the reader is reminded that Joseph received the double honor of his father, Jacob, by having two sons receive equal status with his brothers among the tribes of Israel. With the removal of the tribe of Levi from the lay tribes, this "bonus" to Joseph maintained the sacral number twelve for the fathers' houses.

The order of the tribes is the same in the two census lists, with the exception of the inversion of Manasseh and Ephraim among the Joseph tribes. One observation we may make about this inversion of order is that the tribe of Ephraim was superior in numbers to Manasseh in Numbers 1; the reverse is true in Numbers 26. Later in Israel's history, the tribe of Ephraim becomes the counterpart in the north to the importance of Judah in the south. Yet at this point the tribe of Ephraim is among the smallest (only Simeon with 22,200 is smaller than Ephraim's 32,500). This datum seems to argue against the critical theory from a number of German scholars that the lists in these chapters of Numbers were projections backwards from late in Israel's history (when these lists were manufactured), based on their conceptions of the ideal state of affairs during the times of David and Solomon. Yet these numbers do not accord with any later period of Israel's history; if the numbers do not accord with the time of Moses in some manner, then they are simply manufactured.

There are a couple of unusual things in the roster of the clans of Manasseh. First, only one son of Manasseh is listed; his name is Makir (see Gen 50:23; Num 27:1; 32:39–40; Deut 3:15; Josh 13:31; 17:1, 3). Joshua 17:1–2 suggests that Makir was the firstborn of Manasseh and that Abiezer (= Iezer), Helek, Asriel, Shechem, Hepher, and Shemida were other "sons." These other sons are actually descended from Gilead, son of Makir.

This means that the tribe of Manasseh is distinctive in that it did not divide into subclans until the fourth generation. The line of descent is Joseph – Manasseh – Makir – Gilead – then six sons, including Hepher—from Hepher comes Zelophehad, who has five daughters. The listing of the sons of Gilead is prominent in our text: Iezer, Helek, Asriel, Shechem, Shemida, Hepher (and Zelophehad).

It is the last named that presents the second unusual factor in this listing; Zelophehad, actually the grandson of Gilead, "had no sons, only daughters" (v.33). This becomes the subject matter for chapter 27 (and a follow up in ch. 36).

The family of Makir is developed in 1 Chronicles 7:14–19. Of Manasseh it is said that his Aramean concubine bore him Makir (v.14). Makir then married Maachah, from the people of Huppim and Shuppim, and they became the parents of Gilead. Gilead has six sons: Iezer (see Notes on v.30), Helek, Asriel, Shechem, Shemida, and Hepher. Hepher was the father of Zelophehad.

While the descendants of Jacob have a remarkable propensity to father sons, surely there were daughters along the way! Yet Zelophehad's daughters (Mahlah, Noah, Hoglah, Milcah, and Tirzah, v.33) are nearly the only ones mentioned in this chapter (see v.46). Since the chapter is a roster of men being mustered for war, the lack of the mention of daughters elsewhere can be explained. But it is interesting to see how 1 Chronicles mentions women abundantly, especially in chapters 2 and 7. The purpose of Numbers 26 in listing men for war is granted, but hardly any other mention of women is unsettling. Who was mothering all these sons? The reason to mention Zelophehad's daughters in v.33 is to set the stage for the narrative of chapter 27. And this is a most dramatic stage indeed.

The most significant gain among all the tribes in the desert period is that of Manasseh (52,700, up from 32,200). No reason is known for this dramatic increase.

In Sum: The tribe of Manasseh numbered 52,700 in the second census, an increase of 20,500 from the 32,200 of the first census (a stunning gain of 64 percent). There are two clans, that of Makir and that of his son Gilead; then there are six subclans of the Gileadites. The tribe of Manasseh is in the eighth rank in the first list and the seventh rank in the second, changing places with its brother tribe Ephraim—perhaps because of its phenomenal increase in numbers. The further history of the tribe of Manasseh is found in 1 Chronicles 7:14–19.

Notes

---

30 אִיעֶזֶר (*'î'ezer*, "Iezer"), this first-named son of Gilead, may in fact have been the son of his sister Hammoleketh but was regarded as his "son" for genealogical purposes (see 1 Chron 7:18, where "Iezer" seems to be intended by Abiezer). The genealogies are exceedingly complex in this section.

---

(8) *The tribe of Ephraim*

26:35–37

35 These were the descendants of Ephraim by their clans:
through Shuthelah, the Shuthelahite clan;
through Beker, the Bekerite clan;
through Tahan, the Tahanite clan.
36 These were the descendants of Shuthelah:
through Eran, the Eranite clan.
37 These were the clans of Ephraim; those numbered were 32,500.

These were the descendants of Joseph by their clans.

35–37 The clans of Ephraim are listed in three sons—Shuthelah, Beker, and Tahan—and one subclan through Eran, son of Shuthelah (yet Eran is not mentioned elsewhere).

In Sum: The tribe of Ephraim numbered 32,500 in the second census, a drop of 8,000 from the 40,500 of the first census (a decrease of about 20 percent). There are three clans and one subclan. The tribe of Ephraim is in the seventh rank in the first list and the eighth rank in the second, changing places with its brother tribe, Manasseh. Further history of the tribe of Ephraim is found in 1 Chronicles 7:20–29.

(9) *The tribe of Benjamin*

26:38–41

38 The descendants of Benjamin by their clans were:
through Bela, the Belaite clan;
through Ashbel, the Ashbelite clan;
through Ahiram, the Ahiramite clan;
39 through Shupham, the Shuphamite clan;
through Hupham, the Huphamite clan.
40 The descendants of Bela through Ard and Naaman were:
through Ard, the Ardite clan;
through Naaman, the Naamite clan.
41 These were the clans of Benjamin; those numbered were 45,600.

38–41 The listing of names of sons and clans in the earlier rosters have presented problems of spelling and identification from time to time when the lists in Numbers 26 are compared with similar lists in Genesis and 1 Chronicles. But in the case of the tribe of Benjamin, we come to nearly insurmountable problems of correlation. It appears that the listing of the clans of Benjamin are quite fluid, perhaps depending on differing purposes of our sources, as well as considerable confusion in the transmission of these names. Again, the most hopeful thing one can observe about the confused state of things is that scribes did not attempt to go through these lists to sanitize them of these astringencies.

The lists that are to be compared are from Genesis 46:21; Numbers 26:38; 1 Chronicles 7:6; and 1 Chronicles 8:1–2. Here are parallel tables of these four texts:

Gen 46:21	*Num 26:38*	*1 Chron 7:6*	*1 Chron 8:1–2*
Bela	Bela	Bela	Bela
Beker	(lacking)	Beker	"his firstborn" (see Notes)
Ashbel	Ashbel	(lacking)	Ashbel
Gera (only here)			
Naaman	[Naaman; name of a son of Bela, v.40]	(lacking)	[Naaman; name of a son of Bela, v.3]
Ehi	Ahiram		Aharah
Rosh			Nohah—only here Rapha—only here
Muppim	Shephupham/ Shupham		
Huppim	Hupham		
Ard	Ard [name of a son of Bela, v.40]		

Here are some possibilities:

1. The name Beker may have been misunderstood in 1 Chronicles 8:1 as *bᵉḵōrô*, "his firstborn," leading to the unusual list of ordinals in the rest of the names of that listing.

2. The name Ahiram in Numbers 26:38 (= Aharah of 1 Chron 8:1) may be identified with Ehi of Genesis 46:21; alternatively, perhaps there is a confusion of the two names Ahi and Rosh of Genesis 46:21 in the name Ahiram.

3. Shephupham (MT = Shupham of Sam. Pent., Vulg., Syr.) is confused perhaps with Muppim of Genesis 46:21.

4. Hupham of Numbers 26:39 may equal Huppim of Genesis 46:21; but he may be a descendant, not the son (see 1 Chron 7:12; yet 1 Chron 7:12 may list descendants who have similar names as their forebears; this issue is complex).

5. Ard in Numbers 26:40 is listed as a son of Bela, along with Naaman. Perhaps these men were not born in Genesis 46.

In Sum: The tribe of Benjamin numbered 45,600 in the second census, an increase of 10,200 from the 35,400 of the first census (a gain of 29 percent). There are five clans and two subclans (but the other lists give different figures). The tribe of Benjamin is in the ninth rank in both census lists. The further history of the tribe of Benjamin is found in 1 Chronicles 7:6–12; 8:1–39. This latter extended excursus on the family of Benjamin is occasioned by interest in the line of Israel's first king, Saul (see 1 Chron 8:33).

Notes

38 In the complex listing of the sons of Benjamin, as compared with other lists, one name is omitted in Num 16:38 but found in Gen 46:21 and 1 Chron 7:6, בֶּכֶר (*beker*, "Beker"). In 1 Chron 8:1 the text reads בְּכֹרוֹ (*bekōrô*, "his firstborn").

(10) *The tribe of Dan*

26:42–43

> 42 These were the descendants of Dan by their clans:
> through Shuham, the Shuhamite clan.
> These were the clans of Dan: 43 All of them were Shuhamite clans; and those numbered were 64,400.

42–43 The briefest of all the tribal notations is given for Dan, and only one clan is listed, Shuham. Yet, surprisingly, the total population is quite large, 64,400; only Judah (76,500) is larger. In Genesis 46:23, one son is listed for Dan, Hushim. The relationship of the words Shuham and Hushim is unknown. It is unexpected that such a large tribe would be descended from only one son.

In Sum: The tribe of Dan numbered 64,400 in the second census, an increase of 1,700 from the 62,700 of the first census (a gain of about 3 percent). There is only one clan. The tribe of Dan is in the tenth rank in both census lists. Alone among the tribes the name of Dan is not mentioned at all in the tribal genealogies of 1 Chronicles 1–8 (see also on vv.26–27, the situation with respect to Zebulun).

(11) *The tribe of Asher*

26:44–47

> 44 The descendants of Asher by their clans were:
> through Imnah, the Imnite clan;
> through Ishvi, the Ishvite clan;
> through Beriah, the Beriite clan;

[45]and through the descendants of Beriah:
through Heber, the Heberite clan;
through Malkiel, the Malkielite clan.
[46](Asher had a daughter named Serah.)
[47]These were the clans of Asher; those numbered were 53,400.

44–47 One name has dropped in Numbers 26 from the listing of the names of the sons of Asher in Genesis 46:17 and 1 Chronicles 7:30, the name Ishvah (*yišwāh*). Perhaps he did not found a clan and so is not listed in Numbers. The other sons who are listed are Imnah, Ishvi, and Beriah, besides Heber and Malkiel, the sons of Beriah who founded subclans.

The mention of Serah, daughter of Asher (v.46), is remarkable (and she is mentioned as well in Gen 46:17 and 1 Chron 7:30). The appearance of her name in these lists raises some questions: Is it possible she was the only daughter born to the twelve sons of Jacob, even as Jacob had only one daughter, Dinah? Do sons (or daughters) run in families that prominently? Or were there numerous other daughters from the many wives of these twelve sons of Jacob but only Serah is mentioned? What happened to her since her name is mentioned without any note of marriage or progeny? All this reminds us of how very little we know of women in the patriarchal stories.

Genesis 46:26 adds up the persons who went down to Egypt thus: "all those who went to Egypt with Jacob . . . , not counting his sons' wives." Since they were not descended from Jacob, out of his body, they were not named. By contrast, the mothers of Jacob's twelve sons are named prominently in Genesis 46 (and elsewhere). But there are things we are not told. By Genesis 46 Rachel is dead. But what of Leah, Zilpah, and Bilhah? Did they go to Egypt, or were they already dead? Does Jacob outlive all four wives before he goes down to Egypt?

Further, we learn of the occasional wife who was inappropriate, Judah's Canaanite wife and his daughter-in-law Tamar (see 1 Chron 2:3), and the exceptional, but apparently fitting, foreign wife such as Asenath (Gen 41:50). But we wonder where the other sons got their wives? Were they also women of the land?

We read of Zelophehad who had only daughters and of Sheshan in 1 Chronicles 2:34–35 who also had only daughters. He gives one unnamed daughter in marriage to a named slave, whose son he regards as his grandson!

Again, we think of David (1 Chron 3:1–9) who has six sons at Hebron from six different wives, then four sons by Bathsheba, plus nine others from wives not specified, and unnumbered sons by concubines. But only one daughter is named, Tamar, the sister of Absalom, daughter of Maacah (2 Sam 13:1). This is a ratio of 19:1, by numerous wives! So we ask, Were there many daughters, but was Tamar only mentioned because of the story of Absalom and Amnon, as Dinah may have been mentioned alone of many sisters only because of the story of Shechem and her brothers?

In Sum: The tribe of Asher numbered 53,400 in the second census, an increase of 11,900 from the 41,500 of the first census (a gain of 29 percent). There are three clans and two subclans, and one daughter. The tribe of Asher is in the eleventh rank in both census lists. The further history of the tribe of Asher is found in 1 Chronicles 7:30–40.

(12) *The tribe of Naphtali* 26:48–50

48The descendants of Naphtali by their clans were:
through Jahzeel, the Jahzeelite clan;
through Guni, the Gunite clan;
49through Jezer, the Jezerite clan;
through Shillem, the Shillemite clan.
50These were the clans of Naphtali; those numbered were 45,400.

48–50 The families of Naphtali are descended from four sons, Jahzeel, Guni, Jezer, and Shillem (all mentioned in Gen 46:24 and 1 Chron 7:13).

In Sum: The tribe of Naphtali numbered 45,400 in the second census, a decrease of 8,000 from the 53,400 of the first census (a drop of 15 percent). There are four clans. The tribe of Naphtali is in the twelfth rank in both census lists. The names of the sons of Naphtali, but no further history of the tribe, are found in 1 Chronicles 7:13.

c. *The grand celebrative number, to the praise of the Lord* 26:51

51The total number of the men of Israel was 601,730.

51 Despite all the people who had died during the years of desert experience, the total of the people—601,730—was nearly the same as the total of those who were first numbered. This remarkable fact is to be regarded as the signal blessing of the Lord, in fulfillment of his many promises to give numerical strength to the people descended from Abraham through Jacob (see Gen 12:2). The loss of 1,820 persons from 603,550 mentioned in 1:46 in the first census is a drop of only 0.3 percent—a negligible sum!

This grand total and its integers are in accord with the general pattern of the numbers of the book. The numbers have a wonderful consistency to them, despite the shifting totals among the various tribes (See Notes). It is utterly remarkable that the total number has remained nearly unchanged even though the people have lived under the most trying conditions for a period of thirty-eight years. There has been the dying of all those who were over the age of twenty at the time of the rebellion at Kadesh, and there have been numerous judgments of God that have come on the people because of this and other rebellions. Then there was the harsh reality of living one's lifetime in the Desert of Sinai. Given all these factors, the birth rate is not just equal but prodigious. God's faithfulness to his people is grandly celebrated with this triumphant chapter of census!

The point of this number is principally the praise of the Lord. The number may have been inflated rhetorically; but if so, it is a celebrative inflation, glorying in God and anticipating the time when the numbers of Israel, the people of God, will be like the stars of the heaven for number, countless as the grains of sand on the seashore.

Notes

51 For the large totals of the tribes and the grand total for the full complement of able-bodied men over the age of twenty, see the Introduction, the sections on the large numbers; also see the comment and Notes on 1:46. The numbers in the second list are consistently large as are those in the first census. Any conclusion one draws about the one must impact on the other. Again in this chapter we find numerous problems in the textual transmission of names but none concerning the transmission of these large numbers. If one wishes to argue for text transmission problems as the source of the large numbers, then the errors would have had to come at such an early period that there was no record left of the errors—a most unlikely situation. Again, the numbers are added as real integers; 1,000 is 1 more than 999. Further, the math is correct; the sum of the twelve tribe rosters adds up to the total: 601,730.

---

d. *The allotment of the land on the basis of the names of the families of Israel*

26:52–56

52 The LORD said to Moses, 53 "The land is to be allotted to them as an inheritance based on the number of names. 54 To a larger group give a larger inheritance, and to a smaller group a smaller one; each is to receive its inheritance according to the number of those listed. 55 Be sure that the land is distributed by lot. What each group inherits will be according to the names for its ancestral tribe. 56 Each inheritance is to be distributed by lot among the larger and smaller groups."

52–56 This pericope is an impressive addition to the census record as compared to 1:44–46 and following. In the first census the emphasis was fully on preparation for warfare (see 1:3: "all . . . who are able to serve in the army," and 1:45: "who were able to serve in Israel's army"). The second census begins in the same manner (26:2: "who are able to serve in the army of Israel"), but it ends differently. The second census relates not only to military service in the conquest of the land but to inheritance rights once the land was made theirs. This is a pericope of promise that is designed to impel the people to faithfulness. The listing of names was not only the means for demonstrating God's faithfulness for his people; it was also a basis for an equitable distribution of the land they were about to enter. Larger tribes would receive larger shares, but the decisions of place would be made by lot (v.56). Until the end, Moses was still in charge of these things, another of the sweet-hurts that marked his last days. The distribution of the land was to be based on the dual principles of fairness and lot (with the understanding that the fall of the lot is in the hands of the Lord). The land is God's gift to his people; hence their shares in it are their inheritance from him. So the reason for the mustering of the people was twofold: to prepare them for war and to determine their tribal needs in the land.

e. *The families and numbers of the Levites, the holy tribe of Israel*

26:57–62

57 These were the Levites who were counted by their clans:
through Gershon, the Gershonite clan;
through Kohath, the Kohathite clan;
through Merari, the Merarite clan.
58 These also were Levite clans:
the Libnite clan,
the Hebronite clan,
the Mahlite clan,
the Mushite clan,

the Korahite clan.
(Kohath was the forefather of Amram; 59the name of Amram's wife
was Jochebed, a descendant of Levi, who was born to the Levites in
Egypt. To Amram she bore Aaron, Moses and their sister Miriam.
60Aaron was the father of Nadab and Abihu, Eleazar and Ithamar. 61But
Nadab and Abihu died when they made an offering before the LORD with
unauthorized fire.)

62All the male Levites a month old or more numbered 23,000. They were not counted along with the other Israelites because they received no inheritance among them.

57–58a This pericope corresponds to the separate counting of the Levites in the first census (see 1:47–53; 3:1–39; see also Exod 6:16–25). The Levites are grouped in three clans, Gershon, Kohath, and Merari, with five subclans in this text: Libni (of Gershon, see 3:18; Exod 6:18), Hebron (of Kohath, see 3:19; Exod 6:18), Mahli and Mushi (of Merari, see 3:20; Exod 6:19), and Korah (a descendant of Kohath through Izhar, see Exod 6:21). A comparison of the line of Levi in Exodus 6 shows that not all the sons of Gershon, Kohath, and Merari founded families that were reckoned among the Levites.

58b–61 The parenthetical pericope on Kohath, Amram, and Jochebed is a reminder of earlier sections of the Torah (3:1–10; Exod 6:20), likely inserted here to assert anew the lineage of Aaron and to remind the priests of the debacle of Nadab and Abihu. The record of Amram and Jochebed is compressed, as is generally recognized. Kohath must have lived at least 350 years before Moses, as he was born before Jacob went down to Egypt (see Gen 46:11). Further, there is a family of Amramites that numbered several hundred at the time of Moses (see 3:27). Most probably Amram and Jochebed are celebrated ancestors of Aaron, Miriam, and Moses rather than their immediate parents (see W.H. Gispen, *Exodus*, Bible Student's Commentary, tr. Ed van der Maas [Grand Rapids: Zondervan, 1982], p. 77, n. 10; for Nadab and Abihu, see commentary on Num 3:4; Lev 10:1–3). From the direction of these verses, it is clear that the listing of the families of Levi is focused on the need to document the family line of Aaron, Miriam, and Moses one more time.

A question remains, however. If Amram and Jochebed are not the immediate parents of Aaron, Miriam, and Moses, why are they listed so prominently? Perhaps the issue concerns something of a scandal about their marriage. Exodus 6:20 says that Amram married his aunt. Such a breech of taboo would not soon be forgotten. So scandalized was Israel that the names of these remote persons are preserved, though the immediate parents' names are forgotten. On Amram see also 1 Chronicles 6:1–3; contrast Exodus 2:1, which speaks of the parents of Moses without giving their names. Even in the birth narratives of some of its most illustrious heroes, the Torah does not seem to answer the types of basic questions the modern reader has.

62 The number of male Levites over the age of one month increased from 22,000 in the first census (3:39) to 23,000 in the second (26:62), an increase of 1,000 (about 5 percent). The pericope ends with the restated reason for the separate numbering of the Levites: they were neither part of the army nor would they be inheritors of the land; they were a tribe holy to the Lord. But they are a part of the nation, and their families need to be listed along with the names of the other family names in Israel.

f. *A recapitulation of the point of the census: this is the new generation* 26:63–65

[63]These are the ones counted by Moses and Eleazar the priest when they counted the Israelites on the plains of Moab by the Jordan across from Jericho. [64]Not one of them was among those counted by Moses and Aaron the priest when they counted the Israelites in the Desert of Sinai. [65]For the LORD had told those Israelites they would surely die in the desert, and not one of them was left except Caleb son of Jephunneh and Joshua son of Nun.

63–65 This chapter has a fine style to it, despite the seemingly mundane issues it presents. The second census was, of course, of enormous importance to Israel and a central aspect of the Lord's dealings with her. The style is not ornate nor given to literary flourish; yet in the simplicity of its format, in the sense of order and control, its message is proclaimed.

Verses 63–65 serve as the fitting conclusion to the section begun in vv.1–4a. There are numerous ties: (1) the mention of Moses and Eleazar the priest, (2) the location on the plains of Moab, (3) the words "after the plague" in v.1 tie to the notice in v.64 that not one of the original group of rebels was still alive, save only Caleb and Joshua. The texts lays emphasis on the expression "not one of them" (vv.64–65). This, of course, speaks of the sure righteousness of the Lord. But the survival of Caleb and Joshua reminds us of the grace of the Lord, who keeps his promise to save, even as he remembers his oath to punish.

In fine, it is all of grace, as Moses elaborates in his homily in Deuteronomy. In Deuteronomy 1:31 he speaks of the Lord carrying the people in the desert as a father carries a son; in 2:7 he speaks of God's presence with them throughout the forty years so that they lacked nothing; and in 4:32–40 he speaks of the actions of the Lord in these years as unparalleled in all of human history.

The name of Eleazar is significant in its linking with Moses in v.63. The next verse reminds us of the first census in which Aaron joined Moses in making the tabulation. Of the first generation not one—save only Caleb and Joshua—would enter the land (v.65). Even old Moses was excluded.

2. *The inheritance of women on entering the land* 27:1–11

[1]The daughters of Zelophehad son of Hepher, the son of Gilead, the son of Makir, the son of Manasseh, belonged to the clans of Manasseh son of Joseph. The names of the daughters were Mahlah, Noah, Hoglah, Milcah and Tirzah. They approached [2]the entrance to the Tent of Meeting and stood before Moses, Eleazar the priest, the leaders and the whole assembly, and said, [3]"Our father died in the desert. He was not among Korah's followers, who banded together against the LORD, but he died for his own sin and left no sons. [4]Why should our father's name disappear from his clan because he had no son? Give us property among our father's relatives."

[5]So Moses brought their case before the LORD [6]and the LORD said to him, [7]"What Zelophehad's daughters are saying is right. You must certainly give them property as an inheritance among their father's relatives and turn their father's inheritance over to them.

[8]"Say to the Israelites, 'If a man dies and leaves no son, turn his inheritance over to his daughter. [9]If he has no daughter, give his

inheritance to his brothers. [10]If he has no brothers, give his inheritance to his father's brothers. [11]If his father had no brothers, give his inheritance to the nearest relative in his clan, that he may possess it. This is to be a legal requirement for the Israelites, as the LORD commanded Moses.' "

1–4 The substance of this chapter has a distinctly modern ring to it. Here is a story impinging on the rights of women in early Israel. The issue in the chapter is the question brought to Moses by seven daughters of a man who had no sons. As such, this is a significant chapter in the sociology of early Israel. It is also an important contribution to the biblical theology of the Book of Numbers. While we tend to focus on the fact that it was women who were presenting a claim to Moses, the substance of their claim did not center in gender but only sprang from it. The issue centered in the concept of the land and one's share in it as the spiritual destiny of the redeemed community of Israel.

The five women were daughters of Zelophehad, whose genealogy is traced back to Manasseh (v.1, a reprise of 26:33). In a sense this chapter is an extension of the genealogies of chapter 26, showing how complications may be worked out when the people come to inherit their share in the land of Canaan. The principal concern of Mahlah, Noah, Hoglah, Milcah, and Tirzah was the securing of the inheritance and the preservation of their father's name in the land (v.4). Their action in approaching Moses, Eleazar, and the leaders of the nation was unprecedented, a great act of courage, conviction, and faith.

The women's act of coming near (*qāraḇ*, "to make an approach") to Moses is detailed rather graphically (v.2). They stood before Moses, before Eleazar the priest, and before the leaders and all the congregation at the entrance of the Tent of Meeting (v.3). This march to the central shrine by these women must have been incredible to those who were watching. With the exception of Miriam, sister of Moses and Aaron, we do not read of women coming to such sacral precincts in these ancient narratives.

When the women made their claim to Moses, they specified that their father, Zelophehad, had not died because of participation in the rebellion of Korah (see Num 16) but only because he was part of the entire doomed first generation (v.3). In this they show their understanding of the reality of God's judgment combined with a sense of his mercy. It appears from this verse that the rebels associated with Korah not only lost their lives in the judgment of God on them, but their survivors may have lost their inheritance as well. Here is a particular death notice from among the huge statistic of 26:64. There is something touching in this. But these women did not excuse their father either. These were pious women with a sound understanding of the nature of the desert experience and a just claim for their family. Further, they were women of faith. The people were not in the land yet, but these women knew that they would enter it soon. Their claim to Moses is anticipative of the Lord's deliverance of the people from the awful desert to the Land of Promise.

So the women came with a suit, asking for a decision from the Lord, that their father's name not disappear from among the clans of his family. The tie of name to land in the expectation of Israel is demonstrated clearly here (v.4). One's meaning in the community is dependent on the survival of his name in the distribution of land in the time of conquest.

5 A mark of the leadership of Moses is seen in v.5, where he hears the women's complaint and then takes their case before the Lord. In the MT of this verse, the term "their case" is written with an oversize, darkened nun (the so-called majuscule nun), indicating the suffixed pronoun "their" (fem. pl.). It seems that the scribe used this unusual letter to bring special attention to the fact that this was an appeal from women.

6–11 This section is not only instructive in terms of the issues it presents; these verses also give an indication how case law might have operated in Israel. The general laws would be promulgated. Then legitimate exceptions or special considerations would come to the elders and perhaps be brought to Moses himself. He then would await a decision from the Lord. The language is specific in this regard; Moses did not decide by himself but waited for a decision from the Lord. Then after the decision for the specific case is rendered (see v.7), an application for other situations is also able to be rendered (see vv.8–11).

In this case the Lord gave a favorable decision to these women. In fact, the response of the Lord went beyond their request. In v.4 they requested an *'ªḥuzzāh* ("landed property"). The response of the Lord was for an *'ªḥuzzaṯ naḥªlāh* ("a hereditary possession of landed property," v.7). The point seems to be that not only would they receive the property, they could transfer it to their heirs as well. Thus they share with the sons of other fathers who were deceased. It is as though their father had had sons!

Throughout this section there is a balanced presentation of the grace of God to hear and to review the case as well as a firmness with which the command is worded. The decision is clear, prompt, and exact. This special case is then to be used as a legal precedent for other cases like it. An extension is made of those kinds of application considered binding. The first decision respected the five women; the eventuating law affects all Israel (v.11).

The first in line for inheritance of his father is the father's son. If the father has no son, then his daughter will inherit in his stead. If there is no daughter either, then the inheritance would pass to nearest relatives: brothers, uncles, or other kin. The intent in each case is to keep the inheritance as close as possible to the deceased man's family line. His name and his possession in the land are inseparable.

This decision becomes a *huqqaṯ mišpāṭ*, a statutory legal decision or "requirement" (v.11); compare "their case" of v.5. Moreover, the section closes by saying that the decision was mediated through Moses but originated from the Lord.

Numbers 36 provides an appendix to this account. This deals with the complicating factor of women who are now inheritors of the land and who might marry outside their families and thus muddle the subsequent inheritance claims of Israel.

Notes

---

1 The story of the daughters of Zelophehad is discussed in several critical articles. N.H. Snaith argues that the law really had only to serve as a justification for the settlement of the half-tribe of Manasseh to the west of the Jordan; he regards the law as fiction and as "bad" law ("The Daughters of Zelophehad," VetTest 16 [Jan. 1966]: 124–27). J. Weingreen points out how this section speaks of a new process of law-making in Israel, "a rule of law" ("The Case of the Daughters of Zelophehad," VetTest 16 [Oct. 1966]: 518–22).

7 It seems that the feminine suffixes such as לָהֶם . . . אֲבִיהֶם . . . לָהֶן (*lāhem . . . 'ªḇîhem . . . lāhen,* "[to] them [m. pl.] . . . their [m. pl.] father . . . to them [f. pl.]") are used so

infrequently in Scripture that errors are found from time to time. Numerous MT MSS correct these spelling errors to the feminine gender.

8 תְּדַבֵּר (*tᵉḏabbēr*, "say") is an example of the instructional use of the imperfect.

---

(3) *The successor to Moses*

27:12–23

12Then the LORD said to Moses, "Go up this mountain in the Abarim
range and see the land I have given the Israelites. 13After you have seen
it, you too will be gathered to your people, as your brother Aaron was,
14for when the community rebelled at the waters in the Desert of Zin,
both of you disobeyed my command to honor me as holy before their
eyes." (These were the waters of Meribah Kadesh, in the Desert of Zin.)
15Moses said to the LORD, 16"May the LORD, the God of the spirits of all
mankind, appoint a man over this community 17to go out and come in
before them, one who will lead them out and bring them in, so the
LORD's people will not be like sheep without a shepherd."
18So the LORD said to Moses, "Take Joshua son of Nun, a man in
whom is the spirit, and lay your hand on him. 19Have him stand before
Eleazar the priest and the entire assembly and commission him in their
presence. 20Give him some of your authority so the whole Israelite
community will obey him. 21He is to stand before Eleazar the priest, who
will obtain decisions for him by inquiring of the Urim before the LORD. At
his command he and the entire community of the Israelites will go out,
and at his command they will come in."
22Moses did as the LORD commanded him. He took Joshua and had
him stand before Eleazar the priest and the whole assembly. 23Then he
laid his hands on him and commissioned him, as the LORD instructed
through Moses.

12–14 The conjunction of the story of the daughters of Zelophehad with their request for an inheritance in the land (vv.1–11) and the Lord's words to Moses about his own lack of participation in the land (vv.12–14) is touching indeed. Provisions are made for the exceptions and the irregularities of the inheritance laws, but there is no provision for Moses the (usually) faithful servant of the Lord. His sin at the waters of Meribah at Kadesh (20:1–13) was always before him. Aaron had already died; Moses was soon to die. He would be allowed a glimpse of the land from a distant mountain, but not even he would be allowed a footfall in the land itself.

There is some sense in which we are not sure how to react to the provision of the Lord for Moses to gaze at the land from a distance. On the one hand, this is a provision of mercy, for at least he is able to see the land. Yet this must have been a bittersweet experience. It may have been too hard for Moses even to look, knowing that the land would never be his own. Deuteronomy 3:23–25 describes the pleading of Moses with the Lord for an opportunity to walk through the land. But the Lord would no longer listen; Moses was not allowed even to speak of the issue further (v.26). The mountain from which Moses is to see the land is not specified in Numbers 27; Deuteronomy 3:27 and 34:1 describe it as Mount Nebo and the top of Pisgah (see on Deut 34:1).

The sin of Moses is tied to Aaron in this text as in Numbers 20; hence, both had to die before the people could enter the land. The ominous name "Meribah" is used again in this passage (v.14) to remind us of the rebellion of the leader of the people against the Lord (see on 20:13). The punishment of Moses seems to be a significant element of the *Heilsgeschichte* of Numbers. While Balaam is utterly reprobate and entirely deserving of God's judgment, yet God's judgment comes as well even on Moses because of his rebellion. As in 20:12, the principal error of Moses and Aaron was in not regarding the Lord as holy (see Deut 32:48–51 for a close parallel to this paragraph).

The solemnity of this passage is remarkable. In a context of mercy to the daughters of Zelophehad (vv.1–11) where the righteousness (*ṣᵉḏāqāh*) of the Lord is seen, here we sense something of his holiness (*qōḏeš*). The assault on the holiness of God by Moses and Aaron was disastrous. The fact of Aaron's death adds a level of certainty to Moses' own soon demise.

15–17 Moses now requests, in the light of his own impending death, that the Lord will appoint a successor for him, even as he clearly indicated a successor for Aaron the priest (see 20:22–29). Without such a leader, the people will be like shepherdless sheep, wandering each his own way across the wastelands. In his request to God, Moses uses an unusual form of address: "Yahweh God of the spirits of all flesh" (v.16, lit. tr.; NIV, "the LORD, the God of the spirits of all mankind"; a similar expression is used by Moses in 16:22). This is an expressive title of the Lord that speaks of his ultimate sovereignty over all peoples. If God is sovereign of all, then surely God will wish to show his sovereignty over his people in their evident need for a shepherd to follow Moses.

Thus we see that Moses' reaction to this reassertion of his restriction from enjoying the land is to give a blessing to the Lord and to offer a prayer for his successor. Here is the Moses of old! Gone is his terrible moment of anger. He has the good of the community at heart. He does not grieve at his own loss but desires a successor so that at last the people will be able to enjoy the end of their salvation. In this sense his life will not have been for naught. He does not select his own heir. This is not a hereditary post nor one that was his to dispose—only the Lord can provide a successor to Moses. Since the Lord knows all men, he will be the judge of the inner qualities demanded for the task.

The successor to Moses was not chosen because of a blood relationship to Moses; he was not a king. Nor was he chosen by a popular election; for Moses had not been elected by the people—something they had constantly reminded him! (cf. 14:4, where the people want to select a leader instead of Moses). The successor was to be appointed directly by God. The Lord is King; Moses is only an agent. The successor was not to be a figurehead or a symbol but a leader who goes before his people, leading them in the direction they should go. He is pictured as a shepherd, one needed by the flock. Moses' concern was that his flock not be left without a shepherd.

18–21 The response of the Lord was to take Joshua son of Nun and to consecrate him as the true successor of Moses. As Moses and Aaron needed to determine the true successor of Aaron before his death (20:22–29), so the true successor of Moses needed to be established. Joshua and Caleb were the two heroes in the darkest day of Israel's apostasy (Num 13–14). It was fitting that it was one of these two whom the Lord selected. Further, Joshua had been an aide of Moses from his early youth (11:28), a fact that made him especially well suited to follow his master's steps.

The wording of v.18 is expressive of Moses' own part in the selection process. He was to be the one to single out Joshua; the Hebrew wording for the Lord's command is one that demands personal participation ("you yourself take"; this is an imperative followed by a dative of personal reference). If another had done this, perhaps some might think it was an act against the leadership of Moses. Since he himself was the one to reach out to Joshua, there could only be the sense that this was a deliberate act on his part.

The arresting phrase in v.18 concerning Joshua is that he is "a man in whom is the spirit." The term "spirit" can refer to his own leadership capacity, as would be suggested by the NIV's lower-case reading; perhaps "the spirit [of leadership]" is intended. But it is also possible, as the NIV margin has it, to read the word "Spirit" as a distinct reference to the Holy Spirit. This latter seems to be more likely. The Hebrew term *rûaḥ* is indefinite by spelling but may be regarded as inherently definite when used as a reference to deity. It is possible that this phrase means that Joshua was Spirit-endowed as the leader of the people (see Deut 34:9: "Joshua son of Nun was filled with the [S]pirit of wisdom"), phrasing that is hauntingly suggestive of NT language concerning the Spirit of God (see Acts 6:5).

The succession procedure was to include the laying on of hands, a visual representation of the transfer of power while Moses was still alive (cf. the laying on of hands in the NT, Acts 6:6). This action was to forestall any doubts as to the legitimacy of the transfer of power among the people. This investiture of power (see Deut 34:9, "because Moses had laid his hands on him") was to be done under the most solemn and public of circumstances. It was done before Eleazar and the whole congregation (v.19). Moreover, the transfer was to be put into operation on a gradual but immediate basis. Some of Moses' authority was to be given to Joshua that the people might begin to obey him (v.20). The transition from the leadership of Moses to any successor would be difficult. The change would be made smoother by a gradual shift of power while Moses was still alive.

Joshua was to stand before Eleazar while Moses was alive, that there would be no priestly objections either. Joshua would go before the priest for consultation and for the decision of the Urim (see on Exod 28:30) before the Lord (v.20). Joshua was to begin leading the movement of the congregation as well.

22–23 These verses conclude the pericope on the transfer of power by reporting Moses' complete obedience to the Lord in the matter of Joshua. Moses followed the command of God to the letter. Each time we read of Moses' complete obedience to the Lord in the Book of Numbers, we wistfully glance back to chapter 20, wishing that he had stayed in character there, too.

Notes

17 אֲשֶׁר־יֵצֵא לִפְנֵיהֶם וַאֲשֶׁר יָבֹא לִפְנֵיהֶם (*'ᵃšer-yēṣē' lip̱nêhem wa'ᵃšer yāḇō' lip̱nêhem,* "who will lead them out and bring them in") has a play on the words "to go out" and "to come in," as the next phrases use Hiphil forms of these same words, יוֹצִיאֵם (*yôṣî'ēm,* "to lead them out") and יְבִיאֵם (*yᵉḇî'ēm,* "to bring them in"). The idea of these phrasings is to mirror the activities of Moses who was a faithful leader.

20 The term מֵהוֹדְךָ (*mēhôḏᵉḵāh,* "of your authority") is from *hôḏ,* which may mean "weight," "power," "splendor," or "authority." Here the prefixed partitive *min* suggests the idea "some of your authority." It is not clear in this text whether the idea "some of" was limited and immediate or lasting. That is, it could be that while Moses was alive, "some of" his authority would be given to his assistant so that there would be a gradual shift in leadership, not unlike a coregency of son and father as king. It is also possible that this phrase is used to indicate that no matter how important Joshua became and how significant his role, he is never to be compared to Moses as on the same level. Joshua was the true successor of Moses but never his equal (see Deut 34:10–12). There comes another who is greater than Moses, but his name is not Joshua; his name is Y'shua (see Heb 3:1–6).

23 The Samaritan Pentateuch adds the words "and said to him" to the end of this verse and then interpolates a lengthy section from Deut 3:21–22. This is in keeping with the Samaritian Pentateuch penchant for adding explanatory glosses from other sections of the Torah. See Bruce K. Waltke, "The Samaritan Pentateuch and the Text of the Old Testament," *New Perspectives on the Old Testament*, ed. J. Barton Payne (Waco, Tex.: Word, 1970), pp. 212–39.

---

4. *Commands for the second generation on regular offerings, festival offerings, and vows (28:1–30:16)*

Numbers 28–30 is a section on varied laws that interrupts the narrative flow of this section of the book, much like chapters 5–10 and chapter 15 break the narrative flow of the first sections of the book. The intrusion of laws on holiness, worship, and vows serves to remind the readers that they are reading not only a story of dramatic power but also an account that is profoundly religious in nature. This is not just a story to entertain but an account that serves to present the highest demands of purity, worship, and obedience on the people of God. As the first generation was given numerous laws on worship and behavior in preparation for its entry into the Land of Promise (chs. 5–10), so now the second generation, which is the heir of all, receives its own new *tôrô<u>t</u>* ("laws") on offerings and vows. They will be the people of God in his land; in everything they do they are to reflect his character by obeying his word.

The offerings in chapters 28–29 should be contrasted with the offerings of chapter 15 (see 29:39). These are offerings that are demanded by the Lord, expected by him on a regular basis. Numbers 15 presented supplementary offerings that would be prompted by grateful people who respond out of joyful hearts to the Lord. Both the required offerings and the supplementary gifts were governed by stipulation and regulations, and both needed to be presented with attitudes of wonder and response to the Lord. Perhaps the reason for the insertion of these passages at this time is to indicate a sense of continuity in the impending transition from the leadership of Moses to that of Joshua (27:12–23). The change of leadership does not indicate a change in the worship patterns of Israel; these are confirmed to continue. The modern reader likely has only a vague awareness of the role of sacrifice in the worship patterns of the OT. These extended chapters attest to the all-pervasiveness of sacrifice in the life of the people and the enormity of the work of the priests on their behalf.

Chapters 28–29 follow a clear order and progression. They do not give all new material; much has been given in earlier sections of the Torah. But the repetition and restatement of these sacrificial gifts to the Lord serves to remind the people who were about to enter the land that it was not an ordinary land they were entering, nor were they an ordinary people. The land was God's promised land, and they were covenant people. Everything that they were to become was extraordinary, for they were the people of God. Everything that they were to do was special, for they were in league with him. So offerings pile on offerings, sometimes overlapping in what seems to us today to be a bewildering, benumbing collage. But these offerings were the perpetual reminders of who the people were, who their God is, and the enormity of their need to respond to him in overwhelming gratitude. For what people has ever received the blessings of deity that this people enjoyed? And what god is there who is like their God?

a. *Regular offerings (28:1–15)*

The first part of chapter 28 is given over to lengthy descriptions of the offerings that were to be made to the Lord each day (vv.1–8), each Sabbath (vv.9–10), and each new month (vv.11–15).

(1) *The daily offerings*

28:1–8

> 1The LORD said to Moses, 2"Give this command to the Israelites and say to them: 'See that you present to me at the appointed time the food for my offerings made by fire, as an aroma pleasing to me.' 3Say to them: 'This is the offering made by fire that you are to present to the LORD: two lambs a year old without defect, as a regular burnt offering each day. 4Prepare one lamb in the morning and the other at twilight, 5together with a grain offering of a tenth of an ephah of fine flour mixed with a quarter of a hin of oil from pressed olives. 6This is the regular burnt offering instituted at Mount Sinai as a pleasing aroma, an offering made to the LORD by fire. 7The accompanying drink offering is to be a quarter of a hin of fermented drink with each lamb. Pour out the drink offering to the LORD at the sanctuary. 8Prepare the second lamb at twilight, along with the same kind of grain offering and drink offering that you prepare in the morning. This is an offering made by fire, an aroma pleasing to the LORD.

1–8 This paragraph reiterates the laws of sacrificial worship in the daily offerings in their order (see Exod 29:38–41; Lev 1–7). Verses 2–8 speak of the daily offerings; vv.9–10 of the Sabbath offerings; and vv.11–15 of the monthly offerings. The most significant issue for the modern reader, I suspect, is not in the details of each of these sacrifices nearly so much as in the wording of these commandments. The personal involvement of the Lord, the emphasis on his speaking, and the direction of worship are the paramount issues. The original text of v.2 has some difficulties, but great stress is presented on the pronouns "me" and "my." Here is a translation of vv.2–3a that presents this emphasis:

> Then Yahweh spoke to Moses saying:
> "Command the Israelites, and say to them,
> 'You must be careful to present to me my offering,
> my food of my offerings by fire, my soothing
> aroma, at the appointed time for each.'
> "And you will say to them,
> 'This is the offering by fire that you shall present to Yahweh.' "

Attention to this wording should correct the notion so common among Christians in our day that the OT is filled with the laws of Moses concerning sacrifice and that it was the purpose of Jesus to set us free from such bondage to ritual. Whatever we may think of these laws should be conditioned by the wording of the text. These were not the laws of Moses but the *tôrôṯ* of Yahweh. In fact, to speak of "the law of Moses" is something of a misnomer. It is the law of God, as this wording makes abundantly clear.

Second, we may focus on the regularity of these sacrifices. They form part of the rhythm of life of the redeemed community. Each morning there is sacrifice. Each evening there is sacrifice. On the Sabbath there are special sacrifices, and there are also sacrifices on the first of each month. These will overlap and intertwine—no matter, they are to be so much a part of the life of the people that one would find it quite impossible to think of the worship of God apart from sacrifice.

The Hebrew Scriptures are quite clear that sacrifice that is done apart from obedience is valueless; indeed, sacrifice apart from obedience is an affront to God. It is always true that to obey is better than to sacrifice (see 1 Sam 15:22). Indeed, there are significant texts in Scripture that call sacrifice into question when one is apart from the will of God (see Isa 1:1–18) or when one has lost a sense of purpose in sacrifice (see Ps 40:6–8; Mic 6:6–8). But these various passages were never intended by the Spirit of God to destroy sacrificial worship or to replace it. They have one intent: to keep those who are engaging in sacrificial worship thinking rightly about their service to the Lord.

As we, the modern readers of Numbers, think scripturally, this overwhelming emphasis on sacrificial worship has one intent: to cause each reader to think of the enormity of the offense of our sin against the holiness of God, thus driving the repentant sinner to the foot of the Cross. All sacrifices—whether of the morning or evening, of Sabbath or New Moon—have their ultimate meaning in the death the Savior died. Apart from his death, these sacrifices were just the killing of animals and the burning of their flesh with attendant ceremonies. After his death, sacrifices such as these are redundant—indeed, offensive—for they would suggest that something was needed in addition to the Savior's death. But before his death, these sacrifices were the very means God gave his people in love to help them face the enormity of their sin, the reality of their need for his grace, and—in some mysterious way—to point them to the coming cross of Savior Jesus.

When we look at the daily offerings, we find the following factors are emphasized:

1. The concept of the "appointed time" (v.2). Sacrifices are a part of the rhythm of worship. The ordering of the sacrifices is a fixed element in the ritual of the people. Each day begins and ends in sacrifice; each Sabbath has its special sacrifices, as does each new month. All of time is marked by sacrifice.

2. The concept of the "acceptable gift." Just as there is a time, so there is a specified offering that is to be presented (see Lev 22:17–33). Not just any animal or any amount of flour, oil, and wine may be used; all i according to pattern. The flour is as important as the animal; the wine is as significant as the oil. The sacrifices will not be appropriate if any element is not acceptable or if any element is not in the right proportion. Again, we may err if we try to determine spiritual significance in the varied proportions; the issue in all seems to be one of obedience to the revealed will of God.

3. The concept of a "pleasing aroma to the LORD" (vv.2, 6–7). There is a sense in which these sacrifices bring pleasure to the Lord. Yet as we reflect on them, we realize that it is not the sacrifice that brings him pleasure; it is the offerers who obey him in these demands who please him! This is the clear teaching of Psalm 40:6–8 and Micah 8:6–8. The acrid odor of the burning flesh and attendant grain, oil, and wine are the physical symbols of the spiritual reality; obedient people bring pleasure to the Lord. To bring oneself as a living sacrifice (Rom 12:1–2) is not a distinctly NT teaching, as often averred. It is the clearer statement of that which had always been the major issue in sacrifice from Abel until Christ (see the words of Ps 40:6–8 quoted in Heb 10:5–7).

God looks first on the one who brings the sacrifice (notice the word order in Gen 4:4–5) and then on the sacrifice that person brings. But when all is as it should be, person and sacrifice, then there is a "pleasing aroma" that ascends to the Lord.

4. The sense of the enormity of it all. G.J. Wenham, expanding on an article by Anson Rainey (*Biblica* 51 [1970]: 492), calculates that the yearly sacrifices at a minimum would include the following: 113 bulls, 32 rams, 1,086 lambs, more than a ton of flour, and a thousand bottles of oil and wine (p. 197). This pictures an exceedingly prosperous nation in which agriculture is especially blessed of the Lord. Thus in these required sacrifices there is considerable promise: God will bless his people in such a manner to allow them to do all that he demands.

Notes

---

7 Usually the drink offering is specified to be wine; here it is שֵׁכָר (*šēkār*, "beer"). Wine is the naturally fermented product of grapes and fruit; beer is the naturally fermented drink of grains. The traditional translation "strong drink" (KJV) leads one to think that the alcohol content of *šēkār* was more than that of wine (*yayin*), but that is probably not the case. Often the associations of this word are unsavory, depicting drunkenness and untoward behavior (e.g., Prov 20:1; Isa 5:11; 28:7; Mic 2:11). But the word is also used as a parallel to wine and a common drink of the people (Deut 29:6), a part of the sacred festal meals of Israel (Deut 14:26), and is commended for the weak and the weary (Prov 31:6). Decisions for or against Christian abstinence are best made from other considerations than from the meaning and usage of the several words for wine and beer in the Bible.

---

(2) *The Sabbath offerings*

28:9–10

9 " 'On the Sabbath day, make an offering of two lambs a year old without defect, together with its drink offering and a grain offering of two-tenths of an ephah of fine flour mixed with oil. 10 This is the burnt offering for every Sabbath, in addition to the regular burnt offering and its drink offering.

9–10 The Sabbath offerings were in addition to the daily offerings. The special offerings made on this day mark it out as "holy." This does not mean that the Sabbath was to be the "day of worship." It was to be a day of rest—except for the priests, who had additional service to perform before the Lord. Each day was a day of the worship of God; this is the reason for the daily offerings.

The passages concerning the Sabbath festivals of ancient Israel are brought into focus for the Christian reader by Hebrews 4, where we learn that the Savior Jesus is our Sabbath-rest (vv.1–5). Other significant references in the NT to the Sabbath include Matthew 12:1–14; 28:1; Luke 4:16; John 5:9; Acts 13:42; Colossians 2:16.

(3) *The monthly offerings*

28:11–15

[11]" 'On the first of every month, present to the LORD a burnt offering of two young bulls, one ram and seven male lambs a year old, all without defect. [12]With each bull there is to be a grain offering of three-tenths of an ephah of fine flour mixed with oil; with the ram, a grain offering of two-tenths of an ephah of fine flour mixed with oil; [13]and with each lamb, a grain offering of a tenth of an ephah of fine flour mixed with oil. This is for a burnt offering, a pleasing aroma, an offering made to the LORD by fire. [14]With each bull there is to be a drink offering of half a hin of wine; with the ram, a third of a hin; and with each lamb, a quarter of a hin. This is the monthly burnt offering to be made at each new moon during the year. [15]Besides the regular burnt offering with its drink offering, one male goat is to be presented to the LORD as a sin offering.

11–15 The sacrifices at the beginning of the month were of great proportion. These were times for celebration and the blowing of the trumpets in worship (see 10:10). Whereas two lambs were specified for the daily offerings (and two more on each Sabbath), the animals for the New Moon holocaust sacrifices included two bulls, one ram, and seven lambs. Each animal sacrifice was accompanied with flour, oil, and wine; in addition, a goat also was to be offered as a sin offering. The NIV translates the beginning of v.11 as "On the first of every month." This is the intent, but the Hebrew phrasing is "in the first of your months." As the land is the Lord's gift to his people, so time is his gift to enjoy the land. Each month is a marker of his blessing, a time for special rejoicing. Later in Israel's history, the New Moon festivals may have become opportunities for excess, for licentious behavior. In the Prophets there are times when God says to his erring people, "I hate your New Moons" (cf. Isa 1:14). There is always a latent danger in the most festive occasions to be forgetful of God's intention for us to respond to his wonder. Compare contemporary celebrations of Christmas and Thanksgiving, times where few celebrants give much serious thought to God.

b. *Festival offerings (28:16–29:40)*

The passages demanding regular offerings are followed by the demands of the Lord for the offerings to be made during the great festivals: Passover (vv.16–25), Feast of Weeks (vv.26–31), Feast of Trumpets (29:1–6), Day of Atonement (vv.7–11), and Feast of Tabernacles (vv.12–38); all conclude with a contrast between these sacrifices and those of chapter 15 (see 29:39) and a statement that Moses instructed the people just as he had been commanded by the Lord (v.40). As in the earlier section, there is a sense of order, propriety, and measure to these paragraphs.

(1) *The Passover*

28:16–25

[16]" 'On the fourteenth day of the first month the LORD's Passover is to be held. [17]On the fifteenth day of this month there is to be a festival; for seven days eat bread made without yeast. [18]On the first day hold a sacred assembly and do no regular work. [19]Present to the LORD an offering made by fire, a burnt offering of two young bulls, one ram and seven male lambs a year old, all without defect. [20]With each bull prepare a grain offering of three-tenths of an ephah of fine flour mixed with oil; with the ram, two-tenths; [21]and with each of the seven lambs, one-tenth.

> [22]Include one male goat as a sin offering to make atonement for you.
> [23]Prepare these in addition to the regular morning burnt offering. [24]In
> this way prepare the food for the offering made by fire every day for
> seven days as an aroma pleasing to the LORD; it is to be prepared in
> addition to the regular burnt offering and its drink offering. [25]On the
> seventh day hold a sacred assembly and do no regular work.

16–25 This passage instructs the priests as to the proper preparation for the Passover in the first month of the year. Passover is the spring feast at which the nation celebrates the marvel of redemption from Egypt, the great work of God in freeing the people to worship him and to enjoy him in the land that he was giving them (see commentary on 9:1–14). The focus of these passages in Numbers is on the work of the priests; the participation of the families of Israel is not the concern of these texts. Liberal scholars therefore have regularly styled these sections as P for the putative Priestly source. The Torah has already spoken on the subject of Passover (see commentary on Exod 12:14–20; Lev 23:4–8; also Deut 16:1–8). The Festival of Passover is also associated with the Feast of Unleavened Bread (v.17; see Exod 12:15; Lev 23:4–8). This paragraph is studded with the number seven (and its multiple of fourteen). The Festival of Passover was to be a time during which the people were not to do any work. It was akin to a week of Sabbath in this regard. It is from such a concept that the idea of "holy days" originates; the modern "holiday" is far afield from the original concept. The NT speaks of the Passover celebration and its fulfillment in Christ on several occasions (Matt 26:17; Mark 14:12–16; John 2:13; 11:55; 1 Cor 5:7; Heb 11:28).

(2) *The Feast of Weeks*

28:26–31

> [26]" 'On the day of firstfruits, when you present to the LORD an offering
> of new grain during the Feast of Weeks, hold a sacred assembly and do
> no regular work. [27]Present a burnt offering of two young bulls, one ram
> and seven male lambs a year old as an aroma pleasing to the LORD.
> [28]With each bull there is to be a grain offering of three-tenths of an
> ephah of fine flour mixed with oil; with the ram, two-tenths; [29]and with
> each of the seven lambs, one-tenth. [30]Include one male goat to make
> atonement for you. [31]Prepare these together with their drink offerings,
> in addition to the regular burnt offering and its grain offering. Be sure
> the animals are without defect.

26–31 The Festival of Firstfruits is also called the Feast of Weeks (see Exod 23:16; 34:22). This festival came fifty days after the Feast of Unleavened Bread (see Lev 23:9–22); from this number the Greek term Pentecost was used in the NT period (Acts 2:1). For other texts on the Feast of Weeks, see Leviticus 23:15–22; Deuteronomy 16:9–12. In the NT the association of Pentecost and the beginning of the church is of signal importance (see Acts 2:1–4; 20:16; 1 Cor 16:8).

Each of these feasts is associated in some way with the agricultural year. This has led some scholars to assume that there was a gradual development from a purely agricultural festival to a quasi-agricultural and spiritual festival to a purely spiritual festival. It is preferable to assume that the Lord graciously used the agricultural year with its natural rhythm to stimulate his people in the worship of his name. Thus the association of the agricultural calendar and the spiritual worship were framed together from the beginning by the Lord through his servant Moses.

These texts contain a couple of emphases we should not miss:

1. The special offerings of these feasts are to be made in addition to the regular daily sacrifices (v.31). This means that in the days in which the people were to do no regular labor (v.26), the priests were unusually busy.

2. The animals had to be without any defect at all; this is the final note at v.31. The reminders of this standard point, for the Christian reader, irresistibly to the person of Christ, the one Perfect Sacrifice for the sins of mankind, who "offered himself unblemished to God" (Heb 9:14).

(3) *The Feast of Trumpets*

29:1–6

> 1 " 'On the first day of the seventh month hold a sacred assembly and do no regular work. It is a day for you to sound the trumpets. 2 As an aroma pleasing to the LORD, prepare a burnt offering of one young bull, one ram and seven male lambs a year old, all without defect. 3 With the bull prepare a grain offering of three-tenths of an ephah of fine flour mixed with oil; with the ram, two-tenths; 4 and with each of the seven lambs, one-tenth. 5 Include one male goat as a sin offering to make atonement for you. 6 These are in addition to the monthly and daily burnt offerings with their grain offerings and drink offerings as specified. They are offerings made to the LORD by fire—a pleasing aroma.

1–6 This feast came at the beginning of the seventh month, an exceedingly busy month for the worship of the Lord in holy festivals (see Lev 23:23–25); later in Jewish tradition this feast became the time of the new year (Rosh Hashanah). The blowing of the trumpet on this feast is the blowing of the shophar, the ram's horn, rather than the silver trumpet of Numbers 10.

The contribution of this text in Numbers is to detail to the priests the sacrifices that must be accomplished on this holy day. The sacrifices fall into a certain pattern. On this the first day of the seventh month there was to be the sacrifice of one bull, one ram, and seven male lambs, each along with the requisite grain and libation offerings. The goat for the sin offering accompanies these celebrative whole burnt offerings; and the daily offerings are also to be accomplished. The language is somewhat repetitive in these sections, emphasizing the soothing aroma of the sacrifices and the fact that the male animals must be without defect.

(4) *The Day of Atonement*

29:7–11

> 7 " 'On the tenth day of this seventh month hold a sacred assembly. You must deny yourselves and do no work. 8 Present as an aroma pleasing to the LORD a burnt offering of one young bull, one ram and seven male lambs a year old, all without defect. 9 With the bull prepare a grain offering of three-tenths of an ephah of fine flour mixed with oil; with the ram, two-tenths; 10 and with each of the seven lambs, one-tenth. 11 Include one male goat as a sin offering, in addition to the sin offering for atonement and the regular burnt offering with its grain offering, and their drink offerings.

7–11 The Festival of Trumpets leads into the Day of Atonement, or Yom Kippur, on the tenth day of the seventh month. The name of the day of assembly is not given in vv.7–11, but we pick up this name from the parallel texts in Leviticus. Yom Kippur (properly *yôm hakkippurîm,* "the day of atonings") was a time of confession, contrition, and celebration (see Lev 16; 23:26–32). This is the most solemn of Israel's holy days. It is a time of fasting rather than of feasting, of solemnity rather than rejoicing. The NIV reads, "You must deny yourselves" (v.7; *weʿinnîṯem,* from *ʿānāh* in the Piel); the implication of this verb is that one is to deny oneself by means of fasting (see Lev 16:29, 31; 23:27, 32; Ps 35:13; Isa 58:3, 5). Even today the Day of Atonement is regarded by traditional Jews as the holiest day of the year. Men still fast during this day, and they lie prostrate in their synagogues in a posture of repentance for the sins of the people. In the NT, Yom Kippur is fulfilled in the death of the Savior who made atonement for us (see Rom 3:24–26; Heb 9:7; 10:3, 19–22).

(5) *The Feast of Tabernacles*

29:12–38

12 " 'On the fifteenth day of the seventh month, hold a sacred assembly and do no regular work. Celebrate a festival to the LORD for seven days. 13 Present an offering made by fire as an aroma pleasing to the LORD, a burnt offering of thirteen young bulls, two rams and fourteen male lambs a year old, all without defect. 14 With each of the thirteen bulls prepare a grain offering of three-tenths of an ephah of fine flour mixed with oil; with each of the two rams, two-tenths; 15 and with each of the fourteen lambs, one-tenth. 16 Include one male goat as a sin offering, in addition to the regular burnt offering with its grain offering and drink offering.

17 " 'On the second day prepare twelve young bulls, two rams and fourteen male lambs a year old, all without defect. 18 With the bulls, rams and lambs, prepare their grain offerings and drink offerings according to the number specified. 19 Include one male goat as a sin offering, in addition to the regular burnt offering with its grain offering, and their drink offerings.

20 " 'On the third day prepare eleven bulls, two rams and fourteen male lambs a year old, all without defect. 21 With the bulls, rams and lambs, prepare their grain offerings and drink offerings according to the number specified. 22 Include one male goat as a sin offering, in addition to the regular burnt offering with its grain offering and drink offering.

23 " 'On the fourth day prepare ten bulls, two rams and fourteen male lambs a year old, all without defect. 24 With the bulls, rams and lambs, prepare their grain offerings and drink offerings according to the number specified. 25 Include one male goat as a sin offering, in addition to the regular burnt offering with its grain offering and drink offering.

26 " 'On the fifth day prepare nine bulls, two rams and fourteen male lambs a year old, all without defect. 27 With the bulls, rams and lambs, prepare their grain offerings and drink offerings according to the number specified. 28 Include one male goat as a sin offering, in addition to the regular burnt offering with its grain offering and drink offering.

29 " 'On the sixth day prepare eight bulls, two rams and fourteen male lambs a year old, all without defect. 30 With the bulls, rams and lambs, prepare their grain offerings and drink offerings according to the number specified. 31 Include one male goat as a sin offering, in addition to the regular burnt offering with its grain offering and drink offering.

32 " 'On the seventh day prepare seven bulls, two rams and fourteen male lambs a year old, all without defect. 33 With the bulls, rams and lambs, prepare their grain offerings and drink offerings according to the number specified. 34 Include one male goat as a sin offering, in addition to the regular burnt offering with its grain offering and drink offering.

35" 'On the eighth day hold an assembly and do no regular work.
36Present an offering made by fire as an aroma pleasing to the LORD, a
burnt offering of one bull, one ram and seven male lambs a year old, all
without defect. 37With the bull, the ram and the lambs, prepare their
grain offerings and drink offerings according to the number specified.
38Include one male goat as a sin offering, in addition to the regular
burnt offering with its grain offering and drink offering.

12–38 The seventh month begins with the Feast of Trumpets on the first day, then moves to the Day of Atonement on the tenth day. Then the Feast of Tabernacles began on the fifteenth day and lasted for seven more days (see Lev 23:33–44). Each day of the Feast of Tabernacles (or Booths) had its own order for sacrifice; the small paragraphs in the rest of this chapter note each of these orders. The somewhat repetitive nature of these several paragraphs adds to the solemnity and pageantry of this text, much like the repeated sections in Numbers 7. These texts are not just explanatory, they themselves are a ritual celebration. To read these texts is to enter into a world of rhythm and ritual, where the patterns have a satisfying nature to them.

This Feast of Booths demanded the most animals to be sacrificed. On each of the first seven days, there were two rams and fourteen male lambs sacrificed, along with their requisite grain and libation offerings. In addition, there were thirteen bulls sacrificed on the first day, twelve on the second, and one less on each of the days leading to seven bulls on the seventh day—a total of seventy bulls for the seven days. On the eighth day there were one bull, one ram, and seven male lambs sacrificed along with requisite grain and libation offerings. In each of the days of this festival, there was also a male goat offered as a sin offering, along with the normal daily offerings. This was an exceedingly busy time of sacrificing to the Lord. See also Exodus 23:16; 34:22; Deuteronomy 16:13–15; Zechariah 14:16–19. In the NT the Feast of Booths is mentioned in John 7:2, 37. It was on the last, the most significant day of the feast, that Jesus stood in the temple in Jerusalem and invited the spiritually thirsty to come to him (John 7:37–38).

(6) *Summary*

29:39–40

39" 'In addition to what you vow and your freewill offerings, prepare
these for the LORD at your appointed feasts: your burnt offerings, grain
offerings, drink offerings and fellowship offerings.' "
40Moses told the Israelites all that the LORD commanded him.

39–40 The recapitulation of each of these festivals was a necessary part of the transfer of power from Moses to Joshua. The new community would soon be in the Land of Promise wherein these festivals would take on their full meaning in the life of the people. It would be in the good land where they would be able to bring all these sacrifices to the Lord because of his bounty. The restatement of these various offerings is a mark of faith and trust in the Lord, that at last he will complete his promise to bring his people into the land that is his gift for them.

Verse 39 explains that the sacrifices that have been elaborated on in Numbers 28–29, with special attention to the priestly participation in the worship of God, are in addition to any voluntary offerings that one might bring (see ch. 15), as well as any vow that one might make to the Lord (see ch. 30). Thus we understand that there was to be a regular pattern of sacrifice without regard to the special offerings one might bring because of a heart overflowing with joy to God or because of a desire to make a special need known to him. Sacrifice was a continual process in the courts of the Lord, a theme picked up by the writer to the Hebrews who speaks of "the same sacrifices repeated endlessly year after year" (Heb 10:1). This writer then points to the sacrifice of the Savior Jesus, which was singular and nonrepeatable (v.10), after which he sat down (v.12). No one reading these sections in Numbers would ever imagine a godly priest sitting down; the work was never done. But in Jesus all the work of priestly sacrifice was fulfilled; in him all meaning was realized—and he sits down. Sacrifice of animals, offerings of grain, and libations of wine are all fulfilled in his own work, to the praise of the Father.

Notes

---

39 Here is a tabular listing of the varied offerings mentioned in these two chapters. There are several observations that we may make. All the animals that are to be sacrificed are to be young males and without blemish. The grain offerings are always mixed with oil, and they are in a regular proportion to the animal sacrificed: with a bull one presents three-tenths an ephah of grain, with a ram one presents two-tenths, and with a male lamb one presents one-tenth ephah of flour. The amount of oil is not always noted, but the proportions used with the daily and monthly offerings may be a guide. The libation is not always mentioned. It is not certain that libations accompanied every one of these offerings. In each of the special offerings, the daily and—where appropriate—the monthly offerings are to be made in addition to the special offerings.

Daily offering

Two male lambs (one in morning; one in evening)
Each with grain offering of one-tenth ephah (about two quarts) of fine flour mixed with a quarter hin (about one quart) of oil
Accompanied by a quarter hin (about one quart) of *šēḵār* as libation

Sabbath offering

Two male lambs
Grain offering of two-tenths ephah (four quarts) fine flour, mixed with oil (unspecified amount)
Libation (amount not specified)

Monthly offering

Two bulls, one ram, seven male lambs
With each bull:
grain offering of three-tenths ephah (six quarts) of fine flour, mixed with oil libation of one-half hin (about two quarts) wine
With the ram:
grain offering of two-tenths ephah (four quarts) of fine flour, mixed with oil libation of one-third hin (about two quarts) wine
With each lamb:
grain offering of one-tenth ephah (two quarts) fine flour, mixed with oil libation of one quarter hin (about one quart) wine
One male goat as a sin offering
Plus the regular daily offerings and libations

Passover

Two bulls, one ram, seven male lambs
Grain offerings for each with the same proportions specified with the monthly offerings, each mixed with oil
No mention of libation with these offerings
One male goat as a sin offering
Plus the regular daily offerings and libations
Emphasis on unleavened bread for seven days

Feast of Weeks

Two bulls, one ram, seven male lambs
Grain offerings for each with the same proportions specified with the monthly offerings, each mixed with oil
Each along with libations
One male goat as a sin offering
Plus the regular daily offerings

Feast of Trumpets

One bull, one ram, seven male lambs
Grain offerings for each with standard proportions
No mention of libations
One male goat for sin offering
In addition to daily and monthly offerings, with attendant grain and libation offerings

The Day of Atonement

One bull, one ram, seven male lambs
Same proportion of grain offerings as with the others
No mention of their libations
One male goat as sin offering
Regular daily offerings

The Feast of Tabernacles

On the first day of the feast, the fifteenth day of the seventh month:

Thirteen bulls, two rams, fourteen male lambs
Same proportion of grain offerings as with the others
One male goat as sin offering
Regular daily offerings

On the second day of the feast

Twelve bulls, two rams, fourteen male lambs
Grain offerings and libations, as before
One male goat as sin offering
Regular daily offerings

On each successive day from day three to day seven, one less bull, plus the two rams, the fourteen male lambs, and all attendant sacrifices

On the eighth day

One bull, one ram, seven male lambs
Grain offerings and libations, as before
One male goat as sin offering
Regular daily offerings

40 This verse is given as 30:1 in the MT. This means that each verse in chapter 30 will be one number lower when the English is compared to the Hebrew text. The placement of this verse as the end of chapter 29 is correct; it is the completion of a section, not the beginning of a new unit.

---

c. *Vows (30:1–16)*

The third part of the legislative "intrusion" of chapters 28–30 deals with the issue of vows. Again, there must have been some purpose for inserting this material in the Book of Numbers at this point. I suggest that these chapters are placed here as guarantors of hope: the very fact that plans are being made for the sacrifices and vows that will be performed in the land are sure indicators that God is going to complete his work for his people. All one needs to do is to prepare for the coming battle. For victory under the Lord is the hope for the people of the second generation.

Significantly, the problematic issue in this section (ch. 30) has to do with vows that are made by women. In the male-oriented culture of biblical times, there were numerous complications that would arise when a woman would make a religious vow. There were questions about whether she was a free agent or whether her vow might needlessly entangle her father or her husband. Yet we should not miss the fact that women did make vows, which shows that they really did participate in the worship patterns of Israel. That the vows of women were considered problematic only reminds us of the cultural astringencies of the day. This chapter—as well as chapter 27 on the daughters of Zelophehad—points to change, even though it does not make many changes in its own day. These chapters speak of a gradual shifting from the patriarchy to a more egalitarian relationship between women and men. The change is very gradual in biblical times, but the change is underway.

(1) *The issue of vows to the Lord*

30:1–2

1 Moses said to the heads of the tribes of Israel: "This is what the LORD commands: 2 When a man makes a vow to the LORD or takes an oath to obligate himself by a pledge, he must not break his word but must do everything he said.

1–2 This chapter is a significant OT text on the subject of the vow (see Deut 23:21–23). The principal issue is this: A vow is not to be made rashly (see Eccl 5:1–7), but a vow to the Lord must be kept. The chapter begins with the words "When a man makes a vow to the LORD" (v.2). The Hebrew word *'îš* means "man," but not always "male." This is clearly indicated in the verses that follow, for the ones making the vows in this chapter are not men. The rest of the chapter develops some of the problems that eventuate when women began making vows to the Lord in a society that is male oriented. These ideas are the beginning of a movement to bring more personal freedom to women, but there are also numerous brakes applied here and there. This chapter is one of several that indicates that a change is in the works, even though the change is somewhat far off.

(2) *The vows of a woman who lives with her father*

30:3–5

3 "When a young woman still living in her father's house makes a vow to the LORD or obligates herself by a pledge 4 and her father hears about her vow or pledge but says nothing to her, then all her vows and every pledge by which she obligated herself will stand. 5 But if her father forbids her when he hears about it, none of her vows or the pledges by which she obligated herself will stand; the LORD will release her because her father has forbidden her.

3–5 The vow of an unmarried woman who is still under her father's protection might be nullified by her father. We may presume that this and the following law were designed for the protection of the woman, who in ancient Near Eastern society was subject to strong societal pressures, some of which would leave her without defense. That is, this text is not simply a denial on the part of male leadership for a woman to be able to enter into a vow to the Lord or a contract with another party. But it is a text that protects her from the abuse of others; and it protects her father as well, who might be the one who would have to come up with whatever the vow entails if his daughter is remiss in fulfilling her vow. Again, the very fact that women were making vows in this antique age is a step of great significance. But, as in every step of progress, there were attendant evils as well.

Notes

3–4 (4–5 MT) The phrasing וֶאֱסָרָה אֲשֶׁר אָסְרָה עַל־נַפְשָׁהּ (*weʾesārāh ʾašer ʾoserāh ʿal-napšāh,* "the pledge by which she obligates herself") in v.4 (5 MT) is used to amplify and make more specific the usual term for making a vow, כִּי־תִדֹּר נֶדֶר (*kî- tiddōr neder,* v.3 [4 MT], "surely she had made a vow"; NIV, "makes a vow"). In both cases the verbs are used with their cognate accusatives. The verb *ʾāsar* basically means "to bind" or "to tie"; hence, in the context of making a vow, the idea is "to tie oneself to do something." The full phrase from v.3 could be translated rather woodenly: "and her binding, by which she has bound her own being." This is most serious language indeed!

וְאִשָּׁה . . . בִּנְעֻרֶיהָ (*weʾiššāh . . . binʿureyhā,* "a woman . . . in her youth"; NIV, "young woman") is the manner in which this text speaks of the young, unmarried woman (see also v.16 [17 MT]). The term *binʿureyhā* is an example of a plural noun used as an abstraction ("youth") plus the pronominal suffix. In both cases the phrase is further defined in terms of her living in her father's house.

(3) *The vows of a (newly) married woman*

30:6–8

6 "If she marries after she makes a vow or after her lips utter a rash promise by which she obligates herself 7 and her husband hears about it but says nothing to her, then her vows or the pledges by which she obligated herself will stand. 8 But if her husband forbids her when he hears about it, he nullifies the vow that obligates her or the rash promise by which she obligates herself, and the LORD will release her.

6–8 The vow of a married woman might be nullified by her husband. The comparison of this section with vv.10–15 suggests that these verses relate to the instances of young couples who have recently married, as these are cases where the woman brings a vow into her marriage that may be heavily restrictive on her husband. Again, we may presume that there is something protective in this for the woman (she has an escape clause) as well as for the husband (who would have to pay if the vow was not fulfilled). The woman in this case is treated like a minor child, not having independent authority to enter into a vow or an obligation on her own right. She was either under her father's home or under her husband's home.

It is significant that v.6 suggests that the woman might have made a vow and then subsequently have become married. That she might be released from such a vow is greatly liberating both to her and to her husband. He might not want to take on a obligation that she has entered into before they were married. This is a protective clause. It also works for her in that she might have been pressured into making a vow that was not at all in her best interests to keep. This provision frees her from unnecessary complications to her life as well. In both the case of the married woman and the woman who lives with her father, the vows may be released by another, but only if he acts immediately on the information he has.

(4) *The vows of a widow or a divorced woman*

30:9

> [9] "Any vow or obligation taken by a widow or divorced woman will be binding on her.

9 A widowed or divorced woman is her own agent in the taking of vows. She is no longer under the household of her father, and she is no longer under the household of her husband. This verse is a significant contribution to our understanding of the ramifications of divorce in ancient Israel.

Some people claim that divorce in biblical times was only a certain legal fiction, that the woman was always to be considered the wife of the husband who had dismissed her (see Deut 24:1–4, for the basic text on divorce in the OT). Yet this verse clearly indicates that a divorced woman (*gᵉrûšāh* [v.10], the Qal fem. pass. part. of *gāraš*, "to be driven out"; see also Lev 21:7, 14; 22:13; Ezek 44:22) has the legal status of one who is a widow (*'almānāh*). She has become an independent agent. Like the widow, her former husband is in a sense "dead" to her. Since she has been married, she is not under the protection of her father (unless she were to seek that out again). So, strangely, this woman, along with the widow, is able to negotiate contracts, take vows, make promises—to function like any man in society. This is not to say that she could do anything; certainly some restrictions are placed on her just by virtue of her gender and her status as one who is divorced (see Lev 21:7 again). But even though she is the freest woman around, she is the one most apt to be bound by vows.

(5) *The vows of a married woman*

30:10–15

> [10] "If a woman living with her husband makes a vow or obligates herself by a pledge under oath [11] and her husband hears about it but says nothing to her and does not forbid her, then all her vows or the pledges by which she obligated herself will stand. [12] But if her husband

nullifies them when he hears about them, then none of the vows or pledges that came from her lips will stand. Her husband has nullified them, and the LORD will release her. [13]Her husband may confirm or nullify any vow she makes or any sworn pledge to deny herself. [14]But if her husband says nothing to her about it from day to day, then he confirms all her vows or the pledges binding on her. He confirms them by saying nothing to her when he hears about them. [15]If, however, he nullifies them some time after he hears about them, then he is responsible for her guilt."

10–15 This paragraph illustrates the complications that come in the taking of vows within the woman-man relationship. In contrast to vv.6–8, which deal with young couples in the early stages of their marriage, vv.10–15 deal more with those who have been married for a while. One gains the impression that these several complications may have come much as the case of the daughters of Zelophehad (27:1–11). That is, one case after another presented itself; the resulting chapter is the final codification. We may well presume that in the centuries leading up to the NT, the legal decisions on the subject of vows became even more complex. The words of the Lord Jesus to avoid the complications of these oaths (Matt 5:33–37) are quite liberating. For after a while serious language about holy things would be used in the most trivializing manner possible. So Jesus forswore oaths and vows altogether for his young disciples. He urged them to let their words speak for themselves, apart from the calling of heaven and earth to witness. Actually, this is great grace on his part.

(6) *A summary statement*

30:16

[16]These are the regulations the LORD gave Moses concerning relationships between a man and his wife, and between a father and his young daughter still living in his house.

16 From the summary it is evident that this chapter has to do specifically with the making of vows by women, not the making of vows in general. This chapter is much like chapter 27. It deals with the feminine exceptions to the general rule of men in the age of the patriarchy. Like chapter 27, it deals rather sympathetically with women and presents some small glimmer of light in terms of their growing partnership with men in the praise of God and in their living their lives here on earth as God's gift to them would suggest. But we also recognize that the door to full participation is only cracked briefly in this chapter. That it is cracked at all is the most hopeful sign.

5. *The reprisal against Midian, Moses' last campaign (31:1–54)*

Chapter 31 picks up on the story line of chapter 25, the account of the debauchery of Israel at Baal Peor. We remember that Midian was placed under interdict by the Lord because of their part in the failure of Israel in that ignoble event. The Lord had said to Moses, "Treat the Midianites as enemies and kill them" (25:17). This chapter tells the story of the holy war of Israel, the vendetta of Yahweh, against these enemies of God and his people. That such an idea as "holy war" is distasteful to many believers today is granted. But the reader of Scripture can only come to a sense of its meaning if he or she abandons for a moment the ethical and moral stances of our day and attempts to read it within the standards of the day in which the text stands. This is not to present an idea of moral relativism or to censor the morality of the Bible. It is merely to observe that different conditions obtain in the robust and rugged world of the ancient Near East than we are used to or are comfortable with in our own living. On its own grounds, the frightful events of this chapter are moral and are from God. The most important issue in texts such as this is not to concentrate on the suffering and pain that the chapter describes but to reflect on the holiness of the Lord that the chapter celebrates. In the midst of terrible wrath, God remembers mercy, which is also the story of this chapter, as we shall see.

a. *The report of the battle (31:1–24)*

(1) *The instructions for the battle*

31:1–6

[1]The LORD said to Moses, [2]"Take vengeance on the Midianites for the Israelites. After that, you will be gathered to your people."

[3]So Moses said to the people, "Arm some of your men to go to war against the Midianites and to carry out the LORD's vengeance on them. [4]Send into battle a thousand men from each of the tribes of Israel." [5]So twelve thousand men armed for battle, a thousand from each tribe, were supplied from the clans of Israel. [6]Moses sent them into battle, a thousand from each tribe, along with Phinehas son of Eleazar, the priest, who took with him articles from the sanctuary and the trumpets for signaling.

1–2 This is the last war of Moses before God brings his life to an end. On the expression "to be gathered to your people" (v.2), see Notes on 20:24. Moses does not get to lead the war of conquest in Canaan; that will be for his successor. But at least he is to lead a punitive war against the foes who nearly had destroyed his people, seemingly on the eve of their greatest triumph. This war was to be a war of vengeance against Midian, a holy war of the people of God. The war is announced by the Lord, not Moses. The war was not regarded by Moses as motivated by petty jealousy. It was "the LORD's vengeance" because of the wickedness of the Midianites, who caused the seduction of the Israelites in the pagan worship system of Baal of Peor (25:16–18). The Lord's strong words came specifically to Moses: "avenge an avenging" (v.2). The cognate accusative is a means of emphasis in Hebrew style. The specific mention of Cozbi (see 25:15, 18) heightens the anger latent in this text. See also Deuteronomy 32:43, a text of God avenging the blood of his servants (also Nah 1:2, of vengeance against Nineveh). We may also notice the phrase "avenge the breaking of the covenant" (Lev 26:25).

3–4 On hearing the commandment of the Lord, Moses turns to the people and calls for a strike force, an elite corps of soldiers who will carry out the punitive war. This is a limited, contained, special task calling for a limited army of special forces. One thousand men were to come from each of the tribes of Israel. The entire nation was jeopardized; all the tribes share in vengeance. If the figures of the census of 26:51 are "common numbers," then 12,000 of the 600,000 men makes a very small proportional force (1/50 of the whole). If the number 12,000 is taken from a smaller army of approximately 60,000 men, then the 12,000 would be a relatively small but still significant number (one-fifth of the whole). In any case, it is a part for the whole, a representative army for the whole nation.

5–6 Verse 5 is somewhat celebrative in nature, as is so much of the historical narrative of this book. The "thousand of the thousands" is a nice tie of words, having an almost mystical ring to it. The holy war is a vendetta of God that calls for special uses of numbers and men.

In biblical thought a blood relative may take vengeance on the killer of the slain (see on ch. 35). There is a sense that the Lord is the kinsman of his people who issues a command for his own holy vendetta. The war is one of divine reprisal for the near destruction of his people by the Midianites. The mention of Phinehas in v.6 is especially noteworthy. It was his zeal for the honor of the Lord that led him to spear Zimri and Cozbi in their licentious act at the entrance to the Tent of Meeting (25:8). Now his leadership in the sacral aspects of the battle was to demonstrate that this was truly holy war. He took to the site of the battle the holy implements from the sanctuary and the priestly trumpets for the battle signals (see 10:9). The implements from the sanctuary do not seem to include the holy ark (despite the desire of some to connect this phrasing to the story of the ark in warfare in Josh 6:6 and 1 Sam 4); surely the ark would have been mentioned if it were used in this battle. More likely the priest took small implements from the worship of God in the tent; the focus is on the trumpets. Whatever implements he took with him, the belief was sure: Yahweh was with his people in the sacred place; so he was with his people as they went to war.

The trumpet in this text is the *ḥᵃṣōṣᵉrāh* ("sacred clarion" from 10:8; see also 2 Chron 13:12). This was a long, straight metal tube with a flowing bell; it is distinguished from the *šôp̄ār,* the ram's horn of ancient Israel. The verb root *ḥṣṣr* is denominative, meaning "to sound a clarion" (see 2 Chron 5:13, Piel, and 1 Chron 15:24, Hiphil). The blowing of the sacred clarion was an act of celebrative worship. While the concept is alien to us today, even the warfare that Israel was to engage in was regarded as a sacral act—in some way an act of the worship of God (see Ps 149:6, the praise of God linked to the wielding of a sword). "Onward Hebrew Soldiers" was more than a metaphor for Israel; it was a descriptive reality of army life.

(2) *The report of the victory*

31:7–12

7 They fought against Midian, as the LORD commanded Moses, and killed every man. 8 Among their victims were Evi, Rekem, Zur, Hur and Reba—the five kings of Midian. They also killed Balaam son of Beor with the sword. 9 The Israelites captured the Midianite women and children and took all the Midianite herds, flocks and goods as plunder. 10 They burned all the towns where the Midianites had settled, as well as all their camps. 11 They took all the plunder and spoils, including the people and animals, 12 and brought the captives, spoils and plunder to Moses and Eleazar the priest and the Israelite assembly at their camp on the plains of Moab, by the Jordan across from Jericho.

7 The narrator stresses the fact that this battle was the Lord's; it was not the result merely of human pique. The narrator does not say much at all about the battle, but he is very concerned to detail the aftermath of the victory of Israel. Our modern difficulty to comprehend the concept of holy war and the annihilation of a populace that this would bring about is understandable but somewhat short-sighted. The Lord was about to bring Israel into the land of Canaan to engage in a war of conquest and extermination of all the peoples in that land (see Deut 20:1–16) because of their gross wickedness and the threat they represented to the integrity of the worship of Israel and to their very survival in the land. The cup of the Amorites was now full (see Gen 15:16). Further, the judgment of the Lord on the peoples of Canaan is a paradigm of final judgment, a teaching of both testaments and all orthodox creeds.

So it is that v.7 reports that Israel obeyed the word of the Lord through his servant Moses. They fought as they were taught, an action of faithfulness, courage, and obedient trust. The report that they "killed every man" does not necessarily mean that they killed every individual but that there was a complete defeat, with a focus on the males of the enemy army who were slain. Some of the enemies must have fled. The emphasis in this report is that they killed the men only; this allows for the report of v.9 respecting women and children.

8 Verse 8 lists the notables that the Israelites killed and then impaled (see Notes). The listing of the Midianite kings (Evi, Rekem, Zur, Hur, and Reba) is like a listing of trophies. These five chieftains are memorialized forever as enemies of the Lord who were impotent before his armies. Their wounds and their impaling poles point to ghastly deaths and grisly display. There is here a vindictiveness of the sacred, a display of triumph—a celebration of God who has given glorious victory.

Among the names are two surprises. One is Zur, whom we remember as the father of Cozbi (see 25:15), the Midianite woman who was stabbed to death with Zimri by Phinehas. The supposition we had in chapter 25 that she was a significant person is now confirmed. Cozbi is like Jezebel. She is a priestess-princess of paganism. As in the case of Jezebel, so too her name has been defiled in Israel (Cozbi means "Deception"). We have a name to use for her if we wish to recall her at all, but it is a name of infamy.

The other surprise, of course, is the mention of Balaam. The Hebrew wording is striking: "And Balaam son of Beor they also killed by the sword." Up till now, following the text, we would have had no idea he would appear in Scripture again. The story of chapter 25 lacks the name of the principal instigator of the seduction of the men of Israel to the orgiastic worship of Baal. But here he is found among the dead of the princes of Midian; what trouble Balaam failed to accomplish by the role of the mantic arts he was able to achieve by his advice to the Midianites (v.16; see chs. 22–24).

Balaam's name, amid the recital of the names of the Midianite kings, suggests that he was their advisor, their spiritual guru. Always after a shekel, Balaam had a new gig. It must have seemed ironic to him to have his pay and to know that Israel was in trouble. But the irony has come full circle; he is now dead. There is considerable discussion as to the manner of his death, indicated in this verse. Some feel he may have died in war; others believe that he was executed, that he died a judicial death. It is possible that the second is the case and that after he was run through with a sword he was also impaled with the princes whom he had so misdirected.

9–12 While the men of Midian were killed by the victorious Hebrew soldiers, the women and children were spared by the troops as plunder (v.9). Moses commanded that only the virgin women (who were thus innocent of the indecencies at Peor) could be spared; the guilty women and the boys (who might endanger the inheritance rights of Israelite men) were to be put to death (vv.15–17).

We may make some observations about this shocking situation:

1. Jericho is the first city of cis-Jordan (the near side of Jordan) that Israel will win

by warfare. In the case of Jericho, all the inhabitants and all their possessions were placed under *ḥerem;* all was devoted to the Lord. In the case of Midian, this was a punitive strike; Midian was not the firstfruits of the land. Therefore, there were many items of booty and plunder (including surviving people) to be distributed among the men of the army, as well as among the people who had remained in camp. The burning of the cities was a mark that these were not to be inhabited by the Hebrews; burning them would greatly impede their being reinhabited by enemies.

2. The saving alive of the women and children was likely considered by the soldiers of Israel to be an act of mercy. They could have killed them or abandoned them to their own devices. By sparing their lives the soldiers must have thought they were being magnanimous.

3. There is a sense of poetic justice in that the Midianites had conspired to destroy Israel through licentious behavior of their priestess cult functionaries. Now their wives and daughters were about to be added to the families of Israel. This seems to be a proper despoiling of the enemies.

4. At the same time we see here, and often, how in the ancient Near East (and in the Bible, which is a part of that world) that women and children were regarded as property to be listed with cows, trinkets, and assorted booty. This is the sadness; the times were not merciful to women as persons, except on rare occasions.

Throughout, Phinehas was intensively involved as a priest-warrior. There was a sense in which his father, Eleazar, was still the high priest who functioned in the camp at the altars of the Lord. But Phinehas was more like a field priest who functioned with the armies of Israel to remind them that the Lord was in their midst, fighting for them.

This section is marked by an orderliness that is characteristic of so much of the Book of Numbers and which stands in studied contrast to the horrors the verses present. Verse 8 gives a list of the kings, v.9 a list of the booty, v.10 an accounting of the burnings, and v.12 a list of their possessions. There is also a redundancy of verbs describing the taking of captives ("the Israelites captured," "they plundered," "they burned," "they took," and "they brought"). Verse 12 is particularly triumphant in tone, having a formal pageantry to its cadences. They proved that they can do it. They are not like their parents who could not win wars against their enemies; with only a small fraction of the entire army, they had been able to win a great victory. So they come to Moses, to Eleazar, and to the people who had remained behind in camp. This is not unlike the later Roman victory processionals following a distant campaign by a great general. This is a showing forth to the entire community of what God had done.

There is an episodic nature to the Book of Numbers. In some ways it is like *The Memoirs of Moses in the Desert.* This is shown in the way that this story ties up three loose ends: Cozbi's father, Balaam, and the meaning of the story of Baal Peor. The tone so far in this story is one of victory march. The people must have been thinking, *We are faithful, and so is the Lord.*

Notes

---

8 In the phrase הָרְגוּ עַל־חַלְלֵיהֶם (*hārᵉg̲û ʿal-ḥallêhem,* "they killed . . . with the sword"), the meaning of the word *ḥallêhem* remains debated. The meaning of the noun means "pierced."

It seems preferable to think of "impaling stakes," a brutal, grisly display of vanquished foes that was regarded in the ancient Near East as a potent symbol of their destruction. The body of a man would be thrust down on a sharpened stake that would pierce through his rectum to enter his abdomen. There was a double shame to this action; the awful display of the corpse would also preclude decent burial.

11 בָּאָדָם וּבַבְּהֵמָה (*bā'āḏām ûḇabbᵉhēmāh,* "the people and animals") aptly illustrates how the Hebrew term *'āḏām* ("man") is used in the Bible to speak of persons, rather than necessarily of males. Here it is used specifically of women and children; all the adult males had been slain in the battle and the subsequent judgment.

12 The phrasing אֶל־עַרְבֹת מוֹאָב אֲשֶׁר עַל־יַרְדֵּן יְרֵחוֹ (*'el-'arḇōṯ mô'āḇ 'ᵃšer 'al-yardēn yᵉrēḥô,* "on the plains of Moab, by the Jordan across from Jericho") presents a perspective of Transjordan from cis-Jordan. The expression *'arḇōṯ mô'āḇ* has the sense "over there." Similarly, the reference of the Jordan River to the city of Jericho is also the perspective that later people would have found helpful to visualize the site in mind. The perspective of geography in the Bible regularly centers in the land, even when the people are not there. Everything else is designed to give us a sense of "out there"—a regular metaphor of one at some distance from God's dwelling.

---

(3) *The destruction of the women and boys*

31:13–18

[13]Moses, Eleazar the priest and all the leaders of the community went to meet them outside the camp. [14]Moses was angry with the officers of the army—the commanders of thousands and commanders of hundreds—who returned from the battle.

[15]"Have you allowed all the women to live?" he asked them. [16]"They were the ones who followed Balaam's advice and were the means of turning the Israelites away from the LORD in what happened at Peor, so that a plague struck the LORD's people. [17]Now kill all the boys. And kill every woman who has slept with a man, [18]but save for yourselves every girl who has never slept with a man.

13–18 We are quite shocked when we find the people are facing anger from Moses instead of approval. The meeting outside the camp is an omen; something is unclean. The Bible says that Moses was furious against the officers of the armies. He does not come to bless them in their victory but to vent his rage at the victories. Even in victory the people can grossly err.

Moses asks almost incredulously, "Have you allowed all the women to live?" (v.15). The text has led us down a line that leads to deliberate surprise. We find ourselves as startled by these words, even as some of the soldiers might have been. But then Moses explains: These were the very women whom Balaam had used to bring the seduction of the people of Israel and to provoke the terrible plague that had broken out among the congregation of Israel (v.16). So boys and women were to be killed; there was to be no mercy, no exception (v.17). Only young girls (demonstrable virgins) would be saved alive; only they had not contaminated themselves with the debauchery of Midian and Moab in Baal worship (v.18). The suggestion is that the participation of women from Midian in the debased orgiastic worship of Baal described in chapter 25 was extensive, not selective. Who would know which of these women was innocent of these rituals? The presumption is that each one was guilty in some manner.

Verse 17 is rather powerful in its formation. It is framed with chiasm of the imperative verb "kill." The following format shows the word order, the pungency, of the original:

> And now, kill every male among the children;
> and every woman who knows a man,
> a male sexually, kill!

The brutality demanded by this verse is nearly unimaginable—the killing of boys and babies. One has to ask, What separates this from the Egyptian killing of the Hebrew boy babies in Exodus 1? Since most women were married young in biblical times, most women would have had to be killed as well. Here is the sort of text that troubles us deeply. It is one thing to kill a man. It is one thing to kill a woman in battle. It is one thing even to kill children in a frenzy of hatred. But this verse demands the calm, selective, purposeful killing of women and children after the battle was over.

Verse 18 only increases our sense of unrest in this text. Those girls who were to be kept alive would have to be rather young. Since little girls were preserved, their mothers would have had to be killed.

Such stories are bound to raise questions about the morality of the OT. Ultimately, these questions are darts directed to the person of God. One cannot debate the "morality" of the OT apart from the "morality" of God who is represented in these passages. And once one begins to ask, "Is God moral?" the very question damns the speaker. For who is man to be the instructor of the Lord? (see Job 40:1–2). This is not to say that these passages do not cause us to shriek with inner tension—for they do! But our shout had best not be an arrogant attack on Majesty. Ultimately, people of faith affirm—in the midst of the most negative environment—"The God of Israel will do right."

The only way to understand such a ghastly command is to realize what was at stake in the story of Baal Peor (ch. 25), the incident that gave rise to the holy war in the first place. This story is not just another account of sin and rebellion in the desert. Indeed, if the story of Baal Peor is not an unusual and remarkable account, then the punishment meted out in chapter 31 is not in keeping with the crime.

Numbers 25 is unique. It records an altogether new type of sin and rebellion—one that bears within itself the threat of the doom of the nation as a whole. As we know, from our distance, it was the very type of evil described in chapter 25 that finally destroyed the Hebrew kingdoms in the land. While it is difficult to say such a thing, the destruction of the women and the boys was an act of God's mercy—for Israel. There is a sense of perspective here that is so very difficult to grasp and yet which permeates the Word of God: Divine judgment is sure for the nations who are a threat to the existence of God's people or who have rejected his grace. And that remains true in our own "sophisticated" day. The nations today, and the ungodly among all peoples, are at risk. They know of risk from the possibility of nuclear disaster, from the threat of war, from the tweaks of nature, and from the freaks of chance. But the nations today are at risk from the judgment of God. This is true whether they acknowledge it or not. One day that judgment will come. At that time there will be no weeping over women and boys who died in ancient Midian three and a half millennia ago; at that time the judgment of God will transcend anything ever written in the harshest Scripture. And God will still be merciful and holy, maintaining glory and honor in the midst of havoc and ruin. The God of Israel will still do right.

Notes

---

17 The phrase יֹדַעַת אִישׁ לְמִשְׁכַּב זָכָר (*yōḏa'aṯ 'îš lᵉmiškaḇ zāḵār*, "to know a man," "lying with a male"; NIV, "who has slept with a man") is noteworthy. The word *miškaḇ* is a noun that means "place of lying," "couch," "act of lying." Here it is used idiomatically as an adverb to define further the intention of the line; to the first phrase, "who had not known a man," this word adds the idea "lying with a male." The two phrases together are a definitive statement of virginity. It has been observed that no single word in biblical Hebrew unequivocally means "virgin." A qualifying phrase is needed to make the idea clear. See Cyrus Gordon (UT, #540): "There is no word in the Near Eastern languages that by itself means *virgo intacta*." The noun *miškaḇ* as an adverb indicating sexual behavior is seen also in Judg 21:11–12 and in Lev 18:22; 20:13 (of man-to-man relationship; i.e., sodomy).

---

(4) *The purification of the soldiers*

31:19–20

> [19]"All of you who have killed anyone or touched anyone who was killed must stay outside the camp seven days. On the third and seventh days you must purify yourselves and your captives. [20]Purify every garment as well as everything made of leather, goat hair or wood."

19–20 The "seven days" of v.19 help us to sense the full weight of what the laws of cleanness pertained to, as this was holy war (see 19:11–13). Both people (vv.19–20) and things (vv.21–24) had to be cleansed. The rites of purification from contact with a dead body would demand the waters of cleansing from the ashes of the red heifer (see 19:12). There is an emphatic pronoun at the beginning of this verse: "And you!" All are addressed here who had been involved in the killing of others, even when those who were killed were the enemies of God and man. The death of any person makes one who comes in contact with that corpse unclean, even when the killing was commanded by God. Thus even in a text of judgment, there are still the lessons of ritual cleansing for the people of God.

Notes

---

19 תִּתְחַטְּאוּ (*tiṯḥaṭṭᵉ'û*, "purify yourselves") is a Hithpael imperative from the root *ḥāṭā'* ("to purify oneself from uncleanness"), a verb used of the Levite in 8:21. Those who had had any contact with the dead were impure (see 19:12) and needed to undergo the rite of purification.

---

(5) *The purifying of the goods*

31:21–24

> [21]Then Eleazar the priest said to the soldiers who had gone into battle, "This is the requirement of the law that the LORD gave Moses: [22]Gold, silver, bronze, iron, tin, lead [23]and anything else that can withstand fire must be put through the fire, and then it will be clean. But

it must also be purified with the water of cleansing. And whatever
cannot withstand fire must be put through that water. [24]On the seventh
day wash your clothes and you will be clean. Then you may come into
the camp."

21–24 Purification extends to things as well as to people. Things that are ritually impure will contaminate people who are otherwise clean. Hence it is another mark of the grace of God to provide a means for the purification of goods as well. Metal objects had to be purified by having them pass through fire, then be cleansed with the waters of cleansing. Some of these metal objects that were so cleansed became gifts to the Lord (see v.50). Those items that could not withstand fire had to be cleansed in the water alone. Possibly Paul's description of the bema judgment of the work of believers (1 Cor 3:10–15) is patterned after this passage. In the case of the cleansing of these soldiers, they had to wait until the seventh day, then wash their clothes, and then they could enter the camp. This pattern of seven days of exclusion from the camp because of uncleanness is well established in Israel (see the story of Miriam in ch. 12).

b. *The division of the spoils (31:25–54)*

Another aspect of holy war was the just distribution of the spoils of war, both among those who fought in the battle as well as among those who stayed with the community, with appropriate shares to be given to the Lord, whose battle it was (v.28). This section describes rather elaborately that division process. As in so many such sections in the Book of Numbers, this rather prosaic text reads with a certain grandeur—for it, too, is celebrative. These texts are meant to be read aloud as a declaration of the work of God in the lives of his people. Much like the antiphonal responses in Psalm 136, the patterns of remembrance of the works of the Lord in the deliverance of his people were designed to be recited in a variety of ways.

(1) *The share for the soldiers*

31:25–41

[25]The LORD said to Moses, [26]"You and Eleazar the priest and the
family heads of the community are to count all the people and animals
that were captured. [27]Divide the spoils between the soldiers who took
part in the battle and the rest of the community. [28]From the soldiers who
fought in the battle, set apart as tribute for the LORD one out of every five
hundred, whether persons, cattle, donkeys, sheep or goats. [29]Take this
tribute from their half share and give it to Eleazar the priest as the LORD's
part. [30]From the Israelites' half, select one out of every fifty, whether
persons, cattle, donkeys, sheep, goats or other animals. Give them to
the Levites, who are responsible for the care of the LORD's tabernacle."
[31]So Moses and Eleazar the priest did as the LORD commanded Moses.
[32]The plunder remaining from the spoils that the soldiers took was
675,000 sheep, [33]72,000 cattle, [34]61,000 donkeys [35]and 32,000 women
who had never slept with a man.
[36]The half share of those who fought in the battle was:

337,500 sheep, [37]of which the tribute for the LORD was 675;
[38]36,000 cattle, of which the tribute for the LORD was 72;
[39]30,500 donkeys, of which the tribute for the LORD was 61;
[40]16,000 people, of which the tribute for the LORD was 32.

41 Moses gave the tribute to Eleazar the priest as the LORD's part, as the LORD commanded Moses.

25–41 The Book of Numbers delights in lists, in the numbering of persons and things. Here in this section of the chapter is the command of the Lord to Moses to have the sum taken of the spoils of the battle, both man and beast. The term "man" in this section relates only to the little girls who were spared the *ḥerem;* the animals include sheep, cattle, donkeys, and goats. Eleazar and heads of the father's houses were to aid Moses in taking this toll. The task must have been enormous, given the numbers involved. The purpose of making this sum seems to be twofold: (1) it is a celebrative declaration of the work of God on their behalf; (2) it is a means to assure the equitable distribution of the spoils of war. Dividing the spoils of war was a proverbial symbol for exquisite joy in the ancient world (e.g., Isa 9:3, where it is paired with harvest festival).

The division of the spoil was to be made in two sections, one for those who had fought in the war and the other for the rest of the congregation. The two halves were equal, but their distribution was deliberately unequal—there were far fewer soldiers than those who remained in the camp. Yet it was the soldiers who had risked their lives; so theirs is the larger personal share. The term used for soldiers in v.27 is indicative of the type of man who had been called to serve in the elite corps. They are described as *tōp̱ᵉśê hammilḥāmāh* ("those who are skilled for battle"; cf. Jer 2:8, "those who deal with the law").

Before the men of war could enjoy the spoil that was their allotment, there first had to be a tax set apart that was to be given to the Lord. The ratio in this case was one of five hundred. Again, the soldiers who had risked their lives received larger personal shares (as they were a smaller collective unit than the vast numbers of the congregation), but their share to the Lord was also smaller than the share that was demanded of the people. The proportion to be given to the Lord is termed a "tax" or a "tribute" (v.28, *meḵes,* from the verb *kāsas,* "to compute"; see Exod 12:4). This tribute was given to Eleazar the priest as a sacred offering (*tᵉrûmāh*) to the Lord (v.29).

From the half of the booty that was to be distributed to the members of the congregation, one unit of each fifty was to be given as a tribute to the Lord for the special use of the Levites in return for their sacral service at the tabernacle. Thus the people's tax in this booty is ten times that of the soldiers' share, one-fiftieth as against one five-hundreth.

The instructions that the Lord gave to Moses (vv.25–30) are followed by a report of accomplishment (v.31). In this verse we find again the familiar words of obedience. Each time we read these words of compliance on the part of Moses, we groan within at the thought of the one time that Moses did not do as God had commanded him (ch. 20).

The listing of the plunder as a whole is given in vv.32–35. The numbers were enormous; the victory was staggering. This was just the beginning; on the other side of the Jordan lay the rest of the land of God's promise. The people should have been thinking, *If we received this much booty in a punitive war, just think what will be our portion when we are on the campaign of conquest!*

The table reads:

675,000 sheep (presumably including goats)
72,000 cattle

61,000 donkeys
32,000 young (virgin) women

The half share follows with correct, simple arithmetic:
337,500 sheep (including goats)
36,000 cattle
30,500 donkeys
16,000 young (virgin) women

The Lord's tax (to be given to Eleazar) (ratio of 1 unit of 500):
675 sheep
72 cattle
61 donkeys
32 young (virgin) women

Again, the section concludes with a summary statement of complete obedience on the part of Moses with regard to the presentation of the tax on these items as a sacred contribution to the Lord, by giving these items to Eleazar the priest (v.41).

We may make a few observations about these numbers:

1. They are immense numbers, indicative of a great victory with enormous booty.

2. Though the numbers of the animals and women are rounded off to the thousands, the proportion of 1/500 gets pretty exacting; the supposition is that these numbers may well be "common numbers" rather than inflated sums.

3. The supposition, so often heard, that numbers are not copied well in the Bible is not buttressed in these sections of Numbers. It seems that in this book, at least, the copying of numbers (in the awkward manner of words rather than symbols) was done quite carefully. Perhaps the necessity for the sums and totals to work out correctly was a check against carelessness by later scribes.

As to the use to which the women would be put in the service of the priests, we can only guess. It is possible that they were given menial tasks to do in the service of the Lord, as many commentators suggest (see Exod 38:8). In these women there is something redemptive in the whole dismal record of the defeat of Midian. Though most of their countrymen had been slain, including their parents and brothers, the surviving young girls would eventually become part of the redeemed community. Eventually these few girls became mothers in Israel.

(2) *The share for the people*

31:42–47

[42]The half belonging to the Israelites, which Moses set apart from that of the fighting men—[43]the community's half—was 337,500 sheep, [44]36,000 cattle, [45]30,500 donkeys [46]and 16,000 people. [47]From the Israelites' half, Moses selected one out of every fifty persons and animals, as the LORD commanded him, and gave them to the Levites, who were responsible for the care of the LORD's tabernacle.

42–47 The statistics of the half share for the people follow in much the same procedure as the previous section for the soldiers. The numbers of the half are the same but are listed in a celebrative manner. In this case the tax, which would become a sacred tribute to the Lord, was proportionally higher, 1 unit of 50 (rather than 1 unit of 500).

This would mean the following:

6,750 sheep
720 cattle
610 donkeys
320 young (virgin) women

Again, Moses followed faithfully in the distribution of the Lord's share. In this case it was given to the Levites.

(3) *The extra share for the Lord*

31:48–54

48 Then the officers who were over the units of the army—the commanders of thousands and commanders of hundreds—went to Moses 49 and said to him, "Your servants have counted the soldiers under our command, and not one is missing. 50 So we have brought as an offering to the LORD the gold articles each of us acquired—armlets, bracelets, signet rings, earrings and necklaces—to make atonement for ourselves before the LORD."

51 Moses and Eleazar the priest accepted from them the gold—all the crafted articles. 52 All the gold from the commanders of thousands and commanders of hundreds that Moses and Eleazar presented as a gift to the LORD weighed 16,750 shekels. 53 Each soldier had taken plunder for himself. 54 Moses and Eleazar the priest accepted the gold from the commanders of thousands and commanders of hundreds and brought it into the Tent of Meeting as a memorial for the Israelites before the LORD.

48–54 For a chapter that begins with such a grim story, there is a perfectly lovely ending. This is the account of a spontaneous extra gift of the officer corps to the Lord. Beyond the tax that they were required to give of the animals and persons that had been distributed to them in the sharing of the booty of the war, there were innumerable objects that the soldiers had taken for their own use as they looted the camps (v.53). Now the captains of thousands and of hundreds approached Moses (v.48) and made a magnanimous offering of numerous beautiful objects of gold—armlets, bracelets, signet rings, earrings, and other ornaments (v.50). This gift, they assured Moses, was in gratitude for a most remarkable fact: not one soldier of the elite Hebrew corps had died in the war (v.49)! The only explanation for this is the presence of the Lord among his people in his holy sanctuary (cf. Goldberg, "Gott ist im Israel gegenwärtig im Heiligtum," p. 134).

That no Israelite soldiers were lost was miracle, pure and simple. But it was a miracle that impels response on the part of the people to the Lord. As Walther Eichrodt points out, the important issue in the belief in miracles in the Scripture is not so much in the material facts of the miracles but in that which the miracles present of the person and work of God. He says that the real importance of the miraculous for faith is in "its evidential character," particularly "a clear impression of God's care or retribution within it" (*Theology of the Old Testament*, tr. J.A. Baker [Philadelphia: Westminster, 1967], p. 163).

Of course, the people made a special gift to the Lord. He had made a special gift of life to them. The gifts of the officer corps is reminiscent of the extravagant gifts of the people from the despoiling of the Egyptians (Exod 35). This is a mark of the gratitude of the new generation. Moses and Eleazar the priest took the gold items from them, all of fashioned work (v.51). When they weighed them, they found the cumulative weight to be 16,750 shekels (a weight of about 420 pounds, v.52)! This is an enormous gift—and it came from grateful men to an all-protective God.

Moses and Eleazar brought the gold into the Tent of Meeting, where it became a "memorial" (*zikkārôn*) of the victory that the Lord had won (v.54). We suspect, though the text does not specify this, that the gold would have been melted down and reworked into a suitably fashioned symbol—an extravagant offering to the Lord.

The most interesting phrase in this entire section concerns the motivation of the chiefs. It was "to make atonement for ourselves before the LORD" (v.50). Thus the making of atonement was not prompted by sin or guilt but by overwhelming gratitude. They knew, as all officers know, that every battle is a calculated risk in which some soldiers will die. A good officer will wish to minimize his losses as he maximizes his gain. In this case the gain was overwhelming—complete victory. And the losses were nil—not one Hebrew soldier died. The making of atonement, then, would be an offering of expiation in gratitude to God for the gift he made of the lives of those who ordinarily would have died. This is a payment, if you will, in return for that which they might have lost.

We have no reason to believe that the protection of the lives of every soldier in the wars of Israel ever happened again. This must have been a solitary act in the history of Israel. If so, it is suitably predictive of the army of Christ in his final victory over all wickedness (Rev 19). No doubt in that final battle there will also be no casualties among his forces. So here is a battle at the beginning of the wars of Israel that in one particular points forward to the final battle of Savior Jesus. Gratitude to him shall be at least in the measure of the gratitude of these officers in that olden time.

6. *The settlement of the Transjordan tribes (32:1–42)*

There is a sense of direction and symmetry to the Book of Numbers that is satisfying to the patient reader. Within the book, as we have seen, there are some passages of dramatic encounters, of miraculous acts, of robust theology, and even of comedic drama. There are also texts, such as the present chapter, that are none of these things. Yet the chapter is significant because it deals with the ways the will of God was effected through the tribes of Israel as the new generation was taking its place in the world God had given her. This chapter presents the account of the first tribes making their settlement in the land of their choice. In the case of two and one-half tribes, Transjordan was their inheritance of choice. For them—Reuben, Gad, and the half-tribe of Manasseh—the victories over Sihon and Og (ch. 21) and the punitive victory over Midian (ch. 31) signaled victory aplenty. It was time at last to make a home.

The chapter is most significant in what it presents of the life and character of Moses. Here we find another block to add to our view of his complex humanity—he flashes here in rage, it seems, before he knows fully what is being asked. But his rage is based on a lifetime of disappointment, a generation of waste, and the ever-present desert.

a. *The request of Reuben and Gad to settle in Transjordan (32:1–19)*

(1) *The original request*

32:1–5

1 The Reubenites and Gadites, who had very large herds and flocks, saw that the lands of Jazer and Gilead were suitable for livestock. 2 So they came to Moses and Eleazar the priest and to the leaders of the

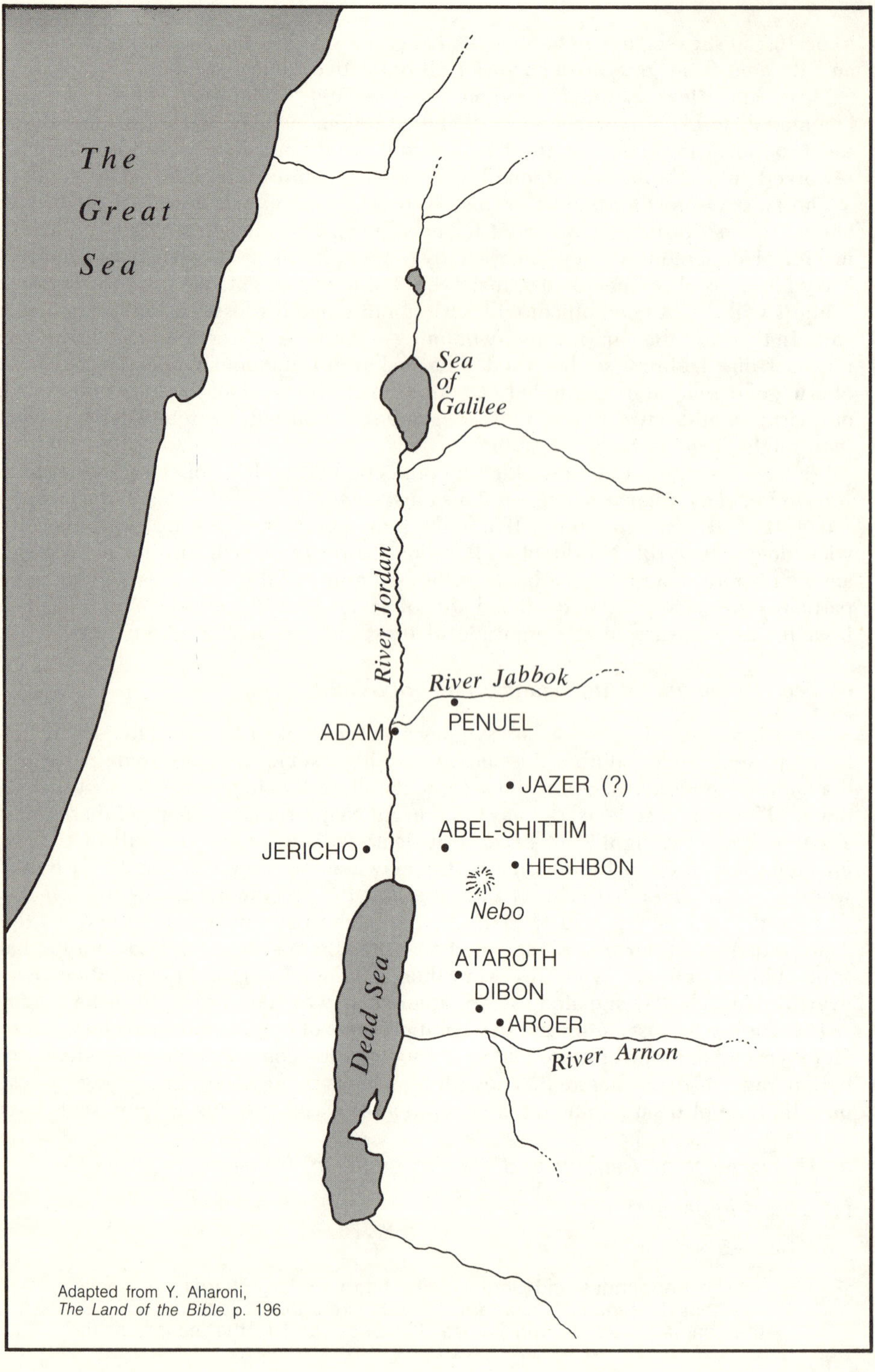

Adapted from Y. Aharoni, *The Land of the Bible* p. 196

community, and said, [3]"Ataroth, Dibon, Jazer, Nimrah, Heshbon,
Elealeh, Sebam, Nebo and Beon—[4]the land the LORD subdued before
the people of Israel—are suitable for livestock, and your servants have
livestock. [5]If we have found favor in your eyes," they said, "let this land
be given to your servants as our possession. Do not make us cross the
Jordan."

The chapter begins as several do, with the approach of petitioners to Moses. They came to him, not because he was king, but because he was the regent of the Lord who mediated the divine word in the league of tribes. As in the case of the daughters of Zelophehad in chapter 27, and as in the instance of the relatives of these women in chapter 36, so the leaders of the tribes of Reuben and Gad made their approach to Moses for the settlement of their land claim. The abundance of fertile grazing land in Transjordan prompted the leaders of these two tribes to request of Moses and Eleazar that they might settle there and not cross the Jordan.

There are several approaches we may take in evaluating the request of these tribal leaders. It is customary among Christian commentators to regard their actions as sinful, an accepting of lesser things rather than having faith to cling on for the best. But it is possible to see in the actions of the men of Gad and Reuben nothing untoward at all, only a pragmatic decision that leads to a remarkable negotiation with the Lord and his servant Moses.

Transjordan, too, was a gift of God won by conquest. When we think of Canaan, we are prone to think of cis-Jordan; Canaan proper is described this way in chapter 34. Yet the full inheritance of the peoples of Israel extended to the regions of Transjordan as well. But it was, in a sense, the fringe of the garment. It was not the heart and soul of the land. To settle in the fringes was a mixed blessing. The people who lived in Transjordan were able to do so by conscious choice. But because they were somewhat removed from the center of the life of the land, they were the most prone to be influenced by outsiders. And clearly they were the most open for territorial expansion by their neighbors. Territorial living has both its advantages and its disadvantages. Ultimately, their request and the Lord's decision through Moses expanded the territory of Israel. If we put the best construction on things, we may see this chapter as a rash adventure in faith rather than a record of rebellion.

As these tribal leaders evaluated the lands they had won from the people of Sihon and Og, they found themselves particularly attracted to these areas. The region and its habitations (Ataroth, Dibon, Jazer, Nimrah, Heshbon, Elealeh, Seban, Nebo, and Beon—cities and regions that are relatively well located; see the accompanying map) looked especially promising to these chiefs. Extensive excavations and surface surveys have been done in these areas of Transjordan in the 1970s and 1980s. The consensus is that these were not regions of a high population density in the period of the Exodus (however this period may be dated); the biblical evidence of this chapter accords well with the archaeological evidence. This was an ideal place for the running of large flocks and herds.

1 Verse 1 is characteristic of well-formed prose structure, exhibiting a chiasm based on the word "herds" or "livestock" (*miqneh*). Here is an attempt to render the order of the words of the verse and its emphasis:

> Now the livestock was great of the people of Reuben,
> and of the people of Gad, it was exceedingly numerous;
> and they saw the land of Jazer

and the land of Gilead,
and they were a region ideal for livestock.

2–5 There is a subtle shift in the wording of v.2 from that of v.1. In v.1 Reuben precedes Gad; in v.2 this order is reversed. Perhaps this is a gentle way to suggest that both tribes had an equal stake in the affair. Only later (see v.33) do we find that some clans of Manasseh were involved as well. The listing of sites within the land they desired (see v.3) adds verisimilitude to their request; specificity of this sort helps the story to be more believable. But these nobles of Gad and Reuben do more than to add place names; they place the issue of the land in the realm of divine gift in v.4:

The land that Yahweh smote
before the congregation of Israel;
It is a land for livestock,
and your servants have livestock.

The repetition of the word "livestock" (*miqneh*) is for emphasis; their herds must have been exceptionally large. The conquest of the Midianite livestock would have further expanded the holdings of these tribes as well as the others. But their language suggests that their holdings in livestock were out of proportion to the other tribes. They needed the room that Transjordan seemed to provide for them. But it is not just the matter of livestock that animates them; it is also the fact that God in his power has provided the land as a gift for his people. The battles of victory over the peoples of Transjordan were the battles of Yahweh. His people were his agents, but the outcome was his.

As we read these verses, we might wonder what the motivation of the two tribes really was. We may wonder how they knew that the region of Transjordan was more suitable for their needs than a share in cis-Jordan. We may wonder if they were selfish, grasping for land ahead of the other tribes. It is also possible that Reuben, at least, was operating under a still-mistaken notion of primogeniture, desiring that the first share of the land be given to him by right of his being the firstborn of the tribal fathers of Israel. Yet, based on their subsequent words in this chapter, we may conclude that none of these issues was paramount. The text breathes a certain naïve transparency, a simplicity and candor that does not seem to admit complex reasoning. We may observe simply: These were two tribes with unusually large holdings of herds and flocks, and they believed that Transjordan was quite suitable for their needs. So the two tribes requested of Moses that the land of Transjordan be given to them as their singular possession, on the basis of any grace that they have found in his sight as his servants (v.5). All seems respectful and deferential in tone and manner.

There is the possibility, however, that these polite words were covering a rebellious spirit. It was not just that they felt they were at home and should be allowed to settle in the place of their choice; these two tribes were possibly abandoning their place in the league as a whole, saying something such as, "We have ours, good luck with yours." This was the way Moses read their words.

Notes

1 יַעְזֵר (*ya'zēr*, "Jazer") is a place name of a region of Transjordan often associated with Heshbon (vv.1, 3, 35; 21:32; Josh 13:25; 21:39 [37 MT]; 2 Sam 24:5) and with vineyards (Isa 16:8–9 = Jer 48:32).

5 The tendency is to view verbs such as יֻתַּן (*yuttan*, "be given") as a Pual imperfect. It is better, however, to parse this verb as a Qal passive jussive: "let [this land] be given [to your servants]."

---

(2) *The angry response of Moses*

32:6–15

[6]Moses said to the Gadites and Reubenites, "Shall your countrymen go to war while you sit here? [7]Why do you discourage the Israelites from going over into the land the LORD has given them? [8]This is what your fathers did when I sent them from Kadesh Barnea to look over the land. [9]After they went up to the Valley of Eshcol and viewed the land, they discouraged the Israelites from entering the land the LORD had given them. [10]The LORD's anger was aroused that day and he swore this oath: [11]'Because they have not followed me wholeheartedly, not one of the men twenty years old or more who came up out of Egypt will see the land I promised on oath to Abraham, Isaac and Jacob—[12]not one except Caleb son of Jephunneh the Kenizzite and Joshua son of Nun, for they followed the LORD wholeheartedly.' [13]The LORD's anger burned against Israel and he made them wander in the desert forty years, until the whole generation of those who had done evil in his sight was gone.

[14]"And here you are, a brood of sinners, standing in the place of your fathers and making the LORD even more angry with Israel. [15]If you turn away from following him, he will again leave all this people in the desert, and you will be the cause of their destruction."

6–7 The response of Moses is an example of his flash point. He rages against the two tribes that they have become no better than their fathers, for they also were not willing to go to the land to fight the battle of conquest. We may wonder at the reason for his anger; it seems to be complex in nature:

1. Moses may have had a suspicion that the real reason for the request of these tribes was that they really did not want to participate in the war of conquest. This suspicion could not have come by their words alone, which seem respectful and reasonable, but by other information he may have had.

2. Moses may have reacted the way he did, not because of their words, but because of the torment within him that must have been welling up constantly, uncontrollably.

3. Moses could not enter the land; could it be possible that these two tribes who could enter the land would not? The words of the tribal spokesmen may have rubbed the wound of his own limitation with abrasive salts.

Moses' words may have been provoked by his anger, but they became the opportunity to review the basic theology of the desert period. He is able to contrast the first and second generation, to warn the second on the basis of the experience of the first. In this case our approach to the Book of Numbers is vindicated by his homily: The old generation is dead; the new generation must be different than their fathers.

In any event, Moses charges these tribal leaders with posing an intolerable situation. By granting them the right to settle outside of Canaan proper, not only will these tribes be lost from the battle plans, but their absence will be a means of hindering the other tribes from crossing the Jordan as well. "Think of it," Moses seems to be saying. "Could we have come this far after so long and still never enter the land?" For him, then, their question seemed not only to be selfish but seditious. The entire nation might have become discouraged (v.7). This would lead perhaps to an ominous replay of the failure of their parents—and this is the thesis of the book: Will the sons behave like the parents, or will they believe and inherit?

8 In v.8 Moses rages, "This is what your fathers did." Moses' fear was that the failure of these two tribes to stay with the whole community in the war of conquest of Canaan would be the beginnings of a general revolt among the people against entering the land. It would be the failure of Kadesh (chs. 13–14) all over again.

In fact, this chapter has numerous word associations with chapters 13–14. In addition to the reporting of the story of those chapters in vv.6–15, there are several terms that cause the reader to juxtapose the chapters. Among the most prominent are the following: (1) the verb "cross over" (*ʿāḇar*)—compare 32:21 ("go over"), 27, 29–30, and 13:32 (untr. NIV); 14:7 ("passed through"), 41 ("disobeying"); (2) the term "children" (*ṭap̱*)—compare 32:16–17, 24, 26, and 14:3, 31; (3) the phrase "the inhabitants of this land" (*yôšᵉḇ hāʾāreṣ*)—compare 32:17 and 14:14. G.J. Wenham (p. 213, no. 1) lists other words as well; these seem the more convincing.

9–13 All this affords Moses the opportunity to preach a brief homily (certainly shortened considerably in this chapter from what he might really have said) on the history of the national experience in the desert. In this preaching Moses presents an example of a biblical use of history for the instruction of the people of God. He speaks with specificity, with passion, with historical insights, and with a contemporary feel—the tying of the experience of the past into the present of his hearers. In some ways this section may be thought of as a model of biblical exhortation. The section is also a splendid review of the core of the history of the narrative of the Book of Numbers. The materials center particularly on the debacle of Numbers 13–14, the rebellion of the first generation at Kadesh Barnea, which led to the divine sentence to spend the rest of their lives in the desert.

The underlying theology is based on the notion that the land is the gift of God. How would it be possible for the Israelites to spurn his gift? Even though their fathers had done this despicable act, is it really possible that such an act of cowardice and ingratitude might be done again? In asking these questions, Moses is developing the central message of this book. The new generation has a new opportunity to be other than their parents. They may be the people who succeed. They do not have to repeat the failure of their parents. But what if they do? This is the hidden horror in Numbers. What if the new generation is no better than their fathers and mothers? Will God then give a third generation an opportunity? Will God keep waiting until he finally has a people who will act on his word? Or is it possible that God can be spurned one time too many, and the Land of Promise will revert to its present, wicked inhabitants? These may be the strong emotions that course through the mind of Moses as he preaches this homily.

The sermon is more than homily. It is also litany. The words of vv.10–12 are a confession of sorts. This is not the confession of faith that begins with "I believe." But it is a litany of experience, beginning with "This we have experienced." The Book of Numbers not only describes worship; it is a book of worship. Remembering failure is also a part of worship (see Ps 95, third strophe for a splendid example). Worship is not just responding to grace; it is also remembering past disaster—and learning to avoid it in the present.

With the words of v.11, we are in the heart of covenant, a covenant that was promised and was rebuffed. But the promise is still there. God's oath to the fathers

Abraham, Isaac, and Jacob is present in his eternity. This is not just a past oath. Since he lives, so does the promise. The only question will be in the generation that stands before him now: Will they be the ones, or must he wait for another? These words are liturgical in form; they are meant to be recited and remembered. The reference to twenty years and upward speaks of the generational change that these emissaries from Reuben and Gad represented.

The promise to Caleb and Joshua is also part of the litany (v.12). This section is like the preaching of the apostles in the early NT. There is a pattern, a *kerygma* of grace and wrath. The NT preaching of the evangelists begins in grace but moves to wrath. The OT preaching of the prophets begins in wrath but moves to grace. In both there is a pattern of historical citation and present adjuration. There is no truly biblical preaching that does not ultimately tie history to the current message; neither the evangelist nor the prophet would draw his message merely from his existential situation.

14–15 Moses' words in vv.14–15 are unusually harsh. In the phrase "brood of sinners" (v.14), he is prescient of the preaching of Jesus (e.g., Matt 12:34; cf. 3:7). There is a moral culpability in the action of disunity that may bring the ruin of God on the entire community. Moses' words in this section are as expressive of his deep, personal feelings as are the words of Paul in texts such as 2 Corinthians 1–3. This is an intensely personal moment for the great prophet of God. Rightly or wrongly, he has been provoked to give vent to his deepest feelings. But the deep feelings were based on his experience—and the deep feelings of God that he has experienced as none other in his day.

Notes

11 The LXX adds an explanatory phrase after the words "twenty years old or more" that serves to explain it more fully: "who know [the difference between] good and evil." This is to suggest that the age of twenty was possibly regarded as an age of adult accountability (not unlike our age twenty-one for one's majority).

13 וַיְנִעֵם (*wayᵉniʿēm*, "and he made them wander") is an unusual use of the verb *nûaʿ*, a word meaning "to quiver," "to wave," "to tremble" (see 2 Kings 19:21 = Isa 37:22; Pss 22:7 [8 MT]; 109:25; Dan 10:10). Here, in 2 Sam 15:20, and in Ps 59:11, the verb has the idea "to cause to wander." The connotation likely ties something of the latent meaning of this verb into this more unusual usage. The time in the desert was wandering, not as an aimless and pleasurable jaunt, but as a journey that is like a quivering, trembling walk.

14 לִסְפּוֹת (*lispôṯ*, "to increase") is by form a Qal infinitive construct of the root *sāp̱āh* ("to snatch away"). But the intent seems to be the root *yāsap̱* ("to add to"); hence the verb should be read as *lāsᵉp̱eṯ*.

The prepositional phrase at the end of the verse, אֶל־יִשְׂרָאֵל (*'el-yiśrā'ēl*), is also unusual. This would normally be translated "to Israel," but the expected meaning is "against" or "with Israel" (as though the preposition were misspelled for *ʿal*). However, the preposition *'el* can sometimes have the idea of "against."

(3) *The assurances of Reuben and Gad*

32:16–19

> [16]Then they came up to him and said, "We would like to build pens here for our livestock and cities for our women and children. [17]But we are ready to arm ourselves and go ahead of the Israelites until we have brought them to their place. Meanwhile our women and children will live in fortified cities, for protection from the inhabitants of the land. [18]We will not return to our homes until every Israelite has received his inheritance. [19]We will not receive any inheritance with them on the other side of the Jordan, because our inheritance has come to us on the east side of the Jordan."

16–19 The response from the men who were addressed so angrily seems to be something like, "You have us all wrong. We are sincere in our desire to find the pleasure of the Lord. We will gladly go with the people into Canaan; only let us prepare temporary pens for our sheep and places to live for our children and our wives. Then we will come; and to them we will return." They say these and similar things (see Notes on v.17) in an attempt to assure Moses that they did not wish to shirk from their part in the conquest of the land. They would join their brothers in battle but wished to leave their families and livestock behind in the portion of their choosing. Their promises are sound; they have met the demands implicit within the charge of Moses.

Many commentators believe that the chiefs of Gad and Reuben are acting disingenuously here, that they are covering their original intention with hastily drawn plans to accede to Moses' desires. Yet it appears to me that it is quite possible that the intentions of these men were honorable from the beginning. It is a possibility that the reaction of Moses to them was based on his own fears of rebellion (and he has been given ample opportunity in the past forty years to develop such a jaundiced view!), rather than a truly rebellious spirit in these men.

If this more positive view is correct, then the comparisons within the chapter, both implicit and explicit, that we may make with chapters 13–14 are dissimilar. In the former generation there was a rebellion that did spell ruin for the nation. But in this generation there is not rebellion, only petition; there is not a lack of faith, only an alternate plan. As long as both parties are clear as to the intention of the whole, then the story of the second generation will wind up quite differently than the account of the first.

Notes

17 The term חֻשִׁים (*ḥušîm*, "ready") is problematic. It may be parsed as a Qal passive participle, masculine plural, from *ḥûš* ("to make haste" or "to be ready"). There are numerous alternative words suggested for this difficult term. Some think this verb should be repointed as an active verb, *ḥûšîm*, rather than the passive, for a more likely spelling. Others emend to *ḥamušîm* (as in Exod 13:18), an adjective plural meaning "in battle array" (see Josh 1:14; 4:12; Judg 7:11). My own choice is for the emendation to *ḥamušîm*.

b. *The decision of Moses for their settlement*

32:20–30

[20]Then Moses said to them, "If you will do this—if you will arm yourselves before the LORD for battle, [21]and if all of you will go armed over the Jordan before the LORD until he has driven his enemies out before him—[22]then when the land is subdued before the LORD, you may return and be free from your obligation to the LORD and to Israel. And this land will be your possession before the LORD.

[23]"But if you fail to do this, you will be sinning against the LORD; and you may be sure that your sin will find you out. [24]Build cities for your women and children, and pens for your flocks, but do what you have promised."

[25]The Gadites and Reubenites said to Moses, "We your servants will do as our lord commands. [26]Our children and wives, our flocks and herds will remain here in the cities of Gilead. [27]But your servants, every man armed for battle, will cross over to fight before the LORD, just as our lord says."

[28]Then Moses gave orders about them to Eleazar the priest and Joshua son of Nun and to the family heads of the Israelite tribes. [29]He said to them, "If the Gadites and Reubenites, every man armed for battle, cross over the Jordan with you before the LORD, then when the land is subdued before you, give them the land of Gilead as their possession. [30]But if they do not cross over with you armed, they must accept their possession with you in Canaan."

20–30 Moses is not easily calmed. He speaks to the people, in a sense, as a father to an errant but repentant child. He gives them words of comfort and also words of strong warning: "Your sin will find you out" (v.23). The language is striking: it is not just that their sin will be discovered but that their sin will be an active agent in discovering them. This is not unlike the picture of sin lying at the door of Cain's life (Gen 4:7). Moses' words of v.20 are especially vivid: "If you are willing to do this thing, then prepare yourselves before Yahweh for war" (pers. tr.).

Moses' adjuration also reminds the people of Gad and Reuben that it is not just their participation that he desires but their commitment to the affirmation of faith. They need to prepare for battle, but they also need to know that the Lord is going to be the one to win the battle (v.21). The actions are the Lord's; the people are partners with him in his holy war. Verse 22 also makes strong emphases on the role of the Lord in the taking of the land. It will be subdued "before the LORD"; they will be innocent from "obligation to the LORD and to Israel[!]," and the land will be their possession "before the LORD."

The bargain was struck, but not without strong warnings of the seriousness of the matter if the people failed to live up to their word. In the permission that Moses grants to them, we sense the negotiation that was possible in Israel, even from the hand of the Lord. The story of Abraham and the Lord bartering over the fate of Sodom (Gen 18:16–33) comes to mind as an example. In a sense the bargain with Moses was a bargain with God. Like the daughters of Zelophehad (ch. 27), these men had come to Moses in order to come to the Lord. When they agree with Moses, they say, "Your servants will do just as my lord commands" (v.25). They are also saying that they will do as our Lord commands. The specifying elements—children, wives, livestock, and cattle—are a part of the bargain. The language is like that of a contract; agreement is full and complete.

Notes

24 The term צֹנָא (*ṣōna'*) is an unusual spelling of the more common צאן (*ṣō'n*); it is used only in Ps 8:7 [8 MT] and here—לְצֹנַאֲכֶם (*leṣōna'akem*, "your flocks").

---

c. *The public declaration of the agreement*

32:31–32

31 The Gadites and Reubenites answered, "Your servants will do what
the LORD has said. 32 We will cross over before the LORD into Canaan
armed, but the property we inherit will be on this side of the Jordan."

31–32 These two verses serve as a public declaration of the decision to which the men of Gad and Reuben had come before the presence of Moses. Now it is made formal and binding before the congregation.

d. *The territories of Reuben and Gad*

32:33–42

33 Then Moses gave to the Gadites, the Reubenites and the half-tribe
of Manasseh son of Joseph the kingdom of Sihon king of the Amorites
and the kingdom of Og king of Bashan—the whole land with its cities
and the territory around them.
34 The Gadites built up Dibon, Ataroth, Aroer, 35 Atroth Shophan, Jazer,
Jogbehah, 36 Beth Nimrah and Beth Haran as fortified cities, and built
pens for their flocks. 37 And the Reubenites rebuilt Heshbon, Elealeh and
Kiriathaim, 38 as well as Nebo and Baal Meon (these names were
changed) and Sibmah. They gave names to the cities they rebuilt.
39 The descendants of Makir son of Manasseh went to Gilead,
captured it and drove out the Amorites who were there. 40 So Moses
gave Gilead to the Makirites, the descendants of Manasseh, and they
settled there. 41 Jair, a descendant of Manasseh, captured their settlements and called them Havvoth Jair. 42 And Nobah captured Kenath and
its surrounding settlements and called it Nobah after himself.

It appears that after the principle of Transjordan settlement was established with the tribes of Reuben and Gad that a portion of the tribe of Manasseh joined with them in their agreement to settle in Transjordan and then to participate in the battle for Canaan. It is possible that the chapter has been compiled from two different records and that the role of the men of Manasseh was present in the beginning of the bargaining in one of the traditions. But since the text as we have it only mentions Manasseh at this late point in the negotiation, it may more likely be that the leaders of Manasseh were hesitant to approach Moses and that they only came forward with their own participation in the plan when the deal was accomplished.

33 So the chapter that began with such hostility on the part of Moses ends with happy portents: The territory of Transjordan becomes part of the new homeland for some of the tribes of Israel. As the representative of God on earth, Moses bestowed the territory of Transjordan to Gad, Reuben, and some of the families of Manasseh.

34–38 Verses 34–38 are the happy record of the rebuilding and settling of the people of the Lord in that portion of the land that he had given to them. It includes as well notices about continuing conquests, a mark of the Lord's continuing pleasure. The listing of towns and cities adds two things to this text, a sense of verisimilitude and a note of celebration. The listing of towns such as Dibon, Ataroth, Aroer, Atroth Shophan, Jazer, and the like are important, not just for cartography, but for theology. This land was now really theirs. The cities that had been destroyed were now being rebuilt, and in some cases they were being renamed (v.38) to show new relationships and to evince the new reality. The old gods are not in control any longer; this is now the land of the people of Yahweh.

39–42 The pericope of vv.39–42 may well be a later addition to this chapter. It features the exploits of the family of Makir, of which the celebrated daughters of Zelophehad were a part (see chs. 27; 36), and their conquest of Gilead, along with the heroic exploits of Jair and Nobah. This is a further expansion of the people in Transjordan. Their territorial aggression was a part of the plan of God in further dispossessing the Amorites from the region. The taking of cities and renaming them after heroic persons is a part of the celebrative nature of the chapter, a projection of what lies ahead on the other side of the Jordan for the people of God.

The settlement of Transjordan was considerably more complex an issue than this chapter presents; here are only a few instances in the process. The point of the chapter is not to give a complete record or to prepare a full mapping of the territory. Rather, the chapter speaks of territorial expansion and the gifting of God.

B. *A Review of the First Generation's Journey and Words of Warning and Encouragement to the Second Generation (33:1–56)*

Numbers 33 is a somewhat curious piece in the book. Principally, it is a listing of places, much like some chapters have been listings of numbers and names. It is the one chapter in which we read that Moses was commanded by the Lord to write an account of his experience in the desert (v.2)—a notice that certain critical scholars find to be the most potent argument against Moses having written anything!

For example, when Gray turns to 33:2, he writes, "In one passage only (33:2) does the book lay any claim to the authority of Moses for its statements; that passage is closely related to others (P) which are clearly of far later origin than the age of Moses, and consequently the Mosaic authorship even of this particular passage cannot be seriously considered" (pp. xxix–xxx). Noth says, "Yet the sentence contained in v. 2a, which follows awkwardly on v. 1, and has occasioned a brief summary of v. 1 in v. 2b, is certainly an addition to what is already a very late passage" (p. 243). (Further discussion on the subject of the Mosaic authorship of Numbers is found in the Introduction: Authorship and Date.) Yet Gray and others notwithstanding, Moses certainly wrote this travel itinerary; this is an explicit statement of Scripture. Gray's rejection of the statement is based on an appeal to prior late-dating of the so-called Priestly document. This is quite simply nothing more than an example of special pleading. Gray argues that Moses cannot have been the author because the book does not assert his authorship; in the one verse where the book does say that Moses wrote a section, Gray dismisses that datum for other reasons. In this manner one can deny just about anything.

Greenstone tells a rabbinic story that points out a reason for the inclusion of this itinerary in the Book of Numbers. He reports, "A king took his son who was ill to a distant place to be cured. On his return, with the son entirely cured, the king points out to him the various places which they had passed through and recalls certain occurrences that happened there. The list was written by Moses at the command of God as a record for future generations (Num. R. 23:3; Tan., Masseė, 2)" (p. 337).

G.J. Wenham has a rather elaborate schematization of the place names in six columns of seven entries each (adding the beginning at Rameses and the ending on the plains of Moab to achieve a total of forty-two places). He finds some interesting correlations between several of these cycles, based, in part, on significant uses of certain numbers in the Bible (1, 3, 4, 7, and 12); see Wenham, pp. 216–30, for his extended discussion.

1. *The stages of the journey in the desert (33:1–49)*

a. *Introduction*

33:1–2

> [1] Here are the stages in the journey of the Israelites when they came out of Egypt by divisions under the leadership of Moses and Aaron. [2] At the LORD's command Moses recorded the stages in their journey. This is their journey by stages:

1–2 The listing of the numerous places (significantly forty in number between Rameses in Egypt and the plains of Moab) in Israel's desert experience appears to be a rather straightforward listing that might easily be charted on a map. The chapter presents numerous difficulties, however, once one brings out the map. Most of the sites were desert encampments, not cities with lasting archaeological evidences. Many of the places in the listing are not recorded elsewhere in Exodus and Numbers (e.g., most of the places in vv.19–29). Some of the places that are mentioned in Numbers are lacking here (e.g., Taberah [11:3; see also 21:19]). Some places that are mentioned in this list are found in a recapitulation in Deuteronomy, though with slightly different spelling and in an irregular order (compare vv.30–34 with Deut 10:6–7); but even these place names are otherwise unknown. G.J. Wenham is correct in describing these data as among the most intractable that are faced by biblical scholars (p. 220).

We may conclude from these factors the following:

1. The recording of the list was done by the hand of Moses at the command of the Lord (v.2).

2. The listing thus should be taken seriously as an accurate reprise of the stages of the journey, despite our difficulty in locating many of the sites today.

3. The numerical factor of forty sites between Rameses and the plains of Moab suggests some styling of the list, which helps to account for the inclusion or exclusion of some sites.

4. As in the case of genealogies in the Torah, not all the factors of ancient significance may be apparent to the modern reader.

5. Ultimately the record is a recital of faith in the Lord's blessing over his people for the extended period of their desert experience. Although certainly not without geographical importance, the listing of the stages of Israel's experience in the desert is fundamentally a religious document, a litany of the Lord's deliverance of his people.

Despite the many places that are mentioned in these verses, this is not really a travel story. One of the most durable formats for literary setting is the travel narrative; such are found in ancient and modern writings. An Egyptian example is called "The Journey of Wen-Amon to Phoenicia," a travel narrative from the Twenty-First Dynasty (11th century B.C.; see ANET, pp. 25–29). In a travel narrative, the journey is the setting for the story, for character development, and for plot conflict and resolution. Numbers 33 has none of this. It is merely an itinerary, the barest listing of places. Even when great events are associated with places, they are only rarely noted in this chapter. The Book of Numbers as a whole is a travel narrative; this chapter is just a routing list.

Notes

---

2 The noun מַסַּע (*massa'*, "stage") is derived from the verb *nāsa'* ("to set out," "to journey"). It presents the stopping places of Israel in the desert, not so much as their sites of dwelling, as though they were there to stay, as it speaks of their places of habitation as staging points for the continuation of their journey. This word thrusts us forward in a recital of a journey that moves to completion.

---

b. *The point of departure*

33:3–4

> 3The Israelites set out from Rameses on the fifteenth day of the first month, the day after the Passover. They marched out boldly in full view of all the Egyptians, 4who were burying all their firstborn, whom the LORD had struck down among them; for the LORD had brought judgment on their gods.

3–4 Only at the beginning of the journey and at one point along the way does the listing of places give way to narrative. The wording of these verses includes both the specific notation as to the time of the Israelites' departure as well as a description of the manner of their leaving Egypt (see Exod 12:37). They left with disdain (see Ps 114:1–2), not watching the burial details of the many grieving Egyptian families whose firstborn had been slain by the hand of the Lord, but relishing the victory that the Lord had won over the gods of the land (v.4). This section is a triumphant taunt; yet even the mention of the dead adds a gentle note of sadness. Rameses (v.3) has traditionally been identified with Tanis (San el-Hajar; cf. Gen 47:11; Exod 1:11). However, evidence now points to Qantir-Khataana-Tell Daba as the correct location (see E.M. Blaiklock and R.K. Harrison, edd., *The New International Dictionary of Biblical Archaeology* [Grand Rapids: Zondervan, 1983], pp. 384, 435). The name Rameses is derived most likely from the great Pharaoh, Rameses II, who is dated centuries later than either the story of Joseph (Gen 47:11) or, we believe, the time of Israel in Egypt (Exod 1:11). This means that we have an example here of a historical up-dating of an ancient place name to a more current, recognizable name for later generations.

The stages of the journey of Israel are grouped in two sections, with an emphasis on the stop at Mount Hor where Aaron the priest died.

Notes

3 In contrast to 15:30, the expression בְּיָד רָמָה (*beyād rāmāh*, "with a high hand") is used in a positive sense as a figure of triumph (NIV, "boldly"). With hand held high, the Israelites left in a deliberate and conscious sense of the presence of the grander, higher hand of the Lord over them in blessing.

c. *The stages of the journey from Rameses to Mount Hor 33:5–37*

5 The Israelites left Rameses and camped at Succoth.
6 They left Succoth and camped at Etham, on the edge of the desert.
7 They left Etham, turned back to Pi Hahiroth, to the east of Baal Zephon, and camped near Migdol.
8 They left Pi Hahiroth and passed through the sea into the desert, and when they had traveled for three days in the Desert of Etham, they camped at Marah.
9 They left Marah and went to Elim, where there were twelve springs and seventy palm trees, and they camped there.
10 They left Elim and camped by the Red Sea.
11 They left the Red Sea and camped in the Desert of Sin.
12 They left the Desert of Sin and camped at Dophkah.
13 They left Dophkah and camped at Alush.
14 They left Alush and camped at Rephidim, where there was no water for the people to drink.
15 They left Rephidim and camped in the Desert of Sinai.
16 They left the Desert of Sinai and camped at Kibroth Hattaavah.
17 They left Kibroth Hattaavah and camped at Hazeroth.
18 They left Hazeroth and camped at Rithmah.
19 They left Rithmah and camped at Rimmon Perez.
20 They left Rimmon Perez and camped at Libnah.
21 They left Libnah and camped at Rissah.
22 They left Rissah and camped at Kehelathah.
23 They left Kehelathah and camped at Mount Shepher.
24 They left Mount Shepher and camped at Haradah.
25 They left Haradah and camped at Makheloth.
26 They left Makheloth and camped at Tahath.
27 They left Tahath and camped at Terah.
28 They left Terah and camped at Mithcah.
29 They left Mithcah and camped at Hashmonah.
30 They left Hashmonah and camped at Moseroth.
31 They left Moseroth and camped at Bene Jaakan.
32 They left Bene Jaakan and camped at Hor Haggidgad.
33 They left Hor Haggidgad and camped at Jotbathah.
34 They left Jotbathah and camped at Abronah.
35 They left Abronah and camped at Ezion Geber.
36 They left Ezion Geber and camped at Kadesh, in the Desert of Zin.
37 They left Kadesh and camped at Mount Hor, on the border of Edom.

5–37 Succoth, Etham, and Pi Hahiroth were in Egypt, to the west of the Sea of Reeds (vv.5–7). The other sites are all in the Desert of Sinai. Here are their staging areas, in the order they are given, their English name, their verse number, a transcription of their Hebrew names (helpful in precision of names), suggested English meanings (many of which are provisional in nature), and further comments about identification, significance, or parallel Scriptures.

1. Succoth (*sukkōṯ*, "Booths," v.5)—see Exod 13:20; Succoth is likely identified with modern Tell el-Maskhutah in the Wadi Tumeilat, about forty miles southeast of Tanis/Rameses.

2. Desert of Etham (*'ēṯām*, meaning unknown, v.6)—see Exod 13:20; the first mention of the pillar of cloud and pillar of fire here.

3. Pi Hahiroth (*pî haḥîrōṯ*, "Mouth of Burning," v.7)—see Exod 14:2, 9; their encampment was near Pi Hahiroth, between Migdol (*migdōl*, "Tower") and the sea, to the east of Baal Zephon (*ba'al ṣᵉp̄ôn*, "Ba'al of the North"). It was from this encampment that they made their miraculous escape across the divinely dried seabed of the Sea of Reeds (see Notes; see Exod 14:2)—the great Exodus (v.8).

4. Marah (*mārāh*, "Bitter Spring," v.8)—see Exod 15:23; the site of the bitter waters cleansed by the Lord through his servant Moses.

5. Elim (*'êlim*, "Place of Trees," v.9)—see Exod 15:27; curiously, this is the only place that is described in this listing.

6. The Red Sea (*yam-sûp̄*, "Sea of Reeds," v.10)—not mentioned in Exodus as an encampment, but a reference to a southwestwardly move before turning eastward to the south-central Sinai.

7. Desert of Sin (*miḏbar-sîn*, meaning unknown, v.11)—see Exod 16:1; their arrival here was on the fifteenth day of the second month; the location seems to be in the south-central Sinai Peninsula.

8. Dophkah (*dop̄qāh*, "Beaten," v.12)—not mentioned in Exod; location is unknown.

9. Alush (*'ālûš*, meaning unknown, v.13)—not mentioned in Exod; location is unknown.

10. Rephidim (*rᵉp̄îdim*, "Spreading," v.14)—see Exod 17:1; it is strange that there is a note about the significance of this site ("no water") when other sites are mentioned without any notice at all.

11. Desert of Sinai (*miḏbar sînāy*, meaning unknown, v.15)—see Exod 19:2; believed to be the southern section of the Sinai peninsula. Here Israel lingered for about eleven months. That the giving of the Torah is not mentioned here is especially surprising. The leaving of Sinai is recorded in Num 10:11–36.

12. Kibroth Hattaavah (*qiḇrōṯ hatta'awāh*, "Graves of Desire," v.16)—Num 11:34; all that is known is that this is a journey of three days from Sinai.

13. Hazeroth (*ḥᵃṣērōṯ*, "Settlements," v.17)—see Num 11:35; 12:16; Deut 1:1; location is unknown.

14. Rithmah (*riṯmāh*, "Binding," v.18)—not mentioned elsewhere; it is a factor of each of the next eleven sites.

15. Rimmon Perez (*rimmōn pāreṣ*, "Pomegranate Breach," v.19)—not mentioned elsewhere.

16. Libnah (*liḇnāh*, "White," v.20)—not to be confused with Libnah in Josh 10:29; not mentioned elsewhere.

17. Rissah (*rissāh*, meaning unknown, v.21)—not mentioned elsewhere.

18. Kehelathah (*qᵉhēlāṯāh*, "Assembly," v.22)—not mentioned elsewhere.

19. Mount Shepher (*har-šep̄er*, "Mount of Beauty," v.23)—not mentioned elsewhere.

20. Haradah (*ḥᵃrāḏāh*, "Frightening," v.24)—not mentioned elsewhere.

21. Makheloth (*maqhēlōṯ*, "Place of Assembly," v.25)—not mentioned elsewhere.

22. Tahath (*tāḥaṯ*, "Lower," v.26)—not mentioned elsewhere.

23. Terah (*teraḥ*, meaning unknown, v.27)—not mentioned elsewhere.

24. Mithcah (*mitqāh*, "Sweetness"[?], v.28)—not mentioned elsewhere.
25. Hashmonah (*ḥašmōnāh*, meaning unknown, v.29)—not mentioned elsewhere. This means that twelve staging places in a row (nos. 14 to 25) are otherwise completely unknown to us.
26. Moseroth (*mōsērôṯ*, "Bands," v.30)—another form of *môsērāh*, mentioned in Deut 10:6 as the place where Aaron died, but see on v.37, below.
27. Bene Jaakan (*b^enê-ya'^aqān*, "Sons of Ya'aqan," v.31)—a place in Edom mentioned in Gen 36:27 and 1 Chron 1:42 as "and Akan." In Deut 10:6 this is called *b^e'ērōṯ b^enê-ya'^aqān* ("The Wells of the Sons of Ya'aqan"; NIV, "the wells of the Jaakanites"), but the order in Deut 10:6 is the reverse of Num 33:30–31. The somewhat extemporaneous nature of Deuteronomy sometimes has events in a less regular order than in the more orderly patterns of Numbers.
28. Hor Haggidgad (*ḥōr haggiḏgāḏ*, "The Hollow of Gidgad," v.32)—called *guḏgōḏāh* in Deut 10:7.
29. Jotbathah (*yoṭḇāṯāh*, "Pleasantness," v.33)—mentioned in Deut 10:7 as a land with streams of water. So we have four places (staging areas 26–29), otherwise unknown, that are mentioned in Deut 10:6–7 with slightly different spellings and some irregularity in order.
30. Abronah (*'aḇrōnāh*, "Regions Beyond," v.34)—not mentioned elsewhere.
31. Ezion Geber (*'eṣyôn geḇer*, "Mighty Trees"[?], v.35)—the well-known oasis near Elath on the Gulf of Aqabah; see Deut 2:8; 1 Kings 9:26.
32. Kadesh (*qāḏēš*, "Sanctuary," v.36)—This is the well-known 'Ain Qedeis oasis, also known as Kadesh Barnea, in the Desert of Zin (see 13:21; 20:1; 27:14; 34:3; Deut 32:51; Josh 15:1; see also Deut 1:46 and Num 27:14). It is over seventy miles from Ezion Geber to Kadesh; numerous intermediate stops would be indicated here. It was here that the revolt against the Lord took place with the evil report of the spies (Num 13–14). God's judgment of a forty-year period of desert waiting was given at Kadesh. It is likely that most of the thirty-eight years of Israel's experience in the desert was spent with Kadesh as their central location. Here also Miriam died (see 20:1).
33. Mount Hor (*hōr hāhār*, "Hor the mountain," v.37)—perhaps Jebel Nebi Hârûm, about fifty miles south of the Dead Sea, southwest of Petra.

Notes

8, 10 The full designation for הַיָּם (*hayyam*, "the sea") is יַם־סוּף (*yam-sûp̄*), traditionally translated "the Red Sea," but more recently "The Sea of Reeds." *Yam-sûp̄* can speak of the Gulf of Aqabah (the northeast branch of the Red Sea) in some contexts (see Exod 23:31; Deut 1:40). When the phrase is used of the body of water where the miraculous crossing occurred, it may speak of an inland lake (marked by reeds) or a part of the northwest branch of the Red Sea, which may have been connected with the Bitter Lakes in ancient times. The phrase is not unambiguous.

15 סִינָי (*sînāy*, "Sinai"), the mountain of God (also known as Mount Horeb), is the most significant mountain locale in the Bible, next to Mount Zion and Jerusalem. Yet it is the most elusive mountain in biblical geography to identify with precision. Not only is the site of the revelation of the Lord to Moses of importance on its own merits; most of the other sites of the desert wanderings and the route that connects them are dependent on where one identifies Sinai. The oldest tradition is Jebel Musa, a mountain of about 8,500 feet in the southern Sinai Peninsula. The broad plain at the base seems to serve as an admirable site for the encampment of the thousands of Israel. H.G. Andersen ("Mount Sinai," ZPEB, 5:447–50) presents a defense of this traditional site. Another suggestion, particularly of some nineteenth-century writers, is Jebel Serbal, a mountain of about 6,700 feet, in the central

Sinai Peninsula. Yet another is Jebel Sin Bisher, a mountain of about 1,900 feet, located about thirty miles southeast of Suez. This last is the suggestion of M. Harel (*Masei Sinai* [Tel Aviv: Am Oved, 1968]) and is cautiously accepted by G.J. Wenham (pp. 220–27). His discussion is a fine summary of the difficulties one faces in this issue.

---

d. *The events at Mount Hor*

33:38–40

38At the LORD's command Aaron the priest went up Mount Hor, where he died on the first day of the fifth month of the fortieth year after the Israelites came out of Egypt. 39Aaron was a hundred and twenty-three years old when he died on Mount Hor.

40The Canaanite king of Arad, who lived in the Negev of Canaan, heard that the Israelites were coming.

38–40 Unexpectedly, it is this staging area of Mount Hor that is singled out for special mention. It becomes the setting for a memorial notice to Aaron the high priest, brother of Moses, who died here at the age of 123. Not only is his age given, but so is the date: the first day of the fifth month of the fortieth year. This is the second date in the list; the first was the date of their leaving Rameses on the fifteenth day of the first month of the first year (v.3). This means that the journeying from Tanis/Rameses to Mount Hor completes the forty years of desert wanderings. The death of Aaron marks a pivotal date in the history of Israel. The death of the priest is regarded as having an atoning effect (see ch. 35). Aaron was three years older than Moses (see Exod 7:7; cf. Deut 1:3; 34:5–7). His death came at a great age—a mark of God's blessing in his life. By the mercy of the Lord, his time was extended to the very last year of Israel's desert experience; his own sin (Num 20) kept him from living into the time of the conquest of the land.

The second notice given with respect to Israel's time at the staging area of Mount Hor is word concerning the king of Arad (v.40). Even the king who dwelled in the Negev of the land of Canaan knew of the coming of the people of Israel; the reference is to the story of 21:1–3, the first of Israel's victories on the military field—promise for a new generation being different than their fathers.

e. *The stages of the journey from Mount Hor to the mountains of Abarim*

33:41–47

41They left Mount Hor and camped at Zalmonah.
42They left Zalmonah and camped at Punon.
43They left Punon and camped at Oboth.
44They left Oboth and camped at Iye Abarim, on the border of Moab.
45They left Iyim and camped at Dibon Gad.
46They left Dibon Gad and camped at Almon Diblathaim.
47They left Almon Diblathaim and camped in the mountains of Abarim, near Nebo.

41–47 The listing of place names continues:

34. Zalmonah (*ṣalmōnāh*, "Resemblance," v.41)—not mentioned elsewhere. There is an es-Salmaneh, about twenty-five miles south of the Dead Sea.

35. Punon (*pûnōn,* meaning unknown, v.42)—perhaps the same as the Edomite site *pînîn,* Gen 36:41; 1 Chron 1:52; located between Petra and Zoar, famous for its mines.

36. Oboth (*'ōbōṯ,* "Water Skins," v.43)—the story of the stay at Oboth is given in 21:10–11; probably the eastern outskirts of Idumea, not far from Moab. The route from Punon to Oboth is not as simple as this listing might suggest. Eugene H. Merrill suggests that the people probably went south from Punon to Ezion Geber, then east and north around Edom along the desert road of Moab ("Numbers," *The Bible Knowledge Commentary: Old Testament,* edd. John F. Walvoord and Roy B. Zuck [Wheaton: Victor Books/SP Publications, 1985], p. 254; cf. 21:4; Deut 2:8).

37. Iye Abarim (*'îyê ha'ᵃḇārîm,* v.44; short form in v.45, *'iyîm;* meaning unknown)—see Num 21:11; a location on the border of Moab.

38. Dibon Gad (*dîḇōn gāḏ,* "Built Up by Gad," v.45)—a city in Moab north of the Arnon (Dhiban); see 21:30; 32:3; also mentioned in the Mesha Inscription.

39. Almon Diblathaim (*'almōn diḇlāṯayim,* meaning unknown, v.46; perhaps "Hidden Figs"; *dᵉḇēlāh* means "a lump of figs")—mentioned in Jer 48:22; a site north of Dibon Gad, location unknown.

40. The mountains of Abarim (*hārê hā'ᵃḇārîm,* "The Mountains Beyond," v.47)—the fortieth station, a mountainous region of northwest Moab just northeast of the Dead Sea; see 27:12. Pisgah and Nebo are two ridges in this mountainous region.

f. *The encampment in Moab as the staging area for the assault on the land of Canaan*

33:48–49

48 They left the mountains of Abarim and camped on the plains of Moab by the Jordan across from Jericho. 49 There on the plains of Moab they camped along the Jordan from Beth Jeshimoth to Abel Shittim.

48–49 At last, after a period of forty years, the people are situated on the plains of Moab across from the city of Jericho—the firstfruits of the land; only the Jordan River separates them now from their goal, the Promised Land. The encampments of the thousands of Israel stretched from Beth Jeshimoth (*Bêṯ hayᵉšimōṯ,* "Place of Desolation"; see Josh 12:3; 13:20) to Abel Shittim (*'āḇēl haššiṭṭîm,* "Field of Acacias"; see Num 25:1, where it is called Shittim; Mic 6:5), in the lowlands of Moab. The distance from these two sites, north to south, was over five miles—a suitable spread for the thousands of the tribes of Israel.

We now may make some concluding observations about this listing of the *massā'îm* ("staging areas") of Israel in the desert:

1. That there are forty places may be significant as a memnonic device; as the people dwelled in the desert for forty years, so there are forty sites of their journeys.

2. Most of the "places" were very temporary abodes; we should not be surprised that they are not easily located on modern maps. They are not made-up places, just encampments in the desert.

3. The principal story line was omitted from this listing; here just the names of the places are important. There is an assumption that one would know the basic associations as the places were listed.

4. The intrusion of the account of the death of Aaron (vv.38–40) is remarkable. This travel account is something of an obituary for Moses, as he was about to die. But in the midst of it he memorializes his brother.

5. The fact that many of the names are not sites that can be located, or that are not found in other passages, is an indication that this is a very ancient text; the notice that

Moses was commanded by the Lord to write it (v.2) is more credible because of our uncertainty over locations.

6. Most significantly, the document talks, not of rebellion, but only of continuity. Were one only to read this list of staging places, he would conclude that Israel marched faithfully from one place to another in an orderly progression from Egypt to Moab. This is the point: the new generation has become the replacement for the old. *It is as though there had never been a first generation.* The people who arrive at Moab are regarded as the people who left Egypt. The plan and purpose of God will be realized, despite the loss (and disappearance!) of an entire generation.

2. *Words of warning and encouragement to the second generation* 33:50–56

> [50]On the plains of Moab by the Jordan across from Jericho the LORD said to Moses, [51]"Speak to the Israelites and say to them: 'When you cross the Jordan into Canaan, [52]drive out all the inhabitants of the land before you. Destroy all their carved images and their cast idols, and demolish all their high places. [53]Take possession of the land and settle in it, for I have given you the land to possess. [54]Distribute the land by lot, according to your clans. To a larger group give a larger inheritance, and to a smaller group a smaller one. Whatever falls to them by lot will be theirs. Distribute it according to your ancestral tribes.
>
> [55]" 'But if you do not drive out the inhabitants of the land, those you allow to remain will become barbs in your eyes and thorns in your sides. They will give you trouble in the land where you will live. [56]And then I will do to you what I plan to do to them.' "

50–54 It is on the basis of triumphalism that the final pericope of this chapter has its meaning. The instructions of the Lord to the new generation come at the climax of the record of their triumphal march. They were now at their last *massa'*, their last staging area. Before them was the land, behind them an exceedingly long and tortuous journey. Now is the time for their obedience that their salvation will be made sure in the new land.

The commands of the Lord to the people are expressed in several significant verbs in v.52: (1) they are to dispossess (Hiphil of *yāraš*) the present inhabitants, (2) destroy (Piel of *'āḇaḏ*) their idolatrous symbols, (3) destroy (Piel of *'āḇaḏ*) all their molten images, and (4) shatter (Hiphil of *šāmaḏ*) their high places. Verse 53 repeats the verb "to dispossess" and then speaks of living in the land as God's divine grant to the people. The land is his to give; he chooses to give the gift to his people. The manner of the distribution of the land was to be by lot, with the assurance that the lot would not be by chance but by the disposition of the Lord. In this way the people would be able to take possession (Hithpael of *nāḥal*, "to possess oneself of something") of the land as a lasting inheritance. As in 35:8, consideration would be given for the size of the clans of Israel (v.54); there was to be no claim of inequity or "influence-peddling"—to use a modern term. Possession would come by the will of God expressed through the fairness of divine lots.

55–56 The positive admonitions of vv.50–54 are followed by a strong warning in vv.55–56. If the people do not succeed in their divine commission to dispossess the pagan inhabitants, they will find two things to be true: (1) the natives who remain will be perpetual trouble to the Israelites' enjoyment of the land, and (2) the Lord will bring on Israel the dispossession he demanded them to accomplish.

The description of trouble is, of course, sadly prophetic. The remaining Canaanites were to be barbs in the eye and pricks in the side (images that Joshua uses in his farewell address; see Josh 23:13). These expressions describe constant annoyance (at the least) to terrible pain (at the most)—a constant harassment. The most chilling words, however, are not the troubles that might come from peoples but that which may come from the Lord:

And it will happen,
  Just as I intend to do to them,
    I will do to you. (v.56)

This is the theology of the land *in nuce*. It is God's land. He will give and take it as he wills.

These words, at the end of the travel itinerary, are most threatening indeed. For the present—that is, the time of the writing of the Book of Numbers—the outcome is uncertain. But the prospects are good. The second generation has fully replaced their erring fathers and mothers. The land lies before them as they wait in the final staging area. There is the Jordan. Over yonder is Jericho, the firstfruits of the land. And with them is the eternal Yahweh!

Notes

52 מַשְׂכִּיֹּתָם (*maśkîyōṯām*, "[their] carved images") is from the word *maśkîṯ*, which means "show piece," "something to be displayed." Here it is used of carved figures, idolatrous symbols of the pagan religious practices of the Canaanite peoples. These would include sexual symbols of the fertility deities that were so pervasive in that region (see Lev 26:1; Ezek 8:12).

The second term, מַסֵּכֹתָם (*massēḵōṯām*, "cast idols") is found also in Exod 32:4, 8; 34:17; Lev 19:4; Deut 9:16.

The third, בָּמוֹת (*bāmôṯ*, "high places") refers to artificial mounds that were used for the worship of the nature gods of the ancient Near East. The licentious system of sexually centered worship was particularly exhibitionist in nature. Ba'al and Asherah were regarded as voyeur deities whose own libidos would be "turned on" by viewing orgiastic rites or sacrificial acts of especial brutality or blood-letting (notice the blood-letting of the pagan priests on Mount Carmel, 1 Kings 18:28). The raised platform was an enhancement "to let the gods" see more clearly. As is well known from the reading of the historical books, Israel adapted the use of *bāmôṯ* for their own local patterns of the worship of the Lord (or for syncretistic systems of worship of the Lord and Ba'al). One of the most resistant of paganisms in Israel's later history, the *bāmôṯ* were the banes of godly kings who fought desperately to destroy these "high places."

C. *An Anticipation of the Promised Land (34:1–36:13)*

These last three chapters of Numbers round out the book. They have about them the sense of appendages. Chapter 33, with its itinerary, final blessing, and warning (vv.50–56), really serves as the climax of the book. The prospects for conquest and the warning of failure are just what the new generation needs to be the people God wants them to be.

Although these last three chapters are somewhat anticlimactic, they also have their role in furthering the general driving force they present to the new generation: "The land is before you for your habitation. For God's sake [and I use the phrase advisedly], do not behave as your fathers and mothers did; move on in faith to take the land he offers. You will not receive the offer of his gift again."

1. *A preview of the land (34:1–26)*

a. *The boundaries (34:1–12)*

(1) *Introduction*

34:1–2

> [1]The LORD said to Moses, [2]"Command the Israelites and say to them: 'When you enter Canaan, the land that will be allotted to you as an inheritance will have these boundaries:

1–2 The listing of the four boundaries in this section of Numbers is given, not only for information purposes, but also to display again the dimensions of God's great gift to his people in the Land of Promise. The initial covenant specified the land in terms of the peoples who lived there (see Gen 15:18–21). This chapter presents the land in terms of an outline of its borders. The language is covenantal in nature; the description is that of a contract. Those who were in the final staging area in the plains of Moab would have their sensibilities greatly encouraged by the dimensions and directions of the land so described. Some critical scholars tend to dismiss this chapter as an unauthentic piece from the vantage of anticipation of the land; rather, they would suggest this is a later projection backward, based on some experience in the land itself. Noth, for example, judges the situation this way: "In short, this whole section presupposes, on the one hand, the Pentateuchal narrative at an already late stage, and on the other, the deuteronomistic historical work, and is, therefore, part of the editorial unification of these two literary complexes" (p. 248).

Yet it is possible to argue that the spies who scouted out the land in chapters 13–14 brought with them sufficient information for Moses to be able to construct this general outline of the land. The manner of the description of the borders certainly accords with what we know of Egyptian concepts of Canaan of the period of the Exodus. The records of the spies presumably would have been kept by Moses. Further, both Caleb and Joshua might have assisted Moses in the construction of this outline of the land. We may further presume that had things gone differently in chapters 13–14, and had the majority report been one of confident expectation and courage, then just such a report as this chapter presents might have been given thirty-eight years earlier. But at last, for the new generation, the report is given—as God's promise.

Moreover, the text itself presents the outlines to have come directly from the Lord to Moses (vv.1–2). Based on the information that Moses had before him from the report of the spies and with the assistance of Caleb and Joshua at hand, the direction of the words of the Lord to Moses would have been understandable and clear.

The presentation of the boundaries follows an orderly format. This is the way of the Book of Numbers. Even when we have difficulty in making identifications of geographical sites (not a very surprising matter, given the nature of the case), we may still be impressed with the order and format of these texts. They were designed to be read aloud. Even geography is a matter of worship, a litany of promise, in the Book of Numbers. This chapter is a celebration of God's gifting, a liturgy of geography. It presents a trust deed, a legal document from God to his people. Prophetically, it points to realization in Joshua 15. The repetition of the phrase "the land of Canaan" in v.2 (Heb.) has something triumphant about it. These chapters were designed to build confidence in the people and also to provoke their continuing worship of the Lord.

Notes

2 In the phrase אֲשֶׁר תִּפֹּל לָכֶם (*'ašer tippōl lāḵem,* "which will fall to you"), the use of the verb *nāp̱al* ("to fall") is a colorful touch; reference is made to the distribution of the land that will be done by lot but that the lot will be the outworking of the will of the Lord. The same wording is found in Judg 18:1; Ps 16:6; Ezek 47:14. The translation "that will be allotted to you" is a more sedate rendering of this phrasing.

(2) *The southern boundary*

34:3–5

3 " 'Your southern side will include some of the Desert of Zin along the border of Edom. On the east, your southern boundary will start from the end of the Salt Sea, 4 cross south of Scorpion Pass, continue on to Zin and go south of Kadesh Barnea. Then it will go to Hazar Addar and over to Azmon, 5 where it will turn, join the Wadi of Egypt and end at the Sea.

3–5 The southern boundary does not run on a straight line on an east-west basis; it forms a rough, broad angle with the southernmost point south of Kadesh. Similarly, the northern boundary forms a rough, broad angle with the northernmost curve extending through Lebo Hamath (v.8) and then reaching into northeastern Syria (v.9) before turning south and west in a swoop to the Sea of Galilee. The resultant picture of the land is somewhat ideal, jewellike. The western and eastern boundaries are formed principally by the waterways; but the north and south are peaked outward, giving a dynamic shape to the outline of the land. However, the land was a real entity, not just an ideal in the mind. Hence the exotic place names that form the outline of the borders are of signal importance.

The line of the border begins with the south, that which was more familiar to the people from their desert environment. There is a sense that movement is from the known to the unknown. The southern border would include part of the Desert of Zin near Edom, with the Dead Sea as the easternmost extension. The line moves southwest through Scorpion Pass, traverses Zin, and extends to the south of Kadesh Barnea. Then the border moves westward and northward passing through Azmon to the Wadi of Egypt on the Mediterranean.

Scorpion Pass (*ma'ᵃlēh 'aqrabbîm,* v.4) is mentioned in Joshua 15:3 and Judges 1:36—likely a very well known feature of the desert. The inclusion of Kadesh Barnea, the site of Israel's long sojourn in the desert (see on 33:36), is arresting. There was a sense in which all those years that they lived in the region of Kadesh, they were living on the fringe of the land. Certainly by their occupation of that region for a generation, it was fitting that it become a hereditary feature of the Land of Promise. The Wadi of Egypt (Wadi el-Arish) is a well-known geographical feature that separates Canaan proper from Egypt as it empties into the Great Sea. This was part of the original promise (see Gen 15:18: "from the river of Egypt").

So with Edom on the east and the Great Sea (the Mediterranean) on the west, with Kadesh Barnea as the southernmost extension of the border, the general sense of the line is fairly clear.

Notes

3 The language used in this chapter—e.g., פְּאַת־נֶגֶב (p^e'*a͟t-nege͟b*, "southern side")—to describe the four sides of the land by their boundaries is similar to that used in Exod 27 to describe the sides of the tabernacle and in Ezek 47 to describe the new (prophetic) borders of the land (see vv.13–20).

(3) *The western boundary*

34:6

[6] " 'Your western boundary will be the coast of the Great Sea. This will be your boundary on the west.

6 The Great Sea is the Mediterranean and its coastlands. Certainly there was no misunderstanding of the western boundary.

(4) *The northern boundary*

34:7–9

[7] " 'For your northern boundary, run a line from the Great Sea to Mount Hor [8] and from Mount Hor to Lebo Hamath. Then the boundary will go to Zedad, [9] continue to Ziphron and end at Hazar Enan. This will be your boundary on the north.

7–9 The northern boundary may be something of a bloated, mirror image of the southern. It does not form a straight line west to east but moves northeast to Lebo Hamath, where it turns, either dropping sharply to the eastern area north of the Sea of Galilee (so Greenstone, p. 384; see also Walter C. Kaiser, Jr., "The Promised Land: A Biblical Historical View," BS 138 [Oct.–Dec. 1981]: esp. p. 304) or, more likely, moving even more northerly as it reaches to the sites of Zedad, Ziphron, and Hazar Enan (towns that Wenham suggests are considerably north and east of Damascus in Syria; pp. 231–33). The Mount Hor of v.7 cannot be confused with the Mount Hor in the south where Aaron died (see 33:37); this is a mountain in the region of Lebanon, perhaps Jebel 'Alekar.

These two constructions of the northern boundary are dissimilar. That which presents Lebo Hamath as the northernmost point (forming a "cap" to the land) is more in line with the historical reality, where Lebo Hamath is presented as the remote north of the land (see Josh 13:5; 1 Kings 8:65 = 2 Chron 7:8; 2 Kings 14:25; 1 Chron 13:5; Amos 6:14). The view that the northern boundary includes much of northeastern Syria seems not to correspond to biblical events but may present the biblical ideal that was never fully realized (see Gen 15:18: "from the river of Egypt, to the great river, the Euphrates"). Had Israel continued to expand under glorious kings such as David and Solomon, then perhaps the completion of the amalgamation of the northern territories as a part of Canaan would have been realized. Certainly the incongruity of this ideal northern boundary with the historical facts of occupation during Israel's history would have been known by people at the time. Finally, the northern border is an eschatological promise.

Notes

7 תְּתָאוּ (*tᵉṯā'û*, "mark out"), which the NIV translates "run a line," is quite problematic. The word in the text appears to be a Piel imperfect from the root תָּאָה (*tā'āh*), but BDB lists it as quite dubious (p. 1060d); similarly, BDB finds quite dubious the supposed Hithpael of *'āwāh* in v.10. The suggested emendation for both verbs is to connect them to the root תָּאַר (*tā'ar*), which in the Piel as a denominative verb may mean "to draw," "to trace an outline." This emendation of difficult words seems to be an appropriate decision. Thus the verb in v.7 should be emended to תְּתָאֲרוּ (*tᵉṯā'ᵃrû*, a Piel imperfect second masculine plural of *tā'ar*, "trace out a line"). The verb in v.10 should be emended to וְתֵאַרְתֶּם (*wᵉṯē'artem*, a Piel perfect second masculine plural of *tā'ar* with waw consecutive, meaning "and trace out a line").

8 In לְבֹא חֲמָת (*lᵉḇō' ḥᵃmāṯ*, "Lebo Hamath"), the term "Lebo" can also be translated "to the entrance of." The phrase seems to be used as a geographical limit (Judg 3:3 NIV mg.).

---

(5) *The eastern boundary*

34:10–12a

[10]" 'For your eastern boundary, run a line from Hazar Enan to Shepham. [11]The boundary will go down from Shepham to Riblah on the east side of Ain and continue along the slopes east of the Sea of Kinnereth. [12]Then the boundary will go down along the Jordan and end at the Salt Sea.

10–12a The line from the northernmost point that traverses to the south finally to join the southern tip of the eastern side of the Sea of Galilee is the most precarious to attempt to draw. Perhaps a grand curve is intended that includes the sweep of much of southeastern Syria. The sites Shepham and Riblah are unknown today. The Sea of Kinnereth (another name for the Sea of Galilee) and the Jordan form the traditional eastern border for the southern part of the line.

(6) *Summary*

34:12b

" 'This will be your land, with its boundaries on every side.' "

12b These are words of grand gifting; the role of God as the Giver of the land cannot be stressed too highly. At no time in Israel's history did she ever realize the full extent of the land as these verses present it (but cf. Josh 23:14). But the ideal was ever there. One day, many Christians believe, the rule of David's greater son, the Lord Jesus, will fulfill each of these promises to overflowing. At that time the boundaries of ancient promise will form living markers for the heart of his reign; yet, ultimately, there is no line that may be drawn to show the full extent of his rule.

b. *The inheritance in Transjordan*

34:13–15

[13]Moses commanded the Israelites: "Assign this land by lot as an inheritance. The LORD has ordered that it be given to the nine and a half tribes, [14]because the families of the tribe of Reuben, the tribe of Gad and the half-tribe of Manasseh have received their inheritance. [15]These two and a half tribes have received their inheritance on the east side of the Jordan of Jericho, toward the sunrise."

13–15 The new realities that the settlement of Reuben, Gad, and the half-tribe of Manasseh in Transjordan brought about (see ch. 32) demand that this section be added. Since the Jordan River is the traditional eastern boundary of the land of Canaan, these tribes are outside the boundaries in a strict sense. Yet it is possible to see them as deliberately extending the borders of the Land of Promise. Again in these verses we find the obedience of Moses to the word of God as he allots the land of Canaan proper to the nine and one-half tribes.

c. *The personnel of the inheritance*

34:16–29

16 The LORD said to Moses, 17 "These are the names of the men who are to assign the land for you as an inheritance: Eleazar the priest and Joshua son of Nun. 18 And appoint one leader from each tribe to help assign the land. 19 These are their names:

Caleb son of Jephunneh,
from the tribe of Judah;
20 Shemuel son of Ammihud,
from the tribe of Simeon;
21 Elidad son of Kislon,
from the tribe of Benjamin;
22 Bukki son of Jogli,
the leader from the tribe of Dan;
23 Hanniel son of Ephod,
the leader from the tribe of Manasseh son of Joseph;
24 Kemuel son of Shiphtan,
the leader from the tribe of Ephraim son of Joseph;
25 Elizaphan son of Parnach,
the leader from the tribe of Zebulun;
26 Paltiel son of Azzan,
the leader from the tribe of Issachar;
27 Ahihud son of Shelomi,
the leader from the tribe of Asher;
28 Pedahel son of Ammihud,
the leader from the tribe of Naphtali."

29 These are the men the LORD commanded to assign the inheritance to the Israelites in the land of Canaan.

16–29 The listing of the new tribal leaders recalls the listing of the leaders of the first generation (1:5–16). This time the promise will be realized; these new leaders will assist Eleazar and Joshua in actually allotting that land.

Following is a list of the leaders' names, along with suggested meanings for the transliterated Hebrew terms. The meanings of these names are somewhat speculative; Hebrew has so many homonyms in its verbal root structure that one is often unsure which presumed root is correctly identified with the name in question. Many of these names are theophoric; that is, they are constructed with a form of the divine name, as a statement of the faith the parents had in the Lord when they assigned these names to their children.

Caleb (*kālēḇ*, "Dog"—see at 13:6) son of Jepunneh (*yᵉp̱unneh,* meaning unknown; perhaps, "He Makes Clear," if related to the Piel of the verb *pānāh*, "to turn," "to make clear"), of tribe of Judah (v.19)—a figure well known to us by this time (see chs. 13–14).

Shemuel (*šᵉmû'ēl*, "His Name Is God") son of Ammihud (*'ammîhûḏ*, "My Kinsman Is Majesty"), of the tribe of Simeon (v.20).

Elidad (*'elîḏāḏ,* "God Loves") son of Kislon (*kislôn,* "Confidence"), of the tribe of Benjamin (v.21) It does not seem possible that this is the same person as the prophet *'elḏāḏ* of 11:26; presumably that Eldad (whose father's name is not given) was already deceased, unless he was very young when the Spirit fell on him in that unusual event.

Bukki (*buqqî,* "Proven"[?]) son of Jogli (*yoglî,* "Led Away"), of the tribe of Dan (v.22).

Hanniel (*hannî'ēl,* "Grace of God") son of Ephod (*'ēp̱ōḏ,* "Ephod," as in the vest of the priest), from the tribe of Manasseh, from the families of Joseph (v.23).

Kemuel (*qᵉmû'ēl,* "God Establishes") son of Shiphtan (*šip̱ṭān,* "Judgment"), of the tribe of Ephraim (v.24).

Elizaphan (*'ᵉlîṣāp̱ān,* "My God Protects") son of Parnach (*parnāḵ,* no meaning known), of the tribe of Zebulun (v.25).

Paltiel (*palṭî'ēl,* "My Deliverance is God") son of Azzan (*'azzān,* "Mighty"), of the tribe of Issachar (v.26).

Ahihud (*'ᵃḥîhûḏ,* "My Brother is Majesty") son of Shelomi (*šᵉlōmî,* "My Peace"), of the tribe of Asher (v.27).

Pedahel (*pᵉḏah'ēl,* "God Ransoms") son of Ammihud (the same name as the father of Shemuel, v.20), of the tribe of Naphtali (v.28).

The chapter ends in the report of accomplishment: "These are the men" (v.29). These are the names of the second generation; the leaders of the earlier listings were now dead. But with the outlines of the land now in mind, and with new leaders of the tribes now in place, certainly soon the new generation will begin its long-anticipated conquest of the land under the hand of God.

Notes

24 The NIV text adds "son of Joseph" to the words "from the tribe of Ephraim"; this is to allow the patterning of the previous verse to be understood. Further, the MT begins adding the word "leader" to each of the names in v.22; it is possible that each verse should have this word included but that it was dropped from vv.19–21.

2. *Levitical cities and cities of refuge (35:1–34)*

The materials of this chapter serve as a further appendage to the major story line of the Book of Numbers; the climax of the theology of the book was found at 33:50–56. Yet there is a logic and a plan to this chapter, especially as it follows on the account of the divine dimensions of the Land of Promise in chapter 34. There is a pattern in the Book of Numbers that deals first with the laic tribes and their concerns and then moves to the holy tribe of the Levites and their concerns. This was true in the census enumerations and in various other sections throughout the book. Chapter 34 presents the ideal dimensions of the whole land of Canaan, including the acknowledgment of the divine sanction of the settlement of the two and one-half tribes in Transjordan. Now it is necessary for Moses to speak more clearly on the prospects for settlement of the Levites. They were not to have a full tribal holding as the other tribes, but they certainly needed places to live. The solution is in the concept of cities spread throughout the entire land, in and among the other tribes. In this way the Levites might serve as a "holy leaven" that permeates the laic tribes with their presence as special representatives of the work of God in their midst. Among the people they will serve as holy guides to the truth and work of God (see Gen 49:7; Lev 10:11; Deut 31:9–13; 33:10).

We should not be surprised that critical scholars do not regard this chapter as an authentic piece from the time of Moses. Because of its connection with Joshua 20–21, where the distribution of the cities of refuge and other Levitical cities is enacted, some scholars regard Numbers 35 to be dependent on rather than anticipatory of Joshua 20–21 (e.g., Noth, p. 253). See commentary on Joshua 21. Other passages that deal with the distribution of land among the families of the Levites include Leviticus 25:32, 34; Joshua 14:4; 1 Chronicles 13:2; 2 Chronicles 11:14; 31:15, 19. Later texts reflecting on these issues include Ezra 2:70; Nehemiah 7:73; 11:3, 20, 36. A prophetic perspective of future Levitical land arrangements is given in Ezekiel 48:8–14.

Despite the fact that the distribution of land for the Levites is such a major theme in Scripture, many critical scholars doubt whether there was any enactment at all of this arrangement in the history of the nation. Noth, for example, concludes (pp. 253–54):

> These considerations are perhaps, however, superfluous, since the whole passage is purely theoretical, as is clear from the prescriptions for the schematic measuring out of the pasture lands. According to these, the "city" with its "wall" must have been only a point without extension (v.5). The idea of cities of residence for the Levites must, in itself, go back to Deuteronomic-Deuteronomistic ideology (so, too, surely the original form in Josh 21); the present elaboration is a very late product.

In response to Noth, we may assert that the provisions of this chapter were indeed an ideal, just as the outlines of the boundaries of the land were an ideal (see Num 33), never fully realized in the historical period. Nonetheless, there were boundaries that corresponded at least in part to the ideal of the boundaries in Numbers; similarly, there were provisions made for the dwellings of the Levites and for the cities of refuge in the historical experience of the people that correspond at least in part to the ideal of this chapter, as Joshua 20–21 details.

a. *The Levitical cities*

35:1–5

> [1]On the plains of Moab by the Jordan across from Jericho, the LORD said to Moses, [2]"Command the Israelites to give the Levites towns to live in from the inheritance the Israelites will possess. And give them pasturelands around the towns. [3]Then they will have towns to live in and pasturelands for their cattle, flocks and all their other livestock.
>
> [4]"The pasturelands around the towns that you give the Levites will extend out fifteen hundred feet from the town wall. [5]Outside the town, measure three thousand feet on the east side, three thousand on the south side, three thousand on the west and three thousand on the north, with the town in the center. They will have this area as pastureland for the towns.

1–3 Since the Levites would not receive an allotment with the other tribes in the land (1:47–53), they would need towns in which to live and to raise their families and places to care for their livestock. The Levites were to be spread throughout the land, not placed in an isolated encampment. Joshua 21 presents the fulfillment (in part) of this command.

This chapter begins in the same pattern as does chapter 34, with a command from the Lord to Moses respecting the provisions the people needed to have in mind as they contemplated the land of Canaan. The notation of their present location across from Jericho (v.1) adds pungency to the account. In their final staging area for their assault on the land, the people needed to have a perspective of how the land was to be apportioned. Some of the cities and territory would be given to the Levites. But this made only a small proportion of the whole; Greenstone estimates that the total holdings of the Levites envisioned here would be a little over fifteen square miles, a very small proportion of the nearly six thousand square miles of Palestine (p. 352).

The Levites were to be given cities along with adjacent open areas for pasture and farming activities. The term the NIV translates "pasturelands" (*migrāš*, from the verb *gāraš*, "to drive out") includes open land for agriculture as well as for herds and flocks (see Josh 14:4; 21:2). These cities were to be for their habitation, and the surrounding area would be for their use. It is not clear that these cities would be inhabited exclusively by Levites, but this seems to be the suggestion of the text—a notice that suggests the arrangement is rather idealistic. We do know of priest-towns, however, in later Scripture. Anathoth is the most celebrated (Josh 21:18; 1 Kings 2:26; Jer 1:1; 32:7–8); yet Bethel (Judg 20:18; 1 Sam 10:3; 2 Kings 17:28), Nob (1 Sam 21:1; 22:19), and Shiloh (1 Sam 1:3) also come to mind. Greenstone concludes: "The exact distribution of the towns and the measurements of the open land as given here may not have been carried out, but there is no reason to doubt the fact that certain definite localities were set aside by each tribe for the priests and the Levites, where they might find homes for their families" (p. 352).

4–5 The description of the allotment of land in each of these cities is not very clear as we compare v.4 and v.5. Verse 4 speaks of a distance of one thousand cubits (NIV converts this to fifteen hundred feet) from the town wall round about for the open land; v.5 speaks of a measurement of two thousand cubits (three thousand feet, NIV) on each side of the city for the open land. These apposite dimensions have caused commentators to exercise remarkable mathematical creativity. We may observe that the placement of these verses in juxtaposition suggests that for the ancients there was a workable solution to what seems to us to be a considerable problem. If these two verses were separated by a large block of material, one might argue that they are contradictory and that it was carelessness on the part of scribes or redactors not to see how they do not meld together. Since they are adjacent, they must work—or the work of the writer was most careless indeed! The situation is not unlike the comparison of Proverbs 26:4–5, verses that seem to be mutually exclusive but which speak in a complementary and comprehensive manner.

The simplest suggestion to these two verses in Numbers is given by Wenham (p. 234). The city is regarded as a point encompassed by a square that is two thousand cubits to a side. From the point of the city, each direction would be one thousand cubits. That this suggests a very small city is not really a difficulty; most of the towns and settlements of the land of Canaan were very small—often just a matter of acres. Again, the small size of the settlements of Canaan fit better with the reduced numbers of Israel that we have suggested in terms of the census listings. If a city were to become larger, then correspondingly larger dimensions could have been added. The point of the verses is not mathematics but simply an adequate provision for the land needs of the people who would live in the cities. One might imagine, were this provision of open lands not made, that a grudging tribe might allow some Levitical families to live within a small settlement but not give them any room (except at great cost) for their flocks, herds, and farming needs. A city apart from arable land and sufficient pasturelands was no great gift.

b. *The cities of refuge (35:6–33)*

(1) *The basic concept of the cities of refuge*
35:6–8

> [6]"Six of the towns you give the Levites will be cities of refuge, to which a person who has killed someone may flee. In addition, give them forty-two other towns. [7]In all you must give the Levites forty-eight towns, together with their pasturelands. [8]The towns you give the Levites from the land the Israelites possess are to be given in proportion to the inheritance of each tribe: Take many towns from a tribe that has many, but few from one that has few."

6–8 Six Levitical cities were to be stationed strategically in the land—three in Transjordan and three in Canaan proper—as cities of refuge, or asylum cities, where a person guilty of unintentional manslaughter might escape blood revenge. Joshua 20 describes the sites that were eventually chosen.

The term "refuge" or "asylum" (*hammiqlāṭ,* v.6) speaks of a place of escape for the one who has committed manslaughter from the avenger of blood who will be out to kill him in retribution. The term used for the man-slayer is *hārōṣeªḥ,* a term that can be used of premeditated murder (see Exod 20:13 = Deut 5:17, the commandment against murder; 1 Kings 21:19; Jer 7:9; Hos 4:2; cf. Deut 22:26). It may also be used of one who has taken human life without premeditation, or inadvertently, as here (Deut 4:42; 19:3–4, 6; Josh 20–21). Further, the same verb may be used to describe the act of the blood-avenger (vv.27, 30).

These six cities of asylum were to be in addition to forty-two cities for the Levites, giving a total of forty-eight cities (v.7). Further, the ideal was that the selection of the cities would be based on the relative size of the holdings of the various tribes and their relative populations (v.8). All this is ideal in nature, but the general application is still clear. The cities that were later selected as the asylum cities are Bezer, Ramoth-Gilead, and Golan in Transjordan, and Hebron, Shechem, and Kedesh in cis-Jordan (see Deut 4:43; Josh 20:7–8; 21:13, 21, 27, 32, 36, 38).

(2) *Further details on the cities of refuge*
35:9–15

> [9]Then the LORD said to Moses: [10]"Speak to the Israelites and say to them: 'When you cross the Jordan into Canaan, [11]select some towns to be your cities of refuge, to which a person who has killed someone accidentally may flee. [12]They will be places of refuge from the avenger, so that a person accused of murder may not die before he stands trial before the assembly. [13]These six towns you give will be your cities of refuge. [14]Give three on this side of the Jordan and three in Canaan as cities of refuge. [15]These six towns will be a place of refuge for Israelites, aliens and any other people living among them, so that anyone who has killed another accidentally can flee there.

9–15 Verse 9 is worded as a new oracle from the Lord. It may be that the chapter is made of varied materials that were worked into a unified whole; it is also possible that the revelation of the Torah on asylum cities came in stages, not unlike the pattern we find elsewhere in Scripture (cf. the two oracles to Abraham following his obedience in the binding of Isaac; Gen 22:11–12, 15–18).

The Lord through Moses commanded the people who were about to enter the land to personally select special cities for asylum of the man-slayer from the avenger of blood. The provision of these cities is stated in v.11 to be for one who has killed another person accidentally (*bišgāgāh*). This is opposite to the sins of the "high hand" of 15:30. Other references to inadvertent sins are found in 15:25; Leviticus 4:2, 22; and Joshua 20:3, 9.

The avenger of blood is a relative of the slain who will take it on himself to protect the family rights, to avenge his relatives of the loss suffered by the family. In fact, the term *gō'ēl*, often translated "redeemer," has this basic idea; the *gō'ēl* is principally the "protector of family rights" (see Lev 25:48; Ruth 3:13). A redeemer is one who redeems the loss sustained by the family. This can be by payment of a price; it may also be in taking of life. In the latter case, one is an "avenger of blood" (*gō'ēl haddām*, vv.19, 21). In his rage against the loss of a family member, the *gō'ēl haddām* might rashly kill the offender before he found out the circumstances of the death. If the death was not premeditated, or was quite accidental, then the killing of the offending party would add wrong to wrong. Basically, then, the provision of the cities of asylum was another instance of the mercy of the Lord in his provisions for the needs of his people in the world setting in which they lived. We notice that this text does not demand that a relative act as a blood avenger; the assumption is that in this culture this is precisely what he will do. Given the culture, then, the provision is merciful and righteous.

There seems to be no significance to the number of the cities (six), but there is certainly a significance to the placement of them. Three would be on each side of the Jordan River, providing accessibility from any point in the land. Also, the inclusion of three cities of asylum in Transjordan serves further to legitimize the holdings of the two and one-half tribes in the expansion territories.

Verse 15 explains that there will be equal access to these cities by all persons who are in the land, free citizen as well as sojourner or even temporary alien. This provision is another aspect of the grace of God who provides one law for all persons who come under the purview of the Torah of his grace.

Notes

---

11 The verb וְהִקְרִיתֶם (*wᵉhiqrîṯem*, "select") is a Hiphil perfect with waw consecutive of the root *qārāh*. In the Qal stem this verb means "to encounter," "to meet." In this formation the verb has the idea "to make a suitable selection," "to make one's choice in." Moreover, the command comes through Moses in a very direct manner: "You [pl.] are personally to select."

---

(3) *Basic stipulations concerning the taking of life and the cities of refuge* 35:16–21

16" 'If a man strikes someone with an iron object so that he dies, he is a murderer; the murderer shall be put to death. 17Or if anyone has a stone in his hand that could kill, and he strikes someone so that he dies, he is a murderer; the murderer shall be put to death. 18Or if anyone has a wooden object in his hand that could kill, and he hits someone so that he dies, he is a murderer; the murderer shall be put to death. 19The avenger of blood shall put the murderer to death; when he meets him, he shall put him to death. 20If anyone with malice aforethought shoves another or throws something at him intentionally so that he dies 21or if in hostility he hits him with his fist so that he dies, that person shall be put to death; he is a murderer. The avenger of blood shall put the murderer to death when he meets him.

16–21 Various descriptions of the taking of life are presented that would indicate willful murder. This is all very practical in intent, as is the listing of stipulated foods for the household in Leviticus 11. Rather than having a vastly complicated system of classifying of animals, for example, all the "housewife" of ancient Israel had to know were two things: Does the animal ruminate, and does it have a cloven hoof? If so, the meat was acceptable for the table; if not, then the meat was to be excluded.

Similarly, as we think of the inordinately complicated system of modern jurisprudence concerning criminal, homicide law, the provisions of this section are rather clear and straightforward. They are based on the notions of evident intent. The manner of a man's death may be suggestive of willful intent or not. If the man was killed by a lethal instrument, then there is a presumption of guilt on the part of the one who killed him. Those instruments might be iron (v.16), a (heavy) stone (v.17), or a wood implement (v.18). In these cases the party was presumed guilty, as the means of death seem purposeful.

Further, if the person died by a physical blow that was made by hatred or in the context of an ambush (v.20), then the party is guilty and must die. For such a one is a killer, not just an inadvertent man-slayer.

Notes

20 יֶהְדָּפֶנּוּ (*yehdāpennû*, "shoves") can be used to describe a mere push or rejection (2 Kings 4:27; Prov 10:3). It is used of the Lord's actions in driving the enemies of Israel from Canaan (Deut 6:19; 9:4). Here the idea is a shove that results in a fatality, perhaps if the one who is pushed falls against a rock. Again, intentionality is the point here. One might shove another playfully and the result be death, or one might shove someone out of violent hatred with the intention of killing him.

(4) *Cases to be decided concerning the taking of life and the cities of refuge*

35:22–32

22 " 'But if without hostility someone suddenly shoves another or throws something at him unintentionally 23 or, without seeing him, drops a stone on him that could kill him, and he dies, then since he was not his enemy and he did not intend to harm him, 24 the assembly must judge between him and the avenger of blood according to these regulations. 25 The assembly must protect the one accused of murder from the avenger of blood and send him back to the city of refuge to which he fled. He must stay there until the death of the high priest, who was anointed with the holy oil.

26 " 'But if the accused ever goes outside the limits of the city of refuge to which he has fled 27 and the avenger of blood finds him outside the city, the avenger of blood may kill the accused without being guilty of murder. 28 The accused must stay in his city of refuge until the death of the high priest; only after the death of the high priest may he return to his own property.

29 " 'These are to be legal requirements for you throughout the generations to come, wherever you live.

30 " 'Anyone who kills a person is to be put to death as a murderer only on the testimony of witnesses. But no one is to be put to death on the testimony of only one witness.
31 " 'Do not accept a ransom for the life of a murderer, who deserves to die. He must surely be put to death.
32 " 'Do not accept a ransom for anyone who has fled to a city of refuge and so allow him to go back and live on his own land before the death of the high priest.

22–32 The cities of refuge were to be established for the person who had committed an act of involuntary manslaughter. But such cases are not always simple to determine, then or now. The killing of an individual by a lethal weapon brings a presumption of guilt on the slayer. Yet it is quite possible that this death was quite inadvertent. In cases of doubt, judgments would have to be made by the people (v.24), presumably by their town elders (the term "assembly" can refer to the whole nation or to any grouping within the nation). The text is not specific, but it would seem that the judgment would be made in the city in which the death occurred. If the council would decide the death was premeditated and deserving of death, then the guilty party would be delivered over to the blood avenger. But if the decision was for his innocence of malice aforethought, then the slayer would have to go to the asylum city to be protected from the avenger. He would be protected from the avenger only so long as he remained within the asylum city (v.26); if he were to leave the city for any reason, the avenger was allowed to slay him without any consequence to his own person (v.27; *'ên lô dām,* "there is no blood guilt"; NIV, "without being guilty of murder").

Most interestingly, the one who sought asylum had to stay in that asylum city if he expected protection until the death of the high priest (vv.25, 28). There was an atoning significance for the entire populace when the high priest (notice the phrasing: "who was anointed with holy oil") would die. If the high priest died during the period of the slayer's exile in the asylum city, then he was not only free to leave the city, but he could resume his normal life again, including his stake in his ancestral land. We understand that in the case of the death of a pharaoh in ancient Egypt, capital crimes would be forgiven. The notice of the death of the Pharaoh of the Oppression (Exod 2:23) was the political factor God provided for Moses to return to Egypt without fear of reprisal for his crime of murder some forty years earlier.

Christian readers of the words of the salvific effect of the death of the high priest find themselves brought to the Book of Hebrews and its presentation of Christ as our High Priest (Heb 5–10). His death as High Priest is the antitype for the atoning deaths of high priests of Israel in antiquity. There can be no salvific merit in the death of a high priest in isolation; only when the death of that high priest is seen in a *heilsgeschichtliche* continuity with the death of Christ—as an arrow pointing forward to the death of the one who really mattered for salvation of the community—can we understand this provision. Hence, even though many shy away from typological relationships between the testaments, this is a connection that we must not miss.

As we think of the application of the death of the high priest to the freedom of the man-slayer, we understand that the sin of killing, no matter how unintended, is most serious indeed. It cannot be passed on without serious consequence. The life of an exile in an asylum city was one of discontinuity and estrangement—but it was life. Then, if the high priest might die during the period of the person's exile, he would be free, not subject again to the avenger of blood. This is a portrait of redemption—a picture of remission of sin. The sins do matter; they do affect one's life—but they may be forgiven and a person may be set free (see also Josh 20:6).

A further provision of mercy in these cases was the necessity for witnesses (v.30). This provision was made to avoid the possibility of an innocent party being accused and sentenced to death on insufficient evidence. Two witnesses (at least) were required to preclude malevolent falsehood from one isolated voice. As we know, even the provision of multiple witnesses will not automatically preclude collusion; witness the shocking perversion of Israel's justice system by the foreign priestess Jezebel in the incident of Naboth (1 Kings 21).

The stipulations concerning ransom payments also are designed as acts of mercy (vv. 31–32). Conceivably, a wealthy person might take the route of paying ransom as a means of getting out of a sticky situation, while the poor person who could not afford a ransom payment would be at the mercy of the avenger or be forced to live years in an asylum city. Hence, no ransom was to be paid by either the deliberate killer or the man-slayer. In Exodus 21:29–30 we read of an exception, in the case of the man whose ox gored a neighbor.

(5) *The divine perspective on murder and the land* 35:33–34

> 33" 'Do not pollute the land where you are. Bloodshed pollutes the land, and atonement cannot be made for the land on which blood has been shed, except by the blood of the one who shed it. 34Do not defile the land where you live and where I dwell, for I, the LORD, dwell among the Israelites.' "

33–34 The underlying theology of this text is most significant: the shedding of man's blood pollutes the land. The crime of murder is not only an offense against the sanctity of life; it is in fact a pollutant to the Lord's sacred land. It is like the blood of innocent Abel screaming out to the Lord (Gen 4:10). Only the blood of Christ will be able to speak a better word (Heb 12:24).

The point of the passage is not just that there be cities for the Levites to inhabit or that there be cities of asylum for the inadvertent man-slayer to find refuge. All the theology of the chapter culminates in the last words of v.34: "For I am Yahweh who dwells in the midst of the people of Israel" (pers. tr.). This is the issue. If God is to be resident among his people, then the land may not be polluted. With all the attention we (rightly) give to issues of ecology and pollution in our own day, there is an act of pollution that far transcends the trashing of rivers, the killing of lakes, the denuding of forests, and the spilling of oils to mar even the seas; this is the abuse of persons. The worst abuse of all is wrongful death. God will not draw near a land where blood is the polluting agent.

3. *A review of the inheritance of women (36:1–13)*

Each of the last three chapters of the Book of Numbers is an appendage; the theological climax of the book comes directly in the last pericope of chapter 33. It is there that the will of the Lord for his people is stated in definitive form as they are about to enter the land. Of the last three chapters, this one is the most transparently additional, as it presents an interesting further development of the account of Zelophehad's daughters (see 27:1–11). Since the Lord had instructed Moses that the women might inherit their father's land, new questions arose: What will happen to the family lands if these daughters marry among other tribes? Will not the original intention of the first provision be frustrated? Such questions led to the decision that marriage is to be kept within one's own tribe so that the family allotments will not "pass from tribe to tribe" (v.9).

Even though we regard this chapter as anticlimactic, this is not to say that it is not instructive. It shows a continuing pattern of the development of Torah in Israel. As the Lord would speak to Moses in general terms, specific cases would arise that would not seem to fit the general framework of the revelation. Moses could address the needs of the people in this instance to the Lord; and then he would receive new instructions that would not only care for the immediate needs but would serve as a further basis for application in Israel. This is the system of case law and precedent in the instruction of Torah.

The present account has three divisions to it, followed by a summary statement (v.13).

a. *Concerns of the Gileadites for the daughters of Zelophehad*

36:1–4

1 The family heads of the clan of Gilead son of Makir, the son of Manasseh, who were from the clans of the descendants of Joseph, came and spoke before Moses and the leaders, the heads of the Israelite families. 2 They said, "When the LORD commanded my lord to give the land as an inheritance to the Israelites by lot, he ordered you to give the inheritance of our brother Zelophehad to his daughters. 3 Now suppose they marry men from other Israelite tribes; then their inheritance will be taken from our ancestral inheritance and added to that of the tribe they marry into. And so part of the inheritance allotted to us will be taken away. 4 When the Year of Jubilee for the Israelites comes, their inheritance will be added to that of the tribe into which they marry, and their property will be taken from the tribal inheritance of our forefathers."

1–4 The setting is grandiloquent in its pageantry, speaking of the importance of the issue. It is the family of the daughters of Zelophehad who bring to Moses their petition. They do not dispute the former decision of the Lord that the daughters may inherit, in the absence of brothers, to carry on their father's line. Their distress is occasioned by the problems that would eventuate if these daughters would marry outside their clan and tribe. The wholesale confusion of title to land would threaten the very base of the concept of tribal inheritance.

At issue is not a complaint or a grievance against women per se so much as a concern for the continuity of the lines of inheritance within the tribes. At the year of Jubilee (*hayyōḇēl,* "the cornet"; see Lev 25:12, 28ff.; 27:17ff.), when all problems of lines of inheritances are to be resolved, this one will not be resolvable because of the twin lines of right to the land, through wives and husbands from different tribes.

So the issue is not antiwoman but a concern for the integrity of the land. At the same time we may observe from the vantage point of the rights of women as equal participants in the community that this chapter in some manner diminishes the slight advance that was made in chapter 27. By this I mean that the women were still not considered as independent entities within the community; their definition continued to be in connection with their husbands (and sons).

Nonetheless, this sequence of events (chs. 27–31) is a significant entry in the history of women's issues. It is two steps forward and one back; but there is movement forward—a countercultural thrust that has the blessing of God.

Notes

3 The two forms of the verb *gāra'*—וְנִגְרְעָה (*wenigre'āh,* "will be taken") and יִגָּרַע (*yiggārēa'*, "will be taken away")—speak of something that abates or is withdrawn. The point, however, is that this is the very verb used in 27:4, on the part of the daughters in their initial complaint. The tie of the chapters is made compelling by this same word.

---

b. *The law for the marriages of the women who inherit familial land* 36:5–9

5 Then at the LORD's command Moses gave this order to the Israelites: "What the tribe of the descendants of Joseph is saying is right. 6 This is what the LORD commands for Zelophehad's daughters: They may marry anyone they please as long as they marry within the tribal clan of their father. 7 No inheritance in Israel is to pass from tribe to tribe, for every Israelite shall keep the tribal land inherited from his forefathers. 8 Every daughter who inherits land in any Israelite tribe must marry someone in her father's tribal clan, so that every Israelite will possess the inheritance of his fathers. 9 No inheritance may pass from tribe to tribe, for each Israelite tribe is to keep the land it inherits."

5–9 Again, in great grace, the word of the Lord came through Moses to present a decision. In this case, as in the case of the daughters of Zelophehad, the petitioners were right; and the issue is decided in their favor. The women are permitted to marry whomever they choose—a surprising turn, as we usually think of women being chosen in biblical times! Perhaps the fact that they inherited land made them active rather than passive agents in marriage. But they must choose their husbands from within their own clans. The issue is not just their personal happiness but the solidarity of the larger family unit. As a man is to cleave to his wife (Gen 2:24), so a person is to cleave to his family inheritance. The destiny of the family in Israel is tied to the land.

The instance of these women becomes a law that is applicable in other similar cases (v.8). The basic issue is to keep the inheritance of a family in the clan and the tribe of the fathers. Verse 9 summarizes the earlier elements and so reinforces them.

c. *The compliance of the daughters of Zelophehad* 36:10–12

10 So Zelophehad's daughters did as the LORD commanded Moses. 11 Zelophehad's daughters—Mahlah, Tirzah, Hoglah, Milcah and Noah—married their cousins on their father's side. 12 They married within the clans of the descendants of Manasseh son of Joseph, and their inheritance remained in their father's clan and tribe.

10–12 In a book in which names of women are given only rarely, the names of these women are repeated: Mahlah, Tirzah, Hoglah, Milcah, and Noah (see again 27:1–11). They were married within their families, paternal "cousins" (*dōḏêhen,* "[sons of] their uncles," v.12). In this manner the inheritance of their father stayed within the clan.

The Book of Numbers, which so often presents the rebellion of God's people against his grace and in defiance of his will, ends here on a happy note. These noble women, who were concerned for their father's name and their own place in the land, obeyed the Lord. There is a nice tie with this concluding section of the Book of

Numbers to the epilogue of the Book of Proverbs. In the acrostic to the wise women (Prov 31:10–31), there is an exemplification of wisdom in action—in the life of a woman. Significantly, in a book so marred by disobedience, there is a final statement of obedience; and it is in the lives of these noble daughters of Zelophehad. We may observe that we would likely never have heard of him had he had sons instead of these daughters!

d. *A summary statement of the law of the Lord*

36:13

13 These are the commands and regulations the LORD gave through Moses to the Israelites on the plains of Moab by the Jordan across from Jericho.

13 The Book of Numbers is far more than a record of commands and regulations. The true climax of the book is in 33:50–56. Yet there is a salutary feeling in this chapter of theoretical issues being put to practical work. There is hope in the actions of the daughters of Zelophehad that they will be representative of the nation: this generation will do well.

There is an unstated supplement to the book. We follow the lead of Olson (see Introduction), who suggests a heading such as this:

[D. *The Prospects for the Second Generation Are for Good, but the Warning From the Experience of the First Generation Must Not Be Forgotten]*

The chapter presents the idea of Psalm 78:8—Let this people not be like their fathers, but let them obey the Lord and enjoy the good land!

Based on the story of the daughters of Zelophehad, the provisional outlook is very good indeed!